COLLEGE BOTANY

COLLEGE BOTANY

Volume I

INCLUDING ALGAE, FUNGI, LICHENS, BACTERIA, VIRUSES, PLANT PATHOLOGY, INDUSTRIAL MICROBIOLOGY AND BRYOPHYTA

(For Undergraduate and Postgraduate Students)

Dr. B. P. PANDEY
M.Sc., Ph.D., FPSI
Former Head
Department of Botany
J.V. College, Baraut, Uttar Pradesh

S. CHAND
PUBLISHING

S Chand And Company Limited

(ISO 9001 Certified Company)

S. CHAND
PUBLISHING

S Chand And Company Limited

(ISO 9001 Certified Company)

Head Office: D-92, Sector–2, Noida – 201301, U.P. (India), Ph. 91-120-4682700

Registered Office: A-27, 2nd Floor, Mohan Co-operative Industrial Estate, New Delhi – 110 044, Phone: 011-49731800

www.**schandpublishing.com**; e-mail: **info@schandpublishing.com**

Marketing Offices:

Chennai : Ph: 23632120; chennai@schandpublishing.com
Guwahati : Ph: 2738811, 2735640; guwahati@schandpublishing.com
Hyderabad : Ph: 40186018; hyderabad@schandpublishing.com
Jalandhar : Ph: 4645630; jalandhar@schandpublishing.com
Kolkata : Ph: 23357458, 23353914; kolkata@schandpublishing.com
Lucknow : Ph: 4003633; lucknow@schandpublishing.com
Mumbai : Ph: 25000297; mumbai@schandpublishing.com
Patna : Ph: 2260011; patna@schandpublishing.com

First Edition 1979
Subsequent Editions and Reprints 1980, 81, 82, 86, 89, 90, 92, 93, 94, 96, 97, 98, 99, 2001, 2007, 2009, 2010, 2011, 2012, 2013 (Twice), 2014, 2015, 2016 (Twice), 2017, 2018, 2019 (Twice), 2020 (Twice), 2021

Low Priced Students' Paperback Edition (LPSPE), 2022
Reprint 2022 (Twice)

Reprint 2023

ISBN: 978-93-550-1092-6 **Product Code:** H6BTY68BOTN10ENAA21L

PRINTED IN INDIA

By Vikas Publishing House Private Limited, Plot 20/4, Site-IV, Industrial Area Sahibabad, Ghaziabad – 201 010 and Published by S Chand And Company Limited, A-27, 2nd Floor, Mohan Co-operative Industrial Estate, New Delhi – 110 044.

Preface to the Fifth Edition

This text book, College Botany, Volume I includes Algae, Fungi, Lichens, Bacteria, Viruses, Fundamentals of Plant Pathology and Bryophyta. This is a compilation work and embodies a fairly comprehensive treatment of the fundamental facts of the subject. The College Botany will serve as an introduction to the subject of botany to the beginners in this field. Several new topics and latest researches have been added in the text. Actually the present edition of the book has been elevated to fulfil the long felt need of the students of graduate, honours and post-graduate level of all Indian Universities. The syllabi of all the universities have been kept in view during the preparation of the text of this edition.

The book has been written in simple, lucid and graspable language, and illustrated with self explanatory labelled diagrams. All diagrams have been provided with detailed legends. Some of the diagrams have been drawn by author himself from the original sources, while the remaining ones have been quoted from the authentic works of various authors.

The book is primarily an elementary text for degree students and not a text for researchers, and therefore, the bibliography has been kept at minimum. In the end of the text a list of important books and periodicals is being given.

In conclusion, I wish to express my deep sense of gratitude and indebtedness to those who helped my directly or indirectly during the preparation of the text of this edition. Especially I am indebted to Dr. (Mrs.) Rajeshwari sharma, Dr. A.K. Sharma and Dr. J. Mohan for their valuable advise and suggestions.

The healthy criticisms and suggestions for the improvement of the book will be of much value to me for the improvement of the subsequent editions.

Subhash Nagar
BARAUT. 250 611.

B.P. Pandey

CONTENTS

ALGAE

CHAPTER 19 277-292

BACTERIAL, VIRAL AND FUNGAL DISEASES OF PLANTS

CHAPTER 20 293-307

PRINCIPLES OF PLANT DISEASE CONTROL

CHAPTER 21 308-322

METHODS OF STUDYING PLANT DISEASES

MICROBIOLOGY

CHAPTER 22 323-359

BACTERIA, MYCOPLASMA, ACTINOMYCETES AND CYANOBACTERIA

CHAPTER 23 360-377

VIRUSES

BRYOPHYTA

THE ALGAE

1
General Topics

INTRODUCTION

"The algae are chlorophyll bearing organisms which possess unicellular sex organs or multicellular ones in which every cell forms a gamete." In this respect the algae differ from all other green plants.

They are aquatic, both marine and fresh water, and occur on and within soil and on moist stones and wood as well as in association with fungi and certain animals. The algae are of great importance as primary producers of energy rich compounds which form the basis of the food cycle of all aquatic animal life. For this purpose the planktonic algae are of special importance, since they serve as food for many animals. It is thought that 90 percent of the photosynthesis on earth is carried on by aquatic plants ; the planktonic (suspended) algae are chiefly responsible for this. While photosynthesizing, they oxygenate their habitat, thus increasing the level of dissolved oxygen in their environment. Certain blue-green algae, like some bacteria, can use gaseous nitrogen from the atmosphere in building their protoplasm, and in this way they increase the nitrogenous compounds in water and soils of their habitat. This activity is called *nitrogen fixation.*

There are approximately 1800 genera with 21,000 species which are highly diverse with respect to habitat, size, organization, physiology, biochemistry and reproduction. **Phycology** is the study of algae and those who pursue such a study seriously are **phycologists.**

HISTORY OF PHYCOLOGY

The algae as such have a history that is as old as that of other plants. The first references to algae are to be found in early Chinese literature but there are also references in Roman and Greek literature. The Greek word for alga was **Phykos** while in Roman times they were called **Fucus** and were used by matrons for cosmetic purposes. The Roman writer Virgil apparently did not have much use for them as he writes of '*nihil vilior alga*'. The Chinese regarded them aesthetically and this is signified in their name **Tsao.** In the eighth century there are references to several kinds of *tsao.* Algae have been known for a long time in Hawaii where they are used as a food and are called **limu.**

In the early centuries writings about algae were restricted either to their use or else to their taxonomy. As with other plants no real progress was made in our scientific knowledge of the algae until the invention of the microscope. As early as the twelfth century, however, algae were being used for manuring purposes on the north coast of France. From here it seems that the practice spread to Great Britain because in the sixteenth century there is reference to their use for the algae for measure may have had something to do with the idea that they were 'bred of putrefaction' as described in 1583 by Cesalpino.

Upto about 1800 A.D. almost all algae were placed in one of four great genera, *i.e., Fucus, Ulva, Conferva* and *Corallina.* In those times *Chara* was grouped with horsetails. In the seventeenth century the utilization of brown seaweeds for fertilizers was known in France. In those days agar making art was newly discovered in China and Japan.

Until the development of the microscope in the middle of the seventeenth century algae were regarded as lacking sexuality. After fifty years of the introduction of the microscope R. Reaumour described the sex organs of *Fucus.* After near-about a century of this discovery, Turner for the first time, described fertilization in *Fucus.*

In the beginning of nineteenth century Vaucher published his *Histoire Confervae d'eau douce* in which confirmation was given of the reproductive process in *Spirogyra.*

Dillwyn, Vaucher and Roth were great algologists of the early years of the nineteenth century. Roth named and described the genera *Hydrodictyon, Batrachospermum* and *Rivularia.* There were several workers in the marine algae too. Between 1805 and 1816, Lamouroux described many new marine genera including *Laminaria* and many tropical green algae. Lyngbye, Bory and Greville did lot of work in Great Britain and on the continent marine algae. Greville named the well known genera, *i.e., Polysiphonia* and *Rhodymenia.* C. Agardh, a Swedish algologist established the importance of cystocarp in Rhodophycean taxonomy and formed the divisions Diatomaceae, Nostochineae, Confervoideae, Ulvaceae, Florideae and Fucoideae. He included many Myxophyceae in Nostochineae and filamentous green algae in Confervoideae. His son J. Agardh described new species and also studied reproduction in *Conferva, Bryopsis, Fucus* and *Griffithsia.*

Thuret, the great French algologist, produced his monograph on fertilization in *Fucus* in 1854-55. In the middle of the nineteenth century an English algologist W.H. Harvey produced a series of marine algal floras – *Phycologia Britannica, Phycologia Australica* and *Nereis Boreali Americana.* In these classical works on marine algae he divided the plants into Chlorospermae, Rhodospermae and Melanospermae. During the same time a German algologist, in Germany, described more new genera and published them in a number of works – *Systema Algarum, Phycologia Generalis* and *Tabulae Phycologicae.*

In the end of the nineteenth century, Areschoug (1866-84) described new genera and species and also investigated zoospore and gamete formation in *Urospora* and *Cladophora* and carried out morphological studies in *Laminaria* and *Macrocystis.* During this period the existing algal classifications were rearranged. The workers realized that the old classifications were unsatisfactory. Between 1875 and 1900 Sirodot reorganized the Batrachospermaceae; Gomont the Myxophyceae ; Phillips the Rhodymeniales and Schmitz the Rhodophyceae. During this period of great discoveries, De Toni published his great work *Sylloge Algarum* which contained all known and described algal species.

At the end of the nineteenth century several important life histories were worked out. In 1897-98, Williams described the complete life history of *Dictyota.* In 1899, Sauvageau worked out the life history of *Cutleria.* In 1882 Berthold studied photoperiodism in *Bryopsis.* In 1894 Bonnier and Mangin did preliminary work of algal respiration.

Taxonomic rearrangement was still in progress. In 1899 Luther established the Heterokontae. In 1902, Blackman and Tansley used up the nature of cilia in their classification. In 1900 Blackman suggested three distinct tendencies in green algae – the **Volvocine, Tetrasporine** and **Chlorococcine.**

In 1910 work on fossil study was started. In 1910 Pia published his studies of fossil algae in Europe. Walcott published the work of fossil study in the United States in 1914. In 1912 Cotton started work on algal ecology. Fritsch and Salisbury and Brenchley started work on soil algae. During this period fresh-water algal ecology also received a great impetus from the work of Transeau in The United States. Kylin, Kniep, Pantanelli and Harder did work on algal plant physiology and biochemistry. Jonsson, Borgesen, Collins and Skottsberg published the important algal floras. In 1915 Laminarian life-cycle was fully established.

Since 1930, the knowledge of the algal cell, the cell wall and cell sap, nuclear division and the structures of flagella has greatly increased especially with introduction of new techniques such as X-ray photography, electron microscopy and improved optical microscopes. Kylin, Papenfuss, Feldmann and Svedelius have given the modern ideas on the classification of Phaeophyceae and Rhodophyceae. Pringsheim has demonstrated the importance of pure algal cultures.

ALGOLOGY IN INDIA

The pioneer work on algology in India was started by M.O.P. Iyengar, Y. Bharadwaja, Ghose and P. Bruhl and K. Biswas in the first quarter of this century. This led to the establishment of two major schools at Madras and Banaras, respectively by M.O.P. Iyengar and Y. Bharadwaja. Recently more algal laboratories have been set up in several universities and research institutes, notably Udaipur, Hyderabad, Delhi, Ranchi, Allahabad, Lucknow, Kanpur, Cuttack, Bombay, Bhavnagar and Mandapam. However, the school of algology at Banaras developed rapidly, and produced several eminent workers, who are busy with the research work on algology throughout the country.

The progress done in the field of algology in India can be categorized in three important phases. In the first phase much work was done on the algal flora, taxonomy and morphology of several freshwater and marine algae. This phase ended in 1938, when the Indian Science Congress celebrated its Silver Jubilee.

In the second phase much has been done in the field of morphology, reproduction, cytology and life-histories of several algae. Cytological studies on green algae were carried out by Y.S.R.K. Sarma (1964). Different aneuploid numbers like 12, 14, 16, 18, and 22 chromosomes have been recorded in different genera of Ulotrichales by Y.S.R.K. Sarma in 1963, and in some members of Oedogoniales by Y.B.K. Chowdhary in 1965.

R.N. Singh isolated several algae from rice fields and established nitrogen fixation by forms like *Aulosira fertilissima*. He (1961) also emphasized the role of this species in the nitrogen economy of Indian agriculture and indicated how the blue green algae can be used in reclamation of alkaline soils (1950). G.S. Venkataraman and his associates (1962, 1969) have shown that artificial inoculation of high yielding rice varieties with nitrogen-fixing blue-green algae increases grain yield. A.B. Gupta and K. Lata (1964) have studied the beneficial effects of extracts of blue-green algae in crop improvement. R.N. Singh (1961) also studied water blooms and water pollution. J.N. Misra (1959, 1966) studied the ecological aspects of marine algae and fresh-water diatoms.

During the second phase of algology in India, a series of monographs on Indian algae were published by the Indian Council of Agricultural Research. These monographs are : 1. **Cyanophyta** by T.V. Desikachary (1959); 2. **Zygnemaceae** by M.S. Randhawa (1959); 3. **Role of Blue green Algae in Nitrogen Economy of Indian Agriculture** by R.N. Singh (1961); 4. **Phaeophyceae in India** by J.N. Misra (1966); 5. **Vaucheriaceae** by G.S. Venkataraman (1962); 6. **Cultivation of Algae** by G.S. Venkataraman (1969); 7. **Charophyta** by B.P. Pal, B.C. Kundu, B.S. Sundaralingam and G.S. Venkataraman (1962); 8. **Chlorococcales** by M.T. Philipose (1967); 9. **Ulotrichales** by K.R. Ramanathan (1964).

In the third phase some very astonishing developments have come in picture. During this phase R.N. Singh (1961) in collaboration with H. Ris studied the ultrastucture of several blue green algae under electron microscope and established their *procaryotic* nature. In 1960, R.N Singh worked out the biochemical mechanism of fixation of nitrogen by blue-green algae. E.R.S. Talpsayi (1962, 1967) studied the phosphorus metabolism and physiology of cellular differentiation in Cyanophyta.

H. D. Kumar, R. N. Singh, H. N. Singh and their associates have added much to our knowledge of the genetics and photobiology of blue-green algae. For the first time in 1962, H. D. Kumar recorded a case of genetic recombination in blue-green alga *Anacystis nidulans*, later on this type of recombination was also reported by R. N. Singh and J. P. Sinha (1965) in *Cylindrospermum majus*. H. D. Kumar (1963, 1964), R. N. Singh and H. N. Singh (1964) studied the photobiology of blue-green algae and isolated X-ray and ultra violet induced mutations. R. N. Singh and D. N. Tiwari (1969) obtained an ultra violet induced mutation in *Nostoc linckia*. R. N. Singh and his students (1966-1971) studied the genetic basis of cellular differentiation in blue-green algae and nitrogen fixation and published several valuable publications. R. N. Singh and P. K. Singh (1967) have isolated a number of blue-green algal viruses, the *Cyanophages*. R. N. Singh and P. K. Singh (1970) reported for the first time transduction of streptomycin resistance and lysogeny with some of these viruses.

HABIT AND HABITAT

Most of the part of the land is covered over either by fresh water or sea water. Besides, several other algae are found in somewhat drier conditions. They are found on the trunks of trees, on telephone wires, on rocks, on walls, in hot springs and in several other unusual habitats. Here some of the algae have been classified according to their habitats. Special emphasis has been given on the occurrence of fresh water algae.

1. **Hydrophytes.** They are more or less completely submerged or free floating on the surface of the water. The hydrophytes may be subdivided into following heads.

(i) **Benthophytes.** Several fresh water and marine algae are found in attached condition. The fresh water such as *Chara, Nitella, Cladophora, Gongrosira, Chaemosiphon* etc., are found attached to some substratum in the bottom of the water. Almost all of brown algae (Phaeophyceae) are found in attached condition to some substrata in the sea.

(ii) Epactiphytes. Such algae grow along the shores of lakes and ponds, and may be delimited from benthophytes with some difficulty. The most important fresh water forms are – *Oedogonium, Chaetophora*, some species of *Spirogyra, Mougeotia*, some diatoms, *Scytonema* and *Rivularia*.

(iii) Thermophytes. Many algae are reported from hot springs. These algae may tolerate the temperature upto 70°C or more than that. According to Copeland, 53 genera and 153 species of Chroococcaceae may survive upto 84°C. Some Oscillatoriaceae may survive upto 85°C. This supports that Myxophyceae (blue-green algae) are primitive.

(iv) Planktophytes. The algae which float on the surface of the water are called 'planktophytes'. They may be of two types, *i.e.*, (a) euplanktophytes (b) tychoplanktophytes.

(a) Euplanktophytes. They are never attached, and from the very beginning are free floating, *e.g.*, diatoms, *Cosmarium, Closterium, Microcystis, Sphaeroplea, Scenedesmus, Pediastrum, Chlamydomonas, Volvox*, other Volvocales and some members of Chroococcales. The above given forms are fresh water in habit.

(b) Tychoplanktophytes. In the beginning such algae are attached, but later on they become detached and free floating, *e.g.*, some species of *Spirogyra, Zygnema, Cladophora, Oedogonium, Rhizoclonium, Mougeotia, Tribonema, Microspora, Cylindrospermum, Tetraspora, Rivularia, Nostoc, Gloeotrichia, Sargassum* etc.

(v) Halophytes. The algae occur in saline waters are known as 'halophytes'. The most striking examples are *Dunaliella* and *Chlamydomonas* which occur in salt lakes, the species of *Scenedesmus, Aphanocapsa, Pediastrum, Aphanothece, Oscillatoria* are found in saline waters; the species of *Enteromorpha* are found in inland astuaries ; many species of Ulvales, Ulotrichales, Conjugales, and Myxophyceae are found near the sea in astuaries.

(vi) Epiphytes. Many algae are found upon other living plants and bigger species of algae. *Aphanochaete, Bulbochaete, Oedogonium* and *Microspora*, are found as epiphytes upon larger species of *Oedogonium, Cladophora, Rhizoclonium, Vaucheria* and *Hydrodictyon* species. *Coleochaete nitellarum* is epiphytic upon species of *Chara* and *Nitella*. Some of the species of *Coleochaete* are epiphytic upon some grasses grown on the banks of the ponds and the hydrophytes such as – *Vallisneria, Typha, Ipomoea* and several other aquatic plants. *Chaetonema* is found epiphytic on the mucilaginous masses of *Tetraspora* and *Batrachospermum.*

(vii) Epizoophytes. Certain algae are found on living aquatic animals such as turtles, mollusc shells, fishes etc. Species of *Cladophora* grow upon mollusc shells. *Protoderma* and *Basicladia* occur on the back of turtles. *Characiopsis* and *Characium* occur on the posterior and anterior legs of Branchipus respectively.

2. Edaphophytes. Such algae are also called terrestrial algae. They are found upon or inside the surface of the earth. They can be (i) saphophytes and (ii) cryptophytes.

(i) Saphophytes. They are surface algae. Most of the species of Myxophyceae are found upon the surface of the soil. Besides, *Mesotaenium, Botrydium, Protosiphon, Oedocladium, Vaucheria, Fritschiella* and many others are met with upon the surface of the wet soil.

(ii) Cryptophytes. Such algae are subterranean in habit and occur inside the soil. The species of Myxophyceae are found in the soil. The species of *Nostoc, Anabaena* and *Euglena* have been reported from the paddy fields, where they also fix the atmospheric nitrogen in the soil to enrich the fertility of the fields.

3. Aerophytes. Such algae are aerial in habitat. They are found upon the trunks of trees, walls, fencing wires, rocks, and animals and so many other aerial substrata.

(i) Epiphyllophytes. Such algae are epiphytic upon leaves of trees. Species of *Trentepohlia* are commonly found upon the bark of trees. They also occur upon rocks and fencing wires. They are abundantly found on the fencing wires of Calcutta botanical gardens. *Phycopeltis* occurs upon *Rubus* ; *Phyllosiphon* on *Arisaema* ; *Rhodochytrium* on *Asclepias* and *Solidago.*

(ii) Epiphloephytes. These algae grow on the bark of trees mixed with many mosses and liverworts. *Phormidium, Scytonema, Haplosiphon* and *Schizothrix* grow on the bark of trees mixed with liverworts.

(iii) Epizoophytes. These algae are found even on the bodies of land animals. Certain Chaetophorales are found even on the hairs of sloth.

(iv) Lithophytes. Many algae grow on the rocks and walls. The species of *Scytonema* grow on the walls in rainy season and the whole wall becomes black spotted. *Vaucheria, Nostoc* and many other algae are also found on wet rocks.

4. Cryophytes. These algae are found on ice and snow. These algal forms cause red snow, green snow, yellow snow, yellowish green snow and violet snow. In European countries, especially in arctic region the green snow is caused by *Chlamydomonas, Ankistrodesmus* and *Mesotaenium;* red snow is caused by species of *Chlamydomonas, Scotiella, Gloecapsa* and diatoms.

Certain species of *Ulothrix, Oedogonium, Pleurococcus* and *Nostoc* cause yellow or yellow green snow.

Alaskan (1942) classified the Cryo algae in four groups:

(i) Those algae which can grow only on ice, *e.g., Ancylonema, Mesotaenium.*

(ii) Those algae which can occur only on snow, *e.g., Scotiella, Chlamydomonas.*

(iii) Those algae which can grow on ice and snow both, *e.g., Cylindrocystis, Trochiscia.*

(iv) Those algae which can grow on ice or snow. These are not true cryophytes, *e.g., Gloeocapsa, Phormidium.*

5. Symbionts or endophytes. Many algae grow in symbiotic association of other plants. The most striking example of symbiosis are lichens. here the algae are found in symbiotic association of fungi. Various Myxophyceae, *e.g., Chroococcus, Nostoc, Microcystis, Gloeocapsa, Scytonema,*

Rivularia etc., have been separated from lichens. Some green algae, *e.g., Coccomyxa, Chlorella, Protococcus, Palmella* etc., are also found as symbionts in lichens.

Besides, several algae are endophytes in the tissue of other plants. *Anabaena azollae* is found inside the leaves of *Azolla* (a Pteridophyte). *Anabaena cycadae* is found in the coralloid roots of *Cycas. Nostoc* has been reported from the tissues of *Anthoceros* and *Notothylas. Nostoc* is found in the leaves of *Sphagnum* (Bryophyta) and several angiosperms. *Chlorochytrium* is endophytic inside *Lemna, Ceratophyllum* and certain mosses.

6. Endozoophytes. Certain algae occur inside the body of animals. *Zooxanthella* is found inside fresh water sponges; *Zoochlorella* is found inside *Hydra viridis.* According to Langeron (1923), about 14 species of Oscillatoriaceae are found in the digestive and respiratory tracts of various vertebrates.

7. Parasites. Certain algae are parasites upon other plants. The most striking example is *Cephaleuros virescens* which causes the havoc of tea foliage in Assam and neighbouring areas, called 'red rust of tea'.

8. Fluviatile algae. Such algae are found in rapidly flowing waters; *Ulothrix* occurs in mountain falls. *Stigeoclonium, Batrachospermum* is reported from the swift running streams of Dehradun and other hilly tracts.

NUTRITION

From the view point of their nutrition the algae are **autotrophic.** They synthesize their food from inorganic materials such as carbondioxide, water and minerals by means of photosynthesis. Chlorophyll is the most common pigment in all the algae, though in many, the green colour of the plastids is masked by other pigments, such as, **fucoxanthin** a yellow pigment which dominates in brown algae whereas **phycoerythrin** and **phycocyanin** pigments are found in red and blue green algae respectively. The algae also synthesize oil and proteins from the carbohydrates which they manufacture and soluble forms of nitrogen and other minerals available in solution in the water in which they are found. The aquatic species of algae obtain water and carbondioxide by osmosis and diffusion processes respectively from the water in which they grow. This way, the process of nutrition in algae is quite similar to that of ordinary green plants.

The algae, like other chlorophyllous plants, require C, H, O, P, K, N, S, Ca, Fe and Mg and also traces of Mn, Bo, Zn, Cu and Co. For certain algae additional elements are required such as Si for diatoms and Mo for *Scenedesmus.*

The algae which grow in an entirely inorganic medium in the presence of light are known as *photoautotrophic.* In other words, using light energy they synthesize their protoplasm from exclusively inorganic sources. Several other algae require in addition certain vitamins, usually B-12, thiamine or biotin and such algae are known as *photoauxotrophic.* A number of algae are heterotrophic. The algae which do not synthesize their protoplasm solely from inorganic sources but require some of the essential elements, usually carbon and nitrogen, are known as *heterotrophic.* Several algae (*e.g.,* species of *Ocaromonas*) digest solid particles of food and are known as *phagotrophic.*

RANGE OF VEGETATIVE STRUCTURE

The whole range of the somatic structure of algae may be divided into following important types.

1. The motile type.
2. Palmelloid and dendroid types.
3. Coccoid forms.
4. Filamentous habit.
5. Siphonous habit.
6. Advanced type.

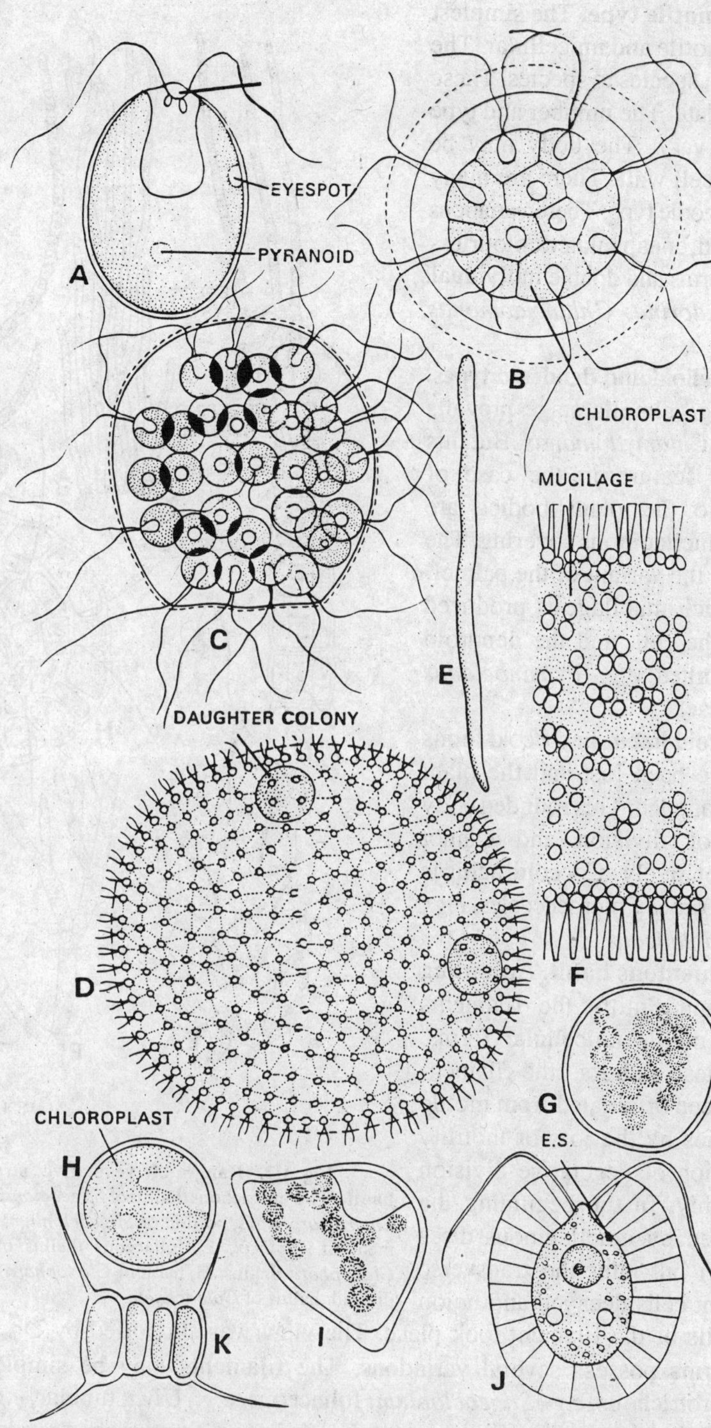

Fig.1.1. Range of vegetative structure. The motile type A-D and J; A motile vegetative cell of *Chlamydomonas;* B, vegetative colony of *Pandorina* sp; C, vegetative colony of *Eudorina unicocca*; D, vegetative colony of *Volvox;* J, Motile cell of *Sphaerella*. The palmelloid type E and F; E, colony of *Tetraspora cylindrica;* F, portion of a colony of *T. cylindrica;* the coccoid type – G-I and K; G, H and I, vegetative cells of *Chlorococcum humicola;* K, colony of *Scenedesmus* sp.

1. The motile type. The simplest type of body is motile and unicellular. The shape varies from species to species. These bodies are flagellate. The number and type of flagella also vary. The body may be naked or with a cell wall. There are many variations in the motile type. These variations may be, amoeboid, encapsulated colourless forms, colonial forms and double individuals, *e.g., Volvox, Eudorina, Chlamydomonas* etc.

2. Palmelloid and dendroid types. For a time being palmella stage prevails in the species of *Chlamydomonas*. But this is a permanent feature in the case of *Tetraspora,* here the plant bodies are surrounded by mucilaginous covering. The dendroid type is the variant of the palmelloid type in which mucilage is produced at the base of the cell, and the dendroid colonies are resulted, *e.g., Prasinocladus* of Chlorophyceae.

3. Coccoid habit. In coccoid forms the flagella have been lost and the plant body becomes rounded. This rounded body has no power of division and cannot reproduce vegetatively. Coccoid habit is very common in order Chlorococcales, *e.g., Chlorococcum humicola.*

4. Filamentous habit. According to Blackman and Smith, the filaments originate from motile unicellular forms. According to these authors, the filamentous habit has been originated from motile unicellular bodies by the loss of motility and the restriction of vegetative division in one plane only. In the beginning the cells were united by mucilaginous discs (false septation) but later the transverse septa of adjacent cells decayed and union between the cells of the filament took place. The view was supported by Dr. F.E. Fritsch. The filamentous forms possess several variations. The filaments may be simple, *e.g., Ultothrix, Spirogyra*; heterotrichous, *e.g., Stigeoclonium;* foliaceous, *e.g., Ulva*; tubular, *e.g., Enteromotpha;* discoid, *e.g., Coleochaete.* The filaments of *Ulothrix* and *Spirogyra* are simple and unbranched. The filaments of *Stigeoclonium* are heterotrichous, *i.e.,* the plant body consists of two systems, one erect and the other prostrate. The prostrate system is comparatively smaller and possesses many erect branches. *Ulva* is a good example of foliaceous variant. The divisions

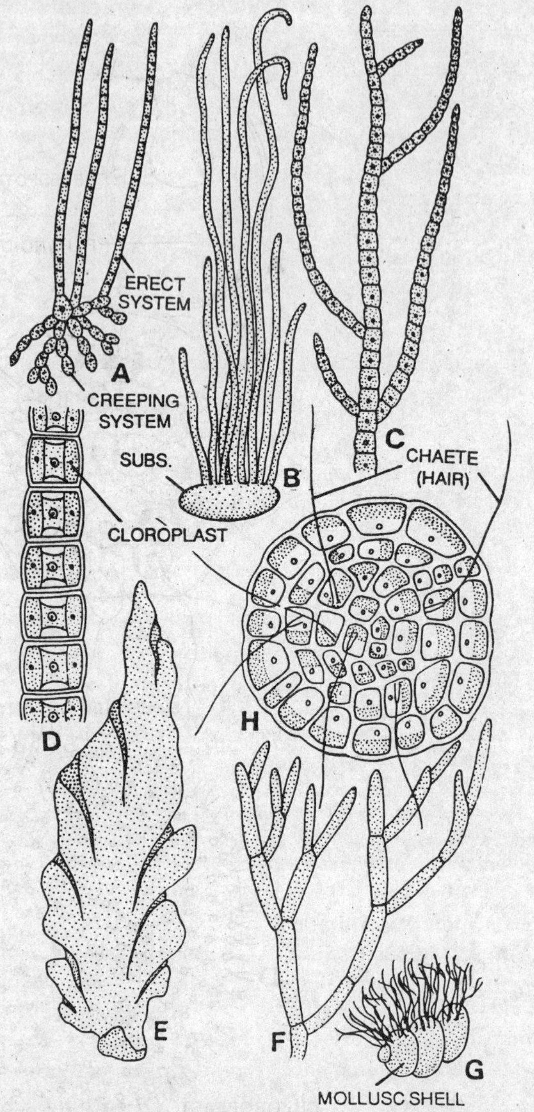

Fig. 1.2. Range of vegetative structure. Filamentous habit. A, heterotrichous thallus of *Stigeoclonium;* B, tubular thallus of *Enteromorpha;* C, portion of *Stigeoclonium;* D, portion of the filament of *Ulothrix;* E, foliaceous thallus of *Ulva;* F, a part of *Cladophora* thallus; G, habit of *Cladophora* (on mollusc shell); H, discoid thallus of *Coleochaete.*

take place in all the planes and a foliaceous structure is developed. The thallus is two celled thick. In tubular variant the thallus is a hollow tube with a wall one cell in thickness, *e.g., Enteromorpha.* The discoid type has been evolved from heterotrichous filament. *Coleochaete scutata* is the well known example of this type. The cells of *Coleochaete* are joined end to end in branching filaments and a discoid habit is attained. The other species *Coleochaete pulvinata* possesses free branches.

5. Siphonous habit. The plant body consists of branching filaments having many nuclei and no partition walls. The cross walls appear only at the time of the formation of reproductive bodies. The well known examples of this type are – *Vaucheria, Codium, Caulerpa* etc., of order Siphonales.

6. Advanced Type. The advanced types, may be uniaxial filamentous type, multiaxial filamentous type and parenchymatous type. In uniaxial filamentous type, the single main axial thread has close branch systems to form more or less compact pseudoparenchymatous thallus, *e.g., Dumontia* of Rhodophyceae. **In the multiaxial filamentous type, there is a number**

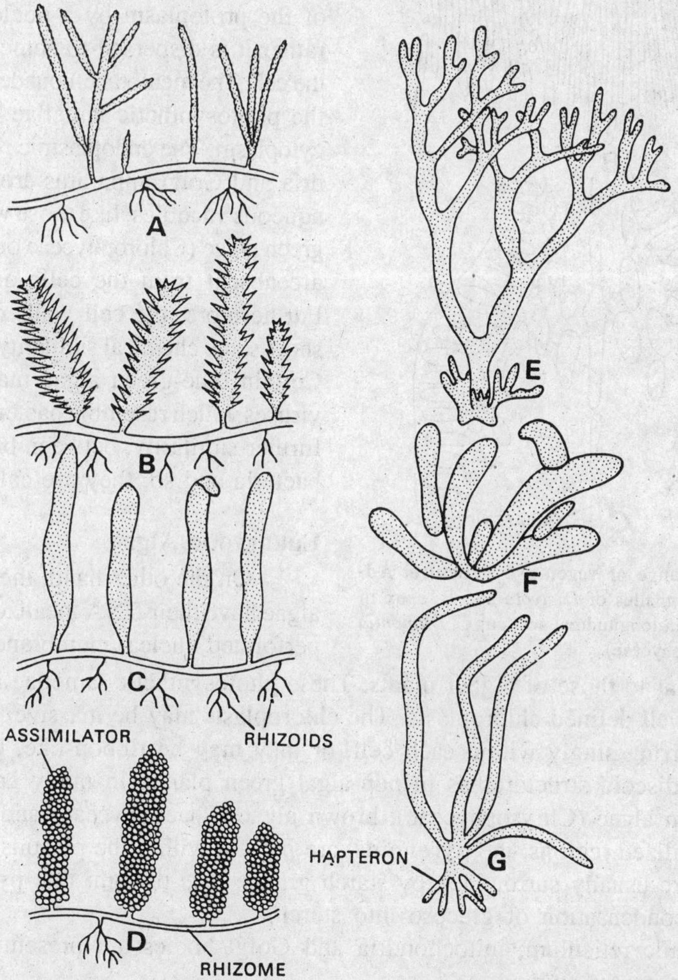

Fig. 1.3. Range of vegetative structure. Siphonous type. A, thallus of *Caulerpa cupressoides;* B, thallus of *C. crassifolia;* C, thallus of *C. prolifera;* D, thallus of *Caulerpa* sp.; F, thallus of *Valonia utricularis;* G, thallus of *Vaucheria* sp.

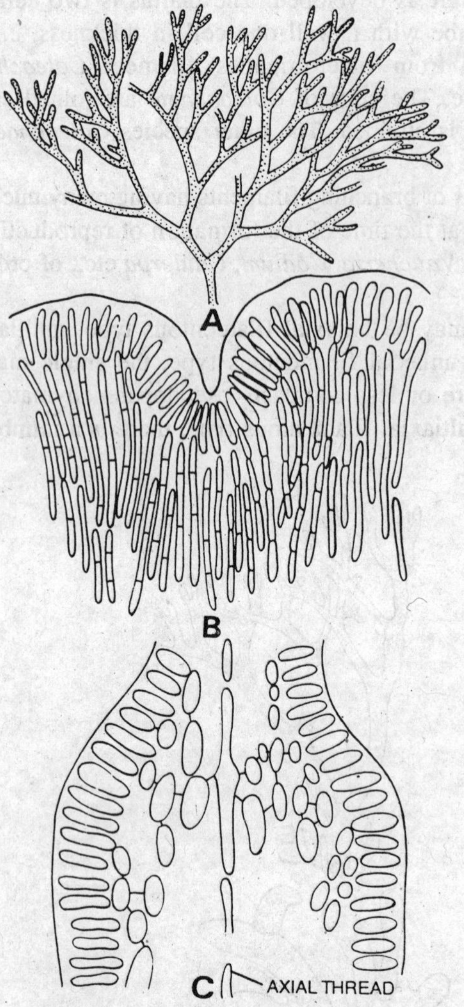

Fig. 1.4. Range of vegetative structure. Advanced type. - A, thallus of *Dictyota* sp.; B, apex of *Scinaia furcellata* in longitudinal section; C, *Dumontia incrassata* (Rhodophyceae).

of axial threads and the branches and all of them form a compact cortex, *e.g.*, *Scinaia furcellata* of Rhodophyceae. Many advanced types are truly parenchymatous, *e.g.*, *Laminaria, Fucus, Sargassum* of Phaeophyceae.

CELLULAR ORGANIZATION

There are two main patterns of cellular organization in algae. They are *prokaryotic* and *eukaryotic*.

Prokaryotic Algae

The blue-green algae (Cyanophyceae or Cyanophycophyta) are prokaryotic algae. In these algae their nuclear materials, deoxyribo-nucleic acid (DNA), is not delimited from the remainder of the protoplasm by a nuclear membrane, but rather it is dispersed to some degree throughout the cell. The membrane-bounded plastids are absent; the photosynthetic lamellae occur freely in the cytoplasm. The endoplasmic reticulum, mitochondria and Golgi apparatus are also absent. Large aqueous vacuoles, like those which occur in many green algae (Chlorophyceae or Chlorophycophyta) are absent from the cells of blue-green algae. Furthermore, the cell walls of blue-green algae show some chemical similarity to those of bacteria. Certain blue-green algae may be infected with viruses which resemble bacteriophages advocates further similarity, between blue-green algae and bacteria and so, they are called **cyanobacteria.**

Eukaryotic Algae

On the other hand, the cells of eukaryotic algae have their DNA localized within a minutely perforated nuclear membrane, their nuclei being essentially similar to those of higher plants. These photosynthetic lamellae are confined within membranes as well defined chloroplasts. The chloroplasts may be massive, parietal or star-like structures, occurring singly within each cell, or they may be ribbon-like, bar-like, net-like or in the form of discoid structures as in non-algal green plants. In many green algae (Chlorophyceae), golden algae (Chrysophyceae), brown algae (Phaeophyceae) and red algae (Rhodophyceae), specialized regions, the **pyrenoids,** are present within the plastids. In the green algae the pyrenoids are usually surrounded by starch grains. It is thought that pyrenoids are centres for enzymatic condensation of glucose into starch.

Endoplasmic reticulum, mitochondria and Golgi bodies are present in the cells of all eukaryotic algae so far studied.

The motile cells of algae may be flagellate. Associated with motility are such strucutres as contractile vacuoles, flagella and stigmas.

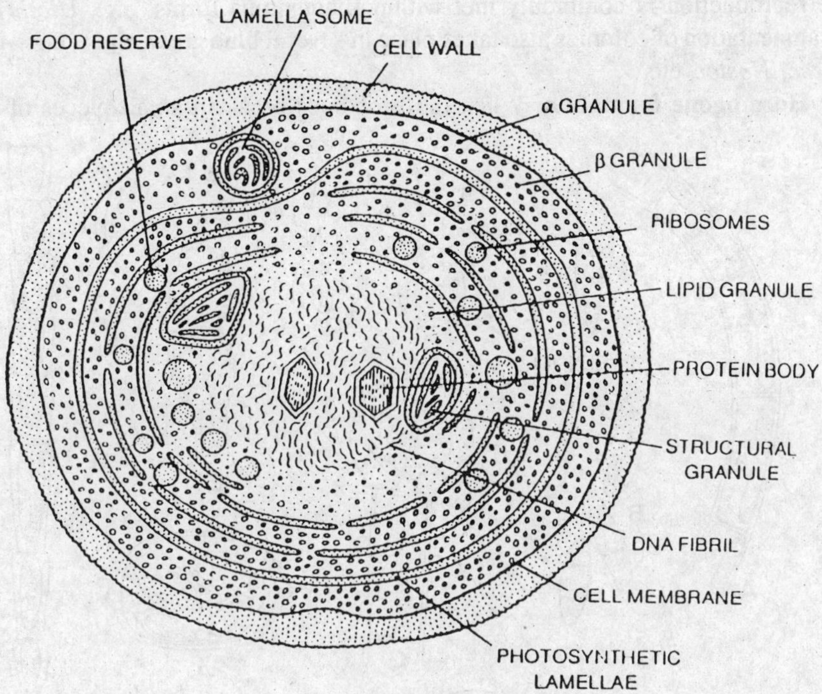

Fig. 1.5. Prokaryotic cellular organization in Myxophyceae. Line diagram of an electron micrograph of typical Myxophycean cell.

REPRODUCTION AND METHODS OF PERENNATION

There are three common methods of reproduction found in algae-(i) vegetative, (ii) asexual, and (iii) sexual. In addition to these methods several perennating bodies also develop which face the adverse conditions.

1. Vegetative reproduction. This may be of several types.

(i) By cell division. The mother cells divide and the daughter cells are produced, which become new plants. This is exclusive type of reproduction in *Pleurococcus,* some desmids, diatoms, *Euglena* etc.

(ii) Fragmentation. The plant body breaks into

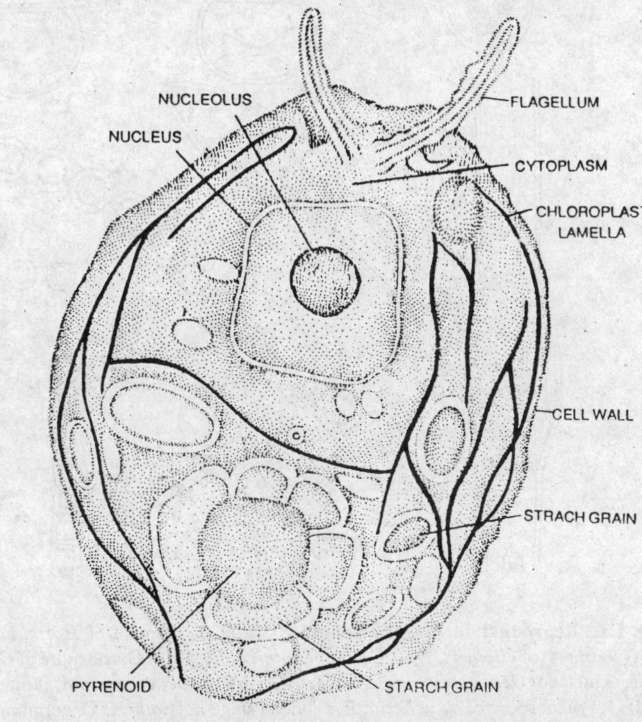

Fig. 1.6. Eukaryotic cellular organization in *Chlamydomonas*. Electron microscopic structure.

several parts or fragments and each such fragment develops into an individual. This type of vegetative reproduction is commonly met within filamentous forms, *e.g., Ulothrix, Spirogyra* etc. The fragmentation of colonies also takes place in several blue green algae, *e.g., Aphanocapsa, Aphanothece, Nostoc* etc.

(iii) Hormogone formation. When the trichomes break in small pieces of two or more

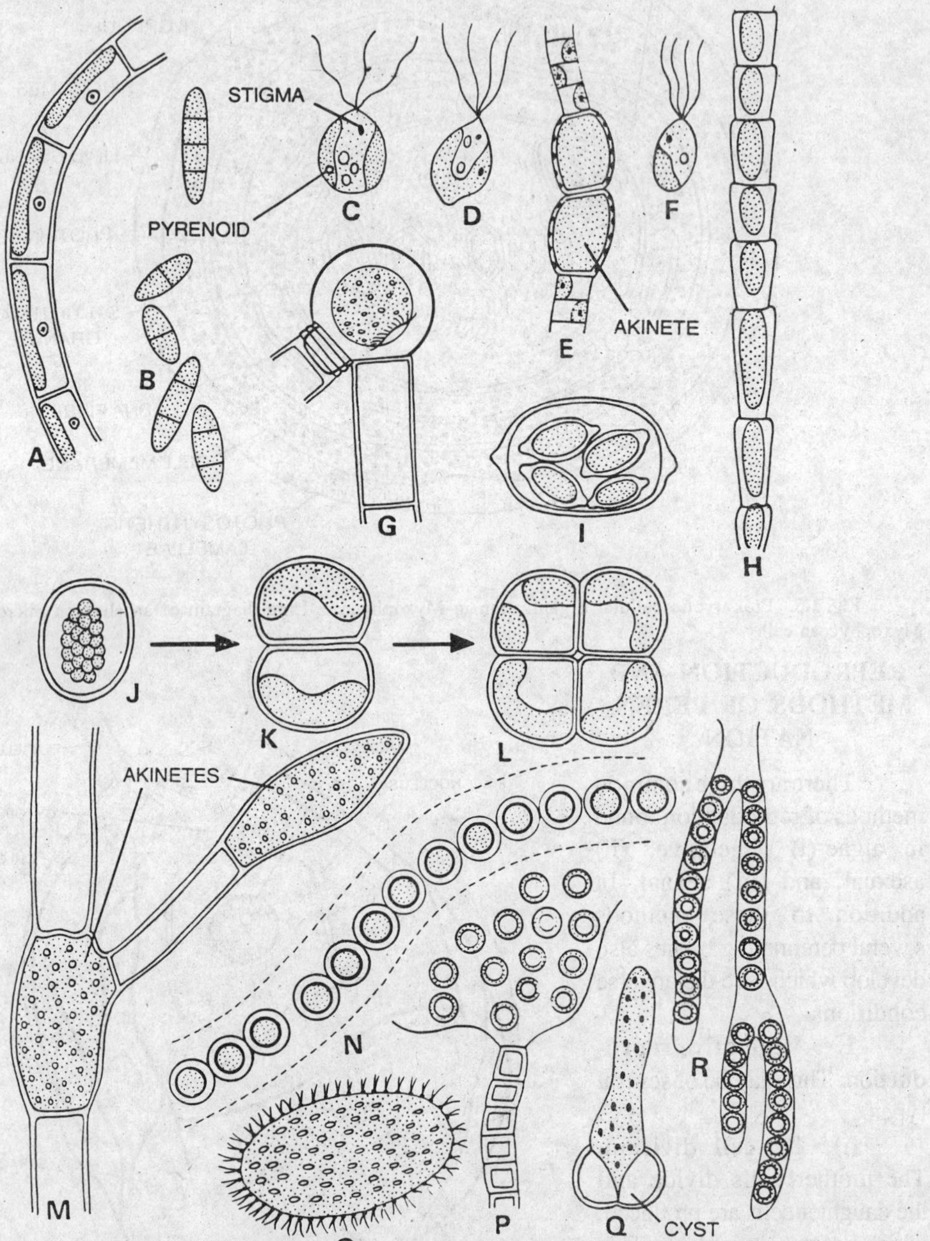

Fig. 1.7. Reproduction. Vegetative and Asexual. A filament of *Hormidium;* B, fragments of same; C, D and F, zoospores (swarmers) of *Ulothrix;* E, akinetes of *Ulothrix idiospora;* G, zoospore of *Oedogonium* sp.; I, autospores of *Oocystis lacustris;* H, akinetes of *Oedogonium;* J-L, cell division in *Pleurococcus* sp.; M, akinetes of *Pithophora;* N, akinetes of *Ulothrix oscillarina;* O, synzoospore of *Vaucheria;* P, palmella stage in *Ulothrix;* Q, germination of cyst in *Vaucheria;* R, akinetes of *Botrydium.*

cells, such pieces are called **'hormogones'**. Each hormogone develops into a new plant, *e.g.*, *Oscillatoria, Nostoc* etc.

(iv) Hormospores or hormocysts. They are thick-walled hormogones, and produced in somewhat drier conditions.

(v) By adventitious thalli. Certain special structures of thalli are formed which help in vegetative reproduction. The well known **propagula** of *Bryopsis, Sphacelaria* and *Nereocystis* are good examples.

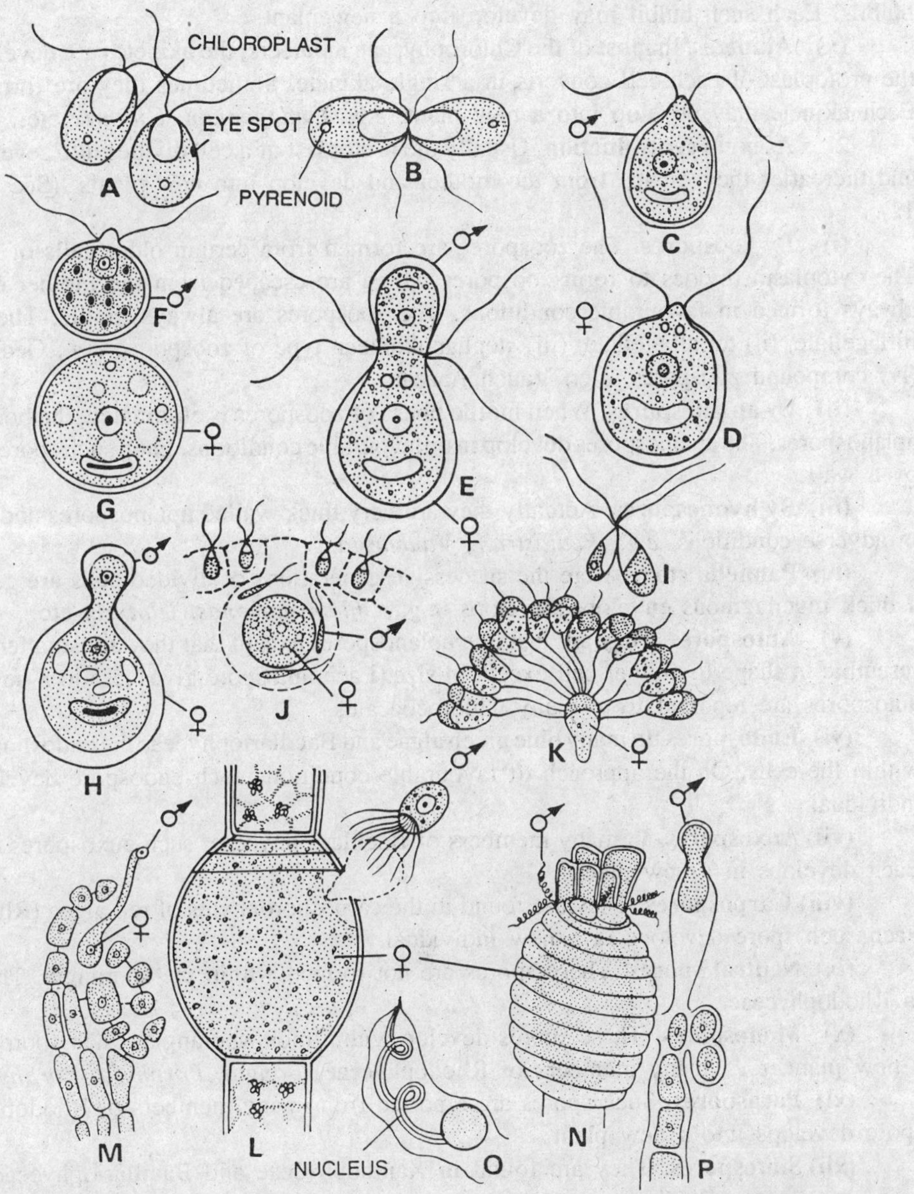

Fig. 1.8. Reproduction. Sexual. A, two gametes of same size (isogametes); B, fusion of same (isogamy); C and D, two gametes of different size (male and female); E, fusion of same (anisogamy); F and G, male and female gametes; H, fusion of same (oogamy); I, anisogamy in *Enteromorpha intestinalis;* J, oogamy in *Volvox;* K, clump formation in *Ectocarpus,* large female is surrounded by male gametes; L, oogamy in *Oedogonium;* M, advanced oogamy in *Polysiphonia;* N, oogamy, in *Chara;* O, antherozoid of *Chara;* P, oogamy in *Batrachospermum.*

(vi) By primary secondary protonema. Such thread-like vegetative bodies develop in the case of *Chara,* which help in reproduction.

(vii) Tubers. Usually these bodies are rounded and filled up with abundance of starch. Each body may give rise to a new plant, *e.g., Chara.*

(viii) Starch or amylum stars. Such special star-shaped starch filled bodies give rise to new plants frequently reported from *Chara.*

(ix) Bulbils. Small bud-like structures. Usually develop on the rhizoids of *Chara* are called bulbils. Each such bulbil may develop into a new plant.

(x) Akinetes. In most of the Chlorophyceae members, the akinetes are developed. Usually the protoplast of each cell converts in a single akinete. Sometimes they are formed in chains. Each akinete may develop into a new plant, *e.g., Oedogonium, Ulothrix* etc.

2. Asexual reproduction. Usually the protoplast of a cell divides into several protoplasts and thereafter they escape from the mother and develop into new plants. (See fig. 1.7 on p. 12).

(i) By zoospores. The zoospores are formed from certain older cells of the filaments. The cytoplasm divides to form zoospores which are escaped from the mother cell. They are always formed in favourable conditions. The zoospores are always motile. They may be (i) biflagellate, (ii) tetraflagellate, (iii) stephanokontean type of zoospores, *e.g.*, Oedogoniales and (iv) compound zoospores, *e.g.*, Vaucheriaceae.

(ii) By aplanospores. When motile phase of zoospores is eliminated, the bodies are called aplanospores. The aplanospores develop in unfavourable conditions. Each such spore is surrounded by a wall.

(iii) By hypnospores. Actually they are very thick-walled aplanospores and develop only in adverse conditions, *e.g., Pediastrum, Vaucheria.*

(iv) Palmella stage. Here the successive generations of divided cells are gelatinized and a thick mucilaginous envelope develops, *e.g., Chlamydomonas, Ulothrix* etc.

(v) Autospores. They are just like aplanospores except that they are smaller in size. They resemble in shape to mother cell except in size. Each autospore gives rise to a new plant. Such autospores are reported from many Chlorococcales.

(vi) Endospores. In many blue green algae and Bacillariophyceae the endospores are formed within the cells. On the approach of favourable conditions each endospore develops in a new individual.

(vii) Auxospores. In many members of Bacillariophyceae, such auxospores are produced. Each develops in a new plant.

(viii) Carpospores. They are found in the carposporophytes of red algae (Rhodophyceae). Each such spore develops in a new individual.

(ix) Neutral spores. These spores are not formed within the sporangia. They are found in Rhodophyceae.

(x) Monospores. These spores develop within monosporangia. Each spore gives rise to a new plant, *e.g.*, many members of Rhodophyceae (*Bangia, Porphyra, Porphyridium* etc).

(xi) Paraspores. Such spores are reported from many members of Rhodophyceae. Each spore develops into a new plant.

(xii) Statospores. They are found in Xanthophyceae and Bacillariophyceae where they act as perennating bodies.

(xiii) Daughter colonies. In many Volvocales and Chlorococcales the daughter colonies are developed asexually, *e.g., Volvox, Hydrodictyon, Pediastrum* etc.

(xiv) Gongrosira stage of Vaucheria. In the aseptate filaments of *Vaucheria,* the protoplast divides into several parts, several hypnospores or cysts are produced and the whole filament looks like an algal form *'Gongrosira'*.

(xv) Microspores. They are produced in many Bacillariophyceae.

3. Sexual reproduction. It is greatly advanced method of reproduction and not known in Myxophyceae (blue green algae). There are two main types, *i.e.,* 1. isogamy and 2. heterogamy.

1. Isogamy. The fusion of similar motile gametes is found in many species. Usually the gametes taking part in fusion come from two different individuals or filaments, sometimes these gametes come from two different cells of the same filament. Thousands of gametes come and aggregate in clumps. (See fig. 1.8 on page 13).

2. Heterogamy. The fusion of dissimilar gemetes is called heterogamy. There are variations of it.

(a) Anisogamy. The motile gametes taking part in fusion may either differ in size (morphological anisogamy) or physiological behaviour (physiological anisogamy).

(b) Oogamy. In this case the male antherozoid fuses with the female egg. This fusion may be of primitive type as found in *Cylindrocapsa,* or advanced type as in *Oedogonium, Vaucheria, Chara, Polysiphonia* etc.

3. Aplanogamy or conjugation. It implies the fusion of two non-flagellate amoeboid gametes (aplanogametes). They are morphologically similar but physiologically dissimilar, *e.g.,* order Conjugales.

In fresh water algae, the sexual reproduction is best means of perennation because it is followed by the formation of thick-walled zygote or oospore.

Conditions for sexual reproduction. (a) The sexual reproduction takes place after considerable accumulation of food material and the climax of vegetative activity is over.

(b) The bright light is the major factor for the production of the gametes.

(c) A suitable pH value is required.

(d) The optimum temperature is necessary.

Parthenogenesis. The female gametes convert into **zygotes** without fusion. The resultants are called **azygospores** or **parthenospores** and the phenomenon 'parthenogenesis'. *e.g., Spirogyra, Oedogonium* and many others.

Autogamy. In this phenomenon the fusion of the daughter protoplasts or of the divided nuclei of a cell without liberation takes place. This process is known in many diatoms and colourless dinoflagellates.

TABLE 1.1

COMPARATIVE ACCOUNT OF RANGE IN CELL ORGANIZATION (CELL WALL AND CYTOPLASM) IN CHLOROPHYCEAE, BACILLARIOPHYCEAE, PHAEOPHYCEAE, RHODOPHYCEAE AND MYXOPHYCEAE

Classes	Cell Wall	Cytoplasm
Chlorophyceae	2 or 3 layered; innermost layer of cellulose and second one of pectic compounds; outermost layer of *Oedogonium* and *Cladophora* is chitinous; callose (in Siphonales); outermost wall layer slimy (in *Spirogyra*).	2 or more contractile vacuoles in motile cells; single large central vacuole in each cell of filamentous forms; vacuole contains cell sap and tannins; cytoplasmic connections present in *Volvox*.

Classes	Cell Wall	Cytoplasm
Bacillariophyceae	Cell wall or protoplast + cell wall = frustule; it consists of two overlapping pieces, upper half **epitheca,** lower half **hypotheca;** it consists of pectin; highly silicified; deposition of silica forms definite patterns in the cell wall; unthickened areas are **punctae;** sometimes round **pits** arranged radially; deep pits are known as areolae; longitudinal **raphe** may or may not be present.	Thick layer of cytoplasm just beneath the cell wall; large central vacuole present; central bridge of cytoplasm in Pennales.
Phaeophyceae	2-layered; inner layer of cellulose and outer layer of mucilaginous substance (algin, fucoidin etc.); callose (in *Laminaria digitata*); special mucilage ducts (in Laminariales).	Less viscous; numerous vacuoles within the cytoplasm of cell; each cell of *Dictyota* and *Fucus* contains single large vacuole; cell sap contains colloidal substances; special bodies, fucosan vesicles present in meristematic, photosynthetic and reproductive cells.
Rhodophyceae	2-layered; inner layer of cellulose and outer of pectic substance; sometimes cell wall contains iodine; cell wall stratified in Ceramiaceae.	Highly viscous; conspicuous central vacuole in Florideae; no central vacuole in Bangiales; cell sap alkaline or neutral, rarely acidic; cytoplasmic pit connections present except in Bangiales; pit membrane remains surrounded by a disc of pectic material.
Myxophyceae	2-layered; inner layer of cellulose and outer of pectic substance; complete cell filled up with cytoplasm.	Complete cell filled up with cytoplasm; outer peripheral pigmented region is **chromoplasm** and the central colourless region the **centroplasm** or central body; cytoplasm is viscous and gel-like; true vacuoles absent; pseudovacuoles present in the chromoplasm of many cells.

TABLE 1.2

COMPARATIVE ACCOUNT OF RANGE IN CELL ORGANIZATION (NUCLEUS, PLASTIDS, PIGMENTS AND PYRENOIDS) IN CHLOROPHYCEAE, BACILLARIOPHYCEAE, PHAEOPHYCEAE, RHODOPHYCEAE AND MYXOPHYCEAE

Classes	Nucleus	Plastids and Pigments	Pyrenoids
Chlorophyceae	Usually cells are uninucleate; multinucleate (in *Cladophora*); coenocytic condition in *Vaucheria*;nucleolus present within nucleus; centrosomes presnet in *Volvox, Cladophora* and *Vaucheria.*	Various types of chloroplasts; chlamydomonad type is common in Volvocales; stellate in *Zygnema;* spiral in *Spirogyra;* reticulate in *Oedogonium, Cladophora;* discoid in *Chlamydomonas alpina.*	Pyrenoids found in chloroplasts of all Chlorophyceae except *Chara, Vaucheria* and *Microspora.*

Bacillariophyceae	Nucleus present in the centre of cytoplasmic bridge; there is a plate-like structure on either side of nucleus; a centrosome present on one side of nucleus; nucleus diploid in many Pennales.	Chromatophores remain embedded in cytoplasmic layer in some forms single chromatophore present; chromatophores of various shapes in different species; golden brown colour; chlorophylls *a* and *c*, xanthaophylls, diatomin, β carotene.	Pyrenoids are without starch sheath and remain embedded in the chromatophore; they function as elaioplasts and form oil.
Phaeophyceae	Usually uninucleate cells, multinucleate condition rare; nucleus quite large in size with less amount of chromatin; one or two nucleoli in each nucleus; nuclei vacuolate in Fucales; extra or intranuclear centrosome; number of chromosomes 8-32.	Chromatophores brown, discoid and parietal one or many chromatophores per cell; chlorophylls *a* and *b*, xanthophylls, carotenoids, phycoxanthin overmasks the other pigments.	Pyrenoids usually attached to the inner margins of chromatophores; usually stalked and attached laterally to the chromatophores.
Rhodophyceae	Cells uninucleate (in Cryptonemiales, Bangiales etc.); cells multinucleate (in Ceramiales, Rhodymeniales etc.); one or more nucleoli in each nucleus; well developed chromatin network.	Single stellate chromatophore in each cell (in Bangiales); in majority of cases the number of chromatophores is more than one per cell; band-like chromatophores in Ceramiaceae; irregularly lobed or discoid, *e.g., Polysiphonia; r*-phycocyanin, *r*-phycoerythrin, xanthophylls, β carotene, chlorophylls *a* and *b* (in traces).	Each chromatophore contains a pyrenoid without starch sheath.
Myxophyceae	True nucleus absent; chromatin present in central body that consists of DNA, RNA and protein.	Chromatophores absent; pigments dispersed in chromoplasm; pigments are phycocyanin, phycoerythrin, carotenes, xanthophylls and chlorophyll *a*.	

TABLE 1.3

COMPARATIVE STUDY OF VEGETATIVE REPRODUCTION IN ALGAE

	Chlorophyceae	Phaeophyceae	Rhodophyceae	Myxophyceae
Cell Division	The mother cells divide to form daughter cells that act as new individuals, *e.g., Pleurococcus*, desmids and diatoms.			Only method of propagation in Chroococcales.

	Chlorophyceae	Phaeophycease	Rhodophyceae	Myxophyceae
Fragmentation	The plant body breaks into fragments each fragment develops into a new plant, *e.g.*, *Ulothrix, Cladophora, Oedogonium, Spirogyra, Vaucheria* etc.	Fragmentation of thalli takes place in many species, *e.g.*, *Sargassum;* special fragments, the **propagula,** occur in *Sphacelaria.*	Fragmentation takes place in majority of Rhodophyceae, *e.g., Polysiphonia, Batrachospermum.*	Fragementation of colony, *e.g.*, *Nostoc, Anabaena* etc; fragmentaion of filaments *e.g.*, Oscillatoriaceae; when trichomes are fragmented **hormogones** are formed, *e.g.*, Nostocales; when large quantity of food material is accumulated in the cells of hormogones, they are called **hormospores** or **hormocysts,** *e.g., Westiella;* each above-mentioned structure develops into a new plant.
Protonema	Development of thread-like bodies that bear new plants on them, *e.g., Chara.*	—	—	—
Stolons	Cell of decaying rhizoids filled up with starch, these structures develop into new plants next season, *e.g., Chara, Cladophora.*	—	—	—
Tubers and Bulbils	Starch filled bodies developing on rhizoids, each such structure develops into a new plant, *e.g., Chara, Cladophora.*	—	—	—
Akinetes	The protoplast of a cell becomes round and thick-walled. Each such structure develops into a new plant in favourable conditions, *e.g., Oedogonium, Ulothrix, Cladophora* etc.	—	—	Akinetes develop in unfavourable conditions; such thick walled akinetes are also known as **arthrospores** or **resting spores,** *e.g., Nostoc.* The akinete develops into new plant in favourable conditions.
Amylum Stars	Star-shaped, starch filled bodies, each such structure develops into a new plant, *e.g., Chara.*	—	—	—

	Chlorophyceae	Phaeophycease	Rhodophyceae	Myxophyceae
Adventitious buds	—	The adventitious buds develop by the division of meristematic cells in young plants, *e.g., Fucus.*	—	—

PIGMENTATION

Various pigments, such as red, yellow, green and blue have been found in various marine and fresh water algae. Usually these pigments are found in special plastids called chromatophores, however, in Myxophyceae the chromatophores are not found, and the pigments are dispersed in peripheral chromoplasm. Only, because of the presence of these conspicuous pigments the algae look variously coloured in their habitats. Besides, several algae are colourless and more or less saprophytic in nature. Colourless algae have been reported from several major groups. There are colourless diatoms, colourless dinoflagellates, colourless Chlorophyceae and colourless Rhodophyceae. The principal pigment chlorophyll has been reported from all major groups of algae. Besides, carotenoids, xanthophylls and phycobilins are also found in various algae.

Principal kinds of algal pigments. There are three main groups of principal algal pigments. They are as follows:

1. The chlorophylls. They are green fat soluble pigments and universally present in green and other algae.

2. The carotenoids. They are fat soluble yellow pigments and present in various groups of algae. They are subdivided into three groups: (i) carotenes; (ii) xanthophylls or oxycarotenes; and (iii) carotenoid acids.

3. The phycobilins. They are water soluble blue and red pigments. The phycobilins are subdivided into two groups, *i.e.,* (i) the phycocyanins and (ii) phycoerythrins.

Properties of chlorophylls. The algal chlorophylls are (i) green, (ii) in solution the chlorophylls are fluorescent and emit red light, (iii) they are also distinguished by strong absorption of the blue-green and green colours.

Properties of carotenoids. As stated the carotenoids are subdivided into three groups, *i.e.,* (i) carotenes; (ii) xanthophylls and (iii) carotenoid acids. The properties are as follows:

1. Carotenes. (i) They are unsaturated hydrocarbons; (ii) they absorb blue and green light and transmit the yellow and red; (iii) they are fat soluble and yellow in colour.

2. Xanthophylls. They are also named as oxycarotenes. They are oxygen derivatives of carotenes and resemble the properties of carotenes.

3. Carotenoid acids. They consist of a chain of carbon atoms. Their properties resemble the properties of other two carotenoids.

Properties of phycobilins. The phycobilins are subdivided into two groups, *i.e.,* (i) phycocyanins and (ii) phycoerythrins.

The phycobilins are proteins. They are soluble in water and insoluble in the fat solvents. They are strongly fluorescent and emit orange or red light.

(1) **Phycocyanins.** They absorb green, yellow, and red light and trasmit the blue.

(2) **Phycoerythrins.** They absorb blue green, green and yellow light and transmit the red.

All the phycobilins are strongly fluorescent and emit orange or red light.

Table 1.4

Pigments	Chloro-phyceae	Xan-thophyceae	Bacillario-phyceae	Phaeo-phyceae	Rhodo-phyceae	Myxo-phyceae
Chlorophylls :						
Chlorophyll a	AAA	AAA	AAA	AAA	AAA	AAA
Chlorophyll b	AA	O	O	O	O	O
Chlorophyll c	O	O	A	A	O	O
Chlorophyll d	O	O	O	O	A	O
Chlorophyll e	O	A	O	O	O	O
Carotenes:						
α Carotene	A	O	O	O	A	O
β Carotene	AAA	AAA	AAA	AAA	AAA	AAA
e Carotene	O	O	A	O	O	O
Flavicin	O	O	O	O	O	A
Xanthophylls :						
Lutein	AAA	O	O	O	AA	O
Zeaxanthin	A	O	O	O	O	O
Violaxanthin	A	O	O	A	O	O
Flavoxanthin	O	O	O	A	O	O
Neoxanthin	A	O	O	A	O	O
Fucoxanthin	O	O	AA	AA	O	O
Neofucoxanthin A	O	O	A	A	O	O
Neofucoxanthin B	O	O	A	A	O	O
Diatoxanthin	O	O	A	O	O	O
Diadinoxanthin	O	O	A	O	O	O
Dinoxanthin	O	O	O	O	O	O
Neodinoxanthin	O	O	O	O	O	O
Peridinin	O	O	O	O	O	O
Myxoxanthin	O	O	O	O	O	A
Myxoxanthophyll	O	O	O	O	O	AA
Unnamed		AA		A		AAA
Phycobilins:						
r-Phycoerythrin	O	O	O	O	AAA	O
r-Phycocyanin	O	O	O	O	A	O
c-Phycoerythrin	O	O	O	O	O	A
c-Phycocyanin	O	O	O	O	O	AAA

AAA–Indicates the principal pigment in each of the four groups of pigments.

AA–Indicates a pigment comprising less than half of the total pigments of the group.

A–Indicates a pigment comprising a small fraction of the total pigments of the group.

O–Indicates absence of a pigment.

Occurrence of principal pigments in algae. All autotrophic algae contain chlorophylls, carotenoids and xanthophylls. The Myxophyceae and Rhodophyceae contain phycobilins which overmask the other pigments. Phycobilins are always associated with other pigments such as chlorophylls and carotenoids.

Occurrence of individual pigments in algae. In **Chlorophyceae** chlorophyll (α chlorophylls), β carotene (carotenoids) and lutein (xanthophylls) are present as principal pigments. Besides, other chlorophylls, carotenoids and xanthophylls are also found.

Xanthophyceae. Chlorophyll, α and β-carotene are present as principal pigments. Xanthophylls are also found.

Bacillariophyceae. Chlorophyll, α and β-carotene are found as principal pigments. In addition to these several xanthophylls have also been reported.

Phaeophyceae. Chlorophyll, α, β-carotene and several xanthophylls are found.

Rhodophyceae. Chlorophyll, α, β–carotene and *r*-phycoerythrin are found as principal pigments. In addition to these chlorophyll *d*, α carotene, lutein and *r*-phycocyanin are also found.

Myxophyceae. Chlorophyll, α, β-carotene and *c*-phycocyanin are principal pigments. Besides, *c*-phycoerythrin and xanthophylls are also found.

ORIGIN AND EVOLUTION OF SEX IN ALGAE

Primarily there are two methods of reproduction in plant, *i.e.*, **asexual** and **sexual.** In asexual type of reproduction no sex is involved and there is no fusion of any kind of gametes or cells. This type of reproduction is being effected by special cells known as **spores.** Each such spore is capable to develop into a new plant. On the other hand, in sexual reproduction the two cells or the gametes unite together, and the zygote is resulted, which develops into a new plant. Normally, the individual gametes are incapable to produce new plants without fusion.

Origin of sex. The most primitive algae, *i.e.*, the members of Cyanophyceae (Myxophyceae), *e.g.*, *Gloeocapsa, Chroococcus* etc., reproduce by means of fusion, whereas *Oscillatoria, Nostoc, Anabaena,* etc., reproduce vegetatively, by means of a group of few cells called **hormogonia,** which later on give rise to new plants by further division. Some members of Cyanophyceae reproduce by means of **arthrospores.** This shows that all the blue-green algae reproduce asexually and the sexual reproduction is altogether absent. In rest of algae, whether unicellular or filamentous, both asexual and sexual methods of reproduction prevail.

It is thought that probably the gametes have been originated from the motile asexual spores or zoospores. Except few cases, the sexual reproduction has not replaced the asexual method but has been added as a supplementary method. The zoospores usually resemble the gametes exc ɔt for their size. For example in algae such as *Chlamydomonas, Ulothrix, Cladophora* etc., it is thought that the zoospores were probably produced before the gametes originated. In above-mentioned and many other filamentous forms, the asexual reproduction takes place by means of uninucleate and biflagellate zoospores which are formed by repeated division of contents of the ordinary vegetative cell. The zoospores are produced, in favourable conditions. In adverse conditions the gametes are formed in the vegetative cells which earlier produced zoospores in favourable conditions. The gametes are quite similar to zoospores but for their size and behaviour. In forms like *Chlamydomonas debaryanum* the zoospores and gametes are quite similar. In *Ulothrix* two types of zoospores, *i.e.*, the micro – and the macrozoospores, are produced and the gametes are produced in the same manner as the zoospores are formed. The microzoospores are quite similar to the gametes. At the end of the season, when the plants run in the shortage of food and other favourable conditions, the cells begin to produce gametes. Cholnosky, however, advocates that the gametes in *Ulothrix variabilis* develop from potential zoospores which fail to escape and undergo more divisions to give rise to the gametes. According to him, the gametes are quite similar except their size and number of flagella. In *Oedogonium,* the gametes and the zoospores are quite similar except their size.

One can conclude, that the gametes are formed as a result of aging of cells and unfavourable conditions. It may be said that the gametes are the reduced type of zoospores. Such reduced zoospores cannot reproduce asexually. They can give rise to a new offspring only with the result of fusion and formation of the zygote. All these examples support that the gametes have been originated from zoospores by means of reduction.

Evolution of sex. The members of Myxophyceae do not show any trace of sexuality. In other classes of algae the sexuality has been established. Now to trace out the evolution of sex in algae, it becomes necessary to know about the nature of the gametes in beginning. It is thought, that in the beginning the gametes were of similar shape and size. These gametes were morphologically identical, but physiologically different, *e.g.*, in *Ulothrix* and certain species of *Chlamydomonas,* the gametes are of plus and minus strains. This is known as **isogamy.** Thereafter **anisogamy** developed. In this process the two uniting gametes are of different sizes, *e.g.,* in *Chlamydomonas braunii* and *Pandorina.* In this condition, the number of divisions in one cell is more or less than the other cell, and therefore, the uniting gametes are unequal in size. Thereafter developed **oogamy.** The oogamy is the highly evolved condition of heterogamy. In oogamy, one cell does not divide at all, it simply increases in size, accumulates sufficient food material and acts as female cell or egg. The other cell divides repeatedly producing small motile cells, acting as male gametes. However, in *Polysiphonia* the resultant male gametes are non-motile. Less evolved oogamy is found in *Chlamydomonas coccifera, Volvox* and *Oedogonium.*

The evolution of sex in algae has not taken place in any one phylogenetic line. This has taken place along several independent lines. The example of this statement is found in Volvocales, where *Gonium* is isogamous, *Pandorina* slightly anisogamous, *Eudorina* and *Pleodorina* marked by anisogamous and *Volvox* oogamous. This *Gonium-Pandorina-Eudorina-Pleodorina-Volvox* series also shows progressive somatic differentiation. It has been assumed that it is correlated with the evolution from isogamy to oogamy through anisogamy. Whereas on the other hand, in another genus of Volvocales, *i.e., Chlamydomonas,* where species within the genus show all gradations from isogamy to oogamy, *e.g., Chlamydomonas snowiae* is isogamous, *C. braunii* is anisogamous and *C. coccifera* is oogamous.

In a few green algae, such as *Spirogyra, Vaucheria, Chara* and in nearly all the brown and red algae a far more advanced condition has been reached. In *Spirogyra,* the two uniting gametes are produced inside the ordinary vegetative cells known as gametangia. The gametangia are not differentiated into male and female structures. Those which receive the contents are supposed to be female ones while those from which the contents pass out are supposed to be male ones. In *Vaucheria* the gametes are borne in well differentiated gametangia, known as antheridia and oogonia. The antheridia produce antherozoids and the oogonium contains an egg. In *Chara,* there is further advancement. Here the sex organs are not developed all over the plant body, but are confined to nodes on the branches of limited growth. The male and female sex organs are highly developed and specialized organs known as globule and nucule respectively. The spermatogenous filaments develop within globule while the nucule possesses an egg.

In brown algae, *Fucus* and *Sargassum* possess fertile conceptacles on the receptacles which contain male and female sex organs. The oogonia may be liberated even before fertilization, and the fertilization takes place in the water. *Fucus* contains eight eggs in its oogonium whereas in *Sargassum* seven eggs degenerate but one. The highest evolution of sex in algae has been seen in the red algae. In *Polysiphonia,* the male spermatia are nonmotile. After their liberation, the spermatia are carried away to the female by means of water currents. From these examples it becomes quite clear, that there is no evolutionary sequence in the evolution of sex in algae. It is thought that it developed and evolved independently in green, brown and red algae.

In conclusion, we can say that the sex has been developed in response to circumstances and gametes have been developed from zoospores by means of reduction. The isogamy gave rise to oogamy through anisogamy. During oogamy the female sex organ increases in size and stores food material to face adverse weather conditions, whereas, the male sex organ gives rise to numerous male gametes which ensure fertilization. The most important feature of sexual reproduction is the union of two gametic nuclei, which results in the formation of a diploid zygote nucleus. Sooner or later reduction division takes place which provides a means of reshuffling of paternal and maternal chromosomes brought together during the act of fertilization.

Asexual reproduction results in organic similarity while sexual reproduction in diversity. The sexual reproduction is not primarily meant for the multiplication of individuals. It is actually meant for reproduction of heritable variations that accelerate the process of evolution.

LIFE-CYCLE PATTERNS IN ALGAE

Many life-cycle patterns are found in algae. However, there is no regular and fixed alternation of generations, as found in higher plants. In blue-green algae, and certain Chlorophyceae (*e.g., Protococcus, Scenedesmus* etc.) which reproduce asexually, there is no alternation of generations.

The representative life-cycle patterns in algae are as follows:

1. Haplontic type. This is the simplest and most primitive type of life-cycle. The other patterns of life-cycle have originated from this type. This type is found in all Chlorophyceae except a few. Sometimes this is called *Ulothrix* or Chlamydomonad type.

In such cases the somatic phase (plant) is haploid (gametophyte) while the diploid phase (sporophyte) is represented by zygote. During germination the zygote (2n) divides meiotically producing haploid (n) zoospores, which develop into individual plants. Here the unicellular (*e.g., Chlamydomonas*) or filamentous (*e.g., Ulothrix, Spirogyra, Oedogonium, Chara* etc.) gametophyte (n) alternates with a one-celled zygote or sporophyte (2n). The haploid filamentous plants are known as *haplonts* which reproduce asexually by zoospores or aplanospores producing the individuals like parents.

2. Diplontic type. This pattern is reverse of haplontic type. In this case somatic phase (plant) is diploid (sporophyte 2n) while the haploid phase (gametophyte n) is restricted to gametes which are produced by meiotic division. After gametic union a diploid zygote is formed, which develops into a diploid (sporophyte 2n) plant by mitotic divisions. The well known examples of this pattern are – *Fucus, Sargassum, Codium, Bryopsis* etc.

3. Isomorphic type. In this type there are two exactly similar (*morphologically identical*) somatic phases (plants) showing alternation of generations. Here the one phase is diploid (sporophyte 2n) while the other haploid (gametophyte n). Among Chlorophyceae this is found in Ulvaceae, Chaetophoraceae and Cladophoraceae. The orders Ectocarpales, Cutleriales, Tilopteridales, Sphacelariales and Dictyotales of Phaeophyceae also exhibit this pattern of life-cycle.

In such cases, the zygote develops into a diploid multicellular plant (sporophyte) by postponement of meiosis. Prior to zoospore (meiospore) formation there is meiosis. These zoospores (n) develop into haploid plants (gametophyte n). The haploid plants produce gametes (n) which after fusion develop into zygotes (2n).

4. Heteromorphic type. This pattern of life cycle is exactly like that of preceding one (isomorphic type) only with the difference that the alternating haploid (n) and diploid (2n) somatic phases (plant) are *morphologically different*. In such cases the diploid multicellular sporophytic plant produces haploid zoospores (meiospores) by meiosis. These zoospores develop into game-

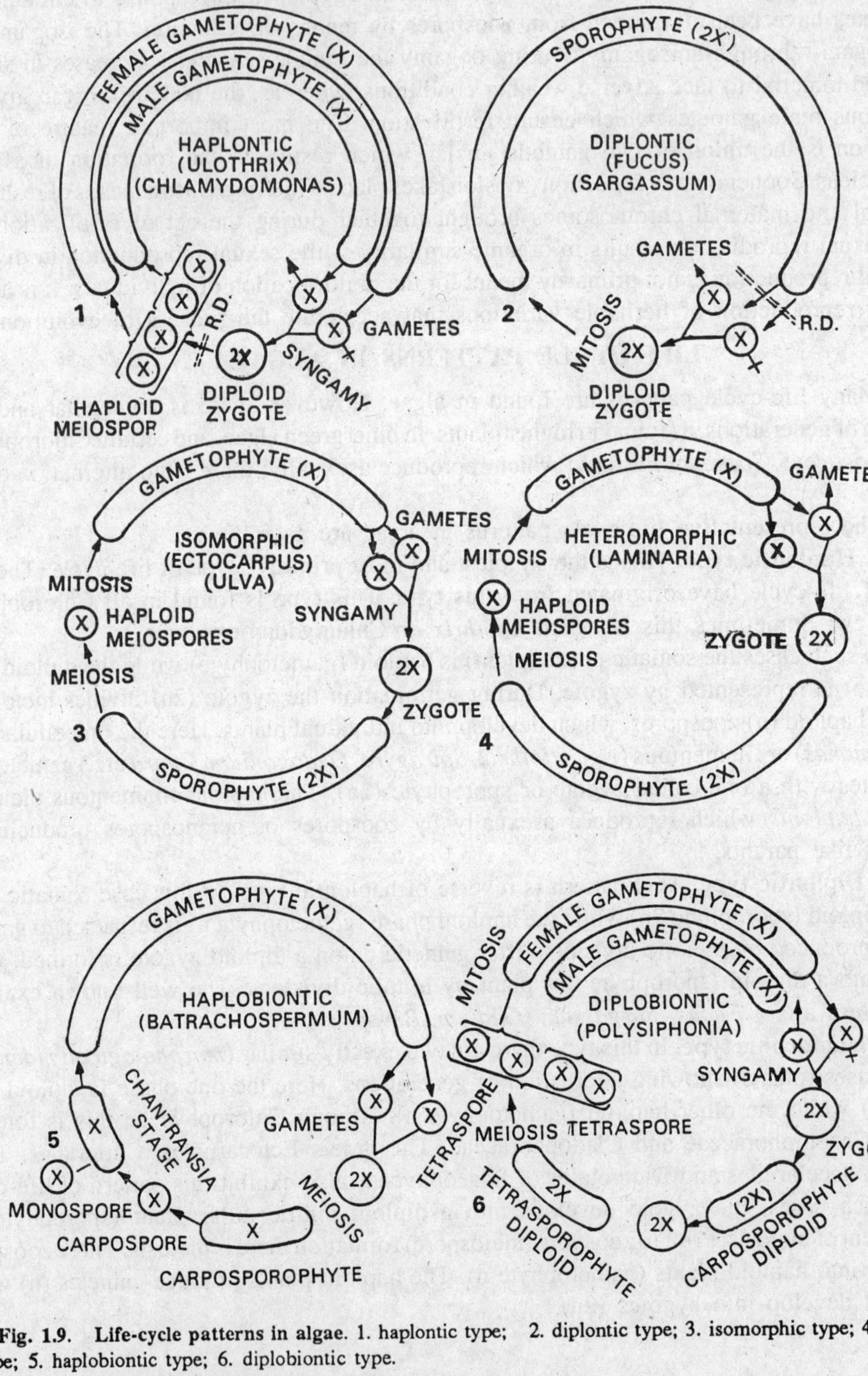

Fig. 1.9. Life-cycle patterns in algae. 1. haplontic type; 2. diplontic type; 3. isomorphic type; 4. heteromorphic type; 5. haplobiontic type; 6. diplobiontic type.

tophytes. Each gametophytic plant (n) produces gametes which after their union form a zygote and the latter develops into a diploid sporophytic plant by mitotic divisions. This pattern is found in Laminariales, Sporochnales, Desmarestiales etc., of Phaeophyceae and *Urospora* of Chlorophyceae.

5. Haplobiontic type. In this pattern there are three phases in the life-cycle. Out of three, two phases are haploid (n) and one diploid (2n). The examples are found among Nemalionales (*e.g., Batrachospermum*) of Rhodophyceae, and *Coleochaete* of Chlorophyceae. For example, in *Batrachospermum* a haploid gametophytic phase produces gametes which on fusion form a zygote (2n). The latter is the only diploid phase which divides meiotically forming a haploid asexual phase known as carposporophyte. The latter reproduces asexually by haploid carpospores which again develop into gametophytes (haploid plants n). Thus two morphologically different haploid phases (gametophyte and carposporophyte) alternate with the zygote (2n).

6. Diplobiontic type. This type of life-cycle is found in almost all Rhodophyceae except Nemalionales. The most common example is *Polysiphonia* of order Ceramiales. Here the life-cycle is triphasic and involves an alternation of two diploid (2n) or sporophytic generations, *i.e.,* carposporophyte and tetrasporophyte with one haploid (n) or gametophytic generation. Thus there are two diploid phases and one haploid phase. The gametophyte produces gametes which unite and form a zygote (2n). Now the zygote divides mitotically forming a carposporophyte (2n) bearing diploid (2n) carpospores. On germination these diploid carpospores form another diploid plant, the tetrasporophyte. The latter produces tetraspores by meiosis. The haploid tetraspores germinate and give rise to haploid gametophytic plants.

Thus, there are several patterns of life-cycle in algae, and there is no regular and fixed alternation of generations, as found in higher plants.

ALTERNATION OF GENERATIONS IN ALGAE

In algae, there is no regular and fixed alternation of generations, as found in higher plants. In all blue green algae, and some Chlorophyceae, such as *Protococcus, Scenedesmus* etc., the reproduction is sexual type, and there is no alternation of generations. In the case of simple unicellular Chlorophyceae, such as *Chlamydomonas, Sphaerella* etc., which reproduce sexually, there is no distinct sporophytic generation. In such cases the zygote is regarded as a sporophyte, because it is diploid (2n) and during germination undergoes reduction division, producing gametophyte. The life cycle of such primitive algae consists of an alternation of generations of one-celled haploid phase with a one-celled diploid phase.

The above-mentioned primitive type of life-cycle is succeeded by such type of cycle in which the haploid phase, *i.e.,* gametophyte is filamentous showing vegetative cell division and alternates with a one-celled diploid phase, *i.e.,* sporophyte, *e.g.,* in *Oedogonium, Ulothrix, Spirogyra, Zygnema* etc. The haploid filamentous plants, are known as **haplonts** reproduce asexually by means of zoospores or aplanospores. In the case of *Bryopsis* and *Codium* of Siphonales, there is an alternation of generations of one-celled haploid phase with diploid coenocyte or siphonous filament, which is supposed to be morphologically equivalent multicellular diploid generation or **diplont.** In the life cycle of certain Ulvaceae and Cladophoraceae there is an alternative of many-celled haploid generation with a many-celled diploid generation. In such cases the two alternating generations are morphologically identical, *i.e.,* **isomorphic,** and cannot be distinguished from each other until the time of reproduction. In Ulvaceae and Cladophoraceae the meiosis in the zygote is delayed and the nuclei in the cell of the diploid plants usually do not divide reductionally until the plant is fully mature. Meiosis may take place in the nuclei of all the cells of diploid plant, such as, in *Ulva* or may be restricted to the terminal actively growing cell, at the branch apices as in *Cladophora.* In one species of *Cladophora, i.e., Cladophora glomerata,* reduction division does not occur in the development of the zoospores. The zoospores remain diploid like the plant that produces them. They are true asexual spores. In *C.glomerata,* meiosis occurs in the development of isogametes, which are consequently haploid. The zygote formed with the result of conjugation is diploid so that the haploid generation is represented only by the isogametes. In this way two types of life-cycles occur in different species of *Cladophora.*

In one of the brown algae, *i.e., Dictyota* the two generations are morphologically identical but physiologically different. In this case a flat ribbon-like sexual plant is identical with an asexual plant. The sexual plants which are haploid and bear antheridia or oogonia, whereas, the asexual plant which is produced from the oospore is diploid and shows reduction division (meiosis) of the spore mother cell during tetraspore formation. The tetraspores are haploid and produce the haploid sexual plants which bear antheridia or oogonia on their germination. Such type of life cycle bears only two phases, *i.e.,* diploid and haploid and is known as biphasic life-cycle. This type of alternation of generations is known as **isomorphic** or **homologous.** The life-cycle of *Ectocarpus* is also of isomorphic type, where the gametophyte and sporophyte are alike.

In other brown algae the two alternating generations are quite dissimilar. For example, in *Laminaria,* the sporophyte is a large complex plant and male and female gametophytes are simple and small. The type of life-cycle is also biphasic but the type of alternation of generations is **heteromorphic,** as the two phases are morphologically dissimilar. In *Fucus,* reduction division (meiosis) occurs during the gamete formation in the antheridia and oogonia and therefore, the eggs and sperms become haploid. Such type of life-cycle is found in animals as well as in higher seed plants where the gametophytes are reduced to a few nuclei.

In the red algae, there is a great variation in the life-histories. In these algae the sexual reproduction and the female sex organs are more complicated. The alternation of generations in the lower genera of red algae such as *Batrachospermum* and *Nemalion* is more or less like that of green algae where the plant body is haploid and, therefore, gametophyte. The zygote formed by the fusion of egg and sperm is only diploid structure. The cystocarp or the fruit body of these algae produced from the oospore, though apparently sporophytic, is haploid because during its formation the zygote nucleus undergoes reduction division. In these lower red algae, there is a definite alternation of haploid to diploid number of chromosomes and back to haploid. In these cases, there is no alternation of gametophytic and sporophytic generations with different functions. Such life-cycle is triphasic, possessing three phases, *e.g., Batrachospermum* plant, cystocarp and zygote. The first two phases are haploid and the last phase is diploid one. This way, there is alternation of two haploid generations (gametophyte) with one diploid (sporophyte) generation. Such life-cycle is known as **haplobiontic** type of life-cycle.

There is distinct alternation of generations in the higher red algae, *e.g., Polysiphonia.* The plants are different in their chromosome numbers as well as in functions. The sexual plants bear male and female sex organs on them, and the asexual plants bear tetraspores. The tetraspores produce male and female plants (gametophytes) on germination with the result of fertilization the number of chromosomes being doubled, *i.e.,* diploid. The diploid zygote produces the asexual plant, *i.e.,* tetraspores, bearing tetrasporangia on germination. The tetrasporangia produce tetraspores. The reduction division takes place during tetraspore formation and therefore, the spores become haploid. Such life cycle is also triphasic involves an alternation of two diploid or sporophytic generations with one haploid or gametophytic generation. Here, the diploid phases are represented by tetrasporophyte and carposporophyte, and the haploid phase by sexual plants. Such life-cycle is known as **diplobiontic** type of life-cycle.

GROWING FRESH WATER ALGAE IN THE LABORATORY

Fresh-water algae are of very general distribution and are found in nearly every type of damp and aquatic habitat. Ditches, ponds, rivers, lakes and marshes of any locality abound in a great variety of forms, both of the unicellular and multicellular type. Some algae grow on damp earth or rocks and some kinds make up the greenish covering which appears on the bark of trees. Most of the more conspicuous forms are independent either free floating or attached in tufts or mats to the substratum, but there are also epiphytic and endophytic species. Many of the smaller forms are attached to the other water plants or are found in the loose sediment and debris of the substratum.

Many kinds of algae are easily cultured in the laboratory. Some kinds will grow well indoors in containers of pond water or in a balanced aquarium; other field collected algae are more difficult to culture and can be maintained over long periods only by the use of nutrient solutions, and the pure culture technique. For most kinds of algae, the jars are good culture containers; some robust forms such as *Spirogyra* and *Cladophora* are best grown in aquarium tanks.

When possible, water should be used in which the algae were growing, since sudden changes in kinds of water are injurious. Where additional water is needed, one should use distilled water. The new water should be added gradually, to compensate evaporation.

One should not put too much material into a jar. Actively growing material will increase and gradually accommodate itself to conditions. The excess in an overabundant supply will be choked off and the consequent decay will cause fermentation and general fouling of the culture, ultimately killing the whole. Likewise, luxuriant forms like *Cladophora* may soon overstock themselves and the excess material must be removed from time to time.

Cultures may be started at any time of the year. In winter, bring in some mud over which the desired form was growing the previous season. Sticks or stones may also be used. Place it in a jar and add tap water, distilled water or rain water as the case may require. Cultures of some forms, such as *Chara* and *Nitella* have been obtained from mud collected several years before. Cultures started in this manner usually yield a variety of material.

The healthy culture should not be thrown out if the algae disappear. Seasons of dormancy occur in nature one should look in the bottom of the jar for spores. After the evaporation of water, the jar should be covered for protection, and kept aside. After a period of a month or two add more water and you will likely have your cultures again. Lengths of dormancy periods vary. In *Volvox* it is quite long; in *Oscillatoria* it is only a couple of months; in *Cladophora* there may be no dormancy. Warm weather makes it difficult to keep some culture of algae in good condition. Refrigeration, after collection, will make it possible to study the material for a week or more instead of just a day or two.

While collecting algae, care must be taken to avoid metal containers, specially on long, warm trips. Ample water must be used if the containers are to be sealed. However, forms like *Spirogyra, Mougeotia, Zygnema, Cladophora, Hormiscia.* and *Vaucheria* may be rolled in wet newspapers or magazines and carried thus.

Blue-Green Algae

Oscillatoria is readily found in stagnant water, watering troughs, damp earth, flower pots, and in many other habitats. It is recognized by its dark blue-green, or blackish colour. *Oscillatoria* is one of the easiest of plants to keep in the laboratory. Place a little of material in a container partly filled with water; cover with a lid to avoid unnecessary contamination from dust. By adding water from time to time to compensate for evaporation, the cultures should keep indefinitely.

Nostoc is frequently found in lakes and also occurs on damp earth. It is easy to maintain in laboratory cultures, and will keep in good condition for a month or more if kept under refrigeration at a temperature of about 40⁰F.

Rivularia is found attached to the leaves and stems of various aquatic plants. It often occurs in laboratory aquaria.

Gloeocapsa is found in gelatinous masses, sometimes floating in ponds, but more often as a coating on wet rocks. It is easily maintained in laboratory cultures.

Green Algae

Volvocales. Most of the members of this group and some of the related families are best growing in pure culture, using nutrient solutions.

For this purpose Knop's solution is recommended. Knop's solution, for forms that prefer an acid medium.

$MgSO_4.7H_2O$ (Magnesium sulphate)	...	0.25 gm.
KH_2PO_4 (Potassium phosphate)	...	0.25 gm.
KCl (Potassium chloride)	...	0.12 gm.
$Ca(NO_3)_2.4H_2O$ (Calcium nitrate)	...	1.00 gm.

To prepare measure out one litre of distilled water and dispense about 250 cc. into each of 4 flasks. Dissolve the chemicals separately in these portions of water and combine into one volume–adding the calcium nitrate last. There should be no evidence of precipitation if the individual solutions are well mixed as they are combined. To complete the medium, add one drop of freshly prepared 1% ferric chloride solution. Experimentation will best determine the most suitable concentration for any particular alga – which may vary from full strength to a 1:10 dilution. The pH of this solution will be about 6.4.

Knop's solution (modified), pH 7.6.

$MgSo_4.7H_2O$ (Magnesium sulphate)	...	0.1 gm.
KH_2PO_4 (Potassium phosphate)	...	0.2 gm.
KNO_3 (Potassium nitrate)	...	1.00 gm.
$Ca(NO_3)_2.4H_2O$	...	0.1 gm.

Prepare as outlined above add one drop of 1% ferric chloride solution.

Cultures may be put up in battery jars. The jars must be covered with plates so that the entrance of gross contaminants may be prevented. All glassware previously used for culturing of algae should first be washed and then steamed 30 minutes to avoid contamination. New glassware may be made ready for use by washing it with detergent and hot water followed by a rinse in weak hydrochloric acid (HCl) solution and a final rinse in tap water. Droppers used for transfers may be steamed and kept in a wide-mouth screw-cap jar.

Store cultures in a room where there is a plentiful supply of daylight, at temperatures not in excess of 80⁰F (optimum 70⁰-75⁰F). If, because of the season or for other reasons it becomes necessary to use artificial light, the fluorescent culture lamp should be used at a distance of about one foot from the culture shelf.

Soil-water medium. This is a modification of the Pringsheim method for culturing the

Volvocales and many of the filamentous forms.

To prepare, soil-water medium, take a gallon battery jar, add 0.5 gm of precipitated calcium carbonate, enough humus or garden soil to make a layer from 1/2 to 3/4 inches deep, and sufficient distilled water to bring the level within an inch of the top. The culture jar, covered with a glass plate, together with its contents, is steamed at normal atmospheric pressure in autoclave or pressure cooker for an hour on each of two consecutive days before inoculation. The most effective light for this type of culture is provided by two 40 Watt fluorescent culture lamps located at a six-inch distance for the first week and at an increased distance of 18 inches subsequently for periods of 16 hours daily–in addition to normal diffuse day light.

Chlorella is free living and also lives in a commensal relationship within tissues or cells of invertebrates (protozoa, hydra etc.) This organism has been extensively studied in connection with photosynthesis and for its potential as a food source. *Chlorella* may be cultured in a variety of nutrients such as acid Knop's solution and soil-water medium. For maximum yield under mass culture conditions, it is necessary to aerate the culture with 5% CO_2, thus keeping the cells in suspension while at the same time, supplying the essential gas. The living cells must be regularly harvested and should be fed fresh nutrients as the culture medium becomes depleted.

Spirogyra is found in the field in the quiet waters of ponds, ditches and lagoons, where it often forms large green mats covering the surface of the water. Occasionally it occurs in running water, while still less commonly it is found attached to rocks and piles. *Spirogyra* is not easily cultured for prolonged periods, but it will sometime grow well in a balanced aquarium, and some species live and increase nicely in soil-water medium.

The related algae, *Mougeotia* and *Zygnema,* can be cultured by the same methods that are used for *Spirogyra.*

Hydrodictyon is found suspended in ponds and lakes. When brought into the laboratory it should be placed in an aquarium which receives an abundance of direct sunlight; then it should grow well. It will also grow in Soil-Water Medium.

Vaucheria. One kind of *Vaucheria* can usually be found in greenhouse, where it forms a green felt on flower pots and damp benches. Such material is usually in the vegetative condition. Another species, *Vaucheria geminata* is often found in ponds and ditches. The species will grow fairly well in laboratory cultures.

The formation of zoospores may be induced by cultivating the material in the dark, using a 2% cane sugar solution. The formation of oogonia and antheridia may be induced by cultivating in bright sunlight, using a 2-4% cane sugar solution. Sex organs will not be formed in partial light or in darkness.

Cladophora is found growing attached to sticks and stones in quiet or running water. For cultures, one should select the forms found in quiet water, and place in one or two gallon aquaria. In larger aquaria *Cladophora* is likely to grow too luxuriantly; even with the smaller containers, care must be taken to remove the excess material from time to time.

Oedogonium. Most species of *Oedogonium* are found in the quiet waters of ponds and ditches. Forms with dwarf males are exceedingly small, and appear as a fuzzy covering on submerged twigs, and various other plants. Larger filamentous species often form floating mats which resemble *Spirogyra,* but they are not so slippery.

Chamberlain reports that in the case of *Oedogonium diplandrum,* "Klebs found that a change from a lower to a higher temperature would induce the production of zoospores. A culture which has been kept in a cold room with a temperature varying from 6 degrees to 0 degree centigrade, when brought into a warmer room with a temperature varying from 12°C to 16°C, produced an abundance of zoospores within two days. Light does not seem to have any influence on the formation of zoospores in this species, but light is necessary for the formation of antheridia and oogonia."

Although *Oedogonium* sometimes grows well in an ordinary aquarium, if it is desired to maintain cultures for the entire year, soil-water medium is recommended.

Pleurococcus. Good material for study can be secured by collecting pieces of tree bark on which this alga is growing. Such material may be stored dry; if placed in a moist chamber for 24 hours, the *Pleurococcus* will begin active growth and is then in good condition to study. It is also possible to grow *Pleurococcus* on nutrient agar slants.

Chara and *Nitella.* Both of these algae are fairly easy to grow in large containers in the laboratory. Prepare an aquarium tank with a couple of inches of sand and pond mud in the bottom and fill with natural pond water. Plant a small amount of freshly-collected material in this and place the container where it will get plenty of light and some direct sunlight.

Mud taken from the bottom of ponds in which *Chara* and *Nitella* are known to grow will often produce excellent new growths.

Diatoms are usually found in large quantities around springs and in pools and ponds, clinging in great numbers to filamentous algae, or forming gelatinous masses on various submerged plants. The surface mud of a pond, ditch or lagoon will always yield some forms. Fresh-water diatoms appear in greatest abundance in the spring, are comparatively scarce in summer, but reappear again in the autumn.

Diatoms show their characteristic movements best when transferred from cooler to warmer water. This phase of motility is therefore well illustrated shortly after being brought into the warm laboratory.

ECONOMIC IMPORTANCE

The importance of algae has not been much realized by a layman but a deep study of the subject shows immense value to human beings. Two aspects of economic importance of algae have been realized, *i.e.,* (A) Harmful aspects and (B) Useful aspects.

A–Harmful Aspects

1. **Harmful to living stock.** The algae are harmful to humanity in several ways. Volvocales, Chlorococcales, Myxophyceae and several others occur in such a great abundance in water, that they colour the whole water either green or blue green and cause the death of fishes. The algae block the gills of the fishes and they respire during night and make the respiration of fishes difficult by complete depletion of oxygen.

Sometimes the algae are found in water so abundantly that they make difficult to drink water of livestock. Some blue green algae have been reported poisonous and they directly cause the death of living stock who drink this contaminated water.

2. **Blocking of photosynthesis.** The epiphytic algae which are found upon other plants and trees block photosynthesis and indirectly harm the trees and plants.

3. **Parasitic algae.** The well known disease 'red rust of tea' is not caused by any parasitic fungus but an algal form *Cephaleuros virescens.* This causes a havoc to tea plants in Assam tea gardens. Besides, this parasitic form attacks several other plants, *e.g., Mangifera, Rhododendron, Coffea* etc. The heavy losses are caused to tea and coffee by this parasitic algal form.

4. **Mechanical injury.** Sometimes the filamentous forms of algae are found in such a great abundance and net-like behaviour, that many fishes and other aquatic animals may get perish in these tangles, and direct death is inflicted upon them.

5. **Contamination of water supply.** Many blue green, green and other algae contaminate the water of city reservoirs. This contamination develops a foul odour in the water and makes

the water unhygienic. The algae also form some mucilaginous secretions which are the seats of harmful bacteria and other pathogens causing several human and animal diseases.

6. Fouling of ships. Some algae are attached to the ships, and this is called fouling of ship. The fouling retards the speed of the ship. To avoid this nuisance the ships are periodically dried up and painted with copper paint.

7. Deterioration of exposed fabrics. Commonly in rainy season, if the wet fabrics are exposed, within a few days a blue green alga appears on it and makes the cloth black spotted and weak. This was a serious problem during the Second World War. This algal growth is usually followed by bacterial infection and the fibres are completely destructed.

B. Useful Aspects

1. Food for sea animals and fishes. The algae are used as a direct source of food by several sea animals and fishes. The marine algae are rich in iodine and several other important minerals. This makes the fundamental source of food for all marine animals, and in this respect sea is the richest food producing area. Marine planktonic diatoms together with Dinoflagellata are of fundamental biological importance since all life of sea is dependent upon them.

2. Mineral contents. High mineral content, upto five percent of the wet material, in which all the mineral elements important in human and animal physiology are found, makes sea weeds a unique supplement for a well balanced diet. Potassium, sodium and chloride are found in the ionic form in sea weeds (Pillai 1956). According to Black (1953), the significance of iodine, as a constituent of food, is that besides being present in organic combination it is also available in part in the readily available form of the precursor of thyroxine, and hence this source of iodine surpasses mineral iodine in drinking water and iodized table salt. The another micronutrients besides iodine which are important in human metabolism are iron, copper, manganese and zinc, and all of them are present as the trace elements of sea weeds. The highest copper content was found in *Sarconema furcellatum* and *Acanthophora spicifera*.

At the present time iodine is produced from brown seaweeds in Japan, France, Norway and Java. However, in Russia it is obtained from a red alga of the Black Sea, *Phyllophora nervosa* which contains from 0.2 to 0.5 percent on the dry matter. About 80 percent of the world's supply comes from nitrate mines in Chile.

3. Direct use of algae as food for man. Since the prehistoric times several sea weeds have been used as direct source of food to human beings. Several fresh water algae have also been utilised in the preparation of various kinds of vitaminized food. As we know well that the fundamental food of sea living stock are algae and they are used as food by human beings. Since the algae are rich in vitamins and minerals, all the deficiencies are overrun by the use of algae as food. The algae (sea weeds) form the most important part of the diet of Japan and China. And some people think that the artistic taste and cultural development of the people of Japan is because of the use of the sea weeds as food. In our country a few species of *Spirogyra* and *Oedogonium* are utilised as food in South India.

Several preparations of algae are used in various countries. Of course Japan tops the list. **Suimono** is a Japanese preparation of dried fish and several sea weeds. **Mitsu** is another Japanese preparation which contains sea weeds, fruits, sugars and dried kidney beans. **Dulse** is an English dish of algae prepared from *Rhodymenia*. **Seatron** is prepared from *Nereocystis* in United States. **Laver** or **Nori** is prepared in Japan from *Porphyra*. **Green Laver** is prepared in South India from *Spirogyra* and *Oedogonium*. **Kompu** is the product of many Laminariales.

Apart from China and Japan, in Malaya, Indonesia, Burma and Thailand, the sea weeds are used as food. *Ulva lactuca* was used in Scotland for the preparation of salad and soups.

Laminaria saccharina, Rhodymenia palmata have been used as food in parts of Scotland and Ireland and *Porphyra* is considered to be a tasteful culinary dish in many parts of England.

Among the more important algal food industries may be mentioned **carrageen.** This is a product of several sea weeds but principally *Chondrus crispus*. Carrageen is used by soaking it in water and mixing it with milk. Carrageen possesses the properties of gelling which is one of the factors which enhances its usefulness. Fruit juice may also be mixed with it forming fruit jelly. It is also employed in the preparation of ice creams and in the confectionery industry.

The sea weeds are also used as food in the regions of Far East and Australia. The inhabitants of the Hawaii island consume large quantities of sea weeds. The indigenous people of Chile use large quantities of *Durvillea antarctica* and some species of *Ulva*. The natives of New Zealand use certain green sea weeds in preparation of salad and soups.

The people of China and Japan consume the sea weeds on large scale. The people living on the sea coasts in these countries commonly use fresh sea weeds as food. In Japan *Porphyra tenera* happens to be one of the most important edible algae and a product by the name of **amanori and Asakusa-Nori** are made from it.

4. As a source of vitamins. The marine algae are the richest source of vitamins. The vitamins A, B and E are found abundantly in sea weeds. The vitamin B essentially required for the development of human body is found in great abundance in almost all Phaeophyceae. The cod liver oil is the rich source of vitamin A, which is acquired from sea weeds. Vitamin E is equally important for human beings which is found in many marine algae.

According to Lundin and Ericson (1956), in the sea weeds of Sweden maximum amount of vitamin B_{12} and folic acid are found in spring and summer and niacin and folic acid in winter. Vitamin B_{12} content and also that of B_1 are higher in green and red algae than in brown algae and that the niacin and vitamin C content appear to be about the same in the above three groups of marine algae. Several vitamins except ascorbic acid have been reported from *Chlorella*. The vitamins found in *Chlorella* are–thiamin, riboflavin, niacin, pyridoxine, pantothenic acid, chlorine, biotin, vitamin B_{12} and lipoic acid.

5. As a source of agar. The best agar is manufactured from *Gelidium* of Rhodophyceae, which is also called vegetative agar, Japan produces the largest quantity of agar. It produces 95% of the World production. Agar is also obtained from several other marine algae, the yield of agar, setting temperature and gel strength of the product from ten species belonging to *Gelidium, Sarconema, Hypnea* and *Gracilaria* were obtained by Thivy (1951). Japan is the chief agar producing country and it exports agar to most of the countries of the world.

The agar is used in several ways. It is employed in the preparation of ice cream, jellies, desserts etc., in sizing the textiles and clearing many liquids. It is also used in preparing shaving creams, cosmetics and shoe polishes. The agar has constantly been used in biological laboratories for media preparation.

In India, agar resources, as annual yield of dry sea weeds of Chilka Lake have been estimated by Mitra (1946) to be about 4.06-5.08 metric tons, of Cape Comorin by Koshy and John (1948). Thivy (1957) about one metric ton, and of the Pamban area as estimated by Thivy (1957) about seven metric tons. Other large quantities are in Kathiawar Peninsula end estuaries, the resources of the Andamans are believed to be considerable..

6. Medicines and minerals. Several diseases caused by vitamin deficiency such as vitex, asthma, tooth decay etc., may be eradicated, if flour of the sea weeds is added to the food. According to Dr. Weston, iodine is the most important element to enable the thyroid glands to secrete the thyrosin which contains 60% iodine. It controls the general development of the animal. Sea weeds are the best source of iodine for human beings. Several important sea weed medicinal preparations are prepared in various countries, *i.e.*, Kelpeck is prepared from kelps in Chicago; Burbank Vegetable tablets are sea weed preparations from United States. Kelpamalt is a sea weed medicinal preparation from New York (U.S.A.); Isokelp is prepared in California; Parakelp and Manamar are other medicinal sea weed American preparations. An antibiotic drug Chlorellum is also obtained from algae.

About fortyfive elements are found in a sea weed *Macrocystis pyrifera*. In addition to these elements vitamins are also found. No other food contains such a great abundance of minerals and vitamins.

Marine algae are specially rich in vitamins A, B, C and E. The diatom *Nitzschia* is very rich in vitamin A and possibly this is the main source of vitamin A that is found in liver oils of many fishes. Vitamin B is also found in certain algae, as for example, *Ulva, Porphyra* etc., and *Alaria valida* is rich in Vitamin C, while some Fucoids and *Porphyra* are even richer.

Besides these several other marine forms are quite rich in minerals and vitamins. Several tribes using the sea weeds directly as food have their people handsome and sturdy.

7. Manufacture of iodine. The World's iodine supply is fulfilled from the sea weeds. Since a century back the iodine manufacture is in progress. Iodine is used in several ways.

8. Alginic acid, algin and mannitol. The alginic acid is manufactured from the cell wall of Phaeophyceae. It is insoluble in water and hard when dry. Sodium alginate is used in sizing material for water proof material, dyes, buttons, handles, combs and many of such things. This is also used as a sterilizer in daily use.

The algin is found in the form of calcium alginate and alginic acid. The Fucaceae are the chief source of algin in India. Yields of algin varying from 15.6 to 19.2 percent on air dry matter were estimated for Fucaceae and 10.4 percent for *Padina*.

A yield of 9.4 percent of mannitol from *Sargassum tenerrimum* and 73% from *S. wightii* have been reported.

9. Manufacture of soaps and alums. By burning sea weeds on the sea coast, the alkalies are prepared from sea weed ashes. These alkalies are employed in the manufacture of soaps and alums.

10. As a fodder for hens and milk cattle. By feeding the milk cattle and hens with sea weeds, iodine quantity of the milk and eggs may sufficiently be increased. In Scotland, New Zealand, Norway, France and United States several sea weeds are utilized for feeding hens and young livestock.

Some countries have even factories to process sea weeds into suitable cattle feed. The manufacture of cattle feed from sea weeds is made principally from brown algae and the processed food is fed to cattle, poultry and even pigs. It has seen recorded that dried sea weeds served as cattle food have enhanced the milk-yielding and egg-laying capacity of cattle and poultry respectively.

11. Manufacture of potash. Species of *Macrocystis* and *Nereocystis* (Phaeophyceae) possess 30% of potash in their dry weight.

12. Used as fertilizers. Due to the presence of potassium chloride (KCI) in sea weeds, they are used as fertilizers in many countries, such as Japan France, United States, England and South India.

Sea weeds are a store-house of the important potash, ionic sulphate, trace elements and growth substances, besides having every other element and radical required by plants. Sea weed manure seems to increase resistance to disease. Most of the nutrients including nitrogen compounds are in ionic form and a quick absorption by crops takes place and relatively little is left to be broken down by soil microflora, thus preventing acid conditions of the soil arising from the fermentation. In general the minerals diffuse out from the sea weed thallus rapidly. Yet another feature is that sea weed manure holds water and air at the same time and improves the soil in both respects. Like other manures sea weeds have a similar role but also contribute the required potassium, sulphur, phosphorus and calcium.

13. Manufacture of light weight buildings. Germany has discovered a process, in which the sea weeds are mixed with cement to make buildings light in weight and good heat resistant.

14. Manufacture of paper. It is probably thought that a rough quality of paper may be manufactured from sea weeds, as yet it is not practised.

15. Ornamental uses. Some algae like *Botrydium* and *Spirogyra* are grown in the garden ponds for their good looking habit.

16. Diatomin earth. In the beds of oceans diatom earth is found. During millions of years immense rocks of diatomaceous earth have been formed. At Lompoc and California the deposits are several hundred feet deep, *i.e.*, 700 feet. At St. Maria oil fields California, the deposits are 3,000 feet deep and miles and miles in length. Diatomaceous earth is very important commercial product and used in several ways. America is the largest producer of diatomaceous earth. This is employed as an absorbent in the manufacture of dynamite. It is used in the filtration of liquid in sugar industry. This earth can resist very high temperatures upto 1,500°C, and used in the manufacture of fire bricks. These bricks are used in the inner lining of the blast furnaces. This is also added in the cement to increase its cementing power. It is used as a mild abrasive for metal polishes. It is also used in the manufacture of tooth pastes and car polishes. It acts as a catalyst carrier in the hydrogenation of vegetable oil. In the manufacture of paints, lipsticks and other cosmetics, it is used in many ways.

17. Nitrogen fixation by blue green algae (cyanobacteria). Many members of blue green algae have the ability to fix the atmospheric nitrogen in the soil. Soil is a living mass and apart from soil particles there are in it a number of bacteria, fungi, algae and protozoa. According to Russel, algae occupy a volume three times that of the bacteria. For a long time it was felt that these are the bacteria in the sheath of blue green algae which fix nitrogen. P.K. De (1939) conclusively proved that blue green algae are the main agents for nitrogen fixation in rice fields, and the part played by bacteria is relatively unimportant. Watanabe (1951) made a far reaching research and proved that *Tolyporthrix tenuis* is a strong nitrogen fixer, and it was also reported that it could fix as much as 780 lbs.of nitrogen per acre per year. Allen (1955) found that *Anabaena cylindrica* fixes 2,900 lb. of nitrogen per acre per year.

The work on this problem has been undertaken at I. A. R. I. New Delhi by G.S. Venkataraman and N. Dutta (1958). They have concluded that many blue green algae are capable of fixing atmospheric nitrogen in the soil. The dominance of the blue green algae, possessing the ability for nitrogen fixation particularly in the tropics, suggests that these organisms are of considerable importance in maintaining soil fertility. By increasing and strengthening the local blue green algal flora of a given habit, it may be possible to increase the fertility of these soils.

18. Reclamation of alkaline usar soils by blue-green algae (cyanobacteria). It has been found that some blue green algae form a thick stratum on the surface of saline usar soils during the rainy season when other plants including crop fail to grow. Various species of *Nostoc, Scytonema, Anabaena* etc., have been found to be plentifully growing on usar soils during the rains. According to Dr. R.N. Singh (1950), these algae can be of use in the reclamation of usar lands. There is successive growth of the algal crop on such soils in a water-logged condition. After a year of such reclamation it has been possible to grow transplanted paddy crop with a yield of as much as 1576-2000 lb. per acre. It has been found that the pH of the soil experimented upon in this matter fell from 9.7 to 7.6. Moreover, there was an improvement in the tilth and exchangeable calcium by about 20 to 33 percent. The water holding capacity increased by about 40 percent.

19. Utilization of *Chlorella*. In recent years the alga *Chlorella* has assumed great importance and it is likely to become even more important in the future. *Chlorella* is rich in proteins, fats and vitamins, and in the presence of nutrients, CO_2 and sunlight, multiplies at an enormous rate. Several countries have been experimenting with the mass production of *Chlorella*. Pilot scale *Chlorella* farms have already been established in America, Japan, Holland, Germany and Israel. Such farms do not require excessive amounts of water and hence would be invaluable to augment food supplies in arid areas. Such 'farms' on a smaller scale could also be used to supply food in space stations of the future and even in the large ships.

Chlorella is also being increasingly used as means of purifying sewage when it is present in large, shallow tanks of effluent (after primary sedimentation of solids) the rapid photosynthesis produces abundant oxygen which is then used by the bacteria responsible for destroying the remaining organic matter. A number of sewage works using *Chlorella* now exist in the U.S.A. and at present largest in the world is opening at Auckland in New Zealand. It would seem that this cheap and effective means of sewage purification is likely to extend in the future.

Chlorella has the distinction of being the most widely studied alga as a potential food source for the world's expanding population. Each quart of a moderately thin suspension of *Chlorella* contains twenty billion cells of the alga. Arthur D. Little has produced *Chlorella* at the rate of 20 grams per square metre per day in his pilot plant established at Massachusetts. This way 17.5 tons of *Chlorella* may be produced per acre per year.

Chlorella has been largely used for studies on photosynthesis because it is easy to grow in various environments and because the chlorophyll and end products obtained during photosynthesis are quite similar to those found in higher plants. In newly grown cultures of *Chlorella*, large amount of protein is formed, but as the culture gets older the fats and carbohydrates are produced abundantly. The nutritional value of *Chlorella* is not only based on its high protein content but also on the fact that it contains the essential amino acids.

Chlorella contains most of the known vitamins such as thiamin, riboflavin, niacin, pyridoxine, pantothenic acid, choline, biotin, vitamin B_{12} and lipoic acid. Phytoplankton is the basic source of vitamins for fish, and makes the basis of food and vitamins for human beings. This has been calculated that a quarter pound of *Chlorella* will fulfil the need of all the vitamins except ascorbic acid, of a man for a day.

The amino acids of dried *Chlorella* are:

TABLE. 1.5

Crude protein	....	44.00%	Methionine	....	0.36%
Arginine	....	2.06%	Phenylalanine	....	1.81%
Histidine	....	0.62%	Threonine	....	2.12%
Isoleucine	....	1.75%	Tryptophan	....	0.80%
Leucine	....	3.79%	Valine	....	2.47%
Lysine	....	2.06%			

Both starch and sucrose have been isolated from *Chlorella*. The dry weight storage of carbohydrates in this alga may be as high as 20 per cent.

Ordinarily the fat contents are 20 to 25 percent. Palmitic acid is the main saturated fatty acid. Most of the fat of *Chlorella* is unsaturated that is as high as 65 percent of the total fat content.

In United States, *Chlorella* has been considered to be used to control the oxygen and carbon in atomic submarines. It has been calculated that one kg. of fresh *Chlorella* can supply the 25 litres of oxygen required hourly by a 70 kg. man, as well as use the carbondioxide liberated by him. In United States, the scientists are experimenting and considering the use of *Chlorella* in spaceships. The algae will supply oxygen and utilize carbon dioxide. Besides this the culture of *Chlorella* would also serve as food and the waste materials of the spacemen would serve as nutrient for algae.

Conclusively, Sir John Murray is of opinion that the sea is as important as the land in the production of food materials. Marine Biology is a new field of study and may lead to the scientists to a new science 'mariculture' parallel to 'agriculture'. Certainly we have not realized the importance of sea vegetation.

CLASSIFICATION

For the first time Aristotle (382-322 B.C.) and his pupil Theophrastus (372-287 B. C.), the father of Botany, classified the plants into three groups, *i.e.*, **trees, shrubs, and herbs.** This classification was based on the form and texture of the plants. Here, they considered the trees to be highest evolved.

In eighteenth century Linnaeus (1707-1778) proposed his artificial sexual system of classification. He divided the plant kingdom into twentyfive orders or classes. In his last order **Cryptogamia,** he placed the plants with concealed reproductive organs (flower etc.). Linnaeus divided his order Cryptogamia into four suborders, *i.e.*, (1) **Filices** (Pteridophytes), (2) **Musci** (mosses and leafy liverworts). (3) **Algae,** (algae, lichens and thallose liverworts), (4) **Fungi.**

The first natural system of classification of the plants was proposed by A. L. de Jussieu (1748-1836) in the end of eighteenth century, who divided the plants into three major groups, *i.e.*, (1) **Acotyledones,** (2) **Monocotyledones** and (3) **Dicotyledones.** His classification was based upon the sexual system of Linnaeus but in improved form. His Acotyledones were like Cryptogamia of Linnaeus.

In 1880, the cryptogamic plants were divided into three major groups, *i.e.*, (1) **Thallophyta** (algae, fungi and bacteria), (2) **Bryophyta,** and (3) **Pteridophyta.**

Before twentieth century only four classes were recognized among algae, *i.e.*, (1) **Chlorophyceae** (2) **Phaeophyceae,** (3) **Rhodophyceae** and (4) **Myxophyceae** or **Cyanophyceae.** Diatoms were then included in Phaeophyceae.

Formerly many zoologists placed many motile (flagellate) algae of today in the class Mastigophora of phylum Protozoa.

Rabenhorst in 1863, for the first time placed the *Chlamydomonas-Volv*ox series in the Chlorophyceae of algae.

In the beginning of the twentieth century the class Xanthophyceae was separated from Chlorophyceae and certain pigmented flagellate types were included in the class. According to Dr. F. E. Fritsch (1935, 1944, 1945) the algae have been divided into following eleven classes:-

1.	**Chlorophyceae**	2.	**Xanthophyceae**
3.	**Chrysophyceae**	4.	**Bacillariophyceae**
5.	**Cryptophyceae**	6.	**Dinophyceae**
7.	**Chloromonadineae**	8.	**Euglenophyceae or Euiglinieae**
9.	**Phaeophyceae**	10.	**Rhodophyceae**
11.	**Myxophyceae**		

FRITSCH'S SYSTEM

Dr. Fritsch's classification is mainly based on the following facts:-

1. Pigmentation
2. The assimilatory food products or metabolic products.
3. Type of flagella.

In addition to above given facts a few minor characters may also be taken into consideration. Here we will consider the characters of few important classes, *i.e.,* 1. Chlorophyceae, 2. Xanthophyceae, 3. Bacillariophyceae, 4. Phaeophyceae, 5. Rhodophyceae and 6. Myxophyceae.

1. Chlorophyceae (360 genera; 5,000 species).

Major Charactersitic Features

(i) The pigments are just like in higher green plants, *i.e.,* chlorophyll *a,* chlorophyll *b,* xanthophyll and carotenes. These pigments are localized in definite plastids or chromatophores.

(ii) The photosynthetic food product is starch, rarely oil as in *Vaucheria.* Usually in the chromatophores the pyrenoids are present. They are organellae for the formation of starch. A part of pyrenoid converts into starch.

(iii) The flagellation is of isokonate type, *i.e.,* both of the flagella are equal in length.

Minor Characteristic Features

(i) Vegetative body may be one to many celled.

(ii) The cell consists of cellulose.

(iii) Sexual reproduction ranges from isogamy to oogamy.

(iv) The life-cycle is mostly of haplontic type.

(v) The parenchymatous cells do not occur.

(vi) Most of the species are fresh water and few are marine.

2. Xanthophyceae (75 genera; 675 species)

Major Characteristic Features

(i) The chromatophores are yellow green, containing chlorophyll *a,* carotenes (β carotene) and xanthophylls in them.

(ii) The starch is not found. The pyrenoids are absent. The chief food products are oils.

(iii) The flagellation is of heterokontae type, *i.e.,* one flagellum is short and other long.

Minor Characteristic Features

(i) The cell wall consists of pectin, and in majority of cases two overlapping halves are present, *e.g., Tribonema.*

(ii) The sexual reproduction is rarely found and is doubtfully established for only one species.

(iii) The resting stages possess two pieced membranes.

(iv) The walls are silicified.

(v) The life-cycle is mostly of haplontic type.

(vi) Majority of the species are fresh water, some are marine.

3. Bacillariophyceae (170 genera; 5,300 species)

Major Characteristic Features

(i) The chromatophores are golden brown or yellow, due to the presence of a pigment called **diatomin.** The other pigments are chlorophyll *a,* carotenes (β Carotene) and xanthophylls.

(ii) The food products are fats or volutins.

(iii) The flagellate bodies are 1 to 2 flagellate.

Minor Characteristic Features

(i) Majority of them are unicellular and, some are colonial.

(ii) The sexual reproduction is of special type resulting in the formation of auxospores.
(iii) They are diplontic.
(iv) They are widely distributed in sea and fresh waters.

4. Phaeophyceae (195 genera; 1,000 species)

Major Characteristic Features

(i) The chromatophores are yellowish brown in colour possessing xanthophylls in abundance in them, chlorophyll *a*, and carotenes (β carotene) are also found.

(ii) The reserve food products are alcohols, mannitol and laminarin.

(iii) The motile reproductive cells are pyriform with two laterally inserted flagella; one of which is of tinsel type. In all except Fucales the anterior flagellum is longer.

Minor Characteristic Features

(i) The unicellular bodies are unknown.
(ii) The special type of granules, which are excretory in nature are vesicles.
(iii) The sexual reproduction ranges from isogamy to oogamy.
(iv) The zygote has no resting period.
(v) The great diversity prevails in the life cycles, possessing clear alternation of generations.
(vi) With the exception of three species, rest are marine.

5. Rhodophyceae (400 genera; 2,500 species)

Major Characteristic Features

(i) The chromatophores possess r-phycoerythrin and c-phycocyanin pigments. The other pigments are chlorophyll *a*, carotenes (β carotene) and the xanthophylls. The plants look reddish in colour.

(ii) The reseve food products are polysaccharides, floridean starch and a soluble sugar called floridoside.

(iii) The flagellation is altogether absent.

Major Characteristic Features

(i) The prominent plasmodesmata are present.
(ii) Sexual reproduction is special and advanced.
(iii) The life-cycle clearly shows alternation of generations.
(iv) About 50 species belonging to near about a dozen genera are fresh water. The rest are marine.

6. Myxophyceae (150 genera; 1,500 species)

Major Characteristic Features

(i) The pigments are not localized in definite chromatophores. The pigments are localized in the peripheral portion of the protoplast. The main pigments are chlorophyll *a*, carotenes (β carotene) and xanthophylls. The overmasking blue pigment is c-phycocyanin. The red pigment c-phycoerythrin is also found in peripheral regions in dispersed condition. This peripheral region with pigments is called chromatoplasm.

(ii) The reserve food products are sugars and glycogen-like compounds called the 'cyanophycean starch,

(iii) The flagella are altogether absent.

Minor Characteristic Features

(i) Sexual reproduction is unknown.
(ii) Majority of them are fresh water forms. Some are found in sea water.

PASCHER'S AND SMITH'S SYSTEM

Gilbert M. Smith (1955) followed A. Pascher's (1914, 1921, 1927) classification with slight modifications. This is as follows—

Division 1. **Chlorophyta**
  Class 1. **Chlorophyceae** (green algae)
  Class 2. **Charophyceae** (stoneworts)
Division 2. **Euglenophyta**
  Class 1. **Euglenophyceae** (euglenoids)
Division 3. **Phyrrophyta**
  Class 1. **Desmophyceae** (dinophysids)
  Class 2. **Dinophyceae** (dinoflagelloids)
Division 4. **Chrysophyta**
  Class 1. **Chrysophyceae** (golden brown algae)
  Class 2. **Xanthophyceae** (yellow greean algae)
  Class 3. **Bacillariphyceae** (diatoms)
Division 5. **Phaeophyta** (brown algae)
  Class 1. **Isogenerateae**
  Class 2. **Heterogenerateae**
  Class 3. **Cyclosporeae**
Division 6. **Cyanophyta** (blue green algae)
  Class 1. **Myxophyceae**
Division 7. **Rhodophyta** (red algae)
  Class 1. **Rhodophyceae**

Algae of uncertain systematic position—
1. **Chloromonadales**
2. **Cryptophyceae**

PAPENFUSS SYSTEM

According to Papenfuss (1953) the algae have been divided into eight phyla. these phyla and classes are as below:

Phylum 1. CHLOROPHYCOPHYTA
  class (a) Chlorophyceae
Phylum 2. CHAROPHYCOPHYTA
  class (a) Charophyceae
Phylum 3. EUGLENOPHYCOPHYTA
  class (a) Euglenophyceae
Phylum 4. CHRYSOPHYCOPHYTA
  class (a) Xanthophyceae
    (b) Chrysophyceae
    (c) Bacillariophyceae
Phylum 5. PYRROPHYCOPHYTA
  class (a) Dinophyceae
    (b) Cryptophyceae
    (c) Chloromonadophyceae
Phylum 6. PHAEOPHYCOPHYTA
  class (a) Phaeophyceae
Phylum 7. SCHIZOPHYCOPHYTA
  class (a) Schizophyceae
Phylum 8. RHODOPHYCOPHYTA
  class (a) Rhodophyceae

Chapman (1962) has also proposed a system of classification based on morphological characters, pigments and biochemical differences. He has placed, Charophyceae, Chlorophyceae, Phaeophyceae and Rhodophyceae under a large group EUPHYCOPHYTA. According to him, these classes of algae are interrelated, and therefore, have been grouped under Euphycophyta. The classification proposed by Chapman (1962) is as follows:

A. EUPHYCOPHYTA
  classes 1. Charophyceae
    2. Chlorophyceae
    3. Phaeophyceae
    4. Rhodophyceae
B. MYXOPHYCOPHYTA
  class Myxophyceae
C. CHRYSOPHYCOPHYTA
  classes 1. Chrysophyceae
    2. Xanthophyceae
    3. Bacillariophyceae
D. PYRROPHYCOPHYTA
  classes 1. Cryptophyceae
    2. Dinophyceae.

MODERN TRENDS IN CLASSIFICATION

The classification of algae has continually been modified since its beginning in the 1753 edition of Linnaeus **Species Plantarum.** In **natural** or **phylogenetic** systems (which represent real evolutionary relationships) of classification, alterations in the classification of algae are made as a result of augmentation of our knowledge. This has resulted in the present, largely **polyphyletic** system (the system having many distinct lines of evolutionary history) in which the algae are grouped in seven to eleven categories of divisional rank. The criteria on which the classification is based are **pigments, reserve food** and **flagellation.** However, our knowlege of the comparative chemistry of the several pigments and storage products is fragmentary, especially in relation to the genetics and evolution of the organisms, that it is quite possible our current polyphyletic groupings may be modified into a more monophyletic system in the future.

At the levels of orders, families and genera it has been noted that (1) In the Chlorophycophyta and Phaeophycophyta, the orders are delimited largely on vegetative or somatic characters, variation in reproduction being treated as of secondary importance. In the division Rhodophycophyta, in contrast, the orders are at present delimited on the basis of the organization of the female reproductive branch, vegetative attributes being secondary. (2) Among the Chrysophycophyta, the families of certain orders are at present delimited on the basis of flagellar numbers while the same criterion is used at the generic level in the unicellular motile Chlorophycophyta. These examples indicate that modern classifications are, at least approximations of relationship.

Like all plants the algae are classified in accordance with the recommendations and prescriptions of the International Code of Botanical Nomenclature. This code recognizes the individual organism as belonging to a species, the species to a genus, the genus to a family, the family to an order, the order to a class and the class to a division.

The following suffixes for use in the classification of algae have been recommended by the International Code of Botanical Nomenclature;

- Division–**phyta**
- Class–**phyceae**
- Sub-class–**phycideae**
- Order–**ales**
- Sub-order–**inales**
- Family–**aceae**
- Sub-family–**oideae**
- Genus–a Greek name
- Species–a Latin name

The algae have been divided into 11 divisions. They are as follows.

1. Cyanophycophyta (Blue-green algae)
2. Chlorophycophyta (Green algae)
3. Charophyta (Stoneworts)
4. Euglenophycophyta (Euglenoids)
5. Xanthophycophyta (Yellow-green algae)
6. Chrysophycophyta (Golden algae)
7. Bacillariophycophyta (Diatoms)
8. Phaeophycophyta (Brown algae)
9. Pyrrophycophyta
10. Cryptophycophyta
11. Rhodophycophyta (Red algae)

Representatives belonging to few important divisions–Cyanophycophyta, Chlorophycophyta, Charophyta, Xanthophycophyta, Bacillariphycophyta, Phaeophycophyta and Rhodophycophyta have been discussed in detail in the present text.

Revision Questions

Long Answer Type

1. How would you define algae? Give characteristic features of this diversified group of plant kingdom.
2. Trace out the history of phycology. Also, mention the Indian work.
3. Write a comprehensive note on habit and habitat of algae.
4. What type of nutrition is found in various groups of algae?
5. Describe the range of vegetative structure in various groups of algae.
6. Give the various modes of reproduction found in algae.
7. Write a detailed note on the methods of perennation in algae.
8. What type of life-cycles are met with in algae?
9. Write a detailed note on pigmentation of algae.
10. Write an essay on the economic importance of algae.
11. Give the modern trends of classification of algae.
12. What criteria have been adopted for classifying algae?
13. Give the outline of Fritsch's system of classification of algae.
14. Give a comprehensive account of origin and evolution of sex in algae.

Short Answer Type

1. Write a note on history of phycology.
2. Write a note on Algology in India.
3. Write notes on – Planktophytes, Cryophytes and Fluviatile algae.
4. Write a brief account of nutrition in algae.
5. Write notes on palmelloid and dendroid types, siphonous type, and advanced type of algae.
6. Write a note on evolution of sex in algae.
7. Write notes on: Heteromorphic and haplobiontic types of life-cycle in algae.

Diagrammatic Type

1. Give the cellular structure of a procaryotic alga.
2. Give the structure of a cell of eucaryotic alga.

Multiple Choice Type

1. Nitrogen fixation in soil is caused by:
   (i) Chlorophyceae, (ii) Phaeophyceae, (iii) Myxophyceae, (iv) Rhodohyceae.
2. Nitrogen fixation in soil is caused by:
   (i) green algae, (ii) brown algae, (iii) blue-green algae, (iv) red algae.
3. R.N. Singh worked on:
   (i) red algae, (ii) brown algae, (iii) blue-green algae, (iv) green algae.
4. Cyanophyta is written by: (i) T.V. Desikachary, (ii) M.S. Randhawa, (iii) R.N. Singh, (iv) J.N. Misra.
5. Zygnemaceae is written by:
   (i) T.V. Desikachary, (ii) M.S. Randhawa (iii) R.N. Singh, (iv) J.N. Misra.
6. Phaeophyceae in India, is written by:
   (i) T.V. Desikachary, (ii) M.S. Randhawa, (iii) R.N. Singh, (iv) J.N. Misra.
7. Role of blue-green algae in Nitrogen economy of Indian Agriculture is written by:
   (i) T.V. Desikachary, (ii) M.S. Randhawa, (iii) R.N. Singh, (iv) J.N. Misra.
8. Cryophytes are found:
   (i) in deep sea, (ii) on sea shore, (iii) on ice and snow, (iv) on humus soil.
9. Chlorophyll is found in:
   (i) blue-green algae, (ii) green algae, (iii) brown algae, (iv) all the above.
10. Amylum stars are found in:
    (i) *Vaucheria*, (ii) *Ulothrix*, (iii) *Chara*, (iv) *Polysiphonia*.
11. Heterocysts are found in:
    (i) Chlorophyceae, (ii) Phaeophyceae, (iii) Rhodophyceae, (iv) Myxophyceae.
12. Diplobiontic type of life-cycle is found in:
    (i) *Vaucheria*, (ii) *Oedogonium*, (iii) *Polysiphonia*, (iv) *Ectocarpus*.
13. Carrageen is obtained from:
    (i) *Chara*, (ii) *Polysiphonia*, (iii) *Sargassum*, (iv) *Chondrus*.
14. Agar-agar is manufactured from:
    (i) *Ectocarpus*, (ii) *Polysiphonia*, (iii) *Spirogyra*, (iv) *Gelidium*.
15. Alginic acid is obtained from:
    (i) Chlorophyceae, (ii) Phaeophyceae, (iii) Rhodophyceae, (iv) Myxophyceae.

16. Diatomin earth is a product of:
(i) Chlorophyceae, (ii) Bacillariophyceae, (iii) Xanthophyceae, (iv) Rhodophyceae.
17. High protein contents are found in:
(i) *Chlorella,* (ii) *Chlamydomomas,* (iii) *Spirogyra,* (iv) *Ulothrix.*
18. Red rust of tea is caused by:
(i) *Puccinia,* (ii) *Ustilago,* (iii) *Melampsora,* (iv) *Cephaleuros.*
19. Red rust of tea is caused by:
(i) Algae, (ii) Fungi, (iii) *Cuscuta,* (iv) *Balanophora.*
20. Point out the algologist:
(i) M.O.P. Iyengar; (ii) Y.Bharadwaja (iii) R.N. Singh, (iv) all the above.

Answers

1 (iii), 2 (iii), 3 (iii), 4 (i), 5 (ii), 6 (iv), 7 (iii), 8 (iii), 9 (iv), 10 (iii), 11 (iv), 12 (iii), 13 (iv), 14 (iv), 15 (ii), 16 (ii), 17 (i), 18 (iv), 19 (i), 20 (iv).

2

Cyanophycophyta–Myxophyceae Blue Green Algae–Cyanobacteria

Characteristic features

Pigmentation. Chlorophyll *a*, β-carotene, Antheraxanthin, Aphanicin, Aphanizophyll, Flavacin, Lutein, Myxoxanthin, Myxoxanthophyll, Oscilloxanthin, Zeaxanthin, Allophycocyanin, Phycocyanin, Phycoerythrin.

Storage products. Cyanophycean starch, proteins.

Flagellation. Absent.

There are about 150 genera and 1,500 species of fresh water, marine and terrestrial algae in this class. The synonyms of the class are Cyanophyceae, Schizophyceae, and Phycochromophyceae.

Occurrence and distribution. The members of this class are worldwide in distribution and occur in all possible kinds of habitats. Majority of the Chamaesiphonales are marine occurring in the littoral and sub-littoral zones, while the majority of Chroococcales, and Hormogonales are fresh water. The red colour of the red sea is due to a blue green alga, *i.e.*, *Trichodesmium erythrium*. This form is found in the bottom of the sea. There are several terrestrial forms which occur on rocks and walls, *e.g.*, *Porphyrosiphon*, *Scytonema* etc. Some are found in the soil upto the depth of 8 feet. Some members of Chroococcaceae, Stigonemataceae and species of *Phormidium* inhabit in hot springs even upto 85°C temperature. Such algae are restricted to Myxophyceae and are called the thermal algae. The salts of calcium and magnesium are precipitated in the bottom by the thermal algae and are called 'travertine'. Calcium carbonate is deposited by *Schizothrix*, *Lyngbya* and *Rivularia* species. Several Myxophyceae live in symbiosis. Some forms are endophytic. *Nostoc* colonies are found inside the tissues of *Anthoceros* and *Notothylas*. *Anabaena cycadeae* is found inside the coralloid roots of *Cycas*. *Anabaena azollae* is found in the tissues of *Azolla*. Many unicellular Chroococcaless are found in the association of unicellular animals such as Rhizopods and Cryptomonas etc. Several Oscillatoriaceae are parasites. About forty species belonging to four genera of Oscillatoriaceae are parasitic inside the alimentary canal of human beings and other animals. Majority of Myxophyceae like soft water and sometimes found in such an abundance that the whole surface of the water becomes blue green in colour. A large part of the free floating population of microscopic organisms which constitute the **plankton** of lakes and oceans is made up of members of Myxophyceae.

Fossils. The fossils of blue green algae are not definitely known from the oldest geological era, *i.e.*, the *Archeozoic*, but immense graphite deposits indicate the presence of organisms whose remains were decomposed by the activity of bacteria. Many impressions have been of blue green algae.

Range of structure. The forms may be found as (i) unicellular individuals, (ii) non-filamentous colonies and (iii) filamentous forms.

1. Unicellular forms. Many members of Chroococcales are truly unicellular in structure, such as *Chroococcus*, *Tetrapedia* and *Gloeocapsa* are widespread unicellular blue-green algae.

2. Non-filamentous colonial forms. The colonies are amorphous. Such colonies are resulted from the confluence of the gelatinous envelopes surrounding the individual cells, *e.g.*, *Aphanocapsa, Aphanothece* etc.

The shape of colony depends upon the plane of division of the cells forming the colony. When the cells divide in one plane the colony becomes plate—like, *e.g.*, *Merismopedia*. When the cells divide in many planes, cubical or three dimensional colonies are formed. Irregular colonies are developed by the irregular divisions of the cells.

3. Filamentous forms. When a single cell divides continuously in one plane the ultimate result is a filament. Such types are commonly known in Oscillatoriaceae. In *Oscillatoria* the filament consists of a trichome surrounded by a sheath. In *Schizothirx* several trichomes are surrounded by a common sheath.

In *Nostochopsis*, the filaments are truly branched.

Leaving aside Oscillatoriaceae, in other filamentous forms the 'heterocysts' are found. The heterocysts may be intercalary or terminal.

Structure of the cell. The cell wall is two layered. The outer layer consists of pectic substance and the inner of cellulose.

The complete cell is filled up with cytoplasm. The protoplast may be differentiated into two regions. The outer peripheral region is called the **'chromoplasm'** and the central colourless region is **'centroplasm'** or **central body.**

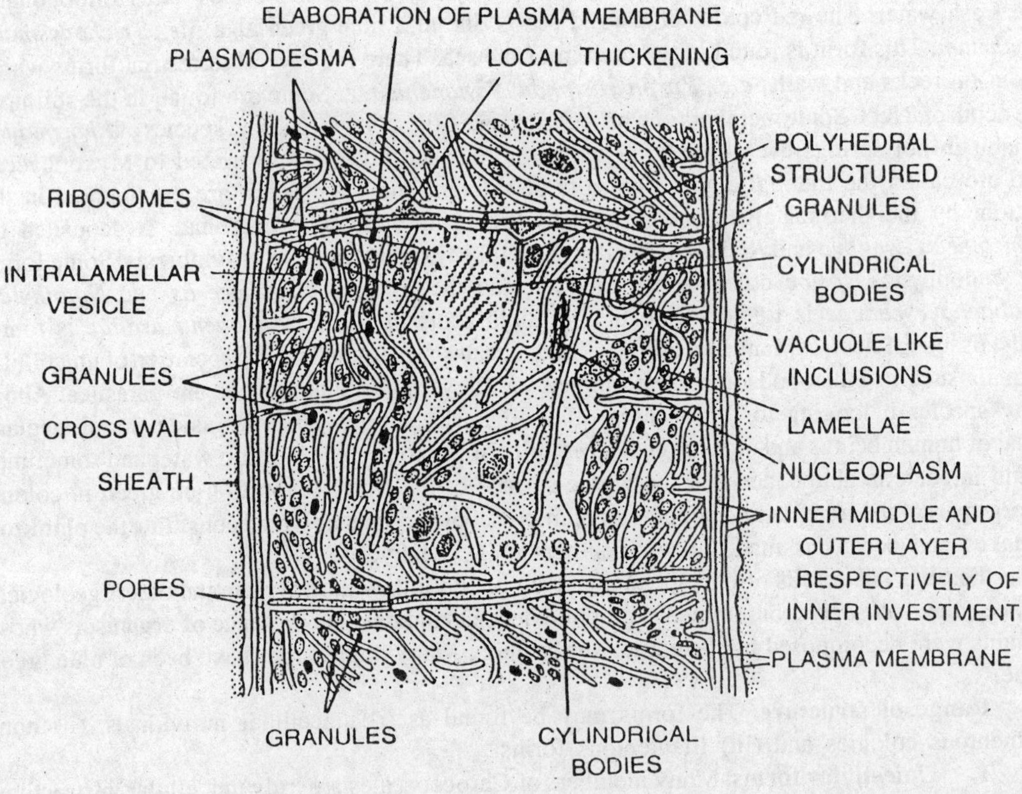

Fig. 2.1. Myxophyceae. Ultrastructure of a cell; a filamentous form.

The coloured peripheral chromoplasm contains many pigments, *e.g.*, phycocyanin, phycoerythrin, carotenes, xanthophylls and chlorophylls in dispersed condition. These pigments are not found in chromatophores as in other algae. In addition to these pigments oil drops and glycogen granules are also found in this region.

The central body or the centroplasm of the cell is colourless. According to one view, the central body is regarded as primitive nucleus having no nucleoli and nuclear membrane. There is no true nucleus. Several stainable chromatin **grains** are dispersed in the centroplasm. According to another view, the central body is a store-house of food material. According to West, the central body is an **incipient nucleus.**

In whole of the cytoplasm there are no vacuoles. It is viscous and gel like. Special pseudovacuoles have been reported from the cells. They are small, irregular bodies and commonly found in chromatoplasm. According to one view these pseudovacuoles are gas filled. According to another view, they are filled with viscous liquid.

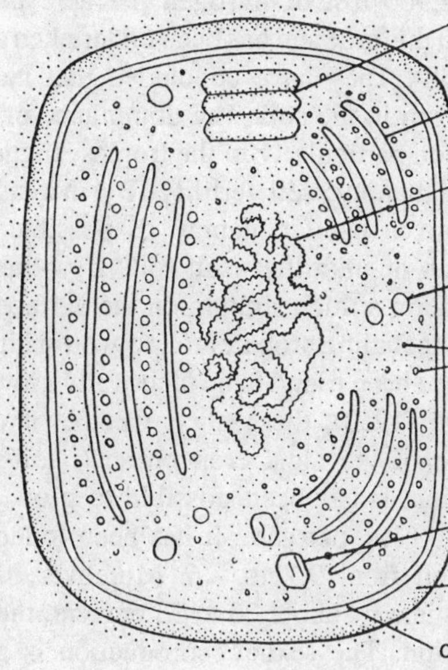

Fig. 2.2. A cyanophycean cell. Ultra-structure

Cytological work. The chromatin found in the central body has been demonstrated to be composed of DNA (deoxyribonucleic acid), RNA (ribonucleic acid), and protein. The DNA molecule determines the structure and heredity of the cell. The isolation of the radicals of nucleic acids (RNA and DNA) from blue green algae gives some substance to the view that a nucleus is present.

Movements of Myxophyceae. In some of the species the trichomes move forward and backward within the sheath, this movement is called 'gliding movement'.

The second type of movement is called the 'oscillation'. This movement is pendulum-like and found in many Oscillatoriaceae. The increase of temperature and illumination accelerates oscillating movement.

Photosynthesis and food products. The process of photosynthesis goes on in blue green algae, in the same manner as in other plants. The storage food products in blue green algae are somewhat different from those of other green plants. The storage product is usually a starch like substance similar to glycogen and is different from the starch produced in other plants. This is known as **Cyanophycean starch.** In many of the Myxophyceae the reserve foods are stored in the form of oils. An amino acid known as diaminopimelic acid is found in the proteins of blue green algae and bacteria but never found in higher plants or animals. This characteristic feature supports the view that both bacteria and blue green algae have common ancestry.

Nitrogen fixation by blue-green algae. Many members of blue green algae have the ability to fix the atmospheric nitrogen in the soil. Soil is a living mass and apart from soil particles there are in it a number of bacteria, fungi, algae and protozoa. According to Russel, algae occupy a volume three times that of the bacteria. For a long time it was felt that these are the bacteria in the sheath of blue green algae which fix nitrogen. P.K. De (1939) conclusively proved that blue green algae are the main agents for nitrogen fixation in rice fields, and the part plåyed by bacteria is relatively unimportant. Watanabe (1951) made a far reaching research and proved that *Tolypothrix tenuis* is a strong nitrogen fixer, and it was also reported that it could fix as much as 780 lbs. of nitrogen per acre per year. Allen (1955) found that *Anabaena cylindrica* fixes 2,900 lbs. of nitrogen per acre per year.

The work on this problem has been undertaken at I. A. R. I. New Delhi by G.S. Venkataraman and N.Dutta (1958). They have concluded that many blue green algae are capable of fixing atmospheric nitrogen in the soil. The dominance of the blue green algae, possessing the ability for nitrogen fixation particularly in the tropics, suggests that these organisms are of considerable importance in maintaining soil fertility. By increasing and strengthening the local blue green algal flora of a given habitat, it may be possible to increase the fertility of these soils.

Reclamation of alkaline usar soils by blue green algae. It has been found that some blue green algae form a thick stratum on the surface of saline **usar** soils during the rainy season when other plants including crop fail to grow on such soils. Various species of *Nostoc, Scytonema, Anabaena* etc., have been found to be plentifully growing on **usar** soils during the rains. According to Dr. R.N. Singh (1950), these algae can be of use in the reclamation of usar lands in the successive growth of the algal crop on such soils in a water-logged condition. After a year of such reclamation, it has been possible to grow transplanted paddy crop with a yield of as much as 1576-2000 lbs. per acre. It has been found that the pH of the soil experimented upon in this manner fell from 9.7 to 7.6. Moreover, there was an improvement in the tilth and exchangeable calcium by about 20 to 33 percent, the water holding capacity of about 40 percent.

Reproduction. The sexual reproduction is altogether absent. The forms reproduce by means of vegetative and asexual methods.

1. Vegetative reproduction. The vegetative reproduction takes place by several methods.

(i) By cell division. This is only the known method of propagation in the order Chroococcales. The cell becomes constricted in the middle and ultimately divides giving rise to two individuals.

(ii) Fragmentation of colony. The colonies are fragmented into small bits. Each such bit develops into a colony by division of the cells in different planes.

(iii) Fragmentation of filaments. In the family Oscillatoriaceae the filaments break into small fragments. The fragmentation may be accidental or otherwise.

(iv) By hormogones. Inside the sheath, the trichomes are fragmented and hormogonia or hormogones are formed. Each such hormogone or hormogonium may develop into a new individual, *e.g.,* many Nostocales.

(v) Hormosphores or hormocysts. During the formation of hormospores, a large quantity of food material is accumulated in the cells of hormogones and they become thick walled, these structures are called the hormospores or hormocysts. Each such structure develops in a new plant on the approach of favourable conditions, *e.g., Westiella.*

(vi) Akinete formation. Sometimes some of the cells of filamentous genera accumulate much of food, become thick-walled and are called the 'akinetes'. These are produced in unfavourable conditions, each such vegetative structure may develop into a new plant, *e.g., Nostoc*. On the approach of favourable conditions the akinetes develop into new filaments; the akinetes are also called the **'arthrospores** or **resting spores'**.

2. Asexual reproduction. The asexual reproduction takes place by means of (i) endospores and (ii) exospores.

(i) Endospores. The endospores are produced inside the cell. During the formation of these spores the cytoplasm of the cell becomes cleaved into several bits. These bits later become endospores and are liberated. Each spore germinates into a new plant, *e.g., Dermocapsa.*

When the endospores are comparatively smaller in size and larger in number in the cell, they are called **'nannospores'**. Such spores develop individually into new individuals, *e.g., Dermocapsa.*

(ii) Exospores. Such spores are produced outside the cell by constriction. In the case of *Chamaesiphon,* the exospores are developed from the terminal end of the plant in continuous succession. The plant is epiphytic upon *Oedogonium.*

Heterocysts. In majority of filaments of Myxophyceae the button-like heterocysts are found. However, they are not found in Oscillatoriaceae. Each heterocyst is a spherical oval structure, with a thick wall of two layers. The inner thin layer is called the inner investment and the outer sheath is called the outer investment. The heterocysts may be intercalary or terminal in position. At the point of contact to the filament there is a pore in the heterocyst. The intercalary heterocyst is bipored and the terminal one is monopored. In the case of *Gloeotrichia, Rivularia, Cylindrospermum* etc., the heterocysts are terminal and monopored. The filaments of *Anabaenopsis* bear heterocysts at their both the terminal ends and are monopored. In *Nostoc* they may be mono- or bipored.

The nature of the heterocyst is also very debatable and controversial. According to Geitler, these bodies are ancient reproductive cells which have now become functionless. In rare cases still today they germinate giving rise to new plants. According to another view, the heterocyst is considered to be the store-house of food material.

Origin and affinities of Myxophyceae. The group is considered to be most ancient because of the presence of many special features such as (a) absence of the chromatophores, (b) presence of incipient nucleus, (c) lack of flagella, (d) lack of reproductive cells and (e) total lack of sexual reproduction.

They are worldwide in distribution and found in every possible type of habitat. An independent origin for the group is almost certain. But the ancestry is not known. The total absence of any swarmer rules out the possibility of flagellate ancestry.

The Myxophyceae also resemble the red algae in the sense that both lack swarm cells, and the blue green algae occasionally possess a red pigment similar to that found in Rhodophyceae.

They resemble bacteria in few respects. They have no nuclei, no sexual reproduction and fix atmospheric nitrogen in the soil like some bacteria, and called cyanobacteria.

Classification. There are five orders in this class. The first three orders are without hormogones and the last two possess hormogones.

1. **Chroococcales.** They are unicellular or colonial; they reproduce by the cell division and endospores.

2. **Chamaesiphonales.** They are unicellular or colonial, epiphyte or lithophytes; they reproduce by endo- or exospores.

3. **Pleurocapsales.** They are non-heterotrichous filamentous types; heterocysts absent; reproduce by endospores.

4. **Nostocales.** They are non-heterotrichous filamentous types; heterocysts present; reproduction by hormogones, hormospores and akinetes.

5. **Stigonematales.** They are non-heterotrichous filamentous types with true branching; mostly heterocysts present; reproduction takes place by hormogones, hormospores and rarely by akinetes.

The order Nostocales is sub-divided into five families–

1. Oscillatoriaceae. *Oscillatoria.*

2. Nostocaceae. *Nostoc*
3. Microchaetaceae.
4. Rivulariaceae. *Rivularia.*
5. Scytonemataceae. *Scytonema.*

Economic importance of Myxophyceae. Some species of blue green algae with gelatinous matrix including *Nostoc*, are boiled in soups and utilized as food. These algae form much of the plankton eaten by fish and the human beings in turn consume the fish. The growth of these algae in abundance makes the water of lakes or rivers unsuitable for human consumption. Excessive growth of some blue green algae such as *Aphanizomenon*, in lakes resulted in the death of innumerable fish from a depletion of the oxygen supply. The species of *Microcystis* and *Anabaena* may even kill the cattle which drink the water polluted with these algae. These algae cause various liver, heart and lung diseases to the cattle which consume the algae with water, and ultimately they die. The active principle in *Microcystis* is described as a potent neurotoxin. If the species of *Oscillatoria* are consumed by human beings along with water, they cause the symptoms of itching, conjunctivitis, blocking of nasal passages and bronchial asthma.

The dominance of the blue-green algae possessing the ability for nitrogen fixation particularly in the tropics suggests that these organisms are of considerable importance in maintaining soil fertility.

ORDER–CHROOCOCCALES

Characteristic features

1. The order contains unicellular forms that are free living and either living singly or united into colonies.
2. Reproduction takes place by means of cell-division in one or more planes. Endospores have been recorded for a couple of the genera, but in these genera they are not regularly formed.

There are 35 genera and about 250 species.

There are two families in this order – 1. Chroococcaceae; 2. Entophysalidaceae.

Family–Chroococcaceae

The majority of the genera of this family are colonial and a few are unicellular. There is no tendency towards the formation of pseudofilament, when the cells are united in colonies.

CHROOCOCCCUS

(*chroo*, colour; *coccus*, berry)

The genus is very widespread, the species being either free floating or soil inhabitants. The cells are single or else united into spherical or flattened colonies each containing a small number of cells, the individual sheaths being either homogeneous or lamellated. The plants which grow in water produce a concentric envelope but when they grow on damp soil, the sheath is often asymmetrical. The outer integument is not very gelatinous and indeed is quite thin in some species. The cell contents are variously coloured and either homogeneous or granular.

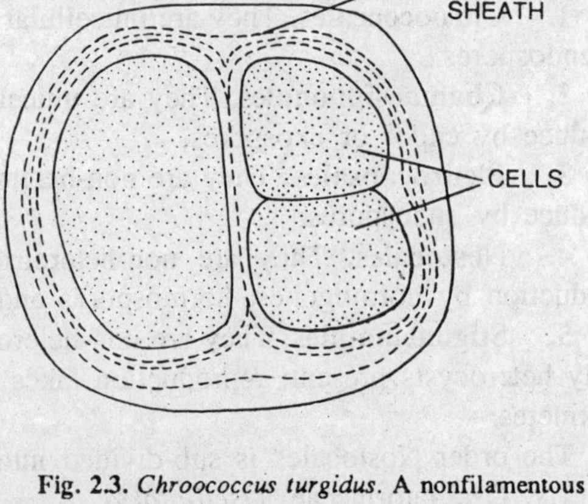

Fig. 2.3. *Chroococcus turgidus.* **A nonfilamentous Myxophyceae showing a colony of three cells.**

Cytological work. Cytologically *Chroococcus turgidus* represents the simplest condition with the metachromatin granules only just differentiated. *Chroococcus macrococcus* is a more complex type. It contains a central body which is said to contain a fine reticulum with chromatin at the nodal points. During cell division the reticulum divides by simple constriction. There is no evidence of mitosis.

GLOEOCAPSA (Family-Chroococcaceae)

This is found growing in extensive strata on damp rocks. This genus resembles *Chroococcus* in having colonies composed of a few spherical cells, each surrounded by a homogeneous to lamellated sheath. The sheath is coloured yellow, brown, red, blue or violet.

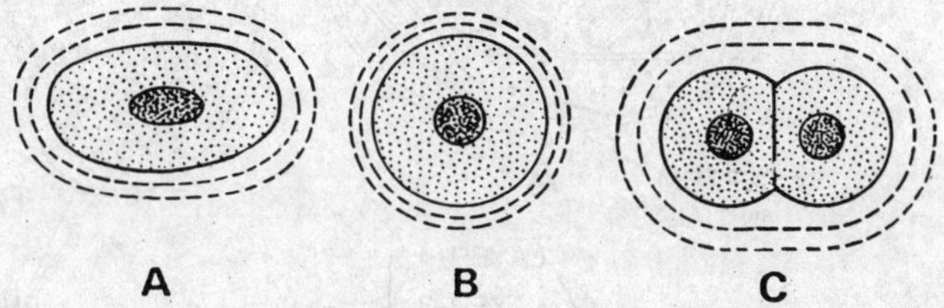

Fig. 2.4. *Gloeocapsa* sp. Non-filamentous blue green algae. A-B, individuals; C, cell division.

Cell structure. Each cell is surrounded by a two layered cell wall. Each cell possesses a colourless central portion, the so-called **central body,** surrounded by an exterior portion, in which the pigment is diffused. The central body seems to represent an incipient nucleus. The central body is not separated from the rest of the cell by a membrane; it has no nucleus; it does not divide mitotically. The colourless granules found in the peripheral region of the cell are said to be of glycogen.

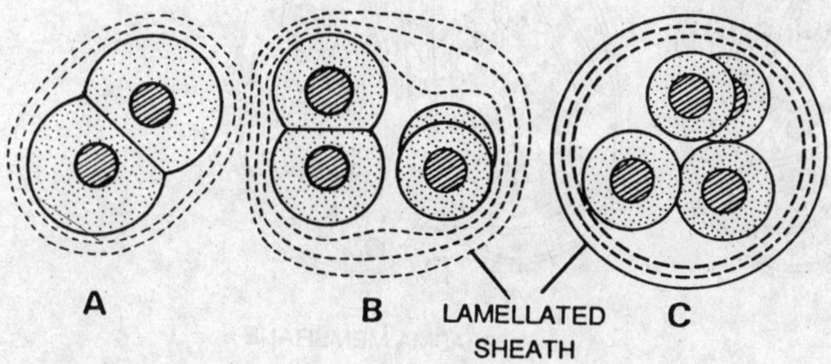

Fig. 2.5. *Gloeocapsa*. Non-filamentous Myxophyceae A-C, various stages of cell division and colony formation.

Reproduction. Only vegetative method of reproduction takes place. The cell becomes constricted in the centre and ultimately divides giving rise to two individuals.

MICROCYSTIS (*micro*, small; *cystis*, bladder)

This is a fresh water genus. They often cause 'water blooms' in hard water lakes. The thallus is free-floating and varies much in shape. It contains a mass of single spherical cells but the sheaths of the individual cells are confluent with the colonial envelope. The gelatinous matrix of the colonial envelope is of watery consistency and the margins of the matrix are usually not evident. The cells frequently contain numerous pseudovacuoles.

Reproduction. The reproduction of individual cells takes place by means of fission in three planes, while reproduction of colony is through successive disintegrations, each portion develops into a new colony. The shape of the colony is primarily determined by the environmental conditions.

Systematic position. Division-Cyanophycophyta; Class-Myxophyceae or Cyanophyceae; Order-Chroococcales; Family-Chroococcaceae; Genera-*Chroococcus, Gloeocapsa* and *Microcystis*

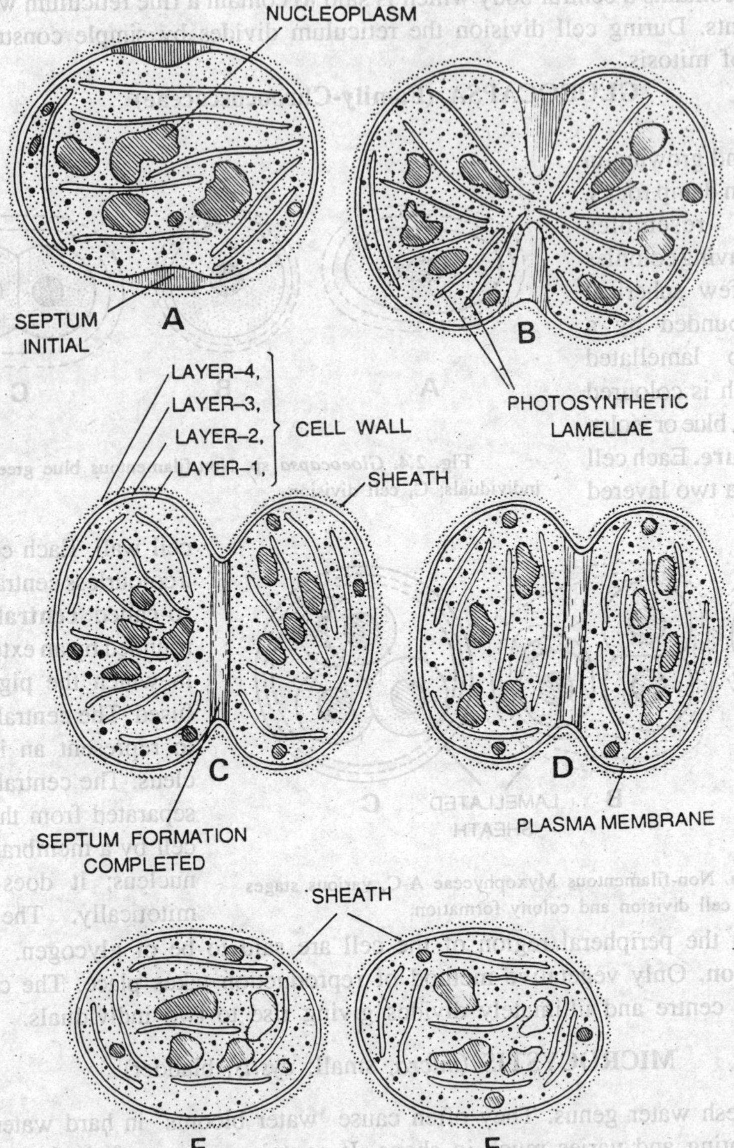

Fig. 2.5. (a). Blue-green algae (Cyanobacteria). A-F, stages in cell division in *Gloeocapsa* spp. (ultrastructure).

ORDER-NOSTOCALES

Characteristic features

(i) Majority of the forms are fresh water in habit.

(ii) The plant body is filamentous. The cells are united end to end in the simple or coiled trichomes ensheathed by an individual or a common sheath.

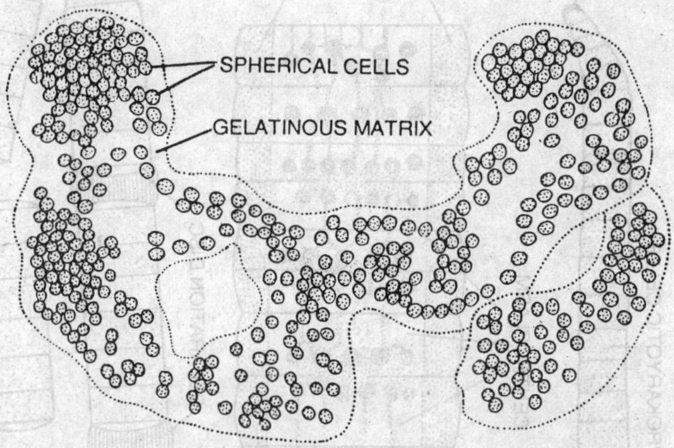

Fig. 2.6. *Microcystis.* A colony containing hundreds of cells.

(iii) The heterocysts may or may not be present.

(iv) Reproduction takes place by means of fragments, hormogonia and akinetes (arthrospores or resting spores).

Classification. There are five families in this order.

1. Oscillatoriaceae
2. Nostocaceae
3. Microchaetaceae
4. Rivulariaceae
5. Scytonemataceae

Family-Oscillatoriaceae

They reproduce by means of hormogonia only, and never form either heterocysts or akinetes. The trichomes are always uniseriate and unbranched. The apical cell is somewhat rounded at its apex while the other cells of the trichome are of same diameter. A majority of genera possess gelatinous, homogeneous or lamellated, hyaline or coloured sheaths about the trichomes. Some genera possess several trichomes within a common sheath; others have one trichome within a sheath.

Genus-OSCILLATORIA

Occurrence. The species of *Oscillatoria* are commonly found in fresh water. They are found in ditches, ponds, pools and even the drains. Some species are also found on damp soil and damp rocks. They are found in the form of scums either in free floating condition on the surface of water or in the bottoms of pools and puddles. Some species are commonly found in polluted water.

Structure. The plant body is filamentous. The filaments are uniseriate and unbranched. Each filament consists of a trichome ensheathed by a gelatinous sheath. The filaments are found either singly or in masses. The cells of the filament are placed end to end like coins. The cells of the broad species are broader than their length, but the cells of narrow species are much longer than their breadth. The terminal cell of filament may be somewhat round at its apex. In *Oscillatoria proboscidea* the apex of the filament forms a proboscis like structure.

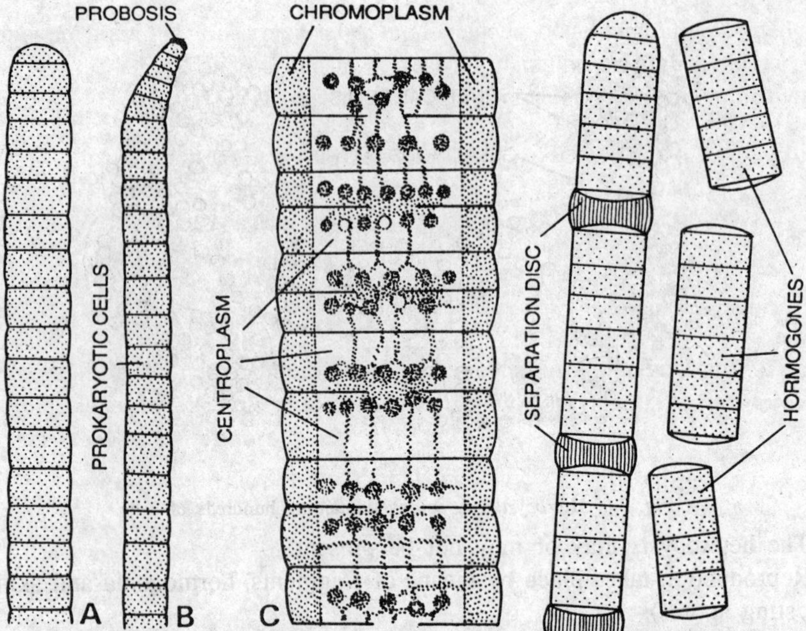

Fig. 2.7. *Oscillatoria* sp. Vegetative structure and vegetative reproduction. A, *O. limosa;* B, *O. proboscidea;* C, cell structure (detailed); D, formation of hormogones; E, hormogones.

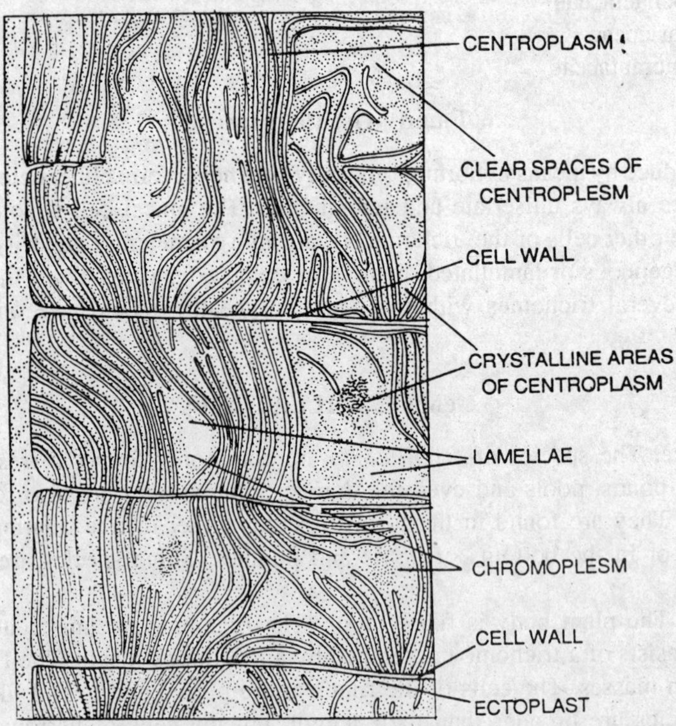

Fig. 2.8. Line diagram of the electron micrograph of *Oscillatoria chalybia* showing membranous nature of the pigment bearing chromoplasm, the centroplasm probably contains DNA is irregular in shape and not separated by a membrane from the chromoplasm. The centroplasm possesses granular background in which are embedded crystalline-like areas and clear spaces.

The cells of the trichome are somewhat rectangular. The protoplast of each cell may easily be differentiated into two regions. The peripheral coloured region is called the chromatoplasm. This region contains many pigments such as phycocyanin, phycoerythrin, carotene, xanthophyll, chlorophyll and food reserves such as glycogen granules etc. In addition to pigments pseudovacuoles are also found in the region. The function of pseudovacuoles is a subject of controversy. The central colourless region of the cells is called the centroplasm or central body. True nucleus is absent. The central body contains chromatin granules in dispersed condition. The central body represents the very primitive form of nucleus. According to West, this is an **incipient nucleus.** There are no nucleoli and nuclear membrane.

The cell wall of the cell is two layered, the outer layer consists of pectic substances whereas the layer next to protoplast consists of cellulose.

Movement of the filament. The filaments of *Oscillatoria* oscillate in pendulum-like fashion. The trichomes are ensheathed with gelatinous matrix and because of the swelling and expansion of this matrix the filaments move like the pendulum of the clock.

Reproduction. The reproduction takes place by vegetative method.

The vegetative reproduction takes place by means of **hormogones.** At various places of the filament colourless biconcave separation discs are formed. The filament breaks at these points giving rise to hormogones. Each hormogone consists of two or more cells. Each hormogone develops into a new plant.

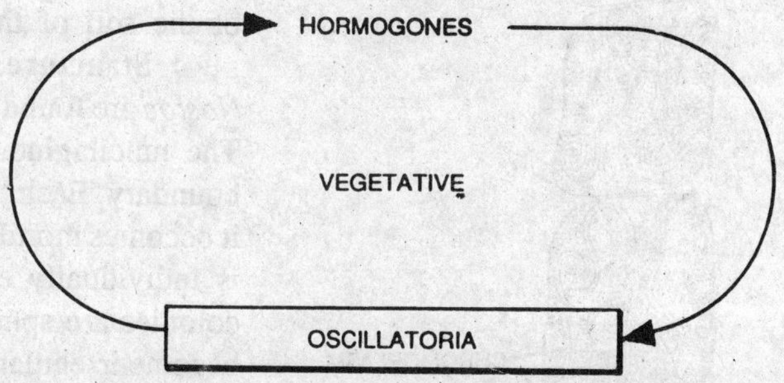

Fig. 2.9. *Oscillatoria* sp. Graphic life-cycle.

Genus-LYNGBYA

The members do not form spores or heterocysts. The trichomes are uniseriate and occur singly in the enveloping sheath.

All cells are capable of division, and reproduction is by hormogones. The enveloping sheath is often thick and coloured.

Family-Nostocaceae

The trichomes of this family are always unbranched, uniseriate and without attenuation at their apices. The trichomes remain always surrounded by a sheath. They may be straight, spiral or twisted. The sheaths surrounding the trichomes are homogeneous. The cells are rounded or barrel-shaped and with or without constrictions at cross walls. The protoplasts of the vegetative cells may possess a homogeneous or granular structure and their colour may be blue green. All genera produce heterocysts, which may be terminal, intercalary, solitary or catenulate. Akinetes are also formed in several genera. They may be adjacent to or away from the heterocysts. The akinetes are longer than ordinary vegetative cells. They may be of different shapes.

Genus-NOSTOC (Family-Nostocaceae)

Occurrence. The species of *Nostoc* occur in fresh water ponds, pools, puddles and ditches. They are found in the form of mucilaginous masses free floating or attached among the grasses or other aquatic plants growing in the ponds. Some species are found on damp soil and some on the wet bark of the trees in irregular mucilaginous masses. Many species grow on the damp soil among mosses. Some species are sub-terranean and found in the soil even in the depth of three feet or more than that. A few species are found in the running streams of mountains. Some species are found in the bottom of the ponds attached to some substratum.

Certain species are endophytic. The colonies of *Nostoc* are found inside the tissues of *Anthoceros*. Certain species are found in the tissues of lichens, *e.g.*, *Nostoc punctiforme* is found in a lichen *Peltigera canina*. Certain species of *Nostoc* are found in paddy fields where they fix atmospheric nitrogen in the soil and enrich the fertility of the soil of the fields.

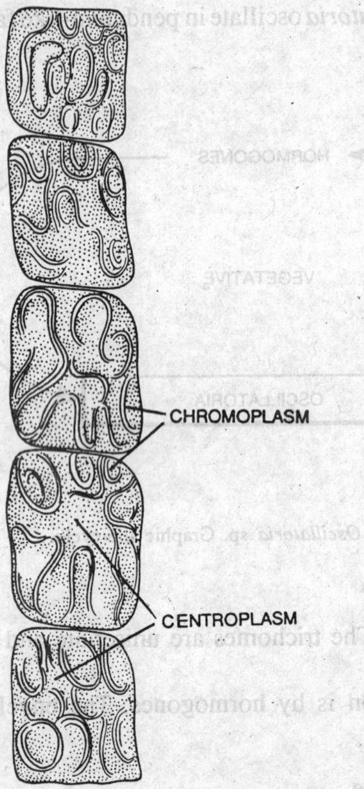

Fig 2.10. *Nostoc muscorum.* Enlargement of several cells showing membranous nature of chromoplasm.

Structure. Innumerable contorted filaments of *Nostoc* are found embedded in the mucilaginous envelope. The mucilaginous envelope forms more or less a firm boundary. Each thread possesses many spherical cells and it becomes moniliform in appearance. Usually each thread is individually ensheathed by a gelatinous sheath. The colonies are spherical in the beginning but later on they become irregular in shape. The colonies of *N. pruniforme* sometimes reach the size of a hen's egg.

The structure of the cell is typical cyanophycean type possessing chromo- and centroplasm. In *Nostoc* the cells are somewhat spherical in outline otherwise the structure is same as in *Oscillatoria.*

Reproduction. The reproduction is vegetative and takes place by means of hormogones, akinetes and rarely heterocysts.

1. **By hormogones.** In favourable conditions the filaments break in small pieces called the hormogones. Each hormogone consists of two or more cells. Usually the filaments break at the heterocysts. Each hormogone is capable to give rise to a new plant. The hormogones may germinate after liberation from the gelatinous matrix or still within it.

2. **Akinetes or arthrospores.** The akinetes are produced in mature colonies. They are formed in unfavourable conditions. The akinetes are developed in between the heterocysts of the filament. Each cell develops into a single akinete. There are much food reserves in each cell and the walls are being thickened. They are also called arthrospores or resting spores. They are perennating bodies. They survive in adverse conditions even for the years. On the approach of favourable conditions they germinate directly or indirectly giving rise to new filaments. The contents of the akinete divide into small bits prior to germination. In many species of *Nostoc* a primary hormogone is produced from the germinating akinete.

3. **Heterocysts.** The reproduction by heterocysts is very rare. The heterocysts germinate in exceptional cases. The contents of the heterocyst of *N. commune* divide giving rise to filament. The newly developed filaments liberate from the heterocysts by breaking their thick walls.

ANABAENA
(Family Nostocaceae)

The filaments of this blue-green alga occur either singly or in floccose colonies and free-floating or in a delicate mucous stratum in permanent and semi-permanent pools. Some species of *Anabaena* are endophytic and live within the roots of *Cycas* and leaves of *Azolla*.

The trichomes are of the same thickness throughout and sometimes slightly attenuated at their apical ends. They are straight, circinate or irregularly contorted and occur singly within a sheath. The sheaths which surround the trichomes are hyaline and generally of watery nature. The sheaths may be broad or narrow, and many planktonic species possess sheaths several times broader than the vegetative cells.

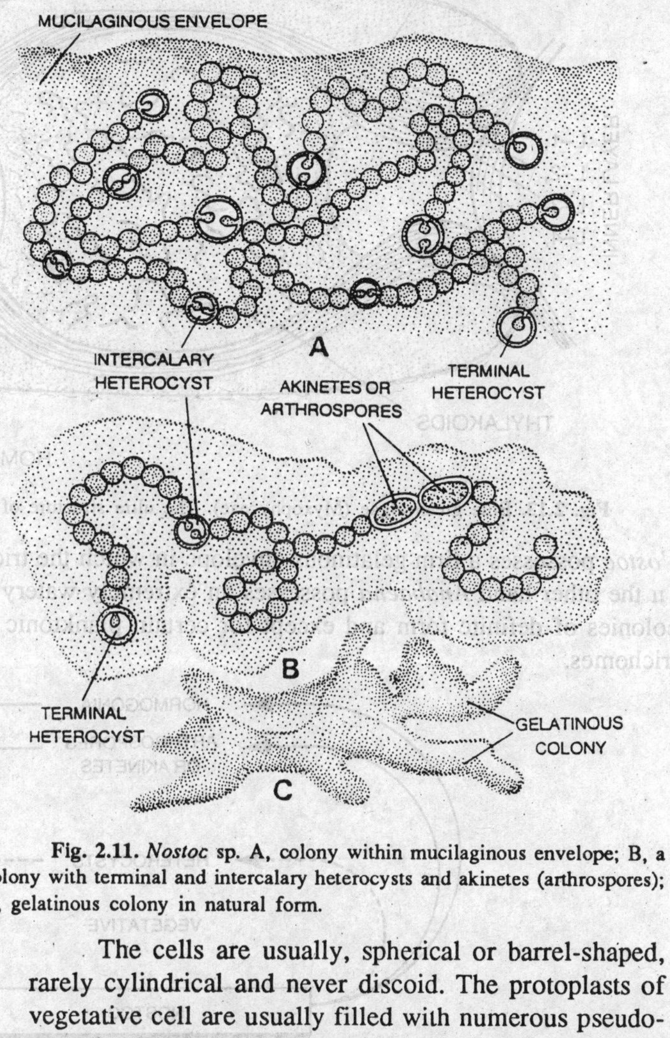

Fig. 2.11. *Nostoc* sp. A, colony within mucilaginous envelope; B, a colony with terminal and intercalary heterocysts and akinetes (arthrospores); C, gelatinous colony in natural form.

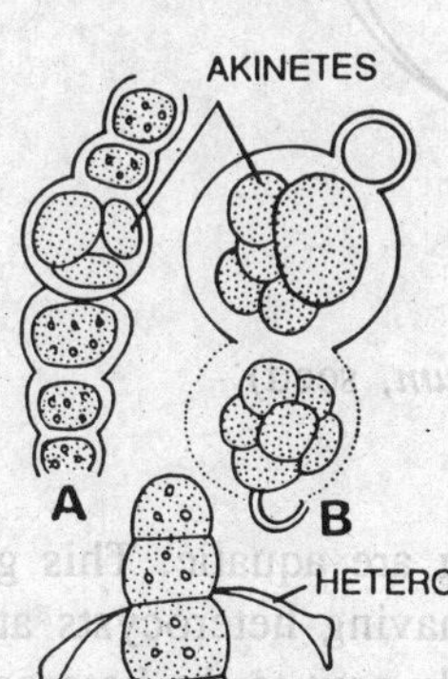

Fig. 2.12. *Nostoc.* A-B. germination of akinetes of *N.muscorum:* C, germination of heterocyst of *N. commune.*

The cells are usually, spherical or barrel-shaped, rarely cylindrical and never discoid. The protoplasts of vegetative cell are usually filled with numerous pseudo-vacuoles. The intercalary heterocysts are of the same shape as vegetative cells, though slightly larger are present in any trichome. They are generally solitary and may be present in any trichome.

Akinetes develop only next to heterocysts, only remote from them or in both positions. The akinetes may be found singly or in very short catenuate series. They are always larger than the vegetative cells and generally cylindrical and with rounded ends.

Reproduction is similar to that of *Nostoc*.

The descriptions of *Anabaena* and of *Nostoc* are quite identical and it seems difficult to distinguish between the two. In actual practice there is no such difficulty, since

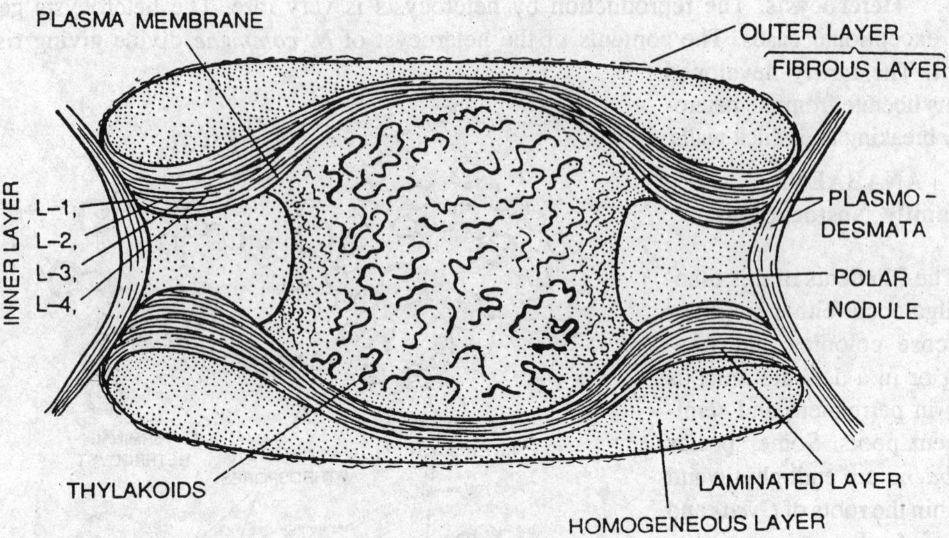

Fig. 2.13. Blue green algae (Myxophyceae). The ultra structure of a heterocyst in L.S. (diagrammatic)

Nostoc possesses a firm gelatinous envelope in which the trichomes are always much contorted, on the other hand *Anabaena* possesses an extremely watery gelatinous sheath and never forms colonies of definite form and except for certain planktonic species, never possesses contorted trichomes.

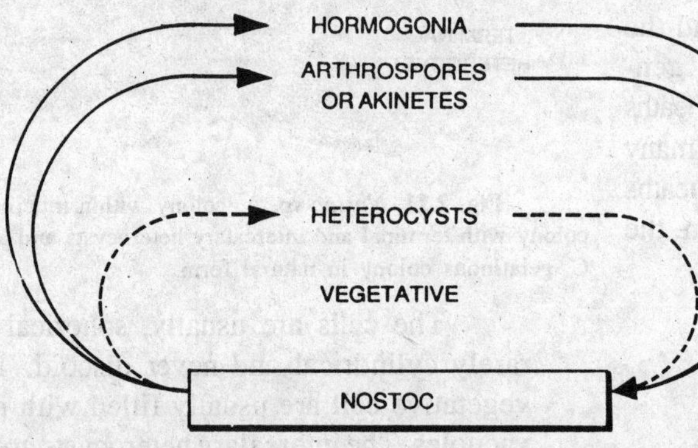

Fig. 2.13 (a). *Nostoc* sp. Graphic life-cycle.

CYLINDROSPERMUM (*cylindro*, cylinder; *spermum*, seed) (Family-Nostocaceae)

Some species of this genus are terrestrial while the remaining are aquatic. This genus may sharply be differentiated from other genera of the family by having heterocysts at one or both ends of the trichomes and by the formation of the akinetes only next to the heterocysts. The trichomes are generally short, straight or curved and of the same diameter of its entire length. Each trichome is surrounded by an extremely mucous sheath. The cells are barrel-shaped or cylindrical and possess rounded ends. Each cell is about twice as long as broad. The akinetes are quite large in size but the heterocysts are approximately the same size as vegetative cells. The outer wall of the akinete is often papillate.

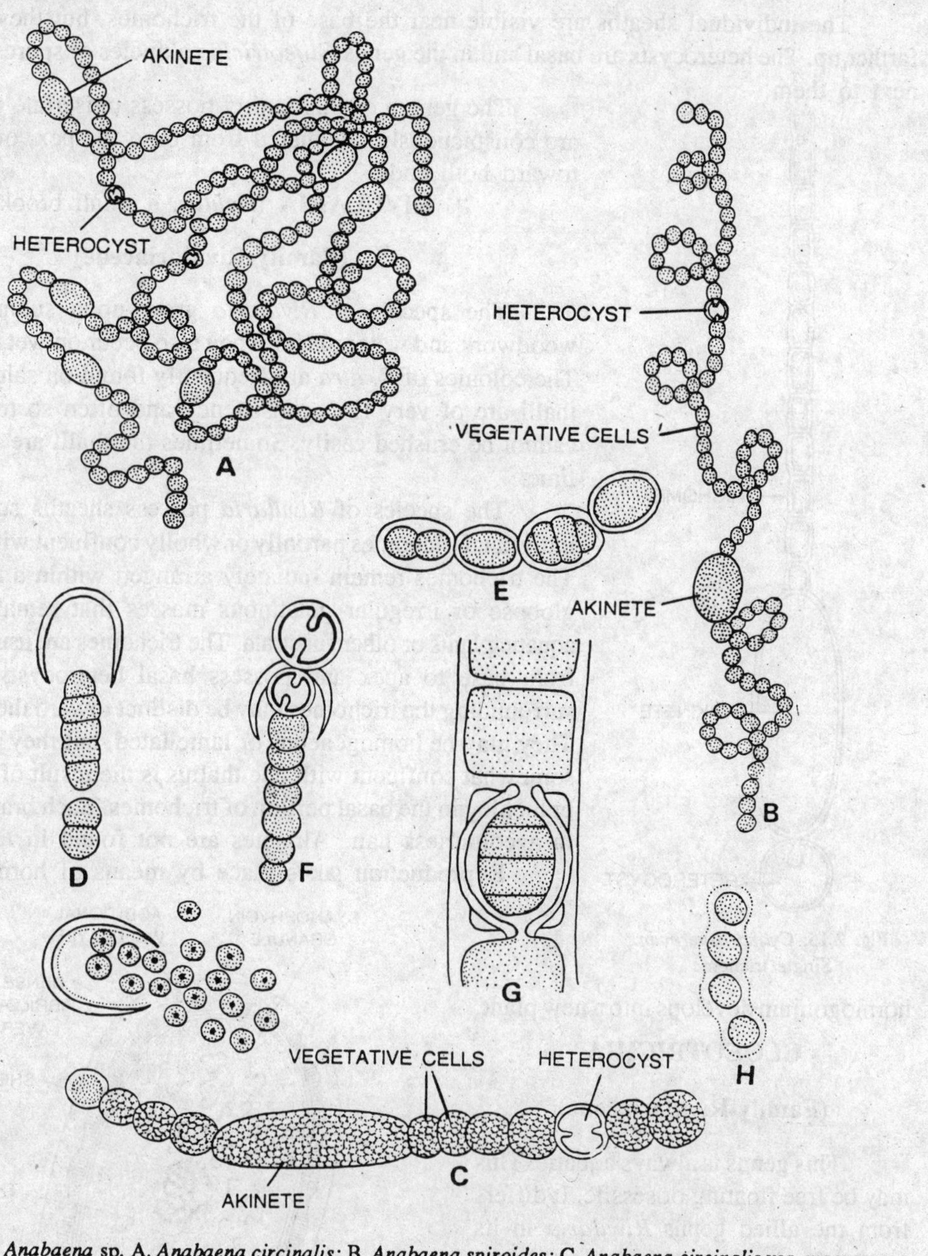

Fig. 2.14. *Anabaena* sp. A, *Anabaena circinalis;* B, *Anabaena spiroides;* C, *Anabaena circinalis* var. *macrospora;* D, germination of akinete in *A. sphaerica;* G, germination of heterocyst in *A. hallensis;* H-I, germination of heterocyst in *A. cycadae;*

Family-Rivulariaceae

The colonies form spherical, hemispherical or irregular gelatinous masses which remain attached to plants or stones or they occur on the soil. The colonies of *Rivularia atra* are very frequently found on salt marshes. Each colony contains numerous radiating filaments with repeated false branching. Each branch terminates in a colourless hair. With the production of mucilage the false branches become displaced and their origin is not easily seen.

The individual sheaths are visible near the base of the trichomes, but they are different farther up. The heterocysts are basal and in the genus *Gloeotrichia* akinetes or spores are produced next to them.

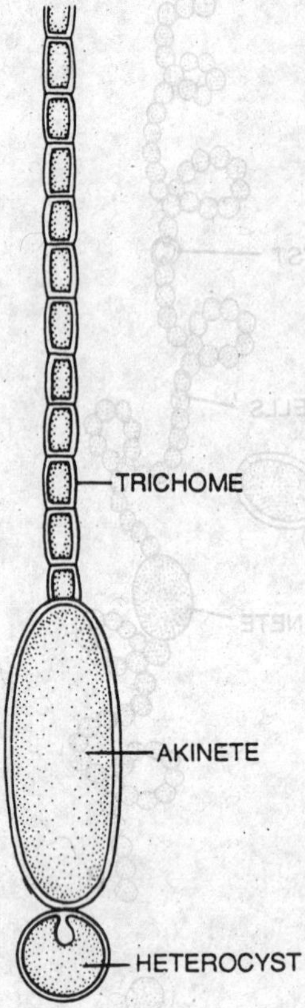

Fig. 2.15. *Cylindrospermum.* Single trichome

The genera of this family possess uniseriate trichomes that are conspicuously attenuated from base to apex, or from middle toward both ends.

RIVULARIA (*rivulus,* a small brook)

(Family-Rivulariaceae)

The species of *Rivularia* grow upon submerged stones, woodwork and water plants. They also occur on wet rocks of cliffs. The colonies of *R. atra* are frequently found on salt marshes. The thalli are of very firm consistency and often so tough that they cannot be crushed easily. Sometimes the thalli are incrusted with lime.

The species of *Rivularia* possess sheaths surrounding the individual trichomes partially or wholly confluent with one another. The trichomes remain radiately arranged within a hemispherical, globose or irregular gelatinous masses that remain attached to aquatic plants or other substrata. The trichomes are usually attenuated from base to apex and possess basal heterocysts. The sheaths surrounding the trichomes may be distinct toward the basal portion. They may be homogeneous or lamellated, but they remain always somewhat confluent with one thallus is the result of repeated false branching in the basal portion of trichomes. Each branch terminates in a colourless hair. Akinetes are not found in *Rivularia.*

Reproduction takes place by means of hormogonia. Each hormogonium develops into a new plant.

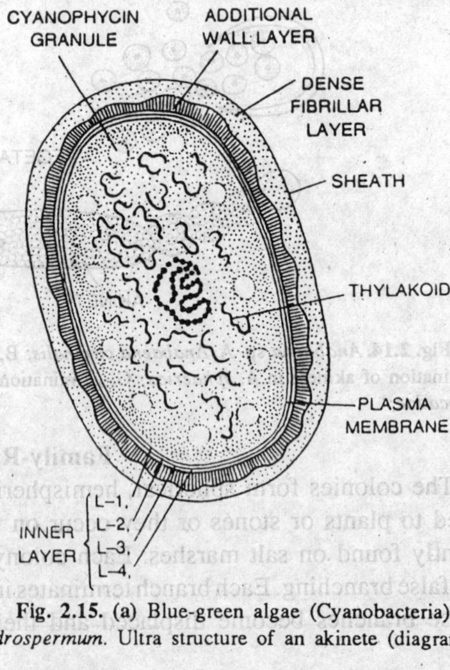

Fig. 2.15. (a) Blue-green algae (Cyanobacteria). *Cylindrospermum.* Ultra structure of an akinete (diagrammatic).

GLOEOTRICHIA

(Family-Rivulariaceae)

This genus is always aquatic. This may be free floating or sessile. It differs from the allied genus *Rivularia* in its regular formation of akinetes and in the gelatinous texture of its thalli.

The trichomes possess regular attenuation from base to apex like *Rivularia,* but they are surrounded by more gelatinous sheaths which are often wholly confluent with one another. The species of *Gloeotrichia* always possess basal heterocysts and sometimes intercalary ones in addition. The elongated akinetes are present at the base of trichomes. There is a single akinete that lies next to heterocyst. If more than one akinetes are found, they are arranged in series of twos or threes.

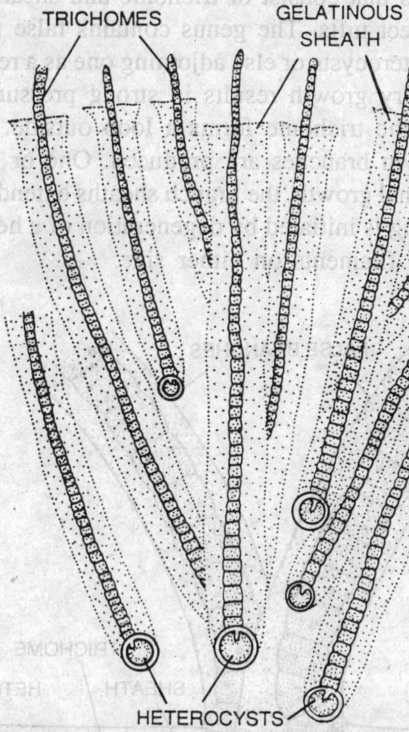

Fig. 2.16. *Rivularia.* Trichome attenuated from base to apex and possess basal heterocysts.

Reproduction takes place by hormogonia and akinetes.

Family-Scytonemataceae

The genera of this family possess uniseriate, falsely branched trichomes of the same diameter throughout their length. The filaments remain surrounded by a firm, well defined, hyaline or coloured and homogeneous or lamellated, sheath. With the result of the segmentation of a trichome into hormogonia, without their liberation from the sheath, the false branching takes place. The ends of the trichomes that develop from hormogonia grow through the old sheath of the parent filament, either singly or in pairs and then secrete a sheath of their own. Akinetes are not found. Heterocysts are always present. In many genera the region of the false branches is correlated with the position of heterocysts.

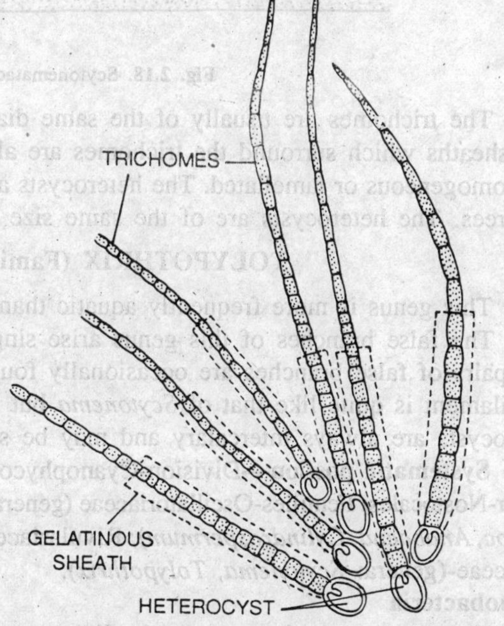

Fig. 2.17. *Gloeotrichia echinulata.* Portion of a sterile colony.

SCYTONEMA (*scyto*, leather; *nema*, thread)

The genus is usually found in subaerial habitats. Some species grow best on damp soil, others on rocky cliffs. The filaments that consist of trichome and sheath possess distinct basal and apical regions forming little erect tufts. The genus contains false type of branching. The branches arise either between two heterocysts or else adjoining one as a result of the degeneration of an intercalary cell. The intercalary growth results in strong pressure being applied to the sheath, which finally ruptures and the trichome forms a loop outside. Further growth results in the breaking of this loop and twin branches are produced. One or both of these branches may subsequently proceed to additional growth, the branch sheaths extending back into the parent sheath. Sometimes the false branching is initiated by degeneration of a heterocyst or a vegetative cell and subsequent growth of two filaments on either side.

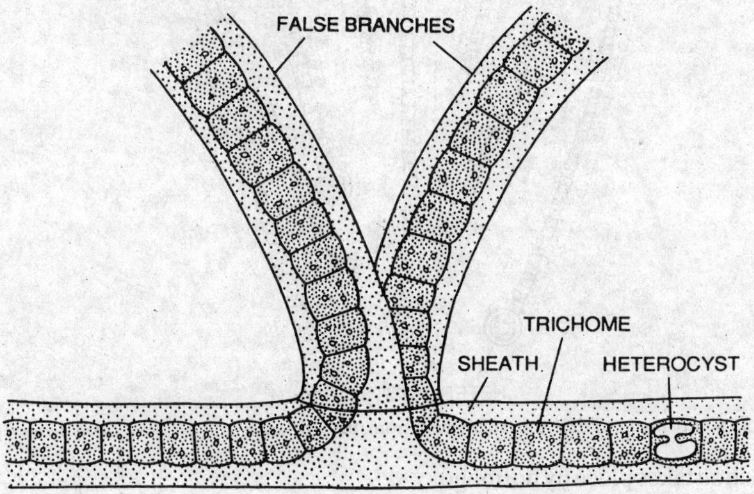

Fig. 2.18. Scytonemataceae. *Scytenema* sp.

The trichomes are usually of the same diameter throughout and with cylindrical cells. The sheaths which surround the trichomes are always firm, hyaline or coloured. The sheaths are homogeneous or lamellated. The heterocysts are intercalary and are borne singly or in twos or threes. The heterocysts are of the same size as vegetative cells. Akinetes are rare.

TOLYPOTHRIX (Family-Scytonemataceae)

This genus is more frequently aquatic than subaerial, usually grows in small clumps or tufts. The false branches of this genus arise singly and immediately adjacent to heterocysts. The pairs of false branches are occasionally found in a filament. The general appearance of the filament is quite like that of *Scytonema* but the sheaths are narrower in *Tolypothrix*. The heterocysts are always intercalary and may be solitary or in series of two to six.

Systematic postion—Division-Cyanophycophyta; Class-Maxophyceae or Cyanophyceae; Order-Nostocales; Femilies-Oscillatoriaceae (genera: *Oscillatoria, Lyngbya);* Nostocaceae (genera: *Nostoc, Anabaena, Cylindrospermum);* Rivulariaceae-(genera: *Rivularia, Gloeotrichia*), Scytonemataceae-(genera: *Scytonema, Tolypothrix*).

Cyanobacteria

There are two main patterns of cellular organization-**prokaryotic** and **eukaryatic**. On the prokaryotic side, there are diverse forms of bacteria and a group generally termed **blue-green algae**. The term algae was applied to these organisms on the basis of their photosynthetic activities before their structural relationship to bacteria was uncovered with the electron microscope; they are, more popularly referred to as **blue-green bacteria** or **cyanobacteria**. The cyanobacteria have been included in Volume 3 of Bergey's Manual. According to Bergey's classification they are **oxygenic phototrophic bacteria.**

In cyanobacteria their nuclear material deoxyribo-nucleic acid (DNA), is not delimited from the remainder of the protoplasm by a nuclear membrane, but rather it is dispersed to some degree throughout the cell. The membrane bounded plastids are absent. Large aqueous vacuoles, like those which occur in many green algae are absent from the cells of cyanobacteria or blue-green algae. The cell walls of cyanobacteria show some chemical similarity to those of bacteria. Certain cyanobacteria may be infected with viruses which resemble bacteriophages advocates further similarity, between cyanobacteria and bacteria.

Revision Questions

Long Answer Type

1. Give the outline classification of Myxophyceae. Mention the characteristic features of the orders. Also assign the genera you have studied to their respective orders.
2. Write an account of blue-green algae and their economic importance.
3. Write a comprehensive account of the methods of reproduction found in blue-green algae.
4. Give the characteristic features of the order Chroococcales. Where the members of this order are met with.
5. How the members of Chroococcales reproduce ? Write a detailed note.
6. Write a comprehensive note on the occurrence, structure and reproduction of *Nostoc*.
7. Write an account of occurrence, structure, ultra structure and reproduction of *Oscillatoria*.
8. Give the important methods of reproduction in blue-green algae giving suitable examples.

Short Answer Type

1. What are Cyanobacteria?
2. Give characteristic features of blue-green algae.
3. Write a note on the reclamation of alkaline usar soils by blue-green algae.
4. Write a note on origin and affinities of blue-green algae.
5. Write notes on: (a) economic importance of blue-green algae, (b) heterocysts, (c) hormogones, (d) hormospores.
6. Write notes on: (a) *Chroococcus*, (b) *Gloeocapsa*, (c) *Microcystis*.
7. Give characteristic features of the order Nostocales.
8. Write short notes on: (a) *Oscillatoria*, (b) *Lyngbya*.
9. Write a note on oxygenic holotrophic bacteria.
10. Differentiate between Cyanobacteria and Bacteria.
11. What pigments are found in blue-green algae?
12. Point out the main differences between *Anabaena* and *Nostoc*.
13. Write notes on: (a) *Cylindrospermum*, (b) *Rivularia*, (c) *Gloeocapsa*, (d) *Scytonema*, (e) *Tolypothrix*.
14. Write notes on: (a) movements of filaments in *Oscillatoria*, (b) hormogones, (c) chromoplasm.
15. Give the important methods of reproduction in *Nostoc*.

Diagrammatic Type

1. Give the ultrastructure of a typical Myxophycean cell.
2. Give the ultrastructure of a cell of *Oscillatoria*.
3. Give the ultrasturcture of a part of *Nostoc*.

Multiple Choice Type

1. The Cyanobacteria are:
   (i) eurkaryotic, (ii) prokaryotic, (iii) eu- and prokaryotic, (iv) none of above.
2. In Cyanobacteria the nucleus is surrounded by
   (i) single-layered membrane, (ii) double-layered membrane, (iii) no membrane, (iv) none of above.

3. The storage products in blue-green algae are:
   (i) mannitol, (ii) cyanophycean starch and proteins, (iii) algin, (iv) agar-agar.
4. Flagellation is not found in:
   (i) Chlorophyceae, (ii) Phaeophyceae, (iii) Charophyceae, (iv) Myxophyceae.
5. The heterocysts are not found in:
   (i) *Oscillatoria*, (ii) *Nostoc*, (iii) *Rivularia*, (iv) *Gloeotrichia*.
6. The pendulum-like movement is found in:
   (i) *Nostoc*, (ii) *Anabaena*, (iii) *Oscillatoria*, (iv) *Rivularia*.
7. The tissue of *Anthoceros* contains:
   (i) *Nostoc*, (ii) *Cylindrospermum*; (iii) *Oscillatoria*, (iv) *Lyngbya*.
8. The roots of *Cycas* contain:
   (i) *Nostoc*, (ii) *Anabaena*, (iii) *Chroococcus*, (iv) *Oscillatoria*.
9. The leaves of *Azolla* contain:
   (i) *Oscillatoria*, (ii) *Anabaena*, (iii) *Rivularia*, (iv) *Gloeocapsa*.
10. Akinete formed only next to heterocyst:
    (i) *Cylindrospermum*, (ii) *Nostoc*, (iii) *Rivularia*, (iv) *Anabaena*.
11. The false branching is found in:
    (i) *Oscillatoria*, (ii) *Scytonema*, (iii) *Cylindrospermum*, (iv) none of above.
12. R.N. Singh is related to:
    (i) Bryophytes, (ii) Brown algae, (iii) Red algae, (iv) Blue-green algae.

Answers

1 (ii), 2 (iii), 3 (ii), 4 (iv), 5 (i), 6 (iii), 7 (i), 8 (ii), 9 (ii), 10 (i), 11 (ii), 12 (iv).

3

Chlorophycophyta-Chlorophyceae (The Green Algae)

Characteristic features

Pigmentation. Chlorophylls a and b, α and β-carotene, Astaxanthin, Lutein, Neoxanthin, Siphonein, Siphonoxanthin, Violaxanthin, Zeaxanthin.

Storage products. Starch, oils.

Flagellation. 1, 2, 4 to many, equal apical or subapical insertion.

There are about 360 genera and 5,700 species.

Occurrence and distribution. About 90% of Chlorophyceae are fresh water and the remaining 10% are marine. Order Conjugales is exclusively fresh water. The algae are common both in quiet and running waters. The species of *Vaucheria* are commonly attached to rocks in mountain cataracts. The species of *Coleochaete* grow on aquatic plants and grasses. The species of *Cladophora* grow even upon mollusc shells. *Trentepohlia* is an aerial alga and grows on rocks and fencing wires. Volvocales and Chlorococcales occur in planktonic habit, *i.e.*, they are free floating. The cryo algae are found upon ice and snow. *Chlamydomonas nivalis* is the main cause of red snow. *Chlorella* is endophytic and grows inside the tissue of *Hydrilla*. *Cephaleuros* is a parasitic form and causes 'red rust of tea.'

Several Chlorophyceae are marine and confined in shallow waters. Many Siphonales are marine. Conclusively, it can be said that the forms of Chlorophyceae are widely distributed and may be expected anywhere.

Range of structure. A sufficiently large range of vegetative or somatic structure is found in Chlorophyceae.

1. Motile forms. There may be motile unicellcular forms, *e.g.*, *Chlamydomonas*. The species of *Phacotus* are motile and unicellular but encapsulated. Several forms are motile colonies, *e.g.*, *Gonium sociale* is a 4-celled colony and *Gonium pectorale* is 16-celled colony. *Pandorina* 8-celled; *Eudorina* 32-celled and *Pleodorina* is 32-128 celled colony. *Volvox* is the highest evolved colonial form and consists of 500-50,000 cells. Only a few cells are reproductive and the rest are vegetative. In one species of *Chlamydomonas* double individuals are found.

2. Palmelloid form. All Tetrasporineae are palmelloid. In the species of *Chlamydomonas* the palmelloid phase prevails temporarily. In *Tetraspora*, this is the permanent phase.

3. Coccoid form. Most of Chlorococcales are coccoid.

4. Filamentous form. Several Chlorophyceae are filamentous. The filaments may be (i) unbranched or (ii) branched. The typical examples of unbranched filamentous forms are Ulotrichales, *Spirogyra, Oedogonium* etc. Branched filaments are found in Cladophorales. Heterotrichous filamentous forms are found in Chaetophorales.

5. Siphonous habit. In such algae the filaments or thalli are branched, multinucleate but without septa. Such types are found in order Siphonles, *e.g.*, *Valonia, Caulerpa, Codium* etc.

6. Uniaxial type. *Chara* is the typical example of this type. Here the ensheathing layer of axis is always one-celled thick.

7. Parenchmatous type. The expanded sheets, which look like parenchyma are also met within Chlorophyceae. *Ulva* possesses two-celled thick expanded sheet.

The cell wall. In Chlorophyceae the cell wall usually consists of 2 or 3 layers. The innermost layer is of cellulose and encircles the protoplast. The second layer consists of pectic compounds of pectose sometimes associated with cellulose. In the case of *Oedogonium* and *Cladophora* the outermost layer of the cell wall is chitinous in nature. In the cell wall of Siphonales and Conjugales the outermost wall layer is covered over with mucilaginous substance and becomes slimy, *e.g., Spirogyra.* Usually calcium silicates and carbonates are deposited on the mucilaginous layer. Some of the more primitive Chlorophyceae lack cell walls and the protoplasts are naked.

The protoplasm. In motile cell two or more contractile vacuoles are found which pulsate alternately and help in excretion. Usually the filamentous forms possess a single large central vacuole in each cell. In some Chlorophyceac, *e.g., Prasiola,* the vacuoles are not found. The vacuole is filled up with cell sap rich in tannins. The cytoplasmic connections are clearly seen in colonial forms such as *Volvox.* Such plasmodesmata are not found in filamentous forms but in *Trentepohlia.*

The chloroplast. In Chlorophyceae a variety of chloroplasts is known. In the genus *Chlamydomonas* various types of chloroplasts are found. The detailed account of the chloroplasts of *Chlamydomonas* will be given in the description of the genus. The typical 'chlamydomonad type' of chloroplast is basin-shaped.

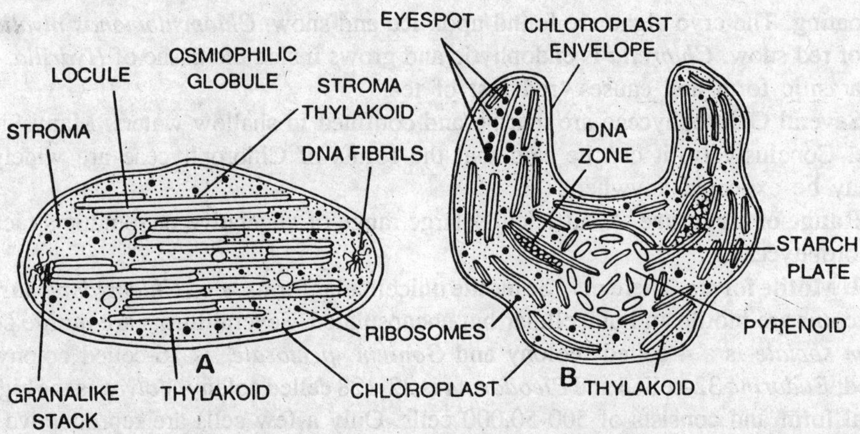

Fig. 3.1. Ultra structures of the chloroplasts of Chlorophyceae (green algae). A, discoid chloroplast showing grana-like arrangement of thylakoid cup-shaped chloroplast of *Chlamydomonas*.

Stellate chloroplasts are found in the cells of *Zygnema* and *thallus Prasiola.* In Oedogoniales and Cladophorales the chloroplasts are reticulate having many pyrenoids in them at anastamoses. In *Spirogyra* the chloroplasts are ribbon-like and 1 -14 in number in each cell. They are spiral and sometimes cut on the margins. In most of the Chlorophyceae one chloroplast is found in each cell but exceptions are there. In *Chlamydomonas alpina* several discoid chloroplasts are developed by breaking a single cup-shaped chloroplast.

In *Mougeotia,* special type of movement of chloroplast is found. Each chloroplast has independent capacity of its movement. The chloroplast rotates to a 90° and exposes its' edge to the light.

The pyrenoids The pyrenoids are found in the chloroplasts of Chlorophyceae with few exceptions as *Chara, Vaucheria, Microspora.*

There are different views about the functions of pyrenoids. According to one view, the pyrenoids are regarded as reserve proteins. According to other view, they are regarded as special organellae of the cells, associated with metabolic activities. According to one rejected view, they are secreting receptacles.

The pyrenoids are crystalloid in structure and sometimes called 'pyrenocrystals'. According to some algologists, the crystals are embedded in a substance.

The compound pyrenoids have been reported from the species of *Tetraspora* and *Enteromorpha.* The compound pyrenoid is surrounded by a starch sheath. There are as many starch grains deposited around the pyrenoid and the whole pyrenoid is surrounded by a starch sheath. Whenever, the starch sheath of starch grains is incomplete around the pyrenoid, the structure is called the 'polar pyrenoid'.

In majority of Chlorophyceae the pyrenoids are responsible for starch formation. In order Siphonales where the pyrenoids are lacking, the starch is formed by leucoplasts in the cytoplasm.

The pigments. The most important pigment of Chlorophyceae is chlorophyll *a*. In addition to it chlorophyll *b,* carotenoids and xanthophyll are also present. Haematochrome is reported from *Trentepohlia* and because of this pigment this looks orange red in colour. Phycoporphyrin is recorded from several Conjugales. Fucoxanthin has been found in *Zygnema pectinatum.* The lutein is among principal xanthophylls.

The nucleus. In majority of Chlorophyceae the cells are uninucleate except Cladophorales where the condition is multinucleate. The multinucleate condition is also seen in Siphonales where the filaments are without septa. Fundamentally the nucleus of Chlorophyceae resembles with the nucleus of higher plants. The nucleolus is deeply stainable and conspicuous. It appears as a central caryosome. The centrosomes have been recorded from Volvocales, *Cladophora* and *Vaucheria.* Mitosis and meiosis occur in all types.

The flagella. The flagella of Chlorophyceae and especially of order Volvocales are

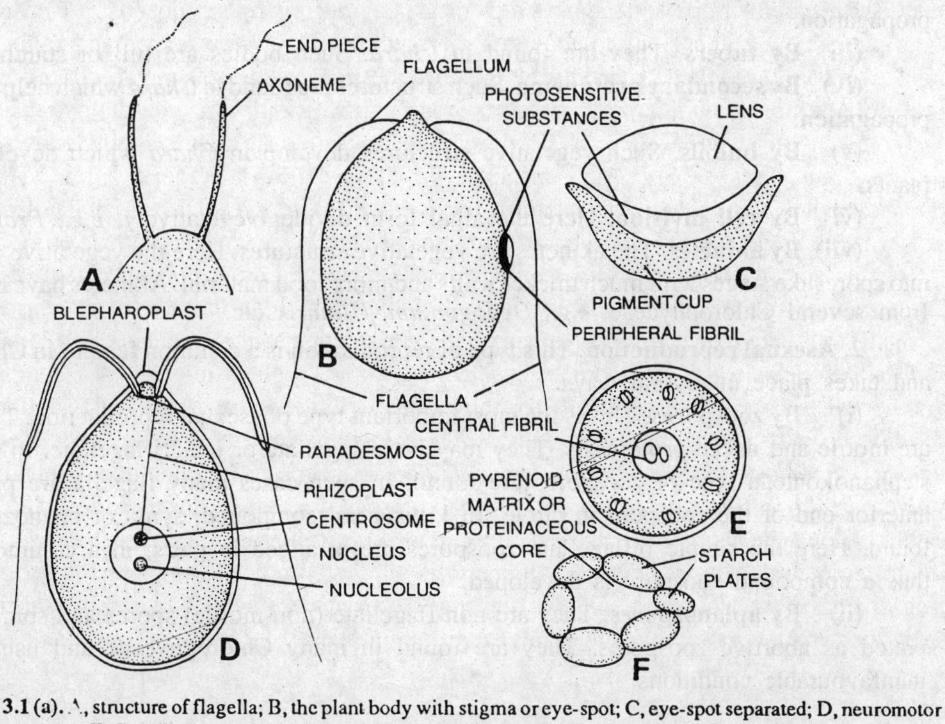

Fig. 3.1 (a). A, structure of flagella; B, the plant body with stigma or eye-spot; C, eye-spot separated; D, neuromotor or flagellatory apparatus; E, flagellum in transverse section (ultra-structure); F, single pyrenoid with starch plates.

produced by an apparatus called **'Neuromotor or flagellar apparatus'.** Usually two flagella occur at the anterior end of the motile body. At the base of each flagellum there is a flagellum producing, **granule** called **'blepharoplast'.** These two blepharoplasts are connected to each other by a thin fibril called paradesmose. One of the blepharoplasts is connected by a long fibre called **rhizoplast** to the centrosome situated inside or outside the nucleus. The whole apparatus is called 'flagellar or neuromotor apparatus'.

In Chlorophyceae both the flagella are of whiplash or acronematic type. The terminal end of the flagellum is thin and uncovered called the **end piece,** whereas the basal part of the flagellum, is comparatively longer and covered by a cytoplasmic coating. This part is called **axoneme.**

Under the electron microscope the flagellum is seen to consist of a peripheral cylinder of 9 doublet fibrils surrounding a central pair of singlet fibrils. This type of arrangement is known as 9+2 arrangement. The entire group of fibrils is enclosed in a double sheath and the two central fibrils have subsidiary (single) sheath of their own.

The eye spot or stigma. Such spots are universally found on the motile organisms of the Chlorophyceae. They are lens-like and sensitive to light. The details of the stigma may be read from order Volvocales.

Contractile vacuoles. The motile bodies of Chlorophyceae possess contractile vacuoles on them. These vacuoles are present on the anterior of the body. They are 2-6 in number. They are pulsating in nature and excretory in function.

Reproduction. Three main types of reproduction are found in Chlorophyceae, *i.e.*, (1) Vegetative, (2) Asexual and (3) Sexual.

1. Vegetative reproduction. This type of reproduction takes place vegetatively by several means.

(i) **By fragmentation,** *e.g.*, in *Spirogyra, Ulothrix, Oedogonium* and several others.

(ii) **By amylum stars.** Such structures are found in *Chara* which help in vegetative propagation.

(iii) **By tubers.** They are found in *Chara*. Such bodies are full of starch.

(iv) **By secondary protonema.** Such structures are found in *Chara* which help in vegetative propagation.

(v) **By bulbils.** Such vegetative structures develop in *Chara* which develop into new plants.

(vi) **By cell division.** Here the algal form divides vegetatively, *e.g., Protococcus.*

(vii) **By akinetes.** The akinetes are vegetative structures. Here the vegetative cells develop into spore-like stages with much thicker walls and more food material. Akinetes have been reported from several Chlorophyceae, *e.g., Oedogonium, Ulothrix* etc.

2. Asexual reproduction. This type of reproduction is a common feature in Chlorophyceae and takes place in several ways.

(i) **By zoospores.** This is the most important type of asexual reproduction. The zoospores are motile and naked protoplasts. They may be biflagellate or quadriflagellate. In *Oedogonium* stephanokontean type of zoospores are found. In such cases many flagella are present at the anterior end of the zoospore in circle. In *Vaucheria,* compound, syn - or coenozoospores are found. Here the simple biflagellate zoospores are arranged in pairs, in a common mass and thus a compound zoospore is developed.

(ii) **By aplanospores.** They are non-flagellate (non-motile) spores and sometimes interpreted as abortive zoospores. They are found in many Chlorophyceae and usually develop inunfavourable conditions.

(iii) Palmella stage. Hundreds and thousands of cells are embedded within a common gelatinous matrix. In *Chlamydomonas* the palmella stage occurs temporarily whereas this is permanent feature in *Palmella.*

(iv) Hypnospores. They are very thick-walled aplanospores. They are perennating bodies. They are found in many green algae, *e.g., Pediastrum.*

(v) Autospores. The autosopres are aplanospores with the shape of mother cells. They are present in order Chlorococcales. When autospores are found in the colonies they are called autocolonies.

(vi) Daughter colonies. In *Volvox* daughter colonies and sometimes even grand daughter colonies are developed asexually.

3. Sexual reproduction. This may be divided into four main sub-types, *i.e.*, (i) isogamy, (ii) anisogamy, (iii) aplanogamy and (iv) oogamy.

(i) Isogamy. This is the simplest and primitive type of sexual reproduction. Two morphologically identical flagellated zoogametes take part in fusion. Usually such gametes come from two different individuals. The resultants are zygospores. Isogamy is found in many Chlorophyceae, *e.g.*, species of *Chlamydomonas, Ulothrix.*

(ii) Anisogamy. Here the gametes taking part in fusion are not identical. The gametes are flagellate. One gamete is smaller and the other larger in size. The smaller one is supposed to be male and the larger female. The resultants are zygospores. The examples of anisogamy are found in several Chlorophyceae, *e.g., Chlamydomonas braunii.*

(iii) Oogamy. This is the highest evolved type. There is union of small flagellated antherozoid with a large non-motile egg. The resultants may be called oospore, *e.g., Volvox, Oedogonium, Vaucheria* and several other Chlorophyceae.

The species may be homothallic (monoecious), *i.e.*, both male and female sex organs are present on the same plant, or heterothallic (dioecious), *i.e.*, male and female sex organs develop on two different thalli.

(iv) Aplanogamy. This is an unusual type found in order Conjugales. Here the amoeboid gametes (aplanogametes) fuse to each other and zygospores are resulted, *e.g., Zygnéma, Spirogyra* etc.

Parthenogenesis. Sometimes the perfect spores are attained without fusion and are called azygospores or parthenospores. Here the female gamete may give rise to a new plant without fusing with male gamete. The process is called parthenogenesis. This process has been recorded from several Chlorophyceae. Sometimes one species of the genus reproduces parthenogenetically and the other species does not, *e.g., Ulva lactuca* is parthenogenetic species and *U. lobata* is not.

Zygote and its germination. The zygote is a very resistant perennating body which usually faces the adverse environmental conditions for its survival. The zygotes of Chlorophyceae may be thin-walled or thick-walled. The thin-walled zygotes germinate within a day or two after their formation. The thick-walled zygotes remain dormant for a short or long period and then germinate.

Iso - and anisogamous species form thick-walled zygotes which possess flagella on them for a short time and the zygote remains motile during this period. Later on, these flagella are withdrawn and the zygote secretes a thick wall around it.

All oogamous species possess non-motile zygotes from the very beginning.

The rest period of the zygotes of various Chlorophyceae varies from genus to genus. The zygotes of *Chlamydomonas* germinate in ten days; those of *Ulothrix* in 5 to 9 months, and the zygotes of *Oedogonium* take the largest period in their germination, *i.e.*, 12 to 14 months.

At the time of the germination of the zygote, meiosis occurs to bring the haploid phase again.

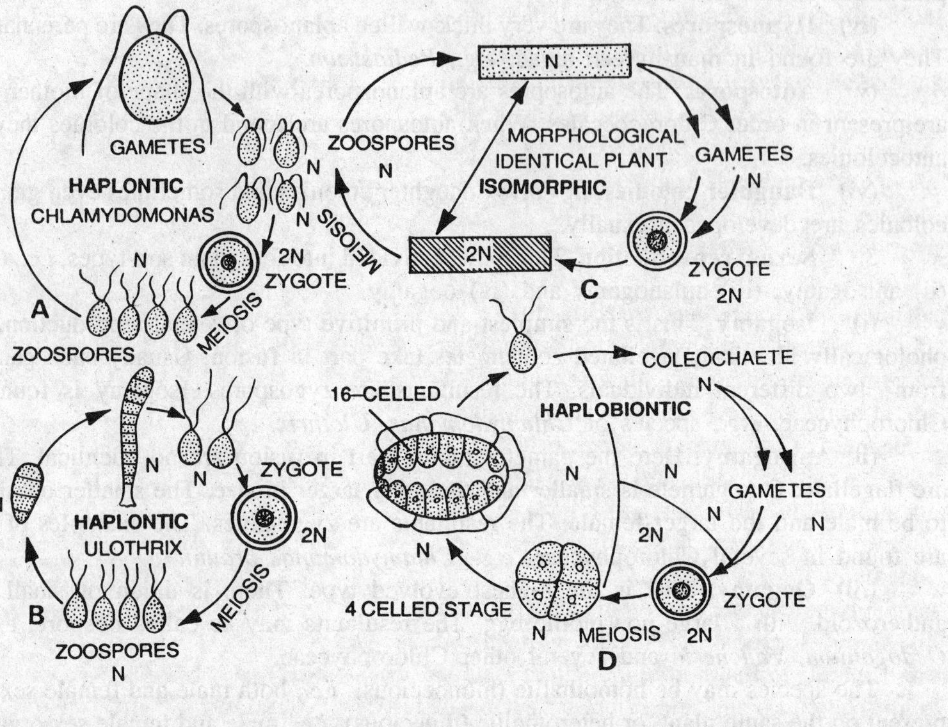

Fig. 3.2. Patterns of life-cycle in Chlorophyceae. A, haplontic type in *Chlamydomonas*; B, haplontic type in *Ulothrix*; C, isomorphic alternation of generations; D, haplobiontic type in *Coleochaete*.

Life cycles. Several types of the cycles are found in Chlorophyceae.

1. Haplontic type. This is also called *Ulothrix* or Chlamydomonad type. Here the zygote is 2x and produces zoospores (x), on germination which develop into individual plants. In this life-cycle the sporophytic or diploid phase is represented by the 2x zygote. This is the simplest and most primitive type of life-cycle. The other life cycles have been originated from this type. This type is found in all Chlorophyceae except few.

2. Isomorphic alternation of generations. In this type there are two exactly similar alternating phases, but one diploid (2x) and the other haploid (x). The haploid plants produce the gametes which after fusion produce zygotes (2x). The zygote is a new plant, which germinates and produces zoospores. Prior to zoospore formation there is meiosis, *e.g.*, Cladophoracese, Ulvaceae, Chaetophoraceae.

3. Heteromorphic alternation of generations. In *Draparnaldiopsis indica* there are two alternating multicellular phases which are haploid (x) and diploid (2x) respectively. These phases are dissimilar in structure.

4. Haplobiontic type. Here there are three phases in the life cycle. Out of three, two phases are haploid and one diploid. The example of this type is *Coleochaete.* Details may be consulted from the description of the genus.

Evolution in chlorophyceae. F.F. Blackman in 1900, reported about evolutionary tendencies in Chlorophyceae. These tendencies are **(1) Volvocine, (2) Tetrasporine and (3) Chlorococcine** tendencies.

In **Volvocine** evolutionary tendency there is an intention of motility by flagella. They do not divide vegetatively.

In **Tetrasporine** tendency there is loss of motility except at the time of reproduction. The cells divide vegetatively besides reproductive divisions.

In **Chlorococcine** tendency there is complete loss of motility. There is no power of vegetative division.

Phylogenetic Relationships in the Chlorophyceae

From the view point of their evolution and phylogenetic relationships three tendencies **volvocine, tetrasporine and chlorococcine** have been taken into consideration. They are as follows.

Volvocine line. The Volvocales possess a unique type of vegetative organization of the individual cells. The group is also specialized for the biflagellate mechanism of motility possessed by the species of the order. There are great differences in the specialization of the cells within the colony and the complexity of the cell within the colony and the complexity of the colony formation. There are also great variations in the reproduction which ranges from isogamy to oogamy through anisogamy. The similarities have been placed in a separate line of evolution which has been known as **volvocine line.**

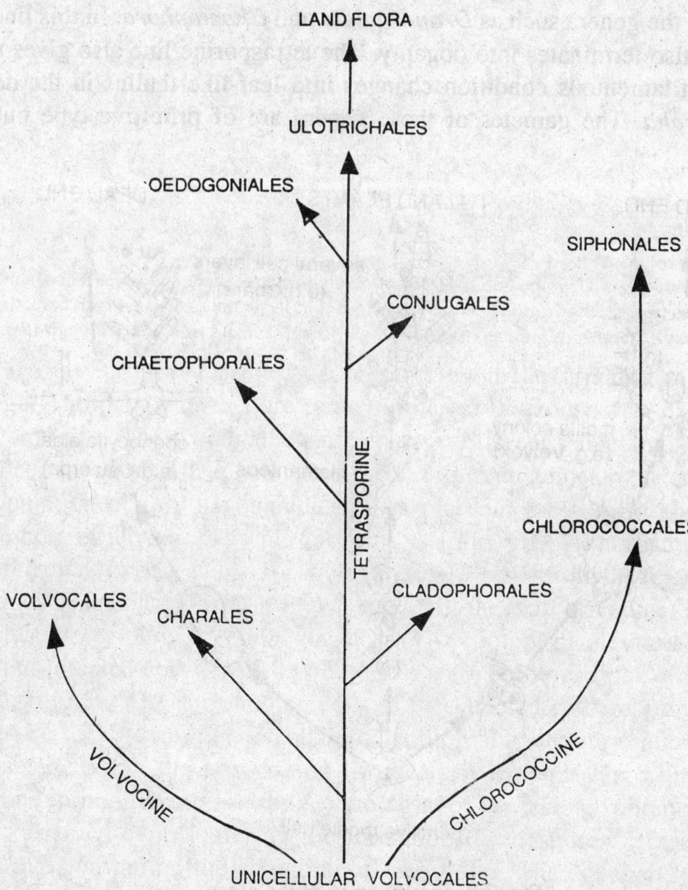

Fig. 3.3. Evolution in Chloropnyceae.

In the order Conjugales, the protoplasts taking part in conjugation are quite similar, and this method of reproduction has been treated as unique among the different groups. The Charales also constitute a unique group on the basis of the complexity of antheridium (globule) and oogonium (nucule), which makes a definite classification of the group difficult. In the order Charales, the vegetative organization is also unique, and because of the presence of all these characteristics sometimes the order is included in a separate class, the Charophyceae. But the cellulose walls, pigmentation and food reserves are clearly of chlorophycean type and therefore, they have been placed in the class Chlorophyceae.

Tetrasporine line. In this line of evolution, the organisms probably began with a unicellular form much like *Chlamydomonas,* but motility was soon restricted to reproductive cells and vegetative body became an unbranched filament like *Ulothrix.* In the tetrasporine line of evolution the members of Ulotrichales play an important role. According to this tendency, the species of *Tetraspora* are supposed to be unicellular members of the Volvocales in which the cells are in an immobile cytoplasmic pseudocilia on the anterior surface. The cell also contains a single nucleus, a cup-shaped chloropolast containing single pyrenoid. The cellular contents of *Tetraspora* indicate a relationship to the Volvocales, and the lack of motility indicates that they have given rise to an unbranched filamentous genus such as *Ulothrix.* The evolution of unbranched filamentous species was followed by the branching filaments. The branching of the filaments becomes more and more complex in the genera such as *Draparnaldia* and *Chaetophora.* In this line of evolution, the simple isogamy also terminates into oogamy. The tetrasporine line also gives rise to another tendency where the filamentous condition changes into leaf-like thallus in the development of *Ulva* and *Enteromorpha.* The gametes of these genera are of primitive type but they show a

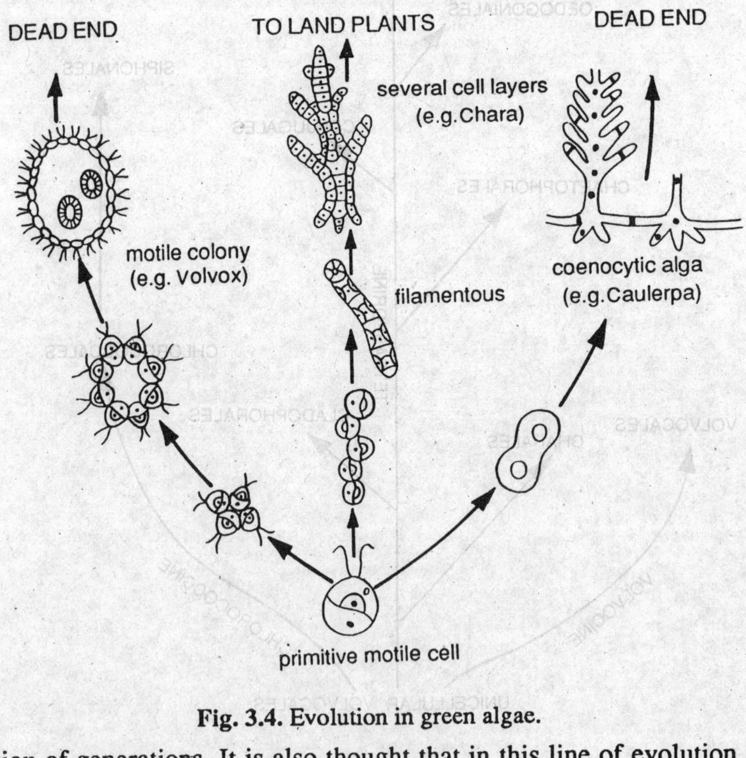

Fig. 3.4. Evolution in green algae.

type of alternation of generations. It is also thought that in this line of evolution a form similar to *Coleochaete* could have given rise to the liverworts.

Chlorococcine line. This line of evolution has been named after *Chlorococcum* and Chlorococcales. In this line, the simple chlamydomonad flagellate type of organism has been thought to be ancestor. Here the line of evolution has proceeded in more than one direction. The motility of the vegetative parts was soon lost and *Chlorella* is an example of this type. The species of *Pediastrum* and *Hydrodictyon* demonstrated the characteristic of being siphonaceous as they possess coenocytic cells and the formation of daughter colonies within the individual cells and the mother colonies. The second divergence of this tendency is shown in *Codium* where the coenocytic cells are found in branched forms. If such a form could have developed a vascular cylinder in its central axis and the sporangia at the apex of its branches, it could have given rise to a plant quite similar to simplest known Tracheophyta. It is believed that the chlorococcine line of evolution is the most logical solution of the relationship of Chlorococcales with the Tracheophyta. They have been treated to be Chlorococcales the ancestors of simplest known Tracheophyta.

Classification of Chlorophyceae. This classification is propounded by Dr. F. E. Fritsch (1944), and based upon the structure of vegetative and reproductive bodies.

There are nine orders in class Chlorophyceae.

1. **Volvocales**
2. **Chlorococcales**
3. **Ulotrichales**
4. **Cladophorales**
5. **Oedogoniales**
7. **Conjugales**
8. **Siphonales**
9. **Charales.**

According to Gilbert M. Smith, the division Chlorophyta is divided into two classes, *i.e.*, **1. Chlorophyceae** and **2. Charophyceae.** In Chlorophyceae there are ten orders whereas Charophyceae contains a single order, *i.e.*, Charales.

Division–Chlorophyta

Class–Chlorophyceae

1. **Volvocales**
2. **Tetrasporales**
3. **Ulotrichales**
4. **Oedogoniales**
5. **Ulvales**
6. **Schizogoniales**
7. **Chlorococcales**
8. **Siphonales**
9. **Siphonocladales**
10. **Zygnematales.**

Class–Charophyceae

1. **Charales**

According to V. J. Chapman (1962) Chlorophyceae has been subdivided into following orders.

Class–Chlorophyceae

1. **Volvocales**
2. **Chlorococcales**
3. **Ulotrichales**

4. **Oedogoniales**
5. **Chaetophorales**
6. **Siphonocladales**
7. **Dasycladales**
8. **Conjugales**

Class–Charophyceae

9. **Charales.**

He has separated the Characeae which comprises of one fresh water order the Charales; from other green algae (Chlorophyceae) because of their remarkable morphological and reproductive features.

Economic importance. The role of green algae is of minor importance as far as the human food is concerned. Occasionally the filamentous genera such as *Spirogyra* and *Oedogonium* are being used in the preparation of soups. The most important green algae with a use as a food today is sea lettuce, *i.e., Ulva lactuca*. This species of *Ulva* and few other species of *Enteromorpha* are used as salads and as an ingredient in soups. Algae may not appear to be of great food value to us at present, but the future of these algae in the human diet seems promising. An adequate world supply of food is becoming a problem every day, and laboratories throughout the world are experimenting with algae as part of diet. In modern days the work *on Chloroella* is in progress. Many countries such as Thailand, Japan, Israel are harvesting thousands of tons of plankton from their nearby seas. This alga has been proved to be substitute for the proteins in human diets.

ORDER VOLVOCALES

There are about 60 genera and 500 species in this order.

Certain important characters of this order are given below :

1. The forms are either unicellular or colonial, *e.g., Chlamydomonas, Volvox, Eudorina, Pandorina, Pleodorina.*
2. The forms either motile throughout life as in sub-order Chlamydomonadineae or forming sedentary colonies of palmelloid forms as in sub-order Tetrasporineae or dendroid forms as in sub-order Chlorodendrineae.
3. Almost all species are fresh water.
4. The chloroplasts are usually basin-shaped each with a single pyrenoid embedded in it.
5. Asexual reproduction is by means of biflagellated zoospores, palmella stages, aplanospores.
6. Sexual reproduction ranges from isogamy to oogamy.
7. The germination of zygote is followed by reduction division.

Classification. The order Volvocales is sub-divided into *three* sub-orders, *i.e.*, 1. Chlamydomonadineae, 2. Tetrasporineae and 3. Chlorodendrineae.

The sub-order Chlamydomonadineae (motile forms) has *four* families, *i.e.*, 1. Chlamydomonadaceae, *e.g., Chlamydomonas, Eudorina, Volvox* etc., 2. Sphaerellaceae, 3. Polyblepharidaceae and 4. Phacotaceae.

The sub-order Tetrasporineae (palmelloid forms) is divided into *two* families, *i.e.*, 1. Tetrasporaceae and 2. Palmellaceae.

The sub-order Chlorodendrineae has only *one family, i.e.*, Chlorodendraceae.

Here the genera, *i.e.*, 1. *Chlamydomonas*, 2. *Eudorina*, 3. *Pandorina*, 4. *Pleodorina*, 5. *Volvox*, included in family Chlamydomonadaceae have been described in detail.

Family-Chlamydomonadaceae

Characteristic features. 1. This family includes all the unicellular Volvocales.

2. Plant body possesses definite cell wall. The cell may be bi - or quadriflagellate.

3. Asexual reproduction takes place by division of the protoplast into two, four or eight daughter protoplasts which form cell walls while still within the parent cell wall.

4. Palmella stages are found in many genera.

5. Sexual reproduction ranges from isogamy to oogamy. Some species are homothallic while other heterothallic.

6. Zygotes are thick-walled and undergo a period of rest before the protoplasts divide to form four or more swarmers.

Genus CHLAMYDOMONAS (*Chlamyda,* cloak; *monas,* single)

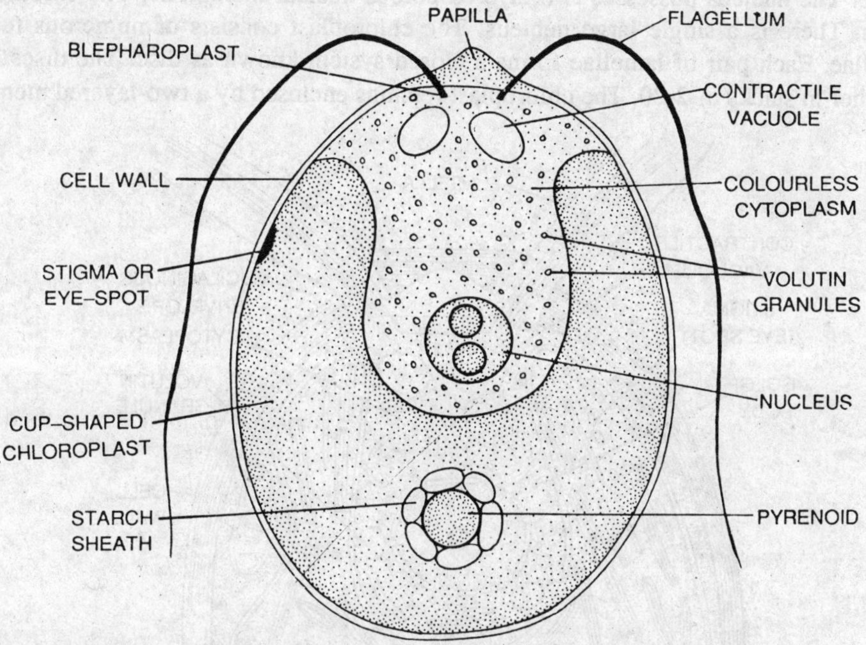

Fig. 3.5. *Chlamydomonas* sp. single cell.

Pascher (1927) has recorded about 150 species of *Chlamydomonas.*

Occurrence. Majority of the species are fresh water. They are found in ponds, pools, lakes, slow running streams and rivers. Sometimes they are found in such a great abundance that the whole water of the pond looks green. *Chlamydomonas ehrenbergii* are found in saline water. *Chlamydomonas nivalis* are found on snow and impart a red colour on the snow causing 'the red snow'. They are usually found in the water rich in ammonium compounds.

Structure. The species of *Chlamydomonas* are unicellular, spherical or ovoid. Usually the wall is thin but in *C. gloeocystiformis* an outer mucilaginous covering is found. The two equal flagella arise from anterior end of the organism. Both the flagella are of whiplash type. A distinct protoplasmic papilla is found at its anterior end. The flagella arise from the granules known, as **blepharoplasts.** A complete 'flagellar or neuromotor apparatus' is found in the organism. The details of this 'apparatus' have already been discussed in the foregoing pages (see page 65). The basal portion of the flagellum is ensheathed by cytoplasm and called **axoneme** whereas the terminal portion is thin and called **end piece.** The two contractile vocuoles are situated at the anterior end in the protoplast usually below the blepharoplasts. The eye spot or stigma is situated on one side of the chloroplast or above it.

Ultra Structure of *Chlamydomonas*

The electron microscopic investigations of the structure of *Chlamydomonas* have revealed many details. The cytoplasm remains bounded by a typical unit cytoplasmic membrane that consists of two opaque layers. In the peripheral cytoplasm of the cell there are a few strands of granular endoplasmic reticulum, free ribosomes and mitochondria. In the cytoplasm within the chloroplast cup lie the mitochondria, volutin granules, a few strands of granular reticulum tubules, free ribosomes and golgi bodies besides the nucleus. The mitochondria possess plate-like cristae. The golgi body is perpendicular in its arrangement. The volutin granules are reserves of phosphate. The nucleus possesses two-layered porous nuclear membrane. The chromosomes are not seen. There is a single large nucleus. The chloroplast consists of numerous tube-like paired lamellae. Each pair of lamellae forms a closed system known as disc. The discs lie one above the other in stacks of 2-20. The chloroplast remains enclosed by a two-layered membrane.

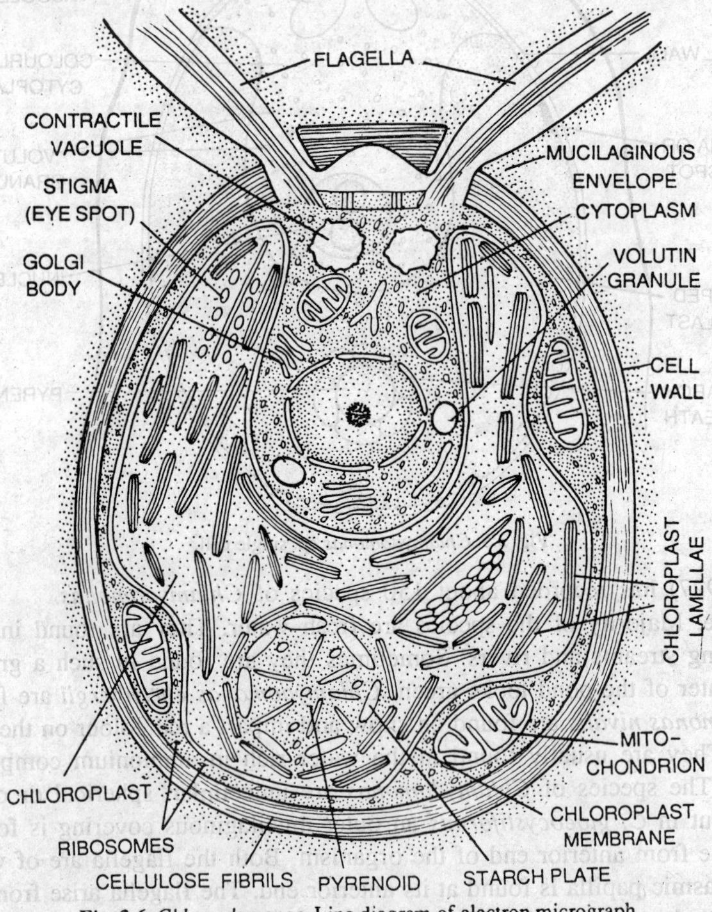

Fig. 3.6. *Chlamydomonas.* Line diagram of electron micrograph. (Ultra microscopic structure)

The space found in between the stacks of lamellae is packed with ribosomes which are smaller in size than those found in cytoplasm. The pyrenoid is also lamellated in nature. The membranous tubular lamellae of pyrenoid are thicker than those of the chloroplast but are continuous with them. The starch plates are synthesized around the pyrenoid. The ribosomes are not found in the pyrenoid. Sager (1965) reported that the pyrenoid consists of a granular core surrounded by lightly packed starch plates. The pyrenoid core is not traversed by lamellae. The eye spot (stigma) consists of two layers of oil droplets containing carotenoid pigments. The flagella pass through the cell wall in fine canals.

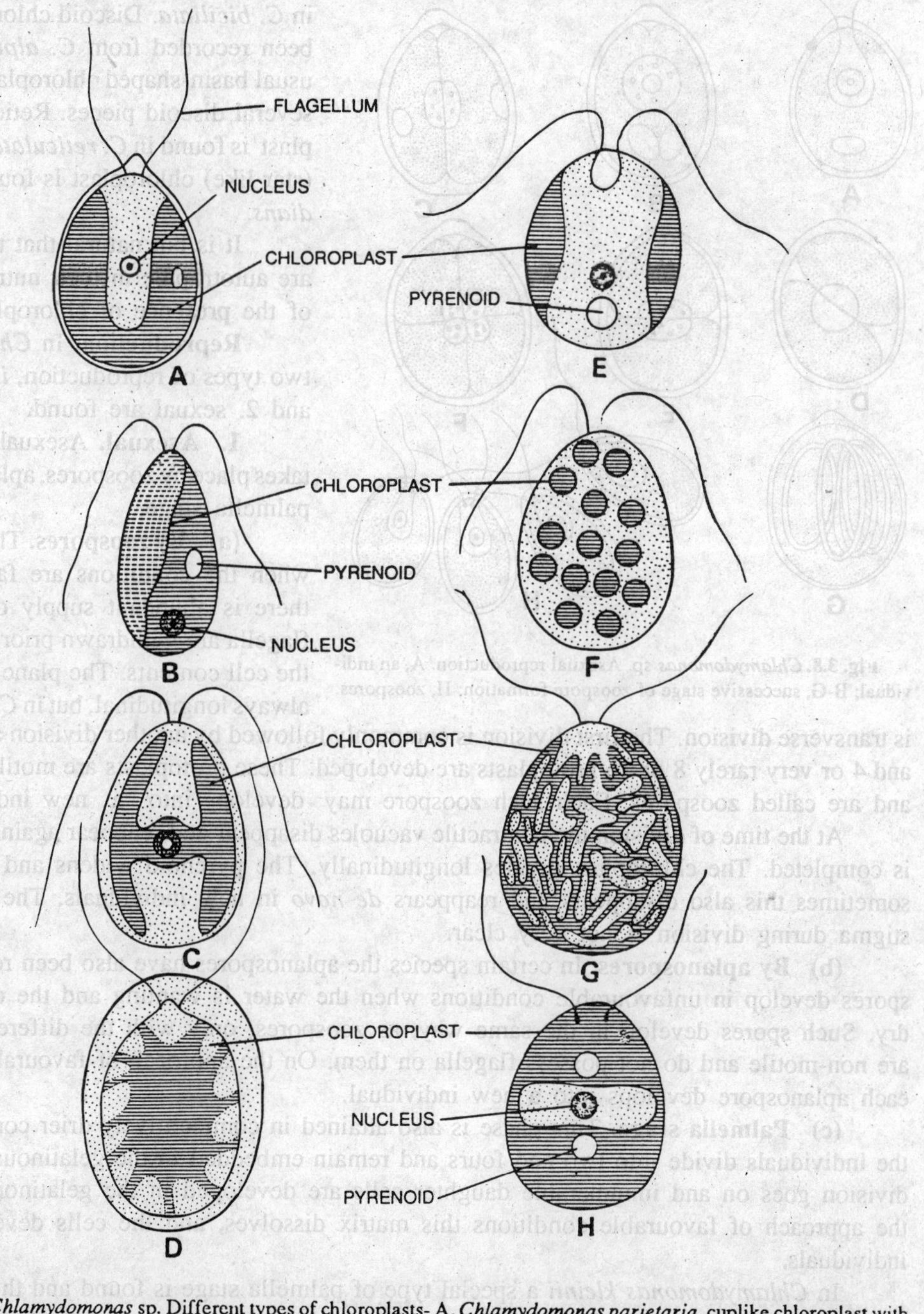

Fig. 3.7. *Chlamydomonas* sp. Different types of chloroplasts- A, *Chlamydomonas parietaria,* cuplike chloroplast with parietal pyrenoids; B, *C. biciliata,* H-shaped chloroplast; D, *C. eradians* stellate chloroplast; E, *C. elegans* flat chloroplast; F, *C. alpina* discoid chloroplasts; G, *C. reticulata,* reticulate chloroplast; H, *C. pertusa* bridge like chloroplast.

Majority of species of *Chlamydomonas* possess cup-shaped chlorolast with a single pyrenoid in each of them. Various types of chloroplasts have been recorded in different species of this genus. In *C. parietaria* the pyrenoid is situated at one side of the cup-shaped chloroplast. In *C. elegans* the chloroplast is flattened. H-shaped chloroplast is found in *C. biciliata*. Discoid chloroplasts have been recorded from *C. alpina*. Here the usual basin-shaped chloroplast breaks into several discoid pieces. Reticulate chloroplast is found in *C. reticulata*. The stellate (star-like) chloroplast is found in *C. eradians*.

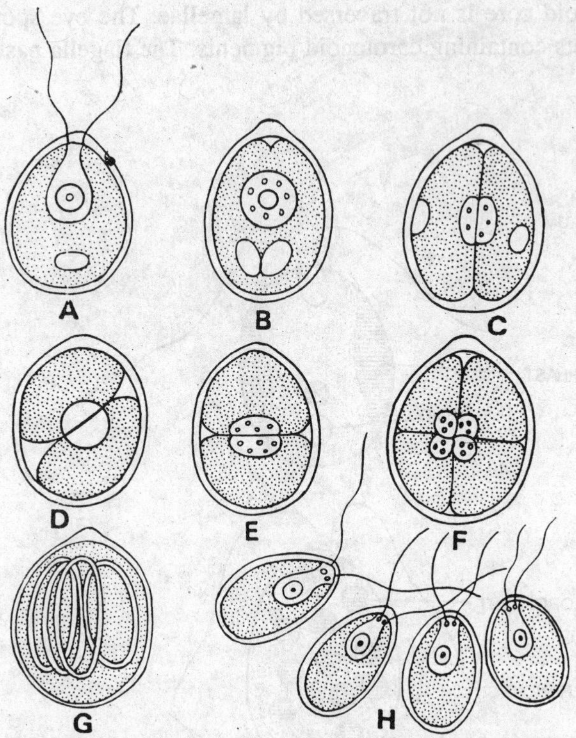

Fig. 3.8. *Chlamydomonas* sp. Asexual reproduction. A, an individual; B-G, successive stage of zoospore formation; H, zoospores.

It is but natural that the organisms are autotrophic in their nutrition because of the presence of chloroplasts.

Reproduction. In *Chlamydomonas* two types of reproduction, *i.e.*, 1. asexual and 2. sexual are found.

1. Asexual. Asexual reproduction takes place by zoospores, aplanospores and palmella stage.

(a) By zoospores. This takes place when the conditions are favourable and there is abundant supply of water. The flagella are withdrawn prior to division of the cell contents. The plane of division is always longitudinal, but in *C. braunii* there is transverse division. The first division is commonly followed by another division at right angles and 4 or very rarely 8 or 16 protoplasts are developed. These protoplasts are motile, biflagellate and are called zoospores. Each such zoospore may develop into a new individual.

At the time of division the contractile vacuoles disappear and reappear again after division is completed. The chloroplast divides longitudinally. The pyrenoid widens and then divides, sometimes this also disappears and reappears *de novo* in new individuals. The behaviour of stigma during division is not very clear.

(b) By aplanospores. In certain species the aplanospores have also been recorded. Such spores develop in unfavourable conditions when the water is wanting and the conditions are dry. Such spores develop in the same way, as zoospores, only with the difference that they are non-motile and do not possess flagella on them. On the approach of favourable conditions each aplanospore develops into a new individual.

(c) Palmella stage. This phase is also attained in comparatively drier conditions. Here the individuals divide into two and fours and remain embedded in the gelatinous matrix. This division goes on and innumerable daughter cells are developed in the gelatinous matrix. On the approach of favourable conditions this matrix dissolves, and the cells develop into new individuals.

In *Chlamydomonas kleinii* a special type of palmella stage is found and the cells divide. On the good supply of water the cells are liberated and become motile individuals.

2. Sexual. The sexual reproduction in the species of *Chlamydomonas* ranges from iso - to oogamy.

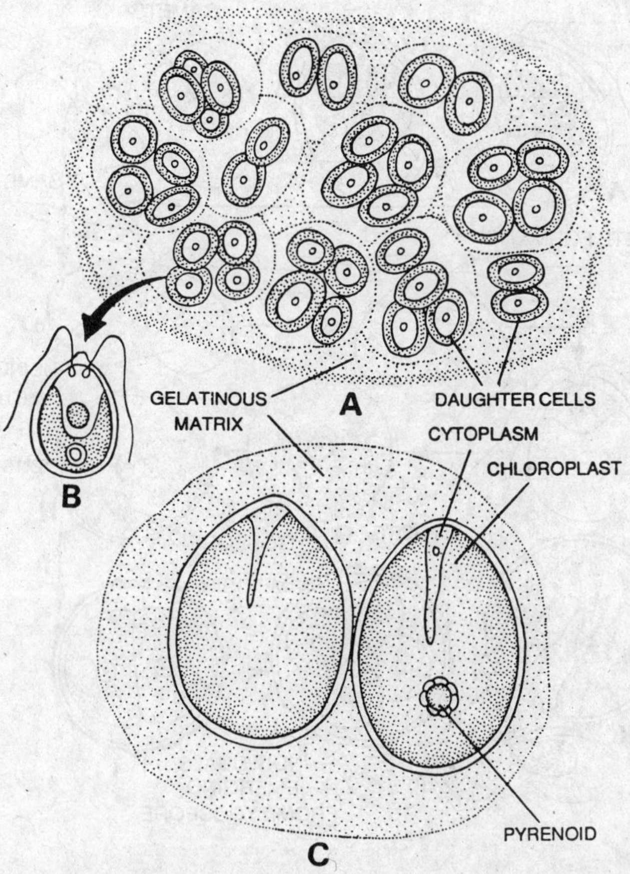

Fig. 3.9. Palmella stage. A, *Chlamydomonas braunii;* B, single chlamydomonad cell; C, *Chlamydomonas frankii.*

(a) Isogamy. The isogamy is recorded in *Chlamydomonas media* and *C. de-baryana*. The contents of an organism divide again and again and 32 or 64 gametes are produced. All gametes are morphologically identical. In majority of cases fusion occurs only in between the gametes from different parent individuals. In *Chlamydomonas media* the gametes are covered by a membrane. This membrane goes away before fusion. The gametes are biflagellate. They move in the water and unite anteriorly or laterally. The resultant of fusion are thick-walled zygospores.

Pascher (1918) has recorded amoeboid gametes taking part in fusion in an undetermined species of *Chlamydomonas.*

(b) Anisogamy. In *Chlamydomonas braunii* the anisogamy is fixed. Here the gametes taking part in fusion are motile and dissimilar. They may be macro - and microgametes. The macrogametes are to be considered as female and microgametes as male. In *C. braunii* 4 macrogametes and 8 microgametes are produced within the parent individuals. With the result of fusion thick-walled zygospores are developed.

3. Oogamy. In *C. coccifera* 16 microgametes are developed in male parent cell. The individuals themselves act as female or macrogametes. The flagella of the female individuals

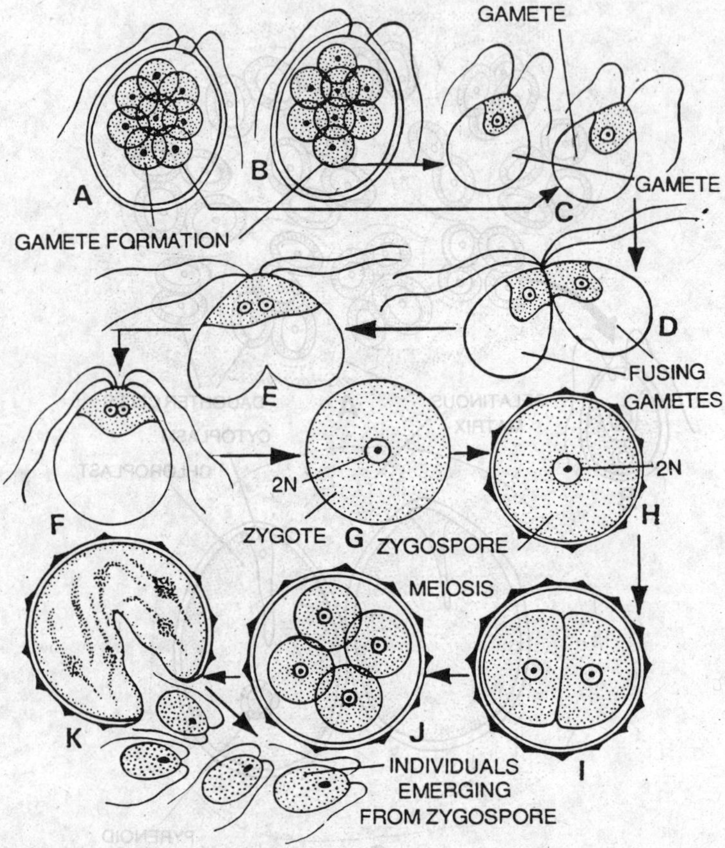

Fig. 3.10. *Chlamydomonas* sp. Sexual reproduction-isogamy A-H, A-B, gamete formation; C, two gametes; D-E, fusing gametes; F, temporary motile phase of quadriflagellate zygote; G, zygote; H, thick-walled ornamented zygospore; I-K, germination of zygospore and formation of zoospores.

are lost and the microgamete attaches to it anteriorly and ultimately the zygospore is produced. This is the primitive type of oogamy.

The oogamy is also found in *Chlamydomonas oogamum.*

Parthenogenesis. Parthenogenesis has also been recorded in some species of *Chlamydomonas*. Here the gametes develop into new individuals without fusion. Actually the female gamtes take part in this process.

Development and germination of zygote. It is not necessary that the plasmogamy is immediately followed by karyogamy. Sometimes, even after the fusion of the gametes the flagella are retained for some time, and the quadriflagellate zygospore moves here and there in the water. Very soon the flagella are retracted and a thick wall is developed around the zygospore. Simultaneously haematochrome also develops and the zygospores become somewhat orange coloured. In some species the outer walls of zygospores are thick and smooth and in others they are thick and ornamented. These zygospores usually pass through a resting period and then germinate.

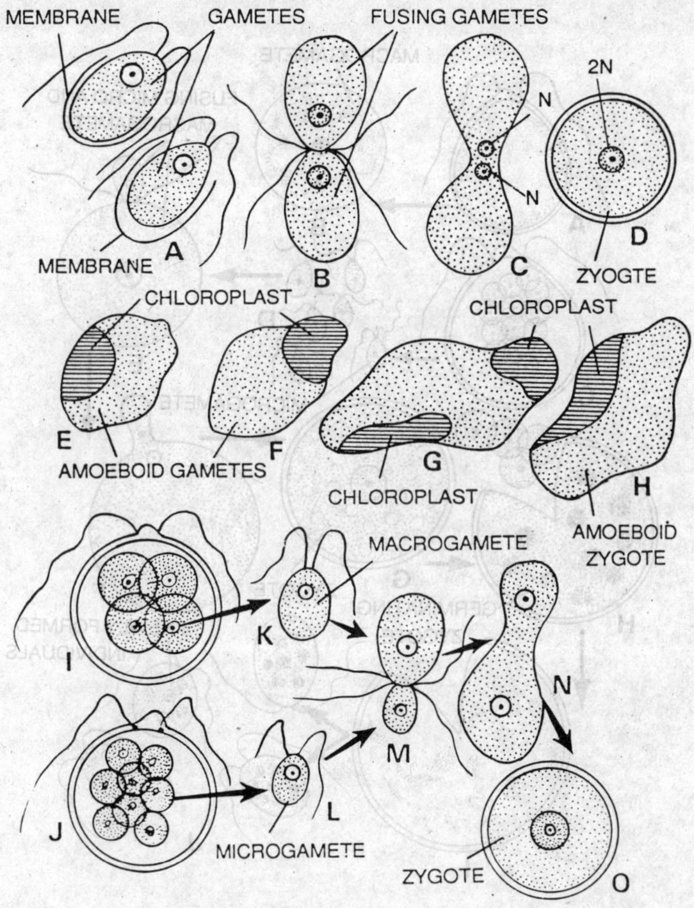

Fig. 3.11. Sexual reproduction in *Chlamydomonas media* A-D. A, membranous gametes lose membrane prior to fusion of isogamete; B-C, fusion of isogametes; D, zygote; E-H, sexual reproduction in an undetermined species of *Chlamydomonas* by means of amoeboid gametes; I-O, anisogamy in *Chlamydomonas braunili.*

At the time of germination the reduction division takes place to bring haploid (x) condition again. The zygote is diploid (2x).

In *Chlamydomonas ehrenbergii,* during germination 4 zoospores are formed. Each develops into a new individual.

Origin of sex. During favourable conditions *Chlamydomonas* produces motile, biflagellate zoospores. Each such spore directly develops into a new *Chlamydomonas* individual. During the process there is no sexual union of gametes, and therefore, this method of multiplication is known as asexual reproduction. In the end of season the environmental conditions become adverse and sexual reproduction takes place. In this phenomenon the fusion of two sex cells (gametes) takes place which results in the formation of a thick-walled zygospore. The resting period of the zygote generally coincides with the unfavourable period. The origin of gametes is, however, known as the origin of sex.

In the process of isogamy, which has been supposed to be the primitive form of sexual reproduction, the uniting gametes are known as isogametes which are motile and identical to

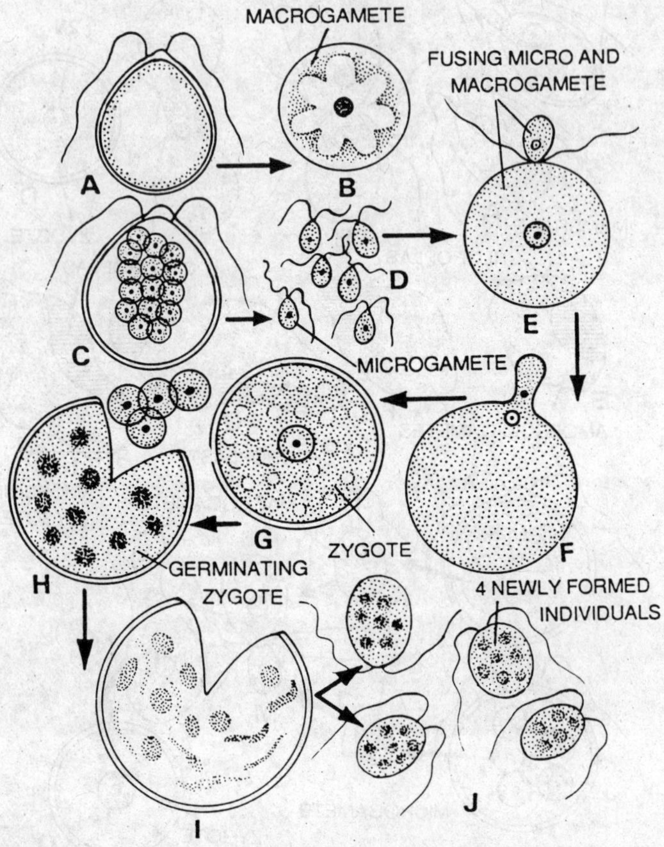

Fig. 3.12. Sexual reproduction by means of oogamy (A-G) in *Chlamydomonas coccifera;* H-J, germination of zygote and formation of new individuals.

each other in every respect. The isogametes and the zoospores resemble each other except for their size and behaviour. The gametes are smaller in size and cannot grow directly into new individuals. The striking resemblance between zoospores and gametes suggests that isogametes have been originated by the subdivision of zoospores into still smaller swarm cells during unfavourable conditions of environment. These reduced zoospores or swarmers are too small and cannot grow directly into new individuals by themselves. Most of them perish and some fuse in pairs forming zygotes. This pairing of reduced zoospores (gametes) increases the vitality and vigour to give rise to a new plant, and the resultant, *i.e.*, the zygospore faces the unfavourable conditions.

The smaller swarmers or reduced zoospores became the gametes and their union the sexual reproduction. This way the sex originated by the accidental fusion of reduced zoospores formed during unfavourable conditions of environment. This process was proved to be an advantage to the species, and therefore, was maintained and fixed under the name of sexual reproduction.

Systematic position—Division-Chlorophycopohyta; Class-Chlorophyceae; Order-Volvocales; Family-Chlamydomonadaceae; Genus-*Chlamydomonas*.

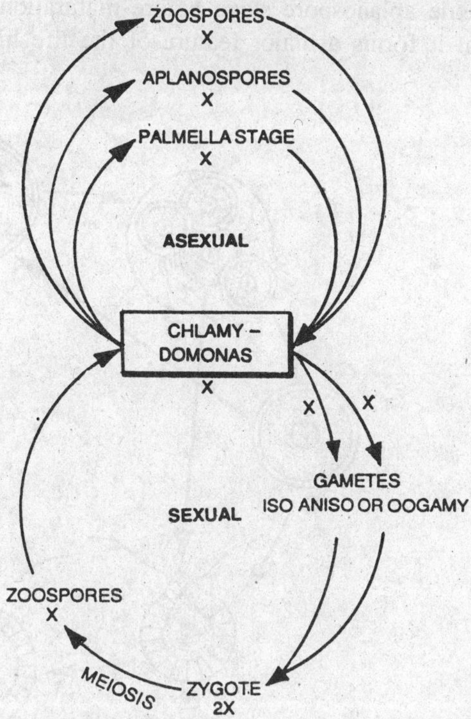

Fig. 3.13. *Chlamydomonas* sp. Graphic representation of life-cycle.

Family-Haematococcaceae

Genus-HAEMATOCOCCUS (*haemate*, orange; *coccus*, berry).

Structure. A characteristic feature of this genus is the area forming the inner wall between the protoplast, which is very similar to that of *Chlamydomonas*. The other characteristic is the presence of firm, outer wall. The area forming the inner wall between the protoplast is filled by a watery jelly and crossing it are cytoplasmic threads which pass from the central protoplast to the cell wall. These are numerous and very fine in *Haematococcus pluvialis*, but are fewer and thicker in other species. The flagella possess a thin tomentum of fine hairs. Contractile vacuoles are not always present, and when present they are inconspicuous. The plastid varies in the different species, and the number of pyrenoids ranges from one in *H. capensis* to many in *H. pluvialis*.

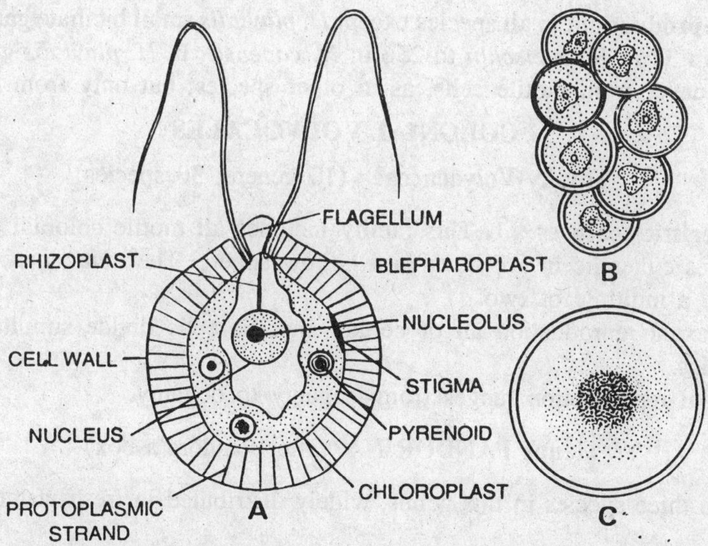

Fig. 3.14. *Haematococcus pluvialis (Sphaerella lacustris)*. A, diagram of single macrozoid; B, eight-celled palmelloid stage; C, encyted plant with haematochrome in centre.

Asexual reproduction. In asexual reproduction the zoospores may pass through a non-motile aplanospore stage before maturation, and this has developed so much in *H. pluvialis* that it forms a maior feature of the life history.

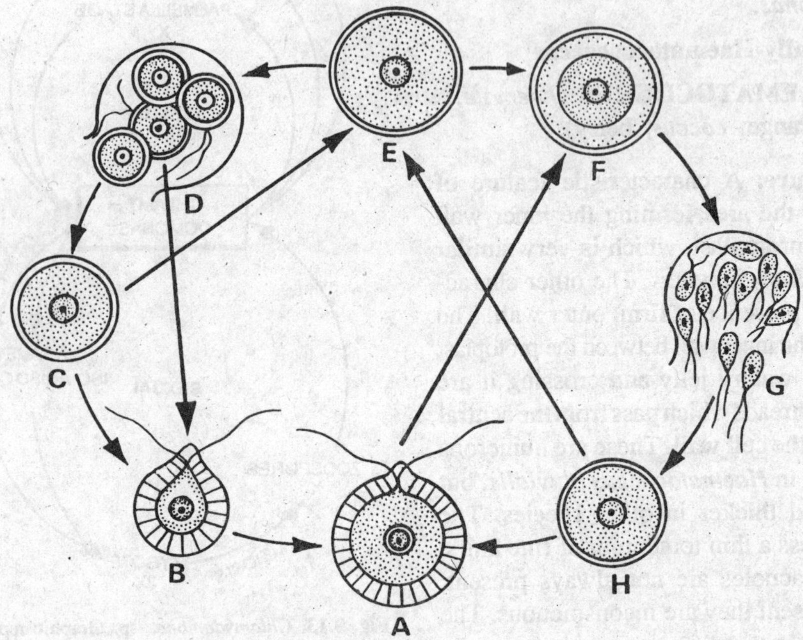

Fig. 3.15. *Haematococcus pluvialis (Sphaerella lacustris).* Diagram showing life-cycle in culture.

Sexual reproduction. In all species except *H. pluvialis* small biciliate gametes are formed, the number from 32 in *H. buetschlii* to 256 in *H. capensis.* In *H. pluvialis* gametes are rarely produced, and never from motile cells, as in other species, but only from resting cells.

COLONIAL VOLVOCALES

Family-Volvocaceae (10 genera; 30 species)

Characteristic features. 1. This family includes all motile colonial genera. The cells of these colonies either lie in a disk or in a hollow sphere. The number of cells in a colony is definite, *i.e.*, a multiple of two.

2. In sexual reproduction all or certain specific cells divide simultaneously forming daughter colonies.

3. Sexual reproduction ranges from isogamy to oogamy.

Genus PANDORINA (after Pandora'a box)

There are three species in this genus, widely distributed in fresh water but rarely found in abundance.

Structure. The coenobia or colonies of *Pandorina* are subspherical to ellipsoidal and possess 4, 8, 16, or 32 biflagellate cells embedded within a homogeneous gelatinous matrix. Sometimes an outer colonial sheath of more watery consistency is also found around the colony. The cells are arranged in a hollow sphere within the colonial envelope. *P. morum,* the commonest species is usually a 16 celled colony. In two species the cells lie so close together that they become laterally flattened by mutual compression. The cells are connected to each other by means of protoplasmic connections. They are obpyriform in structure and possess the two flagella and the eye spot on the broad anterior end. Each cell possesses a massive and cup-shaped chloroplast with one or more pyrenoids.

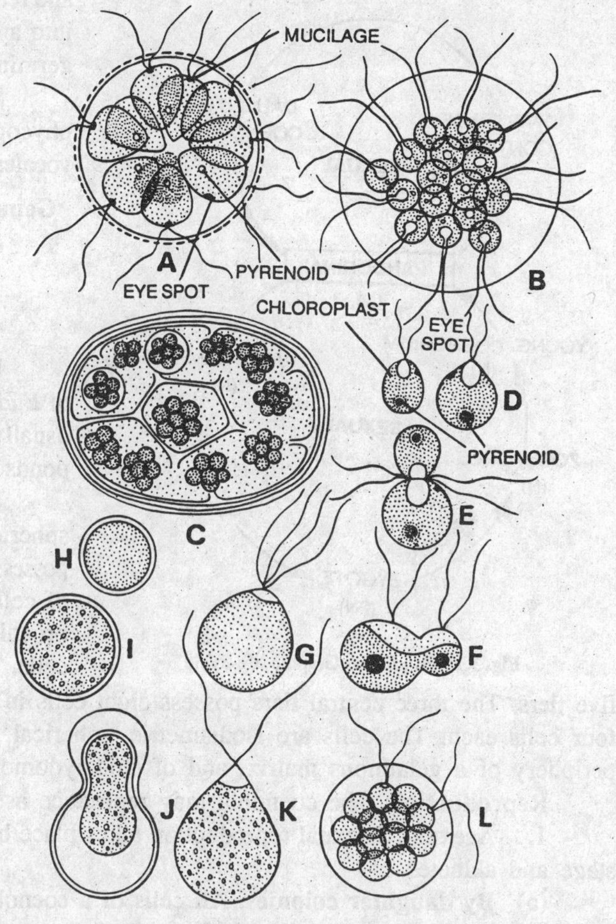

Fig. 3.16. *Pandorina morum.* A, vegetative colony; B, colony of female gametes; C, cells or mother colony forming daughter colonies; D, male and female gametes; E, fusion of gametes (anisogamy); F, plasmogamy; G, flagellated zygote; H, zygote; I, zygote ready for germination; J, germination of zygote to produce zoospore; K, zoospore; L, new colony produced after the division of zoospore.

Asexual reproduction. It takes place by a simultaneous formation of daughter coenobia by all cells of a coenobium. Just before the reproduction a coenobium ceases moving activity and sinks to the bottom of the pond and the colonial envelope becomes more watery and swollen. Each cell forms a typical plakea and the newly developed coenobium becomes bowl-shaped instead of a hollow sphere. The bowl-shaped coenobium becomes inverted forming a sphere in which the phialopore is closed (Morse, 1943; Taft, 1914). After inversion, each cell develops a pair of flagella and the newly developed daughter coenobium escapes by swimming through the gelatinous envelope of the parent coenobium.

Sexual reproduction. *Pandorina* is heterothallic and gametic union is **anisogamous.** Unequal biflagellate gametes are identical with those in asexual reproduction. The coenobium consisting of sex cells, *i.e.,* the gametes escape from the colonial matrix and move about singly (K. I. Meyer, 1935). The male gametes are smaller and swim more actively than female gametes. With the result of the fusion of two unequal gametes quadriflagellate zygote is formed. For a short while this flagellated zygote remains motile but very soon it loses its flagella and secretes a wall around it. The old zygotes possess a smooth wall and protoplast coloured red by **haematochrome.**

Germination of zygote. On the germination of the zygote, the contents of it extrude out in a vesicle and the irregular mass of orange and green protoplast escapes out as a single biflagellate zoospore (Korishkov, 1923). Sometimes, two or three zoospores are produced instead of one. The zoospore swims for a time, retracts its flagella, secretes a gelatinous matrix, divides and redivides forming a plakea which develops into a coenobium. Meiosis takes place during germination of zygote.

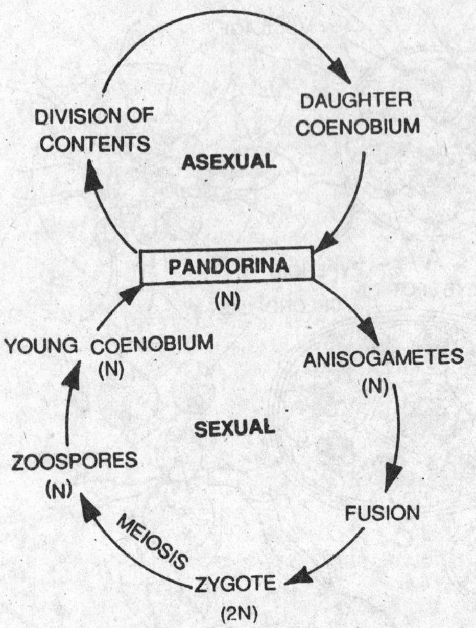

Fig. 3.17 *Pandorina* Graphic life-cycle

Systematic position. Division-Chlorophycophyta; Class-Chlorophyceae; Order-Volvocales; Family-Volvocaeae; Genus-*Pandorina.*

Genus EUDORINA – (ere, well; *dorina*, meaningless)

Family–Volvocaceae

There are 4 or 5 species of *Eudorina.*

Habitat and occurrence. The coenobia of *Eudorina* are found in fresh water. They are usually found in still waters such as lakes, pools, ponds etc.

Structure. The coenobia of *Eudorina* are spherical or broadly elliptical. Each colony possesses 16, 32 or 64 cells. The common number of cells is thirty-two. *Eudorina illinoiensis* is broadly elliptical in shape and possesses 32 cells. The cells of this species are arranged in five tiers. The three central tiers possess eight cells in each whereas the outer tiers consist of four cells each. The cells are isodiametric, spherical, biflagellate, loosely arranged near the periphery of a gelatinous matrix, and of chlamydomonad type.

Reproduction. The coenobia may reproduce asexually and sexually.

1. Asexual. Asexual reproduction takes place by means of daughter colonies, palmella stage and akinetes.

(a) By daughter colonies. All cells of a coenobium are capable to divide and to form new daughter colonies. Sometimes a few cells do not divide. The newly formed daughter colonies escape from the parent coenobium through gelatinous matrix.

(b) Palmella stage. Sometimes, in drier conditions the colonies are gelatinized and the palmella stage is attained. Here the flagella are retracted and the gelatinous palmelloid masses rest upto the approach of favourable conditions. When there is abundant supply of water, the flagella develop again and each motile cell gives rise to a new colony.

(c) By akinetes. Actually they are vegetative bodies. Sometimes, the flagella of the cells are lost, and they act as akinetes. On the approach of favourable conditions each akinete develops into a new colony.

2. Sexual. The sexual reproduction is oogamous. The primitive type of oogamy does occur.

The species of *Eudorina* may be monoecious or dioecious. The female colonies of *Eudorina* are like just the vegetative colonies only with the difference that the cells behave like eggs which are somewhat bigger in size and do not divide. In *E. illinoiensis* the four anterior cells are sterile.

In monoecious species the four anterior cells of the colony give rise to spermatozoids whereas the rest cells act as eggs. In dioecious species the male and female coenobia are separate. In male colonies, the contents of each cell divide again and again forming a bundle of 64 spindle-

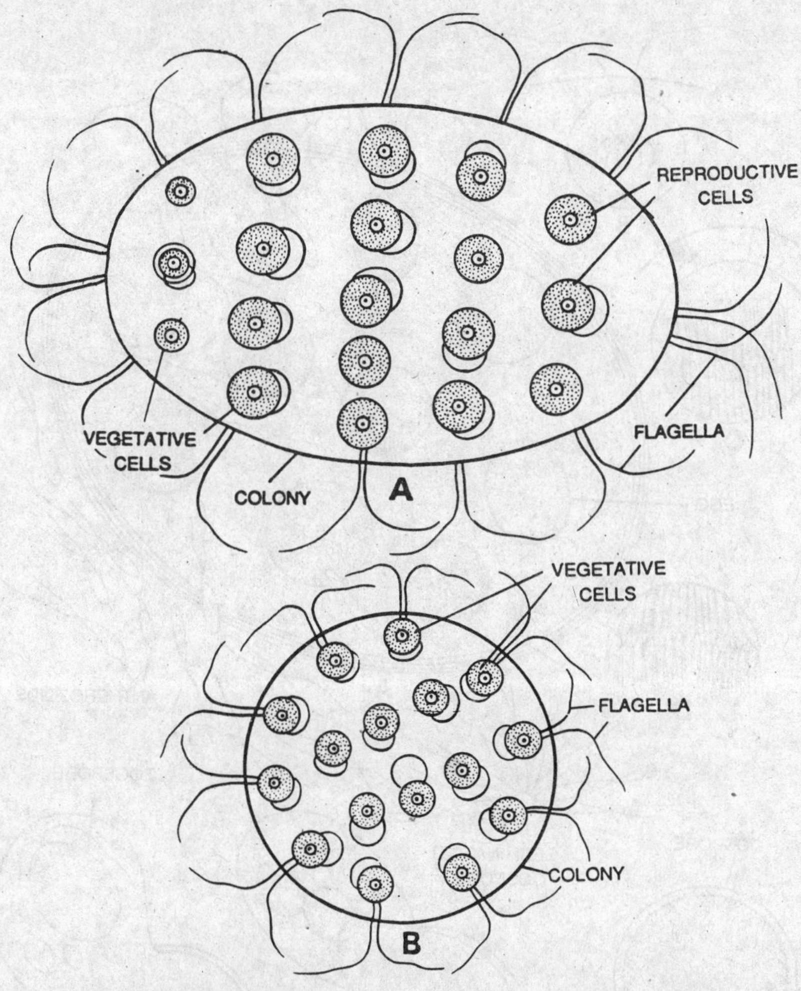

Fig. 3.18. *Eudorina* sp. Vegetative colonies. A, *E. elegans*; B, *E. illinoiensis*.

like antherozoids. These antherozoids are arranged in a flat plate-like structure, which swim collectively as units. The antherozoids arranged in bundles approach the female coenobia. Here the biflagellate spindle-like antherozoids separate from each other. They penetrate the gelatinous envelope of the coenobium. The antherozoid penetrates the egg anteriorly, posteriorly or laterally. They soon retract the flagella. After fusion zygotes are developed. Each zygote secretes a smooth and thick wall around it. On the degeneration of the gelatinous envelope the zygotes are escaped in the water. Very soon the zygotes are impregnated with 'haematochrome' and they become orange red in colour.

Zygote and its germination. The zygote is thick-walled, smooth and orange red in colour. The nucleus is diploid (2x). At the time of the germination it swells to some extent and a vesicle extrudes on one side of it. The contents divide into 4 protoplasts. Leaving one the protoplasts degenerate soon. Reduction division takes place to bring haploid condition again. The surviving single swarmer escapes from the vesicle and gives rise to a new normal coenobium.

Systematic position. Division-Chlorophycophyta; Class-Chlorophyceae; Order-Volvocales;

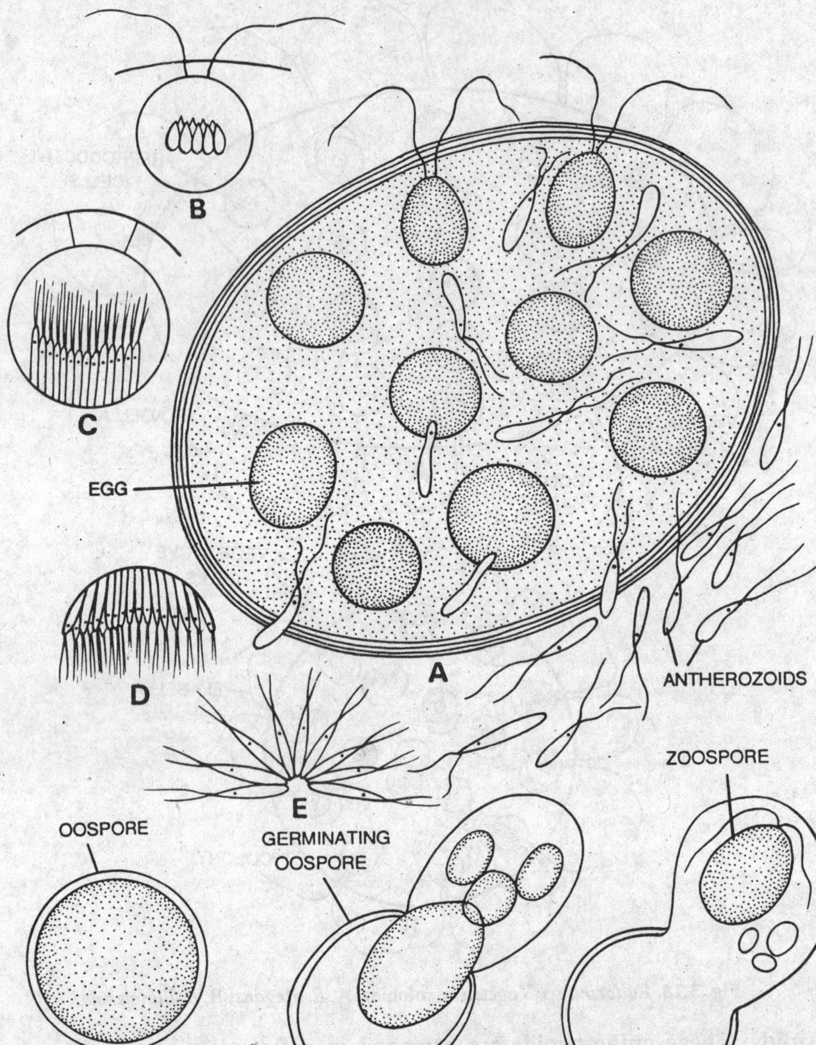

Fig. 3.19. *Eudorina* sp. Sexual reproduction. A, female coenobium with eggs; B-D, development of antherozoids; E, bundle of antherozoids; F, oospore; G, germination of oospore; H, formation of a single zoospore.

Family-Volvocaceae; Genus-*Eudorima*.

Genus PLEODORINA (*pleo*, more; *dorina*, meaningless)

Family-Volvocaceae

Pleodorina is fresh water coenobial alga. There are several species in this genus of which *P. indica* Iyengar has been reported from India. *P. californica* and *P. illinoiensis* are reported from America.

Structure. The coenobia are spherical to broadly ellipsoidal in shape. The coenobia are hollow, the cells forming a single layer in the peripheral mucilage, which is probably in large part composed of the gelatinous walls of the individual cells. The number of cells in a colony is 32, 64, or 128. The cells are arranged at some distance from each other in the homogeneous gelatinous coenobial matrix, *Pleodorina* has more numerous cells which do not show the definite transerve arrangement met with in *Eudorina*. The two flagella of each cell pass out through one or two tubular canals in the external mucilage of the colony. The cells commonly contain a number of pyrenoids. In all other forms which have been described in preceding pages any cell of a coenobium may become reproductive and so there is no differentiation of vegetative and reproductive cells. Such differentiation is found in *Pleodorina illinoiensis* consists of thirty two cells in the front or at anterior end of the colony are small and remain vegetative,while the others are larger and any of them may reproduce the colony. The cells in the anterior end are vegetative. The differentiation of purely vegetative cells is further advanced in *Pleodorina californica*. In this species there are about 64 or 128 cells about half of which may be reproductive, while remaining of the cells located in the anterior end of the colony (coenobium), are small vegetative cells. In *Pleodorina indica* Iyengar the vegetative cells are also scattered among the reproductive cells in the posterior half of the colony. The two types of cells cannot be differentiated in the young coenobia, as all the cells are spherical to ovoid in shape, with an anterior eye spot, a pair of flagella, two contractile vacuoles and cup-shaped chloroplast with a single pyrenoid. On the maturation of the colony, the differentiation of the cells takes place and the reproductive cells (gonidia) become two or three times the diameter of the vegetative cells. They lose their flagella, eye spot and possess massive chloroplast with several pyrenoids.

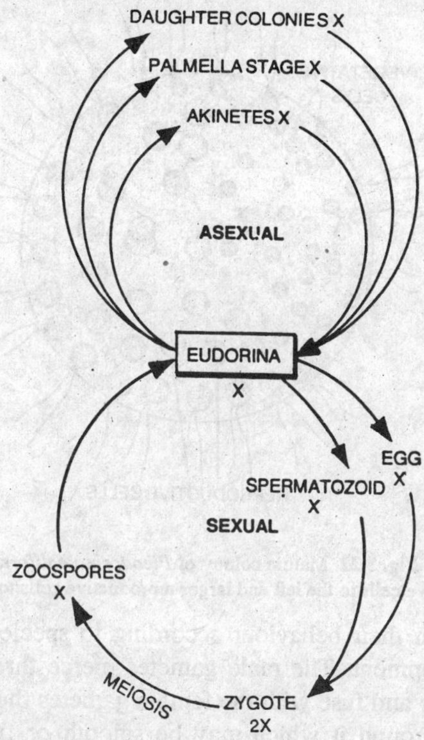

Fig. 3.20. *Eudorina*. Graphic representation of life cycle.

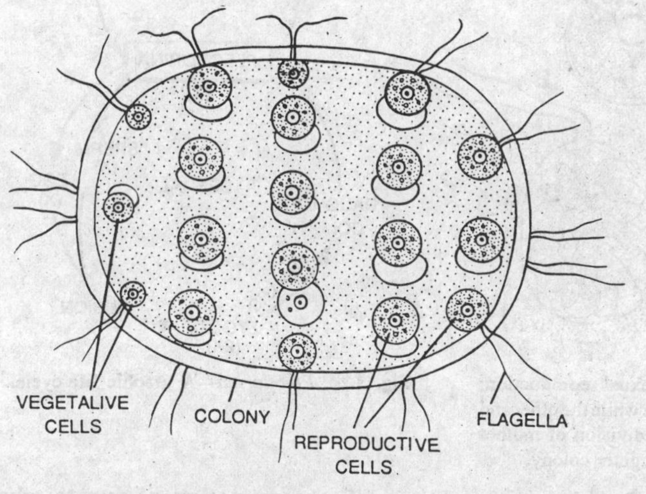

Fig. 3.21. A mature colony of *Pleodorina illinoiensis*. The four small vegetative cells to the left and the remaining cells are reproductive.

Asexual reproduction. It takes place by simultaneous division of all the reproductive cells (gonidia) in daughter colonies. The gonidia producing daughter colonies undergo division within their membrane to form plakeal sequence of cells of the future coenobium. In *Pleodorina* only about half of the cells divide in this way. All the divisions are longitudinal. The normal orientation of the colony by a complete inversion of the young coenobium takes place. The daughter colonies liberate from the parent colony in normal way.

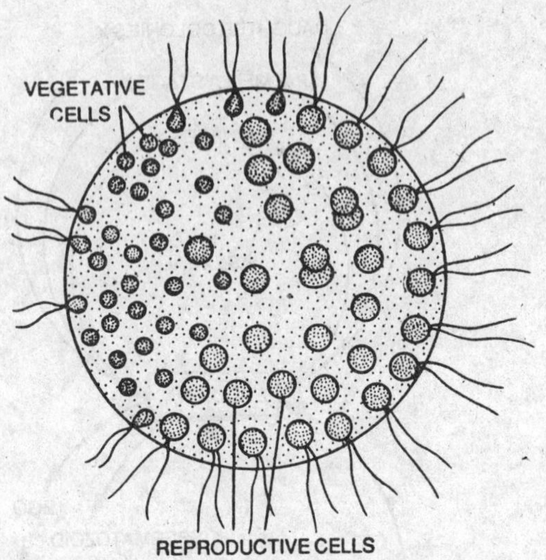

Fig. 3.22. Mature colony of *Pleodorina californica*. Small vegetative cells to the left and larger reproductive cells to the right.

Sexual reproduction. It may be anisogamous or oogamous. Mostly the colonies are dioecious but sometimes it may be monoecious and produce both kinds of gametes (Doraiswami, 1940; Tiffany, 1935). The male gametes are produced in the cluster of sperms in the dioecious species in the same manner as they are produced in *Eudorina*. The male gametes swim about as unit, till they reach the female colony where these units break and the male gametes fuse with the female gametes.

The cells acting as female gametes vary in their behaviour according to species. They may or may not possess their cilia during development. The male gametes pierce through the gelatinous matrix surrounding the female colony and fuse with the female gametes thus effecting fertilization. The zygote secretes a thick wall around it which may be smooth or finely granulate. The zygote undergoes a period of

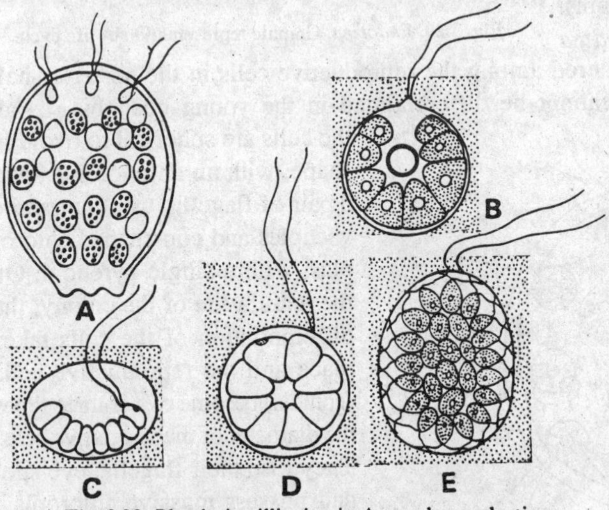

Fig. 3.23. *Pleodorina illinoiensis*–Asexual reproduction; A, the four small anterior cells remain vegetative while the other and larger cells produce daughter colonies; B–E, division of mother cell, while within mother colony, to form a daughter colony.

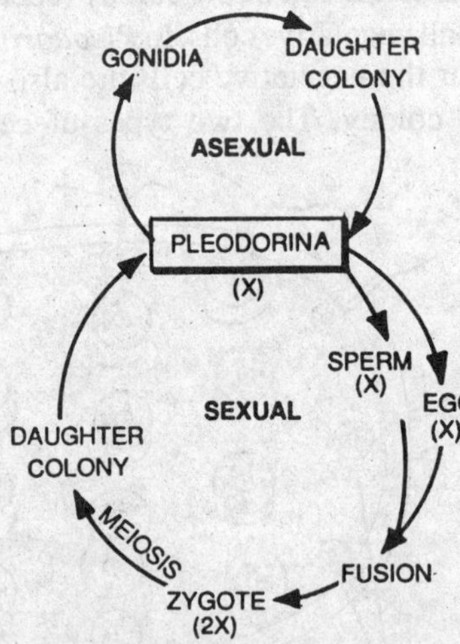

Fig. 3.24. *Pleodorina*—A graphic life-cycle.

rest and its protoplast becomes tinged with haematochrome. The germination of zygote takes place in the manner as that of *Eudorina*.

Systematic position. Division-Chlorophycophyta; Class-Chlorophyceae; Order-Volvocales; Family-Volvocaceae; Genus-*Pleodorina*.

Genus VOLVOX (*Volvere*, to roll)

There are about 20 species.

Habitat or occurrence. All of them are fresh water forms. They are found in puddles, ponds and pools. They are also found in the temporarily formed ponds during rainy season. Sometimes the colonies are found in such a great abundance that the whole water becomes green in colour. The colonies of *Volvox* are motile and met with in rolling condition in the still fresh waters. Sometimes the colonies are intermingled with the tangled masses of other filamentous algae and small aquatic plants.

Structure. The colonies of *Volvox* are hollow. They are spherical or broadly elliptic. The cell number of each colony ranges from 500-50,000. In *Volvox globator* there are 1500-20,000 cells in each coenobium, whereas 500-1000 in *V.aureus*. The inner hollow of the coenobium is filled up with mucilage. The whole coenobium is surrounded by a delicate mucilaginous lamella. The cells are chlamydomonad type. They possess cup-shaped chloroplasts. In each cell there are 2-6 cotractile vacuoles, a single pyrenoid and a stigma. The cells are biflagellate and

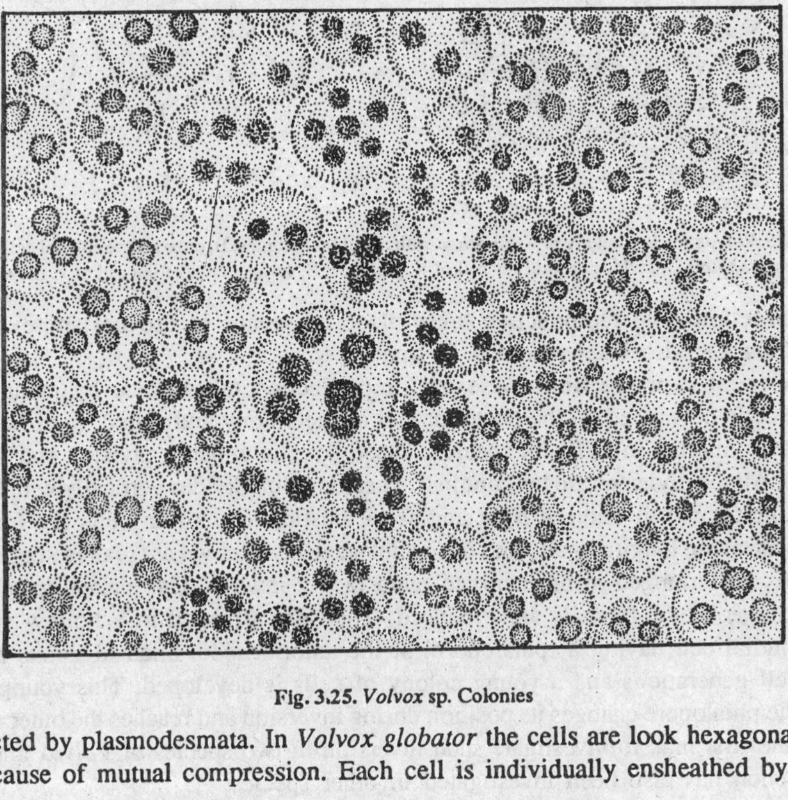

Fig. 3.25. *Volvox* sp. Colonies

interconnected by plasmodesmata. In *Volvox globator* the cells are look hexagonal from upper surface because of mutual compression. Each cell is individually ensheathed by a gelatinous sheath.

Mostly the cells of a mature colony are vegetative and only a few are reproductive. The reproductive cells are devoid of flagella, about ten times bigger than the vegetative cells, and possess many pyrenoids within their chloroplasts. These reproductive cells may be asexual or sexual. When the conditions are favourable asexual reproduction takes place. In the end of the season, when the conditions are comparatively drier, the colonies reproduce sexually.

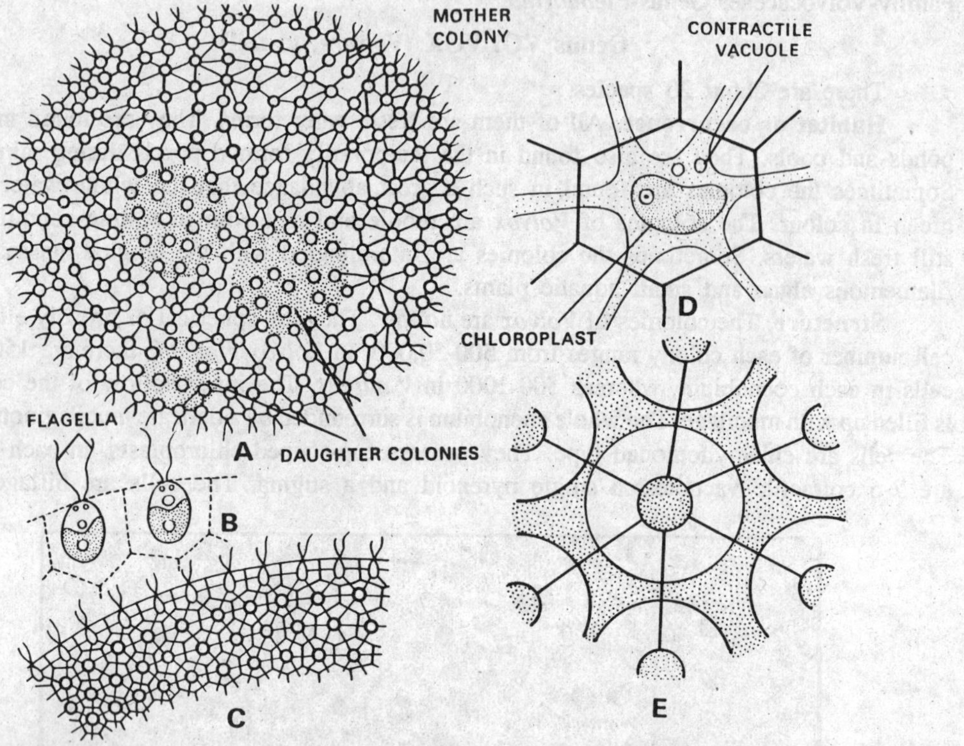

Fig. 3.26. *Volvox* sp. A, a colony of *V. mononae* with daughter colonies; B, enlarged peripheral cells; C, a part of the colony of *Volvox globator*; D, surface view of the cell of *V. globator*; E, surface view of the cell of *V. aureus*.

Reproduction. The reproduction takes place by means of asexual ad sexual methods. Parthenogenesis has also been recorded in some species.

1. Asexual reproduction. Asexual reproduction takes place by means of special reproductive cells developed on the posterior end of the colony and called **'gonidia'**. They may be of 5 to 50 in number in different species. These gonidia undergo division and new colonies are produced. All the divisions are longitudinal. The gonidium divides vertically which is followed by second longitudinal division at right angles to the first. Thus four cells are formed. These four cells divide again longitudinally and the octant stage also known as **'plakea stage'** is attained. Here the cells are arranged in an incurved plate facing inward. The plakea stage is followed by another division and 16 cells are produced. They are arranged in a hollow sphere inside the large gonidial cell having a 'phialopore' at the anterior side. Such divisions are followed by several cell generations and a young colony of cells is developed. This young coenobium inverts and the phialopore changes its position during inversion and reaches the other side. Powers (1908) was the first man to investigate such inversion in two species of *Volvox* and since then this phenomenon has also been investigated in other species.

This invagination or inversion of the young coenobium takes place by a simple method. According to Pocock (1933), a slight constriction develops on the equatorial region of the young colony. Later on the portion of the coenobium opposite the phialopore infolds and gradually the complete inversion of the coenobium takes place. During this process, the phialopore reaches on the outer side of the sphere. Now anterior ends of the cells face outwards. Flagella are developed very shortly after invagination. Such daughter colonies are freed in the hollow of the parent colony of *Volvox*. These daughter colonies move here and there in the hollow for some time, and as soon as the parent colony perishes or it gives way irregularly, they are free, and move in the water as independent colonies.

2. Sexual reproduction. In the species of *Volvox*, the sexual reproduction is **oogamous.** The colonies may be monoecious (homothallic) or dioecious (heterothallic). The coenobia of *V. aureus* are commonly dioecious and rarely monoecious. The coenobia of *V. globator* are monoecious. Commonly the gonidia are not found in sexual colonies. The monoecious coenobia are usually protandrous. *V. aureus* is protogynous. The sexual cells which are comparatively bigger than the vegetative cells are situated in the posterior halves of the colonies. The female cells possess round ova or eggs in them. On maturity, such cells are devoid of flagella. The antherozoids enter the oogonia through neck at the time of fertilization. The oogonia may easily be distinguished from gonidia, that they do not divide like the latter.

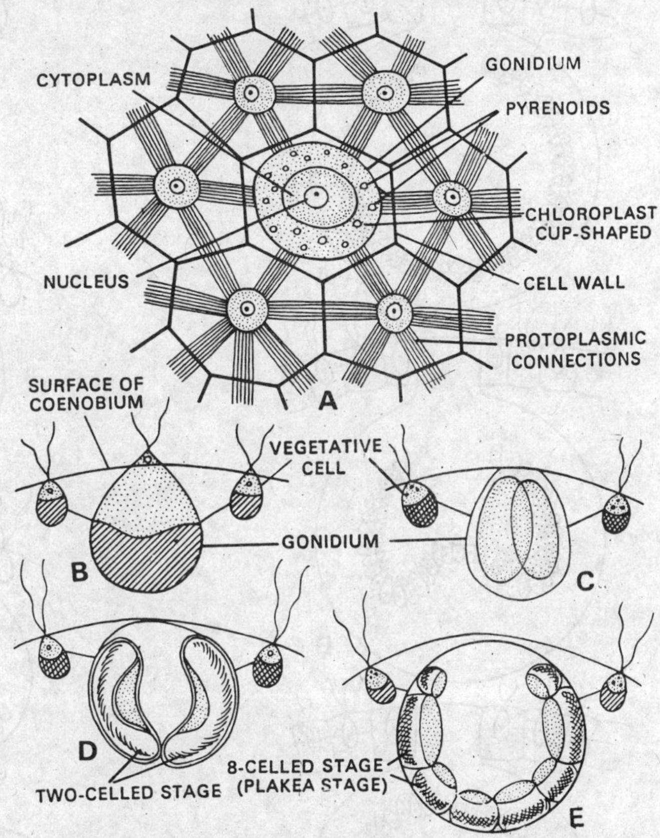

Fig. 3.27. *Volvox* sp. Asexual reproduction. A, a gonidium in the colony in surface view; B, side view of gonidium; C, first division of protoplast; D, two celled stage; E, eight celled stage (plakea stage)

The antheridial cells resemble gonidia, but they are fewer in number. The antheridial cell divides again and again and a plate of 16, 32, 64, 128, 256 or 512 antherozoids is formed. The antherozoids are arranged in a sphere. Usually the inversion of the coenobium takes place. Each antherozoid is spindle-like, biflagellate and with a small pale green chloroplast. The antherozoids are liberated from the cells in the form of bundles. These bundles swim here and there in the water and approaching the eggs. After approaching the female coenobium of oogonia the bundle breaks and the antherozoids are separated from each other.

At the time of fertilization the antherozoids swim around the gelatinous lamella or the coenobium. One or more antherozoids enter through the gelatinous lamella and come in contact of the egg. Only one antherozoid penetrates the egg anteriorly. The flagella are retracted. The male nucleus fuses with the female nucleus, and the **oospore** is developed. The oospores of *Volvox* are commonly spiny. The oospores remain for some time in the hollow of the coenobium after fertilization is over.

Development and germination of oospores. After fertilization a thick wall develops around oospore which usually becomes ornamented. The oospores usually become orange red coloured, because of the presence of **'haematochrome'**. There is always a reduction division during germination. In *Volvox* the contents of the oospore may develop into a large swarmer.

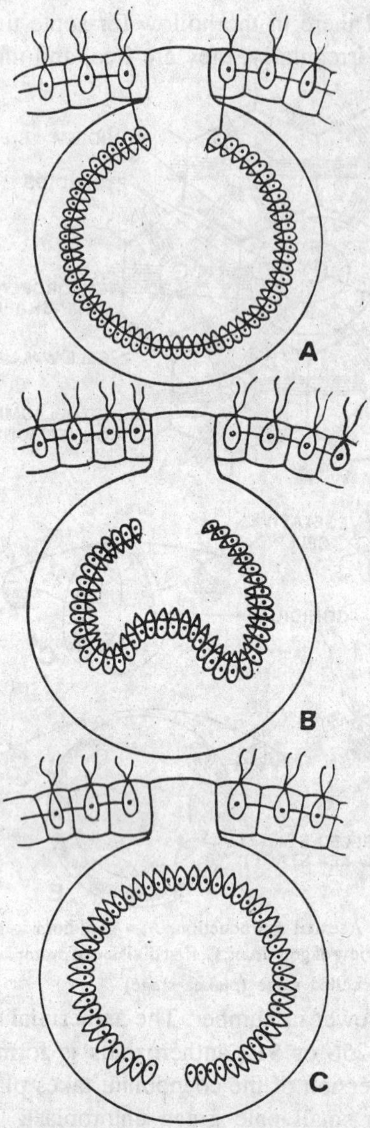

Fig 3.28. *Volvox* sp. Asexual reproduction. A, young colony to invaginate; B, invaginating colony; C, invagination completed. (After G. M. Smith)

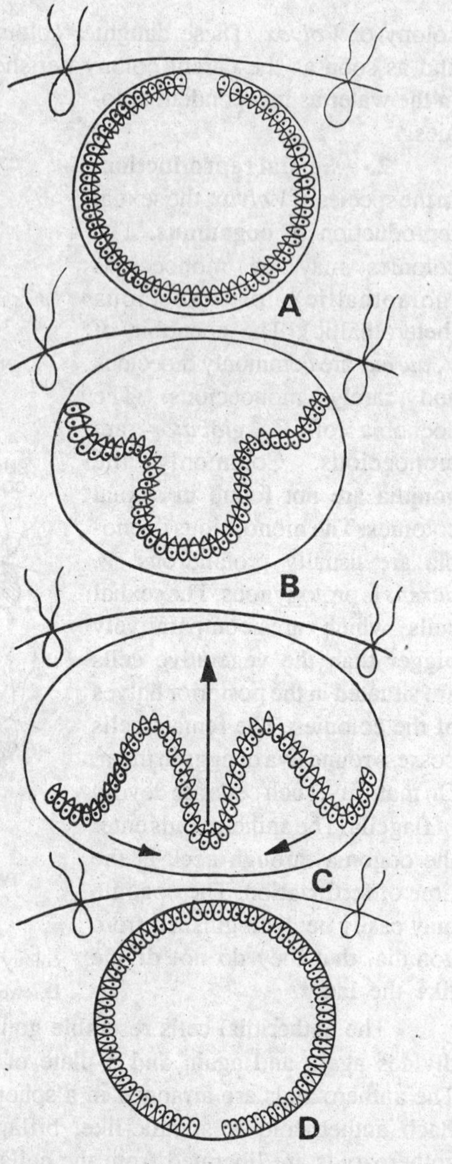

Fig 3.29. *Volvox*. Asexual reproduction. A, young colony to invaginate; B-C, stages of invagination; D, invagination completed. (After F.E. Fritsch)

This swarmer liberates and swims in the water. The protoplast of this swarmer divides again, and a hollow sphere of the cell is developed. Inversion of this hollow sphere also takes place and the newly developed coenobium liberates in the water. According to Miss Pocock, perhaps several swarmers are developed and only one survives from the lot.

Parthenogenesis. Parthenospores have also been recorded in *Volvox aureus.*

Phylogenetic relationships of Volvoclaes. The relationship of the members of the Volvocales is clearly shown by the similar type of vegetative cells found throughout the order. The daughter colony formation and manner of sexual reproduction, although it ranges from isogamy to oogamy are also similar in the order. In this order the motility is preserved throughout. The complexity and differentiation of cell types within the colonies clearly show a line of evolution, known as the Volvocine line of which *Volvox* is the culmination. Botanists are of opinion that this line ended in *Volvox* and did not develop further.

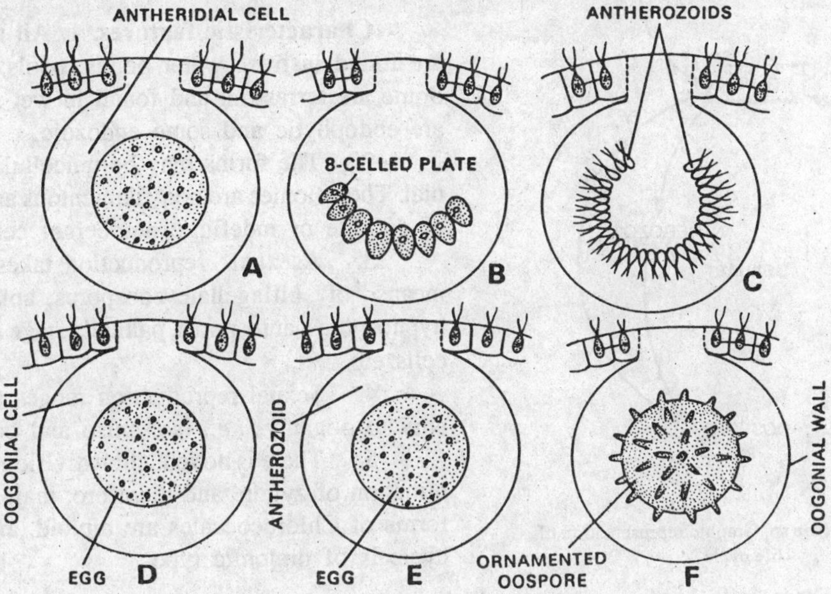

Fig. 3.30. ***Volvox*** **sp. Sexual reproduction. A-C, Development of antherozoids; D, oogonium with egg; E, fertilization; F, ornamented oospore inside oogonial wall.**

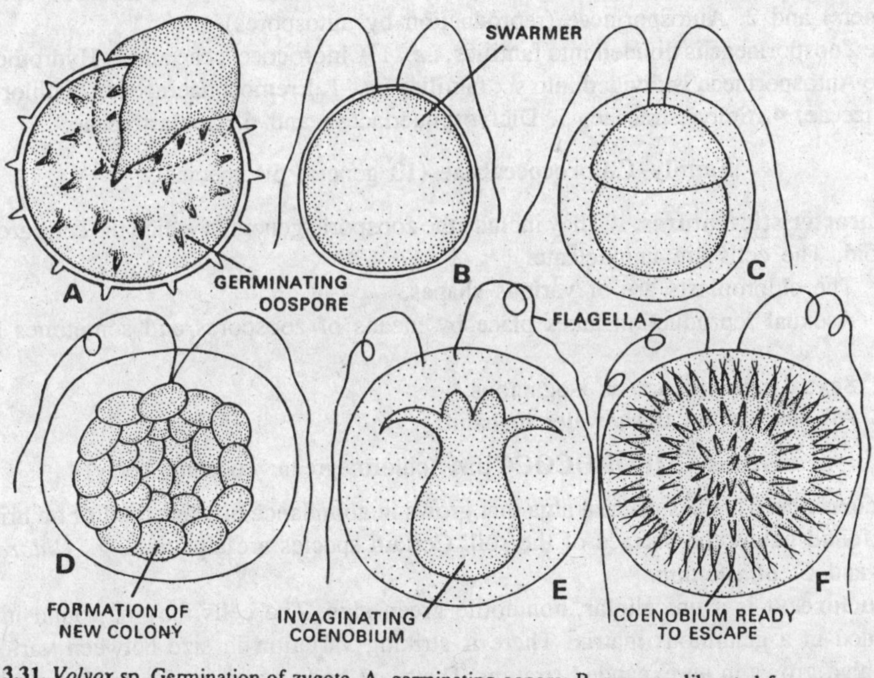

Fig. 3.31. *Volvox* sp. Germination of zygote. A, germinating oopore; B, swarmer liberated from oospore; C, first diviion of the swarmer's protoplast; D, formation of new colony; E, invaginating colony; F, colony ready to eacape.

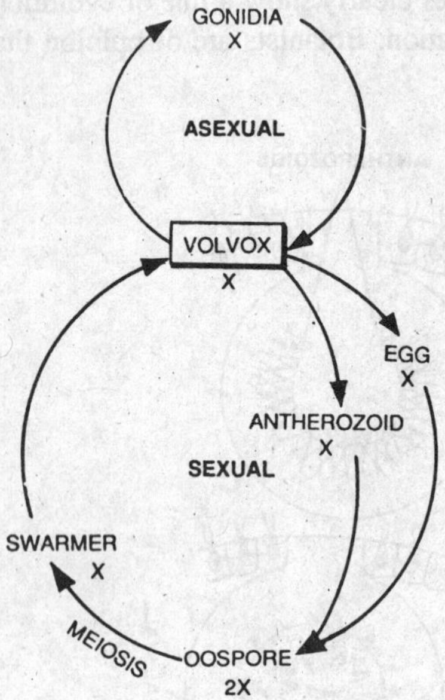

Fig. 3.32. *Volvox* sp. Graphic representation of life cycle.

Systematic position. Division-Chlorophycophyta; Class-Chlorophyceae; Order-Volvocales; Family-Volvocaceae; Genus *Volvox.*

ORDER–CHLOROCOCCALES

Characteristic features. 1. All the species are found in fresh water ponds, pools and lakes. Some are terrestrial and found in wet soil. Some are endophytic and some endozoic.

2. The forms may be unicellular or colonial. The colonies are non-filamentous and consists of definite or indefinite number of cells.

3. Asexual reproduction takes place by means of biflagellate zoospores, aplanospores, hypnospores, autospores, palmella stage and resting cells etc.

4. Sexual reproduction ranges from isogamy to oogamy, *i.e.,* iso, aniso and oogamous.

5. There is no reduction division in the germination of zygote and therefore, majority of the forms of Chlorococcales are diploid, and the life cycle is of diplontic type.

6. There is lack of vegetative cell division.

7. The chloroplasts are cuplike. Each possesses a single pyrenoid.

There are about 100 genera and 800 species in this order.

Classification. The order is divided into two series, *i.e.,* 1. Zoosporineae (reproduction by swarmers) and 2. Autosporineae (reproduction by autospores).

The Zoosporineae is divided into families, *i.e.,* 1. Chlorococcaceae and 2. Hydrodictyaceae.

The Autosporineae is divided into six families *i.e.,* 1. Eremosphaeraceae, 2. Chlorellaceae, 3. Oocystaceae, 4. Selenastraceae, 5. Dictyosphaeriaceae and 6. Coelastraceae.

Family–Chlorococcaceae (10 genera; 50 species).

Characteristic features. 1. They include the zoosporic genera in which the cells are globose and haploid. The cells are uninucleate.

2. The chloroplasts are of various shapes.

3. Asexual reproduction takes place by means of zoospores and sometimes by aplanospores.

4. Sexual reproduction is isogamous.

5. All species are fresh water in habit.

Genus CHLOROCOCCUM (chloro, green; coccum, berry)

Occurrence. This is subaerial alga that grows in abundance on damp soil or on brickwork. It is also found below the surface of the soil. Certain species are aquatic, *e.g., Chlorococcum humicola* and *C. infusionum.*

Structure. It is a unicellular, nonmotile green alga. The cells may be found in masses or embedded in a gelatinous matrix. There is striking variation in size between various cells when the alga grows in an expanded stratum. The plant body consists of a small spherical cell.

The young cells are thin-walled and spherical or somewhat compressed. The old cells possess thickwalls that are often irregular in outline because of the presence of local button-like thickenings. The thickened portions of a wall are often distincdy stratified. The chloroplasts of young ceils are parietal and cup-like. Each chloroplast contains one pyrenoid. In the old cell, the chloroplast usually becomes diffused and contains several pyrenoids. Each cell is uninucleate.

Asexual reproduction. It takes place by the following methods.

1. **Zoospores.** The asexual reproduction by means of zoospores may take place when the cell enlarges in size. Small cells usually produce 8 to 16 zoospores, whereas the large cells form many zoospores. The formation of zoospores takes place by successive bipartition of the protoplast, and as by a progressive cleavage. Each bit of the protoplast develops into a biflagellate zoospore. These zoospores liberate through an aperture in the parent cell wall. After liberation they lose their flagella, become rounded, secrete a wall and develop into vegetative cells.

2. **Aplanospores.** Sometimes instead of the formation of zoospores, the divided contents of old cells develop into nonmotile aplanospores (autospores). The aplanospores face the adverse conditions. On the approach of favourable conditions each aplanospore develops into a new plant.

3. **Palmella stage.** Usually the aplanospores remain within the old parent cell wall until it gelatinizes to form a palmella stage. A palmella stage is produced in the similar way as it is produced in *Chlamydomonas*.

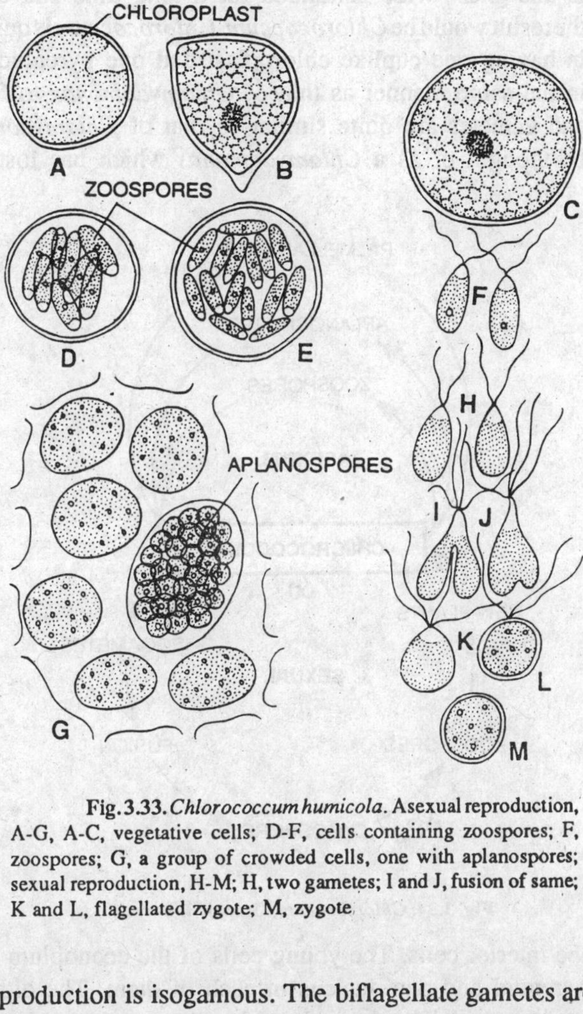

Fig. 3.33. *Chlorococcum humicola*. Asexual reproduction, A-G, A-C, vegetative cells; D-F, cells containing zoospores; F, zoospores; G, a group of crowded cells, one with aplanospores; sexual reproduction, H-M; H, two gametes; I and J, fusion of same; K and L, flagellated zygote; M, zygote.

Sexual reproduction. The sexual reproduction is isogamous. The biflagellate gametes are formed by division of protoplasts of ordinary vegetative cells. The gametes are formed in the same way as zoospores. The gametes escape from the parent cell and fuse in pairs thus producing zygospores. During germination of the zygospore the nucleus divides meiotically after a period of rest and produces several zoospores which develop into new plants.

Systematic relationships. There are three lines of evolution in green algae; the **volvocine** as exhibited by the Volvocales, the **tetrasporine** as shown by the Tetrasporales and the Ulotrichales and **chlorococcine** as shown by the Chlorococcales. The chlorococcine line is like the tetrasporine line as the motility is confined to reproductive cells. In *Chlorococcum*, which is a primitive member Chlorococcales the cells do not divide vegetatively and divisions of the protoplast occurs only in connection with reproduction. In the more highly developed members of the chlorococcine line the cells may be very large and of very intricate form.

It is thought that *Chlorococcum* has been derived through a modification of *Chlamydomonas*. The Volvocales can be thought of as being derived from the motile stage of *Chlamydomonas*, and the Ulotrichales as being due to the developement of the palmella stage. There is often a phase, in *Chlamydomonas*, prior to the division of the protoplast to form zoospores or gametes, where the flagella are retracted and the *Chlamydomonas* cell becomes non-motile for a time. If this phase were continued for a long time and the motile and palmella stages suppressed, the result would be *Chlorococcum*. *Chlorococcum* is quite similar to most species of *Chlamydomonas* in having one cuplike chloroplast and one pyrenoid. The protoplast of *Chlorococcum* divides in the same manner as that of *Chlamydomonas* to form zoospores and gametes. Its zoospores and gametes are quite similar to that of *Chlamydomonas*. In other words, *Chlorococcum* can be thought of as a *Chlamydomonas* which has lost motility except in reproductive cells.

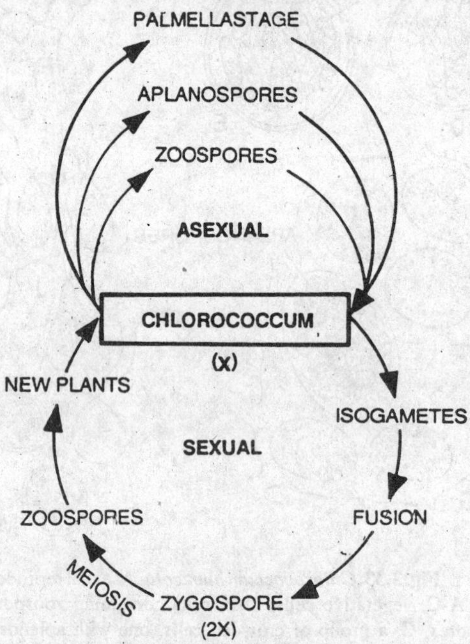

Fig. 3.34. *Chlorococcum*. Graphic life-cycle.

PEDIASTRUM : (*Pedi*, foot; *astrum*, star)

Family-Hydrodictyaceae

There are about 30 species in this genus.

Habit and occurrence. Almost all the species are fresh water. They are found in fresh water ponds, pools, ditches, puddles and lakes in free floating conditions.

Structure. The coenobia of *Pediastrum* are 2, 4, 8, 16, 32, 64 or 128 celled. The cells of the coenobium are polygonal in shape and arranged in a round or stellate plate. The plate is one celled in thickness. The cells are arranged in concentric rings in the plate and each ring consists of definite number of cells. The peripheral cells of colony possess **processes.** Each peripheral cell may bear one, two or even three processes. Such processes are not found in the interior cells. The young cells of the coenobium possess parietal chloroplasts, with a single pyrenoid and one nucleus in each of them. The older cells possess 1 to 4 pyrenoids and two or four nuclei in them. In old cells the chloroplasts are also diffused.

Reproduction. In *Pediastrum*, the reproduction takes place by asexual and sexual methods.

1. **Asexual.** The asexual reproduction takes place by means of (a) zoospores and (b) aplano or hypnospores.

(a) **By zoospores.** Every cell of the coenobium may give rise to zoospores. In the night the contents and the nucleus of the cell divide again and again and by the dawn the zoospores are liberated in a vesicle. The inner wall of the parent cell is extruded in the form of vesicle. These zoospores swim inside the vesicle for some time and ultimately arranged in the form of a coenobium. The zoospores are converted in the shape of the cells of the coenobium. Usually the cells of the 16-celled colonies produce 8 zoospores in each cell. At the time of the liberation

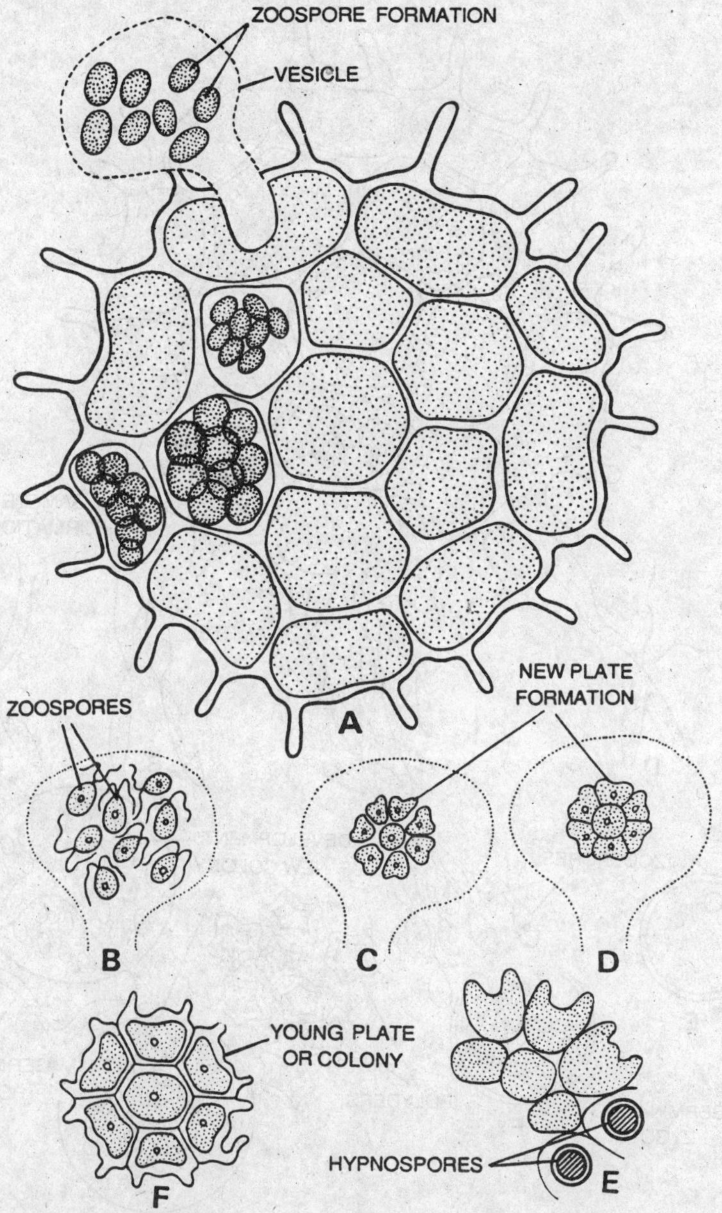

Fig. 3.35. *Pediastrum sp.* – Asexual reproduction. A-B, formation and liberation of zoospores; C-D, formation of new plate; E, hypnospores; F, young colony or plate.

of the zoospores, a slit is developed in the old parent cell and a vesicle comes out through this slit. The zoospores move actively for some time in the vesicle and then are arranged in the form of a plate-like coenobium. The zoospores are metamorphosed in the cells of the new colony and the wall develops around each zoospore.

(b) By aplano - or hypnospores. Very rarely the thick-walled aplano or hypnospores are developed. Single hypnospore develops in a single cell. They are very resistant bodies and may germinate even after a long period of twelve years.

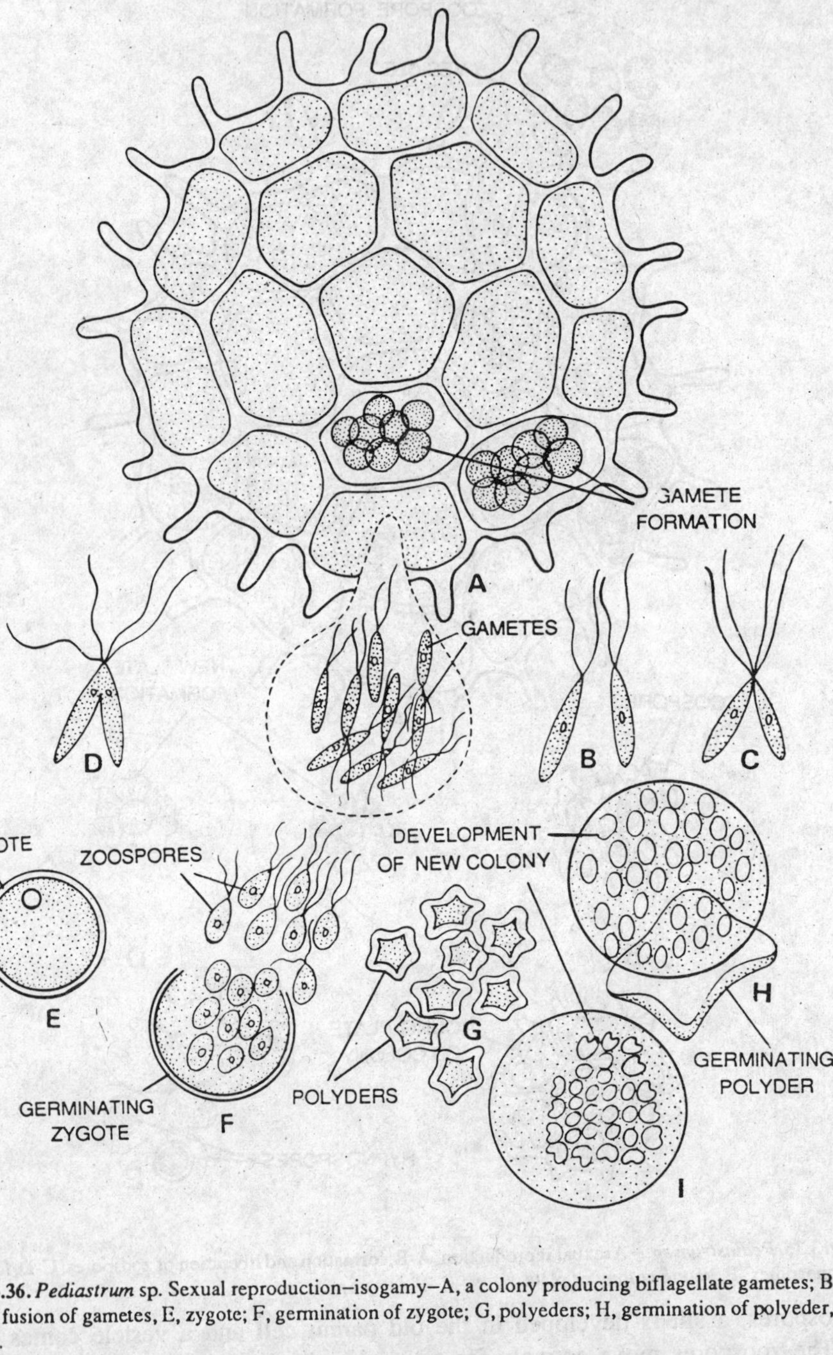

Fig. 3.36. *Pediastrum* sp. Sexual reproduction–isogamy–A, a colony producing biflagellate gametes; B, biflagellate gametes; C-D, fusion of gametes, E, zygote; F, germination of zygote; G, polyeders; H, germination of polyeder, I, formation of new colony.

2. Sexual. The sexual reproduction **takes** place by means of similar motile gametes (isogamy). The gametes are spindle-like and biflagellate. They are produced in the same manner as zoospores. They are differentiated from the zoospores by their spindle-shaped structures. The gametes are fused in pairs and zygotes are produced. The zygote is spherical and somewhat thick-walled.

Germination of zygote. The zygote increases in size and its contents divide to form many biflagellate ovoid zoospores. The zoospores liberate from one side of zygote and swim in the water. On coming to rest they become angular, star-shaped cells called **'polyeders'.** These increase sufficiently in size. The contents of each star-shaped cell divide and zoospores are formed. These zoospores when liberate from a polyeder remain surrounded by a vesicle. This vesicle develops from the inner wall of the polyeder. Ultimately the zoospores arrange in a plate-like structure in a definite pattern inside the vesicle developing a new coenobium.

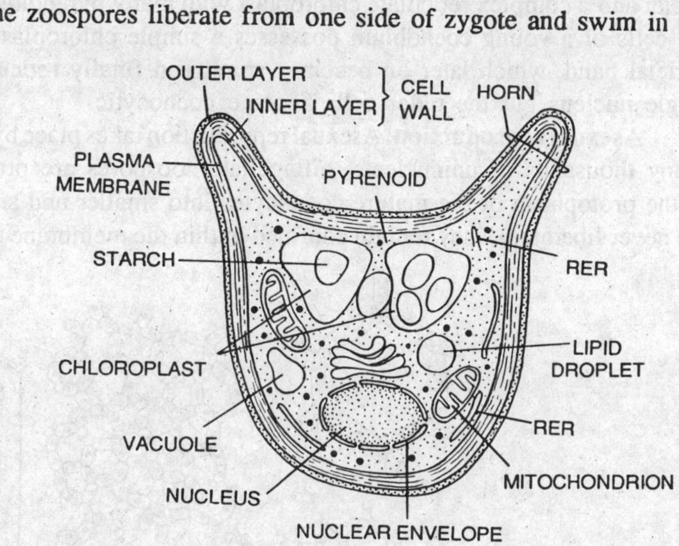

Fig 3.36 (a). *Pediastrum* spp. Ultrastructure of a mature peripheral cell (diagrammatic).

Systematic position. Division-Chlorophycophyta; Class-Chlorophyceae; Order-Chlorococcales; Family-Hydrodictyaceae; Genus-*Pediastrum.*

Genus HYDRODICTYON (*hydro,* water; *dictyon,* net)

Family–Hydrodictyaceae

Occurrence. *Hydrodictyon,* commonly known as water net is a beautiful alga. It is limited in distribution and occurrence but whenever it is found, it occurs in enormous quantities. *Hydrodictyon reticulatum* and *H. indicum* Iyenger are common Indian species.

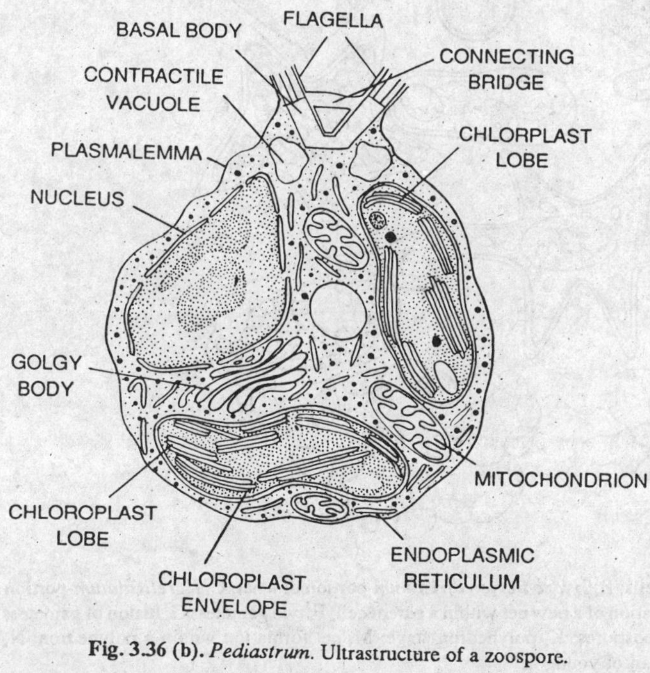

Fig. 3.36 (b). *Pediastrum.* Ultrastructure of a zoospore.

Structure. The coenobium of *Hydrodictyon* is free floating hollow cylindrical network, closed at either end, and reaching a length of as much as 20 cms. *Hydrodictyon indicum* Iyenger is a larger form with bigger cells and meshes and thick lamellated walls. The meshes of the net are pentagonal or more usually hexagonal, the angles being formed by the union of three of the elongate multinucleate cells.

The cells are cylindrical

multinucleate and posses a larger central vacuole. The lining layer of cytoplasm contains the nuclei and a complex reticulate chloroplast with many pyrenoids. According to Lowe and Lloyd, the cells of a young coenobium possesses a simple chloroplast of the shape of an incomplete parietal band, which later on becomes spiral and finally reticulate. The young cells contain a single nucleus but the older cells become coenocytic.

Asexual reproduction. Asexual reproduction takes place by means of biflagellate zoospores. Many thousands of uninucleate, biflagellate zoospores are produced by progressive cleavage of the protoplasm of the mature coenocytes into smaller and smaller fragments. The zoospores are never liberated. They remain confined within the membrane of the parent coenocyte, showing

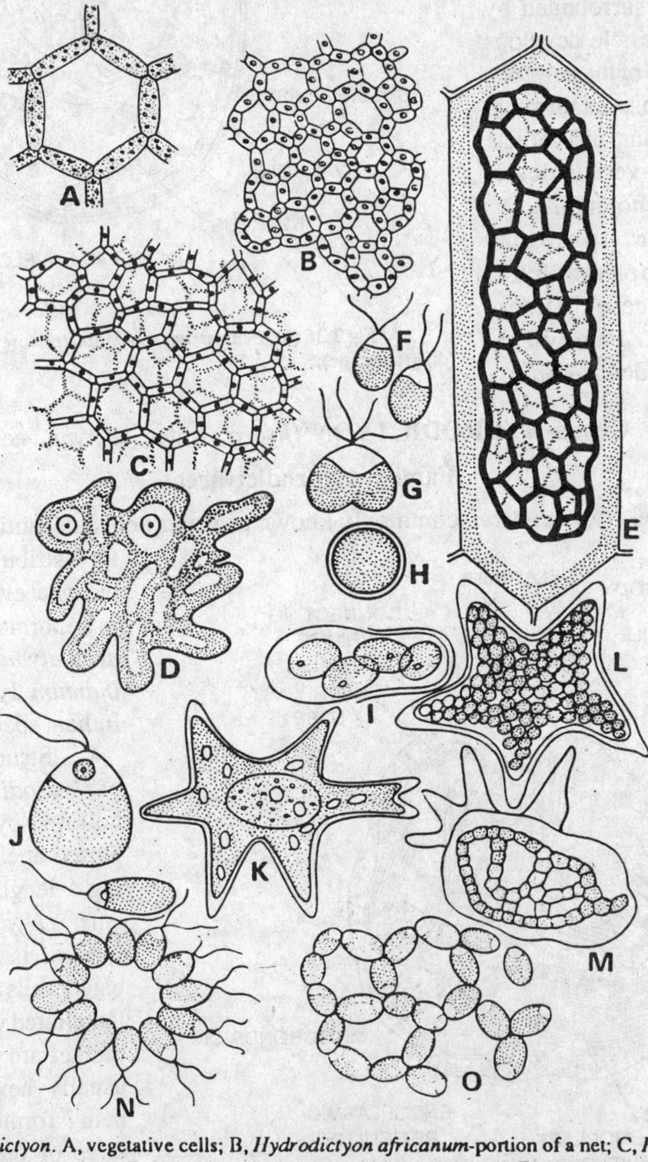

Fig. 3.37. *Hydrodictyon*. A, vegetative cells; B, *Hydrodictyon africanum*-portion of a net; C, *H. reticulatum*-portion of a net; D, part of chloroplast (reticulate); E, formation of a new net within a parent cell; F, two gametes; G, fusion of gametes; H, zygote; I, germination of zygote producing zoospores; K, polyhedron-stage; M, net formation within a polyhedron; N, zoospores arranging to form a net (asexual); O, part of young net.

the usual restricted movements. Ultimately the zoospores withdraw their flagella, secrete membranous walls around them and become arranged to form a new net or coenobium. As a new net is formed within a parent cell, it naturally takes the shape of that cell. A net is liberated by the disintegration of the wall of the parent cell after which the cells of the new net continue to grow.

According to Klebs, the zoospores are permanently connected by short threads, but this is not yet confirmed. The space for the movement of the zoospores is formed by the swelling of the longitudinal walls and a reduction in the size of the vacuole. As soon as the zoospores come to rest they exhibit a tendency to become arranged in straight rows, in three directions at angles of 60° to one another. The zoospores arrange themselves in the pattern of the parent coenobium. *Hydrodictyon* may, therefore, be regarded as a union of individual plants.

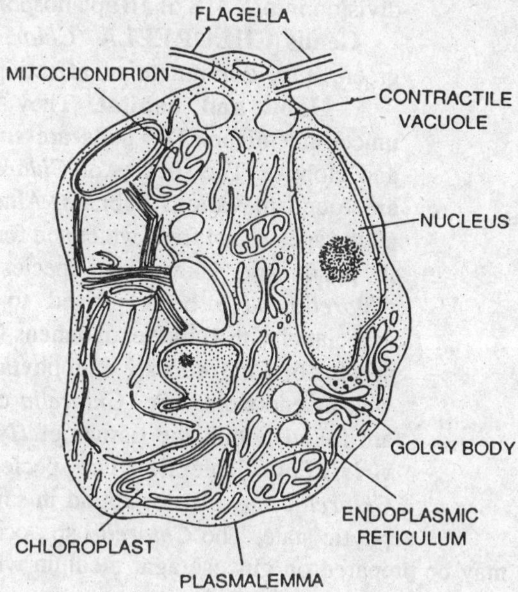

Fig. 3.37 (a). *Hydrodictyon*. The ultra structure of a zoospore (diagrammatic)

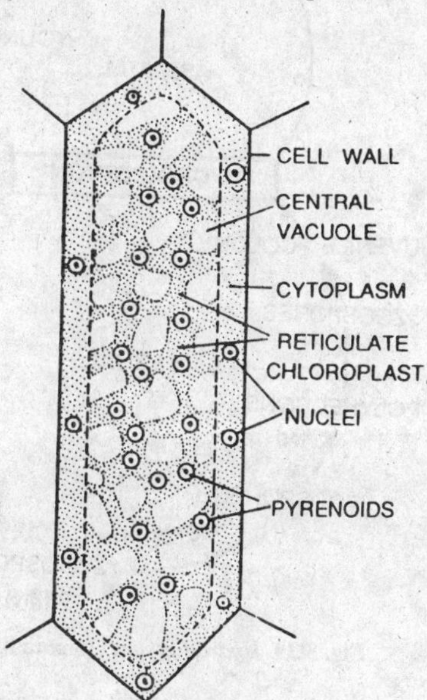

Fig. 3.38. *Hydrodictyon*. Structure of a single cell.

Sexual reproduction. *Hydrodictyon* is **monoecious** and the sexual reproduction is **isogamous.** It takes place by means of biflagellate gametes. The gametes are formed in the same manner as zoospores, but escape through an opening in the wall of the mother cell. Comparatively the gametes are formed in large number (30,000-100,000) and, are therefore, smaller than the zoospores. *Hydrodictyon* is monoecious and even gametes from the same coenocyte may fuse together. Just after fusion the flagella are withdrawn and a spherical zygote covered with a thin membrane is formed. The zygote gradually enlarges in size and stores oil which is coloured red by haematochrome.

Germination of zygote. In *Hydrodictyon patenaeforme* the zygote is motile for a short time, but in *H. reticulatum* and *H. africanum* it is always nonmotile. During germination the zygote enlarges and divides meiotically to give rise to four biflagellate zoospores which, after coming to rest develop into polyhedral cells. These polyhedrons over winter. On the approach of favourable conditions, the contents of each polyhedron produced zoospores. The polyhedron increases greatly in size, and its contents divide to form a considerable number of zoospores. These zoospores surrounded by a vesicle escape from the polyhedron. The zoospores move about in the vesicle. They finally come to rest and within the vesicle form a small irregular net of 200 to 300 cells,which escapes out by the dissolution of the vesicle. Thereafter the new coenobium grows to maturity.

Systematic position. Division-Chlorophycophyta; Class-Chlorophyceae; Order-Chlorococcales; Family-Hydrodictyaceae; Genus-*Hydrodictyon.*

Family-Chlorellaceae

Characteristic features. 1. The cells are globular and nonmotile. They may be solitary or aggregated into groups.

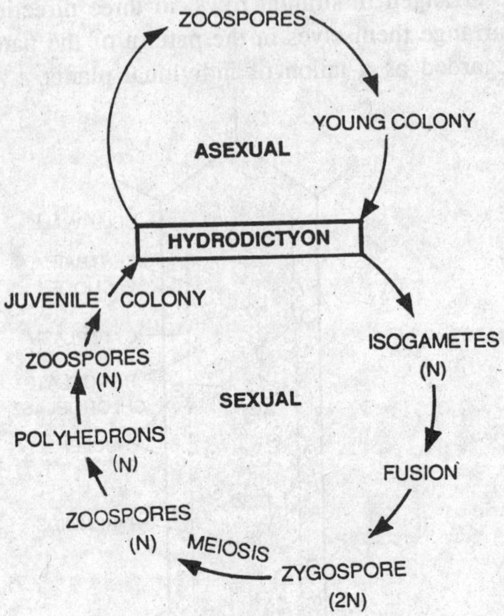

Fig. 3.39. *Hydrodictyon.* Graphic life-cycle.

2. The chloroplasts lack pyrenoids.

3. Reproduction is by means of division into 2, 4, 8 or 16 aplanospores.

Genus CHLORELLA (*Chlor,* green; *ella,* diminutive of affection)

Habit and habitat. They are unicellular algae. The cells are small and globose. The species of *Chlorella* are found in various habitats. Almost all the species are fresh water and found in ponds and lakes. The species of *Chlorella* have been proved to be associated with a number of lichens. The species of *Chlorella* are endophytic as well as endozoic. The *Chlorella* cells are found within the tissues of *Hydra viridis* (a coelenterate). The species of *Chlorella* may also be found in saprophytic state. The *Chlorella* sp., occurs in faecal matter too. The culture of *Chlorella* may be prepared on glucose agar medium where the chlorophyll does not develop in the cells.

Structure. This is unicellular alga. The cell is small and rounded. Each cell is surrounded by a three-layered cell wall. The outer layer if at all present consists of mucilage, the middle layer of pectose and the innermost of cellulose. Each cell contains a cup-shaped (chlamydomonad type) chloroplast. The cell is uninucleate. The contractile vaculoes are not found. The cells lack any type of flagella.

Electron microscopic structure. Much more detail of *Chlorella* cell can be observed with the help of electron microscope. The array of membranes forming a C-shaped profile just inside the cell represents the chloroplast. The chloroplast remains separated from the hyaloplasm by a membrane. The nucleus is bounded by a double envelope which is provided with pores. Mitochondria, dictyospomes and a few vacuoles are present.

Reproduction. The only method of reproduction is by means of aplanospores (asexual method). The protoplast of the parent cell divides to form two, four, eight or sixteen parts. Soon after each part becomes surrounded by a cell wall to form a non-motile cell. These cells resemble the parent cells in all respects except for size.The parental cell wall disintegrates and the small-sized non-motile, rounded daughter cells are released. Very soon they grow to mature size. It is to be remembered that the swarmers are never produced.

Ecology and physiology. Many species of *Chlorella* show saprobic tendency. They grow luxuriantly in organic media, sometime with loss of chlorophyll. Some species occur in the sappy exudations of the trees. According to Artari, Beijerink and Chodat the species of *Chlorella* may be grown on glucose agar medium. *Chlorella rubescens* has been reported to soften or liquefy the gelatin. According to Muenscher (1923), *Chlorella* carries on protein synthesis in darkness when supplied with inorganic nitrogen.

Evolutionary tendency. In *Chlorella* the motile phase has been completely abolished. The unicellular algae totally lack the flagellated bodies. These non-motile unicellular algae have given rise to non-motile colonial forms. There is complete loss of motility and side by side with it a loss of ability to divide vegetatively.

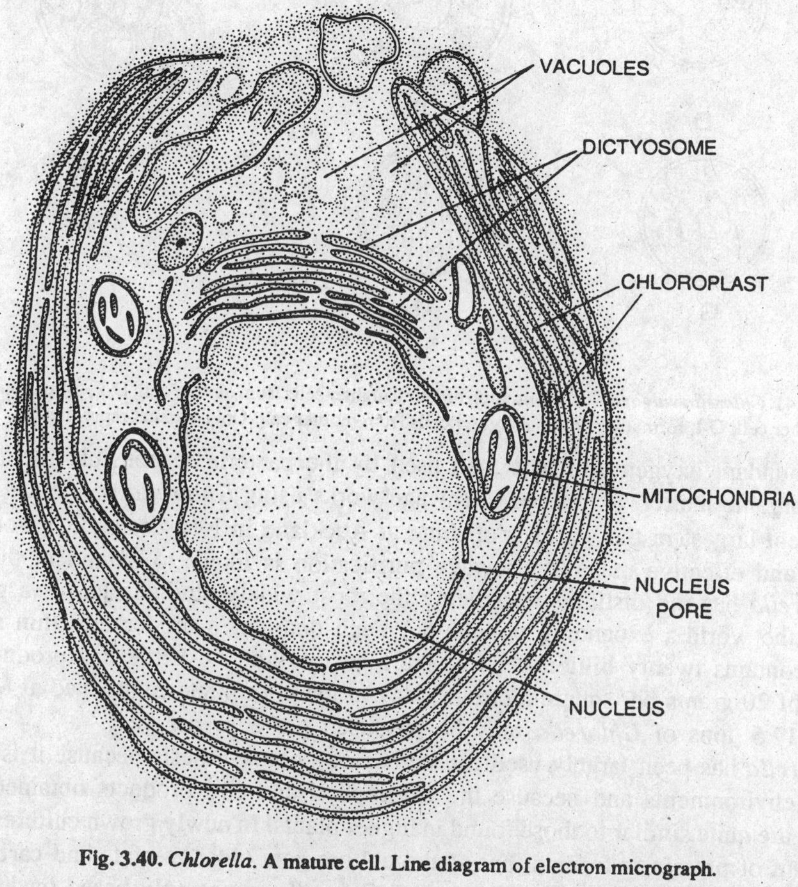

Fig. 3.40. *Chlorella*. **A mature cell. Line diagram of electron micrograph.**

Utilization. In recent years the alga *Chlorella* has assumed great importance and it is likely to become even more important in the future. *Chlorella* is rich in proteins, fats and vitamins, and in the presence of nutrients, CO_2 and sunlight, multiplies at an enormous rate. Several countries have been experimenting with the mass production of *Chlorella*. Pilot scale *Chlorella* farms have already been established in America, Japan, Holland, Germany and Israel. Such farms do not require excessive amounts of water and hence would be invaluable to augment food supplies in arid areas. Such 'farms' on a smaller scale could also be used to supply food in space station of the future and even large space ships.

Chlorella is also being increasingly used as a means of purifying sewage when it is present in large, shallow tanks of effluent (after primary sedimentation of solids) the rapid photosynthesis

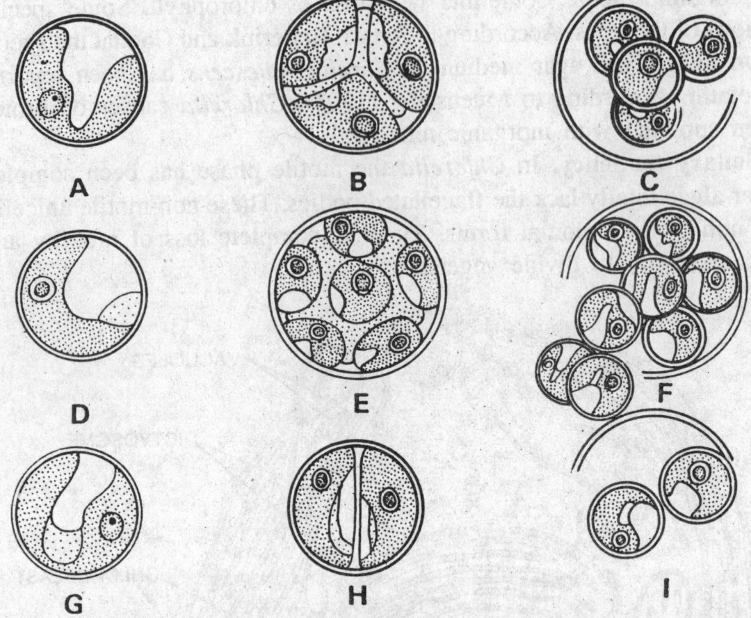

Fig. 3.41. *Chlorella vulgaris.* A-C, formation of four daughter cells from mother cell; D-F, formation of eight daughter cells from mother cell; G-I, formation of two daughter cells from mother cell. Only asexual reproduction.

produces abundant oxygen which is then used by the bacteria responsible for destroying the remaining organic matter. A number of sewage works using *Chlorella* now exist in the U.S.A. and at present largest in the world is opening at Auckland in NewZealand. It would seem that this cheap and effective means of sewage purification is likely to extend in the future.

Chlorella has the distinction of being the most widely studied alga as a potential food source for the world's expanding population. Each quart of a moderately thin suspension of *Chlorella* contains twenty billion cells of the alga. Arthur D. Little has produced *Chlorella* at the rate of 20 grams per square metre per day in his pilot plant established at Massachusetts. This way 17.5 tons of *Chlorella* may be produced per acre per year.

Chlorella has been largely used for studies on photosynthesis because it is easy to grow in various environments and because the chlorophyll and end products obtained during photosynthesis are quite similar to those found in higher plants. In newly grown cultures of *Chlorella*, large amount of protein is formed, but as the culture gets older the fats and carbohydrates are produced abundantly. The nutritional value of *Chlorella* is not only based on its high protein content but also on the fact that it contains the essential amino acids.

Both starch and sucrose have been isolated from *Chlorella*. The dry weight storage of carbohydrates in this alga may be as high as 20 per cent.

Ordinarily the fat contents are 20 to 25 per cent. Palmitic acid is the main saturated fatty acid. The stearic acid forms less than 4 per cent of the total fatty acid. Most of the fat of *Chlorella* is unsaturated that is as high as 65 per cent of the total fat content.

Chlorella contains most of the known vitamins such as thiamin, riboflavin, niacin, pyridioxine, pantothenic acid, choline, biotin, vitamin B_{12} and lipoic acid. Phytoplankton is the basic source of vitamin for fish, and makes the basis of food and vitamins for human beings. This has been calculated that a quarter pound of *Chlorella* will fulfil the need of all the vitamins except ascorbic acid, of a man for a day.

In United States, *Chlorella* has been considered to be used to control the oxygen and carbon dioxide in atomic submarines. It has been calculated that one kg. of fresh *Chlorella* can supply the 25 litres of oxygen required hourly by a 70 kg. man, as well as use the carbondioxide liberated by him. In United States the scientists are experimenting and considering the use of *Chlorella* in spaceships. The algae will supply oxygen and utilize carbon dioxide. Besides this the culture of *Chlorella* would also serve as food and the waste materials of the spacemen would serve as nutrient for algae.

Systematic position. Division-Chlorophycophyta; Class-Chlorophyceae; Order-Chlorococcales; Family-Chlorellaceae ; Genus-*Chlorella*.

ORDER–ULOTRICHALES

This order includes about 80 genera and 430 species.

Characteristic features. 1. Most of the genera are exclusively fresh water. *U. zonata* is found in flowing fresh waters in attached condition. Some genera consist of both marine and fresh water species. Some genera are exclusively marine. Some are found in estuaries.

2. They may be unbranched filaments (Ulotrichaceae) or thalloid sheet-like structures (Ulvaceae).

3. Reproduction takes place by means of 1. vegetative 2. asexual and 3. sexual methods. Vegetative reproduction takes place by fragments and akinetes. They reproduce asexually by bi or quadriflagellate zoospores, aplanospores, hypnospores and palmella stage. Sexual reproduction takes place by isogamous; anisogamous and oogamous methods. Isogamy in *Ulothrix;* anisogmay in *Ulva lobata* and oogamy in *Cylindrocapsa.*

4. During germination of zygote, reduction division takes place to bring haploid condition.

5. The chloroplast may be girdle like (*Ulothrix*), ring-like (*Sphaeroplea*), stellate (*Prasiola*) or plate-like (*Hormidium*). One to many pyrenoids are found in chloroplasts. Single pyrenoid is found in the stellate chloroplasts of *Prasiola*. Two to many pyrenoids are present in the girdle-shaped chloroplasts of *Ulothrix.*

Classification. The order is sub-divided into *three* sub-orders, *i.e.,* 1. Ulotrichineae, 2. Prasiolineae and 3. Sphaeropleineae.

Sub-order Ulotrichineae has *four* families, *i.e.,* 1. Ulotrichaceae, 2. Cylindrocapsaceae, 3. Ulvaceae and 4. Microsporaceae.

Sub-order Prasiolineae has single family, *i.e.,* Prasiolaceae (single genus-*Prasiola*).

Family–Ulotrichaceae (15 genera; 120 species)

Characteristic features. 1. This family includes all the unbranched filamentous genera.

2. The cells are uninucleate with a single girdle-shaped chloroplast.

3. Asexual reproduction takes place by means of bi - or quadriflagellate zoospores. It also takes place by aplanospores or akinetes.

4. Sexual reproduction wherever recorded is isogamous and with a union of biflagellate gametes.

5. All genera are found in fresh water.

Genus ULOTHRIX (*ulo,* shaggy; *thrix,* hair)

The genus includes about 30 species.

Habitat and occurrence. Majoirty of the species are fresh water forms and found in slow running streams. Some species are found in ponds, pools, ditches and water reservoirs of such nature where continuously the water is renewed. The forms are attached to some substrata in earlier stages. *U. zonata* is found in cold waters, *Ulothrix implexa* is a lithophyte in estuaries. *Ulothrix flacca* is found in saline waters whereas some species are marine.

Structure. The plant body consists of unbranched, uniseriate filaments. The cells of the filaments are arranged end to end. They are rectangular or somewhat square in structure. Usually the cells are much broader than their length. Of course, all cells are of same type except the apical and the basal one. The apical cell is somewhat rounded at its terminal end whereas the basal cell is elongated and devoid of chlorophyll. The basal cell is called the **holdfast** which attaches the filament to the substratum.

The cell wall is two layered. The inner layer consists of cellulose and surrounds the protoplast; the outer layer is of pectose. In each cell a single girdle-like and parietal chloroplast is found. There are two to many pyrenoids in each chloroplast. A big nuleues is situated in the central region of the cell called **'primordial utricle'.**

Reproduction. The reproduction takes place by means of vegetative, asexual and sexual methods.

1. Vegetative reproduction. The common vegetative methods are— (a) fragmentation and (b) akinete formation.

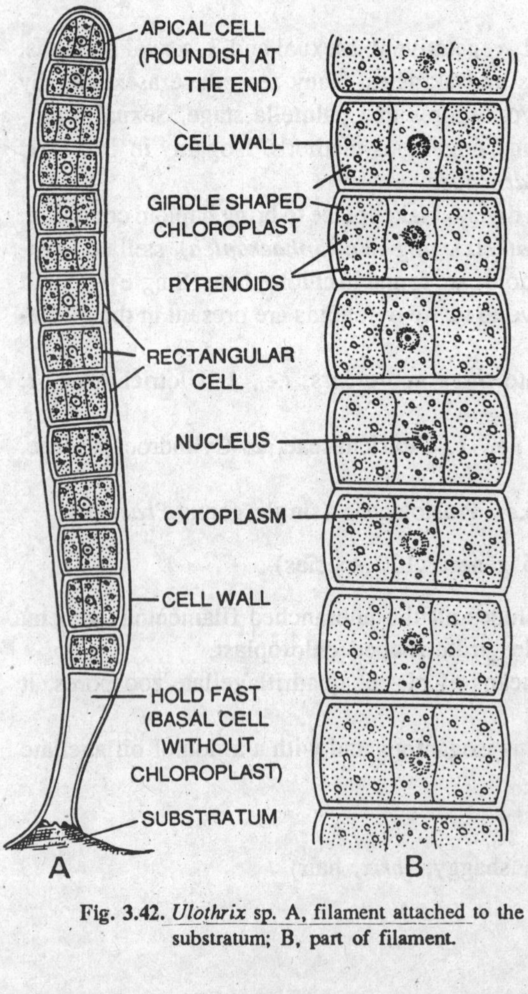

Fig. 3.42. *Ulothrix* sp. A, filament attached to the substratum; B, part of filament.

(a) By fragmentation. The vegetative filaments break into small fragments accidentally. Each fragment is capable to give rise to a new plant.

(b) By akinetes. Some of the vegetative cells of *Ulothrix idiospora* convert into thick-walled akinetes.

The akinetes are produced by thickening and gelatinization of the walls. Much of the food reserves are accumulated within the cells. On approach of favourable conditions each akinete develops into a new plant.

2. Asexual reproduction. The asexual reproduction takes place by means of (a) zoospores (b) aplanospores, (c) hypnospores and (d) palmella stage.

(a) By zoospores. In *Ulothrix* two types of zoospores *i.e.*, (1) macrozoospores and (2) microzoospores are produced according to species. All cells may produce zoospores except the holdfast.

Macrozoospores. The contents of the cell are enriched with food reserves. The protoplast divides in one plane and the next division is at right angles to the first division. In each cell 2, 4 or 8 macrozoospores come out through the lateral wall of the cell and they swim in the vesicle for some time. The vesicle develops from the inner wall of the cell. Very soon this vesicle dissolves and the macrozoospores are set free.

Each macrozoospore is ovoid quadriflagellate, and possesses a band-like chloroplast, pyrenoid and an anterior stigma. The posterior side is somewhat pointed. The zoospores attach themsevles to the substratum anteriorly and the flagella are retracted. With the result of the division of zoospore in one plane the filamentous plant body is developed. The basal cell becomes chlorophyll less elongated holdfast.

Microzoospores. The microzoospores develop in the same way in the cells as macrozoospores only with the difference that they are smaller in size and more in number. In each cell 8, 16 or even 32 microzoospores are produced. Each microzoospore is ovoid and somewhat rounded at its posterior end. It contains a single chloroplast, single pyrenoid, a median stigma and a nucleus in it. Usually they are quadriflagellate and very rarely biflagellate. They also germinate in the same way as macrozoospores.

(b) By aplanospores. Sometime before liberation from the cell, the zoospores secrete a thin wall around each of them and called 'aplanospores'. Some of these aplanospores may germinate *in situ*. Each aplanospore is capable of giving to a new plant. According to West (1916), sometimes the contents of a vegetative cell become rounded and a thick-walled aplanospore develops in the parent cell.

(c) Hypnospores. The thick-walled hypnospores have also been recorded from *Ulothrix*. A single hypnospore develops in a cell. Each such structure is capable of giving rise to a new plant body on the approach of favourable condition by repeated divisions in one plane of the protoplast.

(d) Palmella stage. The palmella stage develops in drier conditions. The cells of the filament divide in all directions and many protoplasts are formed. This is a modification of aplanospore formation where the aplanospores are completely gelatinized and embedded in a common gelatinous matrix. On the approach of favourable conditions each rounded structure develops in a new filament.

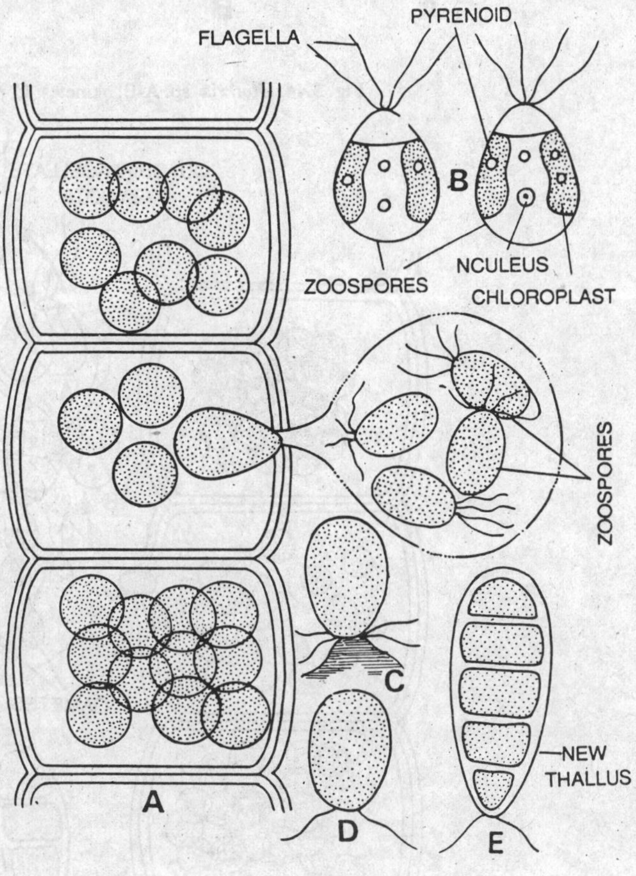

Fig. 3.43. *Ulothrix* sp. Asexual reproduction. A, zoospore formation and liberation; B, quadriflagellate zoospores; C-E germination of zoospore and development of new thallus.

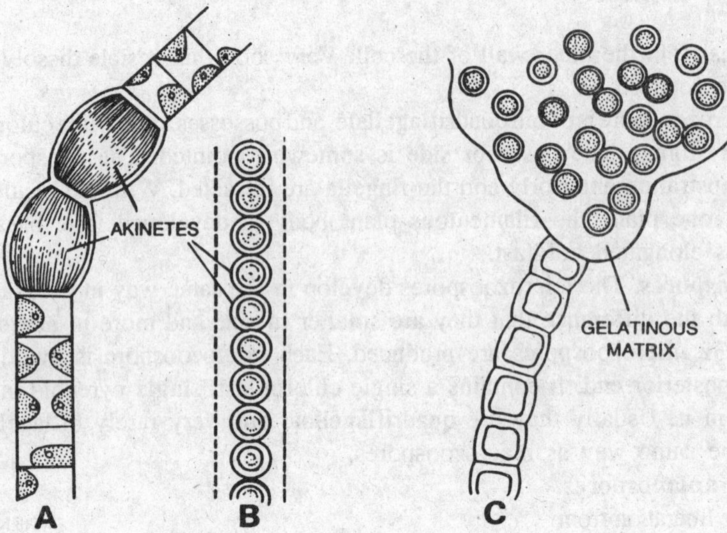

Fig. 3.44. *Ulothrix* sp. A-B, akinetes; C, palmelloid stage.

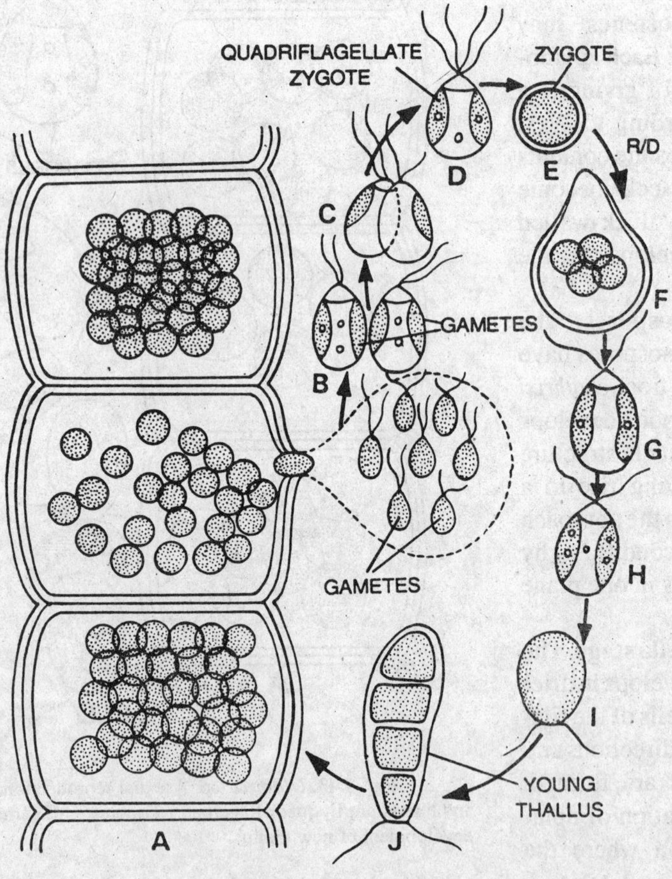

Fig. 3.45. *Ulothrix* sp. Sexual reproduction, isogamy, A, formation and liberation of motile biflagellate gametes; B, gametes; C, fusion of gametes; D, temporary phase of quadriflagellate motile zygote; E, non-motile zygote; F, germination of zygote giving rise to four zoospores; G-H, zoospores; I-J, germinating zoospore.

3. **Sexual reproduction.** The sexual reproduction is isogamous. The species may be homothallic or heterothallic. In homothallic species the isogametes taking part in union usually come from two different cells of the same filament whereas in heterothallic species they come from two different filaments. The sexual reproduction takes place in unfavourable conditions. In each cell of the filament except holdfast, 16, 32, or 64 gametes are produced by successive division, in the same manner as zoospores are produced. The isogametes are ovoid and biflagellate. Each possesses a chloroplast and a single pyrenoid. The stigma is also present. The isogametes come out of the parent cell in a membranous vesicle. Very soon the vesicle disappears and the gametes move freely in water. The gametes fuse in pairs anteriorly and quadriflagellate zygospores are developed. Very soon the cilia of the zygote are withdrawn, it becomes rounded and a thick wall is secreted around it. This zygote rests and accumulates food reserves in resting period.

Germination of zygote. After a definite resting period the zygote germinates. Prior to germination of the zygote increases in size and becomes somewhat deep green or dark in colour. During germination reduction division takes place. The protoplast divides and 4 to 16 aplanospores or zoospores are produced. Each such structure develops into a new filament.

Systematic position. Division-Chlorophycophyta; Class-Chlorophyceae; Order-Ulotrichales; Family-Ulotrichaceae; Genus-*Ulothrix*.

Family-Ulvaceae

Characteristic features. 1. The thallus is either an expanded sheet one or two cells in thickness, or a ribbon-like structure two or more cells in thickness.

2. The cells are uninucleate and possess a single cup-shaped or laminate chloroplast.

3. In the genera *Enteromorpha* and *Ulva* of this family there is an isomorphic alternation of generations with meiosis just before formation of zoospores by the sporophytic generation.

4. Vegetative reproduction takes place by fragmentation.

5. Asexual reproduction takes place by means of quadriflagellate zoospores.

6. Sexual reproduction may be isogamous or anisogamous.

Genus ULVA (latin for a marsh plant)

Occurrence. *Ulva* has about thirty species most of which are exclusively marine. This is also known as 'sea lettuce', commonly found in mid-tidal zone and frequently grows profusely in waters polluted by sewage. A few species grow in brackish waters. *U. indica* is reported from Kumari harbour.

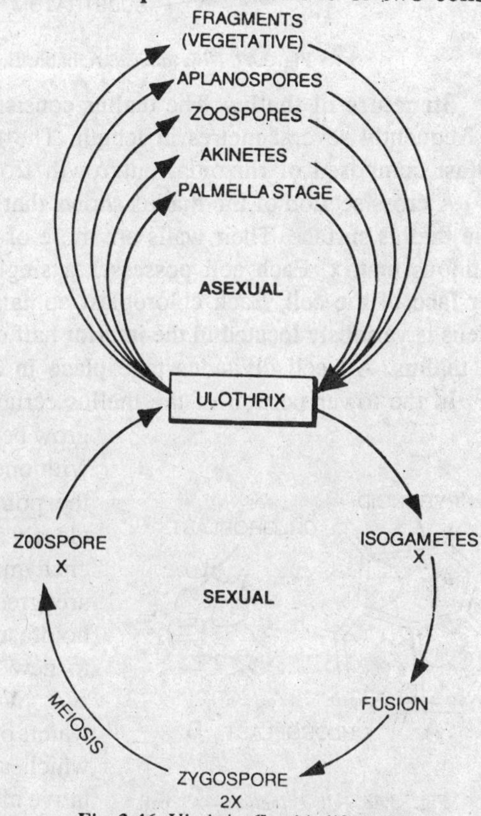

Fig. 3.46. *Ulothrix*–Graphic life cycle.

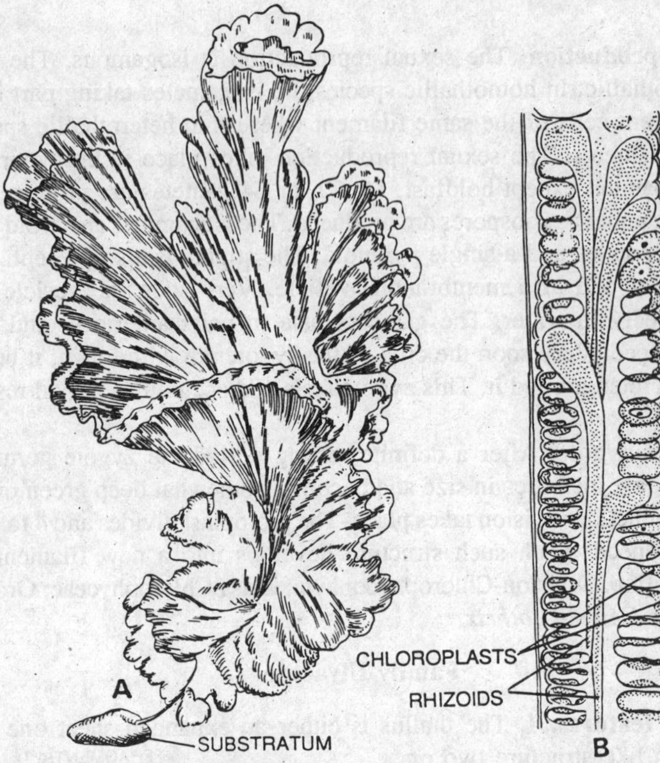

Fig. 3.47. *Ulva lactuca*. A, habit; B, longitudinal section of mature thallus.

Structure of thallus. The thallus consists of large expanded sheet two cells in thickness and frequently several metres in length. The thallus remains attached to the substratum by a holdfast composed of rhizoidal outgrowth from the lower cells.

A cross section of the thallus shows that the cells are isodiametric or vertically elongated to the thallus surface. Their walls are more or less confluent with one another to form a tough gelatinous matrix. Each cell possesses a single cupshaped chloroplast which lies next to the outer face of the cell. Each chloroplast contains one pyrenoid. The cells are uninucleate. The nucleus is variously located in the interior half of the cell. The cell division takes place anywhere in a thallus. All cell divisions take place in a plane perpendicular to the thallus surface.

In the lower portion of the thallus certain cells send out long colourless rhizoids which grow between the two layers of cells and intertwine freely with one another. The rhizoids emerge from thallus near the point of attachment to the substratum and become closely intermingled to one another forming a pseudoparenchymatous holdfast. The emerging portions of rhizoids are green, transversely septate and multinucleate. The holdfast portion of a thallus is perennial and gives rise to new blades each spring (Delf, 1912).

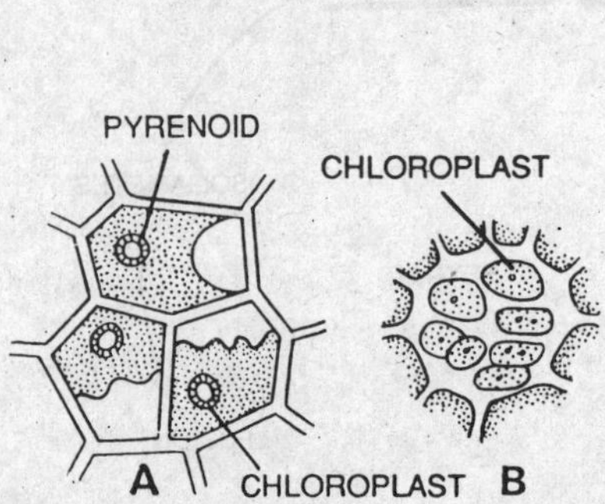

Fig. 3.48. *Ulva lactuca*—A, cell structure; B, small part of thallus.

Vegetative reproduction. *Ulva* growing in quiet waters of estuaries, usually multiply by means of fragments which are accidentally produced from a thallus. Vegetative multiplication also takes place by means of the proliferation of perennial holdfast.

Asexual reproduction. Asexual reproduction takes place by means of quadriflagellate zoospores. The zoospores are formed in ordinary vegetative cells by the dividing up of the protoplast. The divided parts of the protoplast metamorphose into zoospores, which liberate through an opening in the cell wall. The contents of any of the ordinary cells produce 4-8 zoospores. The zoospores are formed at first in the cells near the margin, later on, they are formed in other cells too which are away from the margin. The formation of zoosppores continues until all the

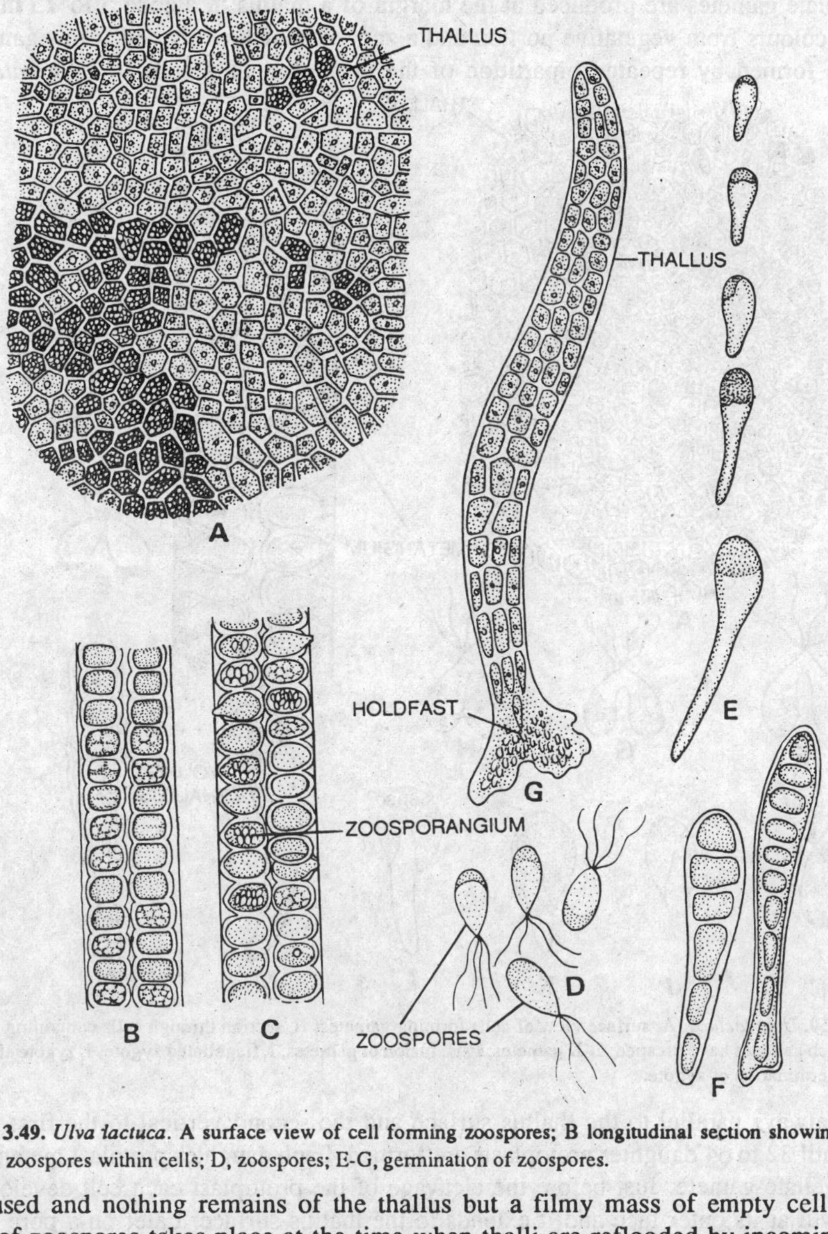

Fig. 3.49. *Ulva lactuca.* **A surface view of cell forming zoospores; B longitudinal section showing cell forming zoospores; C, zoospores within cells; D, zoospores; E-G, germination of zoospores.**

cells are used and nothing remains of the thallus but a filmy mass of empty cell walls. The liberation of zoospores takes place at the time when thalli are reflooded by incoming tides and usually during morning tides (Smith 1947). Sometimes the zoospores are liberated in large quantities and they colour the water green. After swimming for an hour or so, a zoospore comes to rest on some substratum withdraws, its flagella and secretes a wall around it. Soon after, it divides by a transverse wall giving rise to two cells. The lower cell develops into a rhizoidal holdfast and the upper into the blade. Meiosis takes place at zoospore formation and, in all but one of the species investigated, there is a regular alternation of morphologically similar diploid (2x) and haploid (x) generations. In *Ulva linza,* only the diploid generation is known and meiosis does not occur at zoospore formation.

Sexual reproduction. The zoospores develop into sexual plant which produce gametes. The biflagellate gametes are produced at the margin of a thallus in a zone 5 to 15 mm. broad, of different colours from vegetative portion and a zone in which every cell forms gametes. The gametes are formed by repeated bipartition of the protoplast of a cell. In *U. lobata* the first

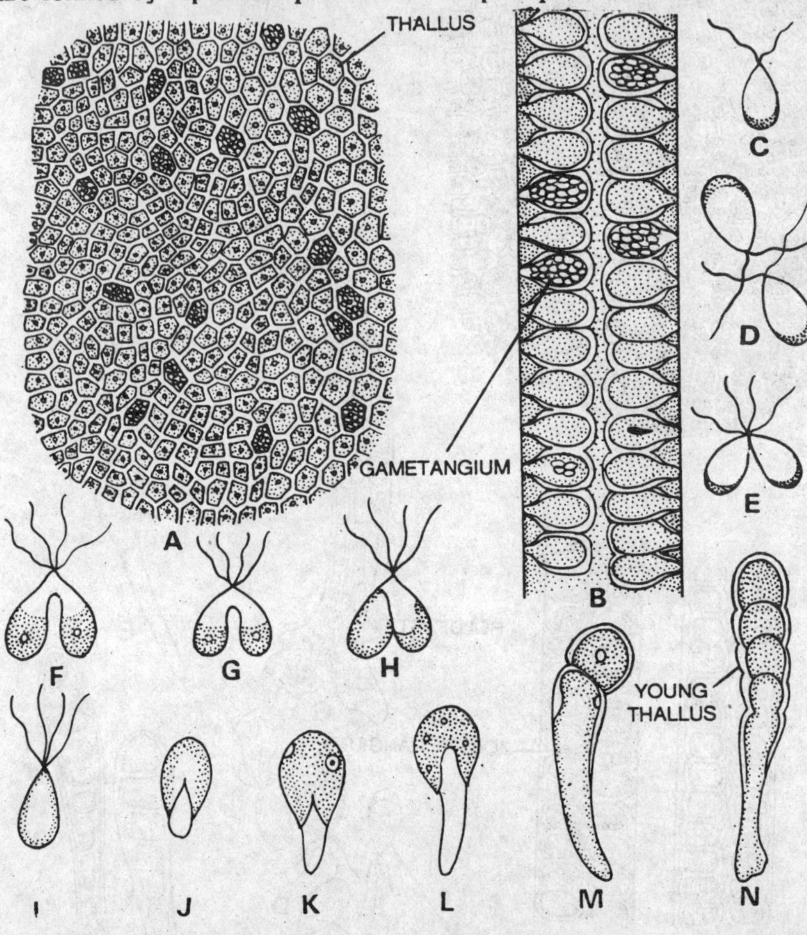

Fig. 3.50. *Ulva lactuca*. A, surface view of cells forming gametes; B, section through cells containing gametes and others from which gametes have escaped; C-D gametes; E-H, fusion of gametes; I, flagellated zygote; J, zygote after losing its flagella; K-N, gemination of zygote.

cleavage is always parallel to the thallus surface and the second vertical to the first. Cleavage continues until 32 to 64 daughter protoplasts are formed. Each daughter protolast metamorphoses into a biflagellate gamete. Just before the cleavage of the protoplast each cell develops a beak like outgrowth at its outer face and it extends to the thallus surface. Later on a pore is formed at the tip of this beak, through which the gametes are liberated. All species so far investigated have been found to be heterothallic. Most of species are isogamous, but three species, including *Ulva lobata* are anisogamous. The gametes are smaller than the zoospores. They are pyriform in shape with a single chloroplast and an eye spot. The gametophytes liberate gametes, at the beginning of each series of spring tides. All the gametes look alike, but really there are two kinds of sexual plants, although they look alike and produce gametes that look alike. This is shown by the gametes in fusing. Gametes from the same thallus or from thalli of the same kind will fuse with each other, while those from different kinds will fuse. The gametes usually show pronounced positive phototaxis, but just after fusion the reaction changes to a negative one.

After fusion of gametes quadriflagellate zygote is formed. It swims for a short time and then comes to rest, withdraws its flagella and secretes a wall around it. Within a day or two the germination of zygote takes place. The division of the zygote nucleus is mitotic. The two daughter cells are formed by means of division of the zygote. One of the two daughter cells

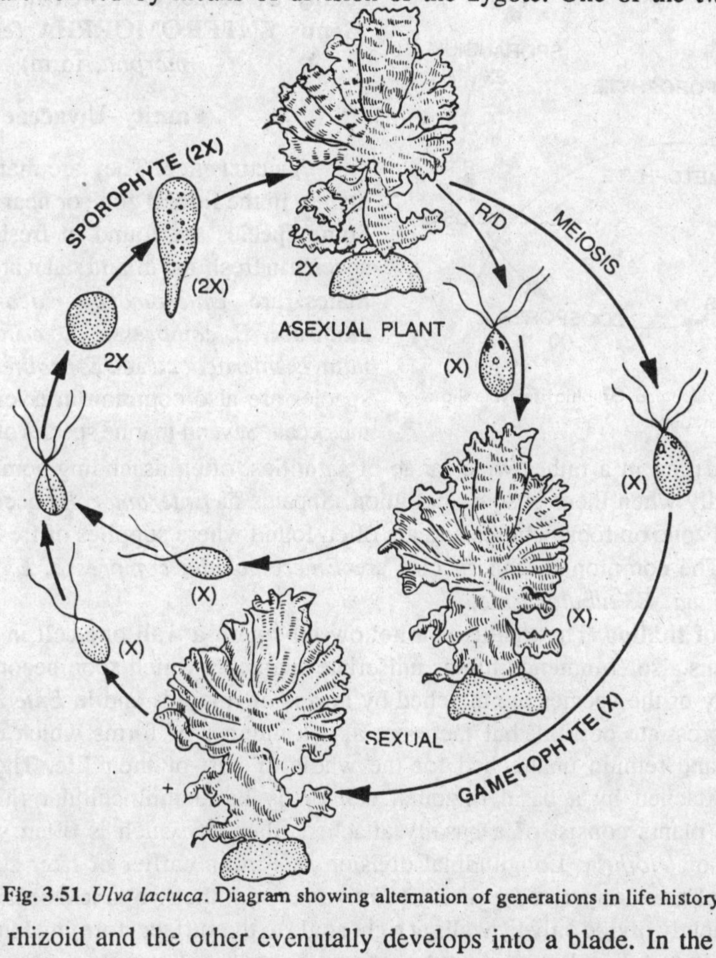

Fig. 3.51. *Ulva lactuca.* Diagram showing alternation of generations in life history.

develops into a rhizoid and the other evenutally develops into a blade. In the development of the blade the first divisions are all transverse and form a filament of several cells, after which both vertical and transverse cell divisions take place. When these plants produce zoospores the number of chromosomes is reduced so that the zoospores have a haploid number and give rise to sexual plants with a haploid number.

Alternation of generations. There is an alternation not only of aseuxal plants but of asexual plants with a diploid number of chromosomes and sexual plants with a haploid number. This phenomenon is known as alternation of generations, *i.e.*, an alternation of a diploid asexual generation (sporophyte) and a haploid sexual one (gametophyte). With the result of the fusion of two gametes the number of chromosomes being doubled and carried over to the cells of the sporophyte. The reduction division takes place when the zoospores are formed. The haploid zoospores give rise to the gametophytes. Both kinds of plants are morphologically identical and therefore, *Ulva* shows an isomorphic alternation of generations.

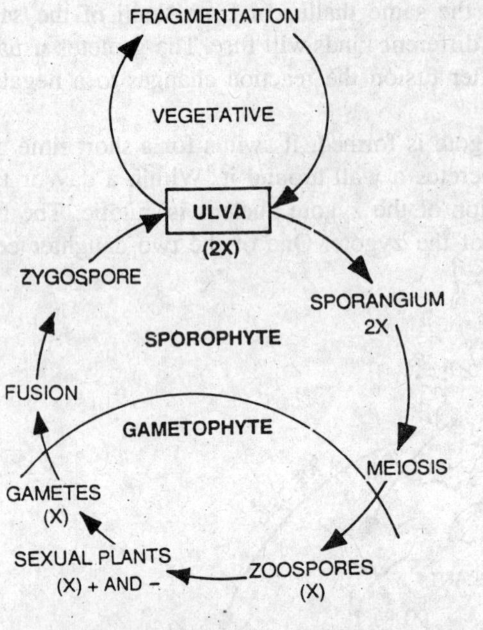

Fig. 3.52. *Ulva lactuca*. Graphic life cycle showing alternation of generations.

Systematic position. Division-Chlorophycophyta; Class-Chlorophyceae; Order-Ulotrichales; Family-Ulvaceae; Genus-*Ulva*.

Genus ENTEROMORPHA (*entero*, entrail; *morpha*, form)

Family–Ulvaceae

Occurrence. They are marine, and occur mainly in the littoral zone or near low-tide level. Some species are found in fresh waters. The species in fresh and inland salt water in the United States are *Enteromorpha acanthophora, E, clathrata, E. compressa, E. crinata, E. marginata, E. micrococca* and *E. prolifera*. Few marine species are also common in rivers flowing into the ocean. Several marine species of *Enteromorpha* are capable of existing in a rather wide range of salinities, often ascending some distance into estuaries, especially when there is some pollution. Species of *Enteromorpha* occur in the upper part of the littoral zone on rocky shores and are often found where supplies of fresh water escape from the cliffs. The common Indian species are *Enteromorpha compressa, E. intestinalis, E. prolifera, E. minima, E. tubulosa* etc.

Structure of thallus. The thallus is a hollow tube with a wall one cell in thickness. The plants of this genus also commence life as uniseriate filaments which soon become multiseriate and tubular. Many of the species are attached by means of rhizoids and in *Enteromorpha nana*, there is a basal prostrate portion, but there are also a number of forms which occur specially on salt marshes and remain unattached for the whole or part of their life. The young plants are sessile and attached by a basal rhizoidal cell or by basal multicellular rhizoids.

The young plants consist of a basally attached filament which is often very much like that of a species of *Ulothrix*. Longitudinal division sets in an earlier or later stages and leads to the formation of a two-layered expanse. In *Enteromorpha*, the two layers separate at an early stage and subsequently divide only by walls at right angle to the surface, forming long intestiniform tubes with a one-layered wall.

The cells are usually placed with their long axes at right angles to the surface of the thallus. Each cell contains a single parietal chloroplast, often with deeply incised or lobed margins and including a single pyrenoid. The chloroplast is usually located on the outer side of the cell, while the nucleus lies adjacent to the inner wall. According to Henkel, the chloroplast in *Enteromorpha intestinalis* always lies against the lower side of the cell. The cell walls are generally conspicuously stratified.

Growth of thallus. In *Enteromorpha*, the growth is partly effected by an apical cell which divides transversely and longitudinally into segments which increase the length of the thallus. The thallus, also enlarges by intercalary division. The branches, common in various species of *Enteromorpha* likewise grow partly with the aid of an apical cell which arises indiscriminately from any cell of the main axis. When the tubular thallus is damaged near the apex the wounded cells put out papillate outgrowths, but if the damage occurs near the base rhizoids are produced.

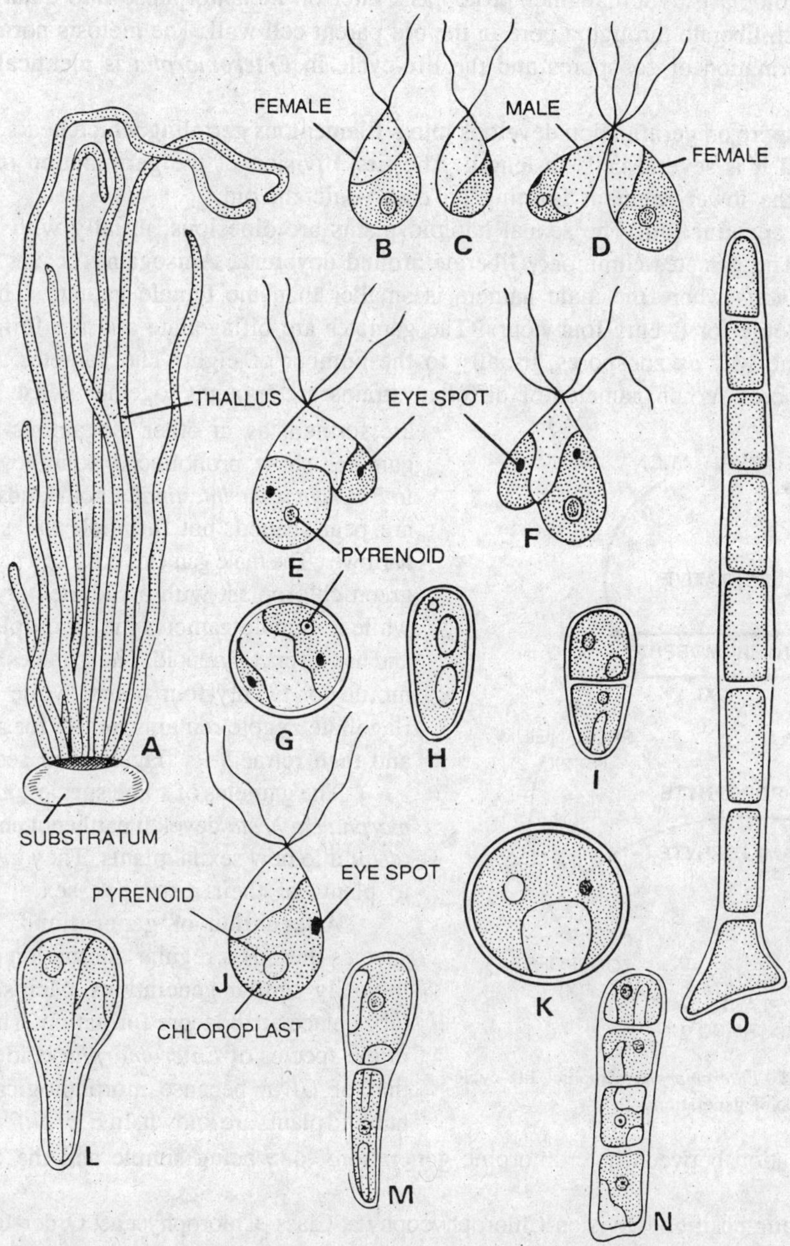

Fig. 3.53. *Enteromorpha intestinalis*—A, habit (thallus); B, female gamete (large); C, male gamete (small); D-F, fusion of gametes (anisogamy), G, zygote; H-I, germination of zygote; J, zoospore; K, zoospore after losing flagella, L-O, germination of zoospore (successive stages).

In certain species the plastids show polarity, *i.e.*, they occur normally in the apical portion of the cell.

Vegetative reproduction. Vegetative multiplication occasionally takes by an abscission of proliferous shoots.

Asexual reproduction. Asexual reproduction takes place by means of quadriflagellate zoospores. The zoospores are formed by repeated bipartition of the protoplast into 4, 8, 16 or 32 daughter protoplasts. The daughter protoplasts later on metamorphose into quadriflagellate zoospores which liberate through a pore in the old parent cell wall. The meiosis normally takes place at the formation of zoospores and the life-cycle in *Enteromorpha* is identical with that of *Ulva*.

The zoospore on germination develops into a filamentous germling which bears a rhizoidal basal cell, until it is several cells in length. The first division of the germination of zoospore is transverse, the lower segment forming an embryonic rhizoid.

Sexual reproduction. The sexual haploid plants are dioecious, usually with isogamous reproduction. The gametes commonly liberate around daybreak. Anisogamy occurs in *Enteromorpha intestinalis* where the male gamete is smaller than the female gamete. The gametes may remain motile for twenty-four hours. The gametes are biflagellate and are formed in any cell in the same way as zoospores, usually to the number of eight. The gametes are smaller than the zoospores. When gametes of different strains are brought together dense aggregates are formed, as in other isogamous algae. The gametes show pronounced positive phototaxis. In *Enteromorpha intestinalis,* both kinds of gametes are pear-shaped, but the male are smaller and narrower. The male gametes possess a pale yellowish green chloroplast with a rudimentary pyrenoid, while in female gametes the chloroplast is green and has distinct pyrenoid. The gametes may remain motile for twenty-four hours, while the quadriflagellate zygote remains motile for a short time and then retracts its flagella and secretes wall.

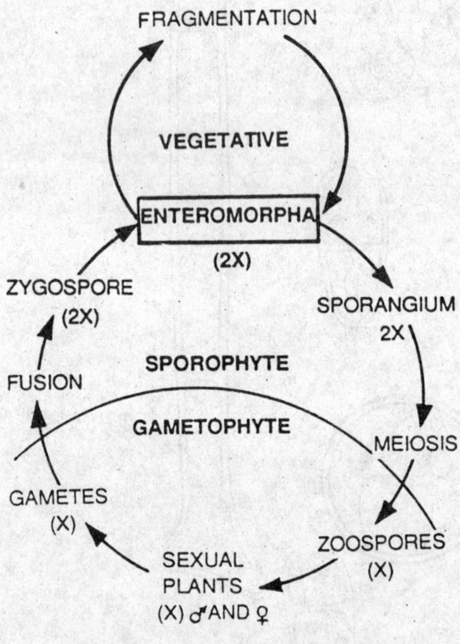

Fig. 3.54. *Enteromorpha*–Graphic life-cycle showing alternation of generations.

The gametes of some species, *e.g.*, *Enteromorpha clathrata* develop parthenogenetically and result into new sexual plants. They give rise only to plants of their respective sex.

Alternation of generations. In most of species there is a regular alternation of morphologically similar generations. Meiosis normally takes place at zoospore formation. The life cycle in the species of *Enteromorpha* is identieal with that of *Ulva,* because morphologically similar haploid plants are known. In *E. prolifera* however, there is alternation between heteromorphic generations, one being simple and the other much branched.

Systematic position. Division-Chlorophycophyta; Class- Chlorophyceae; Order-Ulotrichales; Family-Ulvaceae; Genus-*Enteromorpha.*

ORDER–CLADOPHORALES

This order includes 12 genera and 350 species.

1. Majority of them are found in fresh waters. Some genera are exclusively fresh water, *e.g., Pithophora*. Some genera are exclusively marine, *e.g., Urospora* and *Spongomorpha*. Others are partly marine and partly fresh water, *e.g., Cladophora*. Some species of *Cladophora* are found attached on molusc shells.

2. The filaments may be unbranched, *e.g., Urospora* or richly branched, *e.g., Cladophora*. Branching is always lateral.

3. The cell wall is three layered. The outer layer consists of chitin, the inner of cellulose and the middle of pectin. The cells are multinucleate with the exception of *Spongomorpha* where the condition is uninucleate. The chloroplast is reticulate with many pyrenoids.

4. Reproduction takes place by vegetative, asexual and sexual methods. Vegetative reproduction takes place by cell division, fragmentation, tubers, stolons, akinetes etc. Asexual reproduction takes place by zoospores. The sexual reproduction may be isogamous (*Cladophora*) or anisogamous (*Urospora lubricum*).

5. In Cladophorales there is isomorphic alternation of generations. The sporophytes produce quadriflagellate zoospores on germination and the gametophytes produce biflagellate gametes. In *Cladophora glomerata* the life-cycle is diplontic, and the meiosis takes place prior to gamete formation.

Classification. A single family Cladophoraceae is included in this order.

Family-Cladophoraceae (12 genera; 350 species)

Characteristic features. 1. They possess branched filamentous thalli.

2. The multinucleate cylindrical cells remain united end to end. The chloroplast is a reticulate sheet which surrounds the protoplast. The pyrenoids are found at intersections of reticulum.

3. Asexual reproduction takes place by means of quadriflagellate zoospores, aplanospores or akinetes.

4. Sexual reproduction is isogamous.

5. Sexual genera are exclusively fresh water, others exclusively marine and still others both marine and fresh water species.

Genus CLADOPHORA (*clado*, branch; *phora*, bearing)

There are about 160 species in this genus.

Habit and occurrence. Some species of this genus are marine and some are fresh water. *Cladophora profunda* is found in the bottom of lakes in attached condition. Some species are found on mollusc shells. The fresh water forms are found in streams, ponds and lakes attached to some substrata by rhizoidal bases.

Structure. The plant body consists of branched filaments. Usually the forms of *Cladophora* are found in attached condition.

The basal branched rhizoids remain attached to the substratum and act as holdfast.

Sometimes the branching in *Cladophora* appears to be dichotomous because of a pushing aside process called **'evection'**. The branching is always lateral. The branches arise from the upper ends of the cells.

The cells are elongated and 3 to 20 times longer than the breadth. The cells are arranged end to end. The cell wall is three layered consisting of chitin (outer), pectose (middle) and cellulose (inner) layers. The septa are usually stratified. There is a large central vacuole. The dense cytoplasm is found in peripheral region of the cell. The cell is coenocytic (multinucleate).

The nature of chloroplast is controversial. According to Carter (1919), and others the chloroplast in each cell is single, parietal and reticulate. According to Dr. F. E. Fritsch, the nature of chloroplast in Cladophoraceae is not very clear and can be reached to some conclusion only after studying the chloroplast of young plants, where they are reticulate. So the chlroplast in each cell of *Cladophora* is reticulate and with many pyrenoids.

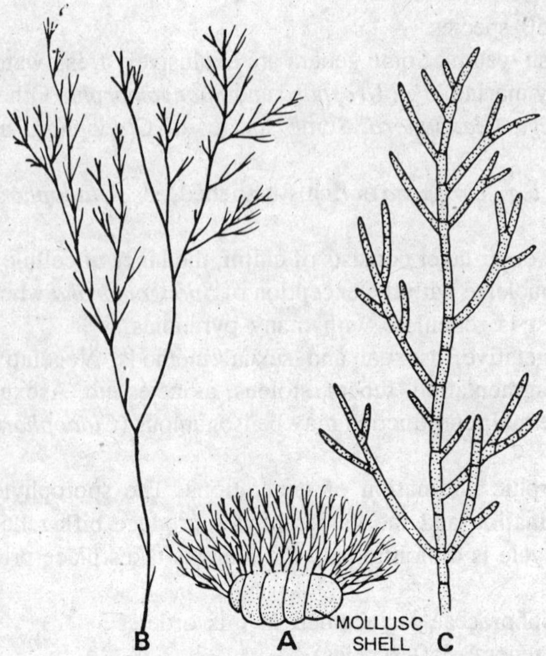

Fig. 3.55. *Cladophora* sp. A, habit (thalli on mollusc shell); B, single plant; C, part of thallus showing branching

In *Cladophora,* the cells have power of multiplication. The protoplast becomes constricted in the centre and ultimately septum develops and two cells are formed.

Reproduction. The reproduction in *Cladophora* may be 1. vegetative, 2. asexual and 3. sexual.

1. Vegetative. The vegetative reproduction takes place by (a) fragmentation, (b) stolons, (c) tubers and (d) akinetes.

(a) Fragmentation. The filaments break in small filaments, each fragment may give rise to a new plant.

(b) Stolons. In *Cladophora,* usually the cells of dying rhizoids are filled up with starch, they survive and give rise to new plants in next season.

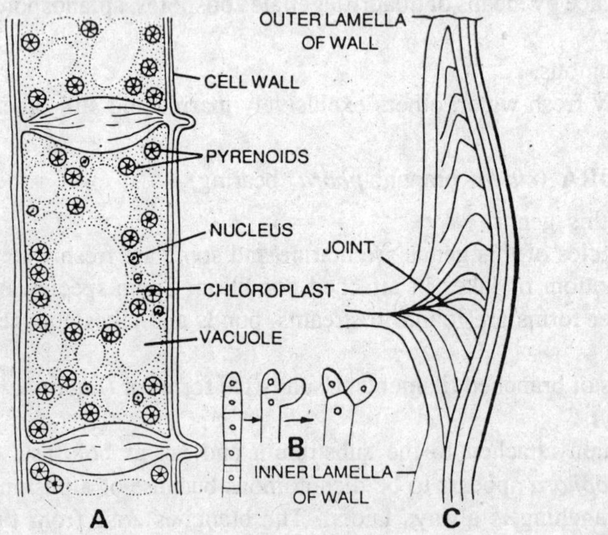

Fig. 3.56. *Cladophora*. A, detailed structure of the cell; B, evection; C, structure of membrane.

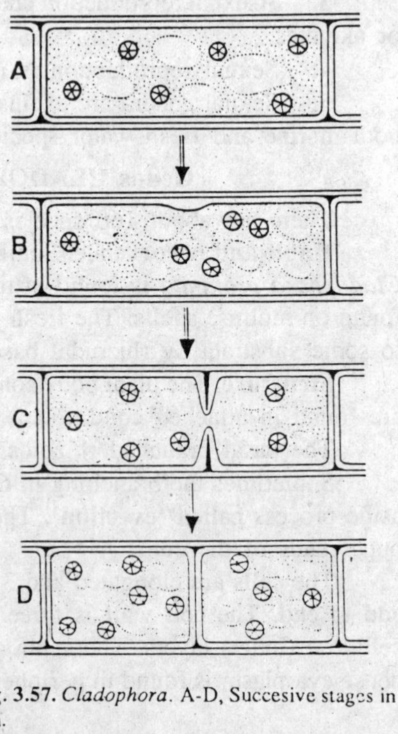

Fig. 3.57. *Cladophora*. A-D, Succesive stages in cell division.

(c) Tubers. Sometimes the rhizoidal branches divide to form multicellular structures called 'tubers'. These structures are filled up with food reserves. In favourable conditions these tubers germinate and produce new plants.

(d) Akinetes. The akinetes are vegetative bodies. The protoplasts of the cell becomes round and thick-walled and known as 'akinete'. Such structures are filled up with food reserves and germinate in favourable conditions.

2. Asexual. The asexual reproduction takes place by means of zoospores. The zoospores are produced inside the cells, called zoosporangia. At the time of zoospore formation the protoplast divides into several bits. Simultaneously the nuclei also divide. Each protoplasmic bit having a nucleus in it metamorphoses into a biflagellate or quadriflagellate zoospore. The zoospore usually develop in the terminal cells of the finer branches. The zoospore formation takes place in basipetal succession. In most of the cases the zoospores are pear-shaped and quadriflagellate but in *Cladophora glomerata* they are biflagellate. The zoospores liberate from the cell through a small lens-shaped area at just below the apical end of the cell. The zoospores move here and there in the water after their liberation. The cilia are retracted. The one-celled structure secretes a wall around it. This structure soon becomes elongated and coenocytic simultaneously a cross wall develops. The upper cell develops into filamentous plant body and the lower cell in rhizoidal system.

3. Sexual. In *Cladophora* the sexual reproduction is isogamous. Almost all the species are heterothallic. The isogametes are formed in the same way as the zoospores are formed. Here the parent cells may be called gametangia instead of zoosporangia. After their liberation from different parents they unite in pairs and the zygotes are resulted. Very soon the flagella are retracted and a wall is screted around the zygote. This zygote germinates immediately and has no resting period. In several species of *Cladophora* the germination of zygote is direct. In many Cladophoraceae there is isomorphic alterantion of generations between asexual and sexual plants. Schussnig has established that in a number of species of *Cladophora* reduction division occurs at the time of zoospore formation and not at the time of gamete formation. In *Cladophora glomerata* the reduction division takes place prior to gamete formation and not at the time of zoospore formation. Here the life-cycle is diplontic.

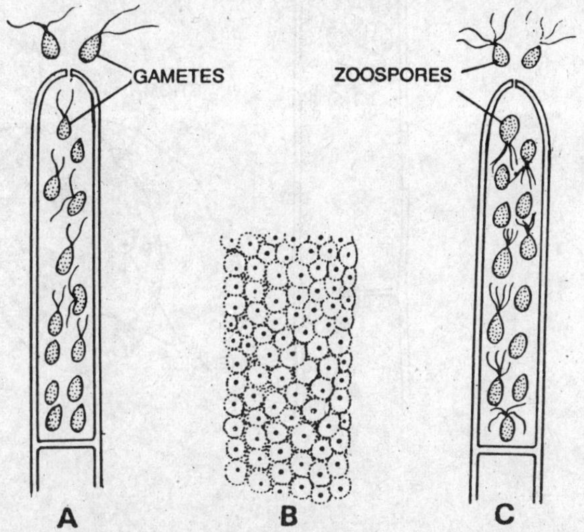

Fig. 3.58. *Cladophora* sp. A, formation and liberation of biflagellate gametes; B, delimitation of zoospores; C, liberation of quadriflagellate zoospores.

The protoplast of the zygote divides meiotically producing 4 quadriflagellate zoospores. Thus four quadriflagellate zoospores are produced which escape through an apical pore. The zoospores swim for some time and flagella are withdrawn. The structure becomes elongated and a wall is secreted around it. It becomes multinucleate and a cross wall develops in it. The lower cell of the germling acts as rhizoidal cell and the upper develops in a new plant.

Alternation of generations. A definite alternation of generations occurs in some species of *Cladophora*. This means that the plants with a 2x number of chromosomes alternate with plants having an x number of chromosomes. The meiosis occurs in the 2x plant, producing

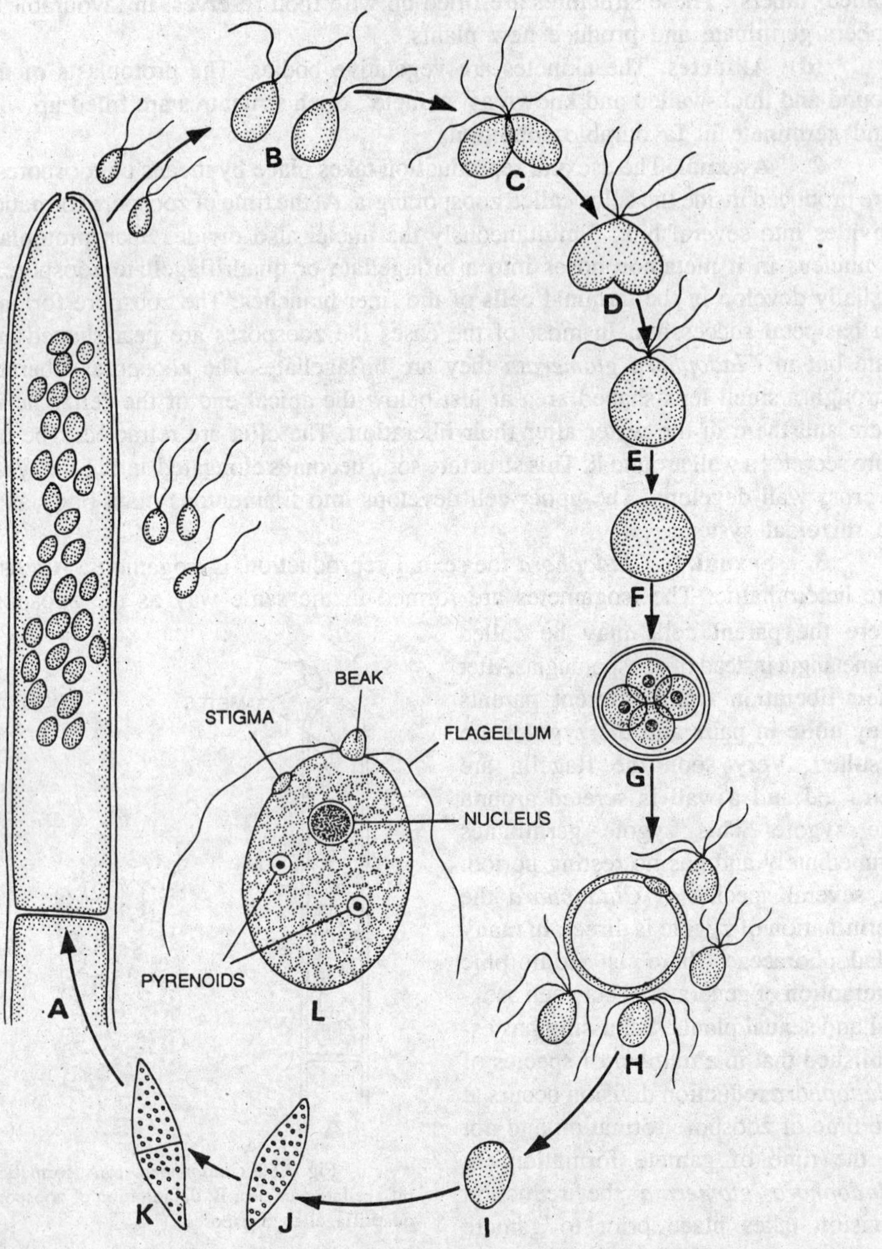

Fig. 3.59. *Cladophora* sp. Sexual reproduction. A, development of isogametes; B, two isogametes; C-D, isogamy; E, motile zygote; F, zygote; G-H, germination of zygote and production of zoospores; I-K, germination of zoospore; L, details of gamete.

meiospores (zoospores), and that the x plant produces gametes. It is thus seen that alternation of generations means that a spore producing generation (*i.e.*, sporophyte) alternates with a gamete producing generation (*i.e.*, gametophyte).

The 2x plant is known as the **diploid plant,** or the diploid generation or the diploid phase; the x plant as the **haploid plant** or generation or phase.

In *Cladophora,* two generations, *i.e.*, x and 2x are indistinguishable morphologically. In other words the x and 2x plants are morphologically indentical. Both contain similar types of chloroplast and dense cytoplasm.

Zoospores (meiospores) are produced in vigorously growing cells near the tips of branches of the diploid plant. Meiosis occurs prior to their formation. The zoospores contain half as many chromosomes in each nucleus as did the cells of the filament which bore them. Here the original filament is diploid while the zoospores are haploid. The zoospores on germination give rise to filaments similar in apperance to the diploid filaments except that the nuclei within their cells contain the haploid number of chromosomes. This haploid filament produces isogametes. The haploid isogametes unite to form a zygote. A new diploid filament develops from the zygote.

This way, two types of life cycle occur in different species of *Cladophora.*

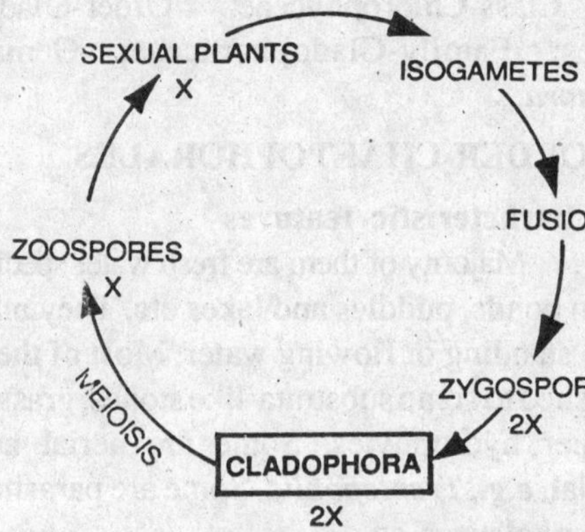

Fig. 3.60. *Cladophora*–Life cycle.

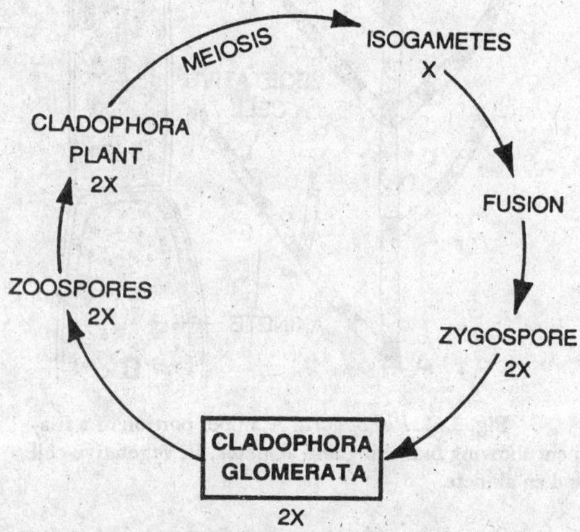

Fig. 3.61. *Cladophora glomerata*–Life cycle.

Systematic position. Division-Chlorophycophyta; Class-Chlorophyceae; Order-Cladophorales; Family-Cladophoraceae; Genus-*Cladophora.*

Genus PITHOPHORA

Family-Cladophoraceae

Occurrence. The species of *Pithophora* are exclusively confined to fresh water. The real home of *Pithophora* is indeed in somewhat stagnant tropical waters.

Structure. *Pithophora* in general appearance looks like *Cladophora* but is easily recognized by the large terminal and intercalary akinetes densely packed with reserve foods. The filaments are freely branched. The branches normally origniate a short distance below the distal end of the cell from which they arise. Commonly the branches are solitary but sometimes they are found in opposite pairs. Some of the species possess rhizoid-like outgrowths at the distal end of certain branches or at the base of a filament.

The cells are cylindrical, and those found at the ends of branches are longer than the other cells of the thallus. The cell walls are quite thick but without the lamellation as found in *Cladophora.* The protoplast is multinucleate. The chloroplast is a reticulate parietal sheet possessing the pyrenoids at the intersections of the reticulum.

Reproduction. The sexual reproduction is altogether absent. The only method of reproduction, apart from accidental fragmentation of filaments is by menas of akinetes.

Asexual reproduction. In *Pithophora* special akinetes are produced by the contraction of a cell towards the upper end which becomes cut off by a transverse septum into a short akinete and a considerably longer vegetative cell. As reported by Ramanathan (1939), the liberation of akinetes takes place by a circumcissal break of the upper part of the wall of the cell beneath it. At the time of germination of akinete, two daughter cells are formed by means of a transverse division. One of the daughter cells develops into a rhizoid and the other into a branched filament.

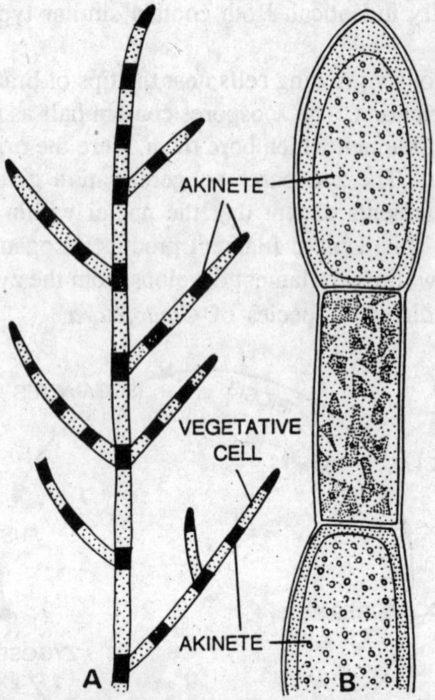

Fig. 3.62. *Pithophora*. A, upper portion of a filament showing branching and akinetes; B, vegetative cell and an akinete.

Systematic position. Division-Chlorophycophyta; Class-Chlorophyceae; Order-Cladophorales; Family-Cladophoraceae; Genus-*Pithophora.*

ORDER-CHAETOPHORALES

Characteristic features

1. Majority of them are fresh water species found in ponds, puddles and lakes etc. They may grow in standing or flowing water. Most of them are attached to some substrata-like stones, grasses and other hydrophytes. Some are aerial and terrestrial, *e.g., Trentepohlia*. Some are parasitic, *e.g., Cephaleuros* sp.

2. The plant is fundamentally a heterotrichous filament and consists of prostrate and erect systems. In some cases the prostrate system is well developed whereas in other cases the

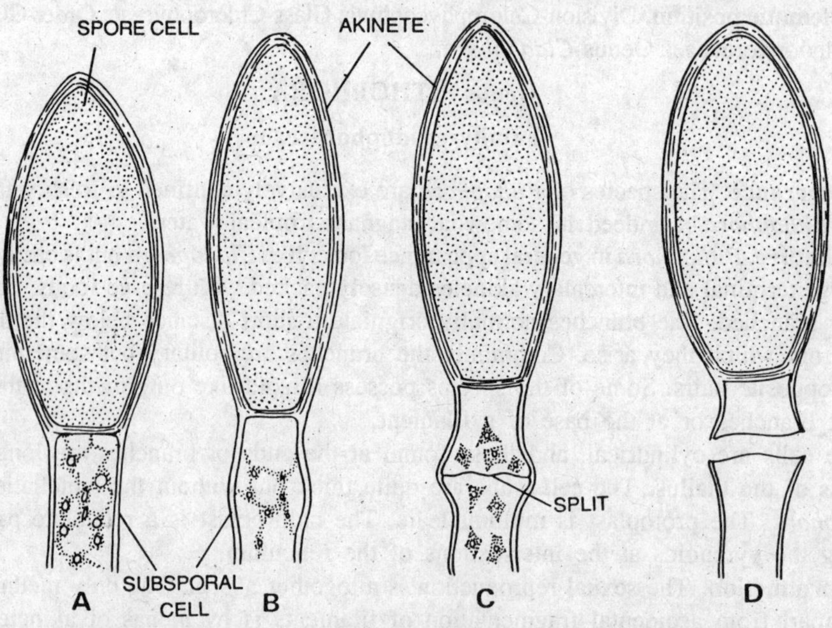

Fig. 3.62 (a). *Pithophora* spp. A-D, splitting and separation of akinete from thallus.

erect system is well developed.

3. The filaments are dichotomously branched and the terminal ends of the branches end in **'chaetae.'**

4. Usually the plant bodies are enveloped in thick mucilaginous envelope.

5. The cell wall consists of two layers, the outer layer is of pectose and the inner of cellulose.

6. Usually several pyrenoids are found in each chloroplast. The cells are uninucleate.

7. Reproduction takes place by vegetative, asexual and sexual methods. Vegetative reproduction takes place by means of cell division, fragmentation and akinetes. Asexual reproduction takes place by micro - and macrozoospores, aplanospores and palmelloid stages. Sexual reproduction ranges from isogamy to oogamy *(Coleochaete.)*

There are 90 genera and about 344 species in this order.

Classification. The order is sub-divided into five families.

1. Chaetophoraceae, 2. Trentepohliaceae, 3. Coleochaetaceae, 4. Chaetosphaeridiaceae and 5. Pleurococcaceae

Family-Chaetophoraceae (50 genera; 225 species)

Characteristic features. 1. They possess branched filamentous thalli. The branches may be free from one another or form pseudoparenchymatous tissue by lateral adjoining.

2. The cells are uninucleate and possess a single laminate chloroplast.

3. The terminal portion of a branch consists of long colourless cells narrower than other cells (hairs).

4. Sexual reproduction is usually isogamous. Sometimes it is anisogamous or oogamous.

Genus CHAETOPHORA

Family–Chaetophoraceae

Occurrence. *Chaetophora* is often found in abundance in standing water, it is also epiphytic upon submerged vegetation or attached to some substrata.

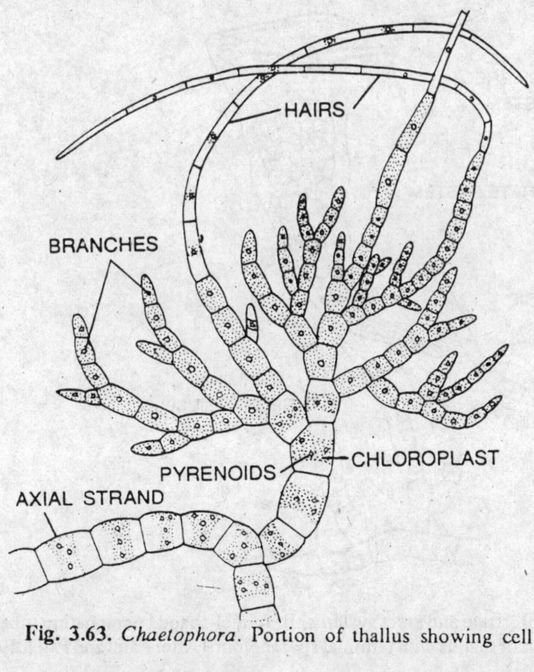

Fig. 3.63. *Chaetophora*. Portion of thallus showing cell

Structure. The thalli are macroscopic. Normally they are of tough consistency and hemispherical; spherical, or elongate and irregularly tuberculate. Spherical colonies possess the branches which radiate from a palmelloid base. The branches are repeatedly branched throughout or at their apices. The branches remain covered with a tough gelatinous covering, and the coverings of adjacent branches may be separate or fused with one another. Very often the basal portion of a colony is found to be impregnated with calcium carbonate, and rarely the entire colony may be strongly calcified. The species which possess the elongate colonies bear the filaments intertwined to form an axial strand which bears many short lateral branches throughout its length. In both spherical and elongated colonies, the terminal branchlets are often extended into large multicellular hairs which taper into a fine point. The prostrate system is feebly developed and often consists only of loosely connected rounded cells.

Reproduction. The reproduction takes place by following methods.

Asexual reproduction. The asexual reproduction takes place by means of quadriflagellate zoospores. The formation of zoospores generally occurs in the main erect system. Usually each cell produces only one to four zoospores and they are mostly liberated through a lateral aperture in the wall. In germination the quadriflagellate zoospores probably normally first form the basal system from which the upright branches later arise. Sometimes the akinetes are produced by cells of the ultimate branchlets but sometimes they are found in any cell of a thallus.

Sexual reproduction. The sexual reproduction is isogamous and takes place by the union of biflagellate gametes. The fate of the zygotes is not known in most cases, but it would seem that commonly at least they germinate directly into new plants.

Systematic position. Division - Chlorophycophyta ; Class–Chlorophyceae ; Order-Chaetophorales ; Family-Chaetophoraceae ; Genus–*Chaetophora*

Genus–FRITSCHIELLA
Family–Chaetophoraceae

The only reported species from India is *F. tuberosa*. For the first time M. O. P. Iyenger

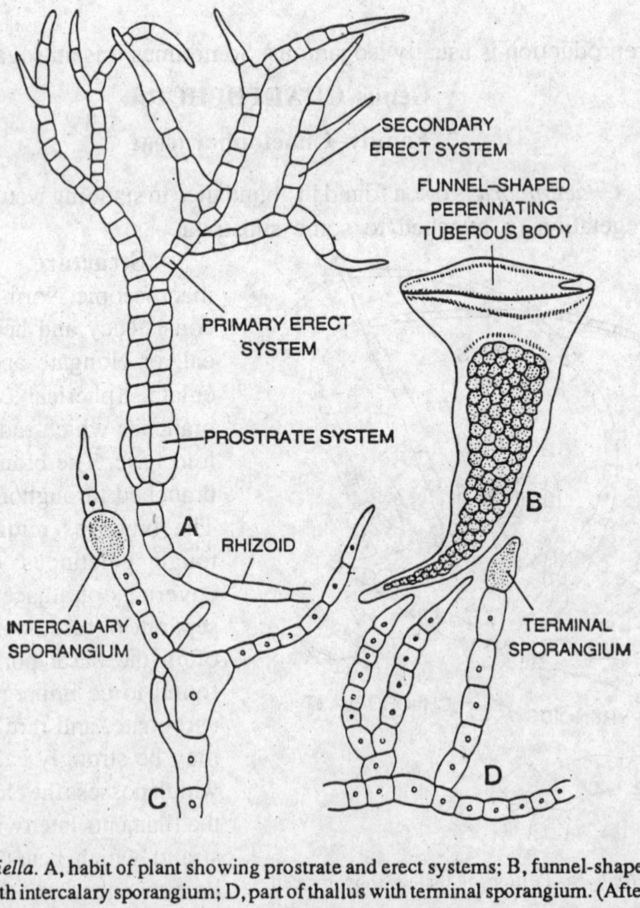

Fig. 3.64. *Fritschiella.* A, habit of plant showing prostrate and erect systems; B, funnel-shaped perennating tuberous body; C, a part of thallus with intercalary sporangium; D, part of thallus with terminal sporangium. (After Patel and Patel, 1969).

collected the plant material in 1932 and named it after the name of his teacher Dr. F. E. Fritsch. The species is commonly found in the moist alkaline soils.

This is a green alga which possesses a heterotrichous system.

The thallus remains differentiated into (a) rhizoidal system, (b) prostrate system, (c) primary projecting system and (d) secondary projecting system.

The rhizoidal system consists of branched, septate and colourless rhizoids that penetrate the soil.

The prostrate system consists of a rounded cluster of cells. This is branched, filamentous, tuberous or parenchymatous and green in colour. Certain nodal initials develop in this system which give rise to rhizoids towards lower side and primary projecting system towards upper side.

The primary projecting system which develops from the prostrate system is erect, filamentous, branched, subaerial and green.

From the branched primary system the branches of projecting secondary system are given out.

The cells of all the systems except that of rhizoidal system are green in colour and possessing parietal chloroplast with many pyrenoids. The cells are uninucleate and filled up with starch.

Reproduction. The reproduction takes place by following methods.

Perennation and vegetative propagation. During adverse and unfavourable conditions the erect and rhizoidal systems commonly degenerate and the alga perennates by its prostrate system. The cells of prostrate system perennate through adverse conditions. However, the nodal regions of prostrate system are capable of independent existence and get detached from the parent thallus by death and decay of internodal regions and serve the function of perennation as well as vegetative propagation.

Sometimes the alga is perennated by means of specially modified tuber-like bodies which remain enclosed in cuticular cell walls. These tubers are formed in prostrate system and are either funnel-shaped or club-shaped. Each such tuber is about 1 mm. in length.

Asexual reproduction. The asexual reproduction takes place by means of quadriflagellate zoospores. The formation of zoospores generally occurs in the main erect system. Usually each cell produces only one to four zoospores and they are mostly liberated through a lateral aperture in the wall. In germination the quadriflagellate zoospores probably normally first form the basal system from which the upright branches later arise. Sometimes the akinetes are produced by cells of the ultimate branchlets but sometimes they are found in any cell of a thallus.

Sexual reproduction. The sexual reproduction is isogamous and takes place by the union of biflagellate gametes. The fate of the zygotes is not known in most cases, but it would seem that commonly at least they germinate directly into new plants.

Systematic position-Division - Chlorophycophyta; Class - Chlorophyceae; Order-Chaetophorales; Family-Chaetophoraceae; Genus-*Fritschiella*.

Genus DRAPARNALDIOPSIS

Family-Chaetophoraceae

Occurrence. This is a fresh water alga found in pools and ponds. It is very commonly found in the ponds of still, clear and shallow waters. Usually it grows upon the leaves of grasses, sedges and many other aquatic angiosperms. The branched, mucilaginous filaments of this alga project outward in water from the plant on which they are found. This genus comprises of two species. *D. alpina* and *D. indica bharadwaja*

Structure. It is a branched, filamentous, green alga. In the beginning the plant body appears to be a small gelatinous ball which later on enlarges in size. The main axis of the filament consists of two types of cells. The smaller cells are nodal cells and the larger barrel-shaped cells are internodal cells. The nodal and internodal cells alternate regularly. From each small nodal cell four laterals are given out. The main axis bears the branches of unlimited growth at the small node. The main axis as well as the branches of unlimited growth bear the branches of limited growth at their nodes. The branches of limited growth are arranged at the nodes at right angles to the main axis. The short branches (of limited growth) do not bear any main axis. The distal ends of these branches terminate in long hyaline hairs. Each chaete consists of one or more elongated cells. Usually the cells of chaete do not bear any chloroplasts.

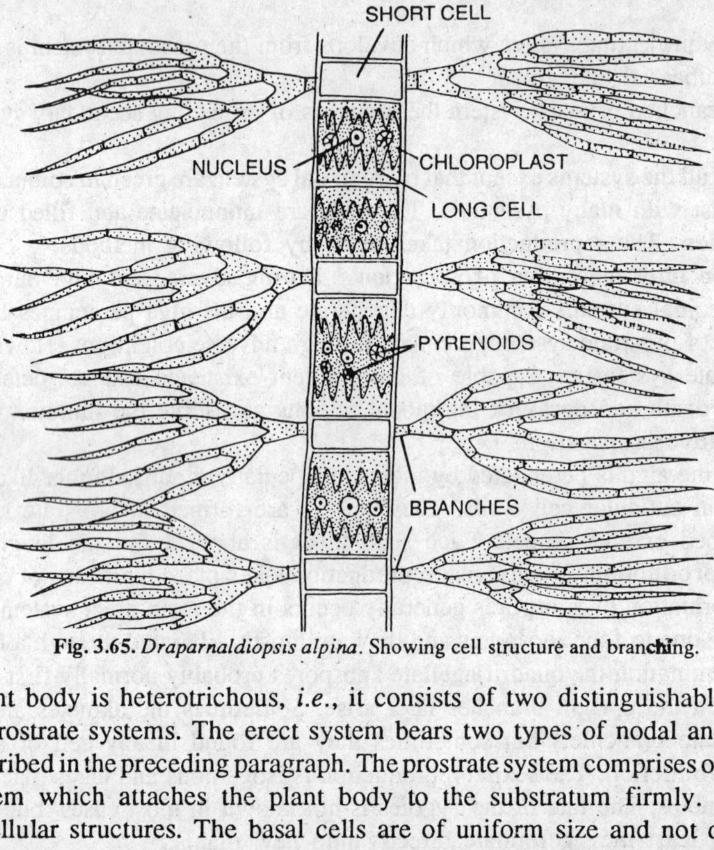

Fig. 3.65. *Draparnaldiopsis alpina*. Showing cell structure and branching.

The plant body is heterotrichous, *i.e.*, it consists of two distinguishable systems known as erect and prostrate systems. The erect system bears two types of nodal and internodal cells as already described in the preceding paragraph. The prostrate system comprises of a well developed rhizoidal system which attaches the plant body to the substratum firmly. The rhizoids are uniseriately cellular structures. The basal cells are of uniform size and not distinguished into nodal and internodal cells. In many cases the branching of rhizoids is so profuse that a cortical envelope develops around the base of the axis. The complete plant body remains embedded within a gelatinous envelope.

The cell wall consists of three layers. The outermost layer consists of mucilage, the middle of pectose and the inner of cellulose. The cells of long axis are barrel-shaped. Each cell contains a girdle-like parietal chloroplast in the shape of a reticulate cylinder. The edges of the chloroplast may be entire or deeply incized. Several pyrenoids are found in each chloroplast. The cells of the branches of limited growth possess similar chloroplasts but with one or two pyrenoids. The cells are uninucleate. The nucleus lies in the peripheral region of the cell and remains suspended with the help of cytoplasmic strands.

Reproduction. In *Draparnaldiopsis,* the reproduction takes place by means of asexual

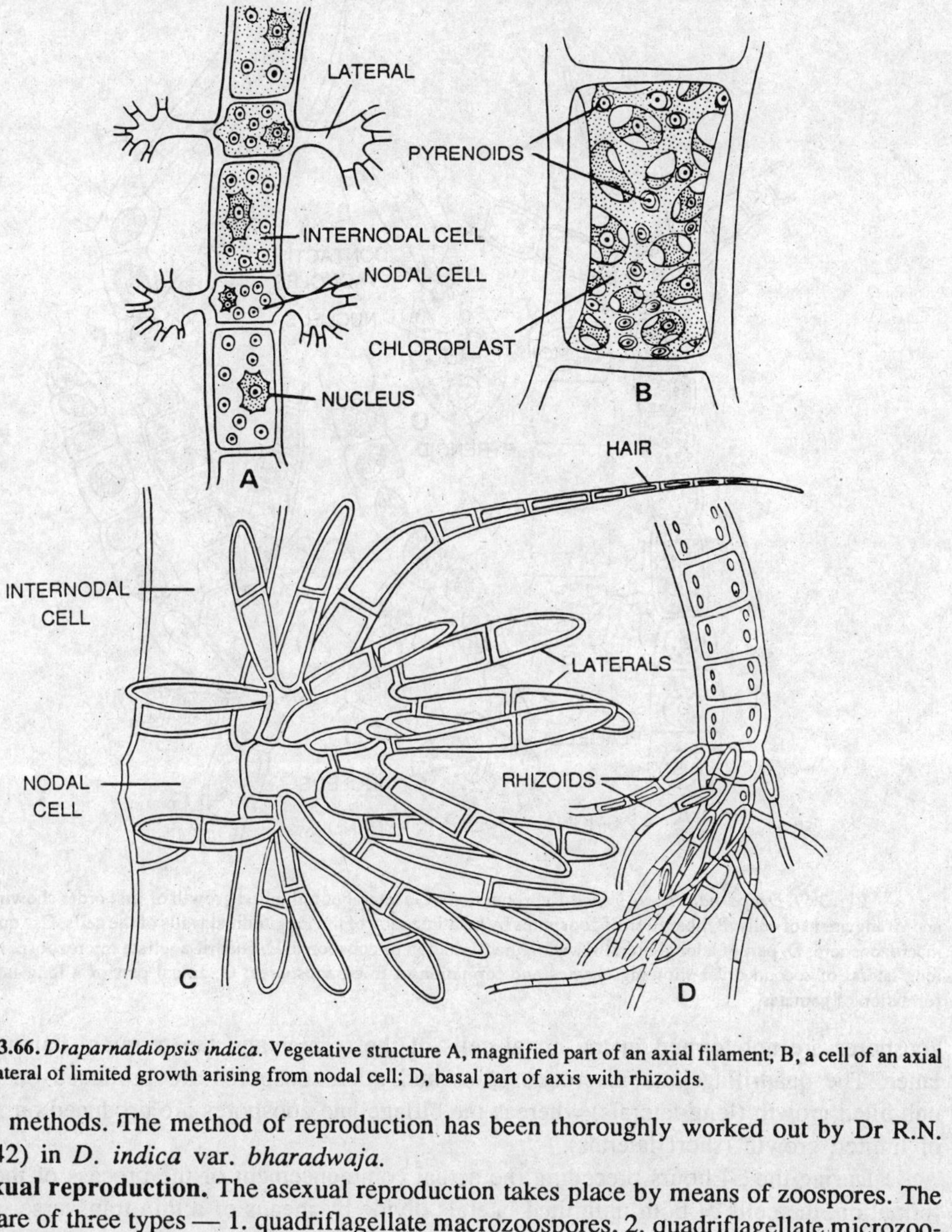

Fig. 3.66. *Draparnaldiopsis indica.* Vegetative structure A, magnified part of an axial filament; B, a cell of an axial filament; C, lateral of limited growth arising from nodal cell; D, basal part of axis with rhizoids.

and sexual methods. The method of reproduction has been thoroughly worked out by Dr R.N. Singh (1942) in *D. indica* var. *bharadwaja*.

Asexual reproduction. The asexual reproduction takes place by means of zoospores. The zoospores are of three types — 1. quadriflagellate macrozoospores, 2. quadriflagellate microzoospores and 3. biflagellate microzoospores. All types of zoopores are formed during rainy season early in the morning. The formation of zoospores starts at about 6 a.m. and continues upto 9.30 a.m.

The pH value of water plays an important role in the formation of zoospores. The alkaline medium is always preferred. The pH value of pond water in nature remains between 7.2 and 7.5 from 6 to 8.30 a.m., which is most suitable for the formation of macrozoospores. After 8.30 a.m., the pH reaches from 7.5 to 8.5 which is suited to the formation of microzoospores.

Production of zoospores and their liberation. The zoospore formation takes place only in the cells of the laterals, *i.e.*, the branches of unlimited and limited growth. However, the

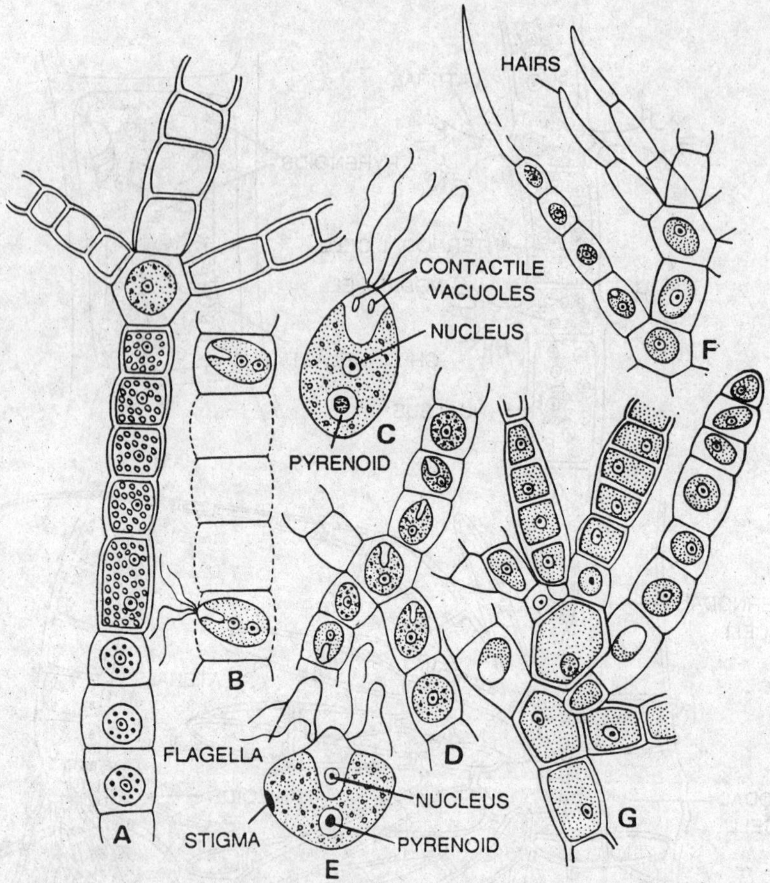

Fig. 3.67. *Draparnaldiopsis indica*-Reproduction. A, a lateral of unlimited growth of first order showing protoplasts and arrangement of cells; B, liberation of zoospores by gelatinization of the longitudinal walls of the cells; C, a quadriflagellate macrozoospore; D, part of a long lateral showing the formation of zoospores; E, quadriflagellate microzoospore; F, part of a long lateral of second order showing chaetes and formation of microzoospores; G, apical part of a long lateral showing formation of gametes.

zoospores are not formed in the nodal cells of the former and the terminal hair cells of the latter. The quadriflagellate macrozoospores and microzoospores are produced on laterals of unlimited growth (long laterals) whereas the biflagellate zoospores are produced on the laterals of limited growth (short laterals).

During the 24 hours preceding the actual commencement of the process of the zoospore formation, the cells of both unlimited laterals divide by means of a thin transverse wall. Three transverse walls do not constrict the filament to the same extent as the original cross walls. A second transverse division and sometimes a third one also occurs. The protoplast begins to round off and recedes from the cell wall so that the filament contains many rounded protoplasts equal in number to the newly formed cells. These protoplasts convert into swarmers by the development of the apical and subterminal flagella. This way the quadriflagellate macrozoospores or microzoospores and biflagellate microzoospores are formed as the case may be.

The liberation of the swarmers takes place by the complete gelatinization of the longitudinal walls of the newly formed cells. The zoospores swim in the water with the help of their flagella after their liberation from the parent filament.

Quadriflagellate macrozoospores. The quardriflagellate macrozoospores are ellipsoid or ovoid in shape. Each such macrozoospore bears four equal, sub-terminal flagella at its anterior end. It possesses a single nucleus and a cup-shaped chloroplast. There is a single pyrenoid on the posterior side of the chloroplast. Two contractile vacuoles are found below the point of attachment of the flagella. There is a medium eye-spot or stigma.

Quadriflagellate microzoospores. They are flattened and bulged in the middle. They appear to be spherical in shape. The chloroplast is cup-shaped and slightly notched. It is also uninucleate and the nucleus lies above the pyrenoid. Each microzoospore bears an apical papilla at its anterior end. The four flagella are inserted around the papilla. They are approximately half the size of the quadriflagellate macrozoospores. The stigma or eyespot lies near the anterior end.

Biflagellate microzoospores. The biflagellate microzoospores vary much in shape and size. They resemble too much to the gametes. They are spherical or ovoid in shape. The two equal flagella remain inserted at the anterior end. It is uninucleate and the pyrenoid lies just above the nucleus. The chloroplast is cup-shaped and notched. The eye-spot or stigma is median. However, the gametes are smaller in size than the biflagellate microzoospores.

Germination of zoospore. The quadriflagellate macrozoospores after swimming for eight hours and the quadriflagellate microzoospores after swimming for 24 hours retract their flagella and come to rest by their anterior ends. The zoospores become rounded and enveloped by a wall. Very soon protuberance is given out and a transverse wall is laid down near its base giving rise to a rhizoidal cell. This rhizoidal cell gives rise to the rhizoidal system consisting of branched rhizoids. The upper cell repeatedly divides transversely to form a three or four celled new filament. Each cell possesses a girdle-like chloroplast with two or three pyrenoids. Dr. R. N. Singh reported that the filaments formed by the quadriflagellate macro-and microzoospores are comparatively bigger and broader than those of produced by the biflagellate microzoospores.

Sexual reproduction. The sexual reproduction takes place by means of gametes. The gametes are formed by the short laterals (branches of limited growth) of the last two orders. This way, there is marked division of labour in the production of different types of swarmers. The gametes, however, are produced on the other plant, which is quite similar to that plant on which asexual swarmers were produced.

The protoplasts of the cells of short laterals divide and develop into gametes. In each cell one to many gametes are developed. The gametes are liberated from the cell by the gelatinization of its longitudinal walls. The gametes may be equal or unequal in size.

Each gamete is biflagellate, ovoid or spherical in shape. The flagella are attached to its anterior end. Each gamete possesses a crescent-shaped chloroplast on its posterior side. A single pyrenoid remains embedded in the chloroplast. A stigma or red eye-spot is found on its lateral side. The gametes swim in the water with the help of their flagella and later on fusion takes place.

Sexual union of the gametes. The two gametes from two different plants come together and fuse. They fuse anteriorly. The gametes taking part in fusion may be of same size or of unequal size. After fusion the flagella are retracted and the zygote is produced which is later on enveloped by a thin wall. The zygote is 2x. The zygote does not go under any period of rest and begins to germinate within a day of its formation.

Germination of the zygote. As the germination starts the zygote becomes ovoid and a hyaline protuberance is given out from its one end. Soon it divides transversely producing two cells. The basal cell is colourless and gives rise to branched rhizoids, the upper cell possesses a chloroplast with one or two pyrenoids, divides repeatedly and new filament is produced. The reduction division takes place to bring the haploid condition again.

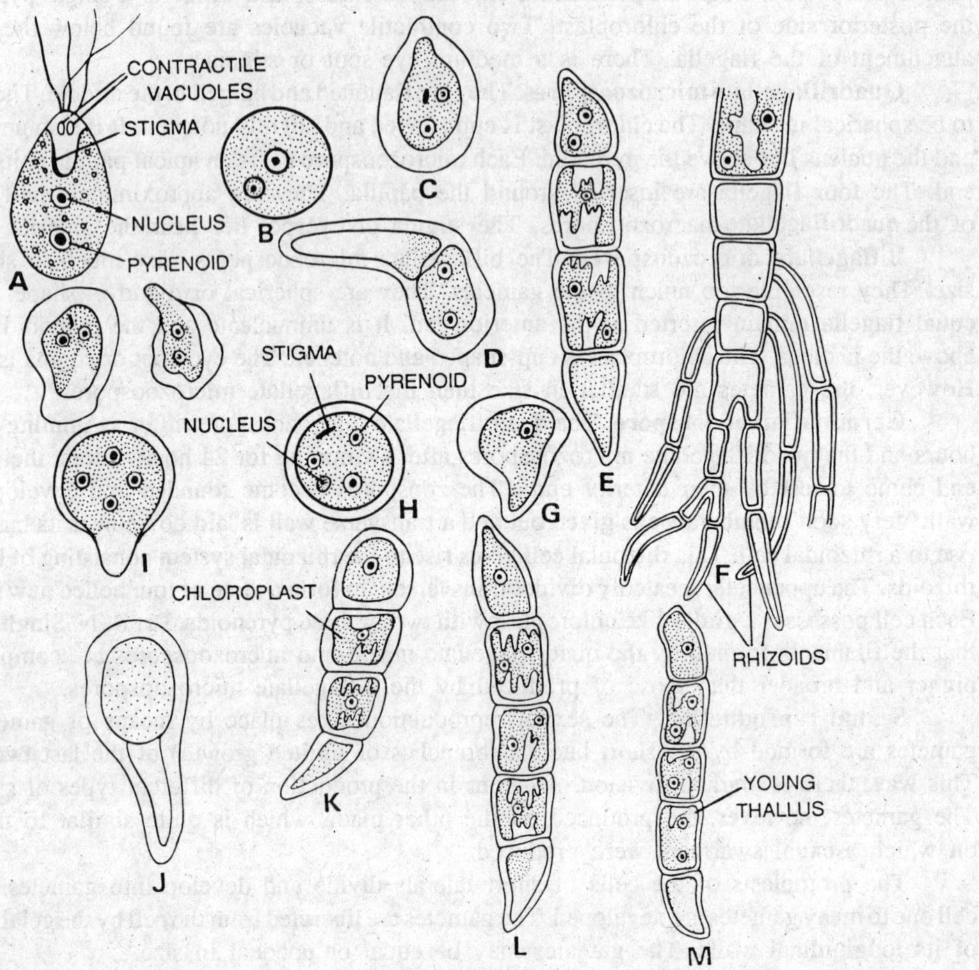

Fig. 3.68. *Draparnaldiopsis indica*. Reproduction. A, quadriflagellate macrozoospore; B, resting macrozoospore, flagella lost; C and D, germination of macrozoospore, E, germling with basal hyaline rhizoidal cell; F, basal part of germling with rhizoids; H, zygote; G-I, J and K, show the germination of zygote; L, germling production on the germination of quadriflagellate microzoospore; M, later stage of the germination of biflagellate microzoospore; figures unmarked on left side show beginning of the germination of quadriflagellate microzoospore and on right the beginning of the germination of biflagellate microzoospore.

Discussion. There are two types of plants in *Draparnaldiopsis indica bharadwaja* one producing the macro- and microzoospores and the other producing gametes. The plants are isomorphic except for the number of chromosomes. The gametophyte possesses x number of chromosomes and the sporophyte 2x. The gametes produced on two different plants take part in fusion and the 2x zygotes are formed. The zygote germinates directly, without going under a period of rest, and 2x sporophyte is produced, which later on gives rise to zoospores. Prior to the formation of zoospores reduction division takes place and the zoospores become x. These zoospores produce gametophytes on germination which when fully grown produce gametes. This

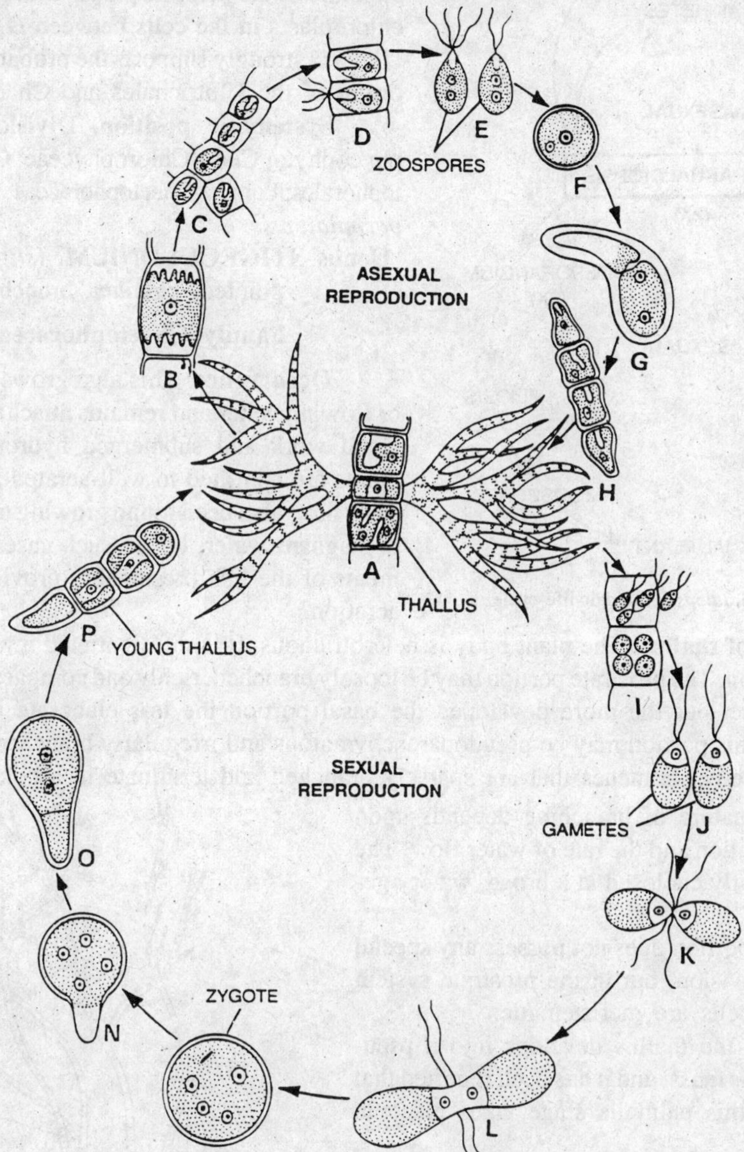

Fig. 3.69. *Draparnaldiopis indica*. Life-cycle—A, part of the filament; B, a single cell; C, formation of zoospore; D, liberation of zoospore by gelatinization; E, quadriflagellate and biflagellate zoospore; F-H, germination of zoospore; I, formation and liberation of gametes; J, biflagellate gametes; K and L, fusion, of gametes; M-P, zygote and its germination.

way, there is an alternation of generations between plants of similar appearance. This is known as 'isomorphic alternation of generations'.

In the production of three types of swarmers, *i.e.*, quadriflagellate macro- and microzoospores and biflagellate microzoospores and gametes, the alga resembles *Ulothrix zonata*. It resembles the other members of Chaetophoraceae, as it produces the large quadriflagellate asexual zoospores. The very close agreement in methods of reproduction and in the simple filamentous structure of the juvenile plants with band-shaped chloroplasts in the cells between *D. indica* and *Ulothrix* strongly supports the probable common origin of the Ulotrichales and Chaetophorales.

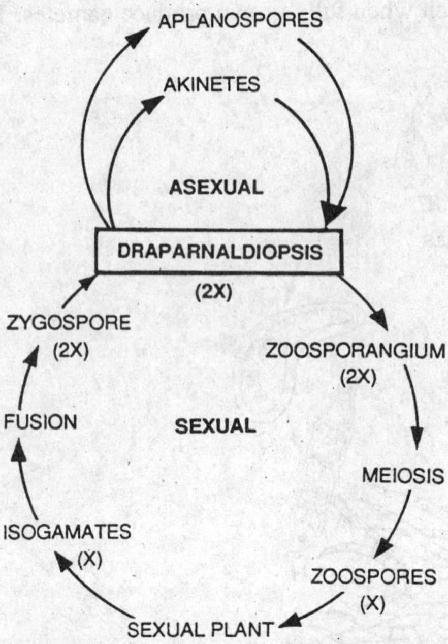

Fig. 3.70. *Draparnaldiopsis*–Graphic life-cycle.

Systematic position. Division- Chlorophycophyta; Class-Chlorophyceae; Order-Chaetophorales; Family-Chaetophoraceae; Genus-*Draparnaldiopsis.*

Genus STIGEOCLONIUM. (*stigeo,* sharp-pointed; *clonium,* branch)

Family–Chaetophoraceae

Occurrence. This alga grows in standing or flowing water and remains attached to stones, wood work and submerged hydrophytes. The plants are confined to well-aerated fresh water. They have also been found growing on fish living in stagnant water, but in such cases the movements of the fish presumably provide adequate aeration.

Structure of thallus. The plant body is heterotrichous. It is differentiated into a prostrate and an erect portion. The prostrate portion may be loosely branched, richly and compactly branched or a compact disc, but the more developed the basal portion the less elaborate is the aerial and vice versa. This portion may be pseudoparenchymatous and irregularly branched. The aerial part bears many erect branches that are sparsely branched and terminate in a colourless hair. The degree and nature of branching depends upon illumination, nutrition and the rate of water flow. The plants are frequently enclosed in a broad, watery gelatinous sheath.

The aerial portion does not possess any special region for cell division, but in the prostrate system only the apical cells are meristematic.

Sometimes the thallus develops into a pseudoparenchymatous mass, and it has been reported that development of this palmella stage takes place in many ways.

The cells possess band-like chloroplasts which usually do not fill the entire cell in the older parts of the thallus. The cells of both the systems and palmella stages are uninucleate and with a single chloroplast. Each chloroplast possesses one or more pyrenoids. In younger cells the chloroplast girdles the whole length of the cell and usually contains one pyrenoid.

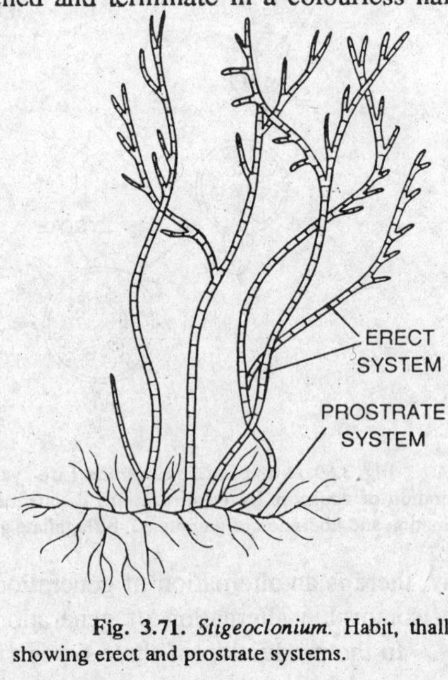

Fig. 3.71. *Stigeoclonium.* Habit, thallus showing erect and prostrate systems.

Reproduction. The reproduction takes place by vegetative, asexual and sexual methods.

Vegetative reproduction. The vegetative reproduction takes place by means of fragmentation. Each fragment develops into a new plant body.

Asexual reproduction. It takes place by zoospore formation. The zoospores are quadriflagellate and are generally formed singly within a cell. The zoospores are of two types (a) large quadriflagellate **macrcozoospores** and (b) smaller quadriflagellate **microzoospores**. In some species the quadriflagellate zoospores of two sizes are formed. For certain of these species the smaller of the two are zoosporic in nature (Juller, 1937), in other cases the smaller of the two are gametes (Godward, 1942).

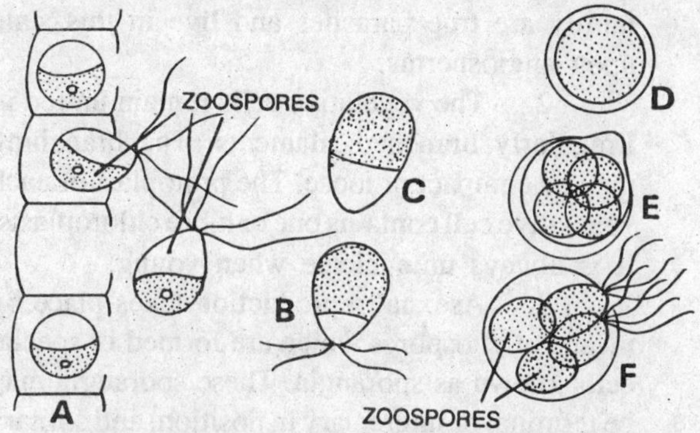

Fig. 3.72. *Stigeoclonium*. A, zoospore formation; B, zoospore; C, germination of zoospore; D-F, germination of zygote and formation of zoospores, meiosis takes place during this process.

After swarming for some time, a zoospore comes to rest at its anterior end, retracts its flagella and secretes a wall around it. Later on it germinates into a germling several ways, according to species. In some species, the one-celled germling grows directly into a vertical filament which later on develops into a prostrate system from its lowermost cells. In other cases the germling first develops into a prostrate system from which erect branches are given out (Fritsch, 1903; Godward, 1942). There are still other cases where the zoospores become amoeboid and remain amoeboid for some time before developing into a new filament (Pascher, 1915).

Aplanospores have also been formed single within a cell. They are usually produced in several successive cells.

Sexual reproduction. The sexual reproduction is isogamous. According to Juller (1937), in some species the biflagellate gametes fuse to form a quadriflagellate zygote whereas in other cases the quadriflagellate gametes fuse and form octoflagellate zygote (Godward, 1942). After a small swarming period, the motile zygote retracts its flagella, rounds up and secretes a wall around it.

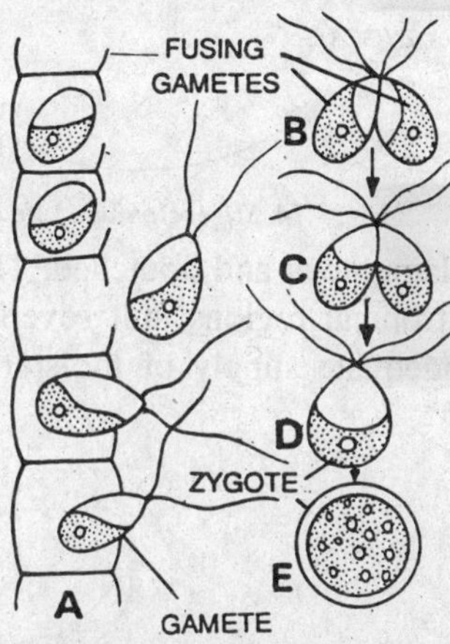

Fig. 3.73. *Stigeoclonium*. A, formation of biflagellate gametes; B-C; fusion of gametes (isogamy); D, quadriflagellate zygote; E, zygote after losing its flagella.

Germination of zygote. The zygote germinates within a day or two, or it enters upon a resting period prior to germination. If the zygote germinates within a day or two, the zygote nucleus undergoes a mitotic division and a short unbranched filament develops which consists of diploid cells.

Alternation of generations. There is heteromorphic alternation of generations. Here the diploid generation produces quadriflagellate zoospores and it is thought that meiosis takes place prior to zoospore formation. The zygotes which enter upon the resting period before their germination produce four quadriflagellate zoospores each of which develops into a gametothallus (Godward, 1942). It is thought that in this case the zygote nucleus undergoes a meiotic division.

Family–Trentepohliaceae (18 genera; 80 species)

Characteristic features. 1. Most of the species are fresh water algae. Some of them are aquatic and others are aerial. Among the aerial algae there are epiphytic species restricted to species of trees. Certain other members of this family are true parasites and live in this state upon angiosperms.

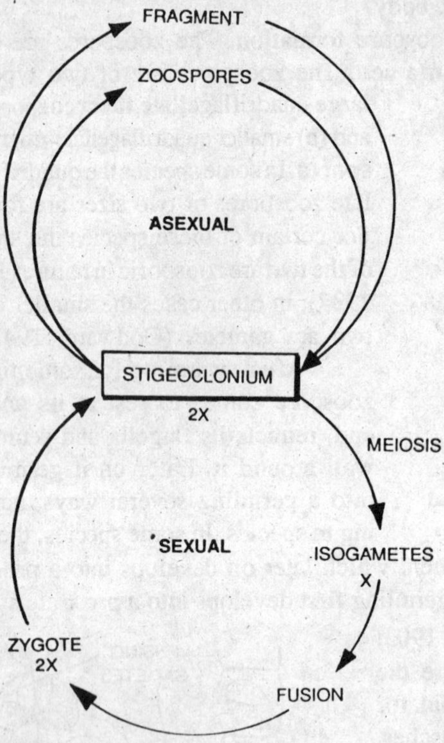

Fig. 3.74. *Stigeoclonium.* Life cycle.

2. The vegetative cells remain united in irregularly branched filaments. The branching may be compact or loose. The protoplast of each vegetative cell contains one or more chloroplasts. It is always uninucleate when young.

3. Asexual reproduction takes place by means of zoospores which are formed in special cells known as sporangia. These sporangia may be terminal or intercalary in position, and solitary or in series.

4. Sexual reproduction is isogamous. The gametes are formed within special cells known as gametangia which may be intercalary, terminal, solitary or in series.

Genus TRENTEPOHLIA (after J. F. Trentepohl)

Occurrence. This genus contains about 50 species. This is strictly an aerial alga. The thallus is filamentous and branched. The species grow as epiphytes or on stones in damp tropical and sub-tropical regions, but several species grow in temperate and sub-arctic regions if there is an adequate supply of moisture. The alga forms a felt-like layer on rocks, on bark of trees

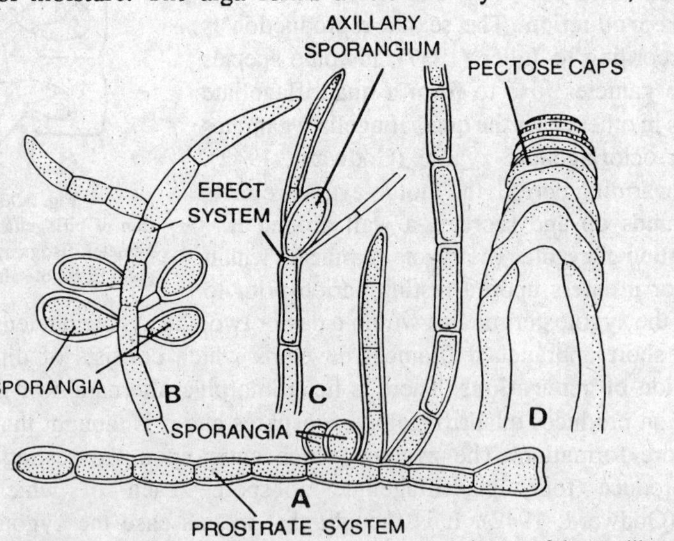

Fig. 3.75. *Trentepohlia.* A—C, prostrate and erect systems, with sporangia, one of them axillary; D, apex of thallus showing pectose caps.

and on the leaves. The filaments have a characteristic yellowish red to brownish red colour due to the presence of β-carotene which is said to be a food reserve accumulated during period of slow growth.

Structure of thallus. The major portion of the plant body is prostrate, and a few short erect branches are given out from it. Sometimes the erect portion is more extensively developed than the prostrate portion. The branching of the erect system may be alternate, opposite or unilateral. The cells which unite end to end are cylindrical to moniliform in shape. They rarely possess a length more than twice the breadth. The cells possess lamellated walls composed of cellulose.

The growth is apical, and the terminal cells often bear a pectose cap or series of such caps which are periodically shed and replaced by new ones. The origin of the cap is not clearly understood but it is thought to be due to a secretion. Its function is supposed to be protective or to reduce transpiration.

Each septum between the cells possesses a single large pit which is penetrated by a protoplasmic strand. The cells are uninucleate when young but become multinucleate when old. There are several parietal chloroplasts in each cell, which may be discoid, spiral or combinations of two, according to species. Usually the chloroplasts are completely overmasked by haematochrome, which colours the entire protoplast a deep orange red.

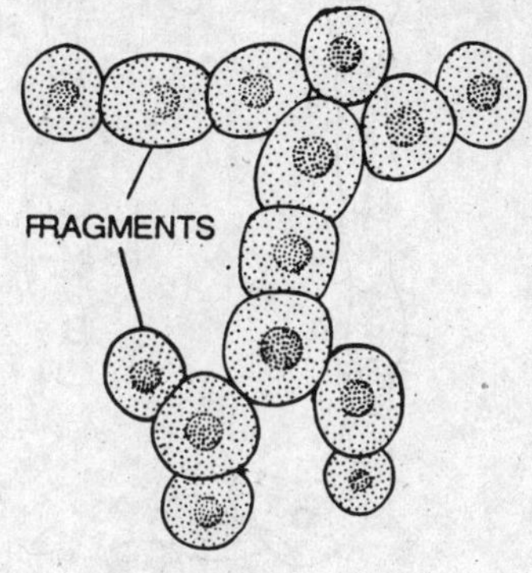

Fig. 3.76. *Trentepohlia*. Vegetative reproduction–fragmentation of prostrate system.

Reproduction. The reproduction takes place by vegetative, asexual and sexual methods. They are as follows.

Vegetative reproduction. The vegetative reproduction takes place by means of fragmentation. Each fragment develops into a new plant body.

Asexual reproduction. The zoospores are produced in two kinds of sporangia. 1. The sporangia which may be intercalary or terminal and remain attached to the thallus; and 2. the stalked sporangia which are always terminal and are shed when mature. In both kinds of sporangia it is more probable that only the latter type of sporangia are sporangial in nature. According to K. Meyer (1937) in majority of species the zoospores are formed within the sporangia are quadriflagellate. The sporangia are detached due to the formation of special wall layers between it and the cell below. After the detachment the sporangia are dispersed by wind. When they come in contact of moisture they immediately produce zoospores, the sessile sporangia invariably produce biflagellate swarmers and in certain cases they have been observed to behave as isogametes.

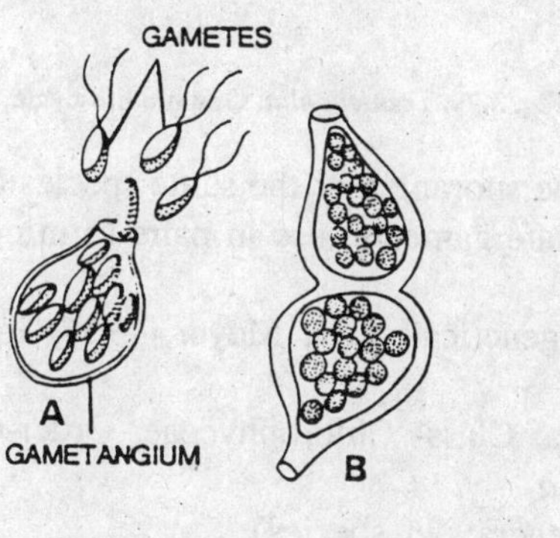

Fig. 3.77. *Trentepohlia*. Sexual reproduction- A, gametangium liberating gametes; B, gametangium with gametes; C, gametes; D, fusion of gametes (isogamy); E, zygote.

Sometimes under certain atmospheric conditions the contents of the sporangium get divided and form aplanospores before the sporangium is detached from the thallus.

Sometimes the akinetes are formed in the cells of the prostrate portion of a thallus and commonly in several successive cells. The akinetes possess thick wall; they germinate directly into new filaments.

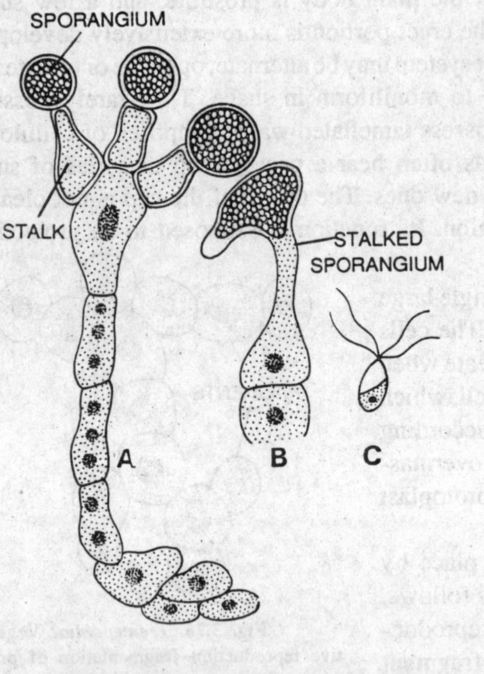

Fig. 3.78. *Trentepohlia*. Asexual reproduction—A, thallus with stalked sporangia; B, single stalked sporangium; C, zoospore.

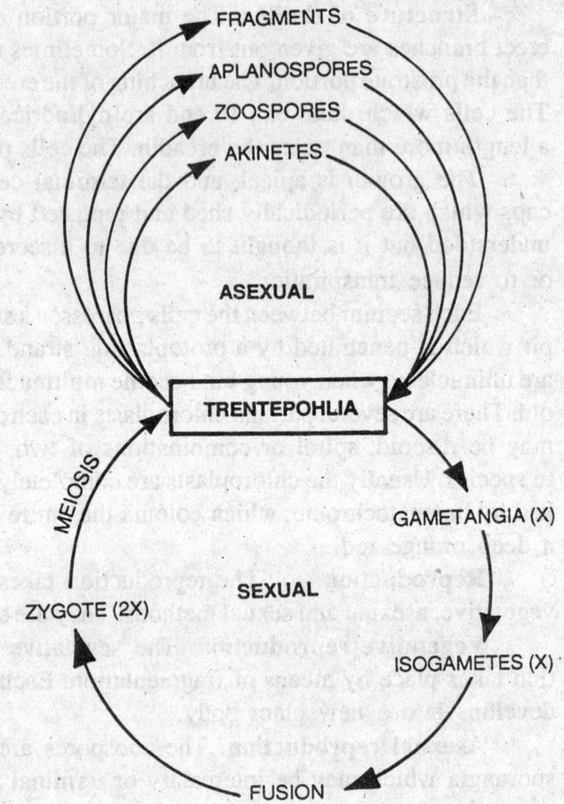

Fig. 3.79. *Trentepohlia*. Graphic life-cycle

Sexual reproduction. The biflagellate gametes are produced within gametangia. The gametangia may be intercalary or terminal but in neither case they shed from the thallus. Generally the gametangia may be distinguished from the sporangia of the same species because of their peculiar shape (K. Meyer, 1937). The biflagellate gametes fuse in pairs forming quadriflagellate zygotes.

In some species the gametes develop parthenogenetically (K. Meyer, 1936) into new filaments.

Systematic position. Division-Chlorophycophyta; Class- Chlorophyceae; Order-Chaetophorales; Family-Trentepohliaceae; Genus-*Trentepohlia*

Family-Coleochaetaceae (10 genera; 25 species)

Characteristic features. 1. The vegetative cells of these algae possess long cytoplasmic setae which remain partly or wholly covered by a gelatinous sheath. All or only few cells of the thallus bear such setae.

2. Some members are unicellular, and others may be multicellular with the cells uniting to form branched filaments.
3. The cells are uninucleate and possess a single parietal laminate chloroplast.
4. Asexual reproduction takes place by means of zoospores.
5. Sexual reproduction may be isogamous or oogamous.

Genus COLEOCHAETE (*coleo*, sheath; *chaete*, hair)

There are about 10 species in this genus.

Habitat and occurrence. This is a fresh water genus, usually occurs epiphytically upon several aquatic plants and larger forms of algae. Some species grow endophytically inside the cell walls of Charales. *Coleochaete nitellarum,* is endophytic in *Nitella.* Majority of the species are epiphytic.

Structure. The thallus of *Coleochaete* is typically heterotrichous, *i.e.,* consists of prostrate and erect systems. The filaments of projecting system in many species, *e.g., Coleochaete scutata,* are arranged so compactly that the whole system looks like a disc or cushion. The branching is dichotomous, which can be clearly seen in the species which possess free branches in projecting system, *e.g., C. pulvinata.* The thalli of *Coleochaete scutata* are usually surrounded by a common gelatinous envelope. Almost in all thalli of the genus some of the cells possess pointed **'chaetae'.** The base of chaete is usually surrounded by gelatinous material. This chaete is the prolongation of the cell wall.

The cell wall consists of two layers. The outer layer is formed of pectose and the inner one of cellulose.

In *Coleochaete* the cells are uninucleate. In each cell there is girdle-like chloroplast which wholly or partially encircles the protoplast. There is a single large pyrenoid in each chloroplast. The motile bodies are biflagellate and lack eye spots.

Reproduction. The reproduction takes place in *Coleochaete* by asexual and sexual methods.

1. Asexual reproduction. The asexual reproduction takes place by means of zoospores. The zoospores are produced in the ordinary cells. A single zoospore may be produced in each cell. The zoospores are large, ovoid and biflagellate. The zoospore liberates through a round

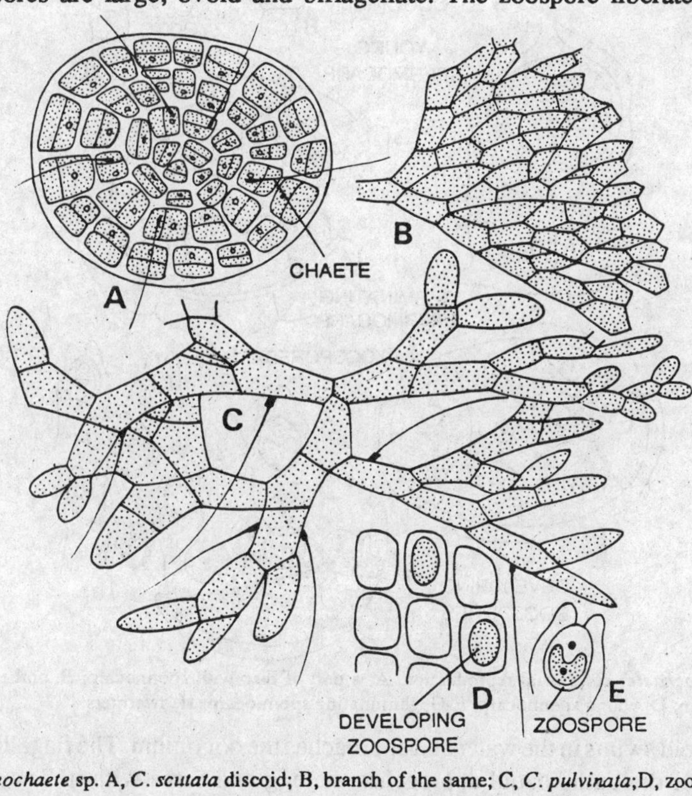

Fig. 3.80. *Coleochaete* sp. A, *C. scutata* discoid; B, branch of the same; C, *C. pulvinata*; D, zoospore formation.

pore formed at the apex of a short papilla of the parent cell. The zoospores swim for an hour approximately and then rest. The cilia are withdrawn and the protoplast of each zoospore becomes rounded and secretes a wall around it. The protoplast of this one-celled germling divides again and again and a multicellular thalloid structure is developed. Some of cells bear setae, and the shape of a cushion-like disc is attained.

According to Wesley (1928), in unfavourable conditions the aplanospores may also be developed. A single aplanospore develops in each cell, and germinates in the manner of zoospore on the approach of favourable conditions.

2. Sexual reproduction. The sexual reproduction in *Coleochaete* is oogamous. The oogamy is of highly specialized type among Chlorophyceae. The plants may be heterothallic (dioecious) or homothallic (monoecious) according to species. The oogonia develop on the terminal ends of the lateral branches of projecting system in *C. pulvinata*. The oogonium is flask-shaped. The basal swollen portion of oogonium contains an egg and chloroplast. The terminal portion is neck-like and called 'trichogyne' containing colourless cytoplasm.

The antheridia develop at the terminal ends of the lateral branches. A single biflagellate antherozoid develops in each antheridium.

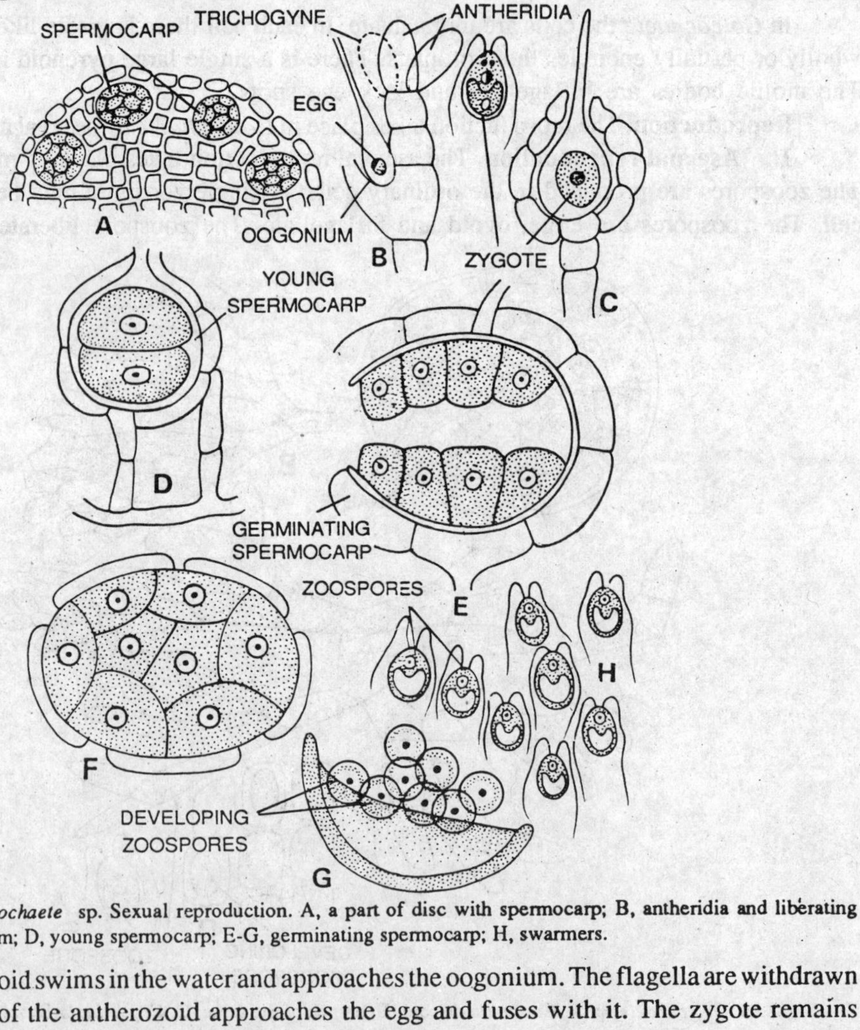

Fig. 3.81. *Coleochaete* sp. Sexual reproduction. A, a part of disc with spermocarp; B, antheridia and liberating antherozoid; C, oogonium; D, young spermocarp; E-G, germinating spermocarp; H, swarmers.

The antherozoid swims in the water and approaches the oogonium. The flagella are withdrawn and the protoplast of the antherozoid approaches the egg and fuses with it. The zygote remains within the oogonium. It increases somewhat in size and a thick wall is secreted around it. Some of the outgrowths develop from the base of the oogonium and a pseudoparenchymatous structure is formed. This round reddish brown body is called **'spermocarp'**. These spermocarps overwinter and only then germinate.

Germination of zygote. The nucleus of zygote divides meiotically and followed by other mitotic divisions. In this way 8-32 protoplasts are developed. Each protoplast metamorphoses into a biflagellate zoospore. After winter the zoospores are liberated from the spermocarp by breaking the spermocarpic wall in irregular way. The zoospores swim here and there, the flagella are withdrawn and each zoospore develops into a new thallus.

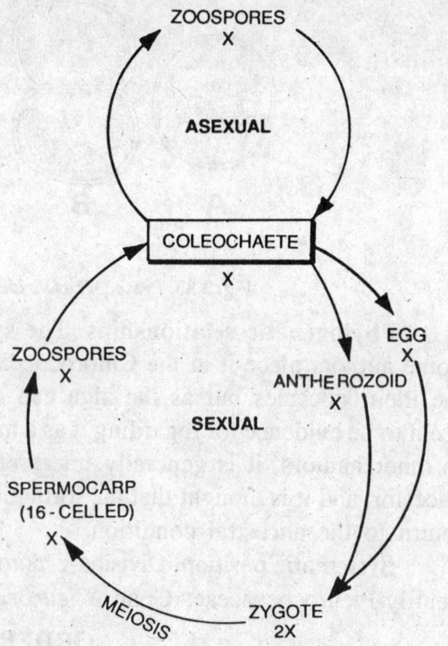

Fig. 3.82. *Coleochaete* sp. Graphic representation of life cycle.

Systematic position. Division-Chlorophycophyta; Class-Chlorophyceae; Order-Chaetophorales: Family-Chaetophoraceae; Genus-*Coleochaete*.

Family–Protococcaceae (Single genus)

Characteristic features. 1. This is a monotypic family with the single genus *Protococcus (Pleurococcus)*.

2. The family includes the forms which may be unicellular or multicellular with the cells united in small packets.

3. This is generally found as a green coating on trunks of trees, on bricks and stone walls and on wood.

4. The reproduction is exclusively by division of vegetative cells.

Genus PROTOCOCCUS (*Pleurococcus-Pleuro*, box; *coccus*, berry)

Occurrence. This is one of the commonest of the algae found in terrestrial situation occurring as thin incrustation on the windward side of tree trunks, stones, walls and railings.

Structure. The plant body is extremely simple. The mature cells are sometimes isolated and more or less spherical, but they are commonly found in groups of two, three or more, owing to their slow separation after division. When the alga grows submerged in water there is a tendency for the cells to remain attached to one another until there are 50 or more cells in a colony and there may be a development of short branched filament. However, such condition is not always produced.

Each cell is surrounded by a cell wall which is usually unthickened. The cells are uninucleate. Each cell contains a hollow parietal laminate chloroplast which is more or less lobed at the margins. Pyrenoids are not found in the chloroplasts.

Reproduction. The reproduction is effected exclusively by vegetative means. It takes place by simple division of cells which is followed by their separation.

This alga does not possess any special resting stage, and therefore, the ordinary cells can withstand long periods of desiccation without injury. The alga can obtain the required water directly from the atmospheric moisture.

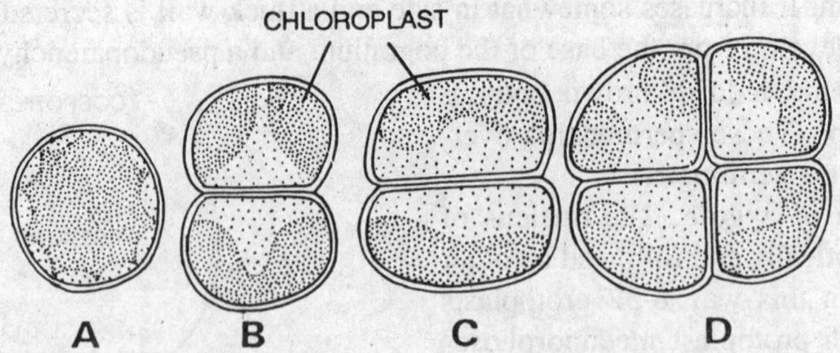

Fig. 3.83. *Protococcus viridis (Pleurococcus viridis)*. A-E, division of cell

Phylogénetic relationships. The systematic position of this alga is varied considerably. Some authors place it in the Chlorococcales while the others have placed it in a special group, the Pleurococcales but as the alga can occasionally develop branched filaments there would seem to be evidence for regarding it as a much reduced member of the Chaetophorales. According to other authors, it is generally interpreted as reduced form from a branching ulotrichaceous ancestor, and it is thought that the formation of pseudobranched filaments represents a temporary return to the ancestral condition.

Systematic position. Division-Chlorophycophyta; Class-Chlorophyceae; Order-Chaetophorales; Family-Pleurococcaceae; Genus-*Pleurococcus* or *Protococcus*.

ORDER–OEDOGONIALES

There are 3 genera and about 350 species in this order.

Characteristic features.

1. Almost all the genera are fresh water.
2. The thallus of *Oedogonium* consists of unbranched threads, whereas the thalli of *Bulbochaete* and *Oedocladium* are branched.
3. The cells are uninucleate, cylindrical and placed end to end.
4. The wall is three-layered, the outer layer consists of chitin, the middle of pectose and the innermost of cellulose.
5. There is special type of cell division and **'caps'** are formed.
6. The reproduction takes place by means of vegetative, asexual and sexual methods.
7. Stephanokontean type of motile bodies are found.
8. Vegetative reproduction takes place by fragmentation and akinete formation.
9. Asexual reproduction takes place by zoospores.
10. Sexual reproduction is oogamous.
11. Life-cycle is simple and haplontic.

Classification. A single family Oedogoniaceae is included in this order.

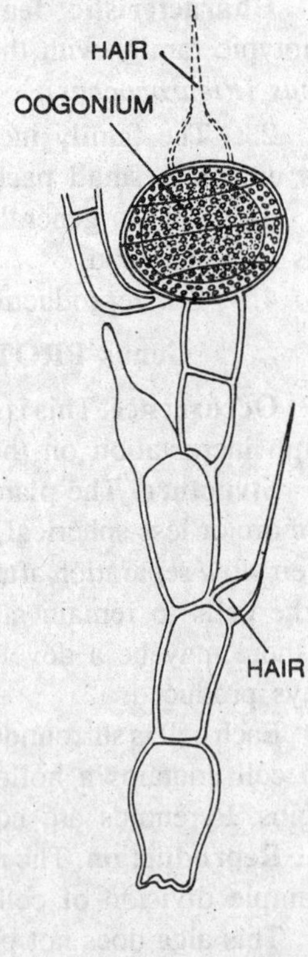

Fig. 3.84. *Bulbochaete*. Portion of a plant.

Family–Oedogoniaceae (3 genera; 350 species)

Characteristic features. 1. They possess simple or branched filaments.

2. The cylindrical uninucleate cells remain united end to end. Unique type of cell division. There is distinctive annular splitting of lateral cell wall.

3. Asexual reproduction takes place by zoospores formed singly within a cell. It also takes place by means of akinetes.

4. Sexual reproduction is always oogamous.

5. All species are fresh water in habit.

Genus OEDOGONIUM (*oedo,* swelling; *gonium*, vessel)

There are 285 species in this genus.

Habitat and occurrence. It is exclusively fresh water in habit. The young filaments are found to be attached to some substrate. On maturity the filaments become free-floating. Sometimes they are epiphytic upon other large sized fresh water algae.

Structure. The filaments of *Oedogonium* are long and unbranched. The basal cell of the young filament is devoid of chlorophyll and attached to some substratum is called the holdfast. The terminal cell of the filament is broadly rounded at its apex. The intercalary cells are cylindrical, uniform in thickness and arranged end to end. These cells possess one or more striations at their apical ends called **'apical caps'**.

The cells are cylindrical and covered with well defined three-layered cell walls. The outer layer consists of chitin, the middle of pectose and the innermost of cellulose.

Each cell contains a large nucleus in it. The nucleus is usually situated in the peripheral cytoplasm of the cell. Each nucleus has well defined chromatin and one or two nucleoli. The chloroplast is reticulate. At the anastamoses of the chloroplast pyrenoids are present. A starch sheath surrounds each pyrenoid.

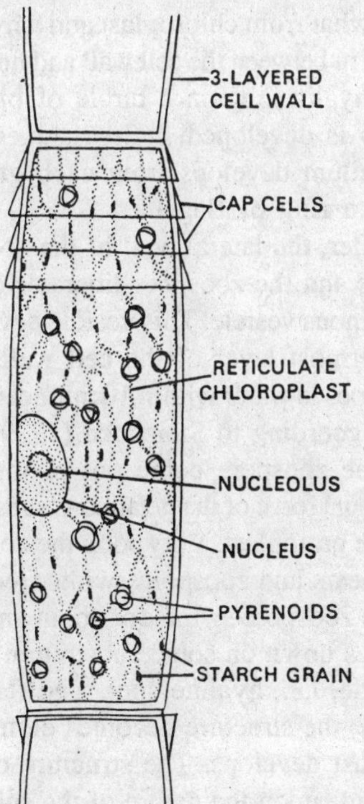

Fig. 3.85. *Oedogonium* sp. Detailed structure of a cell with conspicuous reticulate chloroplast.

Cell division. A special type of cell division is found. This is the peculiar feature of this genus. The following important points are to be considered in the cell division.

1. **Ring formation.** Just before the cell division a ring is developed immediately beneath the upper septum of the cell. According to Wisselingh, this ring consists of cellulose mixed with some starch substances.

2. **Nuclear division.** The nucleus of the parent cell divides into two and simultaneously a septum develops between them. This septum remains unconnected with longitudinal cell walls for some time.

3. **Formation of new cell.** At the level of the ring the cell membrane breaks transversely, the ring stretches gradually and a new cell develops between sheath and cap of parent cell wall. Side by side the septum shifts upwards and acquires a permanent position at the edge of the lower end of the ruptured cell wall

The wall of the upper daughter cell is mainly developed from the stretched ring. At the top of this there is cap developed by original membrane. The cap cells usually divide again and again. Usually the number of cap cells is coincided with the number of cell divisions. The species of *Oedogonium* may easily be recognised because of the presence of these 'cap cells'.

Reproduction. The reproduction takes place by vegetative asexual and sexual methods.

1. Vegetative reproduction. (a) By fragmentation. Reproduction in *Oedogonium* takes place by means of fragmentation. These fragments develop into new individuals. This type of reproduction is especially found in free floating species and rarely in permanent attached forms.

(b) By akinetes. In some of the species the vegetative akinetes are developed. The akinetes are produced in the chains of 10-40 in small and inflated cells. They resemble oogonia in structure. The akinetes are rounded, thick-walled, reddish orange and rich in food reserves. On the approach of favourable conditions they germinate directly into new filaments.

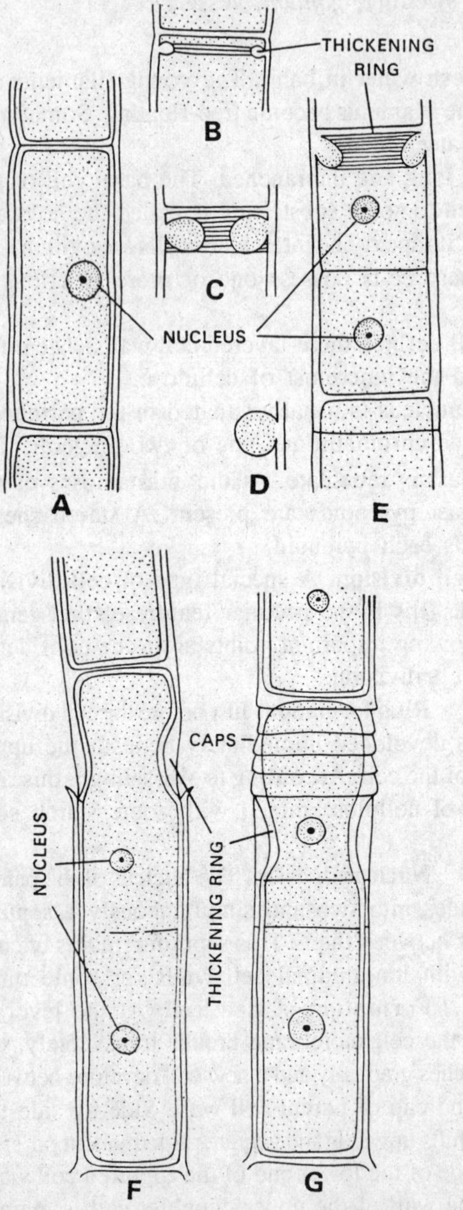

Fig. 3.86. *Oedogonium* sp. Cell division. A, normal cell to divide; B, young thickening ring; C, old thickening ring; D, side view of thickening ring; E, nuclear division and septum formation; F-G, stages of cell division.

2. Asexual reproduction. The species of *Oedogonium* reproduce asexually by stephanokontean type of zoospores. All cells excluding holdfast are capable of producing zoospores. A single zoospore is produced within a cell usually rich in food reserves. This cell is called **'zoosporangium.'**

At the time of zoospore formation the nucleus retracts somewhat from chloroplast and a hyaline region appears in between the cell wall and nucleus. Around this hyaline region a circle of blepharoplast grains is developed. It is assumed that a single flagellum develops from each granule thus forming a ring of flagella.

Soon after, the lateral wall of the zoosporangium splits and the zoospore liberates out in a thin membranous vesicle. This vesicle develops from the innermost layer of the cell wall. The zoospore escapes in water within 10 minuets from the vesicle. According to Steinecke (1929), the vesicle and the zoospore come out of the cell by an imbibitional force of the gelatinous substance secreted by the protoplast. Very soon the delicate vesicle disappears and zoospore swims freely in the water. The zoospore swims for about an hour and then settles down on some substratum from its anterior side, *i.e.*, hyaline spot. The flagella are withdrawn, the structure becomes elongated and the holdfast develops. The structure of the holdfast depends upon the nature of the substratum and species. If the surface of substratum is rough the rhizoidal system is much branched and if it is smooth then the rhizoidal system is unbranched,

3. Sexual reproduction. It is always oogamous. The species may be homothallic or heterothallic. Sexual reproduction may be of **macrandrous or nannandrous type.** It frequently occurs in still water and rarely in flowing waters.

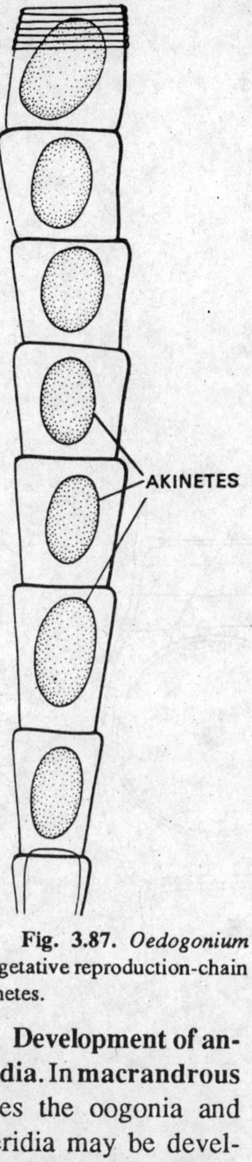

Fig. 3.87. *Oedogonium* sp. Vegetative reproduction-chain of akinetes.

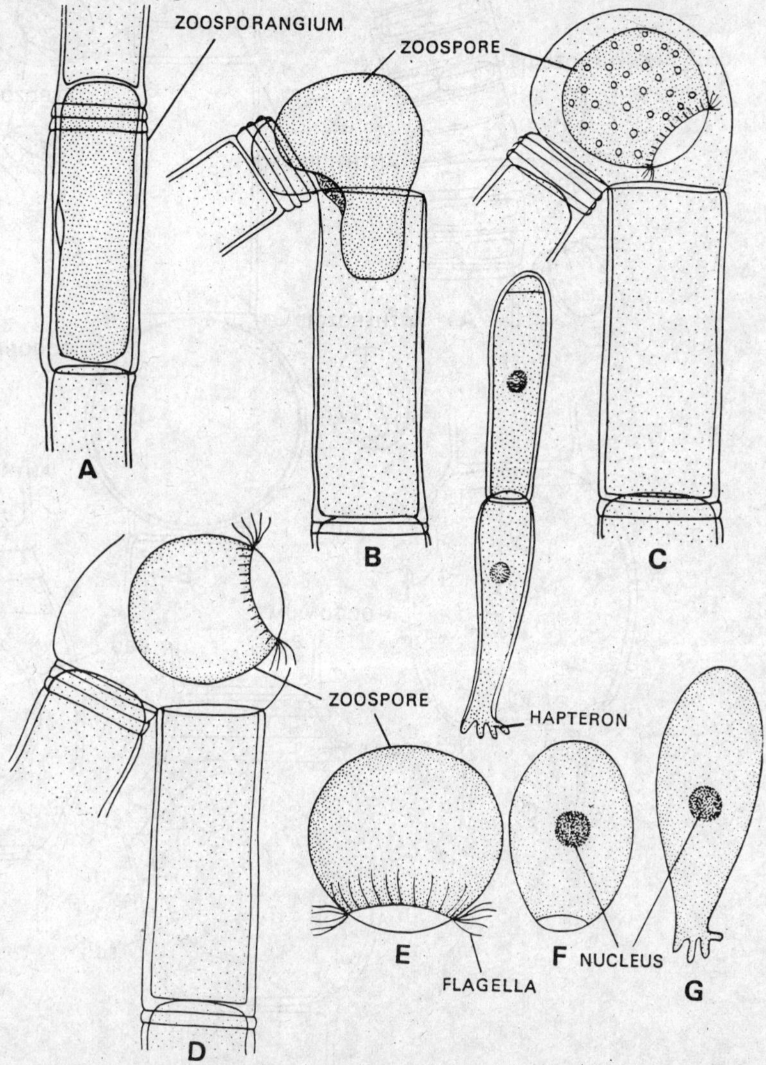

Fig. 3.88. *Oedogonium* sp. Asexual reproduction. By zoospores; A, cell acting as zoosporangium; B-C, formation and liberation of zoospore; D, zoospore liberating out of vesicle; E-G, germinating zoospore and germling; H, two-celled germling.

Development of antheridia. In **macrandrous** species the oogonia and antheridia may be developed on the same filament. (homothallic or monoecious species) or on two different filaments (heterothallic or dioecious species). The antheridia are either terminal or intercalary. They are produced by the division of antheridial mother cell. Any vegetative cell may act as antheridial mother cell. This cell divides into two unequal cells at its upper end forming an antheridium. The lower sister cell divides repeatedly and a chain of 2-40 antheridia is produced. The protoplast of each antheridium metamorphoses in a single antherozoid. Sometimes two antherozoids are produced in one antheridium. The antherozoids resemble zoospores in structure and shape only with the difference that they are somewhat smaller in size and with fewer number of flagella. The antherozoids liberate in the same way as zoospores. They come out in thin membranous vesicles

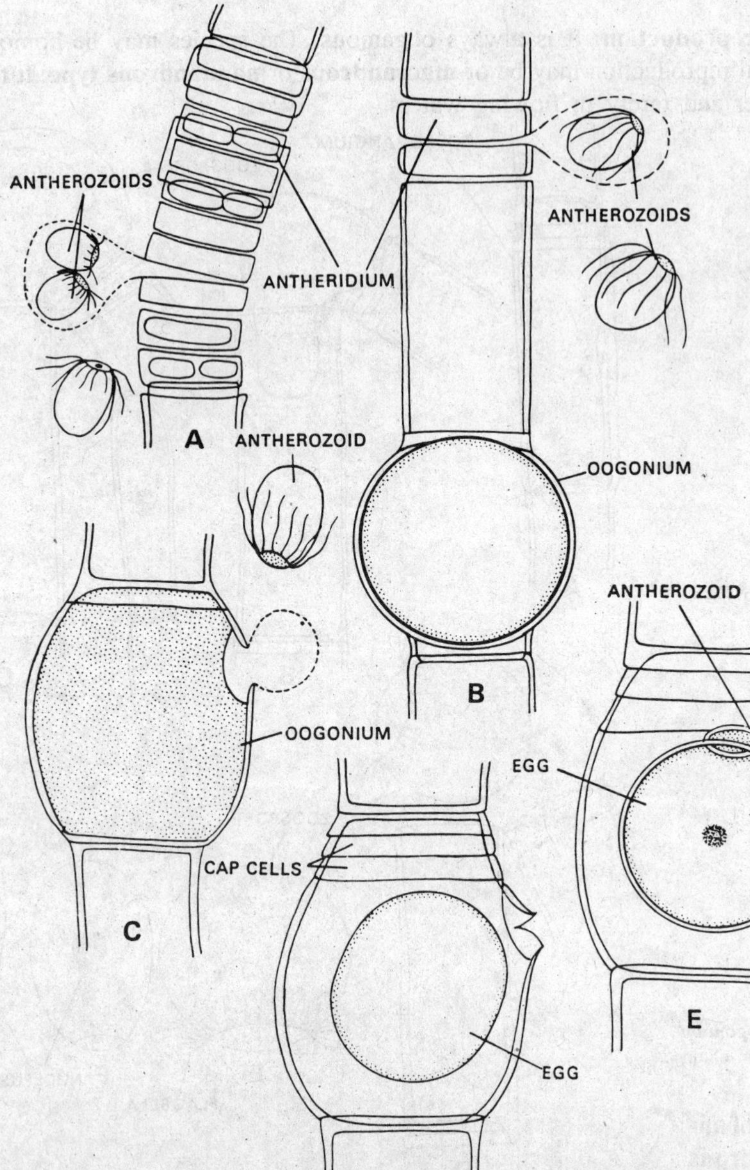

Fig. 3.89. *Oedogonium* sp. Sexual Reproduction-Macrandrous species A, antheridia and liberation of antherozoids; B, a monoecious species having antheridia and oogonium on the same thread; C, mature oogonium ready for fertilization; D, entrance of antherozoid in the oogonium through receptive spot; E, fertilization; F, single antherozoid.

by the split of antheridial wall. Very soon the vesicle disappears and the antherozoid moves freely in the water in any direction.

In **nannandrous** species the antheridia are produced on special dwarf males or nannandria. Majority of the nannandrous species are heterothallic (dioecious), *i.e.*, oogonia are produced on the ordinary filaments and antheridia on special filaments called 'dwarf males' or nannandria. These 'dwarf males' or nannandria originate by the germination of a special type of swarmers known as androspores produced singly in flat cells, *i.e.*, androsporangia formed by repeated

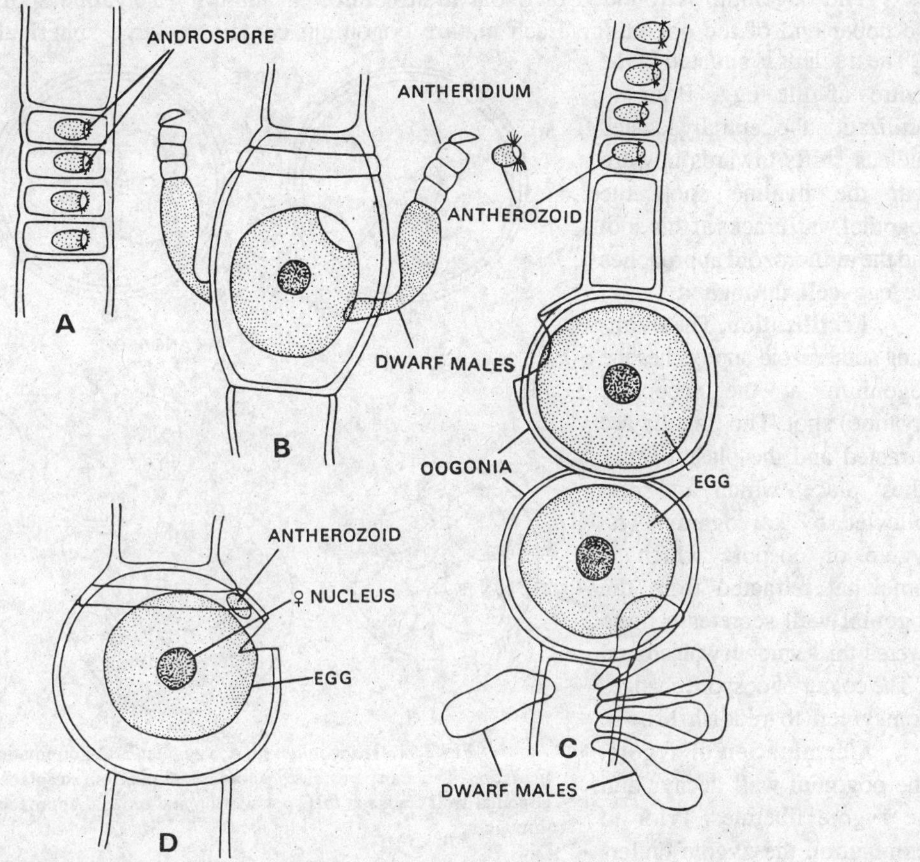

Fig. 3.90. *Oedogonium.* sp. Sexual Reproduction—Nannandrous species; A, androspore formation in androsporangia; B, oogonium with dwarf males and antheridia; C, two oogonia and unicellular dwarf males on supporting (suffultory) cell; D, fertilization.

transverse divisions of the ordinary vegetative cells. The androsporangia may occur on the same filaments on which the oogonia are produced or on different filaments. The androspores resemble in shape and structure to zoospores. They are somewhat smaller than zoospores and larger than antherozoids. After their small swarming period they settle down either on the oogonium or on one of the neighbouring cells. Here the androspore germinates and develops into a dwarf male. The nannandrium consists of one basal cell attached to the oogonlum or adjacent cell, and one or more flat antheridia. In *Oedogonium* the nannandrium consists of an attaching cell only producing two antherozoids develop in an antheridium. The structure of antherozoid is same as that of the antherozoids of macrandrous species. The antherozoids swim here and there in the water after liberation.

Development and structure of oogonia. The development and structure of oogonia of macrandrous and nannadrous species is identical. The oogonia develop by terminal or intercalary oogonial mother cells. The oogonial mother cell divides transversely and the upper daughter cell always develops into an oogonium. Each oogonium always possesses one or more caps at its upper end. The lower daughter cell is called the **'suffultory cell'** which does not develop into an oogonium and thus two oogonia may be seen in continuation on the filament.

The oogonium is rounded or ovoid in structure. On maturity a hyaline spot develops at the upper end of the oogonium. Each mature oogonium contains a large spherical egg cell in it. The nucleus is situated in the centre of the egg. Prior to fertilization the centrally located nucleus shifts towards upward near the hyaline spot, the oogonial wall cracks at this spot and the antherozoid approaches the egg cell through it.

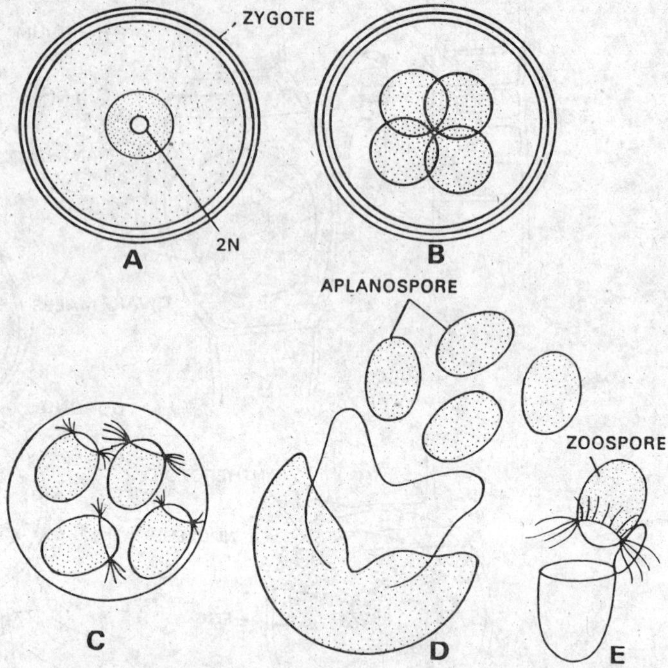

Fig. 3.91. *Oedogonium* sp. A, a zygote; B-C, germination of zygote; D, liberation of aplanospores; E, zoospore comes out from an aplanospore, spot, the oogonial wall cracks at this spot and the antherozoid approaches the egg cell through it.

Fertilization. The swimming antherozoid approaches the oogonium at the receptive (hyaline) spot. The flagella are retracted and the plasmogamy takes place which is soon followed by karyogamy. The zygote or oospore which is somewhat retracted from the oogonial wall secretes a three layered-thick smooth wall around it. The colour of oospore changes from green to reddish brown.

Germination of zygote. The oogonial wall decays and the zygote liberates. Prior to germination the zygote undergoes a period of rest. In the case of the germination of the zygote of *Oedogonium* this resting period ranges from 12 to 14 months. During the resting period there is meiotic division of the zygote nucleus (2x) and four haploid nuclei (x) are formed. The protoplast divides and four daughter protoplasts are developed. Each daughter protoplast metamorphoses in a zoospore. The zygote wall ruptures and the zoospores liberate in the vesicle which later on disappears and the zoospores swim freely in the water. Sometimes, instead of zoospores, four aplanospores are formed. Each aplanospore opens at its anterior end and a single zoospore liberates from it. Each zoospore is capable to give rise to a new filament.

Parthenogenesis. In some of the species, the unfertilized eggs develop into parthenospores. Pathenospores are zygote-like and germinate in the same way without meiosis.

The life cycle of *Oedogonium* is of haplontic type.

Systematic position. Division-Chlorophycophyta; Class-Chlorophyceae; Order-Oedogoniales; Family-Oedogoniaceae; Genus-*Oedogonium*.

ORDER–CONJUGALES OR ZYGNEMATALES

There are 40 genera and about 3,000 species.

Characteristic features

1. This order is exclusively fresh water in habit. Majority of the species are found in fresh water pools and ponds in free floating condition. Some forms are found in wet soil.
2. The forms are unicellular or filamentous. In filamentous forms the cells are arranged

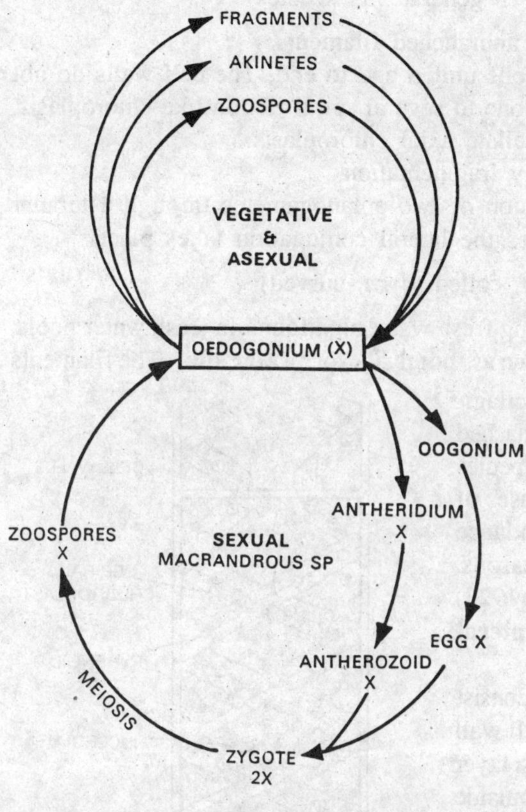

Fig. 3.92. *Oedogonium.* Macrandrous sp., graphic life-cycle.

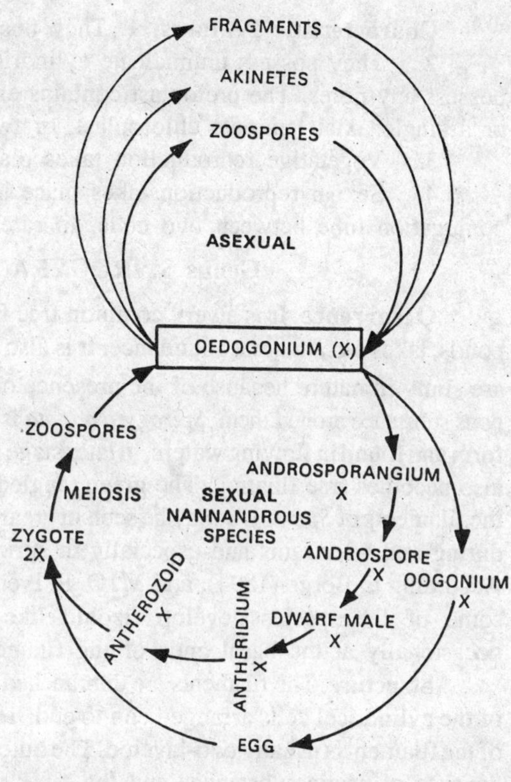

Fig. 3.93. *Oedogonium.* Nannandrous species-graphic life-cycle.

end to end and the filaments are unbranched.

3. The cell wall is two layered. The outer layer consists of pectic substances and the layer just outside the protoplast is of cellulose. The chloroplasts may be spiral, axial or stellate.

4. Asexual reproduction is altogether absent.

5. Sexual reproduction is isogamous and takes place by means of aplanogametes. Motile gametes are altogether absent. Single aplanogamete develops in a cell. Union of gametes takes place by conjugatoin through tubes.

6. The zygospore is thick walled and germinates after passing through a rest period. Meiotic division takes place during germination. The filaments are haploid.

Classification. There are two sub-orders. **1. Euconjugatae** and **2. Desmidioideae.** The sub-order Euconjugatae is sub-divided into two series (a) Mesotaenioideae and series (b) Zygnemoideae.

Series (a) Mesotaenioideae

Family 1 — Mesotaeniaceae

Series (b) Zygnemoideae

Family 2 — Zygnemaceae

Family 3 — Mougeotiaceae

Family 4 — Gonatozygaceae

The sub-order Desmidioideae consists of a single family, *i.e.,* Desmidiaceae.

Family—Zygnemaceae — (13 genera; 533 species)

Characteristic Features. 1. They possess unbranched filaments.

2. They possess uninucleate cylindrical cells united end to end. The cell walls do not possess any pores. The protoplast contains either one to several spiral ribbon-like chloroplasts, or a single axial laminate chloroplast, or two stellate axial chloroplasts.

3. Vegetative reproduction takes place by fragmentation.

4. Sexual reproduction takes place by union of two aplanogametes through a tubular conjugation tube between two cells. In rare cases the lateral conjugation takes place.

Genus SPIROGYRA(*spiro*, coiled; *gyra*, curved)

Occurrence. It is a very common free floating fresh water alga found in fresh water pools, ponds, lakes etc., in great abundance. It is also known as **'pond silk'** or **'water silk'**. The filaments are slimy in nature because of the presence of mucilaginous substance around them. *Spirogyra adnata* is an attached form and found in flowing waters, in later stage this species also becomes free floating. The green tangled masses of the filaments of *Spirogyra* may be seen in great abundance during and after rains and especially in spring seasons. According to Borge (1894), and M. O. P. Iyenger (1923) some of the species develop rizohid like **'haptera'** occasionally at the basal ends of the filaments.

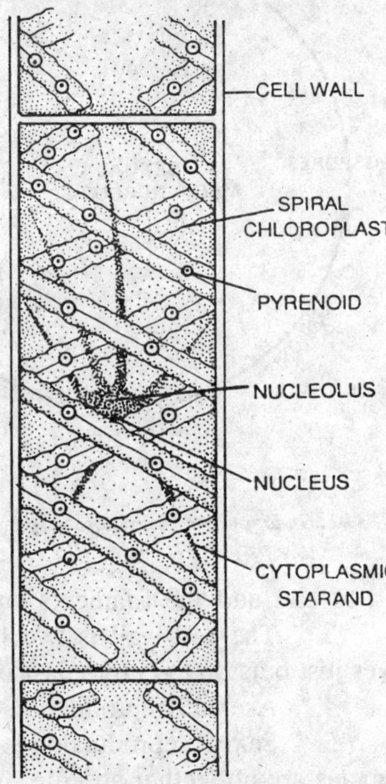

Fig. 3.94. *Spirogyra* sp. Details of a single cell.

Structure. The filaments are unbranched and consist of the cylindrical cells arranged end to end. The cell wall of the filament is usually two-layered. The outermost layer consists of pectic substances and the layer just outside the protoplast consists of cellulose. Each cell is cylindrical and sometimes several times longer than its breadth. The cells are uninucleate. The nucleus is usually situated in the centre of the cell and connected by cytoplasmic strands (primordial utricle) to the dense cytoplasm of the peripheral region. There is a big central vacuole.

In *Spirogyra* the chloroplasts are spiral and band-like. They may be serrated or smooth at the margins. The number of chloroplasts ranges 1-14 in different species. Many pyrenoids are found in each ribbon-like chloroplast.

Reproduction. The reproduction takes place by vegetative and sexual methods. Asexual reproduction is lacking.

1. **Vegetative reproduction.** The vegetative filaments break accidentally into small fragments. Each such fragment may develop into a new filament.

2. **Sexual reproduction.** In *Spirogyra* sexual reproduction takes place by special gametes called **'aplanogametes'**. and the process **'aplanogamy'.** The motile gametes are always lacking. Aplanogamy takes place by conjugation, which may be **scalariform** or **lateral.** In each cell a single aplanogamete is produced which moves in the other cell through a conjugation tube in amoeboid fashion. The species may be homothallic or heterothallic. Scalariform conjugation is the process of reproduction of heterothallic species. Lateral conjugation takes place in homothallic species. In scalariform conjugation the aplanogametes of two filaments unite whereas in lateral conjugation the aplanogametes of two adjacent cells of the same filament unite.

Scalariform conjugation. This type of sexual reproduction is found in majority of the species of *Spirogyra*. Two filaments taking part in conjugation lie side by side. Very soon the outgrowths are given out from the lateral walls of the opposite cells of the filaments. The outgrowths of opposite cells touch each other. Very soon the wall of contact dissolves and a tubular passage is formed between the two opposite cells of the two filaments lying side by side. This tubular passage is called 'conjugation tube'. Simultaneously the contents of the cells retract and aplanogametes

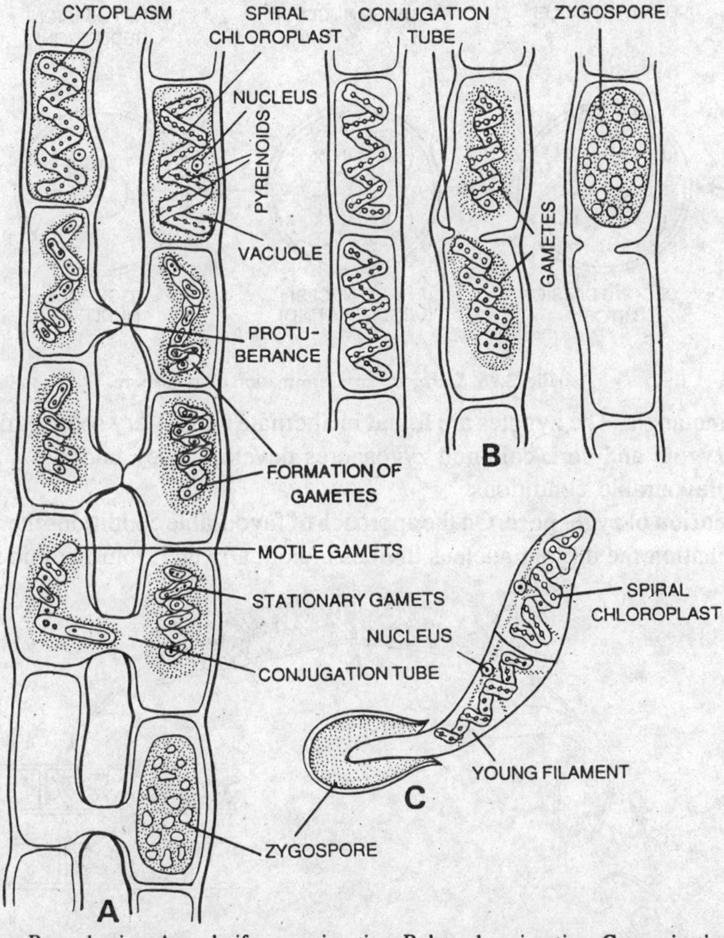

Fig. 3.95. *Spirogyra* sp. Reproduction. A, scalariform conjugation; B, lateral conjugation; C, germination of zygospore.

are developed. A single aplanogamete develops in each cell. The aplanogametes formed in the cells of the one filament pass into the opposite cells of the other filaments through conjugation tubes in amoeboid fashion. The plasmogamy is followed by karyogamy. The transferring aplanogemetes are thought to be male gametes and the receiving aplanogamates are female gametes. Just after fusion the walls are developed around the zygote and they are called zygospores. A single zygospore develops in each cell of the female filament. The wall of the female filament decays and the zygospores are set free in the water, which germinate after a resting period.

Lateral conjugation. This type of conjugation is found occasionally and in homothallic species. Here the aplanogametes of the adjacent cells of the same filament unite. At the septum a tube-like structure develops and through this opening the contents (aplanogamete) of one cell pass into the other. The empty cells are considered as male gametangia and the cells with zygote

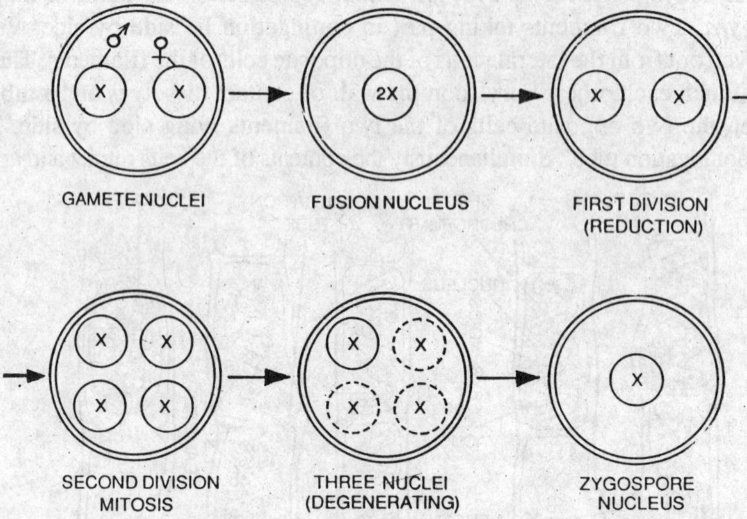

Fig. 3.96. *Spirogyra* sp. Germination of zygospore.

are female gametangia. The zygotes are found in alternate cells. Very soon a thick wall is secreted around each zygote and dark coloured zygospores develop. They undergo a period of rest and germinate in favourable conditions.

Germination of zygospore. On the approach of favourable conditions the zygote germinates. Prior to germination the diploid nucleus divides meiotically and, four haploid nuclei are formed.

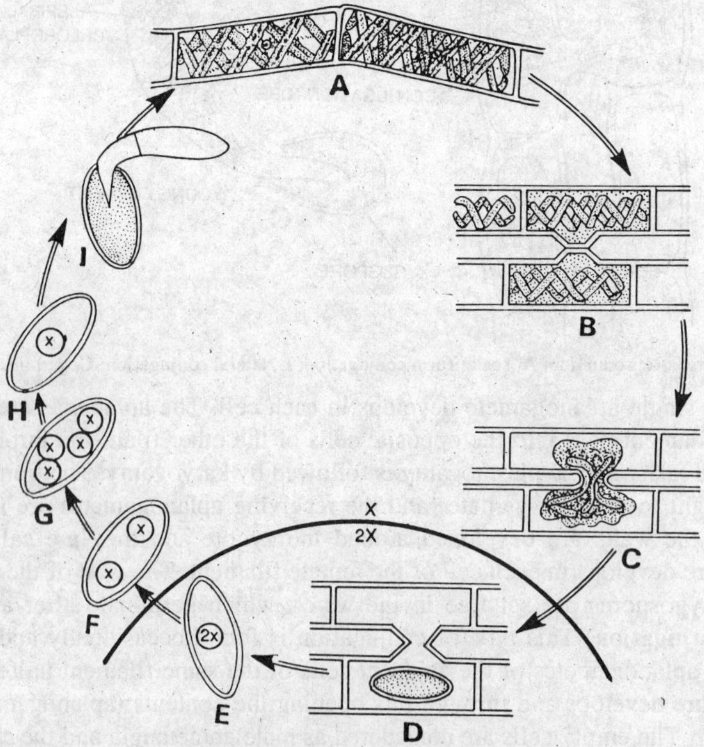

Fig. 3.97. *Spirogyra* sp. Life cycle

Three of the four haploid nuclei disintegrate and only one remains functional. The zygospore wall breaks and the germling comes out which soon develops into a new filament.

Parthenogenesis. The formation of parthenospores or azygospores has been recorded from many species. Here the conjugation does not take place and the contents of the cells become rounded. The walls are secreted around these protoplasts and they are called 'parthenospores' or 'azygospores'. The formation of parthenospores is regular feature in *Spirogyra greenlandica.*

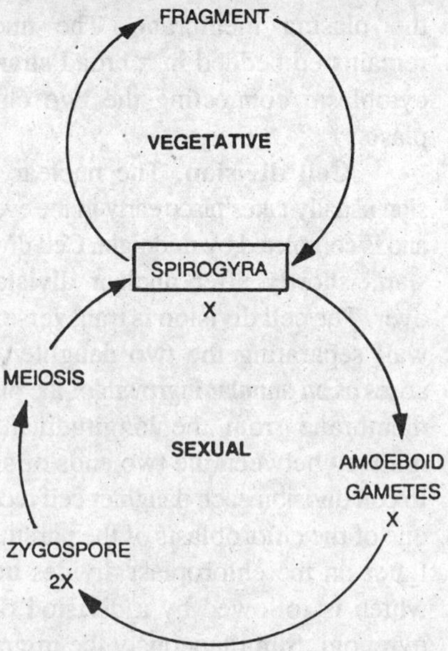

Fig. 3.98. *Spirogyra*—Life-cycle.

Genic action of cytoplasm. In many of the Conjugales, reproduction by conjugation of the protoplasts of cells in the filaments is more than a union of nuclei. Primarily there are plastids which resemble genes in two respects : (1) they are capable of multiplying by division and (2) they are capable of mutation. When the protoplasts of the Conjugales unite there is also an association of **plasmagenes**. The plasmagenes are the units of inheritance which may be compared to nuclear genes found in the cytoplasm. The large chloroplasts break down and lose their shape during formation of gametes and their union, but the zygote contains minute granules which may be called **proplastids** and which may give rise to new plastids. Though the majority of heritable variations are nuclear yet evidences are there which support that cytoplasm also directly participates in some genetic functions. All metabolic activities take place in the cytoplasm of the cell which are controlled by enzymatic action of mitochondria. The genes operate in the cytoplasm, and therefore, the cytoplasm exerts a strong influence on genic action.

Systematic position. Division-Chlorophycophyta; Class Chlorophyceae; Order-Zygenematales; Family-Zygnemataceae; Genus-*Spirogyra.*

Genus ZYGNEMA

Family–Zygnemaceae

Occurrence. *Zygnema*, a genus with about ninety five species is widely distributed green alga. It is commonly found in the fresh water ponds, pools and slow running streams. It occurs in yellowish green free floating masses on the surface of water. Iyenger (1923) reported that a few species growing in quiet water may be sessile and attached to a substratum by lateral or terminal outgrowths known as **haptera** from near the end of a filament or by a tendril-like coiling of a filament.

Structure. The plant body consists of a simple, unbranched filament. The cells are cylindrical which are placed one above the other. The cells are slightly longer than their breadth, usually not more than twice. In few cases the cells are two to five times as long as broad. All cells of a filament are quite similar in their structure. Occasionally certain cells of a filament develop rhizoid-like out growth, *i.e.,* haptera (Iyenger, 1923).

Lateral walls of cell possess an inner layer of cellulose and an outer layer of pectose (Tiffany, 1924). There is never a refolding or replication of transverse walls as is found in certain species of *Spirogyra.*

The cells possess two stellate chloroplasts, each with a single pyrenoid, that lie axial to each other on either side of the nucleus. They are found in the longitudinal axis of a cell. The nucleus lies between the two stellate chloroplasts. A chloroplast possesses many delicate to massive strands extending to the plasma membrane. The nucleus remains embedded in a broad strand of cytoplasm connecting the two chloroplasts.

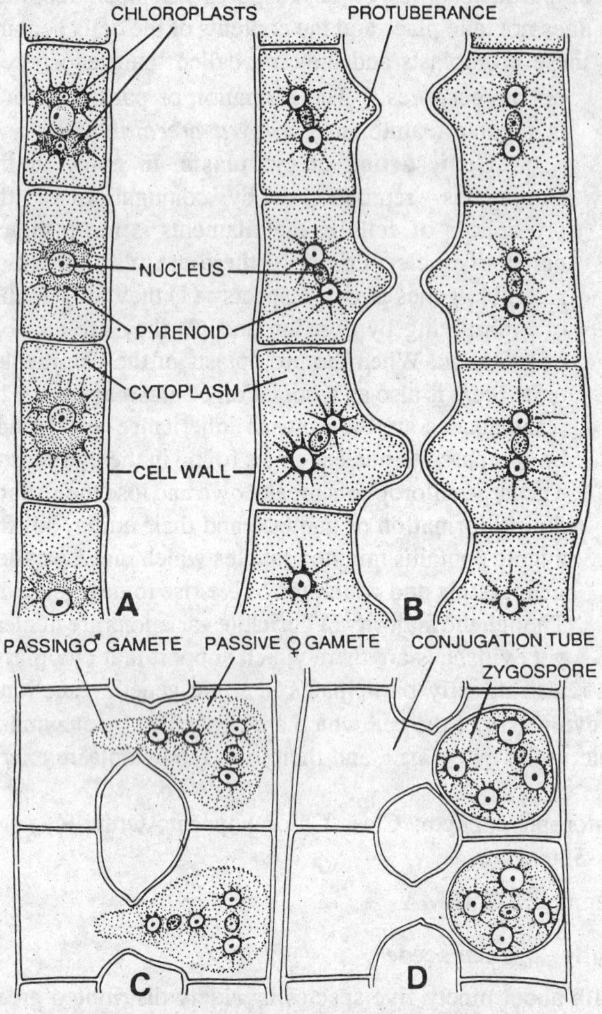

Fig. 3.99. *Zygnema* sp. A, mature vegetative cell of a filament; B-D, stages in scalariform conjugation (sexual reproduction).

Cell division. The nuclear division usually takes place early in the evening and is completed by midnight. Cell division starts shortly after nuclear division is over. The cell division is transverse. The wall separating the two daughter cells arises as an annular ingrowth of the plasma membrane from the longitudinal wall midway between the two ends of a cell. In cell division each daughter cell receives one of the chloroplasts of the parent cell. Later on the chloroplast divides in two which is followed by a division of the pyrenoid. Simultaneously the migration of the nucleus also takes place to a position midway between the two daughter chloroplasts. The number of cells in a filament increases because of cell division.

Reproduction. The reproduction in *Zygnema* takes place by means of vegetative, asexual and sexual methods. They are as follows.

Vegetative reproduction. It takes place by means of accidental fragmentation of filaments. Each fragment by growth and cell division develops into a long filament. When the alga grows in quiet water, the number of filaments increases rapidly. Rarely there is a vegetative multiplication by disjunction into individual cells or into fragments with a few cells each.

By parthenospores or azygospores, akinetes and aplanospores. The cells of *Zygnema* may have a rounding up of the protoplast and a secretion of a thick wall around the contracted protoplast. Such bodies are called **aplanospores.** The aplanospores are found in about a dozen of species, such as *Zygnema himalayense, Zygnema terrestre* etc.

In certain species, the rounded bodies obviously result from failure of a gamete and, therefore, are called **parthenospores** or **azygospores**. Such spores have been reported from *Z .collinsianum.*

The thick-walled akinetes have been reported in the alga. According to Randhawa, the brick-shaped orange coloured akinetes with thick walls are formed in *Zygnema giganteum.* The akinetes are also formed in *Zygnema peliosporium.*

Sexual reproduction. The sexual reproduction takes place by means of conjugation. It is of two types, *i.e.*, scalariform and lateral. These methods are as follows.

Scalariform conjugation. This type of conjugation starts when two filaments lie side by side throughout their entire length. The small dome-shaped protuberances develop from opposite pair of cells and grow towards each other. Each such protuberance elongates in size and ultimately becomes a short cylindrical outgrowth. These outgrowths arising from opposite cells touch each other; the wall of contact is being dissolved and a conjugation tube is formed. In some species both gametes become amoeboid and migrate into the conjugation tube where they fuse with each other to form the zygote. Such species are strictly **isogamous.** In *Zygnema peliosporium* and *Zygnema collinsianum,* the zygote is formed in the conjugation tube. There are other species which are **anisogamous.** In such species one of the gametes (*i.e.*, the male) is actively amoeboid, and the other (*i.e.*, the female) is passive. In such cases the male gamete moves through the conjugation canal and the gametic union takes place in the female gametangium. The zygospore secretes a thick wall and undergoes a period of rest. The zygospores liberate by a decay of the gametangial or the conjugation tube walls. They germinate on the approach of favourable conditions.

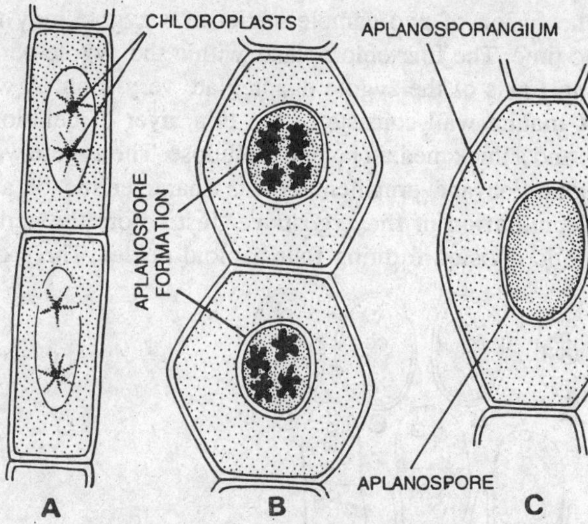

Fig. 3.100. *Zygnema* sp. A-C, formation of aplanospore.

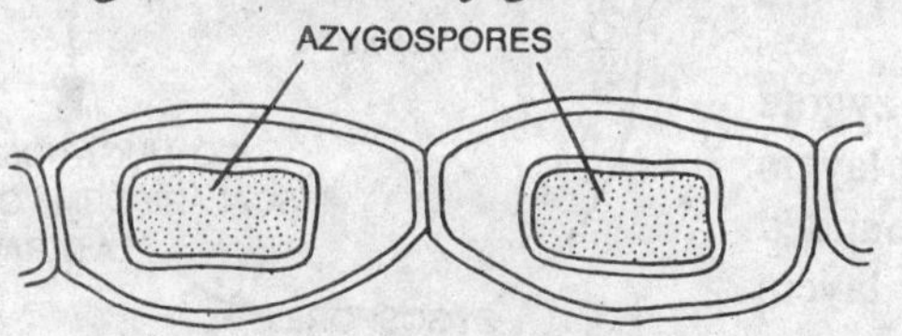

Fig. 3.101 *Zygnema* sp. azygospores.

Lateral conjugation. The lateral conjugation is commonly found in *Zygnema himalayense* and *Z. heydrichii.* Here the adjoining cells of the same filament give out tubular protuberances one on either side of the septum. The lateral protuberances ultimately touch each other and the septum breaks in this region. The contents of one of the adjoining cells, pass into the other where the zygote is formed. The zygote secretes a thick wall around it and undergoes the period of rest.

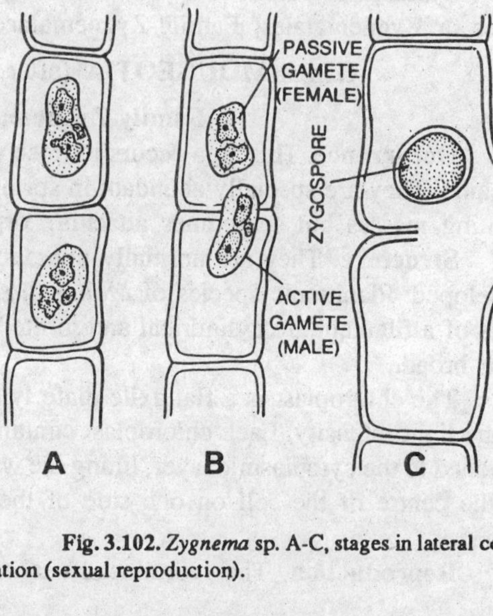

Fig. 3.102. *Zygnema* sp. A-C, stages in lateral conjugation (sexual reproduction).

The sexual reproduction is marked by

a seasonal periodicity and each species usually fruits at a definite time of the year. Majority of the species fruit in spring.

The fusion of two gamete nuclei in a zygote may take immediately or may be delayed for some time. The four chloroplasts within the zygote persist for a time, but two of them lying in the short axis of the zygote disintegrate very soon. A wall develops around the zygote quite early. A mature wall consists of the thin layer of cellulose, a thin outer layer of cellulose or pectose, and a thick median layer of cellulose. The zygote walls become coloured and ornamented. The colouration and ornamentation is characteristic of a zygote of a particular species.

Germination of the zygospore. Just before the germination of the zygote nucleus, there is a meiotic division forming four haploid nuclei. Three of the resultant haploid nuclei degenerate and the fourth remains unchanged until the zygote germinates. During germination the two outermost layers of zygote wall rupture and the protoplast still surrounded by the innermost wall layer escapes from the outer layers or only partially escapes from them. It divides transversely giving rise to two daughter cells which divide and redivide to form a filament.

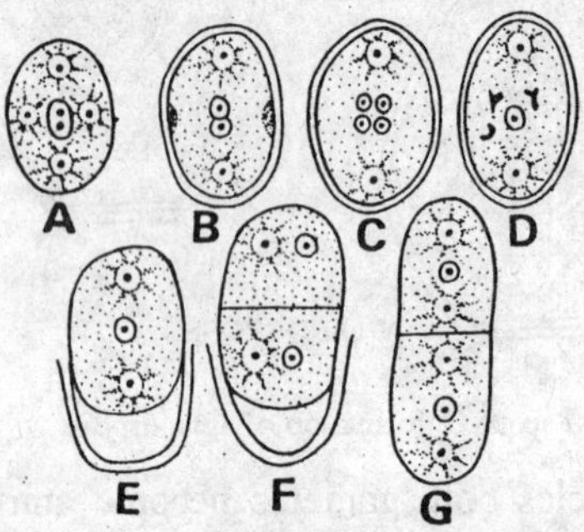

Fig. 3.103. *Zygnema* sp. stages in germination of zygospore.

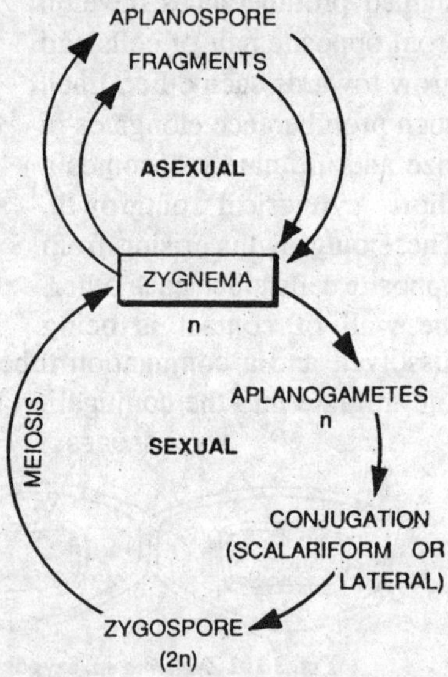

Fig. 3.104. *Zygnema* **sp. Graphic life-cycle.**

Systematic position. Division-Chlorophycophyta; Class - Chlorophyceae; Order-Conjugales or Zygnematales; Family-Zygnemataceae; Genes-*Zygnema*.

Genus MOUGEOTIA (after J. B. Mougeot, a French botanist)

Family-Zygnemaceae (Mougeotiaceae)

Occurrence. This alga occurs in fresh water lakes, ponds, pools, springs and slow running streams. They are specially abundant in spring months, generally occurring as bright green free-floating masses but sometimes attaching organs may be present.

Structure. They are normally unbranched but occasionally short few celled laterals are developed. Planktonic species of *Mougeotia* often have twisted or spirally coiled threads. The cells of a filament are cylindrical and jointed end to end. Each cell is usually four times longer than broad.

The chloroplast is a flat axile plate lying in the centre of the cell and oriented according to the light intensity. Each chloroplast contains two or more pyrenoids. The chloroplast remains attached to the cytoplasmic layer, lining the wall by cytoplasmic strands. There is a single nucleus in the centre of the cell on one side of the chloroplast. The cell wall is usually moderately thin.

Reproduction. The reproduction takes place both by asexual and sexual methods.

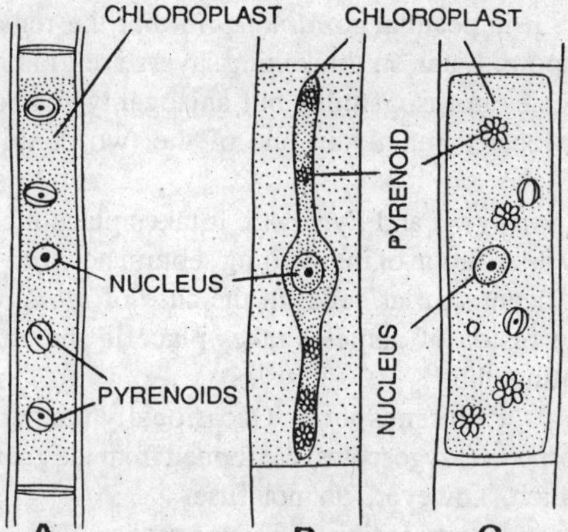

Fig. 3.105. *Mougeotia* sp. A, cell of vegetative filament; B chloroplast within the cell at right angle; C, chloroplast parallel to sun rays.

Asexual reproduction. 1. By fragmentation. The filaments break accidentally into small fragments. Each such piece of filament develops into a new plant. Knee joints or geniculations are also common.

2. By aplanospores. The aplanospores occur quite frequently in this genus. Certain species reproduce by aplanospores and lack zygospore formation.

3. Akinetes. Thick-walled akinetes are formed in isolated cells of the filament.

Sexual reproduction. It takes place by scalariform and lateral conjugation.

Scalariform conjugation. The two filaments lie parallel to each other and the opposite cells of the filaments put out short bud-like protuberances which come in contact and form conjugation tubes. The gametes are produced from only a part of the protoplast of the gametangium. The two gametes fuse

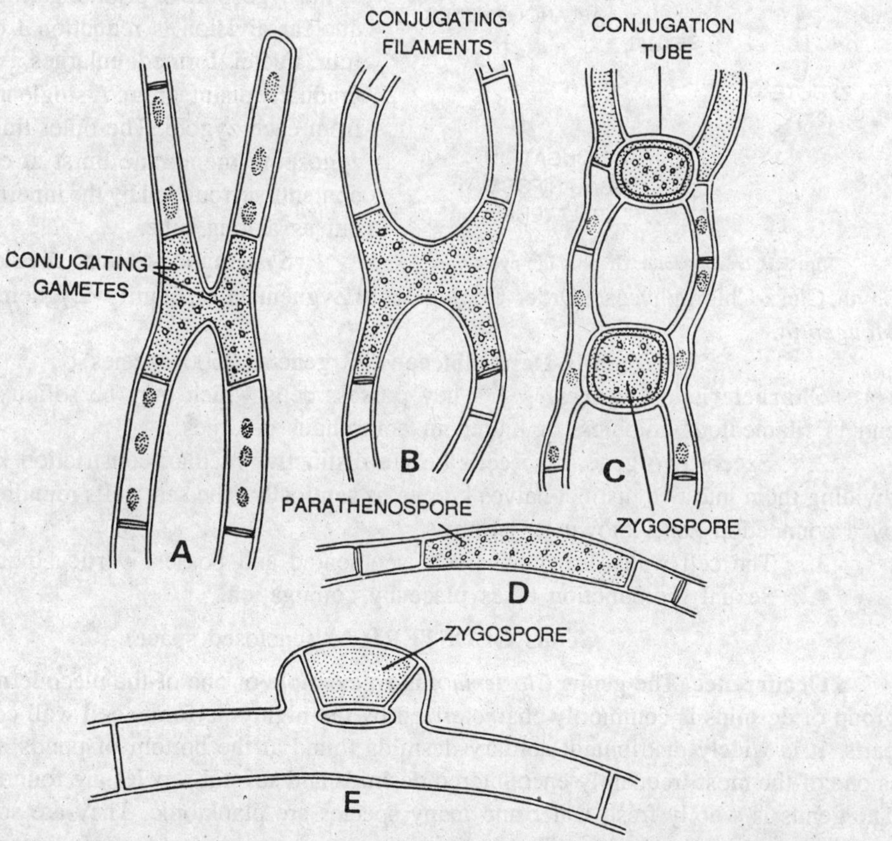

Fig. 3.106. *Mougeotia* sp. A-C, stages showing scalariform conjugation; D, parthenospore; E, lateral conjugation.

in the broad conjugation tube and form a zygote. After fusion the zygote does not immediately secrete a membrane of its own, but becomes separated from the surrounding sterile parts containing the unused cytoplasm by variously oriented walls. It is peculiar to *Mougeotia* that the remains of the gametangia persist around the mature zygospore. Later on thickening layers are gradually secreted internally by the zygote. Most of the species are isogamous but anisogamy is known in *Mougeotia tenuis*. In *M. tenuis*, the zygote is located mainly in one of the two conjugating cells and not in the conjugation tube.

Lateral conjugation. It is similar to that of *Spirogyra* and *Zygnema*. It takes place merely by dissolution of intervening septum between two adjacent similar cells. In the case of *Mougeotia* the fusion of gametes takes place in the conjugating tube.

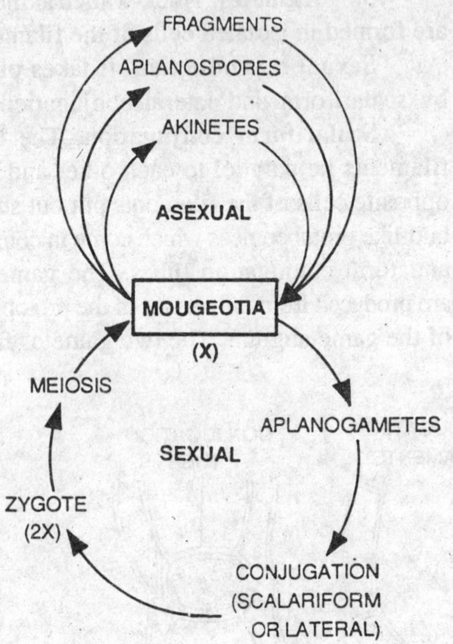

Fig. 3.107. *Mougeotia*. Graphic life-cycle

Parthenospores. Occasionally the parthenospores (azygospores) are formed from the gametes which, however, do not fuse.

Germination of zygospore. The ripe zygospores are usually spherical and possess a thick wall. Nuclear fusion is delayed for some time after the amalgamation of the gametes. The fusion nucleus may divide during the ripening of the zygospore or prior to germination. The first nuclear division is reductional one. One of the four nuclei formed enlarges, while the other gradually disintegrate. A single individual results from each zygote. The outer thick layers of the zygospore membrane burst at one end and the contents surrounded by the innermost layer, grow out as a long tube.

Systematic position. Division-Chlorophycophyta; Class-Chlorophyceae; Order-Conjugales or Zygnematales; Family - Zygnemataceae; Genus-*Mougeotia*.

Family-Desmidiaceae (23 genera; 2500 species)

Characteristic features. 1. They possess cells which may be solitary, united end to end in filamentous colonies, or united in amorphous colonies.

2. Except two genera the cells bear a distinctive median constriction known as **sinus**, dividing them into two distinct halves known as **semicells**. The semicells remain joined together by a connection zone known as **isthmus**.

3. The cell walls are transversely segmented and possess vertical pores.

4. Sexual reproduction takes place by conjugation.

Genus CLOSTERIUM (enclosed space)

Occurrence. The genus *Closterium* is an example of one of the placoderm desmids. This group of desmids is commonly characterized by the highly perforate cell wall composed of two parts. It is widely distributed; solitary desmids found at the bottom of ponds and drains. This is one of the most frequently encountered desmids and several sepcies are found in hard waters. The genus is wholly fresh water and many species are planktonic. They are scarcely found in water containing much lime. The individual species thrive best in soft water.

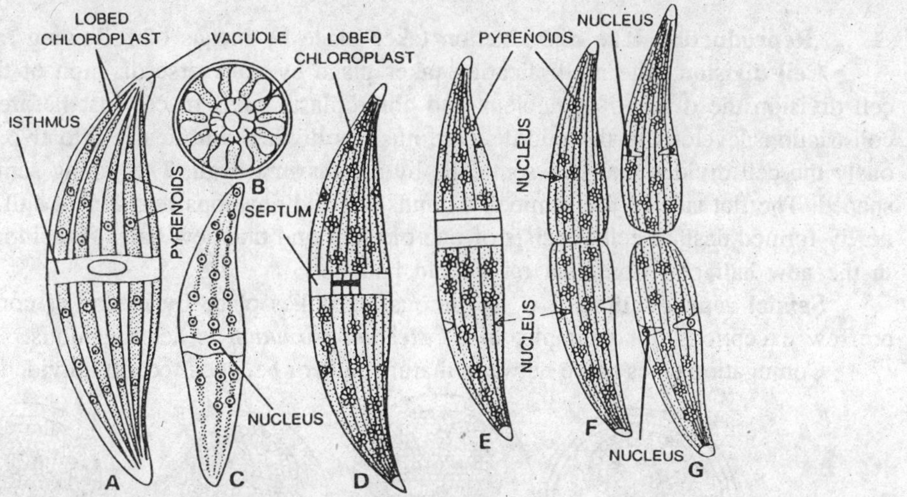

Fig. 3.108. *Closterium ehrenbergii.* A, plant showing the cell contents; B, transverse section of plant showing lobed chloroplast; C, stages showing asexual reproduction; C, a plant cell; D, nucleus in metaphase, septum formation; E, septum nearly complete; F, ends beginning to round off; G, late stage, two cells formed.

Structure. The plant body consists of an elongated, cylindrical cell with attenuated apices. The cells do not possess any median constriction. Most species are distinctly crescent-shaped or arcuate. Each plant body or cell consists of two symmetrical halves known as **semicells.** The two semicells remain connected to each other by **isthmus.**

The attenuated apices of the curved cell possess a vacuole in each apex which contains crystals of gypsum which are probably purely excretory. The pores are being arranged in rows in narrow grooves. The cell movement takes place by the exudation of mucilage through large pores situated near the apices. Each semicell possesses one axial chloroplast which in the form of a curved cone with ridges on it with one to several pyrenoids. The single nucleus lies in the isthmus region embedded in a bridge of cytoplasm connecting the two chloroplasts. The nucleus possesses a conspicuous nucleolus and well defined chromatin network.

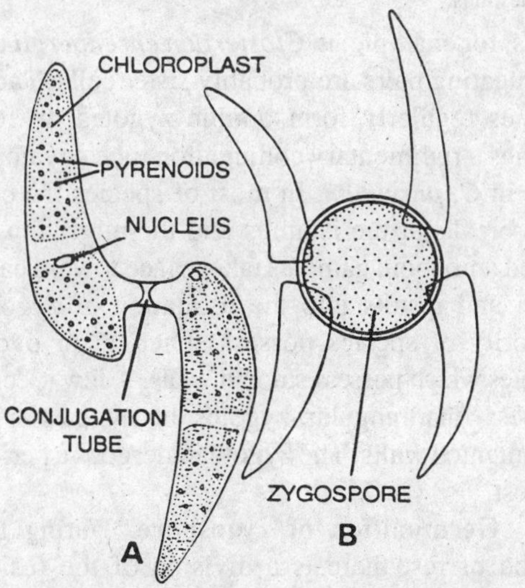

Fig. 3.109. A, *Closterium ehrenbergii* conjugation; B, *Closterium parvulum* zygospore.

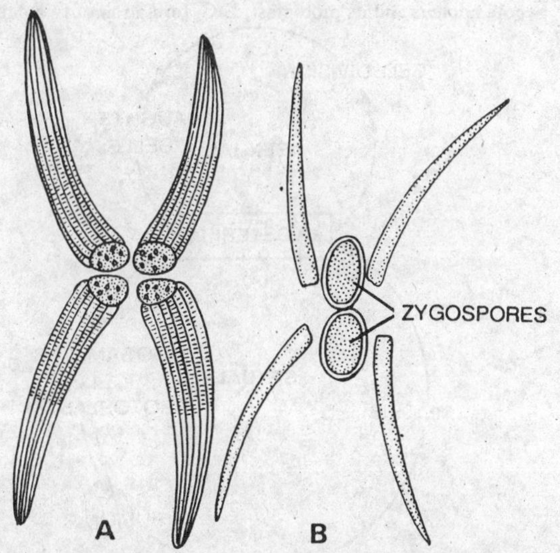

Fig. 3.110. *Closterium lineatum.* A, early conjugation; B, double zygospore.

Reproduction. The reproduction takes place by means of following methods.

Cell division. The multiplication takes place by transverse division of the cell. Prior to cell division the division of nucleus and chloroplasts takes place. Just before cell division a constriction develops in the middle. The nucleus divides mitotically into two, and simultaneously the cell divides into two semicells by a transverse wall. The young semicells are cone-shaped. The flat side of the semicell extends out and develops into a new half. This way each newly formed desmid cell consists of one old half and one new half. The chloroplast develops in the new half cell from that of the old half cell.

Sexual reproduction. It is isogamous and takes place by means of conjugation. There are few exceptions, for example, in *Closterium parvulum* is heterogamous.

Conjugation takes place between mature cells or between recently divided cells. In certain cases, for example, in *Closterium ehrenbergii* the conjugating pairs are probably sister cells. Three species regularly form double zygotes. In few species a rudimentary conjugation tube develops, *e.g.*, in *C. parvulum*. In most of species the cell wall breaks at the isthmus and the migration of naked amoeboid gametes takes place toward each other and results into the formation of zygote. Majority of species possess spherical or ovoid zygotes which possess smooth walls. A few species possess quadrangular zygotes or zygotes with ornamented walls. The zygote undergoes a period of rest.

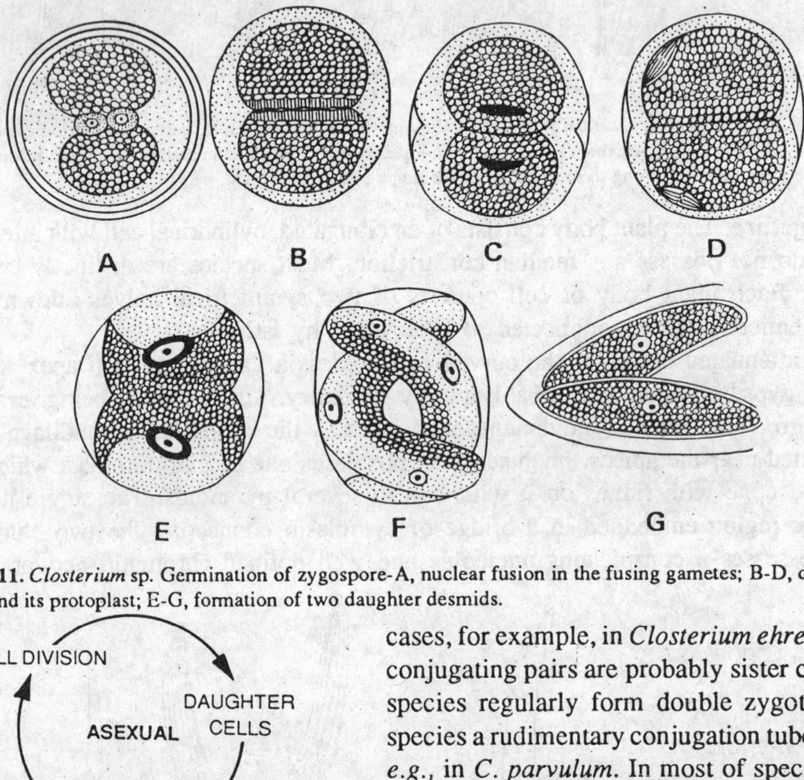

Fig. 3.111. *Closterium* sp. Germination of zygospore-A, nuclear fusion in the fusing gametes; B-D, division of the zygote nucleus and its protoplast; E-G, formation of two daughter desmids.

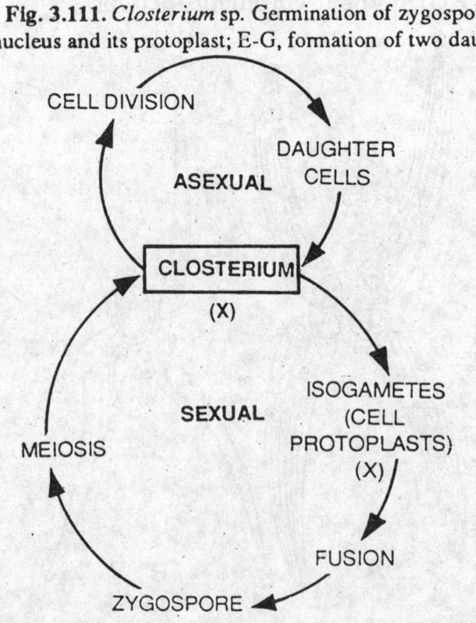

Fig. 3.112. *Closterium*—graphic life-cycle.

Germination of zygospore. During the period of rest there is a division of the fusion nucleus into four daughter nuclei. Two of them partially disintegrate. The remaining two nuclei do not fuse until the beginning of the germination of zygospore. It is thought that these divisions are meiotic, but this has not been demonstrated at least in the case of *Closterium*. During germination of the zygospore the contents divide to form two protoplasts. Each such protoplast contains a single chloroplast and a functional and a degenerating nucleus. Later on the two protoplasts assume the lunar shape and thereafter secretes its own cell wall.

Systematic position. Division-Chlorophycophyta; Class-Chlorophyceae; Order-Conjugales or Zygnematales; Family-Desmidiaceae; Genus-*Closterium*.

Genus COSMARIUM

Family–Desmidiaceae

Occurrence. This is a unicellular fresh water desmid. They occur in ponds rich in decaying organic matter along with other free floating algae. Usually they occur in abundance in mucilaginous masses along the walls of reservoirs and water tanks especially in winter. They are usually found when the waters have a pH of 5 to 6.

Structure. The cells possess an evident median constriction known as **sinus**, dividing them into two distinct halves called **semicells**, which remain joined to each other by a connecting

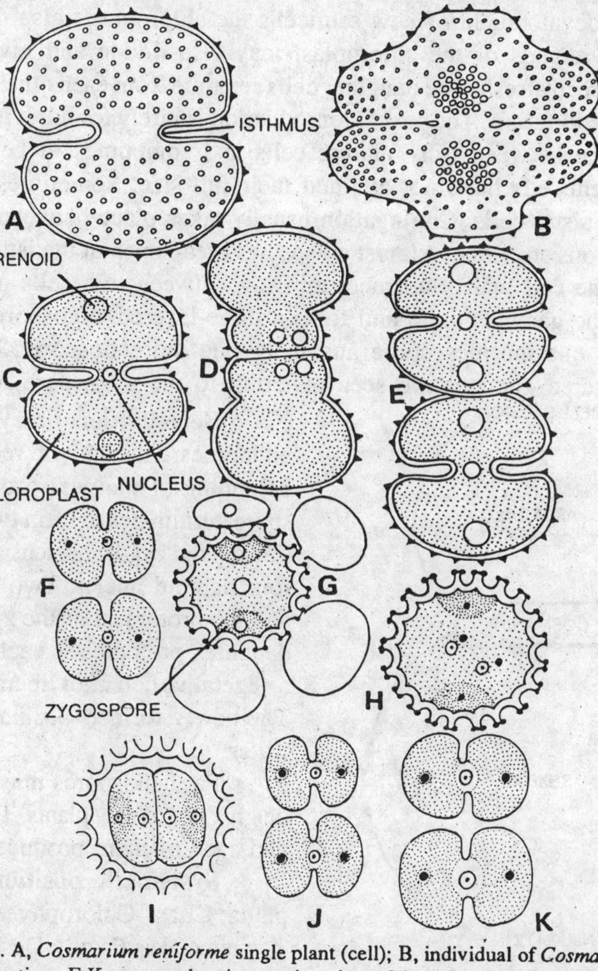

Fig. 3.113. *Cosmarium*. A, *Cosmarium reniforme* single plant (cell); B, individual of *Cosmarium protractum;* C-E, stages showing asexual reproduction; F-K, stages showing conjugation of individuals, formation of zygospore and its germination into new desmids.

zone called the **isthmus**. Each semicell may be circular, elliptical or oval in shape. They possess transversely segmented walls with vertical pores.

The walls of these desmids possess three concentric layers - 1. the outer layer is a gelatinous sheath of pectose that may be narrow or broad; 2. the median layer is somewhat thicker and has a substratum of cellulose which is impregnated with pectic compounds; 3. the innermost layer is thin and composed absolutely of cellulose. The two inner layers possess vertical pores which are arranged in a definite pattern. The pores may be found on all parts of a wall except the isthmus. The single nucleus is found in central region. There is one axial chloroplast in each semicell with one or two pyrenoids. Some species possess two chloroplasts in each semicell. In such cases the chloroplasts usually have them axial and lateral to each other. Some species possess four or more chloroplasts in each semicell where they are parietal in position. Large chloroplasts usually have numerous scattered pyrenoids.

Reproduction. The reproduction takes place by means of asexual and sexual methods.

Asexual reproduction. The asexual reproduction takes place by the division of cells. The isthmus of the cell elongates, which is followed by nuclear division and thereafter cell division. The nucleus divides into two mitotically. The cell divides transversely at the elongated isthmus, after which the portion of the isthmus attached to each semicell enlarges to form a new semicell. During the development of new semicells the chloroplasts also divide in each of original semicells. The pyrenoids of the chloroplast may also divide and give rise to new pyrenoids or they may be formed afresh. The daughter cells separate from each other forming two individuals.

Sexual reproduction. The sexual reproduction is rarely found. It is isogamous. Conjugation usually takes place between fully mature cells and sometimes in between immature cells in which the new semicells have not attained their full size. Sometimes the newly divided conjugating cells are sister cells. Conjugation usually takes place between two cells that lie within a common gelatinous envelope. Almost all species break open at the isthmus and both protoplasts move out from the cell walls and meet midway between two cells or sometimes in the conjugation canal. The gametes unite and form a three-layered zygospore. The outer is known as exospore, middle one the mesospore and inner one the endospore. Sometimes the four semicells of the ruptured gametes are seen adhering to the zygospore for a short time.

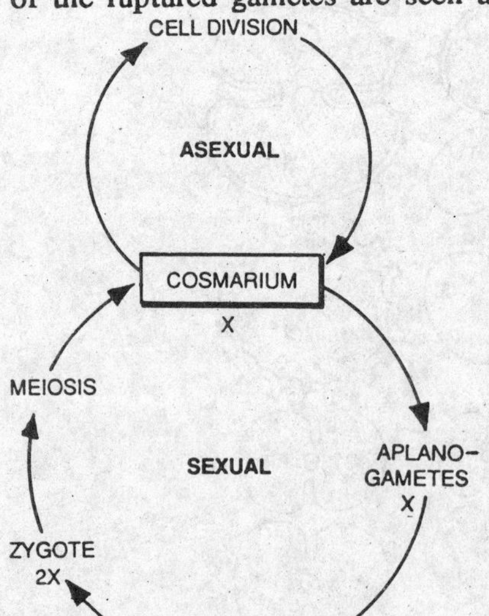

Fig. 3.114. *Cosmarium.* Graphc life-cycle.

Germination of zygospore. The zygospore undergoes a period of rest and germinates at the beginning of the next growing season. Each zygospore germinates to form two new *Cosmarium* plants. The diploid zygote nucleus divides meiotically forming four haploid nuclei. Two of the nuclei disintegrate and the protoplast of the zygospore divides into two daughter protoplasts, each of which develops into a vegetative cell after liberation from the zygote wall. The newly formed *Cosmarium* plants escape in the water.

Parthenospores may also develop which later on give rise to new plants. They behave like zygospores and each of them produces two *Cosmarium* plants.

Systematic position. Division-Chlorophycophyta; CLass-Chlorophyceae; Order - Conjugales or Zygnematales; Family-Desmidiaceae; Genus-*Cosmarium*,

ORDER–SIPHONALES

There are 80 genera and about 505 species in this order.

Characteristic features

1. Majority of the species are marine and found in warm tropical seas. The forms belonging to family Vaucheriaceae are mostly fresh water and found in temperate regions. Some forms are epiphytic and some are endophytic. Some are lithophytes. Three genera of this order are parasitic in habit.

2. Fossil records of Siphonales are found 4,480,000,000 years ago in Palaeozoic period. In the family Dasycladaceae, out of 15 tribes 12 are fossils; out of 58 genera 48 are extinct and 10 are living.

3. The thallus of Siphonales is multicellular but, there is no septation. All forms are coenocytic, tubular and branched.

4. The cell wall commonly lacks cellulose and consists of pectose. In Dasycladaceae there is heavy deposition of lime upon cell walls.

5. The protoplast is peripheral. The nuclei and chloroplasts are embedded in it. The chloroplasts are innumerable. The pyrenoids may or may not be present.

6. In majority of the forms food product is found in the form of starch grains except Vaucheriaceae where oil is found.

7. Reproduction takes place by vegetative, asexual and sexual methods. Vegetative reproduction takes place by fragments and akinetes; asexual reproduction takes place by zoo-spores, aplanospores, cysts, microaplanospores and hypnospores; sexual reproduction ranges from isogamy to oogamy.

Classification. There are 9 families in this order — 1. Protosiphonaceae. 2. Caulerpaceae, 3. Derbesiaceae, 4. Dasycladaceae, 5. Codiaceae. 6. Valoniaceae. 7. Chaetosiphonaceae. 8. Phyllosiphonaceae. 9. Vaucheriaceae.

In the present text family Vaucheriaceae has been treated in division Xanthophycophyta, mainly on the basis of its pigments and absence of starch.

Family-Caulerpaceae (Single genus; 60 species)

Characteristic features. 1. They possess one-celled thallus with a rhizome-like portion which bears root-like structures on its lower face and upright shoot-like appendages on its upper face.

2. The sexual reproduction is isogamous or anisogamous. It takes place by means of biflagellate gametes formed by the division of the protoplast found within the erect shoots.

3. All species are marine and found in warm (tropical) seas.

Genus CAULERPA (*caul*, stem; *erpa*, creep)

Occurrence. This genus has about 60 species. All species are marine and almost all of them found in warm seas. Several species grow at a depth of 75 to 80 metres. Several species are found on the Indian coasts, and can be collected during the winter months. The common Indian species are—*Caulerpa racemosa, C. taxifolia, C. peltata* etc. The Mediterranean *C. prolifera* extends to a depth of 15 metres.

Ecologically the species *of Caulerpa* may be classified as follows—

1. The mud-collecting species which grow as epiphytes upon root of mangrove vegetation.

2. The sand and mud bottom species which grow in shallow or deep water, *e.g., C. crassifolia* and *C. prolifera.*

3. The rock and coral reef species, *e.g., C. racemosa, C. taxifolia.*

Structure. The single-celled thallus of *Caulerpa*, in its size and external structure is comparable to that of a vascular plant with a creeping stolon. The root-like rhizoids and rhizome-like portions are much similar from species to species but there is great variation in form of the erect shoots. The leafy erect shoots of various species resemble to the leafy shoots of cacti, yews, mosses and lycopods.

On the basis of branching system the genus has been divided by Borgesen into three groups. They are as follows.

1. The species growing in much muddy place, possess rhizomes that are vertical or oblique, which enable them to reach the surface even when covered by mud, *e. g., Caulerpa verticillata.*

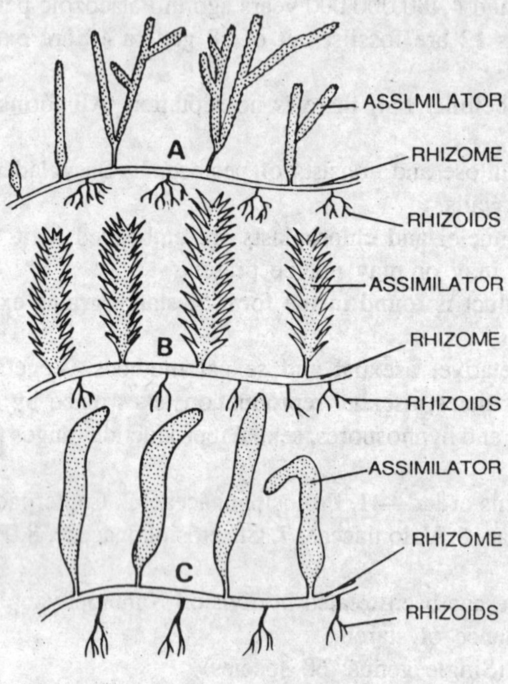

Fig. 3.115. *Caulerpa* thalli. A, *Caulerpa cupressoides;* B, *C. crassifolia;* C, *Caulerpa prolifera.*

2. The rhizome of this type of species first branches at some distance from its point of origin and possesses a pointed apex which helps in boring through sand or mud, *e. g., Caulerpa cupressoides.*

3. In these species the rhizome branches richly immediately from its point of origin. Such species are usually found to be attached to rock and coral reef, *e.g., C. racemosa.*

The form of the thallus in some species is largely dependent upon the conditions of the habitat. The feature is well illustrated by the species *C. cupressoides* and *C. racemosa.*

1. In exposed conditions the plants remain small and stout.

2. In more shelter habitats the shoots become longer and much branched.

3. In deep water the plants become very large and possess richly branched flagellate shoot.

Internal structure. There is no septation. The central vacuole is lined by the cytoplasm with chloroplasts which are devoid of pyrenoids and nuclei being continuous throughout the plant. During night the chloroplasts retreat from the apices of the fronds, the movements due to cytoplasmic currents. In *Caulerpa hypnoides*, however, a small cell is cut off at the tip of each 'leaf'. According to Port (1924), the vacuole contains colloids which coagulate in fixatives. The coenocyte is traversed by numerous cylindrical skeletal strands known as **trabeculae.** The trabeculae are arranged perpendicularly to the surface and most highly developed within the rhizomes. The trabeculae arise from rows of structure known as microsomes. They are at first either free in the interior of the coenocyte or connected with the wall elsewhere. In the adult stage they are always fused to the walls. In the

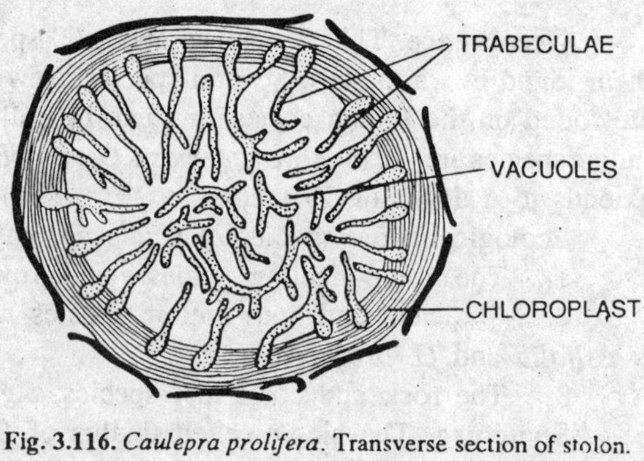

Fig. 3.116. *Caulepra prolifera.* Transverse section of stolon.

flat assimilators the trabeculae run irregularly from surface to surface. The trabeculae are absent or poorly developed in the rhizoids.

The function of the trabeculae is extremely problemetical and may be as follows-

1. They are supposed to be mechanical, and in this case they would provide resistance to high turgor pressures.
2. They are supposed to enlarge protoplasmic surface.
3. They are supposed to be concerned with diffusion, becuase movement of mineral salts is more rapid through the trabeculae than through the cytoplasm.
4. They have no function.

In addition to the trabeculae there are also internal peg-like projections.

Reproduction. The reproduction takes place by asexual (vegetative) and sexual methods. They are as follows.

Asexual or vegetative reproduction. For a long period of time only vegetative reproduction was established for this genus. It takes place by a gradual dying away of the older parts of the rhizomes where ultimately the branches become individual plants. Dispersal is attained by detached fragments which rapidly heal any exposed surface and regenerate new plants when lodged in a suitable position.

Sexual reproduction. In 1928 Dostal reported the discovery of elongated papillae on the assimilators and more rarely on the rhizomes of *Caulerpa prolifera*. He interpreted those structures as possible gametangia. Later on he showed that the swarmers are formed within the assimilators and the papillae only serve for their liberation.

Just before the formation of the papillae the fertile assimilators become variegated in

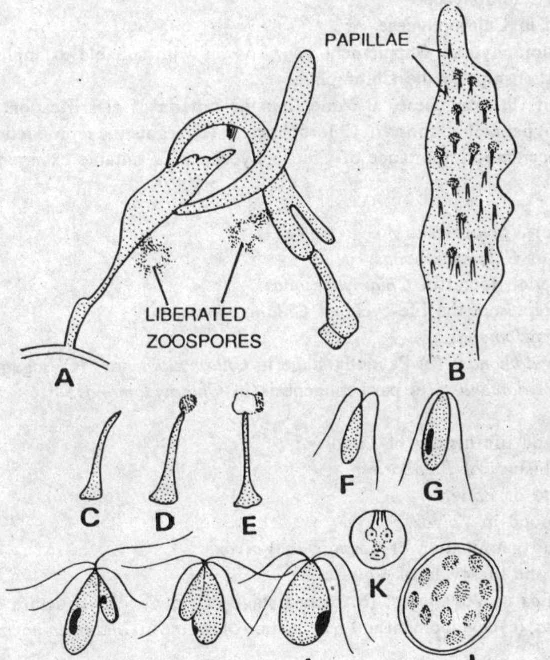

Fig. 3.117. *Caulerpa prolifera*, A, liberation of gametes; B, blade with exit papllae; C-E, development of exit papillae; F, male gamete; G, femalegamete; A-J, stages in union of gametes; K, zygote after losing its flagella; L, two months after germination of zygote.

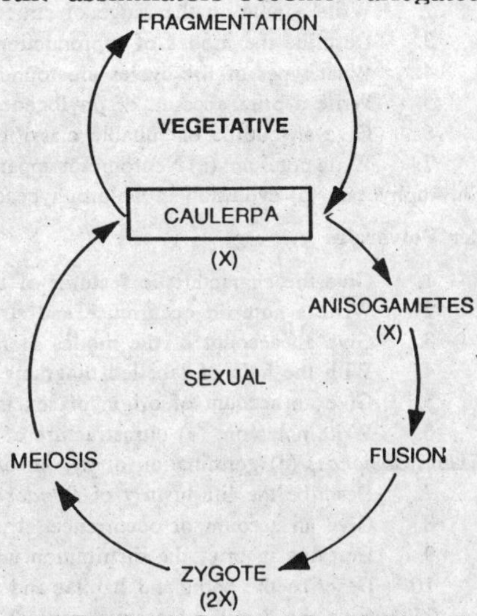

Fig. 3.118. *Caulerpa*. Graphic life-cycle.

appearance, because of massing of the green contents at certain points, while others become yellow in colour. This paling effect is also found in the rhizomes because of the withdrawal of some of their contents. In the green regions the cytoplasm shows a reticulate arrangement and it is here that the uninucleate swarmers are formed. The swarmers liberate rapidly through the apices of the papillae in a mass of mucilaginous matter. The biflagellate gametes escape through the **extrusion papillae** shortly after day-break, sometimes in such a huge quantity that small green clouds appear in the water surrounding the fertile portion of a thallus.

Just before the formation of gametes there is a meiotic division of nuclei in the formation of gametes, therefore, are the only haploid or gametophytic structures in the life-cycle. The thallus is diploid.

All species in which sexual reproduction has been observed so far are heterothallic but one species has been found (Iyenger, 1940) to be homothallic.

The sexual reproduction is anisogamous. The female gamete is slightly longer than the male gamete, but considerably broader. Both male and female gametes are biflagellate, pear-shaped with a single chloroplast and a distinct eyespot. After the liberation of the gametes, fertile parts of the thallus disintegrate and die out. The zygote soon retracts its flagella, secretes a wall around it and becomes spherical. During germination the spherical zygote enlarges and the number of chloroplasts increases to thirty or more (Miyake and Kunieda, 1937). The further development is not followed clearly.

Systematic position. Division-Chlorophycophyta; Class-Chlorophyceae; Order-Siphonales; Family-Caulerpaceae; Genus-*Caulerpa*.

Revision Questions

Class-Chlorophyceae

1. Give the occurrence and distribution of green algae.
2. Write a note on the range of structure in Chlorophyceae.
3. Describe the modes of reproduction found in Chlorophyceae.
4. What types of life-cycles are found in Chlorophyceae. Supplement your answer with suitable examples.
5. Write a brief account of phylogenetic relationships in the Chlorophyceae.
6. Give an outline of suitable classification of Chlorophyceae, also mention the criteria of classification.
7. Write notes on: (a) Neuromotor apparatus; (b) palmelloid forms in Chlorophyceae; (c) vegetative reproduction in Chlorophyceae; (d) evolution in Chlorophyceae; (e) economic importance of Chlorophyceae with suitable examples.

Order-Volvocales

1. Give the characteristic features of the order Volvocales.
2. Write a note on occurrence and structure of *Chlamydomonas*.
3. Give an account of the modes of reproduction found in *Chlamydomonas*.
4. With the help of labelled diagrams only, represent the life-cycle of *Chlamydomonas*.
5. Give an account of origin of sex in *Chlamydomonas*.
6. Write notes on: (a) ultrastructure of *Chlamydomonas;* (b) Palmella stage in *Chlamydomonas;* (c) oogamy in *Chlamydomonas;* (d) germination of zygote of *Chlamydomonas;* (e) parthenogenesis in *Chlamydomonas*.
7. Describe the life-histroy of *Pandorina*.
8. Give an account of occurrence, structure and life history of *Eudorina*.
9. Describe in brief the distribution and life-history of *Pleodorina*.
10. Describe the habit and habitat and structure of *Volvox*.
11. Give the details of asexual reproduction found in *Volvox*.
12. Give an account of sexual reproduction and germination of oospore in *Volvox*.
13. With the help of diagrams only, represent the life-cycle of *Volvox*.
14. Write notes on: (a) phylogenetic relationships in Volvocales; (b) plakea stage of *Volvox;* (c) structure of a mature colony of *Pleodorina;* (d) palmella stage in *Eudorina;* (e) development and germination of zygote in *Chlamydomonas*.

Order-Chlorococcales

1. Give the characteristic features of the order Chlorococcales.
2. Write an account of occurrence and structure of *Chlorococcum*.
3. Describe the modes of reproduction found in *Chlorococcum*.
4. Write a detailed note on systematic relationships in Chlorococcales.
5. Write an account of occurrence and structure of *Pediastrum*.

6. Give a comprehensive account of reproduction and life history of *Pediastrum.*
7. Write a detailed note on occurrence and structure of *Hydrodictyon.*
8. Give an account of the modes of reproduction in *Hydrodictyon*
9. Describe the life-history of *Hydrodictyon.*
10. Give an account of habit and habitat and structure of *Chlorella.*
11. Write notes on: (a) economic importance of *Chlorella*: (b) germination of zygote in *Hydrodictyon;* (c) water-net; (d) reproduction in *Chlorella.*

Order-Ulotrichales.

1. Give the characteristic features of order Ulotrichales.
2. Write an account of occurrence and structure of *Ulothrix.*
3. Describe the modes of reproduction found in *Ulothrix.*
4. With the help of diagrams only, represent the life-cycle of *Ulothrix.*
5. Where does the *Ulva* occur ? Also give the structure of the thallus of *Ulva.*
6. Give an account of the modes of reproduction in *Ulva.*
7. Write notes on: (a) sea lettuce; (b) alternation of generations in *Ulva; (c)* Palmella stage in *Ulothrix;* (d) structure of a cell in *Ulothrix* and *Ulva.*
8. Write an account of occurrence and structure of *Enteromorpha.*
9. Give an account of the modes of reproduction in *Enteromorpha.*
10. Write notes on: (a) growth of thallus in *Enteromorpha;* (b) alternation of generations in *Enteromorpha.*

Order-Cladophorales

1. Give the characteristic features of order Cladophorales.
2. Write an account of occurrence and structure of *Cladophora.*
3. Give an account of the modes of reproduction in *Cladophora.*
4. Write notes on: (a) evection in *Cladohora;* (b) structure of cell in *Cladophora;* (c) cell division in *Cladophora;* (d) vegetative reproduction in *Cladophora*; (e) alternation of generations in *Cladophora.*
5. Write a comprehensive note on occurrence, structure and reproduction of *Pithophora.*

Order Chaetophorales

1. Give the characteristic features of the order Chaetophorales.
2. Write an account of occurrence, structure and reproduction in *Chaetophora.*
3. Write a note on occurrence and structure of the thallus of *Draparnaldiopsis.*
4. Give an account of the modes of reproduction in *Draparnaldiopsis.*
5. With the help of diagrams only, represent the life-cycle of *Draparnaldiopsis.*
6. Give a comprehensive account of occurrence and structure of thallus of *Stigeoclonium.*
7. Write an account of the modes of reproduction in *Stigeoclonium.*
8. Write an account of the occurrence and structure of thallus of *Trentepohlia.*
9. Describe the modes of reproduction found in *Trentepohlia.*
10. Give an account of the occurrence and structure of thallus ot *Coleochaete.*
11. Describe the methods of reproduction in *Coleochaete.*
12. Write notes on: (a) *Cephaleuros;* (b) *Protococcus;* (c) zoospores in *Draparnaldiopsis;* (d) phiyogenetic relationships in Chaetophorales.

Order-Oedogoniales

1. Give the characteristic features of the order Oedogoniales.
2. Write an account of occurrence and structure of thallus of *Oedogonium.*
3. Describe the cell division in *Oedogonium.*
4. Give a comprehensive account of the modes of reproduction in *Oedogonium.*
5. Give a detailed account of sexual reproduction in *Oedogonium.*
6. Write notes on: (a) *Bulbochaete;* (b) structure of a cell of *Oedogonium;* (c) macrandrous and nannandrous types of sexual reproduction in *Oedogonium;* (d) structure and development of oogonium in *Oedogonium.*
7. With the help of diagrams only, represent the life-cycle of *Oedogonium.*

Order-Zygnematales

1. Give the characteristic features of the Order Zygnematales, in brief. Where these algae are found in nature? Name at least three important genera of this order.
2. Why *Spirogyra* is known as pond silk. Mention the structural characters of this alga.
3. Give a comprehensive account of the methods of reproduction found in *Spirogyra.* What type of life-cycle is found in this genus ?

4. How would you differentiate *Zygnema* from *Spirogyra* ? Mention vegetative characters only.
5. Give the characteristic features of *Mougeotia.*
6. Give an account of the methods of reproduction found in *Mougeotia.*
7. What are desmids and where they are found ?
8. Give the important stages of the life-history of *Closterium* or *Cosmarium.*
9. Write short notes on: (a) germination of zygospore in *Spirogyra;* (b) genic action of cytoplasm in Conjugales (Zygnematales); (c) cell structure of *Zygnema;* (d) chloroplast of *Mougeotia*; (e) structure of plant body of desmids.

Order-Siphonales

1. Give characteristic features of the Order Siphonales.
2. Where do the species of *Caulerpa* occur ? Classify them ecologically.
3. Describe the structure and life-history of *Caulerpa.*
4. Give a comprehensive account of the methods of reproduction in *Caulerpa.*
5. Give the structure of thallus (external and internal) of *Caulerpa.*

Multiple Choice Type

1. Unicellular motile alga is:
   (i) *Pandorina,* (ii) *Eudorima,* (iii) *Volvox,* (iv) *Chlamydomonas.*
2. The multicellular filamentous alga is:
   (i) *Ulothrix,* (ii) *Vaucheria,* (iii) *Tetraspora,* (iv) *Pandorina.*
3. The star-shaped chloroplast is found in:
   (i) *Zygnema,* (ii) *Spirogyra,* (iii) *Ulothrix,* (iv) *Cladophora.*
4. The cup-shaped chloroplast is found in:
   (i) *Prasiola,* (ii) *Chlamydomonas,* (iii) *Spirogyra,* (iv) *Ulothrix.*
5. The girdle-shaped chloroplast is found in:
   (i) *Ulothrix,* (ii) *Spirogyra,* (iii) *Zygnema,* (iv) *Chlamydomonas.*
6. The rhizoplast is:
   (i) rhizoid, (ii) rhizomorph, (iii) fibre connecting blepharoplast with centrosome, (iv) fibre connecting two blepharoplasts.
7. The paradesmose is:
   (i) rhizoid, (ii) rhizomorph, (iii) fibre connecting blepharoplasts with centrosome, (iv) fibre connecting two blepharoplasts.
8. Pigment cup is found in
   (i) eye spot, (ii) pyrenoid, (iii) nucleus, (iv) nucleolus.
9. The sea lettuce is
   (i) *Enteromorpha,* (ii) *Ulva,* (iii) *Spirogyra,* (iv) *Sargassum.*
10. The Conjuagles are;
    (i) exclusively fresh water, (ii) exclusively marine, (iii) 50 per cent fresh water, (iv) 90 per cent fresh water.
11. The cause of red snow is:
    (i) *Volvox globator,* (ii) *Ulothrix zonata,* (iii) *Chlamydomonas nivalis,* (iv) none of above.
12. The life-cycle of *Ulothrix* is:
    (i) haplontic, (ii) diplontic, (iii) haplobiontic, (iv) diplobiontic.
13. *Volvox* colonies are found in
    (i) fresh water ponds, (ii) salt lakes, (iii) sea water, (iv) water falls.
14. The structure of *Volvox* is:
    (i) Unicellular, (ii) filamentous, (iii) thalloid, (iv) colonial
15. The plakea stage of *Volvox* consists of
    (i) 2 cells, (ii) 4 cells, (iii) 8 cells, (iv) 16 cells.
16. *Volvox* is a member of the group:
    (i) Rhodophyceae, (ii) Phaeophyceae, (iii) Chlorophyceae, (iv) Myxophyceae.
17. The gonidia of *Volvox* are concerned with:
    (i) sexual reproduction, (ii) asexual reproduction, (iii) vegetative reproduction, (iv) none of above.
18. The sexual reproduction in *Volvox* is:
    (i) isogamous, (ii) anisogamous, (iii) oogamous, (iv) none of above.
19. The alga may be used in space ship as food:
    (i) *Chlorella,* (ii) *Chlorococcum,* (iii) *Chlamydomonas,* (iv) *Haematococcus*
20. The attached form of alga is:
    (i) *Spirogyra,* (ii) *Zygnema,* (iii) *Ulothrix,* (iv) *Mougeotia.*

21. The alga found on mollusc shells is
    (i) *Ulothrix*, (ii) *Chara*, (iii) *Zygnema*, (iv) *Cladophora*.
22. The branched alga is:
    (i) *Ulothrix*, (ii) *Cladophora*, (iii) *Spirogyra*, (iv) *Zygnema*
23. The terminal and intercalary akinetes are found in:
    (i) *Cladophora*, (ii) *Oedogonium*, (iii) *Ulothrix*, (iv) *Pithophora*.
24. The process of 'evection' is found in:
    (i) *Cladophora*, (ii) *Oedogonium*, (iii) Vaucheria, (iv) *Spirogyra*.
25. Sort out the parasitic alga:
    (i) *Cladophora*, (ii) *Pithophora*, (iii) *Cephaleuros*, (iv) *Coleochaete*.
26. *Bulbochaete* is member of:
    (i) Zygnematales, (ii) Oedogoniales, (iii) Cladophorales, (iv) Chaetophorales.
27. Point out the members of order Oedogoniales:
    (i) *Oedogonium*, (ii) *Oedocladium*, (iii) *Bulbochaete*, (iv) all the above.
28. The cap cells are found in:
    (i) *Spirogyra*, (ii) *Vaucheria*, (iii) *Chara*, (iv) *Oedogonium*.
29. The 'pond silk' is:
    (i) *Spirogyra*, (ii) *Vaucheria*, (iii) *Chara*, (iv) *Oedogonium*
30. The 'water net' is:
    (i) *Pediastrum*, (ii) *Hydrodictyon*, (iii) *Cladophora*, (iv) *Pithophora*.
31. Stephanokontean type of zoospores are found in:
    (i) *Vaucheria*, (ii) *Oedogonium*, (iii) *Chara*, (iv) *Ectocarpus*.
32. The nannandria produce:
    (i) oogonia, (ii) akinetes, (iii) zoospores, (iv) antheridia.
33. *Oedogonium* belongs to:
    (i) Chlorophyceae, (ii) Myxophyceae, (iii) Phaeophyceae, (iv) Rhodophyceae.
34. Chloroplast of *Oedogonium* is:
    (i) star-shaped, (ii) spiral, (iii) reticulate, (iv) cup-shaped.
35. The stellate chloroplasts are found in:
    (i) *Spirogyra*, (ii) *Cladophora*, (iii) *Zygnema*, (iv) *Pithophora*.
36. The semicells of the desmids remain joined together by:
    (i) raphe, (ii) sinus, (iii) isthmus, (iv) plasmodesma.
37. The desmids are:
    (i) Chlorophyceae, (ii) Phaeophyceae, (iii) Rhodophyceae, (iv) Myxophyceae.
38. The species of *Caulerpa* are :
    (i) fresh water, (ii) marine, (iii) terrestrial, (iv) 50 per cent fresh water.

Answers

1 (iv), 2 (i), 3 (i), 4 (ii), 5 (i), 6 (iii), 7 (iv). 8 (i), 9 (ii), 10 (i), 11 (iii), 12 (i), 13 (i), 14 (iv), 15 (iii), 16 (iii), 17 (i), 18 (iii), 19 (i), 20 (iii), 21 (iv), 22 (ii), 23 (iv), 24 (i), 25 (iii), 26 (ii), 27 (iv), 28 (iv), 29 (i), 30 (ii), 31 (ii), 32 (iv), 33 (i), 34 (iii), 35 (iii), 36 (iii), 37 (i) 38 (ii).

4

Charophyta–Charophyceae Stoneworts

Characteristic features.

Pigmentation. Chlorophylls *a* and *b*, β-carotene, γ-carotene, lycopene

Storage products. Starch.

Flagellation. 2, subapical equal flagella (on sperm).

ORDER–CHARALES

There are 6 genera and 250 species which are living, rest are fossils. The living members of this order are known as **'stoneworts'**.

Characteristic features

1. The stoneworts usually occur in still and clear waters in attached condition to the mud of the bottom of the pools. They are found in less oxygenated water and best survive in clear and hard waters. Calcium carbonate is deposited on the plant body and the surface of the plant becomes rough.

2. The thallus is attached to the mud by a rhizoidal system. The plant body is erect and possesses nodes and internodes. Secondary laterals, also called **'leaves'** arise from the nodes which are of limited growth. The leaves may or may not be differentiated into nodes and internodes.

3. The reproduction takes place by vegetative and sexual methods. Asexual reproduction is altogether absent. Vegetative reproduction takes place by means of special vegetative bodies such as amylum stars, bulbils, secondary protonema etc. Sexual reproduction is oogamous and takes place by oogonia (nucule) and antheridia (globule).

4. The zygote nucleus divides reductionally producing 4 haploid nuclei. Out of these 4 haploid nuclei one is functional and rest degenerate. The functional nucleus divides into two cells, the lower cell is rhizoidal and the upper one gives rise to main thallus.

Classification. According to Dr. F. E. Fritsch, this is last order of Chlorophyceae. There is a single family Characeae. G. M. Smith has divided his division Chlorophyta in two classes, *i.e.*, 1. Chlorophyceae and 2. Charophyceae. He includes his single order Charales and family Characeae along with other three families in class Charophyceae. He has included all the living genera in the family Characeae. There are about six genera and 250 species in this family.

There are also Characeae known only as fossils. The remaining three families are all fossil. According to Peck (1946) the Charales are known from as far back as the Devonian. The Characeae are known from as far back as the Upper Carboniferous. Another family the Trochiliscaceae, is known only from the Lower Carboniferous and from the Devonian.

Family–Characeae (6 genera; 250 living species)

Characteristic features. They possess an erect branched thallus with regular nodes and internodes. Each node bears a whorl of branches of limited growth, also known as 'leaves'. The branches of unlimited growth may also arise from the axils of the leaves.

2. Many members are calcified.

3. Vegetative reproduction takes place by means of amylum stars, bulbils and protonema-like outgrowths.

4. Sexual reproduction is oogamous. The oogonia are one-celled and surrounded by a sheath of sterile cells. They are borne upon the 'leaves'. The antheridia are one celled and remain united in uniseriate branched filaments. They are surrounded by a common spherical envelope composed of eight cells. These are always borne on the 'leaves'.

5. They are known as stoneworts. They grow submerged in fresh water upon muddy or sandy bottoms of pools and ponds. Few species are found in brackish water.

Genus–CHARA

There are about 90 species in this genus.

Occurrence. The species of *Chara* grow submerged attached to the muddy bottom of the pools and ponds of clear water. They prefer less oxygenated and hard water. The species of *Chara* are not found in the waters where mosquito larvae are present. They form sub-aquatic meadows extending to miles.

The plants of *Chara* are of great ecological value. As they are covered with calcium carbonate deposits, they deposit lot of calcium in the bottom of lake etc., and after a considerable time the whole lake or pond is filled up with calcareous deposits.

Vegetative structure. The plant is always found attached to the substratum by a well developed rhizoidal system. The rhizoids are uniseriately branched and obliquely septate. The rhizoids may or may not be differentiated into nodes and internodes.

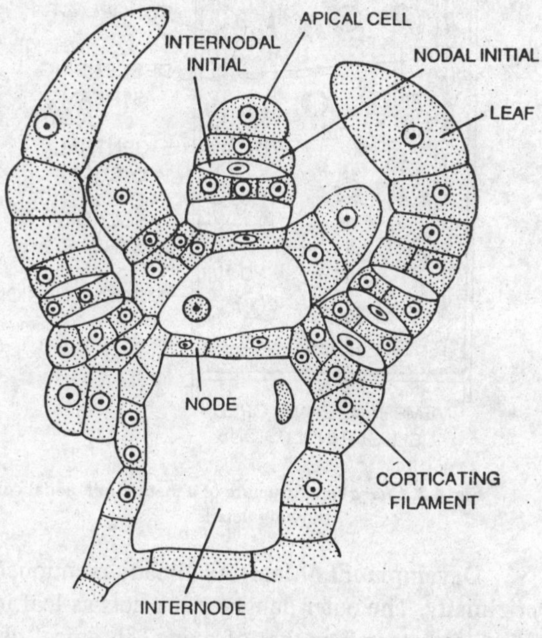

Fig. 4.1. *Chara*. Vertical section of thallus apex.

The axis has nodes and internodes. Several branches of limited growth also known as leaves grow in whorls from the nodes of the axis. These leaves do not grow further after attaining a definite length. The leaves may or may not be differentiated into nodes and internodes. They may be branched or simple. The internodal cell is sufficiently long and ensheathed by a cortex of vertically elongated cells. The cortex is one celled in thickness and consists of the cells of lesser diameter.

Apical growth. The apical growth of the axis takes place by the terminal dome-shaped cell which cuts other derivatives at its posterior face. The derivative of the apical cell divides by a transverse wall producing two daughter cells. The upper daughter cell is the **nodal initial** and the lower one the **internodal initial.** The lower cell (internodal initial) does not divide further and elongates several times of its original length to give rise to an internode. The upper cell (nodal initial) divides by a vertical wall producing two daughter cells. These daughter cells again divide vertically in such a way that two cells remain in the centre called central cells usually surrounded by 6 to 20 peripheral cells. The central cells may or may not divide further.

The peripheral cells divide periclinally. In such a way each peripheral cell divides into two cells. The outer one acts as leaf initial and the inner as nodal which may or may not divide further, if divides the division is vertical.

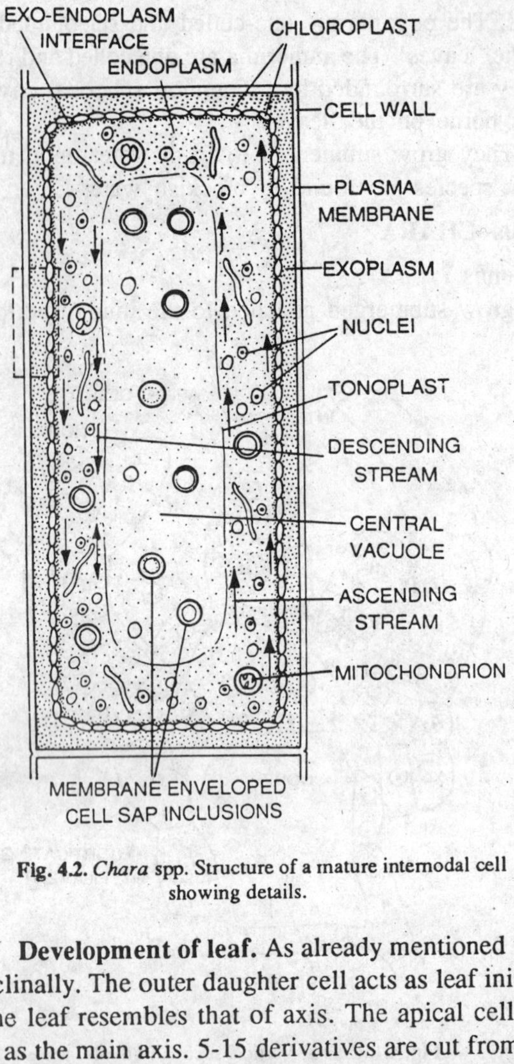

Fig. 4.2. *Chara* spp. Structure of a mature internodal cell showing details.

Development of cortex. The peripheral cells of the nodal regions of the leaves never become apical cells but they may produce one-celled branch known as **stipules,** but this is not necessary for basal node of each leaf. On adaxial side, the upper and lower cells of the basal node protrude. After protrusion a transverse septum is formed at the base of these cells, thus initiating the cortical initials of corticating filaments. This way one of the cortical initials develops towards upper side and the other towards lower side. These cortical initials act as apical cells and give rise to ascending and descending cortical filaments respectively ensheathing the main axis. In young corticating filaments both the nodal and internodal cells are approximately of equal size, but later on the internodal cell and the two peripheral nodal cells elongate sufficiently. The central cell of the nodal region does not elongate. Sometimes one-celled spines develop from this central cell. (See Figs. 4.3 and 4.6).

Development of leaf. As already mentioned the peripheral cells of the nodal region divide periclinally. The outer daughter cell acts as leaf initial and a leaf develops from it. The structure of the leaf resembles that of axis. The apical cell of the leaf cuts the derivatives in the same way as the main axis. 5-15 derivatives are cut from the apical cell. The first derivative becomes the leaf's basal cell. Rest of derivatives divide and give rise to an internodal and nodal initial. The internodal initial gives rise to a comparatively shorter internode than that of axis. The peripheral cells of the nodal region of the leaf do not give rise to the leaves as in the case of axis. Here the peripheral cell gives rise to a single celled structure called the **'stipule'**. The cortex initials found on the leaf give rise to corticating filaments in the same way as on the axis.

Origin of rhizoids. The rhizoids arise from the buried parts of the nodes. The peripheral cells of buried nodes give rise to rhizoids. The rhizoids possess oblique septa. Sometimes the upper and lower parts of the rhizoid at the septum protrude upward and downward in prolonged cells. Each of such prolonged cells may divide further and give rise to secondary rhizoids.

Structure of the cell-nodal cell. There is no large central vacuole. The dense cytoplasm is filled up in the cell. There are numerous discoid chloroplasts, devoid of pyrenoids. There

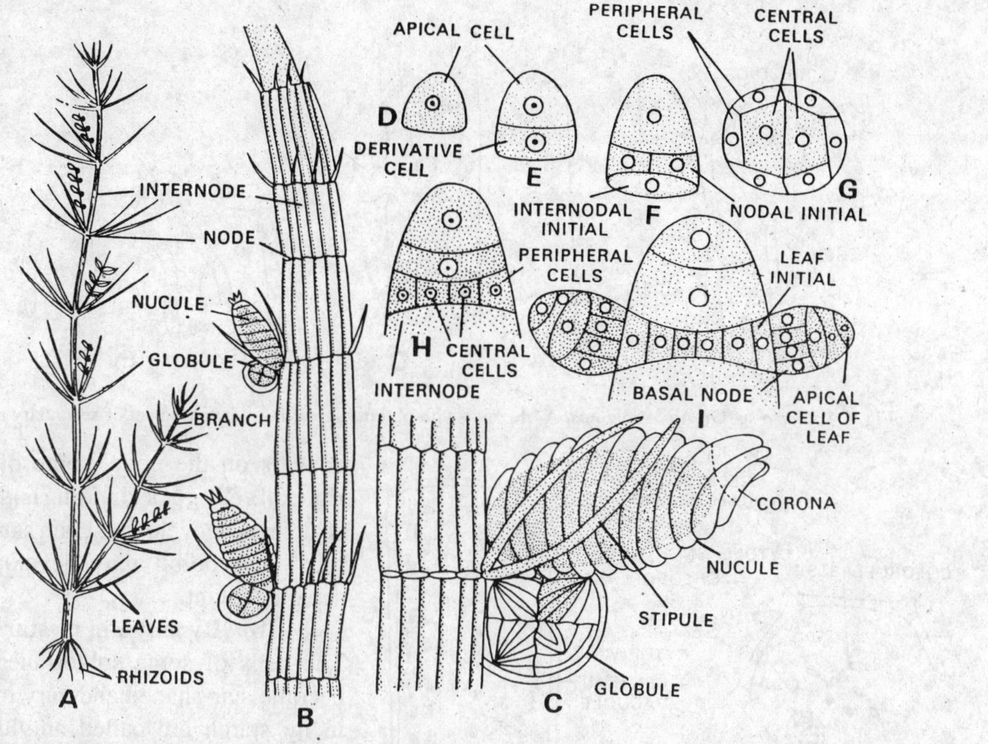

Fig. 4.2. (a). *Chara* sp. A, thallus with rhizoids; B, portion of a leaf bearing mature nucule and globule and stipules; C, nucule and globule magnified; D-I, successive stages of apical growth.

is a single nucleus with many nucleoli. There is well defined chromatin within the nucleus.

Internodal cell. There is a large central vacuole. The cytoplasm is limited to peripheral layer. The cytoplasm is not stationary but always in perpetual rotary motion. The protein bodies are dispersed in the cell sap. The discoid chloroplasts having no pyrenoids are embedded in the peripheral cytoplasm. There are many nuclei. The nuclei have no centrosomes.

The cell wall. The cell wall consists of homogeneous cellulose. It is not multilayered. Outer to the cellulose wall there is a gelatinous layer, and this is the sheath for the deposition of calcium.

Reproduction. The reproduction takes place by vegetative and sexual methods. Asexual reproduction is not found.

1. Vegetative reproduction. The vegetative reproduction takes place by (a) tubers; (b) amylum stars and (c) secondary protonema.

(a) By tubers and bulbils. The tubers are commonly formed on rhizoids or sometimes even on buried nodes. The whole structure is full of starch.

Sometimes the globule divides and becomes multicellular and known as **'simple tuber'**. When the tuber

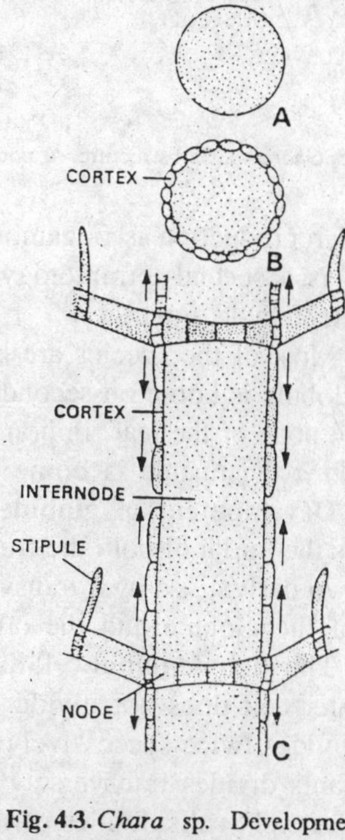

Fig. 4.3. *Chara* sp. Development of cortex and leaf-A, T. S. of *Chara* stem without cortex; B. T. S. of corticated filament; C, L.S. of corticated filament showing development of cortex.

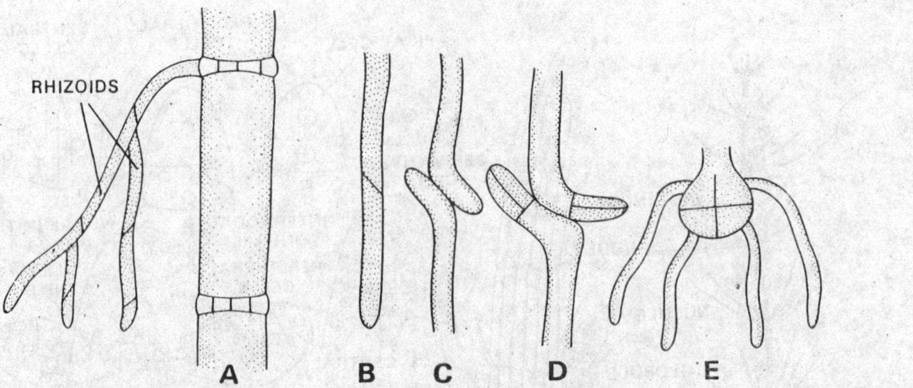

Fig. 4.4. *Chara* sp. Origin of rhizoids. A, rhizoids with oblique septa; B-E, development of secondary rhizoids.

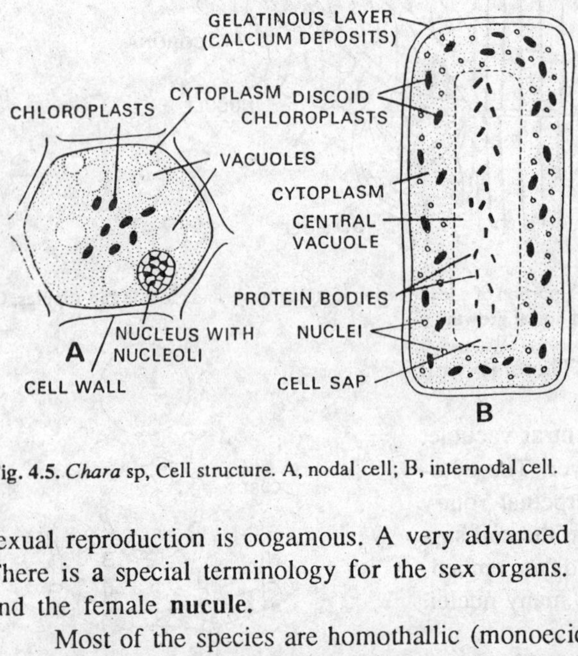

Fig. 4.5. *Chara* sp, Cell structure. A, nodal cell; B, internodal cell.

appears on the node, some of the peripheral cells go on dividing and massive structure is developed. Each starch filled tuber and bulbil may develop into a separate plant.

(b) By amylum or starch stars. The cells of some subterranean nodes become star-shaped and very much laid in by starch are called amylum stars. Each such structure develops into a new plant.

(c) By secondary protonema. The protonema like outgrowths come out from a node. Each such outgrowth is capable to develop into a new plant.

2. Sexual reproduction. The sexual reproduction is oogamous. A very advanced and specialized type of oogamy is found. There is a special terminology for the sex organs. The male fruiting body is called **globule** and the female **nucule.**

Most of the species are homothallic (monoecious) and few are heterothallic (dioecious). The globule is borne on secondary lateral of limited growth. One globule and one nucule borne on one node of the leaf. In homothallic species both the fructifications borne on the same node. In *Chara* the nucule is borne above the globule.

Development of globule. A single superficial nodal cell of the adaxial side of the leaf acts as the initial of both the fructifications, *i.e.*, nucule and globule. This superficial cell divides into two derivatives by a transverse wall. One cell derivative of the superficial cell is the initial cell of the globule and the other is the initial cell of the nucule.

The globule initial cell divides transversely and two daughter cells are formed. The lower daughter cell does not divide further and converts into the pedicel cell. The upper daughter cell divides twice successively and four cells are formed arranged in quadrants. Each of these quadrants divides transversely and eight cells are produced thus attaining octant stage. Each of these eight cells divides periclinally and thus produced eight outer cells which divide further periclinally. The outermost eight cells are called **shield cells.** The middle cells are known as

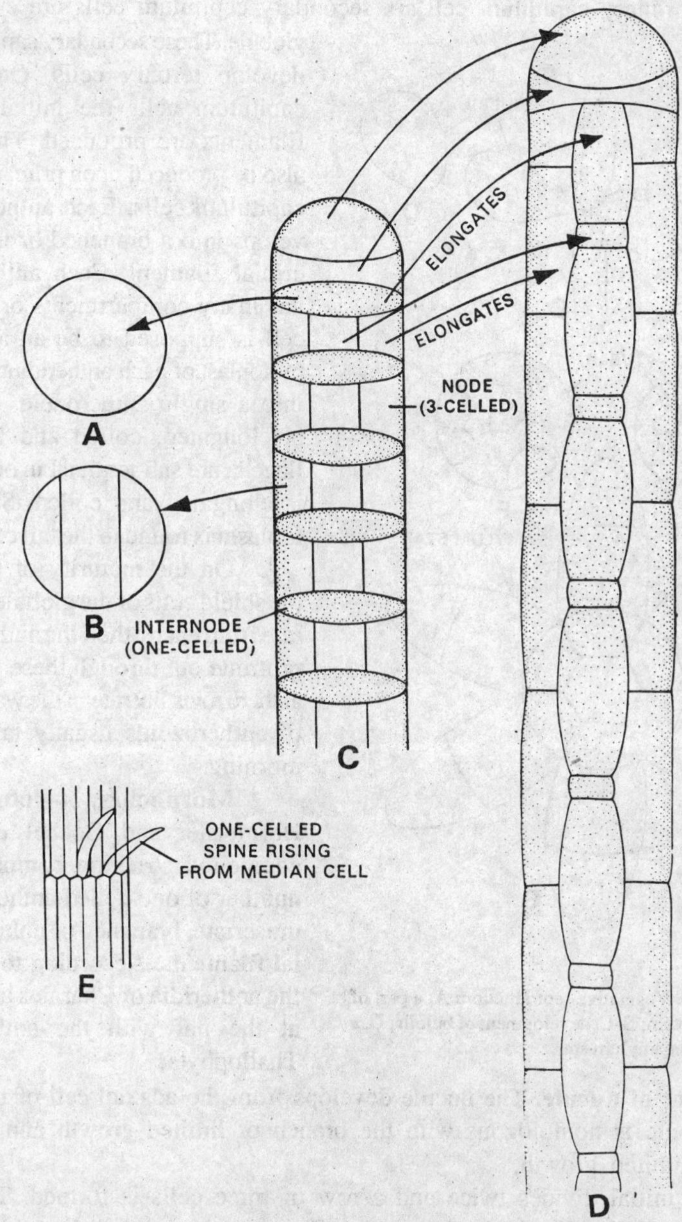

Fig. 4.6. *Chara* sp. A, T.S. of internodal region of young corticating filaments; B, T. S. of nodal region of young corticating filament; C, young corticating filament; D, mature corticating filament; E, one celled spines rising from median cell.

manubrial cells and the innermost eight cells are **primary capitulum cells.** The shield cells become very much enlarged and expanded. The manubrial cells become very much radially elongated, but the primary capitulum cells are arranged compactly to each other in the centre of the globule. The outer walls of the shield cells fold inward and the shield cells appear multicellular structures. The infoldings are incomplete. The shield cells develop red pigments in them and so the globules appear orange red in colour.

From each primary capitulum cell six secondary capitulum cells are cut off inside the globule. These secondary capitulum cells rarely develop tertiary cells. On the secondary capitulum cells the initials of antheridial filaments are produced. These initials may also be produced upon primary or even tertiary capitulum cells. Each antheridial initial develops into a branched or unbranched antheridial filament. Each antheridial filament has many compartments or cells in it. Each cell is supposed to be an antheridium. The protoplast of each antheridium metamorphoses into a single antherozoid. The antherozoid is elongated, coiled and biflagellate. The flagella are sub-terminal in origin. The nucleus is elongated and coiled. Some unused cytoplasm is found in the tail of the antherozoid.

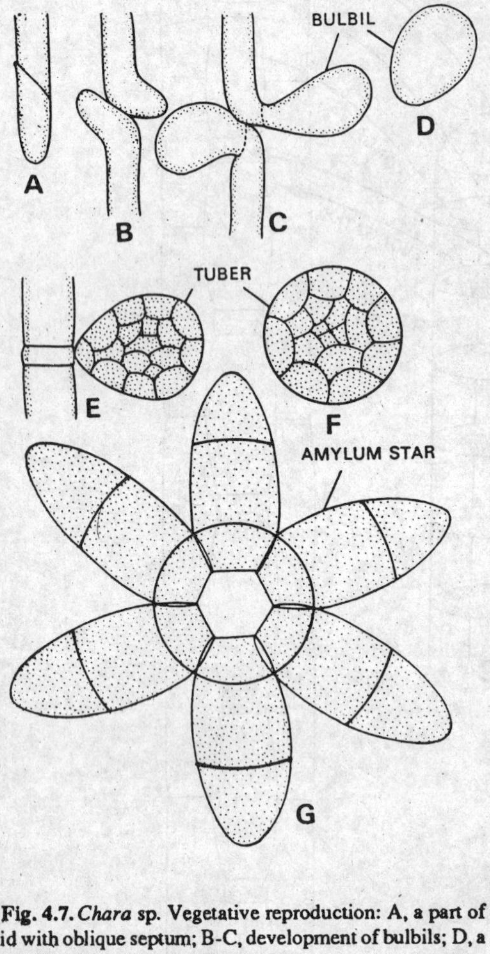

Fig. 4.7. *Chara* sp. Vegetative reproduction: A, a part of rhizoid with oblique septum; B-C, development of bulbils; D, a bulbil; E-F, tubers; G, an amylum star.

On the maturity of the antherozoids the shield cells of the globule somewhat separate from each other, the antheridial filaments protrude out through these openings and the antherozoids liberate in the water. The liberation of antherozoids usually takes place in the morning.

Morphology of globule. According to Hofmeister and Goebel the globule is a compound structure comprising of a large number of one-celled antheridia arranged in uniseriate, branched or unbranched antheridial filaments. According to these biologists, the antheridia of Charales are one-celled and at the par with the antheridia of other Thallophyta.

Development of nucule. The nucule develops from the adaxial cell of basal node of the globule. The globule is homologous with the branch of limited growth and the nucule with the branch of unlimited growth.

The nucule initial divides twice and a row of three cells is formed. The terminal cell acts as oogonial mother cell which elongates sufficiently in vertical direction and transverse wall develops in the lower region of it dividing it into two cells. The lower small cell and the upper one is oogonium which contains an egg. The lowermost cell of the row of three cells does not divide and acts as a pedicel. The middle cell divides vertically in such a way so that a single central cell and five sheath initials are produced. The sheath initials surround the central cell. The sheath initials elongate vertically sometimes even before the vertical elongation of the oogonial mother cell and encircle it. Each of the sheath initials divides transversely forming the upper tier of coronary cells and lower tier of tube cells. The tube cells elongate several times to their original length and become spirally coiled around the oogonium. The coronary

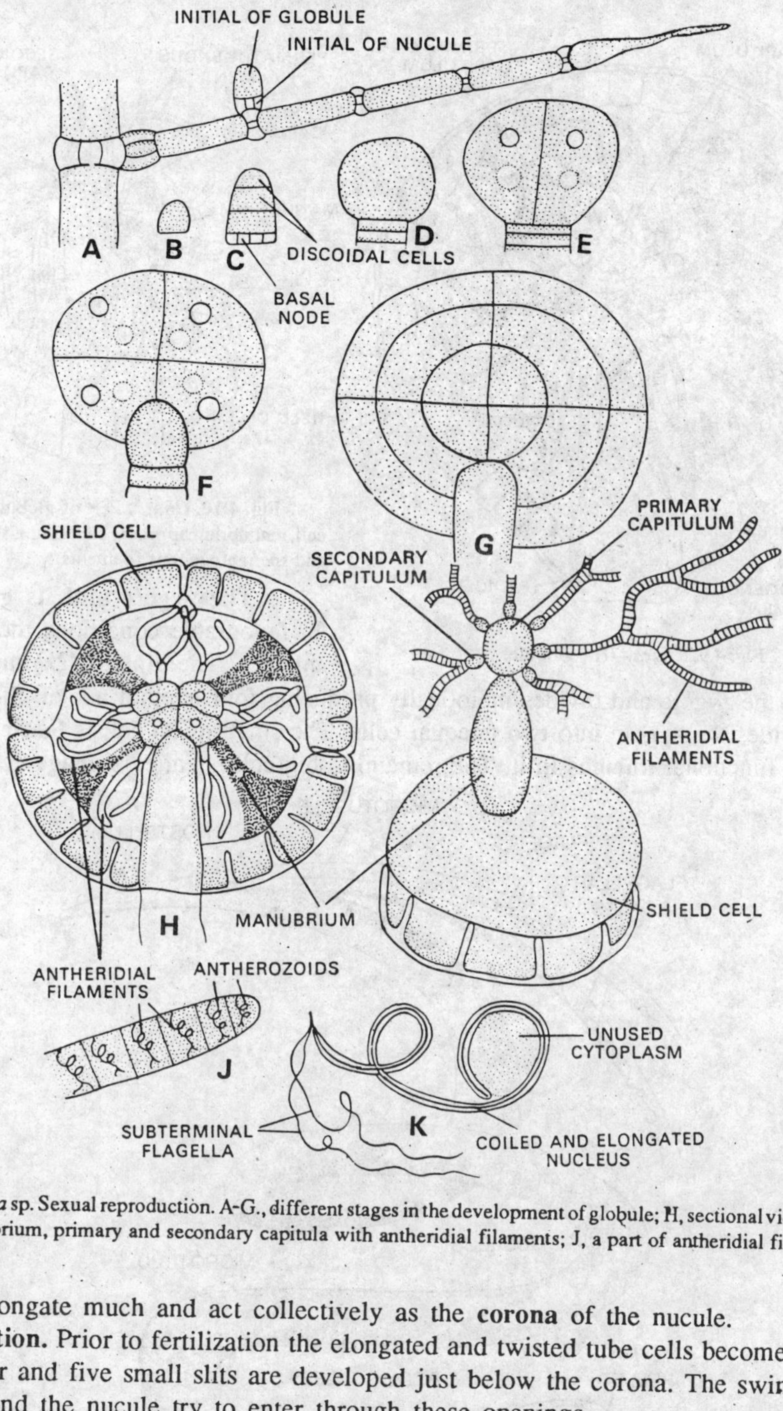

Fig. 4.8. *Chara* sp. Sexual reproduction. A-G., different stages in the development of globule; H, sectional view of globule; I, shield cell manubrium, primary and secondary capitula with antheridial filaments; J, a part of antheridial filament; K, an antherozoid.

cells do not elongate much and act collectively as the **corona** of the nucule.

Fertilization. Prior to fertilization the elongated and twisted tube cells become separated from each other and five small slits are developed just below the corona. The swimming antherozoids around the nucule try to enter through these openings.

The flagella are withdrawn and one of the antherozoids penetrates the egg. The male nucleus travels downwards and fuses with the egg nucleus developing a diploid (2x) nucleus. This diploid nucleus situates in the bottom of the zygote. The zygote settles down in the mud, secretes a thick wall and germinates on the approach of favourable conditions.

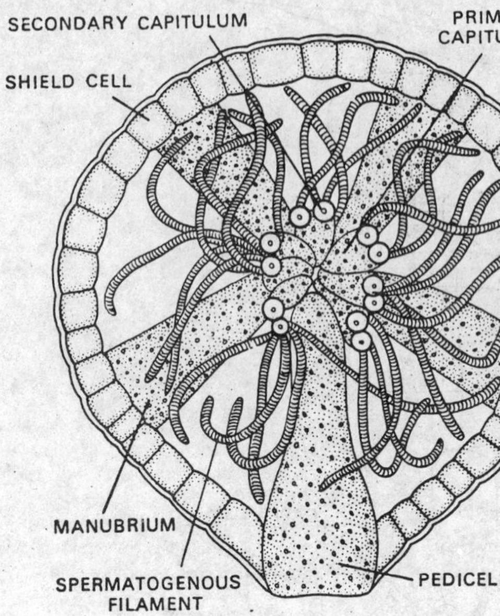

Fig. 4.9. *Chara*—The globule.

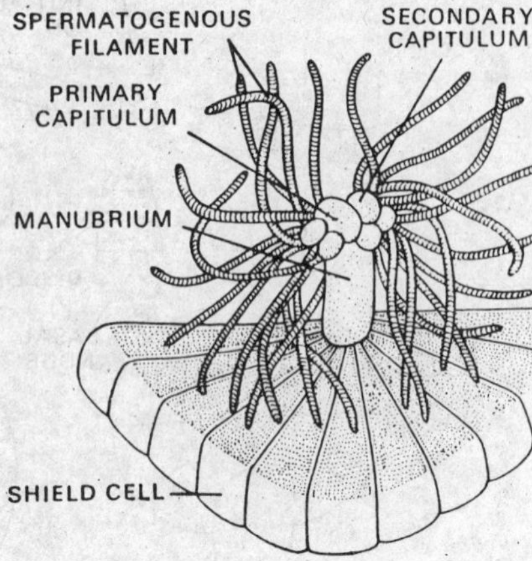

Fig. 4.10. *Chara*. Part of globule showing shield cell, manubrium, primary capitulum, secondary capitula and spermatogenous filaments.

The zygote and its germination. In favourable conditions the zygote germinates. The diploid (2x) nucleus moves to the top of the zygote and divides meiotically producing four haploid nuclei. Simultaneously a septum divides the zygote into two unequal cells. The small distal cell is **lenticular cell** and contains one functional **nucleus** in it. The remaining big cell is called **storage cell,** possessing

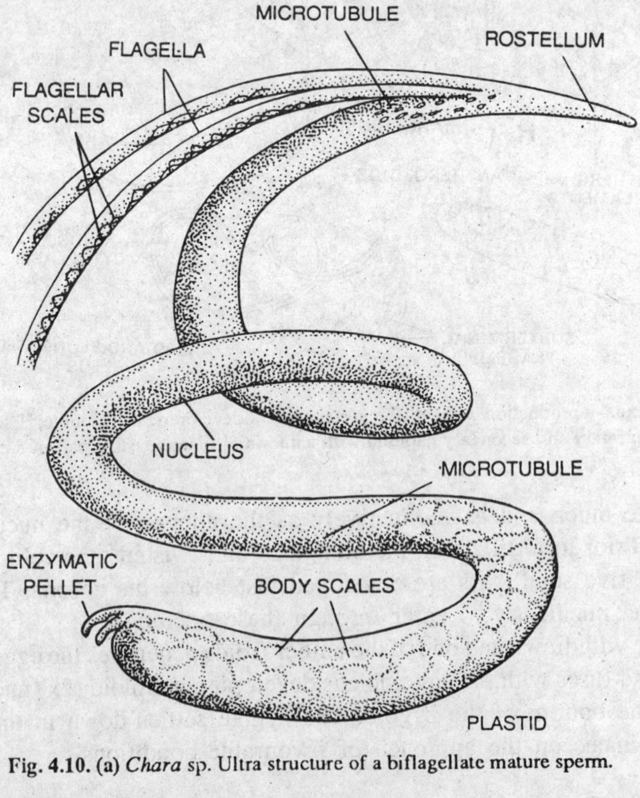

Fig. 4.10. (a) *Chara* sp. Ultra structure of a biflagellate mature sperm.

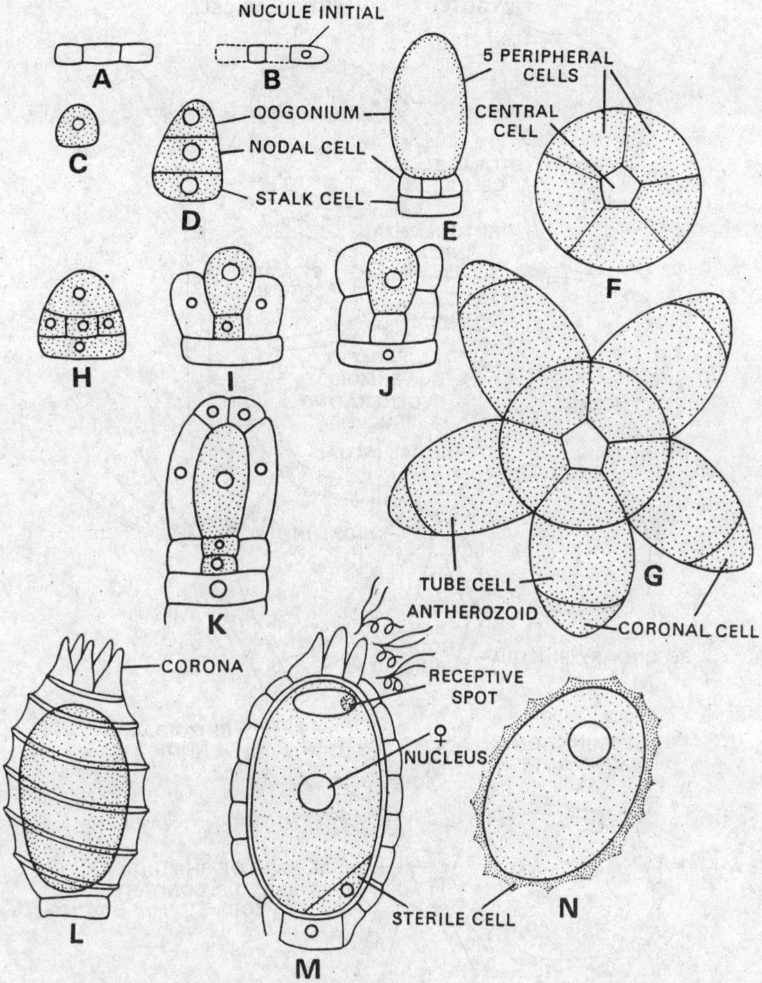

Fig. 4.11. *Chara* sp. Sexual reproduction. A-K, different stages in the development of nucule; L, nucule; M, fertilization; N, zygote.

three nuclei in it which disintegrate very soon. The outer wall of the ornamented zygote cracks and the lenticular cell exposes. The lenticular cell divides by a vertical wall giving rise to a **protonematal initial** and **a rhizoidal initial.** The protonematal initial develops into a primary protonema which later on differentiates into nodes and internodes. The rhizoidal initial gives rise to a colourless rhizoid having nodes and internodes (Fig. 4.12).

From the lowermost node of the protonema the apppendages are given out which develop into secondary protonema or rhizoids. From the second node of the protonema a whorl of appendages is given out. All the appendages except one develop into green filaments. The life cycle is of haplontic type. All phases but zygote are haploid.

Systematic position. Division - Charophyta; Class - Charophyceae; Order - Charales; Family Characeae; Genus - *Chara.*

Advanced features of the Charales. The position of the Charales is controversial on account of the multicellular female organ, the complex antheridium, strong apical growth by vegetative shoots and a degree of specialization which is generally not found in other green algae. The

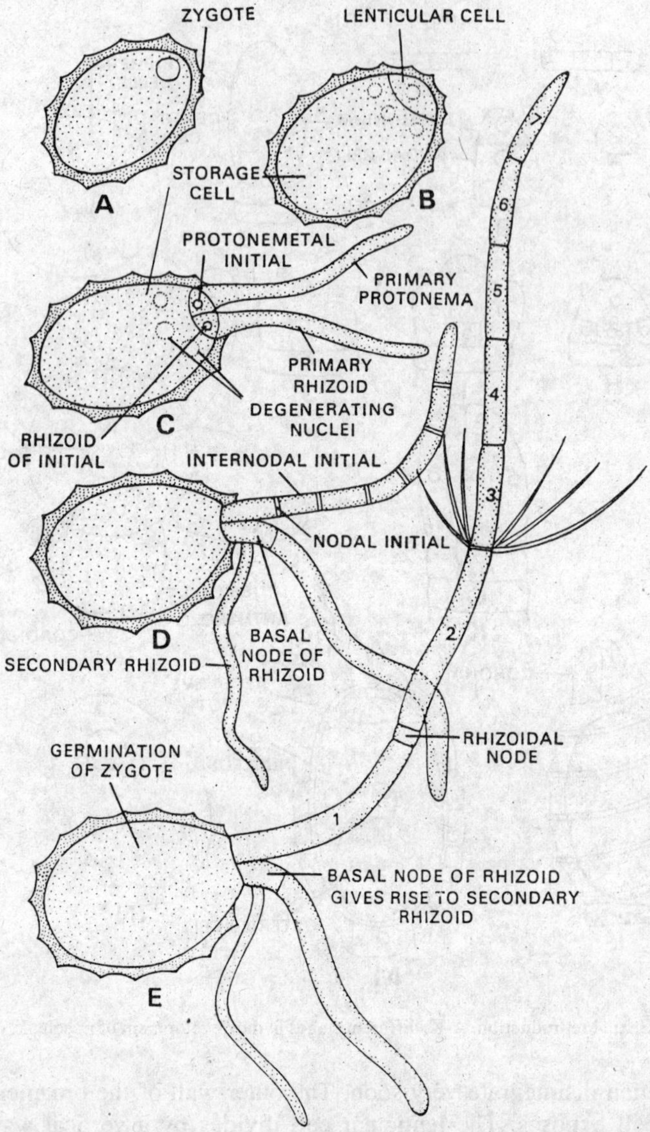

Fig. 4.12. *Chara* sp. Germination of zygote; B, division of nucleus; C-E, different stages in the germination of zygote.

female sex organ possesses a sterile jacket of cells, which is not found in the typical oogonium of other green algae. In 1875, Sachs referred the oogonium of *Chara* as a **nucule.** The presence of sterile jacket of cells is a new thing for the algae whereas on the other hand it is characteristic of the archegonium in the Embryophyta. But the jackets of these two groups are not supposed to be homologous. A parallel or analogous situation is found in the Rhodophyceae, where the female organ is a fairly complex structure.

In the same way the antheridium of the Charales is a much more complex structure than the typical antheridia and does not resemble the antheridia of either Bryophyta or Tracheophyta. Sachs (1875) called the antheridium as a **globule.**

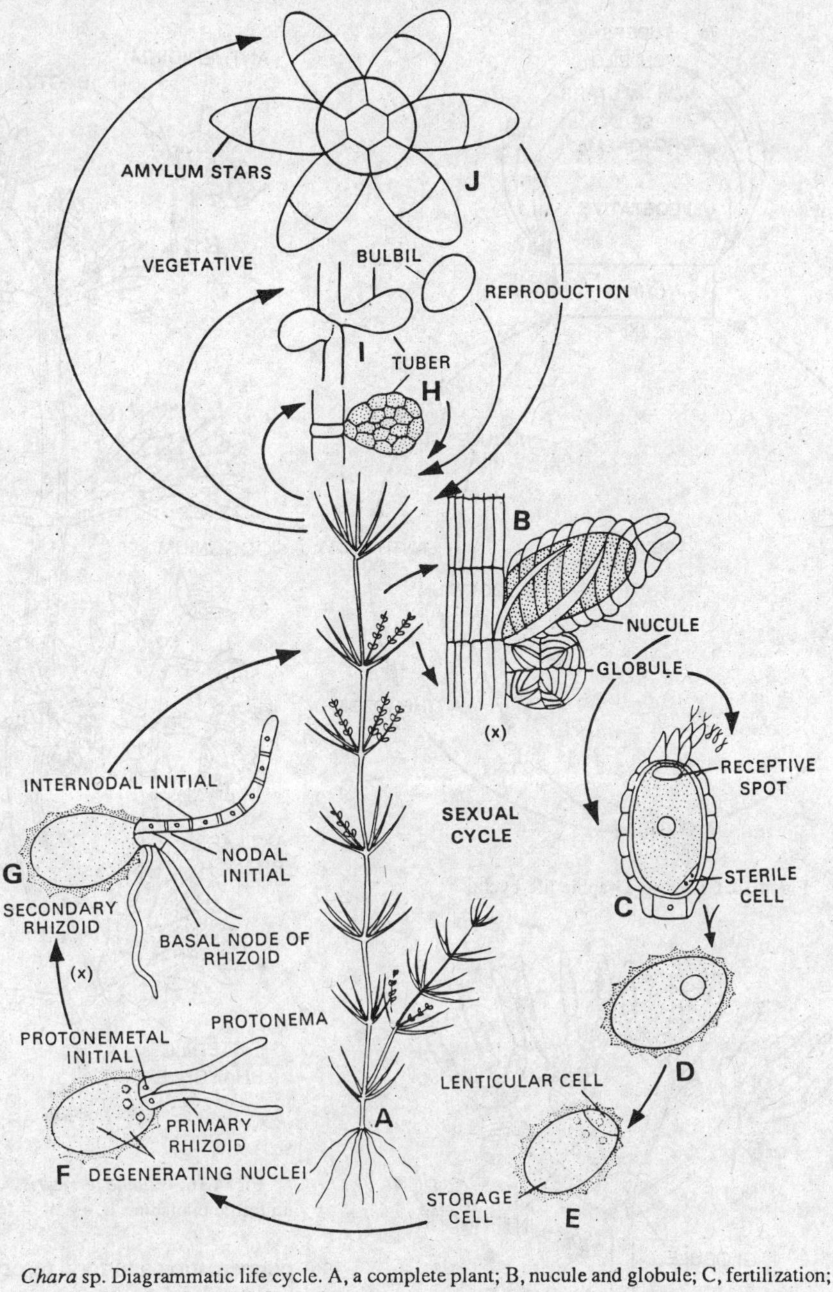

Fig. 4.13. *Chara* sp. Diagrammatic life cycle. A, a complete plant; B, nucule and globule; C, fertilization; D, zygote; E-G, germination of zygote; H, tuber; I, bulbil; J, amylum star.

The Charales have also achieved a degree of specialized apical growth which superficially resembles that of the Equisetales. However, the Charales are devoid of vascular system and they cannot be compared with Equisetales.

The Charales are a unique group so much so that Smith and others have placed this order in a separate class, the Charophyceae. The complex sex organs, *i.e.*, oogonia (nucule) and antheridia (globule) make a definite classification of the group difficult. However, the cellulose wall,

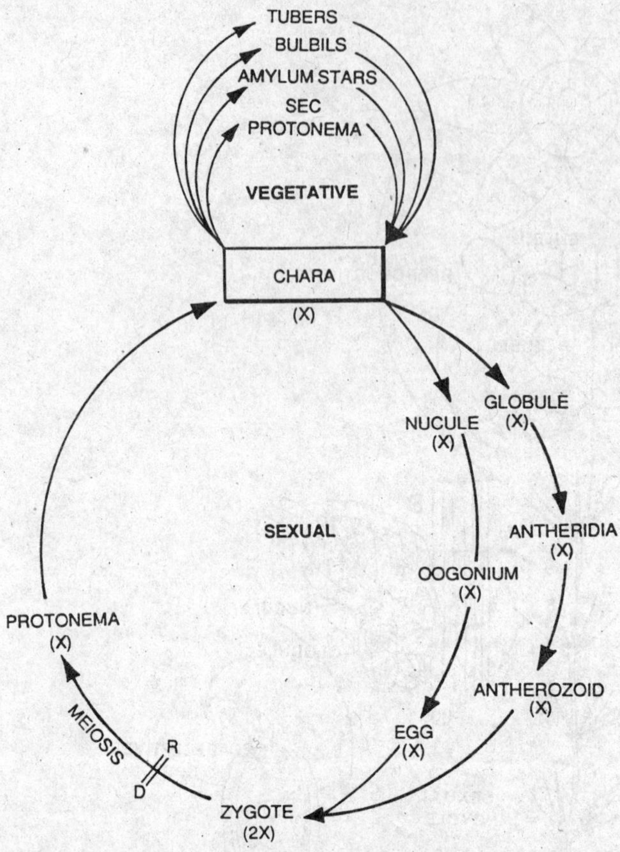

Fig. 4.14. *Chara* sp. Graphic life-cycle.

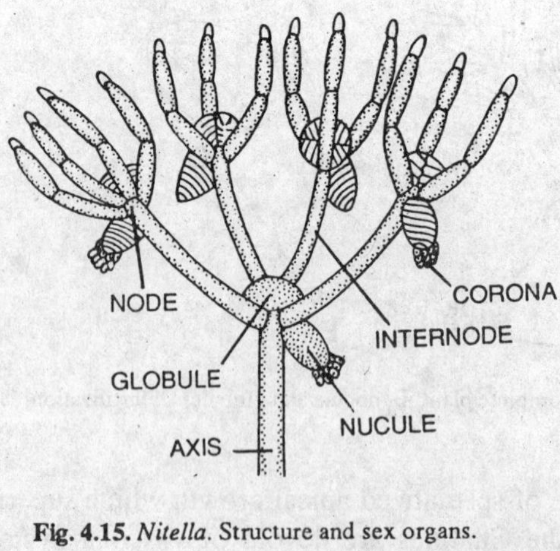

Fig. 4.15. *Nitella.* Structure and sex organs.

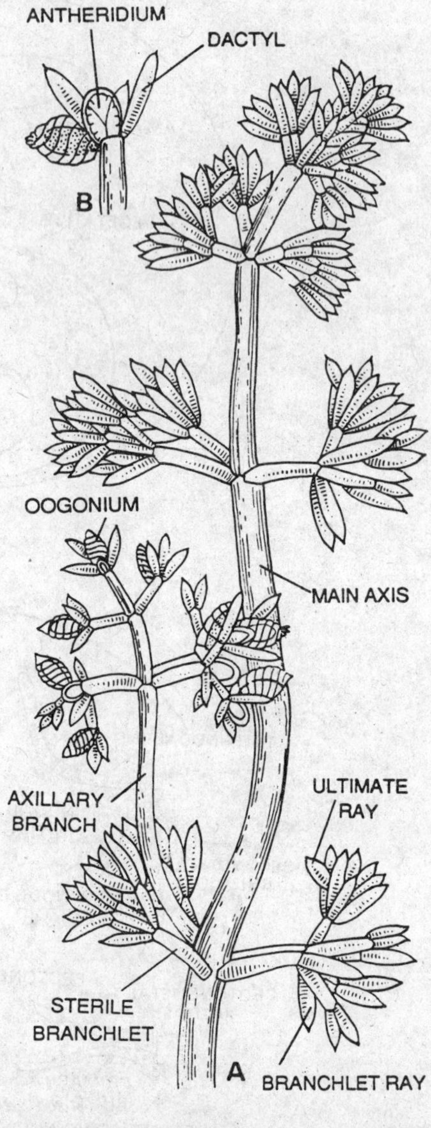

Fig. 4.16. *Nitella terrestris.* A, part of thallus with fertile branchlet; B, a part of fertile branchlet.

pigmentation and food reserves are clearly of chlorophycean type and according to Dr. Fritsch the order has been included in Chlorophyceae.

Genus–NITELLA (a little star)

Occurrence. The species of *Nitella* are commonly found in clear and fresh waters. They remain submerged and found in much deeper water than *Chara*.

External features. The thallus is multicellular and branched. The plant looks like the small plant of *Equisetum,* because of the presence of lateral branches at the nodes. The thallus is differentiated into (a) lower rhizoidal portion and (b) the upper erect and branched main axis.

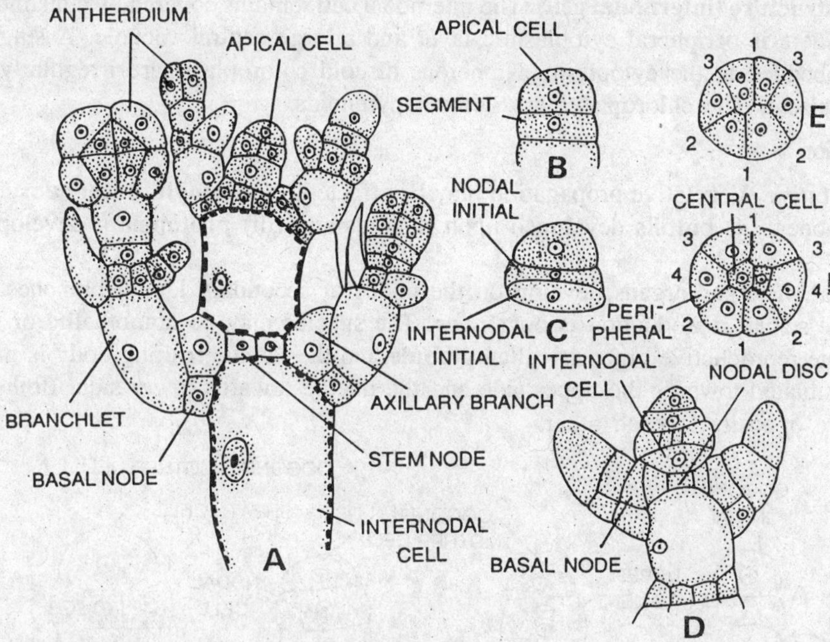

Fig. 4.17. *Nitella* spp. A, apical region of branchlet; B-C, differentiation of nodal and internodel initials; D,L. S. of apex; E-F, cross section of young nodes showing sequence of walls.

The plant remains attached to the muddy soil by means of rhizoids. The rhizoids are multicellular and branched. The rhizoids are given not from the lowermost nodes of the main axis. They possess oblique septa. A quadrant of cells is found at the cross wall of each cell from where the rhizoids are given out. This quadrant is also known as **rhizoidal plate.**

The main axis consists of nodes and internodes arranged alternately. The internodes are long and unicellular whereas nodes are short and multicellular. Internodal cell does not possess cortex. The node of main axis bears branches of limited and unlimited growth in whorls. The branches of limited growth are known as short laterals, and the branches of unlimited growth are long laterals. The branches of limited growth (short laterals) possess nodes and internodes. The nodes of these primary short laterals bear unicellular branches known as **stipules** or **leaves.** The tip of short lateral is tapering. The branches of unilimited growth (long laterals) arise from the node of main axis. They are of similar structure as that of main axis. They possess large number

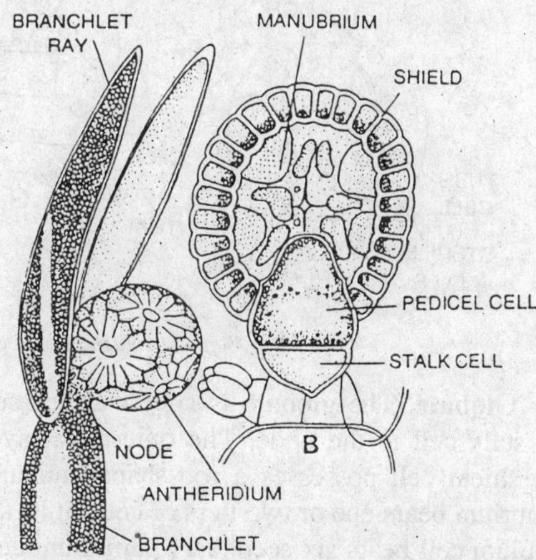

Fig. 4.18. *Nitella* spp. A, fertile branchlet with antheridium at its node; B, details of antheridium.

of nodes and internodes than found on the short laterals. Two to three long laterals are produced from each node of the main axis.

Cell structure (internodal cell). The internodal cell remains covered by a distinct cellulose cell wall. There is peripheral cytoplasmic layer and a large central vacuole. A single nucleus remains embedded in the cytoplasm. Numerous discoid chloroplasts are irregularly dispersed in the cytoplasm. The chloroplasts are without pyrenoids.

Reproduction

Vegetative. Vegetative propagation may be effected by (i) **amylum stars** developed from the lower nodes, (ii) **bulbils** developed upon rhizoids and (iii) **protonema,** developed from a node.

Sexual. The sex organs develop on the nodes of secondary lateral branches of limited growth. The sexual reproduction is oogamous. The species may be homothallic or heterothallic. The male reproductive organ is called **globule** and the female fruiting body is **nucule.** The globule is situated towards the upper side and the nucule towards lower side. Both the fructifications are opposite to each other.

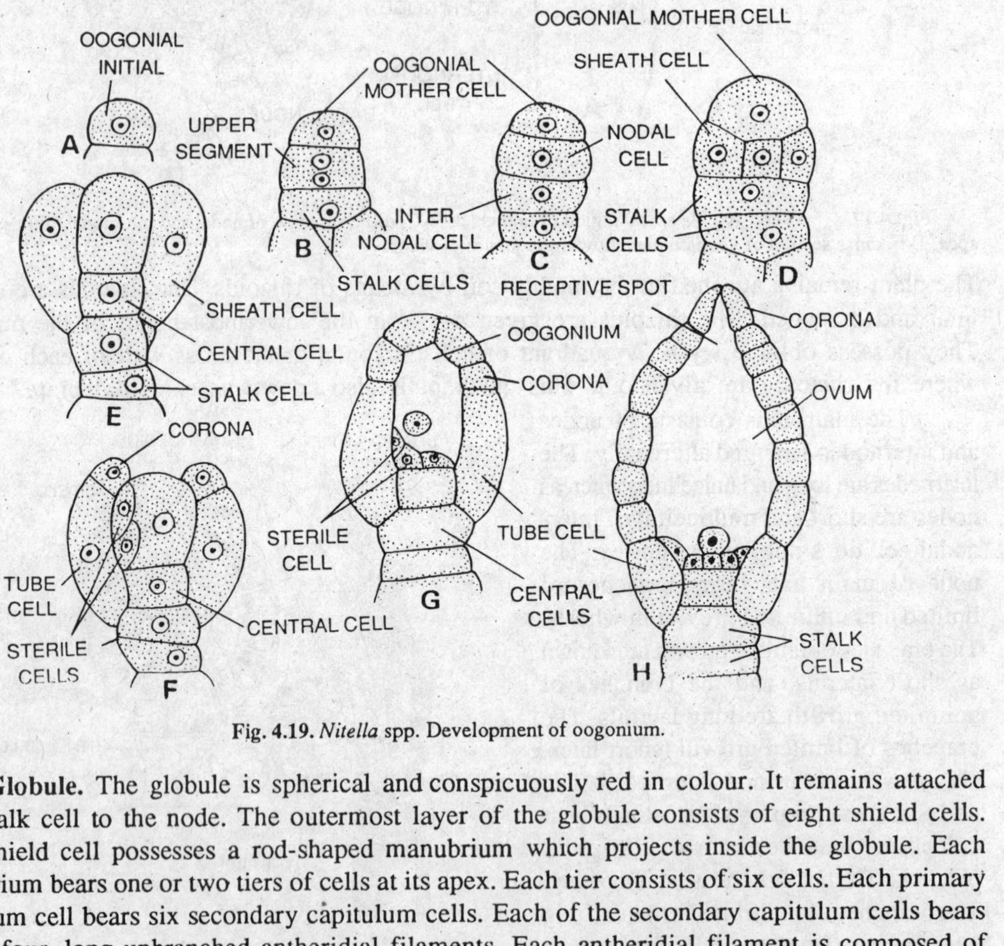

Fig. 4.19. *Nitella* spp. Development of oogonium.

Globule. The globule is spherical and conspicuously red in colour. It remains attached by a stalk cell to the node. The outermost layer of the globule consists of eight shield cells. Each shield cell possesses a rod-shaped manubrium which projects inside the globule. Each manubrium bears one or two tiers of cells at its apex. Each tier consists of six cells. Each primary capitulum cell bears six secondary capitulum cells. Each of the secondary capitulum cells bears two to four, long unbranched antheridial filaments. Each antheridial filament is composed of 100-200 segments. Each cell of the filament acts as antheridium which metamorphoses into a biflagellate antherozoid.

Nucule. The nucule is situated just beneath the globule on the same node (in homothallic species). It is oval to ellipsoidal in shape and greenish to black in colour. There is a corona of ten coronal cells at the apex of the nucule. The corona consists of two tiers and has five cells in each tier. The oosphere is multicellular. It contains a single nucleus and a large amount of cytoplasm. The oosphere is filled up with starch and oil. After fertilization, thick walled oospore is formed. The oospore remains covered by the envelope of conspicuous threads. The silica deposits around oospore.

Development of globule and nucule. As in *Chara*.

Germination of oospore and development of new thallus. As in *Chara*.

Revision Questions

Long Answer Type

1. Give the distinguishing characters of the order Charales.
2. Where do the species of *Chara* occur ? Give vegetative structure of the thallus of *Chara*.
3. Give a comprehensive account of sexual reproduction of *Chara*.
4. Describe the development of *nucule* and *globule* in *Chara*.
5. Give the structure of nodal and internodel cells of Chara.
6. Give the advanced features of the older *Charales*.
7. Write note on (a) apical growth of axis in *Chara*; (b) development of cortex, leaf and rhizoids in *Chara*; (c) vegetative reproduction in *Chara;* (d) structure of nucule and globule in *Chara;* (e) the zygote and its germination in *Chara*.
8. Give the development of cortex, leaf and rhizoids in *Chara*. Also write briefly about its apical growth.
9. Describe the reproductive organs in *Chara*. (Bhopal 1977, 1985).
10. Describe with the help of labelled diagrams, position and structure of sex organs of *Chara*. Discuss its systematic position. (Jiwaji, 1981)
11. Give an illustrated account of structure and development of sex organs in *Chara*. (Bhopal, 1978).
12. Describe the features of special interest in the structure and methods of reproduction in *Chara*. (Agra, 1978, 1981).
13. Describe briefly the structure and development of sex organs of *Chara*. (Agra, 1983).
14. Give the structure and development of globule and nucule in *Chara*.
15. Describe in brief the life-history of *Chara*.
16. Give in brief the life-history of *Nitella*.

Short Answer Type

1. Give the occurrence and vegetative structure of *Chara* or *Nitella*.
2. Write a note on structure of globule in *Chara* or *Nitella*.
3. Write a note on nucule of *Chara*, and compare it with that of *Nitella*.
4. Write a note on apical growth in *Chara*.
5. How the rhizoids originate in *Chara*.
6. Write a note on vegetative reproduction in *Chara*.
7. Give the structure of nodal and internodal cells of *Chara*.
8. How the zygote germinates in *Chara*. ?
9. Give the systematic position of *Chara*. Also mention the advanced features of the order *Charales*.
10. Give the characteristic features of order Charales.

Diagrammatic Type.

1. Draw a diagram to illustrate the structure of globule of *Chara* in longitudinal section. (Meerut, 1982).
2. With the help of diagrams only give the structure of nucule and globule in *Chara*.
3. With the help of labelled diagrams only, give the life-cycle of *Chara*.
4. With the help of diagrams only show the structure and development of sex organs in *Chara* or *Nitella*.
5. Show the structures clearly by labelled diagrams of a branch of *Chara* with sex organs. (Rajasthan, 1981, 1982).

Multiple Choice Type

1. The stoneworts belong to:
   (i) Oedogoniales, (ii) Volvocales, (iii) Charales, (iv) Bryophytes.
2. The vegetative reproductin in *Chara* takes place by:
   (i) amylum stars, (ii) bulbils, (iii) secondary protonema, (iv) all the above.

3. The sexual reproduction in *Chara* takes place by:
   (i) amylum stars, (ii) nucule, (iii) globule, (iv) nucule and globule.
4. The antherozoids of *Chara* are:
   (i) single flagellate, (ii) bi-flagellate, (iii) multiflagellate, (iv) none of above.
5. The *Chara* plants remain covered by:
   (i) potassium carbonate, (ii) sodium carbonate, (iii) calcium carbonate, (iv) none of above.
6. The manubrium is found in:
   (i) nucule of *Chara*, (ii) globule of *Chara*, (iii) bulbil of *Chara*, (iv) amylum star of *Chara*.
7. The chloroplasts of *Chara* are:
   (i) girdle-shaped, (ii) cup-shaped, (iii) spiral, (iv) discoid.
8. The corona is found in:
   (i) nucule of *Chara*, (ii) globule of *Chara*, (iii) bulbil of *Chara*, (iv) protonema of *Chara*.
9. Secondary protonema is found in:
   (i) *Oedogonium*, (ii) *Volvox*, (iii) *Spirogyra*, (iv) *Chara*.
10. Genus *Nitella* belongs to:
    (i) Nemalionales, (ii) Oedogoniales, (iii) Charales, (iv) Cladophorales.
11. The number of coronal cells in nucule of *Chara:*
    (i) 2, (ii) 3, (iii) 5, (iv) 10.
12. The number of coronal cells in nucule of *Nitella:*
    (i) 2, (ii) 3, (iii) 5, (iv) 10.

Answers

1 (iii), 2 (iv), 3 (iv), 4 (ii), 5 (iii), 6 (ii), 7 (iv), 8 (i), 9 (iv), 10 (iii) 11 (iii), 12 (iv).

5

Xanthophycophyta–Xanthophyceae
Yellow Green Algae

Characteristic features.

Pigmentation. Chlorophyll *a*, β-carotene, Lutein, Neoxanthin.

Storage products. Chrysolaminarin, oils.

Flagellation. 2, unequal, apical.

The members of this division were formerly included in the Chlorophycophyta until their distinctive pigmentation, storage products, and flagellation became apparent. The organization of the plant body in this group parallels in part that of the Chlorophycophyta in that both motile and nonmotile unicellular, colonial, filamentous and tubular genera are known.

There are 75 genera and about 375 species in this class.

Characteristic features.

1. **Pigmentation.** They have yellowish green chromatophores containing chlorophyll *a*, chlorophyll *b*, β–carotene and one xanthophyll.
2. **Food reserves.** In this class the food reserves are found in the form of a carbohydrate of unknown combination known as leucosin. Sometimes oil is also found in small quantity. Starch is lacking altogether.
3. **Flagellation.** The motile cells possess two unequal flagella on their anterior ends. The shorter flagellum is of whiplash type and the longer one is of tinsel type. Due to the presence of unequal flagella on swarm cell they are also called **'heterokontae'.**
4. In certain genera, the wall consists of two equal or unequal halves overlapping each other.
5. Asexual reproduction takes place by means of zoospores, aplanospores and special type of statopores.
6. Sexual reproduction is known in only few genera. In majority of cases it is isogamous. In one genus oogamy is also found.
7. Majority of Xanthophyceae are fresh water in habit. They thrive best in soft waters. They may be aquatic, *e.g., Tribonema*, or terrestrial, *e.g., Botrydium.* Few genera are marine.

Classification. There are six orders in this class, *i.e.,* 1. Heterochloridales, 2. Rhizochloridales, 3. Heterocapsales, 4. Heterotrichales, 5. Heterococcales and 6. Heterosiphonales.

1. Heterochloridales

(i) The plant body is flagellated, naked and unicellular.

(ii) Each cell contains two or more discoid or band-shaped chromatophores and one or more contractile vacuoles in the protoplast.

(iii) Reproduction takes place by cell division and in one genus statospores are formed.

(iv) There are 9 genera and about 15 species; 4 genera are marine and rest are fresh water in habit.

(v) Important genus–*Chloromeson.*

2. Rhizochloridales

(i) The plant body is amoeboid in pseudopodia. Sometimes several individuals may become jointed to one another by cytoplasmic bridges, mostly naked or partially surrounded by the **lorica** that may be attached to substratum by stalk.

(ii) Reproduction takes place by cell division, zoospores, aplanospores or statospores.

(iii) The protoplast contains one to many chromatophores. They may be uninucleate or multinucleate.

(iii) There are 7 genera and about 10 species. Majority of them are fresh water.

(v) Important genus–*Chlorachnion*.

3. Heterocapsales

(i) The plant body is palmelloid, *i.e.*, gelatinous colonies are found which may be amorphous or dendroid.

(ii) The cells have the capacity to return directly in the motile condition.

(iii) Reproduction takes place by means of fragments, akinetes and zoospores. The zoospores may divide into new zoospores.

(iv) There are 8 genera and about 9 species. All are fresh water in habit.

(v) Important genus–*Gloeochloris*.

4. Heterotrichales

(i) The plant body is simple or branched filament.

(ii) Reproduction takes place by means of fragmentation, akinetes, zoospores, aplanospores and hypnospores.

(iii) Physiological isogamy is found in one genus, *i.e., Tribonema*.

(iv) There are 8 genera and about 35 species. All are fresh water in habit.

(v) Important genus-*Tribonema*.

5. Heterococcales

(i) They are nonfilamentous and incapable of returning directly to a motile form.

(ii) The cell may be uninucleate or multinucleate. In majority of cases the wall consists of two halves.

(iii) The plant body consists of coccoid or colonial (gelatinous) forms.

(iv) Reproduction takes place by means of zoospores and aplanospores. The aplanospores are autospores. They have no capacity of vegetative cell division.

(v) There are 45 genera, and about 270 species. All are fresh water in habit.

(vi) Important genus–*Botrydiopsis*.

6. Heterosiphonales

(i) All the members are multinucleate, siphonaceous and unicellular in structure.

(ii) Asexual reproduction takes place by means of zoospores, aplanospores and hypnospores. These bodies are coenocytic.

(iii) Sexual reproduction is isogamous.

(iv) There are 3 or 4 fresh water genera.

(v) Important genera–*Botrydium, Vaucheria,*

Here the genera *Botrydium* and *Vaucheria* of order Heterosiphonales have been described in detail.

Phylogenetic Relationships in Xanthophyceae

Luther (1889) for the first time recognized Xanthophyceae as a separate class and named it Heterokontae. He placed the motile genera in one order and the remaining genera in another. Thereafter Pascher (1913) pointed out that evolutionary lines found in the Chlorophyceae are also evident among Xanthophyceae. He also suggested the segregation of Xanthophyceae into orders homologous with those of Chlorophyceae. According to this classification, the Heterocapsales to the Tetrasporales, the Heterotrichales to the Ulotrichales, the Hetercoccales to the Chlorococcales and the Heterosiphonales to the Siphonales. The Rhizochloridales however, does not possess its counterpart among Chlorophyceae.

Genus BOTRYDIUM (a small cluster)

There are six species in this genus.

Occurrence. It is a terrestrial form. It grows on damp soils, drying muddy banks of streams, pools and rivers.

Structure. The body of *Botrydium* is unicellular. It has two distinct parts. The aerial part is rounded, 1 to 2 mm. in diameter and contains typical Xanthophyceae type of chromatophores. The rhizoidal portion found embedded in the mud is colourless and branched.

The outer vesicular portion has a tough wall. Just beneath this wall there is a thin cytoplasmic layer. Several nuclei and chromatophores are embedded in this cytoplasm. The chromatophores are discoid and many. They are interconnected to each other by cytoplasmic strands. Pyrenoids are found in chromatophores of young plants.

The rhizoidal system has no chromatophores but numerous nuclei are found in its cytoplasm. The rhizoids hold the mud or damp soil firmly.

Food reserves. A special type of carbohydrate like substance is found. Starch is always lacking. Occasionally oils have also been recorded.

Reproduction. Reproduction takes place by asexual and sexual methods. Vegetative propagation is not found.

1. Asexual reproduction. Asexual reproduction takes place by means of zoospores, aplanospores and hypnospores.

(a) By zoospores. The zoospores are formed when there is abundant supply of water. The protoplast of the vesicular cell divides again and again and many pyriform and naked swarmers are developed. They escape by the gelatinization of the apical portion of the parent cell. Each zoospore possesses two unequal (heterokontean) flagella. The neuromotor apparatus is not found. Each zoospore gives rise to a new plant.

According to Moewus (1940), these zoospores are gametic in nature and develop parthenogenetically into new individuals.

(b) By aplanospores. The aplanospores are produced when the plant grows on drier soils. The contents of the vesicular portion divide again and again into several protoplasts. Each bit of protoplast contains nucleus in it. Each protoplast becomes rounded, secretes a wall around it and called an aplanospore. In some cases the aplanospores are multinucleate. Each aplanospore gives rise to a new plant in favourable conditions. The aplanospores liberate by the decay of the parent cell wall.

(c) By hypnospores. The hypnospores are much resistant and perennating bodies. Sometimes the aplanospores become thick-walled and called hypnospores. They may be uni - or multinucleate and develop inside the vesicular portion of the plant.

In some cases the protoplasmic contents of the vesicular part are transferred wholly in

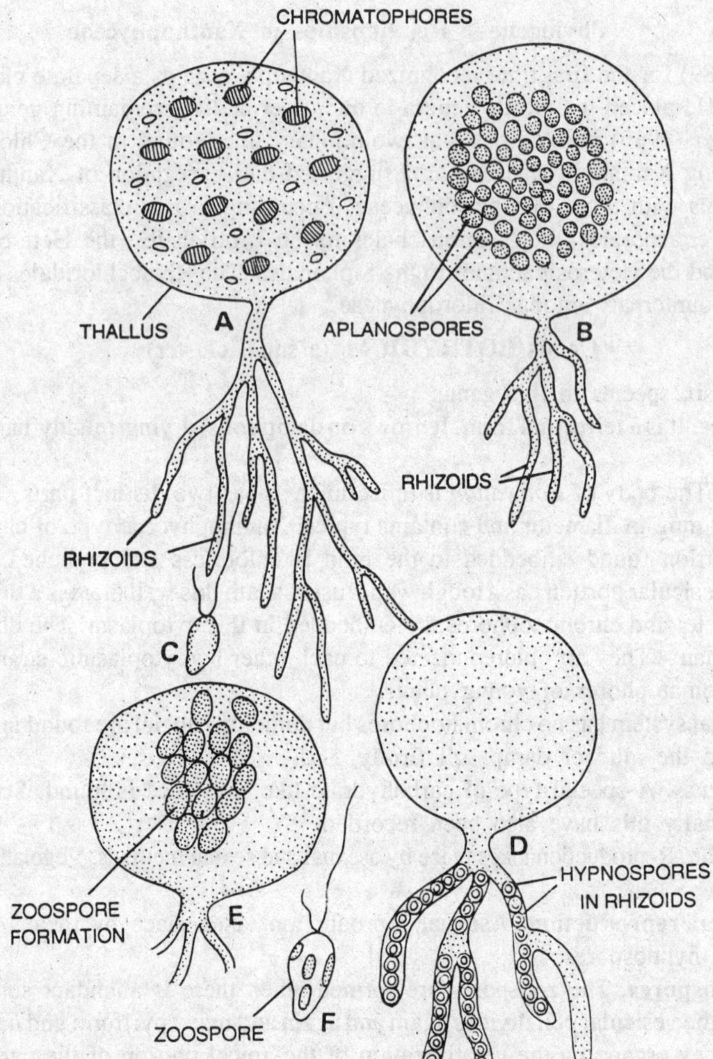

Fig. 5.1. *Botrydium* sp. Vegetative structure and asexual reproduction. A, unicellular plant body; B, aplanospore formation; C, germination of aplanospore; D, hypnospore formation in the rhizoids; E, zoospore formation; F, single zoospore.

the rhizoids. Here these contents divide into multinucleate protoplasts. Each protoplast develops a thick wall around it and becomes rounded.

The uninucleate hypnospores developed directly into new plants, whereas the multinucleate hypnosopores, first give rise to biflagellate zoospores, which develop into new plants.

2. Sexual reproduction. According to Moewus (1950) the sexual reproduction in *Botrydium* may be iso or anisogamous. The gametes are formed in rainy season, inside the vesicular portion. The contents of the globòse body divide into several uninucleate protoplasts. Each protoplast metamorphoses into a gamete. The gametes are biflagellate and of heterokontean type. Each gamete is pyriform, naked and devoid of neuromotor apparatus. The gametes liberate by the gelatinization of the apical portion of the cell wall of the parent cell. After liberation, two gametes fuse together and a tetraflagellate structure develops. The flagella are retracted soon and a rounded zygote develops.

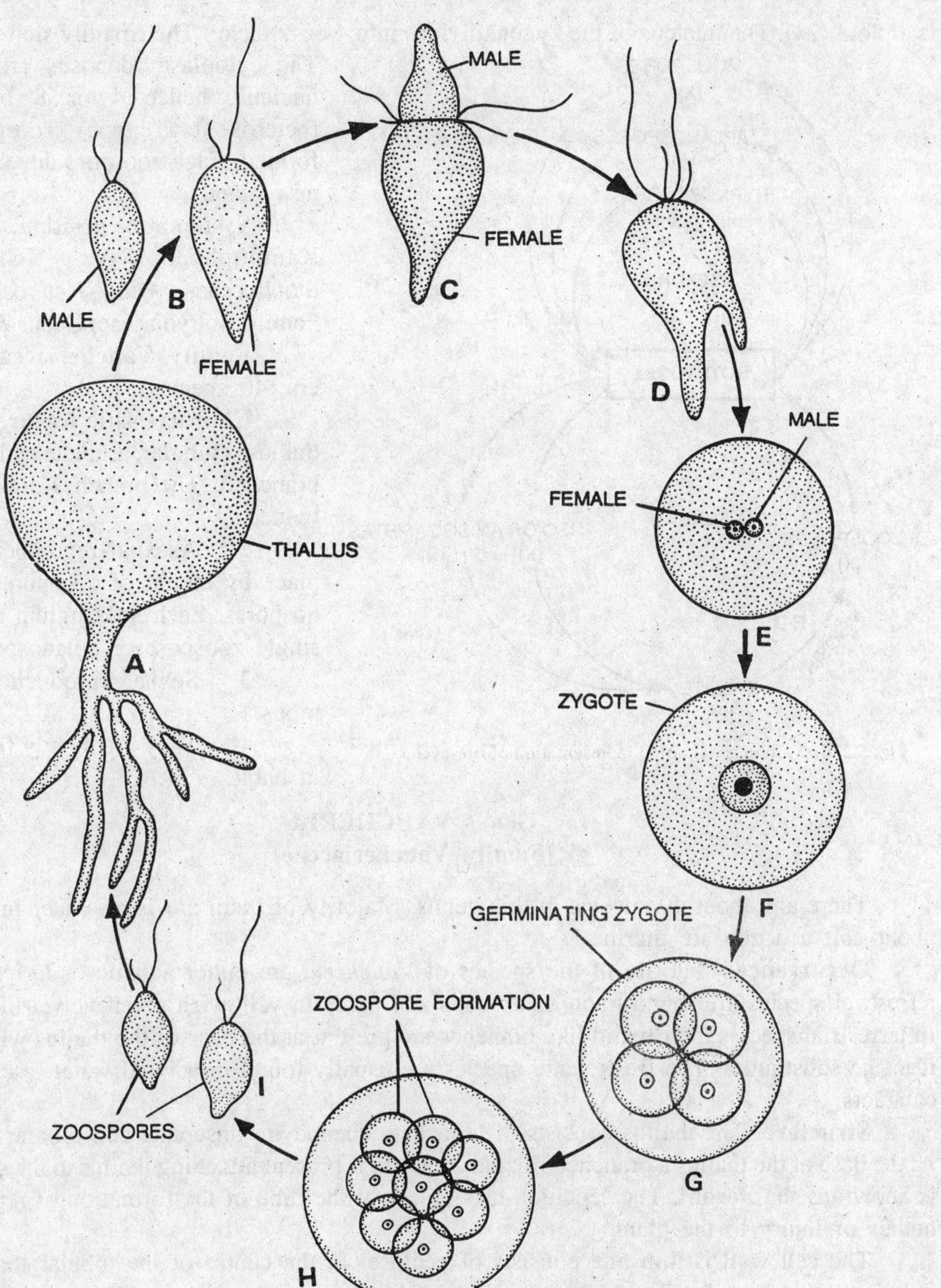

Fig. 5.2. ***Botrydium* sp. Sexual reproduction-A, an individual; B, male and female gametes C-D, union of gametes; E, karyogamy; F, zygote; G-H, germination of zygote and formation of zoospores; I, zoospores.**

After liberation, two gametes fuse together and a tetraflagellate structure develops. The flagella are retracted soon and a rounded zygote develops.

Zygote and its germination. A wall is secreted around the zygote. The zygote nucleus is diploid (2x). The nucleus of the zygote divides into 4 or 8 nuclei. The first division is meiotic.

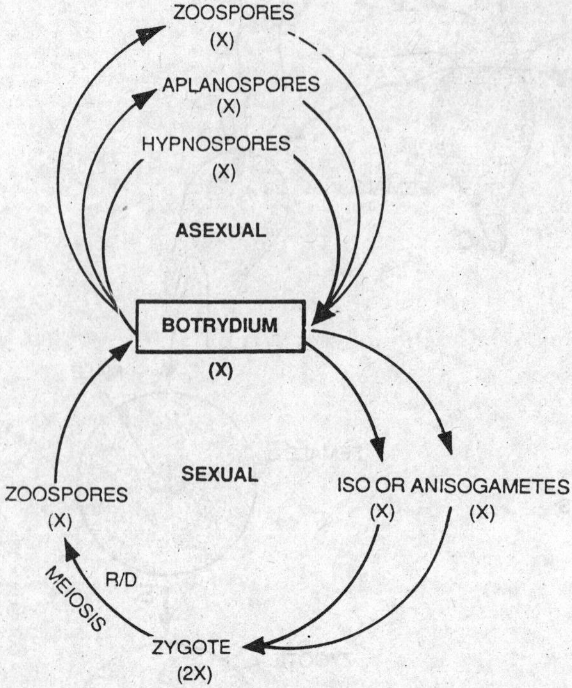

Fig. 5.3. *Botrydium* sp.-Graphic representation of life-cycle.

The cytoplasm deposits around each nucleus, hence 4 or 8 biflagellate (heterokontean type) zoospores are formed. Each zoospore develops into a new plant.

Systematic position. Division-Xanthophycophyta; Class-Xanthophyceae; Order-Heterosiphonales; Family-Botrydiaceae; Genus-*Botrydium.*

Family–Vaucheriaceae (4 genera; 40 species).

Characteristic features.–1. The thallus is tubular, aseptate and profusely branched. The branches are not intertwined.

2. Asexual reproduction takes place by means of zoospores or aplanospores. Each sporangium contains a single zoospore or aplanospore.

3. Sexual reproduction is oogamous.

4. They are mostly fresh water in habit.

Genus VAUCHERIA
(Family–Vaucheriaceae)

There are about 40 species in this genus. Majority of them are fresh water in habit and about half a dozen are marine.

Occurrence. Majority of the species of *Vaucheria* are either aquatic or terrestrial. The terrestrial species are found upon damp soils and muds in yellowish green velvet-like carpets. In terrestrial species the rhizoid-like branches are present at the base of the thallus which attach it to the substratum. The fresh water species are usually found in aerated water, *e.g.*, in water cataracts.

Structure. The thallus consists of branched, coenocytic unseptate and tubular filaments. At the base of the thallus a branched rhizoidal system is present attaching thallus to the substratum is known as **'hapteron'.** The septation takes place at the time of the formation of reproductive bodies or injury to the plant.

The cell wall is thin and consists of pectose. In the centre of the tubular thallus there is a big central vacuole. The cytoplasm is confined to the peripheral region. The numerous discoid chloroplasts are embedded in the cytoplasm towards outside and numerous minute nuclei are found towards the central vacuole. The chloroplasts are devoid of pyrenoids. The starch grains are lacking.

Reproduction. The reproduction takes place by vegetative, asexual and sexual methods.

1. Vegetative reproduction. This type of reproduction takes place by accidental breaking of thalli into small fragments. Each fragment of the filament is capable to give rise to a new plant.

2. Asexual reproduction. The asexual reproduction takes place by several means, *e.g.*, by zoospores, aplanospores, hypnospores etc.

(a) By zoospores. The multiflagellate compound zoospores also known as **'synzoospores'** or **'coenozoospores'** are developed in this genus usually in aquatic forms. A single compound zoospore develops in a single zoosporangium. Any distal branch of the thallus may convert into a zoosporangium. Much of the food reserves, chloroplasts and nuclei accumulate in the distal end of the branch of the thallus. This distal end is comparatively swollen. Very soon a septum appears at the base of this swollen end. The central vacuole disappears, the nuclei and chloroplasts reverse their position, *i.e.*, the chloroplasts shift inwards and nuclei towards periphery just beneath the cell wall. The protoplast retracts from the zoosporangial wall and opposite to each nucleus two flagella are developed.

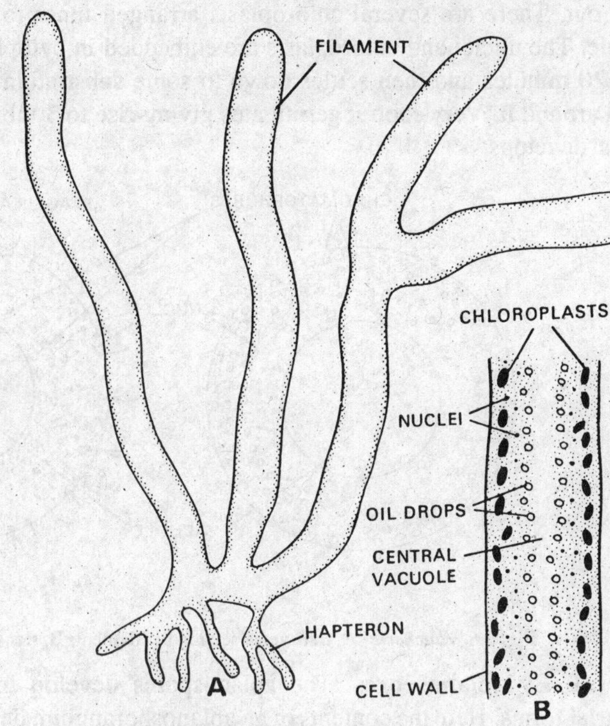

Fig. 5.4. *Vaucheria* sp. Vegetative structure; A, a complete thallus; B, a part of thallus (enlarged).

The terminal portion of the zoosporangium softens and a small pore develops. Through this small terminal aperture the zoospore squeezes out and swims freely in the water. The zoospore

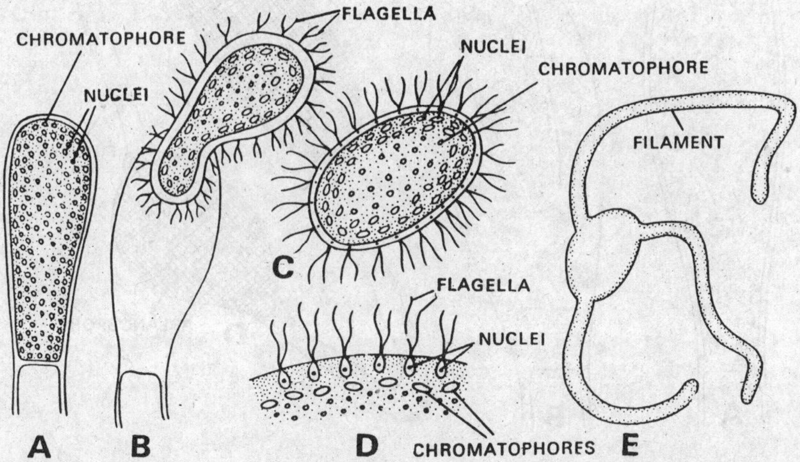

Fig. 5.5. *Vaucheria* sp. Asexual reproduction by zoospore. A, zoosporangium; B, liberation of zoospore from zoosporangium; C, compound zoospore; D, a part of compound zoospore; E, germinating zoospore.

is ovoid or elliptical. It is multiflagellate. From each peripheral nucleus a pair of flagella is given out. There are several chloroplasts arranged inner to the nuclei around the large central vacoule. The nuclei and chloroplasts are embedded in cytoplasm. The zoospore swims for about 15 to 20 minutes and then settles down to some substratum, withdraws its flagella and secretes a wall around it. Very soon it germinates giving rise to 3 tubular outgrowths and a new branched thallus develops.

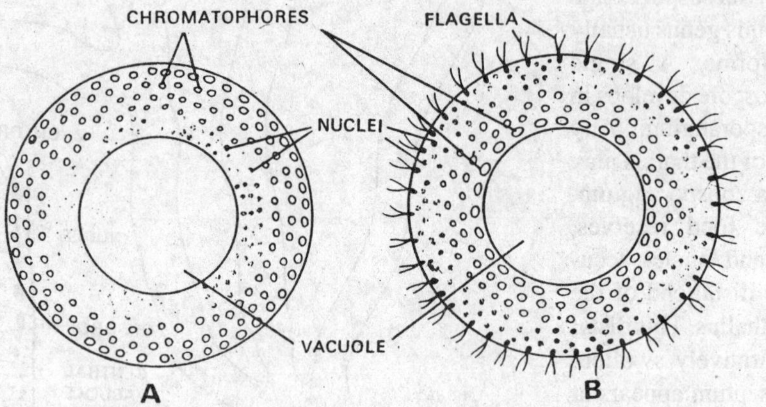

Fig. 5.6. *Vaucheria*. A, transverse section of filament; B, transverse section of synzoospore.

(a) By aplanospores. The aplanospores develop in dry conditions and especially in terrestrial forms. Here the contents of an aplanosporangium develop into a non-motile aplanospore. This aplanospore escapes by the irregular rupture of the aplanosporangium. On the approach

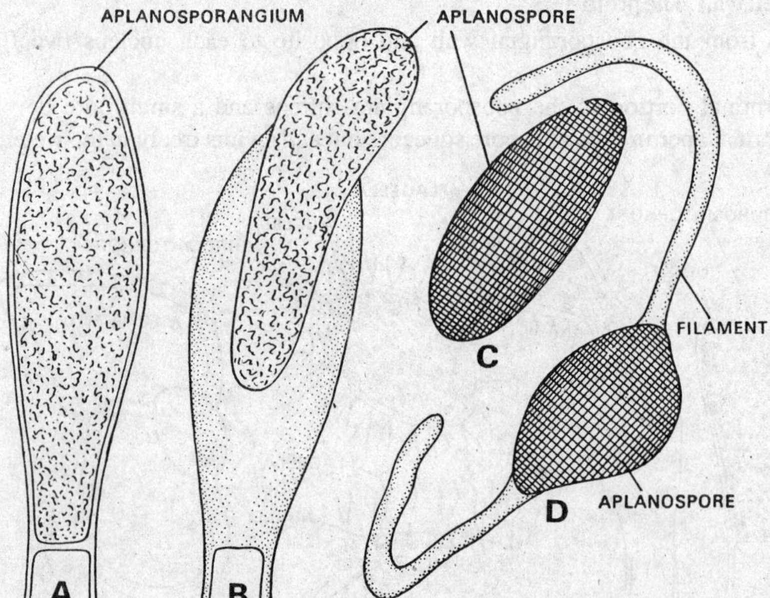

Fig. 5.7. *Vaucheria* sp. Sexual reproduction. A-B, formation of aplanospore in aplanosporangium; C, an aplanospore; D, germination of aplanospore.

of favourable conditions the aplanospore germinates producing tubular outgrowths. They may germinate after liberation or within the aplanosporangium.

(c) Hypnospores and cysts. Sometimes in terrestrial species the segmentation takes place in the tubular branches forming many small compartments. Around the protoplast of each segment a thick wall develops and they are called **'hypnospores'**. The hypnospores either germinate directly producing new thalli or they divide producing thin-walled cyst. Each cyst germinates in a special way. The cyst breaks and a pore develops at one end of it. The protoplast of this comes out in amoeboid fashion, becomes rounded and develops, into a new thallus. The segmented thallus looks like an alga *'Gongrosira'* and this stage is called **'Gongrosira stage.'**

3. Sexual reproduction. The sexual reproduction is oogamous. About all the species reproduce by this method. All the fresh water species are homothallic. The sexual reproduction takes place in the forms growing in damp soil or still waters. It does not take place in running water species. In the monoecious species the oogonia and antheridia develop on the same thallus and in dioecious species these organs develop on two different thalli. Here we will consider the sexual reproduction of fresh water forms (homothallic).

Development of antheridium. Mostly the species are protandrous,*i.e.*, antheridium develops first and oogonium afterwards.

The antheridia develop on the lateral branches at their ends shortly before the formation of oogonia. The part of the thallus giving rise to antheridium possesses abundance of cytoplasm, chloroplasts and nuclei. In most of the fresh water species slender hook-like antheridium develops having a pore at its distal end. A septum develops just beneath the curved portion of the antheridium. The nuclei of the antheridium divide mitotically again and again, and around each nucleus cytoplasm is deposited. Each such small bit metamorphoses in a biflagellate antherozoid. These antherozoids are liberated through the apical round opening of the antheridium. Each antherozoid is spindle-like and the insertion of flagella on it is lateral. According to Couch (1932), the antheridium begins to develop in afternoon and the antherozoids are formed next morning.

Development of oogonium. As mentioned above, the fresh water species are homothallic and the oogonium develops on the same filament just near the antheridium after some time. At the time of the development of oogonium a small mass of colourless multinucleate cytoplasm is accumulated in the thallus just near the antheridium. This colourless

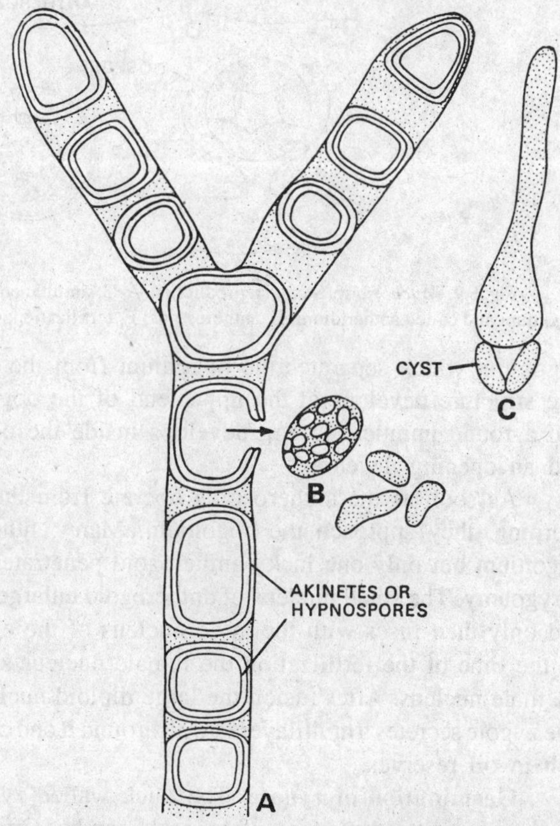

Fig. 5.8. *Vaucheria* sp. Asexual reproducion-A, formation of thick walled akinetes or hypnospores (Gongrosira stage); B, liberation of contents from hypnospore and three amoebae; C, germination of cyst.

mass of cytoplasm is called **'wanderplasm'.** The wanderplasm moves in the apical part of the oogonium developed by the lateral outgrowth of the filament. Gradually the oogonium outgrowth becomes globular and sufficiently large in size. Enough of cytoplasm, many nuclei and numerous chloroplasts migrate in this young globular oogonium. A septum develops at the base of the

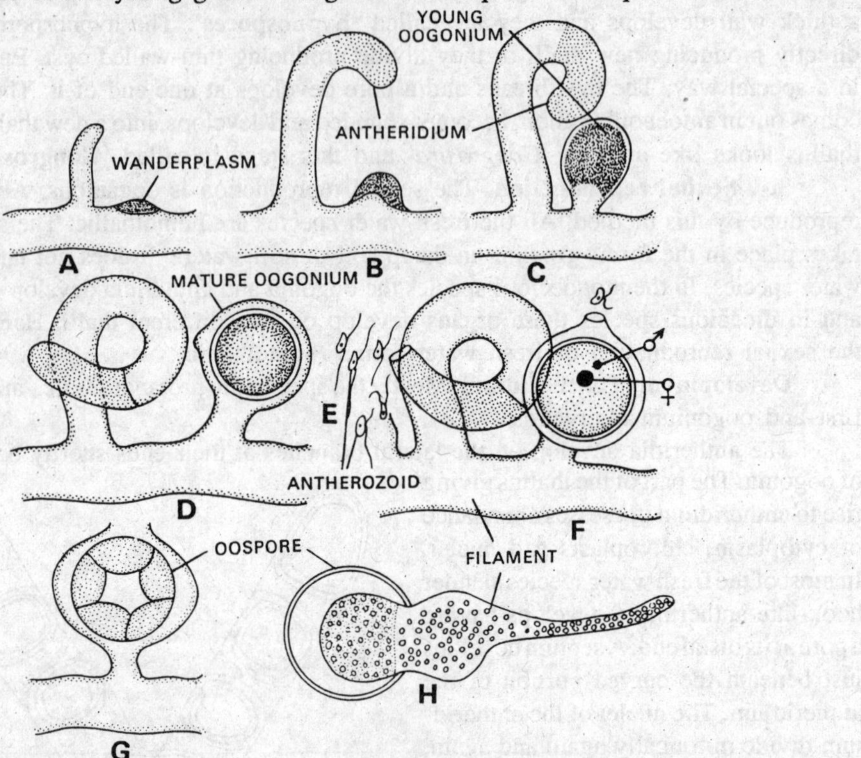

Fig. 5.9. *Vaucheria* sp. Sexual reproduction. A-C, simultaneous development of antheridium and oogonium; D, mature oogonium and coiled antheridium; E, antherozoids; F, fertilization; G, oospore; H, germinating oospore,

oogonium which separates the oogonium from the rest of the plant body. A colourless beak-like structure develops at the upper end of the oogonium. All the nuclei but one disintegrate and a round uninucleate egg develops inside the oogonium. At maturity the beak gelatinizes and an opening develops.

As soon as the antherozoids liberate from the apical opening of the antheridium in the morning, they approach the oogonium. Many antherozoids enter through the opening of the oogonium but only one lucky antherozoid penetrates the egg. The plasmogamy is followed by karygoamy. The small nucleus of antherozoid enlarges and becomes of the size of female nucleus and only then fuses with the large nucleus of the egg. Of course, the fusion takes some time. At the time of the fertilization the female nucleus shifts to the periphery of the egg to receive the male nucleus. After fusion the large diploid nucleus again shifts in the centre of the zygote. The zygote secretes a multilayered wall around it and called the oospore. The oospore is sufficiently rich in oil reserves.

Germination of zygote. The thick walled zygote (oospore) undergoes a resting period. This resting period may be of several months. On the approach of favourable conditions the zygote germinates producing tubular structure which develops into a new thallus. Gross (1937) has given an inconclusive data of the meiotic division of the zygote nucleus during germination.

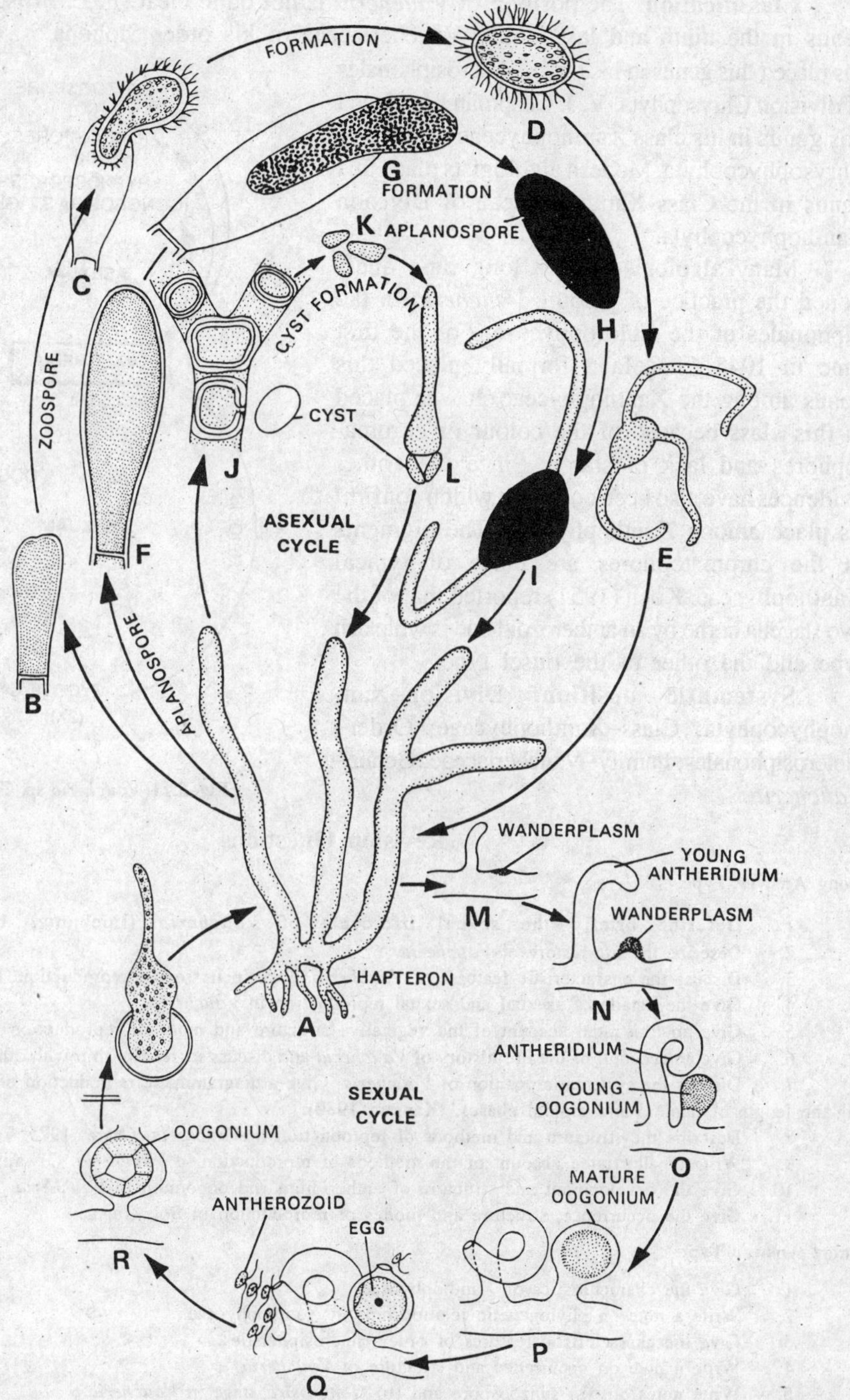

Fig. 5.10. *Vaucheria* sp. Diagrammatic life cycle. A, a complete plant; B-D, formation of synzoospore; E, germination of zoospore; F-G, aplanospore formation; H, aplanospore; I, germination of aplanospore; J-L, cyst formation and its germination; M-O, development of antheridium and oogonium; P, mature antheridium and oogonium; Q, fertilization; R, oospore; S, germination of oospore.

Classification. The position of *Vaucheria* is not quite clear. F. E. Fritsch has placed this genus in the ninth and last family Vaucheriaceae of his order Siphonales. Gilbert M. Smith has placed this genus in his order, Heterosiphonales of division Chrysophyta. V. J. Chapman has placed this genus in his class Xanthophyceae of phylum Chrysophycophyta. Modern algologists place this genus in the Class Xanthophyceae of Division Xanthophycophyta.

Many algologists for a long time questioned the practice of placing *Vaucheria* in the Siphonales of the Chlorophyceae. For the first time in 1945 Chadefaud formally placed this genus among the Xanthophyceae. It was placed in this class because of the colour of chromatophores and lack of starch. Since then other evidences have also been collected which confirm its place among Xanthophyceae. The pigments of the chromatophores are those of typical Xanthophyceae. Koch (1951) reported that of the two flagella borne by an antherozoid one is whiplash type and the other of the tinsel type.

Systematic position. Division–Xanthophycophyta; Class–Xanthophyceae; Order–Heterosiphonales; Family–Vaucheriaceae; Genus–*Vaucheria*.

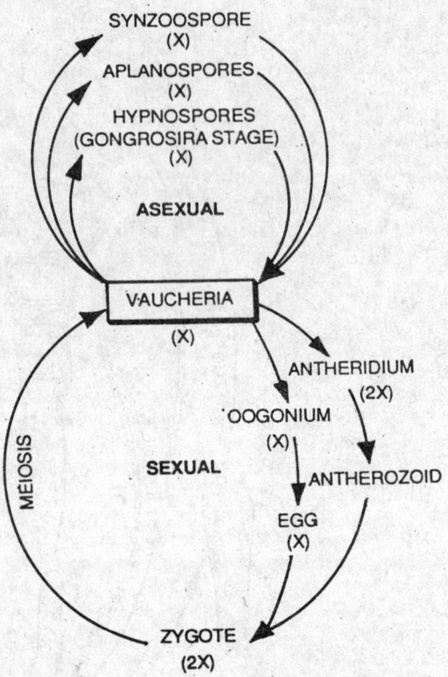

Fig. 5.11. *Vaucheria* sp. Graphic life-cycle.

Revision Questions

Long Answer Type

1. Describe briefly the sexual life-cycle of *Vaucheria* (Lucknow, 1977).
2. Describe the life-history of *Vaucheria*.
3. Discuss the characteristic features of *Vaucheria*. Explain its sexual reproduction. (Allahabad, 1975).
4. Give the details of asexual and sexual reproduction in *Vaucheria*.
5. Give an illustrated account of the vegetative structure and mode of reproduction in *Vaucheria*.
6. Give an account of the life-history of *Vaucheria* and discuss its relationship with other algae. (Agra, 1978).
7. Discuss the systematic position of *Vaucheria*. Give a diagrammatic reproduction of its life-cycle illustrating the length of haploid and diploid phases. (Kanpur, 1980).
8. Describe the structure and methods of reproduction in *Vaucheria*. (Agra, 1975, 76, Saugor, 1981).
9. Write an illustrated account of the methods of reproduction in *Vaucheria*. (Jiwaji, 1976.)
10. Give the development and structure of antheridium and oogonium in *Vaucheria*.
11. Give the occurrence, structure and modes of reproduction in *Botrydium*.

Short Answer Type

1. Give the characteristics of Xanthophyceae.
2. Write a note on phylogenetic relationships in Xanthophyceae.
3. Give the characteristic features of order Heterosiphonales.
4. Write a note on occurrence and structure of *Vaucheria*.
5. Write notes on: (a) synzoospore and (b) *Gongrosira* stage in *Vaucheria*.
6. Give the structure of antheridium and oogonium in *Vaucheria*.
7. Write a note on germination of zygote in *Vaucheria*.
8. Discuss the systematic position of *Vaucheria*.
9. Give the characteristic features of yellow-green algae.

10. Give the structure of plant body of *Vaucheria*.
11. Give the structure and development of oogonium in *Vaucheria*..

Diagrammatic Type

1. Draw well-labelled sketches of sexual reproductive organs of *Vaucheria*. (Bhopal, 1975).
2. With the help of labelled diagrams only give the life-history of *Vaucheria*.

Multiple Choice Type

1. The synzoospores are found in:
   (i) *Chara*, (ii) *Volvox*, (iii) *Oedogonium*, (iv) *Vaucheria*.
2. The chromatophores in synzoospore of *Vaucheria* are found towards.
   (i) centre, (ii) periphery, (iii) both centre and periphery, (iv) none of above.
3. The chromatophores in thallus of *Vaucheria* are found towards:
   (i) centre, (ii) periphery, (iii) both centre and periphery, (iv) in the middle.
4. The *Gongrosira* stage is found in:
   (i) *Oedogonium*, (ii) *Batrachospermum*, (iii) *Ectocarpus*, (iv) *Vaucheria*.
5. The nuclei in synzoospore of *Vaucheria* are found towards:
   (i) centre, (ii) periphery, (iii) both centre and periphery, (iv) none of above.
6. The nuclei in thallus of *Vaucheria* are found towards:
   (i) centre, (ii) periphery, (iii) both centre and periphery, (iv) all of above.
7. Asexual reproduction in *Vaucheria* takes place by:
   (i) synzoospore, (ii) aplanospore, (iii) hypnospore, (iv) all of above.
8. The thallus of *Vaucheria* contains food material in the form of:
   (i) oil globules, (ii) starch grains, (iii) aleurone grains, (iv) none of above.
9. Each sporangium of *Vaucheria* contains:
   (i) single zoospore, (ii) two zoospores, (iii) four zoospores, (iv) sixteen zoospores
10. The thallus of *Vaucheria* is:
    (i) septate, (ii) aseptate, (iii) none of above, (iv) both of above.
11. The synzoospore of *Vaucheria* is:
    (i) biflagellate, (ii) tetraflagellate, (iii) multiflagellate, (iv) all the above.
12. The cell wall of *Vaucheria* consists of:
    (i) pectose, (ii) chitin, (iii) calcium carbonate, (iv) silica.
13. The 'wanderplasm' is found in:
    (i) gonidia of *Volvox*; (ii) nucule of *Chara*, (iii) young oogonium of *Vaucheria*, (iv) oogonium of *Oedogonium*.
14. Formation of thick-walled akinetes or hypnospores in *Vaucheria* is called:
    (i) *Chantrantia* stage, (ii) *Gongrosira* stage, (iii) *Palmella* type; (iv) none of above.

Answers

1 (iv), 2 (i), 3 (ii), 4 (ii), 5 (ii), 6 (i), 7 (iv), 8 (i), 9 (i), 10 (ii), 11 (iii), 12 (i), 13 (iii), 14 (ii).

6

Bacillariophycophyta
Bacillariophyceae–Diatoms

Characteristic features.

Pigmentation. Chlorophyll *a* and *c*, β-carotene, γ-carotene, Fucoxanthin, Diatoxanthin, Diadinoxanthin.

Storage products. Chrysolaminarin, oils.

Flagellation. In male gametes, apical.

There are about 170 genera and 5,500 species of diatoms.

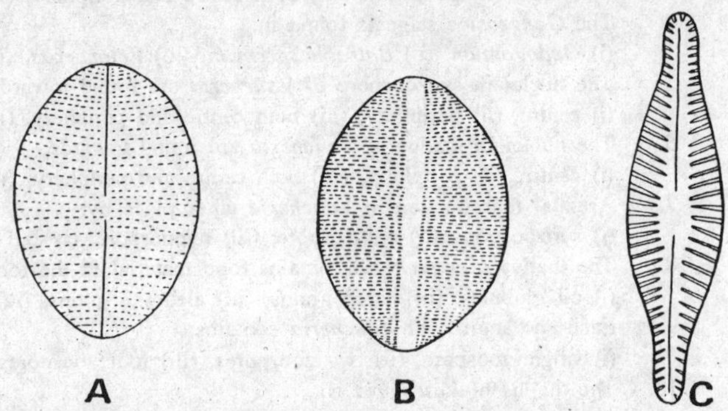

Fig. 6.1. Pennate diatoms. A-B, *Cocconeis pediculus*-two dissimilar valves of a cell; C, *Navicula rhyncocephala.*

Occurrence. The diatoms occur everywhere, where life is possible. Some genera are exclusively fresh water, some are exclusively marine and some are partly marine and partly fresh water. Majority of fresh water species are aquatic and may be attached or free floating. Some diatoms are terrestrial. Some marine diatoms are lithophytes. The aquatic fresh water forms grow in abundance in winter season in cool waters. Some diatoms are epiphytic occurring on other algae such as Phaeophyceae and Rhodophyceae especially in the intertidal zone.

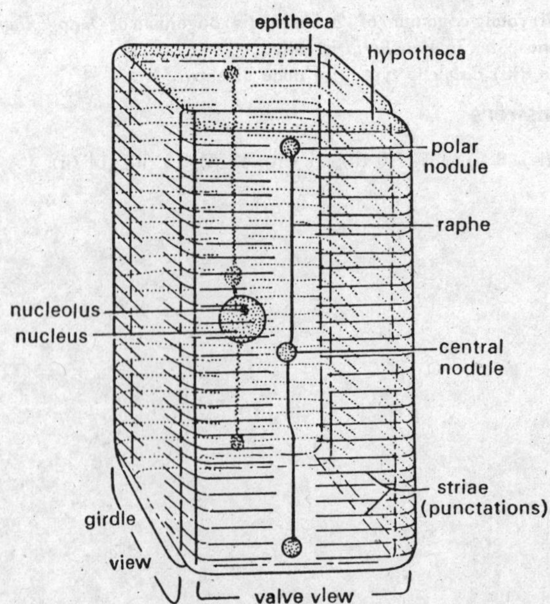

Fig. 6.2. A pennate diatom in three-dimensional aspect.

Structure–the cell wall. This is the most important part of diatoms. All diatoms are colonial or unicellular. The cell wall alone or protoplast+cell wall are known as **'frustule'**. The wall consists of two pieces which overlap each other just like petri dish pieces. The upper half is known as **epitheca** and the inner or lower half as **hypotheca**. The cell can be seen in **valve view** or **girdle view.** The cell wall consists of a substance known as **pectin** without any trace of cellulose or callose. The wall is highly silicified and as to the occurrence of silica there are 3 or 4 views put forth by various scientists.

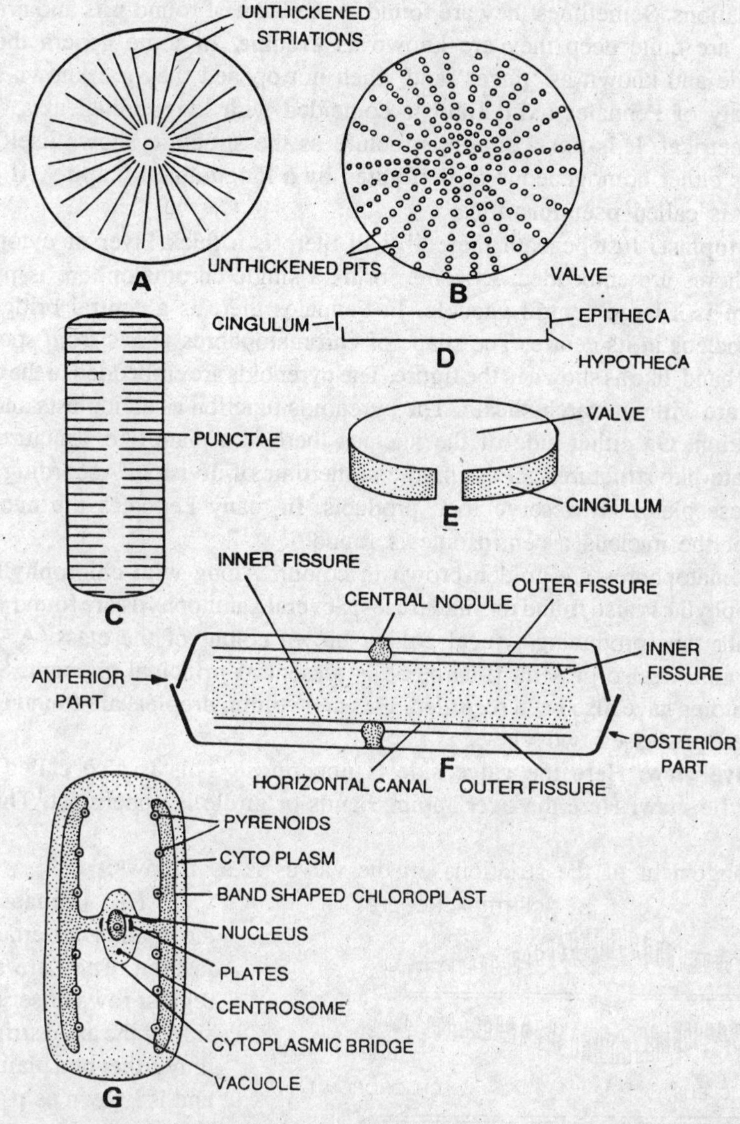

Fig. 6.3. Structure of diatoms. A-C, different types of diatoms; D, side view; E, upper view; F, side view of a diatom; G, structure of protoplast of a diatom.

1. The silica impregnates the pectic material of the cell wall.

2. Mangin (1908) put forward another view that silica combines with pectic acid to form a chemical compound.

3. According to another view, the silicious material forms a layer outer to the organic or pectic cell wall.

4. According to fourth rejected view put forward by Liebisch (1928) the wall does not contain any organic material but only silica.

The silica in cell wall is not deposited smoothly throughout, it is present in such a way that certain patterns are formed in the cell wall. This ornamentation is characteristic for identification of diatoms. The unthickened areas are called **'punctae'**. These unthickened areas are found in the form of striations. Sometimes they are found in the form of round **pits** and arranged radially. When the pits are quite deep they are known as **areolae.** In some genera these areolae are opened to inside and known as **'pores'** and when not opened they are known as **simple pits.**

In majority of Pennales **axial field** is coincided with longitudinal axis. The axial field may be asymmetrical. It is not a simple structure as the structure shows itself. The structure of axial field is either homogeneous or perforated by a longitudinal **'raphe'.** If raphe is absent the axial field is called **pseudoraphe.**

The protoplast. Just beneath the cell wall there is a thick layer of cytoplasm in which the chromatophores are embedded. In some forms a single chromatophore is present. Inner to cytoplasm there is a large central vacuole. In Pennales there is a central bridge of cytoplasm having a big nucleus in its centre. The shape of chromatophores varies from species to species. Sometimes it is band-like as shown in the figure. The pyrenoids are embedded in the chromatophore. The pyrenoids are without starch-sheath. The pyrenoids function as elaioplasts and are concerned with oil formation. On either side of the nucleus there is a plate-like structure. According to some, these plate-like structures act as spindle at the time of division. According to other school of thought, these plates are reserve food products. In many Pennales the nuclei are diploid. On one side of the nucleus a centrosome is found.

The chromatophores are golden brown in colour. Along with chlorophyll *a* as principal pigment chlorophyll *c* is also found in small traces. Several xanthophylls are found which overmask the green colour thus producing typical golden brown colour of the class. A special pigment known as diatomin is also present. β-carotene is present as principal pigment. Some colourless saprophytic diatoms have also been recorded. Fats and volutin droplets are found as food reserves. The diatom cell possesses two views.

(i) **Valve view.** Here the valve side is uppermost. This is also called the top view.

(ii) **Girdle view.** Here the overlapping bands or girdle is uppermost. This is also called the side view.

The arrangement of the striations on the valves is as follows:

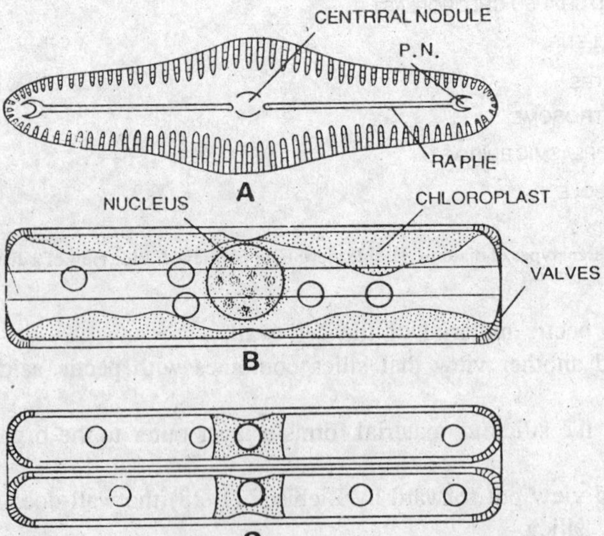

Fig. 6.4. Pennate diatoms. *Pinnularia*. Cellular organization. A surface view of frustule showing raphe, central and polar nodules; B, cell in girdle view showing massive chloroplasts, central nucleus and overlapping of valves; C, girdle view of recently divided cell.

(i) **Pennate type.** In this type the striations are arranged in a pennate fashion. They are arranged in two regular rows or series, one on either side of the axial strip. The axial strip may either be a plain area in between and is known as **pseudoraphe** or it possesses a longitudinal slot called the raphe. The raphe is found to be extended from one end of the valve to the other. The raphe bears three rounded nodules. Each end possesses one nodule and third one is found in the middle. The nodules situated at ends are known as **polar nodules** and the nodule situated in the middle is known as **central nodule.** The nodules are modified from the cell wall. These diatoms are commonly found in fresh water. Such diatoms are known as **pennate diatoms.** These are the members of order Pennales.

(ii) Centric type. In this type the striations are arranged radially. Here the valves are circular and the dots are generally large. Such diatoms are commonly known as **centric diatoms.** They are placed in order Centrales. These diatoms are commonly found in sea water (marine).

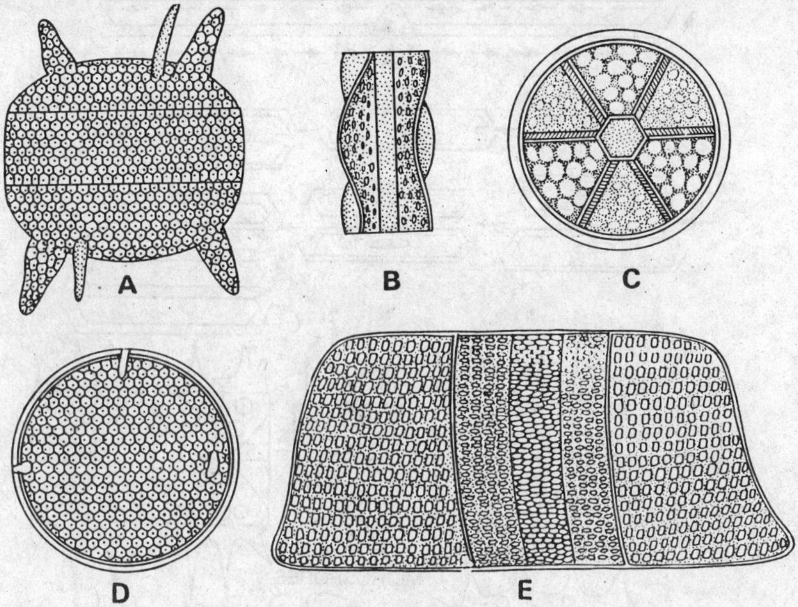

Fig. 6.5. Centric diatoms. A-B, *Biddulphia smithii*. Girdle and valve views respectively; C-D, *Actinoptyhus undulatus*—girdle and valve views, respectively; E, *Isthmia enervis*-girdle view.

Locomotion. Some of pennate diatoms only have a power of spontaneous locomotion. The movement is always by a series of jerks and along to longitudinal axis.

According to Mullar's theory of cytoplasmic streaming, inside the cell there is a cyclosis. In outer fissure there is a backward flow of cytoplasm after reaching to central nodule the cytoplasm moves in two ways.

Reproduction. The reproduction takes place by means of (a) cell division, (b) auxospores, (c) statospores and (d) microspores.

Cell division. This is vegetative method of reproduction. In most of diatoms this takes place in the midnight, but in some in the morning. A diatom gives rise to two small daughter cells after division. Prior to cell division, the protoplast becomes expanded. The chromatophores and pyrenoids divide and become double in number. They divide in longitudinal way. The nucleus divides mitotically. The epitheca and hypotheca become separated by the expansion of cytoplasm. There is a gradual diminution in the progeny of a single diatom cell known as Pfitzer's law. The ultimate smaller individuals lose their capacity of division and individuals will die. Sometimes after division into protoplasts the epitheca and hypotheca do not separate from each other.

The cell division may take place only if the water contains aluminium silicate. Some cells do not divide at all in the absence of aluminium silicate in the water.

By auxospores. Before the minimal size is reached the individuals form the auxospores. The auxospores are always formed after sexual reproduction. There are four principal methods of auxospore formation.

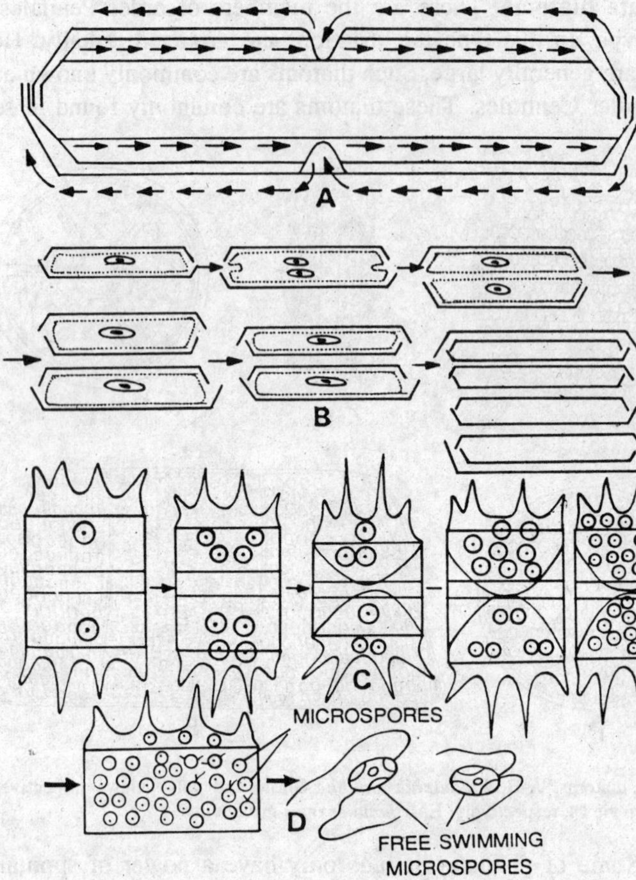

Fig. 6.6. *Diatoms*. A, locomotion; B, cell division; C, statospore and microspore formation; D, microspores.

Auxospore Formation in the Pennales

A. Auxospore formation by gametic union. This is as follows:

(a) Formation of two auxospores by two conjugating individuals. Here two diatom individuals conjugate. The diatoms taking part in conjugation secrete a common mucilage envelope around them. The diploid nucleus of each individual divides meiotically forming four haploid nuclei. Later on two of the four nuclei in each individual disintegrate. Now the protoplast with the two functional haploid nuclei divides into two. This division may be symmetrical or asymmetrical. In the case of symmetrical division the two resultant uninucleate gametes in each conjugate are equal, whereas in the case of asymmetrical division they are unequal. Fusion takes place between the gametes as follows:

(i) The gametes show amoeboid movements. The gametes come out from the parent frustules and unite in pairs. This way two fusion cells or zygotes are formed.

(ii) In this case two gametes formed by one conjugant are amoeboid and of the other conjugant are passive. The amoeboid gametes come out actively from the parent frustule and enter into the shell of the other conjugant to fuse in pairs with the passive gametes. This way two fusion cells or zygotes (2x) are formed in one frustule. The other frustule remains empty.

(iii) Here one of the two gametes is amoeboid and the other one is immobile. The amoeboid gamete of each conjugant comes out of its cell and migrates to the other to fuse with the immobile gamete. Here one zygote (2x) is formed in each frustule.

Now the zygotes (2x) are released out from the enclosing frustules. The zygotes remain dormant for some time. Later on each zygote elongates and functions as an auxospore. The auxospore remains enclosed within a silicified pectic membrane known as **perizonium.** The perizonium is either secreted by the auxospore itself or by the remains of the membrane of the zygote. The auxospore secretes a new frustule around it within the perizonium. The newly formed diatom cell is of normal size. This method of auxospore formation is commonly found in *Cymbella lanceolata.*

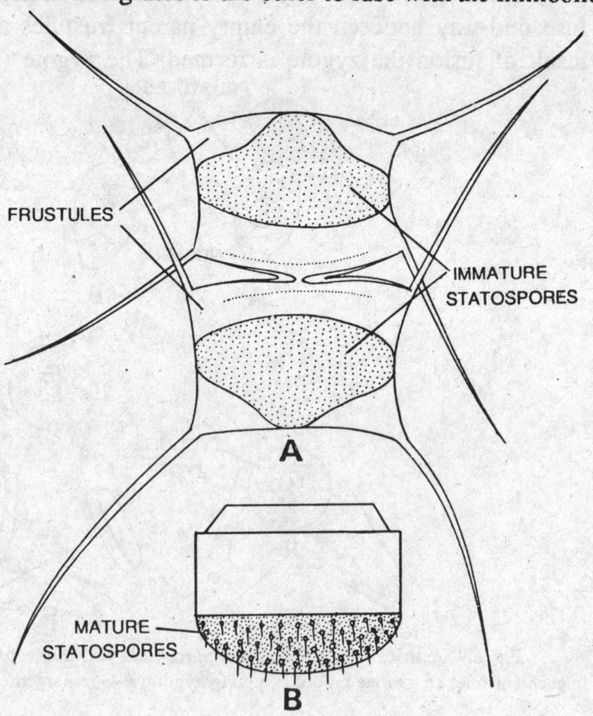

Fig. 6.7. Diatoms. A, statospore formation; B, mature statospores.

(b) Formation of a single auxospore by two conjugating individuals. In this method two diatom individuals come together end to end or laterally and become enveloped in mucilage. The diploid nucleus of each individual taking part in conjugation divides meiotically forming four haploid nuclei. Later on three of the four haploid nuclei of each conjugant degenerate.

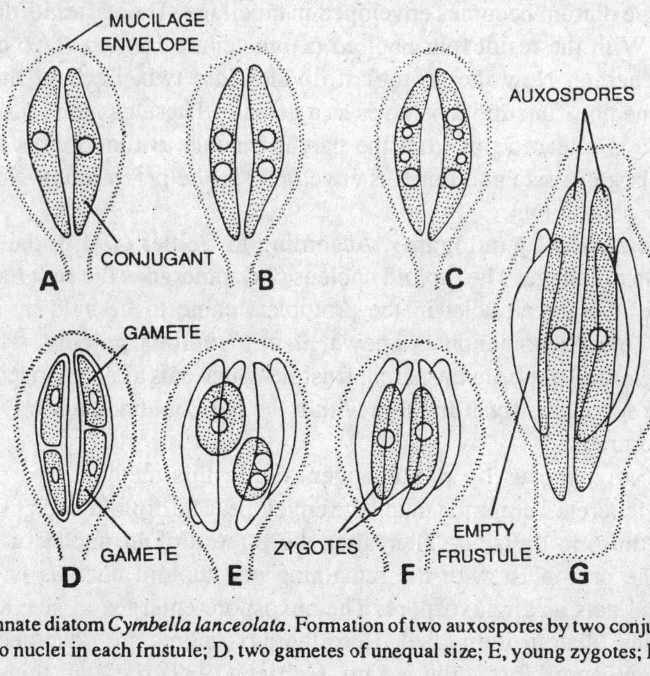

Fig. 6.8. Pennate diatom *Cymbella lanceolata*. Formation of two auxospores by two conjugating cells. A-C, meiosis and degeneration of two nuclei in each frustule; D, two gametes of unequal size; E, young zygotes; F-G, elongation of zygotes to form auxospores.

Only one nucleus survives in each protoplast which functions as the gamete. The two gametes fuse mid-way between the empty parent frustules after their escape from the same. With the result of fusion the zygote is formed. The zygote (2x) or fusion nucleus rests for some time.

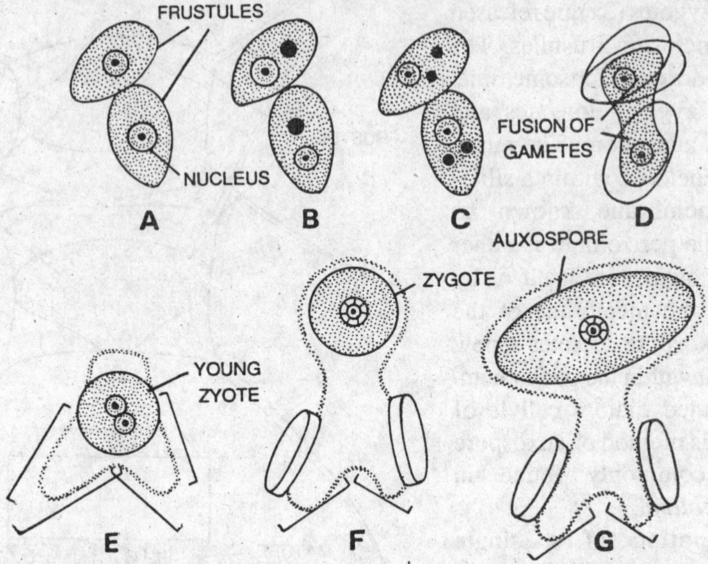

Fig. 6.9. Pennate diatom *Cocconeis placentula* var. *klinoraphis*, A-C, meiosis and degeneration of all but one nucleus in each frustule; D, gamete union; E, young zygote; F-G, enlargement of the zygote to form an auxospore (after Geitler).

Thereafter it elongates in a plane parallel to the long axis of the parent frustules and acts as an auxospore. Now this auxospore secretes a fresh frustule around it inside its perizonium. This method is of isogamous type and commonly found in *Cocconeis placentula* var., *klinoraphis*.

(c) Formation of a single auxospore from a single diatom individual. According to Geitler (1939), a single diatom becomes enveloped in mucilage. Thereafter its diploid (2x) nucleus divides meiotically. With the result four haploid (x) nuclei are formed. Two of the four haploid nuclei partially degenerate. Now the protoplast divides into two. Each of the protoplasts with one functional and one non-functional behaves as a gamete. These gametes fuse together forming a zygote. The zygote is released out from the parent frustule to function as an auxospore. The auxospore becomes large in size and remains enveloped in the perizonium. Now a fresh frustule develops within the perizonium.

Auxospore formation by autogamy. According to Geitler (1939), the single diatom cell becomes enveloped in mucilage. The diploid nucleus (2x) undergoes the first reductional division. Now the two haploid daughter nuclei in the protoplast come to lie side by side in a pair and then fuse together. This phenomenon is known as **autogamous pairing.** The protoplast with a diploid nucleus is released out from the parent frustule which acts as an auxospore. The auxospore increases in size and secretes a fresh frustule within the perizonium. This way, a new individual of normal size is formed.

Formation of auxospores by parthenogenesis. In this method, two diatom individuals come side by side and secrete a common mucilage envelope. The diploid nucleus of each individual undergoes a double mitotic division. Thereafter the three diploid nuclei of each cell become degenerated. Now the protoplast with the remaining one diploid nucleus is released out from its parent frustule and acts as an auxospore. The auxospore enlarges in size and secretes a new frustule forming a new diatom individual. Here the auxospores are developed parthenogenetically. This type of auxospore formation is rare. **Geitler** (1939) reported this type in *Cocconeis* *placentula* var. *lineata.*

Almost all pennate diatoms are monoecious and isogamous except *Rhabodonema adriaticum* which is dioecious and oogamous. Stosch (1958) reports that oogonium produces a single egg. In this dioecious species the male diatom cells produce spermatogonia. The spermatogonia are carried always from one place to another by water currents and become attached to the oogonium by mucilage pads. After attaching themselves to the oogonium the spermatogonia produce non-flagellate, naked, amoeba-like microgametes. The male nucleus passes into the egg cell and fertilization takes place forming a zygote.

Auxospore Formation in the Centrales

In Centrales a single auxospore is formed within a single individual. The auxospore is either formed by autogamy or by oogamy.

Auxospore formation by autogamy. This method of auxospore formation is found in *Melosira nummuloides* and *Cyclotella meneghiniana.* Here the diatom individual secretes mucilage and the thecae are forced apart. Thereafter the diploid nucleus (2x) divides meiotically. With the result four haploid nuclei (x) are formed. Two of the four haploid nuclei degenerate. The remaining two haploid nuclei come together and fuse. This process is known as **autogamy.** Now the protoplast with the diploid nucleus comes out from the parent frustule. This acts as an auxospore. This auxospore increases in size and secretes a fresh frustule inside the perizonium. This way a new diatom cell of normal size is developed.

Auxospore formation by oogamy. In *Melosira varians, Cyclotella tenuistriata* and *Biddulphia mobiliensis* the auxospore formation takes place by sexual process, the oogamy. The diploid diatom individual divides meiotically at the time of gamete formation. The protoplast of the diatom cell divides to form 4 to 128 small uninucleate protoplasmic bits. The number of these protoplasts varies from species to species. The first division is meiotic one. Each haploid (x) protoplast bears a single flagellum. Formerly these small flagellated cells were considered as asexual **microspores.** According to recent research, they have been supposed to be **male gametes** or **spermatozoids.** The diatom cell that produces male gametes is known as spermatogonium.

The female gametes are non-flagellated and are known eggs. A single egg develops in a single female diatom cell or oogonium. This diatom cell is slightly extended with an elongated nucleus. The diploid nucleus of female diatom cell divides meiotically forming four haploid nuclei. Out of these four haploid nuclei three degenerate. The protoplast with the remaining functional nucleus acts as an egg cell.

The male gametes (spermatozoids) are released out from the male cell (antheridium or spermatogonium) and swim to an oogonium. One of the spermatozoids penetrates the egg and fuses with it. The plasmogamy is followed by karyogamy. Now the zygote (2x) escapes from the parent frustule. It acts, as an auxospore or renewal spore. This enlarges in size and the diploid nucleus divides mitotically twice but only one daughter nucleus survives at each division. The auxospore (2x) secretes a frustule inside the perizonium, and a new individual is formed.

Statospores. They are also called hypnospores, endospores or cysts and produced within the frustules of the Centrales. They are thick-walled and formed in pairs or in greater number inside the frustule.

Microspores. The microspores have been reported from Centrales only. They are found in great number but multiple of 2 and 4 upto 128. In *Biddulphia mobiliensis* they are formed by the division of cytoplasm. The division may be simultaneous or successive. The behaviour of nucleus is not clearly understood. The microspores of some genera are biflagellate. If there occurs reduction division, they are gametes; if not then they are zoospores. The microspores found swarming about a round and undivided cell and so there is indication of oogamy but this is only a presumption.

Economic importance of diatoms. Along with Dinoflagellatae they form basic food for sea animals. Besides the cell wall of diatoms is silicified; after the death and decay of diatoms the silicified wall is deposited on the beds of ocean and by the process of silica deposition the beds of silica are formed. Such beds are found in Lompoc, California. The silican earth is miles and miles long and 700 feet in thickness. The thickest deposits are at St Maria oil fields where they are upto 3000 feet in thickness. This diatomaceous earth is used in many small and large-scale industries. It is used in the manufacture of an explosive known as dynamite. This is also used in the filtration work in sugar factories. The fire bricks of diatomaceous earth are manufactured which can resist temperatures upto 1,500°C. They are used in the inner lining of furnaces. By adding 1 to 3% earth in cement, the cementing power is increased a lot. This earth is also used in the manufacture of tooth pastes.

Classification. The present day classification of diatoms is based on Schutt's (1896) classification. It is based on the ornamentation of the cell wall.

There are two orders 1. Centrales and 2. Pennales.

1. Centrales

(i) They are well circular polygonal or irregular. Ornamentation is radially symmetrical around a central point.

(ii) There are no raphe and pseudoraphe.

(iii) There are many chromatophores inside a cell.

(iv) Reproduction takes place by means of statospores, auxospores (singly produced) and microspores.

2. Pennales

(i) Bilaterally symmetrical or even asymmetrical valves are present.

(ii) The ornamentation of the cell wall is bilaterally disposed with respect to a line and never to a point as in Centrales.

(iii) Raphe or a pseudoraphe is present.

(iv) There are only one or two chromatophores per cell.

(v) Reproduction takes place by means of statospores and auxospores.

Phylogenetic Relationships in Bacillariophyceae

It is not very clear whether they arose independently or from some common ancestor. It is speculated that the organisms of Chrysophyceae, Xanthophyceae and Bacillariophyceae also placed under phylum Chrysophyta may have had a common origin in some primitively organized ancestral stock. It is doubtful, that this class has given rise to any of the higher groups of plants beyond thallophytes. It is thought that their evolution is parallel to that of Chlorophyceae. It seems that both of them have been evolved from the flagellated ancestors.

Revision Questions

1. Give the characteristic feature of diatoms.
2. Give the distinguishing characters of Bacillariophyceae.
3. Give the structure of two types of diatoms.
4. Describe the modes of reproduction in pennate type of diatoms.
5. Give the various methods of auxospore formation in Pennales.
6. Give a comprehensive account of auxospore formation in Centrales.
7. Write notes on: (a) economic importance of diatoms; (b) structure of cell wall and protoplast in diatoms; (c) phylogenetic relationship in Bacillariophyceae.

Multiple Choice Type

1. The diatoms are:
   (i) fresh water forms, (ii) marine, (iii) fresh water and marine.
2. The cell wall of diatoms is called:
   (i) epitheca, (ii) hypotheca, (iii) frustule.
3. The cell wall of diatoms consists of
   (i) pectin, (ii) cellulose, (iii) callose.
4. The cell wall is silicified in:
   (i) desmids, (ii) diatoms, (iii) *Vaucheria*, (iv) *Ulothrix*.
5. The 'punctae' are related to :
   (i) *Polysiphonia*, (ii) desmids, (iii) diatoms
6. Sort out the pennate diatom:
   (i) *Biddulphia*, (ii) *Actinoptychus*, (iii) *Isthmia*, (iv) *Pinnularia*.
7. Sort out the centric diatom:
   (i) *Biddulphia*, (ii) *Pinnularia*, (iii) *Cymbella*, (iv) *Cocconeis*.
8. Diatomaceous earth is produced by :
   (i) Chlorophyceae, (ii) Bacillariophyceae, (iii) Xanthophyceae, (iv) Brown algae.

Answers

1 (iii), 2 (iii), 3 (i), 4 (ii), 5 (iii), 6 (iv), 7 (i) 8 (ii).

7

Phaeophycophyta-Phaeophyceae The Brown Algae

Characteristic features

Pigmentation. Chlorophylls *a* and *c*, α, and β-carotenes, Diatoxanthin, Flavoxanthin, Fucoxanthin, Lutein, Violaxanthin.

Storage products. Laminarin, mannitol, oils.

Flagellation. 2, lateral

There are about 195 genera and 1,000 species in this class.

Occurrence. With the exception of three genera, *i.e., Heribendiella, Pleurocladia* and *Bodanella* which are fresh water in habit, rest of all Phaeophyceae are marine and commonly called brown sea weeds. The marine Phaeophyceae occur in littoral zones of arctic and antarctic oceans. As we pass on to the tropics the number of the members of brown algae gradually decreases. Certain forms, such as Dictyotales and *Sargassum* are predominant in warm waters. Almost all of Phaeophyceae are attached; *Sargassum natans* and *Sargassum fluitans* are pelagic, *i.e.*, they are secondary free floating in Sargasso sea of Atlantic ocean.

Most of the Fucaceae are found in the upper littoral zone of the sea. The Laminariales are restricted in the lower littoral zone, whereas the *Sphacelaria* and *Leathesia* are found in midlittoral zone. Certain species of *Sargassum* and *Desmarestia* are found in sub-littoral zones. They are not found below the depth of 25 metres. *Macrocystis* and *Nereocystis* occur in 13 to 20, metre deep waters. These giant kelps are attached to the rocks by their holdfasts. A stipe arises from the holdfast and the large leaf blades and bladders float on the surface of the water. The brown algae are not found below the depth of 110 metres.

Range of somatic structure of Phaeophyceae. No member is unicellular, colonial or unbranched filament. The simplest member is heterotrichous filament, which shows the highest organization in Chlorophyceae is the lowest organization in Phaeophyceae. The various vegetative organizations of the Phaeophyceae may be classified in the following groups.

Ectocarpoid. In *Ectocarpus* the thallus is profusely branched and the cells are joined end to end in a single series. The thallus consists of a prostrate branched portion, from which the erect branched system arises. This is heterotrichous type of organization.

Cable type. This type is represented by *Mesogloea*. Here the thallus consists of several axial strands like a bundle. Some radial branches come out at right angles from these threads, and the whole structure appears like a cable.

Multiseptate cable type. This type is represented by *Chorda filum*. The thallus is formed by many compact filaments. Actually there is no parenchyma but pseudoparenchyma.

Corticated type. *Desmarestia, Arthrocladia* etc., represent this type. Here in the lower region of the plant body the lateral branches become rhizoidal and coil around the main axis to form a compact pseudoparenchymatous cortex around the main axis.

Truly parenchymatous forms. In such forms the thalli are leaf-like or laminate and truly parenchymatous, *e.g., Punctaria*. The members of Laminariales and Fucales possess improved type of parenchyma in them. The plant body of *Macrocystis* is 30 to 50 metres long. It has a

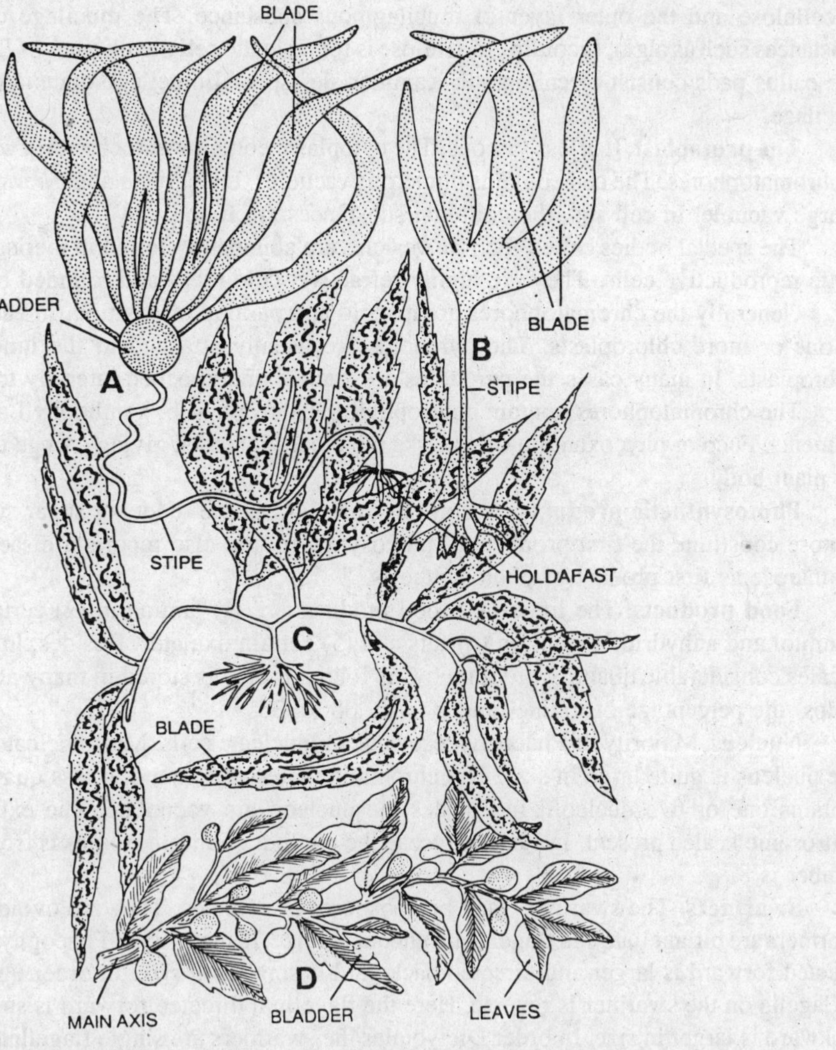

Fig. 7.1. Phaeophyceae. Range of structure. A, *Nereocystis luetkeana;* B, *Laminaria andersonii* (sporophyte); C, *Macrocystis pyrifera;* D, *Sargassum* sp.

dichotomously branched holdfast, a stipe and large leaf blades having gas bladders at their bases. This is the longest known giant kelp.

The plant body of *Nereocystis* is 20 to 25 metres long. It consists of a haptera, a stipe and terminal large gas bladder having many blades on it.

Laminaria, Fucus, Sargassum, Postelsia etc., all possess truly parenchymatous structures.

Internal structure. In *Laminaria,* the stipe consists of epidermis, cortex and medulla. There are 'trumpet hyphae'. At the junction of the mouths of two trumpets a callus pad develops in winter and dissolves in spring. This refreshes the memory of the callus pads of the sieve tubes of higher angiosperms.

Hairs. The hairs are present in all members of Phaeophyceae. They are multicelullar and generally ensheathed at their bases.

Cell structure. The cell wall is two layered. The inner layer outer to the protoplast consists of cellulose and the outer layer of mucilaginous substance. The mucilage contains gum like substances such as algin, fucoidin etc. Callose is found in the cell membranes of *Laminaria digitata*. The callus pads consist of callose. In Laminariales special mucilage ducts are found, secreting mucilage.

The protoplast. It is less viscous. The cytoplasm contains mitochondria which are in contact of chromatophores. The cell contains numerous vacuoles. In *Dictyota* and *Fucus* each cell contains a large vacuole. In cell sap, the colloidal substances are found.

The special bodies called fucosan vesicles are abundantly found in meristematic, photosynthetic reproductive cells. They are highly refractive, colourless and rounded bodies.

Generally the chromatophores are discoid and parietal in position. In each cell, there may be one or more chloroplasts. The pyrenoids are usually attached to the inner margins of the chloroplasts. In many cases the pyrenoids are stalked and attached laterally to the chloroplasts.

The chromatophores contain chlorophyll a, chlorophyll b, xanthophyll and carotenoids as pigrnents. Fuco or phycoxanthin overmasks the other pigments, giving a tinge of brown colour to the plant body.

Photosynthetic products. According to Kylin, simple reducing sugar such as dextrose or pentose constitute the first products of photosynthesis. He also reports a disaccharide known as laminarose as first product of photosynthesis.

Food products. The important food products are (1) laminarin (2) certain hydrolases (3) mannitol and anhydride manniton (4) fats and (5) certain oxalates. Besides, in Laminariales and Fucales considerable quantity of vitamin C is found. Iodine is stored in many algae. In *Laminaria* (kelps) the percentage of iodine ranges from .08 to .35.

Nucleus. Majority of Phaeophyceae have uninucleate cells. Multinucleate condition is rare. The nucleus is quite large in size. The chromatin material is found in less quantity. The nucleus contains one or two nucleoli. In Fucales the nucleoli are vacuolate. The extra or intranuclear centrosome is also present. In Phaeophyceae the number of chromosomes is from 8-32. The basic number is 8.

Swarmers. The swarmers may be zoospores or gametes. They are ovoid or pyriform. The swarmers are biflagellate and flagella are unequal in size. In majority of Phaeophyceae the flagellum directed forward is larger and directed backward is smaller in size. In order Fucales the position of flagella on the swarmer is reverse. Here the flagellum directed forward is smaller and directed backward is larger in size. In order Dictyotales the swarmers are single flagellate. The flagella are attached laterally to the swarmer. Each swarmer contains a large nucleus, 3 or 4 chromatophores, a stigma, a blepharoplast and a plastomere.

Reproduction. The reproduction takes place by 1. vegetative, 2. asexual and 3. sexual methods.

1. Vegetative reproduction. Vegetative propagation takes place by fragmentation of the thalli. In the case of *Sargassum* this type of reproduction is very prolific. In *S. natans* it is found abundantly. This is a free floating species.

In some of the cases special fragments known as **'propagula'** are developed. They occur in *Sphacelaria*.

The **'adventitious buds'** develop in many species of *Fucus*. They develop by the division of meristematic cells in young plants. Each bud develops into a new plant.

2. Asexual reproduction. Asexual reproduction takes place by means of zoospores and aplanospores formed inside the sporangia.

(a) By zoospores. The formation of zoospores is most common in all the members of Phaeophyceae except in *Dictyota* and *Fucus*. The zoospores are pyriform and biflagellate. The anterior flagellum is larger than the posterior one except in Fucales. In Dictyotales single flagellum is found on the zoospore. The zoospores are produced inside the zoosporangia, which may be of two types, *i.e.,* **unilocular sporangia** and **multilocular** or **plurilocular sporangia.**

The unilocular sporangium may be terminal or intercalary in position. In each sporangium 64 or 128 zoospores are produced. At the time of the formation of zoospores reduction division takes place and zoospores are haploid. They germinate into haploid thalli (gametophytes). In some cases as Punctariales, Sphacelariales, Chordales, *Ectocarpus, Pyaeliella* etc., the zoospores behave as gametes and unite in pairs. This is the example of origin of sex.

The plurilocular sporangia are always terminal in position. All the cells of sporangium are diploid and give rise to diploid zoospores. Such zoospores will give rise to sporophytes. The multilocular sporangia are unknown in Fucales and Laminariales.

(b) By aplanospores. Sometimes, in unilocular sporangia instead of producing zoospores the aplanospores may also be produced. They are non-motile and without flagella, *e.g.,* Dictyotales. The first division is always reductional. The aplanospores are always less in number. In *Dictyota* 4 aplanospores and in *Zonaria* 8 aplanospores are produced per sporangium.

3. Sexual reproduction. This ranges from isogamy to oogamy.

(a) Isogamy. This takes place by the fusion of two similar gametes. This is found in many Phaeophyceae such as Ectocarpales, Sphacelariales, Dictyosiphonales etc. The gametophytes may be monoecious or dioecious.

(b) Anisogamy. Here the fusion of two dissimilar gametes takes place. The examples of this type are found in some members of Ectocarpales, *Cutleria, Soranthera* etc. If fusion fails the female gametes may develop parthenogenetically.

(c) Oogamy. In majority of Phaeophyceae the sexual reproduction is oogamous. The species may be homo or heterothallic. The male sex organs are called the antheridia and the female sex organs are called the oogonia. In Dictyotales the antheridia are multicellular structures. Each cell of antheridium gives rise to a spermatozoid. In Desmarestiales and Laminariales the antheridia are unicellular and each antheridium produces a single spermatozoid.

Usually each oogonium produces a single ovum or oosphere, but in *Fucus* eight eggs are produced in the oogonium.

The eggs liberate in the water and only then the fertilization takes place so that the fertilization is external.

In Fucales the sex organs develop inside conceptacles which develop on special reproductive branches called the **'receptacles'.**

Life-cycle. There are three general types of life-cycle found in the class Phaeophyceae (brown algae).

1. An alternation of morphologically similar haploid and diploid generations, as found in *Ectocarpus.*

2. An alternation of morphologically dissimilar (heteromorphic) haploid and diploid generations, as found in Laminariales, *e.g., Laminaria, Nereocystis.*

3. The almost complete suppression of the haploid generation (*i.e.,* diplontic), as in *Fucus.* In this genus only haploid cells are gametes.

Origin of Phaeophyceae. It is very probable that Phaeophyceae are a series of considerable antiquity. The distinct features of Phaeophyceae such as pigmentation, the reserve food products and the type of flagellation are such unique characters that there appear to be no affinities with any other class of algae. The universal presence of a swarmer in the class supports the view of a flagellate ancestry for the class. According to Kylin, the Fucales arose directly unrelated with Phaeophyceae. But according to Gilbert M. Smith, the Fucales arose by dropping off of the gametophytic generation in a complex group of the brown algae with two alternating generations.

Classification. According to Dr. F. E. Fritsch, there are nine orders in this class-1. Ectocarpales, 2. Tilopteridales 3. Cutleriales, 4. Sporochnales, 5. Desmarestiales, 6. Laminariales, 7. Sphacelariales, 8. Dictyotales, 9. Fucales.

The outline of Taylor's system is as follows. About 12 orders are included in this system. The whole class is divided into three sub-classes.

Three sub-classes are:

I. **Isogeneratae.** Isomorphic alternation of generations.

II. **Heterogeneratae.** Heteromorphic alternation of genernaions.

III. **Cylosporeae.** Diplontic type of life cycle.

The sub-class **Isogeneratae** includes 5 orders.

1. **Ectocarpales.** Branched heterotrichous filamentous body; trichothallic growth; reproductive bodies terminal or intercalary, single or in chain; the sporophyte produces zoospores or neutral spors (2x); isogamy.

2. **Sphacelariales.** Growth by single large apical cell segments formed which frequentely divide lengthwise in a regular polysiphonous manner; sporophyte may produce haploid or diploid zoospores; iso or anisogamy.

3. **Tilopteridales.** Thallus freely branched showing trichothallic growth, upper portion monosiphonous; lower portion polysiphonous; sporophytes produce unilocular sporangia only, each containing a single quadrinucleate aplanospore; gametangia are intercalary; doubtful oogamy.

4. **Cutleriales.** Thalluls flattened, blade-like or disc-like, dichotomously branched, trichothallic growth; the sporophyte produces unilocular sporangia only; anisogamy.

5. **Dictyotales.** Erect flattened dichotomously branched parenchymatous thallus; growth by a single apical cell or a marginal row of special cells; the unicellular sporangia of sporophyte each produces 4 or 8 aplanospores; oogamy.

The sub-class **Heterogeneratae** includes two series and six orders.

Series **1. Haplostichineae.** Growth trichothallic; thallus consists of one or more filaments.

Series **2. Polystichineae.** Trichothallic growth absent; longitudinal and transverse intercalary cells form a parenchyma.

Three orders are included in **Series Haplostichineae.**

1. **Chordariales.** Branched filamentous sporophyte; isogamous.

2. **Sporochanles.** Each branch of the sporophyte terminates in a tuft of hairs; growth is trichothallic due to intercalary cell division at the base of each hair; the unicellular sporangia are borne terminally in dense clusters; plurilocular sporangia absent; oogamy.

3. **Desmarestiales.** The thallus has a single filament of each growing apex posterior to which there is pseudoparenchymatous cortication, the thallus is macroscopic; oogamy, gametophyte microscopic.

Three orders are included in **Series Polystichineae.**

1. **Punctariales.** Parenchymatous, sporophyte of medium size; reproductive organs may or may not be borne in sori; the sporophyte reproduces by zoospores; iso or anisogamy, gametophyte microscopic.

2. **Dictyosiphonales.** Profusely branched cylindrical thallus, growth by single apical cells; sporophyte produces unilocular sporangia only; isogamy, gametophyte microscopic.

3. **Laminariales.** Sporophyte differentiated into a holdfast stipe, and blades; growth by intercalary meristem; internal structure of thallus is differentiated into epidermis, cortex and medulla, the medulla shows 'trumpet hyphae' with callus pads; oogamy, gametophyte microscopic; the sporophyte bears only unicellular sporangia in sori.

The sub-class **Cyclosporeae** includes a single order Fucales.

Order-Fucales. Life cycle is diplontic; growth by single apical cell, thallus parenchymatous; unilocular sporangia borne in conceptacles; the egg is liberated in the water prior to fusion.

Economic importance. The people of orient use seaweeds as food than by people anywhere else. The Japanese people begin to collect kelp in July and continue through October. They use more than twenty species of brown algae as food. Many other brown algae are used as fertilizers. The acetic acid is extracted from the seaweed by means of fermentation. With one seaweed the Japanese make **kombu**, which is first dried and then cooked with meat. Sometimes it is powdered and added into soups and sauces. It may also be used as a vegetable, steeped as a beverage, or made into a confection by coating with sugar. In many places *Nereocystis* is used in the preparation of medicines, poultry feed and for the extraction of potash salts. About 30 percent of its dry weight is potassium chloride. The stipe of *Nereocystis* has been used in the preparation of **seatron.**

Macrocystis and *Laminaria* are the chief sources for the extraction of algin. About 44 pounds of algin have been extracted from a ton of kelp. Algin is used in the preparation of paints and varnishes. It is also used in the preparation of ice cream. *Egregia,* a kelp, is used as fertilizer. It contains greater amount of potassium salt and about the same amount of nitrogen. Seaweeds also contain iodine and other salts.

Phylogenetic Relationships in Phaeophyceae

In a number of ways, the Phaeophyceae and Chlorophyceae have been evolved on parallel lines. However, the brown algae possess a more highly differentiated thallus and mostly multicellular reproductive organs. It is also thought that the Phaeophyceae have been evolved like Chlorophyceae from a flagellate ancestor. Although it is quite certain that the divergence from the green line was quite early and gave rise to laterally flagellated progenitors much like the simple forms of Chrysophyceae and Xanthophyceae of today. At present there are no known unicellular Phaeophyceae, but the reproductive cells of today's brown algae indicate that the original brown algae were unicells of this type. The pigments and reserve food substances of Phaeophyceae also resemble with those of Chrysophyceae and Xanthophyceae. Such characteristics suggest the common ancestry of these groups. The thalli of brown algae are highly specialized but the idea of the evolution of higher plants from Phaeophyceae has totally been given up.

Two divergent lines have been established very early in the evolution of Phaeophyceae. One of these lines has given rise to the groups having isomorphic alternation of generations, and the other to the groups having heteromorphic alternation of generations. In both series there was a progressive evolution towards the complexity of the thallus and from isogamous to oogamous type of reproduction. It is thought that the Fucales are at the top of the heteromorphic series.

ORDER–ECTOCARPALES

Characteristic Features

1. The plant body possesses a branched heterotrichous filamentous thallus in which the cell division is not localized.
2. The growth mostly intercalary.
3. The reproductive elements may be terminal or intercalary borne singly or in chains.
4. The plant itself is sporophyte bearing unilocular and neutral sporangia which produce zoospores or neutral spores.
5. The gametophyte produces iso or anisogamous gametes. There are about 50 genera in this order.

Genus ECTOCARPUS

Distribution. *Ectocarpus* is world-wide in distribution and possesses many species. This is most primitive of all the brown algae. The species are commonly found in the colder seas of the temperate and polar regions. They are very common along the Atlantic coast. The plants occur attached to the rocks in the littoral and sublittoral zones. Many species are epiphytic upon the members of Fucales and Laminariales. *E. tomentosus* is an epiphyte upon the species of *Fucus*. *E. fasciculatus* is found growing on the fins of certain fish in Swedish waters.

Structure. The plant body is filamentous and heterotrichous. It is differentiated into prostrate and erect thalli. The prostrate portion is found attached to the substratum and remains creeping on it. The branches of the erect system of the plant are given out from the prostrate system. Comparatively, the prostrate portion of the plant is much branched than that of the erect portion. The ultimate branches of the erect portion are generally thin and pointed. The cells of the branches of the erect portion are uniseriately arranged end to end. The branching is always lateral and the branches arise just beneath the septa. In certain species the older branches are ensheathed or corticated by a layer of the branches of the rhizoids.

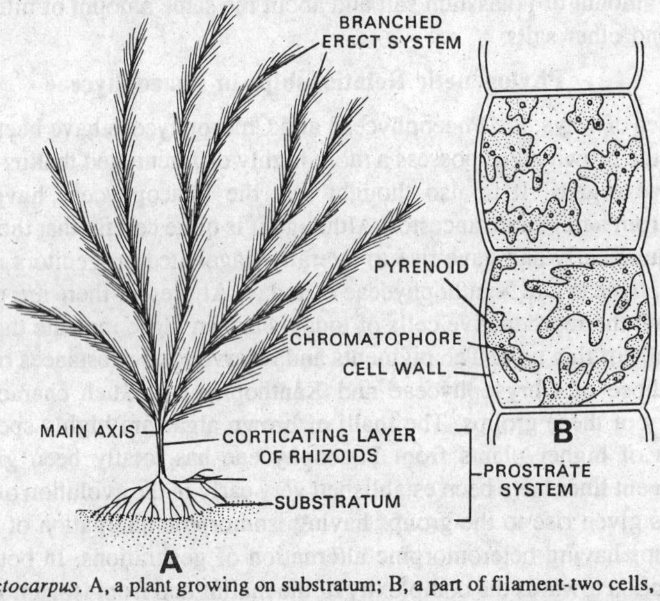

Fig. 7.2. *Ectocarpus*. A, a plant growing on substratum; B, a part of filament-two cells, (magnified)

The cells of *Ectocarpus* are small, cylindrical, uninucleate and with a few band-shaped chromatophores of irregular shape. Sometimes the cells contain many discoid chromatophores. The cell wall is thick and consists of three pectic cellulose layers. The cell wall is mucilaginous. The protoplast is differentiated into a single nucleus and cytoplasm. Naked pyrenoid-like structures are present in the golden-brown chromatophores. The plastids contain chlorohyll a, chlorophyll b, xanthophylls and a brown pigment **fucoxanthin.**

Growth. It is apical in prostrate system and trichothallic, *i.e.*, by means of intercalary meristem located at the base of multicellular hair. The meristematic cells cut off new cells towards the upper side transversely.

Reproduction. The reproduction takes place by means of asexual and sexual methods.

Asexual reproduction. The asexual reproduction takes place by means of biflagellate zoospores known as neutral spores produced within neutral and unilocular sporangia found upon asexual plants (sporophyte) also known as diploid thalli (2x).

Unilocular sporangia. The terminal cell of a short branchlet enlarges in size and develops into an unilocular sporangium. The number of chromatophores increases within the young sporangium, and the young sporangium becomes several fold in size. The single nucleus found within the sporangium divides and redivides and ultimately 32 or 64 nuclei are formed. The first division is reductional one. After the formation of the nuclei, there is cleavage, which results into uninucleate protoplasts. Each such protoplast possesses a chromatophore. Very soon each uninucleate protoplast metamorphoses into a biflagellate zoospore. The zoospores are pyriform in shape. The two unequal flagella are laterally inserted on each zoospore. The longer flagellum is directed

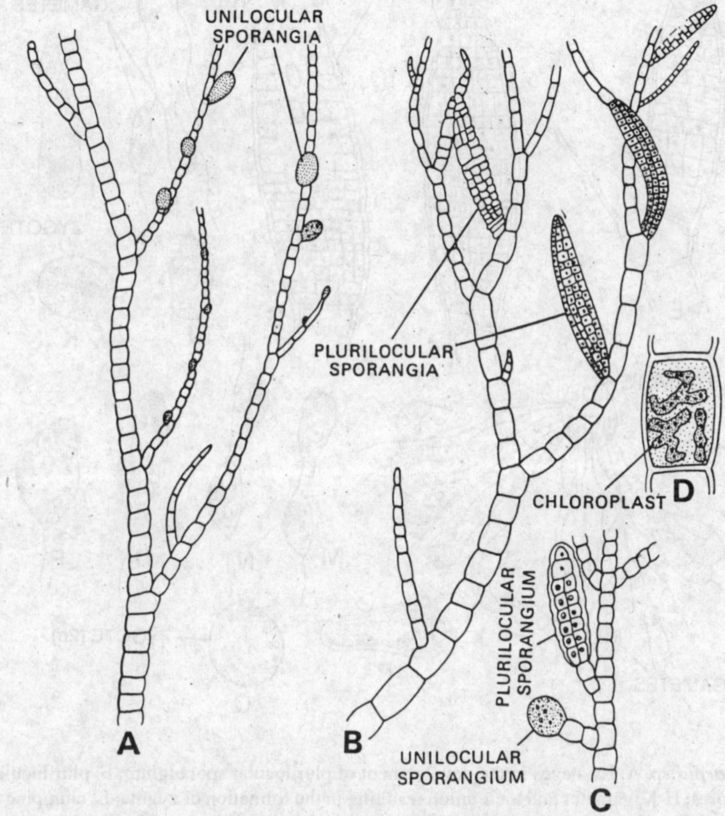

Fig. 7.3. *Ectocarpus siliculosus*. A, a part of the plant with unilocular sporangia; B, a part of the plant with plurilocular sporangia; C, a part of the plant of *E. cylindricus* with both uni-and plurilocular sporangia; D, a cell.

forward and the shorter backward. The zoospores are extruded *en masse* through a small opening found at the distal end of the sporangium. The zoospores of the mass remain inactive about for a minute and thereafter, they become motile and swim here and there in the water. Ultimately the zoospores come to rest on substratum and lose their flagella. The protoplasts become round and give rise to new haploid plants.

Plurilocular sporangia. The plurilocular sporangium develops from the terminal cell of a lateral branchlet. This cell divides several times repeatedly producing a vertical row of 6 to 12 cells. Several other vertical and transverse divisions take place and ultimately several hundred small cubical cells are formed which are arranged in 20 to 40 transverse tiers. There is no reduction division. The protoplast of each diploid cubical cell metamorphoses into a biflagellate neutral

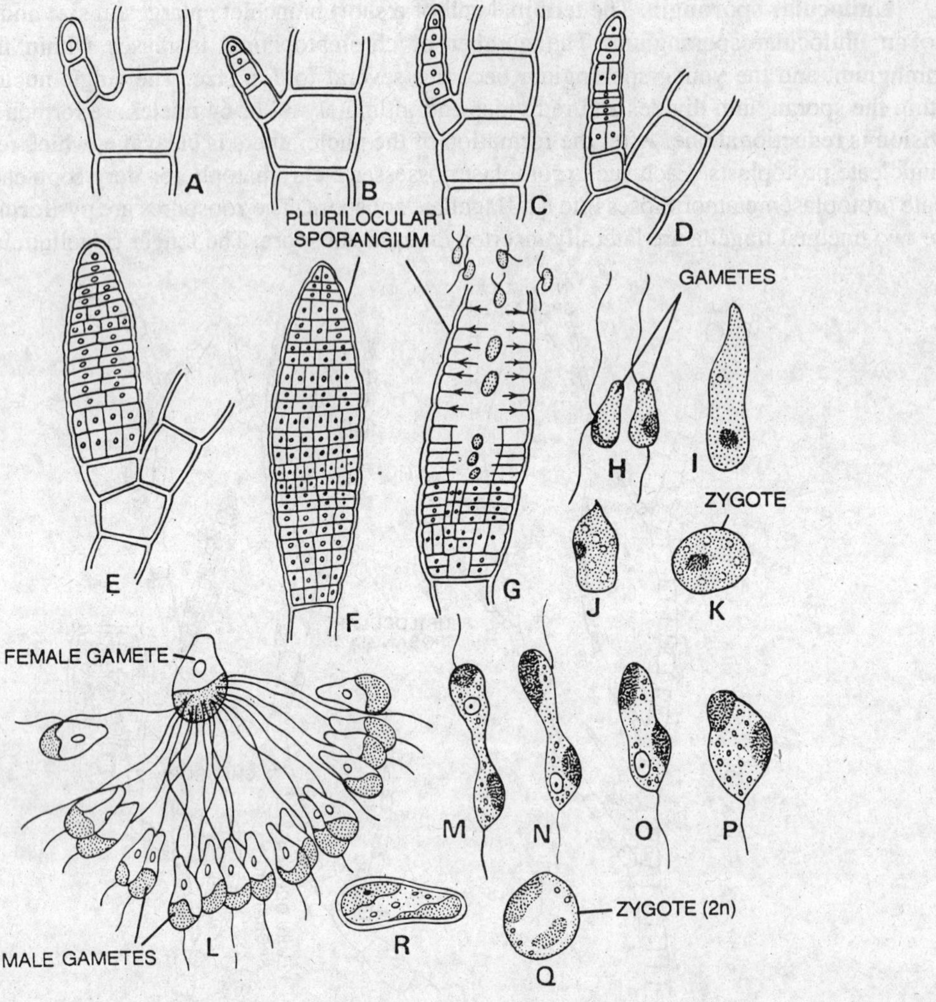

Fig. 7.4. *Ectocarpus* sp. A. E., stages in the development of plurilocular sporangium; F, plurilocular sporangium; G, liberation of neutral spores; H-K, gametes and their union resulting in the formation of zygote; L, clumping of gametes; M-Q, successive stages in the union of gametes and formation of zygote in *E. siliculosus*.

zoospore. The zoospores liberate outside to the sporangium by means of apical or lateral pore. The zoospores resemble in shape to the zoospores produced by unilocular sporangia.

The zoospores swim for a short while and then settle down on some substratum, retract their flagella and directly give rise to new sporophytic (2x) plants. These plants once again bear unilocular and plurilocular sporangia. These sporophytic plants never produce plurilocular gametangia. The plurilocular gametangia are produced upon the plants which are developed from the zoospores of unilocular sporangia.

Sexual reproduction. The sexual reproduction ranges from isogamy to anisogamy. Majority of the species are monoecious. The most thoroughly worked out species *E. siliculosus* is dioecious. The plurilocular gametangia develop from the terminal cell of a lateral branchlet. It divides several times repeatedly producing a vertical row of 6 to 12 cells. This is followed by several other vertical and transverse divisions and ultimately hundreds of small cubical cells are produced arranged in

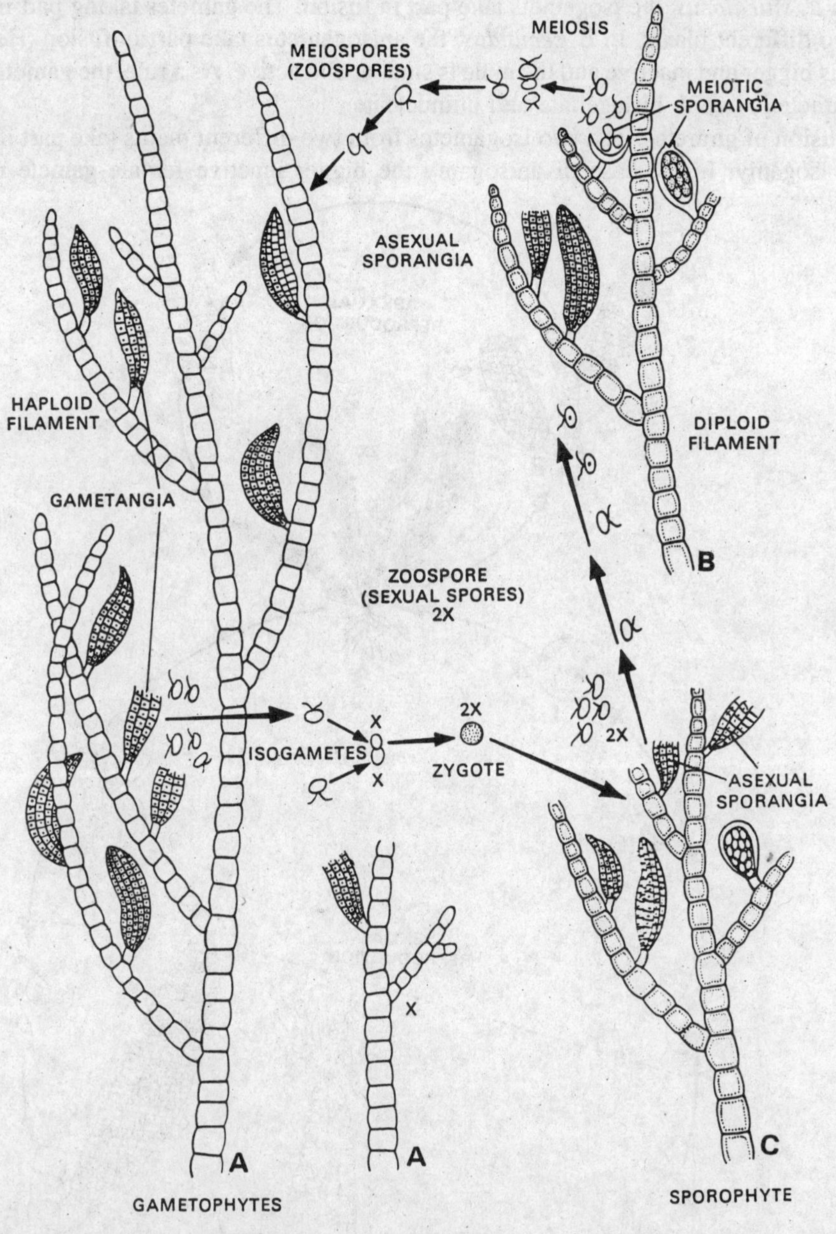

Fig. 7.5. *Ectocarpus*. Stages in life cycle—A and A', gametophyte (haploid filament); B, diploid filament showing meiotic sporangia and zoospores (x) after meiosis; C, sporophyte with asexual sporangia forming zoospores (2x).

20 to 40 transverse tiers. As already stated, the gametes are produced on haploid plants which develop from the zoospores produced in the unilocular sporangia. The gametophytic plants resemble the sporophytic plants in shape but quite different in behaviour. These gametophytes bear plurilocular gametangia. The plurilocular gametangia are quite similar to the plurilocular or neutral sporangia in their shape.

The protoplasts of the cubical cells of the plurilocular gametangia metamorphose into biflagellate gametes which liberate through an apical pore on the gametangium gradually.

In *E. siliculosus,* the isogamets take part in fusion. The gametes taking part in fusion come from two different plants. In *E. secundus,* the anisogametes take part in fusion. Here the female gamete is bigger and inactive and the male is smaller and active. As a rule, the gametes are haploid. Each gamete is ovoid, biflagellate and uninucleate.

Fusion of gametes. The two isogametes from two different plants take part in fusion in the case of isogamy. In the case of anisogamy the bigger inactive female gamete rests and gets

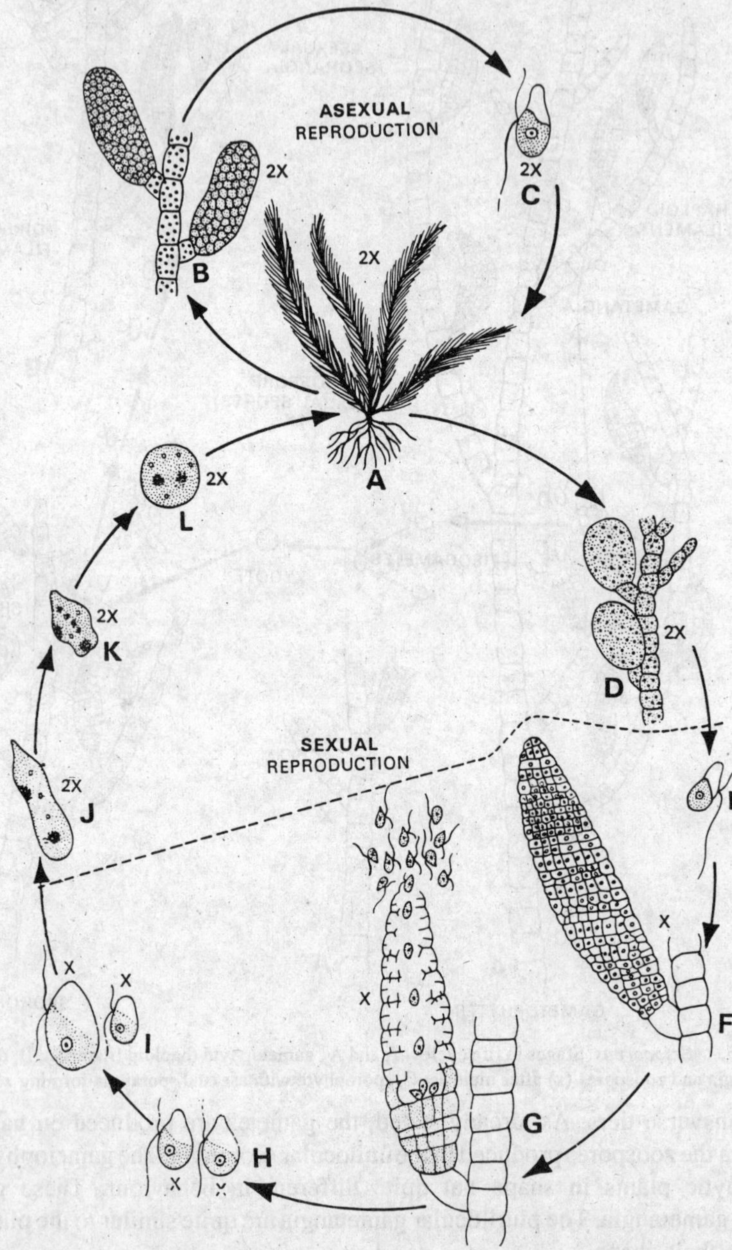

Fig. 7.6. *Ectocarpus*. Life-cycle. A, a plant; B, portion of thallus with plurilocular or neutral sporangia; C, neutral zoospores; D, part of the thallus with unilocular sporangia; E, haploid zoospores; F, plurilocular sporangium; G, liberation of neutral zoospores; H, union of gametes (isogamy); I, anisogamy; J-K, fusion and L, zygote.

surrounded by several actively motile male gametes. Soon after one of the male gametes fuses with the female gamete and the zygote is formed. The zygote germinates into a new diploid plant which produces unilocular or neutral sporangia. All cytological investigations in *E. siliculosus* have revealed that diploid plants bearing unilocular sporangia have a reduction division while those bearing neutral (plurilocular) sporangia have no reduction division.

The diploid zoospores which have been produced from neutral (plurilocular) sporangia germinate into sporophytes bearing unilocular or neutral sporangia. According to Papenfuss (1935), the zoospores produced from unilocular sporangia germinate into gametophytes bearing gametes which may either unite in pairs to produce zygotes, or develop into new gametophytes by means of parthenogenesis. The zygote (2x) on germination produces a sporophyte (2x).

According to Knight (1929), Schussnig and Kothbauer (1934), the zoospores from unilocular sporangia also unite like gametes, but nothing is known about the formation of zygotes.

Alternation of generations and reduplication. The life history of *E. siliculosus* exhibits an alternation of generations of sporophyte (2x) and gametophyte (x). In addition to a regular alternation of generations the reduplication of the sporophyte as well as of gametophyte also takes place. The reduplication of the sporophyte takes place by means of zoospores from neutral sporangia and possibly by a gametic union of zoospores. The reduplication of gametophyte takes place by means of parthenogenetic germination of the gametes.

From the point of view of their environmental conditions such as temperature and light intensity the life history of *E. siliculosus* shows the following variations—

1. According to Kylin (1933), the plants growing in the water of Sweden and according to Knight (1929) the plants growing in the waters of Britain are sporophytic and in any case they do not give rise to the gametophytes.

2. According to Knight (1929), the plants growing in Mediterranean waters near Naples are exclusively gametophytic but according to Schussnig and Kothbauer (1934), the sporophytes have also been seen in these waters. It seems that the zygotes are regularly produced from the gametophytes of Mediterranean waters but these zygotes rarely develop into sporophytes.

3. In United States, near Massachusetts and Woodhole both the gametophytes and sporophytes are found. Here, the life-cycle is isomorphic. The plants are heterothallic.

Systematic position. Division-Phaeophycophyta; Class-Phaeophyceae; Order-Ectocarpales; Family-Ectocarpaceae; Genus-*Ectocarpus*.

ORDER–DICTYOTALES

Characteristic Features.

1. The species possess a well marked regular alternation of two identical generations.

2. The plants are parenchymatous and consist of one or more medullary layers of large cells and a cortical layer of small cells.

3. They are also characterized by apical growth and usually by dichotomous branching in one plane.

4. Asexual reproduction takes place by means of tetraspores produced in superficial tetrasporangia.

5. Sexual reproduction takes place by means of antheridia and oogonia borne in sori on separate plants. It is oogamous.

6. All the organs of reproduction develop from surface cells which enlarge and protrude above the surface of the thallus.

7. The segregation of the sexes takes place at meiosis in tetrasporangia so that two tetraspores give rise to male plants and two to female.

8. They are found both in temperate and tropical seas but occur in abundance in the warmer waters of the tropics.

9. There are 20 genera and about 100 species in this order. The commonest genus *Dictyota* has been described here in detail.

Genus DICTYOTA (like a mat)

Occurrence. This genus has about 35 species. They are widely distributed in warm seas of tropics. *Dictyota dichotoma* is common around the coast of Britain growing in the pools between the lines of high and low tides. Usually they remain attached to rocks in tide pools by a basal **holdfast.** It seems likely that light conditions are involved in the case where single tidal periods are involved.

Morphology. The plant body consists of a strap-like thallus ten to twenty cm., long. The thallus branches repeatedly, each division giving rise to two equal branches. This type of branching is known as **dichotomous.** The basal portion of the thallus forms a disc-like branched holdfast by which the thallus remains attached to the solid substrata.

The strap-like thallus consists of rectangular cells arranged in a single layer, with a superficial layer of smaller cells on each side of the thallus. Small tufts of hairs develop from scattered groups of these surface cells. Viewed in transverse section the thallus is seen to be composed of three layers, a central one of large cells and an upper and lower epidermis of small assimilatory cells from where groups of mucilage hairs arise.

Apical growth. The growth is restricted to the ends of branches. There is a large biconvex apical cell on each branch, which cuts off derivatives at its posterior face. Each derivative divides asymmetrically. This division is always in a plane parallel to the surface of the thallus. The larger of the two daughter cells also divides in the same plane asymmetrically. There are no further divisions parallel to the thallus surface and therefore, thallus does not become more than three cells in thickness.

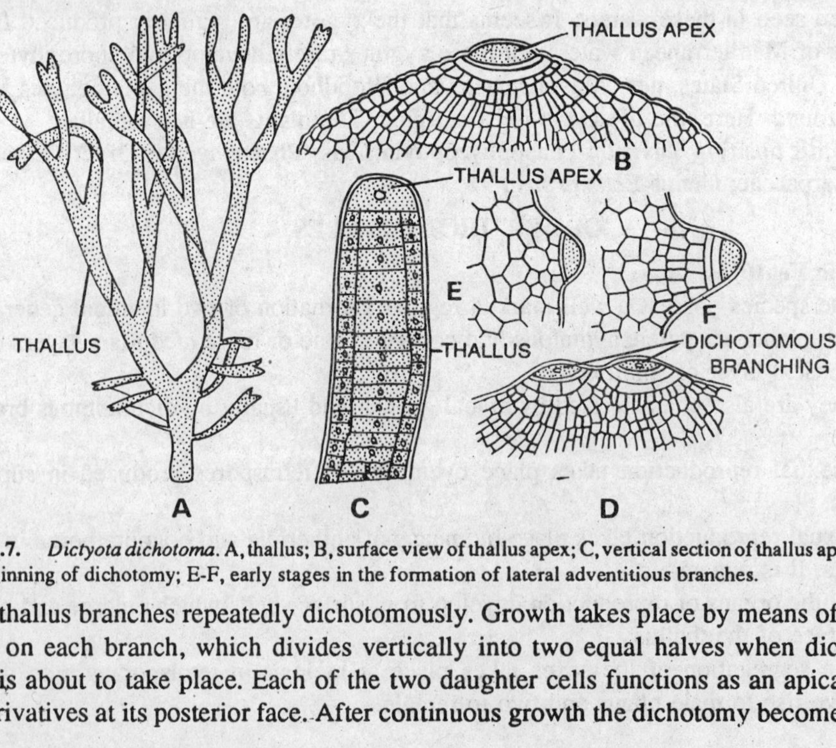

Fig. 7.7. *Dictyota dichotoma*. A, thallus; B, surface view of thallus apex; C, vertical section of thallus apex; D, thallus apex with beginning of dichotomy; E-F, early stages in the formation of lateral adventitious branches.

The thallus branches repeatedly dichotomously. Growth takes place by means of one large apical cell on each branch, which divides vertically into two equal halves when dichotomous branching is about to take place. Each of the two daughter cells functions as an apical cell and cuts off derivatives at its posterior face. After continuous growth the dichotomy becomes distinct, and the two apical cells become far apart from each other.

Reproduction. The reproduction takes place by vegetative, asexual and sexual methods. They are as follows :

Vegetative reproduction. It takes place by the decay of the older parts resulting in the separation of the branches of the thallus. Each such part develops into a new plant. In certain species gemmae like vegetative structures have also been recorded which develop into new plants after detaching from the parent thallus.

Asexual reproduction. The asexual reproduction takes place by means of **tetraspores** produced within the **tetrasporangia.** The tetrasporangium arises from a superficial cell of the thallus, which grows out into a small globular outgrowth from the thallus. The nucleus enlarges in size and divides meiotically producing four haploid nuclei, simultaneously the cytoplasm divides into four portions. No separation walls are formed and the four haploid non-flagellate spores liberate by a breakdown of the sporangial wall. These non-motile spores are known as tetraspores.

On germination, a tetraspore produces a new *Dictyota* plant which resembles the parent plant from which the tetraspores were developed. Two of the tetraspores produce male plants and two female plants.

Development of tetrasporangia. During development of a tetrasporangium, a superficial thallus cell grows out and elongates vertically two to three times its original height and then divides by a transverse division. The lower cell becomes the stalk cell and does not divide further, while the upper cell enlarges in size forming a rounded sporangium. The single nucleus of young sporangium divides meiotically producing four haploid nuclei. The cytoplasm also divides into four and thus four nonflagellate tetraspores are formed. The aplanospores or tetraspores liberate by an apical rupture of the wall of sporangium. There is segregation of sex at time of meiosis and therefore, two of the tetraspores germinate into male gametophytes and two into female gametophytes (Schreiber, 1935).

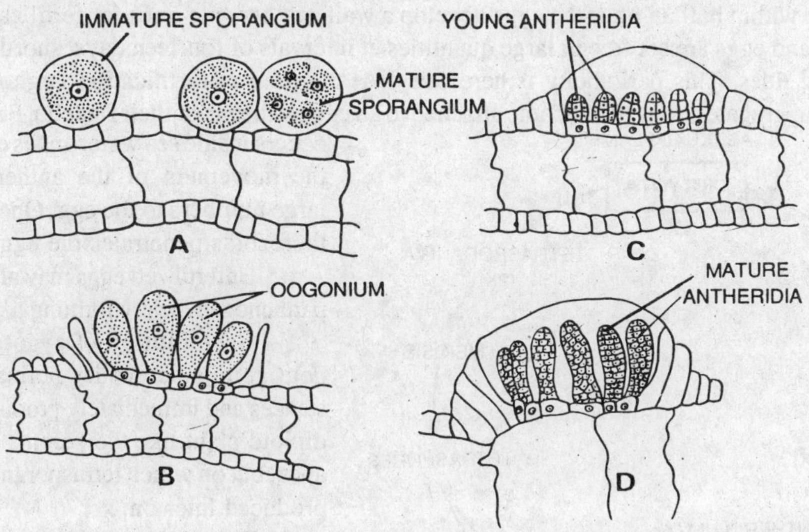

Fig. 7.8. *Dictyota dichotoma.* A transverse section through a portion of sporangial sorus showing immature and mature sporangia; B, transverse section through an oogonial sorus showing oogonia; C, transverse section through antheridial sorus showing young antheridia; D, transverse section through antheridial sorus showing mature antheridia.

Sexual reproduction. The sexual reproduction is oogamous. The sex organs are known as **antheridia** and **oogonia.** The antheridia and oogonia are found to be arranged on surface of the thallus on separate male and female plants respectively. The sex organs borne in elliptical sori on both sides of a thallus.

The antheridium and its development. Each antheridium arises in a male sorus from a superficial cell of the thallus. This cell divides transversely forming a stalk cell and an antheridial initial. The stalk cell does not divide further. The upper cell or antheridial initial enlarges and divides into two cells by vertical division. Both of these cells again divide vertically forming a quadrant of four cells. These cells divide again by vertical and transverse divisions forming ultimately a cellular column that is 20 to 24 cells in height and each tier bears 16 cells. As soon as the cell division stops the protoplasts become rounded and the walls between them are gelatinized. Therefore each protoplast metamorphoses into an antherozoid.

From each mature antheridium about 1500 antherozoids are liberated. There are 100 to 300 antheridia in each sorus and the number of sori on a full-grown plant is 3,000 or more. This way about 500 million antherozoids are produced every fortnight from each mature plant. This means that there are about 6,000 male sperms for each egg. The antherozoids are pyriform and very small in size. Each antherozoid bears two lateral flagella, the one flagellum directed backwards is very much reduced and, therefore, antherozoid appears to be uniflagellate.

Each antheridial sorus remains surrounded by two or three rings of sterile **paraphyses.**

The oogonium and its development. The oogonium also develops from a superficial cell of the female thallus. About 25 to 50 oogonia develop in an oogonial sorus. The superficial cell elongates vertically three to four times of its original height and divides by a transverse wall into two cells, the lower forming the stalk cell and the upper the oogonium. The oogonium enlarges greatly in size and its protoplast develops into a single egg or oosphere, which liberates as a naked mass or protoplasm by the breakdown of the wall of oogonium. Each oogonial sorus is surrounded by a rudimentary involucre.

Fertilization. It takes place immediately after eggs are liberated and if the fertilization does not take place within half an hour the eggs develop a wall and become unfit for fertilization. Both antherozoids and eggs are set free in large quantities at intervals of fourteen days, shortly after the highest spring tides. This periodicity is hereditary. At the time of fertilization large number of antherozoids aggregate about and become attached to an egg by means of their flagella. Fertilization occurs inside sea water and is effected by the movement of the antherozoids in large numbers to the egg. One of the antherozoids penetrates the egg.

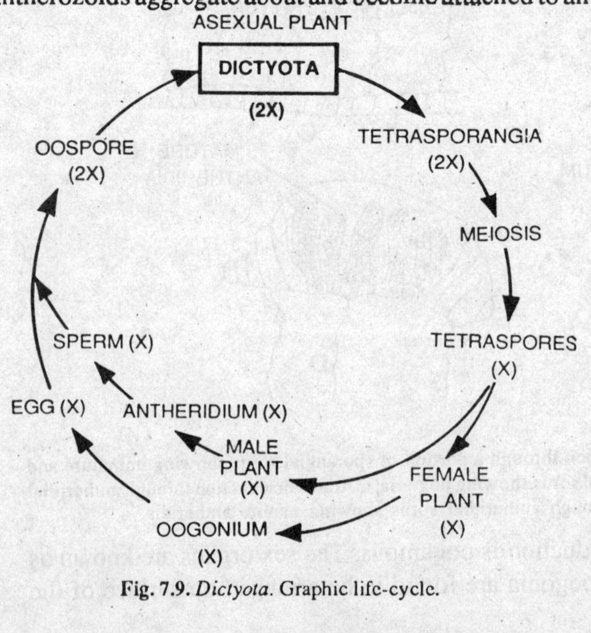

Fig. 7.9. *Dictyota*. Graphic life-cycle.

Unfertilized eggs may also develop parthenogenetically forming azygospores.

Germination of zygote. The zygote germinates under normal circumstances and immediately produces a fresh diploid plant like the parents in appearance, but on which tetrasporangia will be produced later on.

The nucleus of zygote divides mitotically which is followed by a bipartition into two daughter cells, one daughter cell develops into a rhizoid and the other gives rise to the entire sporophyte which later on bears tetrasporangia.

Alternation of generations. This genus exhibits a typical alternation of generations between a diploid tetrasporic plant on the one hand, which is regarded as sporophyte (2x) and two haploid sexual plants, the male and the female which form the gametophytes (x).

Systematic position. Division-Phaeophycophyta; Class-Phaeophyceae; Order-Dictyotales; Family-Dictyotaceae; Genus-*Dictyota*.

ORDER–LAMINARIALES

Characteristic features.

1. There are 30 genera and 100 species in this order.
2. The Laminariales are widely distributed in temperate seas. The bulk of the species being confined to the colder waters of the earth. They are mainly confined to the North Pacific and North Atlantic Oceans.
3. The thallus is nearly always bilaterally symmetrical with an intercalary growing zone. The thallus is large, the order includes the largest of all the sea-weeds such as *Nereocystis* and *Macrocystis;* the latter reaches 200 feet in length and grows at a depth of 60 to 100 feet. The thallus represents the conspicuous generation. In most members the sporophyte is externally differentiated into holdfast, stipe and blades. The sporophytes produce unilocular sporangia only, which remain situated in sori borne upon the blade.
4. The gametophyte is small and filamentous. The sex organs, *i.e.*, antheridia and oogonia are found upon separate plants. The antheridia liberate antherozoids, but the egg even after fertilization remains within or attached to the oogonium.
5. There is a marked alternation of dissimilar generations where the sporophyte is large and conspicuous and the gametophyte is small and filamentous.

Classification. The order has been divided into four families—

1. Chordaceae, *e.g., Chorda;* 2. Laminariaceae, *e.g., Laminaria:* 3. Lessoniaceae, *e.g., Lessonia, Postelsia, Nereocystis, Macrocystis;* 4. Alariaceae, *e.g., Alaria, Undaria.*

Genus LAMINARIA (a thin plate)

Family–Laminariaceae

Occurrence. The genus consists of 30 species. The genus is exclusively marine and occurs in shallow cold waters along rocky shores but just below the low tide level. It is widely distributed in temperate seas, such as North Pacific and North Atlantic oceans. Most of the species are perennial, however, *Laminaria ephemera* is an annual.

Structure of thallus. The sporophyte is differentiated into three distinct parts, *i.e.*, holdfast, stipe and blade. The holdfast may be a solid disc but is usually of forked root-like branches known as **haptera.** The stipe found above the holdfast is always unbranched and either cylindrical or somewhat flattened. The stipe terminates into a single blade which may be entire or vertically incised into a number of segments.

Growth. The growth of sporophyte takes place due to an intercalary meristem found at the juncture of stipe and blade. The stipe increases continuously in length because of meristematic activity. According to Setchell (1905), the length of a mature blade remains approximately constant because increase in length at base equals abrasion at the apex. Most of species are perennial and their blades persist even for five years. *Laminaria ephemera* is an annual. In the perennial species, *e.g., Laminaria digitata* the blades stop growing late in the summer and begin to disintegrate. As the blade disintegrates, the axial portion of the meristem below it begins to elongate. Due to this the cortical portion of the meristem becomes transversely ruptured. Now the exposed axial portion becomes flattened as it increases in length, and ultimately becomes blade-like in structure. The old blade persists for some time upon the apex of the new intercalated blade, but later on the old blade is sloughed off.

Internal structure. Both stipe and lamina in transverse section show a separation into three distinct zones, although these zones are more clearly marked in the stipe because of its greater thickness. These three zones are the **epidermis**, the **cortex** and the **medulla**. Near the apex the blade is only one cell in thickness, but it soon becomes two layered, after which the primary tubes are formed, which make the medulla and separate the two external layers. The epidermis consists of one or two layers of small cubical cells containing many chromatophores. The cortex is formed by division and redivision of superficial cells of a young stipe. It is, therefore, composed of more or less radially arranged vertically elongated cells, the cortex continuously increases in diameter at its periphery as long as the plant remains alive. The cortex may show variation in the size of

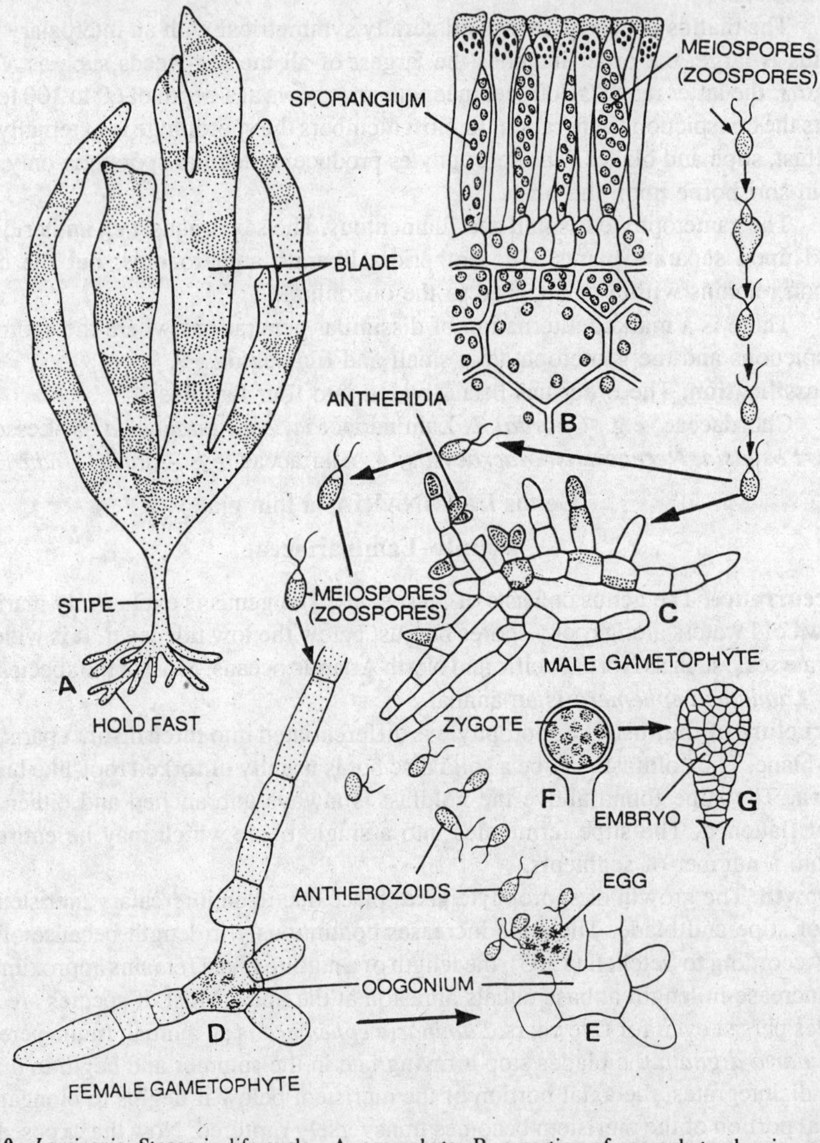

Fig. 7.10. *Laminaria.* Stages in life-cycle—A, sporophyte; B, a portion of sporophyte showing sporangia and zoospores (x); C, male gametophyte; D, female gametophyte; E, fertilization of egg; F, zygote; G, young embryo.

the cells. The cells formed at the end of the growing season are smaller than those formed early in the growing season. For the same reason, the cortex contains one or more concentric rings resembling the annual or growth rings of higher plants. In many species the cortex may contain **mucilage ducts** which form an anastamosing system of canals filled with mucilage. The mucilage ducts are either found just beneath the epidermis or just outside the medulla.

The medulla consists of compact vertical unbranched filaments or hyphae that lie close to one another in the young stipe. In mature stipe the vertical filaments lie apart from one another. The elongated cells of medulla possess pores in the end walls that make them look like the **sieve elements** of vascular plants. The end walls are penetrated by numerous protoplasmic connections. Sometimes sheathed in callus, that later extends to cover both sides of the perforated plate. The cells become long and broad near the transverse wall, thus producing trumpet-like appearance which has given them the name **trumpet hyphae.** The trumpet hyphae possess spiral bands of cellulose thickening of a wood vessel. The function of trumpet hyphae is still uncertain. According to many phycologists, they are meant for conduction of fluids, while according to others they act as storage organs, and still others regard them as organs of support.

The tissues of *Laminaria* show a greater degree of differentiation than we have seen in the other algal groups and the genus seems to have characteristics that might have carried it above and beyond the Thallophyta. So far, there is no evidence that *Laminaria* or any other kelp was ancestral to higher plants.

Reproduction. The reproduction takes place both by asexual and sexual methods.

Asexual reproduction. The sporophytic plants bear clusters of club-shaped zoosporangia on the lamina surfaces. These unilocular zoosporangia are generally formed at a specific season, either summer or autumn. They are borne in extensive sori on both surfaces of lamina. The zoosporangia arise from the superficial cells. Each such cell divides into two, forming a basal cell and a terminal cell. The terminal cell remains assimilatory in the beginning but later on it enlarges in size and becomes club-shaped and is covered by a mucilaginous cap at its top. This is known as **paraphysis.** The mucilaginous caps of all the parphyses adhere and keep them together. Simultaneously the basal cells also enlarge laterally and from its outer ends cut off two cells one on each side of the terminal cell. Both the cells enlarge in size, become oval and convert into two sporangia. The sporangia become club-shaped and about two-third as long as paraphyses. The single nucleus of a young sporangium divides meiotically (Abe, 1939), and the nuclear division goes on until 32 or 64 nuclei have been formed. Thereafter a cleavage takes place forming uninucleate protoplasts. These proto-

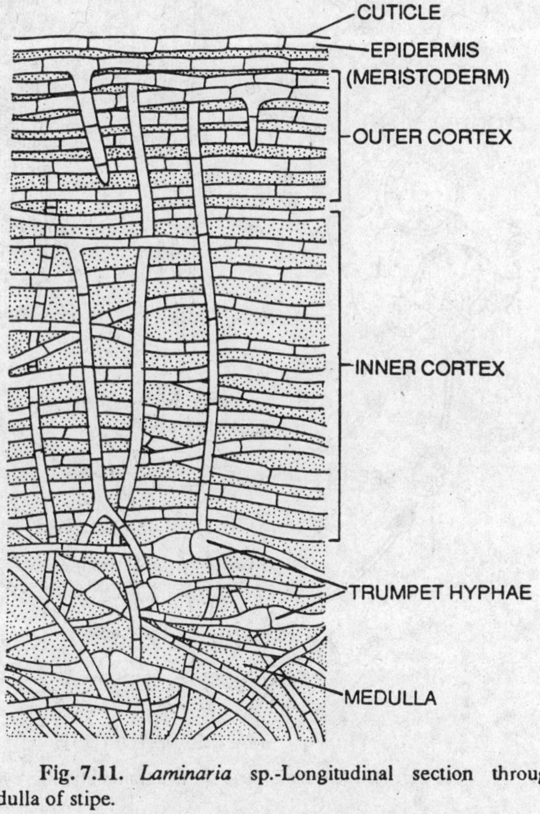

Fig. 7.11. *Laminaria* sp.-Longitudinal section through medulla of stipe.

plasts metamorphose into zoospores. The zoospores liberate through the apex of the sporangium. After liberation the zoospores swim freely in all directions.

The zoospores are pyriform with two long, laterally placed flagella, and each may possess a small eye spot. After swarming for some time, the zoospores retract flagella, become rounded, secrete a wall and soon send forth a germ tube. The nucleus and chromatophores move into the apex of green tube and a transverse wall is formed just posterior to them. The apical cell develops into the cellular gametophyte. During meiosis a genotypic determination of sex takes place. Half of the zoospores develop into male gametophytes and half into female gametophytes.

Sexual reproduction. The sexual reproduction is oogamous. It takes place by the fusion of antherozoids and eggs produced on the male and female gametophytes in sex organs known as antheridia and oogonia respectively. The male gametophyte is a minute branched filament bearing antheridia at the ends of short branches. Each antheridium produces one laterally biflagellate antherozoid (sperm). The gametophyte degenerates after the sperms are shed.

The female gametophyte consists of but a few cells, one or more of which may become an oogonium. The oogonia may be terminal or intercalary. On maturity, a single non-motile egg is liberated through a terminal pore in each oogonium, where it usually remains attached.

It has been demonstrated that the gametophytes will not produce sex organs unless the water temperature is below 15^{0}C. This may account for the abundance of this alga in colder water only.

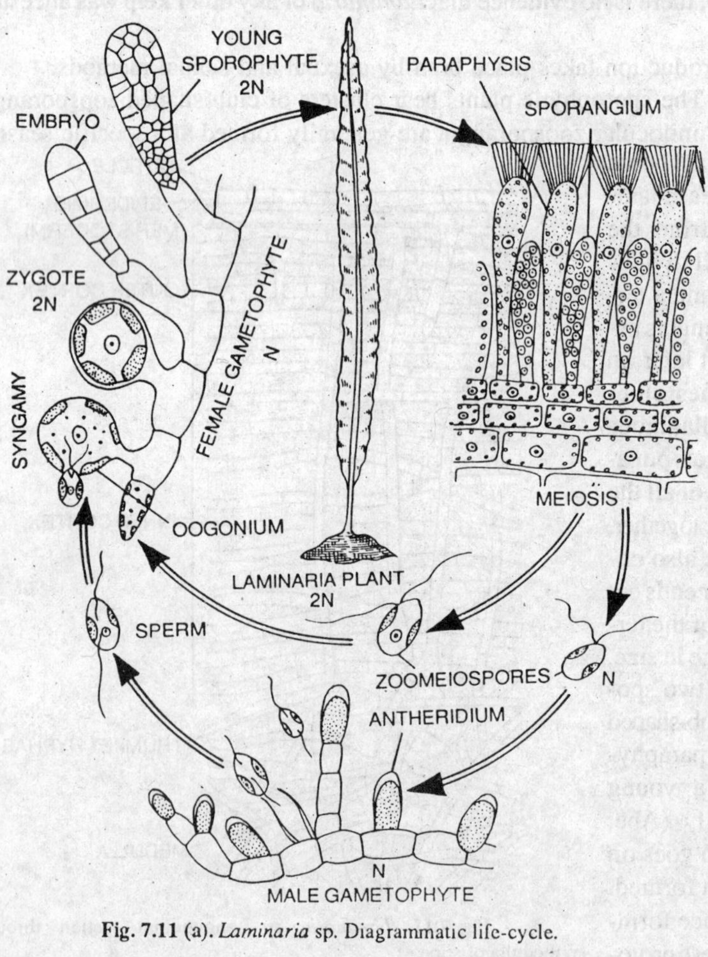

Fig. 7.11 (a). *Laminaria* sp. Diagrammatic life-cycle.

Fertilization. Fertilization is effected in the usual way. An antheozoid swims to and fuses with the egg attached to the oogonial apex. The plasmogamy is followed by karyogamy.

Germination of the zygote. Soon after the formation of the zygote, it begins to develop into a sporophyte. In the beginning it divides transversely several times forming a vertical row of 6 to 10 cells. The median cells of this row thereafter divide vertically, and this is soon followed by vertical division of all cells except the lowermost one. This lowermost cell elongates and develops into a rhizoid. By repeated transverse and vertical divisions in two planes an expanded blade-like sheet of several hundred cells but one cell in thickness, is formed. Several additional rhizoids develop from the lowermost cell of the blade, which anchor the developing sporophyte to the underlying rock. Eventually the cells of the lowermost portion of the blade divide in a third plane and a meristematic region is formed. The upper face of this meristem forms the blade while the lower face gives rise to the derivatives which develop into a stipe.

Alternation of generations. The genus shows a distinct alternation of heteromorphic generations. It is the large sporophytic plant (2x) which is differentiated into holdfast, stipe and blade, while the gametophytes (x) are small, microscopic and seldom more than a few cells in size. The sporophytes reproduce by means of unilocular zoosporangia, usually formed in clusters with paraphyses, on the leaf surface. On maturity the sporangia produce haploid laterally biflagellate zoospores as a result of reduction division (meiosis). After liberation half of the zoospores develop into male gametophytes and half into female gametophytes. The gametophytes bear antheridia and oogonia. The antherozoids and the eggs after fusion produce the zygote (2x) which develops into sporophytic plant bearing sporangia. The gametophytic plants are dioecious and oogamous. *Laminaria* thus shows an alternation of generations comparable with that in *Dictyota*, but in *Dictyota* there is alternation of isomorphic generations while in *Laminaria* there is alternation of hetermorphic generations.

Systematic position. Division-Phaeophycophyta; Class-Phaeophyceae; Order-Laminariales; Family-Laminariaceae; Genus-*Laminaria.*

ORDER–FUCALES

Characteristic features.

1. They are marine and found in the seas of cold water. However, *Sargassum* is found in tropical waters. Most of them are attached to rocks in intertidal zones. Some species of *Sargassum* are floating.
2. The spores behave as gametes. The motile spores develop in microsporangia (antheridia) and called the antherozoids, and the non-motile aplanospores develop in macrosporangia (oogonia), and called the eggs.
3. The anterior flagellum of the swarmer of Fucales is longer than the posterior one whereas in other orders their arrangement is reverse.
4. The plant itself is a sporophyte (2x). The reduction division takes place just prior to

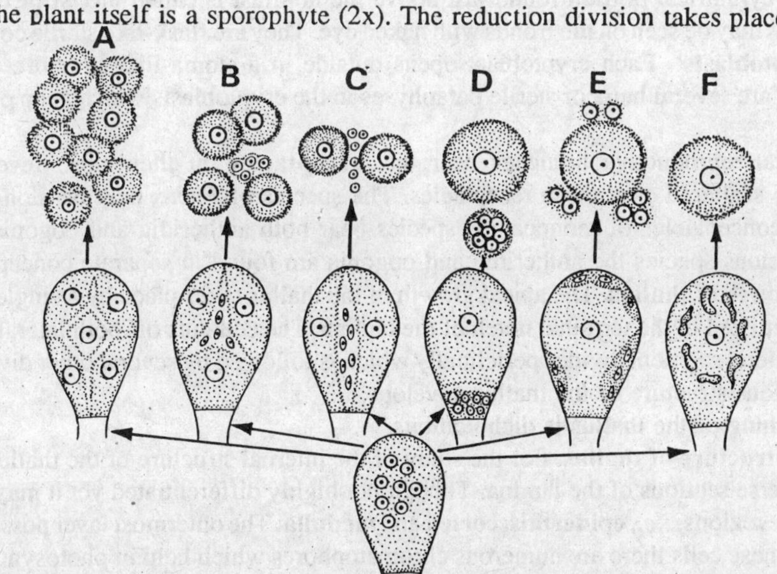

Fig. 7.12. Development of various types of oogonia found in order Fucales. A, *Fucus* type; B, *Ascophyllum* type; C, *Pelvetia* type; D, *Hesperophycus* type: E, *Cystoseira* type; F, *Sargassum* type.

formation of gametes.

5. The developing oogonia undergo a reduction division and the haploid eggs are developed. On comparative grounds this is not oogonium but unilocular sporangium.

6. In all Fucales the oogonia have eight nuclei, but the number of developing eggs is different. In *Fucus* type all eight nuclei develop eggs, this type is most primitive. The other types have been derived from this type. In *Ascophyllum* type 4 nuclei form eggs and 4 supernumerary nuclei. In *Pelvetia* type there are two eggs and six supernumerary nuclei. In *Hesperophycus* type there is one functional large egg and other eggs with 7 degenerating nuclei. In *Cystoseira* type there is one egg and 7 supernumerary nuclei. In most advanced *Sargassum* type there is one egg and 7 degenerating nuclei.

There are about 40 genera and 350 species in this order.

Classification. Seven families are included in this order.

1. Fucaceae, *e.g., Fucus, Pelvetia.*
2. Himanthaliaceae, *e.g., Himanthalia.*
3. Cystoseiraceae, *e.g., Cystoseira.*
4. Sargassaceae, *e.g., Sargassum, Turbinaria.*
5. Hormosiraceae, *e.g., Hormosira.*
6. Durvilleaceae, *e.g., Durvillea.*
7. Ascosiraceae, *e.g., Ascoseira.*

Genus FUCUS

Occurrence. This is a marine genus and occurs in the seas of cold water. The species are widely distributed in the cold waters of Northern Hemisphere. They are found in intertidal zones attached to the rocks on the shores.

External structure of thallus. The thallus of *Fucus* is attached to the rock by a well developed **'holdfast'**. A dichotomously branched leathery thallus called the **frond** or **lamina** is found above the holdfast. The dichotomous branches are flat, ribbon-like and possess distinct midribs in them. In *Fucus vesiculosus* certain air bladders are present upon ribbon-like branches which give buoyancy to the plants. A cylindrical portion found just above the holdfast is called the **'stipe'**. Hundreds of dot-like bodies may be seen on the fronds with naked eye. They are flask-like sterile conceptacles called the **'cryptoblasts'**. Each cryptoblast opens outside in a stoma-like structure the **'cryptostoma'**. There are several hairs or sterile paraphyses in the cryptoblasts which peep out through cryptostomata.

The special reproductive branches bear the **'receptacles'** at their tips. Several fertile conceptacles are scattered over these receptacles. The species of *Fucus* may be monoecious or dioecious. The conceptacles of monoecious species bear both antheridia and oogonia in them, whereas in dioecious species the antheridia and oogonia are found in separate conceptacles.

Apical growth of thallus. The apical growth of the thallus takes place by a single pyramid-like apical cell situated in the terminal notch of the lamina. The cell cuts off both lateral and basal segments. The lateral segment divides periclinally which is followed by several other divisions and the parenchymatous structure of the thallus develops.

The branching of the thallus is dichotomous.

Internal structure of thallus. For the study of the internal structure of the thallus, one has to cut the transverse sections of the lamina. Though not highly differentiated yet it may easily be divided into three regions, *i.e.*, **epidermis, cortex** and **medulla.** The outermost layer possesses thin-walled cells. In these cells there are numerous chromatophores which help in photosynthesis. Just below the epidermis a palisade-like layer is found having numerous chromatophores. The cortex

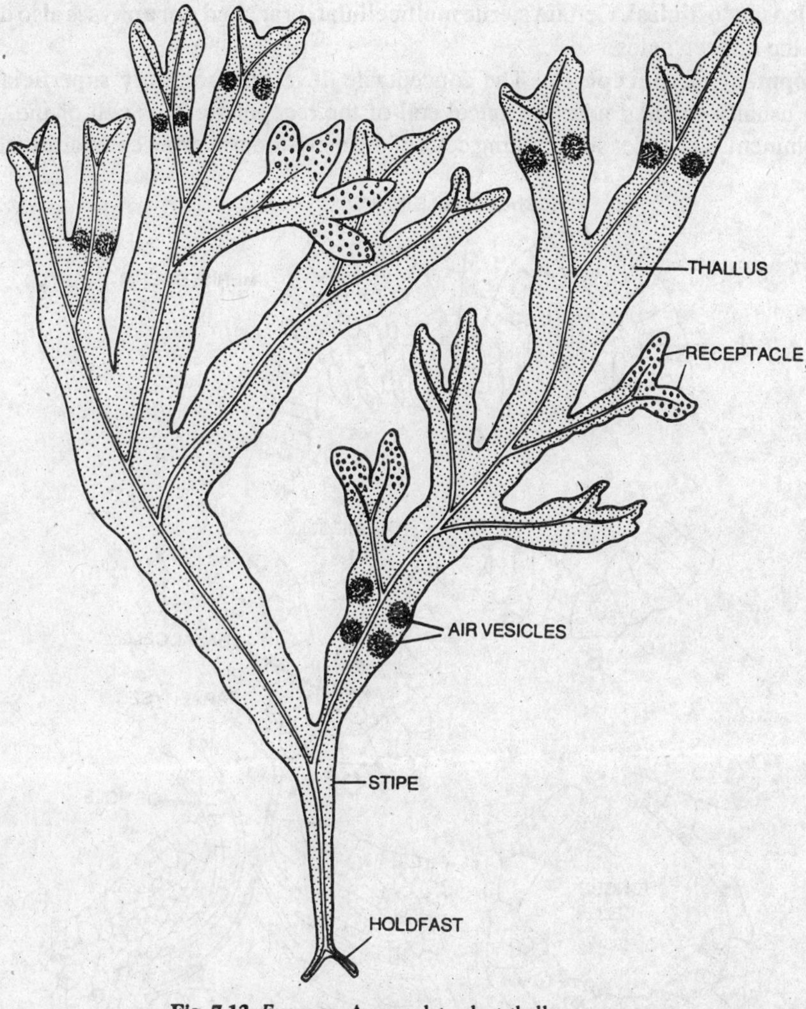

Fig. 7.13. *Fucus* sp. A, complete plant-thallus.

is multilayered parenchymatous tissue next to the epidermis. It is also called the storage tissue. The central region consists of septate, loose, elongated, interwoven filaments. It is supposed to be helpful in conduction.

Reproduction. The reproduction takes place by vegetative and sexual methods.

1. Vegetative reproduction. Vegetative reproduction takes place by means of the small fragments of the thalli. During the process, especially in the case of *Fucus,* certain adventitious buds are produced by the division of the meristematic cells of the young plants. These buds are detached from the young plants and each bud may give rise to a new plant.

2. Sexual reproduction. The sexual reproduction is oogamous. The species of *Fucus* may be homo or heterothallic. The sex organs, *i.e.,* antheridia and oogonia develop in flask-shaped structures called the conceptacles situated on the receptacles. The sex organs develop in different times of the year in different localities even in the same species. In homothallic species the antheridia and oogonia develop in the same conceptacle, *e.g., F. furcatus,* or in different conceptacles of the same plant, *e.g., F. spiralis.* In heterothallic species, *e.g., F.vesiculosus* the conceptacles bearing antheridia and oogonia are situated on different plants. The conceptacles open outside by small openings called the **'ostioles'**. Certain sterile multicellular, branched **paraphyses** also develop from the walls of the conceptacles.

Development of conceptacle. The conceptacle develops from **any** superficial cell of the meristoderm usually situated near the apical cell of the receptacle. This cell of the meristoderm becomes prominent. The other surrounding cells of the meristoderm grow comparatively at a higher

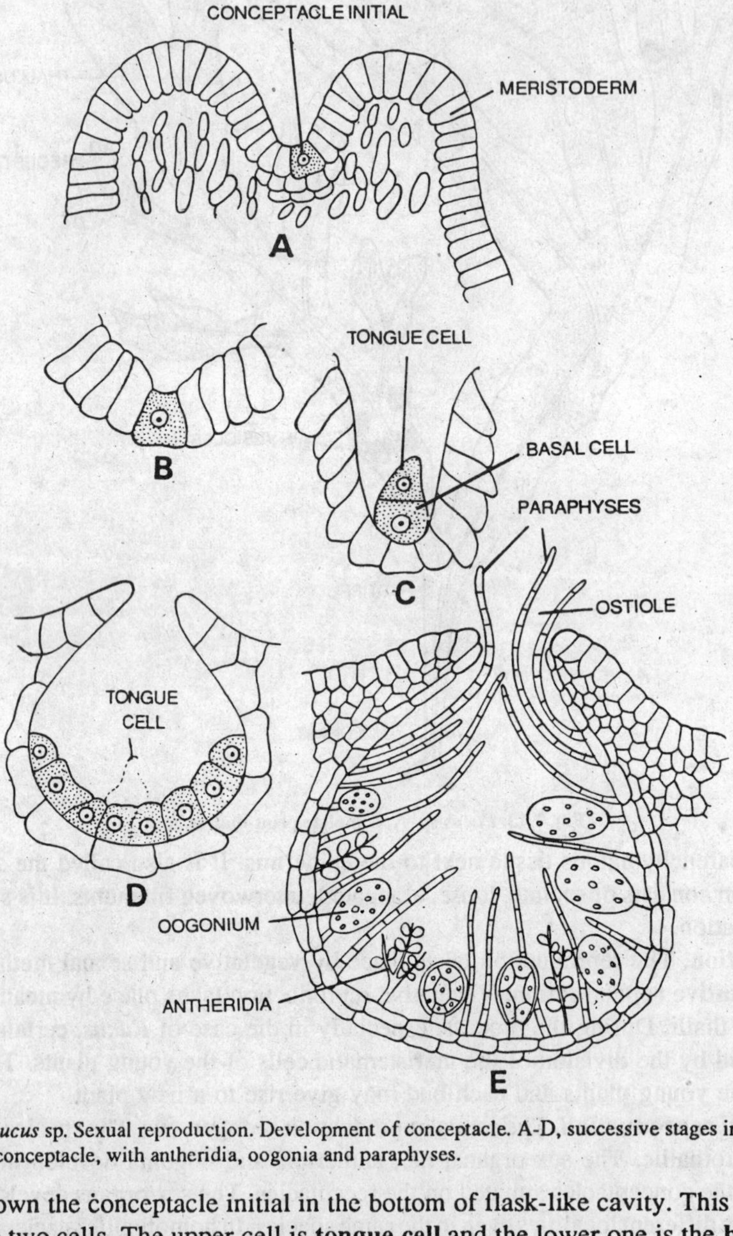

Fig. 7.14. *Fucus* sp. Sexual reproduction. Development of conceptacle. A-D, successive stages in the development of conceptacle; E, a conceptacle, with antheridia, oogonia and paraphyses.

rate and bring down the conceptacle initial in the bottom of flask-like cavity. This initial divides transversely into two cells. The upper cell is **tongue cell** and the lower one is the **basal cell.** The tongue cell does not divide further and gradually degenerates. The basal cell divides and redivides anticlinally and a complete fertile layer of sheet develops. Sometimes the derivatives of the basal cell divide periclinally and two layers developed, but this is not always and essential. This fertile sheet develops antheridia or oogonia on it, as the case may be.

Development of antheridium and structure of antherozoids. The antheridia develop either from the cells of the fertile sheet or at the base of branched paraphyses developed on the fertile sheet. Each antheridium is an elongated structure. The nucleus of young antheridium divides first

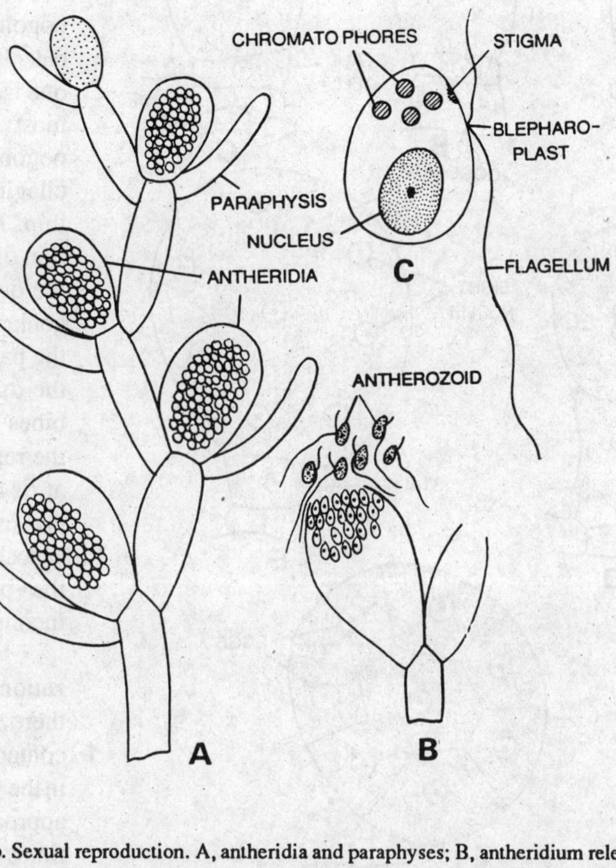

Fig. 7.15. *Fucus* sp. Sexual reproduction. A, antheridia and paraphyses; B, antheridium releasing antherozoids; C, a single antherozoid.

meiotically which is followed by several other mitotic divisions thus giving rise to 64 nuclei. The cleavage of the antheridium takes place and 64 uninucleate protoplasts are developed. These uninucleate protoplasts metamorphose into biflagellate antherozoids, (see fig. 7.15).

The antheridium is two-layered. The outer layer is called the exochite and the inner layer which is somewhat gelatinous is endochite. The exochite bursts at the tip and the antherozoids are liberated still surrounded by thin and gelatinous endochite in the water. Very soon the endochite is gelatinized and the antherozoids become free in the water.

Each antherozoid is ovoid or pyriform. The two unequal flagella are attached to its lateral side. The anterior flagellum is short and the posterior is long. There is a nucleus and few chromatophores in it.

Development and structure of oogonium. Some of the cells of the upper layer protrude upward in the cavity of the conceptacle. These protruding cells are oogonial initials. The oogonial initial divides transversely giving rise to two cells. The upper big cell develops into oogonium and the lower small one acts as stalked cell. The stalked oogonia are intermingled with unbranched uniseriate hair-like paraphyses. The oogonium increases greatly in size. The nucleus of oogonium divides meitotically and then mitotically producing 8 haploid nuclei. The cleavage of the protoplast of the oogonium also takes place and eight uninucleate eggs develop.

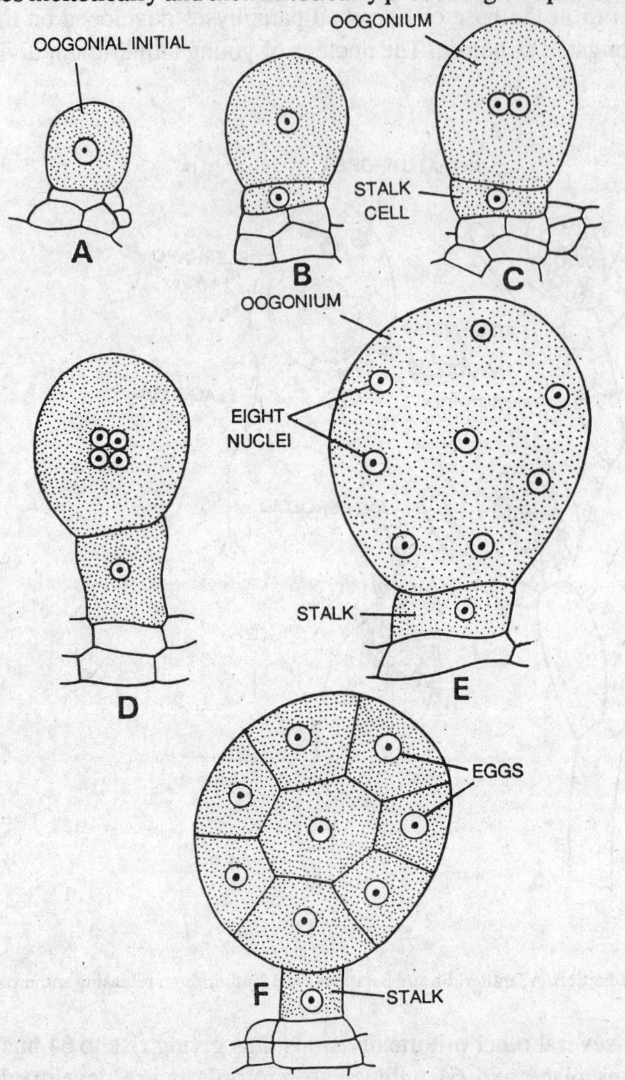

Fig. 7.16. *Fucus* sp. Sexual reproduction. A-F, successive stages in the development of oogonium.

As regards structure of oogonium, it is 3 layered. The outer layer is **exochite,** the middle one is **mesochite** and the innermost is **endochite.** In mature oogonium the mesochite is mucilaginous and the endochite is thin. At the time of the liberation of the eggs the exochite of the oogonium breaks. The oogonium moves passively through the paraphyses and approaches the ostiole. The endochite imbibes water and swells. With the result the mesochite breaks at its apical portion and by the process of invagination of the endochite eggs are liberated when the plants are reflooded by incoming tide.

Fertilization. The fertilization is external, *i.e.,* the antherozoids and the eggs come in contact outside the conceptacle in the water. Many antherozoids approach a single egg. Sometimes the egg appears to be a multiflagellate structure. The egg rotates in the water because of these flagellate antherozoids. Ultimately one of the antherozoids penetrates the egg. About after an hour of fertilization a gelatinous wall is secreted around the zygote. This zygote rests on some substratum for a day and then a rhizoidal protuberance develops on one side of it.

The zygote and development of embryo. The zygote is thick-walled and round. It rests for some time (about a day) and then germinates. It divides transversely into two cells. A protuberance comes out from the lower cell whereas upper cell divides vertically and remains rounded. The lower cell divides transversely. It gives rise to the holdfast. The upper cell divides and redivides by anticlinal and periclinal divisions and develops into the main body of the plant. The two-day old embryo possesses about 4-12 cells whereas four-day old embryo has about 50 cells.

Life cycle. The life cycle of *Fucus* is of diplontic type. There is no alternation of generations. The plant itself is sporophyte (2x). The reduction division takes place prior to the formation of gametes (gametogenesis). The gametophytic phase is represented by eggs and antherozoids.

Systematic position. Division-Phaeophycophyta; Class-Phaecophyceae; Order-Fucales;Family-Fucaceae; Genus-*Fucus*.

Genus SARGASSUM

There are about 150 species in this genus.

Occurrence. All species are marine. Majority of them are free floating on maturity but some are lithophytes when young. The species of *Sargassum* are found in tropical or warm waters. *Sargassum natans* and *S. fluitans* are abundantly found in the Sargasso sea of Atlantic ocean. The name of sea is given after the name of genus. The species of *Sargassum* are commonly met with along the coast of Australia, India and Japan. Some species are found in the waters of West Indies and Florida. The most common centre of the occurrence of the species is supposed to be Southern Hemisphere.

Structure. The plant body is differentiated into a main axis bearing lateral branches on it. In *Sargassum longifolium* the axis bears only flat lateral leaves in the lower portion and in the upper portion the distinct fertile branches are found. In the lower as well as the upper portions the stalked air bladders are present. The air bladder may or may not bear a leaf on its apical end. These bladders give buoyancy to the plants to float. In the upper part of the plant body the axis of the lateral bears several repeatedly branched receptacles. The leaves are usually serrated and with distinct midribs.

The rhizoidal branches are present at the base of the main axis which hold the mud or rock when the plants are young and attached.

Internal structure of main axis. To study the internal

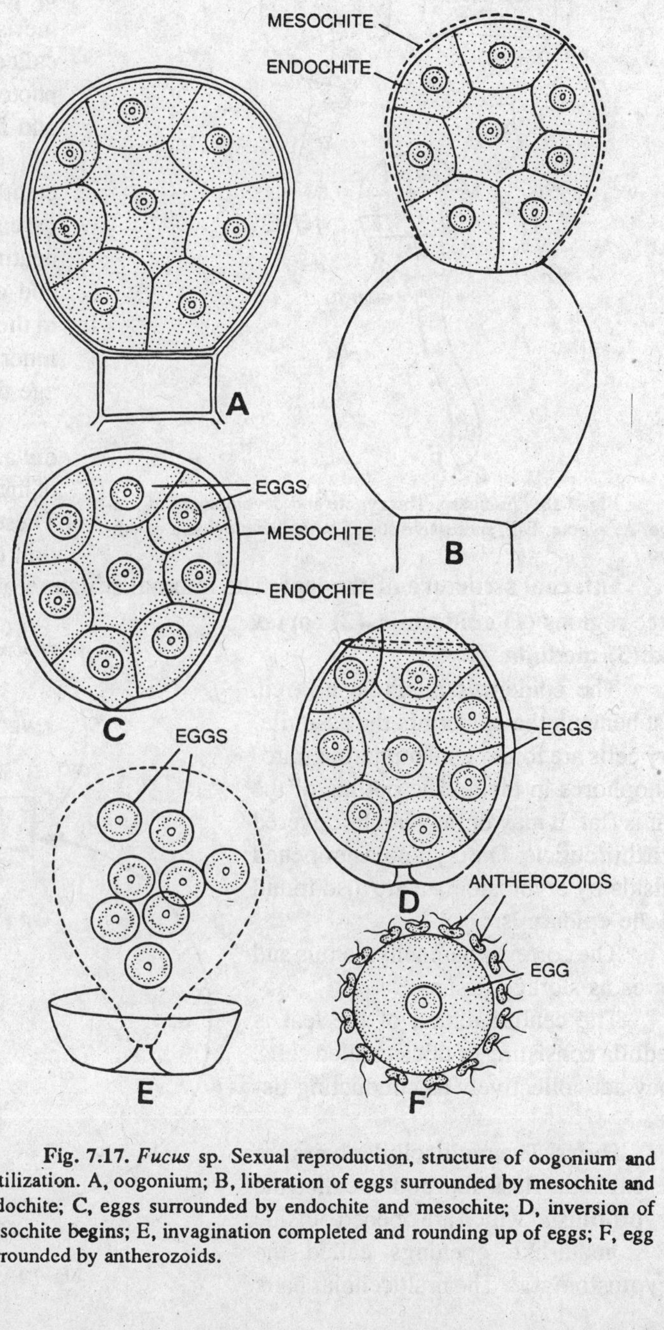

Fig. 7.17. *Fucus* sp. Sexual reproduction, structure of oogonium and fertilization. A, oogonium; B, liberation of eggs surrounded by mesochite and endochite; C, eggs surrounded by endochite and mesochite; D, inversion of mesochite begins; E, invagination completed and rounding up of eggs; F, egg surrounded by antherozoids.

structure of main axis one has to cut the transverse sections of the axis. The axis is differentiated into three parts (1) **epidermis** or **meristoderm, (2) Cortex** and **(3) conducting tissue** or **medulla.**

(1) Epidermis or meristoderm. This is the outermost layer consisting of thin-walled parenchymatous cells with or without a thin cuticle. This layer is meristematic in nature and, therefore, called the meristoderm. The cells are photosynthetic containing chromatophores and fucosan vesicles in them.

(2) Cortex. The cortex is sufficiently broad and consists of thin-walled parenchymatous cells. The cells just beneath the epidermis are photosynthetic and contain numerous chromatophores in them, whereas the cortical cells of the inner region are supposed to be the storage tissue.

(3) Conducting tissue or medulla. The central region of the axis consists of thick-walled cells and known as medulla. These serve the purpose of the conduction of the food.

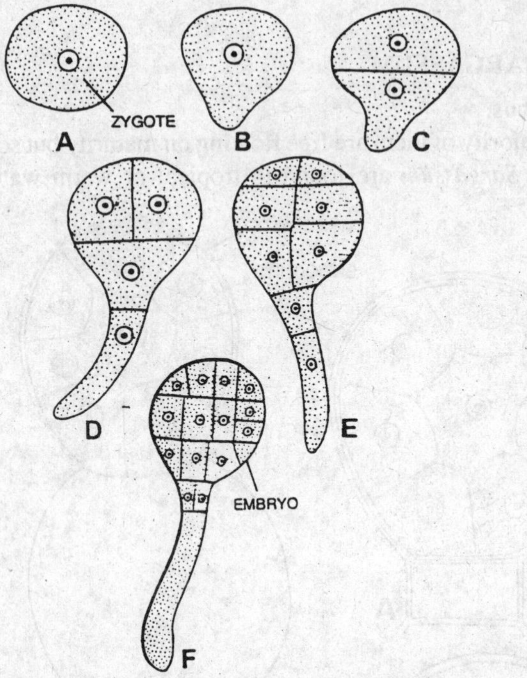

Fig. 7.18. *Fucus* sp. The zygote and development of embryo. A, zygote; B-F, successive stages in the development of embryo.

Internal structure of the leaf. The internal structure of the leaf is also differentiated into three regions **(1) epidermis, (2) cortex** and (3) **medulla.**

The epidermis is single layered. Just beneath the epidermis the assimilatory cells are found with numerous chromatophores in them. The outline of the leaf is flat. It may or may not be covered by a thin cuticle. The cryptoblasts opened outside by cryptostomata are also found on the epidermis.

The cortex is parenchymatous and serves as storage tissue.

The central region of the leaf is medulla consisting of thick-walled cells. They act collectively as conducting tissue.

Hairs. The multicellular hairs are present in the flask-like bodies called the **'cryptoblasts'** which are opened outside by stomata-like openings called the **'cryptostomata'**. The multicellular hairs

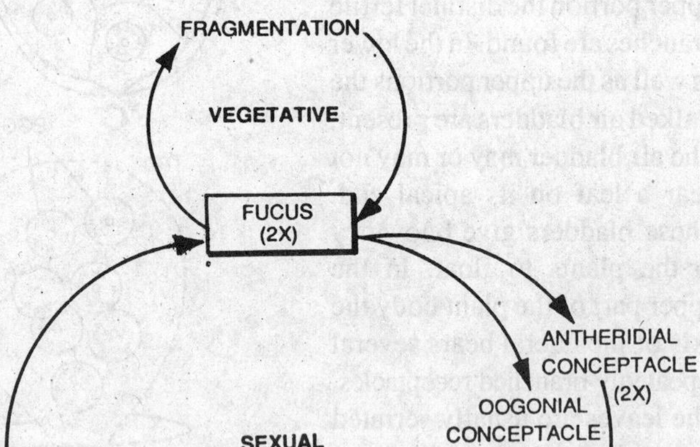

Fig. 7.19. *Fucus* sp. Graphic life-cycle.

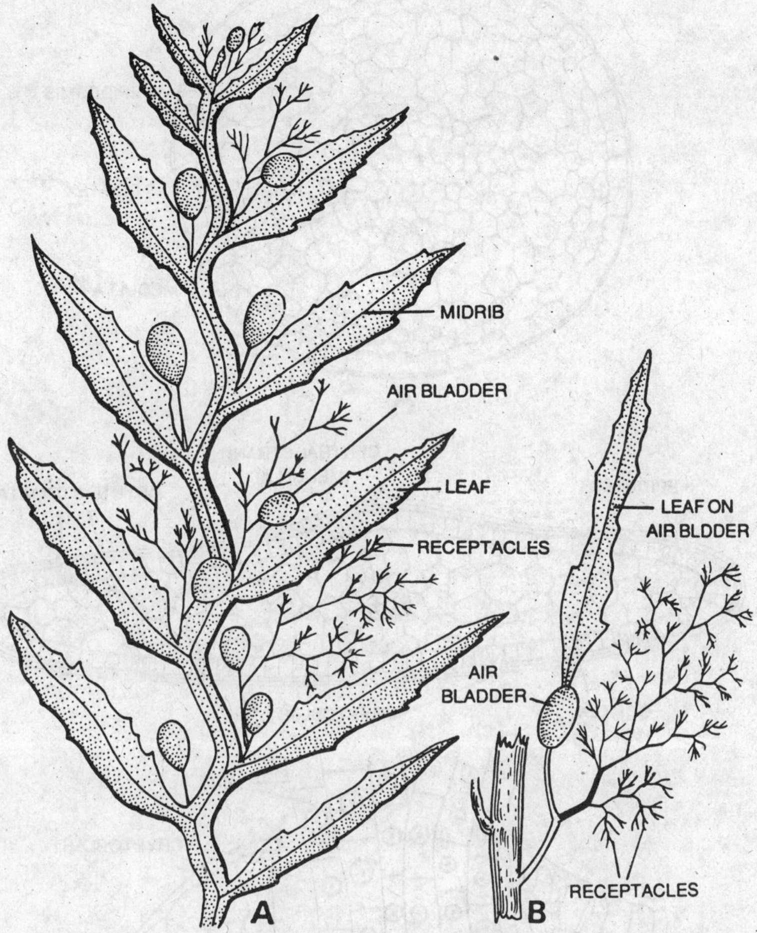

Fig. 7.20. *Sargassum* sp. A, thallus; B, a part of thallus with receptacle and a leaf.

arise from the base and extrude out through the openings. The function and nature of these hairs is a subject of controversy. According to Prof. Lloyd Williams, they are respiratory in function. They also absorb nutritive materials from the water. They also act as protective organs. According to Church, they are mucilage secreting hairs.

Method of the growth of the thallus. The growth of the thallus is initiated by an apical cell found at the tip of the branch. The apical cell is four-sided, pyramid-like which cuts basal and lateral derivatives. The derivatives divide periclinally and anticlinally giving rise to the parenchymatous thallus.

Reproduction. The reproduction takes place by means of vegetative and sexual methods. Asexual method is altogether absent.

1. **Vegetative reproduction.** It takes place by means of fragmentation. In the case of *Sargassum natans* it is very prolific. This is a free floating species. Each fragment develops into a new plant.

2. **Sexual reproduction.** The sexual reproduction is **oogamous.** The male sex organs are called the **antheridia** and the female sex organs the **oogonia.** The species may be homo or heterothallic. In homothallic species the oogonia and antheridia **develop** in the same conceptacle

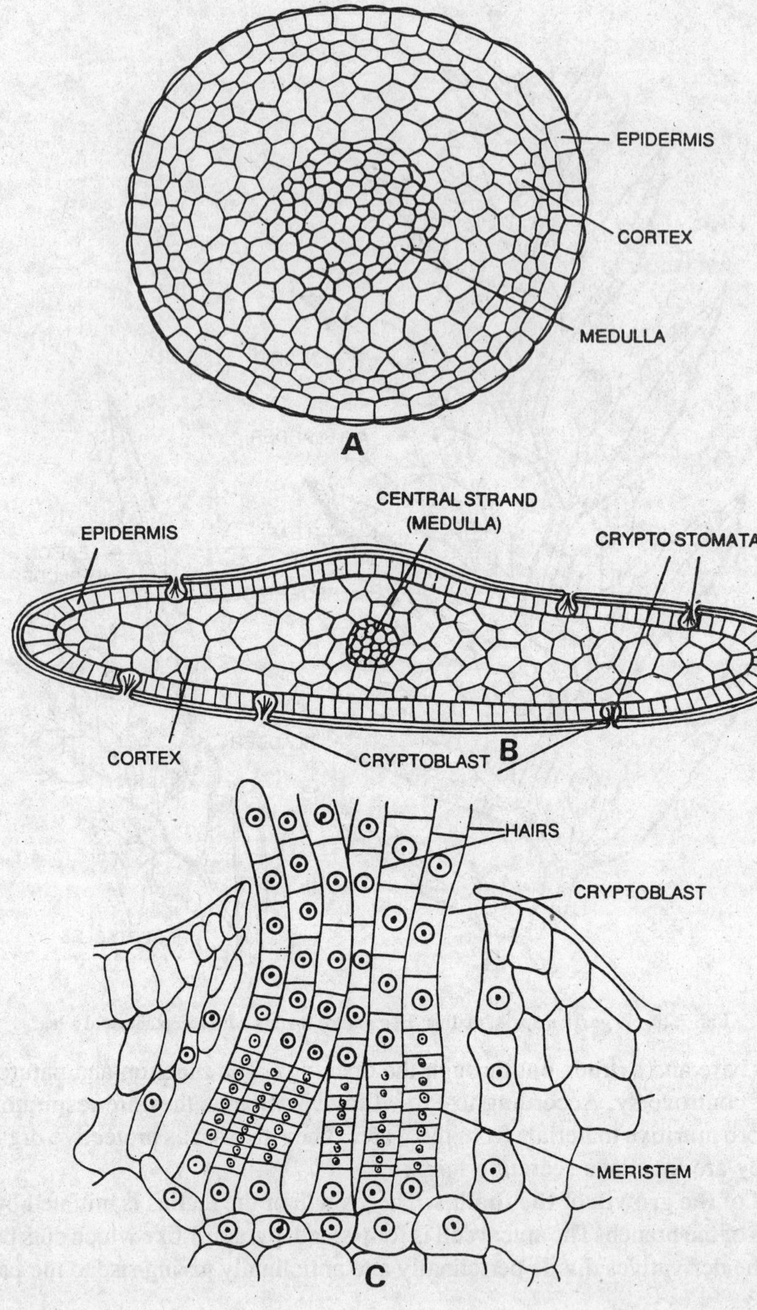

Fig. 7.21. *Sargassum* sp. Internal Structure. A, T. S. of axis; B, V. S. of leaf; C, cryptoblast with sterile hairs.

whereas in heterothallic species in separate conceptacles situated on different plants. The conceptacles are found upon special repeatedly branched reproductive branches, the **receptacles.**

Development of conceptacle. The conceptacle develops from a superficial meristodermal cell. This cell becomes much more prominent. The surrounding cells divide rapidly and the prominent superficial cell goes down in a flask-like cavity. After reaching at the base of the flask this divides transversely giving rise to two daughter cells. The upper cell is the **tongue cell** and

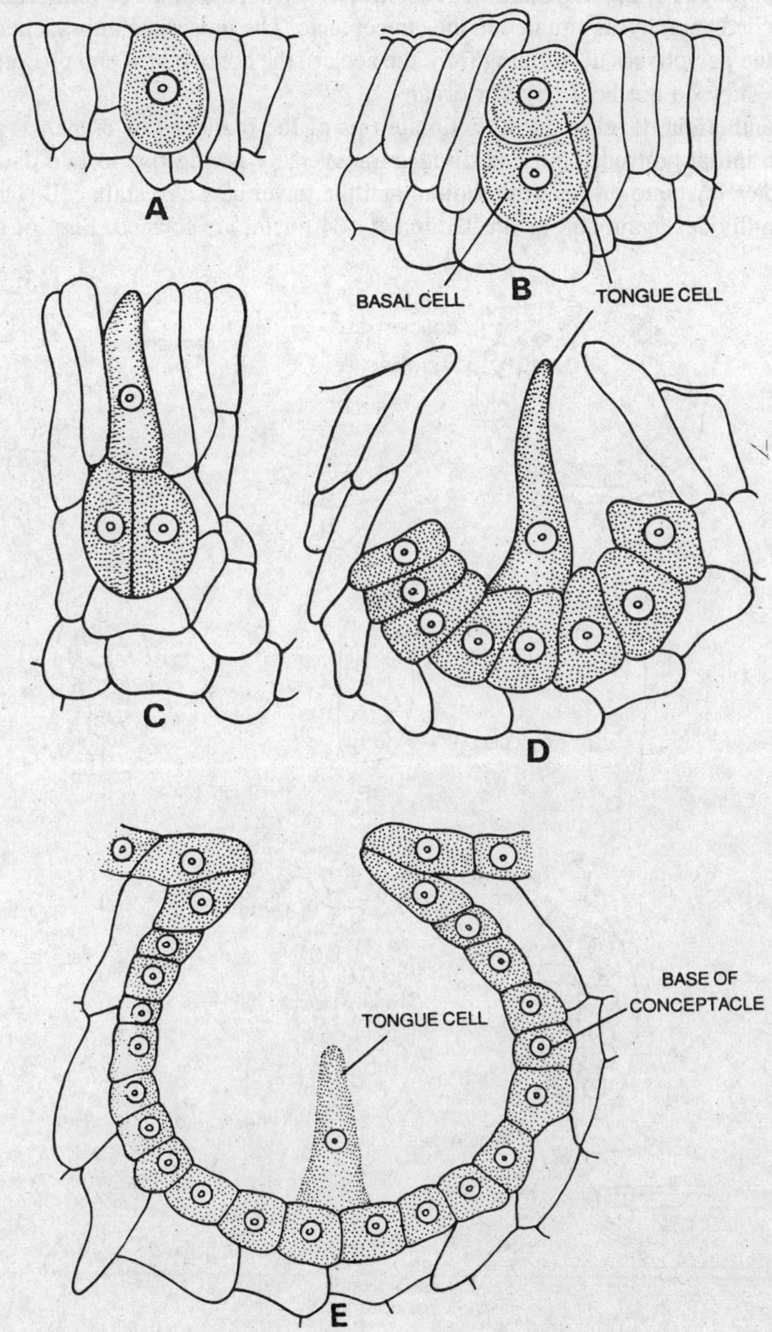

Fig. 7.22. *Sargassum* sp. Sexual reproduction-A-E, successive stages in the development of conceptacle.

the lower one **basal cell.** The tongue cell degenerates very soon. The basal cell divides again and again anticlinally giving rise to a curved row of cells. These cells divide periclinally giving rise to two layers. These layers of the cells represent fertile sheet. The antheridia and oogonia develop on this fertile sheet from the cells of the upper tier.

Development of antheridia and structure of antherozoids. The antheridia are developed on the branched paraphyses situated in the conceptacle. The uniseriate unbranched paraphyses are also called the **periphyses** developing from the neck of the conceptacle and protruding out through the ostiole. They do not bear any sex organs.

The antheridia develop on the ultimate tips of the branches of branched paraphyses. The antheridium initial protrudes out and divides transversely giving rise to two daughter cells. The upper cell develops into proper antheridium and the lower acts as a stalk cell. The nucleus of the antheridium divides again and again. Ultimately 64 nuclei are formed. First of all the reduction

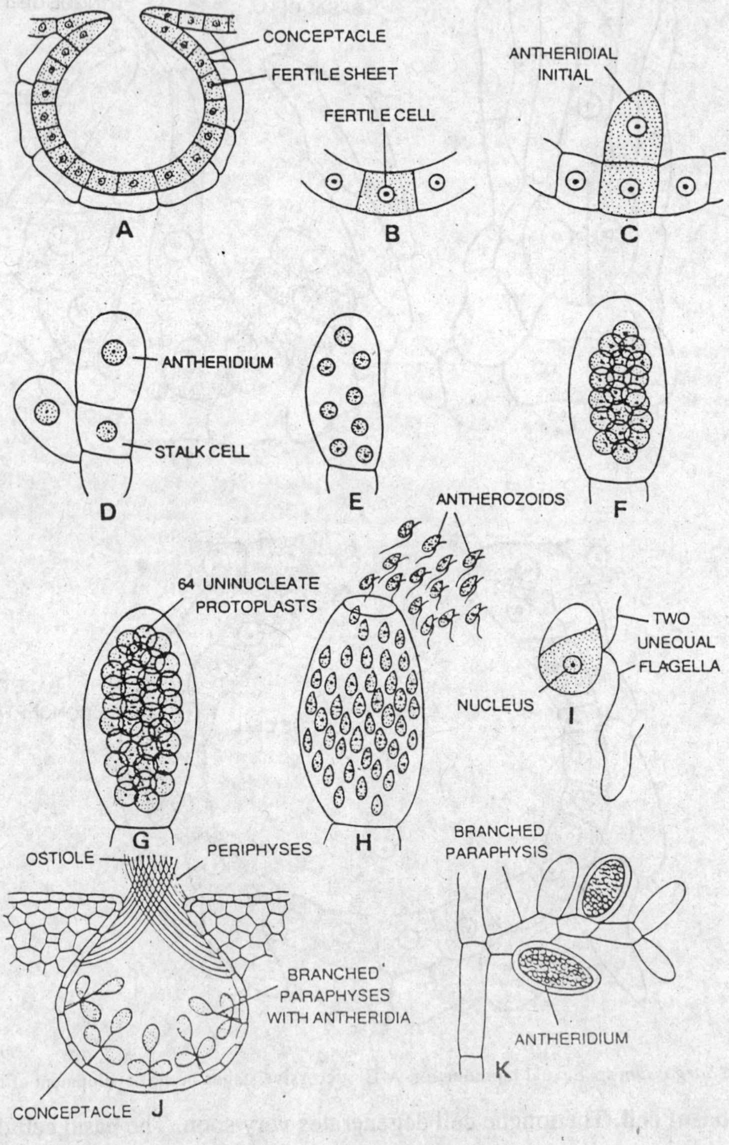

Fig. 7.23. *Sargassum* sp. Sexual reproduction. Development of antheridium. A, V. S. of conceptacle showing fertile layer; B-D, development of antheridium from antheridial initial; E-H, successive stages in the development of antherozoids; I, single antherozoid; J, V. S. of conceptacle showing branched paraphyses and antheridia; K, branched antheridium.

division takes place which is followed by several mitotic divisions. With the result of the cleavage of the contents of the antheridium 64 uninucleate protoplasts are developed. Each such uninucleate protoplast metamorphoses into an antherozoid. On maturity of the antheridium, the apical portion breaks and the antherozoids are liberated in the water.

Each antherozoid is ovoid or pyriform and bears two unequal flagella inserted on the lateral side. The anterior flagellum is shorter than the posterior one whereas in other Phaeophyceae the case is reverse. Each antherozoid contains a large nucleus, a blepharoplast and few chromatophores.

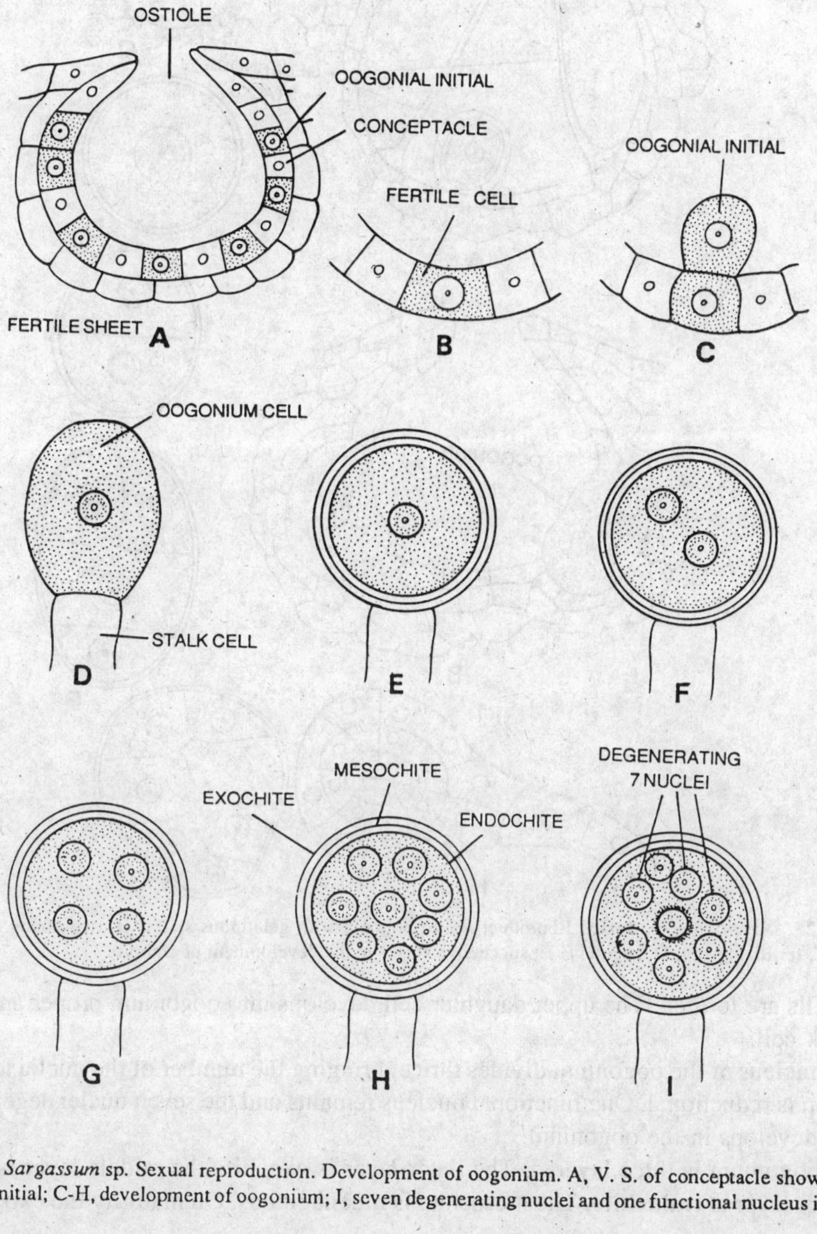

Fig. 7.24. *Sargassum* sp. Sexual reproduction. Development of oogonium. A, V. S. of conceptacle showing fertile layer; B, oogonial initial; C-H, development of oogonium; I, seven degenerating nuclei and one functional nucleus in the three layered oogonium.

Development and structure of oogonium. Some of the cells of the upper tier of the fertile sheet protrude out and act as oogonial initials. Each oogonial initial divides transversely and two

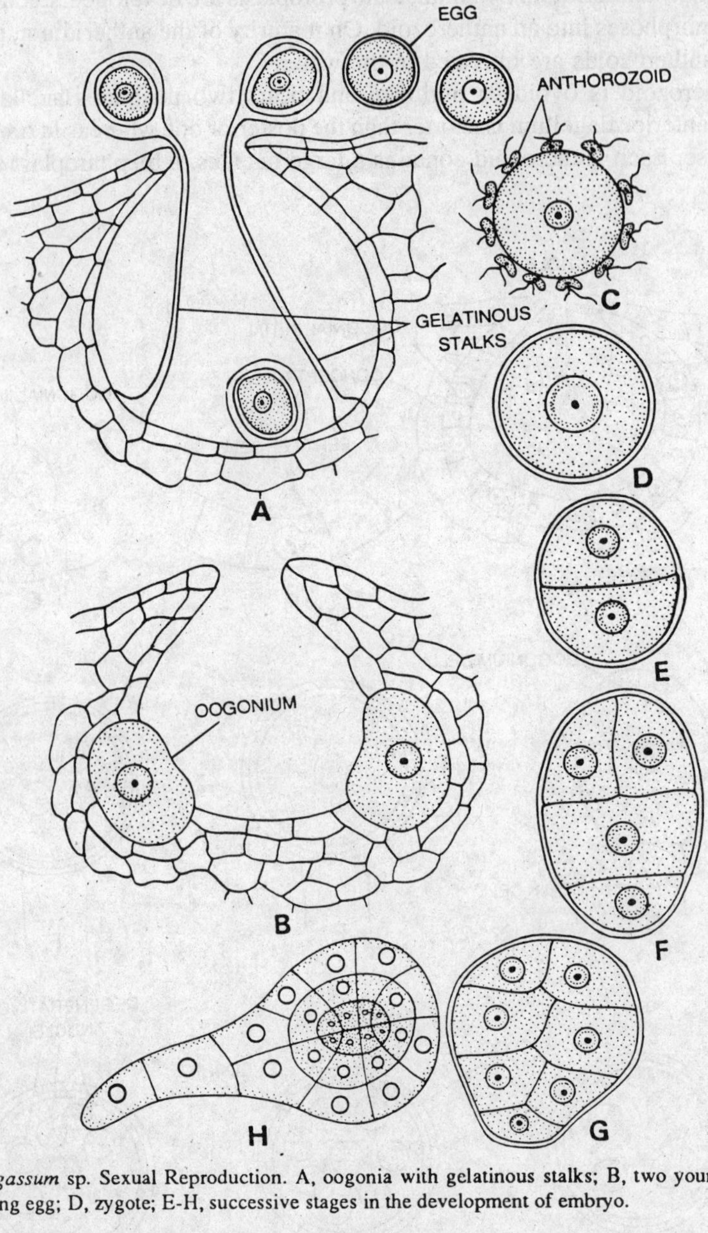

Fig. 7.25. *Sargassum* sp. Sexual Reproduction. A, oogonia with gelatinous stalks; B, two young oogonia in the conceptacle; C, fertilizing egg; D, zygote; E-H, successive stages in the development of embryo.

daughter cells are formed. The upper daughter cell develops into oogonium proper and the lower acts as stalk cell.

The nucleus of the oogonium divides thrice, bringing the number of the nuclei to eight. The first division is reductional. One functional nucleus remains and the seven nuclei degenerate. This single egg develops in the oogonium.

The oogonium is three layered. The outer layer is **exochite,**the middle layer is **mesochite** and the inner layer is **endochite.** The mesochite is mucilaginous. On maturity the exochite breaks

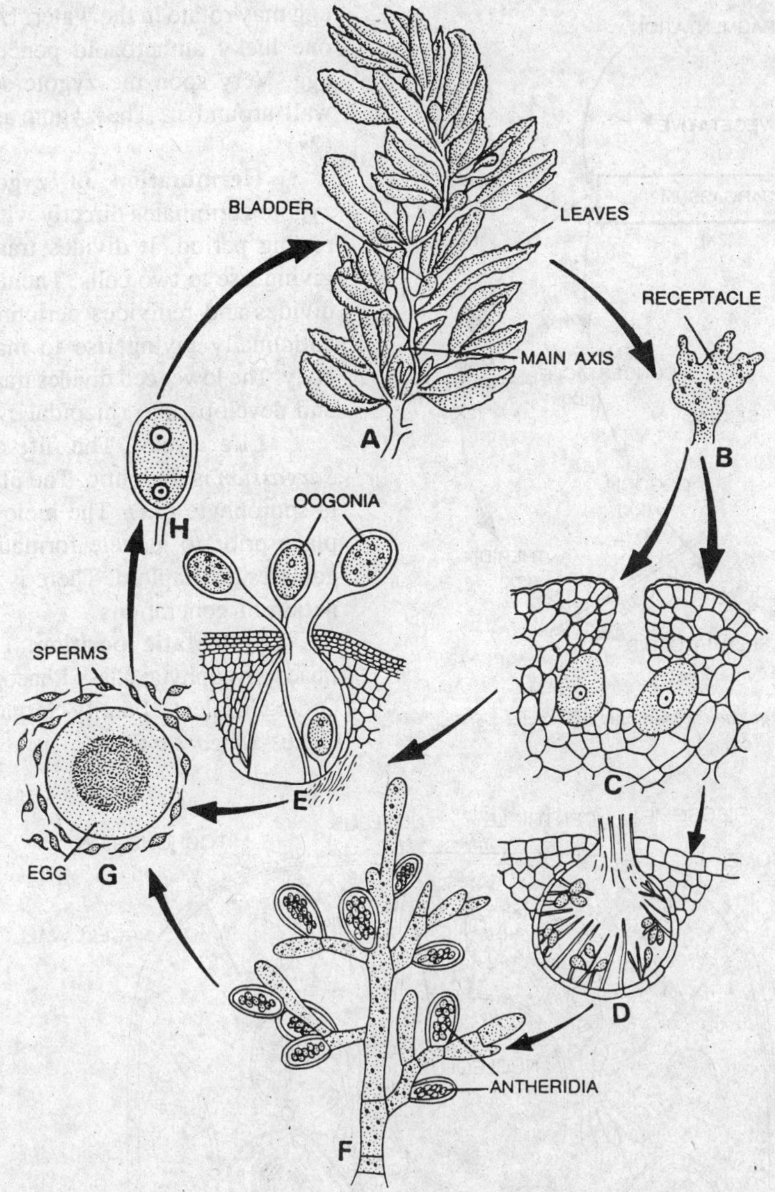

Fig. 7.26. *Sargassum*. Stages in life-cycle. A, thallus; B, receptacle; C, young oogonia; D, conceptacle with antheridia on branched paraphyses; E, oogonia with gelatinous stalks coming out of the conceptacle through ostiole; F, antheridia on branched paraphyses; G. fertilizing egg; H, young embryo (reduction division in the life-cycle at gametogenesis).

and the mucilaginous mesochite forms a long mucilaginous stalk. The oogonia are attached to the base of the conceptacle by long mucilaginous threads.

Fertilization. Later on the endochite also ruptures and the egg is liberated in the water. Several antherozoids approach the egg. Sometimes, because of the presence of the many antherozoids, the egg appears to be a multiflagellate structure. With the help of these antherozoids the egg may rotate in the water. Ultimately one lucky antherozoid penetrates the egg. Very soon the zygote secretes a wall around it. The zygote is diploid (2x).

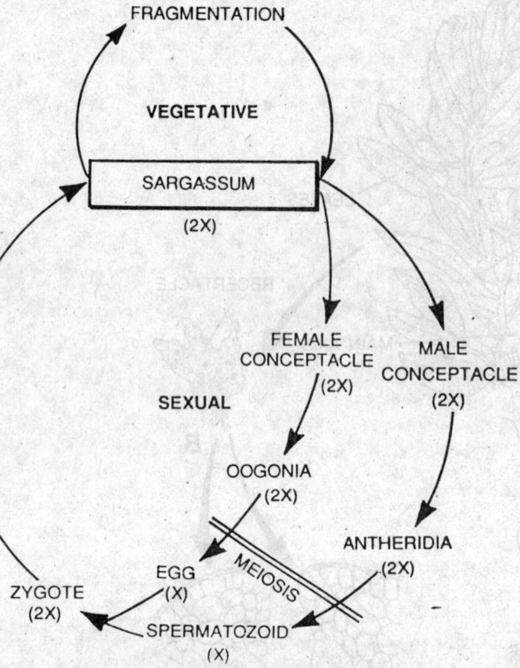

Fig. 7.27. *Sargassum* sp. Graphic life-cycle.

Germination of zygote. The zygote germinates directly without any resting period. It divides transversely giving rise to two cells. The upper cell divides and redivides periclinally and anticlinally giving rise to main plant body. The lower cell divides transversely and develops into rhizoidal system.

Life cycle. The life-cycle of *Sargassum* is diplontic. The plant itself is sporophyte (2x). The meiosis takes place prior to gamete formation. The gametes are haploid. There is no alternation of generations.

Systematic position. Division-Phaeophycophyta; Class-Phaeophyceae; Order-Fucales; Family-Sargassaceae; Genus-*Sargassum*.

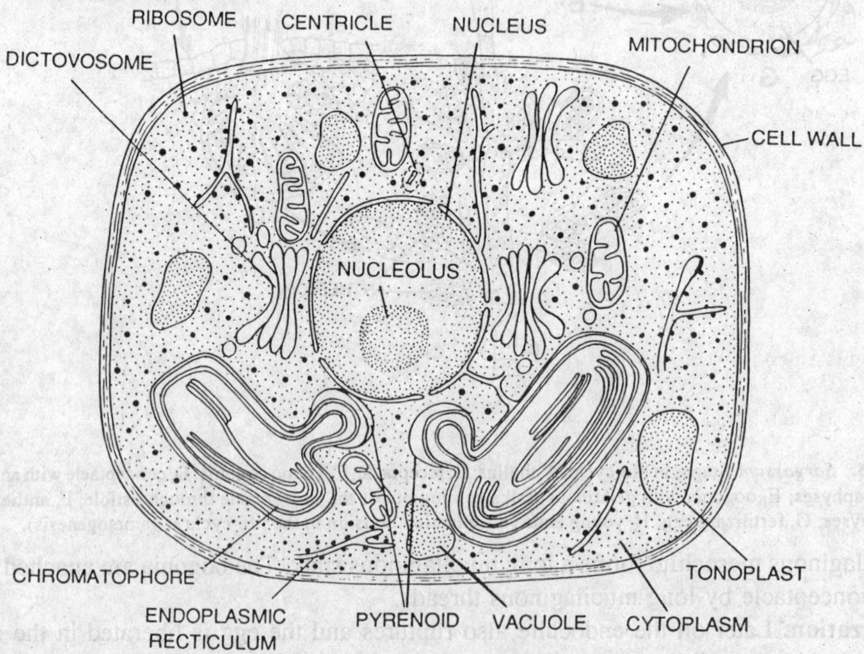

Fig. 7.28. *Phaeophyceae* (brown-algae). Ultrastructure (as revealed by electron microscope) of a cell (diagrammatic).

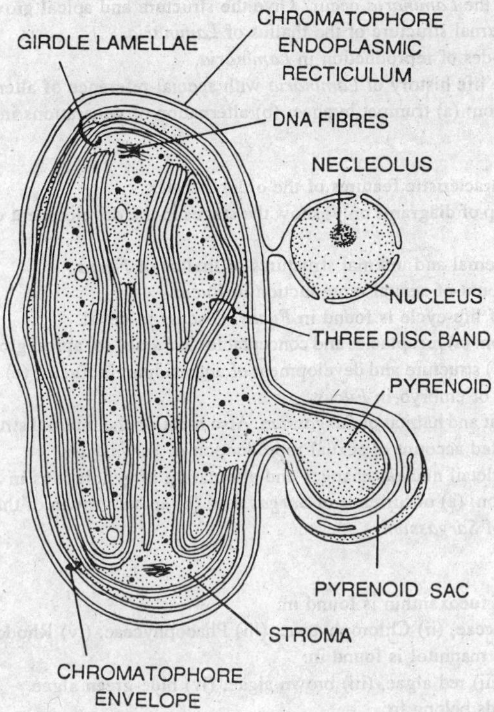

Fig. 7.29. Phaeophyceae (brown algae). Ultra structure of a chromatophore of a cell of brown alga.

Revision Questions

Class. Phaeophyceae

1. Give the characteristic features of Phaeohyceae. Why they are called brown algae ?
2. Where do the brown algae occur? Describe the range of somatic structure of Phaeophyceae.
3. Write a detailed note on pigmentation, food products and flagellation of Phaeophyceae.
4. Mention the modes of reproduction found in Phaeophyceae.
5. Describe in brief the classification of Phaeophyceae.
6. Write notes on: (a) economic importance of Phaeophyceae: (b) phylogenetic relationship in Phaeophyceae.

Order. Ectocarpales

1. Give the characteristic features of the order Ectocarpales.
2. Give the life-history of *Ectocarpus*. Also mention the phenomenon of alternation of generations and reduplication in the life-history of *Ectocarpus*.
3. Give a comprehensive account of the modes of reproduction in *Ectocarpus*.
4. Write notes on: (a) distribution and occurrence of *Ectocarpus;* (b) structure of plant body of *Ectocarpus;* (c) unilocular and plurilocular sporangia; (d) clump formation.

Order Dictyotales

1. Give the characteristic features of the order Dictyotales.
2. Describe in brief the occurrence, morphology and apical growth of *Dictyota*.
3. Give the details of sexual reproduction in *Dictyota*.
4. Give the modes of reproduction found in *Dictyota*.
5. Describe the life-history of *Dictyota* with special reference of alternation of generations.
6. Write notes on: (a) tetrasporangia and their development in *Dictyota;* (b) development of antheridium and oogonium in *Dictyota;* (c) vegetative reproduction in *Dictyota*.

Order Laminariales

1. Give the characteristic features of the order Laminariales.

2. Where does the *Laminaria* occur? Give the structure and apical growth of its thallus.
3. Give the internal structure of the thallus of *Laminaria*.
4. Give the modes of reproduction in *Laminaria*.
5. Describe the life history of *Laminaria* with special reference of alternation of generations.
6. Write notes on: (a) trumpet hyphae; (b) alternation of generations in *Laminaria*.

Order. Fucales

1. Give the characteristic features of the order Fucales.
2. With the help of diagrams only, show the stages in the development of various types of oogonia found in the order Fucales.
3. Give the external and internal structures of thallus of *Fucus*.
4. Give an account of sexual reproduction in *Fucus*.
5. What type of life-cycle is found in *Fucus*. Discuss in detail.
6. Write notes on: (a) receptacles and conceptacles in *Fucus;* (b) apical growth of thallus in *Fucus;* (c) development of conceptacle in *Fucus;* (d) structure and development of antheridium in *Fucus*; (e) structure and development of oogonium in *Fucus;* (f) development of embryo in *Fucus*.
7. Give the habit and habitat of *Sargassum*. Also mention the internal structure of the axis and leaf of *Sargassum*.
8. Give a detailed account of sexual reproduction in *Sargassum*.
9. Describe in detail nuclear changes and alternation of generations in *Sargassum*.
10. Write notes on: (a) occurrence of *Sargassum;* (b) apical growth of thallus in *Sargassum;* (c) development of conceptacle; (d) oogonia of *Sargassum*.

Multiple Choice Type

1. The pigment fucoxanthin is found in:
   (i) Myxophyceae, (ii) Chlorophyceae, (iii) Phaeophyceae, (iv) Rhodophyceae.
2. Storage food mannitol is found in:
   (i) diatoms, (ii) red algae, (iii) brown algae; (iv) blue-green algae.
3. The sea weeds belong to:
   (i) Chlorophyceae, (ii) Myxophyceae, (iii) Bacillariophyceae, (iv) Phaeophyceae.
4. The 'trumpet hyphae' are found in:
   (i) *Polysiphonia*, (ii) *Sargassum*. (iii) *Laminaria*, (iv) *Ectocarpus*.
5. The flagellum directed forward is smaller and directed backward is larger in size, in order:
   (i) Fucales, (ii) Ectocarpales, (iii) Laminariales, (iv) Cutlariales.
6. The iodine is obtained from:
   (i) *Laminaria*, (ii) *Polysiphonia*, (iii) *Sargassum*. (iv) *Ectocarpus*.
7. An alternation of morphologically similar haploid and diploid generations is found in:
   (i) *Ulothrix*, (ii) *Chlamydomonas*, (iii) *Spirogyra*, (iv) *Ectocarpus*.
8. Erect, flattened, dichotomously branched thalli are found in :
   (i) *Ectocarpus*, (ii) *Polysiphonia*, (iii) *Dictyota*, (iv) *Nemalion*.
9. Unilocular and plurilocular sporangia are found in:
   (i) *Polysiphonia*, (ii) *Batrachospermum*, (iii) *Ectocarpus*.
10. Sort out the branched alga:
    (i) *Ectocarpus*, (ii) *Oedogonium*, (iii) *Spirogyra*, (iv) *Zygnema*.
11. Clumping of gametes is found in:
    (i) *Polysiphonia*, (ii) *Ectocarpus*, (iii) *Oedogonium*, (iv) *Volvox*.
12. Motile zoospores are found in:
    (i) *Polysiphonia*, (ii) *Ectocarpus*, (iii) *Spirogyra*, (iv) *Nemalion*.
13. The receptacles are found in:
    (i) *Ectocarpus*, (ii) *Sargassum*, (iii) *Polysiphonia*, (iv) *Nemalion*.
14. The life-cycle of *Sargassum* is :
    (i) haplontic, (ii) diplontic, (iii) haplo-diplobiontic, (iv) none of above.

Answers

1 (iii), 2 (iii), 3 (iv), 4 (iii), 5 (i), 6 (i), 7 (iv), 8 (iii), 9 (iii), 10 (i), 11 (ii), 12 (ii), 13 (ii), 14 (ii).

8

Rhodophycophyta–Rhodophyceae
The Red Algae

Characteristic features.

Pigmentation. Chlorophylls *a* and *b*, α–and β–carotenes, Lutein, Taraxanthin, Allophycocyanin, Phycocyanin, Phycoerythrin.

Storage products. Floridean starch, oils.

Flagellation. Absent.

There are about 400 genera and 2500 species in this class.

Occurrence. Majority of Rhodophyceae are marine and mostly found in sub-littoral zones. When water is clear they can penetrate several metres of depth. Certain species of *Gigartina, Laurencia, Lomentaria* form extensive belts in littoral zones. *Catenella* and *Bostrychia* are found in saline waters. Several Rhodophyceae are found on the roots of mangrove vegetation. The red algae are commonly found in the warmer seas of Australia and Asia. Some species of red algae are found in polar seas in the depth of 30 to 92 metres. Some red algae have been reported even from the depth of 200 metres. Majority of red algae are lithophytes and some are epiphytes, *e.g., Polysiphonia violacea* is epiphytic on *Fucus vesiculosus.* True parasitic forms have also been reported from red algae. *Harveyella pachyderma* is parasitic upon *Gracilaria confervoides. Polysiphonia fastigiata* is parasitic upon *Ascophyllum nodosum.* The photosynthetic tissue is greatly reduced in such forms and sometimes they are quite colourless. About 50 species of 19 or more genera are fresh water in habit. The fresh water species are found in well aerated waters such as water falls. *Batrachospermum* is found in the water falls of Dehradun. *Compsopogon* occurs in the plains of Uttar Pradesh even in the rivers. The other well-known fresh water forms are *Hildenbrandia* and *Lemanea.*

Range of vegetative structure. There is great diversity in the vegetative structure of red algae. They may be of several types.

1. **Unicellular forms.** The species of *Porphyridium* and *Chroothece* are unicellular in structure, but the cells form globose mucilaginous colonies. True unicellular forms are unknown. This is the case of reduction.

2. **Heterotrichous filaments.** Such filaments are commonly found in the species of *Goniotrichum* and *Asterocystis.* In *Asterocystis* the thallus is dichotomously branched.

3. **True parenchymatous forms.** The species of *Porphyra* are *Ulva* like. The Thallus may be one-celled thick (monostromatic) or two-celled thick (distromatic).

4. **Branched filamentous thallus.** All florideae have branched filamentous thalli. In some genera the various branches are free from one another, *e.g., Chantransia,* in other genera they lie more or less intermingled with one another within a common gelatinohs matrix, *e.g., Batrachospermum;* in still other genera they are so closely applied to one another that the thallus seems to be parenchymatous. In the case of *Nemalion, Liagora* etc., the filaments of unlimited growth are formed from protuberances of peripheral cells. The thalli of *Nemaiion, Cumagloia* are pseudoparenchymatous. These constructions are called multiaxial type or fountain type of construction. In *Nemalion* the apical cell forms a hair.

All Rhodymeniales are multiaxial. All Ceramiales are uniaxial. In other orders both types are represented in different families.

Methods of growth of thallus. The growth may be diffused or apical. In the order Bangiales, *Porphyra* and *Asterocystis* any cell of the thallus may divide in any direction. This is called diffused growth. The apical growth is strictly restricted to sub-class Florideae.

Structure of the cell. The cell wall. It is two layered. The outer layer consists of pectic substance and layer next to protoplast of cellulose. Sometimes the cell wall contains iodine in it. In majority of forms a thick cuticle like structure of pectic substance is found. In Ceramiaceae the wall becomes stratified.

Pit connections. The members of order Bangiales lack connections. At the point of contact of two cells there is a pit membrane surrounded by a disc of pectic material. Schimitz reported that these are of cytoplasm.

The protoplasm. The protoplasm is highly viscous. In order Bangiales there is no central vacuole, but in all Florideae the cytoplasm possesses a conspicuous central vacuole. The cell sap is either alkaline or neutral and rarely acidic.

The nucleus. In lower Rhodophyceae the cells are uninucleate, *e.g.*, Cryptonemiales, Bangiales etc. In other cases the cells are multinucleate, *e.g.*, Ceramiales, Rhodymeniales etc. Some of the larger multinucleate cells possess 3000 to 4000 nuclei in each of them. The nuclei are with one or more prominent nucleoli. There is well developed chromatin network.

Chromatophores and pigments. In order Bangiales (lower Rhodophyceae) there is a single stellate chromatophore in each cell. The back cells of *Nemalion* have ridged chromatophores. In majority of Rhodophyceae the number of chromatophores per cell is more than one. They may be band-like, *e.g.*, in family Ceramiaceae, irregularly lobed or discoidal, *e.g.*, in *Polysiphonia.*

In each chromatophore there is a centrally placed naked (without starch sheath) pyrenoid.

The pigments of red algae are r-phycoerythrin (red water soluble pigments), r-phycocyanin (blue water soluble pigment). Chlorophyll a, chlorophyll b (in traces only), xanthophylls and carotenes (β–carotene).

Reserve food products. The most important food product is **floridean starch** (polysaccharide) which is found in the form of small grains usually around the nuclei. These grains are not found within the chromatophores. In many Rhodophyceae a soluble sugar **floridoside** is found. This is galactoside of glycerol. A trehalose polysaccharide water soluble sugar is reported from *Lemanea.* The fats are found in traces.

Reproduction. The reproduction takes place by means of vegetative, asexual and sexual methods.

1. **Vegetative reproduction.** In majority of cases it takes place by fragmentation.

2. **Asexual reproduction.** The asexual reproduction of the gametophytes takes place by **neutral spores, monospores,** and **polyspores.** The neutral spores develop in ordinary cells of thallus, *e.g., Asterocystis.* The monospores are developed in sporangia. A single spore develops in each sporangium, *e.g., Scinaia.* The polyspores are formed in larger number in the sporangium.

The asexual reproduction of the sporophytes takes place by **tetraspores** formed in tetrads in the tetrasporangia, *e.g., Polysiphonia,* and **paraspore** borne inside parasporangium in greater numbers. During the development of tetraspores reduction division takes place. In the development of paraspores there is no reduction division.

3. **Sexual reproduction.** The sexual reproduction is always oogamous. The oogamy is of special type. The sex organs of Rhodophyceae have a distinguished terminology. The male structures are called the **spermatangia** developing non-motile **spermatia** (male gametes) in them. The female sex organ is called the **procarp.** It has a **carpogonium** bearing a receptive structure

trichogyne. The egg develops in the basal swollen part of carpogonium. The **auxiliary cell** may or may not be formed. In Ceramiales the auxiliary cell is formed after fertilization.

Zygote and its germination. In sub-class Bangioideae the zygote divides by vertical and transverse divisions. The number of cells may be 2, 4, or 16. The spores are known as **carpospores.** They are naked and liberated by disintegration of zygote wall and move about in amoeboid fashion. The first division of the nucleus of the zygote is reductional. In sub-class Florideae the carpospores develop indirectly from the zygote.

Life cycle. The life-cycle may be haplontic, haplobiontic or diplobiontic.

Classification. The class Rhodophyceae has been divided into two sub-classes (1) Bangioideae and (2) Florideae.

1. Sub-Class Bangioideae

(i) The growth of thallus is intercalary.

(ii) The zygote directly gives rise to carpospores.

(iii) The cytoplasmic connections between the cells are not obvious.

There is a single order Bangiales in this sub-class.

2. Sub-Class Florideae

(i) The growth of thallus is strictly apical.

(ii) The carpospores are formed indirectly from the zygote.

(iii) The plasmodesmata are very conspicuous.

There are six orders in this sub-class, *i.e.*, 1. Nemalionales, 2. Gelidiales, 3. Cryptonemiales, 4. Gigartinales, 5. Rhodymeniales and 6. Ceramiales.

1. Nemalionales

(i) They are non-tetrasporophytic Florideae.

(ii) Leaving aside a few where an auxiliary cell is found the carposporophyte develops directly from carpogonium.

(iii) The first division of zygote nucleus is reductional.

2. Gelidiales

(i) They are tetrasporophytic.

(ii) The carposporophyte develops directly from carpogonium. Auxiliary cell is not found.

3. Cryptonemiales

(i) They are tetrasporophytic Florideae.

(ii) The auxiliary cell develops on special filament.

4. Gigartinales

(i) They are tetrasporophytic Florideae.

(ii) The auxiliary cell is a vegetative cell of the gametophyte. Either it is borne upon the supporting cell or aloof from carpogonium.

5. Rhodymeniales

(i) They are tetrasporophytic Florideae.

(ii) The auxiliary cell is a special cell differentiated before fertilization.

6. Ceramiales

(i) They are tetrasporophytic Florideae.

(ii) The auxiliary cell is formed subsequently to fertilization directly borne upon supporting cell.

Economic importance of red algae. A few species of red algae also serve as food. They are processed in large quantities. The agar used in bacteriological and mycological media is extracted from red algae. An important genus known as *Porphyra* is used as an important ingredient in soups and is also cooked as a flavouring agent with meat. It is mostly used by Chinese people.

This alga is used on large scale by Japanese. *Gelidium* is also a very important alga. Another most important edible alga is *Chondrus crispus* which is commonly known as Irish moss. This alga is utilized in the preparation of various pharmaceuticals including laxatives and cosmetics. This alga is used as stabilizer in prepared food such as chocolate milk, puddings, jellied fish and similar other products. Another important red alga is *Rhodymenia palmata*. This alga is used as a food and also in the preparation of medicines. This is commonly known as dulse. At the time of famine in Ireland dulse became a very important food there.

Phylogenetic Relationships in Rhodophyceae

The Rhodophyceae are very much obscure in their phylogenetic relationships. The Rhodophyceae are clearly an independent group, however, they possess several characteristics of resemblance with other groups. The Rhodophyceae and Myxophyceae both lack flagellated reproductive cells. They possess similar pigments although one is red and the other blue-green. Both red and blue green algae possess starch variants as reserve foods, *i.e.*, glycogen and floridean starch. Sometimes both the algae possess some food in the form of oil droplets and both may have protoplasmic connections between cells. The Rhodophyceae possess a much more highly specialized vegetative body and specialized reproductive structures quite different and advanced from other groups of algae.

ORDER–NEMALIONALES

Characteristic features.

1. Mostly they are marine, but few exceptions, *e.g.*, *Batrachospermum*.
2. The vegetative structure is both uni and multiaxial.
3. There are no true auxiliary cells in many genera, *e.g.*, *Batrachospermum*, *Nemalion*; while in others, *e.g.*, *Galaxaura* the so-called auxiliary cell may be largely nutritive.
4. In the majority of the genera only haploid plants are represented in the life-cycle but in genus *Galaxaura* there is distinct alternation of generations. Commonly the life-cycle is haplobiontic.
5. The sporophytic phase is being represented by zygote only.
6. The carpospores are haploid and produced in haploid carposporangia.
7. On germination the carpospores produce a juvenile or *Chantransia* stage.
8. The zygote divides meiotically producing haploid carpospores by carposporophyte and have no free living tetrasporophytic generation.
9. Asexual reproduction takes place by means of monospores produced within monosporangia.

There are 35 genera and 250 species in this order. There are eight families in this order. The type genus *Batrachospermum* of Batrachospermaceae has been discussed here.

Family–Batrachospermaceae

Genus BATRACHOSPERMUM (*batracho*, frog; *spermum*, seed).

Occurrence. This is one of the fresh water forms of Rhodophyceae. This alga is found in slow running streams and on the banks of lakes and ponds. It is more commonly found in well aerated waters. The plants are blue-green, olive-green, violet and reddish in colour. The colour varies as a result of the differences in light intensity. The species which grow in deep water are reddish or violet in colour whereas the species growing in shallow water are olive-green in colour. The alga is also known as the **'frog spawn'**. The plants are mucilaginous, moniliform or beaded in appearance to the naked eye. The plants may reach a length of twenty centimetres and may easily be collected from the slow running streams around Dehradun especially in winter season.

Structure. The thallus is filamentous, profusely branched and with a mucilaginous feel. The filament consists of only one axial filament of main axis which has been produced by a single apical cell cutting off the segments parallel to the base. This way, the central filament or main axis consists of a uniseriate row of axial cells. The main axis bears the laterals at various points on its length. These laterals are very short in comparison to the main filament. They are called the branches or the laterals of limited growth.

At the nodal point just beneath the septum, usually four basal cells are formed each producing a whorl of the branches of limited growth. The laterals of limited growth possess constricted cells of moniliform or beaded appearance. The ultimate cells of the branches of limited growth

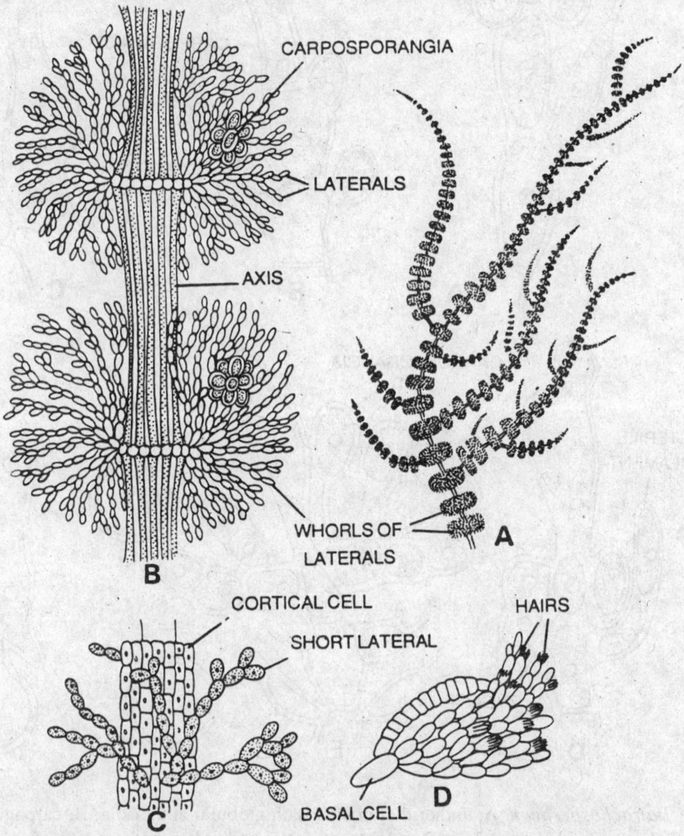

Fig. 8.1. *Batrachospermum.* A portion of plant; B, two whorls of laterals; C, short laterals; D, basal cell with laterals.

usually terminate in unicellular colourless hairs. The clusters of the laterals at nodes are called the glomerules. In addition to the numerous branches of limited growth, resemble the main filament in structure. The basal cells from which the branches of unlimited growth arise also produce filaments growing downward and ensheathing the main axis. They are called corticating filaments and they form the pseudocortex.

The cell wall of each cell is two layered. The outer layer consists of pectin and the inner one of the cellulose. The cells are uninucleate. Each cell contains many (more than one) parietal chromatophores. The cells of *Batrachospermum* do not have pit connections which are common in the other members of Florideae. Each chromatophore contains single pyrenoid.

Reproduction. The reproduction takes place by means of sexual and asexual methods.

Sexual reproduction. The sexual reproduction is advanced oogamous and takes place by means of male and female sex organs known as antheridia and carpogonia respectively. The plants may be monoecious or dioecious.

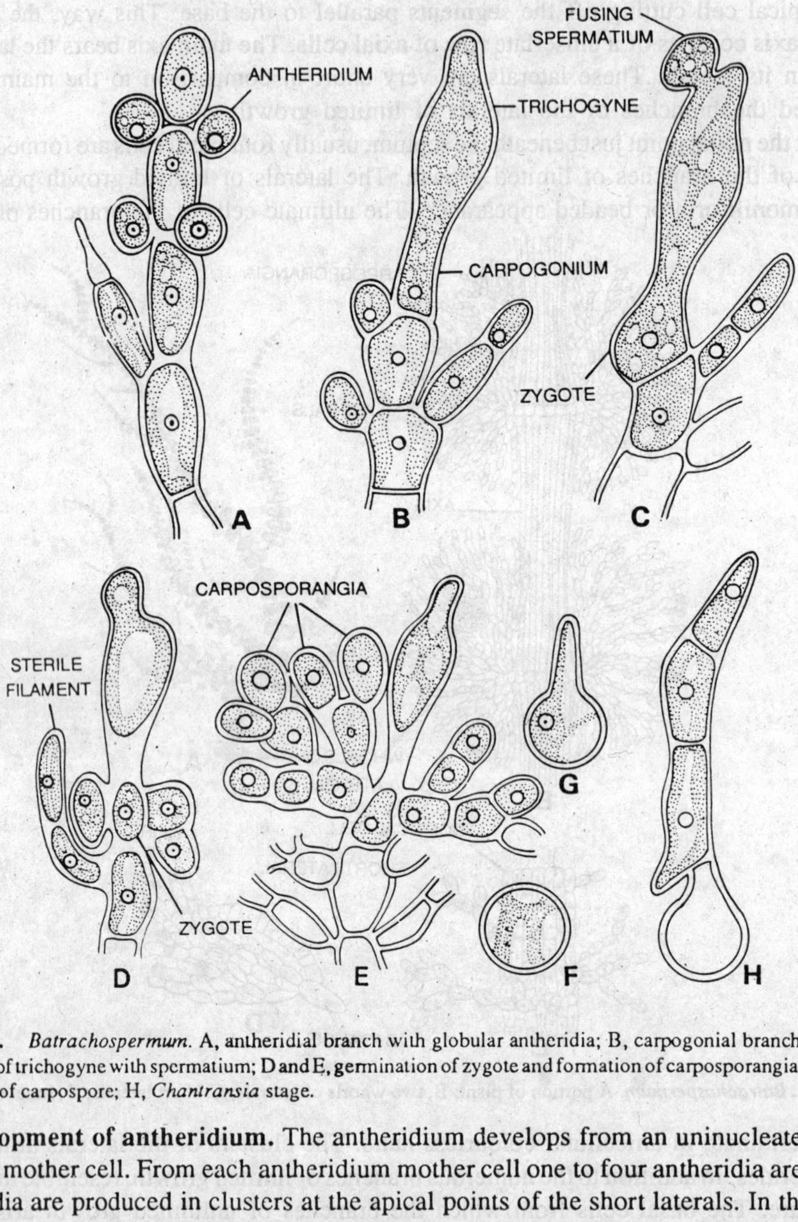

Fig. 8.2. *Batrachospermum*. A, antheridial branch with globular antheridia; B, carpogonial branch with carpogonium; C, fusion of trichogyne with spermatium; D and E, germination of zygote and formation of carposporangia; F, carpospore; G, germination of carpospore; H, *Chantransia* stage.

Development of antheridium. The antheridium develops from an uninucleate, colourless antheridium mother cell. From each antheridium mother cell one to four antheridia are developed. The antheridia are produced in clusters at the apical points of the short laterals. In the beginning they appear as protuberances arising subterminally and successively from different sides of the mother cell. Later on, the small protuberances become spherical.

Each antheridium contains a single spermatium on its maturity. The non-motile, spermatium liberates through a slit formed in the wall of antheridium. The spermatia remain floating in the water.

In *Batrachospermum*, the nucleus divides into two as soon as it contacts the trichogyne. So at the time of the fertilization spermatium contains two nuclei and sometimes known as spermatium complex.

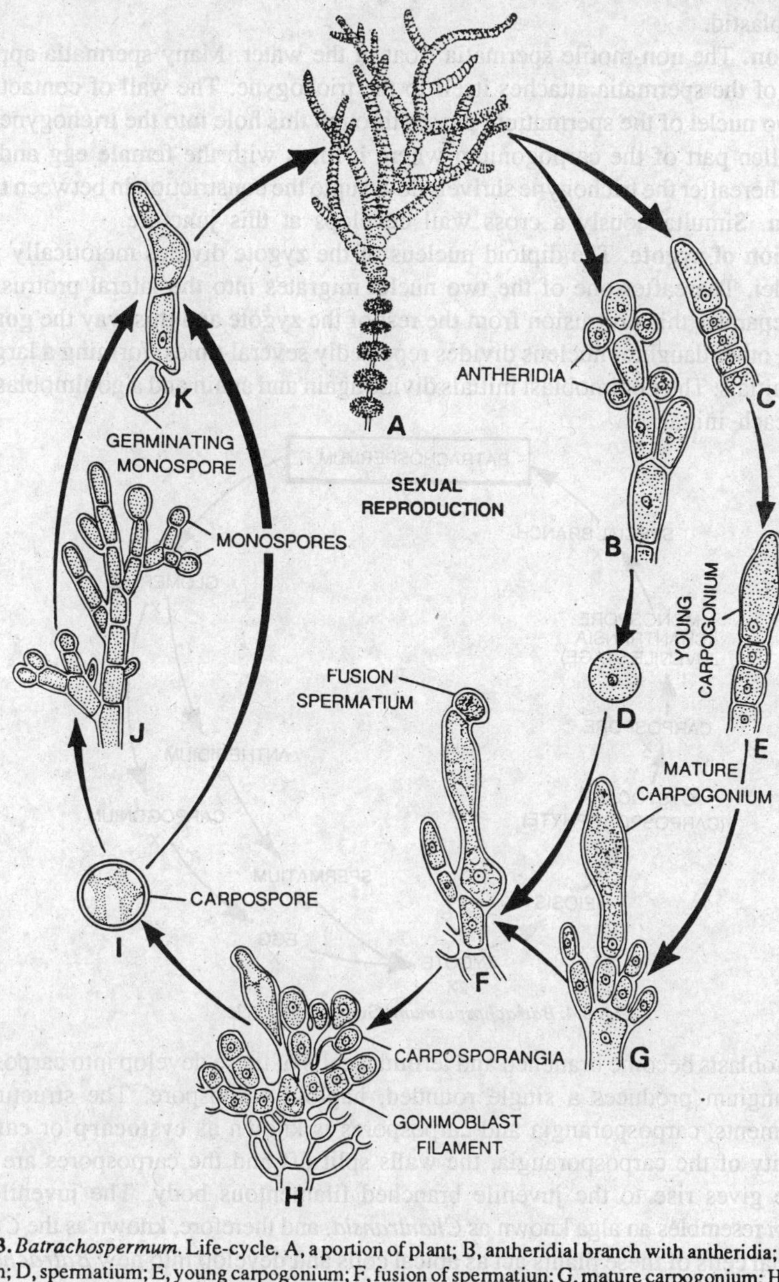

Fig. 8.3. *Batrachospermum*. Life-cycle. A, a portion of plant; B, antheridial branch with antheridia; C and E, formation of carpogonium; D, spermatium; E, young carpogonium; F, fusion of spermatiun; G, mature carpogonium; H, carposporophyte; I, carpospore; J, *Chāntransia* stage producing monospores; K, germinating monospore.

Development of carpogonium. The carpogonia develop on the terminal ends of the short laterals. The terminal cell of the lateral divides into four cells. The uppermost cell develops into the carpogonium.

The carpogonium consists of a swollen basal portion which contains an egg and known as **carpogonium** and an elongated receptive part, the **trichogyne.**The carpogonium is flask-like. In the majority of Florideae the cytoplasm of the carpogonium is colourless, but in *Batrachospermum* it bears a pale plastid.

Fertilization. The non-motile spermatia float in the water. Many spermatia approach the trichogyne. One of the spermatia attaches itself to the trichogyne. The wall of contact dissolves and one of the two nuclei of the spermatium passes through this hole into the trichogyne, reaching in the basal swollen part of the carpogonium where it fuses with the female egg and develops into the zygote. Thereafter the trichogyne shrivels down upto the constriction in between trichogyne and carpogonium. Simultaneously a cross wall develops at this juncture.

Germination of zygote. The diploid nucleus of the zygote divides meiotically producing two haploid nuclei. Thereafter one of the two nuclei migrates into the lateral protrusion of the zygote. A wall separates this protrusion from the rest of the zygote and this way the **gonimoblast initial** is formed, other daughter nucleus divides repeatedly several times, forming a large number of gonimoblast initials. The gonimoblast initials divide again and again and a gonimoblast filament develops from each initial.

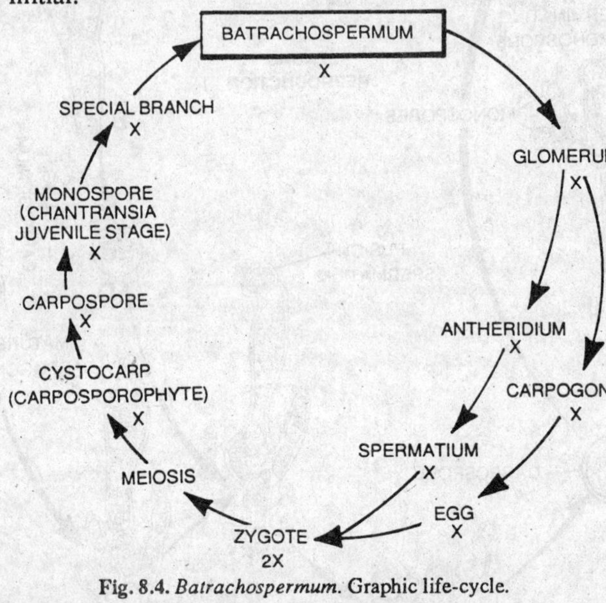

Fig. 8.4. *Batrachospermum.* Graphic life-cycle.

The gonimoblasts become branched and terminal cells of these develop into carposporangia. Each carposporangium produces a single rounded, haploid carpospore. The structure having gonimoblast filaments, carposporangia and carpospores is known as **cystocarp** or **carposporophyte.** At maturity of the carposporangia, the walls split off and the carpospores are liberated. Each carpospore gives rise to the juvenile branched filamentous body. The juvenile form of *Batrachospermum* resembles an alga known as *Chantransia,* and therefore, known as the *Chantransia* stage. The terminal cells of these plants act as apical cells and develop into new *Batrachospermum* plants.

Asexual reproduction. In several species of *Batrachospermum* the short branches of the filaments of *Chantransia* stage produce **monospores.** These monospores again produce *Chantransia* stage, and again the apical cells of this stage produce new plants.

Systematic position. Division-Rhodophycophyta; Class-Rhodophyceae; Sub-class-Florideae;

Order-Nemalionales; Family-Batrachospermaceae; Genus-*Batrachospermum.*

Family–Batrachospermaceae

Genus NEMALION (worm)

Occurrence. *Nemalion* is a marine alga. It is a summer annual which grows in the middle portion of the intertidal zone.

Structure. The thallus is cylindrical sparingly to profusely branched, and of a reddish-brown colour. The generic name, *i.e., Nemalion* is given because of the worm-like appearance of thalli.

Mature portions of the plant body are differentiated into a colourless axial core and a coloured ensheathing layer. The mature portion of the axial core is composed of closely intertwined

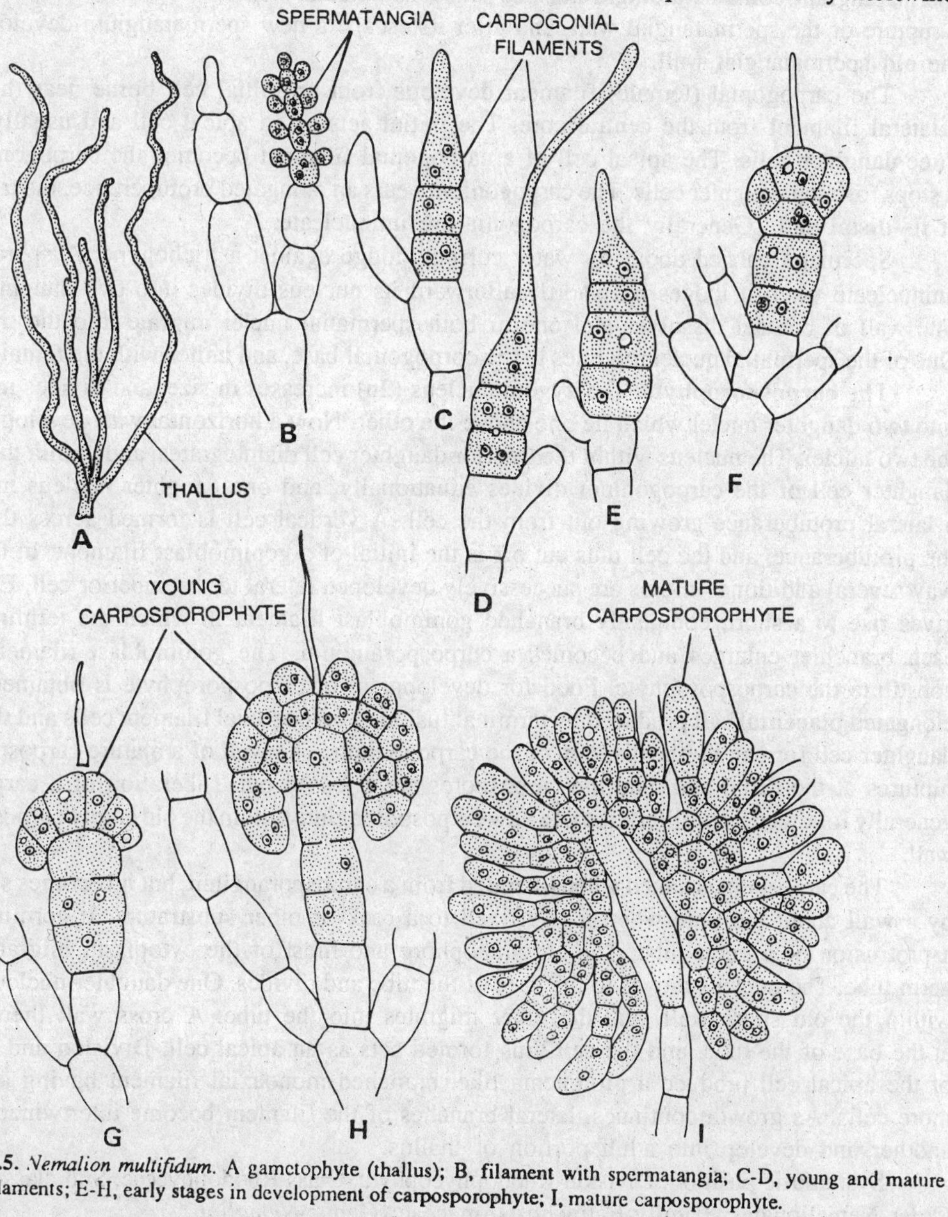

Fig. 8.5. *Nemalion multifidum.* A gametophyte (thallus); B, filament with spermatangia; C-D, young and mature carpogonial filaments; E-H, early stages in development of carposporophyte; I, mature carposporophyte.

longitudinal filaments of elongate cells without chromatophores or nuclei. The ensheathing layer, called cortex, consists of short, erect densely branched, lateral filaments, terminating in elongate hyaline hairs. Medium cells of lateral filaments are barrel-shaped uninucleate and have a single stellate chromatophore containing a conspicuous pyrenoid.

Sexual reproduction. *Nemalion* is homothallic, and rarely heterothallic.

The initial of a spermatangial (male) branch is an ordinary vegetative cell terminating a lateral filament from the central core. This initial cuts off a chain of four to seven derivatives each of which is a spermatangial mother cell. Spermatangial branches are easily distinguishable from vegetative ones because their cells are colourless or have less developed chromatophores. Each spermatangial mother cell generally forms four spermatangia. The spermatium within a spermatangium contains a single nucleus and a rudimentary chromatophore. It is liberated by a rupture of the spermatangial wall, and after its escape a new spermatangium develops within the old spermatangial wall.

The carpogonial (female) filament develops from an initial cell borne near the base of a lateral filament from the central core. The initial acts as an apical cell and usually cuts off three daughter cells. The apical cell of a carpogonial filament becomes the carpogonium after it stops forming daughter cells. The carpogonium bears an elongated protuberance, the trichogyne, at its distal end. Generally the carpogonia are uninucleate.

Spermatia carried about by water currents lodge against a trichogyne. A spermatium is uninucleate when it lodges but shortly afterward its nucleus divides into two daughter nuclei. The wall of contact dissolves and one or both spermatial nuclei migrate into the trichogyne. One of the spermatial nuclei migrates to the corpogonial base, and unites with the female nucleus.

The carposporophyte. The zygote nucleus (2n) increases in size, and divides meiotically into two daughter nuclei which lie one above the other. Now a horizontal wall develops between the two nuclei. The nucleus within the inferior daughter cell disintegrates, and within the superior daughter cell of the carpogonium divides equationally, and one daughter nucleus moves into a lateral protuberance growing out from the cell. A vertical cell is formed across the base of the protuberance, and the cell thus cut off is the initial of a gonimoblast filament. In the similar way several additional initials are successively developed lateral to the superior cell. Each initial gives rise to a short, compactly branched gonimoblast filament in which the terminal cell of each branchlet enlarges and becomes a carposporangium. The gonimoblast filaments jointly constitute the carposporophyte. Food for development of carposporophyte is obtained from an elongated **placental cell** produced by terminal fusion of carpogonial filament cells and the inferior daughter cell formed by the division of the carpogonium. The wall of a mature carposporangium ruptures at the distal end, and the carpospores are released out. Liberation of a carpospore is generally followed by proliferation of a new carposporangium within the old empty carposporangial wall.

The carpospore is naked when liberated from a carposporangium, but it becomes surrounded by a wall about the time when it is affixed to a rock or other substratum. It germinates with a protrusion of a germ tube. The chromatophore and most of the cytoplasm migrate into the germ tube. The nucleus moves to the base of the tube and divides. One daughter nucleus remains within the old spore wall, and the other migrates into the tube. A cross wall then develops at the base of the tube, and the cell thus formed acts as an apical cell. Division and redivision of the apical cell produce a protonema like, branched monoaxial filament having a dozen or more cells. As growth continues, lateral branches of the filament become intertwined with one another and develop into adult portion of thallus.

Systematic position. Division-Rhodophycophyta; Class-Rhodophyceae; Sub-class-Florideae; Order-Nemalionales; Family-Batrachospermaceae; Genus-*Nemalion*.

ORDER-GELIDIALES

Characteristic features.

1. They are only the tetrasporophytic plants of Florideae where the carposporophyte develops directly from the carpogonium.
2. The thallus is compact and all the members are uniaxial in construction.
3. True auxiliary cells are absent but special nutritive cells are formed in association with the carpogonia.
4. This order comprises of plants that provide the best sources of agar-agar in the world.

There are about six genera in this order. The order consists of a single family-Gelidiaceae.

Family–Gelidiaceae

Genus GELIDIUM (congealed)

Occurrence. The species of *Gelidium* are exclusively marine and widely distributed. This is an important alga of considerabie economic importance from which large quantities of agar are extracted.

Structure of thallus. The thallus is cylindrical or somewhat flattened. It is stiff, cartilaginous and often pinnately branched. In many species the branchlets bend away from the main axis in a geniculate way and are constricted in the basal portion. It is perennial and new shoots proliferate from the basal portion of the plant every growing season. The thallus is based primarily upon the uniaxial type of construction.

The thallus possesses a single apical cell at the apex of each branch. The apical cell cuts off derivatives at the posterior face which form a single axial filament of the adult portion. The cells of axial filament, one or two posterior to the apical cell cut off four primary pericentral cells and each of these cells forms a short branched lateral filament. The tips of these lateral filaments adhere to each other and form a pseudoparenchymatous tissue that makes surface of the thallus.

Reproduction. The reproduction takes place both by sexual and asexual methods.

Sexual reproduction. Gametophytes of *Gelidium cartilagineum* are dioecious.

On the branchlets of the male plants the spermatangia are found in elliptical sori also known as nemathecia.

They are found on the flattened sides of the branchlets. Commonly a spermatangial mother cell bears two spermatangia. As soon as the spermatangia are cut off they become transversely divided.

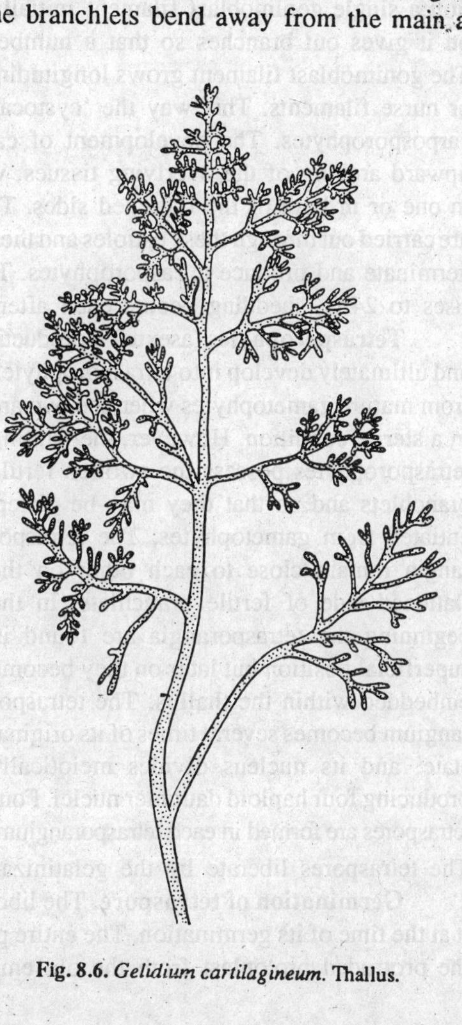

Fig. 8.6. *Gelidium cartilagineum.* Thallus.

The carpogonial filaments develop on the flattened sides of fertile branches of female gametophytes and close to the growing point. The single celled carpogonial filament is found upon the lowermost cells of a vegetative filament developing from the central axis. This single celled carpogonial filament metamorphoses into carpogonium which possesses an elongated trichogyne inflated at its distal end. Side by side of the development of carpogonial filament there develops an outgrowth of small celled filaments from the basal pericentral cells of vegetative filaments. These small-celled special filaments serve as nurse tissue for developing carposporophyte. There is no true auxiliary cell, but the presence of these nurse cells results in the formation of a complex structure composed of several carpogonia and short branches of small nurse cells. Only one of these carpogonia needs to be fertilized.

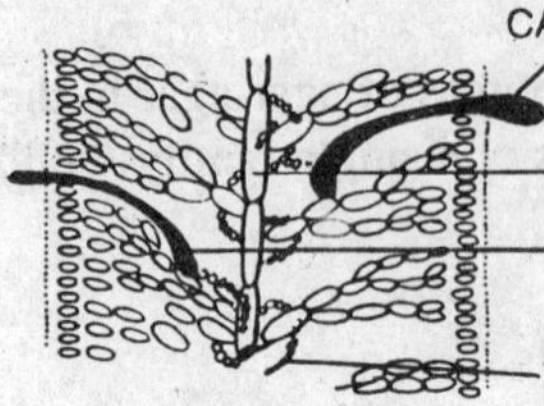

Fig. 8.7. *Gelidium* sp. L. S. of thallus showing carpogonium and the carpogonium producing the first gonimoblast filament.

Post-fertilization stages. After fertilization a single gonimoblast filament initially grows out into the mass of nutritive cell, but later on it gives out branches so that a number of terminal carposporangia are ultimately formed. The gonimoblast filament grows longitudinally along the axial filament and between the nutrient or nurse filaments. This way the 'cystocarp' of *Gelidium* is represented by an aggregation of carposporophytes. The development of carposporangia is simultaneously accompanied by an upward arching of the overlying tissues, which differentiate into an opening known as ostiole in one or in both of the flattened sides. The carpospores liberate from the carposporangia and are carried out through these ostioles and thereafter thrown away by water currents. The carpospores germinate and produce tetrasporophytes. The carpospores are shed when the water temperature rises to 24°C, shedding occurs each afternoon.

Tetrasporophytes (asexual reproduction). On germination the carpospores produce germlings and ultimately develop into tetrasporophytes. The mature tetrasporophytes cannot be distinguished from mature gametophytes when the two are in a sterile condition. However, the fruiting tetrasporophytes possess the swollen fertile branchlets and so that they may be differentiated from gametophytes. The tetrasporangia remain close to each other on the flattened side of fertile branchlets. In the beginning the tetrasporangia are found in superficial position but later on they become embedded within the thallus. The tetrasporangium becomes several times of its original state, and its nucleus divides meiotically producing four haploid daughter nuclei. Four tetraspores are formed in each tetrasporangium. The tetraspores liberate by the gelatinization of the wall of tetrasporangium.

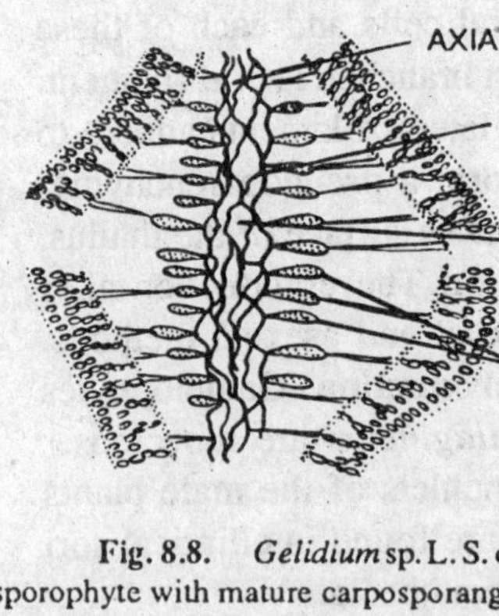

Fig. 8.8. *Gelidium* sp. L. S. of thallus showing carposporophyte with mature carposporangia.

Germination of tetraspore. The liberated tetraspore is naked but it develops a wall around it at the time of its germination. The entire protoplast protrudes out and a transverse wall separates the protruded protoplast from the old empty spore wall. The protruded protoplast divides by a transverse wall and one of the cells develops into a rhizoid. The sister cell produces an apical cell which initiates the growth of the new gametophyte. In heterothallic species two tetraspores develop into male and two into female gametophytes.

The tetraspores are shed when the water temperature rises to 20°C, shedding occurs each afternoon. The growth is slow at first but later becomes very rapid.

→ Male gametophyte (x) Female gametophyte (x) ←
↓ ↓
Spermatangia (x) Carpogonial filament (x)
↓ ↓
Spermatium (x) Carpogonium (x)
↓ ↓
→ Zygote (2x) ←
↓
Gonimoblast filament (2x)
↓
Carposporangia (2x)
↓
Carpospores (2x)
↓
Asexual plant (2x)
(Tetrasporophyte)
↓
Tetrasporangium (2x)
↓ MEIOSIS
Tetraspores (x)

Systematic position. Division–Rhodophycophyta; Class–Rhodophyceae; Sub-class–Florideae; Order–Gelidiales; Family Gelidiaceae; Genus–*Gelidium.*

ORDER–CRYPTONEMIALES

Characteristic features.

1. They are the only tetrasporophytic Florideae which bear an auxiliary cell borne in a special filament of the gametophyte.
2. The auxiliary cell filaments are either remote from or upon the supporting cell of a carpogonial filament.
3. Auxiliary cell filaments resemble carpogonial filaments in that their cells lack chromatophores and are densely packed with protoplasm. Thus they are supposed to be modified carpoginal filaments.
4. The carpogonium is always terminal in position and the auxiliary cell is always intercalary.
5. The plants of this order show a diplobiontic type of life cycle and possess the most elaborate carposporophytes found in the Rhodophyceae.
6. Many of the plants of Cryptonemiales have their cell walls impregnated with lime. In certain extreme cases the whole thallus becomes so encrusted in lime that the plant appears to be petrified and forms an amorphous mass resembling coral. Such calcareous algae make the coral reefs.
7. There are 85 genera and 650 species in this order.

Family–Corallinaceae

1. The sex organs and in certain cases tetrasporangia too are produced in conceptacles opening externally by a circular ostiole.
2. The thallus is heavily calcified. Here, the genus *Corallina* has been discussed:

Genus CORALLINA (coral)

Family–Corallinaceae

Habit and structure. This is an example of fountain type of construction. The original construction is extremely well in this genus.

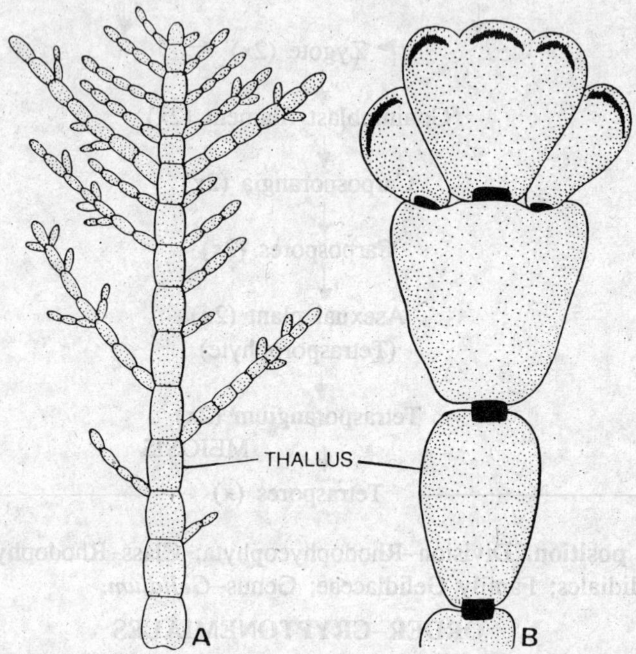

Fig. 8.9. *Corallina officinalis* A, a portion of plant, B, the same enlarged.

The erect plants, which are jointed, cylindrial or compressed arise from calcified encrusting basal discs or prostrate interlaced filaments.

Branching which is frequent, is pinnate. There is central core of dichotomously branched filaments with oblique filaments growing out at the swollen internodes to form a cortical layer, the end cells being flattened, the whole being encrusted by lime except at the joints.

Sexual reproduction. The plants are monoecious or dioecious, the reproductive organs are borne in terminal or lateral conceptacles. The carpogonia, which are not calcified arise from a kind of prismatic disc formed from the terminal cells, these cells also function as auxiliary cells later on. As a result of oblique divisions, one to three embryo carpogonial branches are formed on each mother cell but only one of these finally develops into the mature two-celled carpogonial branch with its long trichogyne.

After fertilization a long or rounded fusion cell is formed by the auxiliary cell, and this contains both fertilized and unfertilized carpogonial nuclei.

The antheridia are much elongated, and after liberation the spermatia round off and remain attached to the antheridial wall by means of a long thin pedicel in *C. officinalis*.

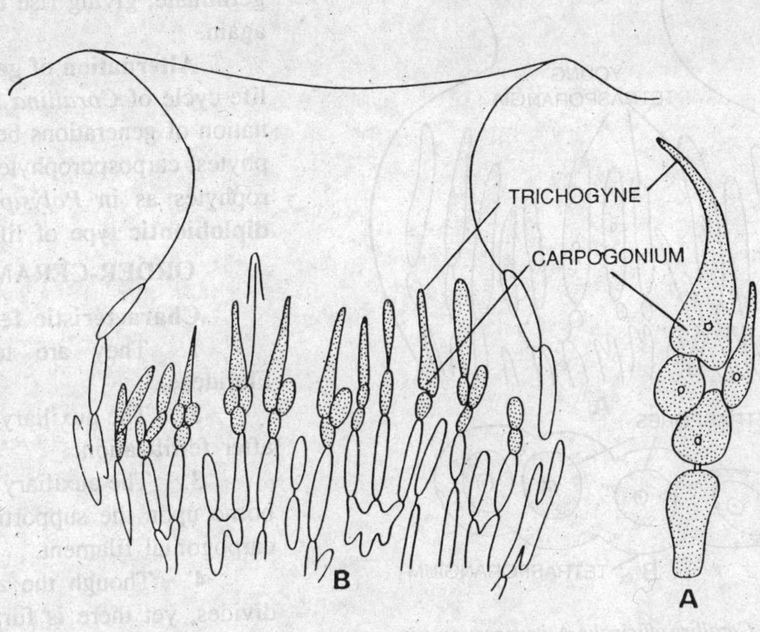

Fig. 8.10. *Corallina officianlis*, A, carpogonial conceptacle; B, single carpogonial branch.

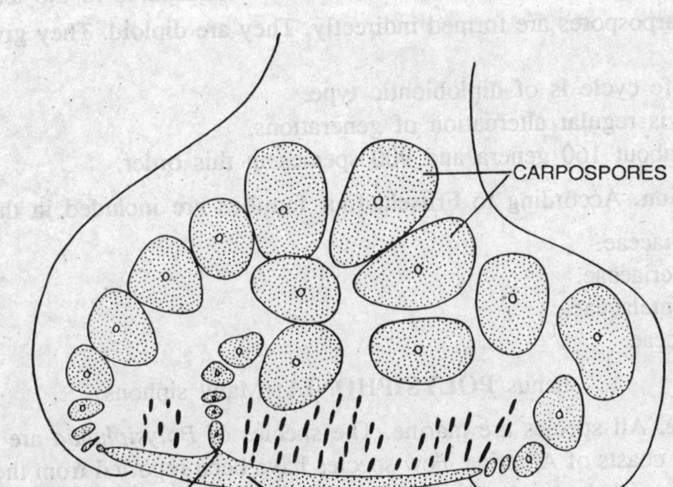

Fig. 8.11. *Corallina officinalis*. Fusion cell, gonimoblasts and carpospores.

Asexual reproduction. The disc cells of the developing asexual conceptacles divide into two, the lower half forming the stalk cell, while the upper becomes the **tetraspore mother cell.** The latter cell becomes clavate in shape. Its nucleus enlarges and divides twice during which meiosis occurs. Wall formation follows meiosis. The walls are laid down one above the other so that a row of four **tetraspores** is produced. The tetraspores are liberated through the ostiole of the conceptacle and float about freely in the water. They become attached to a suitable substratum, such as a rock face, and germinate, giving rise to sexual plants again.

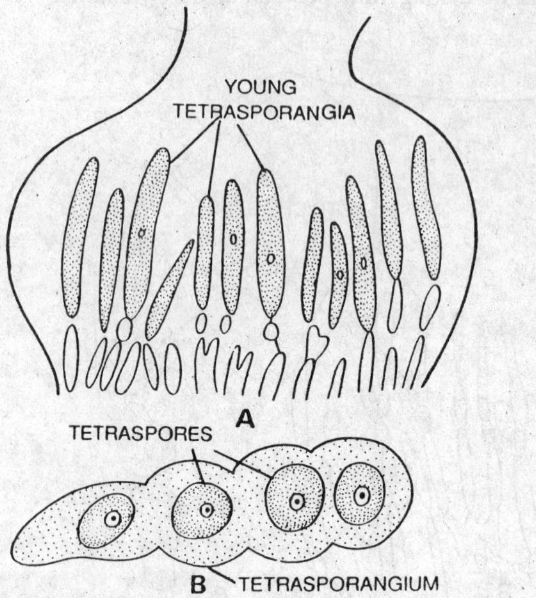

Fig. 8.12. *Corallina officinalis*. A, young tetrasporic conceptacle; B, mature tetraspores within tetrasporangium.

Alternation of generations. The life-cycle of *Corallina* shows an alternation of generations between gametophytes, carposporophytes and tetrasporophytes as in *Polysiphonia.* This is **diplobiontic** type of life-cycle.

ORDER-CERAMIALES

Characteristic features.

1. They are tetrasporophytic Florideae.
2. The auxiliary cell is formed after fertilization.
3. The auxiliary cell is directly borne upon the supporting cell of the carpogonial filament.
4. Though the zygote nucleus divides, yet there is further postponement of meiosis to the formation of tetraspores in the tetrasporangia.
5. The carpospores are formed indirectly. They are diploid. They give rise to tetrasporophytes.
6. The life cycle is of diplobiontic type.
7. There is regular alternation of generations.

There are about 160 genera and 900 species in this order.

Classification. According to Fritsch, four families are included in this order:

1. Ceramiaceae.
2. Delesseriaceae.
3. Rhodomelaceae.
4. Dasyaceae.

Genus **POLYSIPHONIA** (Many siphons)

Occurrence. All species are marine. The species of *Polysiphonia* are abundantly found along the Atlantic coasts of America. Few species have been reported from the coast of Karachi (Pakistan). The species have also been reported from Western Ghats of India. *Polysiphonia platycarpa* is a common Indian species and found in the Kumari harbour. Some species are epiphytic. *Polysiphonia violacea* is epiphytic upon a brown alga *Fucus vesiculosus.* Some species are parasitic too. *Polysiphonia fastigiata* is parasitic upon *Ascophyllum nodosum. Polysiphonia variegata* is found in polluted waters near the estuaries of sea. Some species are very commonly found on the roots of mangrove vegetation.

Structure. *Polysiphonia* varies in colour from red to purple. This colour is because of the overmasking pigment r-phycoerythrin. In addition to this pigment chlorophyll a, β–carotene, xanthophylls and r-phycocyanin are also present.

The thallus of *Polysiphonia* consists of two systems, *i.e.*, (1) the creeping of basal system and (2) the vertical or erect system. The basal system is attached to some suitable substratum by means of a well developed rhizoidal system. The rhizoids are unicellular, thickwalled and possess swollen distal ends which act as attaching discs. The erect or vertical system of the thallus arises from the basal prostrate system. It is much branched and consists of **siphons.**

Superficially the thallus of *Polysiphonia* looks profusely branched, but actually it is not so and composed of several parallel filaments called the **'siphons'**. The cells of the siphons

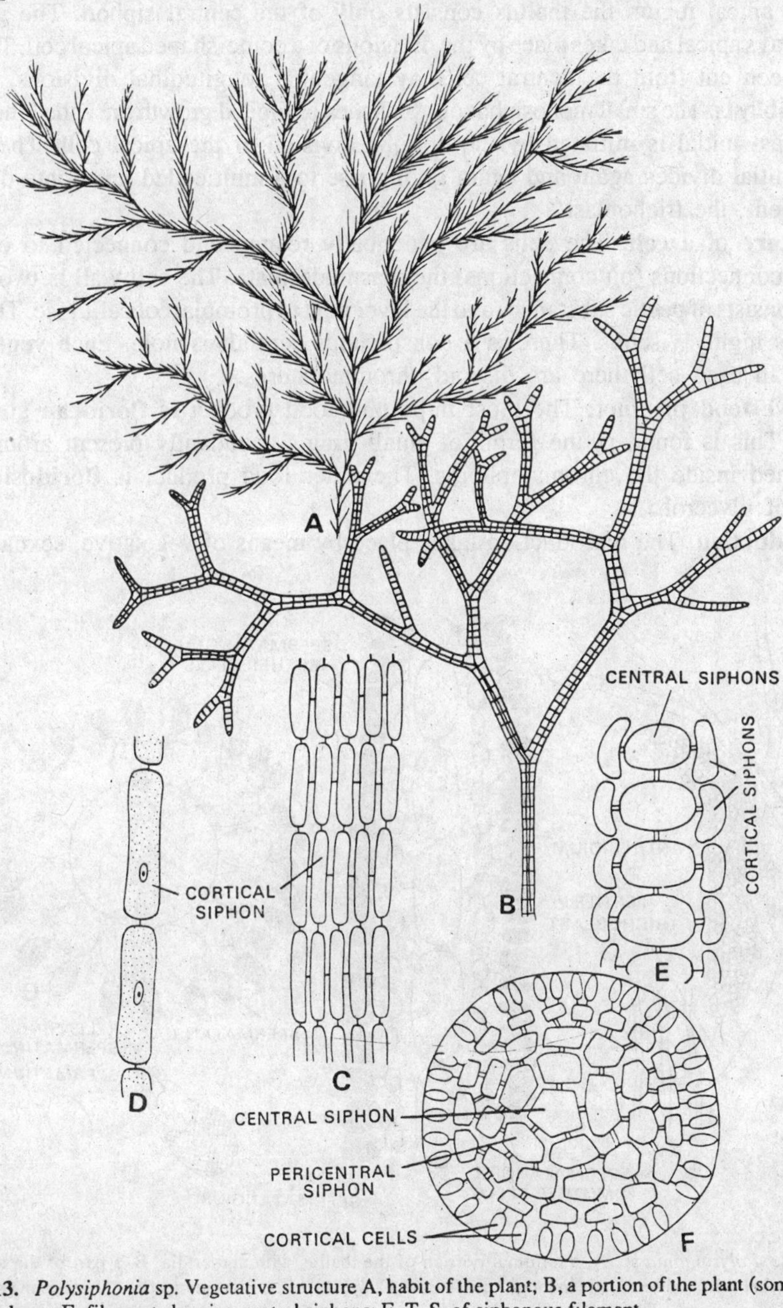

Fig. 8.13. *Polysiphonia* sp. Vegetative structure A, habit of the plant; B, a portion of the plant (somewhat enlarged); C-D, cortical siphons; E, filament showing central siphons; F, T. S. of siphonous filament.

are placed end to end connected to each other by **plasmodesmata.** The cells are genetically related to each other. The siphons may be of two types. There is a **central siphon** surrounded by 4-24 **pericentral siphons.** This number varies from species to species. The cells of the central siphon are somewhat elongated and larger than the pericentral cells.

In the older branches of the thallus, the pericentral cells divide periclinally thus giving rise to comparatively smaller cells. These cells make the cortical region or **cortex.** The protoplasmic connections (plasmodesmata) also develop between them and the pericentral cells.

In the apical region the thallus consists only of the central siphon. The growth of the thallus is always apical and takes place by the divisions of a dome-shaped apical cell. The pericentral cells have been cut from the central cells by tangential longitudinal divisions.

Trichoblasts. The small monosiphonous branches of limited growth are called the **trichoblasts.** The trichoblast initial is initiated by the oblique division of the apical cell. The small apical trichoblast initial divides again and again giving rise to a multicelled uniseriate dichotomously forked filament, the trichoblast.

Structure of a cell. The cells are genetically related and connected to each other by cytoplasmic connections (pit connections) the plasmodesmata. The cell wall is two layered. The outer layer consists of pectic substances and the layer next to protoplast of cellulose. The protoplasm of the cell is highly viscous. There is a conspicuous central vacuole. Each vegetative cell is uninucleate. In each cell there are discoid chromatophores.

Reserve food product. The most important food product is **floridean starch** (a polysaccharide). This is found in the forms of small grains abundantly present around the nuclei but not formed inside the chromatophores. The other food product is **floridoside.** This is a galactoside of glycerol.

Reproduction. The reproduction takes place by means of vegetative, sexual and asexual

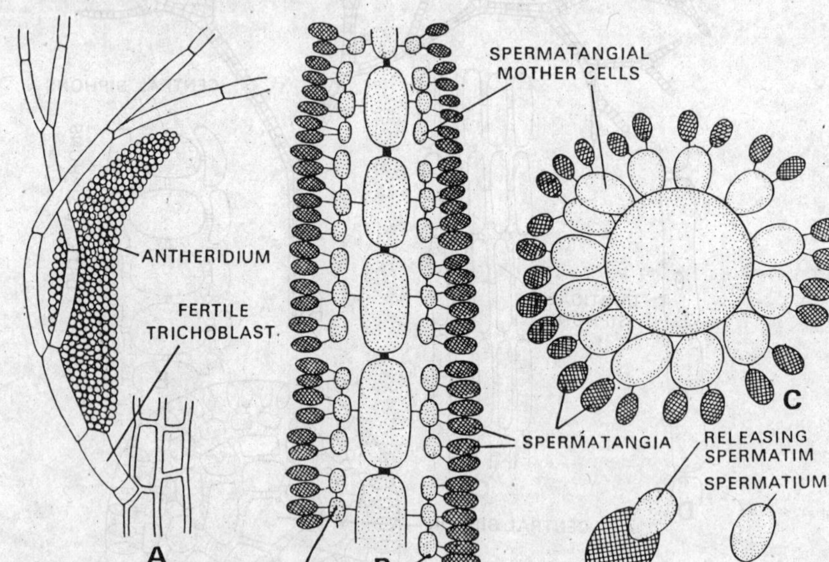

Fig. 8.14. *Polysiphonia* sp. A, a terminal portion of the thallus with antheridia; B, a part of the antheridium with spermatangial mother cells and spermatia in longitudinal view; C, the same in transverse section; D, releasing spermatium from spermatangium.

methods. There are three types of plants, *i.e.*, male, female and tetrasporophyte. The male plants bear antheridia and the female the procarps. The asexual plant or tetrasporophyte produces tetraspores. All the three types are morphologically identical.

Sexual reproduction. The male plants bear the male sex organs the antheridia, and the female plants bear the female sex organs the carpogonia.

Antheridium and its development. The antheridia are borne upon short branches in clusters near the apical portion of the thallus. Each antheridial branch consists of a central trichoblast filament, which produces many lateral pericentral cells. These cells develop antheridial mother cells on them. On each antheridial mother cell two, three or four antheridial cells are developed.

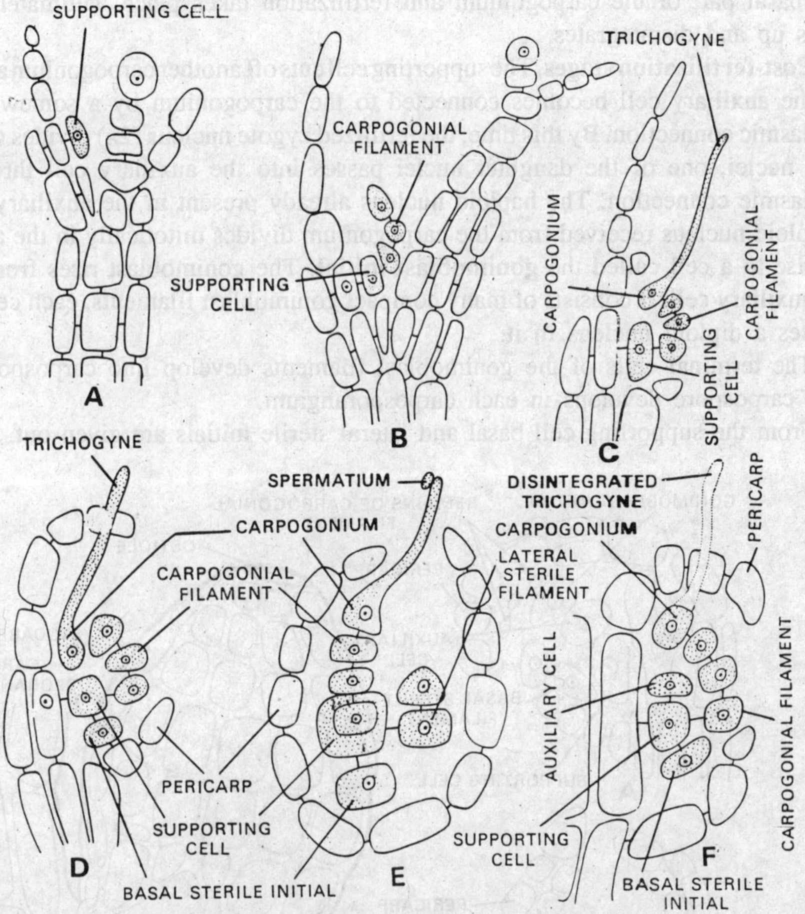

Fig. 8.15. *Polysiphonia* sp. Sexual reproduction: A, longitudinal section of the terminal part of the thallus before the development of carpogonial filament; B, developing carpogonial filament on the supporting cell; C, carpogonial filament; D, basal sterile initials cut off; E, lateral sterile filament cuts off, F, post-fertilization stages and development of auxiliary cell.

These antheridial cells are called the **spermatangia.** A single **spermatium** is liberated from each spermatangium. The new spermatangium may be proliferated from the wall of the old spermatangium. The spermatia are non-motile and uninucleate. They are dependent for their movement upon the mercy of water currents.

Carpogonium and its development. The **procarp** develops from a pericentral cell of greatly reduced trichoblast of female plant. It consists of a row of 3 or 4 celled the **carpogonial**

filament. These cells are connected to each other by usual plasmodesmata. The terminal cell of this filament becomes narrow and elongated. The terminal receptive part is called the **trichogyne** and the basal swollen part bearing female nucleus is called the **carpogonium.**

The basal pericentral cell of the carpogonial branch is called the **supporting cell.** Actually the supporting cell cuts off an initial of carpogonial filament which gives rise to the four celled carpogonial filament.

Fertilization. With the help of water currents the non-motile spermatia are lodged against the receptive trichogyne. The trichogyne is somewhat sticky in nature. The wall of contact dissolves, the male nucleus passes through the trichogyne and ultimately reaches the female nucleus situated in the basal part of the carpogonium and fertilization takes place. Ultimately the trichogyne shrivels up and disintegrates.

Post-fertilization stages. The supporting cell cuts off another carpogonium and the supporting cell. The auxiliary cell becomes connected to the carpogonium by a somewhat wide tubular protoplasmic connection. By this time, the fertilized zygote nucleus (2x) divides mitotically giving to two nuclei, one of the daughter nuclei passes into the auxiliary cell through the tubular protoplasmic connection. The haploid nucleus already present in the auxiliary cell disappears. The diploid nucleus received from the carpogonium divides mitotically in the auxiliary cell and gives rise to a cell called the **gonimoblast initial**. The gonimoblast rises from the upper face to the auxiliary cell. It consists of many compact gonimoblast filaments, each cell of the filament possesses a diploid nucleus in it.

The terminal cells of the gonimoblast filaments develop into carposporangia. A single diploid carpospore develops in each carposporangium.

From the supporting cell basal and lateral sterile initials are given out. The basal sterile

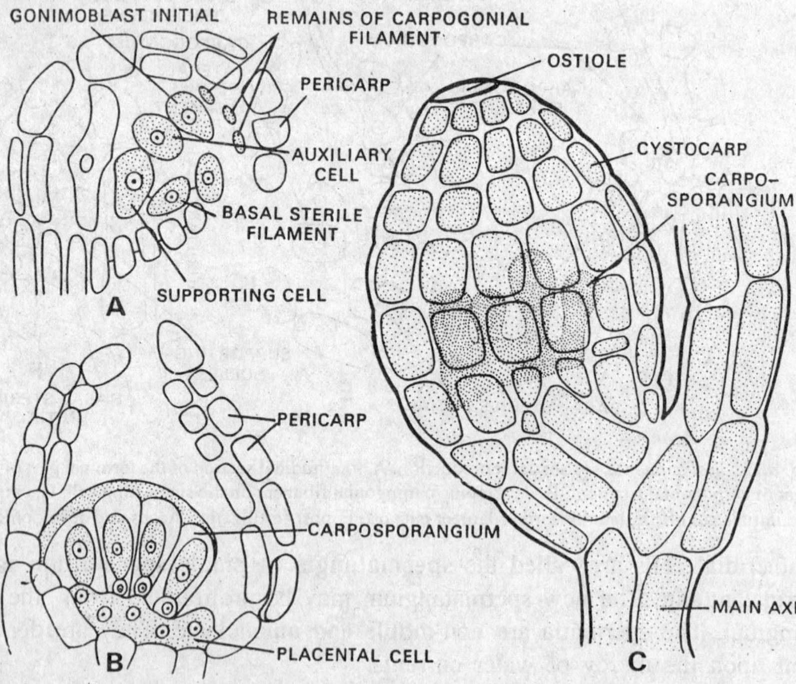

Fig. 8.16. *Polysiphonia*. Post-fertilization stages. A, procarp after formation of first gonimoblast initial; B, Carposporophyte with carposporangia; C, surface view of mature pericarp (cystocarp). After G.M. Smith 1955.

initial divides later on and the lateral sterile initial divides immediately giving rise to 4-10 celled sterile filament. The basal sterile initial gives rise to two cells only.

Ultimately, by the fusion of the supporting cell, auxiliary cell and sterile filaments, a large cell is developed called the **placental cell.** The placental cell is nutritional in function. The carpogonial cells are disintegrated by this time and they do not participate in the development of the placental cell.

A pseudoparenchymatous urn-shaped structure develops around the carposporangia etc. This structure is called the **cystocarp.** It possesses a small terminal opening, the **ostiole.** Each cystocarp contains 50-60 carpospores in it, this structure is **carposporophyte.** The carpospores develop into tetrasporophytes.

Asexual reproduction. The carpospores liberate from the carposporangia and come out in the water through the apical pore of the urn-shaped cystocarp. Each carpospore (2x) develops into a tetrasporophyte. The tetraspores develop in the tetrasporangia situated on the apical branch of the tetrasporophyte. The tetrasporangia develop in several tiers. The fertile pericentral cell which is somewhat smaller than the other cells divides longitudinally and cuts off a daughter cell on its either side. In *Polysiphonia nigrescens* the other daughter cell cuts off two large cover cells on its upper face. In *P. violacea* this cell cuts off two large cover cells and a peripheral cell. The inner half of the pericentral cell divides transversely giving rise to a small cell and the upper tetrasporangium. The sporangial cell increases in size and then the nucleus divides. According to Yamanouchi (1906), this nuclear division is reductional. The cleavage of the protoplast of the tetrasporangium also takes place and four pyramid like-haploid tetraspores are formed in each tetrasporangium. The tetraspores liberate in the water by the rupture of the sporangial wall. According to Lewis (1912, 1914), these tetraspores germinate into gametophytes. Two tetraspores of a tetrad give rise to male gametophytes and two to female gametophytes.

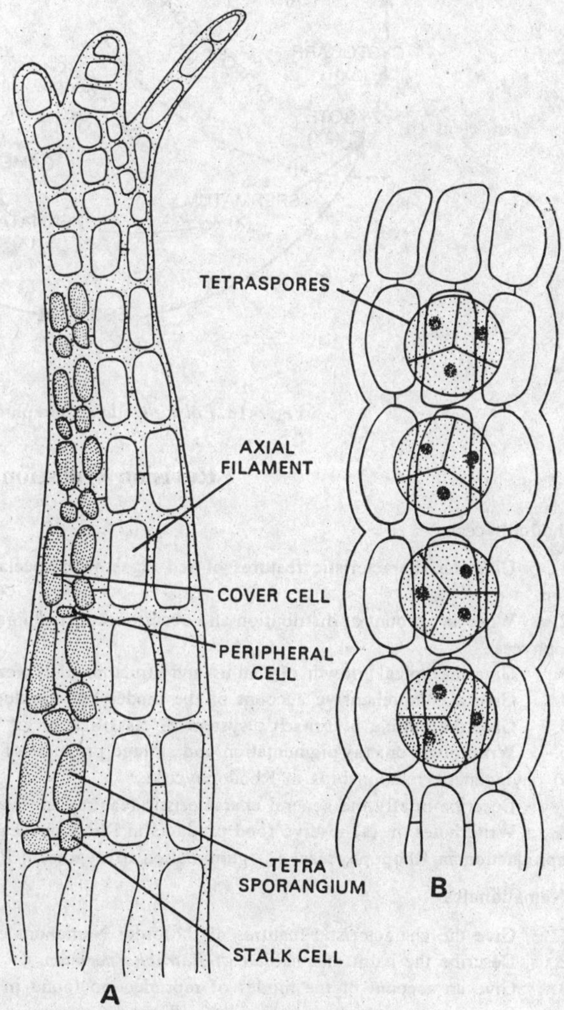

Fig. 8.17. *Polysiphonia* sp. A, development of tetrasporangia; B, tetraspores within tetrasporangia.

Systematic position. Division–Rhodophycophyta; Class–Rhodophyceae; Order–Ceramiales; Family–Ceramiaceae; Genus–*Polysiphonia.*

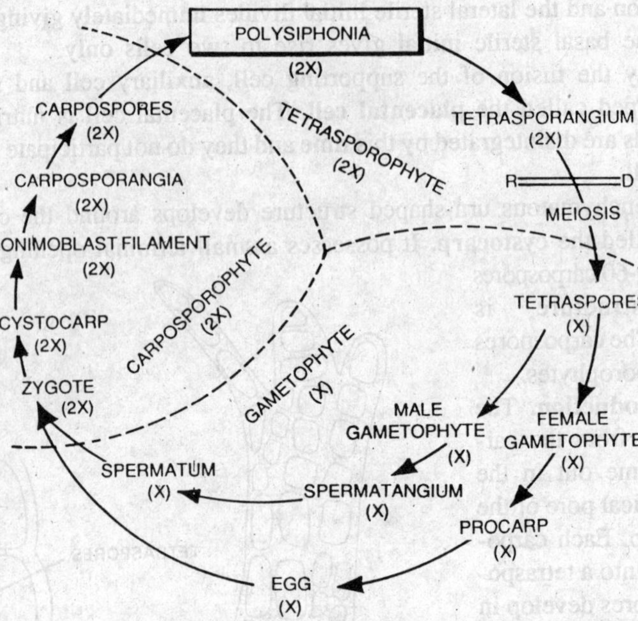

Fig. 8.18. *Polysiphonia* sp. Graphic life-cycle.

Revision Questions

Class. Rhodophyceae

1. Give the characteristic features of red algae with special reference of pigmentation, food products and flagellation.
2. Write an account of distribution and occurrence of red algae. Also mention the range of vegetative structure in Rhodophyceae.
3. Give the apical growth of thallus and structure of typical cell in Rhodophyceae.
4. Give a comprehensive account of the modes of reproduction found in red algae.
5. Give the outline of Fritsch's system of classification of red algae.
6. Write notes on: (a) pigmentation and storage products of Rhodophyceae; (b) economic importance of red algae; (c) phylogenetic relationships in Rhodophyceae.
7. Describe briefly the general characteristic features and classification of Rhodophyceae. (Gorakhpur, 1983)
8. Write notes on (a) reserve food products in Rhodophyceae, (b) asexual reproduction in Rhodophyceae (c) sexual reproduction in Rhodophyceae, (d) germination of zygote in Rhodophyceae.

Order. Nemalionales

1. Give the characteristic features of the order Nemalionales.
2. Describe the habit and habitat of *Batrachospermum.*
3. Give an account of the modes of reproduction found in *Batrachospermum.*
4. Describe the sexual reproduction in *Batrachospermum.*
5. Write notes on : (a) cystocarp of *Batrachospermum;* (b) *Chantransia* stage in *Batrachospermum;* (c) asexual reproduction in *Batrachospermum.*
6. With the help of diagrams only, represent the life-cycle of *Batrachospermum.*
7. Describe the life-cycle of *Nemalion.*

Order. Gelidiales

1. Give the characteristic features of the order Gelidiales.
2. Write a note on habit and habitat of *Gelidium.* Also mention the method of apical growth in thallus.
3. Give an account of modes of reproduction in *Gelidium.*
4. Write an account of sexual reproduction and post-fertilization stages in *Gelidium.*

5. Write notes on: (a) carposporophyte and (b) tetrasporophyte of *Gelidium*.

Order. Cryptonemiales

1. Give the distinguishing features of order Cryptonemiales.
2. Give the details of the somatic structure of *Corallina*.
3. Write an account of sexual reproduction and post-fertilization stages in *Corallina*.
4. Give an account of asexual reproduction in *Corallina*.
5. Write notes on, (a) tetrasporophyte and (b) carposporophyte of *Corallina*.
6. What are 'coral reefs' ? How they are developed ?
7. What type of life-cycle is found in *Corallina* ? Discuss its details.

Order. Ceramiales

1. Give the characteristic features of the order Ceramiales.
2. Mention with the help of diagrams only, the important stages in the life-cycle of *Polysiphonia*.
3. Describe the sexual reproduction in brief, in *Polysiphonia*.
4. Give the occurrence and the structure of thallus of *Polysiphonia*.
5. Mention the post-fertilization stages of *Polysiphonia*.
6. Write notes on: (a) carposporophyte of *Polysiphonia;* (b) tetrasporophyte of *Polysiphonia;* (c) pigmentation and reserve food products of *Polysiphonia;* (d) structure and development of antheridium and carpogonium in *Polysiphonia*.
7. What type of life-cycle is found in *Polysiphonia* ? Discuss its details.
8. Describe in detail the process of sexual reproduction in *Polysiphonia*. (Agra, 1980; Jiwaji, 1985)
9. Describe the structure and reproduction in *Polysiphonia*. Discuss alternation of generations in its life-cycle. (Agra, 1979)
10. Describe the post-fertilization changes in the life-history of *Polysiphonia*. (Osmania, 1984)
11. Trace the development of cystocarp in *Polysiphonia*. (Meerut, 1981; Andhra, 1985)
12. Write a detailed account of tetrasporic plant in *Polysiphonia*. (Jiwaji, 1985)
13. Write a detailed note on carposporophyte in *Polysiphonia*.
14. Write short notes on: (a) Gonimoblast filaments (Jiwaji, 1981); (b) Cystocarp (Jiwaji, 1979).

Diagrammatic Type

1. Draw labelled diagram showing detailed structure of cystocarp. (Lucknow, 1980)
2. Draw labelled diagram of the tetrasporohyte of *Polysiphonia*.

Multiple Choice Type

1. The pit-connections are found in:
   (i) *Chara*, (ii) *Ectocarpus*, (iii) *Polysiphonia*, (iv) *Oedogonium*.
2. Phycoerythrin is found in:
   (i) Chlorophyceae, (ii) Xanthophyceae, (iii) Rhodophyceae, (iv) Bacillariophyceae.
3. *Polysiphonia* is member of :
   (i) Ceramiales, (ii) Gelidiales, (iii) Nemalionales, (iv) none of above.
4. The carpospores are:
   (i) n, (ii) 2n, (iii) nn, (iv) none of above.
5. On germination the carpospores give rise to:
   (i) tetrasporophyte, (ii) gametophyte, (iii) sporophyte, (iv) none of above.
6. Floridean starch is food product of:
   (i) Chlorophyceae, (ii) Rhodophyceae, (iii) Myxophyceae, (iv) Phaeophyceae.
7. The floridoside is found in:
   (i) Chlorophyceae, (ii) Rhodophyceae, (iii) Myxophyceae, (iv) Phaeophyceae.
8. In *Polysiphonia* each spermatangium contains:
   (i) single spermatium, (ii) four spermatia, (iii) many spermatia (iv) none of above.
9. The life-cycle of *Polysiphonia* is :
   (i) haplontic, (ii) diplontic, (iii) haplo-diplobiontic, (iv) none of above.
10. The trichoblasts of *Polysiphonia* are:
    (i) polysiphonous, (ii) monosiphonous, (iii) without siphons, (iv) none of above.
11. The gonimoblast initials give rise to:
    (i) gametophyte, (ii) tetrasporophyte, (iii) carposporangia, (iv) none of above.
12. The cystocarp of *Polysiphonia* develops on:
    (i) male gametophyte, (ii) female gametophyte, (iii) tetrasporophytes, (iv) none of above.
13. The non-motile male gametes are found in:

(i) *Chlamydomonas*, (ii) *Oedogonium*, (iii) *Ectocarpus*, (iv) *Polysiphonia*.

14. The urn-shaped structure in *Polysiphonia* is:
(i) Procarp, (ii) Pericarp, (iii) Cystocarp, (iv) Archicarp.
15. The thalli of worm-like appearance are found in:
(i) *Polysiphonia*, (ii) *Batrachospermum*, (iii) *Sargassum*, (iv) *Nemalion*.
16. Agar-agar is obtained from:
(i) *Polysiphonia*, (ii) *Batrachospermum*, (iii) *Gracilaria*, (iv) *Nemalion*.

Answers

1 (iii), 2 (iii), 3 (i), 4 (ii), 5 (i), 6 (ii), 7 (ii), 8 (i), 9 (iii), 10 (ii), 11 (iii), 12 (ii), 13 (iv), 14 (iii), 15 (iv), 16 (iii).

Question Bank

Long Answer Type

1. Write short essay on economic importance of algae. (Kanpur, 1981)
2. Describe the sexual reproduction in *Oedogonium*. (Kanpur, 1981)
3. Describe the post-fertilization changes in *Polysiphonia*. (Rohilkhand, 1979)
4. Give a brief account of the life-history of *Ectocarpus*. (Rohilkhand, 1979)
5. Describe the structure and method of asexual reproduction in *Volvox*. (Rohilkhand, 1979)
6. Discuss the phenomenon of alternation of generations in the members of Phaeophyceae you have studied. (Kumaon, 1982, 1985)
7. Classify algae upto class level and give salient features of different classes. (Kumaon, 1982, 1986)
8. What is coenobium? Describe asexual reproduction in any motile coenobial form prescribed in your syllabus. (Kumaon, 1982)
9. Write an essay on the origin and evolution of sex in green algae. (Awadh Univ. 1980)
10. Describe the habitat, structure and methods of reproduction in *Oedogonium* or *Chara*. (Awadh, 1980)
11. Give an account of vegetative multiplication and sexual reproduction in diatoms. (Kumaon, 1983)
12. What are the methods of reproduction and perennation in Myxophyceae? Explain. (Kumaon, 1984)
13. Describe the method of sexual reproduction in *Oedogonium*. (Kumaon, 1984)
14. "*Chlamydomonas* throws some light on the origin and evolution of sex in algae." Comment upon the statements. (Kumaon, 1985)
15. What are the prokaryotic and eukaryotic cells ? Which of the two is more primitive type and why ? Give suitable diagrams. (Kumaon, 1987)
16. Describe the various methods of reproduction in *Chlamydomonas*. (Kanpur, 1982)
17. Give an account of habit, structure and methods of reproduction of *Nostoc*. (Kanpur, 1982)
18. List the major classes of algae whose representative genera have been prescribed in your course and describe their distinguishing characters in a tabular form. (Kanpur, 1982)
19. What is diplobiontic type of life-cycle ? Explain with the help of life-cycle of *Polysiphonia*. (Kanpur, 1982)
20. Describe in brief the life-cycle of *Ulothrix*. (Kanpur, 1983)
21. Describe in brief the sexual reproduction in *Vaucheria*. Kanpur, 1984)
22. Give an illustrated account of habit, structure and methods of reproduction of *Oscillotoria*. (Kanpur, 1984)
23. Give an account of life-cycle of *Ectocarpus*, and mention how it is affected by environment. (Kanpur, 1985)
24. Describe the formation of cystocarp in red algae studied by you. (Kanpur, 1985)
25. What are the main features on which the classification of algae is based? Discuss giving suitable examples. (Kanpur, 1986)
26. What do you understand by alternation of generations? Explain this phenomenon with reference to the life-history of *Ectocarpus*. (Kanpur, 1980)
27. Describe the structure of the cell, and asexual reproduction in *Chlamydomonas*. (Rohilkhand, 1980)
28. Describe the characteristic features of blue-green algae. What is their economic importance? (Rohilkhand, 1980)
29. Give an account of the external and internal features of *Sargassum* thallus. (Rohilkhand, 1980)
30. Give an account of thallus structure and sexual reproduction of *Chlamydomonas*. (Rohilkhand, 1982)
31. Write about sexual reproduction in *Vaucheria*. How does it resemble with that of *Cystopus* and mention its significance. Rohilkhand, 1982)
32. Describe thallus structure, and reproduction of *Sargassum*. (Rohilkhand, 1982)

33. Describe thallus structure, and sexual reproduction of *Volvox*. (Rohilkhand, 1983)

34. Give habit, occurrence and reproduction in *Cladophora*. (Rohilkhand, 1986)

35. Give an account of structure, reproduction and systematic position of *Vaucheria*. (Rohilkhand, 1985)

36. What are the common pigments present in algae? State the importance of these pigments in the classification of algae. (Awadh, 1982).

37. Describe the structure and method of sexual reproduction in *Volvox* or *Draparnaldiopsis*. (Awadh, 1982)

38. Describe distinguishing characters of Myxophyceae, Rhodohyceae and Phaeophyceae. (Awadh, 1981)

39. Describe the various modes of perennation in the fresh water algae studied by you. (Awadh, 1985)

40. Describe the mode of sexual reproduction in *Coleochaete* giving suitable illustrations. (Awadh, 1986)

Short Answer Type

1. (a) Describe the structure and development of globule and nucule. In which alga they are found ? (Rohilkhand, 1979)

   (b) Give an account of the morphology of *Oscillatoria*.

2. Write short notes on any four: (a) palmella stage, (b) dwarf male, (c) heterocyst, (d) conceptacle, (e) lateral conjugation in *Spirogyra*. (Rohilkhand, 1979)

3. Describe in detail the following: (a) structure of thallus in *Sargassum*, (b) neuromotor apparatus, in *Chlamydomonas*, (c) reproduction in *Nostoc*. (Rohilkhand, 1981)

4. Write short notes on: (i) *Oscillatoria*, (ii) growth in *Chara* or conjugation in *Spirogyra*, (iii) germination of oospore of *Volvox*. (Rohilkhand, 1982)

5. Write short notes on: (i) palmella stage, (ii) nannandrium, (iii) synzoospore, position and shape of chloroplasts in algae. (Rohilkhand, 1983)

6. Write short notes on any four: (a) vegetative reproduction in *Chara*, (b) dwarf male, (c) gongrosira stage, (d) *Ectocarpus* cell structure, (e) alternation of generations. (Rohilkhand, 1986)

7. Write short notes on: (i) structure of cell in Cynophyceae, (ii) cystocarp of *Polysiphonia*, (iii) heterocyst, (iv) fertilization in *Vaucheria*. (Kanpur, 1981)

8. Describe in brief the following: (a) sexual reproduction in *Oedogonium*, (b) vegetative thallus of *Polysiphonia*. (Knapur, 1983)

9. Write notes on: (a) *Sargassum* thallus, (b) *Stigeoclonium* thallus. (Kanpur, 1984)

10. Write short notes on any three: (i) zoospores of *Vaucheria*, (ii) lateral conjugation in *Spirogyra*, (iii) cell structure in Cynophyta, (iv) coenobium of *Volvox*. (Kanpur, 1985)

Diagrammatic Type

1. Draw the life cycle of *Ectocarpus* with the help of well labelled diagrams alone. (Kanpur, 1981)

2. Illustrate any two of the following with neat and labelled diagrams alone. (a) Structure of cell in Cyanophyceae as seen under electron microscope, (b) asexual reproduction in *Volvox*, (c) stages in scalariform conjugation in *Spirogyra*. (Kanpur, 1982)

3. Illustrate the following with neat and labelled diagrams alone, (a) asexual reproduction in *Vaucheria*, (b) *Chlamydomonas* cell, as seen under electron microscope. (Kanpur, 1983)

4. Illustrate the structure and development of sex organs of *Chara* with neat and labelled diagrams alone. (Kanpur, 1984)

5. With the help of labelled diagrams alone show the structure of thallus and life-cycle of *Polysiphonia*. (Kanpur, 1988)

6. What is heterotrichous form of plant body? With the help of labelled diagrams only show the life-cycle of a green heterotrichous alga. (Kanpur, 1989)

7. What do you understand by cyclosporean kind of life-cycle? With the help of labelled diagrams only show the life-cycle of cyclosporean alga. (Kanpur, 1989)

8. Describe thallus structure of *Polysiphonia*. Give its life-cycle with help of figures only. (Rohilkhand, 1982)

9. Give well labelled diagrams of any four. (i) *Ectocarpus* cell, (ii) vegetative structure of thallus of *Spirogyra*, (iii) *Oedogonium* cell structure, (iv) *Volvox* cell structure, (v) structure of *Nostoc* thallus and cell. (Rohilkhand, 1985)

Multiple Choice Type

1. Organisms which fix atmospheric nitrogen are: (i) mosses, (ii) bacteriophages, (iii) liverworts, (iv) blue-green algae. (C. P. M. T. 1977)

2. *Spirogyra* occurs in: (i) running salt water, (ii) running fresh water, (iii) marine water, (iv) stagnant water. (C. P. M. T. 1977)

3. *Ulothrix* is a green alga because: (i) it has a cell wall, (ii) each cell has a single nucleus, (iii) each cell has a single chloroplast, (iv) it produces gametes. (C. P. M. T. 1978)

4. Blue-green algae are: (i) procaryotes, (ii) eucaryotes, (iii) acellular, (iv) actinomycetes. (C. P. M. T. 1979)

5. The mode of sexual reproduction in *Spirogyra* is: (i) oogamy, (ii) anisogamy, (iii) isogamy, (iv) heterogamy. (C. P. M. T. 1979)

6. Cell wall in algal cell consists of (i) cellulose, (ii) chitin, (iii) cutin, (iv) suberin. (C. P. M. T. 1979)

7. *Spirogyra* resembles *Rhizopus* in having: (i) stored starch, (ii) cellulose cell wall, (iii) single celled gametangia, (iv) single nucleus in each cell. (C. P. M. T. 1980)

8. Algae and other submerged green plants float in water during day time and sink at night because: (i) they come up to enjoy some time, (ii) they lose weight at night, (iii) they become buoyant due to accumulation of O_2 as a result of photosynthesis, (iv) they become light due to food material accumulation. (C. P. M. T. 1980)

9. On germination each zygospore of *Spirogyra* gives rise to: (i) four plants, (ii) three plants, (iii) two plants, (iv) one plant. (C. P. M. T. 1981)

10. Name the organism that lacks archegonium: (i) *Pteris*, (ii) *Funaria*, (iii) *Cycas*, (iv) *Spirogyra*. (C. P. M. T. 1982)

11. *Spirogyra:* (i) the filaments showing lateral conjugation are homothallic, (ii) the filaments showing lateral conjugation are heterothallic, (iii) the filaments showing scalariform conjugation are homothallic, (iv) asexual reproduction occurs by zoospores. (C. P. M. T. 1981)

12. Ability to fix atmospheric nitrogen is found in: (i) leaves of some crop plants, (ii) some marine red algae, (iii) some blue-green algae, (iv) *Chlorella*. (C. P. M. T. 1984)

13. Agar-agar is derived from: (i) fungi, (ii) algae, (iii) *Dryopteris*, (iv) gymnosperms. (C. P. M. T. 1984)

14. In *Spirogyra* pyrenoid is found in: (i) nucleus, (ii) cell wall, (iii) chloroplast, (iv) cytoplasm.

15. Which one of the following is rich in protein: (i) *Ulothrix* (ii) *Spirogyra*, (iii) *Oedogonium*, (iv) *Chlorella*. (C.P.M.T. 1984)

16. *Ulothrix* is considered more advanced than *Spirogyra* because in *Ulothrix:* (i) filament is differentiated into holdfast and apical cell, (ii) chloroplast is parietal and girdle-shaped, (iii) zoospores are formed, (iv) gametes are motile. (C. P. M. T. 1985)

17. The pyrenoids are: (i) protein bodies, (ii) starch bodies, (iii) protein bodies with an envelope of starch, (iv) starch bodies with an envelope of protein.

18. Iodine is obtained from: (i) Bryophytes, (ii) Bacteria, (iii) fungi, (iv) sea weeds. (C. P. M. T. 1987)

19. Parasitic alga is: (i) *Cephaleuros*, (ii) *Ulothrix*, (iii) *Oedogonium*, (iv) *Sargassum*. (C. P. M. T. 1987)

20. The organ by which *Ulothrix* is attached to its substratum is called a: (i) rhizoid, (ii) holdfast, (iii) trichome, (iv) root. (C.P.M.T., 1989)

Answers

1 (iv), 2 (iv), 3 (iii), 4 (i) 5 (iii), 6 (i), 7 (iii), 8 (iii) 9 (iv), 10 (iv), 11 (i), 12 (iii), 13 (ii), 14 (iii), 15 (iv), 16 (i), 17 (iii), 18 (iv), 19 (i), 20 (ii).

General References

(Books)

Alexopoulos, C. J. and H. C. Bold. *Algae and Fungi*. The Macmillan Company, Collier-Macmillan Limited, London, 1967.

Bold, H. C. *Morphology of Plants*. Harper and Row, N.Y., 1970.

Chapman, V. J. *Seaweeds and their uses*. Methuen and Company Limited, London, 1950.

Chapman, V. J. *The Algae*. Macmillan and Company Limited, 1962, New York, St. Martin's Press, 1962.

Dawson, E. Y. *How to Know Seaweeds*. Wm. C. Brown Company, Dubuque, Iowa, 1956.

Dawson, E. Y. *Marine Botany*. Holt, Rinehart and Winston, Inc., New York, 1966.

Desikachary, T. V. *Cyanophyta*. I. C. A. R. New Delhi, 1959.

Fritsch, F. E. *Structure and Reproduction of the Algae*, Vols. I and II. Cambridge University Press, New York, 1935 and 1945.

Jackson, D. F. *Algae and Man*, Plenum Press, New York, 1964.

Kumar, H. D. *A Text Book on Algae*.

Lewin, R. A. (editor) *Physiology and Biochemistry of Algae*. Academic Press, New York and London. 1962.

Misra, J. N. *Phaeophycede in India*. 1962.

Newton, L. *Seaweed Utilization*. Sampson Low, 1951.

Pal, B, P., Kundu. B. C., Sundaralingam, B. S. and Venkataraman, G. S. *Charophyta*.

Prescott, G. W. *How to Know the Fresh-Water Algae*. Wm. C. Brown Company, Dubuque, Iowa, 1954.

Ramanathan, K. R. *Ulotrichales*, I. C. A. R. New Delhi, 1964.

Randhawa, M. S. *Zygnemaceae*, I. C. A. R. New Delhi. 1959.

Round, F. C. *The Biology of the Algae*. St. Martin's Press, New York, 1965.

Smith, G. M. *Marine Algae of the Monterey Peninsula*. Stanford University Press, Stanford, California, 1944.

Smith, G. M. *Freshwater Algae of the United States*. McGraw-Hill Book Co., New York, 1950.

Smith, G. M. *Cryptogamic Botany*, Vol.1. McGraw-Hill Book Co., New York, 1955.

Smith, G. M. (editor). *Manual of Phycology*. Chronica Botanica Co., Waltham, Mass., 1951.

Taylor, W. R. *Marine Algae of the Northeastern Coast of North America*, University of Michigan Press, Ann Arbor, 1937.

Tiffany, L. H. *Algae, the Grass of Many Waters*, Charles C. Thomas, Springfield, Illinois, 1958.

Tilden, J. E. *The Algae and Their Life Relations*. University of Minnesota Press, Minneapolis, 1935.

Venkataraman, G. S., *Vaucheriaceae*, I. C. A. R., New Delhi, 1964.

Venkataraman, G. S., *The Cultivation of Algae*. I. C. A. R., New Delhi, 1969.

Abaxial-(L. *ab,* from; *axis,* axle,) That surface of any structure which is remote or turned away from the axis.

Acropetal-(Gk. *akros,* summit; L, *petre,* to seek.) Ascending; developing successively from an axis so that youngest arise at apex, especially conidia, *e.g., Aspergillus, Penicillium.*

Adaxial-(L. *ad,* to; *axis,* axle,) Turned towards the axis.

Akinete-(Gk, *a,* not; *kinein.* to move.) A resting cell in certain green algae, which will later reproduce.

Algin-(L. *alga,* sea-weed). A mucilaginous substance, alginic acid obtained from certain algae.

Algoid-(L, *alga,* sea-weed; Gk,. *eidos,* shape.) Resembling or of the nature of an alga.

Algology-(L. *alga,* sea-weed; *logos,* discourse.) The study of algae; phycology.

Alternation of generations-The occurrence of one life history of two or more different forms differently produced, usually in alternation of a sexual with an asexual form.

Alveola-(L. *alveolus,* small cavity.) A pit on the surface of an organ.

Amitosis-(Gk. *a,* without; *mitos,* thread.) Direct cell division and cleavage of nucleus without thread-like formation of nuclear material.

Amoeboid-(Gk. *amoibe,* change; *eidos,* shape.) Resembling an amoeba in shape.

Amphibian-(Gk. *amphi,* both; *bios,* life.) Adapted for life either on land or on water.

Amylum-Starch.

Anisogamete-(Gk. *anisos,* unequal; *gametes,* spouse.) One of two conjugating gametes different in form or size.

Anisogamous-(Gk. *anisos,* unequal; *gamos,* marriage.) Differentiated gametes or conjugating bodies.

Anisogamy-(Gk. *anisos,* unequal; *gametes,* spouse). Conjugation between shortly differentiated gametes, heterogamy.

Anterior-(L. *anterior,* former.) Nearer head end.

Antheridium-(Gk. *anthos,* flower; *idion,* dim.) An organ or receptacle in which male sexual cells are produced in many cryptogams; male gametangium; *e.g.,* Phycomycetes and Ascomycetes.

Apex-(L. *apex,* summit.) Tip or summit.

Apical-(L. *apex,* summit.) At top.

Aplanogamete-(GK. *a,* not; *planos,* wandering; *gametes,* spouse.) A non-motile conjugating germ-cell, *e.g., Spirogyra.*

Aplanosporangium-(Gk. *a,* not; *planos,* wandering; *sporos,* seed; *anggeion,* vessel.) A sporangium producing aplanospores.

Aplanospore-(Gk. *a,* not; *planos,* wandering; *sporos,* seed.) A non-motile spore; *e.g., Mucor.*

Aquatic-(L. *aqua,* water.) Living in water; an aquatic plant.

Archaean-(Gk. *archaios,* ancient.) Geological era before Palaeozoic.

Aseptate-(Gk. L. *a,* not; *septum,* partition.) Without any septum.

Asexual-(Gk. *a* without; L. *sexus,* sex.) Having no apparent sexual organs; parthenogenetic or vegetative.

Asexual spore-(Gk. *a,* without; L. *sexus, sex;* Gk. *sporos,* seed.) Asexually developed spore, *e.g.,* conidia of Fungi Imperfecti.

Auxiliary cells-Accessory cells, *e.g., Polysiphonia.*

Auxospore-(Gk. *auxein,* to increase; *sporos,* seed.) Zygote of diatoms, formed by union of two individuals at limit of decrease in size.

Axoneme-(Gk. *axon,* axle; *nema,* thread.) The axial filament of a flagellum. The basal ensheathed portion of a whiplash flagellum.

Azygospore-(Gk. *a,* without; *zygon.* yoke; *sporos,* seed). A spore developed directly from a gamete without conjugation; parthenospore.

Azygote-(Gk. *a,* without; *zygon,* yoke.) An organism resulting from haploid parthenogenesis.

Basipetal-(Gk. *basis,* base; *petere,* to seek.) Developing from apex to base, *e.g.,* conidia of *Aspergillus* and *Penicillium.*

Biflagellate-(L. *Bis,* twice; *flagellum,* whip.) Having two flagella.

Binary fission-Division of a cell into two by an apparently simple division of nucleus and cytoplasm.

Binomial-(L. *bis*, twice; *nomen*, name.) Consisting of two names.

Bioblast-(Gk. *bios*, life; *blastos*, bud.) A hypothetical unit.

Blepharoplast-(Gk. *blepharis*, eyelash; *plastos*, formed.) A basal granule in relation with a motor cell organ, as the flagellum, *e.g.*, many Volvocales.

Botany-(Gk. *botane*, pasture.) The branch of biology dealing with plants, physiology.

Budding-The production of buds.

Capitate-(L. *caput*, head.) Enlarged or swollen at tip.

Carotene-(L. *carota*, carrot.) A yellow pigment synthesized by plants. $C_{40} H_{56}$

Carotenoids-(L. *carota*, carrot; *eidos*, form.) Pigments occurring in plants, including carotenes, Xanthophylls and other fat soluble pigments.

Carpogonium-(Gk, *Karpos*, fruit; *gonos*, birth.) Lower portion of procarp, which contains female nucleus, in some thallophytes; female gametangium in red algae.

Carposporangium-(Gk. *Karpos*, fruit; *sporos*, seed; *anggeion* vessel.) The terminal cells of filaments developed from fertilized carpogonium in certain Thallophyta, (*e. g.*, .red algae).

Carpospore-(Gk. *Karpos*, fruit; *sporos*, seed.) A spore formed at end of filaments of cystocarp, and developed from carpogonium in Rhodophyceae.

Carposporophyte-(Gk, *karpos*, fruit; *sporos*, seed; *phyton*, plant.) The diploid generation of red algae, which consists of filaments forming carpospores at their apices.

Catenulate-Forming a chain-like series.

Cell-(L. *cella*, compartment.) A unit mass of protoplasm, usually containing a nucleus or nuclear material.

Cell sap-Fluid in vacuoles of plant cells.

Cellulose-A carbohydrate forming main part of plant cell walls. $(C_6H_{10}O_5)$ x.

Cell wall-Investing portion of cell.

Central body-Centrosome.

Centriole-The central particle of the centrosome.

Chaeta-(Gk. *chaite*, hair.) A seta or bristle as of Chaetophorales.

Chlorophyll-(Gk. *chloros*, grass green; *phyllon*, leaf.) The green colouring matter found in plants and in some animals; chl. a, $C_{55} H_{72} O_5 N_4$ Mg; chl. b, $C_{55} H_{70} O_6 N_4$ Mg.

Chloroplast-(Gk. *chloros*, grass green; *plastos*, moulded.) A minute granule or plastid containing chlorophylls a and b, found in plant cells exposed to light.

Chorda-(Gk. *chorde*, string.) Any chord-like structure, *e.g.*, *Chorda filum*.

Chromatophore-(Gk. *chroma*, colour; *pherein*, to bear.) A colour or pigment matter in cells.

Cilia-(L. *cilium*, eyelid.) Flagella.

Cingulum-(L. *cingulum*, girdle.) Part of diatom frustule uniting valves.

Clavate-(L. *clava*, club.) Club-shaped; thickened at one end, *e.g.*, sporangiophore of *Albugo*.

Coenobium-(Gk, *koinos*, common; *bios*, life.) A colony of unicells with no marked distinction between vegetative and reproductive units, *e.g.*, Volvocales.

Coenocytic-aseptate and multinucleate.

Conjugation-(L. *cum*, together: *jugare*, to yoke.) The temporary union or complete fusion of two gametes or unicellular organisms, *e.g.*, Conjugales.

Contractile vacuole-a small spherical vesicle found in cytoplasm of Volvocales and other algae.

Cryophytes-(Gk. *kryos*, frost; *phyton*, plant.) Algae, fungi and bacteria on snow and ice.

Cryptocarp-(Gk. *kryptos*, hidden; *karpos*, fruit.) A fruit without a parent reproductive organs.

Cryptonema-(Gk. *kryptos*, hidden; *nema*, thread.) A filamentous outgrowth of paraphysis in a cryptostoma.

Cryptostomata-(Gk. *kryptos*, hidden; *stoma*, mouth.) Non-sexual conceptacles in Fucaceae; singular cryptostoma.

Culture-The cultivation of micro-organisms or tissues in prepared media.

Cuneiform-(L. *cuneus*, wedge; *forma*, shape.) Wedgeshaped.

Cyanin-The blue pigment.

Cystocarp-(Gk. *kystis*, bladder; *karpos*, fruit.) A cyst arising from carpogonial branch and containing spores, in certain Rhodophyceae; cystocarp.

Cytoplasm-(Gk. *kytos*, hollow; *plasma*, mould.) Substance of cell body exclusive of nucleus.

Dendroid-(Gk. *dendron*, tree; *eidos*, form.) much branched.

Diatom-A unicellular form of alga with walls impregnated with silica.

Diatomin-A yellow pigment resembling fucoxanthin, in plastids of diatoms.

Dichotomous-(Gk. *aicha,* in two; *temnein,* to cut) characterized by dichotomy.

Dichotomy-Branching which results from division of growing point into two equal parts: repeated forking.

Dikaryotic-Having dikaryons, diplont.

Dimorphic-(Gk. *dis,* twice; *morphe,* shape.) Having two different forms.

Dioecious-(Gk. *dis,* twice; *orkos,* house.) Having sexes (male and female) separate.

Diploid-(Gk. *diploos,* double; *eidos,* form.) Having a double set of chromosomes; two haploid nuclei make a diploid (2 x) nucleus after fusion.

Dwarf male-small three or four-celled plant formed from androspore of *Oedogonium.*

Ectoparasite-(Gk. *ektos,* outside; *parasitos,* parasite.) A parasite that lives on the exterior of an organism.

Egg-cell-The ovum proper apart from any layer of cells derived from it or from other cells.

Egg-nucleus-The female nucleus.

Ellipsoid-(Gk. *elleipsis,* a falling short; *eidos,* shape.) Oval.

Elliptical-oval-shaped.

Embryo-(gk. *embryon,* embryo.) A young organism in early stages of development.

Endogenous-(Gk. *endon,* within; *genus,* producing.) Originating within the organism.

Endospore-an endogenous spore.

Endozoic-(Gk. *endon,* within; *zoon,* animal.) Living within an animal, *e.g.,* some algae.

Epiphyte-(Gk. *epi.* upon; *phyton,* plant), plant which lives on surface of other plants.

Epitheca-(Gk. *epi,* upon; *theke,* box.) Older half of frustule in diatoms.

Epizoic-(Gk. *epi,* upon; *zoon,* animal.) Living on the body of an animal, *e.g.,* some algae.

Evagination-(L. *e,* out; *vagina,* sheath.) To protrude or evert by eversion.

Evection-(L. *e.* out; *vehere,* to convey.) Displacement of parent cell at septum of a filament, causing dichotomous appearance, as in certain algae, *e.g., Cladophora* sp.

Eye spot-Certain pigment spots in many lower plants, *e.g.,* many Volvocales and other algae.

Facultative-(L. *facultus,* faculty.) Having the power of living under different conditions.

Falcate-(L. *falx,* sickle.) Sickle-shaped.

Family-(L. famila, household.) Term used in classification, signifying a group of related genera, families being grouped into orders.

Fertilization-(L. *fertilis,* fertile.) The union of male and female nuclei.

Filamentous-(L. *filum,* thread.) Thread-like.

Fission-(L. *fissus,* cleft.) Cleavage of cells.

Flagella-Plural of flagellum.

Flagellate-Furnished with flagella.

Flagellum-(L. *flagellum,* whip.) The lash-like process of many motile bodies in Thallophyta and others.

Flora-(L *flos,* flower.) The plants peculiar to a country, area, specified environment or period.

Frond-(L. *frons,* leafy branch.) A leaf-like thalloid shoot, as of lichen.

Fructification-(L. *fructus,* fruit; *facere,* to make.) Fruit body.

Frustule-(L. *frustulum,* small fragment.) The siliceous two-valved shell and potoplasm of a diatom.

Fruticose-(L. *fruticoseus,* bushy.) Thallus of certain lichens; bushy.

Fucoxanthin-(L. *fucus,* sea weed; Gk. *xanthos* yellow.) The main carotenoid pigment of brown algae; $C_{40}H_{56}O_6$.

Gametangium-(Gk. *gametes,* spouse; *anggeion,* vessel.) A structure producing sexual cells.

Gametes-(Gk. *gametes,* spouse.) Cells derived from gametocytes which conjugate and form zygotes.

Gametogenesis-Gamete formation.

Gametophyte-(Gk, *gametes,* spouse; *phyton,* plant.) The gamete-forming haplophase in alternation of plant generations.

Gelatinous-(L. *gelare,* to congeal.) Jelly-like inconsistency.

Genera-Plural of genus.

Geniculate-(L. *geniculum,* little knee.) Bent like a knee joint.

Genus-(L. *genus,* race.) A group of closely related species, in classification of plants and animals.

Germ pore-The exit pore of a germ tube in the spore integument.

Germ tube-Short filamentous tube put forth by a germinating spore.

Globose-(L. *globulus,* globe.) Spherical.

Globule-(L. *globulus,* small globe.) Any minute spherical structure.

Granule-(L. *granulum*, small grain), a small particle of matter.

Haematochrome-(Gk. *haima*, blood; *chroma*, colour.) A carotenoid red pigment of certain algae.

Halophyte-(Gk. *hals*, sea; *phyton*, plant.)- A shore plant.

Haloplankton-(Gk. *hals*, sea; *plangktos*, wandering.) The organisms drifitng in the sea.

Haploid-Having x number of chromosomes.

Haplont-An organism having haploid somatic nuclei.

Heterocysts-(Gk. *heteros*, other; *kystis*, bladder.) Clear cells occurring at intervals on filaments of certain algae, marking limits of hormogonia, *e.g.*, Myxophyceae.

Heterogamy-Anisogamy.

Heterothallic-(Gk. *heteros*, other; *thallos* young shoot.) Having thalli of different sexes; requiring branches of two distinct thalli to form a zygote (2x).

Heterothallism-Heterothallic condition.

Heterotrophic-(Gk. *heteros*, other; *trophe*, nourishment.) Getting nourishment from organic substances, *e.g.*, parasitic plants. Opposite autotrophic.

Holdfast-A disc-like extension of a thallus for attachment.

Holocarpic-(Gk. *holos*, whole; *karpos*, fruit.) Having the fruit body formed by the entire thallus, *e.g.*, certain algae, certain Phycomycetes.

Homothallic-(Gk. *Homos*, same; *thallos*, young shoot.) Having both sexes in the same thallus; forming zygote from two branhces of the same thallus.

Homothallium-Homothallic condition.

Hormocyst-(Gk. *hormos*, chain; *kystis*, bladder) A modified thick-walled hormogonium, in some blue-green algae.

Hormogone-Hormogonium.

Hormogonium-(Gk. *hormos*, chain; *gone*, generation.) That portion of an algal filament between two heterocysts, which breaking away, acts as a reproductive body.

Host-(L. *hospes*, host.) Any organism in which another organism spends part or the whole of its existence, and from which it derives nourishment.

Humus-(L. *humus*, earth.) A dark material formed by decomposition of vegetable or animal matter and constituting part of soils.

Hyaline-(Gk, *hyalos* glass.) Clear, transparent.

Hygroscopic-(Gk. *hygros*, wet; *skopein*, to regard.) Sensitive to, or retaining moisture.

Hypnospore-(Gk. *hypnos*, sleep; *sporos*, seed.) A resting spore.

Hypotheca-(Gk. *hypo*, under; *theke*, box.) Younger half of frustule in diatoms.

Hypovalve-(Gk. *hypo*, under; L. *valva*, fold.) Younger or inner valve in diatoms.

Infection-(L. *inficere*, to taint.) Invasion, or condition caused, by endoparasites.

Invagination-(L. *in*, into; *vagina*, sheath.) inversion, *e.g.*, *Volvox*.

Inversion-(L. *invertere*, to turn upside down.) A turning inward or inside out.

Isogamete-(Gk. *isos*, equal; *gametes*, spouse.) One of a pair of undifferentiated gametes.

Isogamous-(Gk. *isos*, equal; *gamos*, marriage.) Having the gametes alike.

Isogamy-(Gk. *isos*, equal; gamous marriage.) Union of similar gametes.

Isomorphic-(Gk. *isos*, equal; *morphe* shape.) Alternation of diploid and haploid phases in morphologically similar generation.

Karyogamy-(Gk. *karyon*, nucleus; *gamos*, marriage.) Union and interchange of nuclear material after cytoplasmic fusion.

Lamella-(L. *lamella*, small plate.) Any thin plate-like structure.

Leucoplastids-(Gk. *leukos*, white; *plastps*, formed.) Colourless plastids from which amylo, chloro, and chromoplastids arise.

Lithophyte-(Gk. *lithos*, stone; *phyton*, plant.) Plant growing on rocky ground.

Littoral-(L. *litus*, sea shore.) Growing or living at or near the sea-shore.

Lophotrichous-(Gk. *lophos*, tuft; *thrix*, hair) with a tuft of flagella at one pole.

Lutein-(L. *luteus*, orange-yellow.) Xanthophyll or a mixture of xanthophyll and carotene; $C_{40}H_{56}O_2$.

Macrandrous-(Gk. *makros*, large; *aner*, male.) Having large male plants, *e.g.*, *Oedogonium*.

Macrocyclic-(Gk. *makros*, large; *kyhlos*, circle.) Having a long cycle, *e.g.*, *Puccinia graminis*.

Macrogamete-(Gk. *makros*, large; *gametes*, spouse.) The large of two conjugants.

Macroscopic-Visible by the naked eye.

Macrosporangium-A sporangium developing macrospores.

Macrozoospore-Large motile spore.

Medium-(L. *medium*, middle.) Substances in which cultures are propagated.

Meiosis-(Gk. *meion*, smaller.) Process of reduction division of germ-cell chromosomes from diploid to haploid number at maturation.

Meiospores-Haploid spores produced after meiotic division of a diploid cell or zygote.

Meristoderm-(Gk. *meristos*, divided; *derma*, skin.) Outer layer of thallus when thickened by meristematic tissue.

Microbiology-Biology of microscopic organisms.

Microconidium-(Gk. *mikros*, small; *konis*, dust) A comparatively small condition.

Microcyclic-Short cycle with haplophase stage only.

Microgamete-The smaller of two conjugant gametes, regarded as male.

Micron-Micromillimetre, one-thousandth part of a millimetre; symbol.

Mitosis-Indirect nuclear division.

Mitospores-Spores formed after mitotic division of a haploid or diploid parent cell.

Monaxial-(Gk. *monos*, single; *axon*, axis.) Having one line of axis.

Monoclinous-(Gk. *monos*, single; *kline*, couch.) Hermaphrodite; having gametangium and oogonium originating from the same hypha.

Monoecious-Hermaphrodite.

Monotrichous-Having only one flagellum at one pole.

Multiaxial-(L. *multus*, many; *axis*, axis.) Having several axes.

Mycology-(Gk. *mykes*, fungus; *logos*, discourse.) That part of botany which deals with fungi.

Nannandrium-(Gk. *nanos*, dwarf; *aner*, male.) Dwarf male.

Necrosis-(Gk. *nekrosis*, deadness). The death of cells or of tissues.

Nucleoprotein-A compound of protein and nucleic acid.

Nucule-(L. *nucula*, small nut.) Oogonium in Characeae.

Obligate-(L. *obligatus;* bound) parasites which cannot exist independently of a host.

Oidia-Plural of oidium.

Oogamous-(Gk. *oon*, egg; *gamos*, marriage.) Having sexually differentiated gametes.

Oogamy-(Gk. *oon*, egg; *gamos*, marriage.) The union of a non-motile female gamete or egg cell and a male gamete.

Oogonium-The female reproductive organ in certain thallophytes.

Oosphere-(Gk, *oon*, egg; *sphaira*, globe). An egg before fertilization.

Oospore-The zygote or fertilized egg cell.

Order-In classification, group of organisms closely allied, ranking between family and class.

Ostiole-(L. *ostiolum*, little door.) A small opening as of conceptacle.

Ovum-(L, *ovum*, egg.) Mature egg cell.

Palmella-(Gk. *palmos*, quivering.) A sedentary stage of certain algae, the cells dividing within a jelly-like mass and producing motile gametes.

Pandemic-(Gk. *pandemos*, common.) Very widely distributed plants.

Papilla-(L. *papilla*, nipple.) A small projection as on the sporangium of *Phytophthora*.

Papillate-With papilla.

Paradesmose-(Gk. *para*, besides; *desmos*, bond.) A connection between blepharoplasts in neuromotor apparatus.

Paraphysis-(Gk. *para*, besides; *physis*, growth.) A slender filamentous epidermal outgrowth occurring among sporogenous organs; plural; paraphyses.

Parasite-(Gk. *para*, besides; *sitos*, food). An organism living with or within another to its own advantage in food.

Parasitic-An organism living at expense of another, and in or on it.

Parasitism-The parasite living in or on its host.

Parasitology-The science treating of plant and animal parasites.

Pathogen-(Gk. *pathos*. suffering; *genes*, producing.) Any disease producing micro organism.

Pelagic-(Gk. *pelagos*, sea.) Ocean inhabiting.

Perfect-(L. *perfectus*, finished.) Complete; fungi producing sexual spores.

Periplasm-(Gk. *peri*, around; *plasma*, mould.) The region of an oogonium outside the oospore in fungi.

Phialopore-(Gk. *phiale,* bowl; *poros,* channel.) The opening in the hollow daughter colony of *Volvox.*

Phycocyanin-(Gk. *phykos,* sea-weed; *kyanos,* dark blue.) A colouring matter of red algae.

Phycoerythrin-(Gk. *phykos,* sea-weed; *erythros,* red.) The colouring matter of algae.

Phycology-(Gk. *phykos,* sea-weed; *logos,* discourse.) That port of botany dealing with algae.

Phycoxanthin-(Gk. *phykos,* sea-weed; *xanthos,* yellow.) Buff colouring matter of diatoms and brown algae.

Phytology-Botany.

Pigment-(L. *pingere,* to point.) Colouring matter in plants.

Plasmogamy-(Gk. *plasma,* mould; *gamos,* marriage.) Fusion of cytoplasmic substance without nuclear fusion.

Polymorphism-(Gk. *polys,* many; *morphy,* forms.) Occurrence of different forms of spores, in same individual at different periods of life, *e.g., Puccinia graminis.*

Polysiphonic-A filament consisting of several siphons bound together, *e.g., Polysiphonia.*

Procarp-(Gk. *pro,* before; *karpos,* fruit.) The female organ of red algae, a one or more celled structure, consisting of the carpogonium; trichogyne and auxiliary cells.

Protoplasm-(Gk. *protos,* first; *plasma,* form.) Living cell substance.

Pycnia-Plural of pycnium.

Pycnial-Pycnidial.

Pycnidiospore-The spore produced by pycnidium.

Pycnium-(Gk. *pyknos,* dense.) A small flask-shaped spermogonium containing slender filaments which form pycniospores or spermatia by abstriction in life history of wheat rust: receptacle for stylospores in fungi and lichens.

Quadrant-(L. *quadrans,* fourth part.) All the cells derived by divisions from one of the first four cleavage cells.

Receptacle-(L. *recipere,* to receive). Modified end of thallus branch containing conceptacles in algae.

Receptive spot-Small mucilaginous area adjacent to aperture in an ovum at which sperm enters.

Rhizoplast-Rhizoplast

Rhizomorph-(Gk. *rhiza,* root; *morphe,* form.) A root-like strand of hyhpae in certain fungi.

Rhizoplast-Fibrillae connecting blepharoplast and centrosome within or outside the nucleus.

Root nodules-Small swelling on roots of leguminous plants and containing nitrogen fixing bacteria.

Rust-(A. S. *rust,* redness.) A disease of grasses and other plants caused by Uredinales.

Saprophyte-(Gk. *sapros,* rotten; *phyton,* plant.) A plant which lives on dead and decaying organic matter.

Saprophytic-Growing in or on decayed organic matter, as many bacteria and fungi.

Sclerotium-(Gk. *skleros,* hard). Resting, dormant, or winter stage of some fungi when they become a mass of hardened mycelium.

Septate-(L. *septum,* partition.) Divided by partitions.

Septum-A partition separating cells.

Somatic-(Gk. *soma,* body,) purely bodily part of plant.

Spermatia-Pycniospores; a non-motile sperm of red algae: oidia in mushoorms

Spermatozoid-(Gk. *sperma,* seed; *zoon,* animal). An antherozoid; free-swimming male gamete.

Spermogonium-A capsule containing spermatia in certain fungi and lichens; pycnium.

Sporangia-Plural of sporangium.

Sporangiophore-(Gk. *sporos,* seed; *anggeion,* vessel; *pherein,* to bear). A stalklike structure bearing sporangia.

Sporangium-A spore-case, in which spores are produced.

Spore-(Gk. *sporos,* seed.) A highly specialized reproductive cell of plants.

Sporidium-Ascospore, basidiospore.

Sporodochium-(Gk. *sporos,* seed; *docheion,* holder.) A hemispherical aggregate of conidiophores.

Sporophore-A spore bearing structure, in fungi.

Sporophyte-(Gk. *sporos,* seed; *phyton,* plant.) The diploid spore producing phase in alternation of plant generations.

Sterigma-(Gk. *sterigma,* support.) A slender filament arising from basidium or conidiophore and giving rise to spores by abstriction. Plural sterigmata.

Stigma-(Gk. *stigma,* mark) eye spot of some algae.

Stolon-(L. *stolo,* shoot.) A creeping hypha which can form aerial mycelium and rhizoids, *e.g., Caulerpa* spp.

Stroma-(Gk. *stroma*, bedding.) Tissue of hyphae or of fungus cells with host tissue, in or upon which spore bearing structures may be produced.

Subhymenium-(L. *sub*, under; Gk. *hymen*, membrane.) Layer of small cells between trama and hymenium in gill of *Agaricus*.

Substrate-(L. *sub*, under; *stratum*, layer.) Inert substance containing or receiving a nutrient solution.

Suspensor-(L. *suspendere*, to hang up.) A modified portion of a hypha from which a gametangium or a zygospore is suspended, *e.g.*, *Mucor, Rhizopus*.

Swarm spore-Zoospore.

Symbiont-(Gk. *symbionai*, to live with.) One of the partners in symbiosis.

Symbiosis-A condition in which two plants live in mutually beneficial partnership.

Symbiotic-Living in beneficial partnership.

Synzoospore-(Gk. *syn*, with; *zoon*, animal; *sporos*, seed.) A group of zoospores which do not separate (*e.g.*, *Vaucheria*).

Systematic-Throughout the system.

Teleutospore-(Gk. *teleute*, completion; *sporos*, seed.) In Uredinales a spore formed in the end of season; teliospore.

Telia-plural of telium.

Telial-pertaining telia.

Teliosorus-teleutosorus.

Teliospore-teleutospore.

Terrestrial-(L. *terra*, earth.) Organisms living on land.

Tetrad-(Gk. *tetras*. four.) A group of four spores formed by first and second meiotic divisions of spore mother cell.

Tetrasporangium-Sporangium producing tetraspores, as in red algae.

Tetraspore-One of a group of four non-motile spores produced by sporangium of red algae.

Thallus-(Gk. *thallos*, young shoot.) Plant body of Thallophyta. No differentiation in stem, leaves and other vegetative parts.

Thermophyte-(Gk. *therme*, heat; *phyton*, plant.) A heat-tolerant plant, *e.g.*, many Myxophyceae.

Torula condition-yeast-like isolated cells resulting from growth of black mould oidia in sugar solution.

Trabeculae-(L. *trabecula*, little beam.) Primordial lamellae of *Agaricus*.

Trichogyne-(Gk. *thrix*, hair; *gyne*, woman.) An elongated hair-like receptive cell at end of carpogonium of thallophyta.

Trichothallic growth-Growth of filament by division of intercalary meristematic cells.

Ultimate cell-tip cell

Uniaxial-(L. *unus*, one; *axis*, axis) with one axis; monoaxial.

Uredia-plural of uredium.

Uredial-(L. *uredo*, blight.) Uredial stage of rust fungi.

Urediospore-uredospore,

Uredium-A sorus bearing uredospores in rust fungi; uredinium.

Uredosorus-(L. *uredo*, blight; Gk, *soros*, heap.) A group of developing uredospores.

Uredospores-Reddish spores borne on sporophore of rust fungi.

Vacuole-(L. *vacuus*, empty.) One of spaces in cell protoplasm containing cell sap.

Vegetative-(L. *vegetare*, to enliven.) Stage of growth in plants.

Vesicle-(L. *vesicula*, bladder.) A hyphal swelling.

Wilt-a disease caused by *Fusarium* sp.

Xanthophylls-(Gk. *xanthos*, yellow; *pyllon*, leaf) yellow or brown carotenoid pigments found in plastids. $C_{40}H_{56}O_2$.

Zoogloea-(GK. *zoon*, animal; *gloia*, glue.) A mass of bacteria embedded in a mucilaginous matrix, frequently forming an irridescent film; zooglea.

Zoospore-swarm spore of algae and fungi.

Zygospore-(Gk. *zygon*, yoke; *sporos*, seed.) A cell, or resting spore formed by conjugation of similar reproductive cells, as in Conjugales and Zygomycetes.

Zygote-(Gk. *zygotos*, yoked.) Cell formed by union of two gametes or reproductive cells; fertilized ovum.

INDEX

THE FUNGI

1

Introduction

The fungi constitute a large and diverse group of plant kingdom. They resemble algae in many respects and therefore, included in the large group Thallophyta. There are about 50,000 to 100,000 known species of fungi in the world. According to one estimate, there are 4,300 genera and 50,000 species of fungi (Ainsworth, 1961), but this number is constantly increasing because of the never ending search for these organisms, throughout the world. In the five kingdom system of classification, the fungi are treated as a separate kingdom.

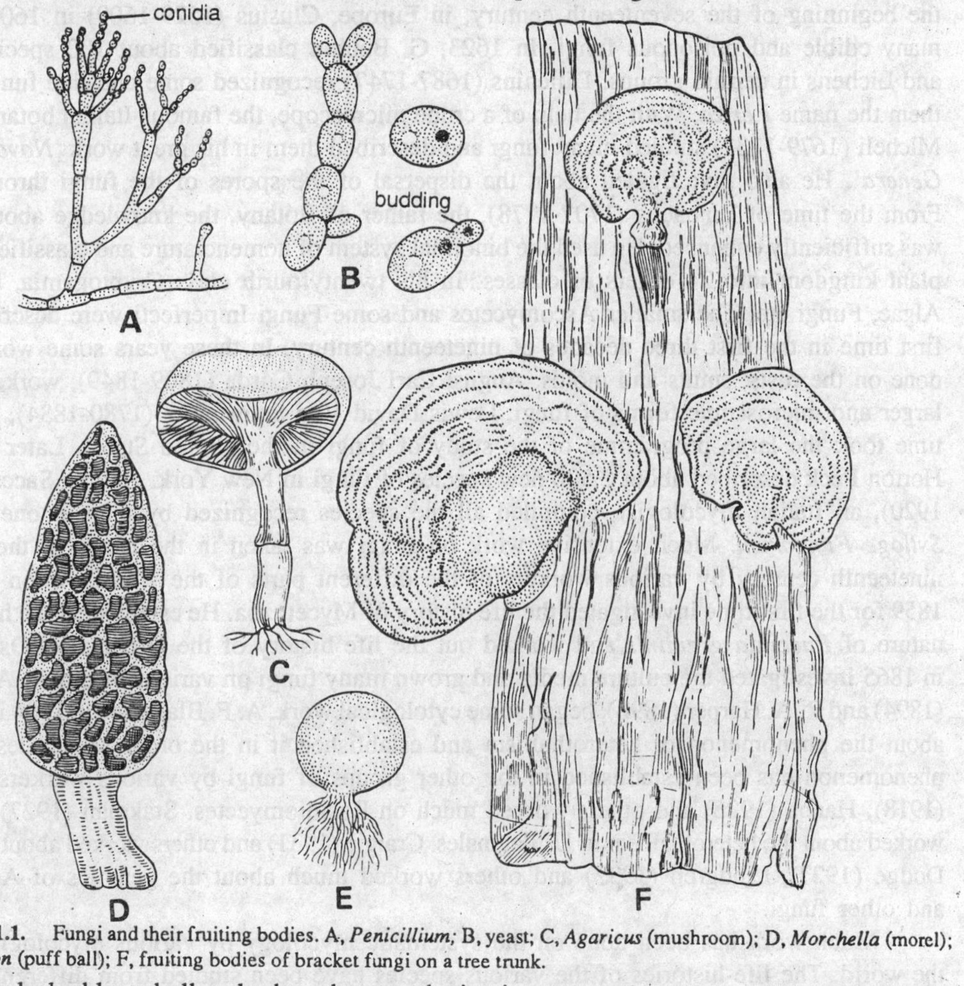

Fig. 1.1. Fungi and their fruiting bodies. A, *Penicillium;* B, yeast; C, *Agaricus* (mushroom); D, *Morchella* (morel); E, *Lycoperdon* (puff ball); F, fruiting bodies of bracket fungi on a tree trunk.

They lack chlorophyll and other photosynthetic pigments and cannot synthesize their food from carbondioxide and water in the presence of sunlight and their mode of nutrition is either saprophytic, parasitic or symbiotic. When fungi live as saprobes they bring about the decay of organic materials, and when they act as parasites they attack living protoplasm and cause diseases of plants, animals and human beings.

The body of fungi is very simple, and in majority of cases consists of a network of branched filaments called the **hyphae.** The tangled mass of hyphae is the **mycelium.** In few cases the mycelium is completely lacking, *e.g., Synchytrium* and in other cases the plant body may be unicellular, *e.g., Saccharomyces.*

The cell wall of the mycelium does not consist of true cellulose. It either consists of chitin or fungal cellulose along with other substances.

The chief food reserves are glycogen and oils. As they are devoid of chlorophyll the starch is not found.

The reproduction takes place by means of vegetative, asexual and sexual methods.

Historical. In ancient times the Roman people knew about some edible and poisonous mushrooms. In those times the Greek word 'mykes' was used for some fungi. Still today the word Mycology (Gr. *mykes* = fungus + *logos* = discourse) stands for the science of fungi. In the beginning of the seventeenth century, in Europe, Clusius (1529-1609) in 1601 described many edible and poisonous fungi. In 1623, G. Bauhin classified about 100 species of fungi and Lichens in certain groups. Dillenius (1687-1747) recognized some cup-like fungi and gave them the name *Peziza.* With the help of a crude microscope, the famous Italian botanist Antonio Micheli (1679-1737) studied many fungi and described them in his great work '*Novo Plantarum Genera*'. He also investigated about the dispersal of the spores of the fungi through the air. From the time of Linnaeus (1707-1778), the father of Botany, the knowledge about the fungi was sufficiently enhanced. He used the binomial system of nomenclature and classified the whole plant kingdom into 24 orders or classes. In his twentyfourth class Cryptogamia, he included Algae, Fungi etc. The smaller Ascomycetes and some Fungi Imperfecti were described for the first time in the first three decades of nineteenth century. In these years some work was also done on the rusts, smuts and molds. August Carl Joseph Corda (1809-1849), worked much on larger and microscopic forms of fungi. Lewis David Von Schweinitz (1780-1834), for the first time took the large programme of the study of fungi in the United States. Later on Charles Horton Peck described about 2,500 new species of fungi in New York. Andrea Saccardo (1845-1920), an Italian mycologist, compiled all the species recognized by then in one work, *i.e., Sylloge Fungorum.* Much extensive work on fungi was taken in the hands in the middle of nineteenth century by various workers of the different parts of the world. Anton de Bary in 1859 for the first time investigated the life history of Mycetozoa. He established the heteroecious nature of *Puccinia graminis* and worked out the life history of the Uredinales. Oscar Brefeld in 1865 investigated the culture media and grown many fungi on various media. P. A. Dangeard (1894) and R. A. Harper (1896), began some cytological work. A. F. Blakeslee in 1904 investigated about the phenomenon of heterothallism and established it in the order Mucorales. Now this phenomenon has been established in the other groups of fungi by various workers. Bensaude (1918), Hanna (1925) and others worked much on Basidiomycetes. Stakman (1927) and others worked about the heterothallism in Ustilaginales. Craigie (1931) and others worked about Uredinales. Dodge (1927), Lindgren (1932) and others worked much about the genetics of Ascomycetes and other fungi.

Much work has been done on the systematic mycology by various mycologists all over the world. The life-histories of the various species have been studied from different classes of the fungi. The extensive programmes of the importance of fungi to human beings have been taken in the hands and several researches have been done for the welfare of the humanity by various fungi.

Indian work. In India serious studies in fungi (mycology) including plant diseases by some of them (plant pathology), started with the establishment of Imperial Agricultural Institute at Pusa, Bihar (now known as Indian Agricultural Research Institute, New Delhi) in the first decade of this century. E. J. Butler, the first Imperial mycologist of Pusa Institute, is regarded as the father of Indian mycology and Plant Pathology. He wrote a classic book entitled '*Fungi and Disease in Plants*'. Some of his contemporary plant pathologists were J. F. Dastur, G. S. Kulkarni and S. L. Ajrekar. By 1930, K. C. Mehta had made name for his studies on the wheat rust problem in India. Other noted Indian mycologists and plant pathologists are – B. B. Mundkur, R. S. Vasudeva, R. N. Tandon, R. Prasada, K. S. Bhargava, T. S. Sadasivan, S. N. Dasgupta, S. Sinha, M. J. Thirumulachar, C. V. Subramanian, D. Suryanarayana, B. S. Mehrotra and L. M. Joshi. At present, the Indian Agricultural Research Institute is an active centre for mycological and plant pathological research.

The fields of the study of fungi. There are several idealistic points of view of the study of fungi such as 1. Plant Pathology; 2. Medical Mycology; 3. Industrial Mycology; 4. Antibiotics Production, *e.g.*, penicillin, streptomycin etc.; 5. Microbiology (study of fungi in relation to chemistry or biochemistry and production of vitamins etc.)

Origin of fungi. There are two important views about the origin of the fungi, *i.e.*, (1) Polyphyletic view and (2) Monophyletic view.

According to first view (polyphyletic) the fungi have originated from various groups of algae by attaining saprophytic or parasitic mode of life. There are several colourless and parasitic algae (*e.g.*, Volvocales and Chlorococcales) which give the idea of the fungi.

According to this view, it is assumed that in the very beginning the whole surface of the earth was covered with water and for the first time the algae appeared which thereafter transmigrated from water to land. During this transmigration many of them died and lost their green colour. A large quantity of dead organic material was available and many of algae converted into saprophytic fungi of today. It is also assumed that the parasitic fungi were the resultants of further transmigration of saprophytic fungi upon other living plants.

According to second view (monophyletic view), the fungi arose independently and not from algae. There are few points in support of this view.

That the sex organs are quite different in two groups.

That the two groups produce diverse forms.

That the fungi were present in the red sandstone of Devonian period which showed the earliest records of the plants.

That the algal and fungal structures are quite different, even on the loss of the chlorophyll of the algae.

That the fungi lack carbohydrates.

That the longitudinal division is absent even in the cell of the highest evolved fungi.

That the chemical composition of the cell wall of two groups is quite different.

However, in the present state of our knowledge, there is no valid reason to assume that all fungi originated from a common ancestor. Many mycologists of present day believe, that all fungi are not related. Some may have arisen from protozoan ancestor and others from a plant-like ancestor, perhaps some primitive alga, which later on assumed a saprobic or parasitic way of life and eventually lost its chlorophyll.

Differences between algae and fungi. The algae and fungi possess the following characteristic features of differentiation:

1. The algae are green thallophytes containing chlorophyll and other pigments; whereas the fungi are devoid of chlorophyll and other such pigments.
2. The algae are autotrophic whereas the fungi are heterotrophic in nutrition; they may

be saprophytic, parasitic or symbiotic.

3. The body of algae may be truly parenchymatous whereas of fungi it is pseudoparenchymatous. The pseudoparenchyma consists of compactly interwoven hyphae.

4. The algal cell wall is composed of true cellulose along with other substances. The fungal walls lack cellulose. They consist of fungal cellulose and chitin.

5. The algae grow in water or on wet substrata whereas fungi are mostly parasites or saprophytes.

6. In algae there is regular increase in the complexity of reproduction from simpler forms to higher forms whereas in fungi there is definite and regular reduction in sexuality from lower to higher fungi.

Occurrence and distribution. The fungi are most diversified in their habitat. They are found in almost all possible types of habitats. They are devoid of chlorophyll and may be saprophytes, parasites or symbionts. Many species of Phycomycetes, are found in the water and are called the **aquatic fungi.** Some fungi are commonly found upon algae and other aquatic plants in epiphytic state. Some species are found on the dead organic materials present in the water. Some species are sub-terranean and found under the surface of the earth.

Many species of the fungi are recognizable only with the naked eye and even from the distance such as mushrooms, morels, puff balls, bracket fungi, cup fungi etc. Whereas on the other hand they are microscopic and may be recognized with great care by the experts of the subject with the help of compound microscope.

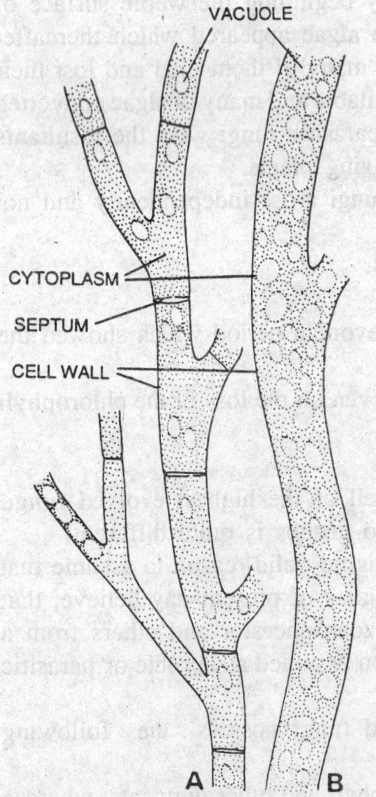

Fig. 1.2. The fungi. vegetative hyphae. A, portion of a septate hypha; B, portion of non-septate hypha.

The parasitic fungi are commonly found upon the hosts, *i.e.*, vascular plants where they cause various diseases and do great harm to the host plants.

Some fungi are found in the alimentary canals of mammals and human beings where they cause the stomach disorders. Some forms cause the skin diseases. In this way we see that fungi are much diversified and accustomed to unusual habitats.

Vegetative structure. Ainsworth (1971) has divided the fungal kingdom into two large divisions – 1. Myxomycota and 2. Eumycota. The Myxomycota includes the class Myxomycetes. In Myxomycetes (the slime molds) the thallus is a naked amoeboid mass of protoplasm. This may be a **plasmodium** (*i.e.*, single large multinucleate protoplast) or a **pseudoplasmodium** (*i.e.*, an aggregation of many small uninucleate protoplasts that retain their individuality).

In the division Eumycota (*i.e.*, true fungi), the thallus has a definite cell wall. In certain fungi the thallus is unicellular (*e.g.*, *Saccharomyces, Blastocladiella*) and the entire surface of the cell is responsible for the absorption of food. The plant body which consists of a single cell, and doesn't bear any additional structures for sucking. The food from the substrate or for reproduction, is called **holocarpic** when a part of the thallus is meant for reproduction, it is **eucarpic.** This eucarpic multicellular vegetative body of the fungus consists of a network of much branched thin filaments called the **hyphae** and the tangled mass of the hyphae is called **mycelium.** The hyphae grow by apical elongation. The hyphae may be segmented or non-segmented. The segmented hyphae possess cross walls in them at regular intervals called the **septa.** The mycelium having septa is called the **septate.** Usually each septum bears a small pore in its centre for the communication of the cytoplasm from one cell to another. The mycelium without septa is called the **aseptate.** The aseptate mycelium possesses many nuclei embedded in the cytoplasm and called the **coenocytic** mycelium. The cells of the septate mycelium may be uninucleate, binucleate, or multinucleate.

The septa in the higher fungi (*i.e.*, Ascomycotina, Basidiomycotina and Deuteromycotina) possess one or more small perforations in the centre to maintain protoplasmic continuity between adjacent cells. This pore is a simple pore in most of higher fungi (all Ascomycotina) but in some (many Basidiomycotina excluding rusts) it is a complex structure called **dolipore.** The electron microscope reveals a curved double membrane on each side of the septum. Because this membrane structure looks like a parenthesis in sectional view, it is known as **parenthosome.** (Fig. 1.3).

Some fungi lack mycelium altogether, *e.g., Synchytrium.*

The cell wall of fungi consists of a chemically different substance from normal cellulose called the **fungal cellulose.** The constituents of the fungal cellulosc appear to be carbohydrates, cellulose, pectose, callose and related compounds mixed with other substances. In higher fungi the walls consist of chitin. The deposits of calcium carbonate and some other salts have also been reported from the cell wall of some fungi. The composition of the cell wall is not a constant feature and changes according to the age of mycelium, temperature, composition and the pH of the media.

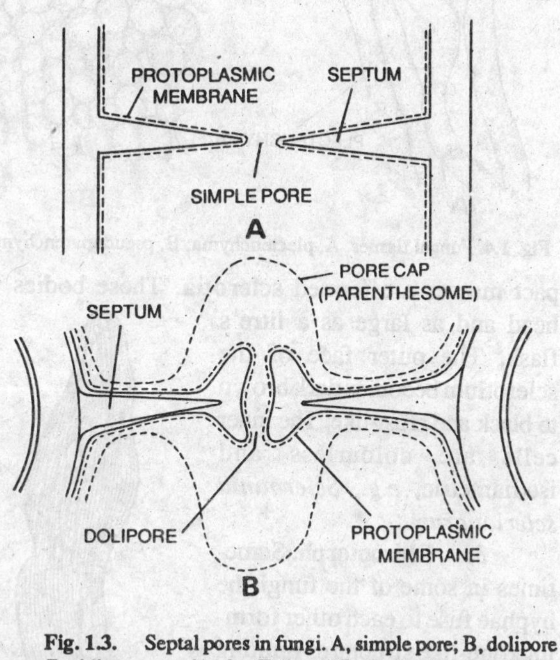

Fig. 1.3. **Septal pores in fungi. A, simple pore; B, dolipore in many Basidiomycetes (A after Talbot 1971; B after Burnett, 1968).**

The cells of a mycelium, as a whole are filled up with colourless cytoplasm. In coenocytic mycelium numerous nuclei are embedded. Many irregular vacuoles also found. The glycogen granules and oil droplets are present as food reserves in the cytoplasm. Most of the parasitic fungi on living plants secrete certain enzymes which dissolve the host cell walls.

Most of the fungi possess hyaline mycelium but some of them possess various coloured pigments. These may be yellow, green, smoky green, orange, brown and red. Certain fungi are named after the colour of their spores, *e.g.*, black molds, green molds and blue green molds. These pigments are nothing to do with the metabolic activity of the fungi.

The mycelium of the lower fungi is aseptate and coenocytic whereas of higher fungi it is always septate and the cells may be uni, bi or multinucleate. In lower fungi the septation takes place only at the time of the formation of sex organs.

There are certain modifications of the mycelium, which are as follows :

1. Plectenchyma. Sometimes the normal hyphae are so compactly interwoven that the whole mass becomes felt like and called the **plectenchyma.** If the hyphae of the mass retain their individuality and do not fuse, the mass is called the **prosenchyma** or **proso-plectenchyma.** And, if the hyphae are completely fused to each other and lost their individuality and the whole mass looks like the parenchyma of the higher plants, it is then called the **pseudoparenchyma** or **para-plectenchyma.**

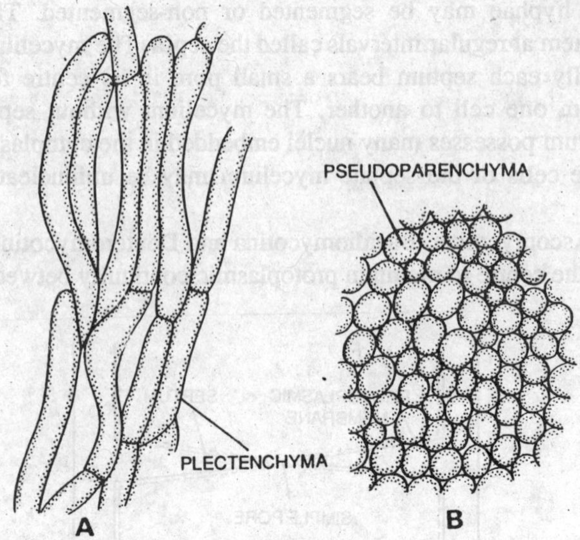

Fig. 1.4. Fungal tissues. A, plectenchyma; B, pseudoparenchyma.

2. Sclerotia. This is another important modified form of the mycelium may also be called a specialized form of plectenchyma. Here the interwoven hyphae of the mycelium become so much compact that the mass becomes rounded and cushion-like. These cushion-like compact masses are termed **sclerotia.** These bodies vary in size. They may be as small as a pin head and as large as a litre's flask. The outer face of the sclerotium becomes dark brown to black and crust-like. The inner cells are colourless and isodiametric, *e.g., Sclerotinia scleriotiorum.*

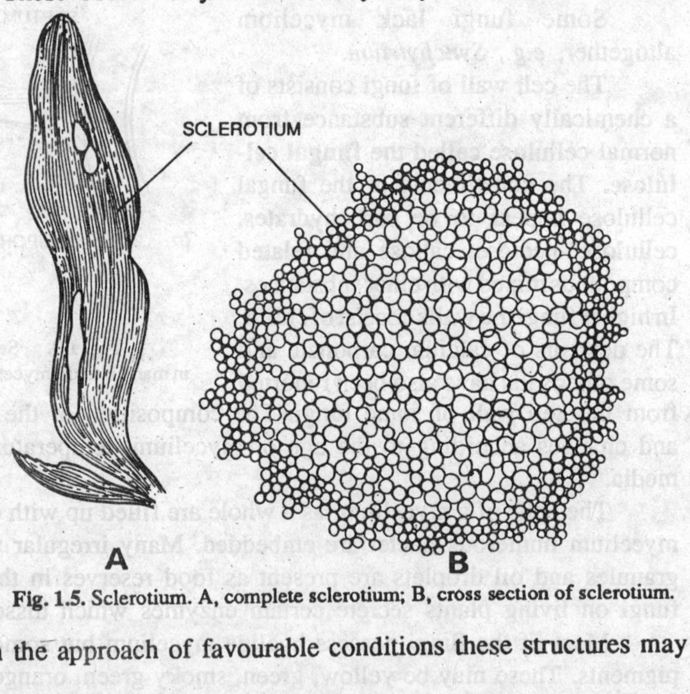

Fig. 1.5. Sclerotium. A, complete sclerotium; B, cross section of sclerotium.

3. Rhizomorph. Sometimes in some of the fungi the hyphae fuse to each other forming rope-like structures running parallel to each other. These thick, gelatinous, dark brown and rope-like coiled structures are called the **rhizomorphs.** They resemble the finer roots of the trees. These structures are perennating and face the adverse conditions. They may survive even for several years. On the approach of favourable conditions these structures may give rise to new mycelia.

4. Sporophores. The sporophores bear spores on them. These are the modified forms of the mycelium. Usually the sporophores are erect and aerial. They arise from the prostrate hyphae. The sporophores may be branched (*e.g., Peronospora*) or unbranched (*e.g., Albugo*). They bear sporangia (*e.g., Albugo*) or conidia (*e.g., Peronospora*) on them. The sporophore bearing sporangia is called the **sporangiophore** and bearing conidia the **conidiophore.** Sometimes the sporophores are found in groups and form **pycnia, sporodochia, hymenia** and **acervuli** in various fungi. (Fig. 1.8)

5. Stroma. They are flat, cushion-like pesudoparenchymatous structures from which usually the sporophores arise.

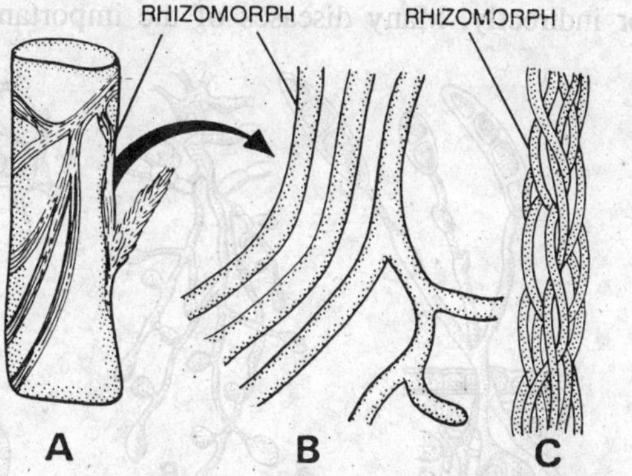

Fig. 1.6. Rhizomorph. A, as seen on root; B, parallel hyphae of rhizomorph; C, rope like structure.

Nutrition. The fungi are chlorophyll-less plants and cannot synthesize their own food unlike green plants from carbondioxide and water in the presence of sunlight. They are so simple in structure that they cannot obtain inorganic food directly from the soil, and therefore they are always dependent for their food on some dead organic material or living beings. The fungi which obtain their food from dead organic materials are called the **saprophytes,** whereas the fungi obtaining their prepared food from living plants or animals are called the **parasites.** The living beings on which the fungi parasitize are called the **hosts.** Some grow in the association of other plants and are mutually beneficial. This association is called the **symbiosis** and the participants are **symbionts.** From the point of view of their nutrition the fungi may be classified as saprophytes, parasites, symbionts and predacious fungi. They are **heterotrophic** and never autotrophic.

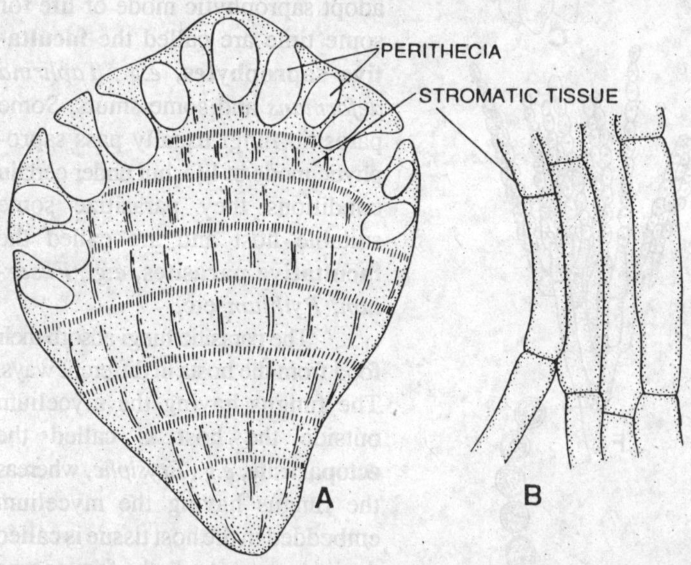

Fig. 1.7. Stroma. A, section through a stroma; B, structural detail of stroma.

(a) Saprophytes. The saprophytic fungi live on dead organic materials produced by the decay of animal and plant tissues. They grow upon dead organic matters such as rotten fruits, rotten vegetables, moist wood, moist leather, jams, jellies, pickles, cheese, rotting leaves, plant debris, manures, horse dung, vinegar, moist bread and many other possible dead organic materials. *Saprolegnia, Mucor, Rhizopus, Penicillium, Morchella, Aspergillus, Agaricus* and many others are good examples of saprophytic fungi.

The saprophytic fungi absorb their food from the substratum by ordinary vegetative hyphae which penetrate the substratum, *e.g., Mucor mucedo.* In other cases of the saprophytic fungi such as *Rhizopus* and *Blastocladiella* the rhizoids develop which penetrate the substratum and absorb the food material. In the case of saprophytic fungi the mycelium may be ectophytic or endophytic. In the case of *Rhizopus* the mycelium is ectophytic whereas the rhizoids remain embedded in the substratum and said to be endophytic.

(b) Parasites. The parasitic fungi absorb their food material from the living tissues of the hosts on which they parasitize. Such parasitic fungi are quite harmful to their hosts and cause many serious diseases. These fungi cause the great losses to the human beings directly or indirectly. Many diseases of the important crops are caused by parasitic fungi. The rusts, smuts, bunts, mildews and many other plant diseases are important examples of fungal diseases of crops. Their mode of life is parasitic and the relation of host and parasite is called the **parasitism.**

The parasites which survive on living hosts and only on living hosts are called the **obligate parasites.** Such parasites cannot be grown upon dead organic culture media, *e.g., Puccinia, Peronospora, Melampsora* etc. The parasitic fungi which usually live on living hosts and according to their need they adopt saprophytic mode of life for some time are called the **facultative saprophytes,** *e.g., Taphrina deformans* and some smuts. Some parasitic fungi usually pass saprophytic mode of life, but under certain conditions they parasitize some suitable host and are called the **facultative parasites,** *e.g., Fusarium, Pythium* etc.

The parasitic fungi absorb their food from the hosts in different ways. The fungus having the mycelium outside the host is called the **ectoparasite,** *e.g., Erysiphe,* whereas the fungus having the mycelium embedded in the host tissue is called the **endoparasite.** In the former type certain cushion-like **appressoria** develop on the surface of the host and from each appressorium a peg-like structure develops which penetrates the host epidermal cell giving rise to a branched or unbranched absorbing organ called the **haustorium.** The haustoria may also develop from the mycelium of endoparasites. The haustoria vary in their shapes. They may be small, rounded, button-like as in *Albugo,* branched and convolute as in *Peronospora* and highly branched as in *Erysiphe.*

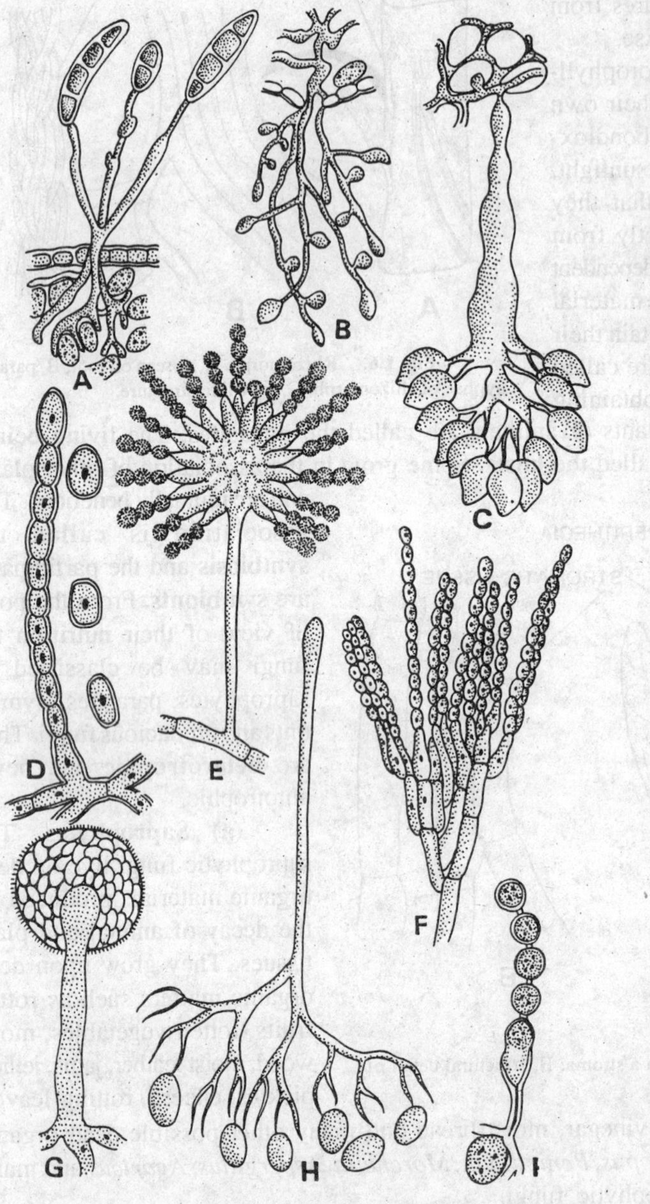

Fig. 1.8. *The Fungi.* Various types of sporophores. A, conidiophores and conidia of *Helminthosporium;* B, sporangiophore and sporangia of *Phytophthora;* C, sporophore and sporangia of *Sclerospora;* D, conidiophore and conidia of *Erysiphe;* E, conidiophore and conidia of *Aspergillus;* F, conidiophore and conidia of *Penicillium;* G, sporangiophore and sporangium of *Mucor;* H, conidiophore and conidia of *Peronospora;* I, sporangiophore and sporangia of *Albugo.*

In the case of rusts and mildews the mycelium remains confined in the pustules and not in the whole body of the plant. This type of fungus is called the **localized fungus.** When the mycelium prevails in the whole of the plant it is said to be **systemic fungus,** *e.g.*, smuts. When the mycelium is confined to the intercellular spaces it is called **intercellular mycelium** and

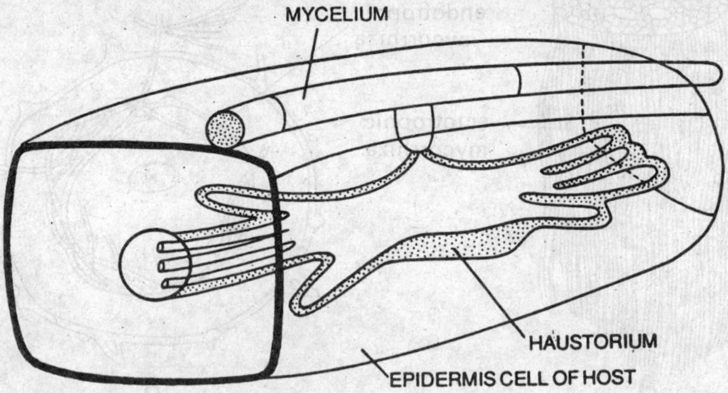

Fig. 1.9. **Haustorium. Three-dimensional diagram of an infected epidermal cell with a branched haustorium of *Erysiphe* spp. (powdery mildew).**

in other cases the mycelium penetrates the host tissue and said to be **intracellular.** Usually the former bears haustoria and the latter does not.

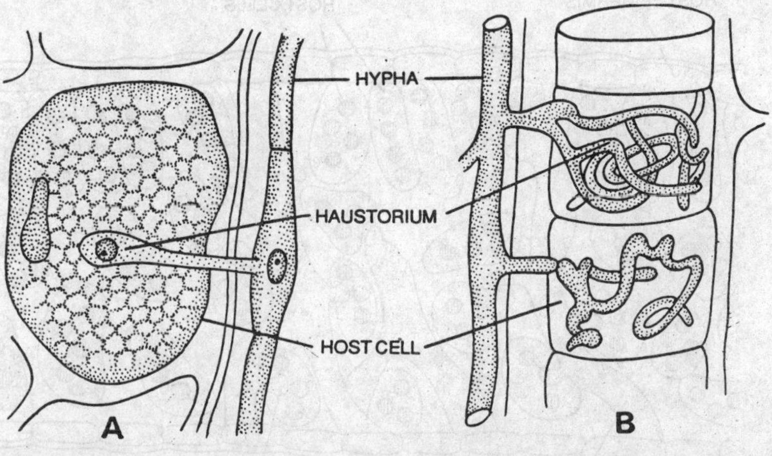

Fig. 1.10. **Haustoria. A, elongated capitate haustorium; B, branched or digitate haustorium.**

(c) Symbionts. Some fungi live in close association of other higher plants where they are mutually beneficial to each other. Such relationship is called the **'symbiosis'** and the participants the **'symbionts'.** The most striking examples are the **lichens** and **mycorrhiza.** The lichens are the resultants of the symbiotic association of algae and fungi. Here, both live together and are beneficial to each other. The algal partner synthesizes the organic food and the fungal partner is responsible for the absorption of inorganic nutrients and water. Certain fungi develop in the roots of higher plants and the mycorrhiza are developed. Here the fungi absorb their food from the roots and in response are beneficial to the plants. The mycorrhiza may be external or internal. The external mycorrhiza also called the ectophytic mycorrhiza are confined to the outer region of the roots whereas the internal mycorrhiza are found deeply in the root cells.

It is to be remembered that in all the cases whether they may be saprophytes, parasites or symbionts, the food is absorbed in the form of solution by cell walls, rhizoids and haustoria.

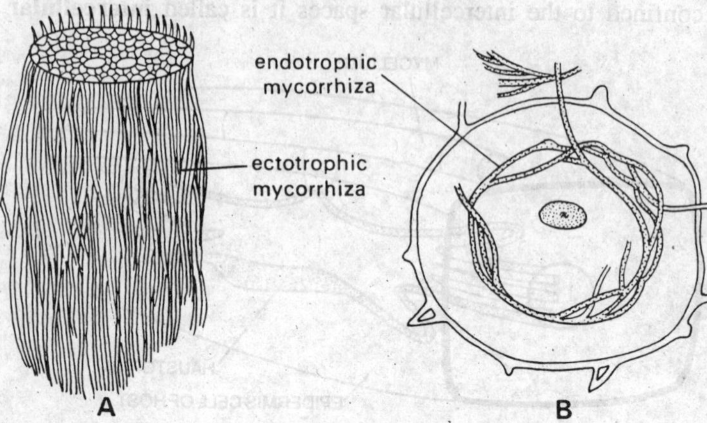

Fig. 1.11. Mycorrhiza. A, ectophytic mycorrhiza, B, endophytic mycorrhiza.

The hyphal cell walls are permeable and the plasma membranes lining to the cell walls are semipermeable. The osmotic pressure of the hyphal cells is higher than that of the host cells

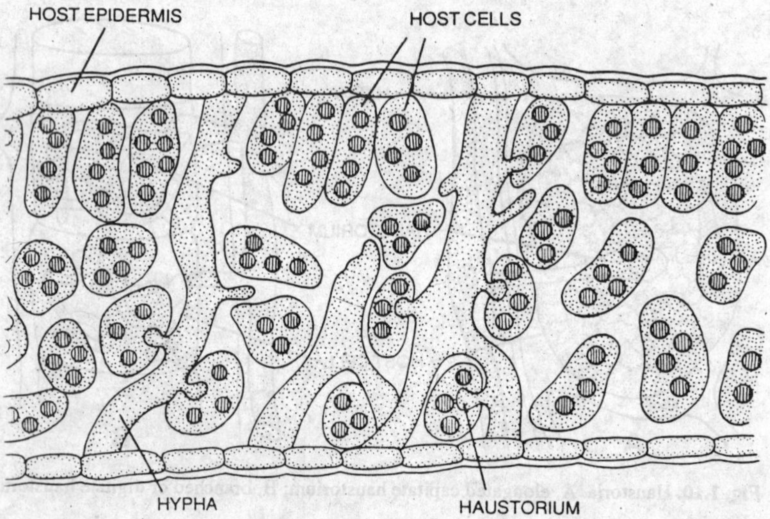

Fig. 1.12. Haustorium. Button-like or globular.

and thus the food materials are absorbed from the substratum and host cells. The fungi secrete some enzymes which dissolve the cellulose walls of the host, hydrolyse the starch and make it available to the fungus.

Many elements such as hydrogen, oxygen, nitrogen, small amounts of potassium, phosphorus and sulphur with the traces of magnesium and iron are required for the growth and other metabolic activities of the fungi. The carbon is always required in its organic form for growth.

When fungi are cultured in the laboratory on synthetic media, the necessary elements may be supplied in the following way: C is usually supplied in the form of a carbohydrate, such as glucose or maltose, sucrose and soluble starch are utilized by many fungi also. N may be supplied in the form of NH_4 salt or as amino acids. Many fungi can utilize NO_3 salts. Each fungus has its own specific requirements which may be known experimentally. Most fungi are able to synthesize the vitamins they need. However, several fungi may need thiamine or biotin or both these substances are generally added to synthetic media.

(d) Predacious fungi. There are many animal trapping fungi which have developed ingenious mechanisms for capturing small animals such as eellworms, rotifers or protozoa which they use for food. The most interesting of these mechanisms is that which utilizes a rapidly constricting ring around a nematode which holds it captive while the hyphae sink haustoria into the body of the victim. Several species of fungi in the genera *Arthrobotrys, Dactylella* and *Dactylaria* employ this method. In the presence of an eelworm population, the hyphae of the fungi produce loops which are stimulated to swell rapidly and close the opening when an eelworm

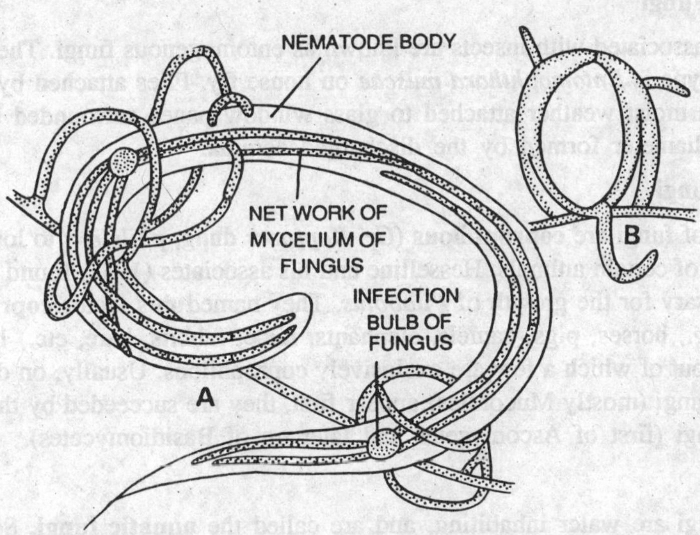

Fig. 1.13. Predacious fungus. ***Arthrobotrys oligospora:*** **A, hyphae growing out of the infection bulb inside the body of the nematode; B, a fully developed network of fungus. (After Duddington, 1957).**

passing through the loop rules against its inner surface. It is assumed that the amount of osmotically active material in the ring cells increases greatly as a result of stimulation and causes water to enter the cells increasing their turgor pressure. The ring cells swell rapidly and the ring closes around the eelworm which is thus held tightly in the trap. Some predacious fungi secrete a sticky substance on the surface of their hyphae to which a passing small animal adheres. Haustorium like hyphae then grow into the body of the animal and absorb food. The animals ultimately die.

Ecological Groups of Fungi

The fungi may be grouped into various ecological groups. Some main ecological groups are as follows:

Soil Fungi

Along with other microorganisms several fungi are also associated with microbiological phenomena in the soil. When the plants grow in the soil their roots are added to the soil system. The greatest microbiological activity remains confined to the surface of the roots, called the

rhizoplane. The soil nearer the roots, under the influence of the exudations of the roots, is called the **rhizosphere.** The fungal flora of the rhizoplane and rhizosphere play an important role in the incidence of root-disease fungi. In many cases the roots of resistant varieties of plants have been found to produce hydrocyanic acid which is however, not produced in the susceptible varieties. It is presumed that this acid has an inverse effect on the pathogenic fungi by preventing them from flourishing near the roots.

Lignicolous Fungi

Lignin is quite resistant to the attack of fungi and other microorganisms. However, certain specific fungi (mostly higher fungi) are responsible for bringing about its distribution. The wood of trees is decayed by such fungi. For example *Polystictus sanguineus* causes the wood decay of the logs of *Shorea robusta* (sal tree).

Entomogenous Fungi

The fungi associated with insects are known as entomogenous fungi. The most important example of this type is *Entomophthora muscae* on house fly. Flies attached by this fungus are generally seen in moist weather attached to glass window panes surrounded by a white halo about 2 cm. in diameter formed by the discharged conidia.

Coprophilous Fungi

A number of fungi are **coprophilous** (*Gr. Kopros* = dung; *philein* = to love), which grow only on the dung of certain animals. Hesseltine and his associates (1952) found in dung a factor which was necessary for the growth of *Pilobolus.* They named this factor **coprogen.** The dung of herbivores (*e.g.,* horses, pigs, camels, elephants, mice, rabbits, hare, etc.) harbours a large number of fungi out of which a few are exclusively coprophilous. Usually, on dung the fruiting bodies of lower fungi (mostly Mucorales) appear first, they are succeeded by the fructifications of the higher fungi (first of Ascomycetes and later on of Basidiomycetes).

Aquatic Fungi

Several fungi are water inhabiting, and are called the **aquatic fungi.** Several members of Chytridiales are found on algae and water molds. The Blastocladiales are chiefly water molds. Most species of Monoblepharidales are aquatic. The Lagenidiales is a small group of aquatic fungi parasitic on algae, water molds, small animals and other forms of aquatic or semi-aquatic life. Though the members of aquatic fungi are found in all fungal groups yet most of them belong to lower fungi.

Cellulose Decomposing Fungi

Some fungi are found on cellulose rich materials such as paper, cotton etc., and cause much damage to paper and textile industry. Some very important cellulose decomposers are *Stachybotrys atra, Chaetomium globosum* etc.

Dermatophytes

These are fungi which cause diseases of the skin of man, animal, or both. The diseases caused by these fungi are grouped under the general term **dermatomycoses** and are commonly known as ring worm, athlete's foot etc. The important genera of these fungi belong to Fungi Imperfecti (Deuteromycotina). Some important genera are–*Trichophyton, Microsporum, Epidermophyton, Keratinomyces* etc.

Respiration. The fungi respire like higher plants. They intake the atmospheric oxygen and release the carbondioxde. The atmospheric oxygen is diffused through the hyphal cell walls.

The fungi and bacteria which require free oxygen for their proper growth are called the **'aerobes'** whereas the micro-organisms which do not require free oxygen and may grow even in the absence of oxygen are called the **'anaerobes'.**

Reproduction. The fungi reproduce by means of vegetative, asexual and sexual methods.

1. **Vegetative reproduction.** The most common method of vegetative reproduction is **fragmentation.** The hypha breaks up into small fragments accidentally or otherwise. Each fragment develops into a new individual. In the laboratory the 'hyphal tip method' is commonly used for inoculation of saprophytic fungus.

In addition to above-mentioned common method of vegetative reproduction the fungi reproduce vegetatively by other means, such as **fission, budding, sclerotia, rhizomorphs** etc.

In fission, the cell constricts in the centre and divides into two giving rise to new individuals.

The budding is commonly found in *Saccharomyces*. The buds arise from the protoplasm of the parent cells and ultimately become new individuals.

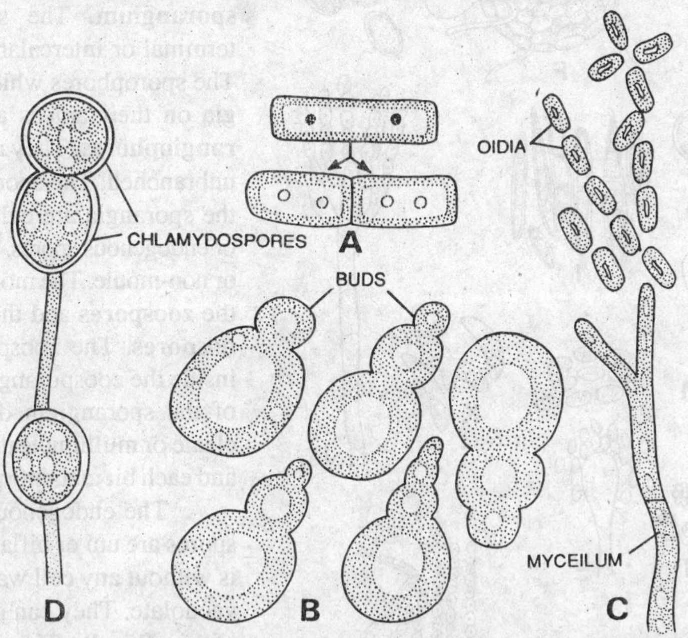

Fig. 1.14. Asexual reproduction. A,transverse cell division (fission); B, budding in yeast cell; C, hypha fragmenting into oidia or arthrospores in *Collybia conigena;* D, chlamydospore formation in *Fusarium.*

The sclerotia are resistant and perennating bodies. They survive for many years. Each sclerotium is cushion-like structure of compact mycelium. They give rise to new mycelia on the approach of favourable conditions.

As mentioned under the modified mycelium, the rope-like rhizomorphs are also resistant to unfavourable conditions and give rise to new mycelia even after several years on the approach of favourable conditions.

2. **Asexual reproduction.** The asexual reproduction takes place by means of spores. Each spore may develop into a new individual. The spores may be produced asexually or sexually and thus named (a) asexual spores and (b) sexual spores. Under asexual reproduction, only asexual spores will be considered.

Asexual spores. They are innumerable and produced on the haplont mycelium in Phycomycetes and Ascomycetes. In Basidiomycetes they are produced on the diplont mycelium. The spores are of diverse type and borne upon special structures called the **sporophores.** These spores are produced asexually and called the asexual spores. Usually the spores are uninucleate and non-motile but multinucleate and motile spores are also found. The fungus producing more than one type of spores is called the **pleomorphic** or **polymorphic.** The spores produced inside the sporangia are termed the **endogenous spores** and the spores developing exogenously on the terminal ends of sporophores are called the **exogenous spores.**

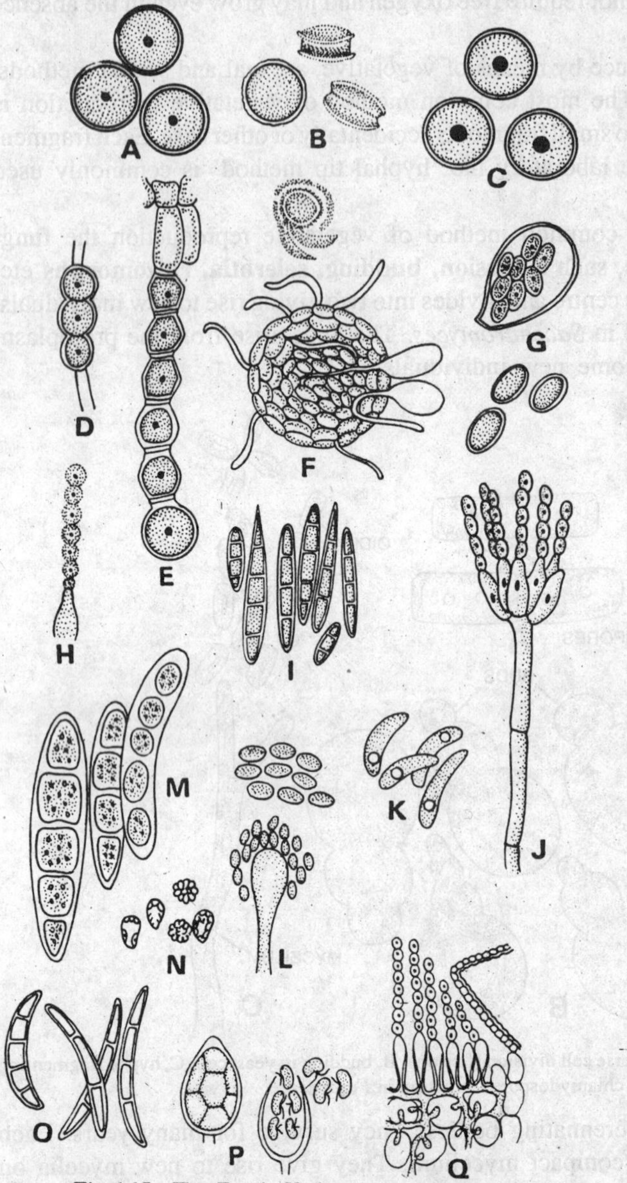

Fig. 1.15. The Fungi. Various types of spores. A, chlamydospores of *Ustilago hordei;* B, ascospores of *Aspergillus;* C, chlamydospores of *Ustilago tritici;* D, chlamydospores of *Fusarium;* E, ascospores of *Erysiphe;* F, cleistothecium of *Erysiphe;* G, ascus and ascospores of *Erysiphe;* H, conidia of *Aspergillus;* I, conidia of *Cercospora;* J, conidiophore and conidia of *Penicillium;* K, conidia of *Colletotrichum* sp; L, aplanospores of *Mucor;* M, conidia of *Helminthosporium;* N, aplanospores of *Rhizopus;* O, conidia of *Fusarium* sp; P, sporangium and zoospores of *Phytophthora* sp; Q, sporangiophores and sporangia of *Albugo.*

Endogenous spores. The endogenous spores are produced within the special spore producing cell the **sporangium.** The sporangia may be terminal or intercalary in their position. The sporophores which bear the sporangia on their apices are called the **sporangiophores.** They may be branched or unbranched. The spores produced inside the sporangia are called the endospores or endogenous spores. They may be motile or non-motile. The motile spores are called the **zoospores** and the non-motile **aplanospores.** The zoospores are produced inside the zoosporangia. The protoplasm of the sporangium divides into uninucleate or multinucleate protoplasmic bits and each bit metamorphoses into a spore.

The endogenously produced zoospores are uni or biflagellate. Each spore is without any cell wall, uninucleate and vacuolate. They can move with the help of their flagella. They are usually kidney-shaped or reniform and the flagella are inserted posteriorly or laterally on them. Such zoospores have been recorded from *Albugo, Pythium, Phytophthora* and many other lower fungi.

The aplanospores are non-motile, without flagella and formed inside the sporangia. They may be uni or multinucleate *(e.g., Mucor, Rhizopus).* These spores lack vacuoles and possess two layered cell walls. The outer thick layer is **epispore** or **exospore** which may be ornamented in many cases. The inner thin layer is **endospore.**

Exogenous spores. The spores producing externally or exogenously are either called the exogenous spores or **conidia**. They are produced externally on the branched or unbranched **conidiophores.** The conidiophores may be septate or aseptate. The conidia borne upon the terminal apices of the conidiophores or the ends of the branches of the conidiophores. The conidia may be produced singly on each **sterigma** or in chains. The conidial chains may be **basipetal** or **acropetal** in succession. The conidia are diverse in their shape and size. They may be unicellular or multicellular, uninucleate or multinucleate. Different genera may be recognized only by the presence of various shaped and various coloured conidia. The conidia of Fungi Imperfecti are multicellular and variously shaped, whereas the conidia of *Aspergillus* and *Penicillium* are smoky green coloured and the fungi are called 'the blue-green molds'.

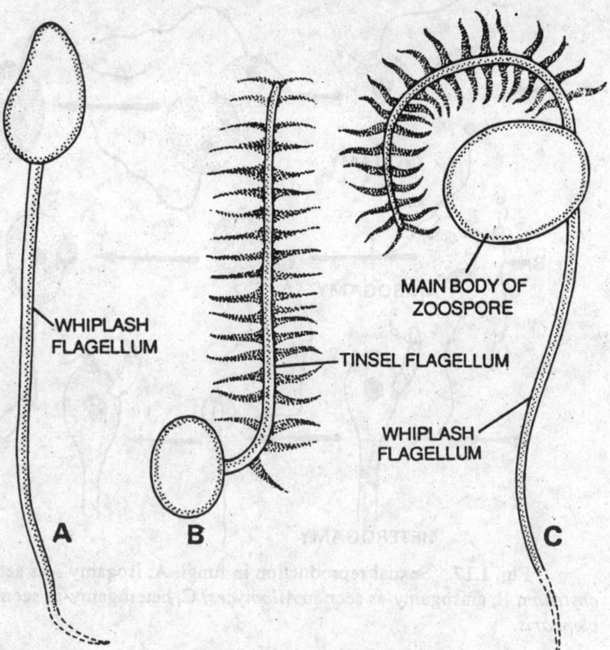

Fig. 1.16. Zoospores. A, posteriorly uniflagellate with a whiplash flagellum; B, anteriorly uniflagellate with a tinsel flagellum; C, biflagellate with an anterior tinsel and posterior whiplash flagellum. (After Couch, 1941).

In other type of exospores, the sporophores develop in groups and form the specialized structure called the **pustules, pycnia, aecidia, acervuli,** and **sporodochia.** The pycnia are flask-shaped producing **pycniospores** in them. The acervuli are saucer-shaped widely open bodies having developed conidia in them on small conidiophores. In mushrooms the sporophores are compactly arranged and form an umbrella-like fructification. The terminal expanded portion bears **gills.** In each gill there are hundreds of sporophores called the basidia bearing basidiospores. The sporophores (basidia) are arranged in hymenia.

3. **Sexual reproduction.** A large number of fungi reproduce sexually. However, the members of 'Fungi Imperfecti, or 'Deuteromycetes' lack sexual reproduction.

Usually two phases are found in the life cycle of the plants. These phases are called haploid and diploid phases respectively. The haploid phase possesses the (x) number of chromosomes in the nucleus, whereas this number becomes (2x) in the diploid phase. The gametes are always haploid (x) and by a sexual fusion they result in diploid (2x) sexual spores, such as **zygospores, oospores** etc. To bring haploid (x) phase once again in the life cycle the reduction division (meiosis) takes place and the number of chromosomes becomes half.

The gametes taking part in sexual fusion may be morphologically or physiologically different. Such two gametes taking part in fusion are of opposite sexes or strains, which may be called male and female sex organs or plus and minus strains. When both the sex organs or strains occur on the same mycelicum, the fungus is said to be **monoecious or homothallic,** and when the male and female sex organs or plus and minus strains occur separately on different mycelia the fungus is said to be **dioecious** or **heterothallic.**

The gametes taking part in fusion are usually formed in the cells of sacs called **gametangia** (singular-gametangium). The morphologically identical male and female gametes are called the **isogametes.** The morphologically dissimilar male and female gametes are called the **heterogametes.** In such cases the male gametes are called the **antherozoids** and the female ones are the **eggs.** The fusion of the plasma of the gametes is called the **plasmogamy,** which is usually followed by the nuclear fusion, *i.e.,* **karyogamy.** The whole process is called the **fertilization.**

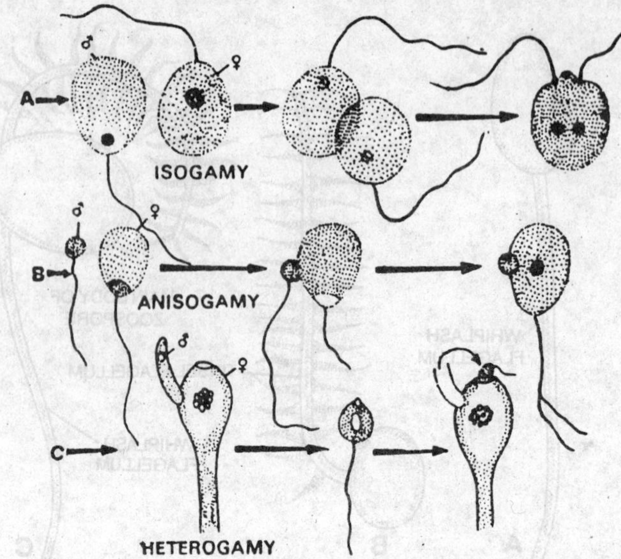

Fig. 1.17. Sexual reproduction in fungi. A, isogamy—as seen in *Synchytrium;* B, anisogamy-as seen in *Allomyces;* C, heterogamy-as seen in *Monoblepharis.*

Sometimes, in some of the fungi, *e.g.,* Phycomycetes and Ascomycetes, the entire contents of the two gametangia fuse with each other, the process is called the **gametangial copulation.** In the members of Phycomycetes and Ascomycetes the gametangia taking part in gametangial copulation are called the **antheridia** (singular-antheridium) and the **oogonia** (singluar-oogonium).

In the lower fungi, there is complete fusion of the nuclei of the two different strained gametes in the sexual union, *i.e.,* karyogamy, whereas in the higher fungi, *e.g.,* Ascomycetes and Basidiomycetes, the fusion of the two nuclei of different strains is delayed and the pairs of the nuclei called the **'dicaryons'** are formed. The mycelium having such pairs of nuclei is called the **'dicaryotic mycelium'.** In the opposite cases where the mycelium possesses single haploid nucleus of either strain in each cell is called the **monocaryotic mycelium.**

The most common methods of sexual reproduction are as follows.

1. Planogametic copulation. This type of sexual reprodction involves the fusion of two naked gametes one or both of them are motile. The motile gametes are known as planogametes. The most primitive fungi produce isogamous planogametes, *e.g., Synchytrium, Plasmodiophora* etc. The anisogamous planogametes are only found in the genus *Allomyces* of order Blastocladiales. In *Monoblepharis* (order Monoblepharidales) the unique condition is present, here the female gamete is non-motile whereas the male gamete is motile. The male gamete enters the oogonium and fertilizes the egg.

2. Gametangial contact. This method of reproduction is found in many lower fungi (class Phycomycetes). In this method two gametangia of opposite sex (oogonium and antheridium) come in contact and one or more gamete nuclei migrate from the male gametangium (antheridium) to the female gametangium (oogonium). In no case the gametangia actually fuse. The male nuclei in some species enter the female gametangium through a pore developed by the dissolution of the wall of contact (*e.g.,* in *Aspergillus, Penicillium* etc.); in other species the male nuclei migrate through a fertilization tube (*e.g., Pythium, Albugo, Peronospora* etc.) After the migration of the nuclei the antheridium eventually disintegrates but the oogonium continues its development in various ways.

3. Gametangial copulation. In this method of sexual reproduction the fusion of the entire contents of two contacting compatible gametangia takes place (*e.g., Mucor, Rhizopus, Entomophthora* etc.)

4. Spermatization. The sexual reproduction in *Neurospora* (Class-Ascomycetes) and other fungi takes place by means of this method. The minute, uninucleate, spore-like male structures are known as spermatia. They are produced in several ways. The spermatia are carried by outer agencies to the receptive hyphae (trichogynes) of female gametangia, to which they become attached. A pore develops at the wall of contact and the contents of spermatium pass into the female gametangium through the receptive hypha.

5. Somatogamy. The sex organs are not produced. The somatic cells take part in sexual fusion, *e.g., Morchella*, many higher fungi.

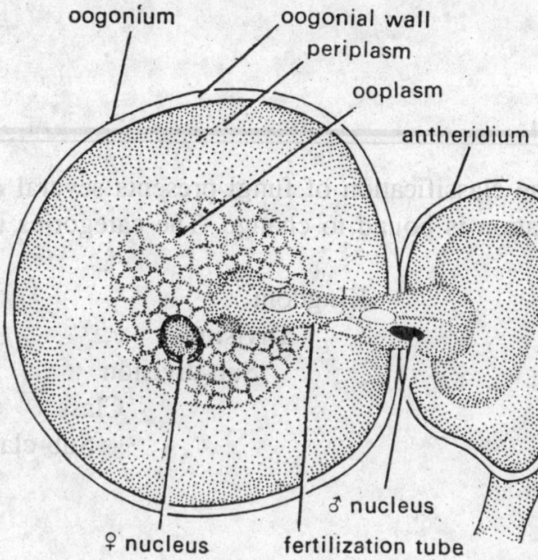

Fig. 1.18. Sexual reproduction. Gametangial contact by means of fertilization tube in *Pythium aphanidermatum*.

Reduction in sexuality. In the series Flagellatae of Phycomycetes (sub-division Mastigomycotina, Ainsworth, 1971) the sex organs are quite conspicuous and called the antheridia (male) and the oogonia (female). The resultants of fusion are oospores. In the series Aplanatae (sub-division Zygomycotina, Ainsworth 1971) the gametangial copulation takes place. The gametangia are represented by + and - signs. The resultants of gametangial union are zygospores. In Ascomycetes (sub-division Ascomycotina, Ainswoth 1971), the sex organs are not so prominent and there is a regular phenomenon of reduction of sexuality. In Ascomycetes, the phenomenon of nuclear fusion is not completely understood as yet. In some of the Ascomycetes (sac fungi) (*e.g., Morchella*) no sex organs are produced and the somatic cells take part in sexual fusion. This process is called the **somatogamy.** In the Basidiomycetes (sub-division Basidiomycotina, Ainsworth 1971) there is further reduction of sexuality. In this class of fungi there are no sex organs and only the fusion of the nuclei of a dicaryon represents the process of sexuality. In the members of Fungi Imperfecti or Deuteromycetes (sub-division Deuteromycotina, Ainswoth 1971) the sexual process is altogether absent and they reproduce asexually by conidia.

2

Classification of Fungi

The classification of fungi presents several difficulties. As the knowledge increases, the classification is bound to change. The categories used in the classification of the fungi are as follows:

Kingdom
Division
Sub-division
Class
Sub-class
Order
Family
Genus
Species

The kingdom is the largest of the categories and includes—divisions, sub-divisions, classes, sub-classes, orders, families and so on down to the species.

According to the recommendations of the Committee on International Rules of Botanical Nomenclature, the names of the divisions of fungi end in **-mycota**, of sub-divisions in **-mycotina**, of classes in **-mycetes**, sub-classes in **-mycetidae**, of orders in **-ales** and of families in **-aceae.** For example, *Puccinia graminis* may be classified as follows :

G. W. MARTIN (1961)

Kingdom	–	Plantae
Division	–	Mycota
Sub-division	–	Eumycotina
Class	–	Basidiomycetes
Sub-class	–	Heterobasidiomycetidae
Order	–	Uredinales
Family	–	Pucciniaceae
Genus	–	*Puccinia*
Species	–	*graminis*

C. J. Alexopoulos (1962)

Kingdom	–	Plantae
Division	–	Mycota
Sub-division	–	Eumycotina
Class	–	Basidiomycetes
Sub-class	–	Heterobasidiomycetidae
Order	–	Uredinales
Family	–	Pucciniaceae
Genus	–	*Puccinia*
Species	-	*graminis*

G.C. Ainsworth (1971)

Kingdom	–	Fungi
Division	–	Eumycota
Sub-division	–	Basidiomycotina
Class	–	Teliomycetes
Order	–	Uredinales
Family	–	Pucciniaceae
Genus	–	*Puccinia*
Species	-	*graminis*

The binomial name of an organism is composed of two words. The first designates the genus and the second denotes the species. The genus name is always capitalized. The specific name starts with small letter.

Binomials when hand written should always be underlined, and when printed should be italicized.

Some mycologists are of opinion that the fungi have evolved from algae by loss of chlorophyll. If this is true, the fungi are plants and are properly placed in the plant 'kingdom'. Mycologists of other school of thought, however, believe that the fungi had a common ancestry, with the protozoa but split off at a very early stage of organic evolution. If this is true the fungi are neither plants nor animals—*they are fungi.* Ainsworth (1971) in his *dictionary of fungi* treated the fungi as a separate and independent kingdom.

The outline of *three* very important and modern systems of classification is being given.

G. W. MARTIN (1961)
Fungal Groups
(Division–MYCOTA)
Chlorophyll always lacking
Sub–divisions

MYXOMYCOTINA
(Assimilative phase a true plasmodium).

EUMYCOTINA
(Plasmodium lacking; thallus sometimes multinucleate or unicellular, but characteristically filamentous).

Sub-division MYXOMYCOTINA
Single Class–MYXOMYCETES
Sub–classes

Ceratiomyxomycetidae
(Spores borne externally on individual stalks each producing on germination a protoplasmic body which is transformed into eight swarm-cells; hypothallus massive, with erect and often branching extensions, the sporophores).

Myxogastromycetidae
(Spores borne internally in fructifications of characteristic form, each spore producing on germination one or two, rarely more, swarm cells; hypothallus rarely prominent, usually inconspicuous, sometimes imperceptible).

Orders:

1. Ceratiomyxales

1. Liceales
2. Echinosteliales
3. Trichiales
4. **Stemonitales**
5. Physarales.

Order-Stemonitales : Spores black, rusty to deep violet in mass; neither peridium nor capillitium calcareous; lime rarely present and then restricted to hypothallus, stalk and columella; 2 families—1. Collodermataceae; 2. Stemonitaceae-described genus: *Stemonitis,*

Sub-division: EUMYCOTINA

Classes

PHYCOMYCETES (Mycelium, when present, either continuous in active assimilative phase, or, if septate, the segments multinucleate, if lacking, reproduction not by budding; perfect stage represented by oospores or zygospores, or by zygotes resulting from union of differentiated gametes; imperfect stage by sporangiophores or modified sporangia or sporangial parts, or by conidia).

ASCOMYCETES (Mycelium septate, the segments 1-2-or few-nucleate, rarely lacking and cell in such case reproducing by budding or very rarely by fission; perfect stage characterized by spores borne in asci).

BASIDIOMYCETES (Mycelium septate the segments 1-2-nucleate; perfect stage characterized by spores borne on basidia).

DEUTEROMYCETES (Mycelium septate with uni- or multinucleate cells: perfect stage not known or at least not normally seen).

Form-class-Lichens : Parasitic on algae, forming with them symbiotic subaerial structures often resembling green plants.

Class–PHYCOMYCETES

Sub-classes

Trichomycetidae
(Thallus filamentous, single or branched, attached to digestive tract or external cuticle of living arthropods by a holdfast or basal cell; mycelium not immersed in tissues of hosts).

Orders:
1. Harpellales
2. Amoebidiales
3. Eccrianales

Oomycetidae
(Thallus mainly saprobic; asexual reproduction by zoospores or by detached zoosporangia; perfect stage represented by oospores produced by fusion of unlike gametangia without differentiated gametes or, less commonly, by fusion of differentiated gametes).

1. Hyphochytriales
2. **Chytridiales**
3. **Blastocladiales**

Zygomycetidae
(Thallus mainly saprobic; asexual reproduction by aplanospores by modified sporangial segments functioning as conidia, or by true conidia; gametangia morphologically similar (sometimes differing in size); perfect stage represented by zygosores).

1. **Mucorales**
2. Entomophthorales.

4. Asellariales
5. Genistellales

4. Monoblepharidales
5. Plasmodiophorales
6. Saprolegniales
7. Leptomitales
8. Lagenidiales
9. Peronosporales

Order—**Chytridiales** : Zoospores posteriorly uniflagellate, usually formed inside the sporangium; thallus holocarpic or eucarpic, in the latter case with one or more reproductive structures attached to the substratum by basal vesicle or rhizoidal system; zoospore usually containing a single conspicuous oil globule. 9 families; **Synchytriaceae** described in the text; described genus-*Synchytrium.*

Order—**Blastocladiales** : Thallus always eucarpic; assimilatory portion hypha-like, scanty or profuse; zoospore without a conspicuous oil, globule; resistant sporangia always present; thin walled zoosporangia usually present: sexual reproduction when known, by isogamous *or* anisogamous planogametes; 3 families—1. Coelomomycetaceae; 2. Catenericeae and 3. **Blastocladiaceae** (described genus *Allomyces).*

Order—**Monoblepharidales** : Thallus eucarpic; assimilative portion hypha-like; resistant sporangia lacking; thin-walled zoosporangia always present, sexual reproduction by union of free-swimming sperm and a non-motile egg, resulting in thickwalled oospore which germinates by a hypha; single family-**Monoblepharidaceae**; described genus-*Monoblepharis.*

Order—**Plasmodiophorales** : Always parasitic, assimilative phase a multinucleate thallus within host cells of plants, mostly vascular, sporulating in place and often causing hypertrophy, both flagella of zoospores of whiplash type; single family-**Plasmodiophoraceae,** described genus-*Plasmodiophora.*

Order—**Saprolegniales** : Parasitic or saprobic; assimilative phase extensive mycelium; anterior flagellum of zoospores always formed within the sporangium diplanetic, monoplanetic or rarely aplanetic; holocarpic or eucarpic; oogonium containing 1-several oospores; 3 families—1. Ectrogellaceae, 2. Thraustochytriaceae and 3. **Saprolegniaceae**; described genera-*Saprolegnia; Achlya.*

Order—**Peronosporales** : Eucarpic; primarily terrestrial, living in soil or parasitic on vascular plants; zoosporangia in latter case, often functioning as conidia; 3 families—**1. Pythiaceae** (described genera: *Pythium* and *Phytophthora*), 2. **Peronosporaceae** (described genus: *Peronospora),* 3. **Albuginaceae** (described genus: *Albugo).*

Order—**Mucorales** : Outer wall of zygospore formed by modification of walls of gametangia; imperfect spores typically sporangiospores; mostly saprobic, 9 families, described family-**Mucoraceae** (described genera *Mucor* and *Rhizopus*).

Class–ASCOMYCETES

Sub-classes

Hemiascomycetidae
(Asci or ascus-like spore sacs formed singly, typically following karyogamy, no ascocarp formed).

Orders :

1. Protomycetales
2. **Endomycetales**
3. **Taphrinales**

Euascomycetidae
(Asci borne in ascocarps)

1. Myriangiales
2. Microthyriales
3. Dothideales
4. Pleosporales
5. Hysteriales
6. Ostropales
7. Coryneliales
8. Coronophorales
9. Laboulbeniales
10. Meliolales
11. **Erysiphales**
12. **Eurotiales**
13. Microascales
14. Onygenales
15. **Hypocreales**
16. Chaetomiales
17. Diaporthales
18. **Xylariales**
19. Phacidiales
20. Helotiales
21. **Pezizales**
22. Tuberales.

Order—**Endomycetales** : Inidividual asci formed; zygote or single cell transformed directly into an ascus; mycelium sometimes lacking, mostly saprobic; 4 families—1. Ascoideaceae. 2. **Saccharomycetaceae** (described genus-*Saccharomyces*), 3. Endomycetaceae, 4. Spermophthoraceae.

Order—**Taphrinales** : Hyphae bearing terminal chlamydospores or ascogenous cells, each of which produces a single ascus, usually forming a continuous hymenium-like layer on often modified tissues of host; parasitic on vascular plants; single family-**Taphrinaceae;** described genus-*Taphrina*.

Order—**Erysiphales** : Mycelium white, without appendages, usually with haustoria; perithecia without ostiole (cleistothecia), bearing appendages; the powdery mildews; single family-**Erysiphaceae,** described genera; *Erysiphe, Sphaerotheca* and *Phyllactinia*.

Order—**Eurotiales** : Ascogenous hyphae filling ascocarp and bearing asci at all levels, perithecia without ostioles (cleistothecia); 2 families—1. Gymnoascaceae, 2. **Eurotiaceae;** described genera: *Aspergillus* and *Penicillium.*

Order—**Hypocreales** : Ascocarp not a mazaedium; perithecia, and stromata if present, bright coloured, soft and fleshy; 2 families—1. Nectriaceae; 2. **Clavicipitaceae** (described genus-*Claviceps*).

Order—**Xylariales** : Perithecia dark coloured and usually possess firm walls; perithecia superficial or embedded in substratum or stroma; asci persistent, paraphyses present, persistent; centrum not pseudoparenchymatous; asci mostly in an hymenial layer lining wall sometimes in a basal cluster, their walls not notably gelatinous; 4 families—1. Sordariaceae; 2. Phyllachoraceae; 3. Diatrypaceae and 4. **Xylariaceae** (described genus-*Xylaria*).

Order—**Pezizales** : Asci operculate, discharging by opening or separation of an apical lid; ascocarp an open apothecium or modified form of it, ascocarp epigeic at least at maturity, 2 families—**1. Pezizaceae** (described genus-*Peziza*) **2. Helvellaceae** (described genus-*Morchella*).

Class–BASIDIOMYCETES

Sub-classes

Heterobasidiomycetidae

(Basidia septate or deeply divided, or arising from a teliospore or cyst; basidiospores often germinating by repetition, by budding, or by the production of conidia).

Orders :

1. Tremellales
2. **Uredinales**
3. **Ustilaginales**

Homobasidiomycetidae

(Basidia simple, cylindrical, uniform, or broadly clavate; cyst not as a rule differentiated; basidiospores on germination, usually producing a mycelium directly)

1. Exobasidiales
2. **Polyporales**
3. **Agaricales**
4. **Lycoperdales**
5. Phallales
6. Hymenogastrales
7. Nidulariales
8. Sclerodermatales

Order—**Uredinales** : Basidiocarps lacking, replaced by sori; accessory spore forms often present; always parasitic on vascular plants; sori, especially of accessory spores, usually yellow or orange, of teliospores dull orange brown to black; tube arising from teliospore cell becoming transversely septate into usually four cells, each cell producing a basidiospore; basidiospores often germinating by repetition but not budding; the rusts; 2 families—1. **Melampsoraceae** (described genus *Melampsora*); 2. **Pucciniaceae** (described genus-*Puccinia*).

Order—**Ustilaginales** : Basidiocarps lacking, replaced by sori; sori usually dull black; promycelium (basidium) septate or not, bearing sessile basidiospores usually capable of germinating by budding, occasionally by repetition or teliospores rarely germinating to produce a mycelium directly; parasitic on vascular plants; the smuts; 3 families—1. Graphiolaceae; 2. **Ustilaginaceae** (described genus-*Ustilago*); 3. **Tilletiaceae** (*Tilletia*).

Order—**Polyporales** : Basidiocarp present, varying from an arachnoid subiculum bearing a loose hymenium to a complex and highly specialized sporocarp; hymenium amphigenous or unilateral, the surface smooth or ridged to warted, spiny or porose, or rarely lamellate, but if porose or lamellate, texture of basidiocarp not soft and putrescent; 6 families—1. Thelephoraceae; 2. Clavariaceae; 3. Cantharellaceae; 4. Hydnaceae; 5. Meruliaceae; 6. **Polyporaceae** (described genus-*Polyporus*).

Order—**Agaricales** : Basidiocarp present, hymemium inferior, borne on lamellae or lining the interior of tubes, in the latter case soft and putrescent; 5 families—1. Boletaceae, 2. Paxillaceae, 3. Russulaceae, 4. Hygrophoraceae, 5. **Agaricaceae** (described genus-*Agaricus*).

Order—**Lycoperdales** : Hymenium present at least in early stages, lining chambers of gleba, gleba powdery and dry at maturity; glebal chambers usually breaking down completely; if persistent, as crumbling masses of spores; spores typically small, pale and accompanied by well-developed capillitium; 3 families—1. Arachniaceae; 2. **Lycoperdaceae** (described genus-*Lycoperdon*); 3. Geastracae.

Order—**Nidulariales** : Gleba waxy, the chamber or chambers thick-walled, each lined by an obscure hymenium and at maturity separating as peridioles which serve as disseminules; 2 families—1. **Nidulariaceae**, (described genus -*Cyathus*), 2. Sphaerobolaceae.

Class–DEUTEROMYCETES

(Fungi Imperfecti)

Orders

Sphaeropsidales	**Melanconiales**	**Moniliales**	**Mycelia sterilia**
(Conidia borne in pycnidia or chambered cavities).	(Conidia borne in acervuli, definitely circumscribed, erumpent)	(Conidiophores if present superficial, entirely free or bound in tufts or pulvinate masses).	(No spores known, mycelium or masses of fungus cells).
Families : 1. Sphaeropsidaceae 2. Zythiaceae 3. Leptostromataceae 4. Excipulaceae	1. **Melanconiaceae** (described genus-*Colletotrichum*).	1. Cryptococcaceae 2. Sporobolomycetaceae 3. Moniliaceae 4. **Dematiaceae** (described genera-*Alternaria, Cercospora* and *Helminthosporium*) 5. Stilbellaceae 6. Tuberculariaceae (described genus-*Fusarium*).	

C. J. ALEXOPOULOS (1962)

Division–MYCOTA

Sub–divisions

MYXOMYCOTINA	EUMYCOTINA

Classes

MYXOMYCOTINA	EUMYCOTINA
1. Myxomycetes	1. Chytridiomycetes
	2. Hyphochytridiomycetes
	3. Plasmodiophoromycetes
	4. Oomycetes
	5. Trichomycetes
	6. Zygomycetes
	Form-class—Deuteromycetes
	7. Ascomycetes
	8. Basidiomycetes

DIVISION—MYCOTA (The Fungi) : Devoid of chlorophyll; the plant body varies from a microscopic unicell to an extensive mycelium; true nuclei with nuclear membranes, nucleoli

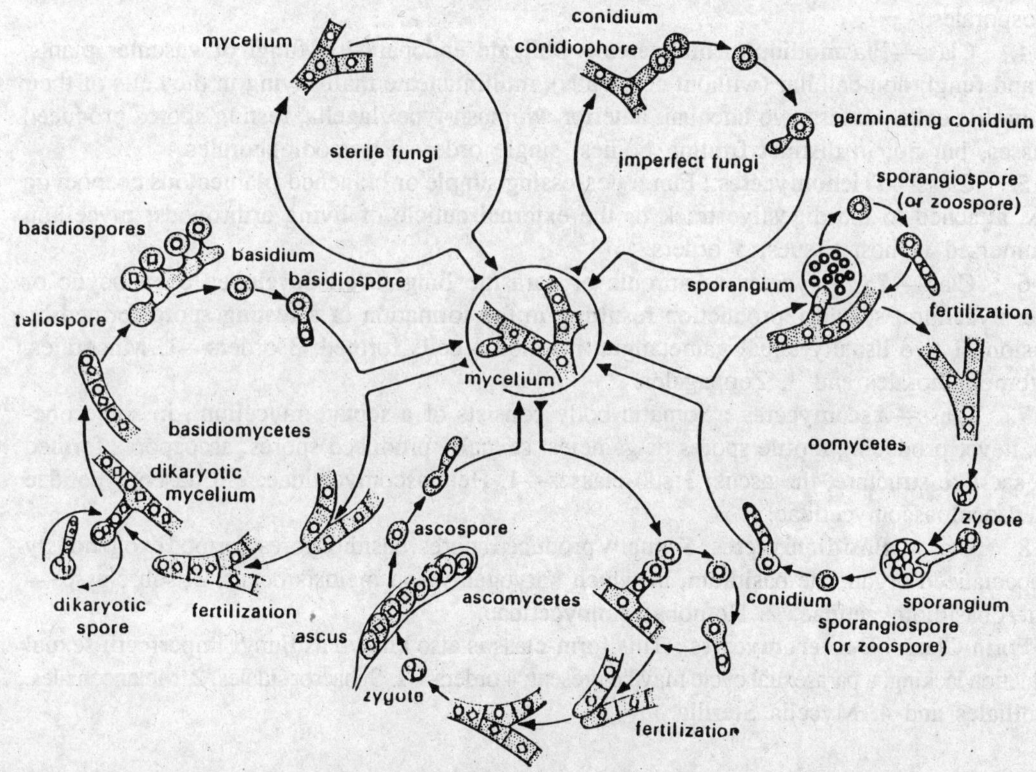

Fig. 2.1. Life-cycles of different classes of fungi.

present; cell walls contain chitin or cellulose, or a mixture of both, and other complex polysaccharides; reproduction asexual and sexual; propagative units—spores, two sub-divisions—1. Myxomycotina and 2. Eumycotina.

Sub-division—MYXOMYCOTINA : The definite cell walls are absent from their amoeba-like bodies; somatic structure, a free-living plasmodium, *i.e,* a multinucleate mass of protoplasm without definite cell walls, the entire plasmodium whose nuclei are diploid (2n), is consumed in the formation of fructifications which bear haploid (n) spores resulting from meiosis; spores are provided with firm walls, flagellated cells are characteristically produced; single class—Myxomycetes.

Sub-division—EUMCOTINA: They are true fungi, the organisms, only with few exceptions provided with cell walls and are typically filaments (some unicellular); reproduction—sexual and asexual; there are eight classes and one form-class.

1. Class—**Chytridiomycetes** : They are posteriorly uniflagellate fungi, motile cells (zoospores or planogametes) produced, each with a single posterior, whiplash flagellum; various types of thalli; 3 orders—1. Chytridiales, 2. Blastocladiales and 3. Monoblepharidales.

2. Class—**Hyphochytridiomycetes :** Aquatic fungi; motile cells possess a single anterior tinsel flagellum; parasitic on algae and fungi or saprobic on plant and insect debris in the water; single order—Hypochytriales.

3. Class—**Oomycetes :** Fungi with well-developed coenocytic mycelium; they reproduce asexually by means of flagellate zoospores, each bearing one tinsel flagellum directed forward and one whiplash flagellum directed backward; zoospores formed in sporangia of various types; perfect spores—oospores; 4 orders—1. Saprolegniales, 2. Leptomitales, 3. Lagenidiales and 4. Peronosporales.

4. Class—**Plasmodiophoromycetes :** Obligate endoparasitic fungi of vascular plants, algae and fungi; non-cellular (without cell walls), multinucleate thalli living in the cells of their hosts, motile cells possess two unequal, anterior whiplash-type flagella; resting spores produced in masses, but not in distinct fruiting bodies, single order—Plasmodiophorales.

5. Class—**Trichomycetes :** Fungi possessing simple or branched filamentous coenocytic thallus, attached to the digestive track or the external cuticle of living arthropods; mycelium not immersed in host tissues; 5 orders.

6. Class—**Zygomycetes :** Saprobic or parasitic fungi, well developed coencocytic or septate mycelium; sexual reproduction resulting in the formation of a resting spore formed by the fusion of two usually equal gametangia; no motile cells formed; 3 orders—1. Mucorales, 2. Entomophthorales and 3. Zoopagales.

7. Class—**Ascomycetes :** Somatic body consists of a septate mycelium, in some one-celled; never producing motile spores or gametes; sexually produced spores, ascospores formed inside sac-like structure, the ascus; 3 sub-classes—1. Hemiascomycetidae, 2. Euascomycetidae and 3. Loculoascomycetidae.

8. Class—**Basidiomycetes :** Sexually produced spores, basidiospores, formed exogenously on a specialized organ, the basidium, in which karyogamy and meiosis occur; 2. sub-classes—1. Heterobasidiomycetidae. 2. Homobasidiomycetidae.

Form-Class—**Deuteromycetes :** This form-class is also known as Fungi Imperfecti; sexual reproduction lacking; a parasexual cycle may be present; 4 orders—1. Sphaeropsidales, 2. Melanconiales, 3 Moniliales and 4. Mycelia Sterilia.

Class–MYXOMYCETES

Sub–classes

Ceratiomyxomycetidae (Spores borne externally on individidual stalks)

Orders

1. Ceratiomyxales.

Myxogastromycetidae (Spores borne internally in fructifications)

Orders

1. Liceales
2. Echinosteliales.
3. Trichiales
4. **Stemonitales** (described in next)
5. Physarales.

Class–CHYTRIDIOMYCETES

Orders

1. Chytridiales (True mycelium lacking, rhizomycelium present in some species).
2. Blastocladiales (True mycelium present, sexual reproduction of fungi by planogametes, thickwalled resistant sporangia characteristically formed).
3. Monoblepharidales (True mycelium present, sexual reproduction by fusion of a male planogamete, with a female aplanogamete, no resistant sporangia).

Class–HYPHOCHYTRIDIOMYCETES

Single order

Hypochytriales

(Aquatic fungi, motile cells anteriorly uniflagellate possessing a flagellum of the tinsel type)

Class–OOMYCETES

Orders

1. Saprolegniales
2. Leptomitales
3. Lagenidiales
4. Peronosporales

Order—**Saprolegniales** : Holocarpic or eucarpic thallus, zoospores always formed within the sporangium, diplanetic, monoplanetic or rarely aplanetic; oogonium not differentiated into ooplasm and periplasm; aquatic; saprophytic except few; 3 families—1. Ectrogellaceae, 2. Thraustochytriaceae and 3. **Saprolegniaceae.**

Order—**Peronosporales** : Eucarpic thallus, monoplanetic; oogonium differentiated into ooplasm and periplasm, terrestrial, parasitic on higher plants; 3 families—1. **Pythiaceae,** 2. **Albuginaceae,** 3. **Peronosporaceae.**

Class–PLASMODIOPHOROMYCETES

Single order

Plasmodiophorales

Always parasitic assimilative phase a multinucleate thallus within host cells of plants (mostly vascular); sporulating in place and often causing hypertrophy, both flagella of zoospores of whiplash type, single family **Plasmodiophoraceae.**

Class–ZYGOMYCETES

Orders

1. Mucorales
2. Entomophthorales (Two families: 1. Entomophthoraceae 2. Basidiobolaceae)
3. Zoopagales (Single family Zoopagaceae)

Order—**Mucorales** : Chiefly saprobic, some weakly parasitic on plants, a few endoparasitic in vertebrates; asexual reproduction by sporangia containing one to many aplanospores, sometimes by conidia; 9-11 families, **Mucoraceae** and **Pilobolaceae** described in the next.

Class–TRICHOMYCETES

Class–ASCOMYCETES

Sub-classes

1. Hemiascomycetidae (Asci naked; no ascocarps; no ascogenous hyphae).
   Orders :
   1. **Endomycetales**
   2. **Taphrinales**
2. Euascomycetidae (Asci usually unitunicate; borne in a cleistothecium, perithecium or apothecium)
   Series
   1. Plectomycetes
      Orders–
      1. **Eurotiales**
      2. Microascles
   2. Pyrenomycetes
      1. **Erysiphales**
      2. Meliolales
   3. Discomycetes
      1. Ostropales
      2. Helotiales
   4. Laboulobeniomycetes
      1. Laboulbeniales
3. Loculoascomycetidae (Asci bitunicate; ascocarp an ascostroma).
   Orders :
   1. Myriangiales
   2. Microthyriales
   3. Hysteriales
   4. Pleosporales
   5. Dothideales

3. Onygenales	3. Chaetomiales	**3. Pezizales**
	4. Clavicipitales	4. Tuberales
	5. Sphaeriales	
	6. Diaporthales	
	7. Hypocreales	
	8. Coryneliales	
	9. Coronophorales	

Order—**Endomycetales** : Asci arising directly from zygotes each derived from the copulation of two cells, or parthenogenetically from single cells; 4 families—1. Ascoideaceae: 2. Endomycetaceae; 3. Spermophthoraceae and 4. **Saccharomycetaceae.**

Order—**Taphrinales** : Product of sexuality a dikaryotic thallus; asci arising directly from cells of this thallus; single family—**Taphrinaceae.**

Order—**Eurotiales** : Ascocarp sessile and without an ostiole; 3 families—1. Ascosphaeriaceae, 2. Gymnoascaceae 3. **Eurotiaceae.**

Order—**Erysiphales** : Ascocarp closed (cleistothecium), typically black or dark coloured, wall appendaged, mycelium largely superficial, single family—**Erysiphaceae.**

Order—**Clavicipitales** : Asci persistent; ascospores thread-like; ascocarp a perithecium with an ostiole; periphyses present; asci with enlarged thickened by apical cap penetrated by a narrow thread-like apical pore; single family—**Clavicipitaceae.**

Order—**Sphaeriales** : Ascocarps and stromata, if present, dark, membranous or carbonous; perithecia, typically white to bright coloured; periphyses and apical paraphyses present; mature asci attached to the inner perithecial wall; 4 families—1. **Sordariaceae,** 2. Phyllachoraceae, 3. Diatrypaceae and **4. Xylariaceae.**

Order—**Pezizales** : Ascocarp an open apothecium or a modified form of it; apothecia above ground (epigeous); asci operculate or sub-operculate; 3. families—1. Sarcoscyphaceae, **2. Pezizaceae** and 3. **Helvellaceae.**

Class–BASIDIOMYCETES

Sub–classes

1. Heterobasidiomycetidae (Basidium septate)
Orders :
1. Tremellales
2. Uredinales
3. Ustilaginales

2. Homobasidiomycetidae (Basidium non-septate)
1. Exobasidiales
Series-Hymenomycetes
2. Polyporales
3. Agaricales
Series—Gasteromycetes
4. Hymenogastrales
5. **Lycoperdales**
6. Sclerodermatales
7. Phallales
8. Nidulariales

Order—Uredinales : Basidiocarp absent; basidium (promycelium) arising from a thick-walled probasidium, a teleutospore; plant parasites; basidiospores produced on sterigmata, forcibly discharged; 3 families—1. **Pucciniaceae**, **2. Melampsoraceae** and 3. Coleosporiaceae.

Order—Ustilaginales : Basidiocarp lacking; mostly parasitic on vascular plants; teleutospores formed in a manner similar to that of chlamydospores; basidiospores sessile, not forcibly discharged, 3 families—**1. Ustilaginaceae, 2. Tilletiaceae** and 3. Graphiolaceae.

Series—Hymenomycetes : Basidiocarp present; hymenium present and exposed before the spores are mature.

Order—Polyporales : Basidiocarp present; hymenium present; hymenium gymnocarpic texture of basidiocarp not soft and putrescent; 6 families—1. Thelephoraceae, 2. Clavariaceae, 3. Cantharellaceae 4. Hydnaceae, 5. Meruliaceae and **6. Polyporaceae.**

Order—Agaricales : Basidiocarp present; hymenium borne on lamellae (gills), or if lining the interior of pores then basidiocarp soft and putrescent; 5 families—1. Boletaceae, 2. Paxillaceae, 3. Russulaceae, 4. Hygrophoraceae and 5. **Agaricaceae.**

Series—Gasteromycetes : Hymenium present or absent, basidiocarps remaining closed at least until the spores have been released from the basidia (*i.e.*, angiocarpic).

Order—Lycoperdales : Gleba powdery; glebal chambers not separating from peridium; hymenium present in early stages; spores mostly light coloured, small; 3 families—1. Arachniaceae, **2. Lycoperdaceae** and 3. Geastraceae.

Order—Nidulariales : Gleba waxy; glebal chambers forming waxy peridioles, or entire gleba separating as a unit from the peridium; 2 families—1. Sphaerobolaceae and **2. Nidulariaceae.**

Form–class-DEUTEROMYCETES
(The Imperfect Fungi)

Orders

1. Sphaeropsidales (Reproduction by means of conidia borne in pycnidia).	2. Melanconiales (Reproduction by means of conidia borne in acervuli).	3. Moniliales (Reproduction by means of conidia borne otherwise, by oidia or by budding).	4. Mycelia Sterilia (No reproductive structures known).
Form-Families			
1. Sphaeropsidaceae 2. Zythiaceae 3. Leptostromataceae 4. Excipulaceae	1. Melanconiaceae Genus-*Colletorichum*	1. Moniliaceae 2. Dematiaceae *Helminthosporium,* *Alternoria,* *Cerospora,* 3. Stilbellaceae 4. Tuberculariaceae Genus—*Fusarium*	Importnat form genera *Rhizoctonia;* and *Sclerotium*

G. C. AINSWORTH (1971)

G. C. Ainswoth (1971-Dictionary of Fungi) has upgraded the fungi upto **Kingdom** level. He has treated the fungi in a separate kingdom, or a sub-kingdom of plant kingdom. The outline of Ainswoth's (1971) classification is given here:

Outline of Ainsworth's (1971) Classification

Kingdom–FUNGI

- Somatic body a mass of free-living plasmodium with no firm wall
  - Division—I MYXOMYCOTA
    Single Class—Myxomycetes
- Somatic body unicellular or multicellular filamentous.
  - II EUMYCOTA

Division II–EUMYCOTA

- Motile cells (zoospores) present; perfect spore, oospore
  - Sub–divisions III MASTIGO-MYCOTINA
- Motile cells absent
  - Perfect stage present
    - Perfect spore zygospore
      - IV ZYGOMYCOTINA
    - Perfect spores, ascospores
      - V ASCOMYCOTINA
    - Perfect spores, basidiospores
      - VI BASIDIO-MYCOTINA
  - Perfect stage absent
    - VII DEUTERO MYCOTINA

Sub-division–MASTIGOMYCOTINA

- Posteriorly uniflagellate zoospore (flagellum whip-lash type).
  - Classes- CHYTRIDIOMYCETES
    - Orders-
      1. Harpochytriales
      2. **Chytridiales**
      3. **Blastocladiales**
      4. **Monoblepharidales**
- Anteriorly uniflagellate zoospore (flagellum tinsel type).
  - HYPHOCHYTRIDI-OMYCETES
    1. Hyphochytriales
- Biflagellate zoos-pores (posterior fla-gellum whisplash type; anterior flagel-lum tinsel type) cel-lulose cell wall.
  - OOMYCETES
    1. **Saprolegniales**
    2. Leptomitales
    3. Lagenidiales
    4. **Peronosporales**
- Biflagellate heter-okontean swarm-ers (zoospore); flagella whiplash type.
  - PLASMODIO-PHOROMY-CETES
    1. **Plasmodio-phorales**

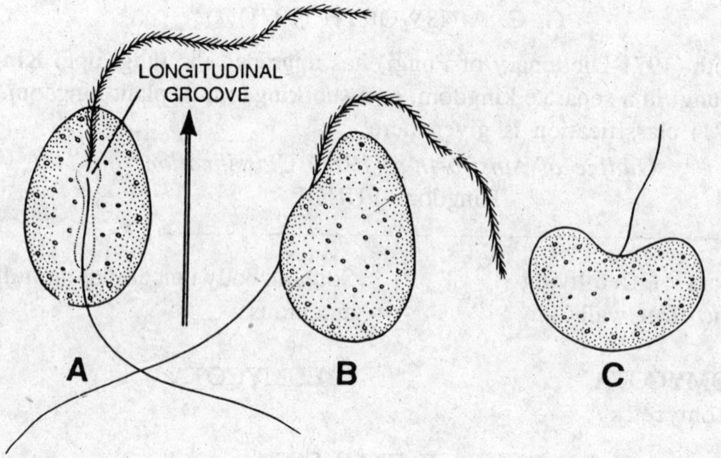

Fig. 2.2. Biflagellate reniform zoospores of Oomycetes in different views (A-C).

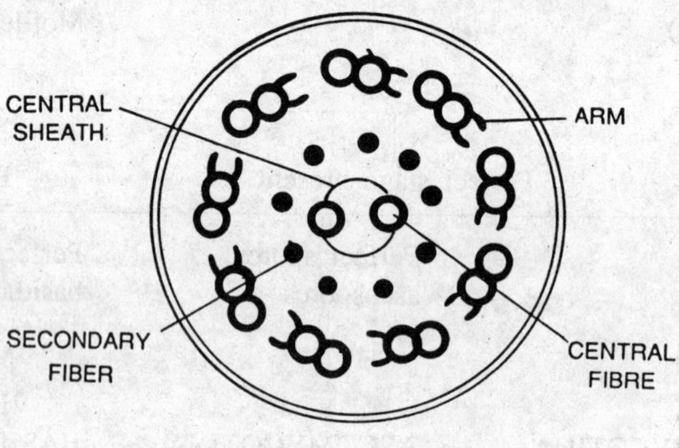

Fig. 2.3. T. S. of the flagellum to show 9 + 2 arrangement.

Sub-division–ZYGOMYCOTINA

Mostly saprophytic; sometimes weak parasites or mycoparasites some attacking insects but then developing mycelium inside instead of only attached to the inner lining of digestive tract; zygospores generally spherical in shape

Classes—

ZYGOMYCETES

Orders–

1. **Mucorales**
2. Entomophthorales
3. zoopagales

Mostly commensals with the guts of arthropods; hyphae attached to inner lining of digestive tract; rarely on external parts of aquatic living arthropods; zygospores where known biploar or biconical

TRICHOMYCETES

1. Harpellales
2. Asellariales
3. Eccrinales
4. Amoebidales

Sub-division–ASCOMYCOTINA

- Ascocarp and ascogenous hyphae absent; thallus mycelial or yeastlike; asci naked — Class 1
- Ascocarp and ascogenous hyphae present; thallus mycelial.
  - Ascus bitunicate; ascocarp an ascostroma. — Class 2
  - Ascus unitunicate; if bitunicate, then ascocarp an apothecium
    - Asci scattered at various levels within a cleistothecium; ascospores aseptate. — Class 3
    - Asci regularly arranged forming a hymenium at the base or periphery of ascocarp.
      - Ectoparasitic on Arthropods; thallus reduced; ascocarp a perithecium; ascus inoperculate. — Class 4
      - Not ectoparasitic on Arthropods.
        - Ascocarp a perithecium; ascus inoperculate. — Class 5
        - Ascocarp an apothecium, often massive; hypogeal or epigeal, ascus inoperculate or operculate. — Class 6

Classes: 1 2 3 4 5 6

Classes	1. HEMIASCOMYCETES	2. LOCULOASCOMYCETES	3. PLECTOMYCETES	4. LABOULBENIOMYCETES	5. PYRENOMYCETES	6. DISCOMYCETES
Orders :	1. **Endomycetales**	1. Myriangiales	1. **Eurotiales**	1. Laboulbeniales	1. **Erysiphales**	1. Helotiales
	2. Protomycetales	2. Microthyriales	2. Microascales		2. Meliolales	2. **Pezizales**
	3. **Taphrinales**	3. Hysteriales	3. Onygenales		3. Coroyophorales	3. Tuberales
		4. Pleosporales			4. **Sphaeriales**	
		5. Dothideales			5. **Clavicipitales**	

Sub-division–BASIDIOMYCOTINA

- Basidiocarps absent, basidium arising from thickwalled probasidium, a teleutospore,
- Well-developed basidiocarp present basidia arranged in a hymenium sapro-

teleutosori on host tissue, parasitic on vascular plants. | phytic, rarely parasitic.

Basidiocarp gymnocarpous or angiocarpous, hymenium exposed throughout its development, *i.e.*, gymnocarpous, hymenium enclosed in the fruit body, *i.e.*, angiocarpous.

Basidiocarp angiocarpous, basidium holobasidium.

Classes 1. TELIOMYCETES | 2. HYMENOMYCETES | 3. GASTROMYCETES

HYMENOMYCETES:

- Basidium phragmobasidium → Sub-classes → PHRAGMOBASIDIOMYCETIDAE
- Basidium holobasidium → HOLOBASIDIOMYCETIDAE

Orders :

TELIOMYCETES:

1. **Uredinales**
2. **Ustilaginales**

PHRAGMOBASIDIOMYCETIDAE:

1. Tremellaels
2. Auriculariales
3. Septobasidiales

HOLOBASIDIOMYCETIDAE:

1. Exobasidiales
2. Brachybasidiales
3. Dacrymycetales
4. Tulasnellales
5. Aphyllophorales (Polyporales)
6. **Agaricales**

GASTROMYCETES:

1. Podoxales
2. Phyllales
3. Hymenogastrales
4. **Lycoperdales**
5. Geitiriales
6. Tulostematales
7. **Nidulariales**
8. Melanogastrales
9. Sclerodermatales

Sub-division–DEUTEROMYCOTINA

Without pseudomycelium or pseudomycelium with yeast-like budding cells; true mycelium absent or underdeveloped.

Mycelium developed assimilatory budding cells absent.

- Sterile mycelium, spores borne on sporophores, sporophores may be grouped together, but pycnia and acervuli are not formed
- Spores or conidia formed in pycnidia or acervuli.

Classes:

BLASTOMYCETES

Orders :

HYPHOMYCETES

1. **Moniliales**
2. Mycelia sterilia

COELOMYCETES

1. **Melanconiales**
2. Sphaeropsidales

3

Class–Myxomycetes

Kingdom–**PLANTAE**
Division–**MYCOTA**
Sub-division–**MYXOMYCOTINA**
Class–**MYXOMYCETES** (The True Slime Molds)
(Alexopoulos, 1962)

G. W. Martin (1961)	**G. C. Ainsworth** (1971)
Kingdom–**PLANTAE**	Kingdom–**FUNGI**
Division–**MYCOTA**	Division–**MYXOMYCOTA**
Sub-di–**MYXOMYCOTINA**	Sub. di–**MYXOMYCOTINA**
Class–**MYXOMYCETES**	Class–**MYXOMYCETES**

Introduction. The slime molds are organisms with characteristics of both plants and animals. According to one school of thought, they are treated as a class coordinate with the Phycomycetes and the other groups of fungi. According to another school of thought, they are believed to be different enough from the fungi. Zoologists often place the slime molds in the protozoan phylum, class Sarcodina with the Amoebae.

The great German mycologist Anton De Bary (1887), considered the slime molds to be animals, or at least more closely related to animals than to plants, and called them **Mycetozoa** (Gr. *mykes,* fungus; *zoon,* animal). He believed that the slime molds originated independently and treated them as separate group. Bessey (1950) followed De Bary in the use of the name Mycetozoa.

C. J. Alexopoulos (1962) has also treated the slime molds in his sub-division, the **Myxomycotina.** However, Ainswoth (1971) has given the place to fungi in a separate kingdom, and simultaneously elevated the slime molds to the division **Myxomycota.** He has also put up a single class—Myxomycetes in his division—Myxomycota.

Thomas H. Macbride (1899) for the first time used the term **Myxomycetes** for the group. Professor G. W. Martin believes that the slime molds have originated from a protozoan-like ancestor. Martin believes that the slime molds have departed sufficiently from the main evolutionary line of the fungi and they constitute a sub-division of their own, the **Myxomycotina.**

Occurrence and distribution. They are frequently found in the rainy season in cool, shady moist places in the woods, on manure, large fungi, decaying logs, dead leaves or other decomposing plant material which holds abundant moisture. A few species occur in open spaces creeping over vegetation especially on the grass lawns. There are about 450 species of slime molds. Most of the species are universally distributed but some are confined to the temperate regions and others to the tropical regions. The slime molds are of little economic value to man.

Characteristic features. These organisms are naked during all stages of development except the spore state. This naked vegetative phase consists of a naked amoeboid multinucleate free living plasmodium. They ingest particles of food and reject the portions remaining after digestion. The plasmodia vary in size from microscopic units to masses of several centimetres. The plasmodia and fructifications of many species of slime molds are very colourful. The fructifications of many species even possess intricate designs.

The spores are produced upon or within aerial sporangia and are more or less dispersed by wind.

Life history of slime molds. After absorbing moisture the spore cracks open its cell wall

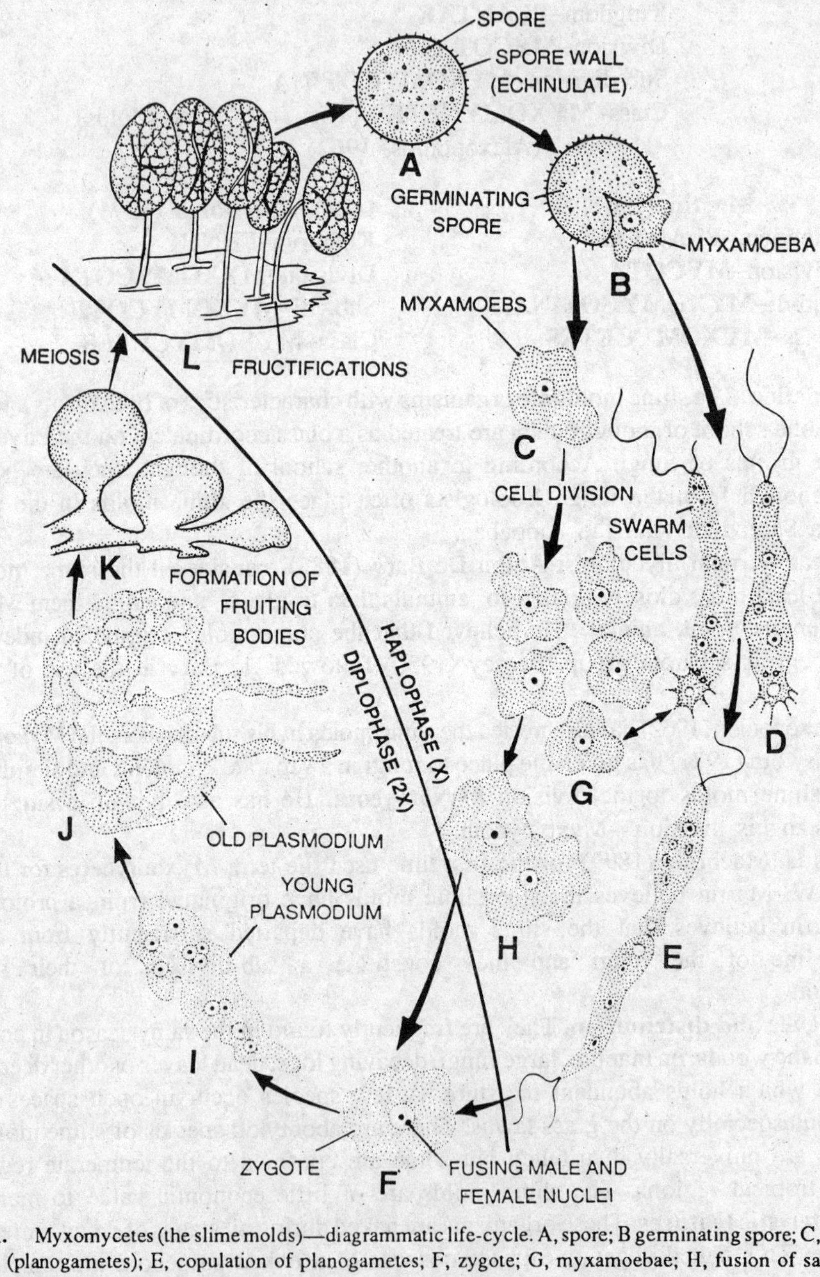

Fig. 3.1. Myxomycetes (the slime molds)—diagrammatic life-cycle. A, spore; B germinating spore; C, myxamoeba; D, swarm cells (planogametes); E, copulation of planogametes; F, zygote; G, myxamoebae; H, fusion of same; I, young plasmodium; J, old plasmodium; K, formation of fruiting bodies; L, fruiting bodies (sporangia).

and escapes one or two naked uninucleate swarm spore or planocyte. The swarm spore is somewhat rounded on its posterior side and tapering to the anterior end from which a single flagellum is given out. In many cases two flagella may also arise. These motile swarm cells ingest food in the manner of *Amoeba* and leave behind the undigested matter. Generally the swarm cells divide by fission several times and then change their form. During this period they retract the flagella, become rounded and produce more conspicuous pseudopodia. These structures are called myxamoebae. Usually they enlarge and divide several times. Now these so called myxamoebae unite by twos, with nuclear fusion forming zygotes. In many genera, *e.g.*, *Reticularia*, *Physarum polycephalum* etc., the myxamoebae are not formed. In such cases the sexual union takes place between two swarm cells. In general the zygote formed by the union of two myxamoebae or of two swarm cells is non-flagellate. The zygote continues its existence as naked amoeba-like cells which ingests its food and enlarges in size. Simultaneously the diploid nucleus divides mitotically. With the result a multinucleate structure is formed which is known as **plasmodium.** Sometimes the zygotes or small plasmodia fuse with other zygotes or plasmodia resulting in a large plasmodium. The plasmodia may ingest and feed upon swarmspores and myxamoebae. The plasmodium creeps through the soil or rotten logs or decaying leaves or some other large fungi etc., digesting the food and increasing in size. The number of nuclei also increases by mitotic division.

The plasmodium creeps on the surface of suitable substratum and there undergoes the changes and ultimately develop the fructifications. These fruiting bodies may be quite separate from each other or they may be crowded together forming a compound structure.

The nuclei now divide meiotically. Each daughter nucleus, together with a portion of cytoplasm is finally covered by a thick wall and metamorphoses into a resting spore.

The resting spores are produced within a fruiting structure covered by a peridium. The spores are generally rounded with a definite ornamented thick-wall. The spores are of various colours, *e.g.*, pale brown and sometimes black. Resting spores are very resistant to adverse conditions. Elliott (1949) reported that resting spores of some species of slime molds may even germinate after 52 years of their formation.

Alternation of generations. The life cycle of slime molds (Myxomycetes) exhibits, alternation of generations. The plasmodium or the vegetative plant body is a sporophyte which contains numerous diploid nuclei. The sporangia borne by plasmodium are also diploid under certain conditions. Reduction division, however, takes place at the time of differentiation of spores. This way, the plasmodium represents the asexual or sporophytic generation. After liberation from the sporangia the spores germinate producing the haploid swarm cells. The swarm cells directly or the myxamoebae produced by them function as gametes. They unite in pairs. Karyogamy follows plasmogamy and the zygote being formed. In zygote the diploid condition is re-established. The haploid spores and the swarm cells represent the gametophytic generation. The zygotes by further growth and mitotic nuclear division become plasmodia. The plasmodium represents the sporophytic generation (2x) while the resting spores and swarm cells represent the gametophytic generation (x). One generation follows the other in a regular sequence and exhibits an alternation of generations in the life-cycle of slime molds.

Genus—STEMONITIS (17 species)

There are 17 species in this genus. 13 species have been recorded from India (Thind 1973).

Life-cycle of *S. herbatica*. The spores of this species are purple-brown, spherical and finely echinulate. The spores can germinate immediately after their formation. After absorbing moisture the spore cracks open its cell wall, and then the protoplast squeezes out. The protoplast is amoeboid in the beginning, but soon after it develops two heterokont whiplash flagella. This swarm cell may have some pseudopodia at its posterior end. These motile swarm cells ingest food in the manner of *Amoeba* and leave behind the undigested matter.

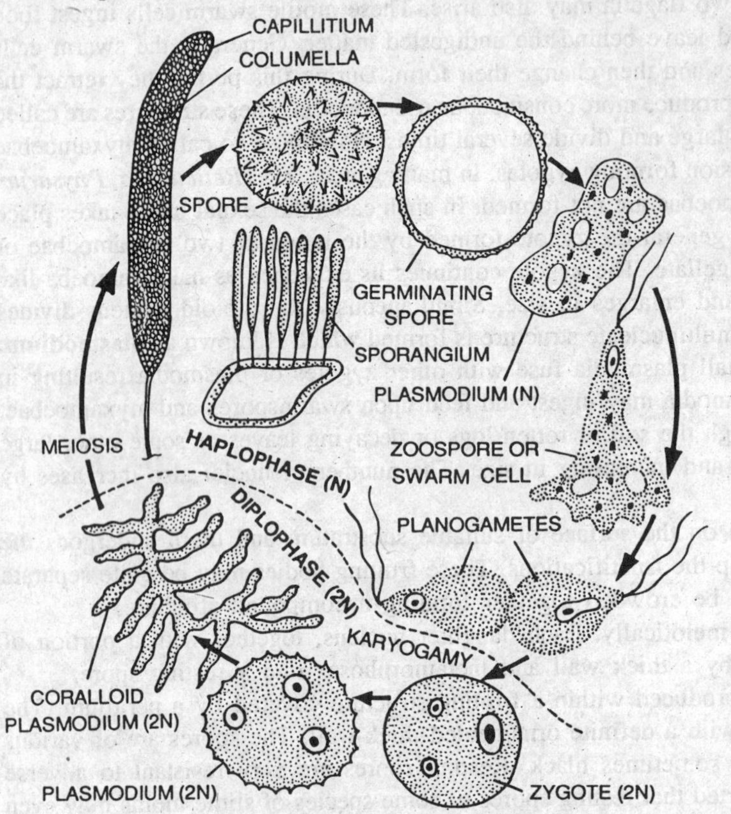

Fig. 3.2. *Stemonitis* sp. Diagrammatic life-cycle.

The swarm cells may divide by fission several times, thus increasing their number. The nucleus of each swarm cell also divides mitotically. Now the sexual union takes place between two swarm cells. The plasmogamy is followed by karyogamy. With the result, a spherical, naked nonflagellate zygote (2n) is formed. The zygote continues its existence as naked amoeba-like cell which ingests its food and enlarges in size. Simultaneously the diploid nucleus (2n) divides mitotically. With the result a multinucleate **young plasmodium** is formed. The young plasmodium enlarges in size by ingesting more and more food material. Sometimes the zygotes or small plasmodia fuse with other zygotes or plasmodia resulting in a large plasmodium. At maturity the plasmodia exhibit characteristic streaming movement through the veins.

The plasmodium undergoes the change and ultimately develop the fructifications. It becomes white to cream coloured and a few dense opaque strands make a coarse network in it. The plasmodium becomes coralloid in appearance, and moves about over the substratum. Within 4-5 hours of its settlement knoblike sporangial initials develop upon it. The protoplasm of the young sporangium becomes highly vacuolated except in a peripheral layer and a columnar tract in the centre. The central portion gives rise to columella. The capillitial threads arise from the columella, thus forming the **capillitium.** The capillitium is net-like, and its surface layer develops into an evanescent peridium.

The spores are formed, as soon as the development of capillitium is completed. During the sporangial development the nuclei divide meiotically. Each daughter nucleus, together with a portion of cytoplasm is finally covered by a thick wall (echinulate) and metamorphoses into a spore. The spores are spherical, uninucleate (n) and provided with fine echines. The spores may be of various colours such as pale, brown or black. The spores are quite resistant to adverse conditions. They germinate on getting suitable conditions.

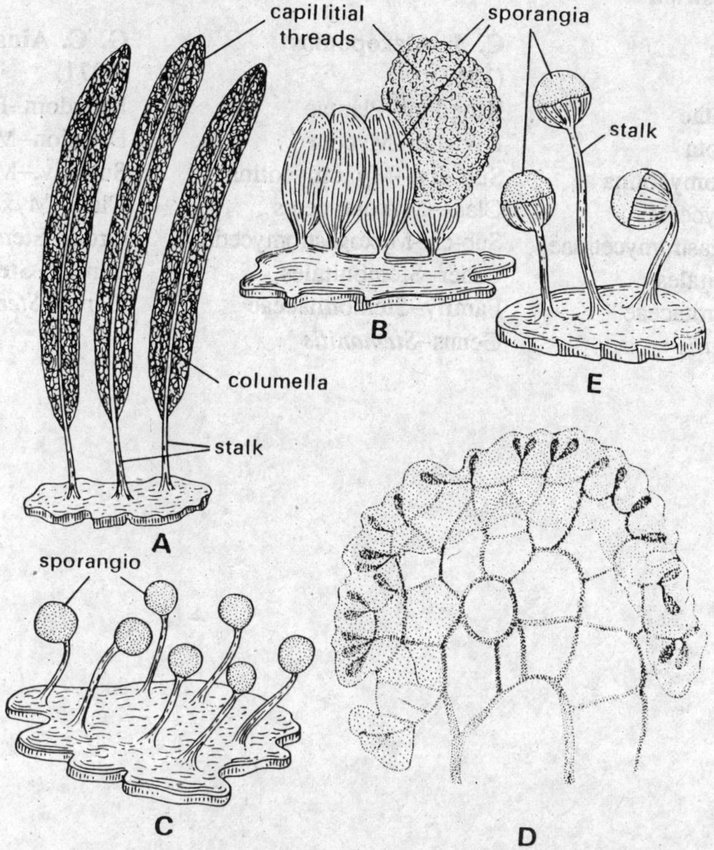

Fig. 3.3. Fruiting bodies (A, B, C and E) and plasmodium (D) of different slime molds (Myxomycetes).

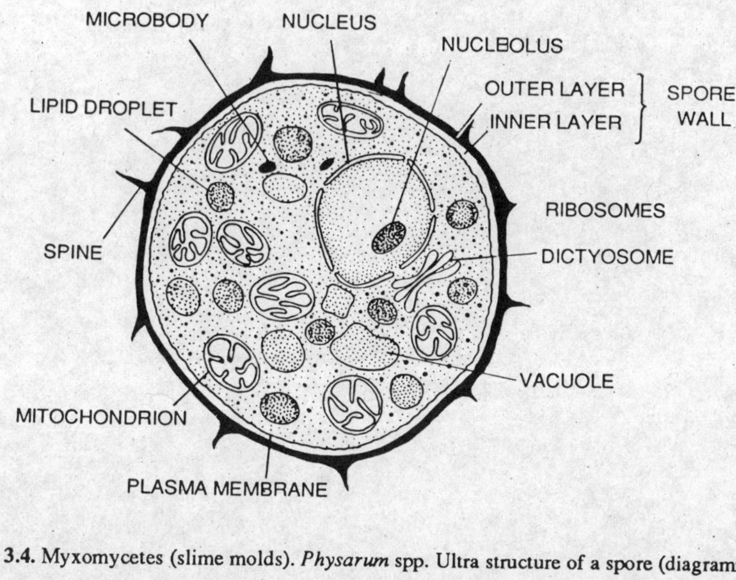

Fig. 3.4. Myxomycetes (slime molds). *Physarum* spp. Ultra structure of a spore (diagrammatic).

Systematic Position

G. W. Martin (1961)	C. J. Alexopoulos (1962)	G. C. Ainswoth (1971)
Kingdom–Plantae	Kingdom–Plantae	Kingdom–Fungi
Division–Mycota	Division–Mycota	Division–Myxomycota
Sub-div.–Myxomycotina	Sub-div.–Myxomycotina	Sub-div.–Myxomycotina
Class–Myxomycetes	Class–Myxomycetes	Class–Myxomycetes
Sub-cl.–Myxogastromycetidae	Sub-cl.–Myxogastromycetidae	Order–Stemonitales
Order–Stemonitales	Order–Stemonitales	Family–Stemonitaceae
Family–Stemonitaceae	Family–Stemonitaceae	Genus–*Stemonitis*
Genus–*Stemonitis*	Genus–*Stemonitis*	

4

Class–Chytridiomycetes

Kingdom–PLANTAE
Division–MYCOTA
Sub-division–EUMYCOTINA
Class–CHYTRIDIOMYCETES
The posteriorly uniflagellate fungi
(Alexopoulos, 1962)

G. W. Martin (1961)	**G. C. Ainsworth (1971)**
Kingdom–**PLANTAE**	Kingdom–**FUNGI**
Division–**MYCOTA**	Division–**EUMYCOTA**
Sub-div.–**EUMYCOTINA**	Sub-div.–**MASTIGOMYCOTINA**
Class–**PHYCOMYCETES**	Class–**CHYTRIDIOMYCETES**

Occurrence. They are typically found in aquatic habitats. However, several of them are found in soil. Some of them parasitize and destroy algae. Members of the genus *Synchytrium* are parasitic on economic plants.

Characteristic features. The most characteristic feature of this class is the production of motile cells (*i.e.*, zoospores or planogametes) each with a single, posterior, whiplash flagellum.

The other characters are—1. The coenocytic structure of the thallus, which may be a multinucleate globose or oval structure, on elongated simple hypha, or a well developed mycelium.

2. The zygote converts into a resting spore or resting sporangium, or it develops into a diploid conenocytic thallus.

3. The chief component of the cell wall is *chitin*.

Somatic structure. The primitive members of this class are unicellular and holocarpic. Such members do not possess any mycelium and sometimes in the early stages of their development they lack cell walls. Certain more advanced species possess a few **rhizoids,** which anchor the unicellular organism to its substratum. The rhizoids are short, possessing thin branches and resemble a root system. Some species produce a many branched **rhizomycelium.** The hypha-like filaments of this system do not contain nuclei. The most advanced members of this class possess a true mycelial thallus. The hyphae are typically coenocytic, but the septa are formed at the base of reproductive organs. Such septa are solid plates. The principal components of a chytrid cell wall is chitin and non-cellulosic alkali-insoluble *glucan*.

Asexual reproduction. The asexual reproduction takes place by means of sporangium and zoospores. The young sporangium is full of protoplasm and contains many nuclei. As the development of the sporangium continues, the entire protoplast divides into numerous minute parts by means of cleavage. Each minute part develops into a uninucleate zoospore. Each zoospore is uninucleate and possesses a single, posterior whiplash flagellum. There is a nuclear cap which partially or wholly covers the nucleus. The most characteristic element of the zoospore is the refractive lipoid globule, which may be quite conspicuous in some species. In some species it is extremely minute but in others it occupies sometimes two-third of the whole body. After discharge the zoospore swims for some time, encysts and withdraws its flagellum and then germinates usually after a short rest period.

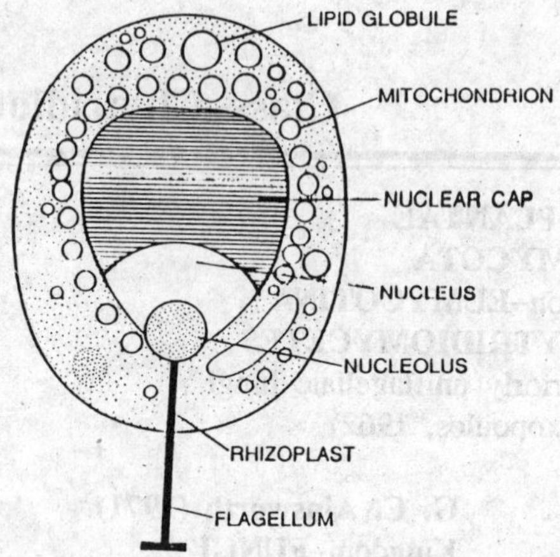

Fig. 4.1. Chytridales. A zoospore. (After Koch, 1961).

Sexual reproduction. Sexual reproduction in this class of fungi is accomplished by any one of the following methods:

(i) *Planogametic copulation.* The conjugation may take place by *isogamous* or *anisogamous* planogametes. In *isogamy* two gametes are morphologically identical, but physiologically dissimilar. They unite to form a zygote, *e.g.*, in *Synchytrium endobioticum.* In *anisogamy* one planogamete is larger than the other. Copulation takes place in water, and a motile zygote is resulted, *e.g.*, in some species of Blastocladiales. In certain other cases a non-motile female gamete and a motile male gamete are fused together to form a zygote. This type of reproduction is found in Monoblepharidales.

(ii) *Gametangial copulation.* In some chytrids, the entire protoplast of one gametangium passes into the other and a zygote is produced.

Classification. The Chytridiomycetes are classified into *three* orders—1. Chytridiales; 2. Blastocladiales and 3. Monoblepharidales (also see chapter two—Classification of Fungi).

ORDER CHYTRIDIALES

(83 genera; 300 species)

Characteristic features

1. The thallus is never a true mycelium.
2. The asexual reproduction takes place by means of posteriorly uniflagellate zoospores. The flagellum is of whiplash type.
3. The sexual reproduction takes place by means of isogamy or anisogamy.
4. There are about 83 genera and 300 species.

Classification. This order has been sub-divided into several families. According to Sparrow (1943), there are nine families. Here, the genus *Synchytrium* of family Synchytriaceae has been discussed in detail.

Family–Synchytriaceae

Characteristic features

1. The family includes holocarpic Chytridiales parasitic on higher plants. *Synchytrium endobioticum* causes the wart disease of potato. Many species are parasitic on mosses, ferns and angiosperms; host plants in wet places are specially liable to attack.
2. The thallus is divided into several reproductive organs, *i.e.*, sporangia or gametangia which are surrounded by a common membrane forming a sorus.

3. Asexual reproduction takes place by posteriorly uniflagellate zoospores.
4. Sexual reproduction takes place by the fusion of uniflagellate isogamous planogametes.
5. According to Sparrow (1960), there are three genera, of which *Synchytrium* is the largest and studied in detail.

Genus—SYNCHYTRIUM (about 200 species—Karling)

Synchytrium is the largest and most commonly known genus of Synchytriaceae and is reported to include almost 200 species. These species are world-wide in distribution and occur in the tropics, temperate zone, and arctic regions as well as low and high altitudes. They have been reported to occur in abundance at sea level and on mountains upto more than 11,000 feet high, whose peaks are covered by snow until late spring and early summer.

All species are parasitic and occur in algae, mosses, ferns and flowering plants. They occur most commonly on flowering plants growing in a moist environment. Since water is essential to zoospore maturation, dissemination and infection, the majority of species have been reported from temporary swamps, ditches and intermittently inundated meadows. Infection usually occurs in the seedling stage of the host; only occasionally the leaves of mature plants become infected immature.

Species of *Synchytrium* may be cosmopolitan in their hosts, also. Upto the present time, they have been reported on more than 1350 different host species in 773 genera and 168 plant families. *Synchytrium endobioticum* for example, is limited to the family Solanaceae.

The species which occur on flowering plants cause the development of the galls—minute, separate and scattered, or conspicuous, composite and confluent, or compound—on the leaves, petioles, flower buds, and stems. These galls may be unicellular or multicellular and are the result of cell enlargement, or cell division, or a combination of both processes. Some species may cause only enlargement of the infected cell alone, while others stimulate adjacent cells to divide and enlarge. In some species, the galls or tumors produced may be so numerous and large that the infected organs become markedly hypertrophied and malformed, *e.g., S. endobioticum.* The aquatic species which parasitize algae may cause marked local enlargement as well as elongation of the infected cell. Most terrestrial species occur on the leaves, petioles, and stems of the host, but some members like *S.fragariae* and *S. endobioticum,* infect the roots and underground stems.

S. endobioticum, causes the destructive wart disease of potatoes. The zygotes of this parasite stimulate the infected cells as well as neighbouring cells to rapid division and enlargement. As the galls become confluent enormous warts, excrescences, and outgrowths may be formed. Frequently, young tubers of susceptible varieties may become so malformed that they are hardly recognizable as potatoes. *S. trichosanthidis* attacks the fruits and leaves of *Trichosanthes dioica,* a cucurbit of much importance as a vegetable in India. The diseased fruits become prematurely yellow and lose flavour, which affects their quality and market value. *S. sesamicola* causes a serious disease of *Sesamum indicum* in India. This species attacks the young axillary shoots near the ground, and they become curled, spindly and malformed, and the leaves become puckered and curled. Severely infected plants fail to bear flowers or capsules and wither away prematurely.

About 60 species of *Synchytrium* have been recorded from this country. Some important species are—*Synchytrium anemones, S, biophyti; S. cajani; S. cassiae; S. cooki; S. crotalariae; S. cyperi; S. desmodicolum; S. dolichi; S. endobioticum; S. fistulosus; S. hibisci; S. indicum; S. khandalensis; S. lagenariae; S. launeae; S. luffae; S. meliloti; S, melongenae; S. oldenlandiae; S. phaseoli-radiati; S. phyllanthi; S. phyllanthicolum; S. piperi; S. rhynchosiae; S. sesami; S. sesamicola; S. thirumalachari; S. trichosanthidis; S. vernoniae; S. viticola* etc.

Synchytrium endobioticum is an obligate parasite of potatoes causing the black wart disease. In India, this disease is found only in Darjeeling district and its surroundings. This is a common disease of potato in United Kingdom and other European countries.

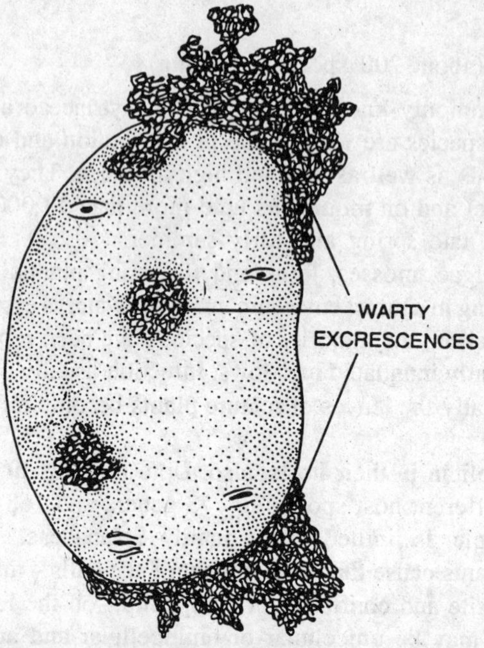

Fig. 4.2. *Synchytrium endobioticum.* Potato wart affected tuber, showing warty excrescences.

This fungus produces large or small greyish yellow, warty excrescences on the tubers and rarely on the leaves. The stolons may also be infected but warty excrescences are not produced. The roots are not infected. However, the growth of the plant is not being attacked. In the last stage the warts rot into a putrid mass, which exudes a dark brown liquid.

Somatic structure. The body of fungus is composed of a single uninucleate cell with a definite cell wall. The organism absorbs its food material from the cell contents of the host. It is incapable of extending to other cells. (See fig. 4.1. on pp. 42).

Asexual stage. In the spring season, the posteriorly uniflagellate zoospores are released from the infected tubers in the soil where they swim in the film of water and ultimately infect the healthy tubers. The zoospore comes in contact of the epidermal cell of the host and dissolves a minute pore. The protoplast enters the minute pore leaving the flagellum outside. After entrance the amoeboid spore settles in the bottom of the cell. Now the protoplast absorbs food from the surrounding host cells and increases sufficiently in size. Its nucleus also increases in size. This becomes rounded and a thick brown wall is secreted around it. This structure is called the **'summer spore'.**

Simultaneously, the host cell becomes hypertrophied, enlarged and pear-shaped. The surrounding cells of the infected cell divide again and again and a rosette of host cells is developed around the infected cell. These rosette cells are somewhat corky and hard in nature.

The summer spore reaches the lower half portion of the infected cell. The infected cell becomes dead by this time. After maturation, the summer spore germinates inside the host cell producing a tube-like structure. Very soon the protoplast is transferred in the upper half of the infected cell, which is surrounded by a thin delicate membrane. The nucleus of the protoplast divides repeatedly mitotically converting the protoplast into a multinucleate **prosorus.** At this stage there are about 32 nuclei in the prosorus.

Now, the prosorus becomes segmented. About 4-9 multinucleate chambers are formed. The nuclei of each chamber divide repeatedly and ultimately 200-300 nuclei are produced in each of the segments or chambers.

Each segment of the prosorus develops into a sporangium or a gametangium. If it is sporangium, the entire protoplast of each sporangium becomes segmented into as many portions as there are nuclei. Each portion is metamorphosed into a posterior uniflagellate zoospore. These posteriorly uniflagellate zoospores are released from the sporangium in the film of water which infect the tubers. The zoospores are only formed in the favourable conditions of water supply and appropriate temperature.

If, on the other hand there is scarcity of water and conditions are much drier, the segments of the prosorus develop into gametangia, and the released motile cells are called the planogametes. These planogametes fuse in pairs and ultimately zygotes are formed.

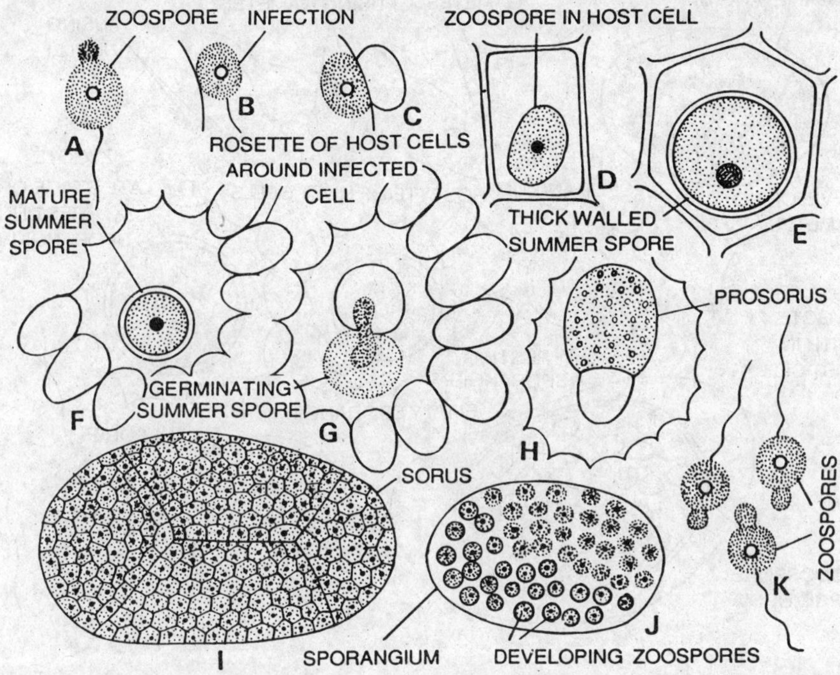

Fig. 4.3. *Synchytrium endobioticum.* Potato wart. A, zoospores; B-C, infection; D, zoospore established in lower half of the host cell; E, thick walled summer spore within host cell; F, mature summer spore, rosette of host cells around infected cell; G, germination of summer spore; H, prosorus; I, sorus; J, sporangium with developing zoospores; K, zoospores (uniflagellate)

According to Miss Curtis (1921), the dry conditions favour the formation of the planogametes.

Sexual stage. The planogametes are quite similar to the zoospores, except that they are somewhat smaller in size. The planogametes from two different gametangia may even of the same sorus copulate in pairs. The planogametes of different gametangia are physiologically different. The copulation of the planogametes takes place in the film of the water found on the surface of the host in the soil. The plasmogamy is followed by karyogamy and the zygote is resulted. The biflagellate zygote swims for some time in the water film, the flagella are withdrawn and it settles on the surface of the host. It makes a pore at the wall of contact and the protoplast is transferred inside the epidermal cell of the host. The protoplast of the zygote soon settles in the bottom of the infected cell where it enlarges in size, becomes thick walled and converts into a **resting sporangium.** The surrounding cells of the infected cell are stimulated and divide repeatedly giving rise to a rosette of the cells. The resting sporangium remains dormant in the winter and becomes active in the next spring. In the next spring a large number of granules which act as zoospore primordia, appear in the cytoplasm of the resting sporangium. Miss Curtis, however, has not observed meiosis during the formation of zoospores. But it is assumed that there is reduction division during the formation of zoospores. The zoospores liberate from the resting sporangium and infect the tubers. These zoospores are somewhat larger in size than the zoospores released from the asexually produced sporangia.

Control. The control measures of 'potato wart disease' are as follows.

In many countries various degrees of quarantine have been practised to reduce spread

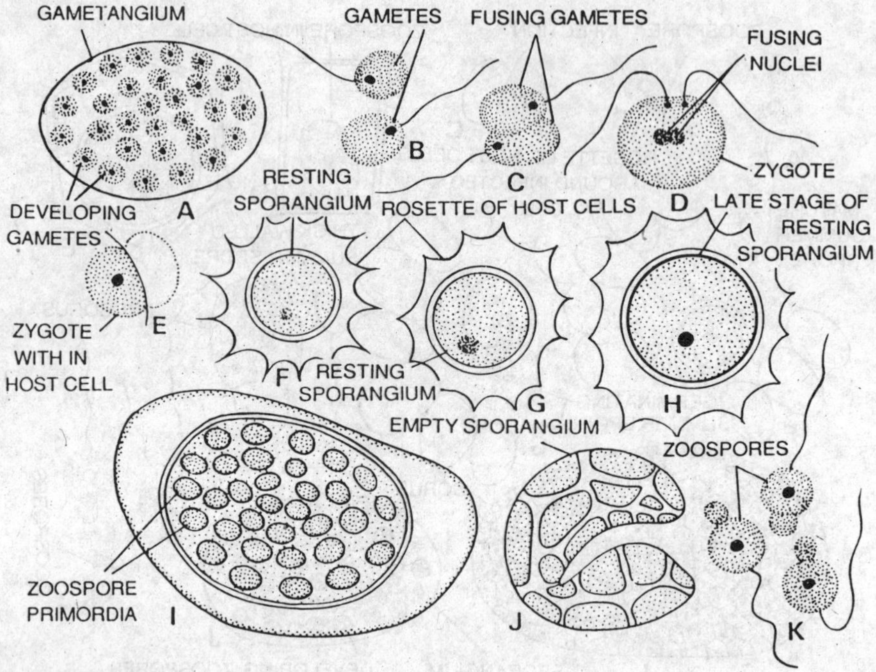

Fig. 4.4. *Synchytrium endobioticum.* Potato wart. A, developing gametes within gametangium; B, gametes; C, pairing of gametes; D, zygote; E, infection by zygote; F, resting sporangium within infected cell, infected cell being surrounded by rosette of host cells; G-H, developing resting sporangium; I, zoospore primordia; J, bursting sporangium and releasing zoospores; K, uniflagellate zoospores.

of the pathogen. The quarantine regulations should be observed strictly. In India, the disease has been confined to the north-eastern Himalayan region (Darjeeling Hills) by prohibiting the introduction of seed potatoes from the region. In U. S. A. and other European countries the experiments on soil have been conducted to eradicate the disease. This procedure, while possible by several means is too costly and impracticable to apply. The only feasible control is to use resistant varieties.

Systematic Position

	G. W. Martin (1961)	**C. J. Alexopoulos (1962)**	**G. C. Ainswoth (1971)**
Kingdom	–Plantae	–Plantae	–Fungi
Division	–Mycota	–Mycota	–Eumycota
Sub-div.	–Eumycotina	–Eumycotina	–Mastigomycotina
Class	–Phycomycetes	–Chytridiomycetes	–Chytridiomycetes
Sub-cl.	–Oomycetidae		
Order	–Chytridiales	–Chytridiales	–Chytridiales
Family	–Synchytriaceae	–Synchytriaceae	–Synchytriaceae
Genus	–*Synchytrium*	–*Synchytrium*	–*Synchytrium*
Species	–*endobioticum*	–*endobioticum*	–*endobioticum*

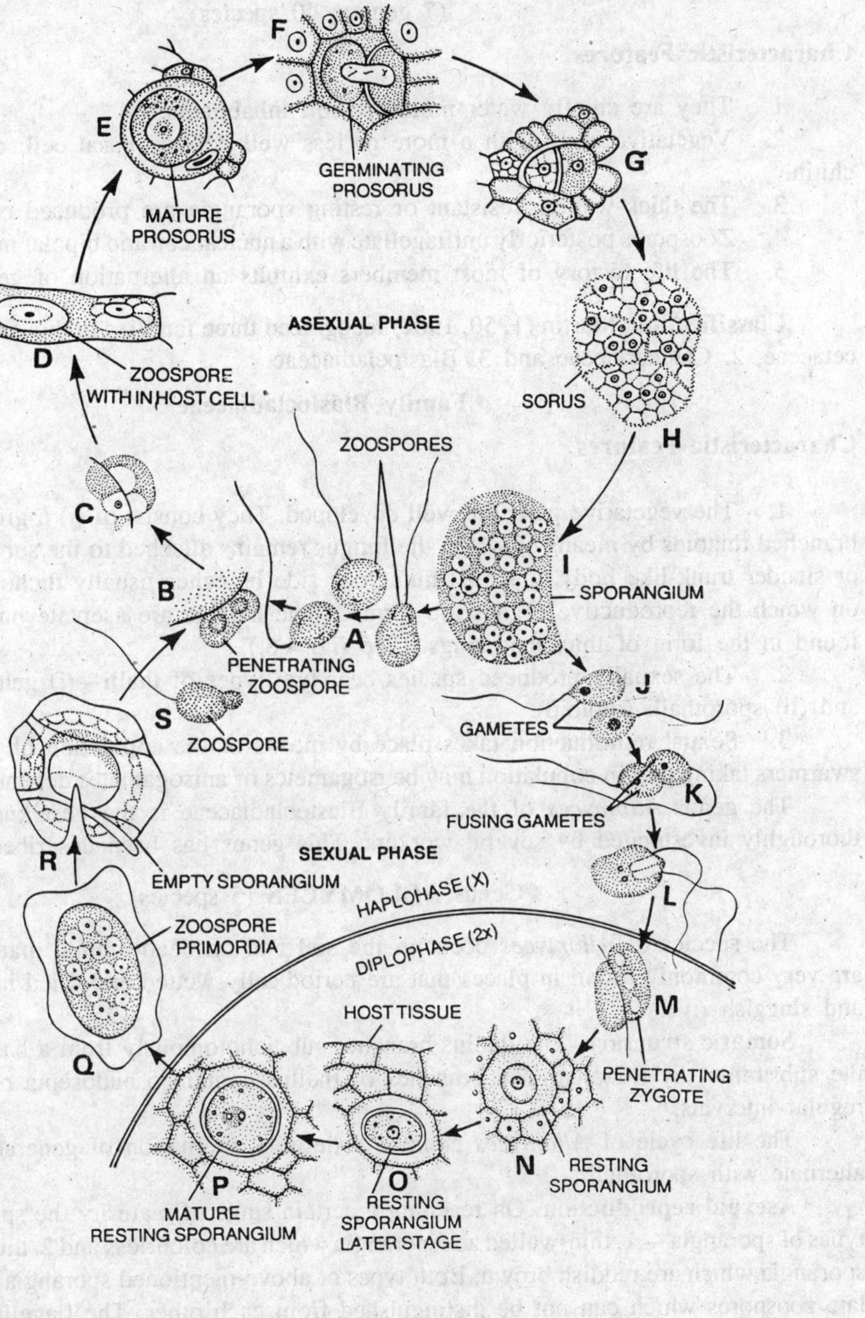

Fig. 4.5. *Synchytrium endobioticum.* Diagrammatic life-cycle; A, zoospores; B, penetrating zoospores on the surface of the host; C, penetration in advanced stage; D, zoospore within host cell; E, mature prosorus; F, germinating prosorus; G, nuclear division; H, sorus; I, sporangium or gametangium; J, planogametes; K, copulation of isogametes; L, motile zygote; M, penetrating zygote after losing flagella; N, resting sporangium; O, resting sporangium in later stage; P, mature resting sporangium; Q, zoospore primordia; R, empty sporangium; S, zoospore.

ORDER–BLASTOLADIALES

(7 genera; 40 species)

Characteristic Features

1. They are chiefly water molds or soil inhabitants.
2. Vegetative body with a more or less well defined basal cell; cell wall chiefly of chitin.
3. The thick-walled, resistant or resting sporangia are produced on the thalli.
4. Zoospores posteriorly uniflagellate with a nuclear cap and bipolar mode of germination.
5. The life history of most members exhibits an alternation of generations.

Classification. Martin (1950, 1961) recognized three families in this order 1. Coelomomycetaceae, 2. Catenariaceae and 3. Blastocladiaceae.

Family–Blastocladiaceae

Characteristic Features

1. The vegetative parts are well developed. They consist of (i) a group of well formed branched rhizoids by means of which the fungus remains attached to the substratum, (ii) a stout or slender trunk-like body, and (iii) numerous side branches usually dichotomously branched on which the reproductive organs are formed. The hyphae are aseptate but pseudoseptae are found in the form of thickened rings. (See fig. 4.6.).
2. The sexually produced species bear two types of thalli—(i) gametothalli (haploid) and (ii) sporothalli (diploid).
3. Sexual reproduction takes place by means of the copulation of planogametes. The swarmers taking part in copulation may be isogametes or anisogametes depending on the species.

The genus *Allomyces* of the family Blastocladiaceae is the best known and has been thoroughly investigated by several workers. This genus has been described here in detail.

Genus ALLOMYCES (5 species)

The species of *Allomyces* occur in the soil and on dead animal matter in water. They are very commonly found in places that are periodically wetted and dried in rice fields, ponds and sluggish rivers.

Somatic structure. The thallus branches subdichotomously from a basal cell attached to the substratum by rhizoids. The branches of thallus contain pseudosepta of cellulin at fairly regular intervals.

The life cycle of *Allomyces* exhibits a definite alternation of generations; gametothalli alternate with sporothalli.

Asexual reproduction. On reaching a certain stage of maturity the sporothalli form two types of sporangia— 1. thin-walled zoosporangia which are colourless and 2. thick-walled resistant sporangia which are reddish brown. Both types of above-mentioned sporangia produce uniflagellate zoospores which can not be distinguished from each other. The flagellum is of whiplash type. The zoospores swim for a while, come to rest, become rounded and apparently absorb the flagellum into the body. Thereafter they germinate at both the ends. One end gives rise to the rhizoidal portion while the other end gives rise to a slender germ tube. The rhizoidal portion of the thallus develops first.

The zoospores produced from the thin-walled zoosporangia are diploid and consequently give rise to sporothalli; the zoospores produced from resistant sporangia are haploid; meiosis takes place during their development and consequently give rise to gametothalli.

Sexual reproduction. The sexual reproduction takes place by means of antheridia and oogonia. The colourless oogonia and orange coloured antheridia develop on gametothalli. The antheridia are smaller and borne on the oogonia as in *Allomyces javanicus*. In *Allomyces arbuscula* the smaller antheridia are borne below the oogonia. Both oogonia and antheridia release planogametes in the water. The female gametes are always larger than the male gametes. Both male and female types of planogametes are posteriorly uniflagellate. The flagellum is of whiplash type in each case.

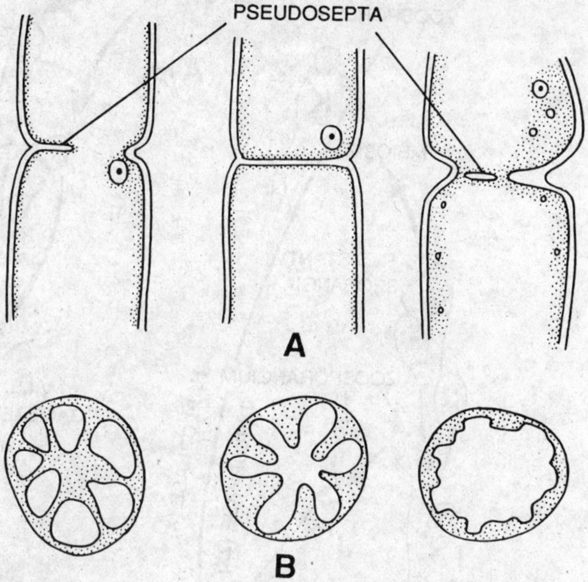

Fig. 4.6. *Allomyces arbuscula*. A, pseudosepta as seen in L.S.; B, same as in T.S.

Soon after their liberation from the gametangia the anisogametes coupulate in water. Karyogamy follows plasmogamy. The motile zygote soon comes to rest and eventually germinates into a sporothallus.

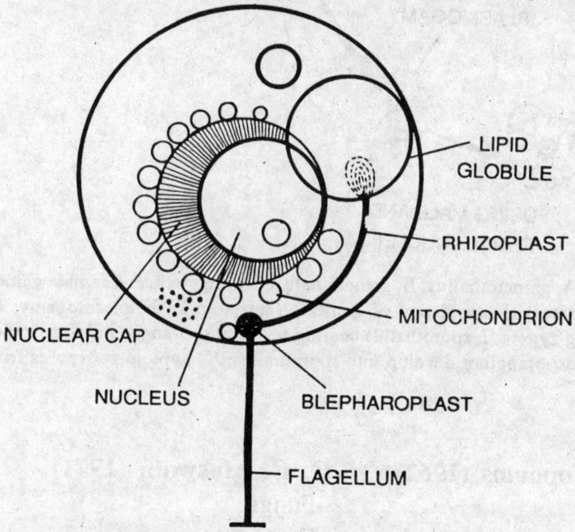

Fig. 4.7. *Allomyces* sp. A zoospore (After Koch, 1961).

Alternation of generations. The life-cycle exhibits distinct alternation of generations. The sporothallus bears two types of sporangia, *i.e.*, thin-walled sporangia and thick-walled resistant sporangia. The zoospores produced from thin-walled sporangia are diploid and consequently give rise to sporothalli; the zoospores produced from resistant spornagia are haploid, meiosis having taken place during their development and consequently give rise to sporothalli. The gametothallus produces male and female planogametes which after copulation develop into a zygote (2x), the zygote gives rise to sporothallus. This shows an alternation of generations.

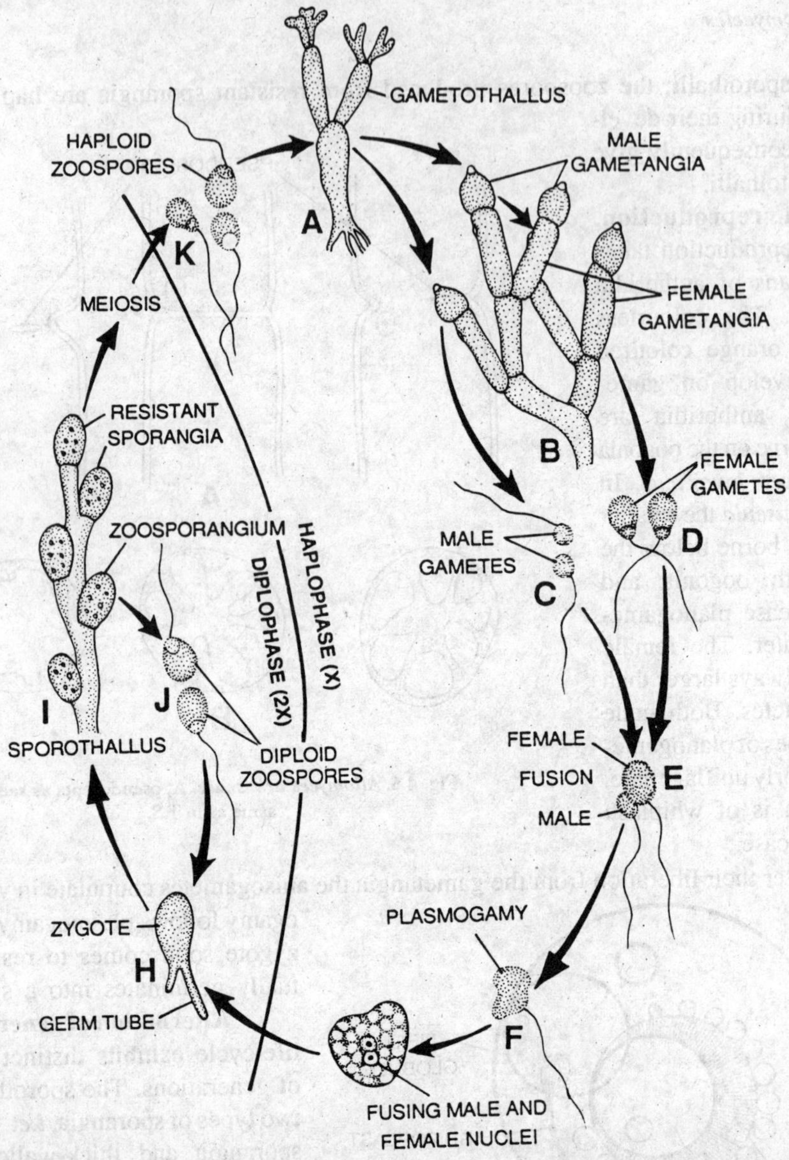

Fig. 4.8. *Allomyces*. Diagrammatic life-cycle A, gametothallus; B, gametothallus bearing male and female gametangia; C, smaller male gametes; D, larger female gametes; E, copulation of gametes (anisogamy); F, plasmogamy; G, karyogamy resulting in zygote formation; H, germinating zygote; I, sporothallus bearing resistant sporangia and thin-walled zoosporangia; J, diploid zoospores from thin-walled zoosporangium develop into sporothallus; K, haploid zoospores from resistant sporangia develop into gametothallus.

Systematic Position

	G. W. Martin (1961)	C. J. Alexopoulos (1962)	G. C. Ainswoth (1971)
Kingdom	–Plantae	–Plantae	–Fungi
Division	–Mycota	–Mycota	–Eumycota
Sub-div.	–Eumycotina	–Eumycotina	–Mastigomycotina
Class	–Phycomycetes	–Chytridiomycetes	–Chytridiomycetes
Sub-class	–Oomycetidae		
Order	–Blastocladiales	–Blastocladiales	–Blastocladiales
Family	–Blastocladiaceae	–Blastocladiaceae	–Blastocladiaceae
Genus	–*Allomyces*	–*Allomyces*	–*Allomyces*

ORDER–MONOBLEPHARIDALES

Characteristic Features

1. They are primarily aquatic fungi usually found in clear water and grow on dead twigs of various trees.
2. They have a well developed mycelium that produces sporangia and sex organs. The sporangia are terminal on the hyphae and elongate. They produce posteriorly uniflagellate zoospores.
3. Sexual reproduction is oogamous, with a single non-motile egg in an oogonium and with motile male gametes.
4. They are the only oogamous Phycomycetes which produce motile antherozoids.
5. In this order the naked zygote may emerge from the oogonium before forming a wall.

Classification. There is but one family the Monoblepharidaceae. It contains 3 genera and 10 species. Some of which are aquatic and others are soil inhabiting.

The life-history of type species *Monoblepharis polymorpha* has been worked out in detail. This has been discussed here.

Genus **MONOBLEPHARIS** Cornu (7 species)
(Family–Monoblepharidaceae)

Occurrence. *Monoblepharis*, the only genus of the family Monoblepharidaceae is usually found in clear waters and growing on dead submerged twigs of various trees, it is also found on some other substrata. These substrata may be the needles of coniferous trees, submerged lichens, fungi and fruits.

Somatic structure. The mycelium is usually attached to the substratum by means of rhizoids. The mycelium consists of profusely branched hyphae which tend to lie free from one another. Sometimes it consists of freely branched hyphae which lie interwoven forming a felted mat. The hyphae are aseptate except where reproductive organs are formed. In *Monoblepharis polymorpha* the mycelium consists of hyphae whose protoplasm is highly vacuolated and, therefore, appears foamy in nature, this foamy appearance is the characteristic of the order.

Asexual reproduction. The elongated, cylindrical zoosporangia are borne singly at the hyphal tips. The zoosporangia are generally no larger in diameter than the somatic hyphae. The sporangia are separated from the rest of hypha by a transverse septum. The protoplast within a sporangium may contain a uniseriate or a multiseriate row of nuclei. In either case the cleavage of the sporangial contents takes place into uninucleate oblique bits of protoplasm which metamorphose into zoospores. The zoospores are posteriorly uniflagellate. The flagellum is of whiplash type. The zoospores escape through a circular pore formed at the apex of the mature sporangium. Through this opening the zoospores creep out one by one in an amoeboid fashion. The zoospores swim through the water for some time before coming to rest. Thereafter they retract the flagella, become rounded and each of them secretes a wall around it. They settle on some suitable substratum and germinate, each by a germ tube forming a new mycelium. In the beginning the mycelium forms two hyphae, one develops into rhizoidal system of the new plant and the other into the remaining part of the thallus.

Sexual reproduction. The sexual reproduction is oogamous. It takes place by means of a single egg (non-motile) in an oogonium and motile male gamete.

The same thallus which produces the zoosporangia produces gametangia when subjected to higher temperatures (Sparrow, 1943). The male and female gametangia are easily distinguishable from each other. The sex organs are formed by the development of transverse walls in the distal portion of a hypha. The cells produced this way alternately develop into antheridia and oogonia.

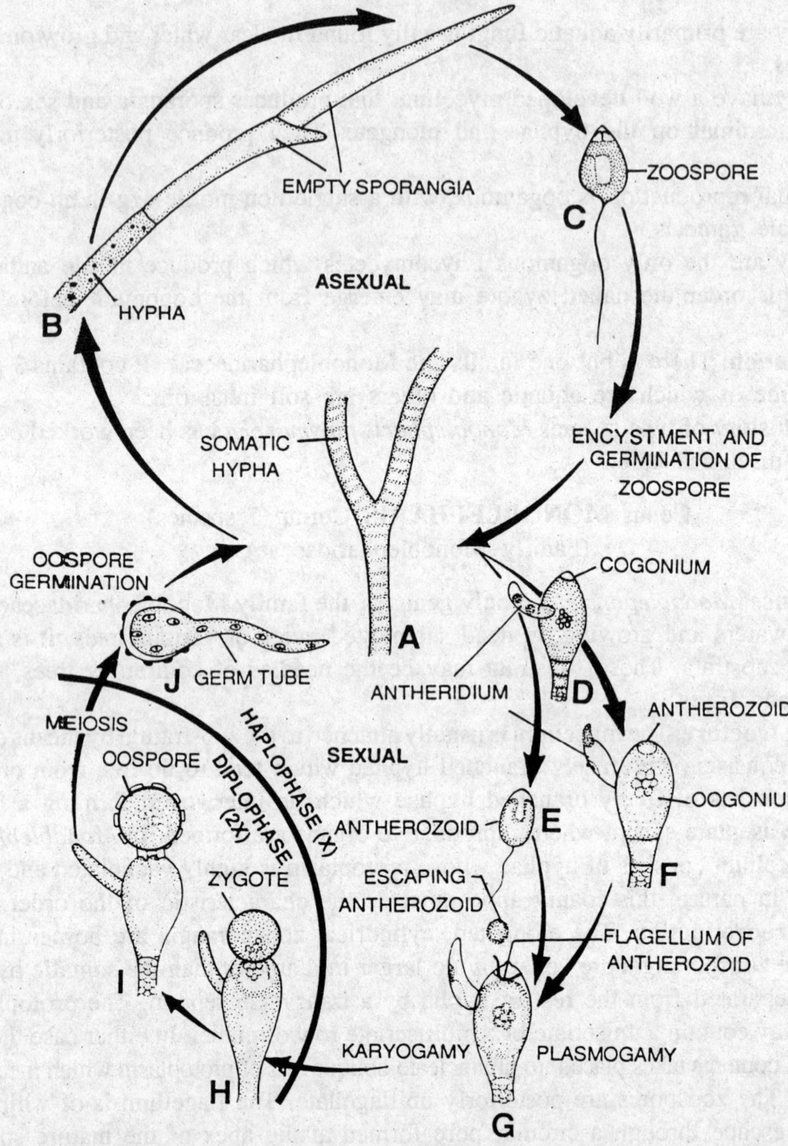

Fig. 4.9. *Monoblepharis*. Diagrammatic life-cycle; A, part of thallus showing characteristic foamy appearance; B, terminal empty zoosporangia; C, posteriorly uniflagellate zoospore; D, antheridium on oogonium; E, antherozoid-posteriorly uniflagellate; F, antherozoid entering the oogonium; G, plasmogamy; H, exuding zygote; I, oospore at apical end of oogonium; J, germinating oospore.

In some species the antheridia lie above oogonia while in others oogonia lie above the antheridia. In *Monoblepharis polymorpha* the narrow, elongated antheridia are borne on the rounded larger oogonia. A number of uniflagellate antherozoids are developed within the antheridium. Usually 4-7 antherozoids are formed within the antheridium but in *M. insignis* 24-32 antherozoids are formed within the antheridium.

The oogonial protoplast is uninucleate from the very beginning and during its development a pore is formed at the apex of oogonial wall. The protoplast becomes globose and forms a uninucleate oosphere.

Fertilization. At the time of fertilization the antherozoids swim or creep with a jerk to the oogonial wall until it reaches the pore. A single sperm enters the oogonium through the opening (papilla), penetrates the oosphere and fuses with it (plasmogamy). The nuclei appraoch each other and soon fuse (karyogamy). Thus formed zygote then emerges from the oogonium and while still attahced to the oogonial wall by a hyaline collar secretes a thick wall around it and converts into an oospore.

The oospore germinates under favourable conditions by means of a hypha which later on develops into a new thallus. During the germination of oospore there is a meiotic division of the fusion nucleus.

Systematic Position

	G. W. Martin (1961)	**C. J. Alexopoulos (1962)**	**G. C. Ainswoth (1971)**
Kingdom	–Plantae	–Plantae	–Fungi
Division	–Mycota	–Mycota	–Eumycota
Sub-div.	–Eumycotina	–Eumycotina	–Mastigomycotina
Class	–Phycomycetes	–Chytridiomycetes	–Chytridiomycetes
Sub-cl.	–Oomycetidae	–	–
Order	–Monoblepharidales	–Monoblepharidales	–Monoblepharidales
Family	–Monoblepharidaceae	–Monoblepharidaceae	–Monoblepharidaceae
Genus	–*Monoblepharis*	–*Monoblepharis*	–*Monoblepharis*

5

Class–Plasmodiophoromycetes

Kingdom–**PLANTAE**
Division–**MYCOTA**
Sub-division–**EUMYCOTINA**
Class–**PLASMODIOPHOROMYCETES**
Endoparasitic Slime Molds
(Alexopoulos, 1962)

G. W. Martin (1961)	**G. C. Ainsworth (1971)**
Kingdom–**PLANTAE**	Kingdom–**FUNGI**
Division–**MYCOTA**	Division–**EUMYCOTA**
Sub-div.–**EUMYCOTINA**	Sub-div.–**MASTIGOMYCOTINA**
Class–**PHYCOMYCETES**	Class–**PLASMODIOPHOROMYCETES**

They are obligate endoparasites of vascular plants, algae and fungi. On being infected an abnormal enlargement of the host cells is caused, which is known as *hypertrophy*. Many species parasitize fresh water algae such as *Vaucheria* or aquatic fungi such as *Saprolegnia, Pythium, Achlya,* etc. Certain other species are found as parasites on aquatic and marsh vascular plants such as *Isoetes, Juncus* etc. *Plasmodiophora brassicae* causes club root or finger-and-toe disease of cabbage and other crucifers.

The somatic phase of this class is a plasmodium which develops within the host cells. Plasmodia give rise to zoosporangia which contain zoospores. Sometimes resting spores are produced by cleavage of the plasmodium into uninucleate portions. No fructifications are produced. However, in some genera the spores are united in spore balls. Each resting spore releases out a swarm cell, on its germination. The swarmers bear two unequal (heterokontean type), anterior flagella, both of the whiplash type.

During nuclear division, an intranuclear spindle is formed on which the chromosomes are found to be arranged in a ring around the nucleus. Later the nucleus begins to elongate and constricts in the centre. The dumbbell-shaped nucleus surrounded by a chromatin ring appears like a cross when viewed from the side, and therefore, to this phase of mitotic division, the name *cruciform* is given. In several members, the so-called *akaryotic phase* has been recorded. In this stage the nuclear body seems to disappear, and the chromatin does not take the usual stain.

Classification. Single order Plasmodiophorales; single family Plasmodiophoraceae (also see chapter two, Classification of Fungi).

ORDER–PLASMODIOPHORALES

(10 genera; 15 species)

Characteristic Features

1. They are endoparasites in higher plants or insects. Some of them are found to be parasitic

on fungi, algae and other cryptogams. They disintegrate the host and bring about the marked changes in its cells.

2. The vegetative body consists of a naked mass of protoplasm, the plasmodium; increase in size is accompanied by nuclear division, and ultimately the thallus breaks up into a number of walled spores. The spores are produced in large numbers inside sporangia.

3. The order includes some of very peculiar cytological phenomena.

4. The order includes a single family Plasmodiophoraceae.

Classification. Many mycologists include this order among the sub-class Archimycetes of class Phycomycetes. Bessey considered Plasmodiophorales before taking systematic study of Phycomycetes. The right place of this order has yet to be finally decided.

Family–Plasmodiophoraceae

Characteristic Features

1. A germinating spore gives rise to a biflagellate heterokontean swarmer. These swarmers behave either as zoospores or as gametes.

2. Sexual reproduction takes place by the union of planogametes.

3. The family includes about eight genera and several species. The best known species of the type genus (*Plasmodiophora*) is *Plasmodiophora brassicae* Woronin, a parasite of various Cruciferae, especially of the genus *Brassica. P. brassicae* causes the club-root or finger and toe disease of cabbage.

The most important and well known species, *i.e., Plasmodiophora brassicae* Woronin has been discussed here in detail.

Genus—PLASMODIOPHORA

Plasmodiophora brassicae Woronin

Plasmodiophora brassicae causes the club root of cabbage. The root decays and ultimately the whole plant decays. The root of the host plants gets swollen into club-shaped malformations

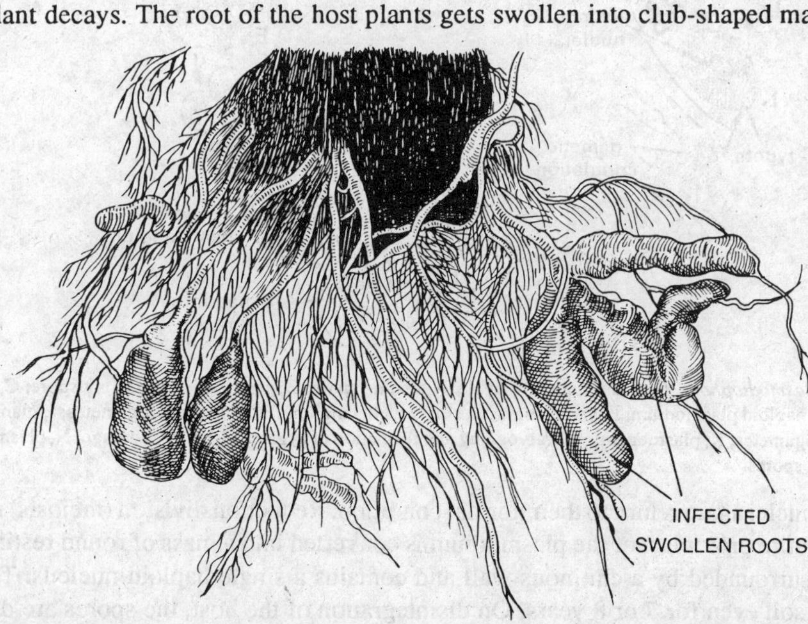

Fig. 5.1. *Plasmodiophora brassicae.* Club root of cabbage; symptoms finger and toe or irregular galls.

and therefore, the disease caused by this pathogen is known as club root of cabbage. There may be a single massive gall or more often several sweet potato-shaped galls, the reason for the name *'finger and toe'*. The parasite within the host cells causes **hypertrophy** or abnormal enlargement of the tissues as well as **hyperplasia,** *i.e.,* repeated division of cells. It is an obligate endoparasite.

Somatic structure. The vegetative or somatic phase of this organism is a plasmodium. It is a multinucleate naked protoplast. The plasmodium is coenocytic, *i.e.,* the nuclei are not separated by walls. The plasmodia are always found within the host cells. A mature plasmodium contains about 30 diploid nuclei. The young plasmodia absorb food and grow in size. The plasmodia may move from the infected large cell of the host into its neighbouring cells making them also infected.

Asexual reproduction. By the time the host dies, the plasmodium matures, it fills the host cells in which this lives. Its nuclei pass through a special phase called **akaryotic phase,** in which the nuclear body seems to disappear and chromatin of each nucleus extrudes out into the cytoplasm.

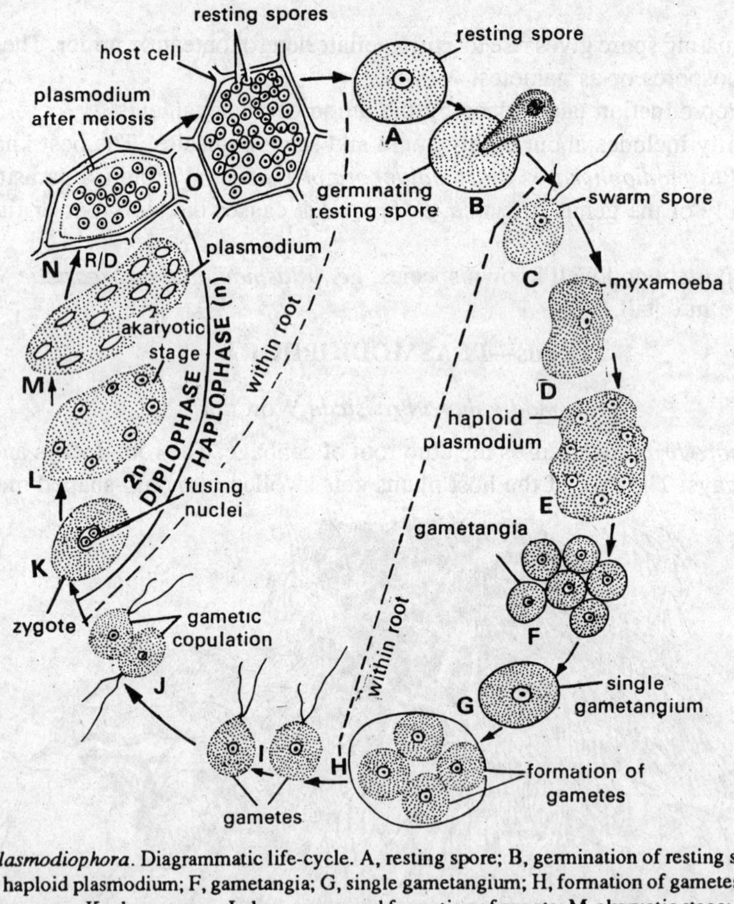

Fig. 5.2. *Plasmodiophora*. Diagrammatic life-cycle. A, resting spore; B, germination of resting spore; C, swarm cell; D, myxamoeba; E, haploid plasmodium; F, gametangia; G, single gametangium; H, formation of gametes; I, planogametes; J, copulation of planogametes; K, plasmogamy; L, karyogamy and formation of zygote; M, akaryotic stage; N, plasmodium after meiosis; O, resting spores.

Very soon the nuclei again return to their normal condition. Reduction division (meiosis) now takes place and the entire protoplast of the plasmodium is converted into a mass of round resting spores. Each spore is surrounded by a chitinous wall and contains a single haploid nucleus. The spores can live in the soil even for 7 or 8 years. On disintegration of the host, the spores are discharged into the soil. Infected soil contains spores. In favourable conditions the spores germinate. The spore wall breaks open and a uninucleate, pear-shaped biflagellate swarm cell or zoospore is released. The flagella are of very different size (heterokont) and both of them of whiplash type. Cook and

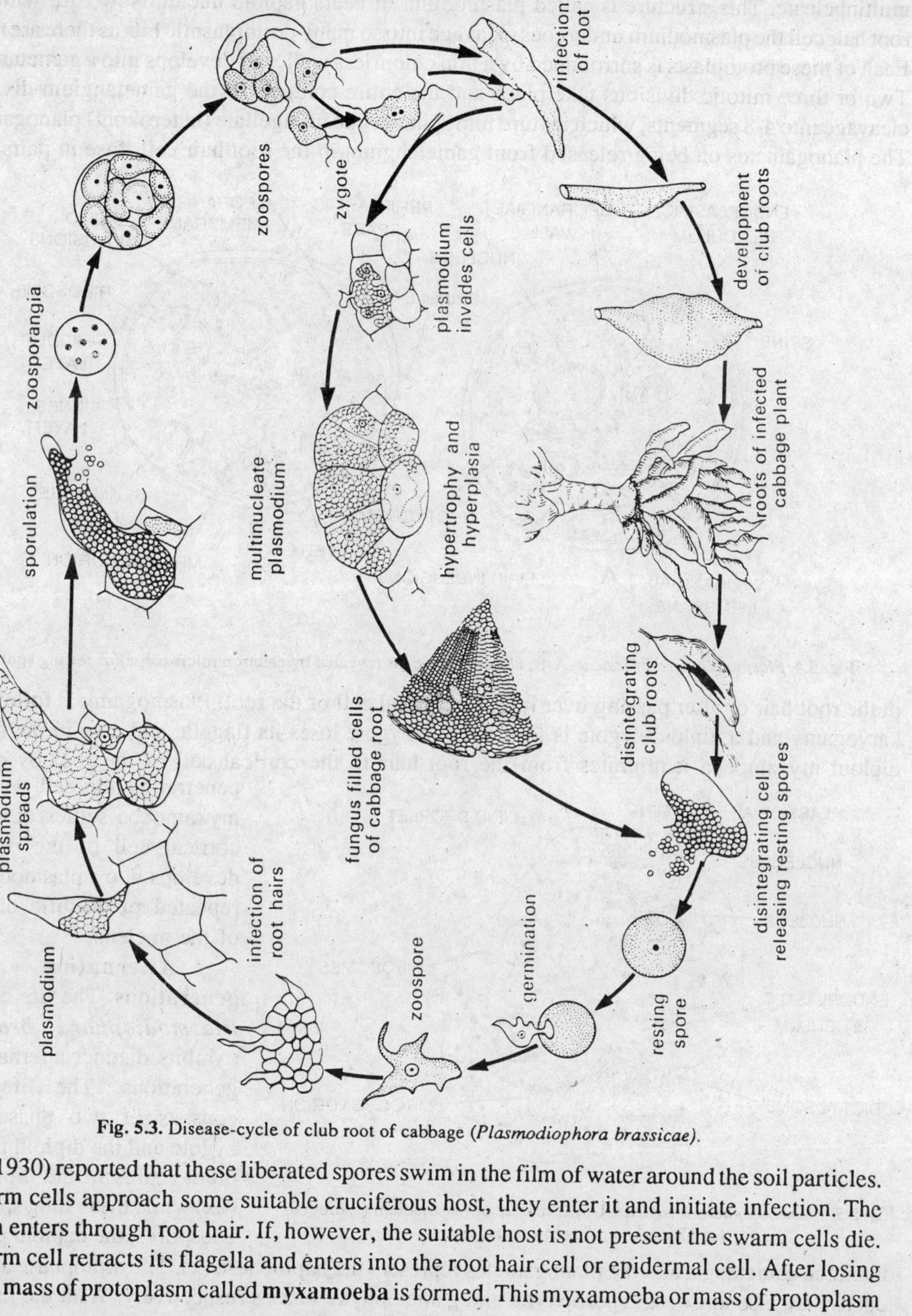

Fig. 5.3. Disease-cycle of club root of cabbage (*Plasmodiophora brassicae*).

Swartz (1930) reported that these liberated spores swim in the film of water around the soil particles. The swarm cells approach some suitable cruciferous host, they enter it and initiate infection. The organism enters through root hair. If, however, the suitable host is not present the swarm cells die. The swarm cell retracts its flagella and enters into the root hair cell or epidermal cell. After losing flagella a mass of protoplasm called **myxamoeba** is formed. This myxamoeba or mass of protoplasm enters the root hair in amoeboid fashion. The cell wall decays with the result of gelatinization and the myxamoeba enters the root hair.

Sexual reproduction. Within the root hair the myxamoeba grows in size, and becomes multinucleate. This structure is called plasmodium. It bears haploid nuclei. Now, still within the root hair cell the plasmodium undergoes cleavage into so many protoplasmic bits as there are nuclei. Each of these protoplasts is surrounded by a thin colourless wall, and develops into a gametangium. Two or three mitotic divisions take place and the entire contents of the gametangium divide by cleavage into 4-8 segments, which mature into spindle-like biflagellate (heterokont) planogametes. The planogametes on being released from gametangium in the root hair cell, fuse in pairs either

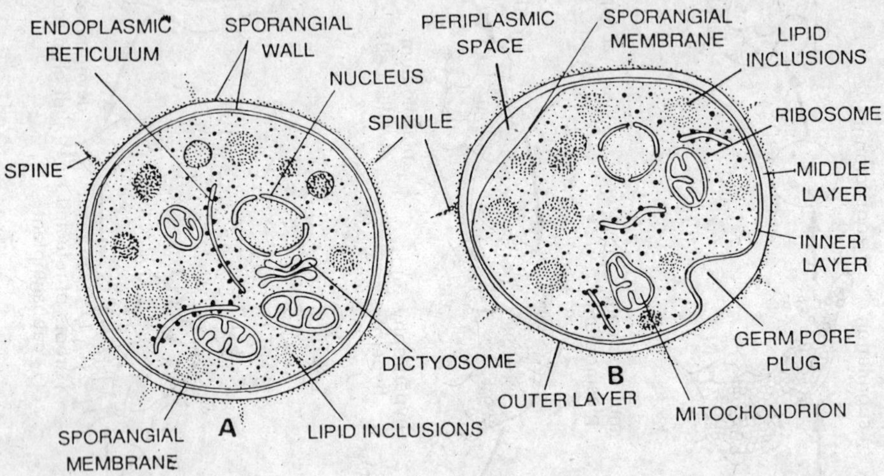

Fig. 5.4. *Plasmodiophora brassicae*. A-B, ultra structure (as revealed by electron microscope) of resting spores.

in the root hair or after passing over into the cortical cell of the root. Plasmogamy is followed by karyogamy and a diploid zygote is formed. The zygote loses its flagella and now in the form of diploid myxamoeba it migrates from the root hair to the cortical cell of the root by directly penetrating the cell wall. The myxamoeba settles down in a cortical cell of the root and develops into a plasmodium by repeated **promitotic** divisions of the nucleus.

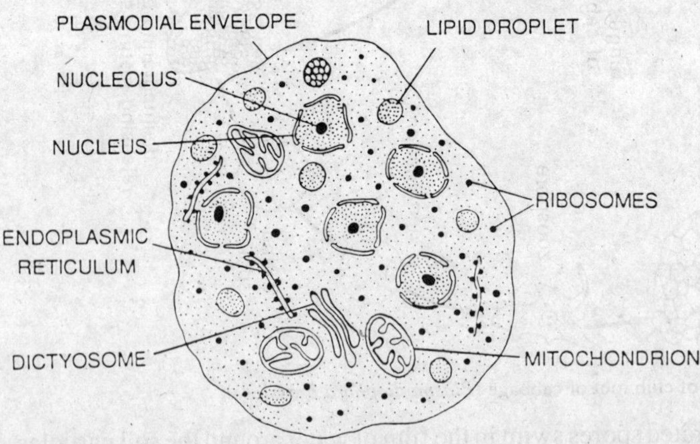

Fig. 5.5. *Plasmodiophora brassicae*. Ultrastructure of plasmodium (sporothallus). Diagrammatic representation.

Alternation of generations. The life cycle of *Plasmodiophora brassicae* exhibits distinct alternation of generations. The life cycle consists of two phases. The zygote and the diploid plasmodium represent the diplophase (2x) while the resting spore, the zoospores, the haploid plasmodium, the gametangia and the planogametes represent the haplophase (x). The diplophase and haplophase are also known as sporophytic and gametophytic phases respectively. With the fusion of planogametes the organism enters into a diplophase. On the contrary, the diploid plasmodium developed from the zygote after reduction division (meiosis) produces haploid resting spores which afterwards give rise to haploid zoospores. With meiosis the diplophase ends, and the haplophase starts; whereas after karyogamy the diplophase starts and haplophase ends.

Control. Since transplants are the most common means of local and widespread distribution of the fungus, it is important to use soil free from the pathogen in propagation of seedlings. Crop rotation has also been suggested. Proper drainage is favoured to lessen the disease. The most important remedy is to use resistant varieties.

Systematic Position

	G. W. Martin (1961)	**C. J. Alexopoulos (1962)**	**G. C. Ainsworth (1971)**
Kingdom	-Plantae	–Plantae	–Fungi
Division	–Mycota	–Mycota	–Eumycota
Sub-div.	–Eumycotina	–Eumycotina	–Mastigomycotina
Class	–Phycomycetes	–Plasmodiophoromycetes	–Plasmodiophoromycetes
Sub-cl.	–Oomycetidae		
Order	–Plasmodiophorales	–Plasmodiophorales	–Plasmodiophorales
Family	–Plasmodiophoraceae	–Plasmodiophoraceae	–Plasmodiophoraceae
Genus	–*Plasmodiophora*	–*Plasmodiophora*	–*Plasmodiophora*

6

Class–Oomycetes

Kingdom–**PLANTAE**
Division–**MYCOTA**
Sub-division–**EUMYCOTINA**
Class–**OOMYCETES**
Water Molds, White Rusts, Downy Mildews
(Alexopoulos, 1962)

G. W. Martin (1961)	**G. C. Ainsworth (1971)**
Kingdom–**PLANTAE**	Kingdom–**FUNGI**
Division–**MYCOTA**	Division–**EUMYCOTA**
Sub-div.–**EUMYCOTINA**	Sub-div–**MASTIGOMYCOTINA**
Class–**PHYCOMYCETES**	Class–**OOMYCETES**

The fungi belonging to this class reproduce asexually by means of biflagellate zoospores. Each such zoospore bears one flagellum of tinsel-type directed forward and the other of whiplash-type directed backward. The zoospores are borne endogenously in zoosporangia of various types.

The most advanced members of the Oomycetes are terrestrial and obligate parasites on vascular plants; several members are aquatic. The spores or spore-like sporangia of such parasites are wind disseminated.

The somatic structures of the Oomycetes range from a primitive unicellular thallus to a profusely branched filamentous mycelium, which grows abundantly in the substratum or in the host plant. Majority of the members are eucarpic. The characteristic components of the cell walls is cellulose.

The reproduction takes place by means of asexual and sexual methods. In all the members of this class the zoospores are produced except in the most advanced species (*e.g., Peronospora* sp.) where the sporangium behaves like a conidium or spore and germinates directly by a germ-tube which gives rise to the mycelium.

Sexual reproduction is always heterogamous. In the primitive Oomycetes, the entire thallus may act as a gametangium. With the result of the fusion of gametes the oospores are resulted except in the most primitive species. The oospores are developed within the oogonia and mature within them. The central part of the oogonium may be differentiated into one or more eggs (oospheres). The oospheres become uninucleate on maturation. In certain forms the oosphere becomes multinucleate and is known as *compound oosphere*.

Classification. There are *four* orders in this class. These orders are-1. Saprolegniales; 2. Leptomitales; 3. Lagenidiales and 4. Peronosporales. Of which the members of Saprolegniales and Peronosporales have been described in this text.

ORDER–SAPROLEGNIALES

(Water Molds)

(29 genera; 90 species)

Characteristic Features

1. Generally they are found in clear waters and called, 'water molds'. Many species are, however, found in soil.

2. Most of the species are saprophytic but some are important parasites. *Saprolegnia parasitica* causes disease of fish and fish eggs. The genus *Aphanomyces* causes root diseases of sugar beets, peas and other crops.

Classification. Sparrow has divided this order into three families—1. The Ectogellaceae. 2. The Thraustochytriaceae and 3. The Saprolegniaceae.

Family–Saprolegniaceae

The Saprolegniaceae is the most advanced family of the order. It contains many species. They possess a thallus composed of richly branched coenocytic hyphae. The remaining two families of the order do not possess any mycelium. The genus *Saprolegnia* may be regarded as typical of the family and has been discussed here in detail.

Genus SAPROLEGNIA (15 species)

Somatic structure. The mycelium is profusely branched and coenocytic. It is easily visible in the form of a colony around some bit of decaying plant or animal tissue in water. The septa are formed in the mycelium only when reproductive organs are produced. These septa separate the reproductive organs from the somatic hyphae, which are generally aseptate.

Asexual reproduction. Long, cylindrical, terminal zoosporangia are typically produced by the species of genus *Saprolegnia.* Generally the zoosporangia are of somewhat greater diameter than the hyphae on which they are produced. The zoosporangium is formed by an accumulation of protoplasm at the end of a hypha.

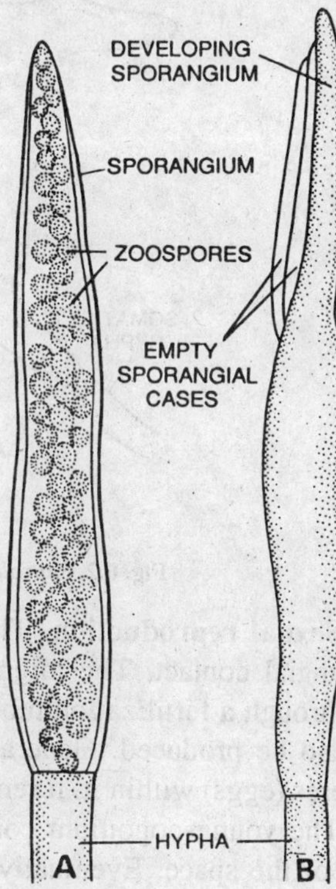

Fig. 6.1 *Saprolegnia*. Asexual reproduction. A, mature sporangium; B, sporangial proliferation showing empty sporangial cases and developing sporangium.

Within the zoosporangium, the zoospores are differentiated by a process of cleavage (Schwarz, 1922). A centrally placed vacuole in the young zoosporangium pushes the cytoplasm and nuclei against the wall, then irregular lines of cleavage appear on the inner face of this peripheral layer and spread radially outwards so that many uninucleate segments are cut out. These segments contract, expelling water from sporangium, and shrinkage occurs. The initials of zoospores become so much crowded together that their outlines become invisible. The cytoplasm again becomes granular, the zoospore initials further shrink, become round off, and are now ready to escape. The zoospores are released through an apical opening formed on the zoosporangium. The zoospores are pyriform with two apical flagella. The zoospores swim for a few minutes and then encyst. After a rest of about twenty-four hours each cyst gives rise to a reniform zoospore with two laterally inserted flagella. These zoospores again encyst and produce a mycelium on germination. The two types of zoospores are formed. The primary zoospores are pear-shaped and bear their two flagella at the apex; the secondary zoospores are reniform and bear their flagella at the concave side of the zoospore. This production of two different types of zoospores by the same fungus is known as **diplanetism.**

Sporangial proliferation is often seen in the species of *Saprolegnia* and related genera. In *Saprolegnia* it takes place as follows: When a sporangium empties its contents of spores, a secondary sporangium often initiates at the basal septum, and develops through the first sporangium. This way, several sporangia may be formed one within the other, each maturing and releasing its spores before the next one is formed. Generally the sporangia remain attached to the somatic hyphae throughout their lives, and even after they have discharged their spores.

Chlamydospores or gemmae. Chlamydospores often called gemmae arise by the condensation of hyphal contents with subsequent deposition of septa cutting off the evacuated position of the hypha. They are generally either singly or in chains. They are separated from each other on maturation and germinate by producing germ tubes.

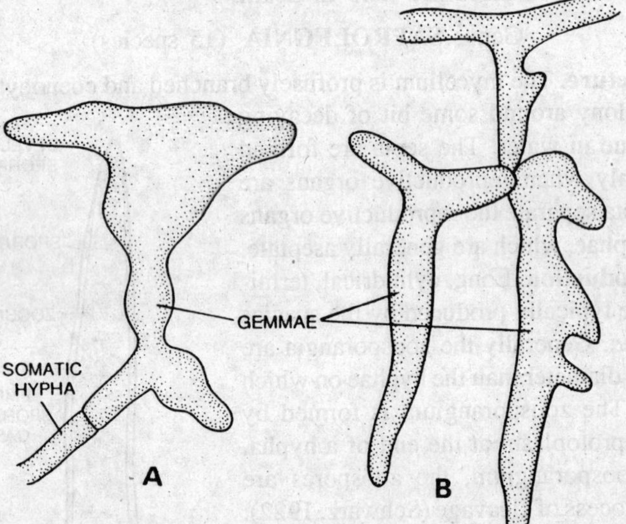

Fig. 6.2. *Saprolegnia*. Asexual reproduction; gemmae (chlamydospores).

Sexual reproduction. The sexual reproduction in *Saprolegnia* takes place by means of gametangial contact. The migration of the male gametes into the female gametangium takes place through a fertilization tube. The sex organs are generally terminal, but intercalary oogonia may also be produced. Generally the oogonium is globose and having one or more globular oospheres (eggs) within it. It remains delimited by a basal transverse septum from somatic hypha.

The young oogonium contains many nuclei and much cytoplasm, at first occupying the whole of the space. Eventually a central vacuole appears, enlarges and presses the cytoplasm and nuclei into a peripheral layer. Many nuclei disorganise and the protoplast becomes cleaved into a number (often five to ten) of uninucleate oospheres; these rounded off and lie free in the oogonium.

The young antheridium contains dense cytoplasm with a few nuclei. The elongated and multinucleate antheridia originate either on the same hyphal branch on which the oogonium is attached, on a different branch or on a different thallus. One or more antheridia become attached to the oogonium. The simple or branched fertilization tubes given out from the antheridium enter the oogonium, passing one nucleus to each oosphere (egg). The male nucleus fuses with the egg nucleus therein.

Fertilized oospheres develop a smooth colourless, thick wall and convert themselves into oospores. The oospore remains surrounded by a thick epispore and a thin endospore. After a period of rest the oospore germinates by means of a germ tube which later on after a short time gives rise to a zoosporangium. Karyogamy has been demonstrated in many species of the genus. In several species oospores develop parthenogenetically. (See life-cycle, p. 64)

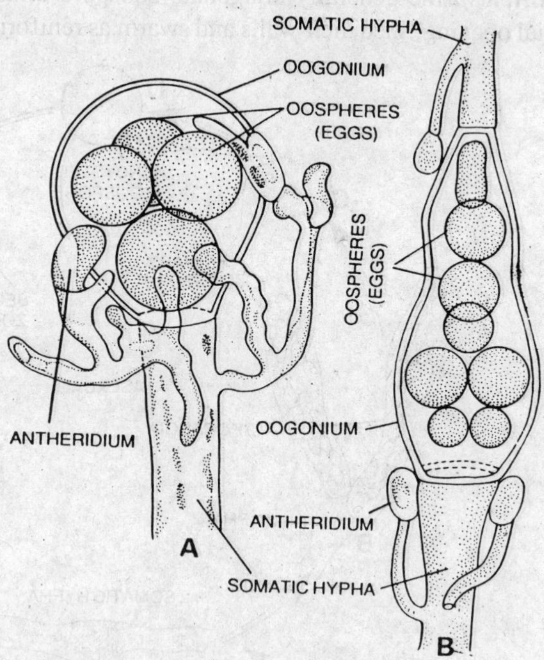

Fig. 6.3. *Saprolegnia*. Sexual reproductiion: A, terminal globose oogonium with antheridia; B, intercalary elongated oogonium with antheridia.

Systematic Position

	G. W. Martin (1961)	**C. J. Alexopoulos (1962)**	**G. C. Ainswoth (1971)**
Kingdom	–Plantae	–Plantae	–Fungi
Division	–Mycota	–Mycota	–Eumycota
Sub-div.	–Eumycotina	–Eumycotina	–Mastigomycotina
Class	–Phycomycetes	–Oomycetes	–Oomycetes
Sub-cl.	–Oomycetidae		
Order	–Saprolegniales	–Saprolegniales	–Saprolegniales
Family	–Saprolegniaceae	–Saprolegniaceae	–Saprolegniaceae
Genus	–*Saprolegnia*	–*Saprolegnia*	–*Saprolegnia*

Genus ACHLYA (35 species)

Habitat. They are mostly saprophytic and rarely parasitic on plant and animal substrata in water or soil. It is found all over the world. It occurs in pools, ponds, streams, stagnant waters, aquaria etc. In laboratory, the fungus can easily be grown on hemp seeds and dead flies.

Mycelium. The mycelium is tubular, slender, coenocytic and less branched which is generally visible as it forms a colony around some bit of decaying plant or animal tissue in water or soil. The septa formed in the mycelium just beneath the reproductive organs separating them from the somatic hyphae, which generally remain aseptate.

Asexual reproduction. Long cylindrical, terminal zoosporangia are produced. Generally, the sporangia are of some greater diameter than the hyphae on which they are produced. The sporangia are renewed by lateral outgrowth of a portion of the hypha next the empty sporangium.

In *Achlya* the generally aflagellate zoospore initials form a small cluster in front of the sporangial opening, shed their walls and swarm as reniform zoospores with lateral flagella, leaving

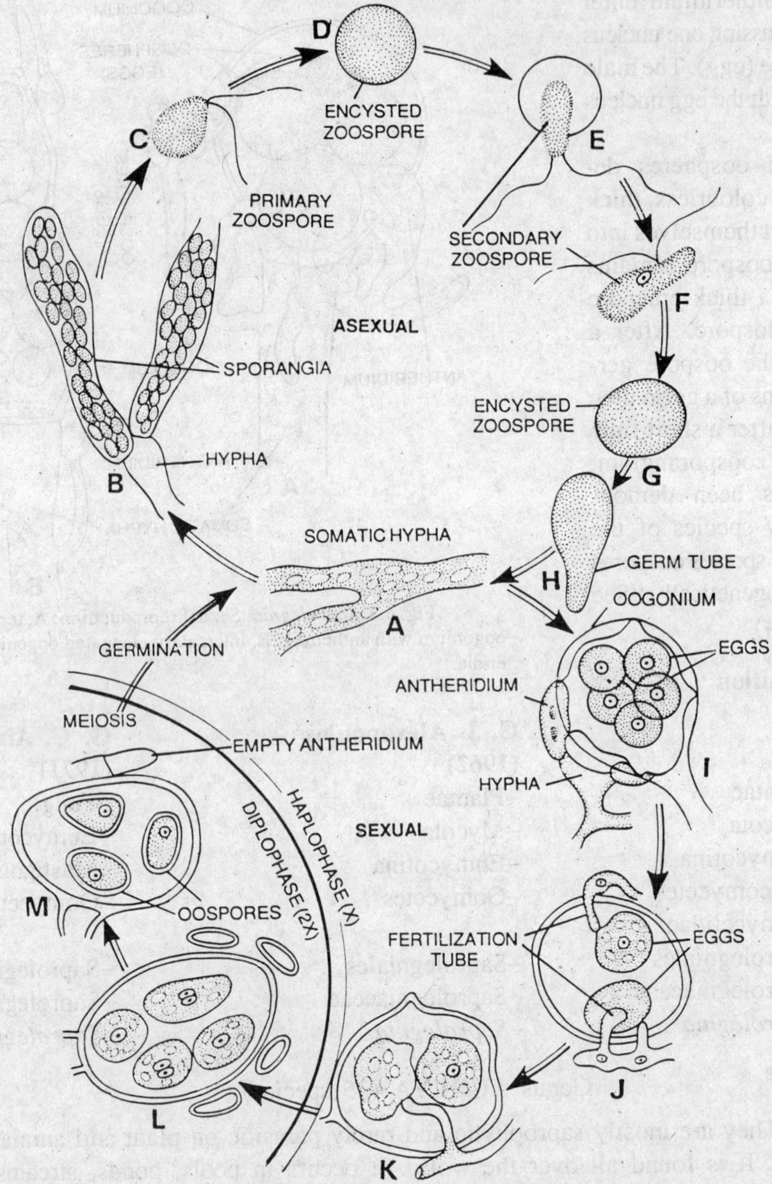

Fig. 6.4. *Saprolegnia*. Diagrammatic life-cycle: A, part of thallus (somatic hypha); B, hypha bearing two apical mature zoosporangia; C, primary zoospore; D, encysted zoospore; E, germination; F, secondary zoospore with laterally attached flagella; G, encysted zoospore; H, germination of encysted zoospore; I, antheridia and oogonium with many eggs; J, penetration of fertilization tube; K, plasmogamy; L, karyogmay; M, oospores which germinate later on producing germ tubes.

the group of empty sheaths before the opening of the sporangia.

Two types of zoospores occur. The primary zoospores are pear-shaped and bear their two flagella at the apex; the secondary zoospores are reniform and bear their flagella at the concave side of the zoospores. In *Achlya* the primary zoosopres encyst just outside the mouth of the sporangium as soon as they are released. Eventually they germinate and release secondary

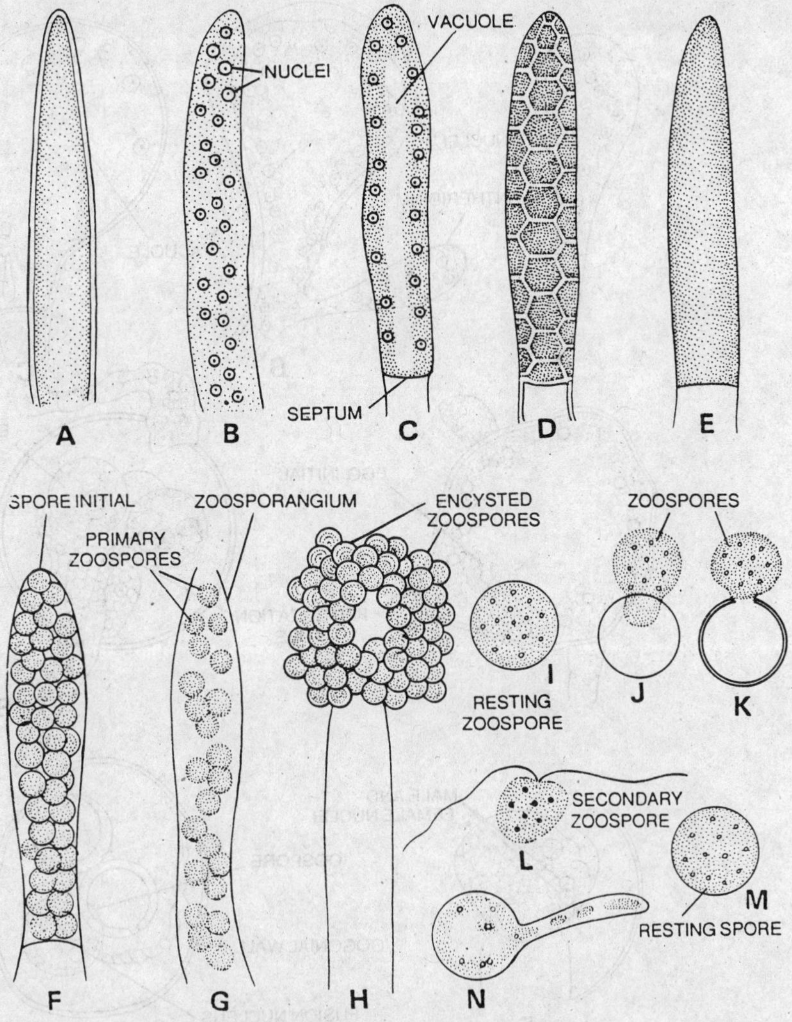

Fig. 6.5. *Achlya* (asexual reproduction). A-B, young sporangium being filled up with multinucleate protoplasm; C, appearance of vacuole and septum formation, protoplasm pushed towards periphery; D, polygonal masses are being formed because of preliminary division; E, homogeneous stage; F, spore initials ready to come out of sporangium; G, primary zoospores and zoosporangium open at apical end; H, encysted zoospores at the sporangial tip in a hollow rounded mass; I, resting spore; J, emergence of zoospore; K, entire mass discharged out; L, motile secondary zoospore; M, resting spore; N, germinating zoospore.

zoospores. Species in which two swarming periods occur involving two types of zoospores, are called **diplanetic** and the phenomenon **diplanetism.** The secondary spores after swimming for some time again encyst. Now these encysted zoospores germinate and produce new mycelia.

Sometimes the chains of thick walled chlamydospores are produced on the hyphae. On the approach of favourable conditions of environment, the chlamydospore germinates and produces new hyphae.

Sexual reproduction. The sexual reproduction takes place by copulation of gametangia. The passage of male gametes into the female gametangium taking place through a fertilization tube. The oogonium is rounded and having one or more globular oospores in it.

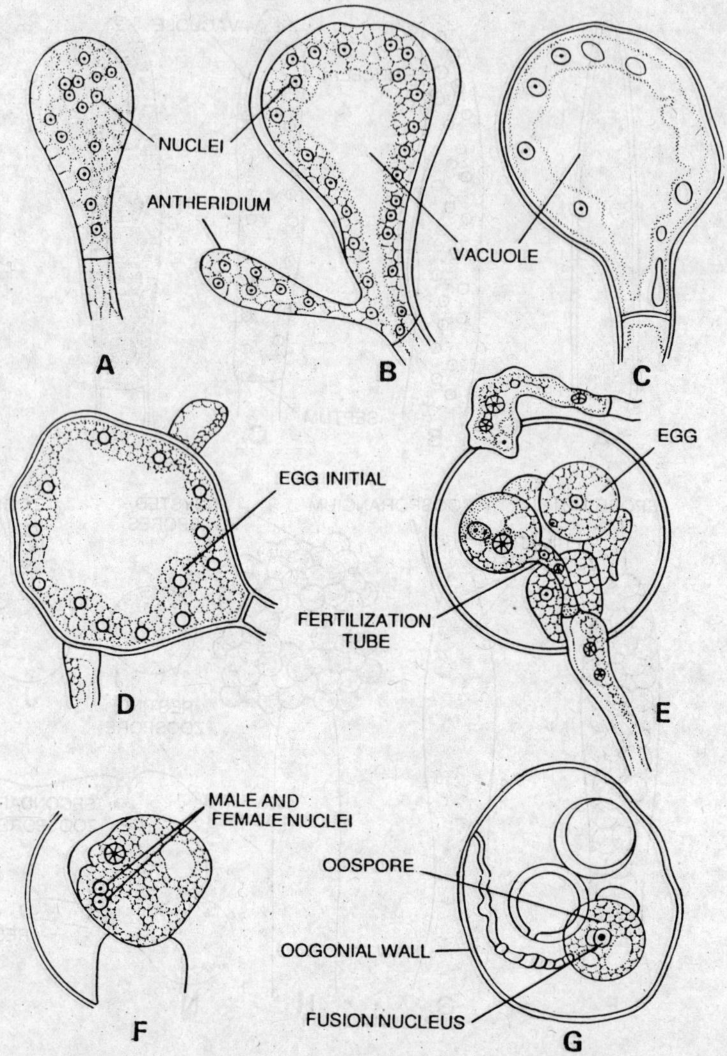

Fig. 6.6. *Achlya* (sexual reproduction). A, young multinucleate oogonium; B, young antheridium develops on the oogonial stalk, oogonium with a big central vacuole; C, dividing nuclei; D, formation of egg initials, each having a single nucleus; E, an oogonium with eggs and fertilization tube developed from antheridium, other antheridium penetrating the wall of oogonium; F, union of male and female nuclei; G, mature oospore containing a single fusion nucleus.

The elongated and multinucleate antheridia originate either on the same hyphal branch on which the oogonium is attached, on a different branch or on an entirely different thallus.

One or more antheridia become attached to the oogonium, pierce it and branched out, sending one branch to each oosphere within the oogonium. One nucleus of the antheridium now passes through each fertilization tube into each oosphere and fuses with the egg nucleus therein.

The fertilized oospheres develop thick walls and are converted into oospores. After maturity of the oospores, the oogonia remain connected with the mycelium until it disintegrates. After a rest of 2-5 months germination takes place with a germ tube, where meiosis occurs. It ends in a sporangium after a short time or develops directly to a mycelium. Meiosis has been recorded in *A. recurva*, *A. megasperma* and *A. colorata* (Ziegler, 1953).

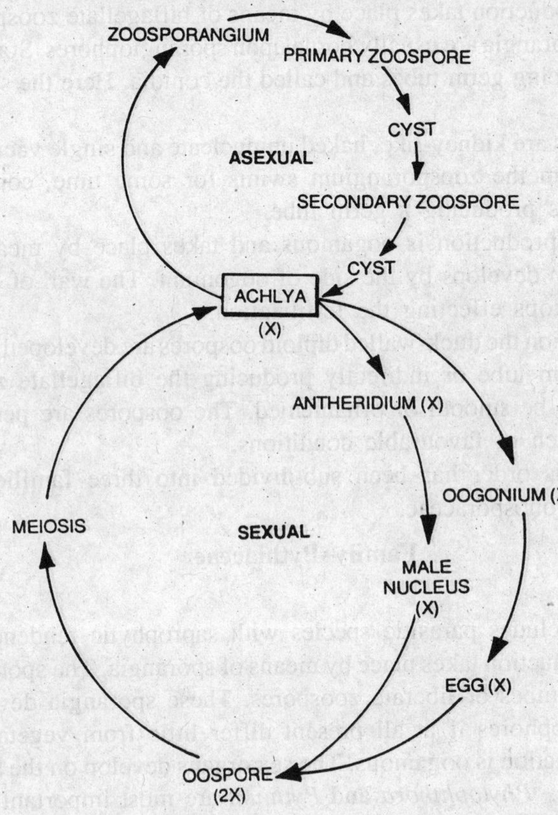

Fig. 6.7. *Achlya*. Graphic life-cycle.

Systematic Position

	G.W. Martin (1961)	C. J. Alexopoulos (1962)	G. C. Ainsworth (1971)
Kingdom	–Plantae	–Plantae	–Fungi
Division	–Mycota	–Mycota	–Eumycota
Sub-div.	–Eumycotina	–Eumycotina	–Mastigomycotina
Class	–Phycomycetes	–Oomycetes	–Oomycetes
Sub-cl.	–Oomycetidae		
Order	–Saprolegniales	–Saprolegniales	–Saprolegniales
Family	–Saprolegniaceae	–Saprolegniaceae	–Saprolegniaceae
Genus	–*Achlya*	–*Achlya*	–*Achlya*.

ORDER–PERONOSPORALES

(15 genera; 550 species)

Characteristic Features

1. Majority of them are parasitic upon aerial portions of herbaceous plants. Besides several

aquatic, amphibious and terrestrial species are found.

2. The mycelium is well developed, branched, aseptate and coenocytic. Majority of the species produce haustoria which obtain nourishment from the host cells. The haustoria are button-like or branched.

3. Asexual reproduction takes place by means of biflagellate zoospores produced within the zoosporangia. The sporangia are usually borne upon sporangiophores. Sometimes the sporangia germinate directly producing germ tubes and called the conidia. Here the sporophores are called the conidiophores.

4. The zoospores are kidney-like, naked uninucleate and single vacuolate. Each zoospore after being liberated from the zoosporangium swims for some time, comes to rest, becomes encysted, and germinates producing a germ tube.

5. The sexual reproduction is oogamous and takes place by means of antheridia and oogonia. The antheridium develops by the side of oogonium. The wall of contact dissolves and a fertilization tube develops effecting the fertilization.

6. After fertilization the thick-walled diploid oospores are developed which may germinate directly producing a germ tube or indirectly producing the biflagellate zoospores. The outer wall of the oospore may be smooth or ornamented. The oospores are perennating bodies and germinate on the approach of favourable conditions.

Classification. This order has been sub-divided into three families: 1. Pythiaceae, 2. Albuginaceae and 3. Peronosporaceae.

Family–Pythiaceae

Characteristic Features

1. The family includes parasitic species with saprophytic tendencies.
2. Asexual reproduction takes place by means of sporangia. The sporangia may germinate directly producing germ tubes or liberate zoospores. These sporangia develop directly on the mycelium. The sporangiophores if at all present differ little from vegetative hyphae.
3. Sexual reproduction is oogamous. The sex organs develop on the apices of the hyphae.

The two genera *viz., Phytophthora* and *Pythium* are most important. These genera have been discussed here in detail.

Genus **PHYTOPHTHORA** (20 species)

(*Phytophthora infestans*)

The most important species *Phytophthora infestans* causes the 'late blight of potato'. This is a havoc for potato crop and causes sufficient damage. The symptoms of the disease appear both upon aerial and underground parts. The whole plant becomes blighted in severe conditions. Dry and wet rots damage the tubers.

The first sign of the disease is appearance of small brown patches on leaves which in cloudy and muggy weather rapidly increase to the whole leaf surface. In bad cases the crown also shows similar symptoms which fall over into a rotten pulpy mass emitting foul odour. On the undersurface of such infected leaves a cottony growth of mycelium consisting of fructification of the fungus is seen. This growth is absent in dry weather. The underground parts especially the tubers are also affected which often remain smaller in size and show dry rot with rusty brown markings in the flesh and brown depressions at certain places, in the skin.

Structure of mycelium. The mycelium is endophytic, branched, aseptate, coenocytic, hyaline, intercellular and nodulated. The rounded or branched haustoria are found which absorb food material from the host cells.

Reproduction. The reproduction takes place by means of asexual and sexual methods.

Asexual reproduction. The asexual reproduction takes place by means of biflagellate zoospores produced inside the sporangia. In favourable conditions the sporangia are produced

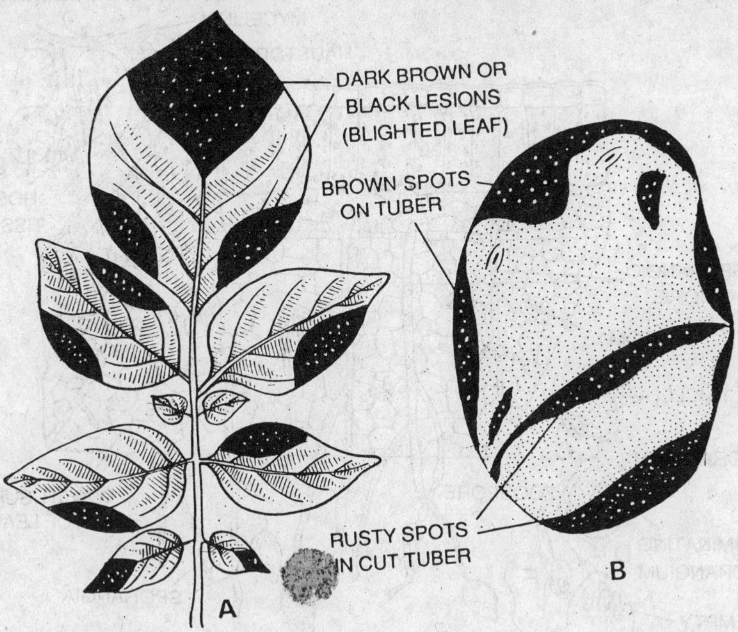

Fig. 6.8. *Phytophthora infestans*. Late blight of potato. A, affected leaf showing characteristic symptoms of disease; B, affected tuber.

on the branched sporangiophores coming out through the stomata in groups on the lower surface of the infected leaves. The sporangia are formed on the branches of the sporangiophores. On

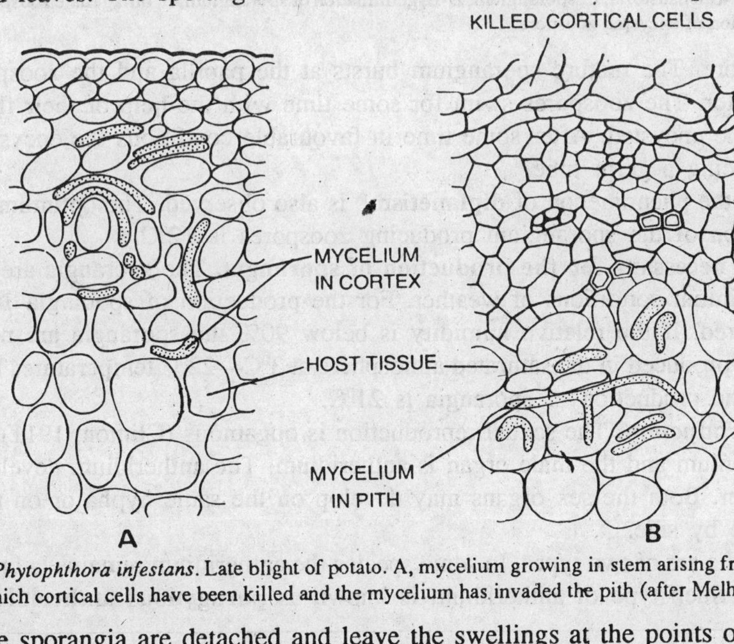

Fig. 6.9. *Phytophthora infestans*. Late blight of potato. A, mycelium growing in stem arising from infected tuber; B, a later stage in which cortical cells have been killed and the mycelium has invaded the pith (after Melhus).

maturation the sporangia are detached and leave the swellings at the points of contact on the sporangiophores.

The sporangia are rounded or lemon-shaped. At the anterior end of the sporangium there is a papilla. On maturation the protoplasm of the sporangium divides into several uninucleate, protoplasts. Each protoplast metamorphoses into a biflagellate, reniform, uninucleate, vacuolate

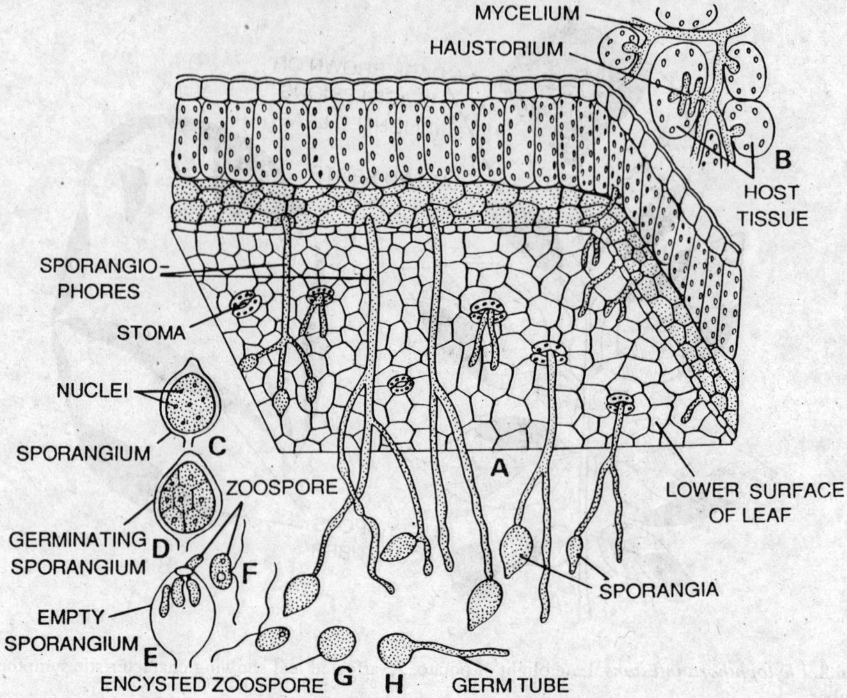

Fig. 6.10. *Phytophthora infestans*. Late blight of potato. A, sympodially branched sporangiophores coming out through stomata on the lower surface of potato leaf, swellings on sporangiophores are distinct, the sporangia are lemon-shaped; B, intercellular mycelium with haustoria; C, sporangium; D-E, germination of sporangium; F, biflagellate zoospores; G, encysted zoospore; H, germination of encysted zoospore.

and naked zoospore. The mature sporangium bursts at the papilla and the zoospores liberate in the film of water. The zoospores swim for some time with the help of their flagella, come to rest and become encysted. After some time in favourable conditions the encysted zoospore germinates producing a germ tube.

Sometimes the phenomenon of **diplanetism*** is also observed. The optimum temperature for the germination of the sporangium producing zoospores is 12°C.

Conditions necessary for the production of sporangia. The sporangia are produced in abundnace in optimum conditions of weather. For the production of sporangia 100% relative humidity is required. If the relative humidity is below 90% the sporangia are not produced. The sporangia are produced in the saturated atmosphere at 3°C—22°C temperature. The optimum temperature for the production of sporangia is 21°C.

Sexual reproduction. The sexual reproduction is oogamous (Clinton, 1911). The female sex organ is oogonium and the male organ is antheridium. The antheridium develops first and the oogonium later. Both the sex organs may develop on the same hypha or on two adjacent hyphae lying side by side.

The antheridia are of two types. In some species the antheridium remains laterally attached to the oogonium. Such type of antheridium is known as **paragynous antheridium.** In other

* *Diplanetism*—Condition of having two periods of motility in one life history as of zoospores in some Flagellatae.

species the antheridium remains attached at the base of oogonium. The development of antheridium in *Phytophthora erythroseptica* is as follows: an antheridium develops on the apex of the hypha,

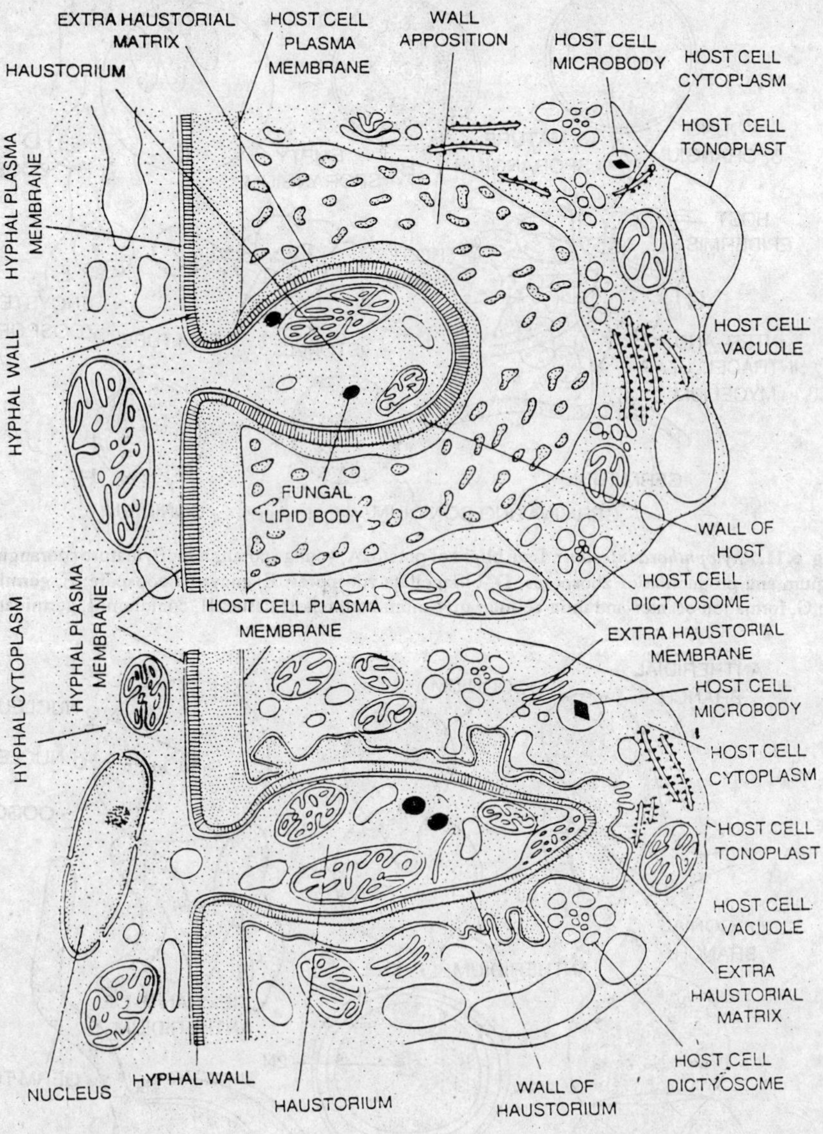

Fig. 6.10. (a) *Phytophthora infestans*. Host parasite relationship. A, infection on partially resistant potato variety; B, infection on susceptible potato variety. Ultrastructure of mycelium and haustoria.

and through this another hypha (female) grows piercing the antheridium above it. This type of antheridium is known as **amphigynous** antheridium. Both types of antheridia are found in different species of *Phytophthora*. After the development of antheridium the oogonium develops. The oogonial hypha penetrates the antheridium and pushes its way otherside the antheridium. The oogonium is pear-shaped. The protoplasm of the oogonium is demarcated into two regions. The outer region is periplasm and the central region ooplasm. The periplasm contains many

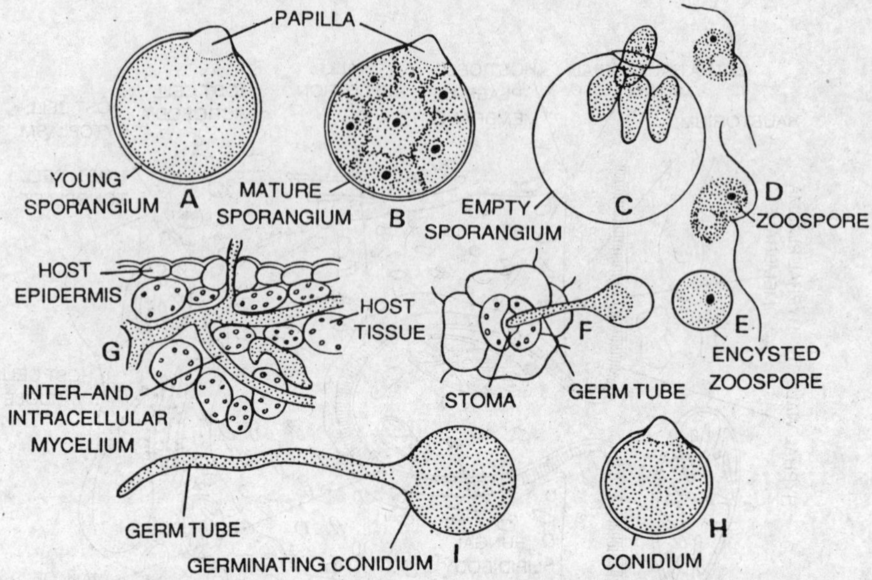

Fig. 6.11. *Phytophthora infestans*. Late blight of potato. A, young sporangium; B, mature sporangium; C, germination of sporangium and production of zoospores; D, biflagellate zoospores; E, encysted zoospore; F, germination of encysted zoospores; G, formation of inter-and intra-cellular mycelium within host tissue; H, conidium; I, germinating conidium.

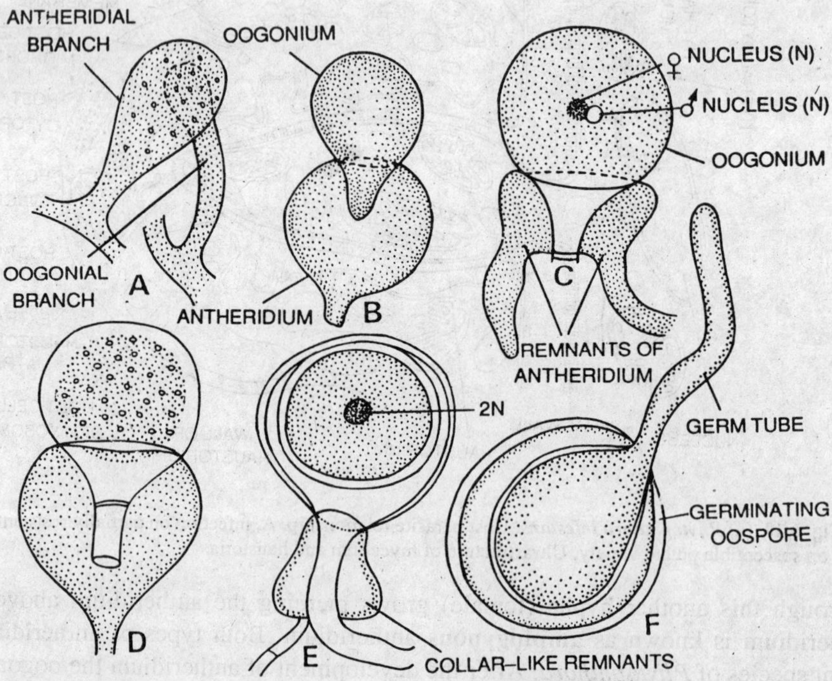

Fig. 6.12. *Phytophthora infestans*. Late blight of potato. A-D, oogonia, antheridia and stages in fertilization; E, oospore within oogonial wall, and remnants of antheridium; F, germination of oospore by germ tube.

nuclei and thin cytoplasm whereas the ooplasm contains dense granular cytoplasm and a single female nucleus in it. The fusion of the male and female nuclei is not clearly understood. It is assumed that the male and female nuclei fuse in the egg after penetration of the oogonium in the antheridium. There is no fertilization tube. After fertilization the thickwalled oospore develops. The oospore is situated inside the oogonium in loose state. Sometimes the parthenospores are also developed without fertilization. The oospore germinates in favourable conditions producing a germ tube, which develops into new mycelium. Reduction division occurs during germination of oospore. They are perennating bodies and face adverse conditions.

In our country the oospores are not found in natural conditions.

The disease may be controlled by the following methods.

1. Selection of healthy tubers for sowing purpose.
2. Proper cold storage of healthy tubers for seeds. Tubers for seed from infected area should not be stored in cold stores as they carry the fungus which remains viable in the store.
3. Spraying of Bordeaux mixture and other fungicides from the time the disease appears till the digging of tubers at intervals of 15 days controls the disease.
4. Proper manuring to increase resistance.
5. Sowing of resistant varieties.

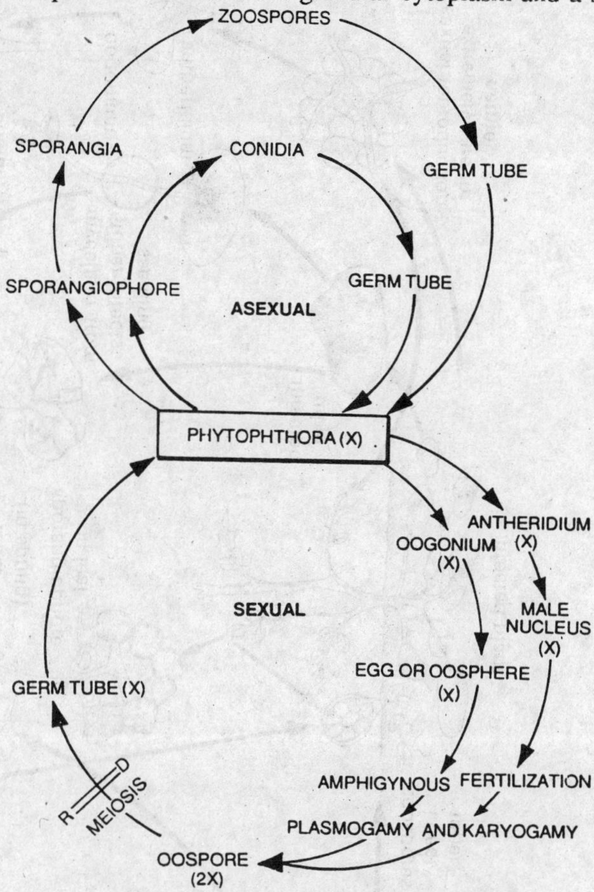

Fig. 6.13. Graphic life-cycle of *Phytophthora*.

Systematic Position

	G. W. Martin (1961)	**C. J. Alexopoulos (1962)**	**G. C. Ainswoth (1971)**
Kingdom	–Plantae	–Plantae	–Fungi
Division	–Mycota	–Mycota	–Eumycota
Sub-div.	–Eumycotina	–Eumycotina	–Mastigomycotina
Class	–Phycomycetes	–Oomycetes	–Oomycetes
Sub-Cl.	–Oomycetidae		
Order	–Peronosporales	–Peronosporales	–Peronosporales
Family	–Pythiaceae	–Pythiaceae	–Pythiaceae
Genus	*-Phytophthora*	*-Phytophthora*	*-Phytophthora*
Species	*–infestans*	*–infestans*	*–infestans*

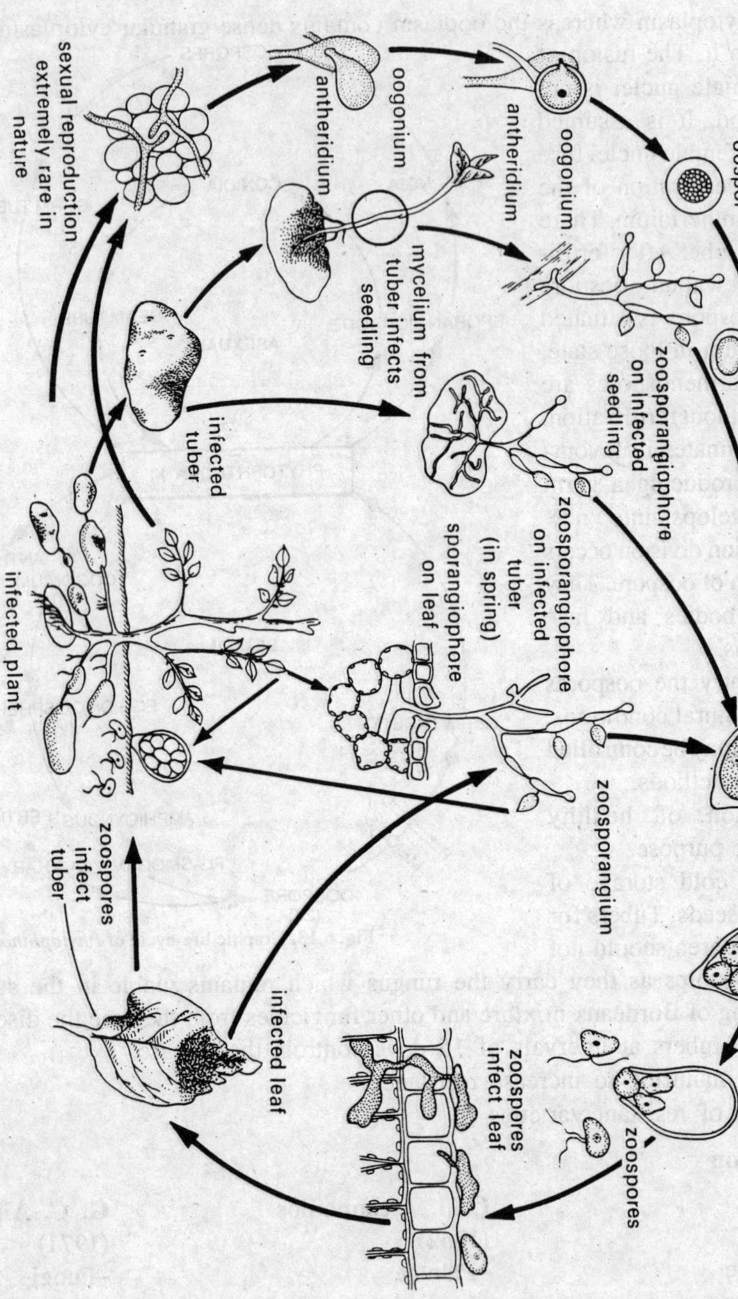

Fig. 6.14. Disease cycle of late blight of potato (*Phytophthora infestans*).

Genus **PYTHIUM** (65 speices)

Habit and habitat. Some of the species of *Pythium* are found in parasitic state on fresh water algae. Several other species found in the damp soil infect the seedlings of certain plants and cause the 'damping off disease' of seedlings.

The damping off disease is characterized by a sudden collapse of the seedlings in the seed bed and their rotting from base to top. Foul odour is emitted by such seedlings and after complete rotting they dry into thread-like structures. Due to the severity of the disease and rapid death of seedlings black patches with dry thread-like seedlings are marked inside the seed bed. The disease initiates from any part of the seedlings, roots, collar, middle of hypocotyl or top of the seedlings but collar is the most common seat of infection. The seedlings are killed or destroyed before actual emergence above the ground level due to pre-emergence damping off.

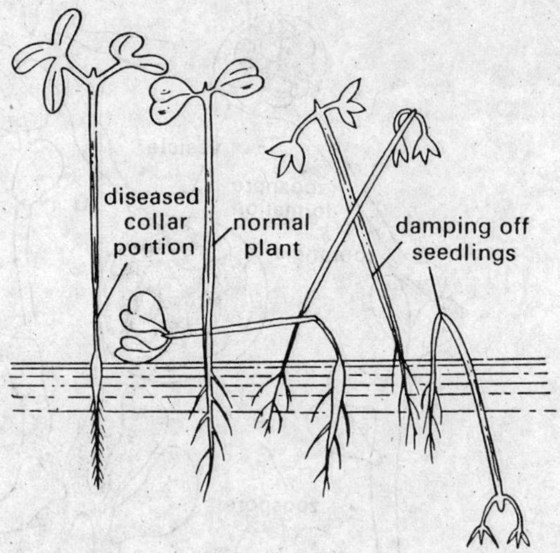

Fig. 6.15. *Pythium* sp. Damping off of seedlings.

Structure of mycelium. The mycelium is profusely branched, aseptate, coenocytic and hyaline. Sometimes the old mycelium becomes septate. When the mycelium is endophytic, it is inter and intracellular. The haustoria are not developed. The food is absorbed by the hyphal walls.

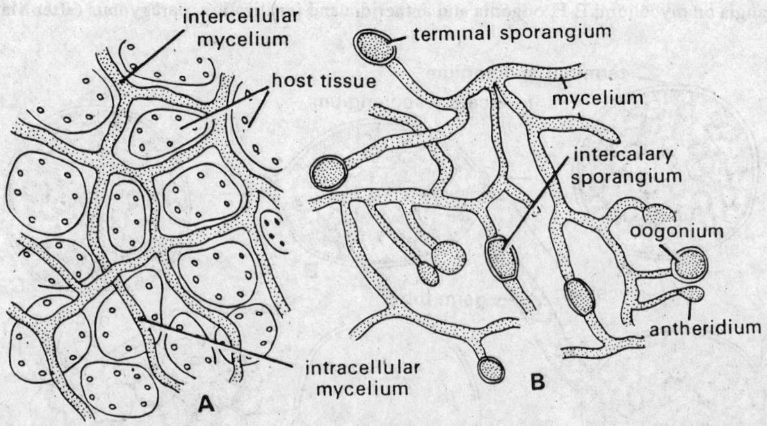

Fig. 6.16. *Pythium* sp. Damping off of seedlings. A, inter and intracellular mycelium within host tissue; B, mycelium and reproductive parts.

Reproduction. The reproduction takes place by means of 1. Asexual and 2. Sexual methods.

1. Asexual reproduction. The asexual reproduction takes place by means of biflagellate zoosopres produced within the zoosporangia. The zoosporangia are formed on aerial sporangiophores. The sporangia may be elongated or rounded. They may be intercalary or terminal in their position.

At the time of the germination the zoosporangium breaks at its anterior end, and the undivided protoplasmic mass comes out through the opening. This rounded protoplasmic mass remains

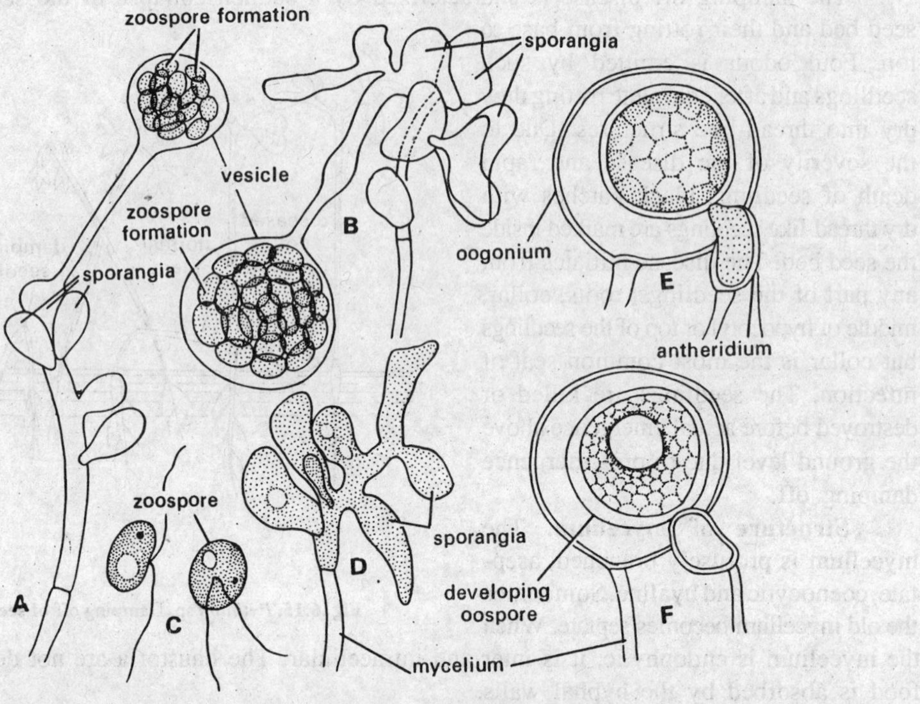

Fig. 6.17. *Pythium aphanidermatum.* Stem rot of papaya. A-B, sporangia and formation of zoospores in vesicle; C, zoospore; D, sporangia on mycelium; E-F, oogonia and antheridia and fertilization, paragynous (after Mathews).

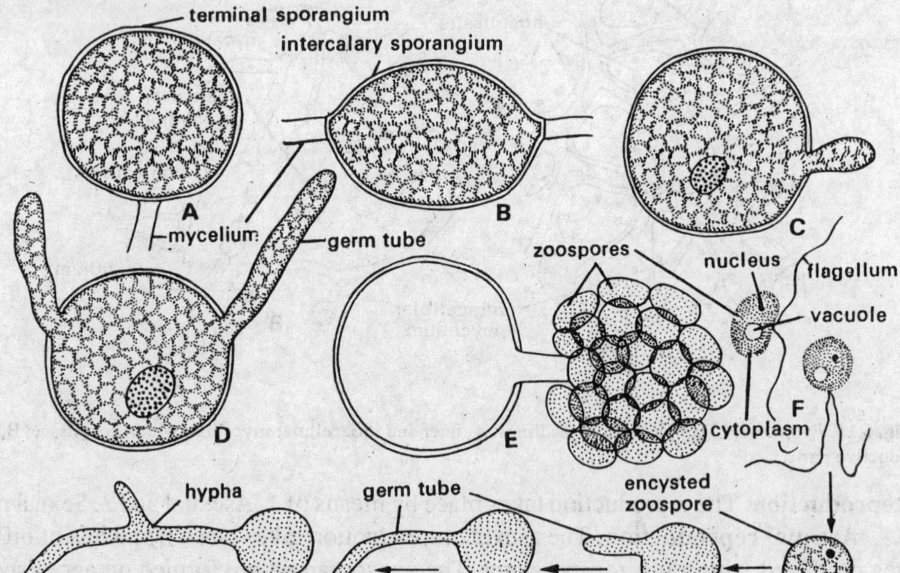

Fig. 6.18. *Pythium de baryanum.* Damping off of tobacco seedlings. A, terminal sporangium; B, intercalary sporangium; C-D, germination of sporangia by germ tubes; E, germination of sporangium by formation of zoospores; F, biflagellate zoospores; G, encysted zoospore; H-J, germination of encysted zoospores by germ tube.

inside the membranous vesicle. This protoplast divides into several small bits, each possessing a nucleus in it. These bits are metamorphosed into zoospores. The vesicle bursts, the zoospores liberate and swim in the film of water.

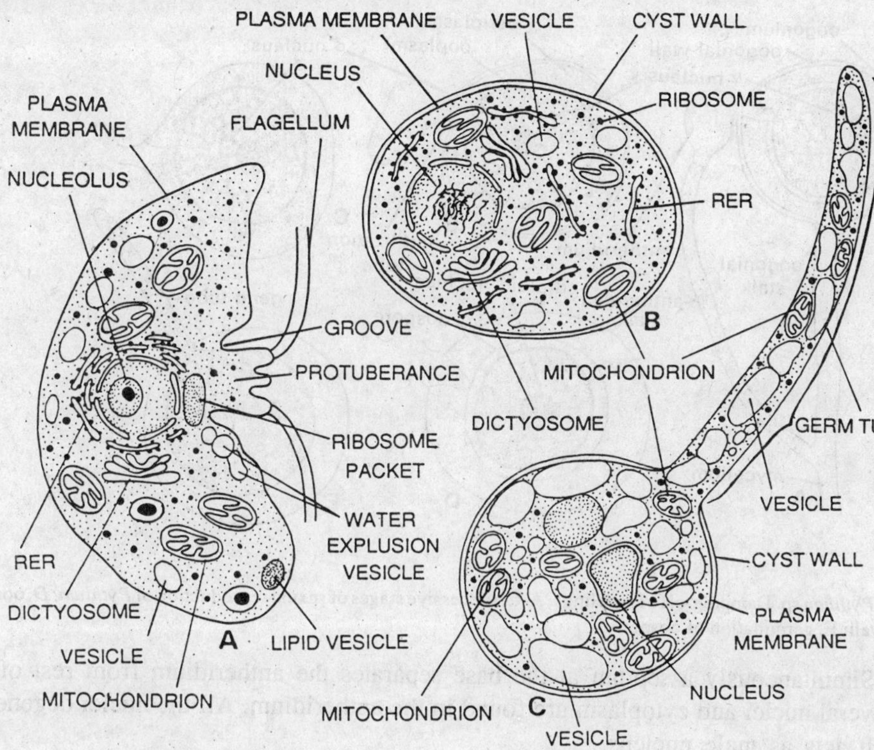

Fig. 6.18. (a) *Pythium* sp. A, ultrastructure of a zoospore; B, ultrastructure of an encysted zoospore; C, ultrastructure of a germinating encysted zoospore.

Each zoospore is reniform, naked, uninucleate and biflagellate. The flagella are laterally inserted. There is a single vacuole in each zoospore. Very soon the flagella are retracted, the protoplasts become rounded and encysted. In the favourable conditions of moisture and temperature the encysted protoplast germinates producing a germ tube developing into a new mycelium.

Sometimes the sporangia behave like conidia and germinate directly producing germ tubes.

2. Sexual reproduction. The sexual reproduction is oogamous. The oogonia are developed on the hyphal ends. The hyphal end becomes somewhat swollen, and many nuclei and abundance of cytoplasm are accumulated in this portion. A septum develops at the base of this portion which separates this rounded oogonium from rest of mycelium. Majority of the species possess smooth walled oogonia. In some cases the oogonia are echinulate, *e.g.*, *Pythium echinulatum*.

In the beginning of the development of the oogonium the nuclei are uniformly distributed in the protoplasm. On the maturation of the oogonium the protoplasm demarcates into outer **periplasm** and the central **ooplasm.** The periplasm is found just beneath the oogonial wall. In this region there are several nuclei and thin protoplasm. The nuclei of periplasm gradually degenerate. The ooplasm contains dense protoplasm and a single female nucleus. This is in the central portion of the oosphere or the egg.

By the side of the oogonium, the antheridium develops on the other hyphal end. The antheridium develops on the same hypha on which the oogonium is developed or on the adjacent hypha. In the development of the antheridium the hyphal end swells somewhat and becomes

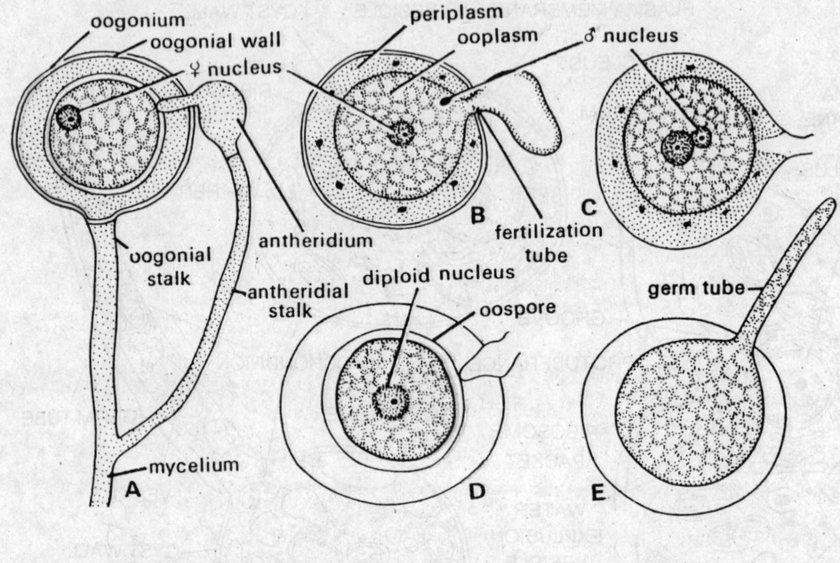

Fig. 6.19. *Pythium* sp. Damping-off of seedlings. A-C, successive stages of sexual reproduction of *Pythium; D*, oospore within oogonial wall; E, germination of oospore.

club-shaped. Simultaneously a septum at the base separates the antheridium from rest of the mycelium. Several nuclei and cytoplasm are found in the antheridium. All the nuclei degenerate but one which acts as male nucleus.

The antheridium attaches itself to the oogonium. The fertilization tube develops from the antheridium which penetrates the oogonium at the wall of contact. The fertilization tube reaches the egg through the periplasm. The male nucleus along with some protoplasm is transferred to the egg through this tube, where it fuses with the female nucleus. Very soon the process of karyogamy is completed and the oospore is formed. The oospore is thick-walled which germinates after going under a rest period.

To bring the haploid condition again, the reduction division (meiosis) takes place during the germination of the oospore.

Germination of oospore. The oospore germinates directly by producing germ tube at high temperatures (28°C). At low temperatures (10-17°C), they germinate indirectly by producing zoospores in the vesicle. The vesicle bursts, zoospores come out and germinate like that of asexual reproduction.

Economic importance. The genus *Pythium* is commonly found in our country. It causes 'damping off of seedlings'. Some of the common diseases found in our country are: 'Damping off of tobacco or chillies' caused by *P. debaryanum;* 'Soft rot of papaya' caused by *P. aphanidermatum;* 'Foot root of ginger' caused by *P. myriotylum;* 'Wheat rot', caused by *P. graminicolum;* 'Rhizome and root rot of turmeric' caused by *P. graminicolum;* (Ramakrishnan and Sowmini, 1954); 'Damping off of potato seedling' caused by *P. aphanidermatum* (Gattani and Kaul, 1951); 'Fruit rot of *Hibiscus esculentus (Abelmoschus esculentus)* caused by *P. indicum* (Balkrishnan, 1948).

Control. The disease is fundamentally soil borne. Attempts should therefore be made tc kill the pathogen inside the nursery soil through soil treatments. Treating the seeds with various

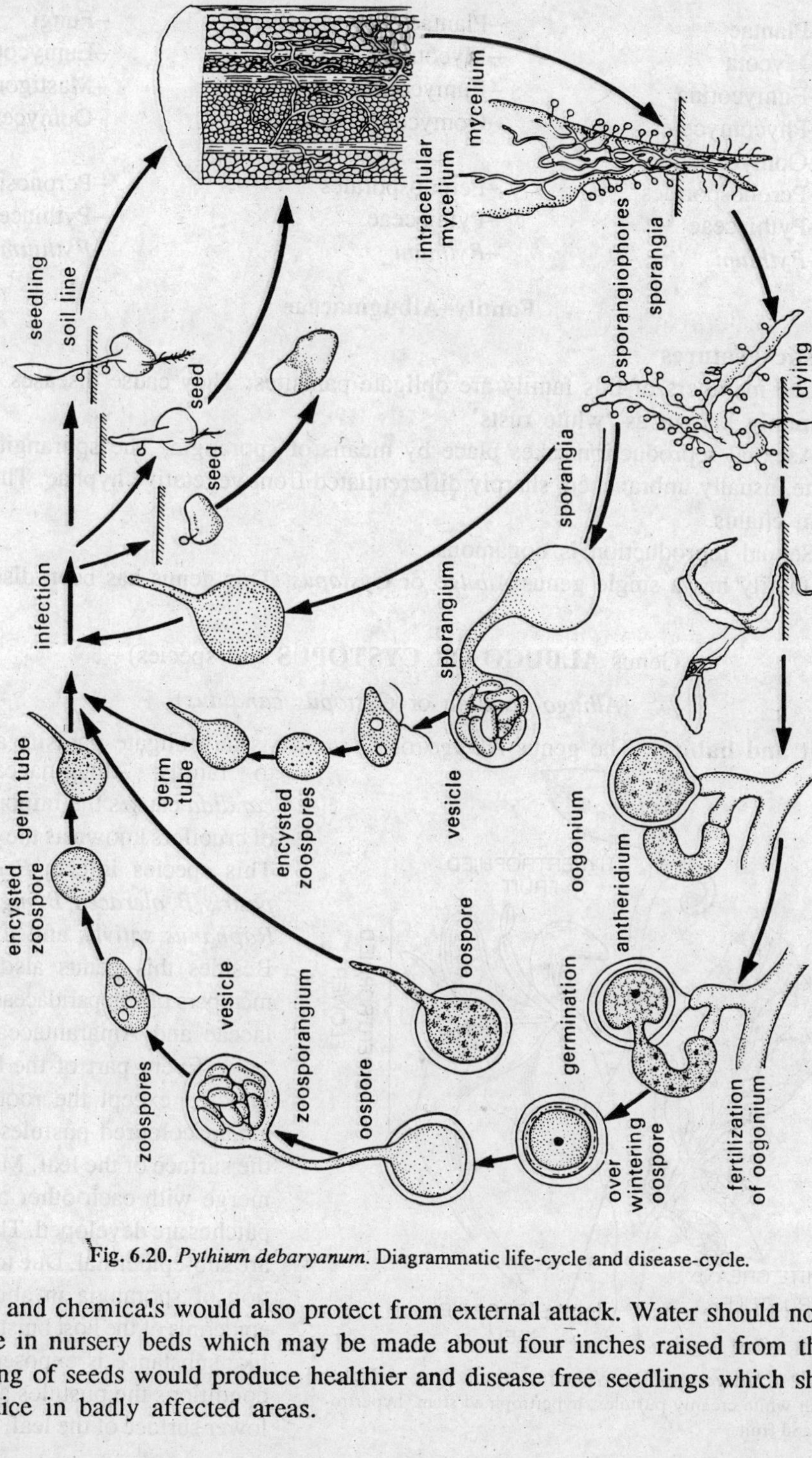

Fig. 6.20. *Pythium debaryanum*. Diagrammatic life-cycle and disease-cycle.

fungicides and chemicals would also protect from external attack. Water should not be allowed to stagnate in nursery beds which may be made about four inches raised from the soil level. Thin sowing of seeds would produce healthier and disease free seedlings which should always be a practice in badly affected areas.

Systematic Position

	G. W. Martin (1961)	C. J. Alexopoulos (1962)	G. C. Ainswoth (1971)
Kingdom	–Plantae	–Plantae	–Fungi
Division	–Mycota	–Mycota	–Eumycota
Sub-div.	–Eumycotina	–Eumycotina	–Mastigomycotina
Class	–Phycomycetes	–Oomycetes	–Oomycetes
Sub-cl.	–Oomycetidae		
Order	–Peronosporales	–Peronosporales	–Peronosporales
Family	–Pythiaceae	–Pythiaceae	–Pythiaceae
Genus	–*Pythium*	–*Pythium*.	–*Pythium.*

Family–Albuginaceae

Characteristic Features

1. The members of this family are obligate parasites. They cause diseases of vascular plants commonly known as 'white rusts'.
2. Asexual reproduction takes place by means of sporangia. The sporangiophores are short, clavate, usually unbranched, sharply differentiated from vegetative hyphae. The sporangia are found in chains.
3. Sexual reproduction is oogamous.

This family has a single genus *Albugo* or *Cystopus*. This genus has been discussed here in detail.

Genus ALBUGO OR CYSTOPUS (30 species)

(*Albugo candida* or *Cystopus candidus*)

Habit and habitat. The genus *Albugo* or *Cystopus* is an obligate parasite and belongs to family Albuginaceae. *Albugo candida* causes the important disease of crucifers known as the 'white rust'. This species infects *Brassica campestris, B. oleracea, B. nigra, B. napus, Raphanus sativus* and *Eruca sativa*. Besides this genus also infects the members of Capparidaceae, Convolvulaceae and Amarantaceae.

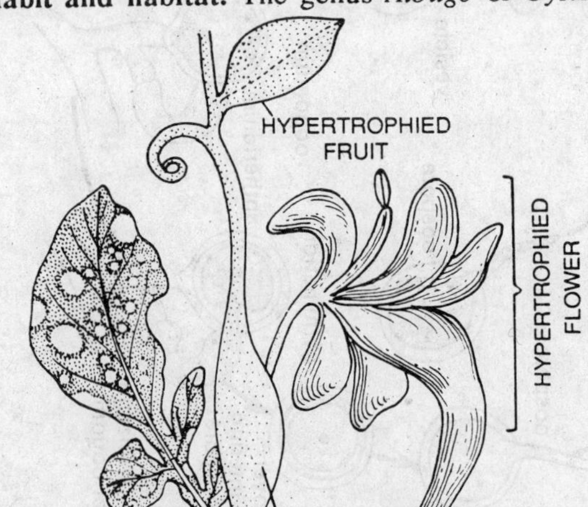

Fig. 6.21. *Albugo candida.* White rust of crucifers—infected twig, leaf with white creamy pustules, hypertrophied stem, hypertrophied flower and fruit.

Every part of the host plant is infected except the roots. White or cream coloured pustules develop on the surface of the leaf. Many pustules merge with each other and irregular patches are developed. These pustules are sub-epidermal. Due to the production of sporangia in abundance, the epidermis of the host bursts and powder like substance is exposed. In normal conditions the pustules appear on the lower surface of the leaf, but in severe conditions of the disease the symptoms appear on both the surfaces. The leaves of some crucifers become thick, fleshy and curled. In severe conditions the leaves remain undeveloped and the plants become dwarf. The stem becomes hypertrophied and the floral parts become withered. The sepals and petals become fleshy and leaf-like. The ovary and stamens become flat, leaf like and sterile. The whole infected flower becomes hypertrophied and several times bigger than the normal size.

Structure of mycelium. The mycelium is endophytic, branched, aseptate, coenocytic, hyaline, intercellular and with knob-like haustoria for the absorption of food material from the host cells.

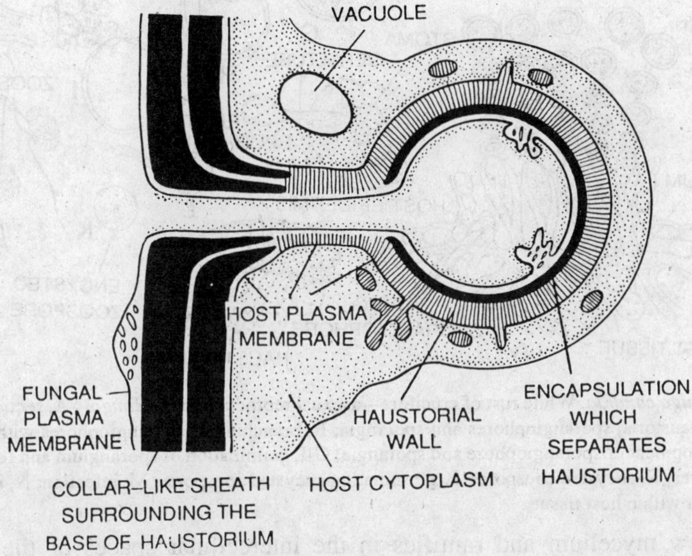

Fig. 6.22. *Albugo candida*. Knob-like haustorium as seen with electron microscope. (After Berlin and Bowen, 1964).

Reproduction. The reproduction takes place by means of asexual and sexual methods.

1. Asexual reproduction. The asexual reproduction takes place by means of biflagellate zoospores formed inside the sporangia. In the very beginning the hyphae accumulate just beneath the epidermis of the infected leaf. From these hyphae, certain thick-walled, clavate aerial sporangiophores come out. In each such sporangiophore there are about a dozen nuclei and sufficient cytoplasm. The terminal end of the sporangiophore becomes constricted and sporangium cuts off. This sporangium contains 5-8 nuclei and cytoplasm. Successively the sporangia develop by constriction method, in basigenous chains. In between each two sporangia a gelatinous pad develops acting as a separator of two sporangia from each other. The sporangium is smooth, double-walled and rounded. When the sporangia are formed in abundance on innumerable sporangiophores, the pressure is caused, the host epidermis ruptures and hundreds of sporangia are seen on the surface of the host in the form of white creamy powder forming pustules. The sporangia are transferred from one place to another by various agencies such as wind, insects, water etc.

On the maturation of the sporangium the protoplast is cleaved into uninucleate protoplasts. Each protoplast metamorphoses into a naked, biflagellate, uninucleate, reniform and vacuolate zoospore. The sporangium bursts anteriorly and the zoospores liberate in the film of water. The flagella are withdrawn and the zoospore becomes encysted. Each encysted protoplast germinates, producing a germ tube on the surface of the suitable host. The germ tube enters through stoma,

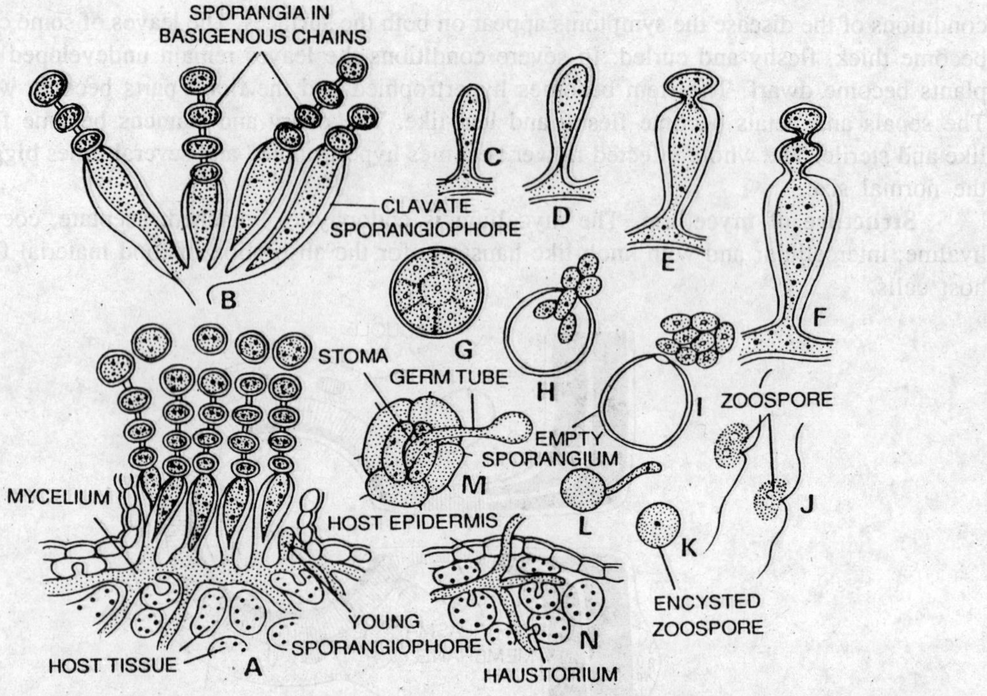

Fig. 6.23. *Albugo candida.* White rust of crucifers—asexual reproduction of *Albugo*—A, section of infected host leaf showing mycelium, haustoria, sporangiophores and sporangia; B, branching of sporangiophores with basigenous chains of sporangia; C-F, development of sporangiophore and sporangia; G-I, germination of sporangium and formation of zoospores; J, biflagellate zoospores; K, encysted zoospores; L, germinating encysted zoospores; M, infection; N, intercellular mycelium and rounded haustoria within host tissue.

develops into new mycelium and ramifies in the intercellular spaces of the host tissue.

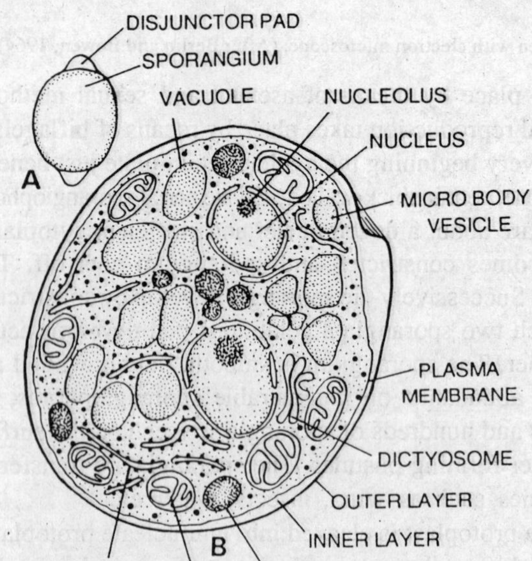

Fig. 6.23 (a) *Albugo candida.* A, sporangium; B, ultrastructure of sporangium (diagrammatic).

Sometimes the sporangia behave as conidia and germinate directly producing germ tubes. The conidia may germinate from 3°C to 25°C temperature, but the optimum temperature is 10°C.

2. Sexual reproduction. The sexual reproduction is **oogamous.** The sex organs develop on the hyphal ends in the intercellular spaces of the deeper tissues of petioles and stems. The female sex organs are oogonia and the male sex organs are antheridia. The oogonium is rounded and the antheridium club-shaped. The developing oogonia and antheridia are separated from rest of the mycelium by septa. The cytoplasm, vacuoles and nuclei are uniformly distributed in the young oogonium. On the maturation of the oogonium the protoplasm of the oogonium differentiates into two regions. The outer region is called the **periplasm**

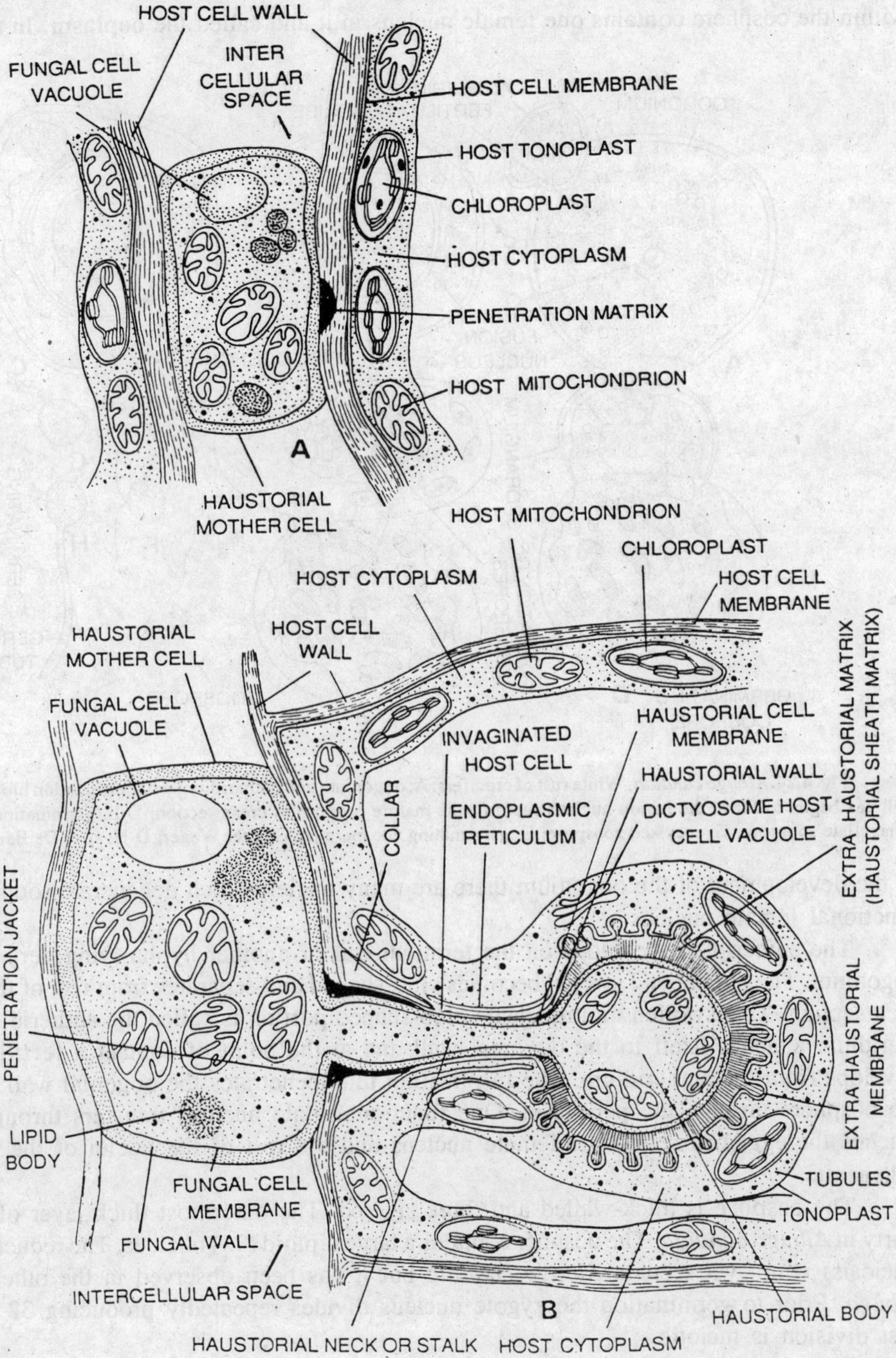

Fig. 6.23 (b) *Albugo candida*. A, part of intercellular mycelium; B, haustorium developed from intercellular mycelium in host cell as revealed under electron microscope.

containing thin cytoplasm, many nuclei and many vacuoles. The central protoplasm with denser consistency surrounded by periplasm is called the **oosphere** or the **egg.** The dense cytoplasm within the oosphere contains one female nucleus in it and called the **ooplasm.** In the beginning

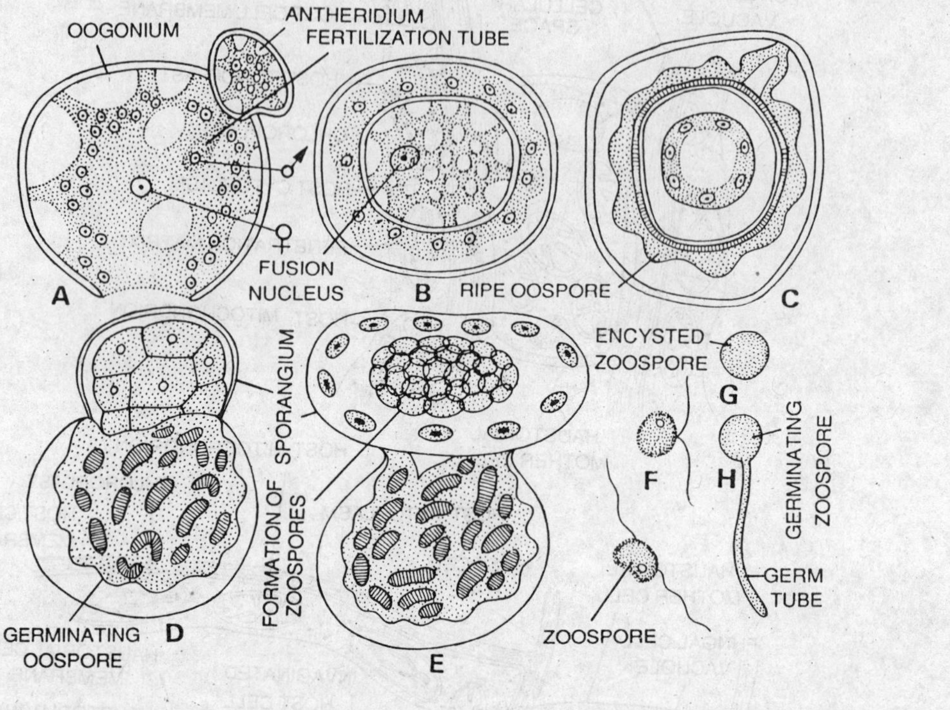

Fig. 6.24. *Albugo candida*. White rust of crucifers. A, oogonium and antheridium with fertilization tube; B, the oospore wall has begun to form, the fusion nucleus seen; C, the mature oospore in cross section; D-E, germination of oospore; F, biflagellate zoospore; G, encysted zoospore; H, germinating zoospore (A-C, after Wager; D-H, after De Bary)

of the development of the oogonium there are many nuclei, which degenerate soon leaving one functional female nucleus.

The antheridium develops on the terminal end of another hypha lying very close to the oogonium. The hyphal end swells, becomes club-shaped and separates from rest of the mycelium by a septum. This swollen multinucleate club-shaped portion is called the antheridium. The antheridium attaches itself to the oogonial wall and at the point of contact a **fertilization tube** develops from the antheridium. The fertilization tube penetrates the oogonial wall and reaches the oosphere through the periplasm. One functional male nucleus transfers through the tube, reaches the egg, fuses with the female nucleus and the rest of the nuclei of the antheridium degenerate.

The **oospore** is thick-walled and three-layered. The outermost thick layer of the wall is warty in *Albugo candida*. The oospore contains a large diploid (2x) nucleus. The reduction division (meiosis) is not yet seen in *Albugo candida* but it has been observed in the other species of *Albugo*. Prior to germination the zygote nucleus divides repeatedly producing 32 nuclei. The first division is meiotic.

Germination of oospore. The oospores are perennating bodies and survive in adverse conditions. The 32 nucleate oospore undergoes a period of rest and germinates on the approach of favourable conditions of moisture and temperature. The outer warty wall of oospore bursts and a thin membrane of sessile vesicle comes out of the oospore. Prior to extrusion of the contents in the vesicle the nuclei undergo the mitotic division repeatedly and a large number of uninucleate bits of protoplast are produced. Each bit metamorphoses into a biflagellate, reniform, naked, uninucleate and single vacuolate **zoospore.** Each oospore produces forty to sixty zoospores. After

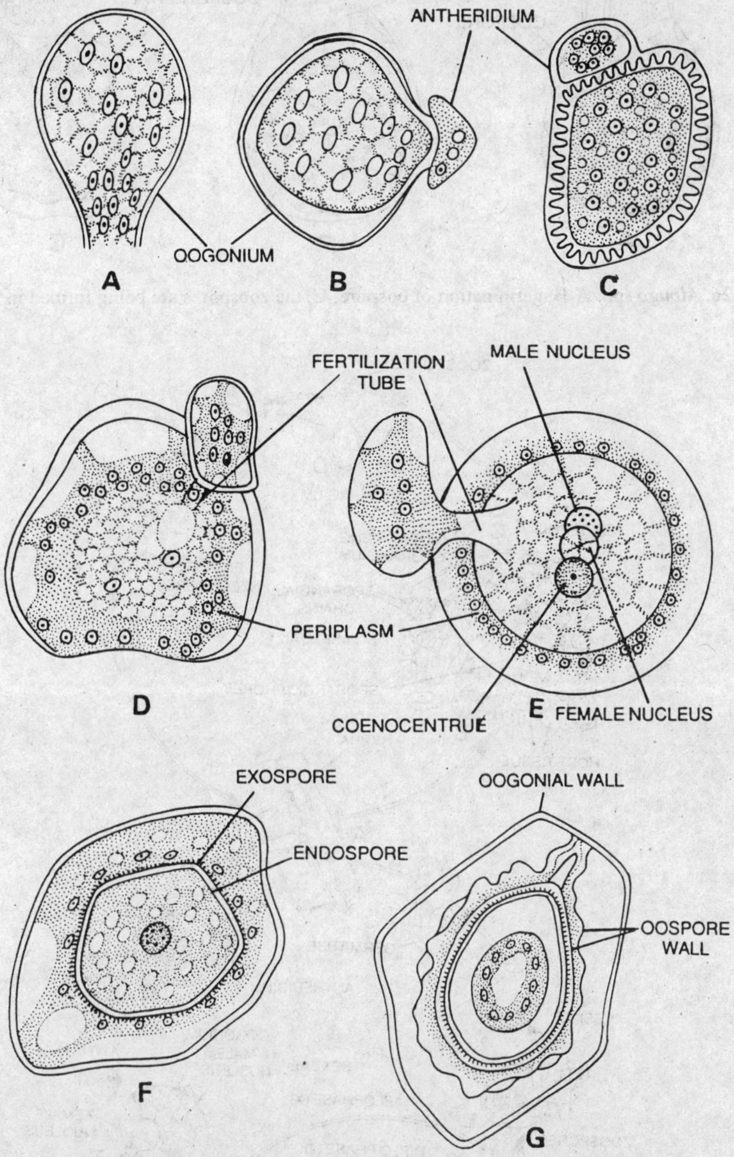

Fig. 6.25. ***Albugo candida.*** A, oogonium with many nuclei; B, formation of the receptive spot towards the attached antheridium; C, nuclei in antheridium and oogonium; D, formation of fertilization tube and migration of the nuclei of oogonium in the peripheral region leaving single female nucleus in the centre of oogonium; E, fusion of male and female nuclei; F, oospore formation and karyogamy; G, mature oospore.

extrusion from the oospore, the vesicle bursts and the zoospores liberate in the film of water where they move about with the help of their flagella. They swim about, encyst and germinate producing the germ tubes on the suitable host. The germ tube enters through the stoma and develops into the new mycelium which ramifies in the intercellular spaces of the host tissue.

The oospores remain dormant in the soil and infect the plants next year.

The disease may be controlled by the following methods:

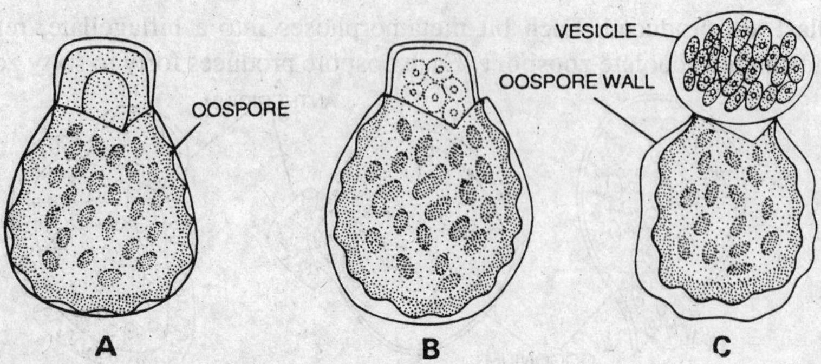

Fig. 6.26. *Albugo* spp. A-B, germination of oospore; C, the zoospores are being formed in the vesicle.

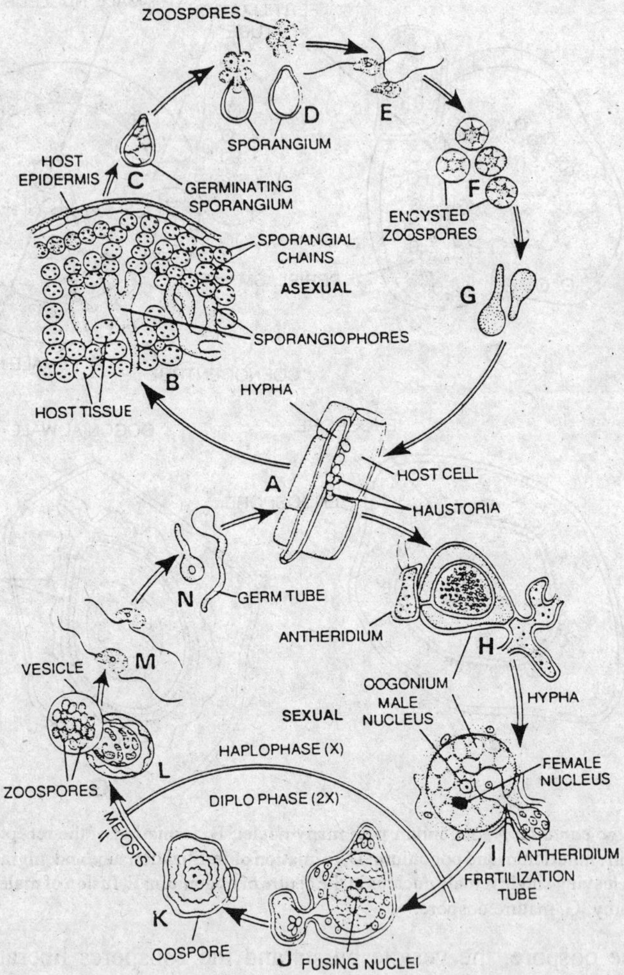

Fig. 6.27. *Albugo*. Diagrammatic life-cycle. A, hypha within host cell showing globular haustoria; B, infected leaf in vertical section showing sporangiophores and sporangial chains; C, germinating sporangium; D, sporangia releasing zoospores; E, zoospores; F, encysted zoospores; G, germination of encysted zoospores; H, antheridium and oogonium; I, plasmogamy; J, karyogamy; K, oospore; L, germination of oospore producing zoospores within vesicle; M, zoospores; N, germination of encysted zoospore.

1. By crop rotation.
2. By eradicating infected plants.
3. By spraying fungicides such as Bordeaux mixture.

Systematic Position

	G. W. Martin (1961)	C. J. Alexopoulos (1962)	G. C. Ainswoth (1971)
Kingdom	–Plantae	–Plantae	–Fungi
Division	–Mycota	–Mycota	–Eumycota
Sub-div.	–Eumyoctina	–Eumycotina	–Mastigomycotina
Class	–Phycomycetes	–Oomycetes	–Oomycetes
Sub-Class	–Oomycetidae		
Order	–Peronosporales	–Peronosporales	–Peronosporales
Family	–Albuginaceae	–Albuginaceae	–Albuginaceae
Genus	–*Albugo*	–*Albugo*	–*Albugo*

Family–Peronosporaceae

Characteristic Features

1. They are obligate parasites. The diseases caused by these fungi are commonly known as 'downy mildews'.
2. Asexual reproduction takes place by means of sporangia or conidia. The sporangiophores or conidiophores are sharply differentiated from vegetative hyphae. The sporangia or conidia are borne simultaneously, either singly or in clusters, at the tips of usually branched sporangiophores or conidiophores.
3. Sexual reproduction is oogamous.

There are several important genera, *viz., Sclerospora, Plasmopara, Bremia, Peronospora.* The genus *Peronospora* has been discussed here in detail.

Genus PERONOSPORA (75 species)

Habit and habitat. The genus is an obligate parasite. Different species of this genus cause the 'downy mildews' of crop plants. *Peronospora parasitica* causes the downy mildew of crucifers; *Peronospora pisi* causes the downy mildew of peas; *Peronospora brassicae* causes the downy mildew of mustard. Besides, several other species cause the downy mildews of many wild plants.

Structure of mycelium. The mycelium is endophytic, branched, aseptate, coenocytic, hyaline, intercellular and with rounded or branched haustoria to absorb food material from the host cells.

Reproduction. The reproduction takes place by means of asexual and sexual methods.

1. Asexual reproduction. The asexual reproduction takes place by means of conidia. The conidia are borne on the terminal ends of the branches of conidiophores. The conidiophores are given out from endophytic mycelium which come out through the stomata in groups. The conidiophore remains unbranched in the lower two-third portion. The remaining one-third of the conidiophore is two to ten times dichotomously branched. The ultimate very fine branches of the conidiophores are called the sterigmata (singular-sterigma) which are soluble in the water. The conidia are borne upon these fine sterigmata. The conidia are oval or elliptical in shape. They are purple, green or red coloured. They are formed in abundance and disseminated by wind. On the approach of favourable conditions of moisture and temperature the conidia germinate on some suitable host producing lateral germ tubes. The germ tubes always come out laterally from the conidia. The germ tube enters the host through stoma and develops into the new mycelium

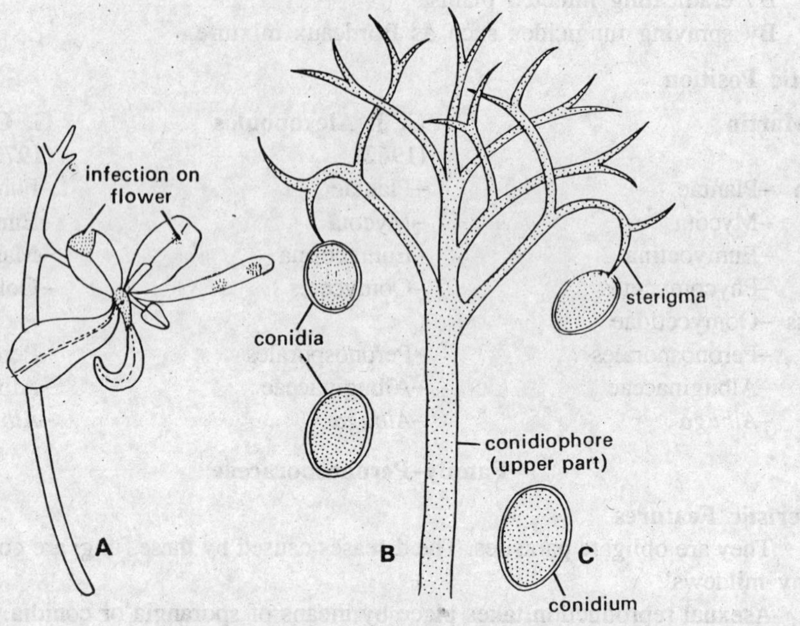

Fig. 6.28. *Peronospora parasitica.* Downy mildew of crucifers. A, distorted mustard flower; B, dichotomously branched conidiophore with conidia; C, conidium.

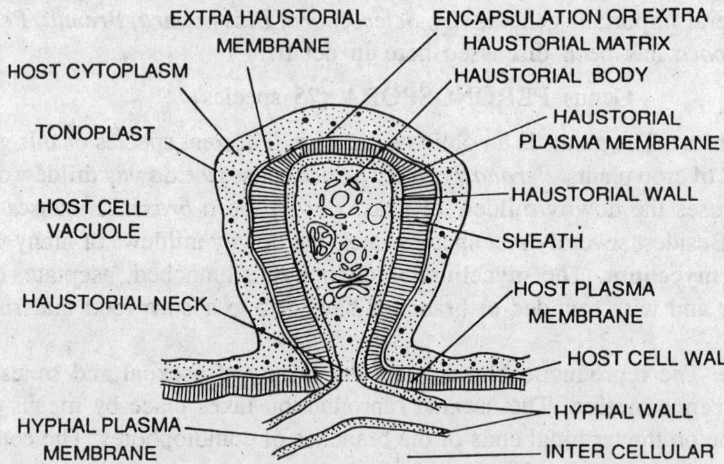

Fig. 6.28. (a) *Peronospora parasitica.* Ultrastructure of haustorium in host cell (diagrammatic).

2. Sexual reproduction. The sexual reproduction is oogamous and takes place by means of antheridia and oogonia. It takes place in unfavourable conditions. The antheridia and oogonia develop on the ends of the hyphae found in the intercellular spaces of the deeper tissues of petioles etc.

Usually the oogonia develop on the hyphal ends. The end of the hypha swells and becomes somewhat spherical. Much of the cytoplasm and nuclei are accumulated in this swollen portion.

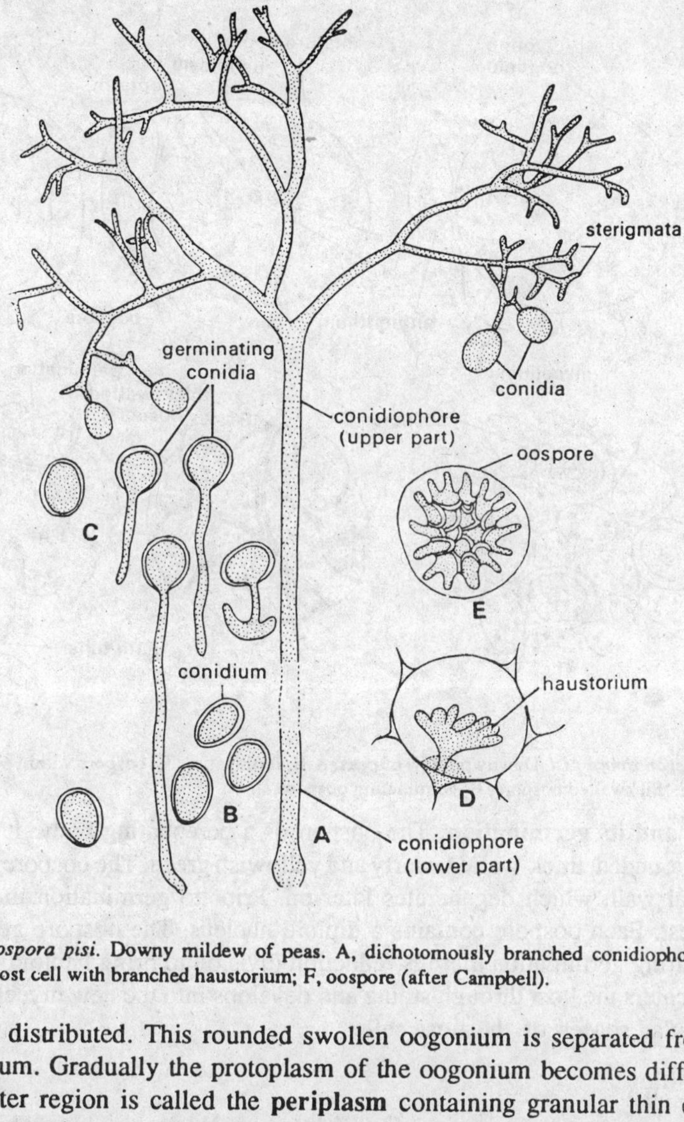

Fig. 6.29. *Peronospora pisi.* Downy mildew of peas. A, dichotomously branched conidiophore; B, conidia; C, germinating conidia; D, host cell with branched haustorium; F, oospore (after Campbell).

They are uniformly distributed. This rounded swollen oogonium is separated from rest of the mycelium by a septum. Gradually the protoplasm of the oogonium becomes differentiated into two regions, the outer region is called the **periplasm** containing granular thin cytoplasm and many nuclei. Very soon these nuclei degenerate. The central portion is ooplasm which is filled up in the oosphere or egg. In this region, in the beginning there are few nuclei, which degenerate leaving one functional female nucleus.

The antheridium develops by the side of the oogonium on the other hypha. The condition of the development of antheridium may be monoclinous or diclinous. The hyphal end swells and becomes club-shaped. This club-shaped antheridium contains many nuclei and cytoplasm in it. This is separated from rest of the mycelium by a basal septum. On the maturation of the antheridium all the nuclei but one degenerate. This is functional male nucleus.

Fertilization. The antheridium attaches itself to the oogonium. At the point of contact the fertilization tube develops from the antheridium. This tube penetrates the oogonial wall and reaches the egg through the periplasm. The male nucleus along with some cytoplasm is transferred to the egg through the fertilization tube, where it fuses with the egg nucleus giving rise to a diploid nucleus. With the result of the fusion the oospore develops.

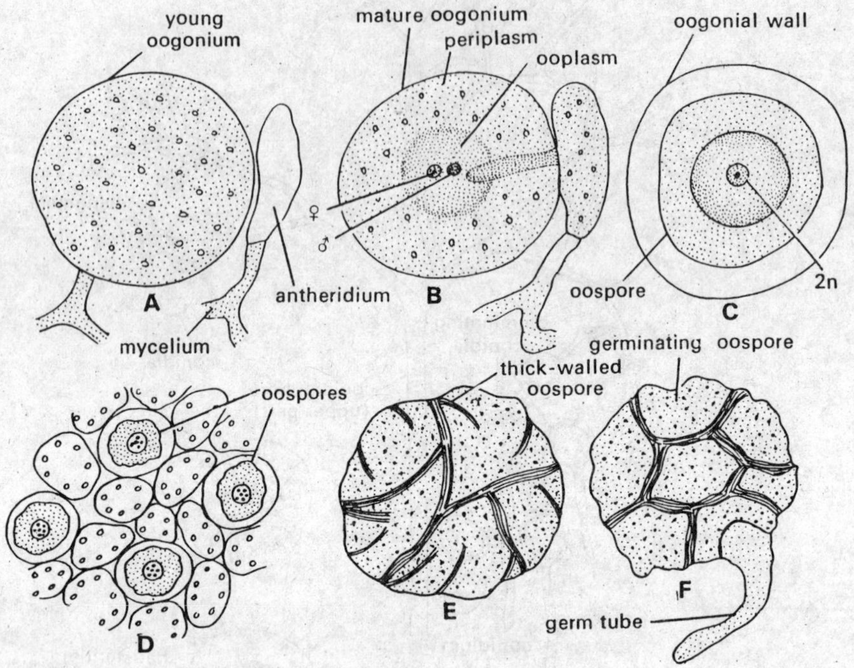

Fig. 6.30. *Peronospora pisi*. Downy mildew of peas. A-B, fertilization; C, oospore within oogonial wall; D, oospores within host tissue; E, thickwalled oospore; E, germinating oospore.

Oospore and its germination. The oospore is a perennating body. It survives in adverse conditions. It is rounded, thick-walled, warty and yellowish green. The oospore remains surrounded by thin oogonial wall, which degenerates later on. Prior to germination the oospores undergo the period of rest. Each oospore contains a diploid nucleus. The oospore germinates producing a germ tube. During germination there is reduction division to bring haploid (x) condition again. The germ tube enters the host through stoma and develops into the new mycelium which ramifies in the intercellular spaces of the host cells.

Systematic Position

	G.W. Martin (1961)	**C. J. Alexopoulos (1962)**	**G. C. Ainswoth (1971)**
Kingdom	–Plantae	–Plantae	–Fungi
Division	–Mycota	–Mycota	–Eumycota
Sub-div.	–Eumycotina	–Eumycotina	–Mastigomycotina
Class	–Phycomycetes	–Oomycetes	–Oomycetes
Sub-Cl.	–Oomycetidae		
Order	–Peronosporales	–Peronosporales	–Peronosporales
Family	–Peronosporaceae	–Peronosporaceae	–Peronosporaceae
Genus	–*Peronospora*	–*Peronospora*	–*Peronospora*

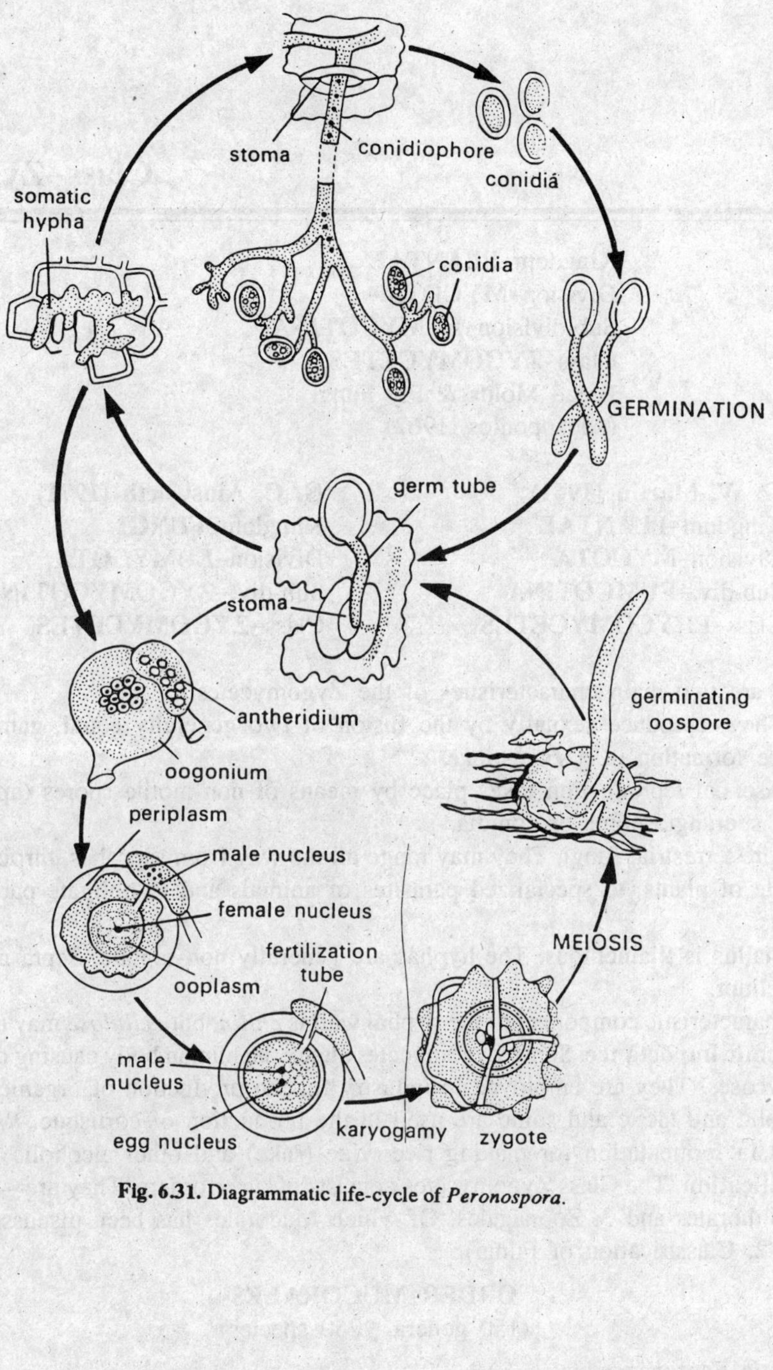

Fig. 6.31. Diagrammatic life-cycle of *Peronospora*.

7
Class–Zygomycetes

Kingdom–**PLANTAE**
Division–**MYCOTA**
Sub-division–**EUMYCOTINA**
Class–**ZYGOMYCETES**
Bread Molds & Fly Fungi
(Alexopoulos, 1962)

G. W. Martin (1961)	**G. C. Ainsworth (1971)**
Kingdom–**PLANTAE**	Kingdom–**FUNGI**
Division–**MYCOTA**	Division–**EUMYCOTA**
Sub-div.–**EUMCOTINA**	Sub-div.–**ZYGOMYCOTINA**
Class–**PHYCOMYCETES**	Class–**ZYGOMYCETES**

There are two main characteristics of the Zygomycetes.

1. They reproduce sexually by the fusion of two generally equal, gametangia which results in the formation of a **zygospore.**
2. Asexual reproduction takes place by means of non-motile spores (aplanospores) in the form of sporangiospores or conidia..

They are terrestrial fungi. They may range all the way from saprobes, through facultative, weak parasite of plants, to specialized parasites of animals and to obligate parasites of other Zygomycetes.

The thallus is filamentous. The hyphae are generally non-septate. Septa may be formed in old mycelium.

The characteristic component of the hyphal wall is *chitin,* but *cellulose* may also be present.

Economic importance. Some Zygomycetes attack the human body causing diseases known as Mucormycoses. They are employed in industry for the production of organic acids such as fumaric, oxalic and lactic and some are used in the production of cortisone. *Rhizopus oryzae* is employed in fermentation for making rice wine (sake) and other alcoholic preparations.

Classification. The Class Zygomycetes consists of *three* orders. They are— 1. Mucorales; 2. Entomophthorales and 3. Zoopagales. Of which Mucorales has been discussed here. (Also see chapter 2, Classification of Fungi).

ORDER MUCORALES

(150 genera ; 250 species)

Characteristic Features

1. Majority of the species are saprophytic growing on dead organic materials. A few species are parasitic. They are called the 'black molds' because of the presence of black spores.
2. The mycelium is profusely branched, aseptate, coenocytic, vacuolate and with oil droplets.

3. Asexual reproduction takes place by means of aplanospores produced inside the globular sporangia borne terminally on aerial sporangiophores.

4. Sexual reproduction takes place by means of aplanogametes (coenogametes) produced singly in the gametangia. Most of the species are isogamous but some species are anisogamous.

5. The perfect or sexual spores are the zygospores resulted by the fusion of aplanogametes.

6. The species may by homothallic or heterothallic.

7. There are about 45 genera and 250 species in this order.

Classification. There are several families of which the family Mucoraceae has been discussed here. It is represented by *Mucor mucedo*.

Family–Mucoraceae

Characteristic Features

1. Most of the species are saprophytic.
2. The sporangiola and conidia are absent.
3. The sporangium possesses a columella. The sporangial wall is thin, fugacious, breaking or deliquescing.
4. Sporangia, chlamydospores or zygospores not enclosed in sporocarps.

The important genera are *Mucor* and *Rhizopus*. They have been discussed here in detail.

Genera MUCOR (60 species) and RHIZOPUS (5 species)

Habit and habitat. These are saprophytic fungi and grow on dead organic material. One can get these fungi in abundance by keeping moist bread under bell jar for two or three days at suitable temperature in the laboratory. The fungal mycelium looks like fine cottony threads on the surface of the bread. This is also called the 'black mold' because of its black spores.

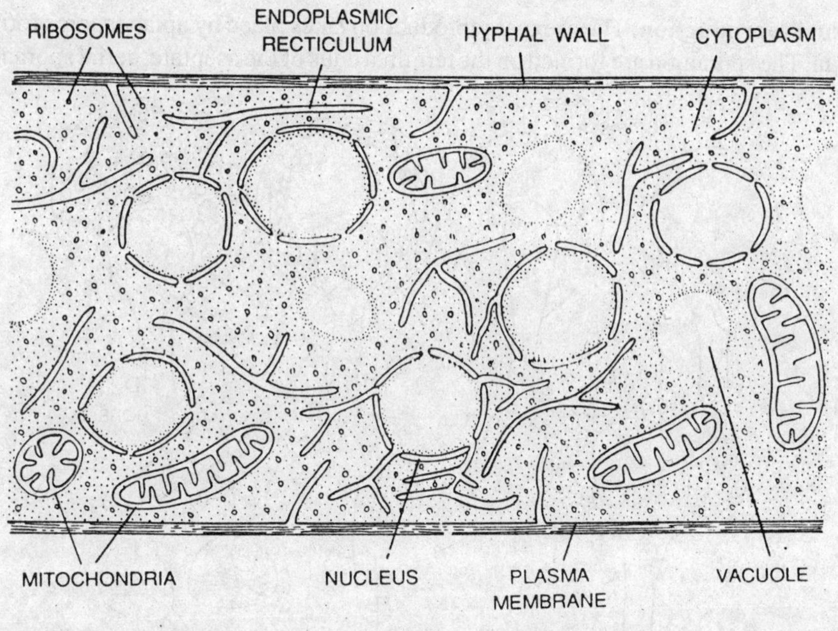

Fig. 7.1. *Mucor* sp. Part of hypha as seen under electron microscope.

Structure of mycelium. The mycelium is white cottony, branched, coenocytic, aseptate, hyaline, vacuolate and with oil droplets.

Reproduction. The reproduction takes place by means of asexual and sexual methods.

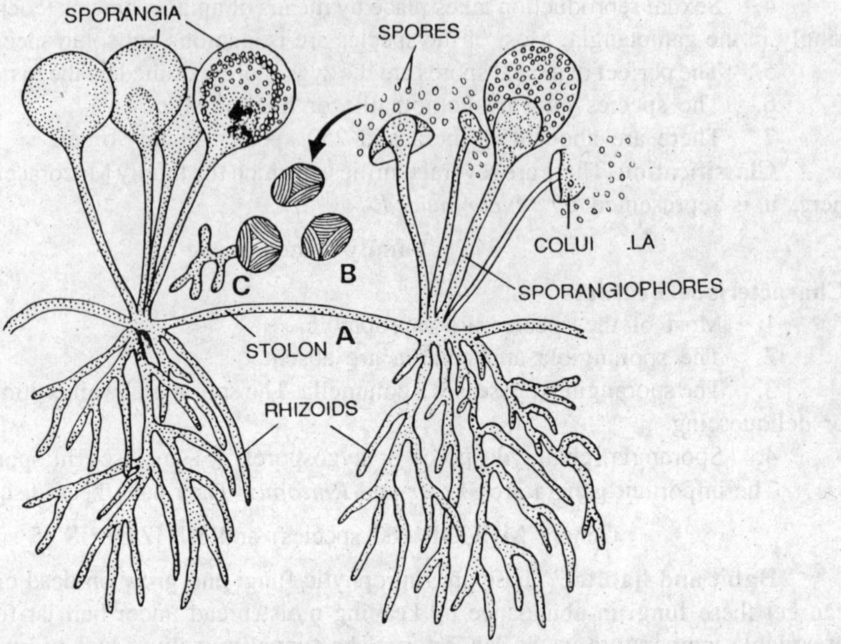

Fig. 7.2. *Rhizopus stolonifer*. A, fascicle of sporangiophores arising opposite the rhizoids, and connected by a stolon with another group; B, spores (aplanospores); C, germinating spore.

Asexual reproduction. The asexual reproduction takes place by aplanospores formed within the sporangia. The sporangia are formed on the terminal ends of the aseptate, aerial sporangiophores.

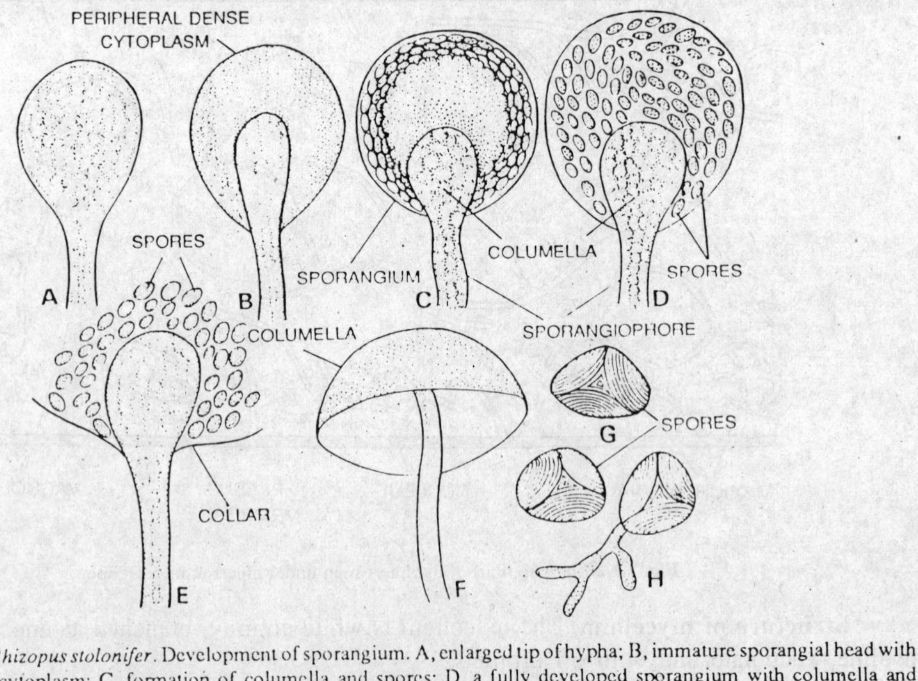

Fig. 7.3. *Rhizopus stolonifer*. Development of sporangium. A, enlarged tip of hypha; B, immature sporangial head with peripheral dense cytoplasm; C, formation of columella and spores; D, a fully developed sporangium with columella and aplanospores; E, dehisced sporangium; F, Columella; G, aplanospore; H, germinating aplanospore.

These sporangiophores directly come out from the mycelium, and there terminal ends swell to develop sporangia. Much of cytoplasm, nutrients, and many nuclei are accumulated in the

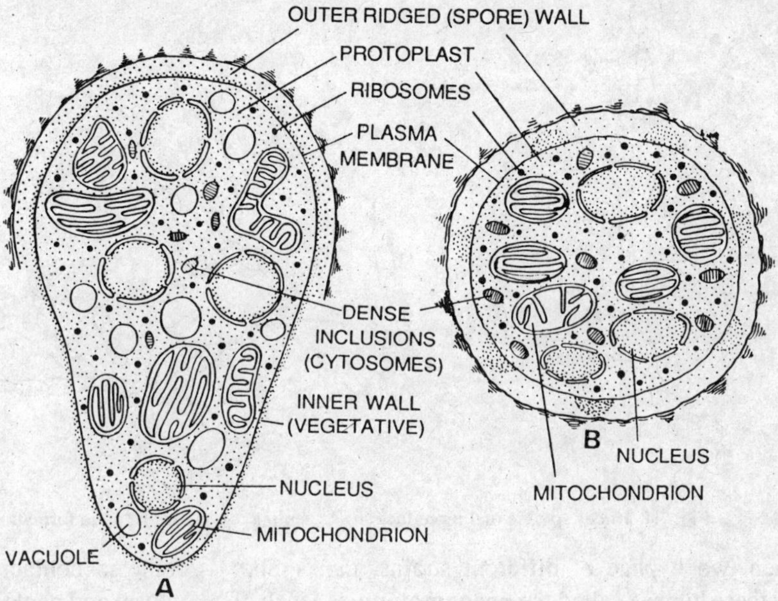

Fig. 7.3. (a) *Rhizopus* sp. A ultra structure of germinating spore; B, ultra sturcture of mature spore.

young sporangia. Usually the protoplasm accumulates just beneath the sporangial wall, and the vacuoles are formed in the central region of the sporangium. There are very few nuclei in the vacuoles. By this time a swollen vegetative columella develops in the centre of this protoplasm. This is absolutely a sterile structure. The protoplasm which surrounds the columella begins to divide in small protoplasmic bits from outside to inside. Each small protoplasmic bit contains 5-10 nuclei in it. They are called the **aplanospores.** On the maturation of the aplanospores the outer wall of the sporangium bursts and the spores are dispersed. The spores are disseminated by wind. Each spore is somewhat triangular, walled and multinucleate. On getting suitable conditions they germinate producing germ tubes developing into new mycelia.

Asexual reproduction also takes place by means of thick-walled intercalary **chlamydospores.** The old mycelium becomes septate, and the protoplasm of each cell becomes rounded and thick-walled. These structures are perennating bodies and survive in adverse conditions. On the approach of favourable conditions, each chlamydospore germinates producing a germ tube, developing into new mycelium on suitable substratum.

The *Mucor* is also asexually reproduced by the formation of **oidia.** These oidia are formed only in the liquid media. They also cause the fermentation in the sugar solution in which they are developed. The mycelium becomes septate, and the thin-walled segments oidia are separated from each other in liquid medium. The oidia increase in number by budding. This state of *Mucor* is called the 'torula condition'. The alcohol is produced during fermentation.

Sexual reproduction. The species of *Mucor* may be homothallic or heterothallic. In the homothallic species the hyphae taking part in sexual reproduction are of the same strain. In other words they may be either of + or of - strains. In the heterothallic species the hyphae taking part in the sexual reproduction are of two different strains, *i.e.*, + and — strains. *Mucor* *hiemalis* is a homothallic species, and *Mucor mucedo* is heterothallic.

In *Mucor mucedo* the sexual reproduction takes place as follows :

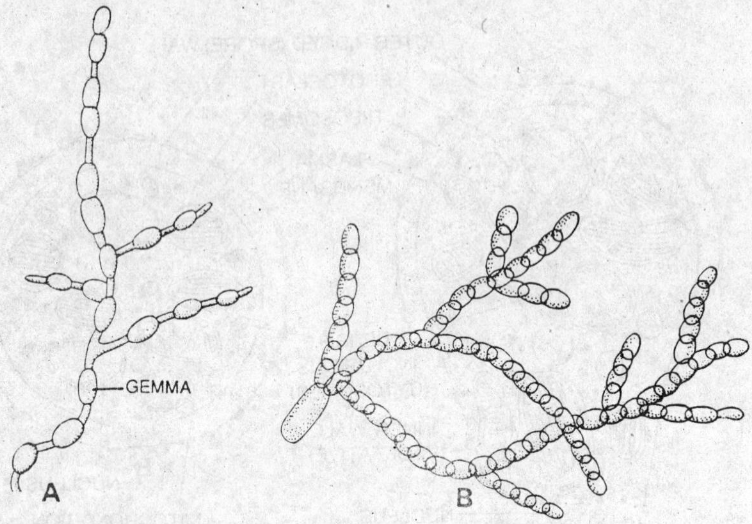

Fig. 7.4. *Mucor* sp. Asexual reproduction. A, gemma formation; B, oidia formation.

When two hyphae of different strains, *i.e.*, + and — come in contact, the outgrowths arise from these hyphae called the **progametangia.** Much of cytoplasm and nuclei are accumulated in terminal swollen ends of these **progametangia.** Very soon the septa are developed just behind the point of contact. The terminal multinucleate segments are called the **gametangia,** and the elongated cells behind the gametangia, the **suspensors.** The gametangia increase in size and the nuclei embedded in the cytoplasm increase in number by repeated mitotic divisions. At the point of contact the gametangial wall dissolves and the **coenogametes** found inside the gametangia are fused. With the result of fusion the **zygote** is formed. The zygospore is black, thick-walled and warty. At the time of the fusion the nuclei of different strained coenogametes form pairs and ultimately fuse forming diploid nuclei. The nuclei which do not form pairs remain haploid and disorganise very soon. The **coenozygospore** is a perennating body and faces adverse conditions. This undergoes the period of rest, which may be of several months. On the approach of favourable conditions the zygote spore germinates.

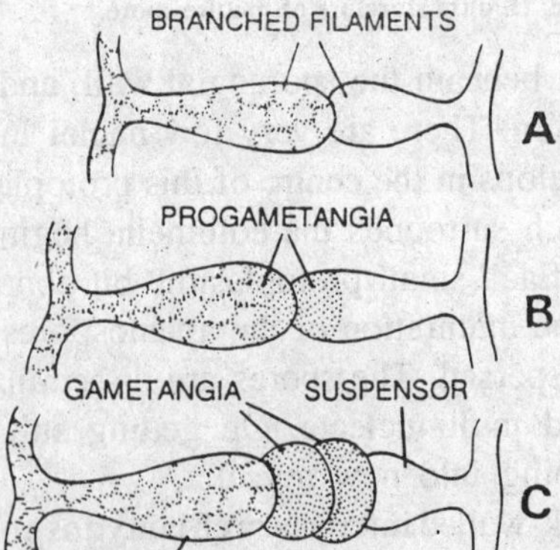

Fig. 7.5. *Rhizopus nigricans*. Sexual reproduction. A-E, successive stages in the formation of zygospore.

Germination of zygospore. In favourable conditions the outer warty wall of the zygospore bursts and a germ tube comes out known as **promycelium.** At the terminal end of this promycelium the **germsporangium** or the **zygosporangium** develops. The apalanospores are produced inside the zygosporangium in the same manner as in asexual reproduction. The sporangial wall of the zygosporangium bursts and the spores are dispersed by wind from one place to another. On getting suitable conditions they germinate producing germ tubes which develop into new mycelia.

Pathenogenesis. Sometimes the gametes behave like zygospores even without fusion. Such spores developed without fusion are called **azygospores** or **parthenospores** and the phenomenon is known as **parthenogenesis.**

Heterothallism. Ehrenbergh (1829), for the first time studied zygospores in the order Mucorales. The American mycologist Blakeslee (1904), reported that in the several genera of the order Mucorales, the zygospores are not formed at all. He also supported his view with facts and reasons, and also investigated that in the same order two types of species are found which may be named as homothallic and heterothallic species. When the two hyphae of the same mycelium produced by a single spore fuse with each other and a zygospore is developed. The species is said to be homothallic, *e.g., Mucor hiemalis.*

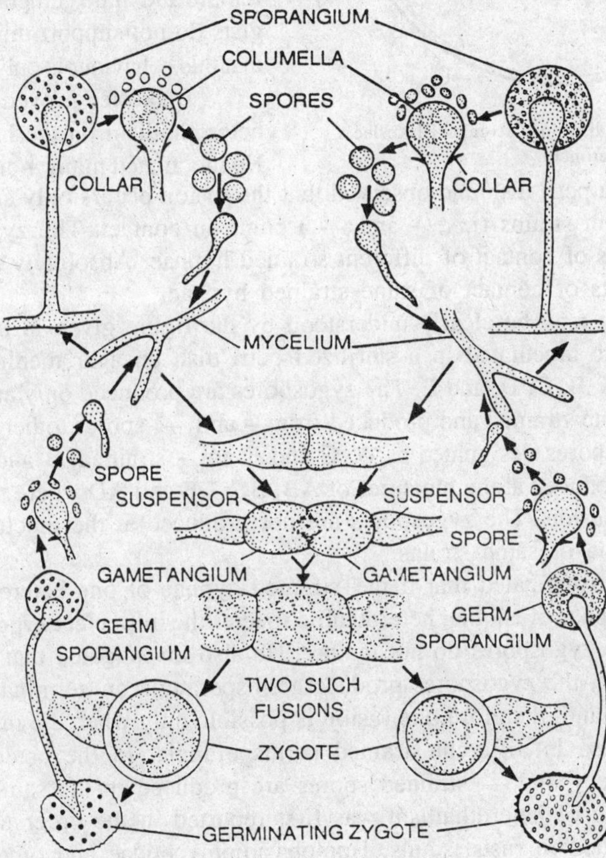

Fig. 7.6. *Mucor* sp. Diagrammatic life-cycle.

Mucor mucedo and *Mucor stolonifer* are the typical heterothallic species. In heterothallic species the fusion can take place only among the different strained hyphae, which develop on different mycelia of different (+ and —) strains. In these species the zygospores cannot be produced by the fusion of two hyphae of the same strain. In 1904 Blakeslee reported that in heterothallic species whenever the mycelia of + and — strains remain apart from each other, the zygospores are not produced and only the sporangia are formed. On the other hand, when + and — mycelia grow together, the fusion takes place and the zygospores are produced. Morphologically the + and — strained mycelia are quite similar in structure, but different in physiological behaviour. In other words, they are morphologically identical and physiologically different. Sometimes, it has also been observed that the growth of the + mycelium is comparatively faster, and the gametangia of + mycelium are bigger than that of the — mycelium, and they can be distinguished as female and male gametangia. Many mycologists do not support this view and advocate that this behaviour is only because of nutrition.

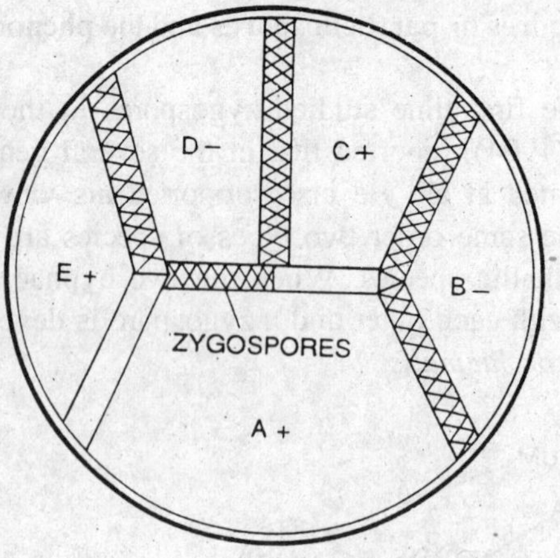

Fig. 7.7. Heterothallism in Mucorales-Blakeslee's experiment.

Blakeslee proved the phenomenon of heterothallism on the basis of experiments. He inoculated many + and — strained spores on the agar media in a petri dish and observed that the fusion occurs only at those points where the hyphae of different strains (*i.e.*, + and —) come in contact. The zygospores were only produced at the points of contact of different strained hyphae. Absolutely no zygospores were produced at the points of contact of same strained hyphae.

This experiment may be clearly understood by the figure given in the text. Five spores of different strains are inoculated in a sterilized petri dish on agar medium at different five points designated as A, B, C, D, and E. The zygospores are produced only at those points where the mycelia are opposite strained and produced from + and — spores, otherwise the zygospores are not formed. The spores designated as A, C and E are + strained, B and D are — strained. The zygospores are produced at the junctures of AB, BC, DE and AD where the opposite strained mycelia take part in fusion. The zygospores are not produced at the junctures of AC and AE because of the mycelia of same strains.

Blakeslee also investigated that if the+strained hyphae of one heterothallic species fuse with the — strained hyphae of another heterothallic species the **imperfect zygospores** are resulted. In such conditions the zygospores do not mature. He also investigated that in the heterothallic species *Mucor mucedò,* the zygospores produce germsporangia on germination, which contain single strained spores, and, therefore, the fusion is possible only when the mycelia are produced from the spores formed in different strained germsporangia. In the heterothallic species of *Phycomyces nitens* the + and — strained spores are produced in the same germsporangium.

The phenomenon of heterothallism was first reported in the order Mucorales, but now this has been established in rusts, smuts, Homobasidiomycetidae and other fungi.

Systematic Position

	G. W. Martin (1961)	**C. J. Alexopoulos (1962)**	**G. C. Ainsworth (1971)**
Kingdom	–Plantae	–Plantae	–Fungi
Division	–Mycota	–Mycota	–Eumycota
Sub-div.	–Eumycotina	–Eumycotina	–Zygomycotina
Class	–Phycomycetes	–Zygomycetes	–Zygomycetes

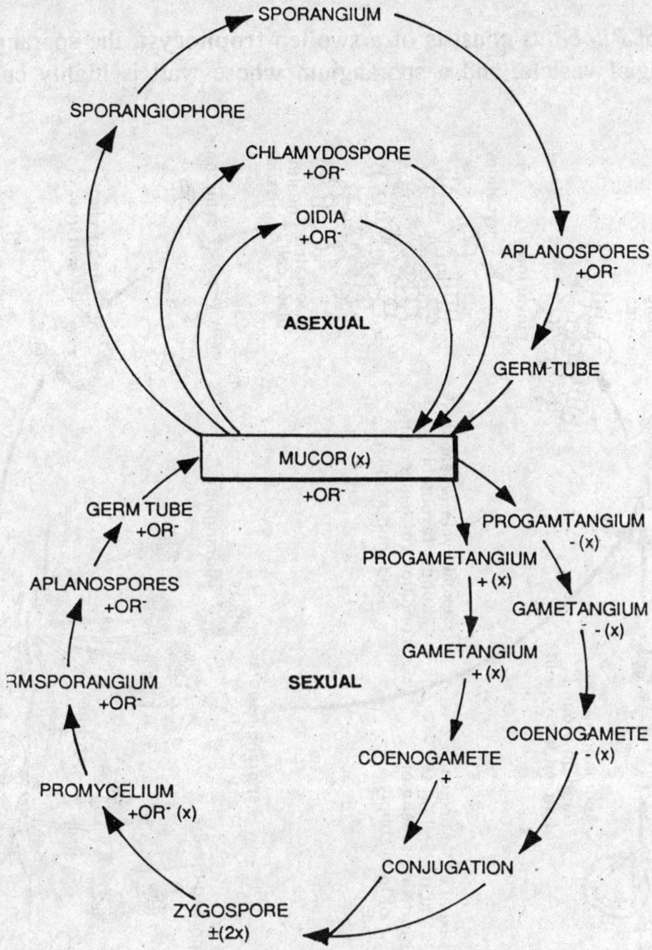

Fig. 7.8. Graphic life cycle of *Mucor.*

Sub-cl.	–Zygomycetidae		
Order	–Mucorales	–Mucorales	–Mucorales
Family	–Mucoraceae	–Mucoraceae	–Mucoraceae
Genera	*–Mucor and Rhizopus*	*–Mucor and Rhizopus*	*–Mucor and Rhizopus*

Genus PILOBOLUS (25 known species)

Pilobolus, a coprophilous fungus, commonly occurs in horse and cow dung. About 10 species are found in India, of which *Pilobolus longipes, P. kleinii* and *P. crystallinus* are most common. *Pilobolus* grows in the laboratory only on media containing dung decoctions. Hesseltine and his co-workers (1952) found in dung a factor which was necessary for the growth of *Pilobolus.* They named this factor 'coprogen'.

Somatic structure. The thallus consists of mycelium; the hyphae are aseptate, branched, coenocytic, hyaline and remain submerged in the substratum.

Asexual reproduction. The asexual reproduction takes place by means of aplanospores produced within the sporangia. Some hyphae become upright, and come out of the substratum.

The sporangiophore of *Pilobolus* consists of a swollen **trophocyst,** the sporangiophore proper, a swollen sub-sporangial vesicle, and a sporangium whose wall is highly cutinized.

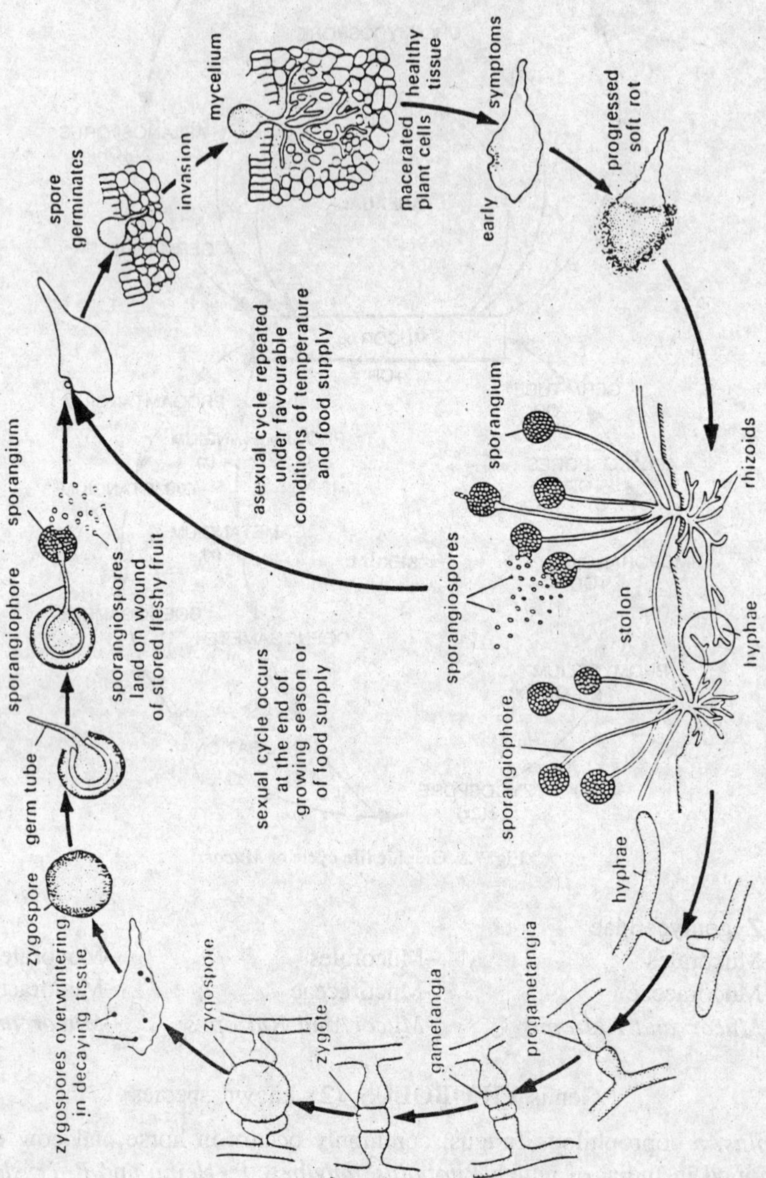

Fig. 7.9. Diagrammatic life-cycle of *Rhizopus*.

The sporangiophores of *Pilobolus* are positively phototrophic and shoot their sporangia toward light. This is a useful adaptation which helps in dissemination of spores. Buller (1934) states that *Pilobolus* can shoot its sporangia vertically upward to a height of six feet. The entire sporangium is violently shot off the sporangiophore and adheres to the first solid object it strikes.

The sporangium contains several thousand of spores.

In *Pilobolus,* discharge of sporangia is an interesting phenomenon. The swelling of sub-sporangial vesicle helps a lot in sporangial discharge. This vesicle is turgid and contains a liquid under pressure. The sporangium is released violently and is carried at a speed of 10 — 20 feet per second through the air (Buller, 1934). As the sporangium strikes a solid object, it gets attached to it by a mucilaginous substance. Ordinarily the sporangia are not detached from the vegetation. When the herbivores eat such herbs, the spores are released from the sporangium in the alimentary canals of animals and are disseminated through animal dung.

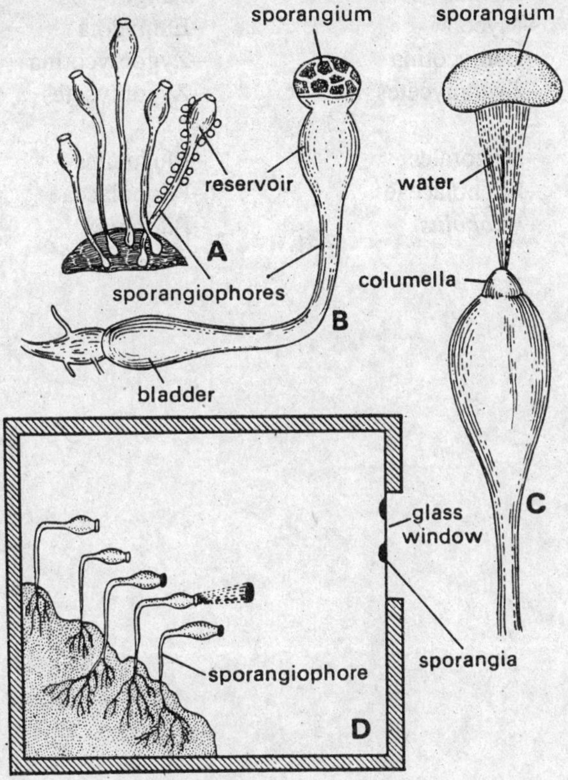

Fig. 7.10. *Pilobolus*. Different stages and asexual reproduction. A, sporangiophores on substratum; B, mature sporangium on sporangiophore; C, sporangium shot off; D, during growth sporangiophores bending towards light.

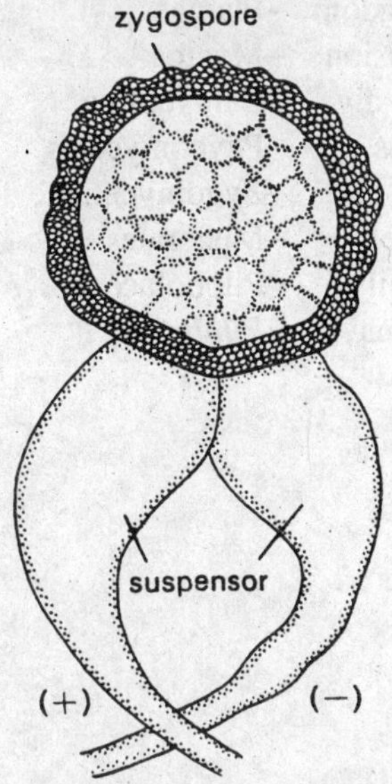

Fig. 7.11. *Pilobolus*. Sexual reproduction, and formation of thick-walled zygospore.

Sexual reproduction. The sexual reproduction is rarely found in *Pilobolus*, and takes place in abnormal and adverse conditions. Most species are heterothallic. Two compatible neighbouring hyphae become club-shaped, rich in protoplasm and are called **progametangia.** They grow up right and lie side by side to each other. The multinucleate gametangia develop on the terminal parts of the progametangia by transverse septation. The sexual reproduction takes place by the copulation of two multinucleate gametangia which are in the main similar in structure, but may differ in size. When the gametangia are formed, the walls between them dissolve and the contents mix. The cells of the two gametania thus actually fuse into one cell, in which karyogamy takes place. This cell develops into a **zygospore** by the deposition of a thick wall around its protoplast. The zygospore germinates either by a germ tube or germsporangium. The meiosis takes place during germination.

Systematic Position

	G. W. Martin (1961)	C. J. Alexopoulos (1962)	G. C. Ainsworth (1971)
Kingdom	–Plantae	–Plantae	–Fungi
Division	–Myctoa	–Mycota	–Eumycota
Sub-div.	–Eumycotina	–Eumycotina	–Zygomycotina
Class	–Phycomycetes	–Zygomycetes	–Zygomycetes
Sub-cl.	–Zygomycetidae	–	–
Order	–Mucorales	–Mucorales	–Mucorales
Family	–Pilobolaceae	–Pilobolaceae	–Pilobolaceae
Genus	–*Pilobolus*	–*Pilobolus*	–*Pilobolus*

8

Class–Ascomycetes

Kingdom–**PLANTAE**
Division–**MYCOTA**
Sub-division–**EUMYCOTINA**
Class--**ASCOMYCETES**
The Sac Fungi
(Alexopoulos, 1962)

G. W. Martin (1961)
Kingdom–**PLANTAE**
Division–**MYCOTA**
Sub-Div.–**EUMYCOTINA**
Class–**ASCOMYCETES**

G. C. Ainsworth (1971)
Kingdom–**FUNGI**
Division–**EUMYCOTA**
Sub-div–**ASCOMYCOTINA**
Classes– **1. HEMIASCOMYCETES**
2. LOCULOASCOMYCETES
3. PLECTOMYCETES
4. LABOULBENIOMYCETES
5. PYRENOMYCETES
6. DISCOMYCETES

According to Ainswoth and Bisby (1950) there are about 1820 genera and 15,500 species. They are included in 'the higher fungi'. The asci (singular-ascus) containing ascospores are uniformly present in all Ascomycetes. The ascospores are produced after a meiotic division, and, therefore, they are haploid. Usually the number of ascospores in each ascus is four or eight. In exceptional cases the number may be as less as two or as high as 16, 32, 64, 128 or more than that.

Occurrence. The fungi of this class may be parasitic or saprophytic. The mycelium of the parasitic fungi is usually endophytic but sometimes ectophytic as in Erysiphales. The parasitic Ascomycetes cause many diseases to the crop plants and fruit trees.

The saprophytic Ascomycetes are found in diverse habitats. They grow on moist rotten logs, plant debris, humus soil, and several other dead organic substrata. Some of the Ascomycetes produce macroscopic mushroom like fructification, *e.g., Morchella* etc. The other saprophytic Ascomycetes, *e.g., Aspergillus, Penicillium* etc., grow upon rotten vegetables, rotten fruits and other such dead organic substrata and called the blue and green molds. The penicillin drug is extracted from *Penicillium* species. The species of *Saccharomyces* are also of industrial importance. Some of them are facultative saprophytes.

Somatic structure. Except for some, such as yeasts, the vegetative body of an ascomycete consists of a well developed mycelium. The mycelium is branched and septate. The cells of the hyphae may be uninucleate, binucleate or multinucleate. There is a central pore in each septum through which the cytoplasm and nuclei are communicated from one cell to another.

Sometimes the mycelium possesses densely interwoven hyphae and the pseudoparenchymatous sclerotia.

Asexual reproduction. The asexual reproduction in Ascomycetes takes place by several methods, *e.g.*, by fission, fragmentation, budding, chlamydospores and conidia. The methods of fission and budding are exclusively reserved for the yeast and some other Ascomycetes.

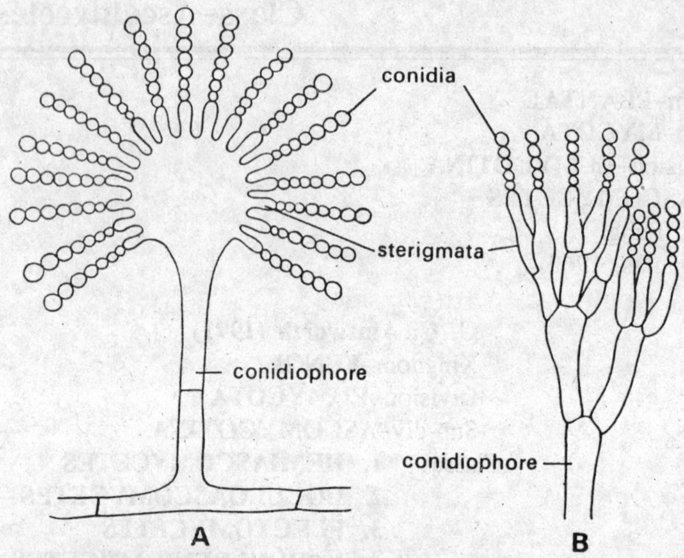

Fig. 8.1. Asexual reproduction by conidia in *Aspergillus* (A) and *Penicillium* (B).

Chlamydospores. The chlamydospores have been reported from many Ascomycetes. They are commonly formed by rounding up of the protoplasm of the terminal and intercalary cells of the hyphae. These structures are thick-walled and act as perennating bodies. Much of the food reserves are accumulated in them. They undergo a period of rest prior to their germination.

Conidia. The most important method of asexual reproduction is by means of exogenously produced conidia. The conidia are produced on the conidiophores in basigenous or acrogenous chains. Sometimes the conidiophores are aerial and in other cases they are arranged in saucer-shaped acervuli. In certain cases the conidiophores are found within the flask-like structures the 'pycnia' and called pycniosporophores. In such cases the conidia are known as 'pycnidiospores'. The pycnia are open at their apical ends by ostioles.

Arrangement of conidiophores. The conidia are generally produced on conidiophores. The conidiophores may be produced free from each other, or they may be organized into definite fruiting bodies. The most common fruiting bodies are of following types.

1. **Pycnidium.** This type of fruiting body is a hollow, commonly globose or flask-shaped structure whose pseudoparenchymatous walls are lined with conidiophores. In such case the conidia are known as **pycniospores** or **pycnidiospores.** The pycnidium opens by an opening called **ostiole.**

2. **Acervulus.** This type of fruiting body develops a mat of hyphae, below the epidermis of cuticle of the host plant and giving rise to short conidiophores closely packed together. On maturation such structure becomes saucer-shaped and looks like a flat open bed of conidiophores with conidia at their tips. The acervuli are usually formed by the parasitic fungi.

3. **Sporodochium.** The conidiophores may also be cemented together to form complex structures known as sporodochia. This is a hemispherical or barrel-like asexual fruiting body. The lower part of sporodochium consists of a cushion-like stromatic mass of hyphae. The conidiophores arise from the surface of the stroma. The conidiophores makes the upper part of the sporodochium.

4. **Synnemata.** Here the conidiophores remain arranged very close to each other. The conidiphores may be branched or unbranched. They are generally united along greater part of their length to form the asexual fruiting body known as **synnema** (*e.g.*, *Arthrobotrym* sp.).

The conidia vary in shape, size and colour. The conidia of *Aspergillus* and *Penicillium* are spherical and smoky green. They may be smooth (*e.g., Penicillium*) or echinulate (*e.g.,*

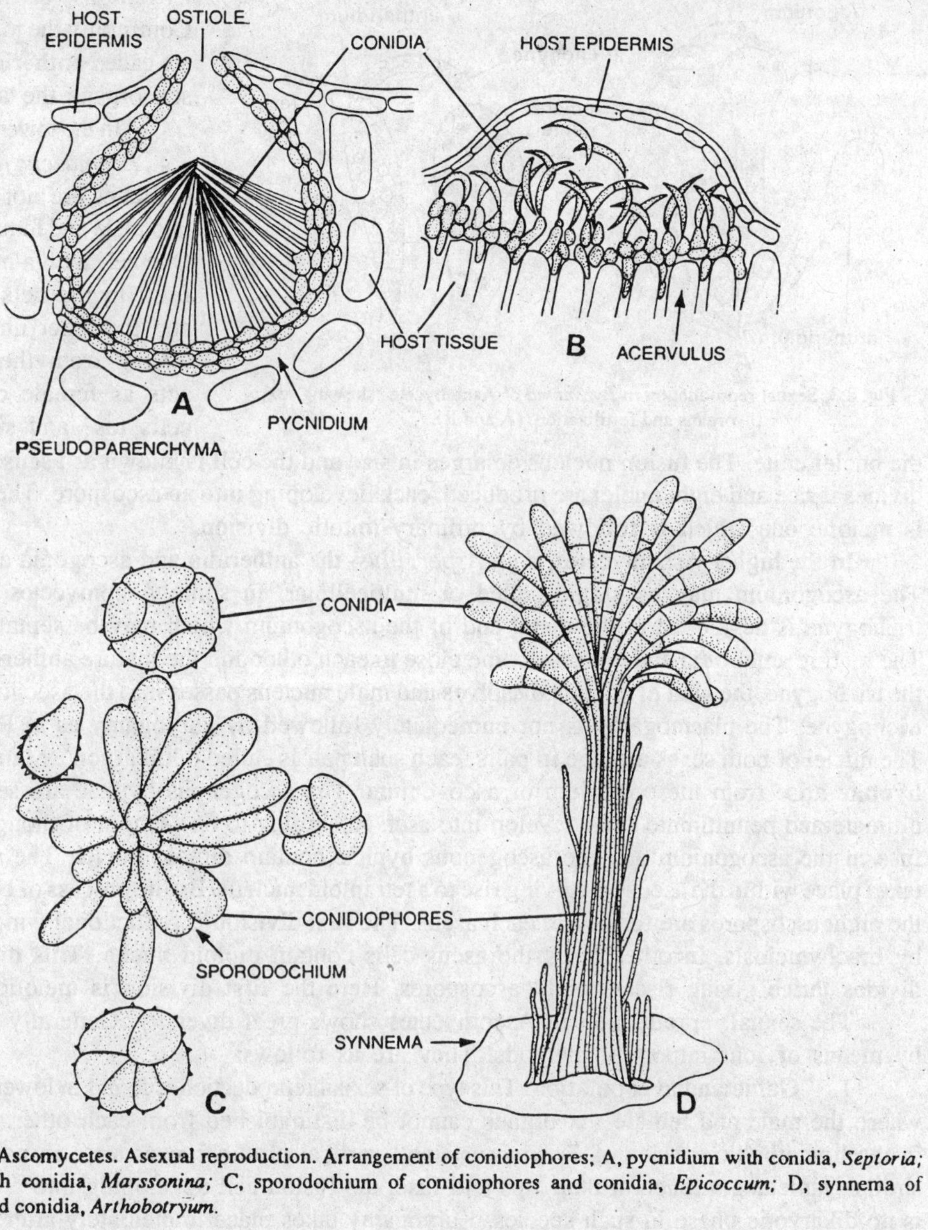

Fig. 8.2. Ascomycetes. Asexual reproduction. Arrangement of conidiophores; A, pycnidium with conidia, *Septoria;* B, acervulus with conidia, *Marssonina;* C, sporodochium of conidiophores and conidia, *Epicoccum;* D, synnema of conidiophores and conidia, *Arthobotryum.*

Aspergillus). They may be uninucleate (*e.g., Penicillium*) or multinucleate (*e.g., Aspergillus).* In *Erysiphe* the conidia are barrel-shaped. The conidia germinate immediately after their detachment from the conidiophores when they fall upon suitable substratum in appropriate atmospheric conditions producing germ-tubes. They remain viable only for a short time.

Oidia. In some ascomycetous fungi the hyphae break into small fragments. Such small, globose structures are known as **oidia.** They separate from each other and act as spores. Such structures are found in *Oospora, Monilinia* etc.

Sexual reproduction. The sexual reproduction takes place by the union of two compatible nuclei. The species are either homothallic or heterothallic, and therefore, the fertilization is either isogamous or heterogamous. Commonly the male sex organs are called **antheridia** and female sex organs the **ascogonia.**

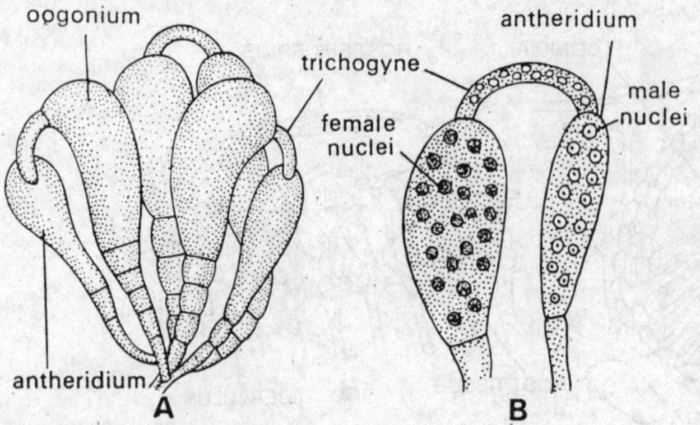

Fig. 8.3. Sexual reproduction in *Pyronema* of Ascomycetes showing sex organs and fertilization. (A and B).

In the lower Ascomycetes, *e.g., Eremascus fertilis,* the sex branches are not distinguished into male and female sex organs. One cell with a nucleus arising from hypha acts as male cell and the other uninucleate cell arising from the same hypha acts as female cell. The two cells fuse and simultaneously the nuclei unite. The fusion nucleus enlarges in size and the cell is known as **ascus.** This nucleus divides thrice and eight nuclei are produced, each developing into an ascospore. The first division is meiotic one which is followed by ordinary mitotic division.

In the higher Ascomycetes, *e.g., Aspergillus,* the antheridia and ascogonia are developed. The ascogonium may be single celled or multicellular. In some Ascomycetes the receptive trichogyne is developed at the distal end of the ascogonium which may be septate or aseptate. The mature antheridia and oogonia come close to each other and the mature antheridium touches the trichogyne, the wall of contact dissolves and male nucleus passes into the ascogonium through trichogyne. The plasmogamy is not immediately followed by karyogamy as in Phycomycetes. The nuclei of both sexes arrange in pairs, each such pair is called a 'dikaryon'. Many **ascogenous hyphae** arise from the oogonium or ascogonium. The ascogenous hyphae are septate and the ultimate and penultimate cells develop into asci. According to one school of thought, the nuclei fuse in the ascogonium and the ascogenous hyphae contain diploid nuclei. The second fusion takes place within the ascus cell giving rise to a tetraploid nucleus. By the process of **brachymeiosis** the eight ascospores are formed in each ascus. The first division is reductional which is followed by brachymeiosis. In other cases the ascus cells contain diploid nuclei. This diploid nucleus divides thrice giving rise to eight ascospores. Here the first division is meiotic one.

The sexual reproduction in Ascomycetes shows great diversity. Generally it takes place by means of four important methods. They are as follows:

1. Gametangial copulation. This type of sexual reproduction is found in lower Ascomycetes where the male and female sex organs cannot be distinguished from each other. For example, in the homothallic species of *Eremascus* small vertical protuberances arise in pairs. Two such similar gametangia touch at their tips and fuse, the fusion cell developing into an ascus. There is no dikaryotic phase in such species. Karyogamy takes place immediately after plasmogamy. The somatic cells of yeasts act as gametangia; two of them fuse forming a zygote which later on directly converts into an asucs.

2. Gametangial contact. Some species of Ascomycetes produce morphologically differentiated gametangia known as antheridia (male) and ascogonia (female). The antheridium and ascogonium come in contact; the wall of contact dissolves and the male nucleus from antheridium passes through the lateral pore into the ascogonium. No fertilization tubes are formed but sometimes the ascogonium is provided with a trichogyne which acts as a receiving organ and receives the male nucleus. In certain cases the antheridia are formed but they are non functional; in other cases the antheridia are not even formed. For example, in *Penicillium* sp., the antheridium is non-functional, and the ascogonial nuclei themselves become arranged in functional pairs.

3. Spermatization. In certain species the antheridia are not formed, and the male nuclei reach ascogonia by means of spermatia, microconidia or conidia. The spermatia are minute, spherical, specialized uninucleate male sex cells. They come in contact of the receptive organs and empty their contents into them. The nuclei of spermatia migrate to the ascogonium through the pores of septa. On maturation the spermatia become detached and carried by some external agency such as insects, wind or water to the receptive organs (trichogynes or somatic hyphae).

4. Somatogamy. Sometimes, in some Ascomycetes the fusion of somatic hyphae of two compatible mycelia takes place and the nuclei migrate to the ascogonia through the septal pores. This type of sexual union is known as **somatogamy** or somatogamous copulation.

Ascus formation. As mentioned above the ultimate and penultimate cells develop into asci. The terminal cell of ascogenous hypha is binucleate. One nucleus of the pair is male and

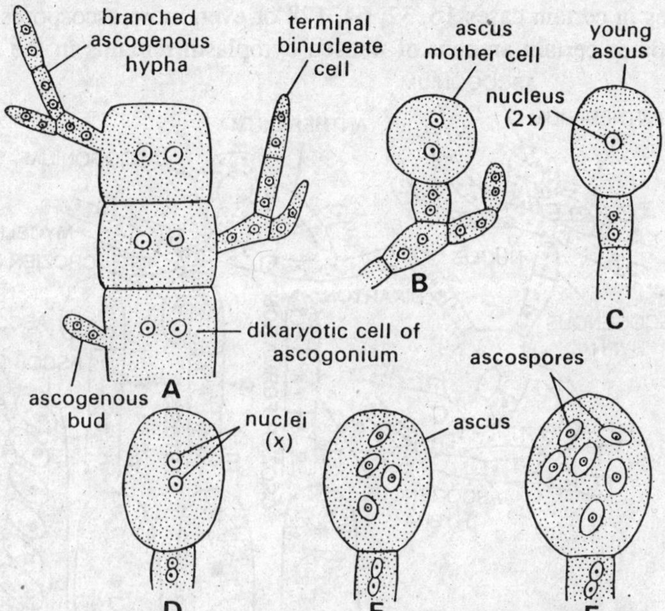

Fig. 8.4. Formation of ascus and ascospores in *Penicillium.*

the other female. The terminal cell becomes curved on one side like a **crozier.** Simultaneously this enlarges in size. Both the nuclei of the pair (dikaryon) divide mitotically and four daughter nuclei are produced, the transverse septa develop in the crozier cell. This results in the formation of a uninucleate terminal cell, binucleate penultimate middle cell and uninucleate basal cell. The penultimate or middle cell is also known as **arch cell** or **crook cell.** The arch cell contains two nuclei of different parentage, one male and the other female. The arch cell acts as ascus mother cell and ultimately develops into an ascus. Both the nuclei of the dikaryon fuse and a diploid (2x) nucleus is formed. This is the process of karyogamy and represents fertilization. The fusion nucleus or synkaryon represents the diploid phase. This is a temporary phase. Very soon the cell containing this nucleus elongates and the fusion nucleus divides. The first division is meiotic. This is followed by two mitotic divisions. In this way eight nuclei are produced.

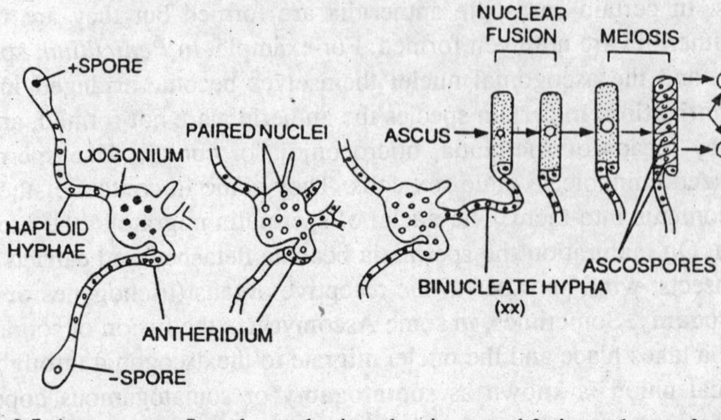

Fig. 8.5. Ascomycetes. Sexual reproduction: showing sexual fusion and ascus formation.

Around each nucleus the cytoplasm is deposited and eight ascospores are formed within the ascus. Sometimes in certain cases 16, 32, 64, 128 or even more ascospores are produced within an ascus. Sometimes certain amount of unused cytoplasm remains in the ascus and called the

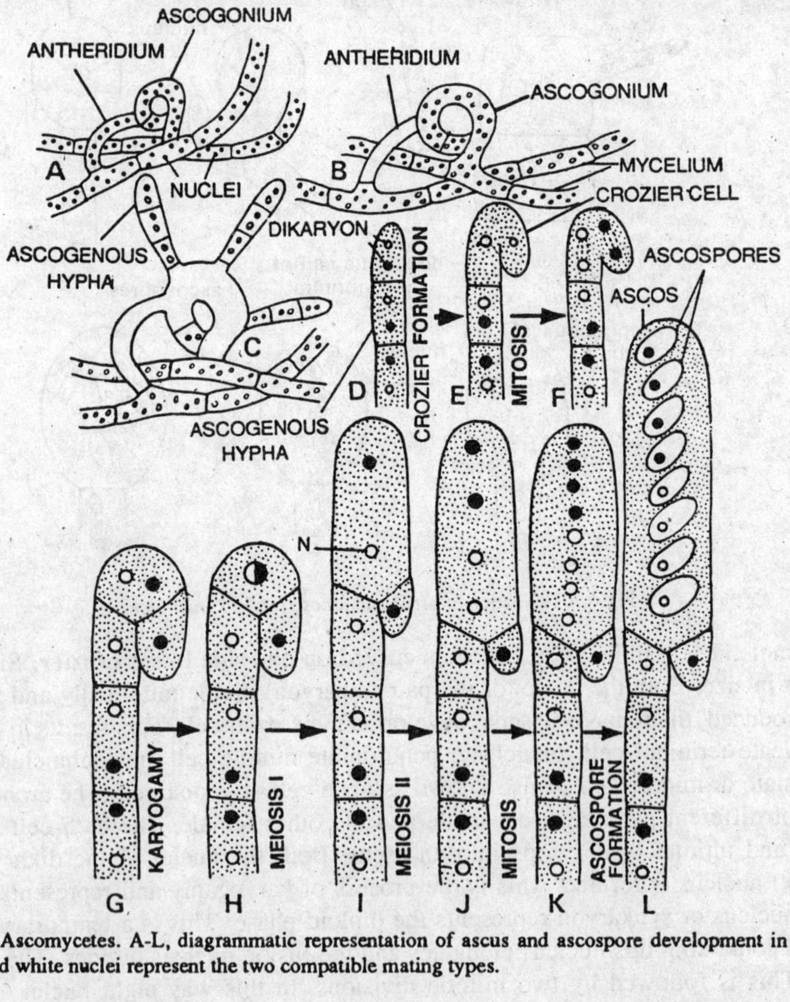

Fig. 8.6. Ascomycetes. A-L, diagrammatic representation of ascus and ascospore development in a heterothallic species. Black and white nuclei represent the two compatible mating types.

epiplasm. The epiplasm contains glycogen and other food materials and serves as nutrition supply for the development of the ascospores within the asucs.

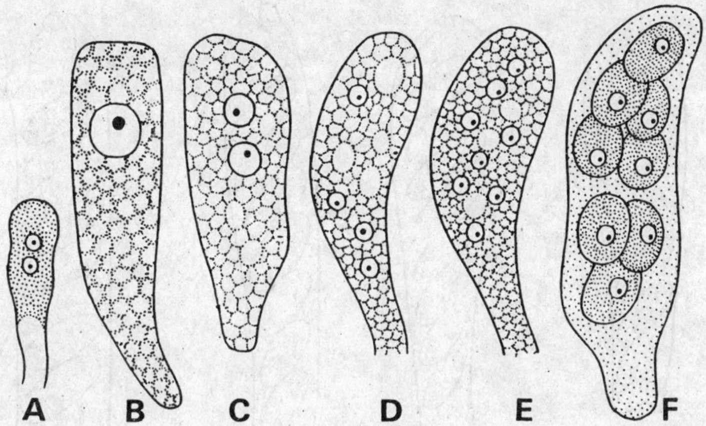

Fig. 8.7. Stages in the development of ascus and ascospores (A-F).

The asci vary in their shape. They may be spherical, clubshaped, oval or cylindrical with a more or less elongated base. The ascospores within the ascus may be arranged in uniseriate, biseriate, fasciculate or in inordinate manner.

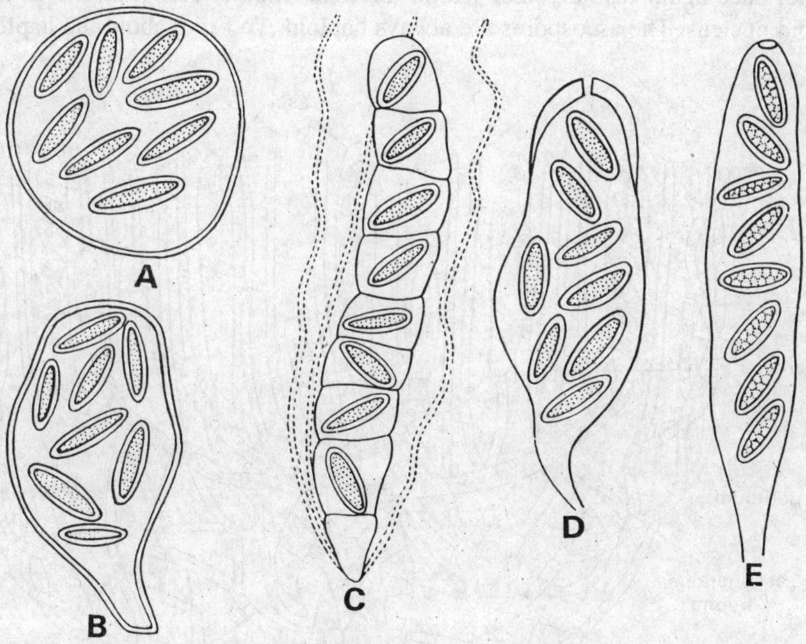

Fig. 8.8. Different types of asci. A, globose; B, ovate; C, septate; D, clavate; E, cylindrical.

The dehiscence of ascospores from asci differs from species to species. In majority of Ascomycetes the ascospores are released with a jerk from asci. The explosions take place successively. In certain cases the asci are provided with opercula. The operculum opens and the ascospores are released.

Cytology of ascus. Nuclear fusion, however, was first observed by Dangeard in 1894, not in the oogonium but in the ascus. As regards the cytology of ascus there are two schools

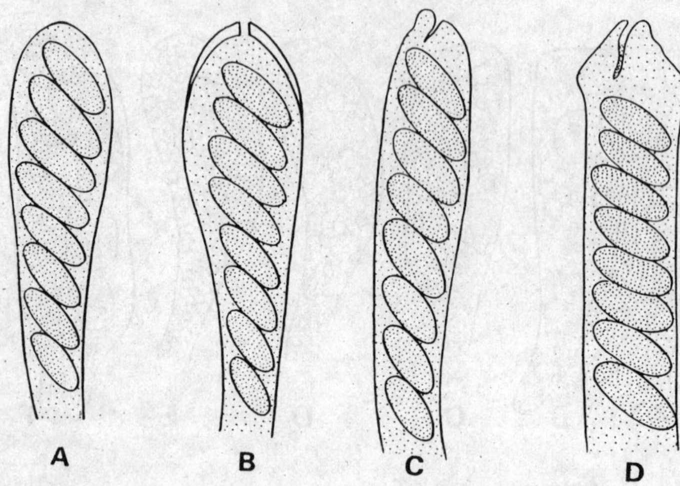

Fig. 8.9. Types of ascal openings. A, absent B; porous; C, operculum; D, slit.

of thought. According to one school of thought, the male and female nuclei fuse in the ascogonium and therefore each of the cells of the ascogenous hyphae contains a pair of diploid nuclei. These diploid nuclei once again fuse together within the ascus mother cell resulting in the formation of a tetraploid nucleus. The ascospores are always haploid. To bring about the haploid condition

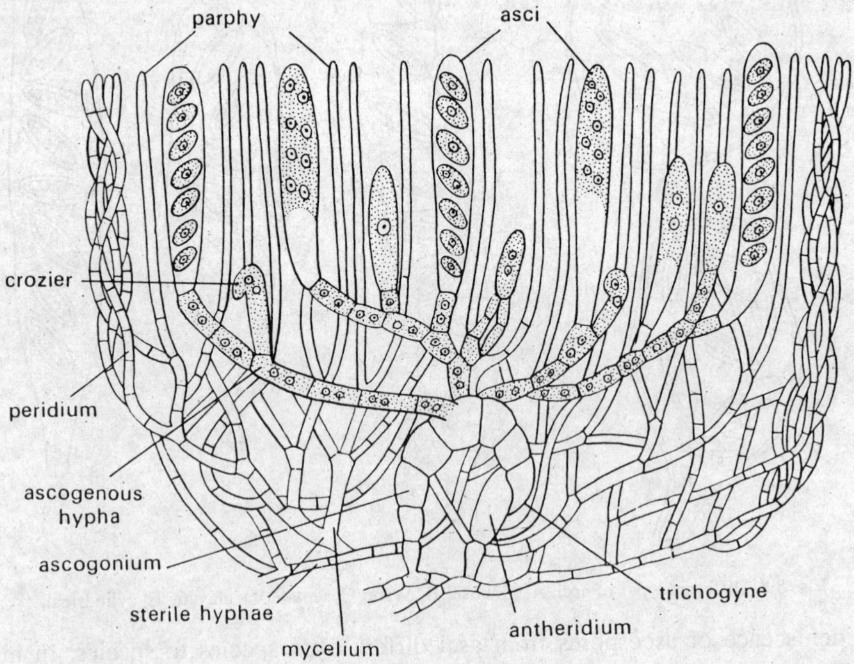

Fig. 8.10. Development of apothecium.

of ascospores, there must be double reduction in the number of chromosomes during the three successive divisions of the tetraploid nucleus. It is held that meiosis takes place twice, *i.e.*, first and third divisions are meiotic. This double reduction division is known as **brachymeiosis.** However, this view is not accepted by modern mycologists.

According to other school of thought, the nuclear fusion does not take place within the ascogonium. In this case the male and female nuclei are found in pairs in the ascogonium. Such pairs are known as **dikaryons.** Generally the fusion of male and female nuclei occurs in the ascus mother cell. Here the fusion nucleus is diploid. The fusion nucleus divides meiotically producing four nuclei, which divide mitotically forming eight nuclei. The resulting ascospores are haploid. This view is generally accepted by present mycologists.

The fruiting bodies or **ascocarps** of Ascomycetes are mainly of three types. They are **1. apothecium, 2. perithecium,** and **3. cleistothecium.**

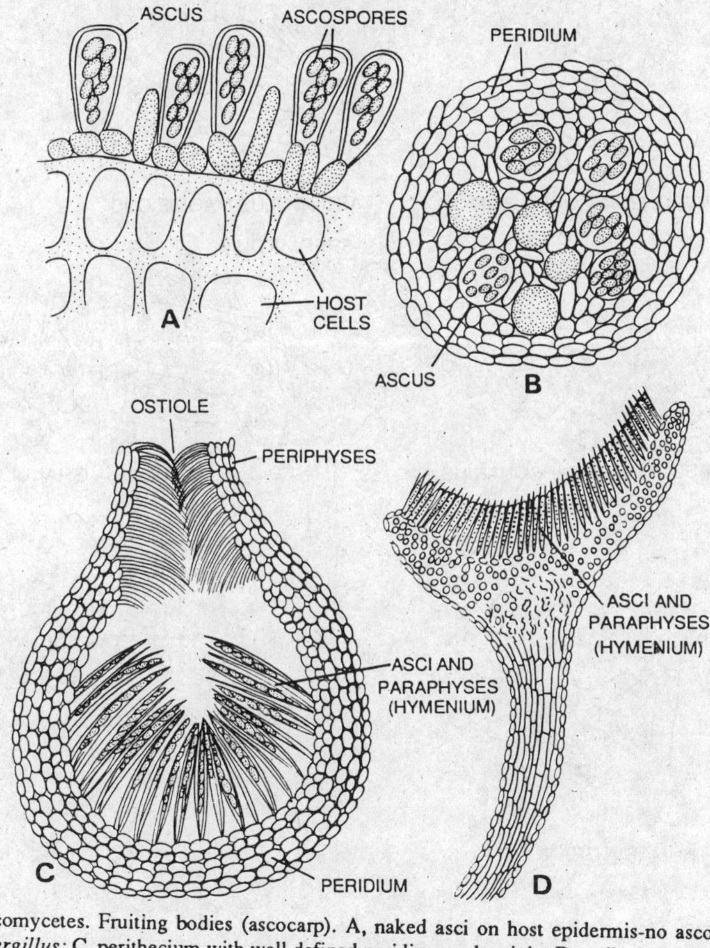

Fig. 8.11. Ascomycetes. Fruiting bodies (ascocarp). A, naked asci on host epidermis-no ascocarp, *Taphrina;* B, cleistothecium of *Aspergillus;* C, perithecium with well defined peridium and ostiole; D, stalked saucer-like apothecium.

Apothecium. In apothecium the hymenium remains exposed even on the maturation of the asci. They are saucer-shaped. The sterile structures called **'paraphyses'** are found intermingled with asci in the hymenium. Perhaps they are protective in function.

Perithecium. The perithecia are spherical or flask-like. The perithecium is covered by a **peridium** except at ostiole. The discharge of ascospores takes place through this narrow opening called the **ostiole.** The asci are found on the ascogenous hyphae present in the round bottom of the perithecium.

Cleistothecium. The cleistothecium is a closed body. Actually this is perithecium without an ostiole. The asci are filled up in these closed bodies. The cleistothecium is covered by a peridium layer. The appendages may or may not be present on the surface of cleistothecium.

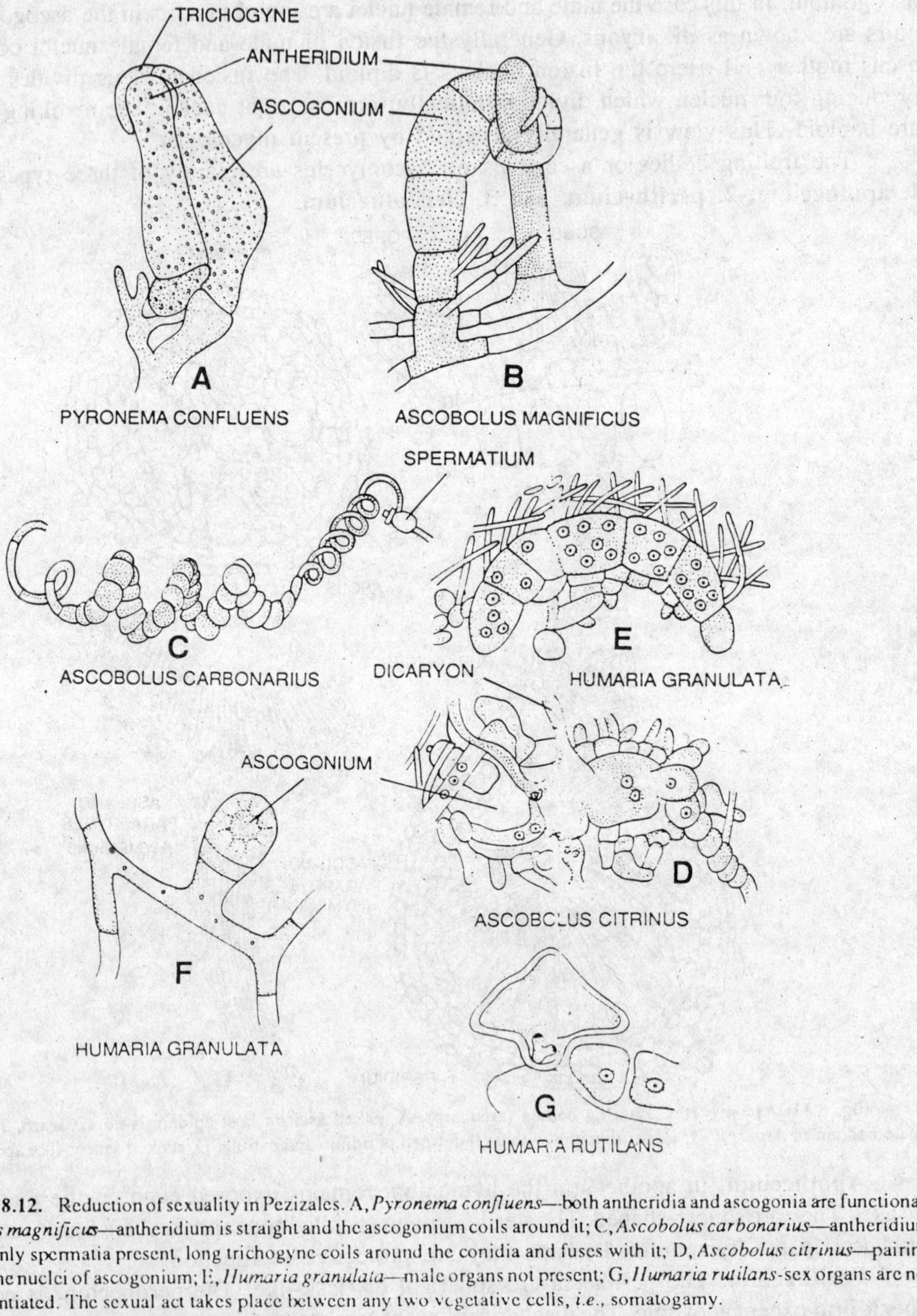

Fig. 8.12. Reduction of sexuality in Pezizales. A, *Pyronema confluens*—both antheridia and ascogonia are functional; B, *Ascobolus magnificus*—antheridium is straight and the ascogonium coils around it; C, *Ascobolus carbonarius*—antheridium absent and only spermatia present, long trichogyne coils around the conidia and fuses with it; D, *Ascobolus citrinus*—pairing in between the nuclei of ascogonium; E, *Humaria granulata*—male organs not present; G, *Humaria rutilans*-sex organs are not at all differentiated. The sexual act takes place between any two vegetative cells, *i.e.*, somatogamy.

The ascospores. They are usually elliptical, but in some species spherical and in some long and narrow. They contain densely granular cytoplasm and frequently oil drops. The epispore may be smooth or ornamented. They may be hyaline, opaque, colourless or variously coloured. The young spore is commonly unicellular and uninucleate, though in some species it contains two nuclei. Nuclear division and wall formation takes place during development. The mature spores are found to be arranged in a row or a mass of cells. Each spore germinates by putting out a germ tube. Most spores germinate immediately after their liberation from ascus.

Economic importance. The class is sufficiently important from the economic point of view to the human affairs. Some of the Ascomycetes are of immense value to the man. The fermenting activities of the yeast are the basis of baking and brewing industries. The vitamins are extracted from yeast and tablets are prepared. The wonder drug penicillin is produced from the species of *Penicillin* such as *P. notatum* and *P. crysogenum.* Morels are edible fungi. The mushroom-like morels are used as vegetables. They are very costly and sold at the rate of two-thousand rupees or more per kilogram. On the other hand some fungi of this class are quite harmful. The species of *Aspergillus* cause the human diseases such as aspergillosis, mycoses and tokelan. Some species of *Aspergillus* destroy the foodgrains in storage. The species of *Penicillin* cause the rotting of the fruits. Many important diseases of cereals and fruit trees are caused by the various fungi of this class. Powdery mildew of wheat (*Erysiphe gramineum),* leaf curl of peaches (*Taphrina deformans*) and many other diseases are caused by various fungi of this class. The species of *Chaetomium* are responsible for the destruction of fabrics containing cellulose. *Claviceps purpurea* causes the ergot of rye. The sclerotia of this fungus contain alkaloids and are used in the preparation of medicines. They are deadly poisonous to human beings and animals if consumed.

Phylogeny of Ascomycetes. Two widely divergent hypotheses have been propounded to account for the derivation of the Ascomycetes— 1. the rhodophycean or floridean hypothesis and 2. the phycomycetean hypothesis. For the first time in 1875, Sachs proposed the rhodophycean hypothesis. This hypothesis is based on the similarities between the reproductive structures of Ascomycetes and Rhodophyceae (the red algae). These similarities are— (a) ascocarp and cystocarp, (b) the trichogyne apparatus in each, (c) the nonmotile spermatia of each and (d) the resemblance of ascogenous hyphae and gonimoblast filaments.

In 1887, for the first time de Bary proposed the phycomycetean hypothesis. He maintained that the primitive Ascomycetes are those in which the asci are directly formed from the zygote, as they are in *Dipodascus* and *Eremascus.* The advocates of this hypothesis regard analogous structures among Ascomycetes and Florideae as being parallel developments and not as being derived one from the other.

Both hypotheses emphasize morphology as a basis for phylogenetic development and fail to stress physiology.

Reduction of sexuality in Ascomycetes. In *Aspergillus* both antheridia and ascogonia are present. But the nuclear fusion even in *Aspergillus* is not clearly understood. In *Lachnea stercorea* the fusion between trichogyne and antheridium takes place, but there is not migraton of male nuclei into the ascogonium. In *Lachnea cretea* there is further reduction and antheridia are altogether absent. Here fusion may take place among female nuclei within ascogonium. In *Humaria granulata* the antheridium and the receptive part trichogyne are altogether absent. The extreme cases of reduction in sexuality are *Humaria rutilans* and *Morchella,* where sex organs are totally obliterated, and there is a fusion between vegetative cells.

Classification. According to Gwynne-Vaughan and Barnes, the class Ascomycetes is sub-divided into the three sub-classes.

1. **Plectomycetes.** Ascocarp, if present either with no definite ostiole, or shield-shaped, or with asci irregularly arranged.

2. **Plectomycetes.** Ascocarp flask-shaped when ripe; asci in parallel series.

3. **Discomycetes.** Ascocarp wide open when ripe; asci in parallel series.

According to latest trend, the Ascomycetes have been divided into two sub-classes— 1. Hemiascomycetidae (Hemiascomycetes) and 2. Euascomycetidae (Euascomycetes). (Also see chap. 2 for details).

1. **Hemiascomycetidae.** Asci naked; ascocarp absent.

2. **Euascomycetidae.** Asci produced in an ascocarp.

9

Sub-Class–Hemiascomycetidae

Sub-class–**HEMIASCOMYCETIDAE**
Yeast and Leaf Curl Fungi
(Alexopoulos, 1962)

G.W. Martin (1961)	**G.C. Ainswoth (1971)**
Sub-class–**HEMIASCOMYCETIDAE**	Class–**HEMIASCOMYCETES**

The sub-class Hemiascomycetidae is also known as Protoascomycetidae. They include either very primitive Ascomycetes or degenerate forms. The characteristic features of these fungi are as follows—

1. The mycelium is poorly developed or altogether absent.
2. The ascogenous hyphae are not found.
3. The asci are naked and not enclosed inside an ascocarp.
4. The ascocarps are not formed.

The sub-class Hemiascomycetidae includes three orders— 1. Protomycetales, 2. Endomycetales and 3. Taphrinales.

Protomycetales. The spore-sac is compound also known as synascus in which numerous asci are produced.

Endomycetales. The individual asci are formed. Plant body is greatly reduced often to a single cell. With the result of sexual fusion an ascus is produced. The asci are produced directly from zygotes.

Taphrinales. The individual asci are formed. The product of sexuality is a dikaryotic thallus. The asci are directly produced from the cells of this thallus.

ORDER–ENDOMYCETALES (43 genera; 150 species)

Characteristic Features

1. The order includes both saprophytic and parasitic fungi.
2. The plant body is greatly reduced, often to a single cell, *e.g.,* in yeasts.
3. The zygote derived from the copulation of two cells, becomes directly transformed into an ascus. In other forms a single cell becomes an ascus parthenogenetically. In still other forms the diploid zygote gives rise to a large number of diploid cells by budding, which, develop into asci.

Classification. According to G. W. Martin (1961), the order includes four families— 1. Ascoideaceae, 2. Endomycetaceae, 3. Spermophthoraceae and 4. Saccharomycetaceae.

Family—Saccharomycetaceae (10 genera; 100 species)

The asci are eight or few spored. The gametangia are not found. The copulation takes place by means of somatic cells.

The thoroughly worked out genus *Saccharomyces* of the family Saccharomycetaceae has been discussed here in detail.

Genus SACCHAROMYCES (30 species)

Occurrence and habit. Usually the yeasts grow in such organic materials where the sugar is found in abundance. They grow in toddy juice, grape juice and sugarcane juice very easily.

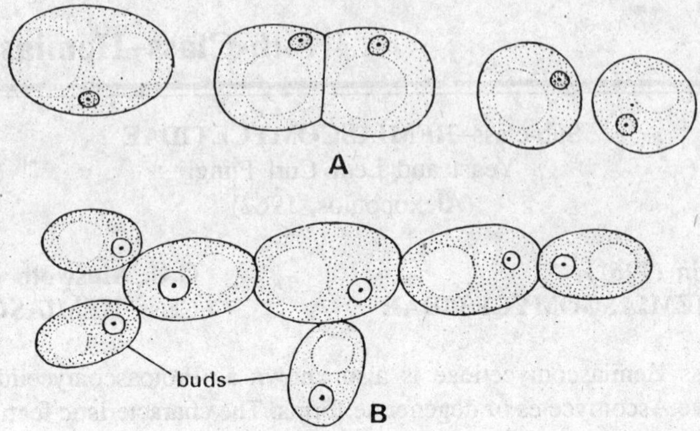

Fig. 9.1. Yeasts showing fission (A), and budding (B).

The yeasts convert the sugars into alcohol by fermentation and only because of this quality they are used in making alcohols, wines and beer etc. They are used in the bakeries to produce loafs. The spongy nature of the loaf is because of the presence of carbon dioxide. This carbon dioxide is released during fermentation.

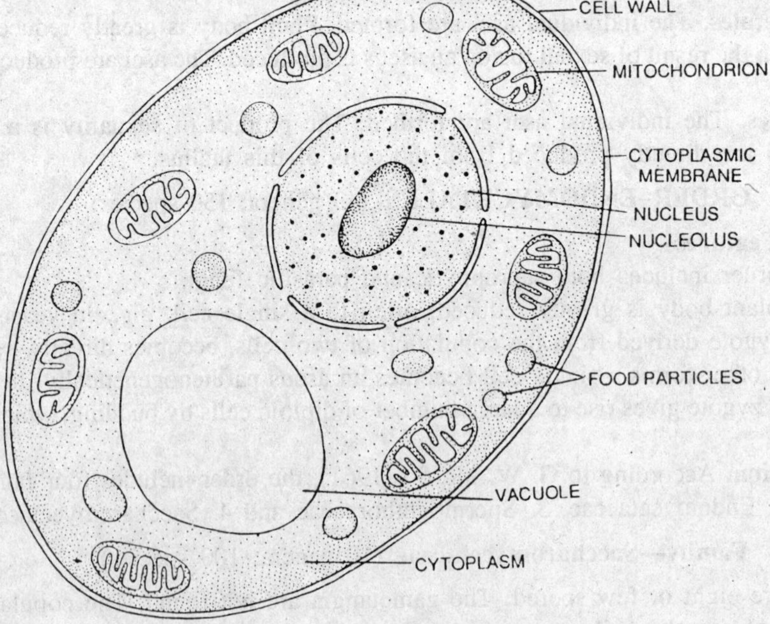

Fig. 9.2. Electron micrograph of single yeast cell.

Some yeasts occur as parasites, *e.g., Monosporella* is parasitic on the intestines of *Daphnia,* a crustacean; species of *Nematospora* are found to be parasitic on tomato, beans etc. Certain yeasts are found in symbiotic relationship with certain bacteria and moulds, *e.g.*, to prepare the sake wine in Japan, the fermentation is brought about by *Saccharomyces sake* (yeast) in association with *Aspergillus oryzae* (mould).

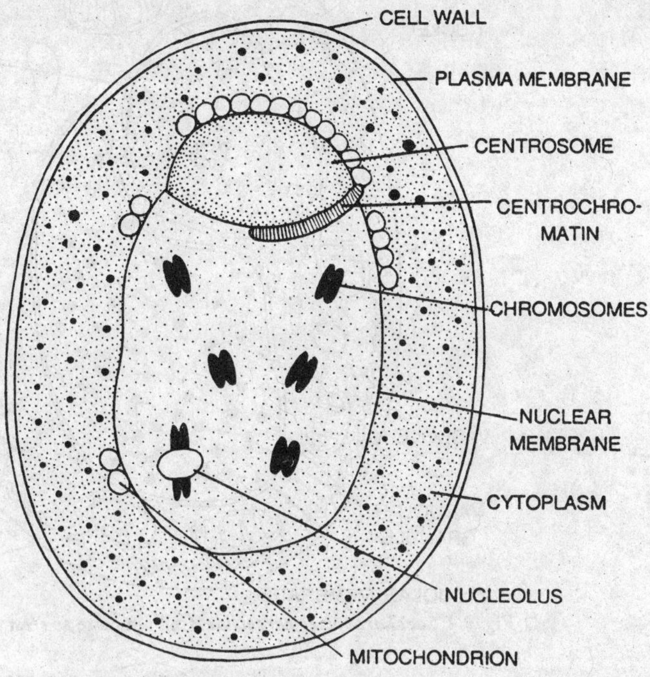

Fig. 9.3. A yeast cell. (After Lindgren).

Structure. The yeast organisation are unicellular. All the metabolic activities are furnished by this single cell. These cells are microscopic and may be seen under the high power lens of the microscope as pin heads.

Each yeast cell is oval or spherical. The cell wall consists of a hard substance, the chitin. The cytoplasm is filled up in the cell. In the most common species *Saccharomyces cerevisiae* there is large rounded colourless area lying towards a pole of the cell. According to Lindgren (1949) and others this has been considered as a nucleus, but according to De Lamater (1950) this is the vacuole and the nucleus is the smaller body which lies on the side of the vacuole. If the former view is correct, the nucleus contains a big vacuole. The nuclear vacuole possesses a chromatin network and a small nucleus situated on one side. The glycogen granules, the oil droplets and the compounds of proteins are found embedded in the cytoplasm.

The cytology of yeast cells remained a topic of controversy for many years. Dangeard, Janssens, Le Blanc and others showed some nucleus like bodies to be present in the cell. This was assumed that a **diffused nucleus** of dispersed particles was present within the cells. Eischenschitz reported that these grains were abundantly found in the vacuole. This concept was recognized by Wagner (1898) and again by Wagner and Peniston (1910). These scientists described the nucleus as **vacuole nucleare,** *i.e.,* a vacuole filled up with chromatin particles and carrying a distinct nucledus towards its outside. Now this account is of historical value only.

Electron Microscopic Structure

The electron microscope has now revealed astonishing details within the yeast cell : Yotsuyanagi, Y. (1959), Hashimoto, T. (1960), Naylor, H.B., Conti, S.F. and Thyagarajan, T.R. (1962).

The detailed electron microscopic structure of the yeast cell is as follows.

The cell remains surrounded by a definite two-layered cell wall. The cell wall consists of chitin and some other substances. Just beneath the cell wall there is cytoplasmic membrane. There is a distinct nucleus within the cell. The nucleus is spherical to ovoid and remains surrounded by a double membrane which is interrupted by 'pores'. A distinct nucleolus is also present within

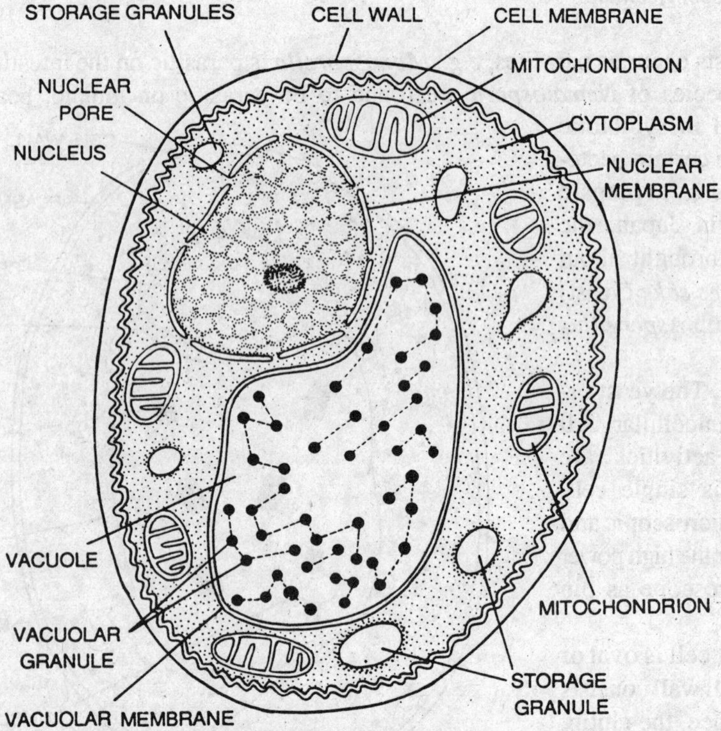

Fig. 9.4. ***Saccharomyces cerevisiae*. Cell structure as seen under electron microscope.**

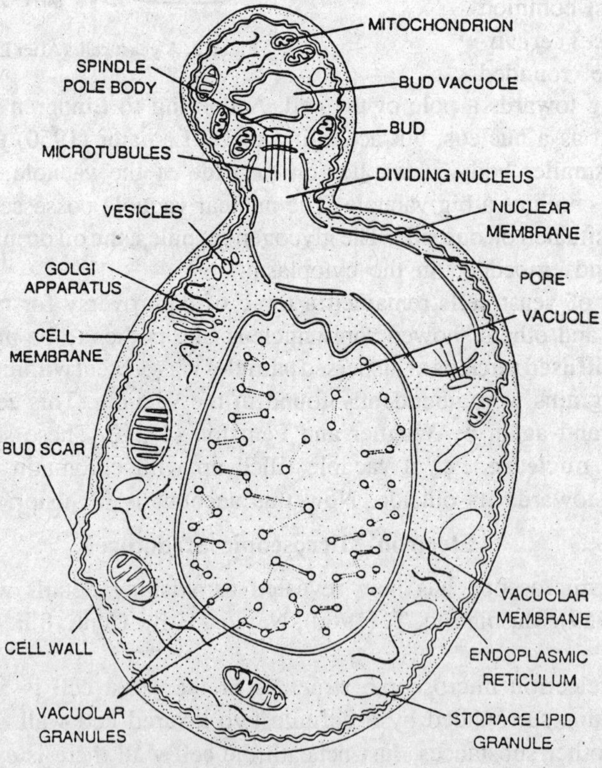

Fig. 9.5. Ultra structure of a budding yeast (*Saccharomyces cerevisiae*).

the nucleus. The nucleolus is a spherical dense body and remains surrounded by its own membrane. Certain vacuole-like areas of lesser density are also found within the nucleolus. The granular and homogeneous nucleoplasm is filled up within the nucleus. There occur some irregular areas within the nucleus, which contain fibrils and correspond to the chromosomes of yeast cell. There is a distinct vacuole found within the cell that remains filled with a granular material, the volutin and is separated from the remaining cell by a membrane of its own. As assumed earlier the vacuole is not integral part of nuclear apparatus. The other cytoplasmic inclusions are mitochondria, endoplasmic reticulum and ribosomes. The number of mitochondria within a cell is 4-20. Certain other inclusions such as food particles of lipids, proteins, glycogen etc., are also found.

Reproduction. The reproduction of yeasts takes place by means of 1. vegetative, 2. asexual and 3. sexual methods.

Vegetative reproduction. The vegetative reproduction takes place by means of 'budding'.

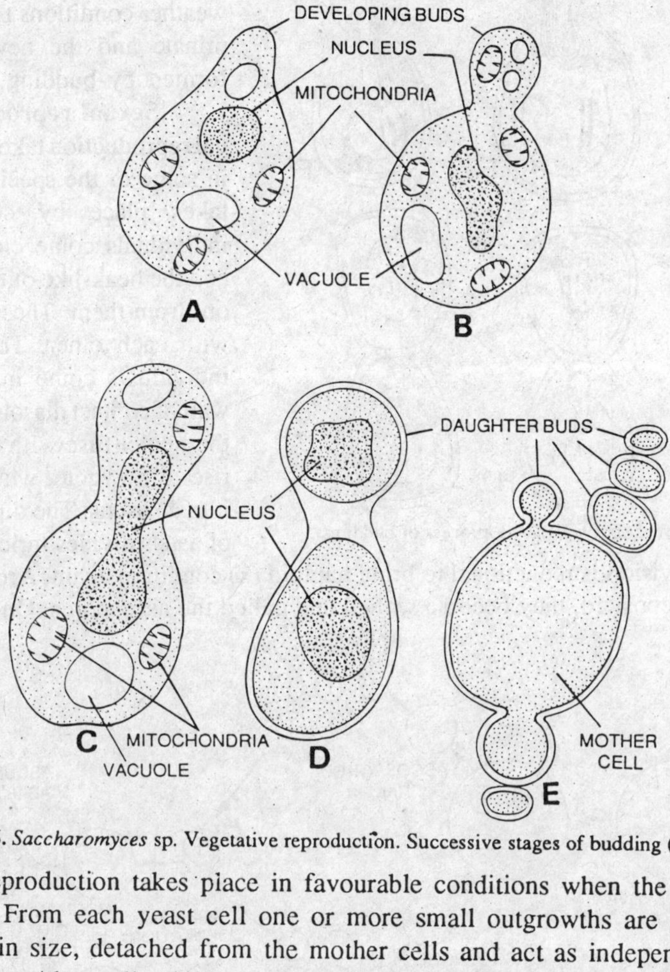

Fig. 9.6. *Saccharomyces* sp. Vegetative reproduction. Successive stages of budding (A-E).

This method of reproduction takes place in favourable conditions when the yeast cells grow in sugar solution. From each yeast cell one or more small outgrowths are given out, which gradually enlarge in size, detached from the mother cells and act as independent individuals. The nucleus of the mother cells divides amitotically and transfers to the daughter cell. Several other outgrowths develop from the newly formed outgrowths, and sometimes the chains of the cells are seen. Very soon the yeast cells are detached from each other and act as new independent individuals.

Asexual reproduction. This type of reproduction probably takes place in adverse conditions, especially when there is scarcity of nutrients and abundance of oxygen. The yeast cell enlarges in size and called the 'ascus.' The nucleus of the ascus divides twice producing four nuclei. Now around each nucleus the cytoplasm deposits and the four ascospores are formed. Sometimes eight ascospores may also be produced. Each ascospore is surrounded by a thick wall. These spores are perennating bodies. They remain dormant in adverse conditions. On the approach of favourable conditions they germinate. The ascus wall bursts and the ascospóres liberate in the atmosphere. They are dispersed by wind from one place to another. On getting suitable media and appropriate weather conditions the ascospores germinate and the new individuals are formed by budding.

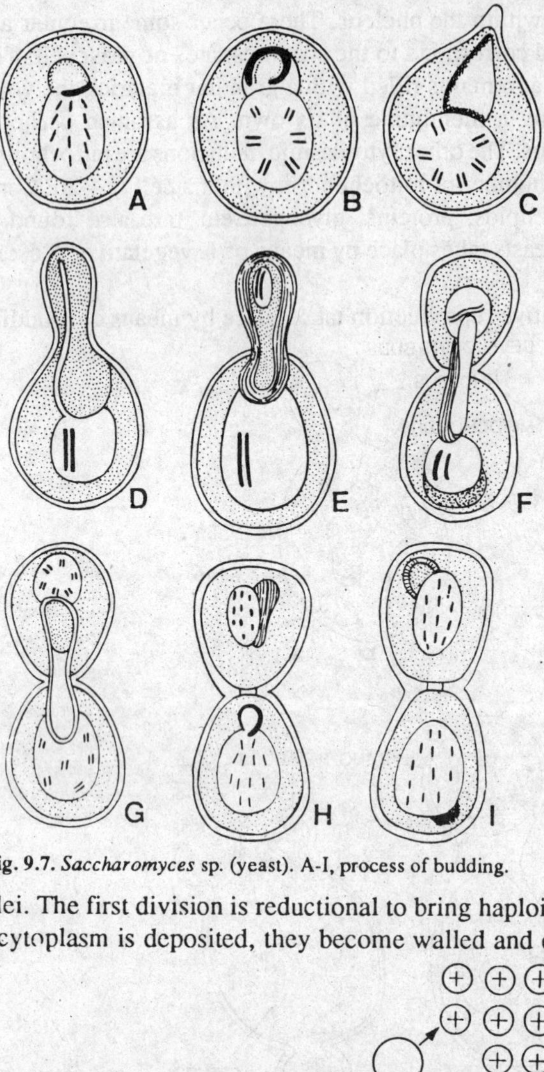

Fig. 9.7. *Saccharomyces* sp. (yeast). A-I, process of budding.

Sexual reproduction. The sexual reproduction takes place very rarely in some of the species of yeasts. This takes place by conjugation. Two individuals come close to each other and the beak-like outgrowths are given out from them. These outgrowths fuse with each other. The nuclei of both individuals come in these beaks, the wall of contact dissolves and ultimately the nuclei fuse with each other giving rise to a zygote, which soon converts into an ascus. The diploid nucleus (2x) of asucs divides thrice producing eight nuclei. The first division is reductional to bring haploid (x) condition again. Around each nucleus the cytoplasm is deposited, they become walled and called the ascospores. On bursting the wall

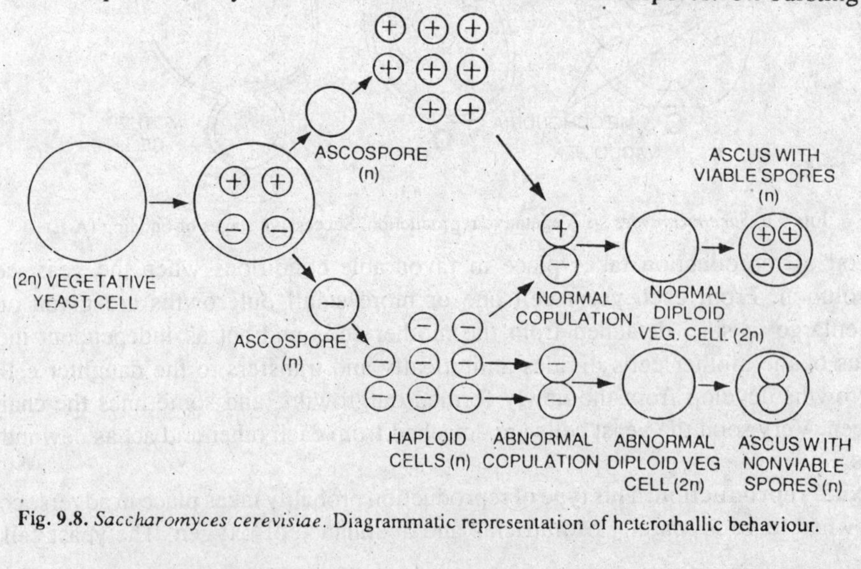

Fig. 9.8. *Saccharomyces cerevisiae*. Diagrammatic representation of heterothallic behaviour.

of ascus the ascospores are liberated. On getting suitable conditions they germinate and the new individuals are produced by budding.

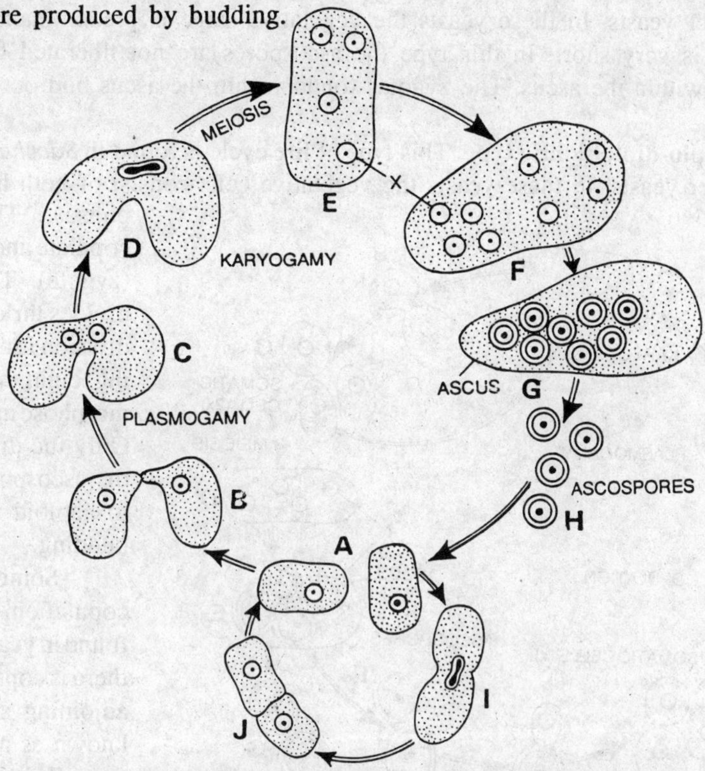

Fig. 9.9. Haplobiontic type of life-cycle in *Schizosaccharomyces octosporus*.

Guilliermond (1940) has recognized three main types of life cycles in the yeast. These life cycles are known as— 1. haplobiontic, 2. diplobiontic and 3. haplo-diplobiontic.

1. Haplobiontic type. This type of life cycle is found in *Schizosaccharomyces octosporus* and some other yeasts. In these yeasts the vegetative stage is predominantly haploid and the diploid stage is very short. The diploid stage is represented by the zygote cell only which undergoes meiosis immediately after nuclear fusion. Here each somatic cell acts as a potential gametangium. During sexual union two cells fuse (plasmogamy) and this is followed by the fusion of the two nuclei (karyogamy). The fusion or zygote nucleus divides thrice of which the first division is meiotic one. Now the zygote cell becomes ascus containing eight ascospores. After their liberation from the ascus the ascospores behave as vegetative cells.

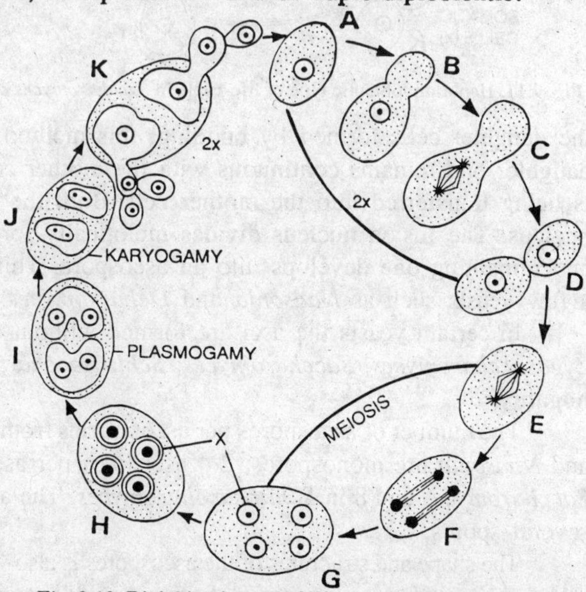

Fig. 9.10. Diplobiontic type of life-cycle in *Saccharomycodes ludwigii*.

2. Diplobiontic type. This type of life-cycle is found in *Saccharomycodes ludwigii* and some other yeasts. In these yeasts the vegetative stage is predominantly diploid and the haploid stage is very short. In this type the ascospores are not liberated from the ascus but they copulate within the ascus. The zygotes found within the ascus bud out diplobiontic vegetative cells.

3. Haplo-diplobiontic type. This type of life cycle is found in *Saccharomyces cerevisiae* and some other yeasts. In these yeasts the vegetative cells consist of both haploid and diploid phases. The haploid cells copulate and form a diploid cell (zygote). The zygote nucleus divides thrice of which the first division is meiotic one, producing eight nuclei which metamorphose into eight ascospores. Only the diploid cells produce the ascospores which give rise to haploid vegetative cells by budding.

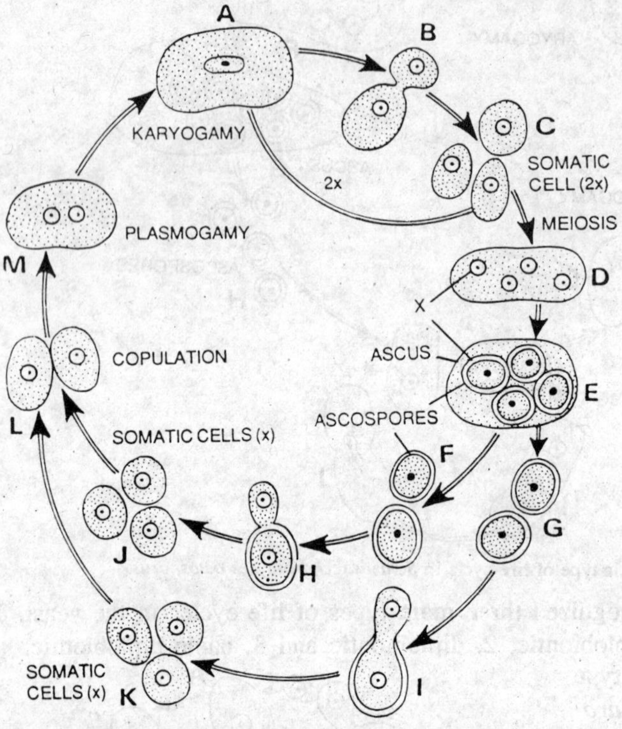

Fig. 9.11. Haplo-diplobiontic type of life-cycle in *Saccharomyces cerivisiae.*

Some more types of copulation methods are also found in yeasts. In certain yeasts there is copulation between two adjoining sister cells ; this is known as **adelphogamy.** Here the cells involved in copulation do not separate after fusion and remain united to form short chains, *e.g., Schizosaccharomyces mellacei* and *S. pombe*. Another type of copulation takes place between the mother and the daughter cells formed by budding; this method is known as **pedogamy.** In this type the daughter bud remains continuous with the mother cell and the nucleus from the daughter bud is being transferred into the mother cell. Both the nuclei fuse together forming diploid (2x) nucleus. The fusion nucleus divides meiotically forming 4 nuclei, three of which degenerate and remaining one develops into an ascospore. This process shows anisogamy and occurs in a few yeasts such as *Nadsonia* and *Debaryomyces.*

In certain yeasts the asci are formed without copulation of two cells, *e.g.,* in species of *Zygosaccharomyces, Saccharomyces, Schizosaccharomyces.* This process is known as **parthenogamy.**

The number of ascospores per ascus varies from genus to genus, *e.g.,* the asci of *Monospora* and *Nadsonia* are monospores; 2-4 ascospres per ascus in *Debaryomyces* and *Hensenula;* 4 in *Saccharomyces* and 8 in *Schizosaccharomyces.* The ascus in *Kluyveromyces polysporus* contains several spores.

The shape and structures of the ascospores is also variable, *e.g.,* the ascospores of *Saccharomyces* and *Schizosaccharomyces* are globose or ovoid; rough and warty of *Debaryomyces;* hat-shaped and flat on one side of *Hansenula;* needle-like and tapering at one end of *Nematospora.*

Fermentation. When the yeast cells grow in the sugarcane juice, toddy juice, or grape juice, then because of the activity of zymase enzyme the fermentation takes place. The sugar decomposes producing alcohol and carbon dioxide. In the abundance supply of oxygen the alcohol is formed in less quantity. On the other hand when there is scarcity of oxygen the large quantity of alcohol is produced.

The conversion of sugars into alcohol is termed **alcoholic fermentation.** The alcohol forming yeasts that grow at the top of the fermenting liquid are known as 'top yeasts'. The other yeasts which grow in the lower portions are known as 'bottom yeasts'. Though yeasts grow in less supply of oxygen yet fermentation does not take place in total absence of oxygen and most of the yeasts are intermediate between aerobic and anaerobic types. During fermentation besides the production of alcohol and carbon dioxide other substances like glycerol, ethers, fatty acids, acetic acid and succinic acid are also produced in small quantities.

The important fermenting yeasts are the wine yeast (*Saccharomyces ellipsoides);* the beer and bread yeasts (*S. cerevisiae);* the ginger beer yeast (*S. piriformis*); the sake wine yeast of Japan (*S. sake*); African beer yeast (*S. pombe*) etc.

The yeasts are rich in enzymes and vitamins and therefore, they make a valuable food and useful as medicine. The cubes or cakes with inactive starch as the base are made from the yeasts. Yeast tablets cure the stomach troubles. Certain pathogenic yeasts have also been reported.

$$C_6H_{12}O_6 + \text{Zymase} \rightarrow 2C_2H_5OH + 2CO_2 + \text{Zymase} + \text{Energy.}$$

Systematic Position

	G. W. Martin (1961)	C. J. Alexopoulos (1962)	G. C. Ainsworth (1971)
Kingdom	–Plantae	–Plantae	–Fungi
Division	–Mycota	–Mycota	–Eumycota
Sub-div.	–Eumycotina	–Eumycotina	–Ascomycotina
Class	–Ascomycetes	–Ascomycetes	–Hemiascomycetes
Sub-cl.	–Hemiascomycetidae	–Hemiascomycetidae	
Order	–Endomycetales	–Endomycetales	–Endomycetales
Family	–Saccharomycetaceae	–Saccharomycetaceae	–Saccharomycetaceae
Genus	–*Saccharomyces*	–*Saccharomyces*	–*Saccharomyces*

ORDER – TAPHRINALES (6 genera; 125 species)

Characteristic Features

1. The fungi of this order are found to be parasitic on vascular plants.
2. The ascospores like yeast cells, multiply by budding. On artificial media no mycelium is formed.
3. These fungi produce a definite, true mycelium.
4. The ascus is not produced directly from a zygote cell resulting from the copulation of two cells. It is produced from a special, binucleate, ascogenous cell developed from the mycelium.
5. The asci are cylindrical in form, parallel in arrangement, and unprotected by a sheath.
6. No sex organs are known.

Classification. This order includes a single family, the Taphrinaceae with a single genus *Taphrina*.

Genus **TAPHRINA** (100 species)

This genus comprises of about 100 species which parasitize on vascular plants. They cause malformations of the tissues they attack and produce disease symptoms such as leaf curl, puckering pockets. blisters and witches broom. *Taphrina deformans* causes the peach leaf curl. *Taphrina pruni* causes plum pockets, *Taphrina cerasi* causes witches broom of cherries, and *T. coerulescens* causes curling and puckering of oak leaves. *Taphrina maculans* commonly causes leaf spots of *Curcuma amada, Curcuma angustifolia* and *Curcuma longa* (Vern. **Haldi**) in several parts of our country.

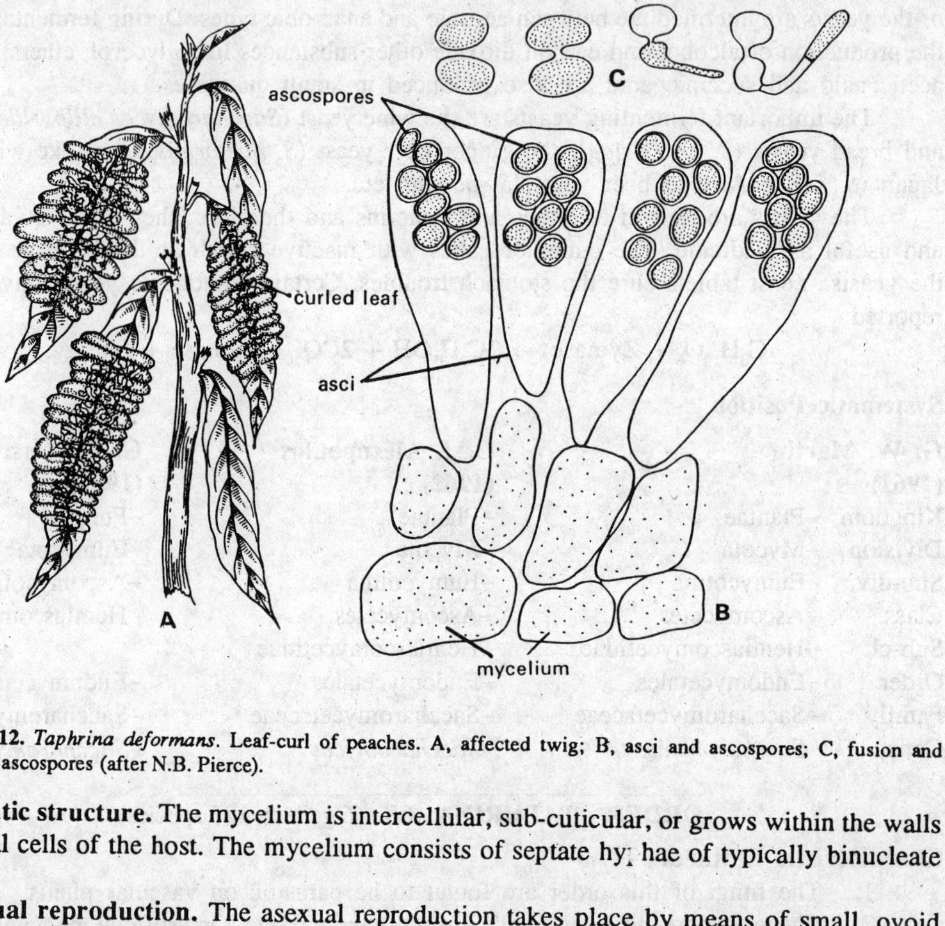

Fig. 9.12. *Taphrina deformans*. Leaf-curl of peaches. A, affected twig; B, asci and ascospores; C, fusion and germination of ascospores (after N.B. Pierce).

Somatic structure. The mycelium is intercellular, sub-cuticular, or grows within the walls of epidermal cells of the host. The mycelium consists of septate hy; hae of typically binucleate cell.

Asexual reproduction. The asexual reproduction takes place by means of small, ovoid or globose, uninucleate, haploid yeast like blastospores which bud directly from the ascospores. The blastospores, may produce more blastospores by budding or they germinate directly producing mycelium which infects the host.

Sexual reproduction and life-cycle. They do not produce any sex organs. In *Taphrina epiphylla* and *T. klebahni,* the copulation of conidia developed from ascospores by means of budding takes place. According to Miss Ella Martin (1940), no plasmogamy takes place in *Taphrina deformans,* and the karyogamy occurs between sister nuclei.

As soon as the ascospores are formed they produce small, spherical or ovoid blastospores by means of budding. The blastospores are uninucleate and haploid. Sometimes the blastospores produce secondary blastospores on the host surface. In other cases they germinate directly producing

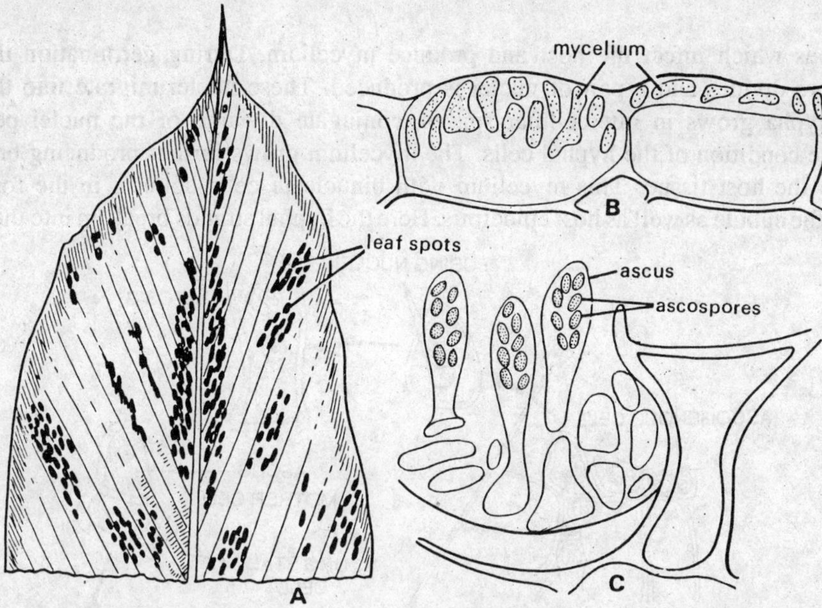

Fig. 9.13. *Taphrina maculans.* Leaf-spot of turmeric. A, affected leaf; B, mycelium; C, asci and ascospores (after Butler).

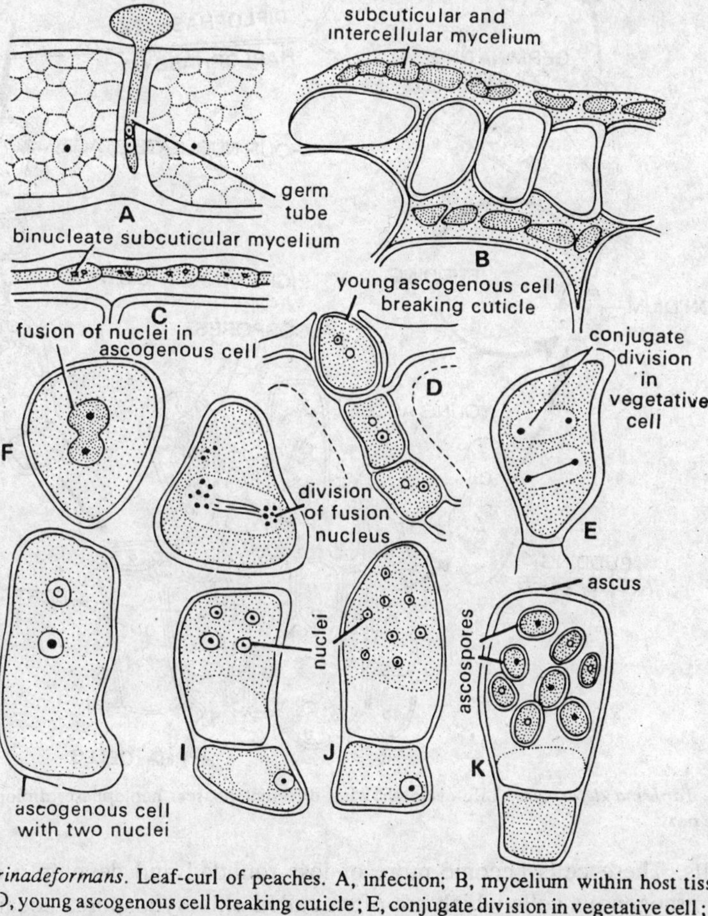

Fig. 9.14. *Taphrinadeformans.* Leaf-curl of peaches. A, infection; B, mycelium within host tissue; C, binucleate subcuticular mycelium; D, young ascogenous cell breaking cuticle ; E, conjugate division in vegetative cell ; F, fusion of nuclei in ascogenous cell ; G, division of fusion nucleus; H, elongating, ascogenous cell containing two nuclei; I, four nucleate ascus; J, eight nucleate ascus; K, ascus containing eight ascospores (after Martin).

germ tubes which infect the host and produce mycelium. During germination the nucleus of blastospore divides and a pair of nuclei is produced. These nuclei migrate into the germ tube. As the hypha grows in intercellular spaces, conjugate division of the nuclei perpetuates the binucleate condition of the hyphal cells. The mycelium grows further producing branches which penetrate the host tissue. This mycelium with binucleate cells collects in the form of a layer between the cuticle as well as host epidermis. Here the hyphal strands break up into their component

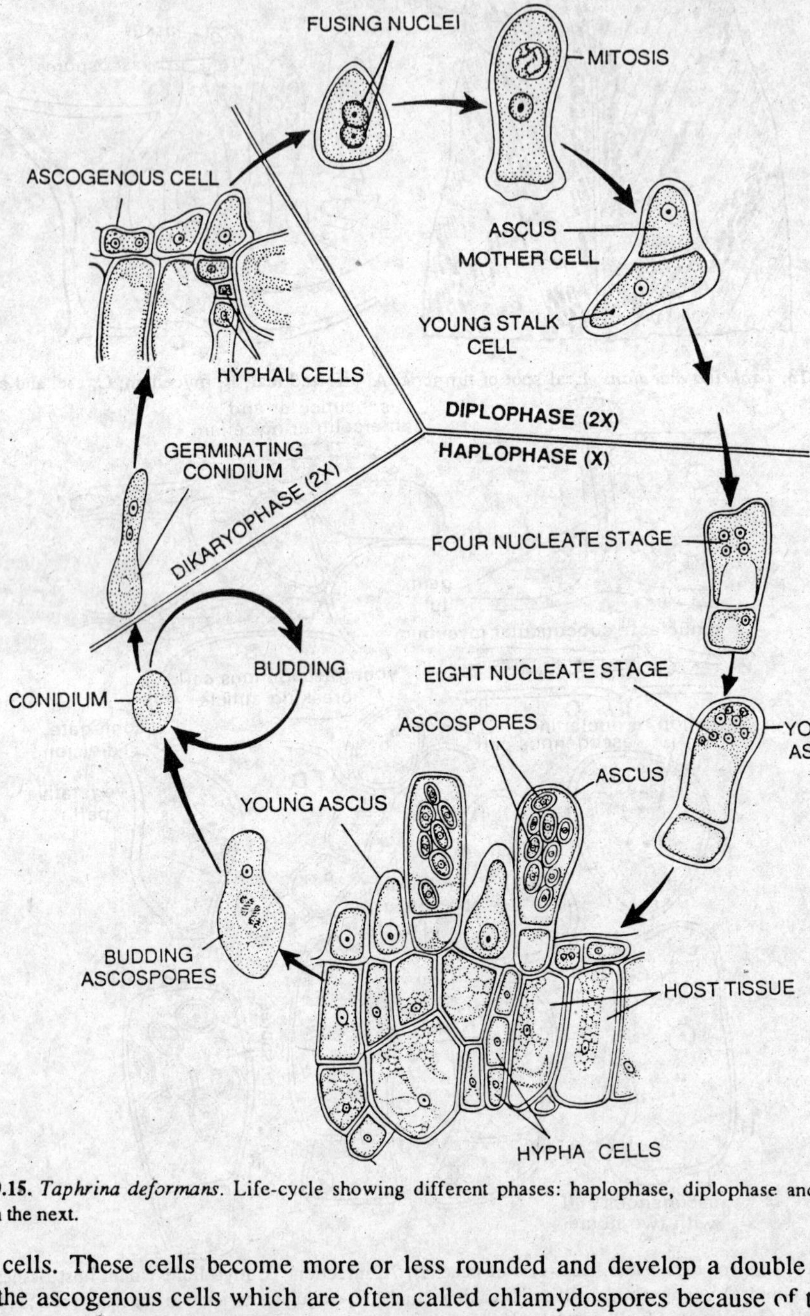

Fig. 9.15. *Taphrina deformans*. Life-cycle showing different phases: haplophase, diplophase and dikaryophase. Description in the next.

binucleate cells. These cells become more or less rounded and develop a double wall. These are called the ascogenous cells which are often called chlamydospores because of their method of formation. The dikaryon fuses within each ascogenous cell. The nuclei fuse forming a diploid nucleus. By this time the cell begins to elongate. During the period of elongation the diploid nucleus divides mitotically producing two nuclei. One daughter nucleus remains near the base of the ascogenous cell while the other moves towards its tip. Thereafter a transverse septum develops between these two nuclei. This septum divides the cell into basal stalk cell and an upper ascus mother cell. The diploid nucleus of the ascus mother cell divides meiotically which is followed by a subsequent mitotic division forming eight haploid nuclei. Each nucleus metamorphoses into an ascospore, and the ascus mother cell converts into an ascus, and the asci exert pressure on the host cuticle from below and eventually gives way and exposes a compact surface layer of asci, the hymenium on the host epidermis. No fruiting bodies or ascocarps are formed. The asci remain naked and release the ascospores in the air. The mature ascospores immediately after their liberation from the asci bud out numerous blastospores. The blastospores eventually produce germ tubes which infect the host. In many species the ascospores bud while they are inside the ascus.

Systematic Position

	G. W. Martin (1961)	**C. J. Alexopoulos (1962)**	**G. C. Ainsworth (1971)**
Kingdom	–Plantae	–Plantae	–Fungi
Division	–Mycota	–Mycota	–Eumycota
Sub-div.	–Eumycotina	–Eumycotina	–Ascomycotina
Class	–Ascomycetes	–Ascomycetes	–Hemiascomycetes
Sub cl.	–Hemiascomycetideae	–Hemiascomycetidae	
Order	–Taphrinales	–Taphrinales	–Taphrinales
Family	–Taphrinaceae	–Taphrinaceae	–Taphrinaceae
Genus	–*Taphrina*	–*Taphrina*	–*Taphrina*

10

Sub-class–Euascomycetidae

Blue Molds, Perithecial Fungi, Cup Fungi and Morels
(Alexopoulos, 1962)

G. W. Martin (1961)	G. C. Ainswoth (1971)
Sub-class–EUASCOMYCETIDAE	Classes–PLECTOMYCETES
	PYRENOMYCETES
	DISCOMYCETES

Characteristic Features

1. The asci are usually unitunicate, *i.e.*, an ascus in which both the inner and outer walls are more on less rigid and do not separate during spore ejection.
2. The asci typically develop from special sexually produced ascogenous hyphae and in the majority of species are enclosed in a true ascocarp—the cleistothecium or apothecium.
3. They develop functional sex organs, but sexual degeneration is found at least in few groups.

Classification. This sub-class has been divided into three series— 1. Plectomycetes, 2. Pyrenomycetes and 3. Discomycetes.

Series–**Plectomycetes** or Class-**Plectomycetes** (Ainsworth, 1971)

Characteristic Features

1. The asci do not develop on any kind of special structures like hymenium or sporophores. They can develop from any part of mycelium.
2. The sexual reproduction results in the formation of asci and ascospores. The asci are globose or broadly club-shaped. They arise at different levels in the ascocarp. They are irregularly arranged.
3. The cleistothecia are formed which contain asci and ascospores. The asci release the ascospores by deliquescing in the ascocarp. Usually the cleistothecia do not possess definite pore.

Classification. The series has been divided into two orders—
1. Eurotiales and 2. Erysiphales.

ORDER—EUROTIALES (60 genera; 120 species)
(Aspergillales)

Characteristic Features

1. Majority of them are saprophytic and known as green or blue green molds.
2. The hyphal ends penetrate the substrata to absorb the nutrition. The haustoria are not developed.
3. The conidia are formed in basigenous chains on conidiophores. The conidiophores may be septate or aseptate and branched or unbranched.

4. Sexual reproduction takes place by means of antheridia and ascogonia, resulting in the formation of asci and ascospores, within the cleistothecium in scattered condition. The outer wall of the cleistothecium is pseudoparenchymatous and called the 'peridium'. The asci are formed from ascogenous hyphae of various lengths and are found to be scattered at various levels within the ascocarp. There is no definite hymenial layer.

5. This order is sub-divided into two (Martin, 1961) to seven (Bessey, 1950) families.

Family–**Eurotiaceae** (Aspergillaceae).

The family is characterized by having well-formed cleistothecia with definite peridia. The peridium consists of pseudoparenchyma formed by the compactly interwoven sterile hyphae. The conidial stages of the form genera *Aspergillus* and *Penicillium* are quite distinct and characteristic.

Genus **ASPERGILLUS** (20 sp.)
(*Eurotium*)

Occurrence. This is a saprophytic fungus. One can get the culture of *Aspergillus* by keeping a moist bread under the bell jar for few days at suitable temperature in the laboratory. In the beginning the white cottony mycelium appears, and afterwards on the same bread *Aspergillus* appears which can be very easily recognised by the presence of its smoky, green conidia. This

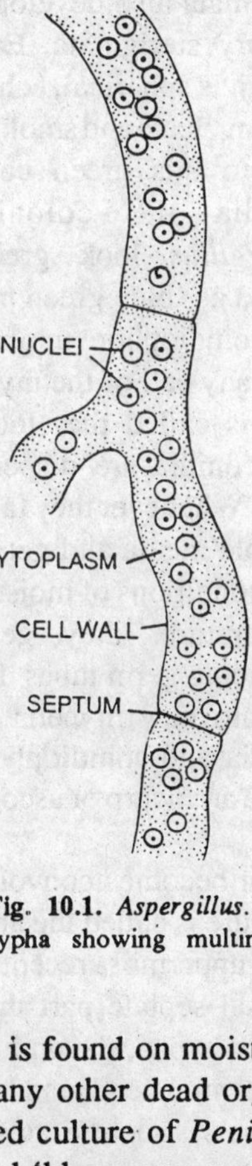

Fig. 10.1. *Aspergillus*. Mycelium. Hypha showing multinucleate cells.

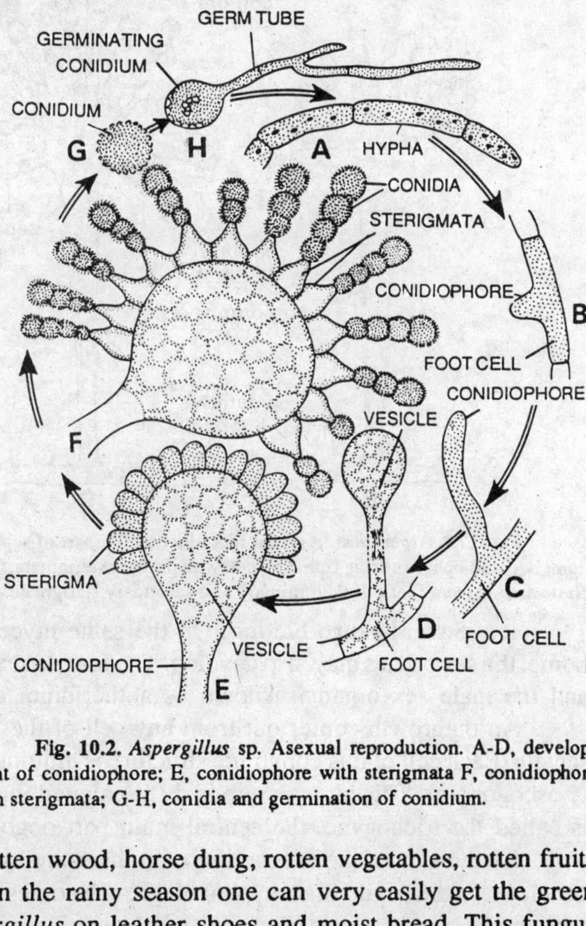

Fig. 10.2. *Aspergillus* sp. Asexual reproduction. A-D, development of conidiophore; E, conidiophore with sterigmata F, conidiophore with sterigmata; G-H, conidia and germination of conidium.

fungus is found on moist leather, moist rotten wood, horse dung, rotten vegetables, rotten fruits and many other dead organic materials. In the rainy season one can very easily get the green coloured culture of *Penicillium* and *Aspergillus* on leather shoes and moist bread. This fungus is called 'blue green mould', because of the presence of its smoky green conidia in abundance.

Some species of *Aspergillus* cause the diseases of animals and human beings. The diseases known as 'mycoses' and 'aspergillosis'are caused by this fungus. The 'tokelan' disease resembling ring worm is also caused by the same fungus.

Mycelium. The mycelium is found on the surface of the substratum. The hyphal ends penetrate the substratum and absorb food material. The mycelium is cottony, profusely branched, brownish and septate. Each cell is coenocytic having oil globules and protoplasm in it. The cytoplasm of one cell to another is communicated through a central septal pore.

Reproduction. The reproduction takes place by means of asexual and sexual methods.

1. **Asexual reproduction.** The asexual reproduction takes place by means of conidia. The conidia are produced on the conidiophores. Each conidiophore is aseptate and globular at its terminal end. The swollen terminal portion is called the vesicle. Many bottle-shaped multinucleate primary sterigmata are produced on this vesicle. In certain species, the secondary sterigmata also develop on the primary sterigmata. Each conidium is spherical, echinulate, multinucleate and smoky green. Due to this green colour of conidia the colonies of *Aspergillus* look green and named as 'blue green moulds'. The conidiophore may develop from any cell of the mycelium. This is called the 'foot cell'. The conidia are dispersed by wind. Whenever they fall on the suitable media and get favourable conditions of moisture and temperature, they germinate producing germ tubes developing into new mycelia.

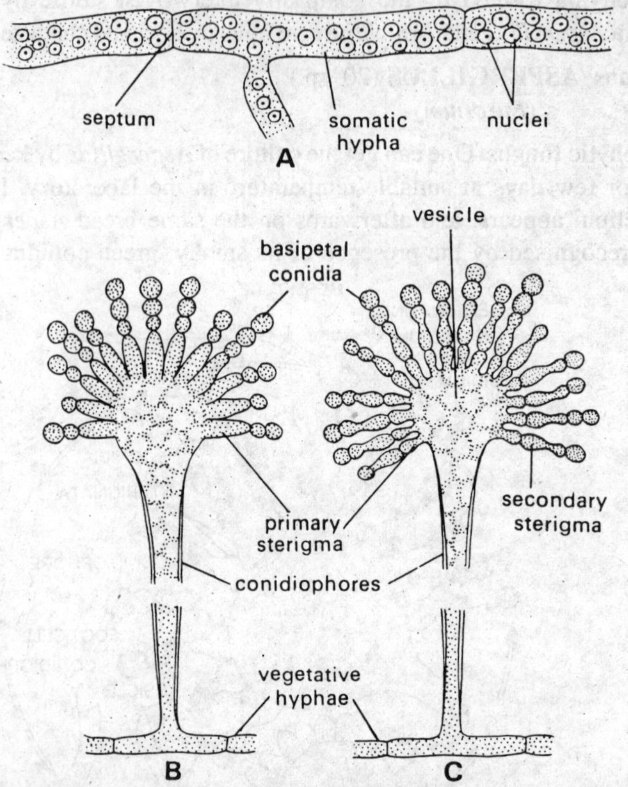

Fig. 10.3. *Aspergillus.* Asexual reproduction. A, part of septate mycelium; B, conidiophore arising from foot cell with primary sterigmata; C, conidiophore arising from foot cell with primary and secondary sterigmata.

1. **Sexual reproduction.** On the same mycelium where conidia and conidiophores are borne, the sex organs may also develop. The female sex organ is called the archicarp or ascogonium and the male sex organ is known as antheridium or pollinodium.

An outgrowth comes out from any cell of the hypha, which soon becomes convolute and septate. Each cell of this convolute structure is multinucleate. This structure is called the archicarp or ascogonium. This ascogonium is differentiated into three parts. The uppermost receptive part is called the trichogyne, the central main part oogonium, and the basal septate part the stalk.

By the side of the ascogonium, on the same hypha or on the other hypha, the antheridium develops. In the beginning a hyphal outgrowth comes out, swells at the terminal end, and becomes septate. This structure is also multinucleate. The uppermost cell of this structure acts as the main antheridium and the lower cell as the stalk. The antheridial stalk gradually increases in size and coils around the ascogonium. Ultimately the main antheridium reaches the trichogyne. The wall of contact dissolves and the protoplasm of the antheridium along with nuclei passes

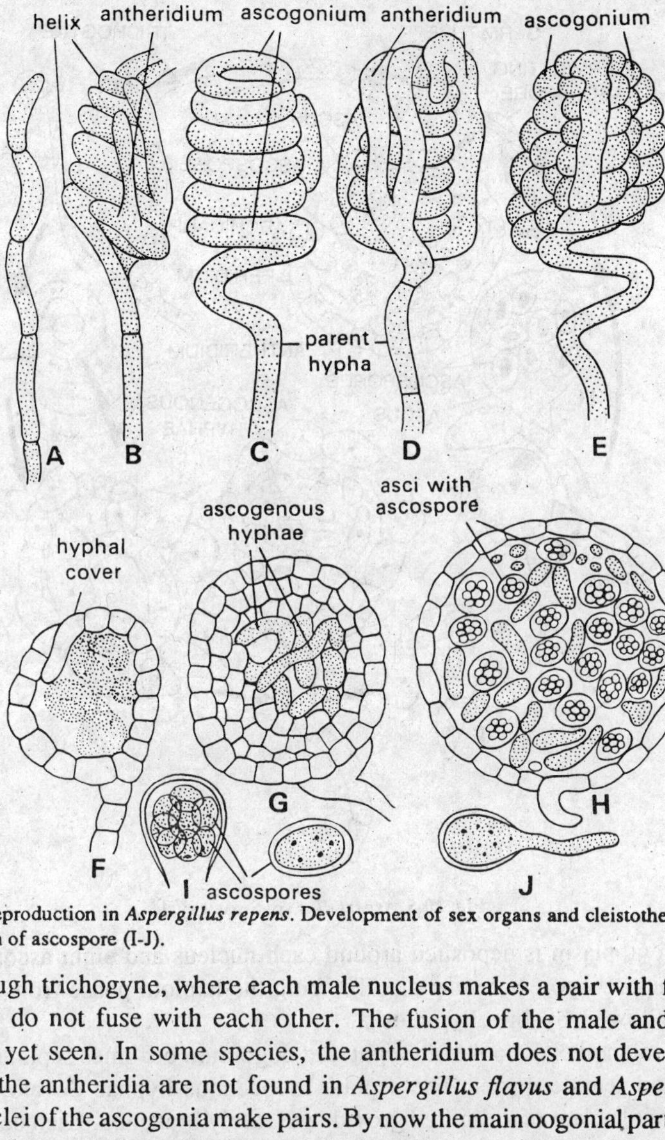

Fig. 10.4. Sexual reproduction in *Aspergillus repens*. Development of sex organs and cleistothecium (A-H); ascus, ascospores and germination of ascospore (I-J).

to the oogonium through trichogyne, where each male nucleus makes a pair with female nucleus, but the paired nuclei do not fuse with each other. The fusion of the male and female nuclei in *Aspergillus* is not yet seen. In some species, the antheridium does not develop. According to Dangeard (1907), the antheridia are not found in *Aspergillus flavus* and *Aspergillus fischeri*. In such species the nuclei of the ascogonia make pairs. By now the main oogonial part of ascogonium becomes septate and the ascogenous hyphae develop on this part. The ascogenous hyphae are also septate. The asci develop from the ultimate and penultimate cells of the ascogenous hyphae. Each ascus contains 4-8 ascospores in it. By this time several sterile hyphae develop on septate stalk, which surround the ascogonium completely.

Development of ascus. The mycologists have different opinions about the development of the ascus.

According to one school of thought the male and female nuclei found in the pairs, in the ascogonium fuse with each other and the diploid (2x) nuclei are formed. By now the oogonium becomes septate and bears septate ascogenous hyphae on it. Each cell of the oogonium bears two diploid (2x) nuclei and each of the ascogenous hypha contains two diploid nuclei. The diploid nuclei of the ultimate and penultimate cells of the ascogenous hyphae fuse and give rise to tetraploid (4x) nuclei in these cells. This tetraploid nucleus (4x) divides thrice. The first division is reductional (meiotic) which is followed by brachymeiosis. In this way eight nuclei

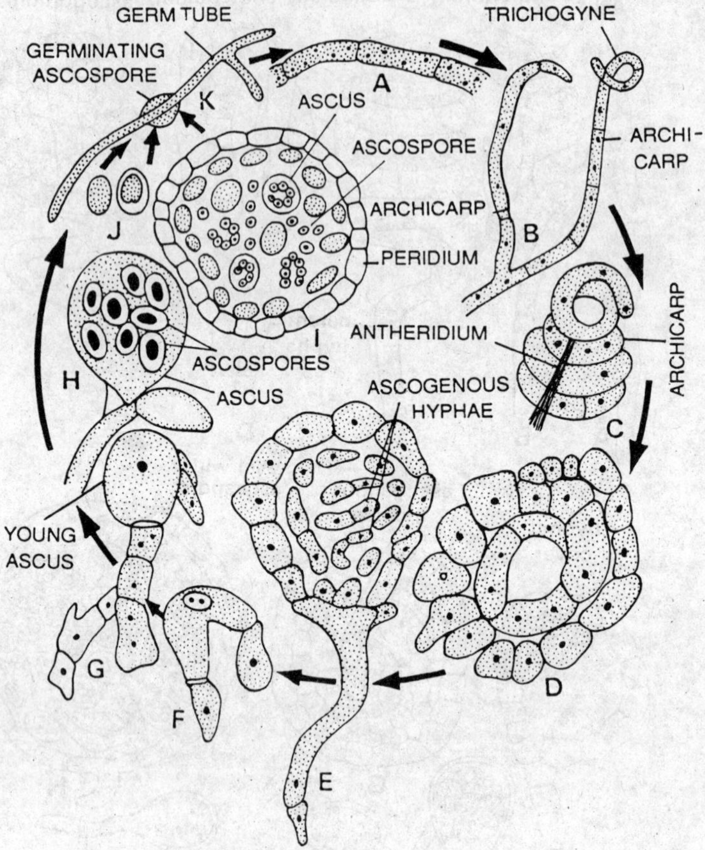

Fig. 10.5. *Aspergillus* sp. Sexual cycle.

are formed. The cytoplasm is deposited around each nucleus and eight ascospores are produced in each asucs. The ascospores are haploid. To bring the haploid phase from tetraploid condition the meiosis is followed by **brachymeiosis.**

According to another school of thought, the oogonium becomes septate and each cell bears a pair of male and female nuclei. The septate ascogenous hyphae develop on the oogonium. The ascogenous hyphae are of unlimited growth and rarely branched. Each cell of the ascogenous hyphae contains a pair of male and female nuclei. The paired nuclei of the ultimate and penultimate cells become fused with each other, and a diploid (2x) nucleus develops in each cell. This diploid nucleus divides thrice and eight nuclei are formed. The first division is reductional. The nuclei, thus formed are haploid (x). The cytoplasm is deposited around each nucleus and eight ascospores are formed in each ascus.

The asci are spherical or pyriform. Each mature ascospore is elliptical, echinulate and biconvex.

Development of cleistothecium. Several sterile hyphae arise from the septate stalk of ascogonium. These sterile hyphae surround completely the ascogonium, the ascogenous hyphae and the asci. A two-layered pseudoparenchymatous peridium develops from the sterile hyphae

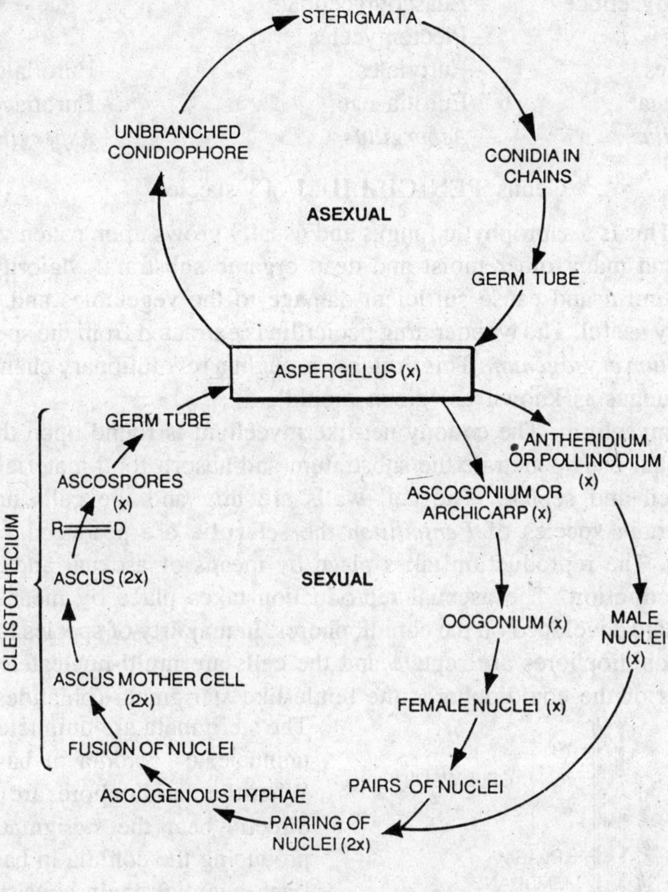

Fig. 10.6. Graphic life-cycle of *Aspergillus.*

which completely surround the ascogonium and its other parts. The inner layer of the peridium acts as nutritional layer which provides food to ascospores whereas the outer layer is protective in nature. This rounded closed pseudoparenchymatous structure is known as **cleistothecium.** On the maturation of the cleistothecium, all parts of ascogonium, ascogenous hyphae and walls of asci disorganise and free ascospores remain scattered within the cleistothecium. The outer wall of the cleistohecium secretes some oily substance and appears yellowish in colour. The cleistothecia are perennating bodies. They survive in adverse conditions. They rupture by the pressure of outer agencies. The ascospores are liberated and dispersed by the wind. On getting the suitable media and optimum weather conditions, they germinate producing germ tubes developing new mycelia on the surface of the substratum.

Systematic Position

	G. W. Martin (1961)	**C. J. Alexopoulos (1962)**	**G. C. Ainsworth (1971)**
Kingdom	–Plantae	–Plantae	–Fungi
Division	–Mycota	–Mycota	–Eumycota
Sub-div.	–Eumycotina	–Eumycotina	–Ascomycotina
Class	–Ascomycetes	–Ascomycetes	–Plectomycetes

Sub-cl.	–Euascomycetidae	–Euascomycetidae	–
Series	–	–Plectomycetes	–
Order	–Eurotiales	–Eurotiales	–Eurotiales
Family	–Eurotiaceae	–Eurotiaceae	–Eurotiaceae
Genus	–*Aspergillus*	–*Aspergillus*	–*Aspergillus*

Genus **PENICILLIUM** (13 species)

Occurrence. This is a saprophytic fungus and usually grows upon rotten vegetables, rotten fruits, rotten meat and many other moist and dead organic substrata. Majority of the species of this genus are harmful and cause sufficient damage to the vegetables and fruits, but some of the species are very useful. The wonder drug penicillin is extracted from the species *Penicillium notatum* and *Penicillium crysogenum.* This drug has brought a revolutionary change in the science of medicine. This fungus is known as 'green mould'.

Structure of mycelium. The cottony net-like mycelium is found upon the surface of the substratum. The hyphal ends penetrate the substratum and absorb food material. The mycelium is profusely branched and septate. The cell walls are thin and the cells are binucleate or multinucleate. In certain species of *Penicillium* the **sclerotia** are produced.

Reproduction. The reproduction takes place by means of asexual and sexual methods.

Asexual reproduction. The asexual reproduction takes place by means of uninucleate conidia. The conidia are developed on the conidiophores. In majoirty of species the conidiophores are branched. The conidiophores are septate and the cells are multi-nucleate. On the terminal ends of the branches of the conidiophores the bottle-like sterigmata (phialides) are produced. The sterigmata are uninucleate and bear the uninucleate conidia in basigenous chains. When the conidiophores are unbranched, they directly bear the sterigmata on their ends producing the conidia in basigenous chains. Each conidial chain consists of hundred or more conidia. Each conidium is smooth, uninucleate and green. Due to the presence of innumerable green conidia the fungus is called the 'green mould'. The conidia are dispersed by wind and carried from one place to another. Whenever they get suitable media and appropriate conditions for germination, they germinate producing germ tubes developing into new myclia.

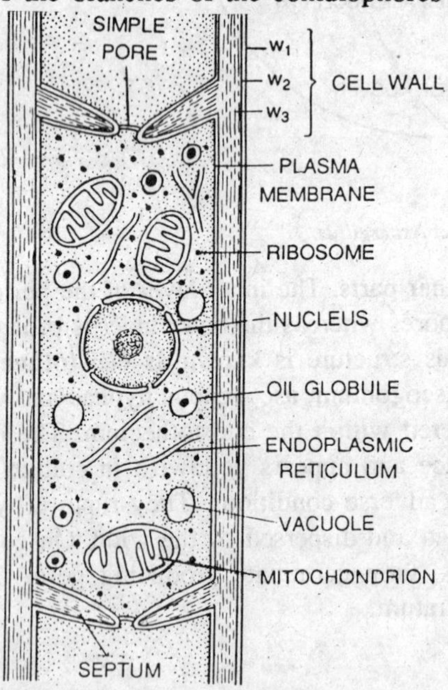

Fig. 10.7. *Penicillium* spp. Ultra structure of a cell (diagrammatic)

Sexual reproduction. Almost all the species of *Penicillium* are homothallic. Only one species is heterothallic. The structure of the sex organs and the production of asci on ascogenous hyphae differ from species to species. In the beginning of the development, the ascogonium is uninucleate, but gradually this nucleus divides mitotically and 2-64 nuclei are produced. A thin-walled uninucleate antheridial branch grows upward coiling around the ascogonium. This antheridial branch bears at its terminal end a small, swollen, uninucleate antheridium. The terminal end of the antheridium attaches itself to the ascogonium, the wall of contact dissolves and a pore develops. Actual process of fusion has not yet been seen and nothing has been confirmed about the sexual fusion. By this time the sterile hyphae surround

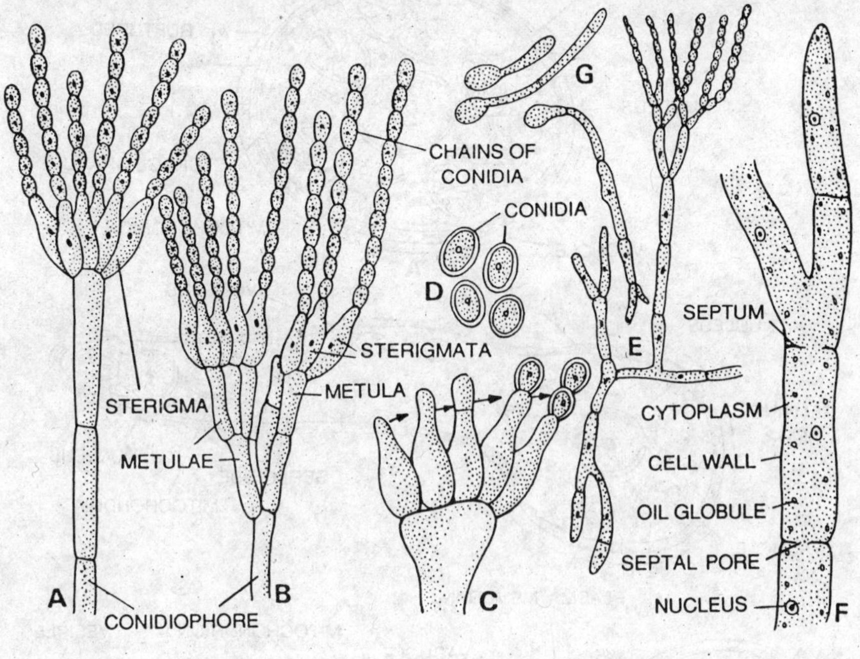

Fig. 10.7 (a). *Penicillium* sp. Asexual reproduction. A, sterigmata and conidial chains arising on unbranched conidiophores; B, sterigmata and conidial chains developing on branched conidiophore; C, formation of conidia on sterigmata; D. conidia; E, conidiophore developed on mycelium; F, part of mycelium; G, germinating conidia.

the fused antheridium and ascogonium, and the central sterile portion of the cleistothecium develops. Now the ascogonium becomes septate and each cell contains a pair of male and female nuclei. In this way a series of binucleate cells is developed. From some of the cells of this row, the branched and septate ascogenous hyphae develop. The cells of ascogenous hyphae are binucleate. The ultimate and penultimate cells of the ascogenous hyphae develop into asci. Each ascus contains eight ascospores in it.

The male and female nuclei found in the pairs in the ultimate and penultimate cells of the ascogenous hyphae fuse with each other and diploid nuclei are resulted. Now these cells with diploid nuclei are called the ascus mother cells. The diploid nucleus of each ascus mother cell divides thrice and the eight nuclei are formed. To bring the haploid phase the first division is reductional. The cytoplasm deposits around each nucleus and eight ascospores are produced in the ascus. In each ascus there are 4 ascospores of + strain and 4 of — strain.

The ascospores are uninucleate, ellipsoidal, biconvex and echinulate. The cleisothecium is a perennating body. Whenever this bursts, the ascospores liberate and disperse by the wind. On getting suitable media and favourable conditions of moisture and temperature, the ascospores germinate producing germ tubes developing into new mycelia.

In the species of *Penicillium* two types of cleistothecia are produced. In one type of cleistothecia the peridium consists of hyphae and in the other type the peridium is pseudoparenchymatous. In the latter type a single ascus develops on the terminal end of the ascogenous hypha.

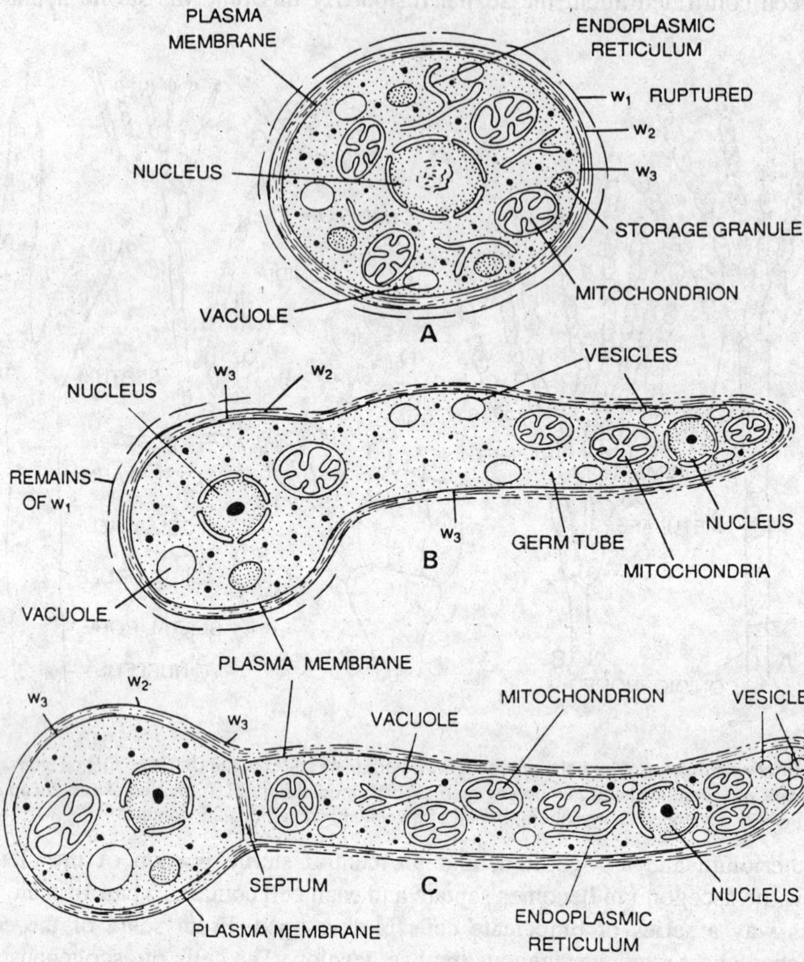

Fig.10.7 (b). *Penicillium* sp. A, ultra structure of a conidium; B, early stage of the germination of conidium showing emergence of germ tube (ultrastructure); C, development of primary septum (ultrastructure).

Systematic Position

	G. W. Martin (1961)	C. J. Alexopoulos (1962)	G. C. Ainswoth (1971)
Kingdom	–Plantae	–Plantae	–Fungi
Division	–Mycota	–Mycota	–Eumycota
Sub-div.	–Eumycotina	–Eumycotina	–Ascomycotina
Class	–Ascomycetes	–Ascomycetes	–Plectomycetes
Sub-cl.	–Euascomycetidae	–Euascomycetidae	
Series		–Plectomycetes	
Order	–Eurotiales	–Eurotiales	–Eurotiales
Family	–Eurotiaceae	–Eurotiaceae	–Eurotiaceae
Genus	–*Penicillium*	–*Penicillium*	–*Penicillium*

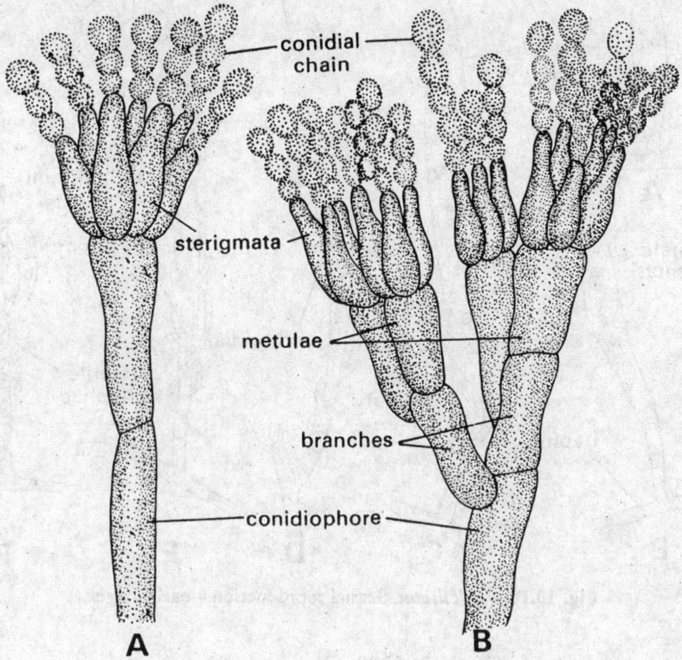

Fig. 10.8. Monoverticillate (A) and biverticillate (B) conidiophores of *Penicillium.*

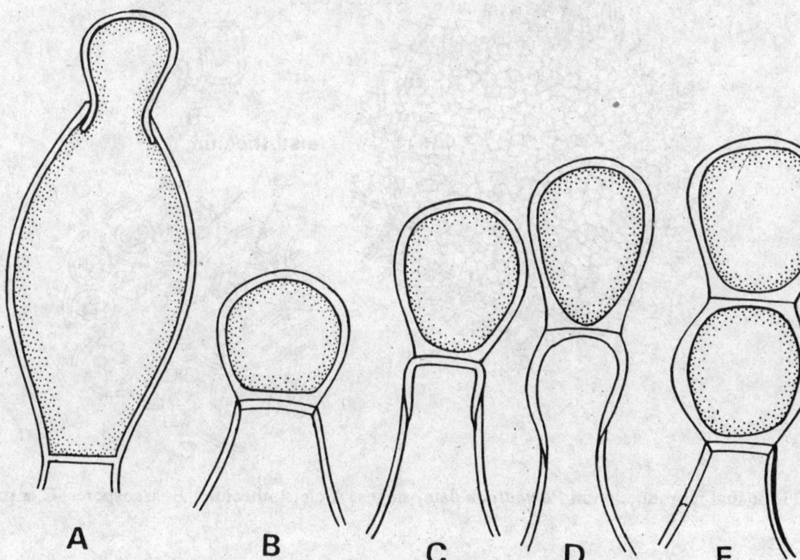

Fig. 10.9. *Penicillium* sp. A-F, stages in the formation of conidia.

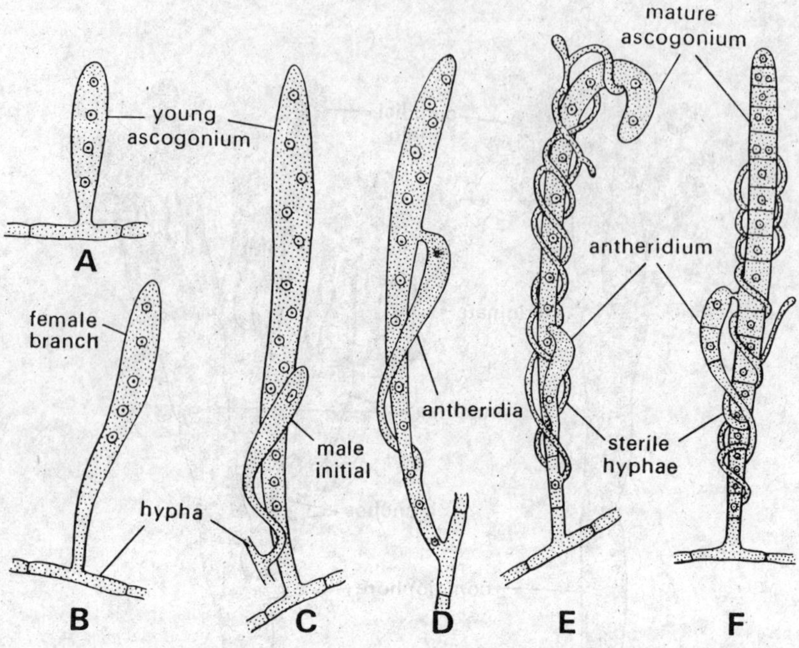

Fig. 10.10. *Penicillium*. Sexual reproduction—early stages.

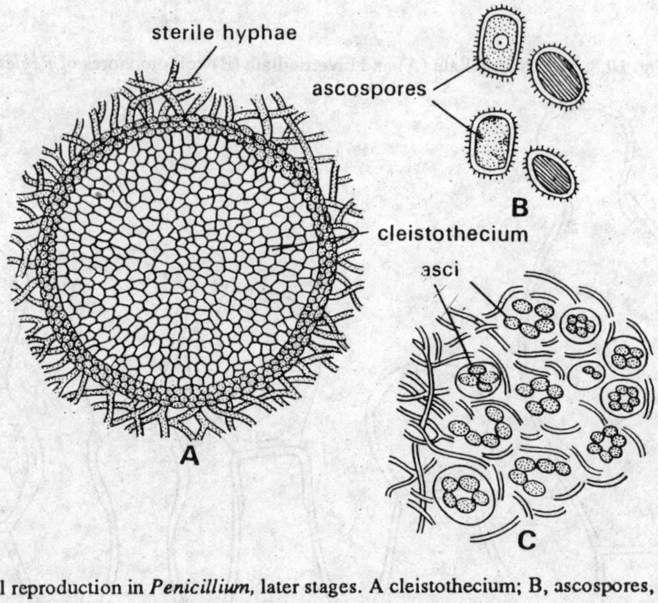

Fig. 10.11. Sexual reproduction in *Penicillium*, later stages. A cleistothecium; B, ascospores, C, a part of cleistothecium.

Class–Pyrenomycetes
(*Ainsworth*, 1971)

Characteristic Features

1. The club-shaped or cylindrical asci are arranged in a hymenial layer (hymenium) which lines the base and often the sides of the inner wall of perithecium. Sometimes the asci are arranged in basal tufts.

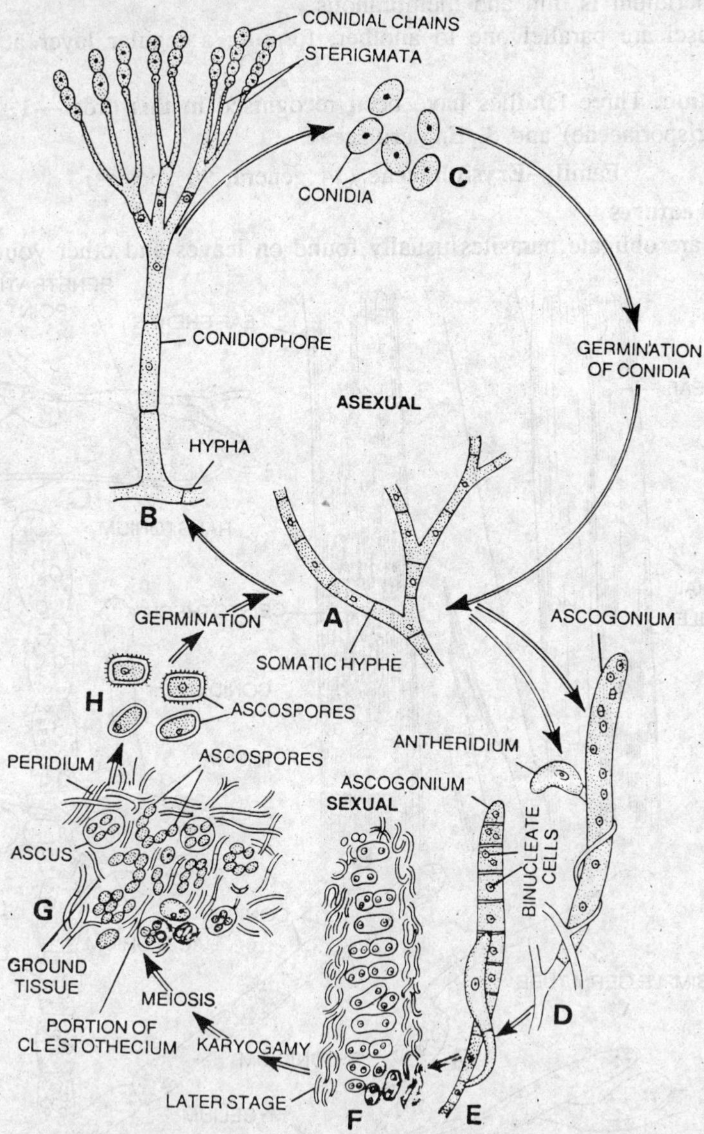

Fig. 10.12. *Penicillium.* Diagrammatic life-cycle. A, branched and septate mycelium; B, septate and branched conidiophore with sterigmata and conidia; C, uninucleate, smooth conidia; D, antheridium and ascogonium; E, gametangial contact and pairing of nuclei; F, later stage; G, portion of cleistothecium; H, ascospores.

2. Usually the asci are persistent.
3. The perithecium may or may not be embedded in a stroma.
4. In every situation the perithecium has a definite peripheral wall of its own.

Five orders are included in this class. They are : Erysiphales; Meliolales; Coronophorales; Sphaeriales; Clavicipitales.

ORDER—ERYSIPHALES (60 genera; 1000 species)

Characteristic Features

1. An abundant, superficial mycelium is present which may be colourless or dark coloured.
2. The perithecia are spherical, ovoid or flattened and are usually without an ostiole.

3. The peridium is thin and membranous.

4. The asci are parallel one to another, forming a regular layer at the base of the fructification.

Classification. Three families have been recognised in this order—1. Erysiphaceae, 2. Meliolaceae (Perisporiaceae) and 3. Englerulaceae.

Family–**Erysiphaceae** (14 genera, 90 species)

Characteristic Features

1. They are obligate parasites usually found on leaves and other young tissues of the host plant.

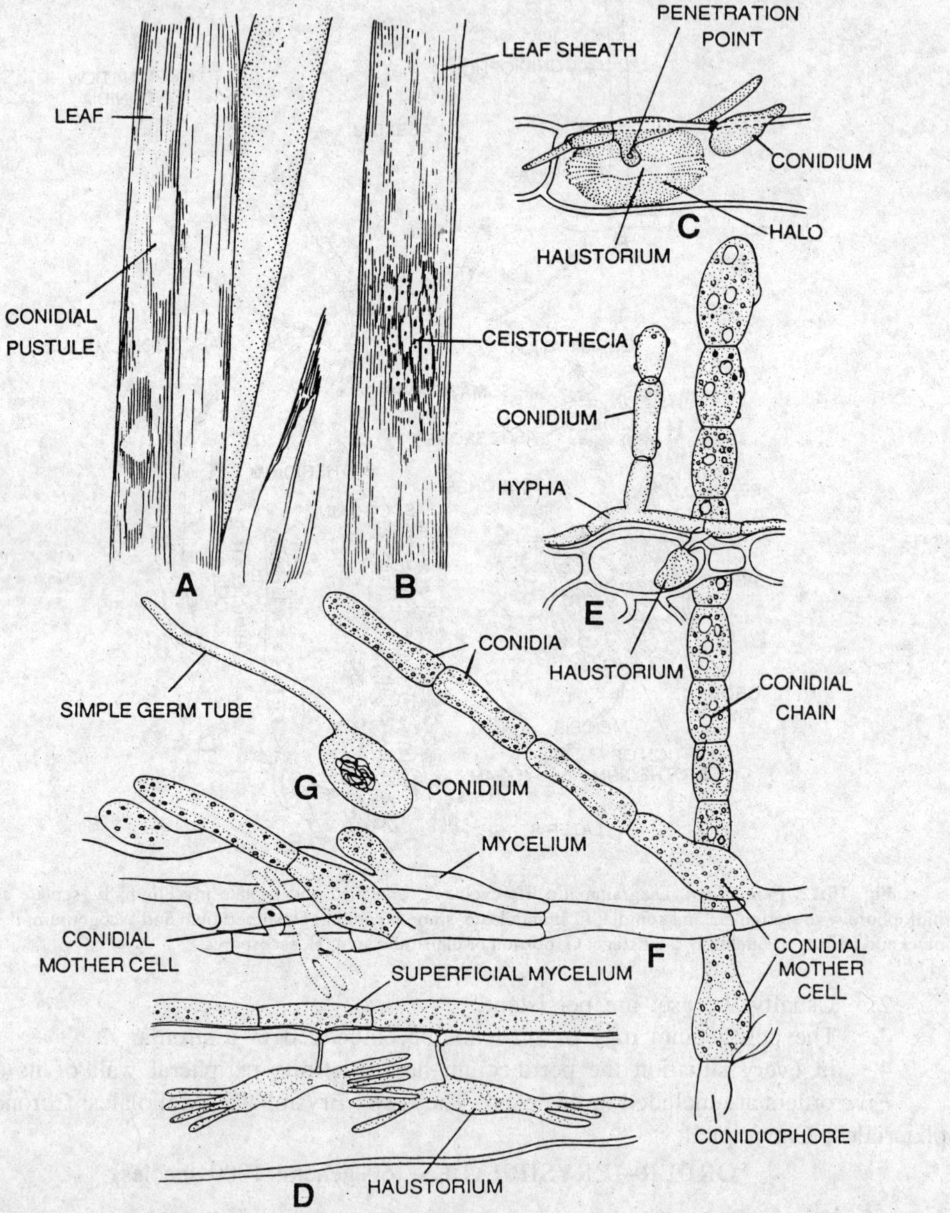

Fig. 10.13. *Erysiphe graminis tritici*. Powdery mildew of wheat. A-B, infected leaf; C-D, epidermal cell of host with haustorium; E-F, conidiophore with conidial chain and conidia; G, germination of conidium.

2. The mycelium is ectophytic and consists of uninucleate cells. It produces haustoria which enter the spongy tissue of the leaves through stomata.

3. They reproduce asexually by one-celled conidia found in chains in such great abundance over the host surface that they appear as a white powdery covering and commonly known as 'powdery mildews'.

4. A single ascus or many asci are found within a cleistothecium. The cleistothecia are provided with specialized appendages.

The most important genus *Erysiphe* of this family has been discussed here in detail.

Genus ERYSIPHE (10 species)

The species of this genus are obligatae parasites on the leaves, young shoots and inflorescence of flowering plant. Powdery mildew of wheat and barley is caused by *Erysiphe graminis.*

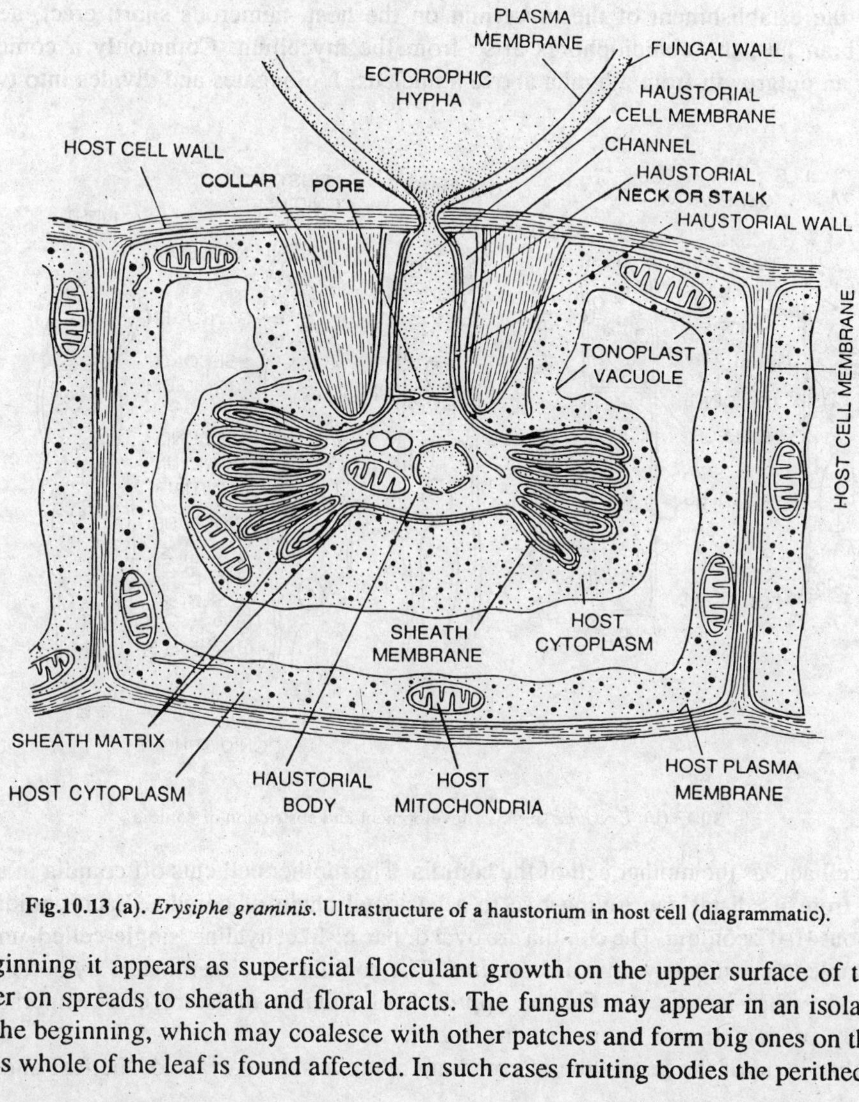

Fig.10.13 (a). *Erysiphe graminis*. Ultrastructure of a haustorium in host cell (diagrammatic).

In the beginning it appears as superficial flocculant growth on the upper surface of the levels, which later on spreads to sheath and floral bracts. The fungus may appear in an isolated white patch, in the beginning, which may coalesce with other patches and form big ones on the leaves. Sometimes whole of the leaf is found affected. In such cases fruiting bodies the perithecia appear like black dots. *Erysiphe polygoni* occurs on the leaves and stems of a considerable variety of hosts.

Mycelium-somatic structure. The mycelium is ectophytic (superficial) and consists of uninucleate cells. It forms a white, web-like coating over the leaf and sends haustoria into the epidermal cells of the host. Usually the haustorium is branched, forming finger-like processes, and frequently provided with an external disc or appressorium, from which the haustorium proper arises and pushes into the epidermal cell. As a rule the fungus does not penetrate deeper in the tissue, but in *Erysiphe graminis* endophytic growth is induced if the conidia germinate on wounded leaves.

Asexual reproduction. The asexual reproduction takes place by means of hyaline, one-celled conidia borne on short, erect, unbranched conidiophores, arising from the superficial mycelium. The conidia are produced in such great abundance over the surface of the leaf that they appear as a white powdery coating. The conidia are produced in rows (chains) on unbranched, aseptate, uninucleate conidiophores.

After the establishment of the mycelium on the host, numerous short, erect, aerial and unicellular branches, the conidiophores arise from the mycelium. Commonly a conidiophore develops as an outgrowth from a hypha above a nucleus. It elongates and divides into two cells.

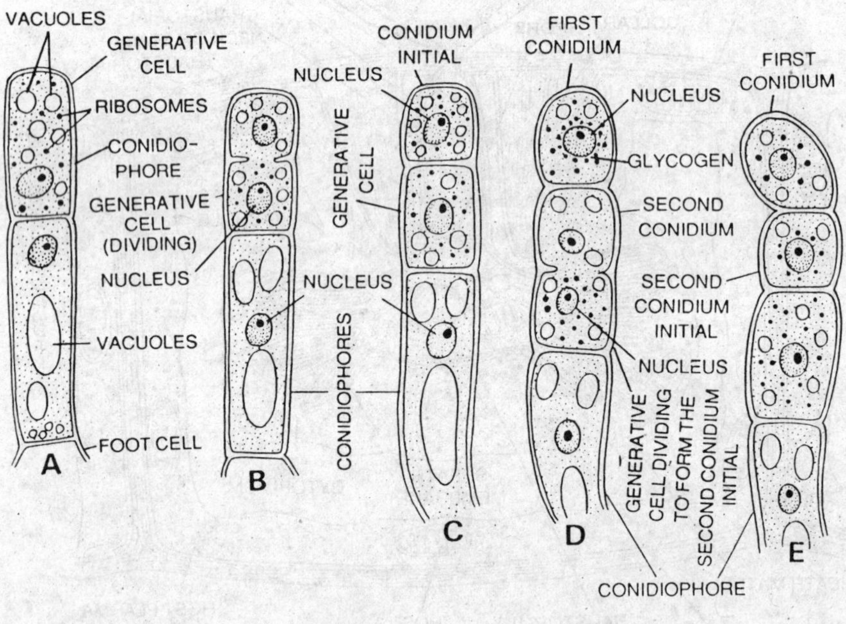

Fig. 10.13 (b). *Erysiphe* sp. A-E, development and abstriction of conidia.

The upper cell acts as the mother cell of the conidia. The mother cell cuts off conidia in acropetal succession from its distal end giving rise to a basipetal chain of conidia. Each conidial chain contains about 10-12 conidia. The conidia are oval or barrel-like, hyaline, single-celled, unicellular and are capable to germinate within a short time. The conidia are disseminated by outer agencies such as wind, water insects etc. On the approach of suitable moisture and temperature they germinate by producing one or more germ tubes.

The distal end of the germ tube of conidium appresses the surface of the leaf and develop into a flat appressorium. A peg-like structure arises from the appressorium and penetrates the epidermal cell of the host. The distal end of this peg-like structure swells up into a vesicle which gives rise to finger-like branches of the haustoria.

Sexual reproduction. The sexual organs arise as lateral branches from the mycelium and projected at right angles to the infected surface. The oval, uninucleate oogonium is found to be situated on a stalk cell. The antheridium is much smaller and is borne on an elongated, narrow stalk. The antheridium also contains a single nucleus. The wall of contact between antheridium and oogonium dissolves, the male nucleus passes into the oogonium, and unites

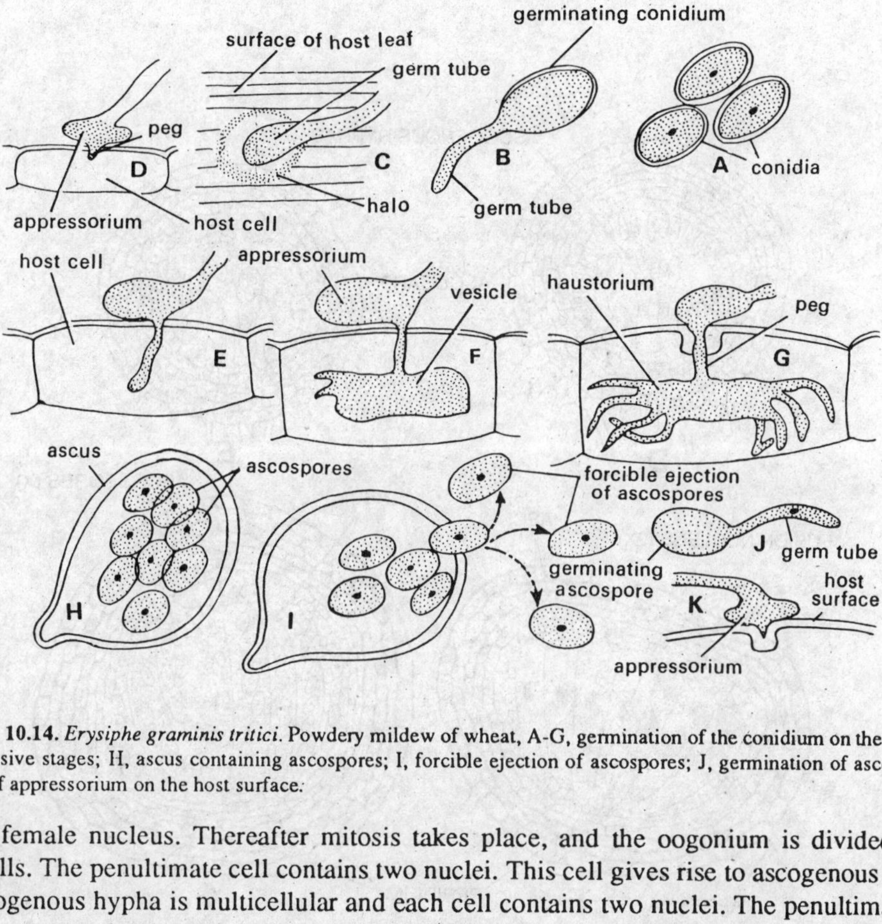

Fig. 10.14. *Erysiphe graminis tritici.* Powdery mildew of wheat, A-G, germination of the conidium on the surface of host, successive stages; H, ascus containing ascospores; I, forcible ejection of ascospores; J, germination of ascospore; K, formation of appressorium on the host surface.

with the female nucleus. Thereafter mitosis takes place, and the oogonium is divided into a row of cells. The penultimate cell contains two nuclei. This cell gives rise to ascogenous hyphae. Each ascogenous hypha is multicellular and each cell contains two nuclei. The penultimate cells of the ascogenous hyphae act as ascus mother cells. The two nuclei of each ascus mother cell fuse together forming a diploid nucleus. This fusion nucleus divides thrice producing eight nuclei of which the first division is meiotic one. These eight haploid nuclei metamorphose into eight ascospores. The asci are oval and contain elliptical ascospores. On maturity the ascospores are forcibly released from the asci. The ascospore germinates on the surface of the host producing a germ tube.

Development of the cleistothecium. While the process of sexual union is going on the basal cells of the ascogonium give rise to sterile branched hyphae which engulf the fruiting body and makes its pseudoparenchymatous, brittle peridium. Some of the cells of peridium give rise to simple hypha-like appendages which remain interwoven with mycelium.

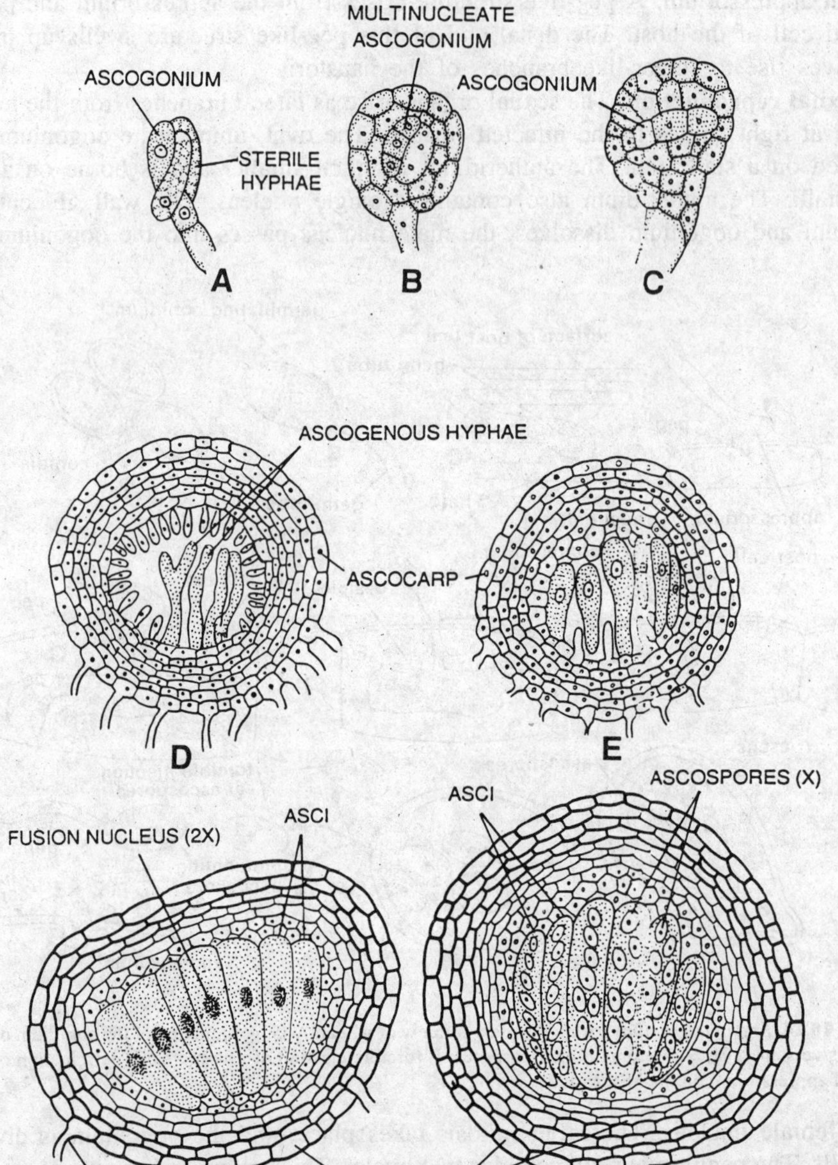

Fig. 10.15. Sexual reproduction. A, coiling of male and female branches; B, fertilization; C, fertilized ascogonium; D-F, successive stages in the development of cleistothecium; G, mature cleistothecium in sectional view.

The cleistothecia generally, appear in the late summer. The cleistothecia are round or sub-globose, bright reddish brown and about 200μ in diameter. Each cleistothecium is furnished with simple or branched appendages.

During development the wall of the ascocarp (cleistothecium) is differentiated, into inner and outer layers. The inner layer consists of thin-walled cells rich in cytoplasm; it supplies the food material to the developing asci. The function of the outer layer is protective; from this layer the characteristic appendages are developed.

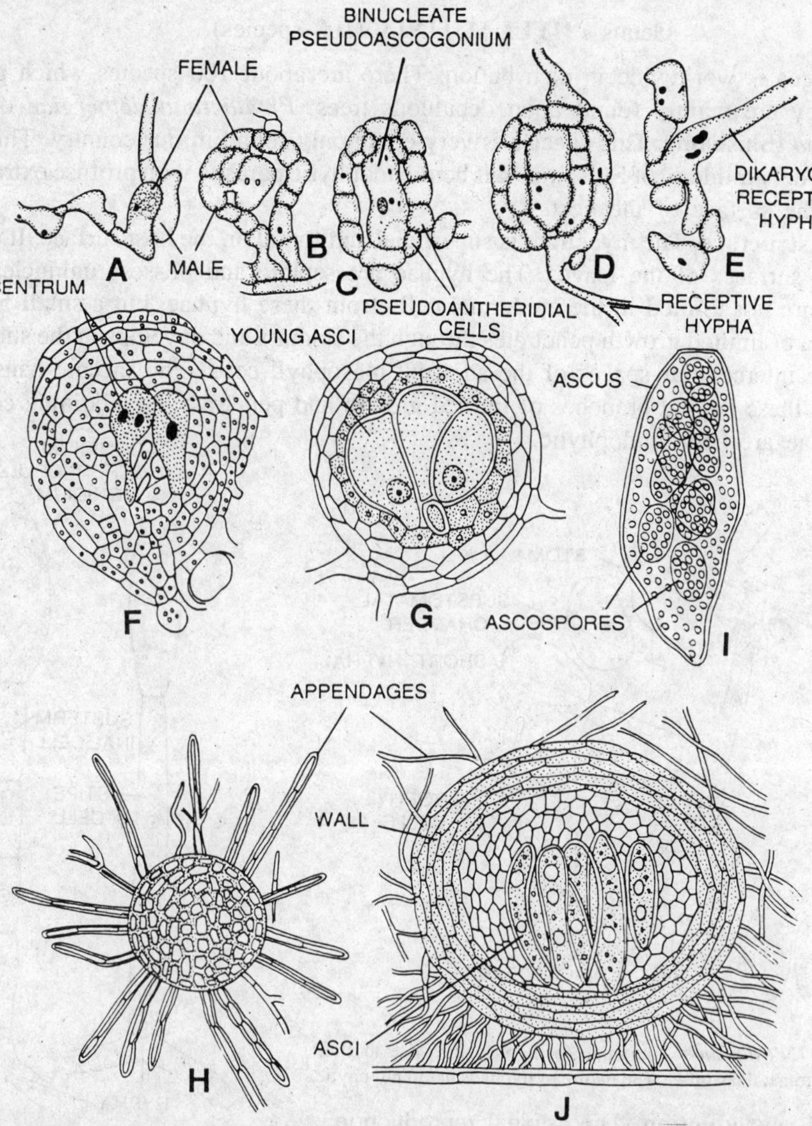

Fig. 10.16. *Erysiphe*. Sexual reproduction. A-E, early stages, F-G developing cleistothecium; I, ascus with ascospores; J and H, cleistothecia.

Systematic Position

	G. W. Martin (1961)	**C. J. Alexopoulos (1962)**	**G. C. Ainsworth (1971)**
Kingdom	–Plantae	–Plantae	–Fungi
Division	–Mycota	–Mycota	–Eumycota
Sub-div.	–Eumycotina	–Eumycotina	–Ascomycotina
Class	–Ascomycetes	–Ascomycetes	–Pyrenomycetes
Sub-Cl.	–Euascomycetidae	–Euascomycetidae	–
Series	–	–Pyrenomycetes	–
Order	–Erysiphales	–Erysiphales	–Erysiphales
Family	–Erysiphaceae	–Erysiphaceae	–Erysiphaceae
Genus	–*Erysiphe*	–*Erysiphe*	–*Erysiphe*

Genus PHYLLACTINIA (100 species)

This fungus is worldwide in distribution. There are about 100 species which parasitize the plants. They are mainly found upon deciduous trees. *Phyllactinia delbergiae* occurs on *Delbergia sissoo* (**Shisham**). This species is very commonly found in our country. This fungus causes the 'powdery mildew' of **Shisham**. It is hemiendophytic parasite with profuse extramatrical mycelium on the surface of the host.

Somatic structure. The mycelium is superficial and found on the host surface. It is mainly found on both surfaces of the leaves. The hyphae are septate and possess uninucleate cells. The haustoria are not formed in the epidermal cells from these hyphae, but a small 5-7 celled branch of hypha of limited growth penetrates through the stomata and develops in the substomatal chamber in the intercellular spaces of the adjacent mesophyll cells. The saccate haustoria are produced from these hyphal branches of limited growth and penetrate the adjoining cells. This way, the hyphae are hemi-endophytic.

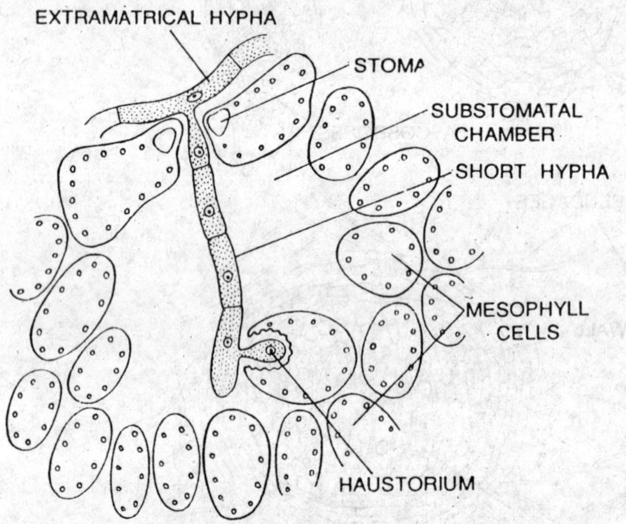

Fig. 10.17. *Phyllactinia*. Extramatrical hypha gives rise to short hypha in the sub-stomatal chamber. The nature of hypha is hemiendophytic.

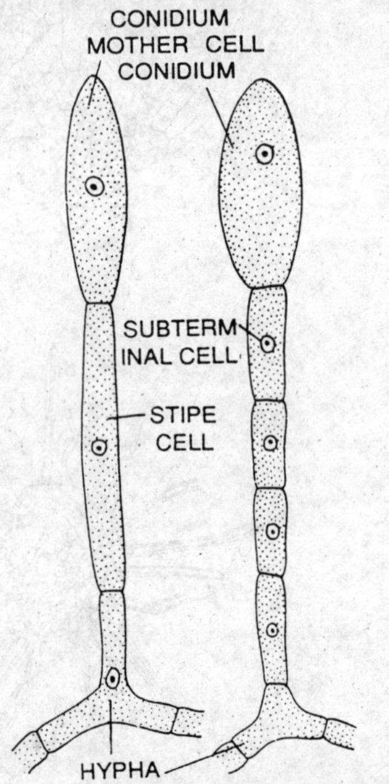

Fig. 10.18. *Phyllactinia*. Development of conidium.

Asexual reproduction. The asexual reproduction takes place by means of conidiophores and conidia. The conidiophores develop vertically from the superficial mycelium. They are formed abundantly first on both surfaces of the leaves, but afterwards on the initiation of the development of cleistothecia their development is confined on the lower surface of the host leaf. The young conidiophore divides transversely into two cells. The upper cell is **conidium—mother cell** and the lower, a **stipe cell**. The conidium mother cell divides once again forming two cells—the upper one acts as conidium and the lower one as **subterminal cell.** When this conidium is shed off, the subterminal cell divides again forming another conidium similarly. This way the conidia are formed, singly and not in chains. The conidia are formed abundantly in favourable conditions.

The conidia are single celled, clavate, hyaline, uninucleate and thin walled. They are dispersed by wind. Each conidium germinates into a new mycelium.

Sexual reproduction. The male and female sex organs are known as **antheridium** and

ascogonium respectively. They arise on superficial hyphal branches that lie close to each other. Both the sex organs are single-celled and uninucleate. The nucleus is being received by the division of the initial nucleus in the respective sex organs. The ascogonium is thick and ovoid while the antheridium is slender and clavate. Both the sex organs are closely appressed to each other. The separation wall between the two dissolves and the male nucleus migrates into the ascogonium. Both the nuclei form a pair and divide. The fertilized ascogonial cell also divides

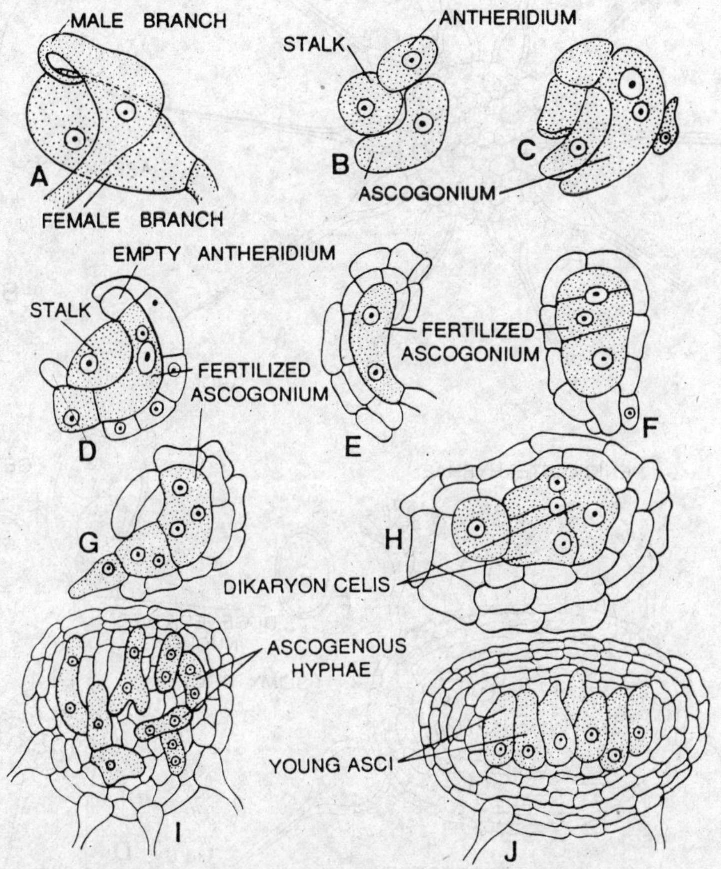

Fig. 10.19. *Phyllactinia.* Sexual reproduction. A-B, development of male and female sex organs, *i.e.*, antheridium and ascogonium C, fertilization; D, fusion of nuclei (karyogamy); E-G, fertilized ascogonium H, dikaryon cells; I, developing cleistothecium with ascogenous hyphae; J, young cleistothecium with young asci,

to form a row of 3-5 cells, of which the penultimate cell is dikaryotic. This cell contains two nuclei one from each of the sex organs. The ascogenous hyphae are produced on this cell. The asci are developed from these ascogenous hyphae. Simultaneously the hyphal branches arise upwards from the basal cell of the ascogonium to form a 2-3 layered sheath round the developing **cleistothecium (ascocarp).** Within the developing cleistothecium the two nuclei of the dikaryon fuse together inside the young ascus, to form a diploid nucleus. This diploid nucleus (2x) divides thrice to form eight nuclei, the first division being reductional one ; six of the nuclei are being disorganized and the ascospores are formed round only two nuclei. Thus the mature ascus contains only two ascospores. Many clavate asci are found to be situated in a parallel layer on the base of the cleistothecium.

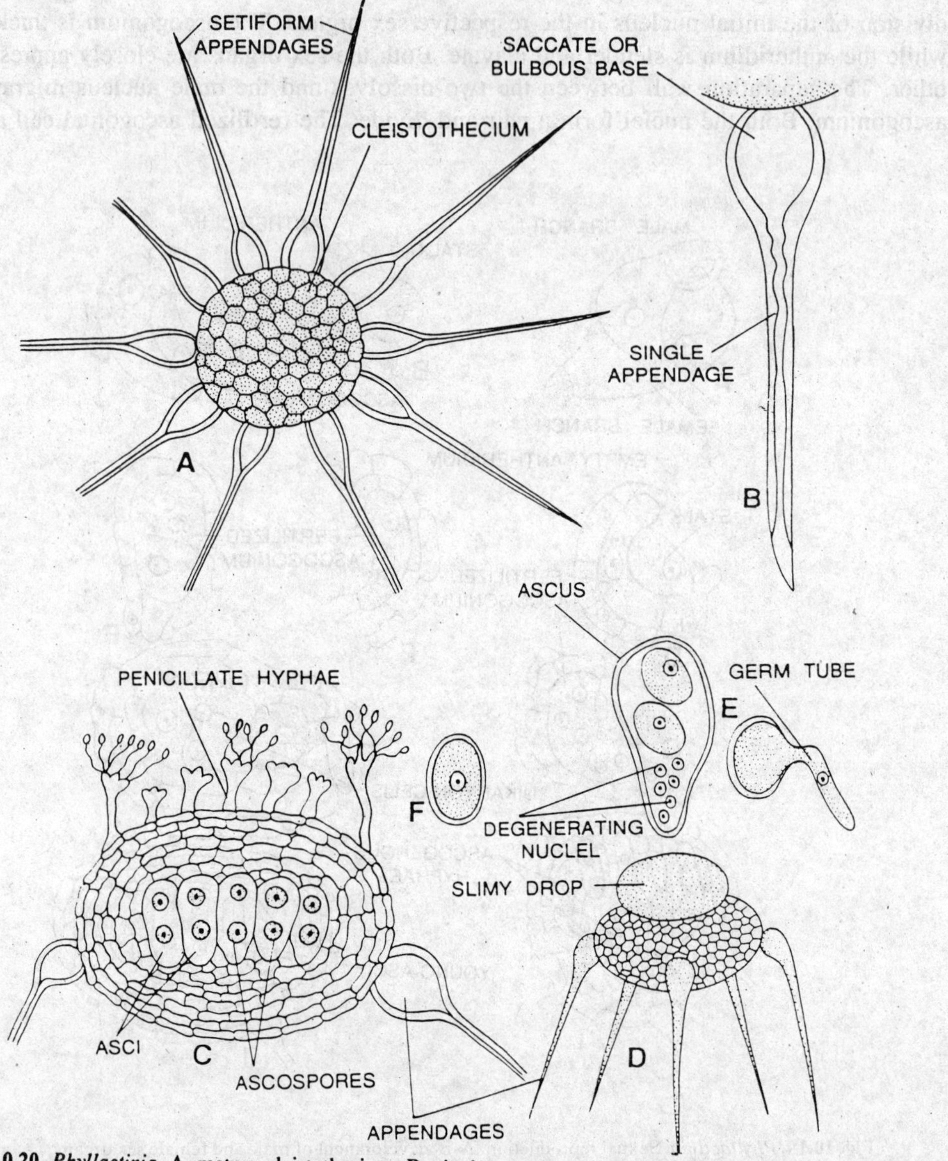

Fig. 10.20. ***Phyllactinia.*** **A, mature cleistothecium; B, single appendage to cleistothecium with bulbous base; C, sectional view of mature cleistothecium showing asci and penicillate hyphae; D, raised cleistothecium with appendages and slimy drop; E, an ascus containing two ascospores and six degenerating nuclei and a germinating ascospore.**

The characteristic appendages arise from the outermost layer of the cleistothecium around its equatorial plane. The appendages are long, unbranched, setiform, stiff structures with a bulbous base. The upper portion of this bulbous structure is thick-walled and the lower portion is thin-walled. In dry weather conditions the lower portion of appendages becomes flaccid and bends downward like a joint. Thus the cleistothecium is raised up as it on stilts. In addition to these appendages a crown of penicillately branched hyphal cells is found on the top of the cleistothecium. These hyphal cells are hygroscopic in nature and swell up to form an apical slimy drop which on drying up fixes the cleistothecium firmly on the surface of the host.

The wall of cleistothecium ruptures irregularly. The asci are escaped out and from which the ascospores are liberated. The ascospores are ovate to elliptical or sometimes spherical. They are uninucleate and smooth. The ascospores, germinate to produce new mycelia when fall upon suitable host. The new mycelium soon becomes ready to produce conidiophores and conidia.

Systematic Position

	G. W. Martin (1961)	**C. J. Alexopoulos (1962)**	**G. C. Ainsworth (1971)**
Kingdom	–Plantae	–Plantae	–Fungi
Division	–Mycota	–Mycota	–Eumycota
Sub-div.	–Eumycotina	–Eumycotina	–Ascomycotina
Class	–Ascomycetes	–Ascomycetes	–Pyrenomycetes
Sub-cl.	–Euascomycetidae	–Euascomycetidae	–
Series	–	–Pyrenomycetes	–
Order	–Erysiphales	–Erysiphales	–Erysiphales
Family	–Erysiphaceae	–Erysiphaceae	–Erysiphaceae
Genus	–*Phyllactinia*	–*Phyllactinia*	–*Phyllactinia*

Genus **SPHAEROTHECA**

This genus is also a member of family Erysiphaceae. Eight species of this genus have been recorded from this country. Of which the most common species is *Sphaerotheca fuliginea.* This species mainly occurs on cucurbits, such as *Luffa, Lagenaria* and *Cucurbita.* Another species *S. pannosa* occurs on the roses in the hilly regions. They cause the powdery mildews.

Somatic structure. The mycelium is superficial and commonly found on the surface of leaves of host plant. The mycelium is branched and septate. The septa are provided with septal pores. The cells are uninucleate. At the point of contact with host plant, the haustoria are developed from the mycelium. The haustoria are generally lobed or branched.

Asexual reproduction. The asexual reproduction takes place by means of conidia developed on short, erect conidiophores in basigenous chains. The conidia are barrel-shaped, hyaline, and uninucleate. The conidia are dispersed by wind and are carried from one place to another. When comes in contact with host leaf, the conidium germinates by producing a forked germ tube.

Sexual reproduction. The sex organs develop on hyphal tips of mycelium. The uninucleate antheridia and ascogonia develop from closely situated neighbouring hyphae. The nucleus of male branch divides and the antheridium is separated at the apex. Antheridium is somewhat more slender than the ascogonium and these organs closely approach each other. This development takes in a similar way as that in *Erysiphe.* The wall of contact dissolves, and the antheridium nucleus passes into the ascogonium through a pore. The plasmogamy takes place, and the pair of male and female nuclei settles down in a cell of ascogonium. The antheridium now disintegrates, and the fertilized ascogonium gives rise to a row of cells by subsequent divisions. The penultimate of this row of cells is dikaryotic, whereas the other cells are uninucleate. This dikaryotic cell acts as ascus mother cell, which develops into an ascus. Karyogamy occurs, which results in the formation of a zygote nucleus. This is followed by meiosis, and thus eight haploid nuclei are formed. The cytoplasm is being deposited around each nucleus, and eight ascospores are developed. Each ascus is somewhat ovoid, broadly elliptic to subglobose, and contains eight ascospores in it. A hyphal sheath engulfs the developing asci. The cleistothecium develops in the similar way as in *Erysiphe.*

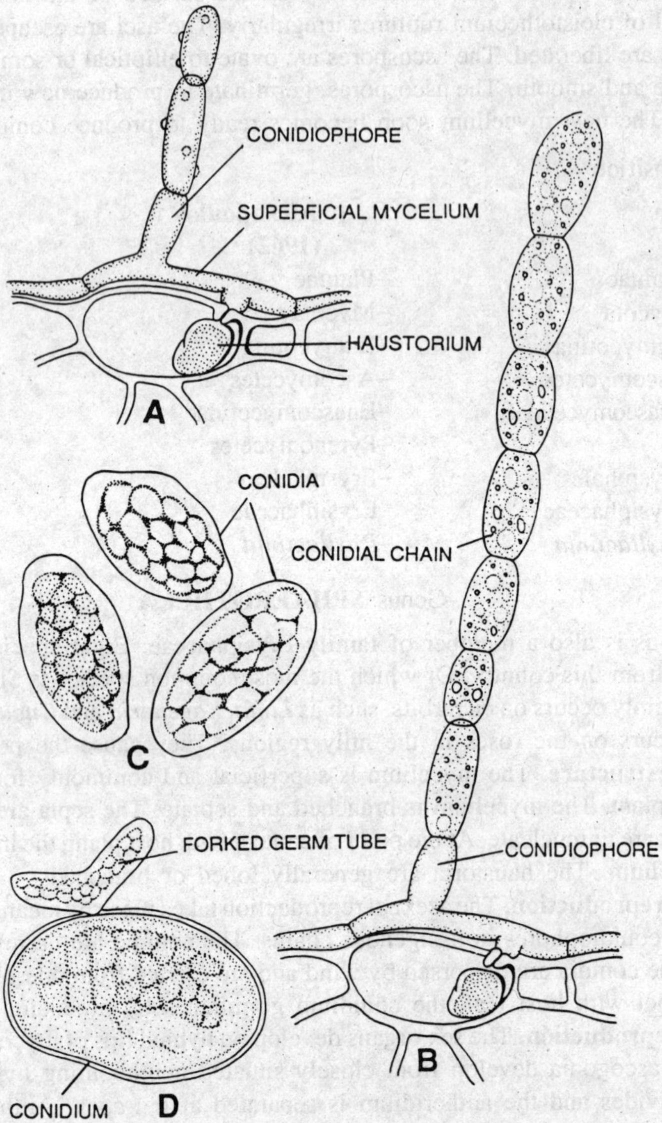

Fig. 10.21. *Sphaerotheca* sp. A, superficial mycelium, conidiophore, developing conidia and simple haustorium within host epidermal cell; B, conidiophore bearing conidial chain; C, conidia; D, germinating conidium.

The mature cleistothecium is globose, dark brown and provided with simple mycelial appendages. The cleistothecial wall is two-layered, and each layer consists of several cells in thickness. The outer cells are dark, polygonal and uninucleate while the inner cells are binucleate. Each cleistothecium contains a single ascus. The ascus is released out on the disintegration of cleistothecial wall.

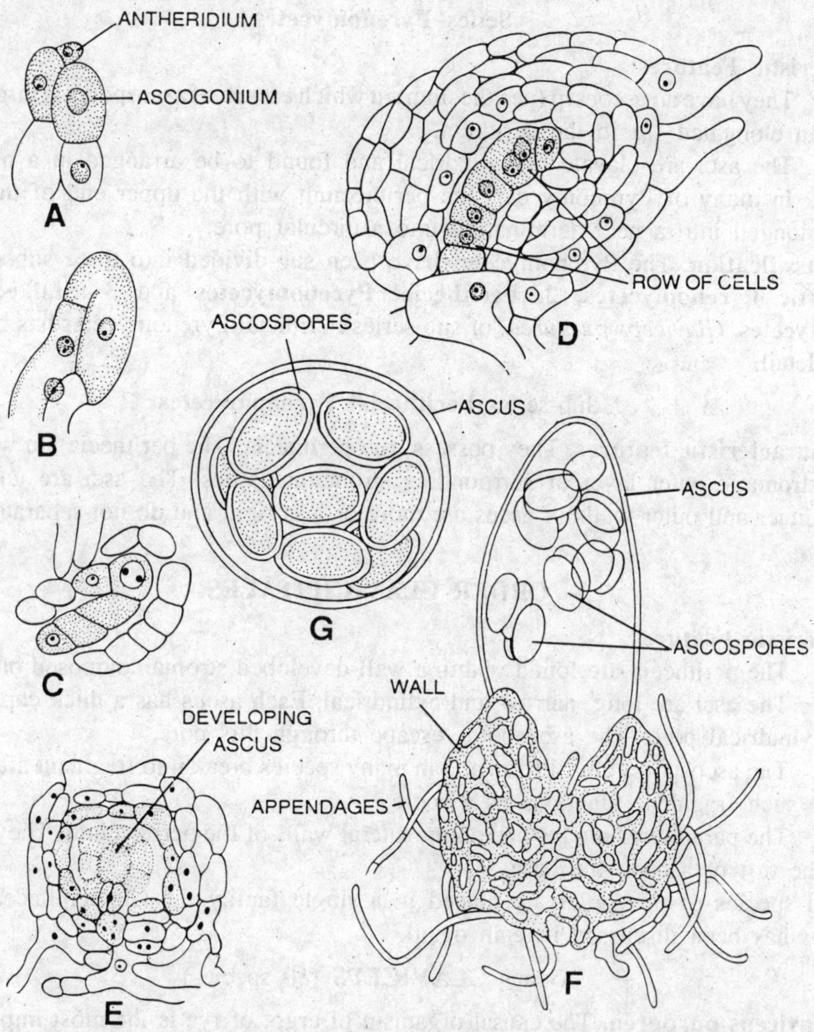

Fig. 10.22. *Sphaerotheca* **sp. Sexual reproduction. A-E, fusion of male and female nuclei formed within antheridium and ascogonium, and development of cleistothecium; F, cleistothecium bursts and releases out a single ascus containing eight ascospores; G, a globose ascus containing eight ascospores.**

Systematic Position

	G. W. Martin (1961)	C. J. Alexopoulos (1962)	G. C. Ainsworth (1971)
Kingdom	–Plantae	–Plantae	–Fungi
Division	–Mycota	–Mycota	–Eumycota
Sub-div.	–Eumycotina	–Eumycotina	–Ascomycotina
Class	–Ascomycetes	–Ascomycetes	–Pyrenomycetes
Sub-class	–Euascomycetidae	–Euascomycetidae	–
Series	–	–Pyrenomycetes	–
Order	–Erysiphales	–Erysiphales	–Erysiphales
Family	–Erysiphaceae	–Erysiphaceae	–Erysiphaceae
Genus	–*Sphaerotheca*	–*Sphaerotheca*	–*Sphaerotheca*

Series–**Pyrenomycetes**

Characteristic Features

1. They have an ascocarp (perithecium) in which escape of ascospores is through a circular pore or an elongated slit in the peridium.
2. The asci are clavate or cylindrical and found to be arranged in a parallel series.
3. In many of Pyrenomycetes the perithecium with the upper end of the peridium is to be prolonged into a neck terminating into a circular pore.

Classification. The Pyrenomycetes have been sub-divided into three sub-series—1. **Ascostromatic Pyrenomycetes,** 2. **Perithecial Pyrenomycetes** and 3. **Stalked Perithecial Pyrenomycetes.** *Claviceps purpurea,* of sub-series Perithcial Pyrenomycetes has been discussed here in detail.

Sub-series **Perithecial Pyrenomycetes**

Characteristic features. They possess true perithecia. The perithecia are with or without marked stromatic outer layer or surrounding stromatic tissues. The asci are unitunicate, *i.e.*, both the inner and outer walls of ascus are more or less rigid and do not separate during spore ejection.

ORDER CLAVICIPITALES

Characteristic Features

1. The perithecia are found within a well-developed stroma composed of fungal tissue.
2. The asci are long, narrow and cylindrical. Each ascus has a thick cap perforated by a long cylindrical pore. The ascospores escape through this pore.
3. The ascospores are filiform and in many species break into fragment after their escape and each such fragment functions as a spore.
4. The paraphyses are formed on the lateral walls of the perithecium. They are not found among the tuft of asci at the base.

All species of this order are placed in a single family the Clavicipitaceae. The genus *Claviceps* has been discussed here in detail.

Genus **CLAVICEPS** (10 species)

Claviceps purpurea. The causal organism of ergot of rye is the most important species. The genus includes six species parasitic on members of Gramineae. The species of *Claviceps* possess filiform ascospores. These thread-like ascospores are forcibly discharged from the perithecia and infect the host plants only at the time of flowering. After reaching the flower the ascospores send germ tubes into the ovary and cause infection. Eventually the developed mycelium destroys the ovary tissue and replaces them in the flower by a soft, white cottony mat of mycelium. This mycelial mat soon becomes covered by a palisade-like layer of short conidiophores which cut off minute, oval conidia at their tips in acropetalous succession. These conidia are found to be mixed with a nectar-like sticky substance. The insects visit the flowers in search of this nectar and disseminate the conidia to other healthy flowers where they cause infection.

Now the mycelial mat which has produced conidiophores on it begins to harden and converts into a hard pink or purplish pseudoparenchymatous mass of mycelium, the **sclerotium.** During harvest many sclerotia fall to the ground where they overwinter. Next spring the sclerotia germinate producing several long stalked, dark purple stromata with spherical heads. A number of minute cavities are formed within and beneath the stromatic heads. These cavities remain surrounded by pseudoparenchymatous tissues of stromatic heads. Each such cavity contains a multinucleate

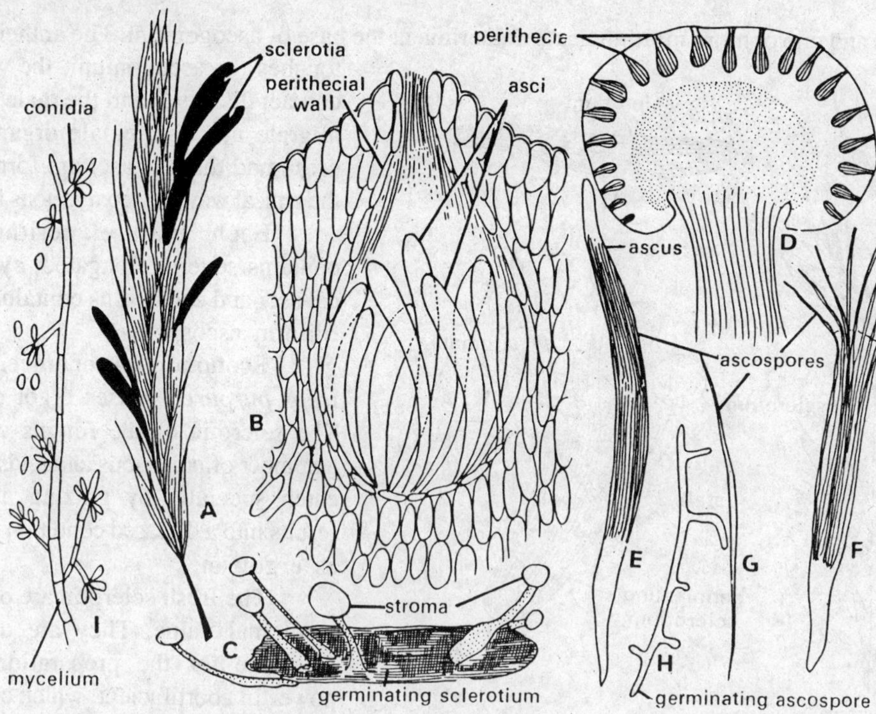

Fig. 10.23. *Claviceps purpurea*. Ergot of rye. A, infected ear with sclerotia; B, perithecium; C, germinating sclerotium which has given rise to several stromata; D, median longitudinal section of stroma showing perithecia; E, ascus with needle-like ascospores; F, ascus discharging ascospores; G, single needle-like ascospores; H, germinating ascospores; I, mycelium with conidiophores and conidia.

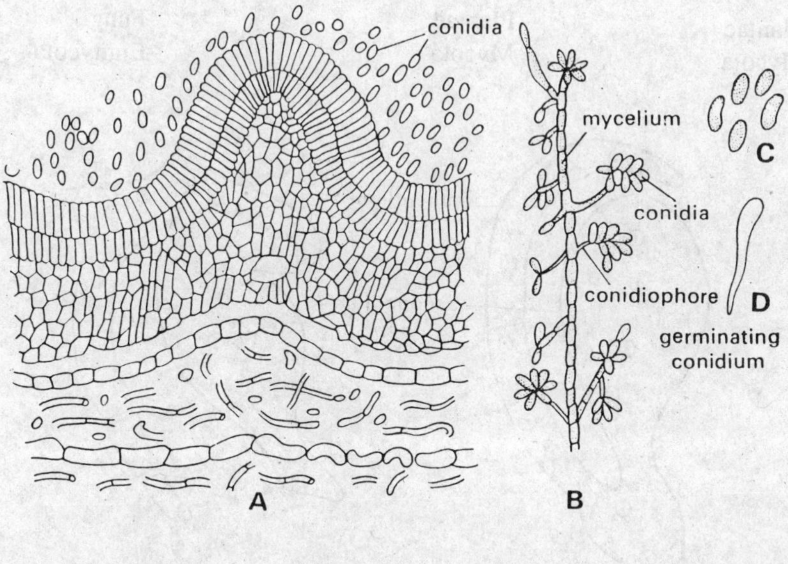

Fig. 10.24. *Claviceps purpurea*. A, sectional view of the ovary of host showing mycelium and conidia; B, hypha with conidiophores and conidia; C, conidia; D, germinating conidium.

ascogonium and one or more multinucleate antheridia at the base of ascogonium. The antheridium touches the ascogonium; the wall of contact dissolves and the male nuclei migrate into the female organ. It is presumed that the asci are formed in the typical way of ascomycetous fungus.

Each mature perithecium contains several elongated, cylindrical asci and each ascus contains eight filiform ascospores.

Economic importance. *Claviceps purpurea* causes ergot of rye. The sclerotia of the fungus contain a number of poisonous alkaloids, when eaten specially by grazing animals results into a diseased condition known as **ergotism.**

The fresh sclerotia are of great medicinal value. They are used in medicine for the preparation of a powerful abortifacient, which controls haemorrahage during child birth. It is also used in inducing uterine contractions during child birth.

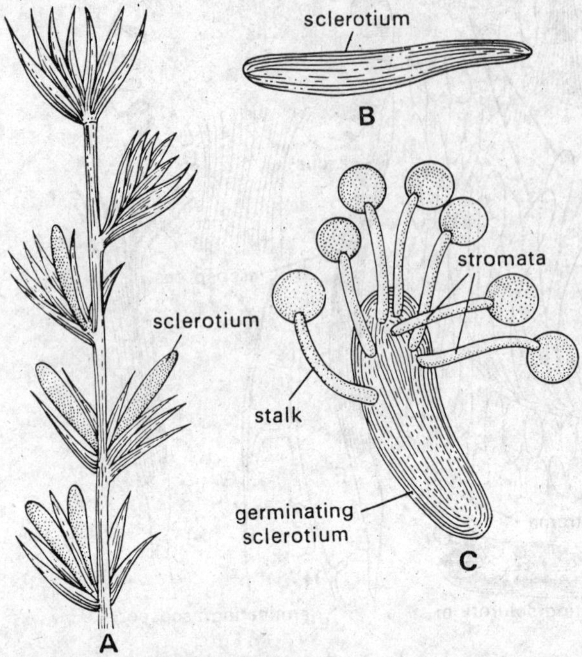

Fig. 10.25. *Claviceps purpurea.* A, ergot of rye showing sclerotia; B, sclerotium; C, germinating sclerotium.

Systematic Position

G. W. Martin (1961)	C. J. Alexopoulos (1962)	G. C. Ainsworth (1971)
Kingdom –Plantae	–Plantae	–Fungi
Division –Mycota	–Mycota	–Eumycota

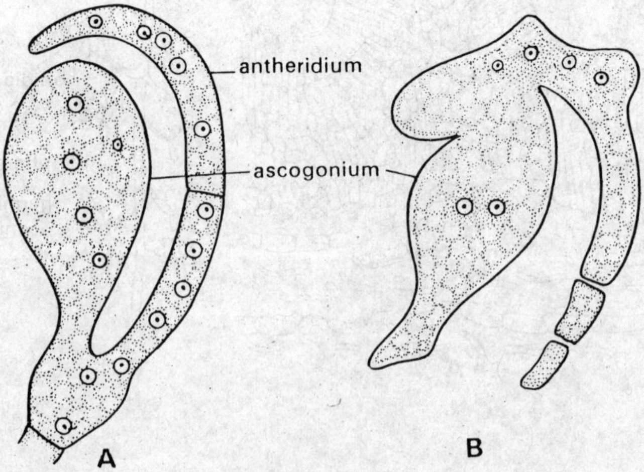

Fig. 10.26. *Claviceps purpurea.* Sexual reproduction (A-B).

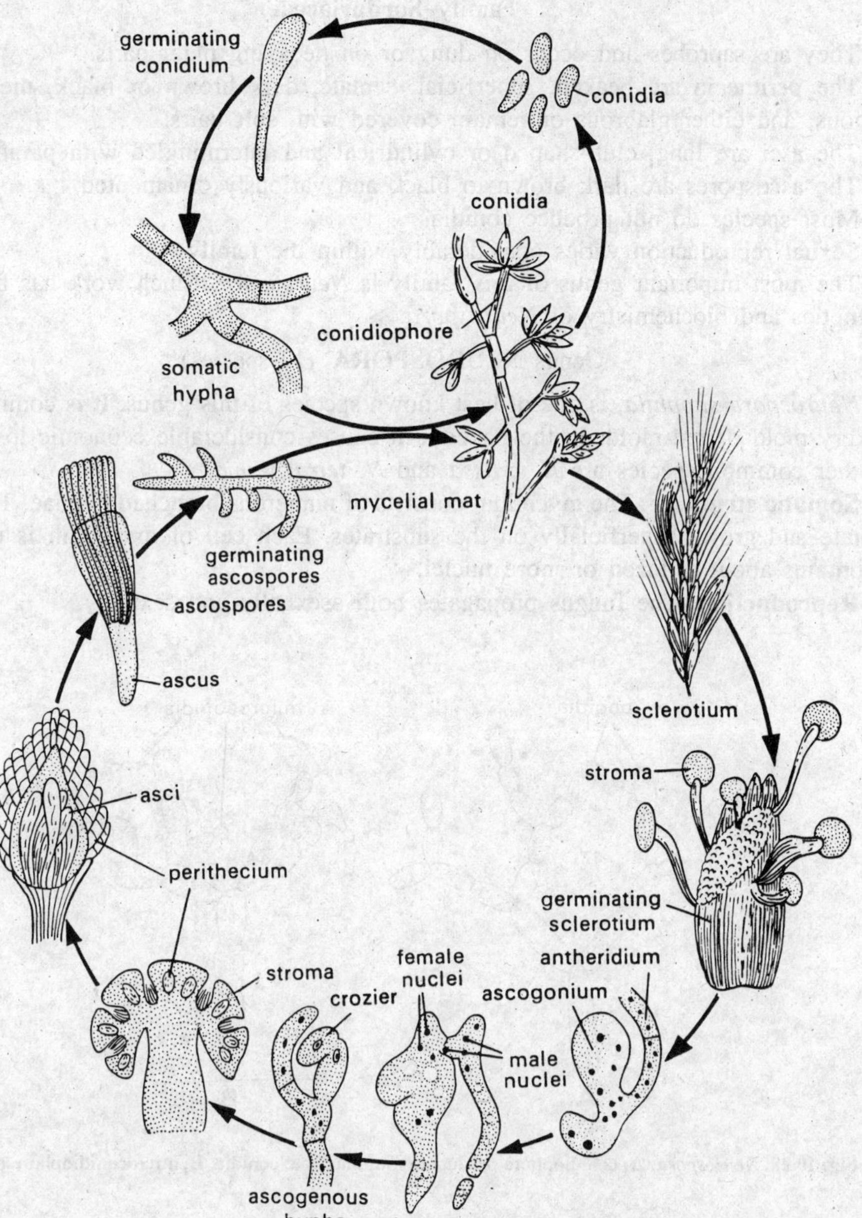

Fig. 10.27. *Claviceps purpurea*. Diagrammatic life-cycle.

Sub-div.	–Eumycotina	–Eumycotina	–Ascomycotina
Class	–Ascomycetes	–Ascomycetes	–Pyrenomycetes
Sub-Cl.	–Euascomycetidae	–Euascomycetidae	–
Series	–	–Pyrenomycetes	–
Order	–Hypocreales	–Clavicipitales	–Clavicipitales
Family	–Clavicipitaceae	–Clavicipitaceae	–Clavicipitaceae
Genus	–*Claviceps*	–*Claviceps*	–*Claviceps*

Family–Sordariaceae

They are saprobes and occur on dung or on decaying plant parts.

The perithecia are beaked, superficial, septate, dark brown or black, membranous or carbonous, and either glabrous or remain covered with soft hairs.

The asci are long, club-shaped or cylindrical and intermingled with paraphyses.

The ascospores are dark brown to black and variously ornamented.

Most species do not produce conidia.

Sexual reproduction varies considerably within the family.

The most important genus of this family is *Neurospora.* Much work has been done on the genetics and biochemistry of *Neurospora.*

Genus NEUROSPORA (12 species)

Neurospora sitophila, is one of best known species of this genus. It is commonly known as bakery mold or red mold. In the bakeries it causes considerable economic loss to owners. The other common species are *N. crassa* and *N. tetrasperma.*

Somatic structure. The mycelium consists of numerous branched hyphae. The mycelium is septate and grows superficially on the substrates. Each cell of mycelium is multinucleate and contains about a dozen or more nuclei.

Reproduction. The fungus propagates both asexually and sexually.

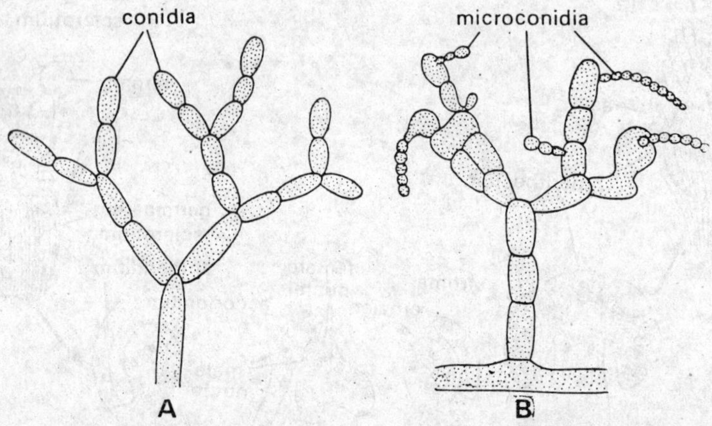

Fig. 10.28. *Neurospora*. A, conidiophore producing multinucleate conidia; B, microconidiophore producing microconidia.

Asexual reproduction. The asexual reproduction takes place by means of unicellular conidia. The conidia look pink-coloured in mass and formed acropetally on branched conidiophores. These conidia are often called **macroconidia.**

Uninucleate **microconidia** are also produced. They are produced in chains on microconidiophore. These conidia may produce mycelia on their germination, or they act as male cells (spermatia).

Sexual reproduction. The female structure is known as **protoperithecium.** In the very beginning a multinucleate, coiled ascogonium is formed. The ascogonia produce long hyphal branches which act as trichogynes. Later on the ascogonia become 5 to 10 celled by transverse septa. Each cell is multinucleate. The side branches of ascogonium develop into a pseudoparenchymatous hyphal ball. The globose structure, thus developed, is known as *protoperithecium*.

No antheridia are produced. The male elements are represented by microconidia (spermatia). The microconidium fuses with the tip of trichogyne. The male nucleus thus migrates through the trichogyne and reaches into the ascogonium. This way, the plasmogamy is resulted by spermatization.

After the process of spermatization, the ascogenous hyphae are developed on the ascogonium. Ultimately in a typical ascomycete method, the asci and ascospores are produced.

During the development of the ascogenous hyphae, the mycelial sheath enveloping the ascogonium develops on the wall of the perithecium. The mature perithecium is globose, pyriform or flask-like and dark-coloured. The neck of the perithecium is extended into an ostiole. The neck is lined by periphyses. However, the asci are not intermingled with paraphyses.

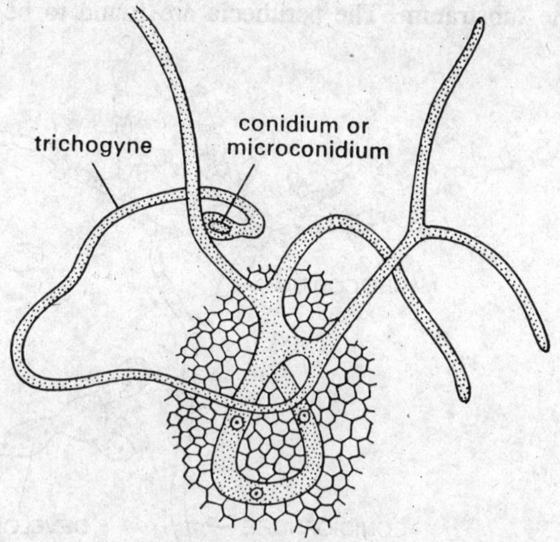

Fig. 10.29. Sexual reproduction in *Neurospora*. An ascogonium with a conidium attached at the tip of trichogyne.

The perithecium contains numerous octosporous asci. The asci are cylindric and long-stalked. The ascospores are dark brown or black with ridges or the outer wall. The ascospores are arranged uniseriately in the ascus. Four ascospores in each ascus are of *plus* strain and four of *minus*.

Genetical studies. The genetical studies on *Neurospora* initiated by Dodge and Shear have opened up new vistas in understanding the laws of heredity, gene-control of enzyme, biochemical actions and other biological processes. The advantage of this fungus as a tool for cytogenetical studies over other plants and animals, is the rapidity with which it can grow and reproduce. For these reasons the *Neurospora,* has become the *Drosophila* of the fungus world. Most of the genetical and biochemical studies have been done in *N. sitophila, N. tetrasperma* and *N. crassa.* In *N. tetrasperma* each ascus contains only four ascospores and each ascospore contains two of the original eight ascal nuclei. Normal spores of this species produce self-fertile mycelium on germination.

ORDER SPHAERIALES (430 genera; 6,600 species)

Characteristic Features

1. The perithecia are dark coloured and usually possess firm walls.
2. The perithecia of the simplest forms are borne singly, free or partly embedded in the substratum.
3. The majority of species are saprophytes and serve as a useful purpose in bringing about the first stages of decay in wood or strand.

Classification. They include over 6,600 species. These species are grouped in several families. The genus *Xylaria* of the family Xylariaceae has been discussed here in detail.

Family–Xylariaceae

Characteristic Features

They occur chiefly on wood. They form the highest development of the order Sphaeriales.

They possess superficial stroma. The stromata of the genus *Hypoxylon* remain partly sunk in the substratum. The perithecia are found to be arranged just below and at right angles to the

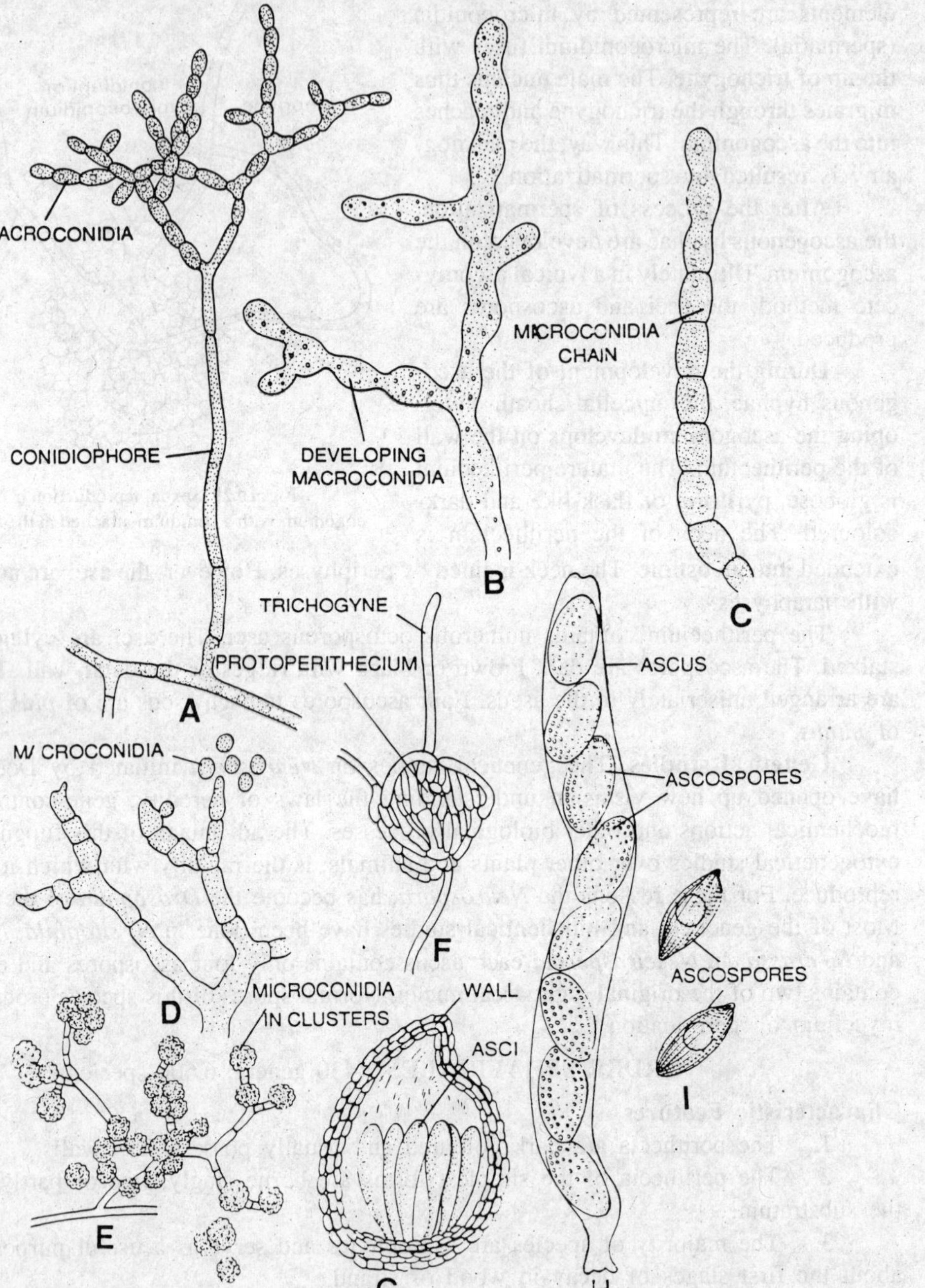

Fig. 10.30. *Neurospore crassa*. A, conidiophore bearing macroconidia; B-C, macroconidia; D-E, microconidia; F, protoperithecium; G, L.S. of perithecium; H-I, ascus and ascospores.

surface of the stroma. Prior to the development of the perithecia the conidia are formed which often cover young stromata with a white or brown coloured powder.

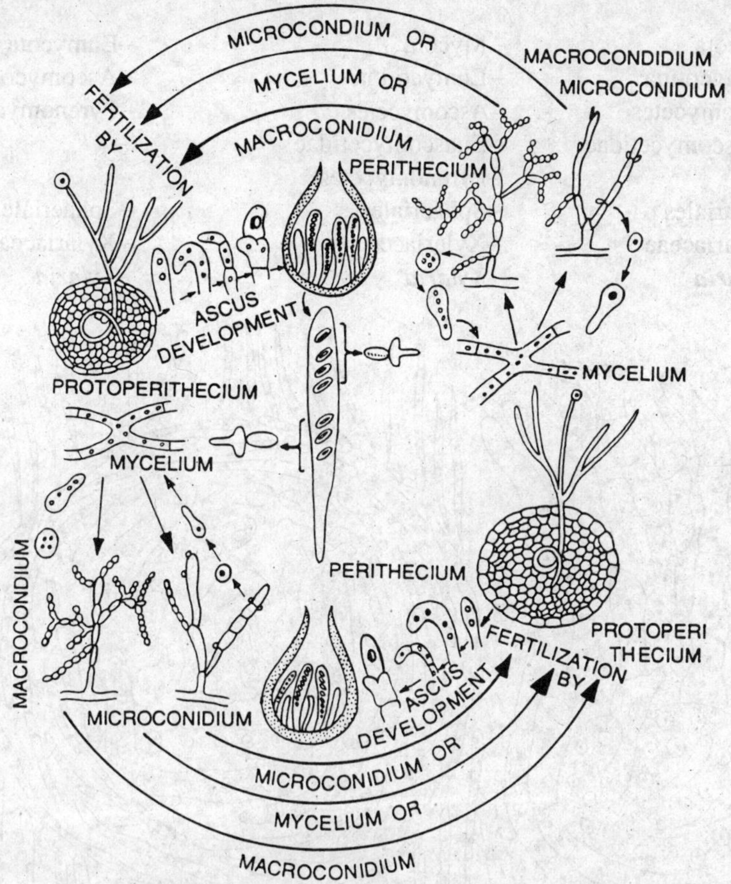

Fig. 10.31. *Neurospora sitophila*. Diagrammatic life-cycle.

Genus XYLARIA (100 species)

The species of *Xylaria* are usually saprophytic on wood substrata such as logs, stumps, branches etc. *Xylaria mali* causes black rot of apple trees.

The stromata are erect slender or stout, clavate or cylindrical with simple or branched expansions.

The perithecia are found to be arranged on the periphery just below and at right angles to the surface of the stroma. Prior to the development of the perithecia the conidia are formed. The conidia often cover young stromata with white or brown coloured powdery substance. The young stromata remain covered by a layer of conidiophores from which the small, oval conidia are abstricted. The conidia form a white coating in marked contrast to the exposed portions of the black stroma. The sectional view of the conidial stroma of *Xylaria* exhibits nests of small hyphae which show the first indications of perithecia. Still earlier a stout hypha with large nuclei, presumably a female branch, is seen, however, in *Xylaria* it has no function.

The asci are cylindrical and clavate. The ascospores are ellipsoidal, single-celled and brown or black in colour.

Systematic Position

G. W. Martin (1961)	**C. J. Alexopoulos (1962)**	**G. C. Ainsworth (1971)**
Kingdom –Plantae	–Plantae	–Fungi

Division	–Mycota	–Mycota	–Eumycota
Sub-div.	–Eumycotina	–Eumycotina	–Ascomycotina
Class	–Ascomycetes	–Ascomycetes	–Pyrenomycetes
Sub-cl.	–Euascomycetidae	–Euascomycetidae	–
Series	–	–Pyrenomycetes	–
Order	–Xylariales	–Sphaeriales	–Sphaeriales
Family	–Xylariaceae	–Xylariaceae	–Xylariaceae
Genus	–*Xylaria*	–*Xylaria*	–*Xylaria*

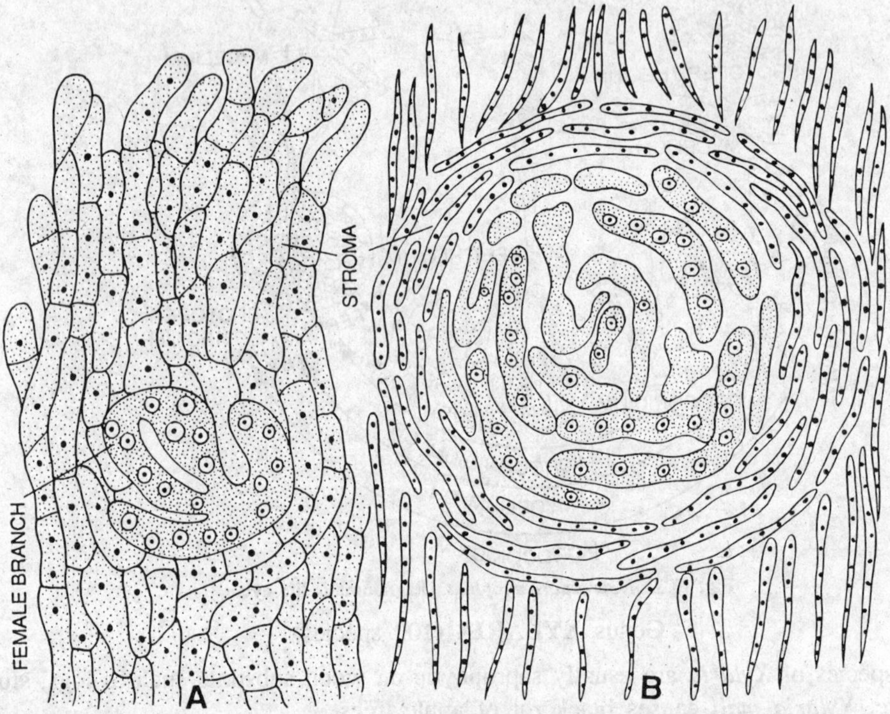

Fig. 10.32. *Xylaria.* A, stroma with female branch; B, sectional view of fruit body (young perithecium).

SeriesDiscomycetes OR
Class—Discomycetes (Ainswoth, 1971)

Characteristic Features

The apothecia of series Discomycetes are open and more or less cup-shaped at maturity. They possess incurved margins, which unfold on the maturation of the apothecium to expose the hymenial layer. They produce their apothecia on the ground, on buried sticks, rotten logs, overwintered leaves or fruits, or on animal dung. The apothecia of some species are variously coloured such as red, yellow or orange; some are brown and few are black. Besides the typical cup or disc-like forms of the apothecia there are sponges, bells, saddles, tongues and brain-like fruiting bodies. However, all these apothecia are open and bear their asci on the surface or in large open cavities. The apothecium possesses a sheath of interwoven hyphae which is pushed open by the growth of the paraphyses so that it forms the outer wall of the cup. The lower part of the cup is filled by the hypothecium, a weft of some vegetative and some ascogenous hyphae. These give rise to the sub-hymenium. The later formed paraphyses and young asci arise from the sub-hymenial layer. The asci and paraphyses constitute the hymenium, which remains spread over the surface of the interior of the cup. The asci are club-shaped or cylindrical. They possess simple or branched paraphyses at the apices among them. The asci usually open by a lid (operculate type) or by the ejection of a plug (inoperculate type). The distinction between these modes of dehiscence has been used as a basis of classification.

Classification. Many authors divide the series Discomycetes into three orders 1. Pezizales, 2. Helotiales and 3. Tuberales.

ORDER PEZIZALES (65 genera; 500 species)

They are characterized by their fleshy or sometimes leathery ascocarp, bounded, except in the family Pyronemaceae, by a definite peridium which remains closed in the beginning but later on pushed open by the growth of a mass of paraphyes, giving the mature ascocarp its typical cup or saucer shape. The fungi of this order are known as the cup fungi. The apothecia are found above the ground (epigean) with or without the stalks.

The asci open by a lid (operculate). The ascospores are ellipsoidal and one-celled.

Most of them are saprophytic grow on dead and decaying wood, on soil rich in organic matter and on dung of animals.

There is a clear tendency towards the reduction of sexuality. In some cases both antheridia and ascogonia are present. In other cases the non-functional antheridia are found. In the extreme cases such as *Morchella* neither the antheridia and nor the ascogonia are present. In such cases the fusion of vegetative nuclei represents the sexual process and asci are produced.

Classification. According to Gaumann, the following families are included in the order Pezizales. 1. Pyronemaceae. 2. Pezizaceae and 3. Helvellaceae.

Family–Pyronemaceae

The Pyronemaceae are characterized by the incomplete development of the peridium and usually compound ascocarps are present. The important genus *Pyronema* has been discussed here in detail.

Genus PYRONEMA (2 or 3 species)

This genus has two or three species, *Pyronema confluens* is the best known species.

Occurrence. All species are saprobic and commonly found on burnt soil. *Pyronema confluens* commonly occurs on burnt ground, decaying leaves and charred wood.

Mycelium. The mycelium is colourless and superficial. It is found as a white cottony layer on the surface of the ground. It is profusely branched and the hyphae are composed of short cells with 6 to 12 nuclei in each.

Asexual reproduction. The asexual spores are not produced regularly; sometimes erect hyphae of a mycelium form chains of oidia.

Sexual reproduction. The sexual reproduction takes place by means of antheridia and ascogonia. The species is homothallic, *i.e.,* the antheridia and ascogonia are produced on the mycelium developed from a single ascospore. Both antheridia and ascogonia are multinucleate. They develop on separate hyphae. The hyphae on which the sex organs are developed are short, erect, dichotomously branched and two or four cells in height. The multinucleate terminal cell of one dichotomy develops into an ascogonium while the multinucleate terminal cell of the other dichotomy develops into an antheridium. On maturity the antheridium becomes club-shaped and its nuclei divide again and again until about hundred or more nuclei are formed. The ascogonium becomes sub-globose and also contains about hundred or more nuclei. The ascogonium produces a curved tubular apical outgrowth, the **trichogyne.** The tip of the trichogyne grows toward the antheridium and becomes applied to the upper end of it. The walls of contact between the two dissolve, the nuclei within the trichogyne disintegrate and an incomplete transverse wall

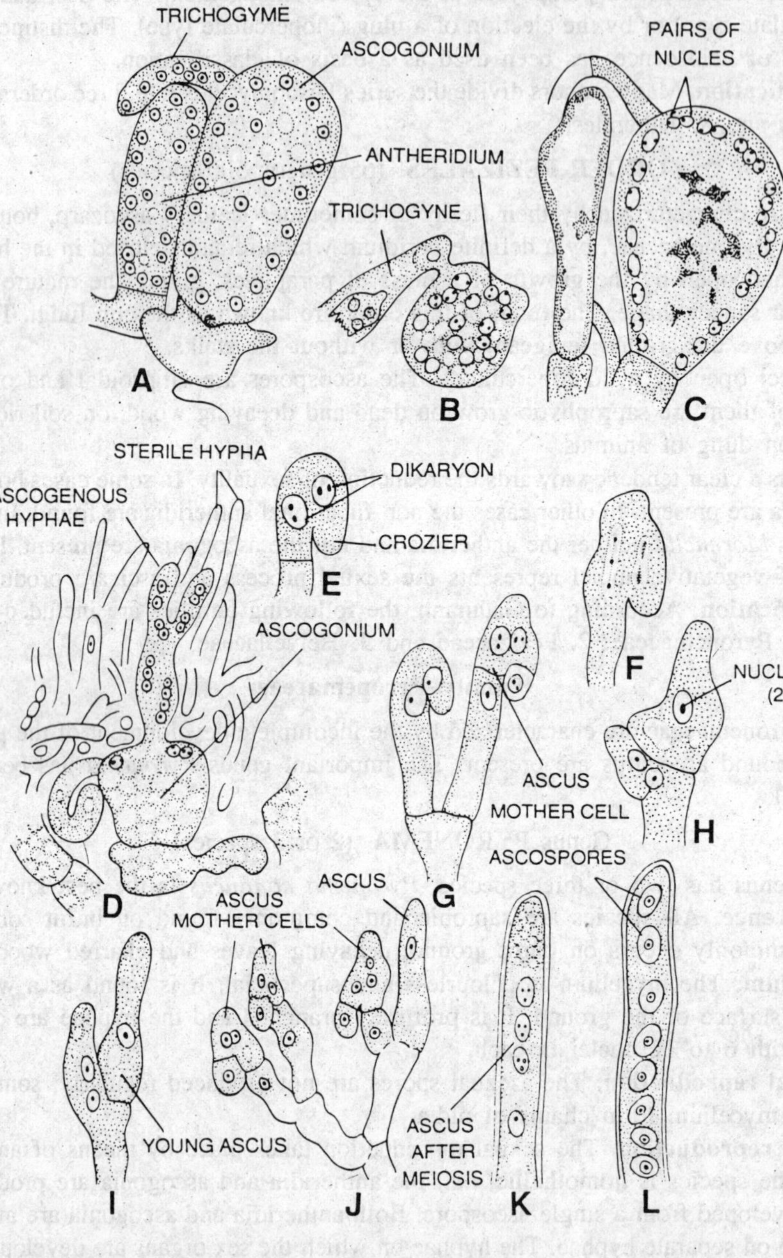

Fig. 10.33. Ascomycetes. Sexual reproduction and development of ascus in *Pyronema* sp. A, antheridium and ascogonium; B, plasmogamy; C, pairing of nuclei; D, formation of ascogenous hyphae; E, crozier formation; F, conjugate nuclei divide mitotically; G, ascus mother cell; H, ascus mother cell with fusion nucleus (2x); I, young ascus; J, ascus mother cell and young ascus; K, ascus after meiosis; L, formation of ascospores.

develops at the base of the trichogyne. Most of the cytoplasm and majority of nuclei of the antheridium migrate into the ascogonium through the central pore in the septum at the base of the trichogyne. Thereafter the septal pore in between the trichogyne and the ascogonium becomes blocked.

According to many mycologists (Claussen, 1912; Dangeard, 1907; and Hirsch, 1950), the fusion of male and female nuclei in pairs does not take place. However, the male and female nuclei in the ascogonium become arranged in pairs forming **dikaryons.** The karyogamy takes place only in the ascus mother cell which turns afterwards in the young ascus. Now the ascus mother cell contains a diploid nucleus or a synkaryon.

After a short time of the entry of cytoplasm and nuclei from the antheridium, numerous knob-like outgrowths, the primordia ascogenous hyphae are produced from the upper half of the ascogonium. Each of these primordia develops into an elongated tubular ascogenous hypha which in the beginning remains multinucleate and without cross walls. The ascogenous hyphae may divide at their tips. Later on the transverse walls are developed in the ascogenous hyphae dividing them into sexual cells. The cells towards the apical end of the ascogenous hyphae are binucleate. The ascogenous hyphae recurve at their tips to form a **crozier** in which the ascus is formed from the binucleate penultimate cell. The dikaryon found within the apical cell of the ascogenous hyphae divides simultaneouly producing four nuclei. Thereafter the walls appear in between the sister nuclei so as to form a terminal uninucleate cell, a subterminal binucleate cell and an antepenultimate uninucleate cell. The subterminal binucleate cell, also known as **arch** cell behaves as the ascus mother cell. The two nuclei of the arch cell fuse together within the young ascus cell forming a diploid fusion nucleus or the **synkaryon.**

The fusion or diploid nucleus divides thrice, forming eight haploid nuclei. Each nucleus metamorphoses into an ascospore. The ascospores are haploid. The synkaryon divides meiotically

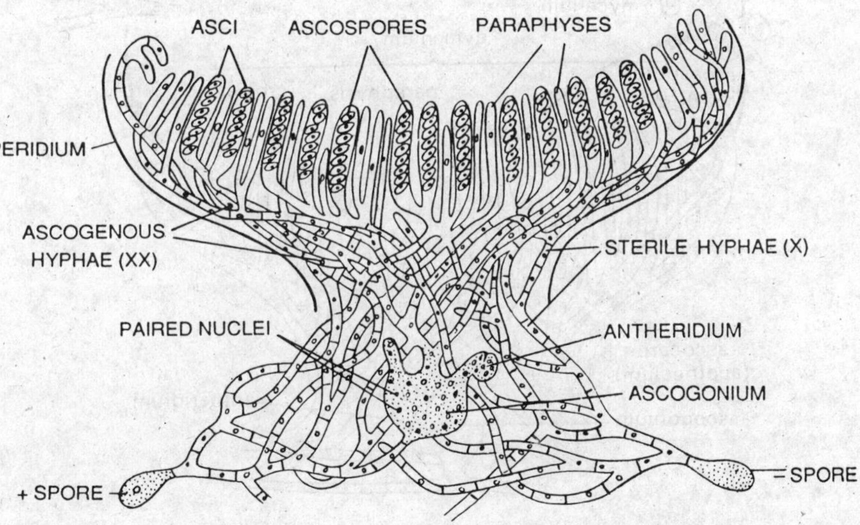

Fig.10.34. Ascomycetes. *Pyronema* sp. Young apothecium.

and thereafter mitotically producing eight haploid nuclei. On maturation the asci elongate and become club-shaped. Under suitable conditions each ascospore germinates and forms a haploid mycelium.

Development of fructification (apothecium). During the sexual process, many sterile hyphae grow out from the cells found below the ascogonium. These sterile hyphae form a loosely interwoven envelope around the united sex organs and ascogenous hyphae. The mature fructification, the apothecium of *Pyronema* is concave, and not markedly cup-shaped as in other Pezizales. The

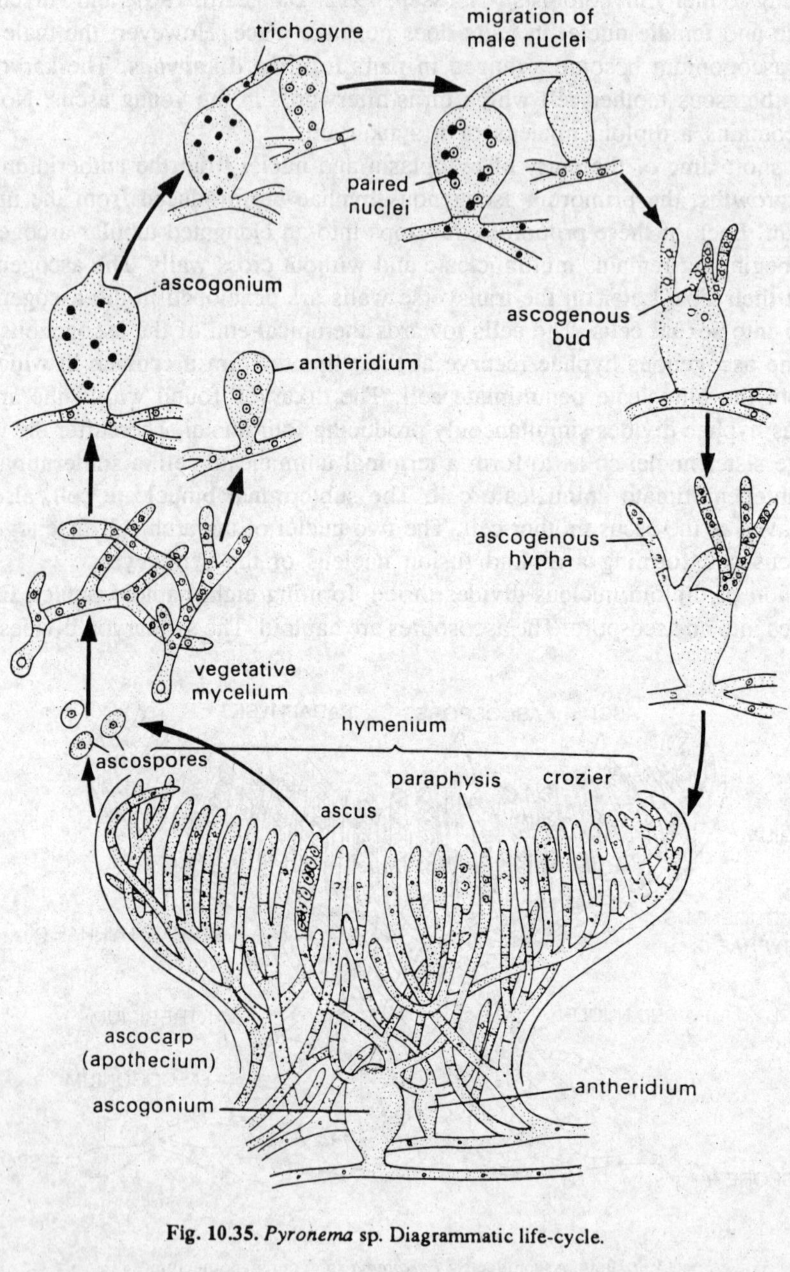

Fig. 10.35. *Pyronema* **sp. Diagrammatic life-cycle.**

concave fertile layer consists of vertical cylindrical asci and paraphyses which remain intermingled. The fruit body is pink coloured and 2 to 3 mm., in diameter.

Sometimes the sterile hyphae surrounding one pair of united sex organs also become intertwined with the sterile hyphae of the other developing ascocarp in the vicinity. This way, sexual ascocarps become enveloped in a common sheath forming a compound fruit body.

Systematic Position

	G. W. Martin (1961)	C. J. Alexopoulos (1962)	G. C. Ainsworth (1971)
Kingdom	–Plantae	–Plantae	–Fungi
Division	–Mycota	–Mycota	–Eumycota
Sub-div.	–Eumycotina	–Eumycotina	–Ascomycotina
Class	–Ascomycetes	–Ascomycetes	–Discomycetes
Sub-cl.	–Euascomycetidae	–Euascomycetidae	–
Order	–Pezizales	–Pezizales	–Pezizales
Series	–	–Discomycetes	–
Family	–Pezizaceae	–Pezizaceae	–Pezizaceae
Genus	–*Pyronema*	–*Pyronema*	–*Pyronema*

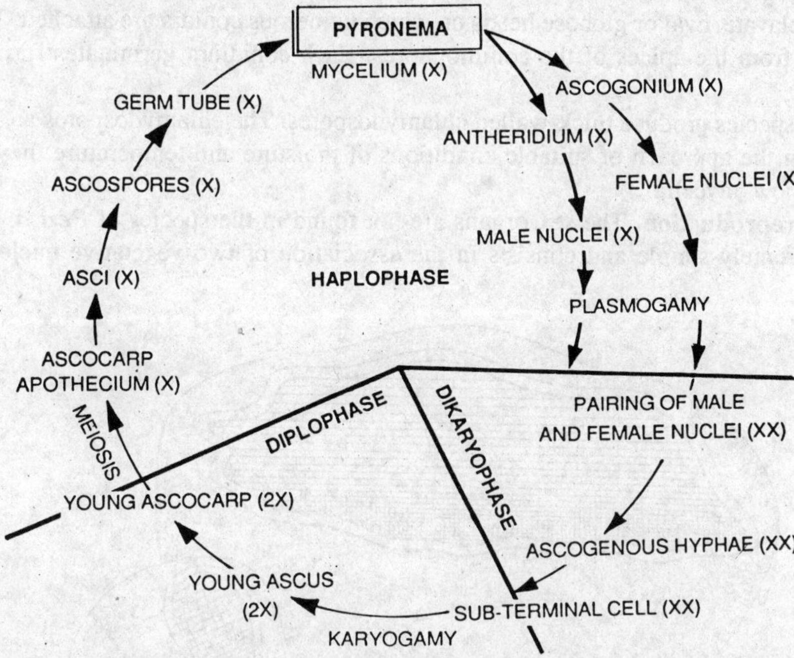

Fig. 10.36. *Pyronema*, Graphic life-cycle.

Family–Pezizaceae

They possess epigenous apothecia. The apothecia are mostly cup, disc or lentil shaped. They are sessile in some species while stalked in others. The apothecia are minute to very large. They are bright coloured to dark brown, smooth velvety, hairy or bristly. The peridium is well developed. It is either fleshy or waxy in texture. The ascospores are uniseriately arranged in asci.

Most of them are coprophilous. The species of many genera grow exclusively on dung, and some of them may even be specialized as to the animal on whose excreta they grow.

Most of the Pezizaceae do not possess any conidial stage. However, conidia have been found in *Peziza repanda* and *Peziza vesiculosa*.

Genus **PEZIZA** (50 species)

Peziza vesiculosa is one of the larger cup fungi. The cup-shaped, fleshy ascocarp with no hairs are found to be crowded together on mature piles, well fertilized gardens, green houses etc. *Peziza badia* is commonly found on the ground in deciduous forests and open places. *P. repanda* is found on rotten logs in woods. The apothecia of the fungus are whitish or pale brown and exhibit minute pustules on the surface.

Somatic structure. The mycelium is well developed and consists of network of septate hyphae with uninucleate cells except in the fructification. The hyphae are found within the substratum and therefore, they are not visible from outside. They absorb the nutrition from the substratum.

Asexual reproduction. Most of the Pezizaceae are not known to reproduce asexually. However, conidia have been found in *Peziza repanda* and *Peziza vesiculosa.* In *Peziza pustulata,* the conidiophores are found which bear heads of conidia developed from surface hyphae. The conidia are exogenously formed from three to four-celled conidiophores. The apices of them form narrow, clavate, oval or globose heads on which numerous conidia are attached. The conidia are abstricted from the apices of the conidiophores. Each conidium germinates forming a new mycelium.

Certain species produce thick-walled chlamydospores. The chlamydospores are intercalary in position. On the approach of suitable conditions of moisture and temperature they germinate and produce new mycelia.

Sexual reproduction. The sex organs are not found in the species of *Peziza.* The sexual process is extremely simple and consists in the association of two vegetative nuclei in a pair;

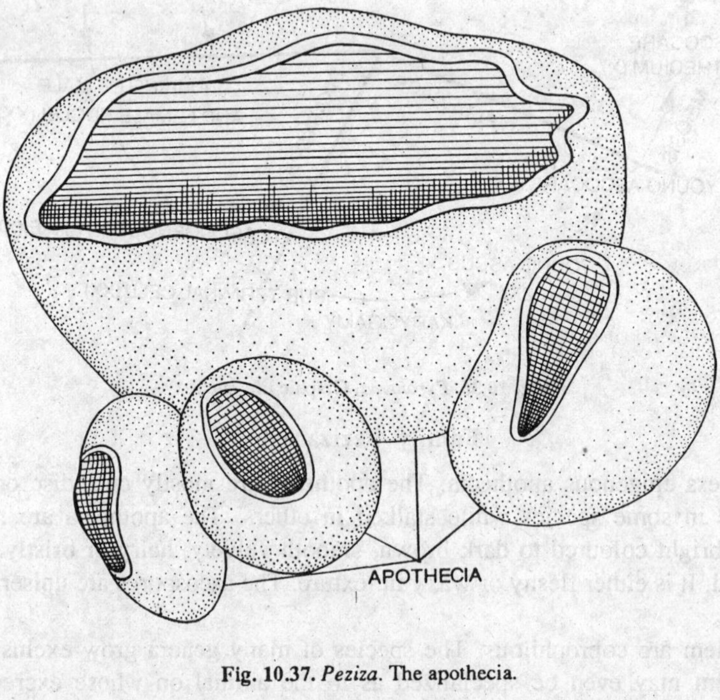

Fig. 10.37. *Peziza.* The apothecia.

the compatible nuclei are brought together by means of somatogamy. The vegetative cells are seen to possess the nuclei associated in pairs. These dikaryotic cells rise to ascogenous hyphae.

The ascogenous hyphae become many celled by septa. The cells are binucleate. The terminal or sub-terminal cell of ascogenous hyphae acts as an ascus mother cell which develops into an ascus. The two nuclei of the ascus mother cell fuse together forming a synkaryon. This fusion nucleus divides meiotically and thereafter mitotically forming eight haploid nuclei which become ascospores. The asci are clavate, erect and lie side by side. They are intermingled with paraphyses.

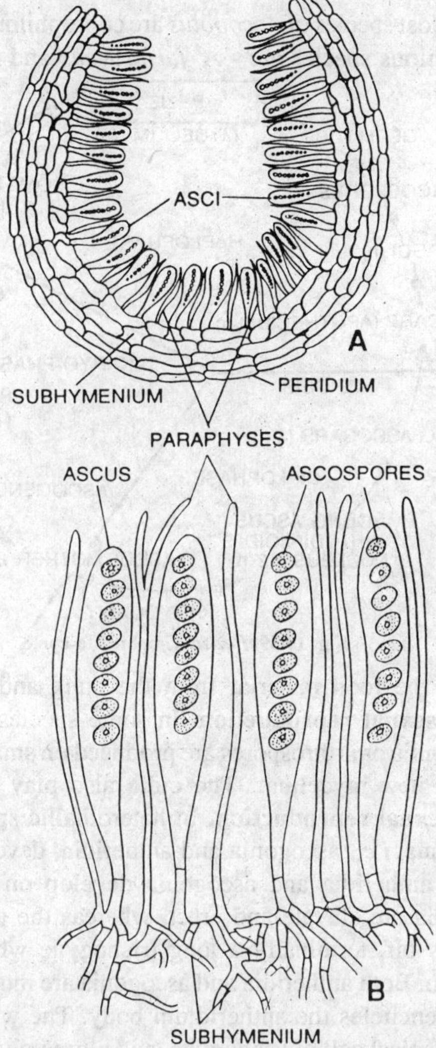

Fig. 10.38. *Peziza.* A, vertical section of mature apothecium; B, a portion of apothecium showing asci, ascospores and subhymenium.

Apothecium. The apothecial cups of *Peziza vesiculosa* are brown, 2 to 3 inches broad, and are commonly contorted and crimpled. The hymenial surface of *P. venosa* is convoluted. In sectional view the apothecium exhibits three layers. The uppermost layer is the hymenium; middle one the sub-hymenium and the outermost layer, the excipulum. The hymenium consists of erect asci and paraphyses; the sub-hymenium of the weft of hyphae and ascogenous hyphae; and the excipulum consists of pseudoparenchymatous tissue formed of compactly interwoven hyphae.

Asci and ascospores. The asci are clavate and form palisade-like layer lining the cavity of the ascocarp. Each ascus contains 8 ascospores. On maturation, the ascospores are shot off from asci and disseminated by wind. Each ascospore is haploid, smooth and elliptical. On germination it produces the haploid mycelium.

Systematic Position

	G. W. Martin (1961)	**C. J. Alexopoulos (1962)**	**G. C. Ainsworth (1971)**
Kingdom	–Plantae	–Plantae	–Fungi
Division	–Mycota	–Mycota	–Eumycota
Sub-div.	–Eumycotina	–Eumycotina	–Ascomycotina
Class	–Ascomycetes	–Ascomycetes	–Discomycetes
Sub-cl.	–Euascomycetidae	–Euascomycetidae	–
Series	–	–Discomycetes	–
Order	–Pezizales	–Pezizales	–Pezizales
Family	–Pezizaceae	–Pezizaceae	–Pezizaceae
Genus	–*Peziza*	–*Peziza*	–*Peziza*

Genus ASCOBOLUS

Most species of *Ascobolus* are coprophilous and grow upon dung of herbivores. The common coprophilous species are - *A. furfuraceus* and *A. immersus*. These species are heterothallic. On the other hand *A. crenulatus* is a homothallic species. About a dozen species have been reported from this country mostly found on dung of herbivores. The common Indian species are—*A. denudatus*, *A. lignata* and *A. magnificus*.

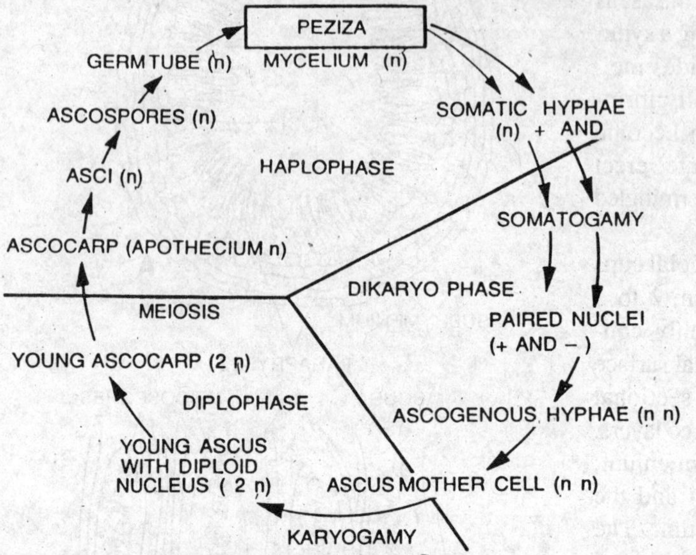

Fig. 10.39. *Peziza*. Graphic life-cycle.

Somatic structure. The mycelium is commonly found within the substratum, and forms a complex hyphal mass. The mycelium is branched, septate and possesses multinucleate cells. The aerial cup-like apothecia are generally seen on the surface of substratum. The complex hyphal mass absorbs the food material from the dung and supplies to fruiting bodies (apothecia).

Asexual reproduction. In some species of *Ascobolus*, such as *A. furfuraceus*, the thin-walled oidia or arthrospores are produced on small hyphal branches in chains. They may germinate to form new mycelium. The oidia also play role in sexual reproduction.

Sexual reproduction. In heterothallic species (*e.g.*, *A. magnificus*), the female and male sex organs, *i.e.*, ascogonia and antheridia, develop on two compatible mycelia. The sex organs, that is, antheridia and ascogonia develop on different branches of compatible mycelia. The antheridia are clavate and erect, whereas the ascogonia are coiled. The ascogonium elongates, and cuts off, terminally a long trichogyne which becomes seven or more celled structure by septation. Both antheridia and ascogonia are multinucleate. The trichogyne reaches the antheridial tip and encircles the antheridium body. The wall of contact dissolves and the male nuclei pass into the apical cell of trichogyne, and ultimately reach the ascogonium. Female nuclei also divide, and form pairs with male nuclei. The ascogenous hyphae develop from the periphery of fertilized ascogonium. At usual, eight-spored asci are developed. The ascospores are single-celled, double-walled, ellipsoidal and dark brown in colour.

With the result of sexual reproduction the apothecia are developed. The apothecia of *A. furfuraceus* are yellowish in colour, saucer-shaped and about 5 mm in diameter. The surface of mature apothecium is provided with purple dots on its maturity. The mature asci are elongated above the general level of hymenium. The cylindrical asci remain mixed with paraphyses. Each ascus is provided with an operculum at its apical end. The ellipsoid ascospores have a mucilaginous epispore. Each ascospore gives rise to new mycelium on its germination.

Systematic Position

G. W. Martin(1961)		**C. J. Alexopoulos (1962)**	**G. C. Ainsworth (1971)**
Kingdom	–Plantae	–Plantae	–Fungi
Division	–Mycota	–Mycota	–Eumycota

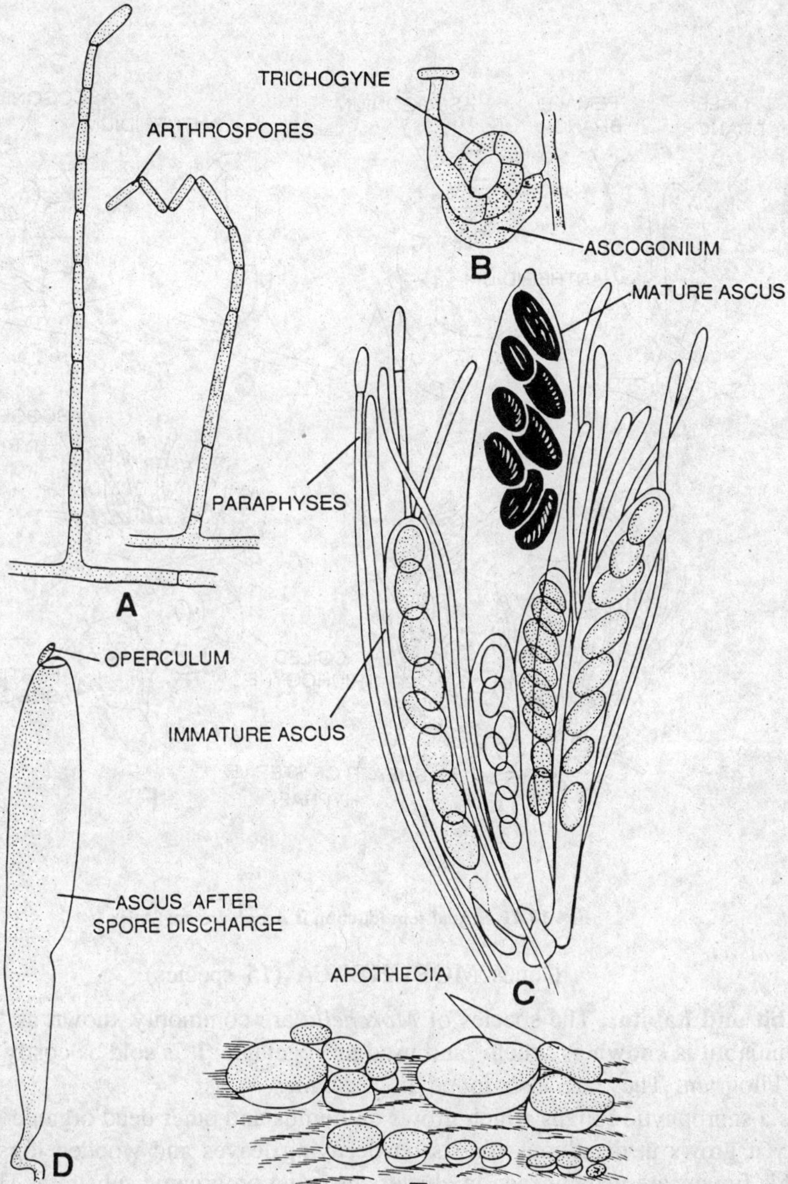

Fig. 10.40. *Ascobolus furfuraceus*. A, arthrospores (oidia); B, ascogonium with trichogyne; C, asci with ascospores, and paraphyses; D, dehisced ascus; E, apothecia on substratum.

Sub.div.	–Eumycotina	–Eumycotina	–Ascomycotina
Class	–Ascomycetes	–Ascomycetes	–Discomycetes
Sub-cl.	–Euascomycetidae	–Euascomycetidae	–
Order	–Pezizales	–Pezizales	–Pezizales
Family	–Pezizaceae	–Pezizaceae	–Pezizaceae
Genus	–*Ascobolus*	–*Ascobolus*	–*Ascobolus*

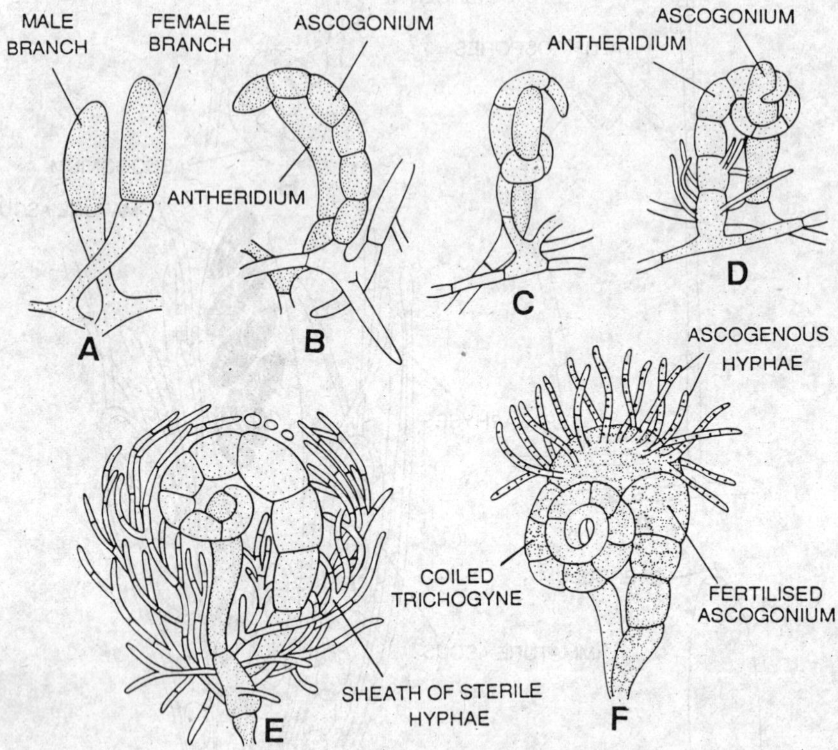

Fig. 10.41. Sexual reproduction is *Ascobolus* sp. (A-F)

Genus MORCHELLA (15 species)

Habit and habitat. The species of *Morchella* are commonly known as 'morels'. In H.P. and the Punjab it is known as 'guchi' and used as vegetable. It is sold as costly as two thousand rupees a kilogram. They are also found in Kashmir.

It is a saprophytic fungus which grows on humus and other dead organic substances. Very commonly it grows in deciduous forests on decaying leaves and wooden logs. The fructifications of this fungus are usually seen in clusters growing on organic substrata. The fructifications of this fungus are most delicious of the edible fungi. In Uttar Pradesh and Punjab this fungus is cooked with rice and vegetables and delicious dishes are prepared. Sometimes they are called the 'mushrooms'. Actually they are not true mushrooms. The true mushrooms are the members of Homobasidiomycetes.

Structure of mycelium. The mycelium of the fungus is found in masses in the humus soil. It is inconspicuous, septate and profusely branched. It penetrates the humus soil several inches deep. Prior to the development of fructifications the hyphal masses develop just below the surface of the soil. When abundance of food and moisture are found in the soil, the fructifications develop from the hyphal masses. The fruiting body is called the ascocarp. The ascocarp is composed of the compactly arranged interwoven hyphae. The fruiting body develops within a few hours.

The fructification. The fructifications of the different species of morels differ in size and external morphology. The fruiting body of *Morchella esculenta* is found upon a cream coloured,

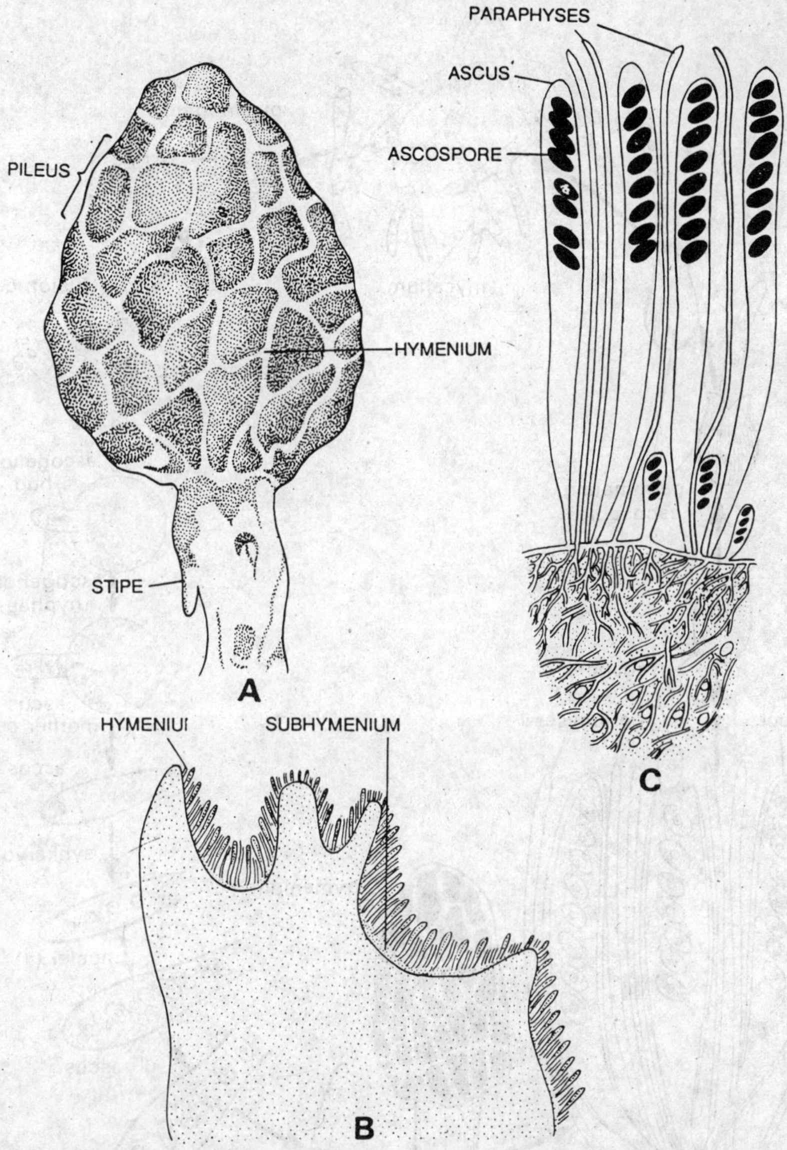

Fig. 10.42. *Morchella*. A, a fructification with stipe and pileus; B, sectional view of a part of pileus showing hymenium and subhymenium; C, paraphyses and asci with ascospores.

thick hollow and fleshy stalk about two or three inches in height and one half to one inch in diameter. The stalk bears at its terminal end more or less a conical hollow cap with ridges and depressions on it. It is as long as the stalk but sufficiently broader in diameter. In the beginning of the development of the fruiting body the cap is quite smooth but afterwards the ridges and depressions are brown.

Internal structure of ascocarp. The stipe or stalk consists of compact interwoven hyphae and looks in sectional view as pseudoparenchymatous structure. In the depression of the ascocarp the hymenial layers are present which consist of innumerable elongated, cylindrical asci containing ascospores. The paraphyses remain intermingled with asci. On the maturation of the asci, they

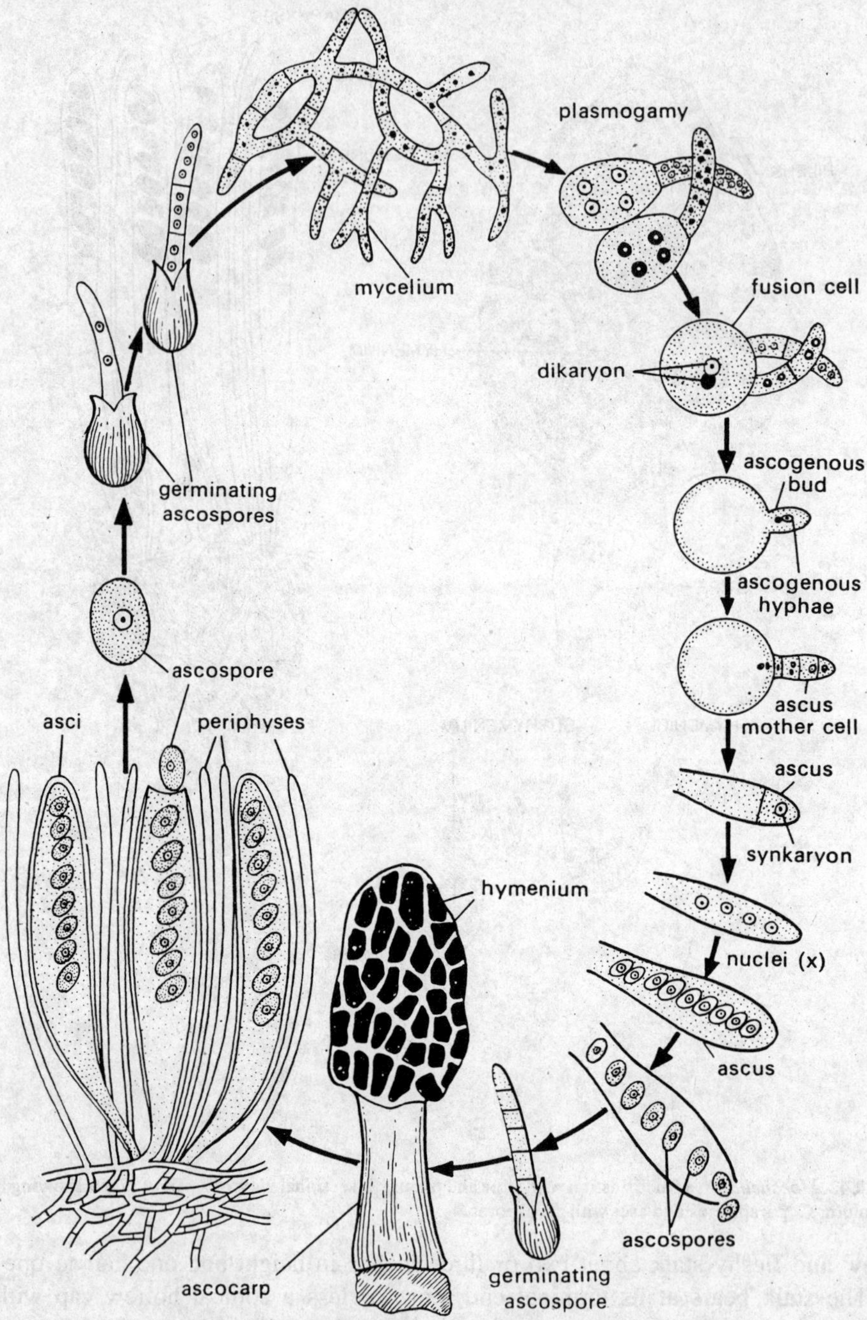

Fig. 10.43. *Morchella* sp. Diagrammatic life-cycle.

become elongated and break at the tips with the release of ascospores with a slight jerk. The ascospores are dispersed by wind. On the approach of suitable media and favourable conditions, they germinate producing germ tubes developing new mycelia.

Sexual reproduction. The sexual reproduction in *Morchella* is very much reduced or altogether absent. The sex organs are not found. The nuclei found in the vegetative hyphae,

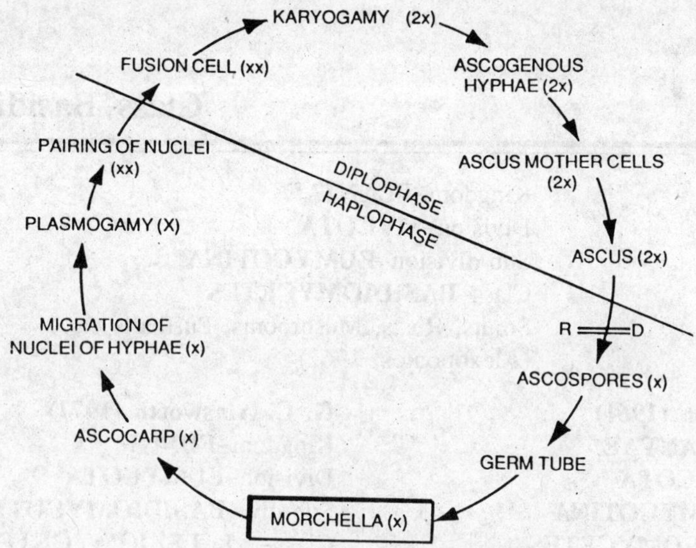

Fig. 10.44. Graphic life cycle of *Morchella*.

however, fuse together. The two adjacent lying vegetative hyphae come together, the walls of contact dissolve and the nuclei of two different hyphae come in pairs and conjugate. This type of sexual reproduction is known as **somatogamy.** The ascogenous hyphae develop. The terminal cell of the ascogenous hypha behaves as ascus mother cell. The diploid nucleus divides thrice and 8 ascospores are developed in the ascus. The first division is reductional.

Systematic Position

	G. W. Martin (1961)	**C. J. Alexopoulos (1962)**	**G. C. Ainsworth (1971)**
Kingdom	–Plantae	–Plantae	–Fungi
Division	–Mycota	–Mycota	–Eumycota
Sub.div.	–Eumycotina	–Eumycotina	–Ascomycotina
Class	–Ascomycetes	–Ascomycetes	–Discomycetes
Sub-cl.	–Euascomycetidae	–Euascomycetidae	–
Series	–	–Discomycetes	–
Order	–Pezizales	–Pezizales	–Pezizales
Family	–Pezizaceae	–Helvellaceae	–Helvellaceae
Genus	–*Morchella*	–*Morchella*	–*Morchella*

11

Class–Basidiomycetes

Kingdom–**PLANTAE**
Division–**MYCOTA**
Sub-division–**EUMYCOTINA**
Class–**BASIDIOMYCETES**
Smuts, Rusts, Mushrooms, Puffballs etc.
(Alexopoulos, 1962)

G. W. Martin (1961)	**G. C. Ainsworth (1971)**
Kingdom–**PLANTAE**	Kingdom–**FUNGI**
Division–**MYCOTA**	Division–**EUMYCOTA**
Sub-div.–**EUMYCOTINA**	Sub-div.–**BASIDIOMYCOTINA**
Class–**BASIDIOMYCETES**	Class– **1. TELIOMYCETES**
	2. HYMENOMYCETES
	3. GASTROMYCETES

This class consists of higher fungi. There are about 550 genera and 20,000 to 25,000 species.

Introduction. The Basidiomycetes include the fungi that bear their spores exogenously on **basidia.** The basidia may occur singly or be variously arranged on hymenia. On the basis of morphology and arrangement of basidia, the Basidiomycetes are divided into two sub-classes,

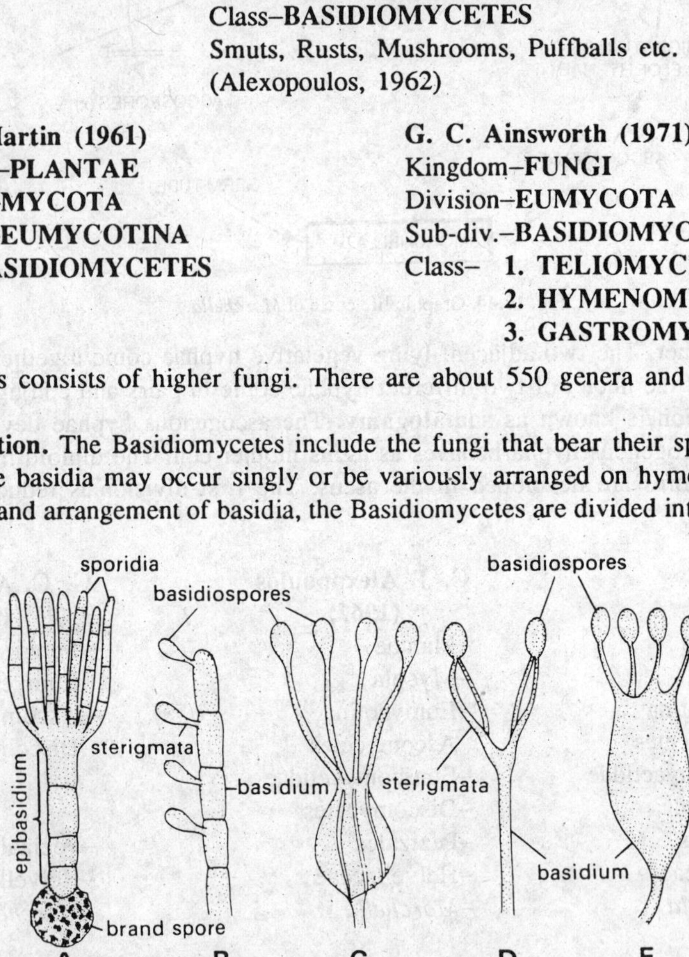

Fig. 11.1. Different types of basidia. A, stichobasidial type with a cluster of sporidia; B, stichobasidial type; C, chiastobasidial type; D, tuning fork type; E, holobasidial type.

the Heterobasidiomycetidae (Heterobasidiomycetes) and Homobasidiomycetidae (Homobasidiomycetes). The Heterobasidiomycetidae include the fungi commonly known as smuts, rusts and jelly fungi, and the Homobasidiomycetidae include the gill, pore, leathery and coral fungi, puff-balls, stinkhorns and bird's nest fungi. The fungi of sub-class Heterobasidiomycetidae are **gymnocarpous,** *i.e.*, their basidia arise on the free surface of the fructification. The Homobasidiomycetidae are further sub-divided into two series, the Hymenomycetes and the Gastromycetes. The Gastromycetes include those fungi whose hymenia formed within the basidiocarp (fruit body), and therefore, they are known as **angiocarpous.** The Hymenomycetes include those fungi which possess transitional conditions of gymnocarpy and hemiangiocarpy.

Somatic structure. The mycelium is well developed and filamentous. It consists of septate hyphae which penetrate into the substratum and absorb nourishment. The mycelium is usually white, yellow or orange and generally spreads out in a fan-shaped growth. In a few species a number of hyphae run parallel to each other and get joined together to form thick strands of mycelium. These structures are known as **rhizomorphs.** The rhizomorphs remain enveloped in a shealth of cortex and behave in the manner of a unit of tissue.

The mycelium of the Basidiomycetes passes through three stages of development, the primary, secondary and tertiary.

The primary mycelium usually develops from the germination of the basidiospore. It may be multinucleate at first, but later on, due to the formation of transverse walls, it divides into uninucleate cells. In certain species the primary mycelium is septate and uninucleate from the beginning. The primary mycelium may give rise to conidia or oidia and never forms basidia and basidiospores.

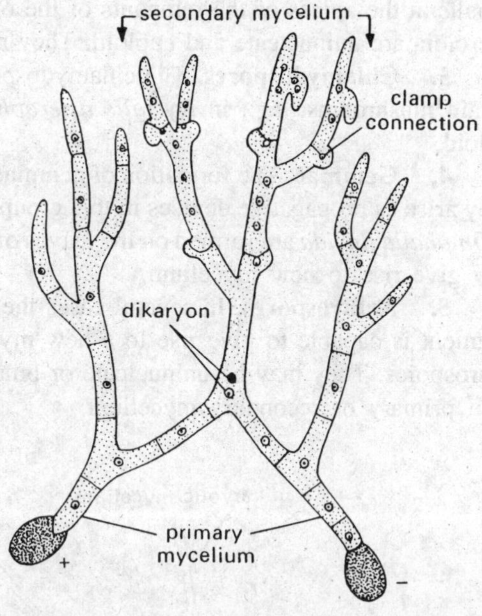

Fig. 11.2. Basidiomycetes. Primary and secondary mycelium.

The secondary mycelium consists of binucleate (dikaryotic) cells. It originates from primary mycelium. It originates from the primary mycelium as follows.

(i) The protoplasts of the opposite strained (+&–) uninucleate cells of the primary mycelium fuse. The walls of contact between the two cells dissolve and the protoplasts from two opposite strained cells fuse together. Now the two (+&–) nuclei lie side by side. This process is **plasmogamy.** The binucleate cell thus formed may develop directly into a secondary hypha.

(ii) Two basidiospores or spermatia of opposite strains come together and conjugate. The binucleate (+ –) structure formed this way gives rise to secondary mycelium.

(iii) Sometimes the germinating oidium of one strain fuses with a cell of primary mycelium of opposite strain. The binucleate cell thus formed gives rise to secondary mycelium.

(iv) Sometimes a germinating basidiospore of one strain fuses with haploid cell of basidium of opposite strain. Thus formed the binucleate cell gives rise to secondary mycelium.

The secondary mycelium always gives rise to brand spores or teleutospores, which on germination produce basidia or promycelia.

Asexual reproduction. The asexual reproduction takes place by means of conidia, oidia, chlamydospores and gemmae. The methods are as follows:

1. Conidia. The basidiospores of many smuts bud indefinitely in yeast-like fashion, and these buds like conidia may eventually serve to initial infection. The uredospores of rusts are like conidia in their origin and since they function in dissemination may also be considered conidia. The basidiospores of many jelly fungi germinate by producing sprout cells which eventually develop mycelia. These conidia develop on secondary (dikaryotic) mycelium.

2. Oidia. Brodie (1931) showed lateral oidiophores arising from mycelium in *Coprinus logopus*. The oidiophores become segmented basipetally into ellipsoidal oidia which mass together in balls at the apices of the remnants of the oidiophores. These oidia may function as conidia. The oidia are uninucleate and haploid. They produce monokaryotic mycelium on germination.

3. Chlamydospores. The chlamydospores are formed as the upper surface of pileus of certain mushrooms, *e.g.*, in *Nyctalis asterophora* and *N. parasitica.* The chlamydospores are diploid.

4. Gemmae. The formation of gemmae has been reported from several Hymenomycetes. They arise as propagative devices in this group. According to Buller (1934), the stalked gemmae of *Omphalia flavida* are formed on the leaves of coffee and other tropical species. On germination they give rise to new mycelium.

5. Arthrospores. In several cases the mycelium breaks up into small fragments. Each fragment is capable to give rise to a new mycelium. These mycelial fragments are called the arthrospores. They may be uninucleate or binucleate, depending on whether they are produced from primary or secondary mycelium.

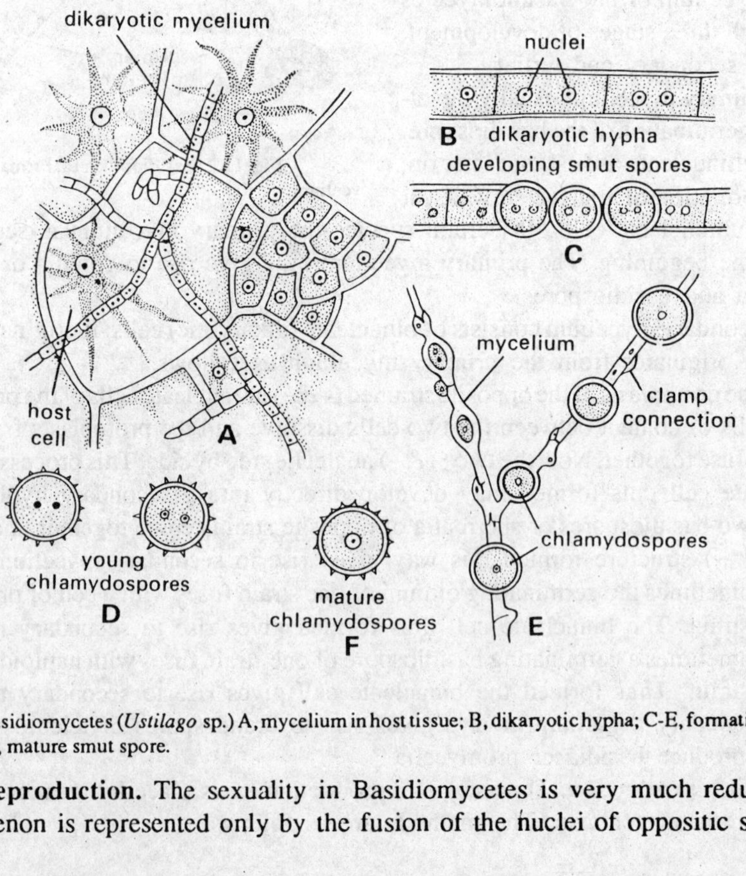

Fig. 11.3. Basidiomycetes (*Ustilago* sp.) A, mycelium in host tissue; B, dikaryotic hypha; C-E, formation of smut spores from a mycelium; F, mature smut spore.

Sexual reproduction. The sexuality in Basidiomycetes is very much reduced, and the sexual phenomenon is represented only by the fusion of the nuclei of oppositic strains (+ and

—). Unlike, Phycomycetes and Ascomycetes the distinct male (antheridium) and female (oogonium or ascogonium) sex organs are never produced. The monokaryotic phase changes into a dikaryotic phase by means of **dikaryotization.** In the ultimate stages of the development of teleutospores and chlamydospores, the opposite strained nuclei get fused, resulting in the diploid nuclei. The diploid spores produce **promycelia** or **basidia** on germination. During this process the first division is reductional one, and the four nuclei of the basidium are haploid. The basidiospores are haploid, uninucleate and single-celled structures. The basidiospore on germination produces haplont mycelium either of + or — strains. The phenomenon of heterothallism is quite conspicuous. The basidiospores produce monokaryotic hyphae, which dikaryotize by the process of dikaryotization and the dikaryotic hyphae are produced. Each pair of the opposite strained (+ and —) nuclei in each cell of the dikaryotic mycelium is known as a **dikaryon.** Ultimately the two nuclei of a dikaryon fuse and a diploid spore develops.

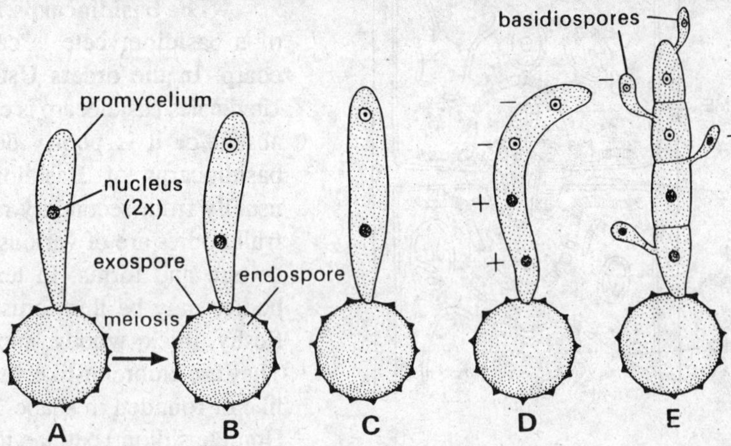

Fig. 11.4. Basidiomycetes (*Ustilago* sp.), germination of smut spore and development of basidium.

The formation of dikaryotic mycelium has already been discussed under the sub-heading—somatic strucuture.

Clamp connections. One or more species of all orders of Basidiomycetes except rusts (Uredinales) form clamp connections. During division of cells of the secondary mycelium in most of Basidiomycetes from the middle region of the terminal cell of the dikaryotic hypha a tubular outgrowth is given out. The outgrowth curves downward making a hook-like structure, touches the cell wall and called the **clamp connection.** Both the opposite nuclei of the terminal cell divide producing four nuclei, two of + and two of — strain. Now one of the daughter nucleus of upper two nuclei passes through the clamp and moves in the basal part of the cell, and one of the daughter nucleus of the two lower nuclei moves upward in the cell. The wall of contact dissolves where the clamp touches the wall, and the nucleus comes through the clamp in the lower region of the cell. Now the clamp begins to degenerate and a septum appears at this point, which divides the mother cell into two cells,

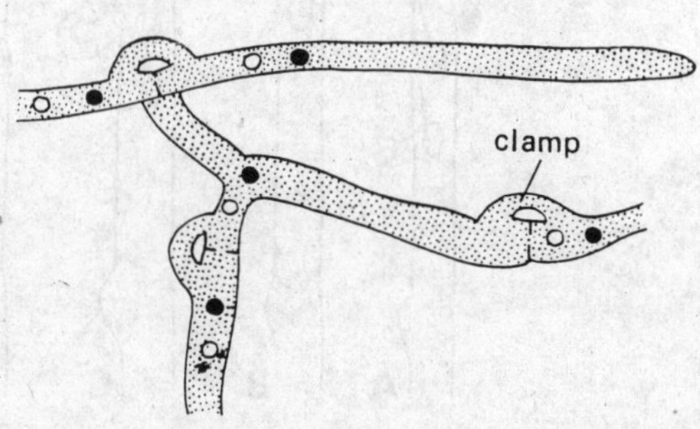

Fig. 11.5. Basidiomycetes. Dikaryotic mycelium with clamp connection.

each possessing two nuclei of opposite strains, this way, one dikaryotic cell gives rise to two dikaryotic cells. The newly developed cells become elongated and the terminal cell is again ready for division and the hypha increases in length continuously.

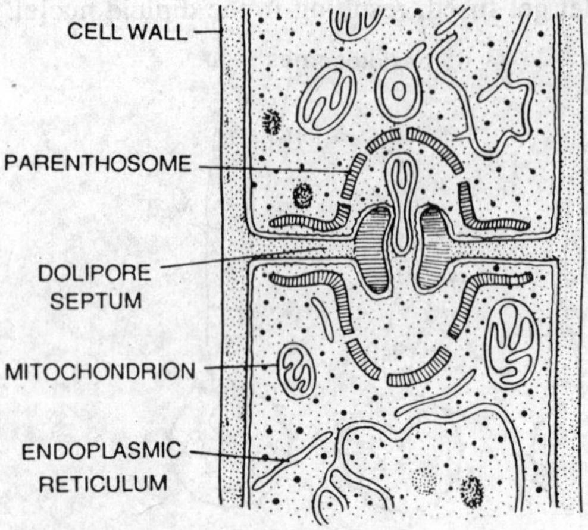

Fig. 11.6. Basidiomycetes. Ultra structure showing dolipore septum in sectional view (diagrammatic).

The basidiocarps. The fruit body of a basidiomycete is called a basidiocarp. In the orders Ustilaginales and Uredinales basidiocarp is either altogether absent or it is poorly developed. The basidiocarps of Basidiomycetes arise usually from secondary mycelium. The fruit bodies are of various shapes, sizes, texture and forms. In texture the fruit bodies may be thin, crust-like, papery, fleshy, thick, woody, spongy or corky. They are umbrella-like, fan-like, button-like or rounded in shape. In most of the Homobasidiomycetidae the basidiocarp (fruit body or sporophore) is large, often with a central stalk, the **stipe,** distinct from the **pileus** or cap and with the fertile region limited to the surface of **lamellae or gills,** or to the interior of deep pores or of closed chambers. Many Basidiomycetes such as mush-

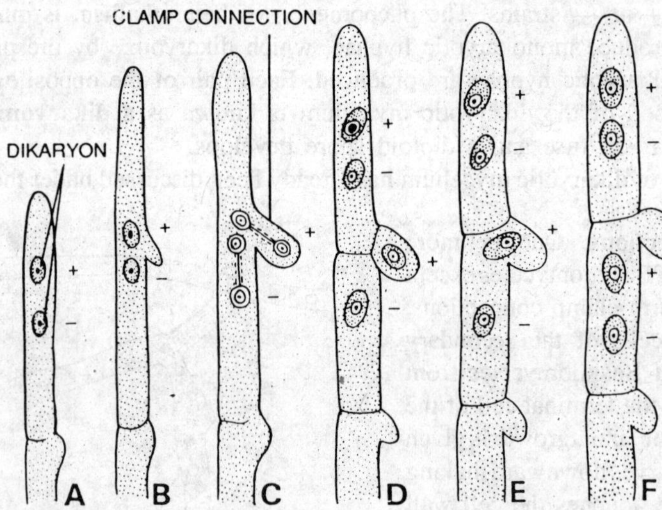

Fig. 11.6 (a). Basidiomycetes. Stages in the formation of clamp connection.

rooms, shelf fungi, coral fungi, puff balls, earth stars, stink horns and bird's nest fungi bear basidiocarps. The main body of the fungus in each case is the extensive mycelium.

The basidiocarps may be open from the very beginning, exposing their basidia outside, or they may open at a later stage, or even remain closed. In species (*e.g., Lycoperdon*) where fruit bodies remain closed the spores liberate only when the basidiocarps are disintegrated or it breaks accidentally.

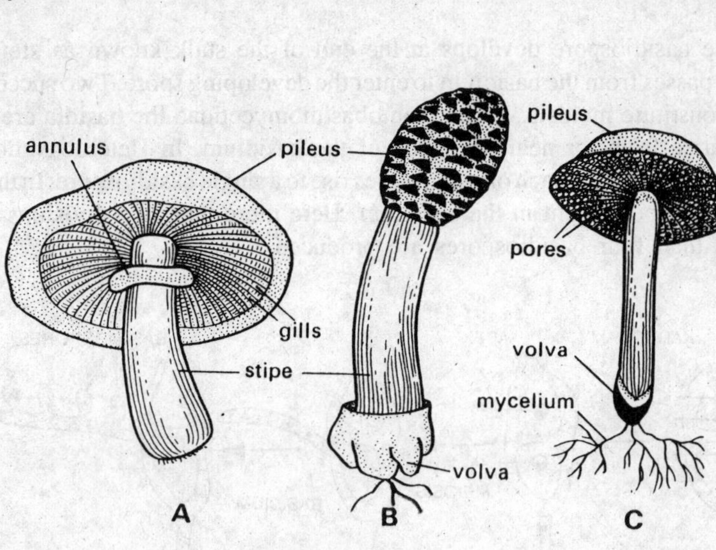

Fig. 11.7. Basidiomycetes. Basidiocarps of *Agaricus* (A), *Phallus* (B), and *Boletus* (C).

The basidia are formed in definite layers called hymenia. The hymenium consists of basidia and sterile paraphyses. In some species the sterile processes among the basidia become much larger than the basidia are called **cystidia.**

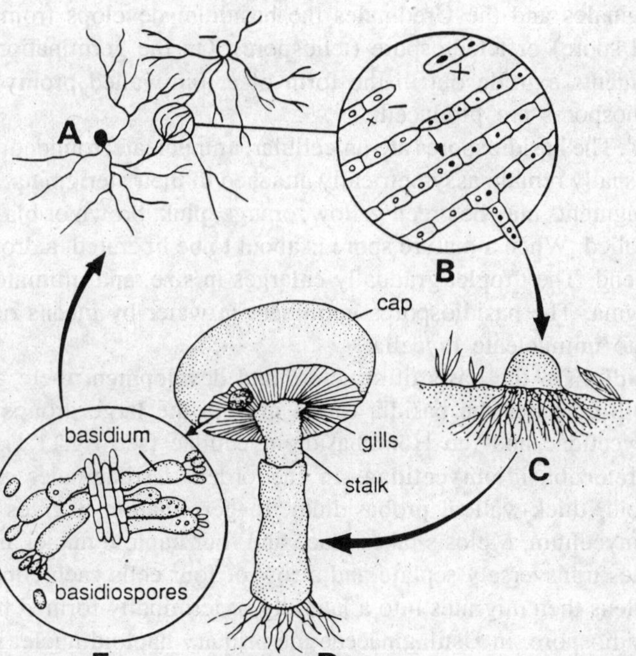

Fig. 11.8. Basidiomycetes. Life-cycle of mushroom (*Agaricus*) A-B, mycelium; C, button stage; D, fruit body; E, part of gill showing basidium and basidiospores.

Basidium. The basidiospores are borne externally on the mother cell, or **basidium.** The young basidium contains two nuclei, these fuse, the fusion nucleus divides forming the nuclei of the spores. The basidiospore develops at the end of the stalk known as **sterigma,** through which the nucleus passes from the basidium to enter the developing spore. Two successive divisions in the basidium constitute meiosis. In the Homobasidiomycetidae the basidia are without septa, and four spores arise from, or near, the apex of the basidium. In Heterobasidiomycetidae the basidium divides into four cells, each of which gives rise to a single basidiospore. In the Ustilaginales septa may or may not be present in the basidium. Here more than two divisions follow nuclear fusion, and more than four basidiospores are produced.

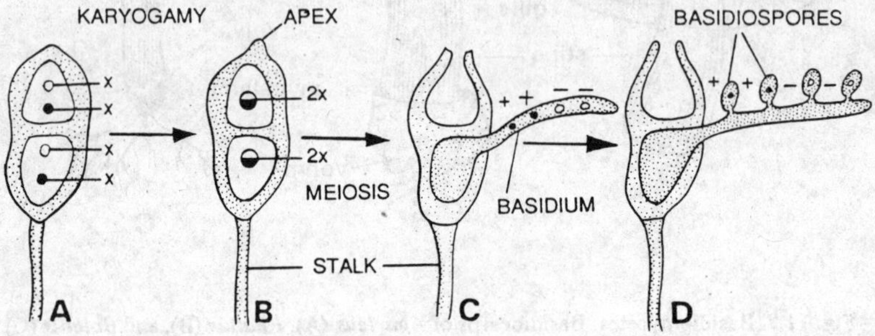

Fig. 11.9. *Puccinia* sp. A, young teleutospore; B, mature teleutospore; C, germinating teleutospore with young basidium; D, germinating teleutospore with basidium and basidiospores 2+ and 2—.

In the Ustilaginales and the Uredinales the basidium develops from a thick-walled chlamydospore (brand spore) or teleutospore (teliospore). On the germination of brand spore or teleutospore the contents extrude out in the form of a thin-walled promycelium or basidium on which the basidiospores are produced.

Basidiospores. The basidiospores are unicellular, uninucleate, rounded, or oval and haploid. The basidiospores usually remain assymetrically attached to their sterigmata. They are colourless or pigmented. The pigments may be green yellow, orange, pink, brown or black. They are usually smooth and thick-walled. When a mature spore is about to be liberated, a droplet of water begins to form at its basal end. The droplet gradually enlarges in size, and ultimately the basidiospore is shot off the sterigma. The basidiospores germinate in water by means of germ tubes which later on develop into uninucleate mycelia.

Types of basidia. On the basis of structure and development there are several types of basidia. Here we will consider the basidia found in both the large groups of Basidiomycetes the Heterobasidiomycetidae and the Homobasidiomycetidae (see fig.11.1).

Basidia of Heterobasidiomycetidae. In the orders Ustilaginales and Uredinales, the teliospore is a diploid, thick-walled, probasidium. In germination it gives rise to a structure, the basidium or promycelium. Meiosis takes place and four haploid nuclei are formed thereafter the basidium becomes transversely septate and a row of four cells each containing one nucleus is formed. Each nucleus then migrates into a laterally or terminally formed bud, which becomes abstricted into a basidiospore. In Ustilaginaceae the primary haploid nuclei within the basidium may continue to divide, and as a result many basidiospores may be produced.

Another type of basidia are found in the order Tremellales. In these fungi the spherical or elongate basidium becomes divided by a vertical septum after division of the primary diploid nucleus. After division of each of these nuclei another vertical septum at right angles to the first is laid down, so that the basidium as seen from the above is cruciately divided. Each quadrant bears a slender sterigma on which a single haploid basidiospore is produced.

In the group Dacryomycetales of Heterobasidiomycetidae there are basidia of still another

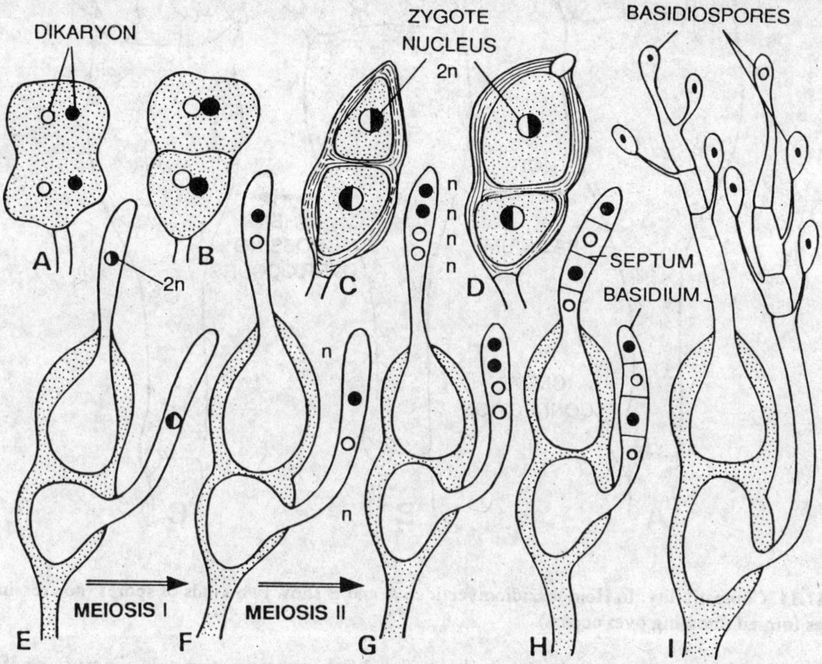

Fig. 11.10. *Puccinia graminis*.A-C, formation of teliospore; D, mature teliospore; E-I, germination of teliospore resulting in the formation of basidium and basidiospores.

type. Here the primary diploid nucleus divides twice forming four haploid nuclei. A tuning fork shaped process arises at the apex of the basidium. Two of the nuclei migrate into basidiospores situated at the apices of the tuning fork basidium and the remaining two nuclei, disintegrate.

Basidia of Homobasidiomycetidae. The basidia of Homobasidiomycetidae are of another type. In the series Hymenomycetes the basidia are slender clavate to broadly clavate whereas in the series Gastromycetes the basidia are globular. The diploid nucleus divides twice forming four haploid nuclei. Usually four sterigmata arise from the apex of the basidium and a uninucleate basidiospore is borne on each sterigma.

Compatibility. About 90% speices of Basidiomycetes are heterothallic, *i.e.*, they require the union of two compatible thalli for sexual reproduction. In about thirty-seven per cent of heterothallic species the sexual compatibility is governed by one pair of factors. As located on the same locus on different chromosomes and behave in the same manner as do the heterothallic, species in Mucorales. Such species are called **bipolar.** The remaining sixty-three per cent of heterothallic species are **tetrapolar,** *i.e.*, sexual compatibility is governed by two pairs of factos **Aa Bb** located on different chromosomes and segregating independently. This way, four types of basidiospores are produced by tetrapolar species, *i.e.*, **AB, Ab, aB, ab.** If crossing over does not take place between the mating type loci and their centromeres, then only two types of basidiospores will be formed:

AB AB ab ab OR **Ab Ab aB aB**

If crossing over takes place for one mating type locus, four types of spores will be formed:

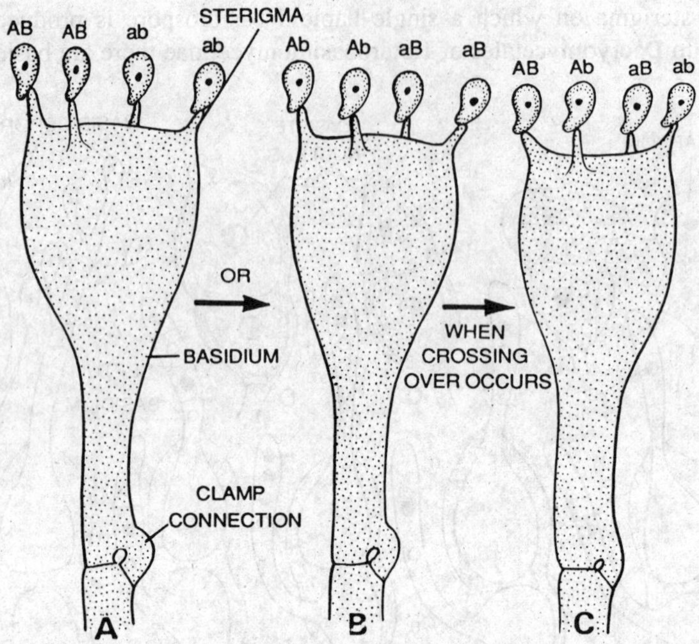

Fig. 11.11. Compatibility. In Homobasidiomycetidae A and B show two kinds of spores (no crossing over); C, four types of spores formed (crossing over occurs).

AB Ab aB ab. If crossing over takes place for both mating type loci, two or four types of spores may be formed on the basidium.

Origin and phylogenetic relationships. At one time the opinion was divided as to whether the Basidiomycetes descended from the Phycomycetes or the Ascomycetes. In recent decades the mycologists argue for phylogenetic relationship between Basidiomycetes and Ascomycetes. Kneip (1915) suggested the origin of Basidiomycetes from Ascomycetes on the basis that the hyphae of Basidiomycetes with clamp connections are homologous with the crozier formation in early development of asci. According to Kniep (1915), the apparently terminal binucleate cell which develops into a basidium is actually a penultimate cell which lies posterior to a terminal uninucleate cell. Here the fundamental change in evolution of an ascus into basidium would be a change from an endogenous to an exogenous method of spore formation.

Evolution within the Basidiomycetes. According to some mycologists (Bessey, 1950; Dietel, 1928; Jackson, 1944), the Basidiomycetes with phragmobasidia are most closely related to the ancestral Ascomycetes. These mycologists interpret that the Uredinales were the first Basidiomycetes to appear. According to other (Alexopoulos, 1952; Martin, 1945), the Auriculariales are the most primitive of phragmobasidial Basidiomycetes. According to another school of thought (Gaumann, 1949, 1953; Gaumann and Dodge, 1928), the Basidiomycetes with holobasidia are more primitive and closer to ancestral Ascomycetes. Many modern mycologists are of opinion that the Basidiomycetes with phragmobasidium are more primitive and called the Heterobasidiomycetidae. The Basidiomycetes with holobasidia are supposed to be advanced and are called the Homobasidiomycetidae.

Economic importance. Majority of the species of this class are harmful. They cause various diseases to the plants of economic value. The most important diseases are smuts and rusts. Many bracket fungi do the great harm to the timber. Some species of Homobasidiomycetidae are deadly poisonous (*e.g., Amanita*). On the other hand some mushrooms are edible and sold very costly for eating purposes *(e.g., Agaricus campestris)* .

Classification. The outline of Gwynne-Vaughan and Barnes (1926) classification is as follows.

Class—BASIDIOMYCETES
(Sexually produced spores, basidiospores, formed exogenously on an organ, the basidium).

Sub-classes—	1. HEMIBASIDIOMYCETES (Number of basidiospores indefinite)	2. PROTOBASIDIOMYCETES (Number of basidiospores definite, usually four; basidium septate).	3. AUTOBASIDIOMYCETES (Number of basidiospores definite, usually four; basidium aseptate).
Orders—	1. Ustilaginales	1. Uredinales. 2. Auriculariales. 3. Tremellales.	1. Hymenomycetales. 2. Gasteromycetales.

Majority of modern mycologists believe that the phragmobasidial (basidium septate) forms are more primitive, being more closer to the ancestral Ascomycetes. The outline of the modern classification is as follows—

Class–BASIDIOMYCETES

Sub-classes–	1. HETEROBASIDIOMYCETIDAE (Basidium septate or deeply divided; or consisting of a teleutospore germinating into a promycelium; basidiospores usually capable of germinating by repetition).	2. HOMOBASIDIOMYCETIDAE (Basidium not septate or deeply divided; basidiospores usually germinating by germ tube).	
Series-		1. Hymenomycetes.	2. Gastromyctes.
Orders—	1. Ustilaginlaes. 2. Uredinales. 3. Tremellales.	1. Agaricales	1. Hymenogastrales. 2. Nidulariales. 3. Lycoperdales. 4. Sclerodermatales.

12

Sub-class–Heterobasidiomycetidae

Rusts and Smuts
(Alexopoulos, 1962)

(G. W. Martin 1961)	(G. C. Ainsworth 1971)
Sub-class–**HETEROBASIDIOMYCETIDAE**	Class–**TELIOMYCETES** and sub-class–**PHRAGMOBASIDIOMYCETIDAE** of class–**HYMENOMYCETES**

Characteristic Features.

1. The basidium is transversely or vertically septate or incised at the apex.
2. The mature basidium typically consists of two portions; a basal hypobasidium and an elongated tube or inflated protuberance, the epibasidium, which typically bears basidiospores on sterigmata.
3. Many basidiospores show germination by repetition. Here the basidiospores on germination produce secondary basidiospores which are shot off in the same manner as were the original spores.
4. In many of them a thick-walled probasidium also known as teleutospore or brand spore is found. The probasidium may undergo a number of morphological changes before it becomes differentiated into a mature basidium. Eventually the probasidium is transformed into hypobasidium which gives rise to the epibasidium.
5. Many members are without a fruit body or basidiocarp (*e.g.*, Ustilaginales and Uredinales) but some of them possess well developed fruit bodies (*e.g.*, Tremellales).

Classification. Martin (1961) has divided the sub-class into three orders—1. Ustilaginales (the smuts); 2. Uredinales (the rusts); and 3. Tremellales (gelatinous Basidiomycetes).

ORDER USTILAGINALES (The Smuts)

(42 genera; 700 species)

Characteristic Features

1. They cause the plant diseases known as 'smuts' and 'bunts'. The black powder of spores is known as 'smut' or 'soot' and because of this reason the diseases caused by Ustilaginales are called 'smuts'.
2. The smuts are parasitic on various plants, but they are not obligate parasites. They are facultative saprophytes.
3. The mycelium is inter and intracellular. The intercalary, thick-walled, round, dark brown chlamydospores or brand spores are produced on dikaryotic or secondary mycelium.
4. On germination, the chlamydospore produces a tube-like structure known as promycelium or basidium.
5. The basidium is either septate or aseptate, and from each cell of basidium, the ba

sidiospores or sporidia are produced in basigenous chains. The basidiospores are not borne on sterigmata. They are not violently discharged.

6. The smuts have a simple life-cycle in comparison to rusts.
7. They lack fruit bodies or basidiocarps.
8. Clamp-connections are more common in smuts.
9. There are about 40 genera and 700 species in this order.

Fig. 12.1. Smuts caused by *Ustilago* sp. A, covered smut of barley; B, loose smut of wheat; C, covered smut of oats.

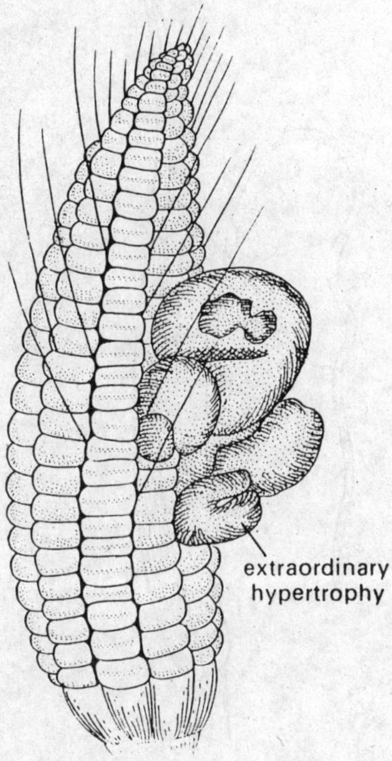

Fig. 12.2. Corn smut (*Ustilago maydis*).

Classification. The order Ustilaginales is sub-divided into three families: 1. Ustilaginaceae, 2. Tilletiaceae and 3. Graphiolaceae.

Family—Ustilaginaceae

The basidiocarps are absent. The promycelium or basidium is septate. The basidiospores are produced laterally from each cell of promycelium. The important genera— 1. *Ustilago* 2. *Sphacelotheca* and 3. *Tolyposproium*, Genus *Ustilago* has been discussed here in detail.

Genus **USTILAGO** (300 species)

Habit and habitat. There are about 300 species of this genus. Majority of them are parasitic upon vascular plants. Some species are parasitic upon cereals. They cause the 'smut diseases' of various crop plants. The diseases caused by this genus are of much economic value as they damage the various crops and cause sufficient losses to the country. In Uttar Pradesh and Punjab the diseases caused by this fungus are known as **'kangiari', 'karanjwa', 'kandua'** etc.

Mycelium. The mycelium is branched and septate. There is a central septal pore in each septum through which the cytoplasm of one cell can move in other cell. The mycelium is endophytic, inconspicuous, hyaline and intercellular. Usually the haustoria are developed which absorb the food material from the host cells. However, the host cells are not destroyed. The mycelium is either localized or systemic.

According to nuclear behaviour of the cells of the fungus in the life cycle, there are two phases of the mycelium. They are primary and secondary mycelia.

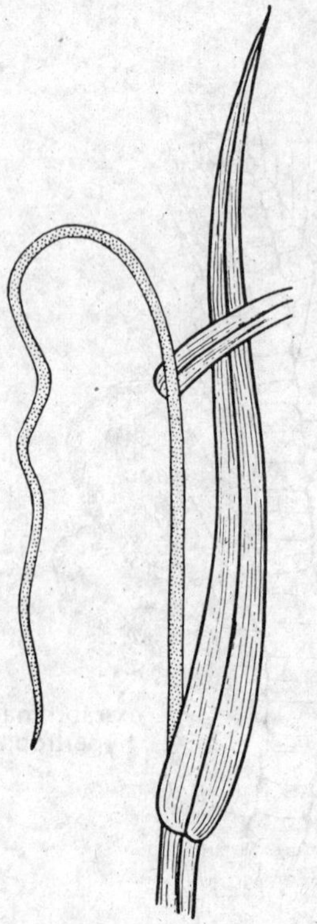

Fig. 12.3. Whip smut of sugarcane (*Ustilago scitaminea*)

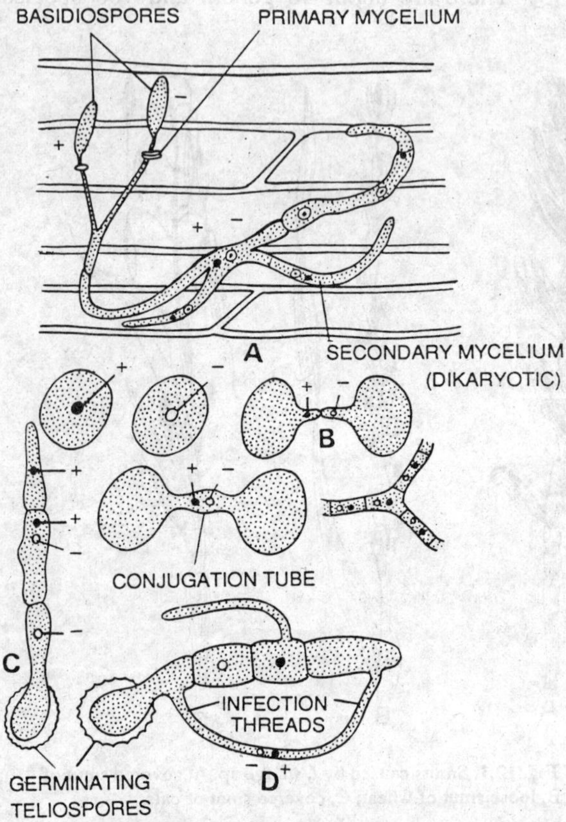

Fig. 12.4. *Ustilago*. Dikaryotization in different species. A, *Ustilago maydis*; B, *U. hordei*; C, *U. carbo*; D, *U. tritici*.

Primary mycelium. Each segment of the primary mycelium contains a single nucleus. The nuclei are haploid and the mycelium is **monokaryotic.** The monokaryotic mycelium develops from the basidiospore, and according to the sexual behaviour of the nucleus it is either of + or of - strain.

Secondary mycelium. Very soon the primary mycelium converts into the secondary mycelium. Each cell of the secondary mycelium is binucleate, but both the nuclei of the pair are haploid and of opposite strain, *i.e.*, + and -. This pair of opposite strained nuclei is called the **'dikaryon'**, and the mycelium containing such pairs in its cells the **dikaryotic mycelium.** The phenomenon of the conversion of primary mycelium into secondary mycelium is called the **dikaryotization** or **diploidization.** The dikaryotization takes place by different methods. In *Ustilago maydis* the two hyphae of opposite strains come in contact, the walls of contact dissolve and the nuclei of a cell of monokaryotic hypha are transferred to the adjacent cells of the other monokaryotic hypha, giving rise to a dikaryotic cell, which develops into new dikaryotic mycelium. In *Ustilago tritici* the infection threads develop on the different strained cells of basidium which furnish the phenomenon of dikaryotization. In *Ustilago hordei* the dikaryotization takes place by the fusion of germ tubes developed from two basidiospores of opposite strains.

Spores. The dikaryotic phase of mycelium is found within the host tissue. Unless and until the infected stem is cut in sections, one cannot detect the presence of the fungus. The

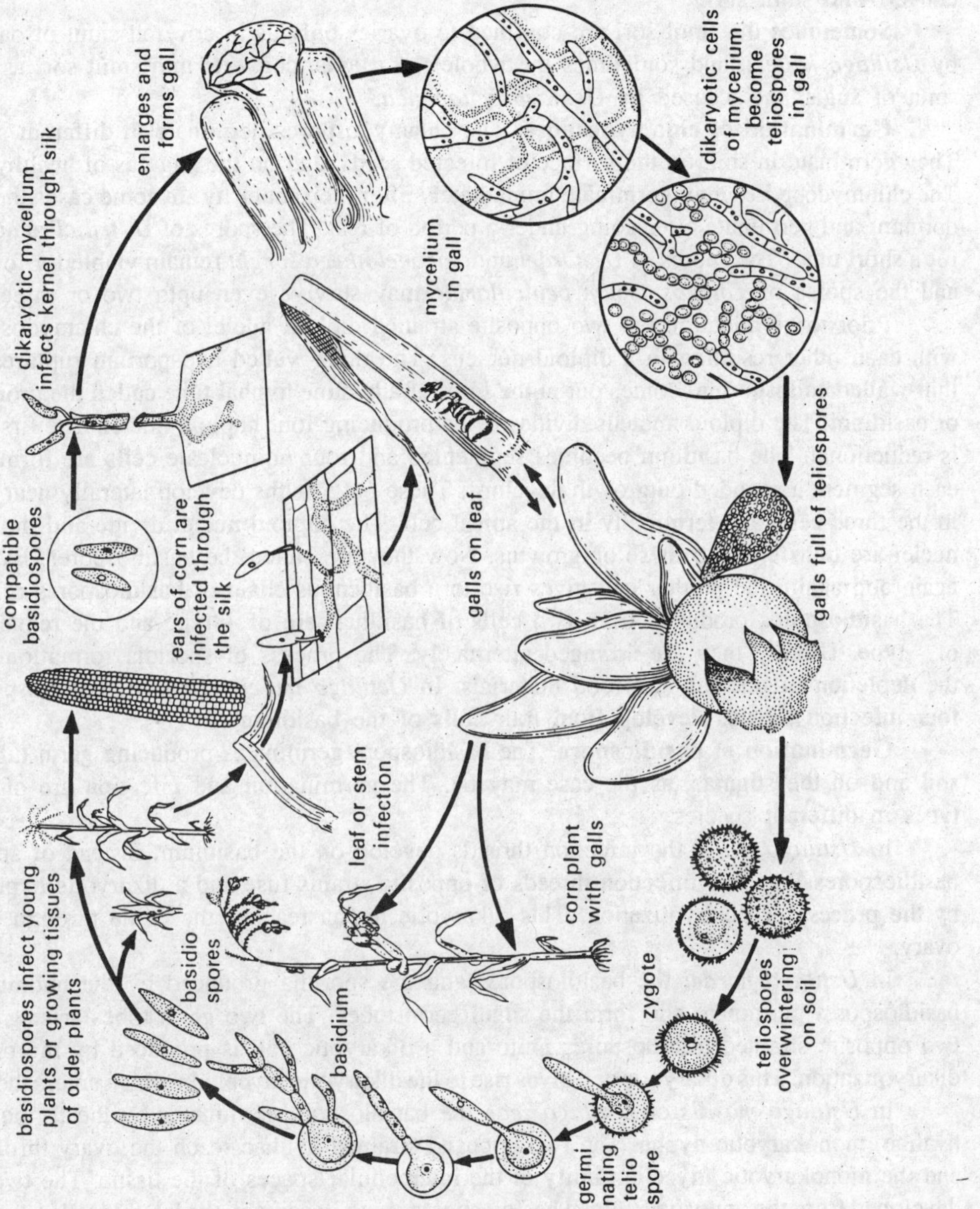

Fig. 12.5. Disease-cycle of corn smut (*Ustilago maydis*).

mycelium is found in endophytic state in the stem, leaves etc. But it is found in abundance in the inflorescence, flowers and specially in the ovaries. In the ovaries the mycelium becomes closely septate and several small cells are produced. The small cells become swollen, rounded, thick walled and olive green or brownish in colour. These perennating structures are called either

chlamydospores, smut spores or **brand spores.** The outer thick wall of the chlamydospore, which may be smooth or echinulate, is exosporium and the inner thin wall the endosporium.

The chlamydospores are produced in abundance and look like black powder. The spores are found in sori. Leaving awns aside, the rest of the parts of the inflorescence of the cereals convert into smut sori.

Sometimes the smut sori are confined to ovaries only as in covered smut of oats caused by *Ustilago kolleri*, and sometimes the whole floral axis, converts into smut sori as in 'whip smut of sugarcane' caused by *Ustilago scitaminea*.

Germination of chlamydospore. The chlamydospores germinate in different situations. They germinate in soil, on the surface of infected seeds, and on the stigmas of healthy flowers. The chlamydospores may germinate immediately after their maturity. In some cases they remain dormant and germinate after going under a period of rest. The spores of *U. tritici* remain viable for a short time. The spores of *U. hordei* and *Sphacelotheca sorghi* remain viable for few months and the spores of *Tolyposporium penicillariae* may survive even upto two or three years.

Prior to germination the two opposite strained diploid nuclei of the chlamydospore fuse with each other resulting in a diploid nucleus. The thick-walled exosporium ruptures and the thin-walled endosporium comes out in the form of a hyaline hyphal tube called the promycelium or basidium. The diploid nucleus divides twice producing four haploid nuclei. The first division is reductional. The basidium becomes segmented and four uninucleate cells are formed. From each segment a rounded outgrowth develops. These outgrowths develop laterally near the septa in the three cells and terminally in the apical cell. The haploid nuclei divide and the daughter nuclei are transferred to these outgrowths. Now they are called the basidiospores. By dividing again and again, the mother cell gives rise to a basigenous chain of basidiospores or sporidia. The basidiospores produced from two cells of basidium are of + type and the remaining two of - type. Usually they are arranged alternately. The process of sporidia formation stops on the depletion of nucleus and food materials. In *Ustilago tritici* instead of basidiospores only four infection threads develop from four cells of the basidium.

Germination of basidiospore. The basidiospore germinates producing germ tubes in the soil and on the stigmas, as the case may be. The germination and infection are of different types in different species.

In *Ustilago tritici* the infection threads develop on the basidium, instead of sporidia or basidiospores. The two infection threads of opposite strains fuse and a dikaryotic hypha results by the process of dikaryotization. This dikaryotic hypha reaches the ovule through style and ovary.

In *Ustilago hordei* the basidiospores and the sporidia produced by the budding of the basidiospores germinate and form the small germ tubes. The two germ tubes arising from the two opposite strained basidiospores unite and a dikaryotic cell is produced by the process of dikaryotization. This dikaryotic cell gives rise to the dikaryotic mycelium which enters the embryo.

In *Ustilago maydis* or *Ustilago zeae* the basidiospore germinates by the formation of a hyaline, monokaryotic hypha. The two opposite strained hyphae reach the ovary through style and the monokaryotic mycelia ramify in the intercellular spaces of the tissue. The two hyphae developed from the opposite strained basidiospores come in contact, the lateral walls are dissolved and the dikaryotization takes place, giving rise to a dikaryotic cell which develops the dikaryotic mycelium.

Heterothallism. In the life cycle of *Ustilago maydis*, prior to the chlamydospore formation, it is most essential that the infection takes place by two opposite strained basidiospores. But it has also been observed that even after the infection by two basidiospores the chlamydospores are not formed. From this very point it is quite clear that the chlamydospore formation is based upon the sexual nature of the mycelia developed from the different basidiospores. The chlamydospores are produced only in those conditions when the monokaryotic hyphae giving rise

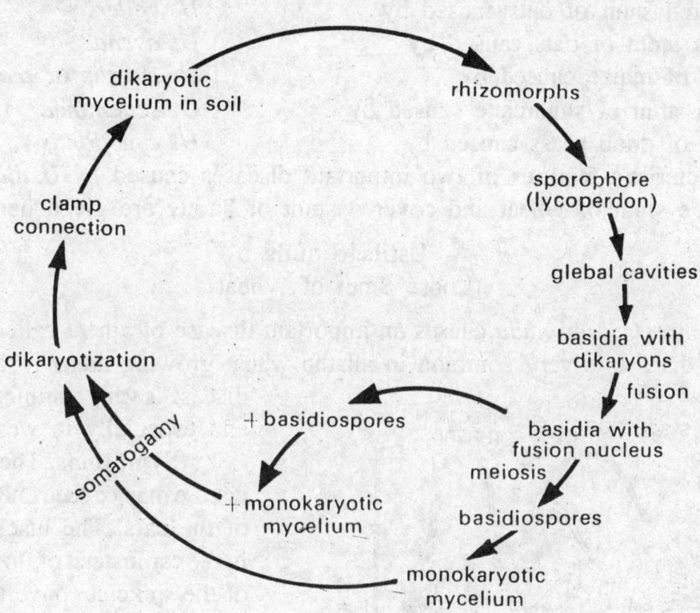

Fig. 12.6. *Ustilago*. Graphic life-cycle.

to a dikaryotic cell by the process of dikaryotization are developed from the opposite strained (+ and -) basidiospores. The monokaryotic hyphae of similar strains cannot go under dikaryotization and the chlamydospores are not produced. It is very clear from this example that the monokaryotic primary mycelia, taking part in dikaryotization are always of different strains. Such fungus is called the heterothallic and the phenomenon heterothallism.

Sexuality. From the study of life-cycle of the different species of *Ustilago,* it is quite clear that the sex organs such as antheridia, oogonia, ascogonia etc., do not occur in any case. The phenomenon of heterothallism is found in the species of *Ustilago*. The basidiospores are haploid and give rise to haploid mycelia. The dikaryotization takes place by the fusion of the two hyphae produced by two opposite strained basidiospores and dikaryotic mycelium results on which the chlamydospores are produced in chains. Prior to the germination of the chlamydospore both the opposite strained (+ and -) nuclei of it fuse giving rise to a diploid nucleus (2 x). This nucleus further divides twice producing 4 haploid nuclei (x) in the promycelium or basidium. The first division is reductional (meiosis). Morphologically, the basidiospores and the hyphae produced from them cannot be considered as sex organs. They are quite identical in outer appearance. The formation of diploid nucleus in the chlamydospore, and the production of 4 haploid nuclei in the basidium by meiosis, advocate the view that the two nuclei of a dikaryotic cell in *Ustilago* are of opposite sexual behaviour, *i.e.,* + and - strains. These nuclei behave as the sex organs of Phycomycetes and Ascomycetes. It is very obvious that the sexuality is very much reduced in *Ustilago* and can be represented only by the opposite strained nuclei present in dikaryotic cell.

The different species of *Ustilago* cause various important crop diseases.

1. Loose smut of wheat caused by *Ustilago nuda*
2. Covered smut of barley caused by *U. hordei*
3. Loose smut of barley caused by *U. nuda*
4. Covered smut of oats caused by *U. kolleri*
5. Loose smut of oats caused by *U. avenae*
6. Smut of maize caused by *U. maydis* or *zeae*
7. Whip smut of sugarcane caused by *U. scitaminea*
8. Smut of doob grass caused by *U. cynodontis*

The characteristic features of two important diseases caused by *Ustilago nuda* and *U. hordei, i.e.*, loose smut of wheat and covered smut of barely are given here.

Ustilago nuda

(Loose Smut of Wheat)

Distribution. *Ustilago nuda* causes an important disease of wheat called the 'loose smut of wheat'. This disease is very common in all the wheat growing areas of our country. This disease is very common in Uttar Pradesh and especially in western districts.

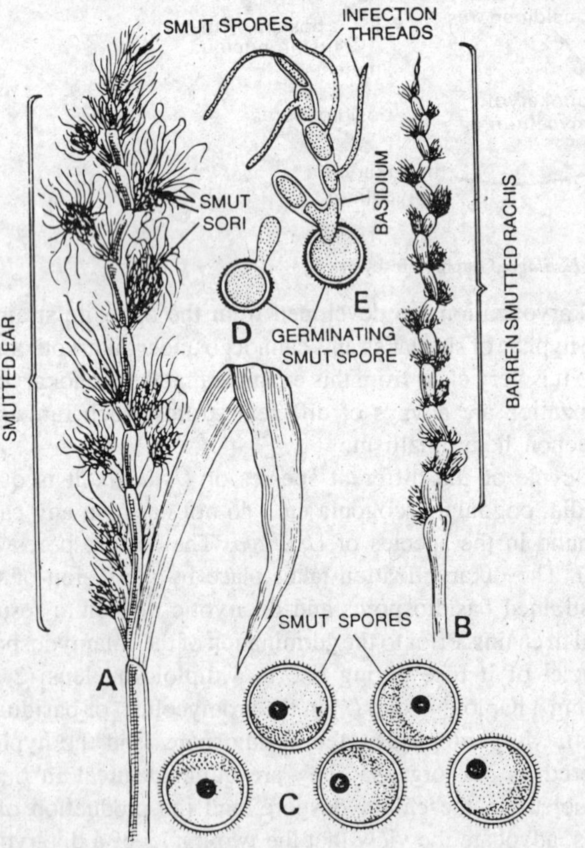

Fig. 12.7. Loose smut of wheat (*Ustilago nuda*). A, smutted ear; B, barren smutted rachis; C, smut spores; D-E, germinating smut spore showing basidium and infection threads.

Symptoms. The symptoms of the disease may be seen only on the emergence of the ears. The black powder is seen in the ear instead of flowers. All the parts of the spikelet convert into smut spores except awns. In the beginning the smut sori are covered with thin silvery membrane, but very soon this membrane disintegrates and the smut spores (chlamydospores) are liberated in the atmosphere. These spores are blown off by wind and other agencies and the rachis remains barren.

Chlamydospore and its germination. The innumerable chlamydospores develop on the mycelium found in the intercellular spaces of the host. The chlamydospores are very minute, round and pale olive in colour. The outer wall of it called exospore is thick and echinulate, whereas the inner wall endospore is thin and smooth. On maturity the two opposite strained nuclei of each chlamydospore fuse and a diploid (2x) nucleus is resulted. The chlamydospores are carried by wind, insects and other agencies to the stigmas of the flowers where they germinate producing basidia or promycelia. The exosporium ruptures and the basidium comes out in the form of a tube.

The diploid nucleus divides twice giving rise to four haploid nuclei. The first division is reductional. The basidium becomes segmented and the four uninucleate cells are produced, two of + and

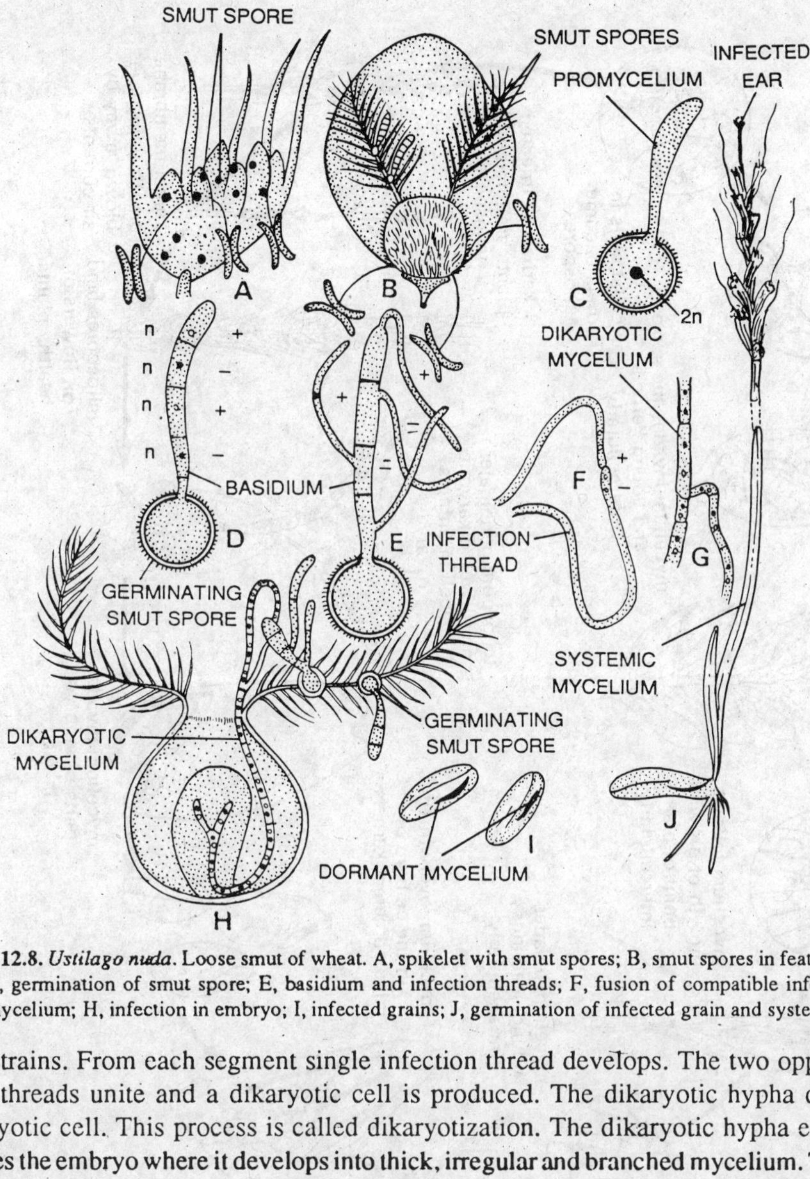

Fig. 12.8. *Ustilago nuda*. Loose smut of wheat. A, spikelet with smut spores; B, smut spores in feathery stigma of the flower; C-D, germination of smut spore; E, basidium and infection threads; F, fusion of compatible infection threads; G, dikaryotic mycelium; H, infection in embryo; I, infected grains; J, germination of infected grain and systematic infection.

two of - strains. From each segment single infection thread develops. The two opposite strained infection threads unite and a dikaryotic cell is produced. The dikaryotic hypha develops from this dikaryotic cell. This process is called dikaryotization. The dikaryotic hypha enters the style and reaches the embryo where it develops into thick, irregular and branched mycelium. The mycelium remains dormant in the embryo. The seeds with dormant mycelia in their embryos look quite healthy in outer appearance.

Germination of infected seeds. The dormant mycelium situated in the embryo of the seed becomes active at the time of the germination of the infected seed and grows along with the apex of the coleoptile. The optimum temperature for the growth of the mycelium ranges from 20°C to 25°C. The fungus is systemic and the mycelium is found throughout in the stem. On the emergence of the ears the mycelium travels in the floral parts and becomes very active. The thousands of chlamydospores are produced in sori on the floral axis. All the floral parts become infected and turned into smut sori, except awns. The haustoria are not produeed on the mycelium. The food is absorbed by diffusion method.

Recurrence of disease. In *U. nuda* the dormant mycelia perennate inside the embryos

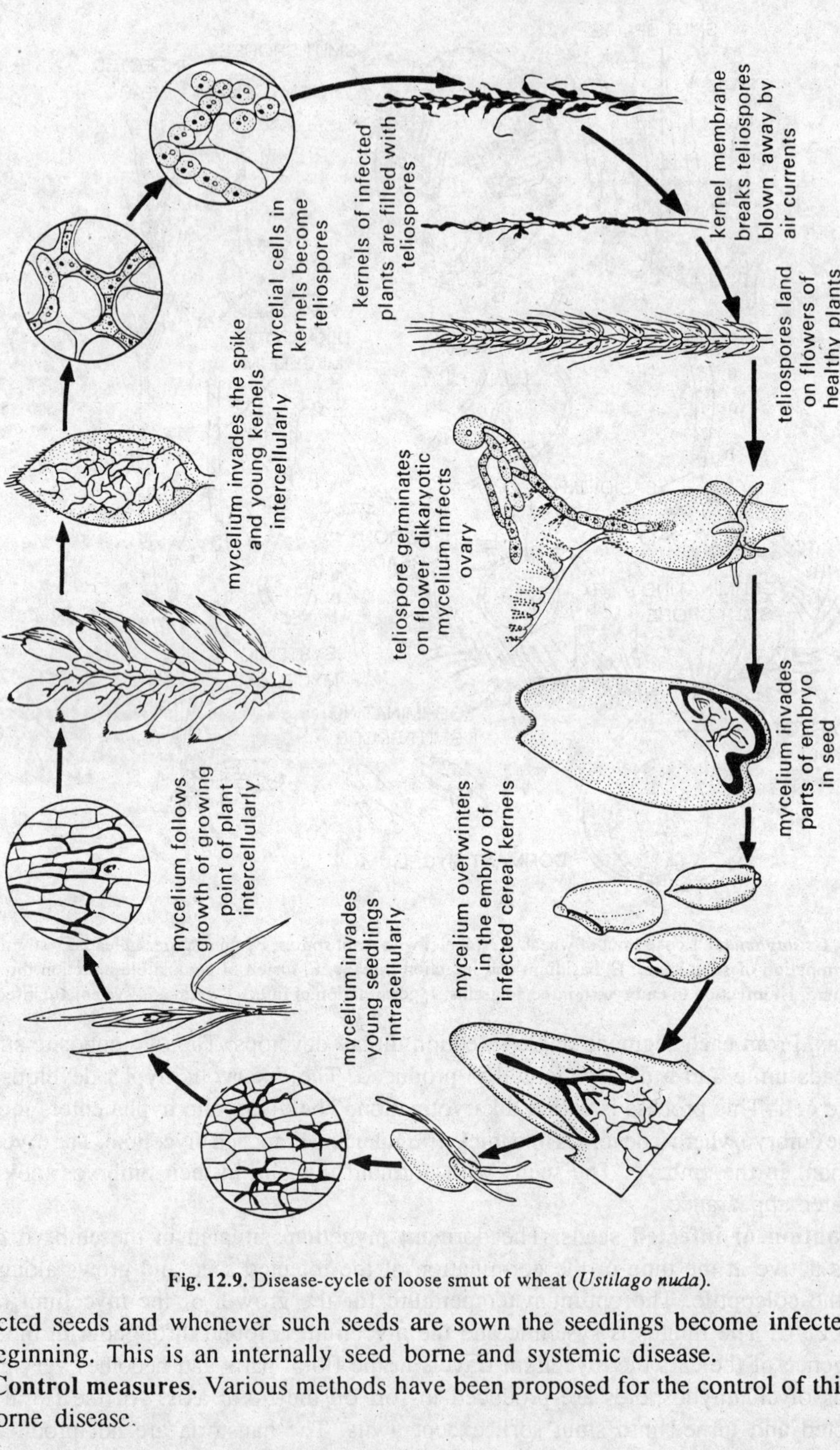

Fig. 12.9. Disease-cycle of loose smut of wheat (*Ustilago nuda*).

of infected seeds and whenever such seeds are sown the seedlings become infected from the very beginning. This is an internally seed borne and systemic disease.

Control measures. Various methods have been proposed for the control of this internally seed borne disease.

1. Rogueing. The infected plants must be uprooted and burnt taking outside the fields. This method of control can easily be practised, because of the earlier emergence of the infected ears from the boot leaves.

2. Seed selection. As this is a seed borne disease, the seeds must be selected from healthy crops.

3. Hot water treatment. To activate the dormant mycelia, the seeds are soaked for four or five hours in the water at normal temperatures ranging fom 26°C to 30°C. Thereafter, the seeds are transferred in hot water at 54°C for ten minutes. The activated mycelium dies at this temperature. These grains may be used as seeds. The temperature of the water should not exceed in any case, because the embryo of the seed dies at 56°C. This method is not practicable in our country because of its complexity.

4. Solar treatment. This is the modification of hot water treatment. Luthra and Sattar proposed this treatment for Punjab, Sind (Pakistan) and Uttar Pradesh. The seeds are soaked in water from 8 a.m. to 12 noon at normal temperatures in the months of May and June. Thereafter the seeds are dried up on the floors in the open sun in very thin layers up to 4 p.m. The dormant mycelium becomes active on soaking the seeds in the water for 4 hours, and dies when the seeds are dried in thin layers in the hot sun and the seeds become disinfected. The method of control may easily be practised in our country.

5. Resistant varieties. This is the simplest and most important method of the control of any disease. Every year many resistant varieties are developed at research centres and distributed to the farmers for sowing purposes.

Systematic Position

	G. W. Martin (1961)	**C. J. Alexopoulos (1962)**	**G. C. Ainsworth (1971)**
Kingdom	–Plantae	–Plantae	–Fungi
Division	–Mycota	–Mycota	–Eumycota
Sub-div.	–Eumycotina	–Eumycotina	–Basidiomycotina
Class	–Basidiomycetes	–Basidiomycetes	–Teliomycetes
Sub-cl.	–Heterobasidiomycetidae	–Heterobasidiomycetidae	–
Order	–Ustilaginales	–Ustilaginales	–Ustilaginales
Family	–Ustilaginaceae	–Ustilaginaceae	–Ustilaginaceae
Genus	–*Ustilago*	–*Ustilago*	–*Ustilago*
Species	–*nuda*	–*nuda*	–*nuda*

Ustilago hordei

(Covered Smut of Barley)

This disease is commonly found in all the countries growing barley.

As soon as the ears of the infected plants come out the first symptoms may easily be seen. The smutted ears come out of leaf sheaths, which may easily be recognized from long distances. All the ears of a diseased plant become infected and all the grains turn into smut sori. The smut sori are always covered with a white, shining, silvery membrane. This membrane is partially developed from host tissue and partially from fungus. Due to this compact covering, the chlamydospores are not blown off, and the disease is called the 'covered smut'.

The silvery membrane of the smut sorus ruptures in the threshing yard, and the released smut spores stick to the rough skinned grains of barley.

Every chlamydospore is rounded, brown and smooth. In masses the spores appear black, but actually they are brown in colour. Whenever, the infected grains of barley germinate, the

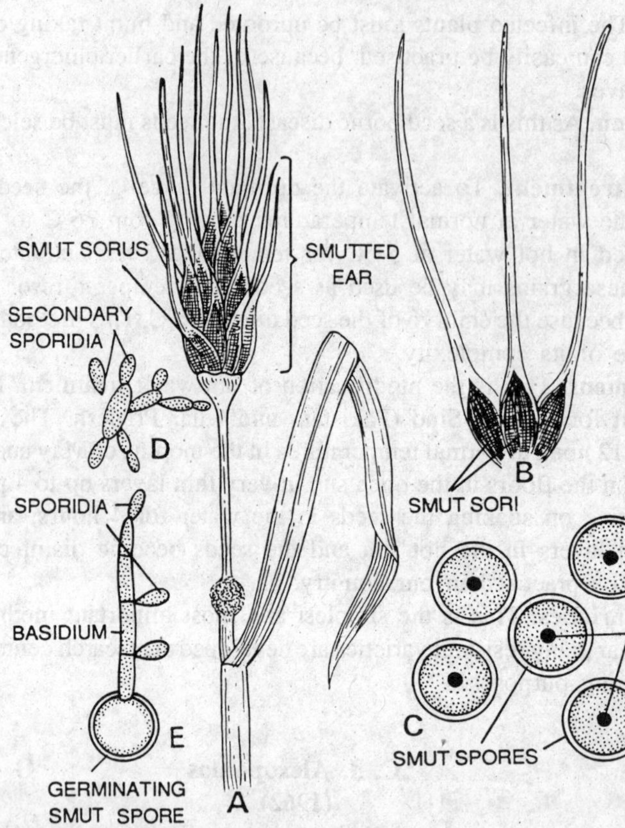

Fig. 12.10. *Ustilago hordei*. Covered smut of barley. A, smutted ear; B, smut sori covered with white silvery membrane; C, smut spores; D, secondary sporidia; E, germination of smut spore producing promycelium and sporidia.

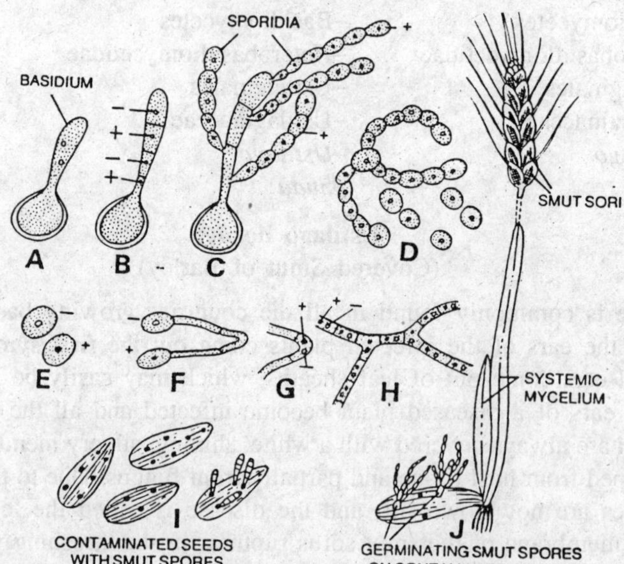

Fig. 12.11. *Ustilago hordei*. Covered smut of barley. A-C, germination of smut spore, and formation of basidium and sporidia; D, secondary sporidia; E-H, process of dikaryotization; I, contaminated grains, smut spores and germinating smut spores; J, germination of contaminated grain and infection.

chlamydospores attached to them germinate simultaneously. Every chlamydospore produces a promycelium or basidium on germination. The diploid nucleus of chlamydospore divides meiotically giving rise to four haploid nuclei. The basidium becomes septate and basidiospores or sporidia are produced on the cells of basidium. From two cells of the basidiospores of + strain and from other two cells the basidiospores of — strain develop. Every sporidium or basidiospore is uninucleate and single celled which produces many spores by budding. The two sporidia of

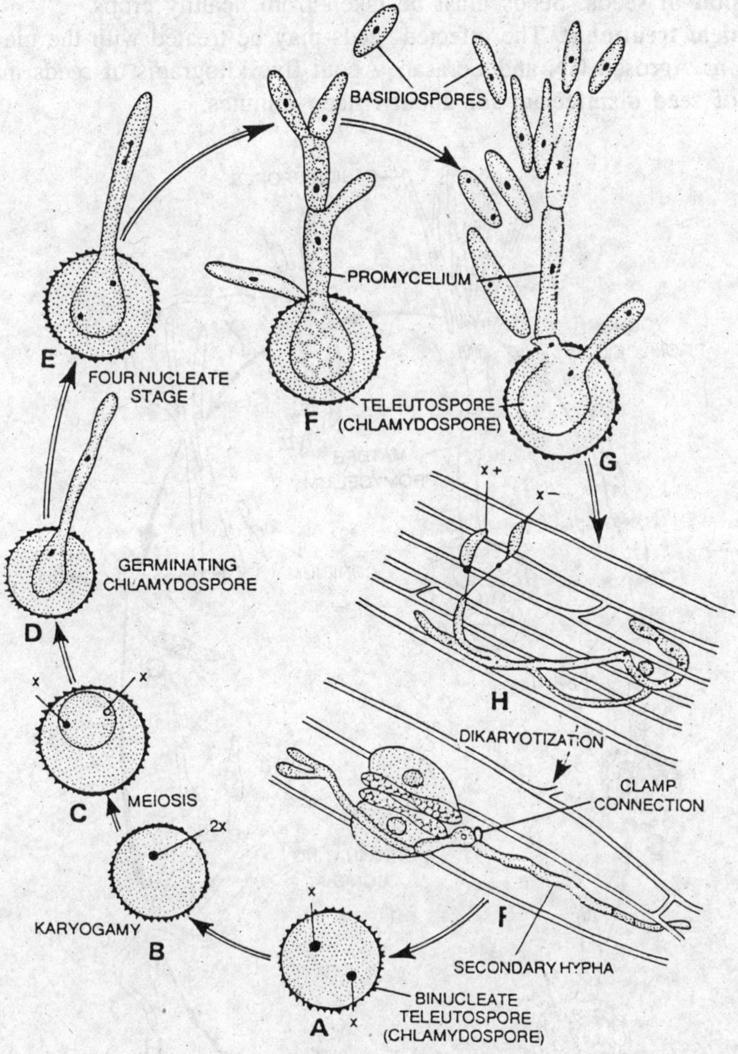

Fig. 12.12. Diagrammatic life-cycle. *Ustilago.*

opposite strains fuse, and a dikaryotic hypha results. This hypha enters the coleoptile through hypocotyl region of germinating seed, and grows upwards in the seedling. The mycelium develops first in stem and on the emergence of ear it becomes most active in floral parts. The mycelium within the floral part becomes closely septate and small cells are developed. The chlamydospores are always protected with thin, shining, white silvery membrane within ovary and are termed as smut sori.

This is an externally seed borne and systemic disease. Every year the disease recurrence takes place by the contaminated seeds. The mycelium develops from the very beginning, along with coleoptile and ultimately reaches the ear.

At the threshing time the smut sori break, the spores come out, and make the seeds contaminated again.

The following control measures have been suggested:

1. **Rogueing.** The infected plants may be uprooted and burnt.
2. **Selection of seeds.** Seeds must be taken from healthy crops.
3. **Chemical treatment.** The infected seeds may be treated with the mercuro-organic compounds such as Agrosan GN and Cerasan. About five kilograms of seeds may be treated with ten grams of seed disinfectant for about fifteen minutes.

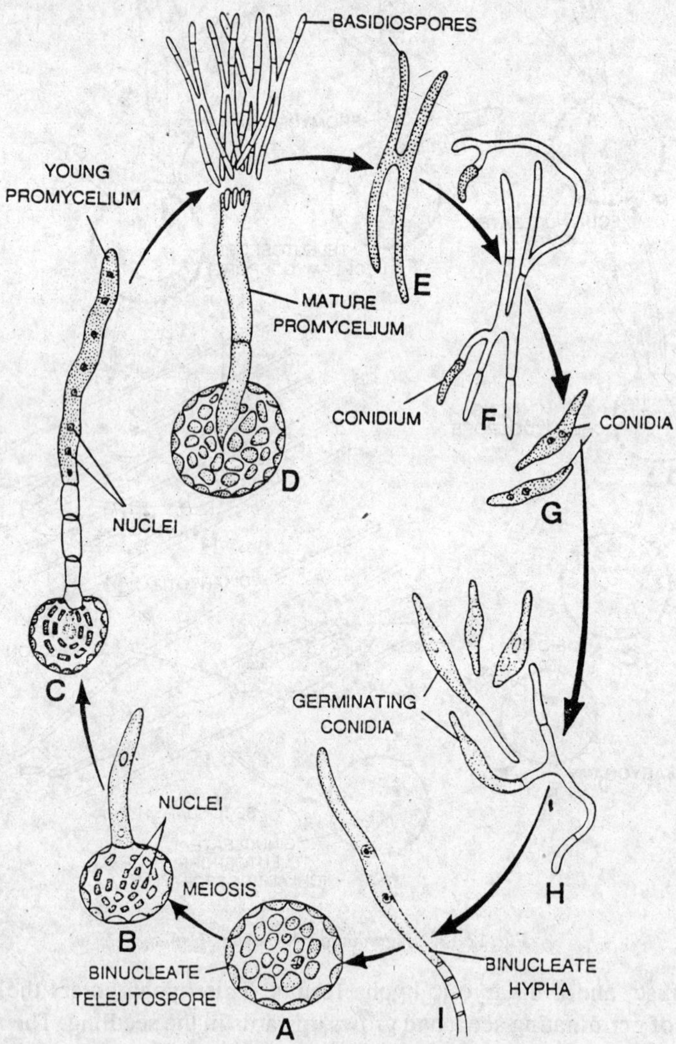

Fig. 12.13. *Tilletia caries*. Diagrammatic life-cycle. A, teleutospores; B, germination of teleutospore; C, formation of promycelium; D, formation of basidiospores and H-pieces; E, H-pieces; F, germination of H-piece and formation of conidia; G, binucleate conidia; H, germinating conidia; I, hypha.

4. **Resistant varieties.** The resistant varieties must be sown.

Systematic Position

	G. W. Martin (1961)	**C. J. Alexopoulos (1962)**	**G. C. Ainsworth (1971)**
Kingdom	–Plantae	–Plantae	–Fungi
Division	–Mycota	–Mycota	–Eumycota
Sub-div.	–Eumycotina	–Eumycotina	–Basidiomycotina
Class	–Basidiomycetes	–Basidiomycetes	–Teliomycetes
Sub-cl.	–Heterobasidiomycetidae	–Heterobasidiomycetidae	–
Order	–Ustilaginales	–Ustilaginales	–Ustilaginales
Family	–Ustilaginaceae	–Ustilaginaceae	–Ustilaginaceae
Genus	–*Ustilago*	–*Ustilago*	–*Ustilago*
Species	–*hordei*	–*hordei*	–*hordei*

Family–**Tilletiaceae**

The basiodiocarps are absent. The promycelium or basidium is non-septate. The basidiospores are found to be borne in a terminal cluster. Genus *Tilletia* has been discussed here in detail.

Genus **TILLETIA** (40 species)

This genus is representative of the genera with epibasidia which are not transversely divided into uninucleate cells. The genus contains about 40 species. This genus causes the bunt of wheat.

Germination of teleutospores. The diploid nucleus of the mature teleutospore undergoes meiosis at the time of germination. A mitotic division typically follows and results in the formation of eight haploid nuclei which migrate into the promycelium. In *Tilletia caries* 8 to 16 nuclei are developed within the short one-celled promycelium. At the apex of the promycelium a number of filamentous cells are produced, each of which contains a single nucleus. The promycelium in contrast to that of Ustilaginaceae, does not become septate. The basidiospores are of at least two strains, half of **A** and half of **a**, factor for sexual compatibility. The basidiospores, which are still attached or after they have been dislodged, copulation tubes are formed between two compatible basidiospores connecting them in H-pieces.

Dikaryotization. Immediately after the formation of H-pieces, plasmogamy follows. It takes place between the two members of H-piece, one protoplast migrating through the tube into the other basidiospore making the cell binucleate. This binucleate cell gives rise in crescent-shaped conidia generally on sterigmata. The nuclei divide conjugately and one pair passes into the conidium. The mycelia delimit binucleate conidia until the available nutrient is exhausted.

Germination of conidium. After their discharge the conidia germinate and develop binucleate mycelia which infect the host. Eventually this mycelium produces the teleutospores (chlamydospores).

Systematic Position

	G. W. Martin (1961)	**C. J. Alexopoulos (1962)**	**G. C. Ainsworth (1971)**
Kingdom	–Plantae	–Plantae	–Fungi
Division	–Mycota	–Mycota	–Eumycota
Sub-div.	–Eumycotina	–Eumycotina	–Basidiomycotina
Class	–Basidiomycetes	–Basidiomycetes	–Teliomycetes

Sub-cl.	–Heterobasidiomycetidae	–Heterobasidiomycetidae	–
Order	–Ustilaginales	–Ustilaginales	–Ustilaginales
Family	–Tilletiaceae	–Tilletiaceae	–Tilletiaceae
Genus	–*Tilletia*	–*Tilletia*	–*Tilletia*

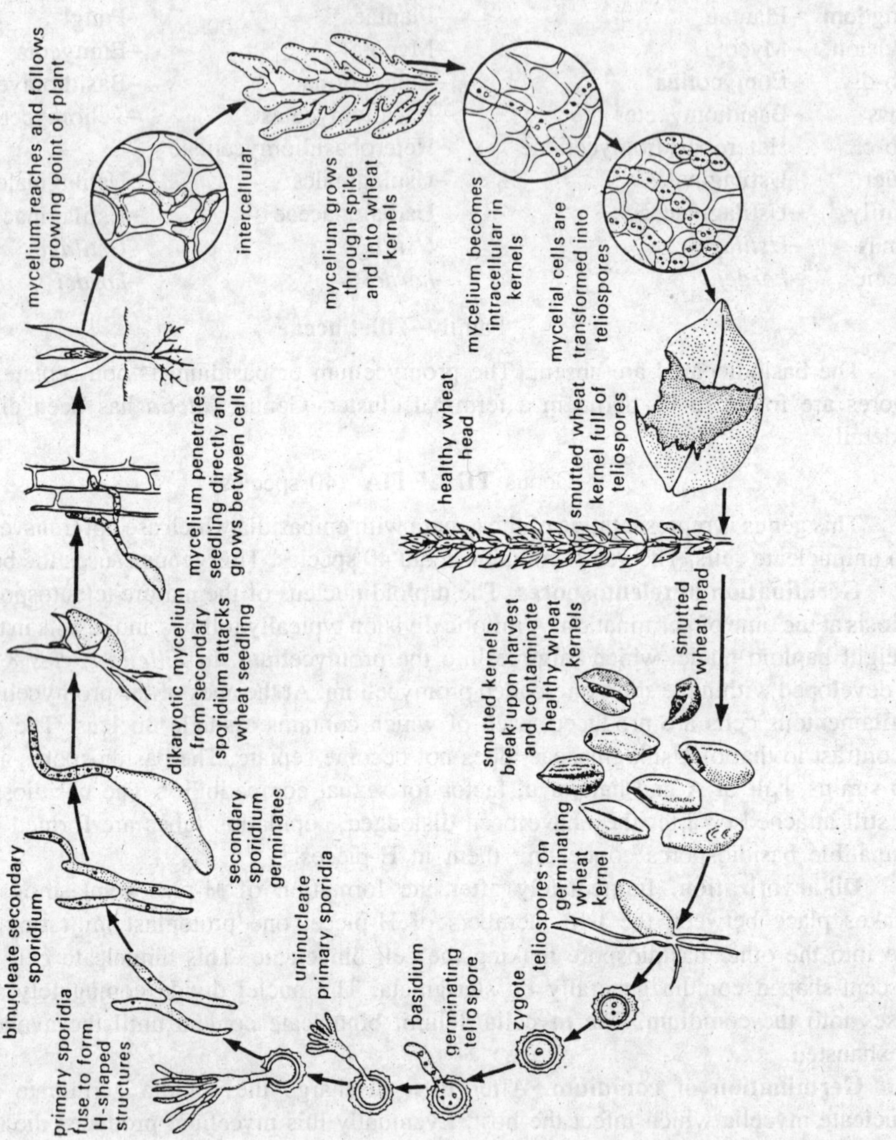

Fig. 12.14. Disease-cycle of bunt of wheat (*Tilletia caries*).

ORDER **UREDINALES** (The Rusts)
(130 genera; 3,600 species)

Characteristic Features

1. This order consists of obligate parasites. They are called the 'rust fungi'.
2. The mycelium is intercellular with round or branched haustoria.

3. Five types of spores are met with in the life histories of various genera of this order. They are pycniospores (o), aeciospores (i), uredospores (ii), teleutospores (iii), and basidiospores or sporidia (iv).

4. The rusts producing many types of spores are known as 'polymorphic' or 'pleomorphic'.

5. Leaving aside basidiospores the rest of the types of spores develop in definite sori, they are, pycnia, aecia, uredia and telia.

6. The rusts may be short-cycled (microcyclic) or long-cycled (macrocyclic)

7. They may be heteroecious (*e.g., Puccinia graminis*) or autoecious (*e.g., Melampsora lini*).

8. During dikaryotization the spermatium (pycniospore) of one strain fuses with the flexuous hypha of opposite strain, and dikaryotization takes place.

Classification. This order is divided into five families, (i) Pucciniaceae, (ii) Cronortiaceae, (iii) Melampsoraceae, (iv) Coleosporaceae, (v) Endophyllaceae.

There are about 130 genera and 4,600 species.

Family–**Pucciniaceae**

The teleutospore forms a septate promycelium (basidium) upon germination. The teleutospores are free or variously united, but never in the form of layer or crusts. The teleutospores

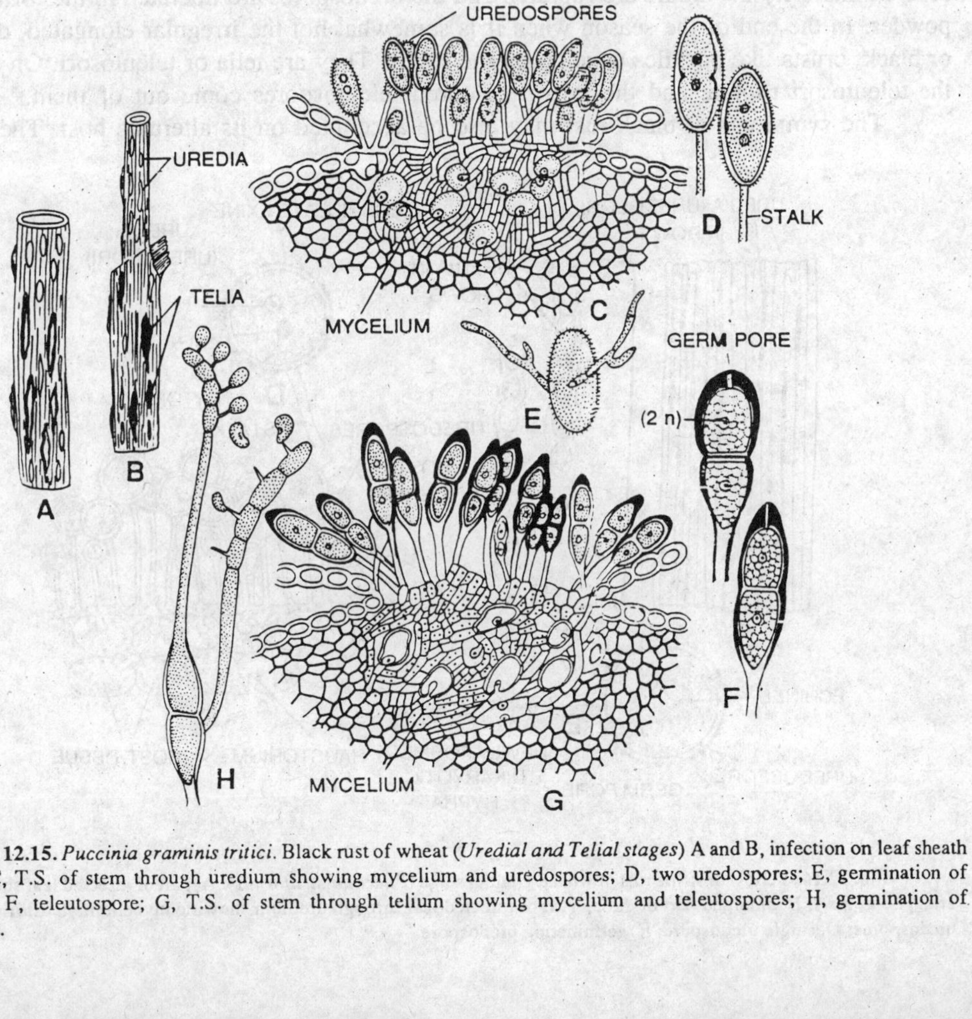

Fig. 12.15. *Puccinia graminis tritici.* Black rust of wheat (*Uredial and Telial stages*) A and B, infection on leaf sheath and stem; C, T.S. of stem through uredium showing mycelium and uredospores; D, two uredospores; E, germination of uredospore; F, teleutospore; G, T.S. of stem through telium showing mycelium and teleutospores; H, germination of teleutospore.

are usually stalked. The promycelium is external. The important genus *Puccinia* has been discussed here in detail.

Genus PUCCINIA (3,000-4,000 species)
(*Puccinia graminis*)

The different species of *Puccinia* cause the diseases known as the rusts on various host plants. *Puccinia* is an obligate parasite which survives only on living host plants. The rusts are known as **rati, ratwa, gerua, gerui, gherir, tombora** in local languages in the different parts of our country. The characteristic feature of rusts is the presence of the pustules of rusty appearance on the surface of the host plants.

In our country the wheat crops are highly infected by the different species of *Puccinia.* The black or stem rust of wheat is caused by *Puccinia graminis tritici;* the yellow or stripe rust of wheat is caused by *Puccinia striiformis;* the brown, orange or leaf rust of wheat is caused by *Puccinia recondita.*

Symptoms. The symptoms of the black or stem rust of wheat (*Puccinia graminis tritici*) are commonly found on the stem but the symptoms also appear on the leaf sheath, leaf blade and even on the ears. The uredia developed by *P. graminis tritici* are oblong and reddish brown which unite to each other. These uredosori or uredia represent the uredial stage of the black rust. On maturity the uredia are ruptured and the uredospores are liberated in the form of brown powder. In the end of the season when it is somewhat hot the irregular elongated, dark brown or black, crusts like pustules develop on the stems. They are telia or teleutosori. On maturation the teleutosori rupture and the brown coloured teleutospores come out of them.

The symptoms of black rust may also be accounted on its alternate host. The groups of

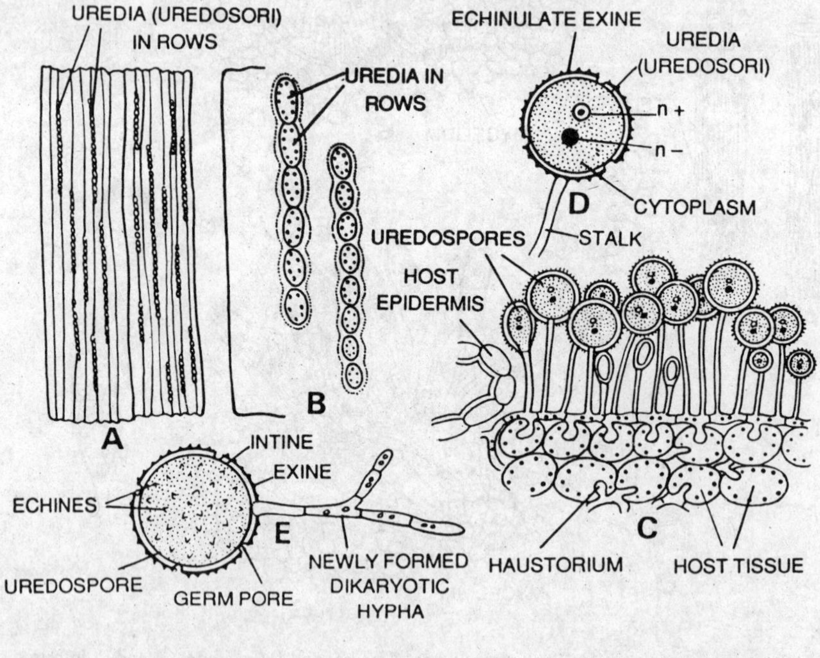

Fig. 12.16. Yellow or stripe rust of wheat. Uredial stage (*Puccinia striiformis*). A, part of infected leaf showing uredia arranged in rows; B, enlarged part of A; C, V.S. of infected leaf through uredium showing mycelium, haustoria and stalked uredospores; D, single uredospore; E, germinating uredospore.

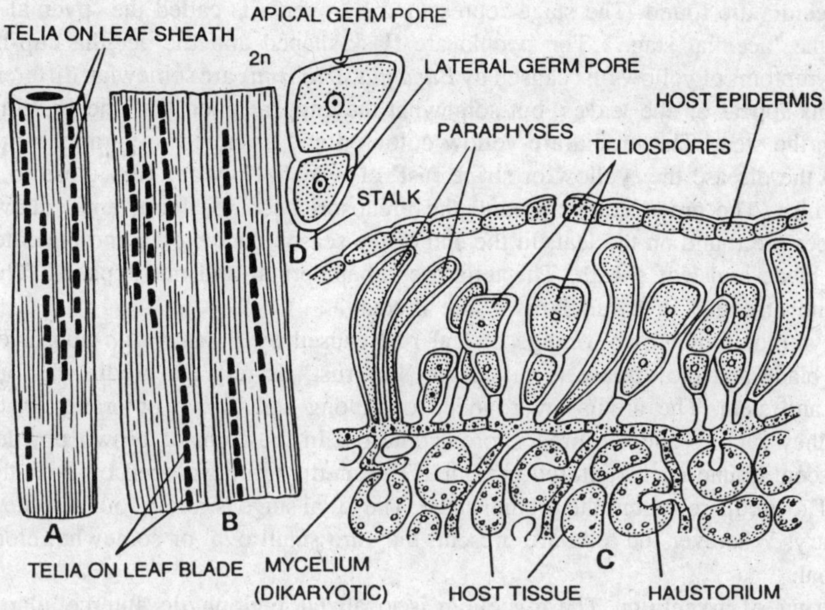

Fig. 12.17. Yellow of stripe rust of wheat (*Puccinia striiformis*). A, telia on leaf sheath; B, telia in stripes on leaf blade; C, V.S. of infected leaf through telium showing its subepidermal state, teliospores, paraphyses, mycelium and haustoria; D, single teliospore.

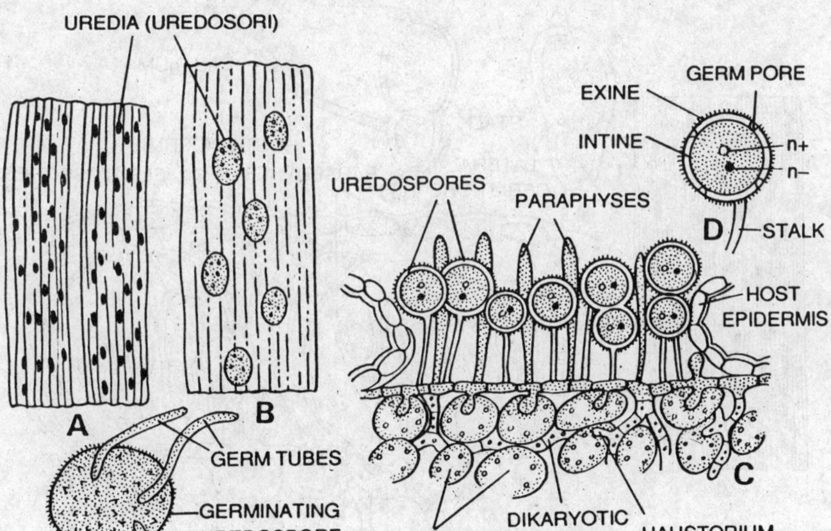

Fig. 12.18. Orange, brown or leaf rust of wheat (*Puccinia recondita*). A, a part of infected leaf with scattered uredia; B, magnified part of same; C, V.S. infected leaf through uredium showing stalked uredospores, paraphyses, mycelium and haustoria; D, single uredospore; E, germinating uredospore.

pycnia are found on the upper surface of *Berberris* leaves, whereas on the lower surface the groups of aecidia are found. The stage represented by pycnia is called the 'pycnial stage' and by aecidia the 'aecidial stage'. The pycnia are flask-shaped and the aecidia cup-like.

The symptoms of yellow rust caused by *Puccinia striiformis* are somewhat different. Usually the symptoms appear on the leaves, but somewhat they appear upon leaf sheath, glumes, awns and even on the stem. The uredia are yellow coloured and arranged in parallel stripes, giving the name to the disease the 'yellow or stripe rust' of wheat. They are very close to each other but do not fuse. The green colour around the uredosori becomes faint, and yellow coloured parallel stripes are found on the leaf. In the end of the season dark brown and black telia appear on the leaf blade and leaf sheath. The telia are subepidermal and not exposed. The telia are elongated and arranged in parallel rows like uredia.

The symptoms of brown, orange or leaf rust caused by *P. recondita* appear exclusively on the leaf blade and the disease is called the 'leaf rust'. Rarely the uredia are found on the leaf sheath and stem. The uredia are rounded or oblong and brown or orange in colour. On maturation they rupture and the uredospores come out in the form of brown powder. Usually a fringe is seen around each ruptured uredium. The uredia are developed on both the surfaces of the leaf. The uredia represent the uredial stage. The telial stage is rarely found in the conditions of our country. Wherever the telia are present, they are small oval or somewhat elongated and sub-epidermal.

Structure of mycelium. The mycelium is localized, endophytic, intercellular, branched, septate and well developed. There is a single central septal pore in each septum for the communication of the cytoplasm from one cell to another. In certain phases of the fungus the mycelium is

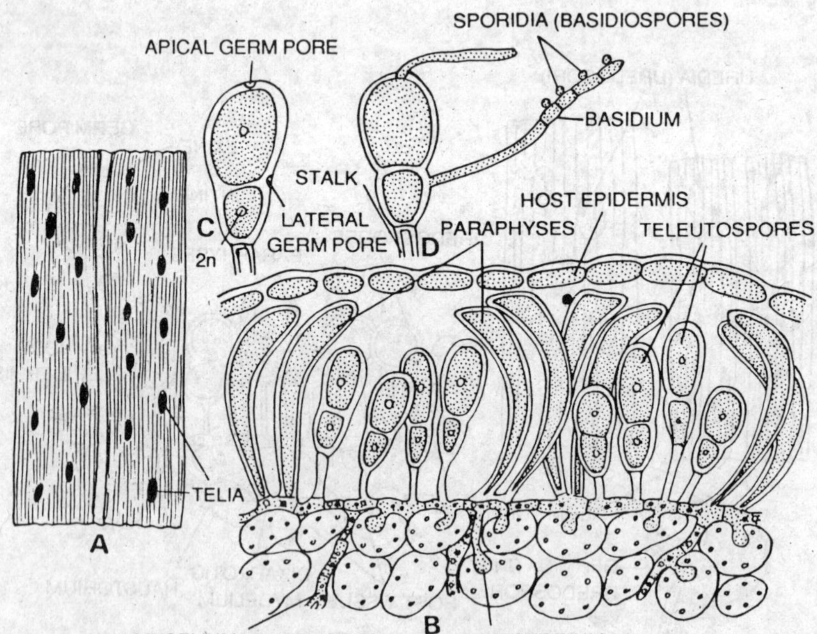

Fig. 12.19. Orange, brown or leaf rust of wheat-telial stage (*Puccinia recondita*). A, a part of infected leaf showing telia; B, V.S. of infected leaf through telium showing teliospores, paraphyses, mycelium and haustoria; C, single teliospore; D, germinating teliospore.

monokaryotic whereas in other phases it is **dikaryotic.** To absorb food material from host cells the haustoria are developed which may be knob-like, finger-like or convolute. In rare cases the hyphae penetrate the cell walls and the mycelium becomes intercellular.

The dikaryotic or secondary mycelium is confined to primary host, *i.e.,* wheat and the monokaryotic or primary mycelium is found on the secondary or alternate host, such as *Berberris* sp., in the case of black rust, and *Thalictrum* sp., in the case of brown rust. The alternate host of yellow rust has not been discovered so far. Such fungi which complete their life cycles on two different hosts, not related to each other in any way, called the **heteroecious** fungi and the phenomenon **heteroecism.** The black rust is heteroecious rust and completes its life-cycle on two different hosts called primary and alternate hosts such as wheat and barberry bushes respectively which are not at all related to each other in any way.

Spores. Several types of spores are found in the life history of *Puccinia graminis tritici.* They are pycniospores, pycnidiospores or spermatia, aeciospores or aecidiospores; uredospores, urediospores or uredeniospores; teliospores or teleutospores and; basidiospores. *Puccinia graminis* is said to be a **polymorphic** fungus, because of the presence of several types of spores and the phenomenon is called the "polymorphism".

Uredospores. The mycelium of *Puccinia* is dikaryotic in the primary host, *i.e.,* wheat. The hyphae accumulate in abundance just beneath the host epidermis. Many vertical hyphae arise from this accumulated mycelium. The terminal cell of each vertical hypha swells and becomes rounded or elliptical. These vertical hyphae are called the sporophores. The terminal cells develop into uredospores. The uredospores always develop in groups or sori called the uredosori. On maturity of the uredospores the host epidermis ruptures due to the pressure exerted by sporophores, and the uredospores liberate outside the uredosori. The uredospores are dispersed by wind and other agencies.

Each uredospore of *Puccinia graminis tritici* is stalked, oblong or elliptical. The exosporium of the spore is echinulate, thick and brown. The four equidistant germpores are arranged on the equator of it. The endosporium is thin and smooth. Each uredospore is dikaryotic (xx).

The uredospores of *Puccinia striiformis* causing yellow rust of wheat are stalked, yellow, round or somewhat oval. The exospore of the spore is hyaline, thick and echinulate. Six to

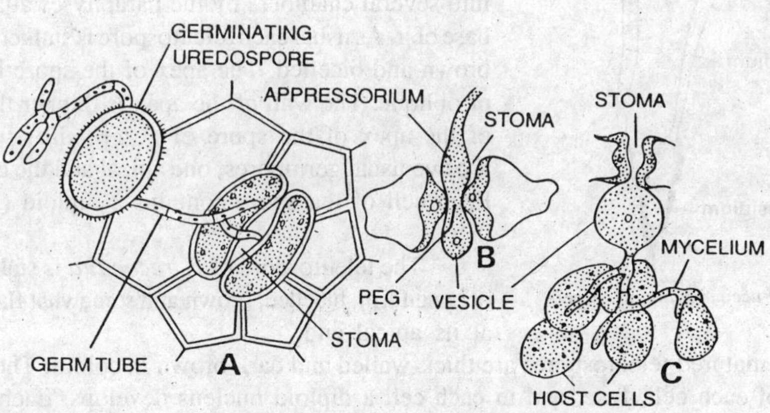

Fig. 12.20. Black or stem rust of wheat (*Puccinia gramins tritici*). A, germination of uredospore on host surface; B, formation of appressorium and vesicle; C, development of mycelium.

ten germ pores are found scattered on the exospore. The endospore is thin and smooth. As usual the spore is dikaryotic (xx).

The uredospores of *Puccinia recondita* causing brown or leaf rust of wheat are stalked, brown and approximately rounded in structure. The exospore is thick, echinuclate and brown. About six germpores are scattered over it. The spore is dikaryotic (xx).

On getting suitable conditions of moisture and temperature for germination, they germinate producing germ tubes. The uredospore germinates on the epidermis of the host. More than one germ tubes come out of the germpores from a single spore. On approaching the stomata these germ tubes form appressoria. From the centre of the appressorium a peg-like structure develops and enters the stoma. The terminal portion of this peg swells into a vesicle. Many branched hyphae arise from this vesicle and ramify in the intercellular spaces of the host tissue, giving rise to normal knob-like or branched haustoria for the absorption of the nutrition from the host cells. The uredial stage is several times repeated prior to the development of teliospores (telial stage) in the same season.

Teleutospores. After the formation of the uredospores for sufficiently a long period on the dikaryotic mycelium, the teleutospores develop in the same sori. These spores are called the **teleutospores,** the stage, **telial stage** and the sori in which the spores develop, the **teleutosori** or **teliosori.** In the transitional stages both the uredospores and teliospores are found in the same sori. But later on the telia develop independently having only teleutospores in them. The telia are dark brown or black coloured.

The telia of black rust (*P. graminis tritici*) are exposed, irregular, elongated, dark brown or black. The crust-like pustules develop on the stems. On maturation, the teleutosori rupture and brown coloured teleutospores are released. Each teleutospore is stalked, dark brown and double celled. The exospore is thick and dark brown in colour. The apex of the teleutospore is either rounded or pointed. There is one germpore at the apex in the upper cell. The lower cell of the spore possesses a lateral germpore. In each cell of a mature teleutospore, there is a conspicuous diploid nucleus (2x).

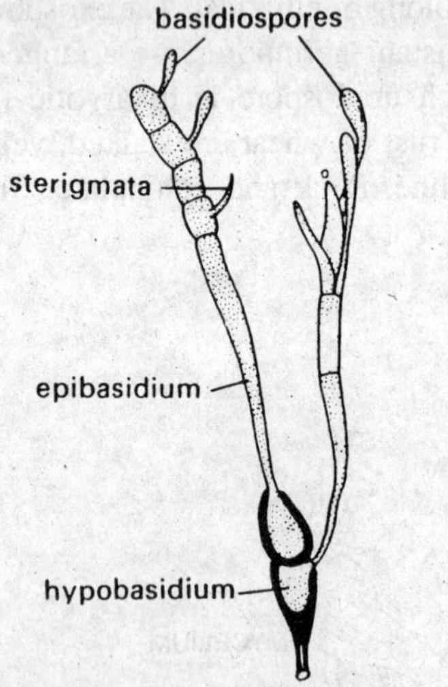

Fig. 12.21. *Puccinia graminis.* A germinating teliospore.

In *Puccinia striiformis* (yellow rust) the telia are sub-epidermal. They are somewhat elongated and arranged in parallel rows like uredia. The telium is divided into several chambers by the paraphyses attached to the base of it. As usual each teleutospore is stalked, elongated, brown and bicelled. The apex of the spore is either flat or oblique. The wall of the apex is thinner than the wall of the apex of the spore of *P. graminis tritici*. There are two usual germpores, one apical and the other lateral. Each cell of the spore contains a diploid (2x) nucleus in it.

The teleutospore of *P. recondita* is stalked, oblong or cuneiform, bicelled, brown and somewhat flat or rounded at its apical end.

The fully matured teleutospores are thick-walled and dark brown in colour. The two nuclei of a dikaryon of each cell, fuse, and in each cell a diploid nucleus develops. Each cell of the mature teleutospore contains a diploid nucleus. After the formation of the teleutospores they need a dormancy period prior to their germination. This is the resting period.

After the harvest, the teleutospores scattered in the soil undergo a period of rest. Prior to germination of the teleutospore the freezing temperature for a long period is essentially an important factor. The teleutospores germinate producing promycelia or basidia on which basidiospores are developed.

On the approach of the favourable conditions, the dormant protoplasm of the resting teleutospores becomes activated and the tubular promycelia or basidia come out of the germpores of each cell of the teliospore. The diploid nucleus is transferred in the basidium where it divides twice giving rise to four haploid nuclei. The first division is reductional. Each basidium becomes segmented forming four uninucleate cells. A sterigma comes out from each of the cells. In the lower three cells, the sterigmata arise just beneath the septa, and in the upper cell at the apex. On the terminal end of each sterigma a small, rounded sporidium or basidiospore develops. A single basidiospore develops on each sterigma and four basidiospores are produced on the basidium, 2 of + strain and two of — strain. The promycelial cells become depleted after the formation of basidiospores. Usually the opposite strained nuclei of the basidium are arranged

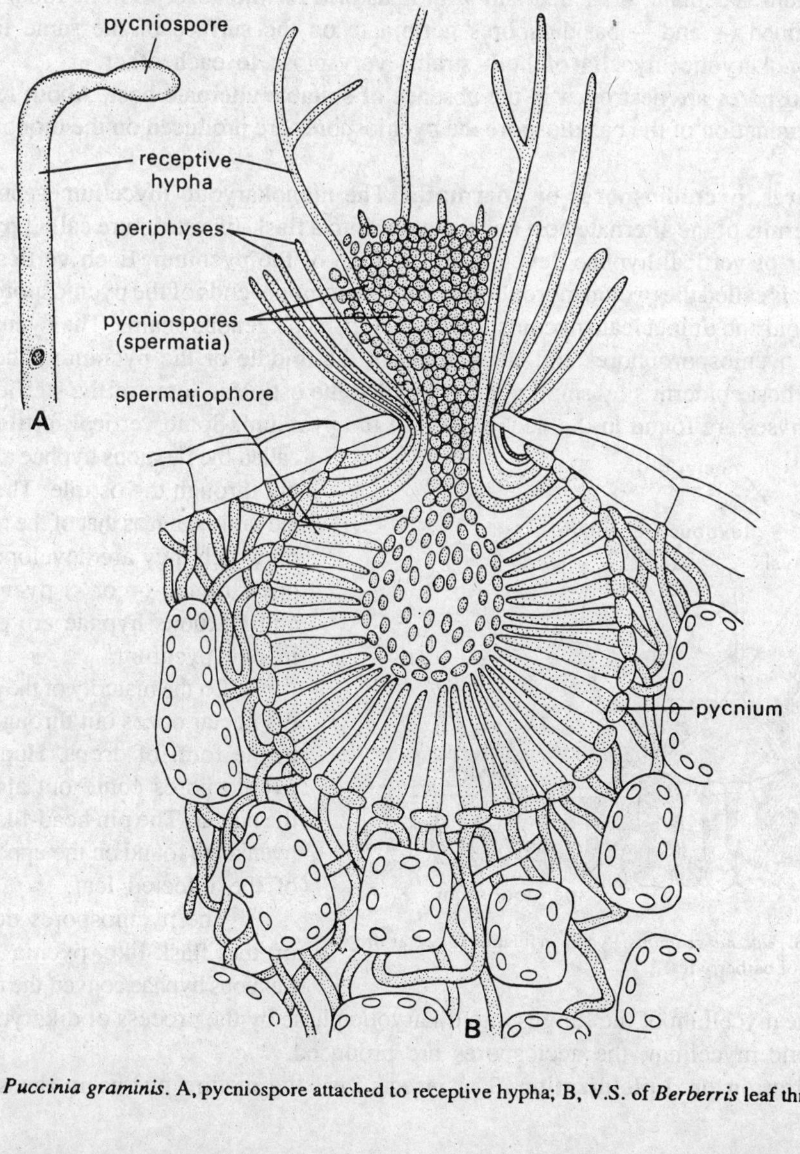

Fig. 12.22. *Puccinia graminis*. A, pycniospore attached to receptive hypha; B, V.S. of *Berberris* leaf through pycnium.

alternately in the segments. *Puccinia* is a heterothallic fungus.

After detaching from the sterigmata of the basidium, the basidiospores are carried over to the alternate host, where they germinate, producing monokaryotic mycelia. The + strained spores give rise to + mycelia and the — to - mycelia. The alternate host of *Puccinia graminis tritici* causing black rust of wheat is *Berberris* sp., and of *Puccinia recondita* causing brown rust of wheat is *Thalictrum* sp. The alternate host of *P. striiformis* causing yellow rust is still unknown. Sometimes when suitable alternate host is not available, these spores give rise to secondary basidiospores which also germinate in the same way. A germ tube comes out from the basidiospore, swells at its terminal end, the nucleus along with cytoplasm transfers to this swelling and the secondary basidiospore develops.

Germination of basidiospore. After reaching the host surface, the basidiospores germinate producing germ tubes. The germ tube directly penetrates the epidermis, enters the host tissue, develops into monokaryotic mycelium which ramifies in the intercellular spaces of the alternate host. The mycelium is septate, branched and with haustoria for the absorption of food. Usually the opposite strained (+ and -) basidiospores germinate on the surface of the same host leaf and produce monokaryotic mycelia of both strains very close to each other.

The basidiospores are destroyed in the absence of suitable alternate host. About four days later after the germination of the basidiospore the pycniospores are produced on the monokaryotic mycelium.

Pycniospores, pycnidiospores or spermatia. The monokaryotic mycelium accumulates beneath the epidermis of the alternate host and develops into a flask-like structure called **pycnium.** A hymenial layer of vertical hyphae develops at the base of the pycnium. Each vertical hypha of this hymenium is called the pycniosporophore. From the terminal ends of the pycniosporophores, round, oval, haploid and uninucleate pycniospores develop in basigenous chains. The pycniospores detach from the pycniosporophores and accumulate in the middle of the pycnium. The pycnia open outside the host epidermis by small openings called the ostioles. Some of the sterile hyphae called the paraphyses are found in the neck region of the pycnium. Some vertical fertile hyphae called the flexuous hyphae also come out through the ostiole. They are of the same strain as that of the mycelium on which they are developed. Only one strained (+ or -) pycniospores and flexuous hyphae are produced in one pycnium.

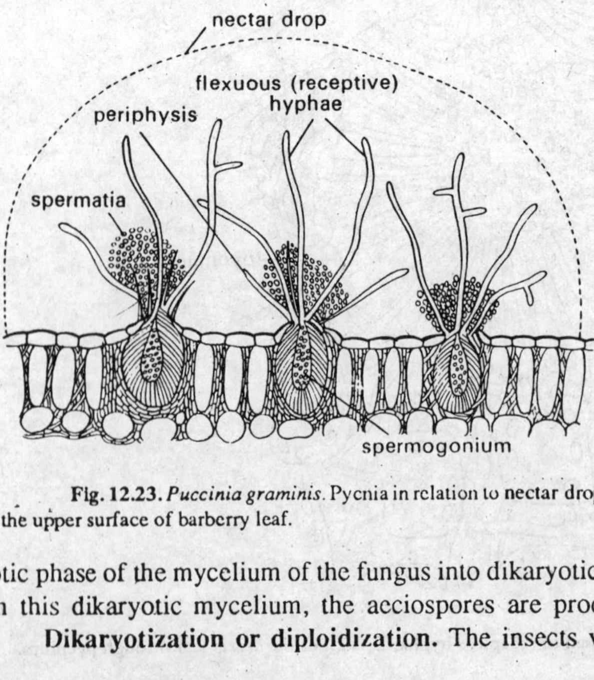

Fig. 12.23. *Puccinia graminis*. Pycnia in relation to nectar drop on the upper surface of barberry leaf.

On the maturity of the pycnium, the nectar oozes out through ostiole in the form of drops. Hundreds of pycniospores come out along with the nectar. The pin head-like yellow pycnia are found on the upper surface of the infected leaf.

The pycniospores developed in the flask-like pycnia and the flexuous hyphae convert the monokaryotic phase of the mycelium of the fungus into dikaryotic phase by the process of dikaryotization. On this dikaryotic mycelium, the acciospores are produced.

Dikaryotization or diploidization. The insects visit the mature pycnia in the search of nectar oozing out through the ostioles. The pycniospores found around the ostioles stick to their legs and proboscis and are transferred from one pycnium (+) to another (-). When the opposite strained pycniospores and the flexuous hyphae come in contact, the wall of contact dissolves and the nucleus of pycniospore moves downward in the flexuous hypha through septal pores.

Simultaneouly, just beneath the pycnium, on the lower surface of the same leaf, the monokaryotic mycelium accumulates in the substomatal chamber and intercellular space. The aecidia are produced from this mycelium, after dikaryotization, and thus called the aecidial primordia or protaecia. The nuclei of the pycniospores, after passing through the pores reach in the cells of the protaecia and dikaryotize all of them.

Besides this phenomenon, sometimes the pycniospores fuse with the sterile paraphyses. Sometimes, the opposite strained monokaryotic hyphae found in the intercellular spaces fuse with each other and the dikaryotization takes place. The nuclei of the cells of one hypha are transferred into the adjacent cells of opposite strained another hypha.

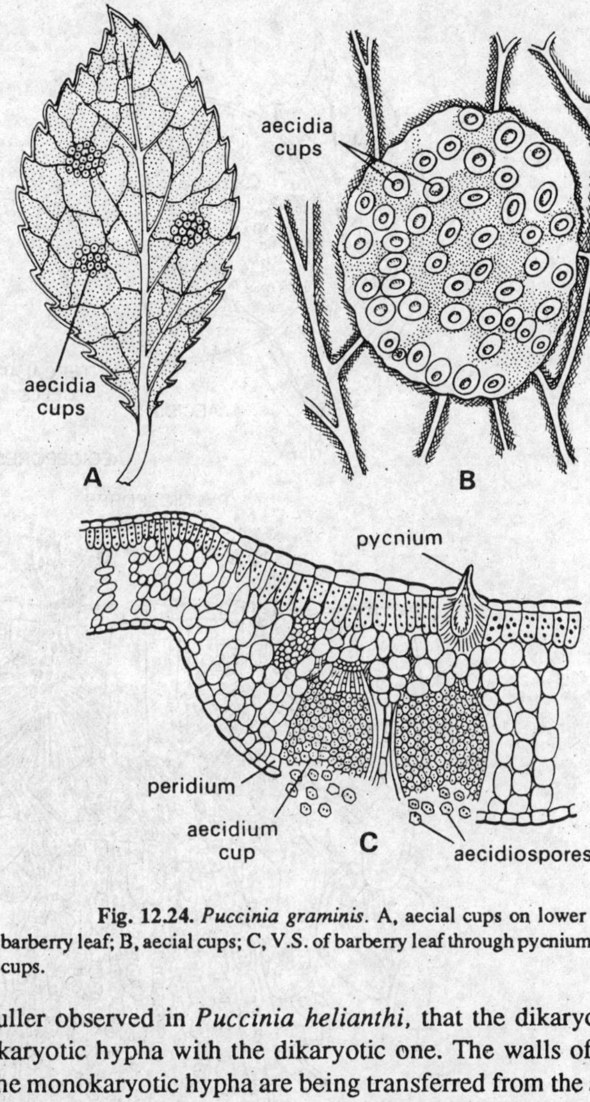

Fig. 12.24. *Puccinia graminis*. A, aecial cups on lower surface of barberry leaf; B, aecial cups; C, V.S. of barberry leaf through pycnium and aecial cups.

The great mycologist, A. H. R. Buller observed in *Puccinia helianthi*, that the dikaryotization takes place by the fusion of monokaryotic hypha with the dikaryotic one. The walls of contact dissolve, and the nuclei lacking in the monokaryotic hypha are being transferred from the adjacent cells of the dikaryotic hypha, and dikaryotization takes place. This special process of dikaryotization is known as **Buller phenomenon.**

Aeciospores or aecidiospores. Just after dikaryotization the hyphae of protaecia form a stromatic layer. The cells of the stroma become dikaryotic. They are surrounded by the monokaryotic hyphae and a pseudoparenchymatous structure is developed. The basal cells of this pseudosparenchymatous structure are somewhat longer than the lower cells. All the cells are monokaryotic.

The dikaryotic cells surrounded by pseudoparenchyma develop vertically elongated downwards in a thick stromatic layer, called the **hymenium.** The hymenium consists of aeciospore mother cell. The aeciospores develop first from the cells of the central region and afterwards from peripheral region of the hymenium. From the outermost mother cells of the hymenial periphery several cells are developed. The lateral walls of these cells fuse to each other and the peridium is developed. The cells of the peridium divide continuously in the transverse plane, increasing the height of

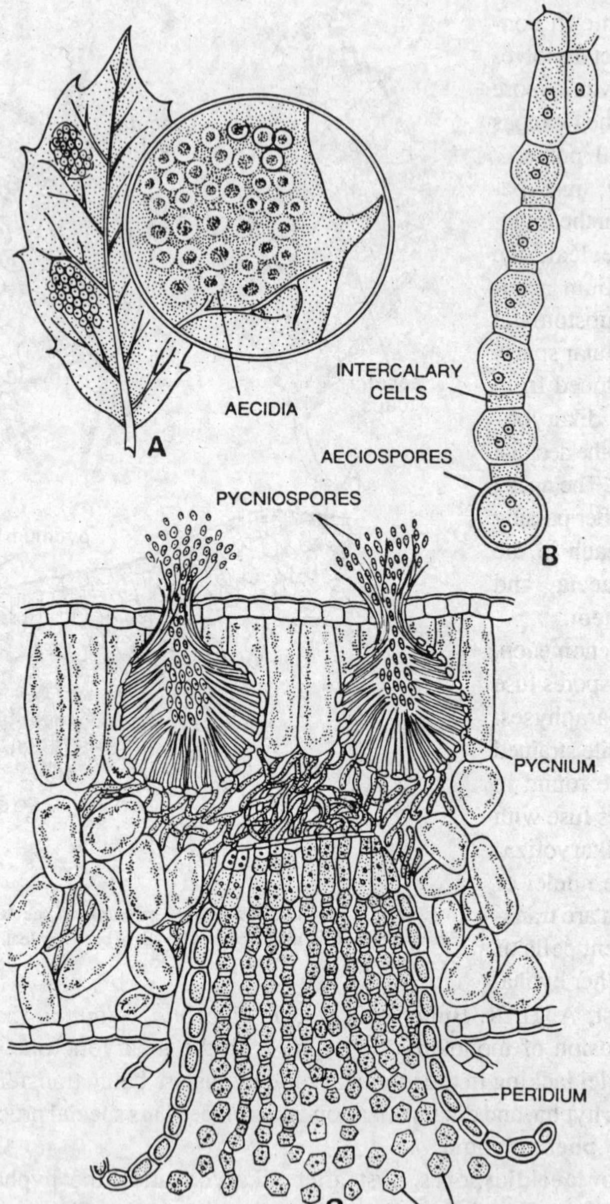

Fig. 12.25. *Puccinia graminis tritici* on *Berberris*. Black rust of wheat. A, infected leaf of *Berberris* showing aecidia; B, a chain of aeciospores; C, V.S. of infected *Berberris* leaf through pycnia and aecidium.

the peridium. The aeciospore mother cells elongate and divide at their apical ends giving rise to a layer of the cells at their apices. The terminal cell separates from the aeciospore mother cell by a septum and two cells develop one larger in size and the other smaller. The terminal large cell develops into the aeciospore whereas the smaller cell acts as intercalary or disjunctor cell. The intercalary cells are sterile. The nucleus of aeciospore mother cell divides again and again giving rise to the basigenous chain of aeciospores and intercalary cells. On the maturation

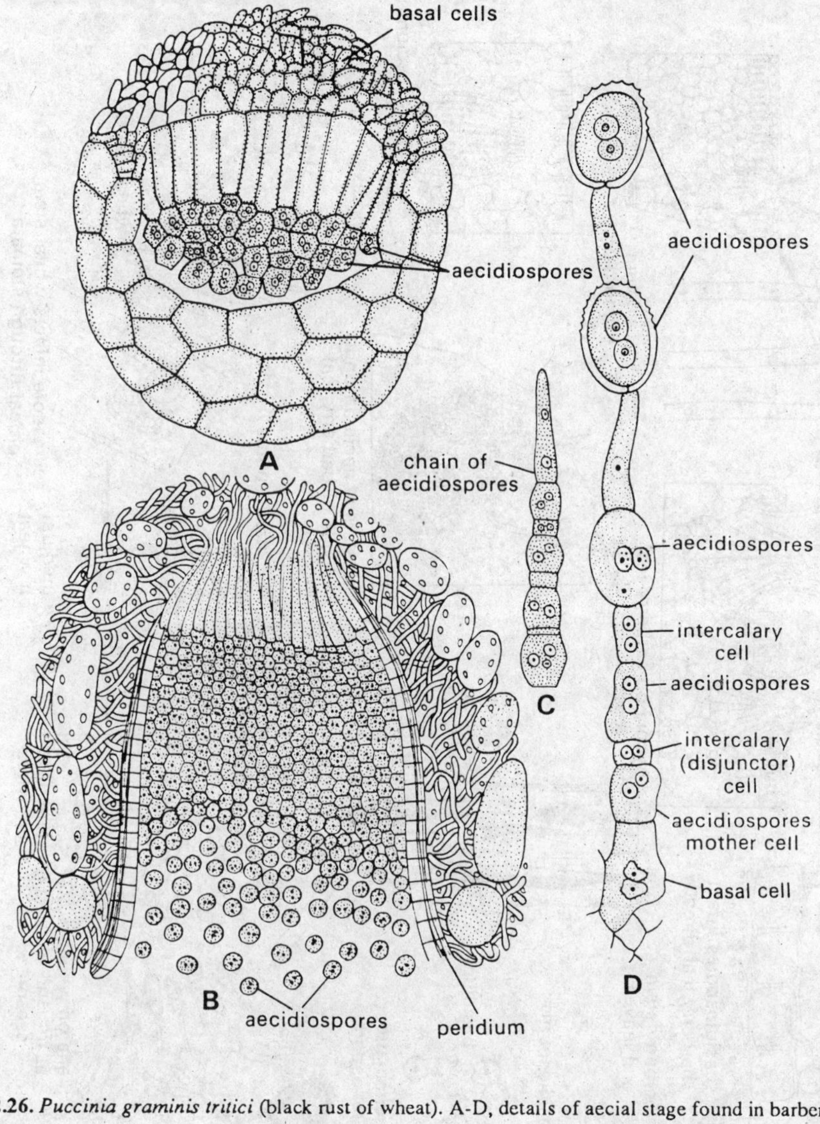

Fig. 12.26. *Puccinia graminis tritici* (black rust of wheat). A-D, details of aecial stage found in barberry leaf.

of the aeciospores, the intercalary or disjunctor cells degenerate and the aeciospores become free.

The aeciospores develop first in the centre and thereafter in the peripheral region, and, therefore, the hymenial layer is thicker in the central region than the periphery and a dome-shaped structure covered by peridium is formed. Very soon the peridium ruptrues, due to the pressure exerted by the aeciospores and the whole structure called aecidium looks like a bell. The aeciospores are dispersed by wind, insects, water and other suitable agencies.

Each aeciospores is rounded, unicellular, dikaryotic (xx) and double walled. The exospore is smooth or sometime echinulate. One or more germ pores are found on it. They are orange coloured and become polygonal because of mutual pressure.

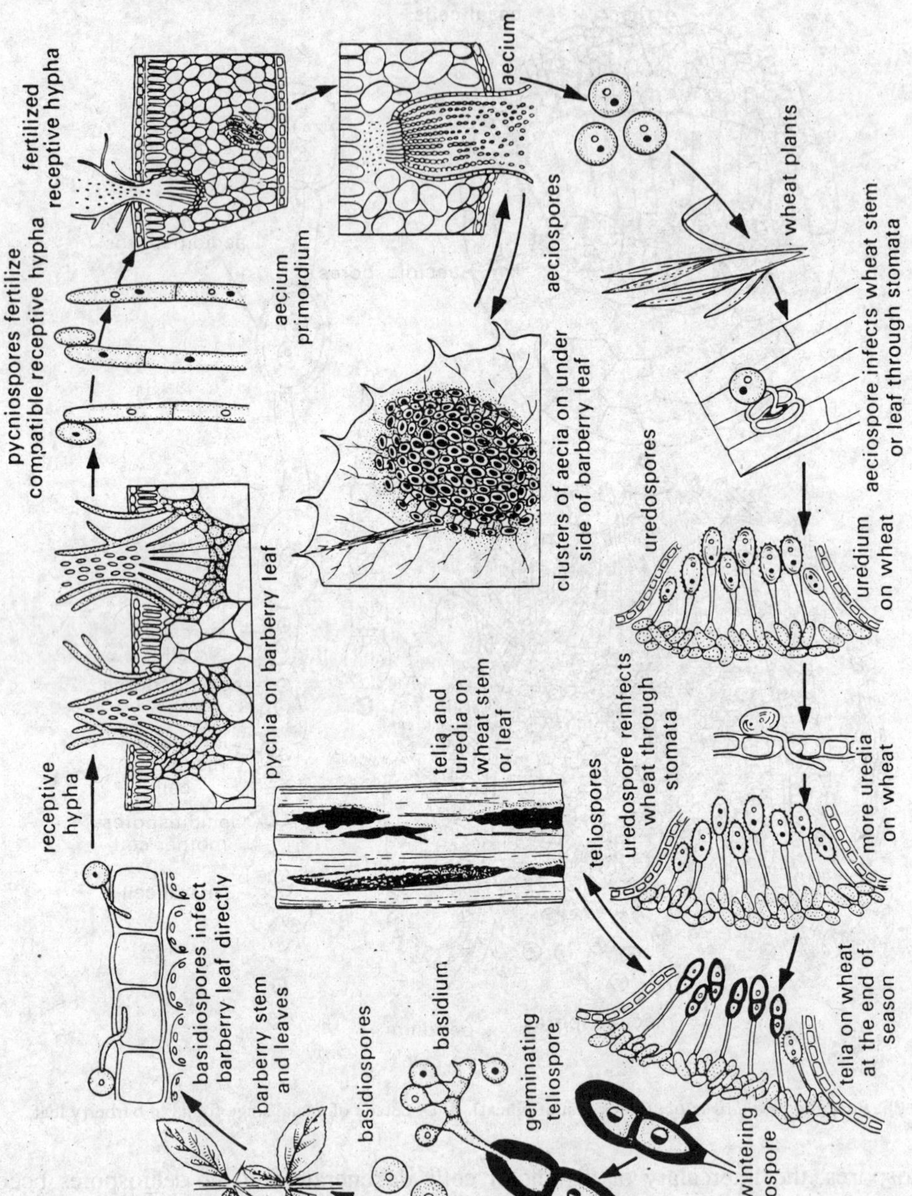

Fig. 12.27. Disease-cycle of black or stem rust of wheat caused by *Puccinia graminis tritici*.

The aeciospores do not infect the host on which they are produced. They infect the primary host. In the case of *Puccinia graminis tritici* aeciospores produced on *Berberris* sp., infect the wheat plants and not *Berberris* in any case. The aeciospores germinate producing a germ tube which comes out through the germ pore and enters the stoma of host leaf where it develops, into new mycelium. The mycelium ramifies in the intercellular spaces of the host tissue. It is dikaryotic and branched. This is secondary mycelium, this dikaryotic mycelium produces uredospores and teleutospores in usual way.

The life-cycle of *Puccinia graminis tritici* completes on two different hosts called primary and secondary or alternate hosts and therefore, this is a heteroecious fungus. The uredial and telial stages are found on the primary host, the basidiospores are found in the soil, and the pycnial and aecidial stages are found upon the alternate host.

Systematic Position

	G. W. Martin (1961)	C. J. Alexopoulos (1962)	G. C. Ainsworth (1971)
Kingdom	–Plantae	–Plantae	–Fungi
Division	–Mycota	–Mycota	–Eumycota
Sub-div.	–Eumycotina	–Eumycotina	–Basidiomycotina
Class	–Basidiomycetes	–Basidiomycetes	–Teliomycetes
Sub-Cl.	–Heterobasidiomycetidae	–Heterobasidiomycetidae	–
Order	–Uredinales	–Uredinales	–Uredinales
Family	–Pucciniaceae	–Pucciniaceae	–Pucciniaceae
Genus	–*Puccinia*	–*Puccinia*	–*Puccinia*

Puccinia graminis tritici is a **heteroecious** rust, requiring two host plants, barberry and wheat. The pycnial (0) and aecidial (1) stages are found on the alternate host, the barberry, whereas the uredial (2) and telial (3) stages develop on the wheat. The sporidia or basidiospores (4) develop in the soil.

Life-cycle of *Puccinia* sp., and rust recurrence in India. The life-cycle of the pathogens causing rusts of wheat is interesting and complicated. They usually pass their life-cycle on two different hosts, wheat and barberry (black rust) or *Thalictrum* (brown rust) which are abundantly found in hilly regions but in India this course is not followed by the rust pathogens. The knowledge regarding the rust cycle in India was solely due to the researches carried out by K. C. Mehta. He showed that barberry shrub plays insignificant role in causing initial outbreaks of black rust in the plains. The summer heat in the plains that follows the wheat harvest kills all the uredospores of the three rusts. Consequently there is no local source of infection when the crop is sown in the plains in the next season. On the other hand in the hills all the three rusts have been found to over summer on stubbles, self-sown wheat and out of season crops at different altitudes ranging from 4,000 to 8,000 feet above sea-level. Crops in the hills get infected rather early in the season in the neighbourhood of these rusted volunteer self-sown wheat plants and the spores are then disseminated and carried down by the air currents to the foot of the hills where they cause infection to the crop present there, and from this the crops in the plains get infected. In general, rusts appear earlier in places at the foot of hills than those situated farther away in the plains. Spores of all these three rusts have been caught on aeroscope slides at a large number of stations in the plains before the appearance of the rusts showing clearly that the spores of rusts are introduced in the plains by wind coming either from the hills or passed over areas where rusts had appeared earlier.

In addition to over summering in the hills on self-sown wheat plants two important foci exist according to Mehta where due to early crop there is plenty of rust every year at the time wheat is sown in the neighbouring plains. These are central Nepal in the north and the Nilgiri and Palini hills in the south. The infection focus in Nepal is important for Uttar Pradesh as it is source of disease in the crops of the plain along the Nepal border.

Recent work. In 1974, L. M. Joshi and his associates reported that black rust develops at an early date in south India which then serves as inoculum reservoir in the form of uredospores for rest of the country.

Brown rust of wheat has two foci of infection, the Himalayas in the North, and Nilgiri and Palini hills in the South. It is the most widely prevalent rust. The uredospores get transported by upper winds from Nilgiris and Palini hills and then are washed down over Central India (Madhya Pradesh) by rains. The northern infection moves slowly southwards until the two populations merge.

The air borne inoculum of brown rust as well as black rust and its deposition from southern hills (Nilgiri and Palini hills) has been traced by wind trajectories and weather satellite cloud images. From recent investigations of Nagarajan and Singh (1975), it appears that the Tropical cyclones have a great bearing on the deposition of spores in Central India (Madhya Pradesh) within a time span of about 70 hours. The cyclonic disturbances occurring in the Bay of Bengal/ Arabian Sea in late October or early November set a pattern of favourable winds which carry the inoculum (uredospores) of black and brown rusts from Southern foci to the target area in Madhya Pradesh along with rain clouds. It has been found that the invisible spore cloud movement can be successfully tagged with the visible cloud movement seen in satellite television cloud photographs. This method has shown that the uredospores are transported from Nilgiris by upper air wind and are deposited over Central India (Madhya Pradesh) along with rain. From these secondary foci, it spreads to other foci making a nation-wide appearance.

Yellow rust is restricted in its distribution and appearance in epidemic form only to north-western regions. Normally the rust appears in the foot-hills and plains in December or first fortnight of January, when conditions in plains are favourable and rapid multiplication of inoculum (uredospores) takes place.

Spread of disease. The initial infection of few odd plants in any field in the plains is sufficient to spread the disease. The disease soon spreads from one field to another by the dissemination of spores by air currents. Every rust pustule contains 30,000 to 80,000 spores and each such spore (uredospore) is capable of causing infection. They are easily carried away by wind and lodge on leaf and other green surface of the plant. In presence of moisture, the spores germinate and cause infection. The new pustules are developed within 10-14 days of infection. Usually four or five short cycles are repeated during the season. The greater the number of these short cycles, the greater would be the damage to the crop.

The multiplication and spread of the rusts in the plains depend on the weather conditions specially the rain or heavy dew on the leaves of the wheat plants. Heavy dew for a long period or rain, moderately high temperatures and strong wind for dissemination of spores on the susceptible varieties are the important factors for rust epidemics.

Loss due to rusts. Rust pustules cover a greater part of photosynthetic area and thus hinder the plant in its food manufacturing process. When pustules burst through the epidermis, the water is lost by transpiration resulting in partial sterility, poorly filled ears and shrivelled grains. If rust becomes severe before milk stage of the crop, the losses are always great even resulting in crop failures.

Comparison of the Symptoms of Three Wheat Rusts

Table: 12.1.

Black rust (*Puccinia graminis tritici*)	**Yellow rust** (*P. striiformis*)	**Brown rust** (*P. recondita*)
Attacks the stem most severely, than the leaf sheaths leaf lamina and ears.	Attacks the leaf lamina most severely, stem and ears.	Attacks the leaf lamina almost exclusively, rarely the sheaths. very rarely the stems.
Uredosori large elongated running together and bursting early forming the large fragments of the epidermis in doing so. Colour dark brown, becoming darker gradually as teleutospores are formed in the same sori (pustules). Found on all green parts of the plants.	Uredosori (uredopustules) small, oval, do not usually run together, burst late and with little fringes of the epidermis. Almost always arranged in long stripes. Colour lemon yellow. Found on all green parts of the plant.	Uredosori (uredopustules) small but often larger than in yellow rust, oval or round do not usually run together, burst early with a fringe of broken epidermis around them. Always scattered the surfaces of leaf lamina. Colour bright orange when fresh. Found chiefly on upper surface of leaves.
Telia or teleutosori (teleutopustules) much elongated and black in colour. Burst rather early. Found on all green parts of the plants, but least on the leaf blades.	Telia or teleutosori (teleutopustules) like uredosori but more flattened dull black, and often run together. Donot burst through the epidermis (subepidermal). Arranged in rows. Found chiefly on under surface of leaves but also on all green parts of the plants..	Teleutosori (teleutopustules) often absent, when present resemble uredosori (uredopustules) but more flattened and dull black. Do not burst through the epidermis (sub-epidermal). Found chiefly on under surface of leaves, very rare else where.

Physiologic races. Stakman (1926) and his co-workers have defined physiologic specialization as "presence of entities within morphologic species, not readily distinguishable by structure, but differing from each other physiologically". These entities are–pathogenicity, host morphology, biochemical properties, cultural variability, spore germination and ecological relationships. These entities have been designated variously such as–physiologic races, biologic species, biologic forms, specialized races, parasitic strains, racial strains, physiologic forms, etc. Each physiologic race is denoted by a specific number such as–*Puccinia graminis tritici* 15, Eriksson (1894) termed these races as '*formae speciales*'. Specialization of parasitism of an extreme type is known as *biotype* and is denoted by an epithet such as 42A, 42B, etc.

Since 1930, twenty physiologic races and eight biotypes of black rust (*Puccinia graminis tritici*–11, 14, 15, 17, 21, 24, 34, 40, 42, 72, 75, 117, 122, 184, 194, 196, 222, 295, X and Y, 15-C, 21-A, 21-A-1, 21-A-2, 34-A, 42-A, 42-B, 117-A), seventeen physiologic races and three biotypes of brown rust (*Puccinia recondita*–10, 11, 12, 16, 17, 20, 26, 61, 63, 70, 77,

106, 107, 108, 131, 162 and race D; 162-A, 162-B and 107-A), and fourteen physiologic races of yellow rust (*Puccinia striiformis*–13, 14, 19, 20, 24, 31, 38, 57, A, D, E, F, G, and H) have been identified. In recent years several new races have been identified. New races are known to arise through hybridization, mutation and introduction from neighbouring countries.

However, the barberries do not play any part in the annual recurrence of the rust in India, but they may be instrumental in creating new races by hybridization. Then it becomes necessary to eradicate the barberry bushes from pockets of infection in the hills.

Control measures. On the basis of the study of the life cycle of the rusts (*i.e.*, black brown and yellow) and their annual recurrence in the Indian plains, a few important methods have been suggested. They are–A, clean-up campaign; B, cultural practices; C, chemical treatment and D, Resistant varieties.

A. *Clean-up-campaign.* In India, K.C. Mehta as a result of his extensive study of wheat rusts (*i.e.*, black, brown and yellow) recommended the vigorous destruction of self-sown plants and tillers which carry over the rusts in uredo-stage and which are responsible for infection of the crop in the plain. He had also recommended the suspension of the first crop (sown during April - June) in Nilgiris and Palini hills and postponement of sowing in the central Nepal to the normal period that is October.

A great doubt has been expressed on the above measures for their practicability and economic soundness. There are certain out of season and self-sown grasses (collateral hosts) which occur on the hills and are affected by the same rust as wheat and barley and they may serve as centres of foci of infection. There are places in the hills which are unapproachable where complete eradication of rusted plants is difficult. There is another factor that seems to mitigate against a thorough clean-up is the short period between the harvest of one season and the sowing of the next which is a monsoon period (July - September) during which it may not be possible to carry the eradication campaign effectively.

B. *Cultural practices.* Certain modification in cultural practices, *viz.*, cultivation of early maturing varieties, early sowing, judicious manuring and irrigation help in minimising the incidence of rusts.

(a) *Cultivation of early maturing varieties.* Varieties of wheat which mature early should be sown so as to avoid the critical period that is milk stage of the crop from the attack of the rusts, the black rust assumes serious intensity during the month of February and if the crop has passed its milk stage at this time it will suffer negligible losses. There are certain varieties of wheat in Uttar Pradesh which come into full flowering as early as middle of January and thus are able to escape the attack of rust at their critical period. The varieties which come late into full flowering are the worst sufferers of the disease.

(b) *Early sowing.* Sowing of wheat varieties a bit earlier than normal is another good method to escape the severe rust incidence at the milk stage of the crop. The early sown wheat flowers early and also matures early. Even the moderately late varieties when grown early would flower and mature early and would thus escape the severity of the rust at the critical stage.

The best time of wheat sowing in Uttar Pradesh is the later half of October. The wheat can, however, be grown profitably if sown a bit earlier. Early sowing can easily be accomplished where irrigational facilities are available. Late sowings in November and December are never recommended and often result in huge losses in yield due to the severity of rust attacks. The practice of early sowing should, therefore, be adopted to save enormous losses of the valuable national food.

(c) *Proper manuring.* Manuring is an important factor governing the incidence of rusts. Nitrogenous manures in general are known to increase the susceptibility of the crop towards diseases by delaying maturity. The nitrogen requirement for wheat in Uttar Pradesh is about 50 lbs. per acre. Over dosages of nitrogenous manures are therefore, not only uneconomical but induce the crop being affected by rusts. The rust resistance is increased by the application of potassic manures to the crop. Phosphatic manures, *e.g.*, bone meal, superphosphate etc., are good as a top dressing to the wheat crop.

(d) *Proper irrigation*. High humidity favours the rusts and, therefore, irrigation is an important factor which governs the rust appearance. Heavy irrigation at the time of rust appearance only favours the speedy development and spread of rusts. Irrigation therefore, should be given timely and properly. Light irrigation during January and February help in keeping the rusts under control.

C. *Chemical treatment*. The control of rusts by chemicals is not a new idea and dates back to at least 1900. Since then the efficacy of sulphur was proved in the field in Canada and it was recommended that 3 to 5 applications at the rate of 30 lbs. per acre per application would control stem rust and increase the yield from 25 to 100 per cent depending on the severity of the rust. Trials conducted at Kanpur have shown that increase in yield of wheat can be attained by four dustings of finely powdered sulphur (400 meshes per square inch) at the rate of 30 lbs. per acre at the interval of 10 days. Similar results were also obtained in Madhya Pradesh. The cost involved was, however, prohibitive and was not commensurate with the gain. The use of sulphur in the control of rusts on a wide scale, therefore, has never been recommended.

Search for chemicals that would be effective in small quantities has led to the formation of such fungicides as *Dithane, Zineb* and *Actidione*. Extensive tests in different countries indicate that rust can now be controlled economically with the help of these compounds provided that weather conditions do not become very adverse during these operations. Dithane has been used successfully and economically in the control of rusts in Japan. Four to five applications of *Nabam* and *Zinc sulphate* gave effective control of wheat rusts in Canada and the cost of the chemicals was about one-third of sulphur. *Actidione* is a promising antibiotic in the control of rusts as a systemic fungicide. It has been demonstrated that certain sulpha compounds including sodium salts of sulphadiazine, sulphapyrazine, sulphapyridine and gantrisin are effective against black rust even as post infection sprays. Certain naphthoquinones and phenols also exert a fungicidal action at low concentrations on cereal stem rust. Parzate liquid with zinc sulphate has been found to be effective in reducing rust infection appreciably under artificial conditions at I. A. R. I. New Delhi.

D. *Resistant varieties*. The best control of wheat rusts lies in evolving resistant varieties. In India systematic work on the breeding of rust resistant wheats was started by B.P. Pal in 1935 in collaboration with K.C. Mehta and several rust tolerant varieties have by now been released for general cultivation. These varieties have done very well in different states and given much higher yield than the local varieties even under epidemic conditions.

The breeding for resistance and chemical protection must make parallel contribution in order to get the best out of improved varieties. It is much more economical and effective to use the fungicide on resistant varieties than on local varieties. Since the annual rust recurrence in India takes place through the agency of uredospores in the hills, K.C. Mehta had emphasized the importance and urgency of breeding rust resistant varieties and gave priority to the hills which act as foci of infection.

Varieties like HD 2009, HD 2204, HD 2135, HD 2278, HD 2281, Sonalika and WH 147 are resistant to rusts upto some extent.

Family–Melampsoraceae

The teleutospore forms a septate promycelium upon germination. The telutospores laterally united into layers, crusts or columns. The teleutospores are sessile, single-celled and sub-epidermal.

Genus **MELAMPSORA** (80 species)

Melampsora lini is an obligate parasite. It infects linseed and causes 'rust of linseed'. Unlike *Puccinia* it has no alternate host and all the stages in the life-cycle of the rust are found on the same host. The life-cycle is polymorphic or macrocyclic and consists of four stages-pycnial, aecial, uredial and telial. When life cycle is completed on one host it is called **autoecious.**

The leaves and stems of affected plants become covered with bright orange pustules. The pustules are called uredia which contain the uredospores and occur on both sides of the leaves. Later on the elongated brown pustules on the stem turn to black which are called telia and contain teliospores. Telia are observed very rarely on the leaves. The pods also get infected. All parts of the plant except roots are affected by the disease.

Mycelium. The mycelium is intercellular, branched, septate, dikaryotic, and subepidermal, and usually found within the parenchymatous tissues of the host.

The uredosori (uredia) are small, bright orange, scattered or in groups; rounded on leaves

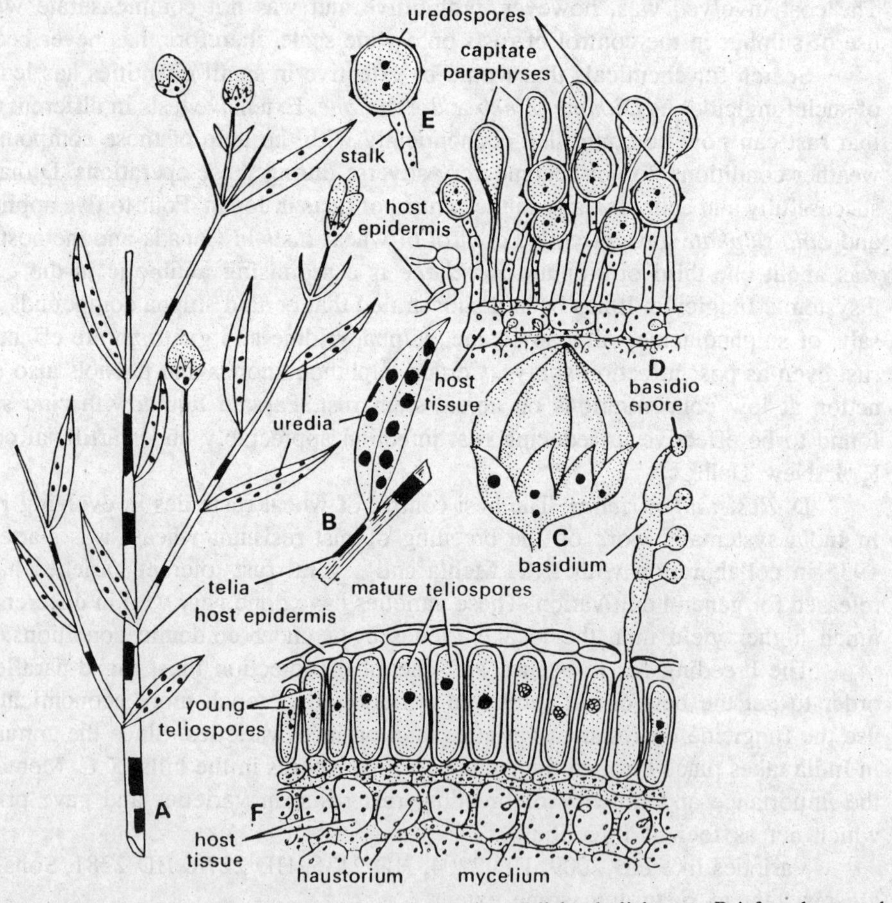

Fig. 12.28. *Melampsora lini.* Rust of linseed. A, infected twig showing uredial and telial stages; B, infected stem and leaf showing magnified uredia and telia; C, infected capsule showing uredia; D, section of infected leaf showing stalked uredospores and capitate paraphyses; E, single uredospore with multicellular stalk; F, section of infected stem showing subepidermal telium, sessile teliospores, mycelium and haustoria, and a germinating teliospore.

and elongated or oblong on stems. Each uredium contains numerous uredospores. The globose and echinulate uredospores are found at the tips of long multicellular sporophores, which remain intermingled with capitate paraphyses. On maturity the uredospores and paraphyses cause a pressure and the host epidermis bursts releasing uredospores outside which are dispersed by wind, insects, water and other outer agencies. On the approach of suitable conditions temperature and moisture the uredospores germinate producing germ tubes. The devleoping mycelium is dikaryotic.

The uredospores cannot withstand the scorching heat of Indian plains and, therefore, they die. They survive in the hills at 7,000 feet a. s. l.

In the end of season the crust-like reddish brown or black telia are formed on the stems. The telia are subepidermal and contain numerous teliospores. The teliospores are sessile, cylindrical, unicellular, reddish brown in colour, and palisade-like in arrangement. They can withstand the adverse conditions for a long time and possess a long dormant period. Prior to their germination they require freezing temperature. In India the teliospores cannot withstand scorching heat, and die (Prasada, 1948).

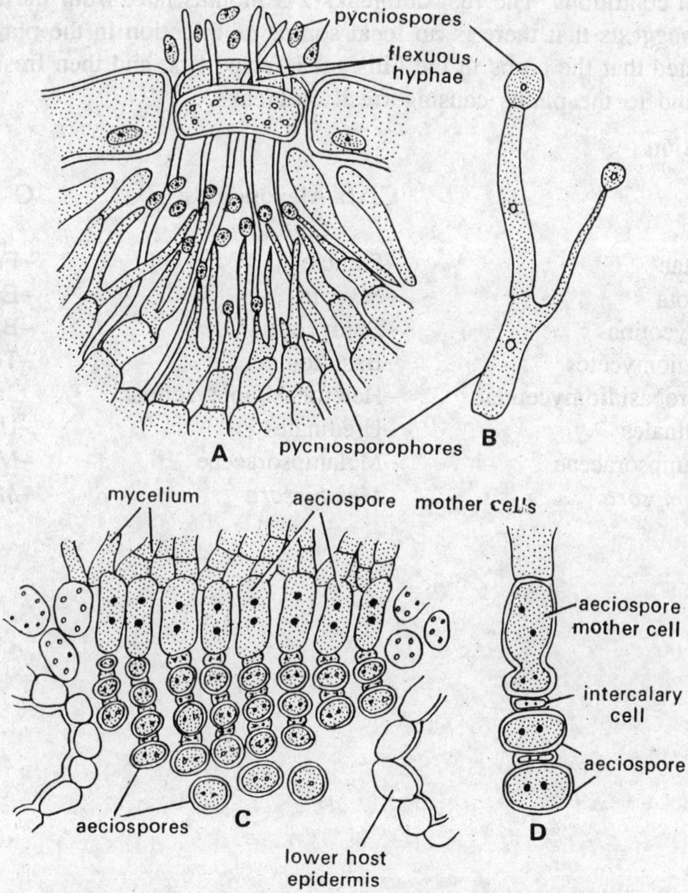

Fig. 12.29. *Melampsora lini*. Rust of linseed. A, flask-like pycnium with pycniosporophores, pycniospores and flexuous hyphae; B, pycniosporophore and pycniospores; C, aecium containing chains of aeciospores; D, production of aeciospores on an aeciospore mother cell.

The teliospores remain viable at 4,000 feet above sea level. In our country the pycnial and aecial stages are rarely found in nature.

The teliospores germinate with the production of basidiospores which infect the leaves causing pycnia and aecia and subsequently uredia and telia.

The small, rounded or oval inconspicuous yellow pycnia are found on both the surfaces of the leaf. They have been seen in green house experiments. The pycnia are composed of pycniosporophores and paraphyses. The pycniosporophores bear pycniospores at their apical ends.

After the formation of pycnia, nearabout a fortnight later the aecia are formed. The aecia are found on the lower surface of the leaf. The aecia are small, orange coloured and scattered. They do not bear peridia and paraphyses. The aeciospores are polygonal and binucleate.

On germination each aeciospore gives rise to a dikaryotic mycelium.

Recurrence. In India, linseed is a winter crop sown in October and harvested in March/April, therefore the teliospores have to over summer and not to over winter as in United States. According to R. Prasada, the teliospores lose their viability during the summer and therefore, the teliospores do not play any significant role in the carry over of the disease from year to year under Indian conditions. The rust outbreaks 2-3 months later from the date of sowing in the plains. This suggests that there is no local source of infection in the plains from previous crops. He suggested that the crops in the hills get infected first and then fresh uredospores are blown by the wind to the plains causing fresh outbreaks.

Systematic Position

	G. W. Martin (1961)	**C. J. Alexopoulos (1962)**	**G. C. Ainsworth (1971)**
Kingdom	–Plantae	–Plantae	–Fungi
Division	–Mycota	–Mycota	–Eumycota
Sub-div.	–Eumycotina	–Eumycotina	–Basidiomycotina
Class	–Basidiomycetes	–Basidiomycetes	–Teliomycetes
Sub-Class	–Heterobasidiomycetidae	–Heterobasidiomycetidae	–
Order	–Uredinales	–Uredinales	–Uredinales
Family	–Melampsoraceae	–Melampsoraceae	–Melampsoraceae
Genus	–*Melampsora*	–*Melampsora*	–*Melampsora*

13

Sub-class–Homobasidiomycetidae

Mushrooms, Shelf Fungi, Puffballs, Bird's Nest Fungi etc.
(Alexopoulos, 1962)

G. W. Martin (1961)	**G. C. Ainsworth (1971)**
Sub-class–**HOMOBASIDIOMYCETIDAE**	Sub-class–**HOMOBASIDIOMYCETIDAE** of class–**HYMENOMYCETES** and class–**GASTEROMYCETES**

Characteristic Features

1. This sub-class consists of mushrooms, toad stools, bracket fungi, puff balls, shelf fungi, earth stars, stink horns, bird's nest fungi etc.
2. The mycelium is found in the hidden substrata in tangled masses. The clamp connections and rhizomorphs are commonly present in the mycelium. The mycelium is dikaryotic.
3. The fructifications or sporophores are seen above the ground.
4. The basidia are unseptate and arranged in hymenia. Each basidium bears four basidiospores at terminal end on sterigmata. The basidia are palisade-like and intermingled with paraphyses.
5. This sub-class is divided into two groups or series. (i) Hymenomycetes and (ii) Gastromycetes.
6. According to Gaumann (1952), Wolf and Wolf (1947) and Alexopoulos (1956), the group Hymenomycetes consists of single order Agaricales.

Series–Hymenomycetes

The Basidiocarp is present. It varies from an arachnoid subiculum to a very complex sporocarp. The hymenium is present. It becomes exposed before the spores are mature. There is a single order–Agaricales.

ORDER **AGARICALES** (275 genera; 7,000 species)

1. The order consists of mushrooms, toad stools, puff-balls etc.
2. The sporophores (fructifications) are macroscopic.
3. The basidia are arranged in hymenia intermingled with paraphyses. The basidiospores are disseminated with a jerk and alternately.
4. The hymenial layers may be protected in gills or exposed.
5. According to Wolf and Wolf (1947), there are six families in this order. (i) Exobasidiaceae, (ii) Theleophoraceae, (iii) Clavariaceae, (iv) Hydnaceae (v) Polyporaceae and (vi) Agaricaceae.
6. There are about 7,000 species in this order.

Family–Polyporaceae (33 genera; 1000 species)

They are also called the **pore fungi**. The hymenial layer lines the inner surface of the tubes. The tubes open on the under surface of the pileus which look like pores. The mature basidiocarp becomes woody, corky or leathery. The young fruit bodies (basidiocarps) are soft and pliable. The polypores are the common wood rotting fungi and they destroy timber. They are commonly found upon the trunks of fallen trees.

Genus **POLYPORUS** (250 species)

This genus includes a large number of species of pore fungi. All species may cause decay of timber, some of being specially destructive to beams, floors and lumber piled in yards. They possess shelving or stalked fructifications. The fruit bodies are fleshy when young but become hardened, leathery or corky at maturity. The pore layer is usually quite different in texture and colour from remainder of the pileus.

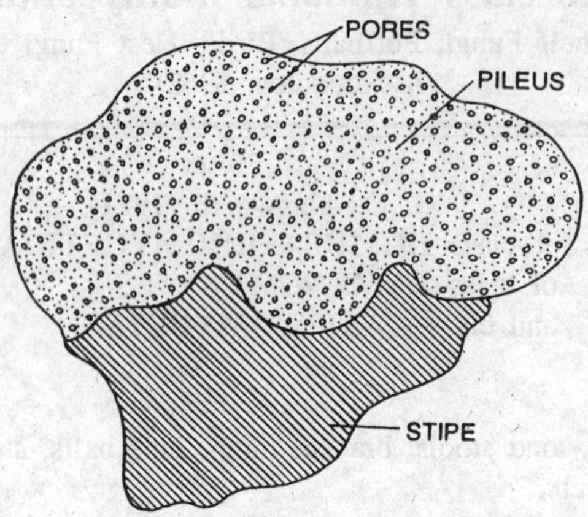

Fig. 13.1. *Polyporus.* Fruit body (basidiocarp).

The most common members of this genus are *Polyporus versicolor* and *Polyporus pargamenus.* They cause decay of many species of deciduous woody plants. *Polyporus sulphureus* occurs at the base of deciduous trees, especially oaks. It produces large, fused imbricated shelves that are conspicuous because of their bright sulphur-yellow to orange colour. *Polyporus cinnabarinus* produces bright, cinnabar-coloured brackets, especially on decaying oak branches. *Polyporus sapurema* from Brazil and *Polyporus mylittiae* from Australia produce giant sclerotia.

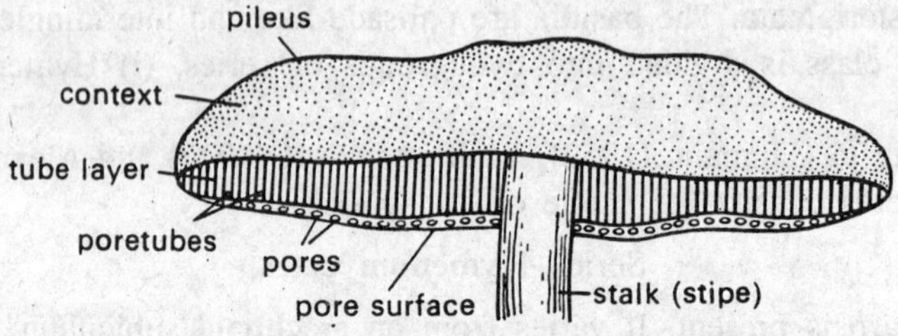

Fig. 13.2. *Polyporus* sp. Basidiocarp with pileus and stipe.

Somatic structure (mycelium). On germination the basidiospores give rise to primary mycelium. In the beginning the mycelium develops in the soil near the host roots. Very soon it attacks the roots and develops beneath the bark. The mycelium is inconspicuous and subterranean. The primary mycelium consists of uninucleate cells. Eventually the cells become dikaryotic by the process of dikaryotization. The newly formed dikaryotic cells elongate and divide by the formation of clamp connections. The secondary mycelium is dikaryotic. On the severity of the parasitism the mycelium forms a complete, thick layer of hyphae around the central woody cylinder.

Fruit body (basidiocarp). The basidiocarp develops from the secondary (dikaryotic) mycelium. In the beginning it appears to be a rounded button-like structure of hyphae. It develops from the subterranean mycelium. The knot of hyphae grows in size and bursts through the bark. Later on it differentiates into a short stalk also known as **stipe** and a rounded cap-like structure, the **pileus.** On maturation the soft basidiocarp becomes woody, corky or leathery.

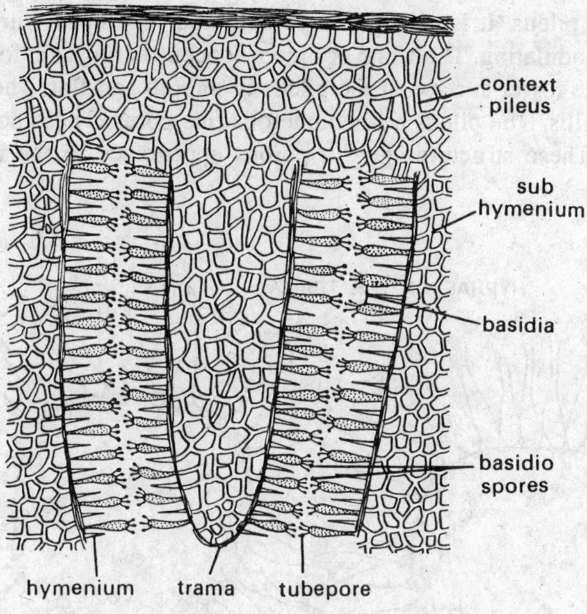

Fig. 13.3. *Polyporus* sp. V.S. through a part of pileus.

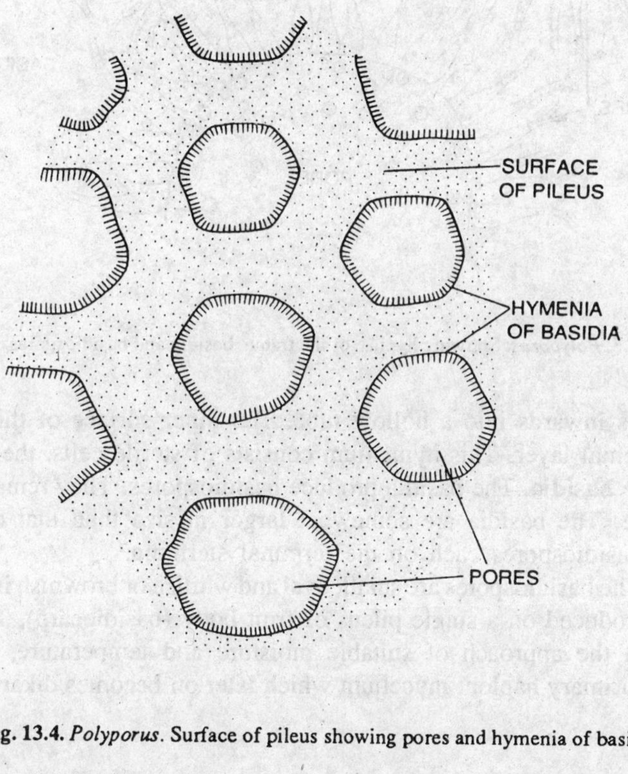

Fig. 13.4. *Polyporus*. Surface of pileus showing pores and hymenia of basidia.

The stipe of basidiocarp is 2-6 inches long and brown or dark brown in colour. It consists of innumerable hyphae arranged together in a compact mass. The stipe bears at its apex an expanded structure, the pileus. It is usually brown coloured. The upper surface of pileus is flat and smooth or slightly undulating. The white or brown concentric rings are found in the peripheral region of the pileus. The lower surface of the pileus is smooth and flat. The lower surface does not bear any radiating gills. The pileus bears numerous fine pores. These pores are the openings of many small tubes. These structures give a porous appearance to the under-surface of the

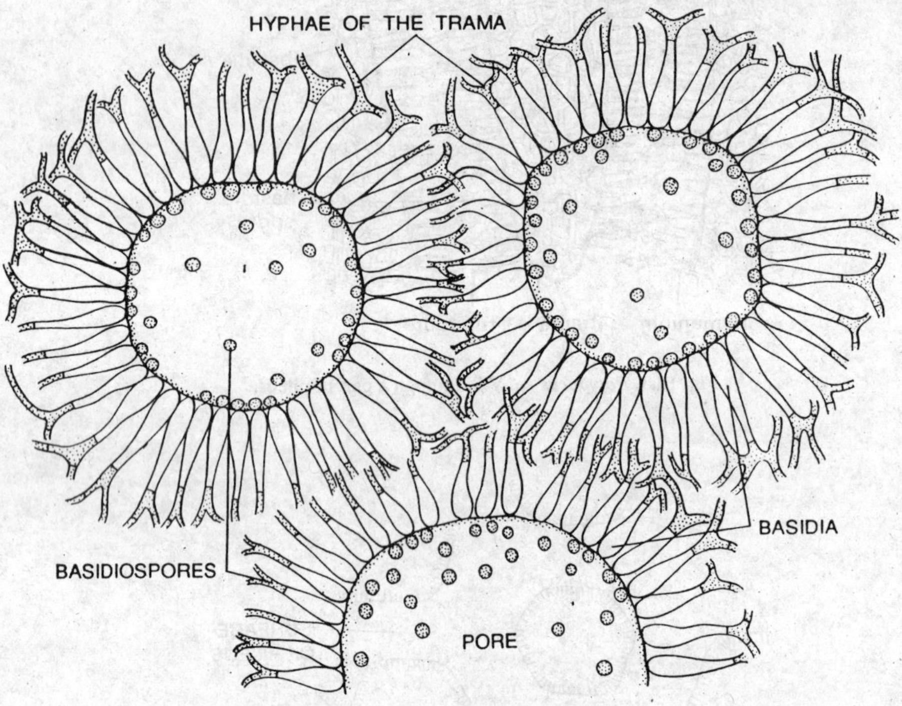

Fig. 13.5. *Polyporus.* Showing hyphae of the trama, basidia and basidiospores.

pileus. Each pore leads inwards into a hollow tube. The inner surface of this hollow tube is lined by a fertile hymenial layer. This hymenium consists of sterile cells, the **cystidia** and the fertile clavate cells, the **basidia.** The basidia produce basidiospores. They remain projected into the hollow of the tube. The basidia are somewhat larger in size than that of cystidia. Each basidium bears four basidiospores each on the terminal sterigma.

Basidiospores. The basidiospores are small, oval and whitish or brownish in colour. Millions of basidiospores are produced on a single pileus of fruit body (basidiocarp). They are released through the pores. On the approach of suitable moisture and temperature, the basidiospore germinates producing primary haplont mycelium which later on becomes dikaryotic after fusion of hyphae.

Systematic Position

	G. W. Martin (1961)	**C. J. Alexopoulos (1962)**	**G. C. Ainsworth (1971)**
Kingdom	–Plantae	–Plantae	–Fungi
Division	–Mycota	–Mycota	–Eumycota
Sub-div.	–Eumycotina	–Eumycotina	–Basidiomycotina
Class	–Basidiomycetes	–Basidiomycetes	–Hymenomycetes
Sub-cl.	–Homobasidiomycetidae	–Homobasidiomycetidae	–Holobasidiomycetidae
Order	–Polyporales	–Polyporales	–Aphyllophorales (Polyporales)
Family	–Polyporaceae	–Polyporaceae	–Polyporaceae
Genus	–*Polyporus*	–*Polyporus*	–*Polyporus*

Family–Agaricaceae

They include the majority of mushrooms. They bear their basidia on gills or lamellae. The gills are neither waxy and nor may easily be separated from context of the pileus. The

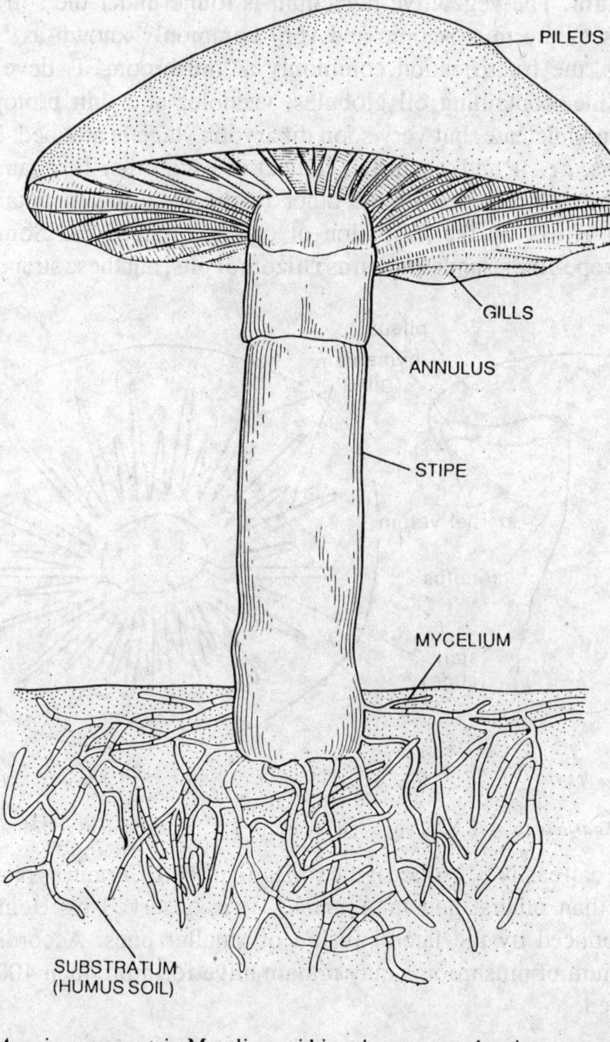

Fig. 13.6. *Agaricus campestris.* Mycelium within substratum; and various stages of fructification.

gills are narrow in section. The basidiocarp is fleshy. The hymenium lining both the sides of gills.

Genus **AGARICUS** (60 species)

Habit and habitat. *Agaricus campestris* or *Psalliota campestris* is a saprophytic fungus, commonly known as 'mushroom'. It grows on damp and dead organic substances such as humus, horse dung, damp rotten logs of wood, trunks of trees and meadows rich in decaying organic matter. The mushrooms are commonly seen growing on grasslands and other places rich in humus soil during rainy season. Some mushrooms are edible but some of them are deadly poisonous. So one must be very cautious about their selection for eating purposes. The common edible mushroom *Agaricus campestris* is cultivated in South India and other places. The group in which *Agaricus* is found includes many other forms commonly known as mushroom and toadstools.

As regards its somatic structure the mushroom can be subdivided into two main parts, one part known as vegetative mycelium, is found living within the soil or humus and the other part, fructification or proper mushroom is aerial and above the soil. This portion is edible and bears the gills and spores.

Vegetative mycelium. The vegetative mycelium is found under the soil in thick, tangled wooly masses. Such masses are microscopic and very commonly known as **'spawns'.** On the maturation of such mass, the fructification commonly a 'mushroom' is developed on it. The hyphae are septate, hyaline, containing oil globules, vacuoles and thin protoplasm. The cells of the hyphae at first are uninucleate, but very soon dikaryotic stage is attained. The two adjacent hyphae of different strains, *i.e.*, + and - come in contact of each other fuse, and a nucleus from one hypha passes into the adjacent cell of the other hypha resulting in dikaryotization. Now the dikaryotic mycelium grows by the formation of clamp connections. Some of the hyphae are interwoven into thick rope-like strands known as **rhizomorphs**, but these strands or rhizomorphs

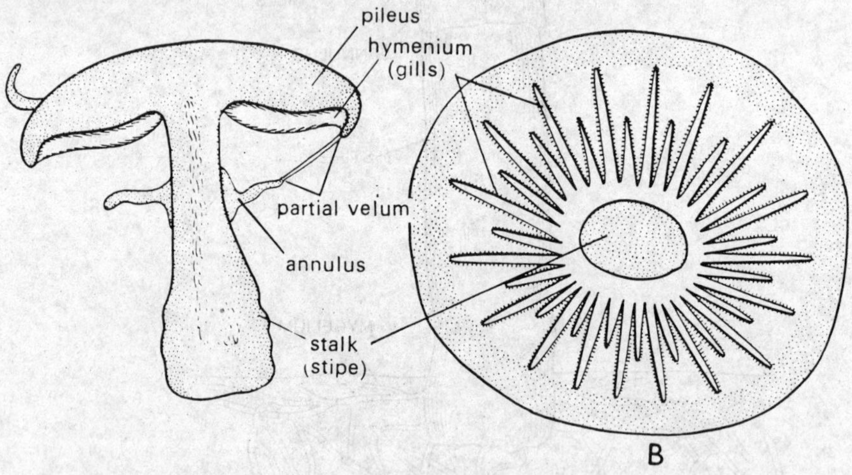

Fig. 13.7. *Agaricus* sp. A, L.S. of stipe and pileus; B, T.S. through pileus and stipe.

and other separate hyphae can easily be broken if the soil is disturbed. Certain hyphae of rhizomorphs are of greater diameter than others, and in *Agaricus,* it is observed by Hein (1930) that the large hyphae can be produced by the lateral fusion of smaller ones. According to Jones and Buller (1949), the mycelium of mushrooms may remain alive for more than 400 years and every year the crop is produced.

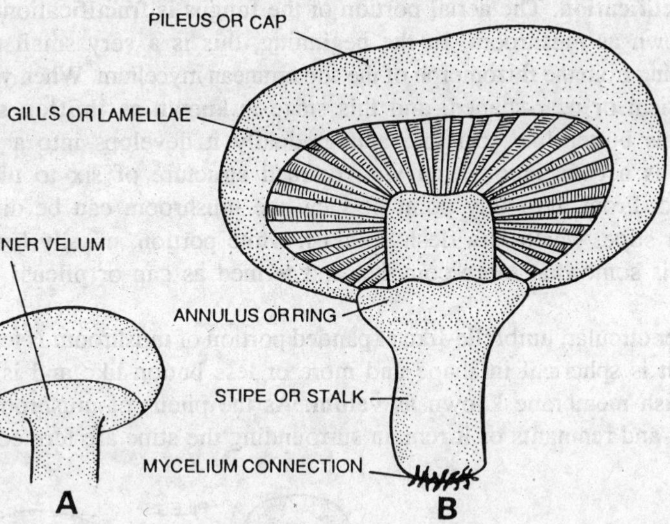

Fig. 13.8. *Agaricus*. A young basidiocarp; B, mature basidiocarp (sporophore).

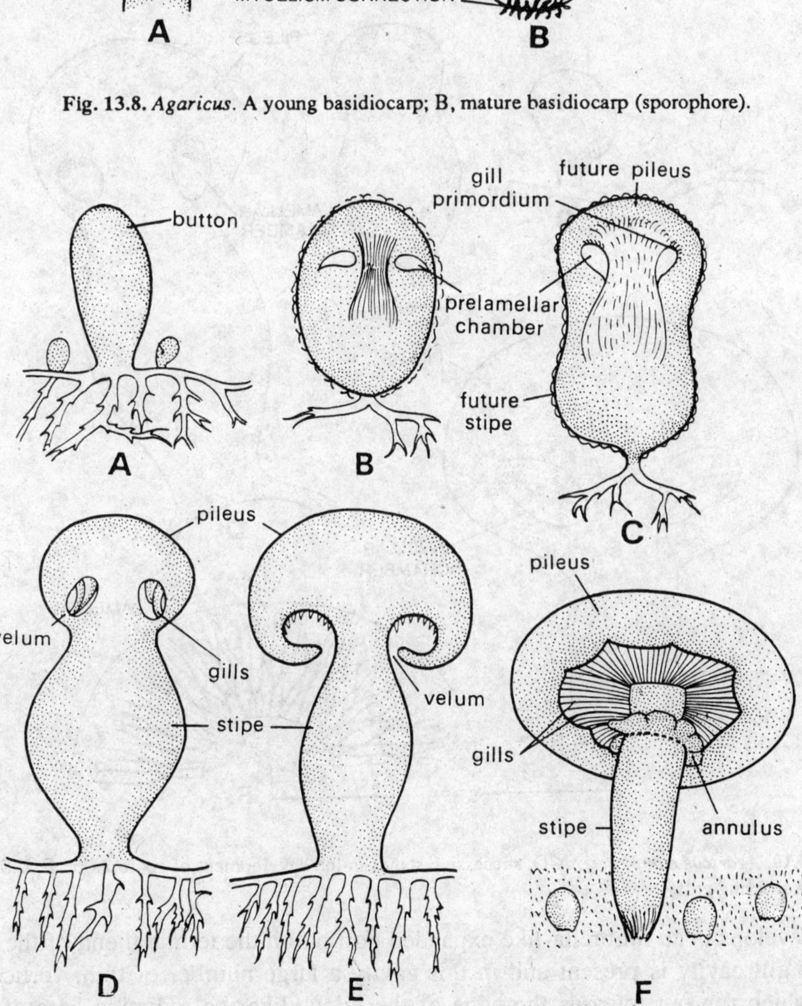

Fig. 13.9. *Agaricus campestris*. Development of fruiting body (basidiocarp) A-F.

The fructification. The aerial portion of the fungus is fructification or fruiting body, and commonly known as mushroom. In the beginning, this is a very small tiny knot of compact hyphae developing from the rhizomorph of the subterranean mycelium. When young, the fructification is small, spherical or pear-shaped, and this stage is known as **'button stage'.** A constriction develops on this button-like structure and gradually it develops into a mushroom proper or sporophore. It is a conspicuous and well defined structure of six to nine centimetres when fully developed. From the study point of view the mushroom can be divided into two parts, (1) the stalk or stipe, which is a fleshy pinkish white portion, usually broader at the base, (2) the other part is somewhat more complex and termed as cap or pileus. The description is as follows.

The upper circular, umbrella-like expanded portion of mushroom is termed as cap or pileus. When young, it is spherical in shape and more or less button-like and is completely enclosed by a thin whitish membrane known as **velum.** As the pileus of mushroom grows in size; the velum ruptures and remnants of it remain surrounding the stipe are termed **annulus.** Ultimately

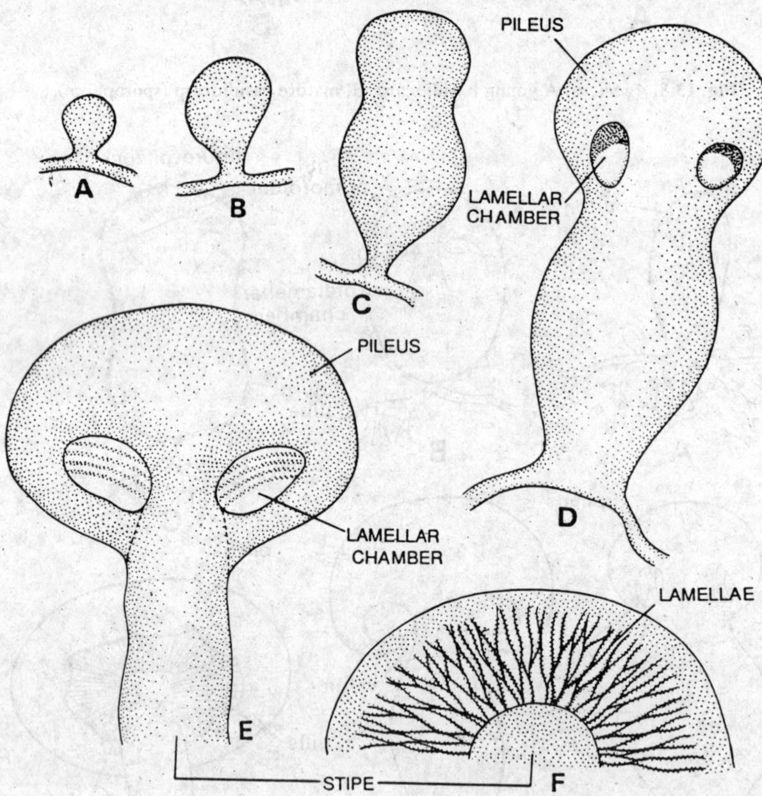

Fig. 13.10. *Agaricus campestris*. A-D, successive stages in the development of sporophore; E, L.S. of sporophore; F,V.S. of pileus showing gills.

the pileus develops in an umbrella-like expanded portion on the terminal end of the stipe. Under the pileus a gill cavity is present and in this cavity a large number of thin, vertical, plate-like structures which run out towards the edge of the pileus like the radiating bars of a wheel are termed **gills or lamellae.** They vary in number from 300 to 600 in each pileus. On both the surfaces of each gill thousands of spores are produced.

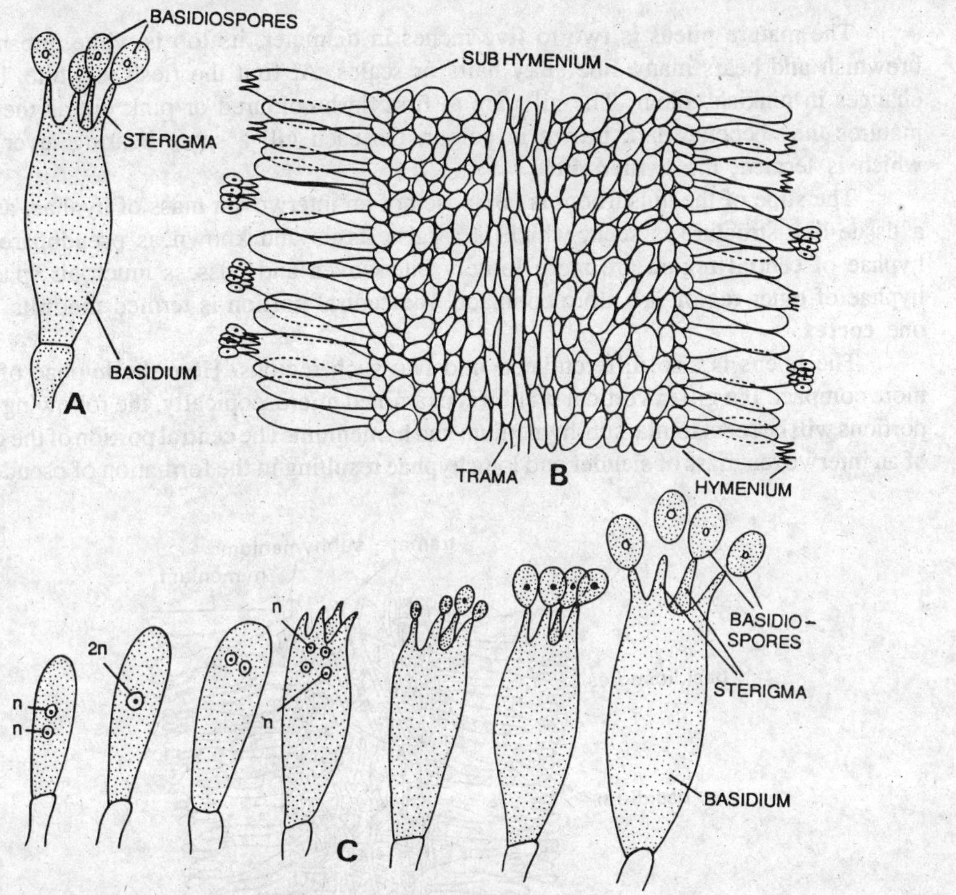

Fig. 13.11. *Agaricus campestris*. A, a basidium and basidiospores; B,V.S. through gill showing the hymenium of basidia and paraphyses; C, development of basidium and basidiospores.

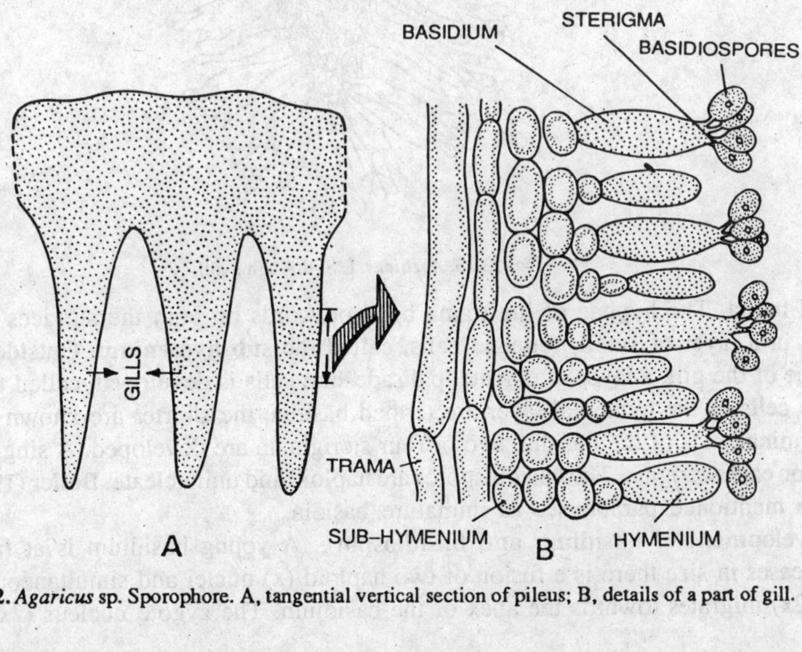

Fig. 13.12. *Agaricus* sp. Sporophore. A, tangential vertical section of pileus; B, details of a part of gill. (After Buller, 1922).

The mature pileus is two to five inches in diameter, its top is white, cream coloured or brownish and bears many fine silky hairs or scales. At first the flesh is white, but later on it changes in pinkish colour. The gills are at first flesh-coloured or pink but as the fructification matures they become dark brown in colour. On each gill a spore bearing layer is developed which is termed, the **hymenium.**

The stipe of the mushroom is composed of an interwoven mass of hyphae, and in sections a tissue-like structure is seen, which is a false tissue and known as pseudoparenchyma. The hyphae of central region are more loosely interwoven and possess much air spaces while the hyphae of outer region are more compact. The central portion is termed **medulla** and the outer one **cortex.**

The pileus is also differentiated into two such regions. Here the hyphae of the gills are more compact. If a gill in vertical section is examined microscopically, the following three distinct portions will be seen: trama, sub-hymenium and hymenium. The central portion of the gill consisting of an interwoven mass of slender and long hyphae resulting in the formation of pseudoparenchyma

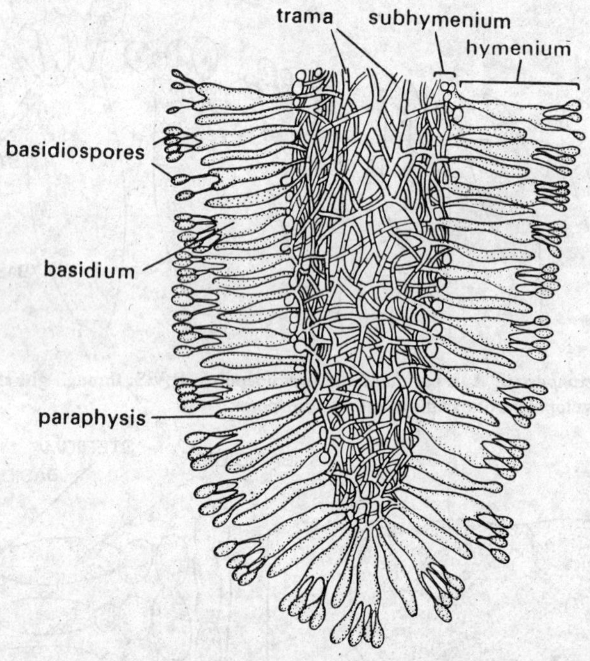

Fig. 13.13. *Agraicus*. L.S. through a gill.

is termed trama. The hyphae of the trama bend outwards on both the surfaces of the gill and terminate in a layer of small, rounded cells, called the **sub-hymenium.** Outside to it, on both the surface of the gill, a layer of clavate, palisade-like cells is developed, called the **hymenium.** The large cells of the hymenial layer are termed basidia, the shorter are known as paraphyses. At the terminal ends of the basidia, two or four sterigmata are developed. A single basidiospore develops on each sterigma. The basidiospores are haploid and uninucleate. Buller (1922), described the above mentioned paraphyses as immature basidia.

Development of basidium and basidiospore. A young basidium is at first binucelate. As it increases in size there is a fusion of two haploid (x) nuclei and simultaneously the zygote nucleus (2x) migrates towards the apex of the basidium. The zygote nucleus (2x) soon divides meiotically into four daughter nuclei, each with x chromosomes. After completion of the nuclear divisions there is a development of slender projections, known as **sterigmata,** at the terminal end of the basidium. The sterigmata may be two or four in number. Each sterigma swells at

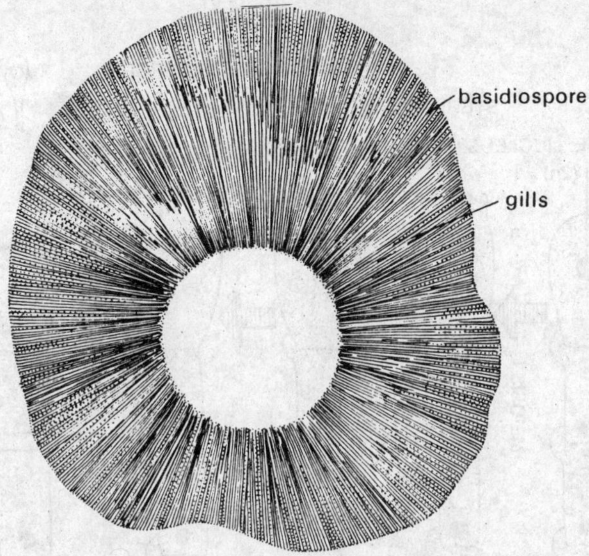

Fig. 13.14. *Agaricus campestris*. Spore print on paper from a mature pileus.

the distal end, and a nucleus from the basidium migrates into the cell thus cuts off is a basidiospore. A small lateral outgrowth known as hilum is developed near the juncture of the basidiospore and the sterigma. A small droplet of liquid appears upon the hilum, about one-fifth of the size

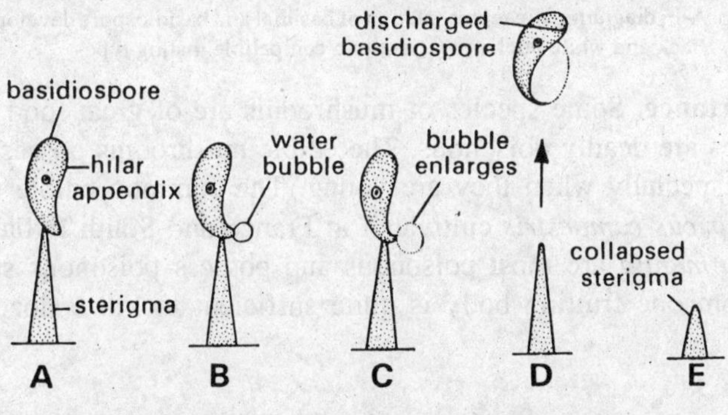

Fig. 13.15. *Agaricus*. A-E, water drop to release basidiospore.

of spore, and the basidiospore along with the drop of liquid suddenly shoots off from the sterigma. The mechanism of this explosive abscission is however, not yet known. The four basidiospores of a basidium are shed in a regular sequence. The spores are discharged one by one continuously at the intervals of few seconds or one or two minutes. The basidia of the hymenium also mature in succession. According to the species, the period of spore discharge from a pileus may last for hours, days or weeks. The number of basidiospores discharged from a certain species of mushroom is estimated at the rate of a million per minute for more than 50 hours.

As soon as the basidiospores are discharged from basidium they germinate on the advent of favourable conditions giving rise to primary monokaryotic, branched, hyaline and septate mycelium. Later on the hyphae of two different strains, *i.e.*, + and - anastamose with each other and the dikaryotic mycelium develops, which gives rise to spawn and fructification.

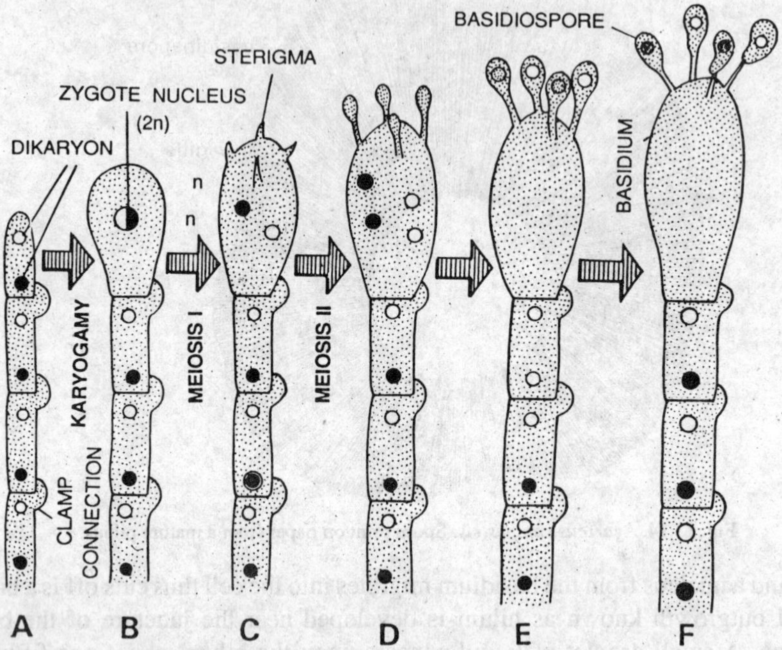

Fig. 13.16. *Agaricus* sp. A-F, diagrammatic representation of basidial and basidiospore development, without crossing over in a heterothallic species. Black and white nuclei represent two compatible mating types.

Economic importance. Some species of mushrooms are of great food value white on the other hand some species are deadly poisonous. The edible mushrooms possess good flavour. All puff balls are edible, especially when they are young. The common edible mushroom is *Psalliota campestris* or *Agaricus campestris* cultivated in France and South India and sold in sealed tins. Some species of *Amanita* are most poisonous and possess poisonous substance known as muscarine obtained from one fruiting body is quite sufficient to kill a dozen or more people.

Systematic Position

	G. W. Martin (1961)	**C. J. Alexopoulos (1962)**	**G. C. Ainsworth (1971)**
Kingdom	–Plantae	–Plantae	–Fungi
Division	–Mycota	–Mycota	–Eumycota
Sub-div.	–Eumycotina	–Eumycotina	–Basidiomycotina
Class	–Basidiomycetes	–Basidiomycetes	–Hymenomycetes
Sub-cl.	–Homobasidiomycetidae	–Homobasidiomycetidae	–Holobasidiomycetidae
Order	–Agaricales	–Agaricales	–Agaricales
Family	–Agaricaceae	–Agaricaceae	–Agaricaceae
Genus	–*Agaricus*	–*Agaricus*	–*Agaricus*

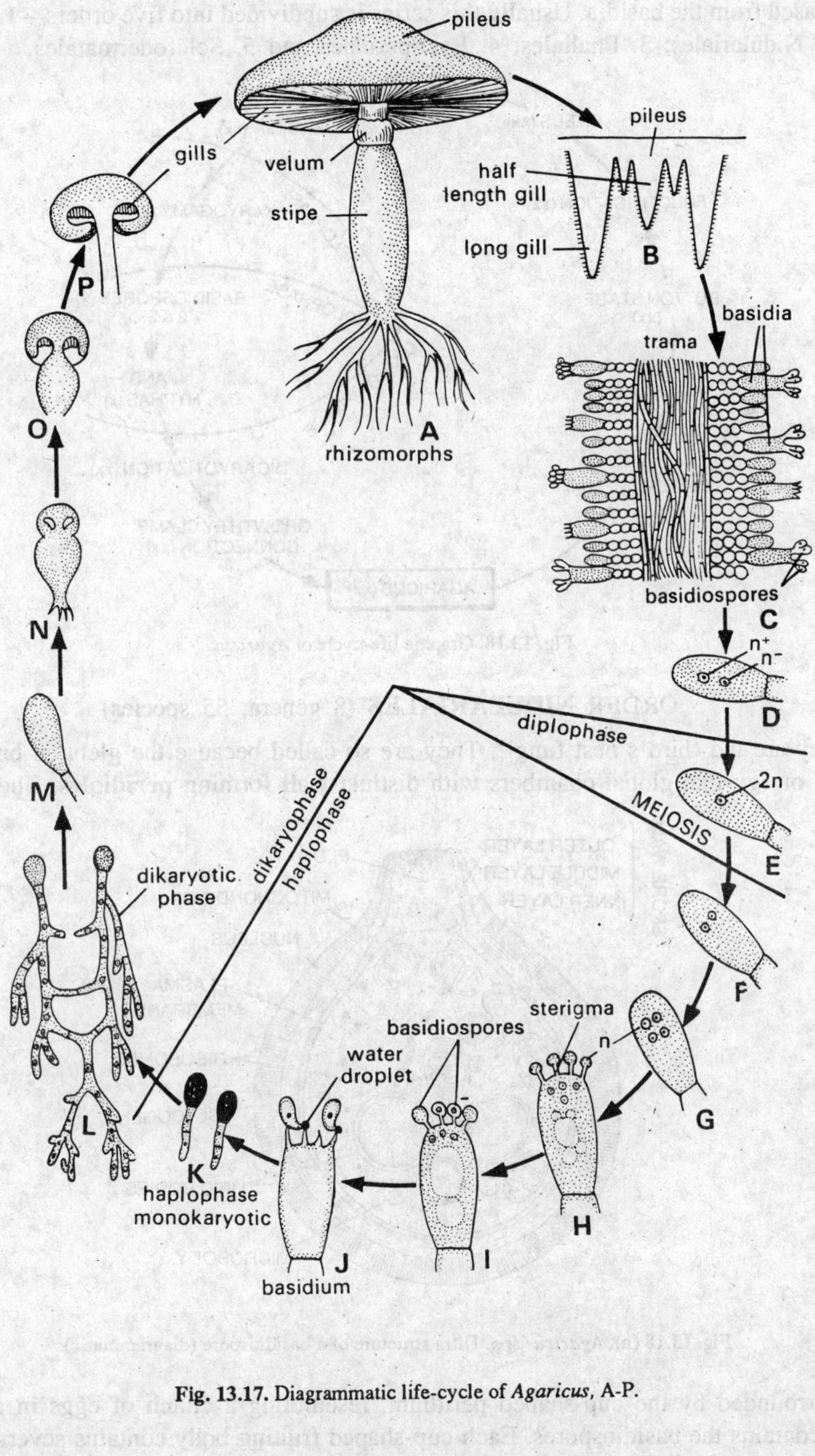

Fig. 13.17. Diagrammatic life-cycle of *Agaricus*, A-P.

Class–Gastromycetes

The basidiocarp is present. The basidiocarps remain closed at least until the spores have been released from the basidia. Usually this series is subdivided into five orders—1. Hymenogastrales; 2. Nidulariales; 3. Phallales; 4. Lycoperdales and 5. Sclerodermatales.

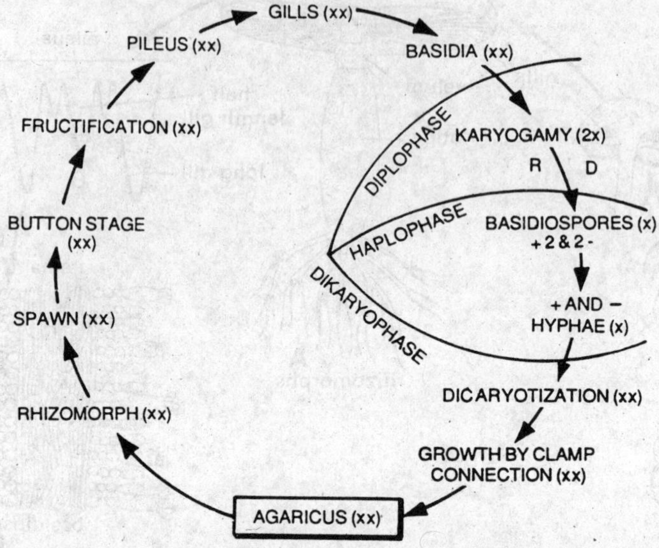

Fig. 13.18. Graphic life-cycle of *Agaricus*.

ORDER NIDULARIALES (8 genera; 55 species)

They are the 'bird's nest fungi'. They are so called because the gleba is broken up into a number of egg-like global chambers with distinct wall forming **peridioles.** These peridioles

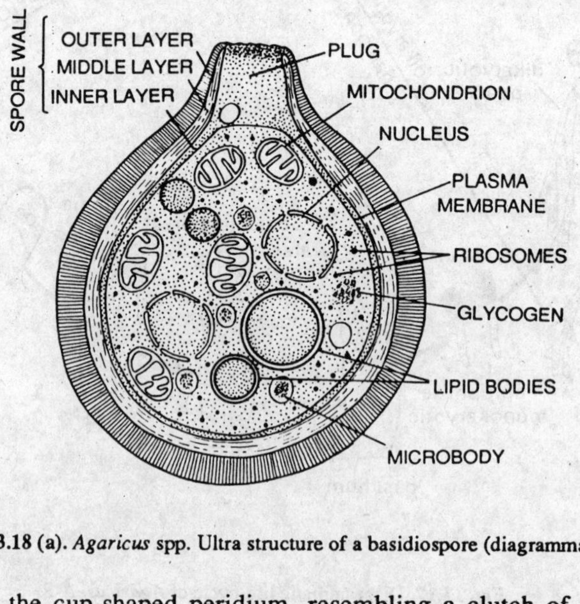

Fig. 13.18 (a). *Agaricus* spp. Ultra structure of a basidiospore (diagrammatic).

remain surrounded by the cup-shaped peridium, resembling a clutch of eggs in a nest. Each peridiole contains the basidiospores. Each cup-shaped fruiting body contains several peridioles.

The Nidulariales comprise but a single family, with four genera-*Nidula, Nidularia, Cyathus* and *Crucibalum.*

Family–Nidulariaceae
Genus CYATHUS (40 species)

In *Cyathus,* the fruit body is deep and of the shape of an inverted bell. The peridioles within this cup-like fruit body are dark grey or black. Each peridiole remaining attached to the inner surface of the cup by means of a slender mycelial connection, the **funiculus.** On getting

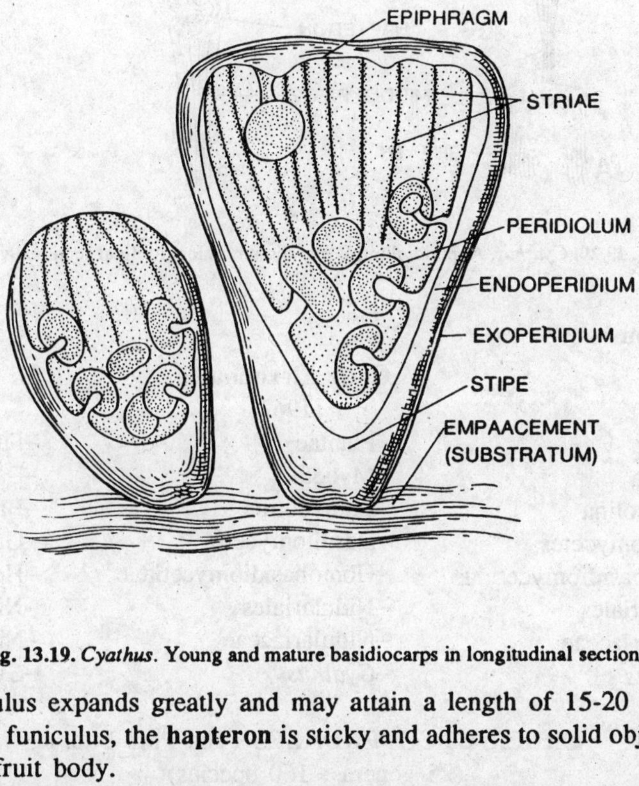

Fig. 13.19. *Cyathus.* **Young and mature basidiocarps in longitudinal sections.**

moisture the funiculus expands greatly and may attain a length of 15-20 cm. This way, the base of the cordlike funiculus, the **hapteron** is sticky and adheres to solid objects when released from the cup-like fruit body.

The wall of peridium is three layered. The central layer consists of pseudoparenchymatous tissue.

The basidiospores are sessile. In *Cyathus,* very frequently there are more than four basidiospores on each basidium. The basidiospores remain interspersed with numerous sterile threads within the peridioles.

Dissemination of peridioles. Brodie (1951) has explained that the cups of the genus *Cyathus* act as splash cups from which raindrops, during a heavy storm when strike with a velocity of six metres per second, the peridioles are ejected out to a distance of 3-4 feet. The **purse** of the funiculus bursts because of the force of ejection and the funicular cord and hapteron are released. The sticky hapteron adheres to some solid object.

The basidiospores germinate producing haploid mycelia, which by mating develop into dikaryotic mycelia and fruiting bodies.

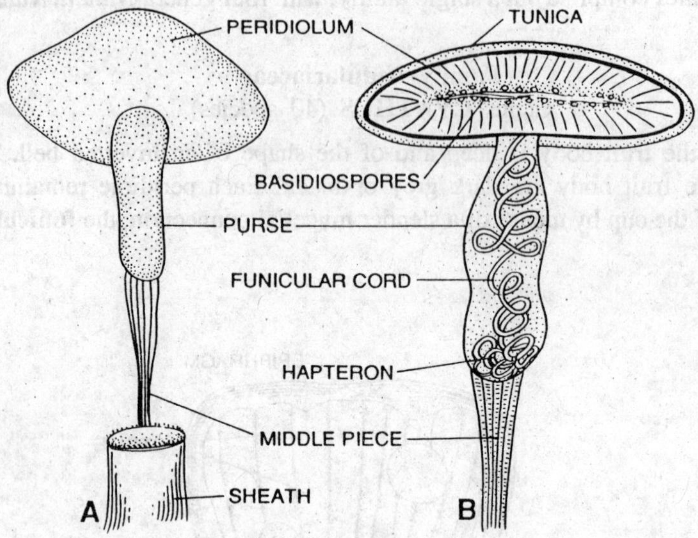

Fig. 13.20. *Cyathus*. A, peridiolum; B, peridiolum in longitudinal sectional view.

Systematic Position

	G. W. Martin (1961)	C. J. Alexopoulos (1962)	G. C. Ainsworth (1971)
Kingdom	–Plantae	–Plantae	–Fungi
Division	–Mycota	–Mycota	–Eumycota
Sub-div.	–Eumycotina	–Eumycotina	–Basidiomycotina
Class	–Basidiomycetes	–Basidiomycetes	–Gasteromycetes
Sub-cl.	–Homobasidiomycetidae	–Homobasidiomycetidae	–Holobasidiomycetidae
Order	–Nidulariales	–Nidulariales	–Nidulariales
Family	–Nidulariaceae	–Nidulariaceae	–Nidulariaceae
Genus	–*Cyathus*	–*Cyathus*	–*Cyathus*

ORDER **LYCOPERDALES** (The Puff Balls)

(25 genera ; 160 species)

The gleba are powdery at maturity. The spores are commonly small and light coloured. At maturity the gleba are surrounded by a peridium of two to four layers. Martin (1961) subdivided the order into three families–1. Arachniaceae; 2. Lycoperdaceae and 3. Geastraceae.

Family–Lycoperdaceae

They are common puff balls and grow upon decaying vegetable materials. All species are edible. The fruit bodies are enclosed by two layers of peridium.

Genus **LYCOPERDON**

Lycoperdon is one of the puff balls. It possesses a gleba of **lacunose type** where numerous small cavities, each lined with a hymenium develop within the gleba. The fruit body (basidiocarp or puff-ball) is globose to pyriform in structure. Basidiocarps are rarely more than 8 cm, in diameter. The base of fruit body is sterile and possesses a double-layered peridium. The outer layer is rough and scaly, and withers on maturity and the inner layer also known as **endoperidium** forms an apical pore through which the spores escape.

Mycelium and rhizomorphs. Swartz (1929) recorded that the basidiospores germinate only after they have been alternately moistened and dried several times. On germination, the basidiospore gives rise to a primary mycelium having uninucleate cells. The dikaryotic secondary mycelium develops from primary mycelia. The hyphae of secondary mycelium are found in a branching system of rhizomorphs. The rhizomorphs are composed of three concentric layers- an outer cortex of loose hyphae, a sub-cortex of compact hyphae, and a central core of parallel hyphae.

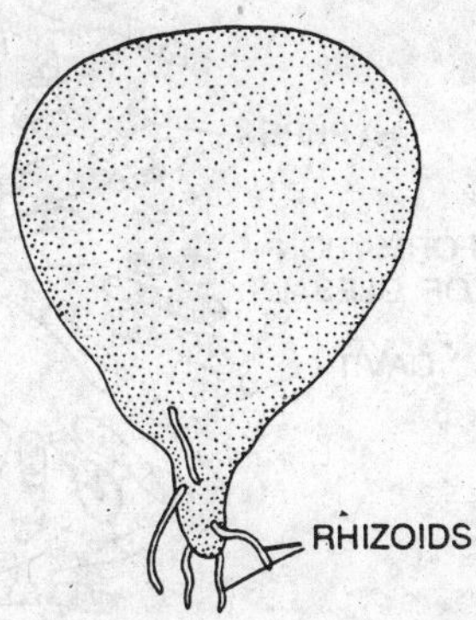

Fig. 13.21. *Lycoperdon* (puff-ball). Basidiocarp.

Basidiocarps. The primordia of basidiocarps usually arise terminally or sometimes laterally on a rhizomorph. The basidiocarps are formed by an outgrowth of hyphae from the central core of rhizomorph. The young primordia which are about 0.5 mm. in diameter are of homogeneous structure. Later on when they become somewhat larger in size they show a beginning of a differentiation into peridium consists of an outgrowth of a compact palisade-like layer or hyphae over the entire surface of the primordium. The outer portion of a young peridium also known as **exoperidium** becomes pseudoparenchymatous and the inner portion known as **endoperidium** remains palisade-like. When basidiocarp increases

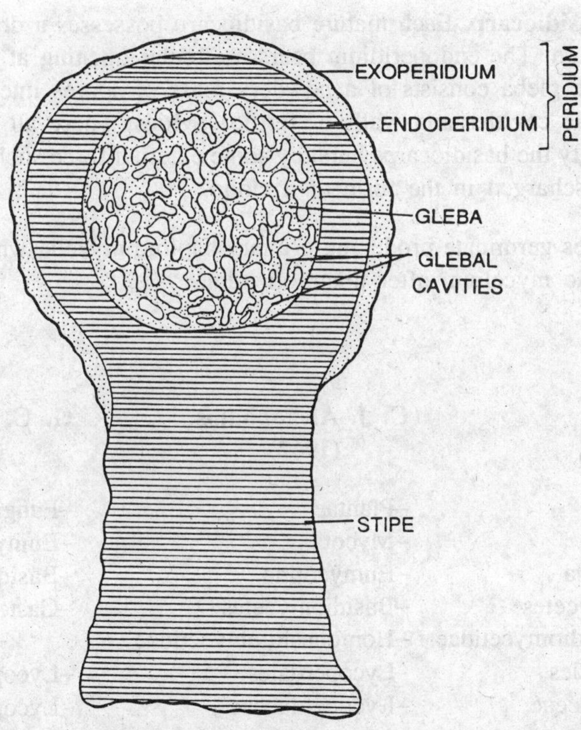

Fig. 13.22. *Lycoperdon*. Longitudinal view of basidiocarp showing gleba and glebal cavities.

in size several cracks are formed on the exoperidium and it separates into layers. Prior to the differentiation of exoperidium and endoperidium the inner region remains homogeneous mass of interwoven hyphae. Thereafter at several places in this tissue small regions are developed where hyphae are separated from one another forming small cavities which contain very loosely interwoven hyphae having several broken ends. Now the hyphae become palisade-like and encircle each of the cavities. As the fruit body (basidiocarp) increases in size several new cavities are formed. The first formed cavities become irregularly lobed, elongated and large in size. The basidia develop from the encircling palisade-like layer. The cavities which develop afterwards remain small, spherical and sterile.

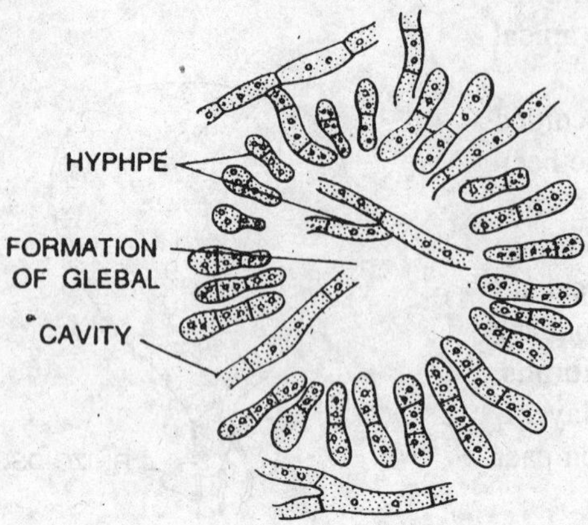

Fig. 13.23. *Lycoperdon*. Arrangement of hyphae prior to formation of glebal cavity.

Basidia and basidiospores. The two nuclei of each basidium fuse together forming a fusion nucleus (2x). The fusion nucleus divides meiotically forming four haploid nuclei. Usually four sterigmata and four basidiospores are formed on basidium but sometimes only three or two of them are formed. The basidiospores are globose and possess ornamented spore walls. On maturity the basidiospores are shed within the cavity.

Structure of basidiocarp. Each mature basidiocarp possesses a dry and leathery sterile jacket, the endoperidium. The endoperidium bears a circular opening at its apical end. In the mature basidiocarp the gleba consists of a powdery mass of spores intermingled with sterile hyphae, walls of sterile cavities and walls of fertile cavities. These all jointly constitute the **capillitium.** On maturity the basidiocarps burst by some external force such as wind and animals and the spores are discharged in the form of a cloud.

The basidiospores germinate producing primary haploid mycelia which later on give rise to secondary dikaryotic mycelium after dikaryotization.

Systematic Position

	G. W. Martin (1961)	**C. J. Alexopoulos (1962)**	**G. C. Ainsworth (1971)**
Kingdom	–Plantae	–Plantae	–Fungi
Division	–Mycota	–Mycota	–Eumycota
Sub-div.	–Eumycotina	–Eumycotina	–Basidiomycotina
Class	–Basidiomycetes	–Basidiomycetes	–Gastermoycetes
Sub-cl.	–Homobasidiomycetidae	–Homobasidiomycetidae	–
Order	–Lycoperdales	–Lycoperdales	–Lycoperdales
Family	–Lycoperdaceae	–Lycoperdaceae	–Lycoperdaceae
Genus	–*Lycoperdon*	–*Lycoperdon*	–*Lycoperdon*

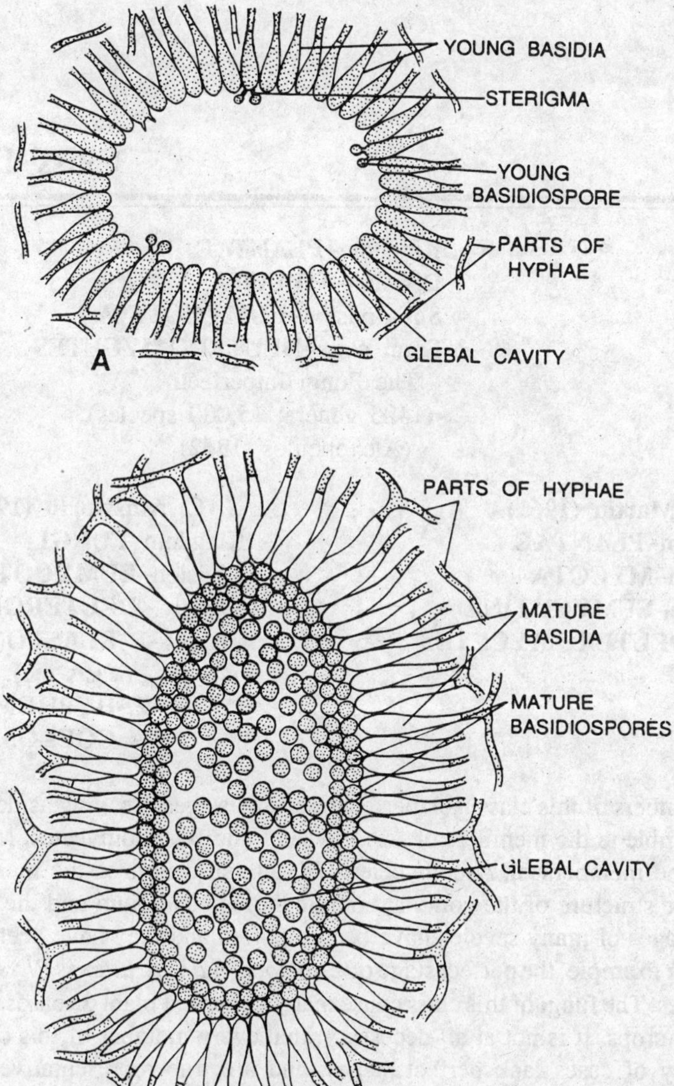

Fig. 13.24. *Lycoperdon*. A, glebal cavity with young basidia; B, glebal cavity with mature basidia and basidiospores.

14

Class–Deuteromycetes

Kingdom–**PLANTAE**
Division–**MYCOTA**
Sub-division–**EUMYCOTINA**
Form class–**DEUTEROMYCETES**
The Fungi Imperfecti
(1425 genera; 15,000 species)
(Alexopoulos, 1962)

G. W. Martin (1961)
Kingdom–**PLANTAE**
Division–**MYCOTA**
Sub-div.–**EUMYCOTINA**
Class–**DEUTEROMYCETES**

G. C. Ainsworth (1971)
Kingdom–**FUNGI**
Division–**EUMYCOTA**
Sub-div.–**DEUTEROMYCOTINA**
Classes–**1. BLASTOMYCETES ?**
(Yeasts etc).
2. HYPHOMYCETES
3. COELOMYCETES

The members of this class lack perfect or sexual stages. Leaving aside the sexual structures, the fungi resemble to the members of Ascomycetes and Basidiomycetes. Majority of these fungi resemble to the members of Ascomycetes. The classification of the members of this class is based upon the structure of the conidia, conidiophores, mycelium and the formation of conidia. The perfect stages of many species have been reported and they have been shifted to their class and genera. For example, the perfect stage of *Colletotrichum falcatum* is *Physalospora tucumanenis* of Ascomycetes. The fungi of this class cause many important plant diseases which cause sufficient damage to the crops. It is not at all necessary, that every member of this class possesses perfect stage. Majority of cases lack perfect stages, and are true representatives of this class.

Vegetative mycelium. The mycelium is endo or ectophytic, inter or intracellular, branched, hyaline or brown, septate and geniculate.

Asexual reproduction. It takes place by means of (a) conidia, (b) chlamydospores. The conidia are commonly found on conidiophores. The chlamydospores are perennating bodies and intercalary in origin.

Sexual reproduction. This is completely lacking.

Classification. This class is subdivided into four orders. 1. Sphaeropsidales; 2. Melanconiales; 3. Moniliales and 4. Mycelia sterilia.

Sphaeropsidales. The conidia are found within the flask-like pycnia. The pycnia are spherical hollow sporocarps. The conidia are borne on stalks, the conidiophores; 600 genera and 5,500 species.

Melanconiales. The conidia are found within acervuli. The acervuli may be regarded as pycnidia without their walls. It consists of an erumpent, cushion-like mass of hyphae possessing conidiophores, conidia, and sometimes setae are also present.

Moniliales. The conidia and conidiophores are not enclosed either in pycnidia or in acervuli.

Mycelia sterilia. The conidia are not formed. They produce sclerotia, rhizomorphs and various other forms of mycelia without spores.

Class Deuteromycetes

Order	Moniliales				Melanconiales
Families	Dematiaceae			Tuberculariaceae	Melanconiaceae
Genera	*Alternaria*	*Cercospora*	*Helminthosporium*	*Fusarium*	*Colletotrichum*
Disease	Early blight of potato	Tikka disease of groundnut	Stripe disease of barley	Wilt of arhar	Red rot of sugarcane
	A. solani	*C. personata*	*H. gramineum*	*F. udum*	*C. falcatum*

ORDER MELANCONIALES (105 genera; 1000 species)

Characteristic Features

1. There are about 150 genera and 1,000 species.
2. The mycelium is endophytic, branched, septate, brown or hyaline, geniculate, inter and intracellular.
3. The conidia and conidiophores are found in acervulus without peridium.
4. The acervuli are sub-epidermal and covered by the fringe of host epidermis.
5. The conidiophores are simple, hyaline or black.
6. The chlamydospores have also been reported.
7. The order consists of a single family, the Melanconiaceae.

Family–Melanconiaceae

Genus COLLETOTRICHUM (11 species)

(*Colletotrichum falcatum* Went)

Occurrence and symptoms. This fungus causes a disease called the 'red rot of sugarcane'. The symptoms of this disease appear on all parts of the plant, except roots. Particularly these symptoms appear on the stem and midrib of the leaves. The infected stem becomes somewhat greyish in colour and shrinks at nodes. The leaves become chlorotic, wither and droop downwards. The whole stem becomes rot. If, one examines the longitudinally cut stem, the long red stripes are quite visible, which are cut by transverse white patches, this is a characteristic feature of the disease. In the depressions, formed on the nodes of the infected stem, small black dots **acervuli** are seen. The red patches are developed on the midrib of the leaf. The straw coloured lesions develop in these red patches. The small black dots, called acervuli are found in these lesions. The presence of acervuli is also a characteristic feature of the disease. A foul odour emits from the infected plants, in the fields. The sucrose is converted in alcohol, because of this fungus.

Mycelium. It is endophytic and found within the host tissue. It is inter and intracellular. It consists of slender hyphae, profusely branched, hyaline, septate and with oil globules. The presence of oil globules in the mycelium is the peculiar feature of this fungus.

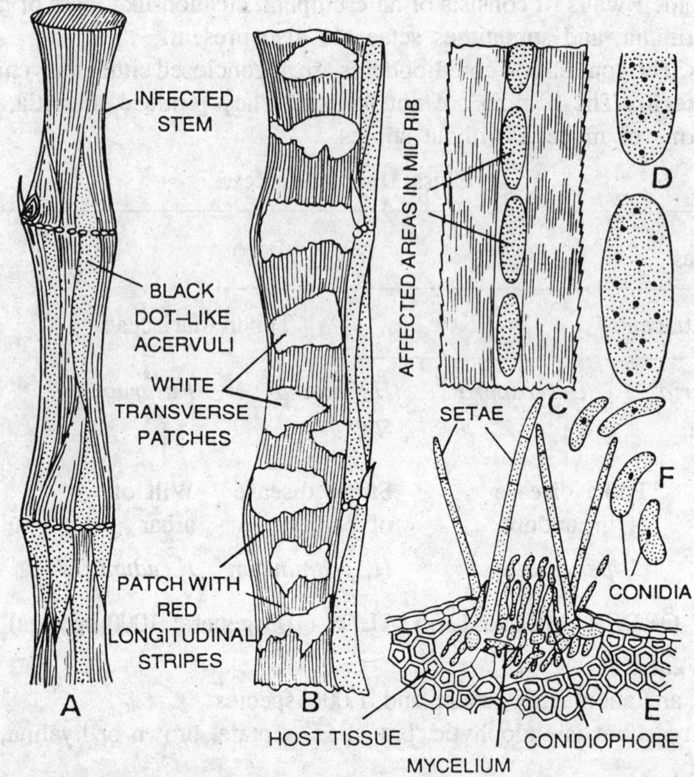

Fig. 14.1. *Colletotrichum falcatum.* Red rot of sugarcane. A, infected stem showing black dot-like acervuli; B, L. S. of infected stem showing red longitudinal stripes and white transverse patches; C, infected leaf showing black dot-like acervuli on straw coloured mid-rib patches; D, magnified straw coloured mid-rib patches acervuli; E, section of infected leaf through acervulus showing mycelium, conidiophores, conidia and setae.

Reproduction. The reproduction takes place by asexually developed conidia on conidiophores.

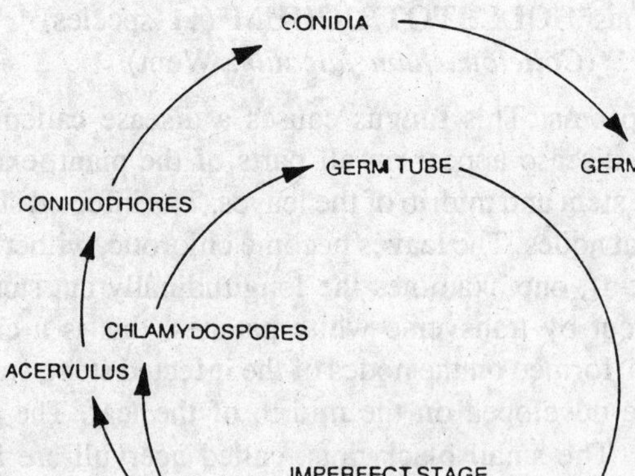

Fig. 14.2. Graphic life cycle of *Colletotrichum.*

Conidiophores and conidia. The conidiophores and conidia are found in acervuli. When a vertical section of infected leaf is cut through an acervulus, the conidiophores and conidia may easily be seen. Usually the conidiophores are single celled, aseptate, 20 μ long and 8μ broad. Each conidium is falcate, single celled, aseptate, hyaline, 20-60 μ long, 5 to 7 μ broad and with a single oil droplet. Some long pointed setae are also found in acervulus. The setae are brown, septate, 100 to 200 μ long and slender.

Perfect stage. The perfect stage of *Colletotrichum falcatum* is represented by *Physalospora tucumanensis* Spegazzini, which is a member of the order Sphaeriales of class Ascomycetes.

Systematic Position

	G. W. Martin (1961)	**C. J. Alexopoulos (1962)**	**G. C. Ainsworth (1971)**
Kingdom	–Plantae	–Plantae	–Fungi
Division	–Mycota	–Mycota	–Eumycota
Sub-div.	–Eumycotina	–Eumycotina	–Deuteromycotina
Class	–Deuteromycetes	–Deuteromycetes	–Coelomycetes
Order	–Melanconiales	–Melanconiales	–Melanconiales
Family	–Melanconiaceae	–Melanconiaceae	–Melanconiaceae
Genus	–*Colletotrichum*	–*Colletotrichum*	–*Colletotrichum*

ORDER MONILIALES
(780 genera; 10,000 species)

Characteristic Features

1. There are about 780 genera and 10,000 species in this order. This order is also known as Hyphomycetes.
2. The mycelium is branched, septate, geniculte, hyaline or brown, inter and intracellular.
3. The conidia develop on the apices and branches of conidiophores. The conidiophores are small, aerial, branched and sometimes arranged in stromatic structures.
4. The important families of this order are Dematiaceae, Moniliaceae, Stilbellaceae and Tuberculariaceae.

Family–Dematiaceae (265 genera; 1,750 species)

The hyphae are dark black. The conidia are typically dark. Sometimes hyphae are dark and conidia are clear, or the conidia are dark and hyphae are clear. Majority of forms are saprobic, but some are plant parasites and a few are parasitic on animals and man. Three genera, *Alternaria, Cercospora* and *Helminthosporium* have been discussed here in detail.

Genus ALTERNARIA (50 species)
(*Alternaria solani*)

Occurrence and symptoms. This fungus causes an important disease of potato known as 'early blight of potato'. In the beginning the yellowish brown spots develop on the leaves. Some of the spots are small in size while some are bigger. They are scattered on the surface of the leaf. Usually the spots are rounded, but the spots developed near about the stout veins are somewhat angular, because of the check of the fungal growth across the stout veins. In severe conditions the whole surface of the leaf is covered with such spots or lesions. The spots are merged to each other and with the result large black or dark brown spots are developed. If we study these spots with the help of hand lens, they look like **'target boards'**, this symptom of the disease is called the **'target board effect'**.

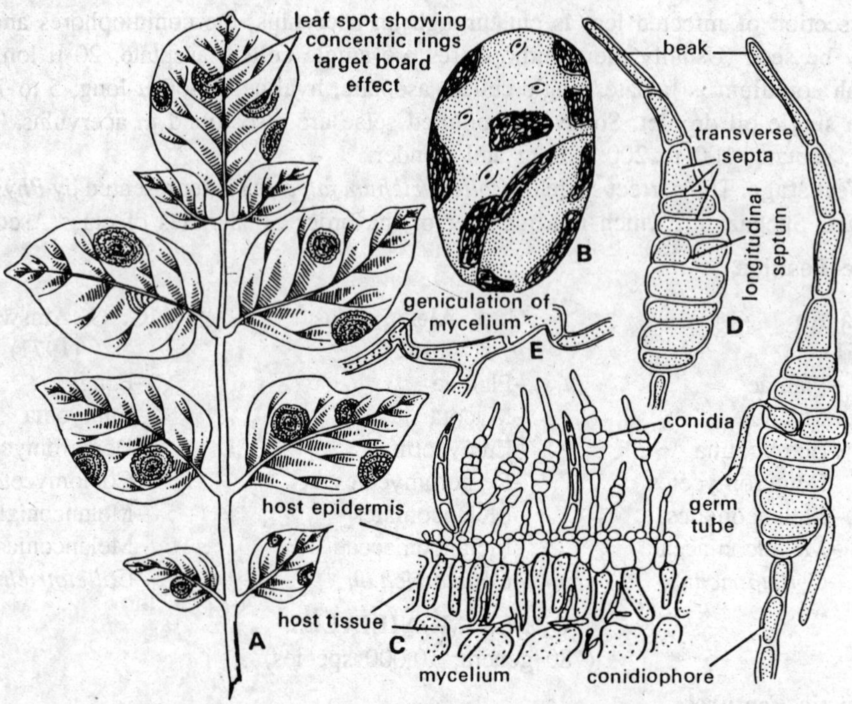

Fig. 14.3. *Alternaria solani.* Early blight of potato. A, affected leaf; B, affected tuber; C, section of infected leaf showing mycelium, conidiophores and conidia; D, conidium and germinating conidium; E, mycelium.

In severe conditions the other parts of the plant such as petioles, stems and tubers are also affected. The peel of infected tuber becomes dark brown, and the irregular or rounded spots develop on it. The pulp of the potato just below the peel becomes rusty or brown in appearance.

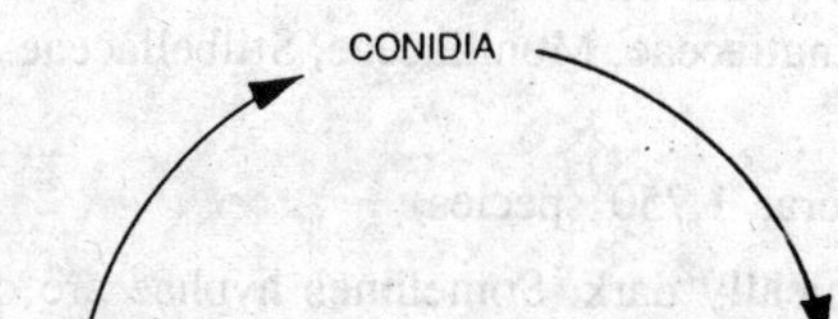

Fig. 14.4. Graphic life-cycle of *Alternaria.*

Mycelium. One can get the mycelium by teasing the infected leaf. The mycelium is endophytic, branched, septate, inter and intracellular, geniculate, light brown and without haustoria.

Reproduction. The fungus reproduces only by asexual method.

Conidiophores and conidia. Only asexual reproduction takes place. The asexual bodies are conidia, developing on the terminal ends of the conidiophores. Each conidiophore bears a single conidium at its terminal end. The conidiophores are aerial and septate.

The conidia are elongated and septate. Each conidium is 5 to 10 times septate. The septation takes place in both transverse and longitudinal directions. The apex of the conidium, is slender, elongated and beak like. Sometimes the germ tubes may also be seen coming out from the cells of the conidium under microscope.

Systematic Position

	G. W. Martin (1961)	**C. J. Alexopoulos (1962)**	**G. C. Ainsworth (1971)**
Kingdom	–Plantae	–Plantae	–Fungi
Division	–Mycota	–Mycota	–Eumycota
Sub-div.	–Eumycotina	–Eumycotina	–Deuteromycotina
Class	–Deuteromycetes	–Deuteromycetes	–Hyphomycetes
Order	–Moniliales	–Moniliales	–Moniliales
Family	–Dematiaceae	–Dematiaceae	–Dematiaceae
Genus	–*Alternaria*	–*Alternaria*	–*Alternaria*

Genus **CERCOSPORA** (1270 species)

(i) Cercospora personata *(ii) Cercospora arachidicola*

Occurrence and symptoms. A popular disease of groundnut is caused by two different species of this fungus. All the parts of the plant found above the ground level are infected,

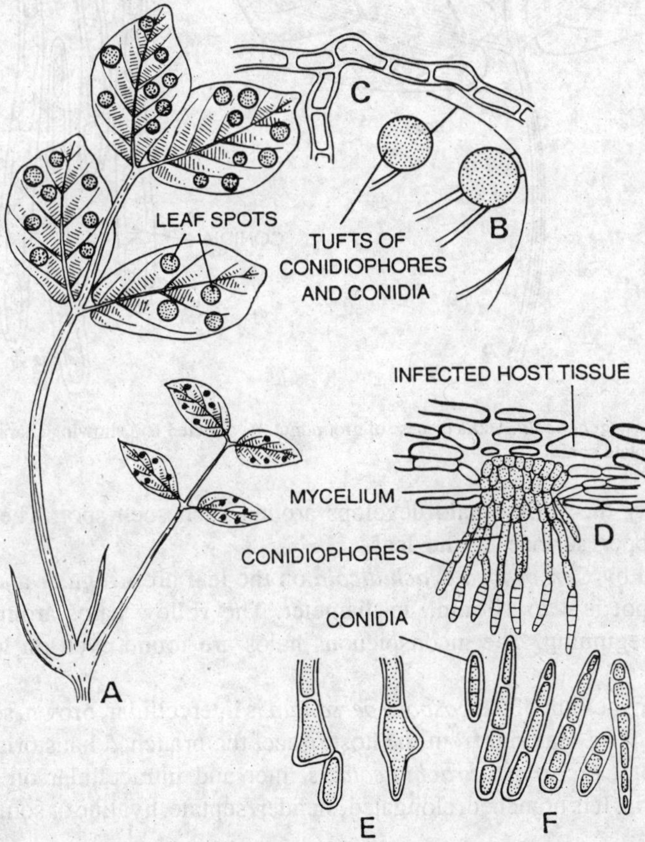

Fig. 14.5. *Cercospora personata.* Tikka disease of groundnut. A, infected leaf showing characteristic leaf spots; B, round spot surrounded by halo, tufts of conidiophores denoted by dots; C, geniculate mycelium; D, V.S. of infected leaf showing mycelium, conidiophores and conidia; E, apices of conidiophores; F, conidia.

but especially the spots caused by the disease appear on the leaves. In the month of July, when the plants become at least two months old, the symptoms begin to appear and this process continues upto maturity. The disease is caused by two different fungi called *Cercospora personata* and *Cercospora arachidicola* respectively. It is very clear that the symptoms caused by these two different fungi are different in nature and appearance. In our country, usually the disease is caused by *Cercospora personata*. The symptoms developed by *Cercospora arachidicola* are rarely seen.

The spots caused by *Cercospora personata* on the leaves are rounded and 1 to 6 mm. in diameter. The spots are dark brown or black and found on both the surfaces of the leaf.

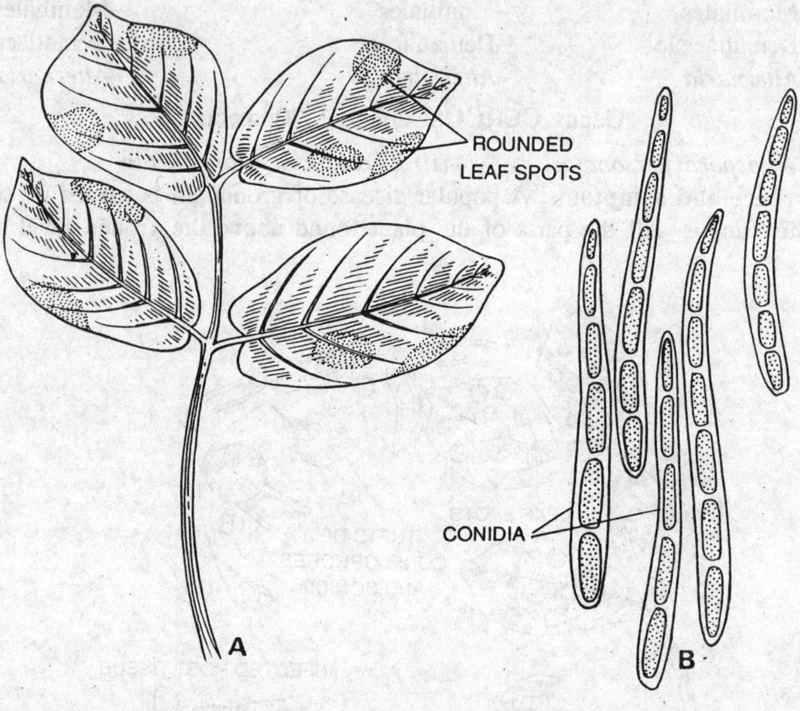

Fig. 14.6. *Cercospora arachidicola*. Tikka disease of groundnut. A, affected leaf showing characteristic round spots; B, elongated, transversely septate conidia.

Afterwards, on maturity the yellow halo develops around each such spot. These yellow halos are confined to the upper surface of the leaf.

The spots caused by *Cercospora arachidicola* on the leaf are irregular and comparatively bigger in size. Each spot is 4 to 10 mm., in diameter. The yellow halos around the spots are found from the very beginning. The inconspicuous halos are found even on lower surface of the leaf.

Mycelium. The mycelium of *Cercospora personata* is intercellular, brown, septate, branched and slender. To absorb food material from the host tissue, the branched haustoria are developed.

The mycelium of *Cercospora arachidicola* is inter and intracellular on the host tissue. It is without any haustoria. It is branched, elongated, slender, septate, hyaline or somewhat brownish in colour.

Reproduction. The reproduction takes place by asexual method.

Conidiophores and conidia. The conidiophores of *Cercospora personata* are 24 to 54 μ long and 5 to 8 μ broad. They are aseptate or 1 to 2 times septate. The conidiophores are geniculate (knee like). The conidia are developed on such geniculate structures. The conidia are situated on the terminal ends of the conidiophores. Each conidiophore bears a single conidium. The conidiophores are arranged in stroma. The conidia are cylindrical, obclavate, 18 to 60 μ long and 5 to 11 μ broad. Each conidium is 1 to 7 times transversely septate.

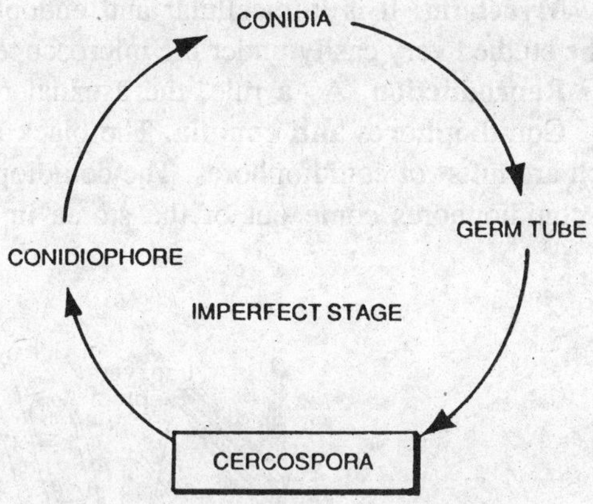

Fig. 14.7. Graphic life-cycle of *Cercospora*.

The conidiophores of *Cercospora arachidicola* are yellowish brown and geniculate. The conidium is attached to the conidiophore on such geniculate structure. The conidiophores are 22 to 41 μ long, 3 to 5 μ broad, aseptate. The conidia are yellowish in colour, obclavate, 31 to 108 μ long 3 to 6 μ broad and curved. Each conidium is, 3 to 12 times septate.

Perfect stages. (i) The perfect stage of *Cercospora personata* is *Mycosphaerella berkeleyji* W.A. Jenkins.

(ii) The perfect stage of *Cercospora arachidiola* is *Mycosphaerella arachidicola* W.A. Jenkins.

Systematic Position

	G. W. Martin (1961)	C. J. Alxopoulos (1962)	G. C. Ainsworth (1971)
Kingdom	–Plantae	–Plantae	–Fungi
Division	–Mycota	–Mycota	–Eumycota
Sub-div.	–Eumycotina	–Eumycotina	–Deuteromycotina
Class	–Deuteromycetes	–Deuteromycetes	–Hyphomycetes
Order	–Moniliales	–Moniliales	–Moniliales
Family	–Dematiaceae	–Dematiaceae	–Dematiaceae
Genus	–*Cercospora*	–*Cercospora*	–*Cercospora*

Genus **HELMINTHOSPORIUM** (175 species)

(*Helminthosporium gramineum*)

Occurrence and symptoms. This imperfect fungus causes the disease of barley known as **'stripe disease of barley'**. When the plants are of about two months, the symptoms appear on the leaves. These symptoms appear first on the lower leaves. In the beginning the yellow spots develop on the leaf sheath, and gradually develop towards the apex of the leaf. These spots fuse to each other and long stripes develop. Though these stripes begin to develop from the lower leaves, yet they are more conspicuous at the apices of the leaves. Ultimately the stripes become dark brown in colour. These stripes bear black dot-like structures in them, which represent the tufts of conidiophores coming out of the stomata. The stripes are brownish at their margins but dark brown in the centre. The infected leaf is turned along these stripes in long thread-like structures. This symptom is called the 'leaf shredding'. Only because of the presence of these stripes, the disease is called **'stripe disease'**. The ears also become dark brown in colour, and the grains become as light as straw.

Mycelium. It is intracellular and endophytic. It is branched sub-hyaline and septate. It can be studied very easily under the microscope, by cutting the infected leaf in vertical sections.

Reproduction. As a rule, the asexual reproduction takes place only.

Conidiophores and conidia. The black dot-like structures are seen in the brown stripes, which are tufts of conidiophores. The conidiophores are long, aseptate, hyaline and geniçulate. The conidiophores come out of the stoma in the groups of 3-5. On the terminal end of the

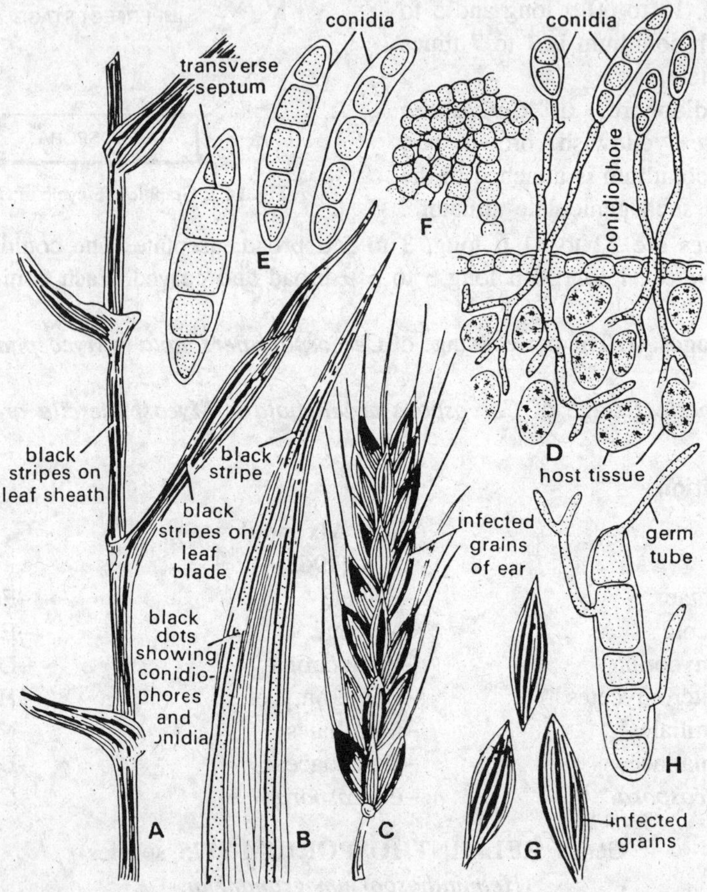

Fig. 14.8. Stripe disease of barley (*Helminthosporium gramineum*). A, infected twig; B, infected apical portion of leaf showing characteristic stripes with dot-like tufts of conidiophore; C, infected ear; D, V.S. of infected leaf showing mycelium, conidiophores and conidia; E, septate conidia; F, mycelium; G, infected grain; H, germinating conidium.

conidiophore a hyaline or yellowish brown conidium develops. The conidium is straight or somewhat curved. Each conidium is several times septate. On germination the germ tubes emerge out from the conidium.

Perfect stage. The perfect stage of *Helminthosporium gramineum* Rabh, is *Pyrenophora graminea* Ito and Kuribay.

Systematic Position

G. W. Martin (1961)		**C. J. Alexopoulos (1962)**	**G. C. Ainsworth (1971)**
Kingdom	–Plantae	–Plantae	–Fungi
Division	–Mycota	–Mycota	–Eumycota
Sub-div.	–Eumycotina	–Eumycotina	–Deuteromycotina
Class	–Deuteromycetes	–Deuteromycetes	–Hyphomycetes.
Order	–Moniliales	–Moniliales	–Moniliales
Family	–Dematiaceae	–Dematiaceae	–Dematiaceae
Genus	–*Helminthosporium*	–*Helminthosporium*	–*Helminthosporium*

Family–Tuberculariaceae (155 genera; 500 species)

A hyphal body is present which is more or less globose and sessile. This structure is known as sporodochium which is characteristic of family. The form genus *Fusarium* is the largest among the family. This genus has been discussed here in detail.

Genus **FUSARIUM** (65 species)
(*Fusarium udum*)

Occurrence and symptoms. This fungus causes a disease of pigeon peas (**arhar**) called the **'wilt of arhar'.** When the plants of pigeon peas (**arhar**) are 5-6 week old, they are infected. Their leaves become yellow and withered. Gradually the plant is wilted and ultimately dried up. Actually this is not because of scarcity of water or frost. But the plants are dried because of toxic effect of the fungus. If one studies the root of an infected plant after pulling it out from the soil, the black coloured streaks are seen on it. In the beginning these streaks are quite narrow but later on they become sufficiently broad. These black streaks may also be seen on the stem even upto sufficient height. The branching arising from these black streaks (vascular tissues) are wilted and withered. This is called 'partial wilting'. Mostly the complete plants are infected and wilted. The vascular tissues become blocked, because the fungus is filled up in these vessels. This fungus plugs the vessels

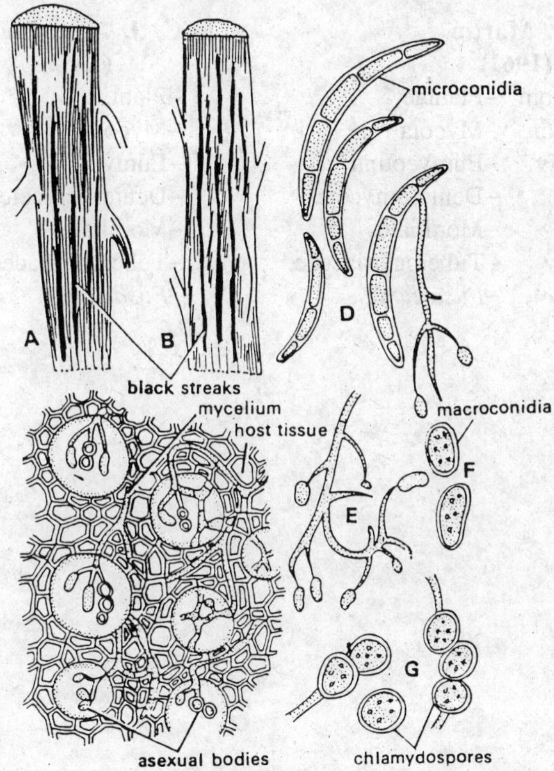

Fig. 14.9. *Fusarium udum.* Wilt of pigeon pea. A, L. S. of infected root, showing black vascular streaks; B, L.S. of infected stem showing black vascular streaks; C, T. S. of infected root showing mycelium, microconidia, chlamydospores in vessels; D, macroconidia and its germination; E, microconidia on conidiophore; F, microconidia; G, formation of chlamydospores.

and the ascent of water and salts is checked, and the plants begin to wilt. The mycologists of today think that certain toxins are secreted by this fungus, which kill the tissue of the host and the plant is wilted.

Mycelium. This fungus is a facultative parasite, and can survive in the soil in the absence of host. The mycelium is confined to the vascular tissue of the host plant. It is inter and intracellular, hyaline, branched, geniculate and septate.

Reproduction. The reproduction takes place by asexual method only.

Conidia and chlamydospores. Usually the conidiophores are not found. There are three types of spores which are found in the mycelium. These spores may be (1) microconidia, (2) macroconidia and (3) chlamydospores.

The microconidia are developed in the vessels of the host plant. They are small, oval or somewhat curved, unicellular or 1-2 times septate, 5-15 μ long and 3-4 μ broad.

The macroconidia are somewhat larger in size. They develop on the stroma of the mycelium found on the bark of the stem. They are long, curved backward, pointed at their ends and septate. Each such conidium is 15-20 μ long and 3-μ broad. Sometimes small conidiophores are also developed.

The chlamydospores are usually found in chains. They are confined in the xylem vessels. They are round, small and thick walled.

Systematic Position

	G. W. Martin (1961)	**C. J. Alexopoulos (1962)**	**G. C. Ainsworth (1971)**
Kingdom	–Plantae	–Plantae	–Fungi
Division	–Mycota	–Mycota	–Eumycota
Sub-div.	–Eumycotina	–Eumycotina	–Deuteromycotina
Class	–Deuteromycetes	–Deuteromycetes	–Hyphomycetes
Order	–Moniliales	–Moniliales	–Moniliales
Family	–Tuberculariaceae	–Tuberculariaceae	–Tuberculariaceae
Genus	–*Fusarium*	–*Fusarium*	–*Fusarium*

15

Economic Importance of Fungi

The fungi are related to both the useful and harmful activities to which the man is directly concerned. Several fungi are directly used as foodstuffs. Many mushrooms are edible and served as delicious dishes. The fungi, like yeasts are responsible for fermentation. The baking industry is dependent on the enormous budding of the yeast cells. Contrary to the useful activities the fungi act as great enemy to the human beings. Some of the mushroom-like fungi are highly poisonous and known as toadstools. If somehow, or other they are eaten as mushrooms, the death is sure. Many saprophytic fungi cause the sufficient damage and decay to the foodstuffs. Several fungi attack the paper wood pulp and give a death blow to the paper industry. Some fungi directly attack the book paper and cause sufficient damage. Many fungi cause the sufficient damage to the woollen and cotton textiles. Some fungi are the greatest enemy of the timbers, and cause the decay of the same. As we know, many of the parasitic fungi are responsible for hundreds of diseases of economic plants. Several fungi cause severe human and animal diseases. Conclusively, this can be said very safely that the fungi are our friends on one side and the greatest foes on the other side.

USEFUL ASPECTS

Direct utilization of fungi as food. Many Agaricales and Helvellales are directly used as food. There is a non-poisonous edible toadstool, *i.e., Coprinus* sp. found in lawns in the rainy season. *Agaricus campestris* is edible mushroom and cultivated for its fructifications. The fruiting bodies are quite fleshy and eaten directly as vegetable or with rice as **'pulao'**. These mushrooms are being successfully cultivated in South India. *Morchella esculenta* is another important edible fungus. It is found in Kashmir, Himachal and Punjab plains. Its local name is **'guchi'** and sold as costly as rupees two thousand or more per kilogram. *Torulopsis utilis,* is used for the large-scale production of yeast for food purposes. *Saccharomyces cerevisiae* is used in bread making industry.

Used as manures. The fungi with bacteria take part in the decay of organic plant and animal waste which is very essential for removing debris from our environments, for supplying carbon dioxide necessary for photosynthesis by green plants, and for providing humus, an important soil constituent for healthy plant growth.

Processing of food. A few species of *Penicillium* are being used in processing of food. *Penicillium camemberti* involved in ripening of Camembert cheese and *P. roqueforti* in ripening of Roquefort cheese. Danish blue cheese and the Italian Gorgonzola are also ripened with *Penicillium.* In Java, *Aspergillus wentii* is employed in processing soybeans, because of its ability to loosen the hard tissues of the bean.

Production of antibiotics. *Penicillium* is best known to the non-botanist because it is the source from which the antibiotic penicillin is extracted. Penicillin was first discovered in *Penicillium notatum* Westling and for a time this was the species from which penicillin was extracted. Later investigation has shown *P. chrysogenum* Thom to be better for this purpose, and irradiation of it with X-rays and ultraviolet light has induced mutants with an even higher content of penicillin. In India at Pimpri and Rishikesh there are big factories of antibiotics.

Beer and wine. Strains of *Saccharomyces cerevisiae* are commonly used in the manufacture of beer. **Taette** is an alcoholic beverage prepared from milk. Yeasts cause the characteristic changes in flavour. **Sake** is widely used alcoholic beverage of Japan. It is a yellow rice wine containing 14 to 24 percent of alcohol. An alcoholic fermentation ensues in which several yeasts may be active. *Saccharomyces sake, S. tokyo* and *S. yeddo* are some of the yeasts characteristic of sake. In Japan *Aspergillus oryzae* is used to make sake, and to manufacture various fermented foods.

Preparation of medicines. The famous drug, ergotine, which has long been used as a drug for obsteric purposes to induce uterine contractions in cases of delayed childbirth; ergot is obtained from *Claviceps purpurea,* the causal organism of plant disease, ergot of rye. This is found in Nilgiris and South India. The other fungi, *Ashbya gosypii* and *Eremothecium ashbyii* are used in the synthesis of vitamin B-riboflavin. *Saccharomyces cerevisiae* are employed in the synthesis of yeast tablets, rich in vitamins. *Saccharomyces cerevisiae,* are used in alcoholic fermentation.

Preparation of various acids. *Aspergillus niger* is however, employed in the production of gallic acid. The same fungus has also been employed in the production of citric and gluconic acids. Molliard (1922), found that gluconic acid was synthesized along with citric acid and oxalic acids by *Aspergillus niger. Aspergillus itaconicus* is used in the synthesis of itaconic acid. *Aspergillus terreus* also produces itaconic acid along with fumaric, succinic and oxalic acids. Kojic acid is obtained from the mycelium of *Aspergillus oryzae, A. glaucus, A. tamarii* and *A. flavus.* Many species of *Penicillium* are capable of producing organic acids, such as citric, fumaric, oxalic, gluconic and gallic.

Synthesis of enzymes. Many important and useful enzymes have been synthesized from various fungi. The enzyme tyrosinase is obtained from *Neurospora crassa. Saccharomycees cerevisiae* synthesizes invertase enzyme. *Aspergillus oryzae* has been employed in active enzyme preparation. *A. niger* produces starch digesting enzymes. *Aspergillus versicolor* synthesizes an enzyme capable of destroying tartrates and recommended its use in the commercial preparation of grape juice.

Production of esters. According to Birkinshaw and others (1931), the ethyl acetate was synthesized by *Penicillium digitatum.*

Production of pigments. A maroon coloured pigment, **fumigatin** is produced by *Aspergillus fumigatus.* The red pigments, **catenarin** is produced by *Helminthosporium* sp. Another important blue-purple pigment, **spinulosin** is produced by *Penicillium spinulosum.* A number of pigments have been isolated from yeasts, particularly from species of *Rhodotorula* and *Cryptococcus.*

HARMFUL ASPECTS

Plant pathogens. Various parasitic fungi act as causal organisms and infect hundreds of species and varieties of plants of the economic value. A list of few important diseases of the plants of economic importance, with their causal organisms is given below.

Name of Disease	Name of Crop	Causal organism
1. Club root	Cabbage	*Plasmodiophora brassicae*
2. Wart disease	Potato	*Synchytrium endobioticum*
3. Damping off	Various seedlings	*Pythium* sp.
4. Late blight	Potato	*Phytophthora infestans*
5. While rust	Crucifers	*Albugo candida* or *Cystopus candidus*

Name of Disease	Name of Crop	Causal organism
6. Downy mildew	Peas	*Peronospora pisi*
7. Downy mildew	Grapes	*Plasmopara viticola*
8. Powdery mildew	Grapes	*Uncinula necator*
9. Powdery mildew	Peas	*Erysiphe polygoni*
10. Powdery mildew	Wheat	*Erysiphe graminis*
11. Loose smut	Wheat	*Ustilago tritici*
12. Covered smut	Barley	*U. hordei*
13. Loose smut	Barley	*U. nuda*
14. Covered smut	Oats	*U. kolleri*
15. Loose smut	Oats	*U. avenae*
16. Whip smut	Sugarcane	*U. scitaminea*
17. Grain smut	Jowar	*Sphacelotheca sorghi*
18. Smut of	Bajra	*Tolyposporium penicillariae*
19. Black rust	Wheat	*Puccinia graminis tritici*
20. Brown rust	Wheat	*P. recondita*
21. Yellow rust	Wheat	*P. striiformis*
22. Rust of	Linseed	*Melampsora lini*
23. Early blight	Potato	*Alternaria solani*
24. Tikka disease	Groundnut	*Cercospora personata*
25. Red rot	Sugarcane	*Colletotrichum falcatum*
26. Flag smut	Wheat	*Urocystis tritici*
27. Leaf curl	Peach	*Taphrina deformans*

Besides, there are hundreds of other diseases which cause heavy losses to the pulses, vegetables, cereals, fruits and other important crops.

Decay of timber. Many species of *Polyporus* and other Basidiomycetes cause the damage and decay to the timber wood and sufficient losses are caused.

Destruction of textiles. According to Prindle (1935), the species of the genera *Alternaria, Penicillium* etc. are especially destructive to woollen textiles. According to Duske (1943), the rayon is destroyed by the genera of *Aspergillus* and *Penicillium.* According to Hardy (1943), the chief destructing fungi to the textiles are *Mucor, Aspergillus, Fusarium* and *Trichoderma.* The deterioration of cotton in storage is caused chiefly by a species of *Stachybotrys.* He also investigated that the greatest amount of damage to textile materials is due to *Chaetomium globosum.*

Destruction of paper industry. Many fungi cause damage to the paper pulp-wood, *e.g., Polyporus adustus, Polysticus hirsutus* etc. Many species of Basidiomycetes cause wood decay if suitable environmental conditions prevail. Many fungi destroy the paper of books and newspapers in moist condition. The fungi such as *Chaetomium, Aspergillus, Cephalothecium, Stachybotrys, Alternaria, Fusarium, Cladosporium, Stemphyllium, Dematium* cause sufficient damage to paper industry.

Spoilage of foodstuffs. *Penicillium digitatum* is responsible for the rotting of citrus fruits. According to Thom and Ayers (1916), many fungi, such as *Mucor, Aspergillus, Penicillium, Oidium* and *Fusarium,* cause damage to the milk and milk products. To avoid this damage to the milk normal pasteurization (*i.e.,* heating milk to 145^{0}F.) is necessary before distribution to the consumer. *Oidium lactis* develops the fishy odour of the butter and causes the damage to the butter. *Mucor mucedo* and *Aspergillus* are responsible for the bread spoilage.

Spoilage of meat. Many fungi are reported from the meat which cause sufficient spoilage to it, usually in tropical conditions. According to Yesair, *Mucor* sp., *Penicillium* sp., *Neurospora* sp., *Fusarium* sp., *Oidium* sp. and *Aspergillius* sp., are commonly met with on meat and cause damage to it.

Medical mycology. Several important human diseases are caused by different species of fungi. *Aspergillus fumigatus* and *A. glaucus* are responsible for the lung disease 'aspergillosis.' The disease 'mycosis' and 'tokelan' are caused by other species of *Aspergillus.* Several other animal and human diseases are caused by various fungi.

The dermatophytes are fungi which cause diseases of the skin of man. The diseases they cause are grouped under the general term **dermatomycoses** and are commonly known as ringworm, athlete's foot etc. *Epidermophyton flocossum* causes chronic infections commonly called athlete's foot. *Microsporum* generally infects the scalp of children, causing a condition called by medical personnel *tinea capitis.* The form genus *Trichophyton* also a cause of athlete's foot and other skin diseases is the largest of the form genera of dermatophytes. Several form-genera of the Moniliaceae which include serious human pathogens are *Blastomyces, Histoplasma, Geotrichum* and *Sporotrichum. Blastomyces dermatitidis* causes North American **blastomycosis.** South American **blastomycosis** caused by *Blastomyces braziliensis* is confined to South America and some parts of Central America. It is confined to the skin and mucous membranes around and in the mouth. Certain form species of *Geotrichum* are known to be pathogenic to man. Four forms of **geotrichosis** have been described–oral, intestinal, bronchial and pulmonary. *Sporotrichum schenkii* is the cause of **sporotrichosis** to man and animals.

MUSHROOMS AND THEIR CULTIVATION

Direct utilization of fungi as food. Many Agaricales and Helvellales are directly used as food. There is a non-poisonous edible toadstool, *i.e., Coprinus* sp. found in lawns in the rainy season. *Agaricus campestris* is edible mushroom and cultivated for its fructifications. The fruiting bodies are quite fleshy and eaten directly as vegetable or with rice as **'pulao'**. These mushrooms are being successfully cultivated in South India. *Morchella esculenta* is another important edible fungus. It is found in Kashmir and Punjab plains. Its local name is **'guchi'** and sold very costly. *Torulopsis utilis,* is used for the large-scale production of yeast for food purposes. *Saccharomyces cerevisiae* is used in bread making industry.

Of the many mushrooms that can be cultivated, only three kinds namely button mushroom (*Agaricus bisporus*), straw mushroom (*Volvariella volvacea*) and oyster mushroom (*Pleurotus sajorcaju*) are suitable for growing in India where suitable environmental conditions exist. The following account deals with cultivation of Button Mushroom (*Agaricus bisporus*).

Growing Season

Agaricus bisporus being a temperate mushroom grows best during winter throughout the plains of North India. It can however, be grown throughout the year in hills. The most suitable temperature for the spread of mycelium is 24-26^{0}C. Temperature ranging from 16-18^0 C is essential for the formation of fruit bodies. Higher temperatures are harmful but the lower temperature retards the development of both mushroom mycelium and fruit bodies.

Mushroom House

The mushroom house can be any available room, shed, basement, garage etc. The growing house should be well ventilated and not stuffy.

Compost

The cultivated mushroom is grown on a special compost. Two types of composts, natural and synthetic are used for growing this mushroom.

Composting Yard

The compost should be prepared on well cleaned concrete or *pucca* floor, which should be on a higher level so that the run-off water does not collect near the heap. Composting is usually done in the open, but it has to be protected from rain by covering it with polythene sheet. It can also be done in a shed with open sides or a large room to shelter it from rain.

Synthetic Compost

The following ingredients are required :

Wheat straw (chopped 8-20 cm. long)	250 Kg.
Wheat/Rice bran	20 Kg.
Ammonium sulphate/calcium ammonium nitrate	3 Kg.
Urea	3 Kg.
Gypsum	20 Kg.

This will make compost sufficient for 15-16 trays of size 1m × 1/2m × 15 cm.

Ten kg molasses and/or 60 kg chicken manure can also be used if available.

Procedure for Long Method

Mixing the materials and making pile : Day-0

The straw is uniformly spread over the composting yard in a thin layer and wetted (thoroughly by sprinkling water). All ingredients such as wheat bran, fertilizers etc., except gypsum are mixed thoroughly in the wetted straw, which is finally heaped into a pile about one metre high, one metre wide and as long as to hold the entire quantity of straw mixture. The pile can be made with hand or stack mould. The straw should be firmly but not compactly compressed into the mould.

It is essential to open the entire pile and remake it a number of times according to the following schedule :

1st turning	4th day
2nd turning	8th day
3rd turning	12th day, add 10 kg. gypsum.
4th turning	16th day, add 10 kg. gypsum.
final turning	20th day, spray 10 ml malathion in 5 litre water (any other available pesticide like, DDT, BHC, Lindane can also be used).

At each turning water should be sprinkled to make up the loss of water due to evaporation. If it is desired to add molasses, then 10 kg molasses diluted 20 times with water should be poured over the straw mixture during the first turning. Sixty kg chicken manure if available can also be added at the time of start of pile, *i.e.*, 0-day to improve the quality of the compost.

Natural Compost

It is prepared from horse dung which must be freshly collected and not have been exposed to rain. It should not contain admixture of dung of other animals. Chopped wheat straw (1/3, or more of weight of horse dung) is mixed with the horse dung to which 3 kg urea and/or 100-110 kg poultry manure per tonne is usually added. Horse dung and straw mixture is uniformly spread over the composting yard and sufficient water is sprinkled over it so that the straw becomes sufficiently wet so that it takes no more water. The manure is then heaped in a pile as for synthetic compost. After 3 days when the manure in the heap gets heated up due to fermentation and gives off an odour of ammonia, it is opened up and repeated 3 or 4 times after an interval of 3-4 days. Twenty five kg gypsum per tonne is added in two instalments at 3rd and 4th turning. At the final turning 20 ml malathion diluted in 10 litres of water is sprayed into the manure.

Filling

The compost when ready for filling and spawning has a dark brown colour and no trace of ammonia. There is no unpleasant odour but it smells like a fresh hay. The pH is neutral or near neutral. The compost should not be too dry or too wet at the time of filling in the trays which can be determined by the palm test. For this purpose a small quantity of compost is taken into the hand and pressed lightly, if a few drops of water ooze of the fingers then it is of right consistency. If relatively dry then the water should be made up by sprinkling. If too wet, the excess water may be allowed to evaporate. The prepared compost is now filled in trays, which may be of any convenient size but its depth should be 15-18 cm. A standard size of tray 1 m × ½ m × 15 cm. The tray should be made of soft wood and provided with the pegs at the four corners so that they can be stacked one over the other leaving sufficient space between the two trays for various operations. The tray is completely filled with the compost, lightly compressed and the surface levelled.

Spawning

Spawning means sowing the beds with the mycelium (spawn) of the mushroom. Spawn can be had from mushroom Laboratory College of Agriculture, Chambaghat, Solan at a nominal cost. Small quantity of spawn is also available from the Division of Mycology, Indian Agricultural Research Institute, New Delhi. The grain spawn is scattered on the surface of the tray bed which is covered with the thin layer of compost. Spawning can also be done by mixing the spawn with compost before filling it in trays. Five hundred gram spawn (two ½ lit bottles/polypacks) is sufficient for five trays of standard size. After spawning the compost surface is covered with old newspaper sheet, which is wetted by sprinkling water to provide the humidity but not water is directly added to the compost during spawn running.

The trays after spawning are stacked vertically one over the other in 4-5 tiers. One metre clear space may be left in between the top tray and ceiling. There should be about 15-20 cm space between the two trays.

The room should be maintained at 25°C or near about. The humidity should be built up by frequently watering the floor and walls. The room may be kept closed as no fresh air is needed during the spawn run. White cottony mycelium spreads and permeates through the compost.

Eventually the compost surface gets covered with the mycelium. It takes 12-15 days for complete spawn run. Low temperature prolongs the spread of the mycelium.

Casing

After the spawn run is complete as is evident by white mouldy growth, the surface of the compost is covered with 3 cm layer of casing soil. A suitable casing soil can be prepared by mixing equal part of well rotten cowdung (finely crushed and coarsely sieved) and garden soil. The casing material should possess high water holding capacity, good pore space and pH should not be lower than 7.4. The casing material is sterilized to kill insects, nematodes and molds. Sterilization can be accomplished either by steaming or by treating with formalin solution. For one cubic metre of casing soil, half litre of formalin diluted with 10 litre of water is sufficient. The casing soil is spread over a plastic sheet and treated with formalin by sprinkling. The treated soil is piled up in a heap and covered with another plastic sheet for 48 hours. The soil is turned frequently for about a week to remove all traces of formalin which can be tested by smelling it. After casing, the temperature of the room is maintained for further three days, after which it must be lowered to below 18°C. At this stage lot of fresh air is needed and therefore, the growing room should be ventilated by opening windows etc.

Cropping and Harvesting

The first flush of the pin heads becomes visible 15-20 days after casing or say about 35-40 days after spawning. Small white buttons develop 5-6 days after pin head stage. The right stage of harvest is when the cap is still tight over the short stem. In case the buttons are allowed to mature, the membrane below the cap will rupture and the cap will open up in umbrella-like shape. Such mushrooms are considered be the inferior. Harvesting is done by holding the cap with forefingers slightly pressed against the soil. The soil particles and mycelial threads clinging to the base of the stalk are chopped off. Mushroom can also be harvested by cutting off with a sharp knife at soil level.

Yield

The average yield of 3-4 kg per tray is considered normal. However, if compost is carefully prepared, spawn reliable and favourable temperature prevailing during the growing period, then a yield of 5-6 kg per tray is possible. Partial or complete failure may also happen due to negligence.

Storage :

The mushrooms are best consumed fresh. Storage in refrigerator for a few days is possible. The mushrooms should be placed between moist paper towel for storing in a refrigerator.

16

Heterothallism, Parasexuality and Sex Hormones in Fungi

HETEROTHALLISM

Heterothallism. Ehrenbergh (1829), for the first time studied zygospores in the order Mucorales. The American mycologist Blakeslee (1904), reported that in the several genera of the order Mucorales, the zygospores are not formed at all. He also supported his view with facts and reasons, and also investigated that in the same order two types of species are found which may be named as homothallic and heterothallic species. When the two hyphae of the same mycelium produced by a single spore fuse with each other and a zygospore is developed, the species is said to be homothallic, *e.g., Mucor hiemalis.*

Mucor mucedo and *Mucor stolonifer* are the typical heterothallic species. In heterothallic species the fusion can take place only among the different strained hyphae, which develop on different mycelia of different (+ and –) strains. In these species the zygospores cannot be produced by the fusion of two hyphae of the same strain. In 1904 Blakeslee reported that in heterothallic species whenever the mycelia of + and – strains remain apart from each other, the zygospores are not produced and only the sporangia are formed. On the other hand, when + and – mycelia grow together, the fusion takes place and the zygospores are produced. Morphologically the + and – strained mycelia are quite similar in structure, but different in physiological behaviour. In other words, they are morphologically identical and physiologically different. Sometimes, it has also been observed that the growth of the + mycelium is comparatively faster, and the gametangia of + mycelium are bigger than that of the – mycelium, and they can be distinguished as female and male gametaniga. Many mycologists do not support this view and advocate that this behaviour is only because of nutrition.

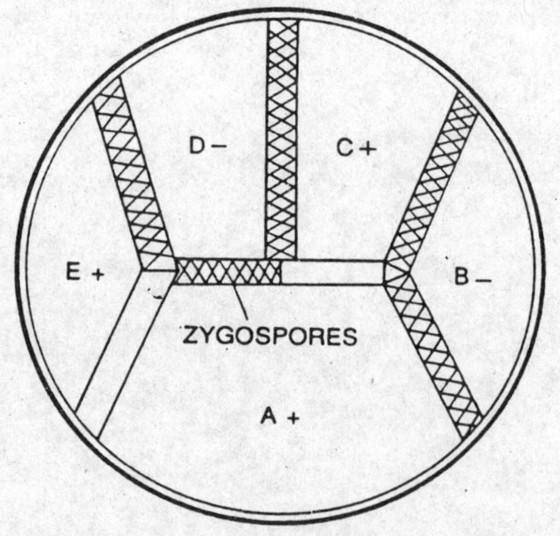

Fig. 16.1. Heterothallism in Mucorales-Blakeslee's experiment.

Blakeslee proved the phenomenon of heterothallism on the basis of experiments. He inoculated many + and – strained spores on the agar medium in a petri dish and observed that the fusion occurs only at those points where the hyphae of different strains (*i.e.,* + and –) come in contact. The zygospores were only produced at the points of contact of different strained hyphae. Absolutely no zygospores were produced at the points of contact of same strained hyphae.

This experiment may be clearly understood by the figure given in the text. Five spores of different strains are inoculated in a sterilized petri dish on agar medium at different five points designated as A, B, C, D and E. The zygospores are produced only at those points where the mycelia are opposite strained and produced from + and – spores designated as A, C and E are + strained, B and D are – strained. The zygospores are produced at the junctures of AB, BC, DE and AD where the opposite strained mycelia take part in fusion. The zygospores are not produced at the junctures of AC and AE because of the mycelia of same strains.

Blakeslee also investigated that if the + strained hyphae of one heterothallic species fuse with the – strained hyphae of another heterothallic species the **imperfect zygospores** are resulted. In such conditions the zygospores do not mature. He also investigated that in the heterothallic species *Mucor mucedo* the zygospores produced germsporangia on germination, which contain single strained spores, and, therefore, the fusion is possible only when the mycelia are produced from the spores formed in different strained germsporangia. In the heterothallic species of *Phycomyces nitens* the + and – strained spores are produced in the same germsporangium.

The phenomenon of heterothallism was first reported in the order Mucorales, but now this has been established in rusts, smuts, Homobasidiomycetidae and other fungi.

PARASEXUALITY

Some fungi do not go through a true sexual cycle, but derive many of the benefits of sexuality through **parasexuality** (Gr. *para* = beside + sex). This is a process in which plasmogamy, karyogamy and haploidization take place, *but not at specified points in the thallus or the life cycle*. For example, the Deuteromycetes (Fungi Imperfecti) are fungi in which sexual reproduction does not take place and in which the parasexual cycle is of paramount importance. However, some fungi which reproduce sexually also exhibit parasexuality. The parasexuality has been reported also in *Aspergillus nidulans* (of Ascomycetes).

Parasexuality was first discovered in 1952 by Pontecorvo and Roper of the University of Glasgow in *Aspergillus nidulans*, the imperfect stage of *Emericella nidulans*. Since then parasexual phenomena have been identified in several imperfect fungi (the Deuteromycetes) which possess no sexual stage, as well as in Basidiomycetes and in Ascomycetes other than *Emericella nidulans*.

According to G. Pontecorvo (1956, 1958), the sequence of events in a complete parasexual cycle is as follows :

1. Formation of heterokaryotic mycelium.
2. Fusion between two nuclei.
   (a) Fusion between like nuclei.
   (b) Fusion between unlike nuclei.
3. Multiplication of diploid nuclei side by side with the haploid nuclei.
4. Occasional mitotic crossing-over during the multiplication of the diploid nuclei.
5. Sorting out of diploid nuclei.
6. Occasional haploidization of the diploid nuclei.
7. Sorting out of new haploid strains.

However, in *Penicillium chrysogenum* and *Aspergillus niger*, neither of which is known to reproduce sexually, diploidization and mitotic crossing-over occur much more frequently, so that the importance of the parasexaual cycle in the Fungi Imperfecti (Deuteromycetes) may be as great as that of the sexual cycle in other fungi, from the stand point of the evolution of the species.

SEX HORMONES

Twenty years after Blakeslee's discovery of heterothallism, Burgeff (1924), in a series of experiments demonstrated that a diffusible substance is probably responsible for the initiation of sexual reproduction in the Mucorales. This was the first demonstration of a hormonal sexual mechanism in the fungi. Burgeff, working with a number of species, showed that, when + and – strains were separated by a collodion membrane, hyphae of opposite strains were still attracted toward each other. Subsequent work by other investigators (Plempel, 1957, 1960; Plempel and Braunitzer, 1958) has expanded upon Burgeff's discovery, and is giving us some knowledge as to the nature of hormones involved and their method of operation.

There are strong indications that a complicated hormonal mechanism operates in initiating plasmogamy, at least in some Ascomycetes. For example, the trichogynes are attracted to compatible male sex cells (spermatia) and will change their direction of growth in response to the proximity of sex cells.

In *Allomyees* (of order Blastocladiales and class Chytridiomycetes), attracted by the sexual hormone **sirenin** produced by the female gametes (Machlis, 1958), the male gametes copulate with the latter in parts very soon after their release from the gametangia.

THE LICHENS

17

Form Class–Lichens

Definition. A lichen is a plant consisting of two separate plants, a fungus and an alga, so closely associated with each other as to appear a single plant. The algal cells of the association are always enveloped by the fungus. The combined growth of both partners results in a constant definite form and internal structure of the lichen. This group has about 400 genera and 15,000 species and is treated separately instead of its connection with fungi or algae. The science of lichens is termed **lichenology** and one who studies this science is known as **lichenologist.**

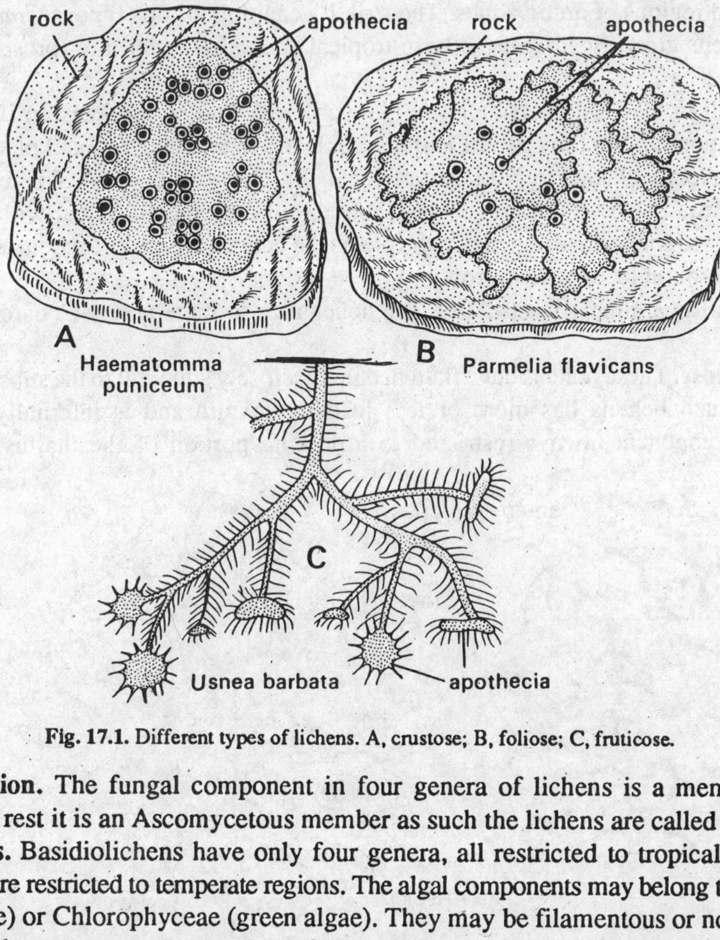

Fig. 17.1. Different types of lichens. A, crustose; B, foliose; C, fruticose.

Composition. The fungal component in four genera of lichens is a member of Basidiomycetes and in rest it is an Ascomycetous member as such the lichens are called **Basidiolichens** and **Ascolichens.** Basidiolichens have only four genera, all restricted to tropical regions, while the Ascolichens are restricted to temperate regions. The algal components may belong to Myxophyceae (blue green algae) or Chlorophyceae (green algae). They may be filamentous or non-filamentous. Basidiolichens always possess a member of Myxophyceae. Some lichens have been observed, where fungi are associated with autotrophic bacteria. Each lichen is always formed of the same fungal and algal components and has constant internal structure and habit.

Nature. The nature of lichens is a subject of controversy. According to some authors, the fungal-algal partnership is of parasitic nature, while others believe, they are symbiotic in nature. In many lichens, the haustoria and appressoria from the fungus penetrate into the algal cells. This is a very strong point in support that the relationship between fungus and alga is of parasitic nature. They are of the view, "a lichen is a fungus which lives during all or a part of its life in a parasitic relation with an organic or inorganic substratum".

Others believe that the partnership (**consortium**) between a fungus and an alga is of symbiotic nature. Fungal hyphae absorb moisture from a spongy structure which retains it, and give support to the alga. The alga in return synthesizes the carbohydrates necessary for both the partners. This type of symbiosis is known as **heliotism,** (=master and slave).

The fungus separated from the lichen never grows to maturity. On the other hand the alga can live independently apart from the lichen but it grows better in the symbiotic association.

Habit and habitat. Lichens grow in the presence of sufficient moisture, cold or moderate temperature, direct sunlight and pure atmosphere. They grow on the leaves, tree trunks, old logs, floor of forests and on exposed rocks. Some lichens are cushion-like masses on bare rocks in extremely cold regions of arctic zones. The striking example of this type is *Cladonia rangifera* Web. Some lichens grow most luxuriently in tropical and subtropical rain forests, in abundance of moisture.

The rainfall in the Eastern Himalayas is much more than in the Western Himalayas. The lichens are more common in the Eastern Himalayas. Darjeeling, Gangtok, and places upto 10,000 feet en route to Jemu glacier in Sikkim are ideal for lichen collection. There, almost every rock, tree fence, road side wooden poles and house walls are seen covered with various forms of crustose, fruticose and foliose lichens. In the plains the lichens are almost absent as the conditions are entirely unfavourable for their growth.

Structure. Regarding their structure, the lichens are of three types–**Crustose, Foliose** and **Fruticose.**

1. Crustose. These lichens have flattened thalli, closely adherent to the substratum. Thallus of majority of such lichens has more or less leathery texture and is internally differentiated with the algal component always restricted to a definite portion of the thallus. Some lichens

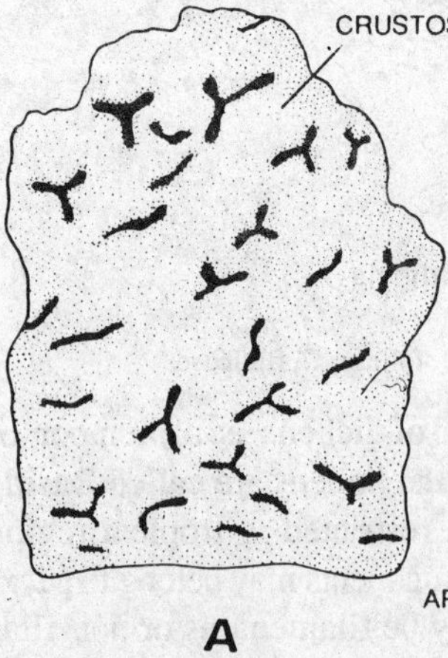

Fig. 17.2. A, Crustose lichen;

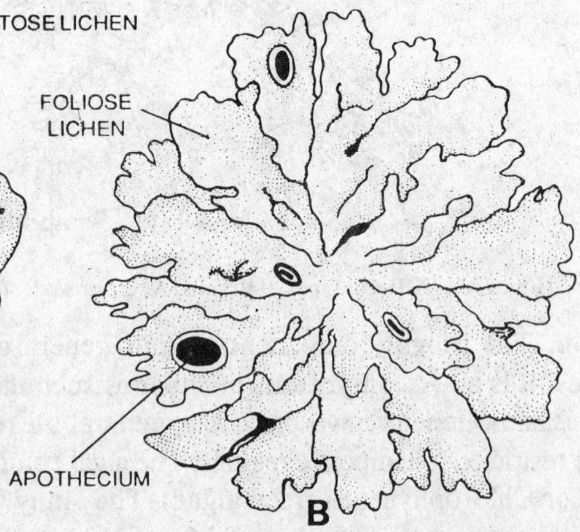

Fig. 17.2. B, Foliose lichen.

have gelatinous thallus, in which alga and fungus are uniformly distributed through a gelatinous matrix. Lichens vary in form, colour and thickness. Thalli of these lichens may remain partly or fully submerged in the substratum on which they grow. In the cases where body is fully embedded, only the fruiting bodies (ascocarps) of the fungus appear on the surface of the substrate.

2. Foliose. These lichens possess leaf-like thalli with lobed or irregularly folded margins. Some parts of thallus are more or less firmly attached to the substratum by means of hyphal outgrowths, **rhizines** from the lower surface. Rhizines may consist of separate single branched or unbranched hyphae, or of several parallel hyphae closely adhered to each other to form strands. A foliose lichen like *Gyrophora* may be attached to the substratum by a single rhizine growing from the centre of the thallus or a lichen may be attached by several rhizines.

3. Fruticose. These lichens have much branched, cylindrical, ribbon-like, flattened or sometimes filamentous thalli. They are much branched, and appear shrubby, and so the name **fruticose** (*frutex* = shrub) is given to them. They may be erect (*Cladonia*) or pendant (*Usnea*). Their thalli are attached to the substratum by the basal portion only which is composed of strands of densely packed hyphae.

Fig. 17.3. Fruticose lichen.

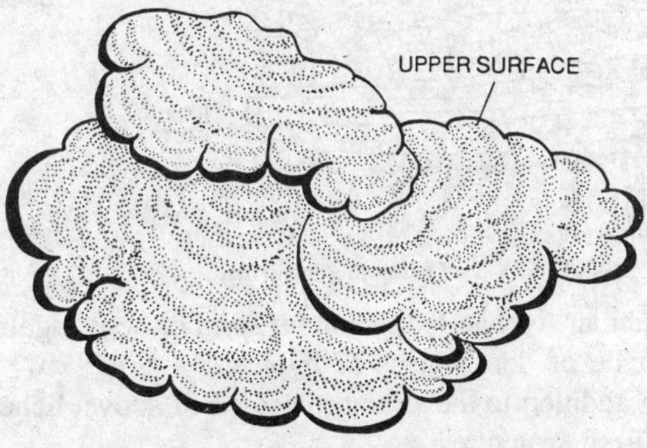

Fig. 17.4. Basidiolichen (*Cora puvina*)

The lichens are variously coloured commonly bluish-green or greyish-green. Many lichens are yellow, orange, reddish, brownish or black due to the presence of additional pigments.

Internal structure. The gelatinous thalli of crustose lichens have algal and fungal components uniformly distributed through a gelatinous matrix. Thalli of such lichens are not differentiated into layers of tissues and therefore, known as **homomerous.** Thalli or most foliose and fruticose lichens are differentiated into several layers of tissues, and therefore known a **heteromerous.** Thalli of foliose lichens have four layers of different tissues. The uppermost layer, **upper cortex,** is composed of more or less vertical hyphae. The intercellular spaces between the hyphae are either absent or filled with gelatinous substance. An epidermis-like layer formed of closely packed hyphae may or may not be present external to the upper cortex. Beneath this cortical layer is **algal layer.** In this layer algal cells lie intermingled with the loosely interwoven

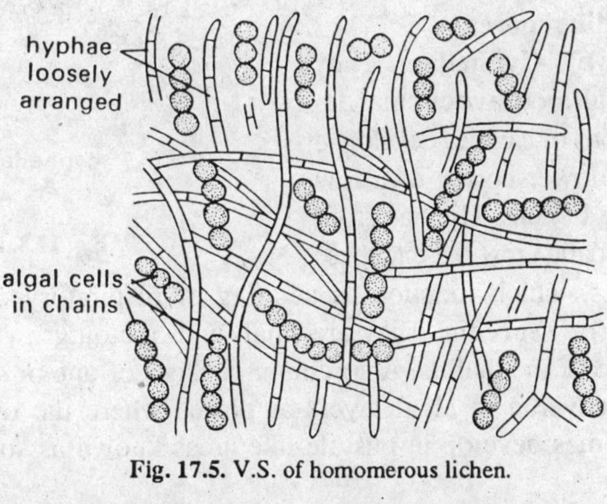

Fig. 17.5. V.S. of homomerous lichen.

fungal hyphae. At one time these algal cells were thought to be reproductive cells of lichens and were known as **gonidia,** and therefore, even today the algal layer is often called **gonidial layer.** Beneath the gonidial layer is **medulla** composed of very loosely interwoven hyphae with very large interspaces. Below medulla is the **lower cortex.** It is made of compact hyphae which may be parallel to perpendicular to the surface of the thallus. The interspaces between the hyphae are either absent or filled with gelatinous material. The rhizines grow out from the underside of the lower cortex and attach the thallus to the substratum. Basidiolichen has uppermost layer of loose perpendicular hyphae **(superior layer)**, below it **algal layer** and the lowermost is the **inferior layer** made of dense mass of hyphae.

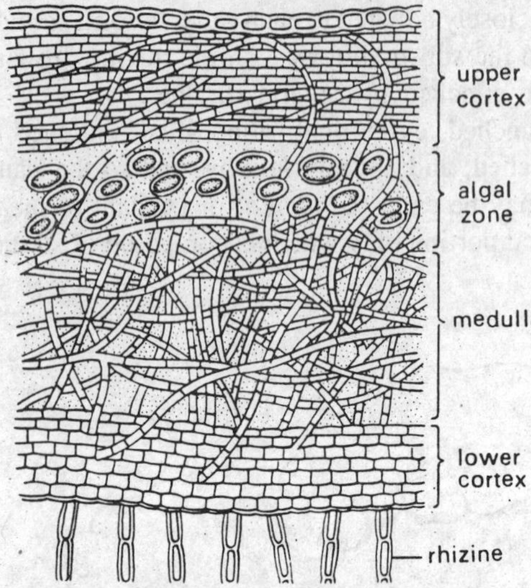

Fig. 17.6. V.S. of heteromerous lichen.

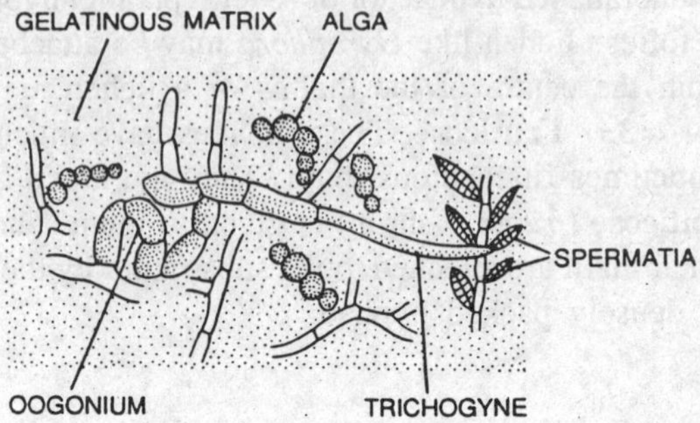

Fig. 17.7. V. S. thallus-crustose lichen.

In addition to the structure described above, lichens bear certain peculiar vegetative structures. These structures are:

(a) Breathing pores. In the upper cortex of some foliose and fruticose lichens, the hyphae are very loosely interwoven to facilitate the gaseous exchange between the thallus and the atmosphere. These localized areas may be depressions or conelike and are known as **breathing pores.**

(b) Cyphellae. They are small, concave circular depressions or cavities developed in the lower cortex of a few foliose lichens. Hyphae from the medulla grow out into these cavities, which function as aerating or respiratory organs.

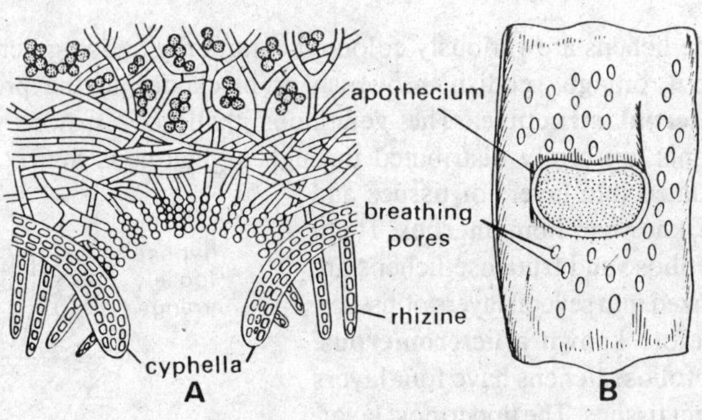

Fig. 17.8. Lichens. A, cyphellae; B, breathing pores.

(c) Soredia. They are small bud-like outgrowths, recognisable as greyish powder on the surface of the thallus. A soredium consists of one or more algal cells enclosed by a few hyphae. They develop in algal layers at places where the over lying upper cortex is absent. Soredia sometimes develop in pustule-like areas known as **sorelia.** Each soredium develops into a new thallus.

(d) Isidia. They are the small papillate outgrowths from the upper surface of the thallus. They consist of an external cortical layer and an internal algal layer. Their primary function

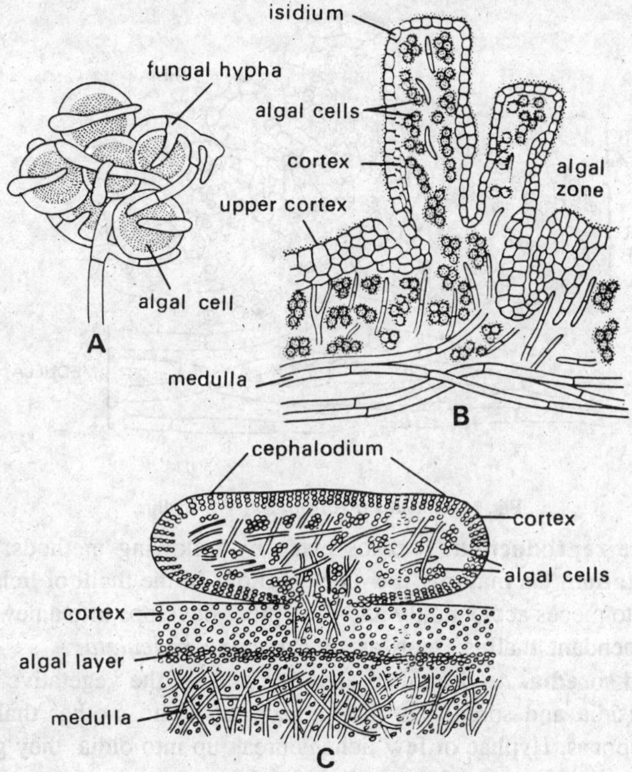

Fig. 17.9. Lichens. A, soredia; B, isidia; C, cephalodia.

is to increase the photosynthetic surface of the thallus, but sometimes they get detached from the thallus and serve as vegetative reproductive bodies.

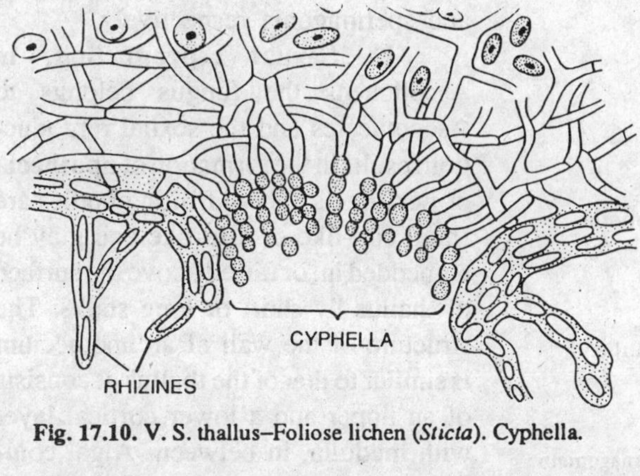

Fig. 17.10. V. S. thallus–Foliose lichen (*Sticta*). Cyphella.

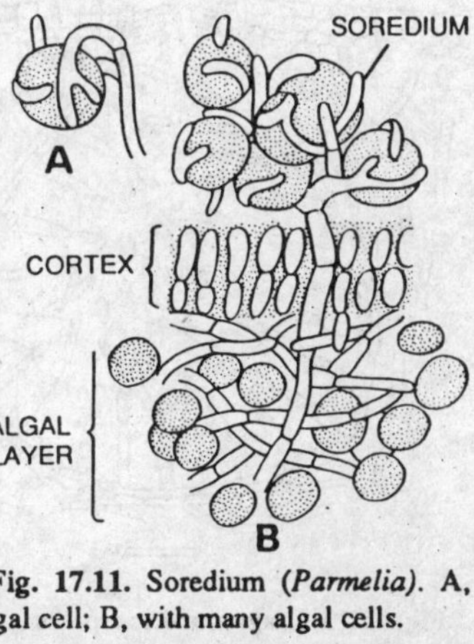

Fig. 17.11. Soredium (*Parmelia*). A, with single algal cell; B, with many algal cells.

(e) Cephalodia. They are external or internal gall-like outgrowths, generally of dark colour. They consist of fungal hyhae enclosing algal cells different from those of the thallus.

Reproduction. Commonly lichens reproduce vegetatively and sexually, but in some Ascolichens asexual spores are also formed.

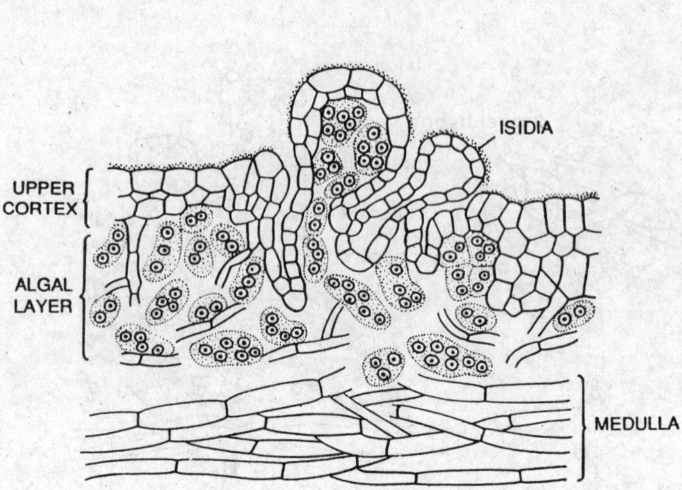

Fig. 17.12. Isidia (*Peltigera* sp.) V.S. thallus.

A. Vegetative reproduction. It takes place by following methods:

1. Fragmentation. On maturity the older portions of the thalli of lichens die and decay. The thallus breaks into pieces accidentally and each piece develops into a new plant. This occurs more frequently in pendant thallus, such as of *Ramalina reticulata.*

2. Isidia and soredia. As described above (c and d), the vegetative reproduction takes place by means of isidia and soredia as they detach from the mother thalli.

B. Asexual spores. Hyphae of few lichens break up into oidia, they germinate into new fungal hyphae and each oidium produces a lichen when comes in contact with suitable alga. Many lichens produce large number of small spore-like structures, **pycniospores,** within flask-shaped **pycnia,** immersed within the thallus. These structures when act as male gametes are known as spermatia and spermagonia respectively.

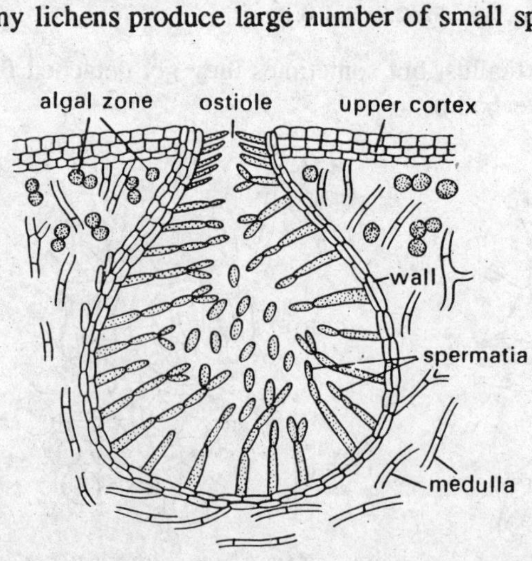

Fig. 17.13. Diagrammatic representation of spermagonium (pycnium) of *Physcia.*

C. Sexual reproduction. In Ascolichens the fungus belongs to Ascomycetes and the sexual reproduction results in the formation of **apothecia** or **perithecia.** These fruiting bodies are small cup-like or disc-like and may be embedded in, or raised above the surface of thallus by short or long stalks. The structure of the wall of an apothecium is similar to that of the thallus, it consists of an upper and a lower cortical layer with medulla, in between. Algal components may not be present in the vegetative part of the apothecium. The bottom of the cup, or the surface of the disc is the fertile part of the apothecium and is lined by the **hymenium.** Hymenium consists of asci and paraphyses growing vertically. Paraphyses contain a reddish oily substance in them and never project beyond

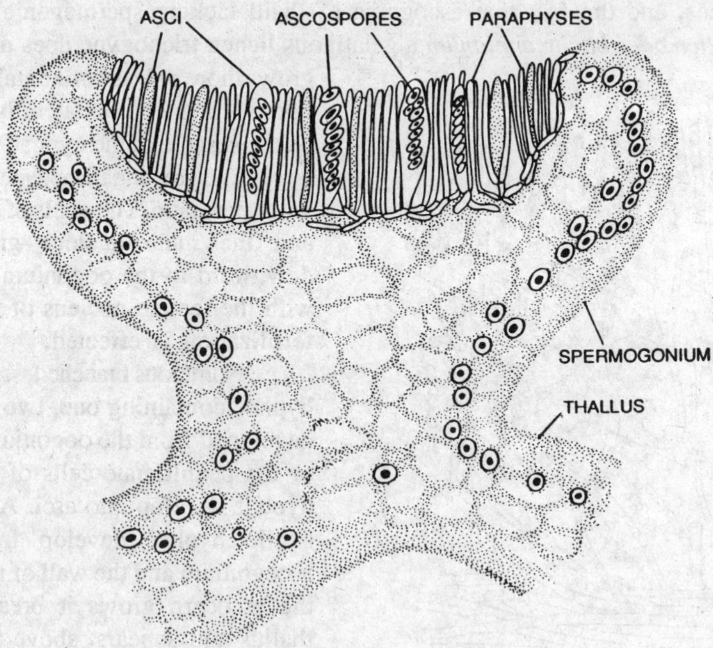

Fig. 17.14. V. S. apothecium (*Physcia*).

asci. Each ascus contains eight ascospores, which become two celled prior to dissemination. Asci are the resultants of sexual union.

Sex organs. The female reproductive organ is an **ascogonium** (carpogonium) which develops from hypha deep in the algal layer. It is a long multicellular hypha, the coiled base of it is the **oogonium** and the straight portion above it the **trichogyne.** The trichogyne in some species

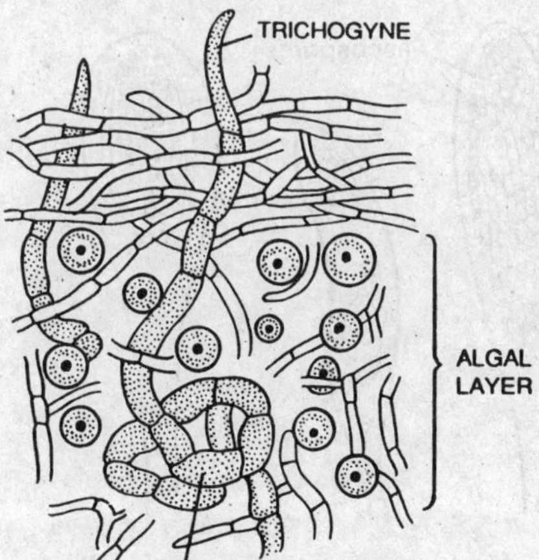

Fig. 17.15. V. S. thallus (*Physcia*).

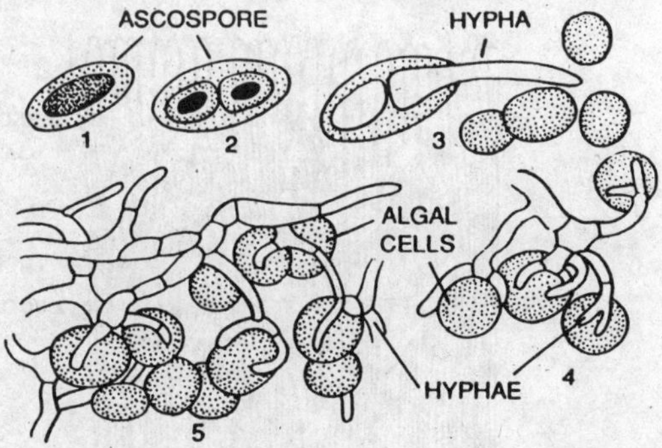

Fig. 17.16. Germination of ascospores and its association with algal cells to form lichen.

projects beyond thallus. More than one ascogonia may develop at a point where an apothecium is later formed but only one becomes fertile.

The male reproductive body is **spermagonium** (pycnium). It is flask-shaped cavity immersed in the thallus and opens to the exterior by small **ostiole.** The fertile hyphae lining the inner surface of the spermagonium produce large number of small non-motile gametes **spermatia.** The spermatia are functional male gametes. The spermatia are lodged against the sticky protruding tips of trichogynes, and the fact that ascogonia of thalli lacking spermagonia rarely produce ascocarps. In *Collemodes bachmannianum* a gelatinous lichen trichogyne does not protrude, but grows more or less horizontally in the thallus. Spermatia are borne laterally and terminally on the surface of the hyphae with the thallus.

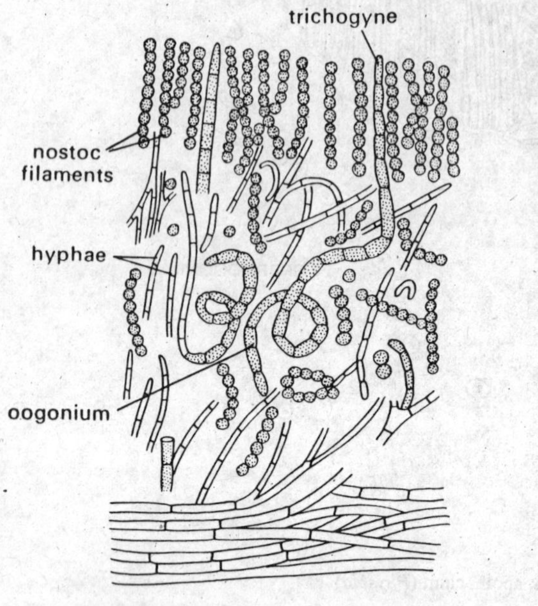

Fig. 17.17. V. S. of lichen thallus showing symbiotic components and trichogyne.

The growing trichogyne comes in contact with spermatia. The walls of contact dissolve and the male nucleus gradually passes downward to the oogonium, where it fuses with the female nucleus of the egg and the fertilization is effected.

Numerous branched, septate ascogenous hyphae containing one, two or many nuclei developed from the oogonium. The ultimate or the penultimate cells of the ascogenous hyphae develop into asci. At the same time sterile hyphae develop from below the ascogonium and the wall of the ascocarp. As the ascocarp grows it breaks through the thallus and appears, above the surface as a cup or disc or remains embedded.

The development of asci and ascospores resembles to that of typical Ascomycetes. Spores are shed only during moist weather. On germination, a spore produces a germ tube which grows in all directions, and as soon as it comes in contact with a suitable alga, additional branches are formed to engulf the

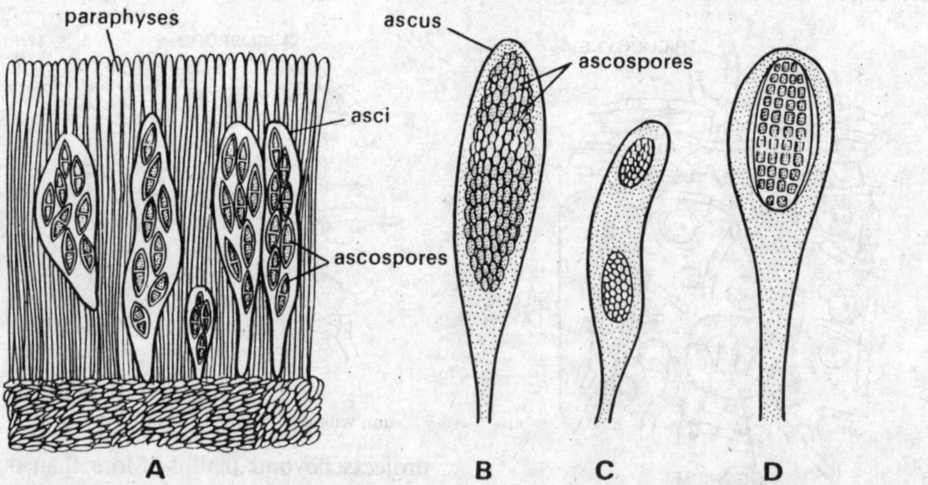

Fig. 17.18. Lichens. A, V.S. of *Physcia* thallus showing asci, ascospores and paraphyses; B, ascus with numerous ascospores; C, bi-spored ascus; D, single spored ascus.

alga. Combined growth of the fungus and the the alga continues and results in a lichen. In absence of a suitable alga the germ tube dies.

Basidiolichens reproduce by basidiospores produced on basidia as in typical Basidiomycetes. Lower surface of the thallus bears **subhymenium,** and basidia are arranged palisade-like on the lowermost face of each subhymenium. Each basidium bears four basidiospores at the tips of sterigmata.

Economic importance. Many lichens are economically important in following ways:

1. Ecological importance. Many crustose lichens growing on rocks dissolve and disintegrate them into soil particles. Limestone rocks are dissolved by the action of certain chemicals, secreted by the lichens and the disintegration of rocks is due to stresses and strains induced by contraction and expansion of the gelatinous thalli. When lichens die and decay, they form humus soil together with rock particles, mosses, ferns and other plants grow on it. Thus they prepare ground for succession of vegetation.

2. Food for man and animals. In Iceland *Cetraria islandica* commonly known as **"Iceland moss"** is grounded up and mixed with wheat flour. A leathery lichen *Umbillicaria,* commonly known as **"root tripe"** has been eaten by travellers in arctic regions in danger of starvation. Two species of *Lecanora* have been used as food in the barren plains and mountains of Western Asia and Northern Africa. Certain classes of East Siberian inhabitants use lichens as vegetable diet. In Madras state a species of *Parmelia* known in Telugu as "rathapu" or rock flower has been used in curry preparation and is famous for its delicacy.

Cladonia rangifera, commonly known as **"reindeer moss"** grows in dense tufts of upto 12 inches height in extremely cold regions. It is a food for reindeers and cattle.

3. Medicinal importance. *Peltigera canina,* the dog lichen was used as medicine for hydrophobia in ancient days and *Lobaria pulmonaria,* the **lungwort** was used for the diseases of lungs.

4. Chemical uses. The lungwort lichen was also used in tanning, in perfumery and as a substitute for hops in brewing. The cell walls of the fungi of certain lichens contain colouring matters. Species of *Rocella* and *Lecanora* yield a most important colouring matter known as Orchil or Cudbear. This is used in colouring woollen and silk fabrics.

PLANT PATHOLOGY

18

Plant Diseases and Their Classification

INTRODUCTION

Plant pathology. The word *pathology* has been derived from two Greek words–*pathos*=suffering and *logos* = discourse or to speak. Plant pathology, is therefore, *a discourse on the suffering plant.* It covers the field of the suffering plant. Thus *the field of plant pathology comprises both the art of treating the sick plant and the science of understanding the nature of the diseased plant.* This is a science which is related with almost all the disciplines of life and environmental sciences.

Definition of plant disease. A suffering plant is diseased; then question arises, what is disease? Very often the disease is considered a condition, but it is not so, because the condition results from the disease and both are not synonymous. Condition seems to be complex of symptoms. Sometimes the disease of the plant is named after certain peculiar symptoms, *e.g.*, mosaic, disease where the leaves are yellowed and mottled, but the symptom and the disease cannot be synonymous. In still other cases the disease is confused with pathogen and very erroneously one says that loose smut of wheat is *Ustilago tritici* or black rust of wheat is *Puccinia graminis tritici.* All this makes the definition of plant disease quite confusing. However, J.C. Horsfall and A.E. Dimond (1959) have concluded that *"disease is a malfunctioning process that is caused by continuous irritation. Of course, this process must result in some suffering. And hence, disease is a pathological process".*

In other words, *disease is a complex phenomenon and, is an interaction among the host, the parasite and the environment. It can* also be defined as a *disturbance in the rhythmical equilibrium of a host in respect of structure or physiology or both, and may lead to the death of a part of or the entire host or reduce the economic value of its produce.*

CLASSIFICATION OF PLANT DISEASES

The plant diseases may be classified in several ways. In one way they may be classified according to their causal agents such as diseases incited by Myxomycetes, Oomycetes, Ascomycetes, Basidiomycetes and Deuteromycetes; diseases incited by bacteria; diseases incited by virus; diseases incited by mycoplasma; diseases incited by nematodes; diseases incited by algae; diseases incited by angiosperms.

Sometimes the diseases are grouped according to the host plant, *e.g.*, cereal diseases; diseases of legumes and pulses; diseases of vegetables; diseases of cash crops; diseases of fruits etc.

In the other way, the diseases may be classified according to their symptoms, *e.g.*, root rots, powdery mildews, downy mildews, rusts, smuts, wilts, leaf blights, hyperplastic diseases hypoplastic diseases, necrotic diseases, damping off diseases, canker diseases, mosaic diseases etc.

The diseases can also be classified according to the parts of plants affected such as diseases of roots, diseases of stems, diseases of leaves, diseases of flowers, diseases of fruits etc.

Parasitic and virus diseases are often classified according to their occurrence into three groups–(1) **endemic,** (2) **epidemic** or **epiphytotic** and (3) **sporadic.**

Endemic diseases. The endemic disease is more or less constantly present from year to year in a moderate to severe form in a particular area. In such cases the pathogen or virus is well established and survives from one crop season to the next in soil, on crop refuge or in wild hosts. It is also implied here that environmental conditions remain favourable for the development of inoculum and for the infection and spread of disease. The common examples of endemic diseases are–flag smut of wheat in the Punjab plains; onion smut, cabbage yellows, club root of cabbage etc.

Epidemic or epiphytotic diseases. The disease which commonly occurs widely but periodically is termed an *epidemic*. The term *"epidemic"* has been derived from a Greek word meaning "among the people" and in the strict sense applies to diseases of man. The term *epiphytotic* has been coined for the plant diseases. The epiphytotic diseases are usually very responsive to environmental conditions. Epiphytotic diseases occur where the environmental conditions are favourable but pathogen occurs irregularly. Late blight of potato is an epiphytotic disease because of its sensitivity to environmental factors such as temperature and humidity.

Sporadic diseases. When the epiphytotics occurs at very irregular intervals and locations and in relatively few instances, it is termed *"sporadic"*.

A particular disease may be endemic in one region and epidemic in another

Diseases Classified According to Major Causal Agents

In this category the diseases can be classified under three heads, *viz.* (1) Nonparasitic diseases; (2) Parasitic diseases and (3) Virus diseases. In nonparasitic diseases, no living organism is involved and they are noninfectious, whereas in parasitic diseases, the causal agent is a living entity and the disease is infectious. The diseases may be summed up as follows—

Plant Diseases

Nonparasitic | Parasitic | Virus

Nonparasitic — *Diseases incited by:*

1. Low temperatures
2. High temperatures
3. Unfavourable oxygen relations
4. Unfavourable soil-moisture relations.
5. Accumulation of injurious impurities
6. Lightening injury
7. Mineral deficiencies
8. Mineral excesses
9. Injurious atmospheric gases etc.

Parasitic — *Diseases incited by animal parasites:*

1. Insects.
2. Nematodes
3. Protozoa
4. Birds
5. Rhodents and other animals

Parasitic — *Diseases incited by plant parasites:*

1 Bacteria
2. Fungi
3. Algae.
4. Phanerogams

DISEASE INCITING ORGANISMS

The plant diseases are caused by several micro-organisms and other agencies. According to their causal agents, they may be grouped as follows: 1.*The Diseases Caused by Animate*

Pathogens; 2. The Diseases Caused by Virus Pathogens and 3. *The Diseases Caused by Inanimate Pathogens.*

1. **Animate Pathogens**
   (1) Diseases incited by **Fungi.**
   (2) Diseases incited by **Bacteria**
   (3) Diseases incited by **Mycoplasmas** (MLO's).
   (4) Diseases incited by **Algae.**
   (5) Diseases incited by **Phanerogams**
   (6) Diseases incited by **Nematodes**
2. **Virus Pathogens**
3. **Inanimate Pathogens.** Low temperature effects; high temperature effects; light effects; nutritional disorders; effects of atmospheric impurities etc.

1. ANIMATE PATHOGENS

Fungi

The *fungi* (singular, *fungus*) constitute a large and diverse group of plant kingdom. They are plant-like, spore-bearing organisms which lack chlorophyll and other photosynthetic pigments and cannot synthesize their food from carbondioxide and water in the presence of sunlight. Consequently, they depend on other organisms for their nutrition. They may live as saprobes which bring about the decay of organic materials, or as parasites which attack living protoplasm and with the result cause diseases of plants, animals and human beings. They possess a well defined nucleus and reproduce asexually and sexually by spores. The plant body of fungus is quite simple and in most of cases consists of a network of branched filaments called the *hyphae*. The tangled mass of hyphae is the *mycelium.* They may be unicellular or multicellular filamentous with a firm wall which consists of chitin or fungal cellulose, along with other substances. However, in some it may be a mass of protoplasm with no firm wall. The chief food reserves are glycogen and oils. Since they are devoid of chlorophyll they lack starch.

There are about 50,000 to 100,000 known species of fungi all over the world.

The modern mycologists exclude the bacteria from the fungi. They place all the fungi including the slime molds in the division **Mycota** which is split into two sub-divisions:

1. **Myxomycotina.** Vegetative body a mass of free living protoplasm with no firm wall.

Class. *Myxomycetes.* Vegetative phase a naked amoeboid, multinucleate, free living plasmodium preceded by a flagellate swarm spore state; fructification with an enveloping wall, peridium.

2. **Eumycotina.** Vegetative body unicellular or multicellular filamentous; reproducing asexually or sexually by spores.

Classes. *Chytridiomycetes, Plasmodiophoromycetes, Oomycetes, Zygomycetes etc.,* (The Lower Fungi). Vegetative body in some one-celled but mostly a mycelium, often non-septate; sexual reproduction planogametic to aplanogametic.

Class. *Ascomycetes* (Higher Fungi) Vegetative body consisting of a septate mycelium, in some one-celled; never producing motile spores or gametes, sexually produced spores, ascospores, formed within an organ, the ascus.

Class. *Basidiomycetes* (Higher Fungi) Sexually produced spores, basidiospores, formed exogenously on an organ, the basidium.

Class. *Deuteromycetes* (Fungi Imperfecti): Reproducing by asexual spores.

Bacteria

Bacteria were probably first seen by Antoni Van Leeuwenhoek (1632-1723) of Holland.

The extensive research of Louis Pasteur in the 1870's and 80's, which revealed the importance of bacteria as agents of disease and decay, stimulated Robert Koch, Ferdinand Kohn, Joseph Lister and others, and the science of *bacteriology*, blossomed rapidly in the later part of the nineteenth century. This was announced for the first time in 1878 by T.J. Burrill of Illinois that bacteria cause diseases in plants. He showed that fire blight of pears and apples was caused by a bacterium. Since then a large number of bacterial plant diseases have been studied. The bacterial plant pathogens are usually facultative parasites.

Bacterial cells are very small, from less than 1 to 10 microns (μ) in length and from 0.2 to 1 μ in width. The majority of bacterial species exist as single celled forms, but some occur as filaments of loosely joined cells. Because of their small size and general similarity of structure, the classification of bacteria usually depends on physiologic or biochemical characters rather than morphologic ones. There are rodlike *bacilli*, spherical *cocci* and *spiral* forms.

The bacterial cell has a cell membrane and is covered by a strong, rigid, cell wall which contains an amino acid, *diaminopimelic acid* (found only in bacteria and in blue green algae) and a derivative of glucose called *muramic acid*. Electron micrographs reveal that cell walls may be constructed of units 50 to 140 mμ in diameter that are arranged in a regular hexagonal or rectangular pattern. Most bacteria have a slimy capsule composed largely of polysaccharides outside this cell wall which serves as an additional protective layer. The cytoplasm of bacterial cells is dense and contains granules of glycogen, proteins and fats but lacks mitochondria and an endoplasmic reticulum. The ribosomes occur free in the cytoplasm and are not bound to membranes. The DNA is present in a distinct nuclear region but there is no nuclear membrane surrounding it. Cocci usually have one nuclear region per cell, rodlike bacilli usually have two or more per cell.

Bacteria generally reproduce asexually, by simple fission – the cell simply divides into two cells. Cell division involves a mitotic process similar to that of higher forms. Cytologic observations and genetic studies indicate that something like sexual reproduction involving the fusion of two different cells and a transfer of hereditary factors, occurs in bacteria infrequently.

According to Bergey's Manual, bacteria belong to class Schizomycetes. The class is divided into several orders, but plant pathogenic forms are confined to Eubacteriales and Actinomycetales. A few families of order Eubacteriales contain pathogenic genera. They are – *Pseudomonadaceae, Rhizobiaceae, Corynebacteriaceae* and *Enterobacteriaceae*. Similarly Streptomycetaceae of order Actinomycetales contains two plant pathogenic species under the genus *Streptomyces*.

Mycoplasma

Mycoplasma is a new discovery in plant pathology. Before 1967 this was thought that plant diseases were caused only by fungi, bacteria, nematodes and viruses. However, in 1967 a team of Japanese workers proved that the plant diseases under the *yellows* group of viruses have been caused by *mycoplasma*, which possess different characteristics from those of viruses.

For the first time in 1898, Nocard and Roux had discovered *mycoplasma* as a disease incitant in animals. They also recorded – that mycoplasma was similar to virus in size and could be grown in artificial culture. *Mycoplasma mycoides* (causal agent of pneumonia) was cultured by that time.

As mentioned above, mycoplasma causes *yellows* disease in plants. Since 1967 most of the plant diseases of yellows group have been reported to be caused by mycoplasma. Some important mycoplasma diseases occurring in this country have been reported from Indian Agricultural Research Institute, New Delhi. These diseases are : *Little leaf of brinjal; Citrus greening; Sandal spike; Grassyshoot of sugarcane; Rice yellow dwarf; Cotton little leaf or cotton stenosis; Sesamum phyllody and some others.*

Mycoplasma has been isolated in pure cultures from insects, diseased mammals and infected plants. Mycoplasma is grown in highly specific culture medium containing sterol.

The mycoplasma is non-motile, gram-negative and contains both DNA and RNA. The respective cells of mycoplasma remain surrounded by proteinaceous membranes. Mycoplasma reproduces by budding and binary fission. Mycoplasma varies in its shape. The spherical forms measure 80-150 mμ. The plemorphic forms measure 210-435 mμ and the large plemorphic forms measure upto 1000 mμ. The filamentous forms with branching structures have been reported.

The mycoplasma structures also known as *Pleuropneumonia-like organisms* (PPLO) or *mycoplasma-like organisms* (MLO), were discovered in the phloem of plants infected with aster yellows and certain other yellows-type diseases. The group of very small, bacteria-like micro-organisms is supposed to be a link between viruses and bacteria.

Algae

A number of parasitic algae have been described. Among these may be cited the green alga *Cephaleuros* which is an intercellular parasite in the leaves of a number of angiosperms, such as *Magnolia, Rhododendron, Camellia sinensis* (tea) and *Piper nigrum* (pepper). Several genera of parasitic algae are known. However, there have been no definitive studies of the nutritional relationships between these parasites and their hosts. Till now much work has been done on "red rust of tea" caused by a green alga *Cephaleuros virescens.*

Phanerogamic Parasites

Some angiosperms obtain their food by living as *parasites,* which are distinguished as *total* or *partial,* according to whether they get the whole or part only of their food. The plants which have no chlorophyll are necessarily total parasites, since they can not synthesize carbohydrates.

Dodder (*Cuscuta*). This is a total stem parasite and belongs to the angiospermic Family Convolvulaceae. Common species are *C. reflexa, C. hyalina* and *C. chinensis.* The seed, which contains a filiform embryo embedded in endosperm, germinates when the plants which serve as hosts have already developed their shoots. The dodder stem twines round the host plants and develops *haustoria* which penetrate into the tissues of the host. The xylem and phloem of these organs fuse with the xylem and phloem of the host and thus the parasite obtains supplies of organic food as well as of water and salts. Ultimately the host plant dies.

Broomrape (*Orobanche cernua*). This is a total root parasite. Its roots are attached to, and absorb both inorganic and organic food from the roots of host plant. It belongs to the angiospermic Family Orobanchaceae. It grows on the roots of solanaceous (*e.g., Nicotiana tabacum*) and cruciferous (*e.g.,* cabbage) crops, and cause much damage to them.

Species of *Viscum, Dendrophthoe* and *Santalum* are partial stem parasites. The seeds of *Viscum, Dendrophthoe* etc., germinate on a branch of a suitable host, and the woody tissues of the two plants become continuous. They cause damage to the fruit trees such as Mango, Guava, Pear, etc.

Several members of Family Scrophulariaceae are partial rootparasites. Examples are provided by some species of *Striga.* They possess cholorophyll and have ordinary roots, but where their roots come into contact with the roots of a suitable host, suckers are formed which attack themselves to these roots from which they absorb food. *Striga lutea* is often found parasitic on the roots of *Sorghum,* where it may cause a serious diminution in the yield.

Nematodes

The nematodes are round worms which live in soil or water. Many of them are free-living and others are parasitic on animals and plants. They are the only plant parasites belonging to the animal kingdom that are studied in plant pathology. Several species of nematodes attack and parasitize man and animals on which they cause various diseases. Many species are known to feed on living plants as parasites and cause various plant diseases. The parasitic nature of nematodes in plants was first discovered by Berkeley in 1855. Most of the species of nematodes known as plant pathogens fall under the order Tylenchida of class Nematoda and phylum Nemathelminthes.

Morphology. The nematodes are eel-shaped round in cross-section, covered with an impermeable, smooth or transversely striated cuticle, beneath which is a subcuticular layer, and beneath the latter is a muscular layer. They are without appendages. The body of nematode usually tapers at each end. Plant parasitic nematodes are small, 300-1000 μ with some upto 4 mm. long and 15 to 35 μ wide. At one end is the mouth, having papillae, leading to a buccal cavity which in turn leads to the oesophagus. A valve is situated at the junction of oesophagus and intestine. The intestine opens into the rectum and anus at the posterior end of the body. In the body cavity between wall and organs is a colourless liquid. The reproductive systems are well developed. Female nematodes possess one or two ovaries, an oviduct and uterus with a terminal slit-like vulva. The reproductive structures of male nematode are similar to those of female but have a testis, seminal vesicle, and ejaculatory duct terminating in a common cloaca with the intestine. Many species of nematodes are bisexual. They lay eggs at the rate of 300 to 500 per female. The females of some species become swollen at maturity and possess pyrifom or spherical bodies.

2. VIRUS PATHOGENS

Viruses

Viruses are submicroscopic entities which multiply only inside living cells and possess the ability to cause disease. All viruses are parasitic in cells and cause diseases to all forms of living, organisms, from single-celled plants or animals to large trees and mammals. More than a thousand viruses are known. More than half of all viruses attack and cause diseases of plants.

3. INANIMATE PATHOGENS

A disease has been defined in the broad sense as any departure from the normal in structure or in function. This is not always found necessary that the disease should be caused only by *animate* and *virus pathogens*. "Sometimes deleterious changes in the external or internal environment of plants may bring about permanent effects and produce symptoms which justify their designation as those of disease (J.C. Walker, 1950)." Much losses have been caused to economic crops by means of such so called 'physiologic diseases' which may be caused through the effect of adverse environment without the involvement of the parasite. Such physiologic diseases may be caused by *low-temperature effects; high-temperature effects; light effects; soil-moisture disturbances; oxygen relations; effects of atmospheric impurities; lightning injury* and *nutritional disorders.*

SYMPTOMS OF PLANT DISEASES

"The diagnosis of a disease means the discovery of its identity or nature. Symptoms are the outward signs by which a diagnosis is assisted (Butler, 1918)". They are as follows:

Symptoms Caused by Fungi

Withering and wilting. The first indication of fungus infection is often the *withering* of a whole plant or of some part of it (*e.g.*, in green ear disease of *bajra* caused by *Sclerospora graminicola*). The term *wilting* is applied to those cases where a whole plant dries up more or less suddenly from fungus attack at the roots or base of stem (*e.g.*, in wilt of pigeon pea caused by *Fusarium udum*). Drying of a branch occurs sometimes in early stages of wilt of pigeon pea. The wilts are primarily diseases of roots, as the pathogens attack them in seedling stage. Sometimes the leaves show the symptoms of mottling, as in cotton wilt caused by *F. oxyspora.* The fungus plugs the xylem vessels and interferes with the free flow of sap.

Pallor. This is due to destruction of chlorophyll in the leaves. It is common sign of the presence of a parasite in or on the pale area. For example, the upper surface of the infected leaf of pea by downy mildew shows the yellow patch. Sometimes it is caused by stem attack lower down, all the leaves above the point infected being discoloured (*e.g.*, in red rust of tea caused by an alga *Cephaleuros* sp.). Pallor is also due to water logging, iron deficiency etc.

Damping off. This is applied to the sudden collapse of seedlings, which are affected at the base of the stem and fall over from weakening of the tissues at this point. Species of *Pythium* and *Rhizoctonia* are most important damping off causing fungi.

Leaf spot. Various types of leaf spots are produced by many fungi. These spots are very varied in colour, according to the plant and parasite. The pallid spots are commonly seen in the mildews and in early stages of several other parasitic attacks.

Yellow spots are generally caused by rusts. Very often they change their colour to brown or black at a later stage. They are often raised and covered. When uncovered, the spores are exposed as powdery or rusty substance. Red spots are found in some rusts (*e.g.*, aecidial stage of black rust of wheat on barberry). In the red rust of tea (caused by an alga) the spots are raised. Brown spots are the commonest, and are the result of the cells being killed. Black spots are found in late stages (telial stages) of rusts and in many Ascomycetes (*e.g.*, *Phyllachora* on *doob* grass). Concentric bands of colour (target board effect) are generally seen in different shades of brown, in spots caused by several species of *Alternaria.*

Shot-hole. In certain cases the dead tissue of the spot is shed, and a circular perforation known as shot-hole is left. They are common in fruit trees such as peach and plum. The fungi responsible for causing shot-holes are mainly the species of *Cercospora, Phyllosticta* etc.

Scab. This is applied for cracking of the outer layers of fruits or tubers. The broken skin becomes dry, flaky and corky. The scales of apples and pears are caused by the species of *Venturia* and that of peaches by *Cladosporium.*

Cankers. This is applied to the open wounds, often of a spreading nature, and sometimes surrounded by a raised, tumour-like margin are generally found on woody stems. Cankers may encircle the entire plant, killing the upper part of the host. They are usually caused by parasites that attack the bark and reach as far as the cambium. The tissues outside this layer are killed and sloughed off, leaving a wound exposing the wood. The canker causing fungi are *Nectria* (Ascomycetes,) *Gymnosporangium* (Basidiomycetes) etc.

Rotting. This is often caused by the species of *Phytophthora* (wet and dry rot of potato) and *Pythium* (stem and foot rot of papaya). Hymenomycetes cause wood rots in tree stems. Still more common rots are prevalent of fruits, bulbs and tubers. The rot may be wet or dry. Rots of pulpy fruits are usually wet. They are generally caused by species of *Penicillium.* Rots of woody and pithy stems are often dry (*e.g.*, red rot of sugarcane and tree rots).

Gummosis and fluxes. It is applied to several diseases of trees which are characterized by an exudation from the bark of the stem. The chief characteristic is the production of a clear amber coloured exudate on the surface of the affected parts of a plant, which later sets into a solid mass. The symptoms of gummosis are commonly found in cherry, peach and citrus trees.

Leaf and fruit dropping. In many cases the leaves are dropped down by the action of leaf parasites such as *Cercospora personata, Hemileia vastatrix.* Dropping of fruits is caused by the attack of *Phytophthora* on palms and some other cases.

Galls and tumours. Abnormal outgrowths are often produced on the herbaceous parts of the plants and also sometimes on woody stems and on roots and tubers. The roots in club root of cabbage or other cruciferous plants are converted into swollen structures of the type of *finger and toes*. This disease is caused by *Plasmodiophora brassicae*. The potato wart caused by *Synchytrium endobioticum* is another suitable example. Sometimes large rounded tumours, several inches across, are developed (*e.g.*, in maize smut caused by *Ustilago maydis*). Gall formation in mustard roots by *Urocystis brassicae* is another good example.

Hypertrophy. The increase of the size of the affected parts of the plant takes place due to the enlargement of component cells. This is known as *hypertrophy*. If hypertrophy takes place because of increased cell division forming a large number of component cells, it is termed hyperplasia. When young stems and flowering parts of *sarson* plants are infected by *Albugo candida*, the fungus becomes systemic in the tissue and stimulates hypertrophy and hyperplasia. This results in enlarged and variously distorted organs.

Atrophy. In certain cases the parts of plants are being arrested in their growth, and sometimes they are even entirely suppressed. This symptom is known as atrophy. For example, when the *sarson* plant is attacked by *Peronospora brassicae*, the floral buds are being suppressed.

Anthracnoses. In these cases the collenchyma and cambium are destroyed. The lesions are sunken in the centre and provided with raised margins. The symptoms are found in grapes, beans, chillies etc. The causal fungus is *Colletotrichum*.

Blights and blasts. Here the tissues of the affected parts are being destroyed. They involve destruction growing succulent tissues, like shoots, leaves, blossoms and twigs. The common blights are: shoot-blight, twig-blight, late-blight, early-blight etc.; blast of rice caused by *Pyricularia oryzae*.

Witches brooms. These symptoms appear on some trees and shrubs. The branch from which they arise is often swollen, and the shoots usually all turned upwards, short and with small leaves such as witches broom of mango.

Proliferation. It occurs in the ears of *Bajra* attacked by *Sclerospora graminicola*, the central axis of flower converts into a stunted leaf shoot, and the attacked organs of the flower are proliferated.

Transformation of organs. In such cases one kind of floral part converts into another type or into ordinary leaves. The stamens may become leaf-like in *bajra* affected by *Sclerospora graminicola. Albugo candida* may cause petals to become sepal like, the stamens may become carpel-like, and the carpels may become leaf-like.

Symptoms Caused by Bacteria

The symptoms of disease caused by bacteria are in main, similar to those caused by many fungi. The disintegration of parenchyma may be produced by species of *Pythium* as well as by species of *Bacterium*.

Curling, spotting and blotching of leaves are caused by bacteria, fungi and viruses.

Cankers and proliferation of shoots are also caused both by bacteria and fungi. *Corynebacterium fascians* causes proliferation.

Stunting and wilting are caused by fungi, bacteria and viruses.

Crown gall (*Bacterium tumefaciens*) and leafy gall (*Corynebacterium fascians*) are caused by bacteria.

The formation of pale chlorotic areas surrounding leaf spots are indications of bacterial attack, for example, in the halo blight of beans.

In the early stages of bacterial infection of green parts such as leaves, pods etc., the spots are of a darker green than the unattached tissue and are often surrounded by a pale-yellow zone, *i.e.*, halo blight. The darker green of the infected area exhibits a water soaked appearance.

The parenchyma is attacked in the soft rot of carrots or in the black leg of potatoes.

In cucumber wilt, the xylem is invaded and blocked, and thus the wilting results.

Bacterial canker of tomatoes, and citrus canker are well known.

The other common symptoms produced by bacterial attack are–blight, fire blight, angular leaf spot, black rot, ring rot, hairy rot, scab etc.

Symptoms Caused by Plant Viruses

Plant viruses can be recognized easily by the symptoms they produce on the host. Sometimes the same virus can cause widely different symptoms on different host plants, and the symptoms may vary in the same plant according to its age, nutrition and other environmental factors. Symptoms may sometimes be produced by a mixture of two or more viruses on the same plant. A few more common and easily detectable symptoms are given here:

Chlorosis. Due to the presence of plant viruses, the chlorophyll of the green parts disappears at places, leaving yellowish spots, this is known as *chlorosis*. The presence of yellow spots at places, in the green tissues appears like a *'mosaic'* pattern and therefore, the diseases with such symptoms are known as *'mosaic'* diseases. The viruses causing most mosaic diseases are mechanically transmitted and usually have aphid vectors in nature. Generally they do not stop flowering or affect the dormancy of buds.

Yellows. When the chlorophyll disappears completely (chlorosis, yellowing, bronzing or reddening) from the host tissue, the organs turn yellow and the symptoms are known as *yellows*. These viruses are generally transmitted by leaf-hoppers, and they are relatively sensitive to heat treatment.

Vein clearing and vein banding. The disappearance of chlorophyll along the veins of the leaves is known as *vein clearing* and when chlorophyll surrounding the veins disappears the symptom is known as *vein banding*.

Necrosis. The brownish spots due to the death and ultimate drying of the tissue are known as necrotic spots and the phenomenon is known as *necrosis*. Necrotic spots are also known as *lesions*.

Ring spots. These symptoms are characterized by the appearance of chlorotic or necrotic rings on the leaves and sometimes also on the fruit and stem. Most ringspot-causing viruses are being transmitted by nematodes.

Other symptoms. Bunchy top, galls, hypertrophy, atrophy, rolling (leaf roll of potato), curling (leaf curl of potato), crinkling of leaves, stunting (corn stunt) and dwarfing (barley yellow dwarf) of plants are various other symptoms usually produced on the host plants by viruses.

19

Bacterial, Viral and Fungal Diseases of Plants

BACTERIAL DISEASES OF PLANTS

Diseases Incited by Bacteria

Brown Rot of Potato
(a bacterial disease)

Pathogen. *Pseudomonas solanacearum* Smith.

Systematic position of pathogen. Class-Schizomycetes.

Distribution. This disease is prevalent in tropical and subtropical countries of the world. The disease has been recorded from the United States, South America, Africa, Europe, Australia, Japan, Thailand, Indonesia and India.

Symptoms. The wilting and collapsing of plants is frequently seen. The name "*brown-rot*" refers to the brown stain formed in the xylem of the vascular bundles in most affected plants. In infected plants stems and tubers are cut across, the bacteria exude in drops. In later stages, the pith and cortex are invaded. Large cavities filled with bacteria develop in the pith region whereas the cortex disintegrates. The skin of infected potato tubers becomes discoloured.

The pathogen. Many species of Solanaceae such as potato, tomato and tobacco are being infected by *Pseudomonas solanacearum* Smith. Infection generally takes place through injured roots and sometimes through the wounds in the stem and through the stomata. Potato tubers are being infected by the stolons. The bacterium is a small rod-shaped organism 1 to 1.5 μ long and 0.5 μ broad. It possesses a polar flagellum.

Nature and recurrence of disease The disease is both tuber-borne and soil-borne. Tubers dug out from the infested field carry infection. The mildly attacked seed tubers sprout and the plants developed from them become infected and wilt soon. Soilborne infection is also common. The bacteria remain viable for 16 months in soil and for 9 months on diseased plants.

Predisposing factors. The high temperature (20^0-38^0C) and high soil moisture (50-100 per cent water holding capacity) favour the disease incidence.

Control measures. *Clean seed.* The disease-free seed tubers should be obtained from disease-free fields.

Fallowing. After deep ploughing the fields should be left under direct sun in the summer months.

pH of soil. By increasing pH of soil the disease may be reduced to some extent.

Resistant varieties. Resistant varieties should be grown.

Ring Rot of Potatoes
(a bacterial disease)

Pathogen. *Corynebacterium sepedonicum* (Spiekermann and Kotthof) Scaptason and Burkholder.

Systematic position and pathogen. Class-Schizomycetes.

Distribution. This disease was first investigated in Germany. The disease is prevalent in the United States, Canada and Northern Europe. The disease is less frequent in India.

Symptoms. The wilting of the foliage takes place late in the season, and may affect the whole or only a part of the plant. The wilted leaflets turn yellow and die. The wilting progresses from lower leaves to upwards. The stems also tend to wilt to some extent.

The more characteristic symptoms appear on the tubers of an infected plant. Some of the tubers of an infected plant become completely disintegrated. If cut in equal halves, diseased tubers show a creamy yellow or light brown, cheesy rot in the tissue surrounding the vascular bundles. Usually there remains a distinct gap between the cortex and the vascular system of the infected tuber, and the "*ring rot*" refers to this feature. The eyes are also being infected and killed, and the whole tuber is being affected. Sometimes the pith disintegrates more rapidly than the cortex and a shell is left. Such hollow tubers are frequently found in storage and less commonly in the field.

The pathogen. The bacterial ring rot of potatoes is caused by *Corynebacterium sepedonicum*. The disease is systemic. The bacteria may pass along the stolons to the newly formed tubers which thus become infected. The tuber may be completely disintegrated. However the pathogen does not survive for long in the soil. The disease does not spread from plant to plant in the field and no other plant is being attacked.

Nature and recurrence of disease. This is a seed-borne disease. The slightly infected tubers act as chief source of inoculum, especially when cut seed tubers are sown. Such cut tubers may give rise to several diseased plants, which will produce some infected tubers. Sometimes the healthy seed tubers may also become contaminated on the outside from the decomposing mass of rotting tubers in store or from sacks.

Control measures. *Clean-seed.* The seed tubers should be selected from disease-free areas. Outwardly contaminated seed tubers may be sterilized by immersion in 1:1000 mercuric chloride for 5 minutes, or in 5 per cent lysol for 10 minutes.

VIRAL DISEASES OF PLANTS

Diseases incited by Virus

Mosaic Diseases of Potato

(*virus diseases*)

Mild mosaic. The mild mosaic of potato is generally caused by *virus X* or *virus A*. The symptom may be noticed if the leaf is held against transmitted light or against a white background. Mild mosaic does not cause much reduction in leaf size or loss of vigour. The fall in yield is also not very high.

Rugose mosaic. The Rugose mosaic of potato is caused by the combination of the *virus X* and *A*. It is one of the commonest disease of commercial stocks in India. In this mosaic there is extreme distortion of leaves, caused by heavy corrugation of the interveinal tissue of the leaf. The infected plants usually exhibit extensive necrotic lesions on the foliage. The foliage is very brittle and the leaves drop from their bases.

Potato crinkle. The potato crinkle is caused by the combination of *virus X* and *virus A*. The crinkled plants exhibit a prominent, blotchy type of mottling. The mottling of leaves is invariably accompanied by leaf distortion, leaves showing varying degrees of waviness, undulating margins etc. Affected plants, in general, are dwarfed and bushy with pale, puckered leaves which curve downwards. A diffused, slightly yellowish spotting occurs in the leaves which later changes to a rusty-brown discolouration before the plants die. Potato crinkle usually causes reduction in vigour, and, the affected plants seldom produce economic yields.

Leaf Roll of Potato

Causal agent. Leaf roll virus, Y, X and A *Solanum virus* 14 (Appel & Quanjer).

This disease is responsible for heavy losses in the yield of potato in India.

Symptoms. The symptom of the leaf-roll affected plants is an upward rolling of the leaflets along the midribs. This symptom particularly appears in the lower leaves of the affected plant. The rolled leaves are thick, harsh and leathery. The leaves become brittle and their tissue breaks easily. On certain varieties, a reddish bronze colouration may develop along the tips and edges of the rolled leaves. The rolling of leaves depends chiefly upon, the stage of infection and vertical responses.

If the plants are infected late, they usually show a little rolling, often confined to the upper leaves. However, during the second year when the disease is already present in the tuber, rolling of leaves finds full expression in the growing plant. This is the secondary stage.

Yield. Leaf roll affected plants generally yield a low crop of somewhat small sized tubers. This is mainly because leaf-roll causes the necrosis on the death of the phloem elements concerned with the translocation of food material from the leaves to the tubers.

Transmission of virus. The natural spread of virus in the field is through the agency of insects, the principal vector being the peach aphis *Myzus persicae*. A peculiar biological relation exists between the virus of leaf roll and the insects responsible for its transmission. An incubation period of 48 to 54 hours within the body of the vector seems to be necessary before the virus becomes sufficiently potent to bring about infection. The new brood can become infective only after feeding upon plants affected with leaf roll. A close relationship thus exists between virus and vector.

Nature and recurrence of disease. The leaf roll of potato is seed-borne. Tubers infected with the virus when planted give rise to shoots in which leaf rolling is a characteristic symptom and such tuber offers a ready means of perpetuating the disease in the progeny, so that successive crops *run out* within a comparatively short time.

Control measures. *Seed selection.* For the eradiaction of potato leaf-roll the selection of healthy seed is of primary importance. To fulfil the need seed growing areas should be situated where the aphids concerned are least likely to breed. Since the aphis *Myzus persicae* survives on peach, the seed crops should not be established where peach trees are near.

Inspection and certification. The annual inspection of potato crops and certification have proved to be helpful in keeping the potatoes free from virus troubles.

Resistant varieties. The resistant varieties should be developed and distributed among farmers.

FUNGAL DISEASES OF PLANTS

Late Blight of Potato

Pathogen. *Phytophthora infestans* (Mont.) de Bary.

Systematic position of pathogen. Class-Oomycetes (lower fungi); Order-Peronosporales; Family Pythiaceae.

This is undoubtedly, the most serious of all potato diseases, when conditions are favourable for its development. It attacks and kills the tops of the potato plant and invades the tubers causing either a *dry* or *a wet rot*.

Historical. When the cause of the disease was uncertain, it was prevalent in North America. The disease appeared in epidemic form in Europe in 1845 and led to the cause of famous famine of Ireland. The likely home of the disease is Mexico, where it is endemic on wild native species allied to the cultivated potato. In India, the disease was first observed in the Nilgiri Hills between

1870 and 1880. Thereafter, it was observed in Darjeeling district in 1883. The disease appeared in Hooghly district of West Bengal during 1899-1900. Later on, the disease was observed in the vicinity of Bhagalpur in 1913. Till 1950, the disease was not supposed to be of major importance in the plains of northern India. But now it is one of the most serious of all potato diseases in the plains of northern India. From the very beginning, the disease has been of major importance in the hills, at elevations of 6,000 feet and above, as the crop is grown there in rainy season, which happens to be the most favourable time in the hills for the spread of the disease.

Distribution. The late blight of potato is world-wide in distribution. Formerly this disease was prevalent in the hilly regions of northern India, but now it is of common occurrence in the plains of northern India. The famous famine of Ireland of 1845-46 was mainly due to the failure of potato crop which constituted the staple food of the people of that country. In northern India, the disease was introduced in the plains because of the introduction of the cold stores of potato, which maintained the desirable temperature and moisture for the survival of pathogen of disease.

Symptoms. The symptoms generally appear on the above ground parts of potato plant but later on the underground parts such as tubers are also infected. First of all small brown patches appear on the leaves, which in suitable weather conditions of temperature and moisture, increase rapidly and involve the whole surface of the plant. In bad cases the symptoms extend to the stalk quickly. With the result the entire crown may fall over in a rotten pulp in few days. The influence of weather has remarkable effects on the spread of disease. In dry clear weather, the spots remain small, brown and dry while the stem may escape altogether. In warm muggy weather, the colour of spots rapidly changes to black and the stems are being infected, and a pronounced smell of decaying vegetable matter is given off. This smell is considered one of the most marked features of the disease.

In severe cases, the tubers are also being infected. In dry soils the disease progresses slowly, and a *dry rot* is resulted. The skin of such tubers becomes slightly sunken and dark in colour. The rusty brown appearance can be observed just beneath the skin of tuber. The symptoms of dry rot may or may not appear at the time of digging of tubers but it develops during first or second month of the storage of tubers. When the soil is moist the tissues of the underlying tubers become softened, and the *wet rot* occurs.

The pathogen. The late blight of potato is caused by *Phytophthora infestans* (Mont) de Bary. The mycelium of this fungus is branched, hyaline, aseptate and measuring 4-8 μ in diameter. To absorb the food material, it sends out the globular or branched haustoria in the host cells. The haustoria are commonly seen in tubers.

The aerial sporangiophores are given out through the stomata in the group of 4 or 5. Sometimes the sporangiophores come out piercing the epidermal cells of the host. The sporangia develop at the tips of the branches or sporangiophores. As soon as a sporangium is formed the branch grows further just beneath it and a new sporangium is formed. The continuity of this process is maintained for a long time, and the nodular swellings are left at those points where earlier sporangia were formed. Generally nine or ten such swellings are seen on a branch. The sporangia are ovoid or lemonshaped. Each sporangium bears a papilla at its apical end. The sporangia are hyaline and measuring 22–32μ × 16–24μ. On maturity of the sporangium, the zoospores are formed within it. The papilla bursts, and the zoospores escape through it. Each zoospore is reniform, biflagellate, naked, uninucleate and single vacuolate. The flagella are retracted, the zoospores become encysted and they germinate, sending out a germ-tube. Sometimes the sporangia behave as conidia and germinate directly, forming a germ tube at the apex.

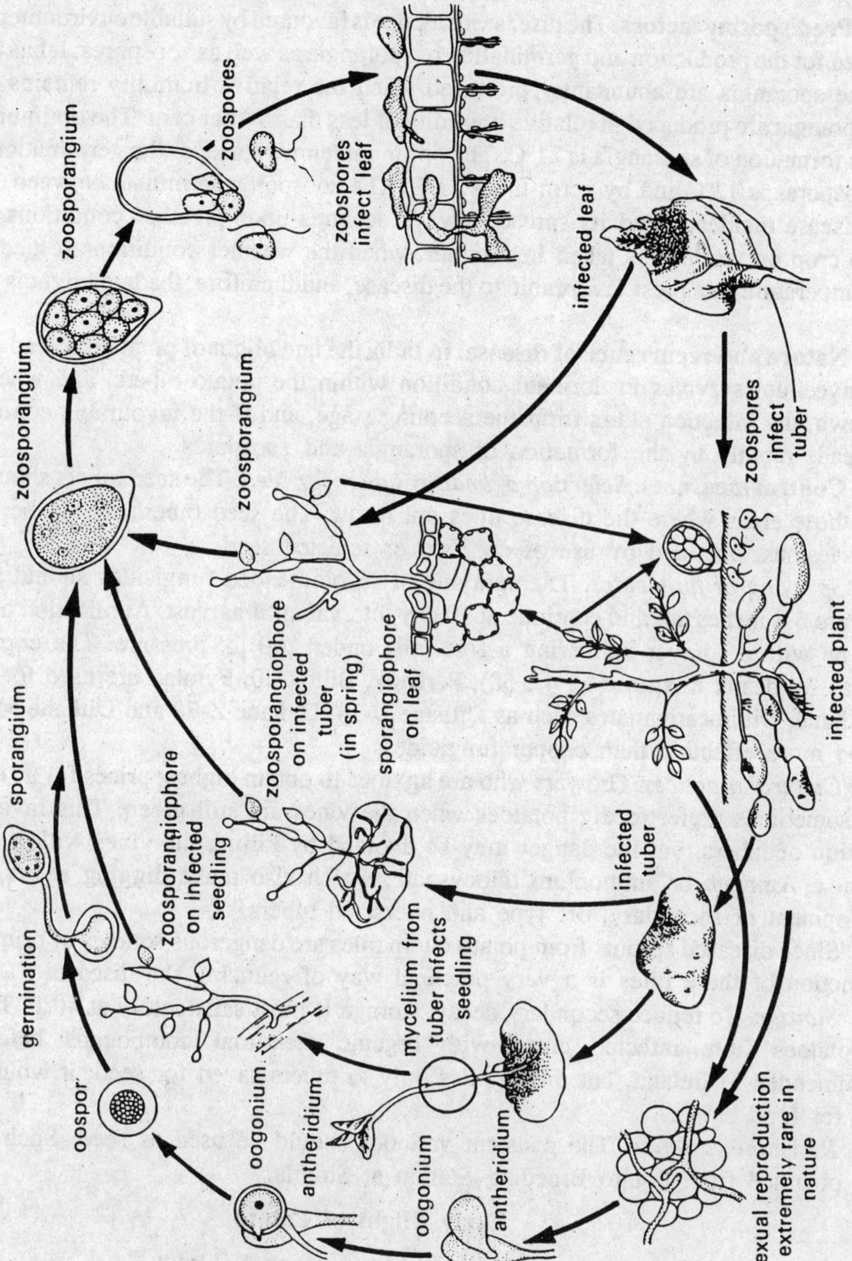

Fig. 19.1. Late blight of potato caused by *Phytophthora infestans*. Diagrammatic disease-cycle.

Sexual reproduction is oogamous, and takes place by means of oogonia and antheridia. The antheridium develops first. Later on the oogonium penetrates the antheridium from one side to the other and fertilization is effected. Such fertilization is known as *amphigynous*. The oogonia are ovoid or spherical, smooth, reddish brown and measuring 31-46μ in diameter. The oospores lie loosely within oogonia. Each oospore is thick-walled and about 30μ in diameter. The oospore germinates by producing a germ-tube.

Predisposing factors. The disease incidence is favoured by suitable environmental conditions required for the production and germination of sporangia as well as zoospores. It has been observed that the sporangia are abundantly produced when the relative humidity remains 100 per cent. No sporangia are produced at relative humidity of less than 90 per cent. The optimum temperature for the formation of sporangia is 21°C. The optimum temperature for the germination of sporangia by zoospores is 12°C and by germ-tubes 21°C. The zoospores germinate between 3°C and 22°C. The disease incidence and its spread, always depends upon weather conditions. In India, the potato crop on the hills is taken in summer, when the weather conditions (especially moisture and temperature) are most favourable to the disease, and therefore, the late blight is quite frequent there.

Nature and recurrence of disease. In India the late blight of potato is a seed-borne disease. The mycelium survives in dormant condition within the potato tubers, and when such tubers are sown, the infection starts from the seedling stage, and if the favourable conditions prevail, it spreads rapidly by the formation of sporangia and zoospores.

Control measures. *Selection of healthy tubers for seed.* The seed tubers should be obtained from those areas where the disease does not occur. The seed tubers should be free from late blight lesions, obtained by use of certified or selected seeds.

Spraying of fungicides. The spraying of recommended fungicides should start when the vines are 6-8 inches tall and continue at 10 day interval until harvest. Application of the fungicide must be with a sprayer delivering a fine mist under 200 lb. pressure. The copper fungicides such as Bordeaux mixture (4 : 4 : 50), Perenox, Blitox-50, Fytolan are used for spray. On the other hand, Dithiocarbamates such as Dithane D-14, Dithane Z-78 and Dithane M-22 have been proved more effective than copper fungicides.

Cultural practices. Growers who are anxious to obtain highest prices for an early harvested crop sometimes prefer to dig potatoes when the vines are still green. This favours late blight infection of tubers, but the danger may be avoided by killing the vines with a herbicide such as sinox, Ammate or ammonium thiocyanate, which also make digging easier and avoid the development of secondary, off type and oversized tubers.

Since diseased sprouts from potato dump piles are dangerous sources of primary infections, destruction of these piles is a very practical way of reducing the disease.

Storage. To reduce secondary decay; storage is most satisfactory at 40°F. Tuber treatment of potatoes from infected crops with organic mercurial compounds before storage is recommended in Ireland, but this applies only to tubers saved for seed; it would render them unfit for food.

Resistant varieties. The resistant varieties should be used as seed. Such varieties have been obtained from Potato Breeding Station at Shimla.

Early Blight of Potato

Pathogen. *Alternaria solani* (Ell. & Mart.) Jones & Grout.

Systematic position of pathogen. Class-Deuteromycetes; Order-Moniliales; Family-Dematiaceae.

The early blight of potato is one of the most destructive fungal disease, in India.

Distribution. This disease seems to have originated in the United State of America. Now this disease is world-wide in distribution, and has been recorded from Canada to New Zealand and from Japan to South Africa. In India, it occurs in the Indo-Gangetic plain and the Nilgiris.

Symptoms. The disease appears first as yellowish spots on leaflets of potato. Later on the spots become dark brown to black. Some of the spots are small in size while some are bigger. They remain scattered on the surface of the leaflets. Usually the spots are rounded or oval, but the spots formed in the vicinity of the stout veins, become somewhat angular, because of the arrest of the fungal growth across such veins. In severe state of disease the whole surface of the leaflets is being covered with such spots or lesions. Sometimes the spots are merged with each other forming bigger lesions. If we study the lesions with the help of hand lens, the concentric ridges may be seen on each such spot, producing a characteristic *'target-board effect'*. There is usually a narrow chlorotic zone around the spot, which fades into the normal green. Lowest leaves are affected first, as a rule, and the disease progresses upward. The leaves of potato dry up and droop.

In severe conditions of the disease the other parts of the plant such as petioles, stems and tubers are also affected. The skin of infected tuber becomes dark brown, and the irregular or rounded spots develop on it. These spots are slightly sunken, and vary in size upto 2 cm in diameter. The pulp of the tuber just below the infected skin becomes rusty or brown in appearance. Fissures may develop in mature lesions.

The pathogen. The early blight of potato is caused by *Alternaria solani (*Ell. & Mart.) Jones & Grout. The pathogen was first described by Ellis and Martin in 1882. The mycelium is septate, branched and becomes dark coloured with age. The conidiophores, rising from the older diseased host tissues are short and dark-coloured. Conidia are beaked, muriform, dark-coloured borne singly or in chains of two (in pure culture). The conidia measure 145 to 370 by 16 to 18μ and are divided by 5 to 10 transverse septa, some of the broader compartments being sometimes further divided by a longitudinal wall. The lower part of the conidium is brown, the beak almost colourless. Germination can take place from any cell of conidium, the germ-tubes enter the leaf both through the stomata and directly into the epidermal cells.

Nature and recurrence of disease. This is a soil-borne disease. The mycelium remains viable in dry infected leaves for a year or more, and the conidia remain viable for seventeen months. Hence the disease is readily perpetuated from season to season.

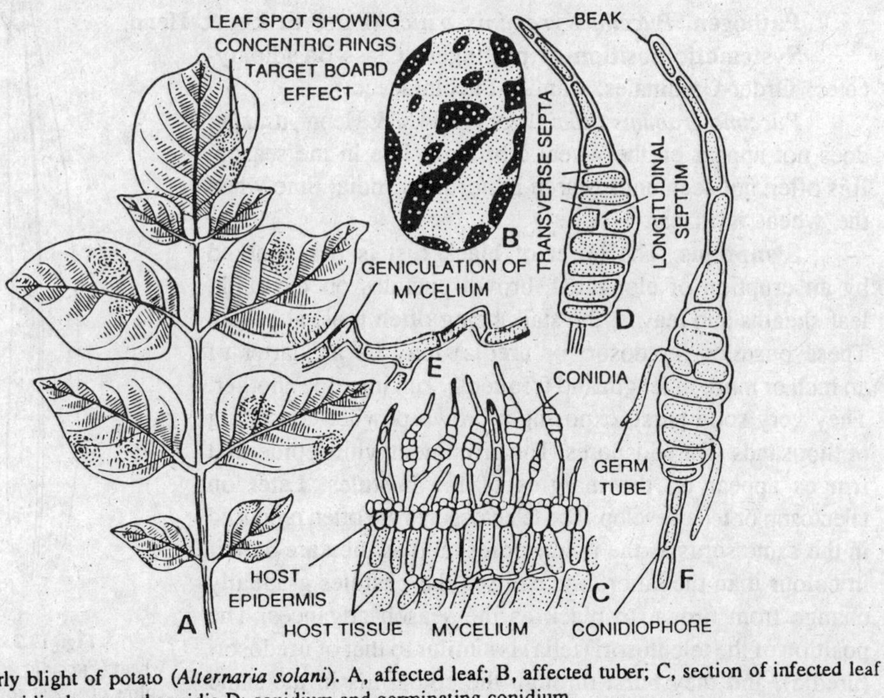

Fig. 19.2. Early blight of potato (*Alternaria solani*). A, affected leaf; B, affected tuber; C, section of infected leaf showing mycelium, conidiophores and conidia D; conidium and germinating conidium.

Predisposing factors. The optimum temperature for germination of conidia is 28-30°C. Heavy dews with frequent rains are essential for abundant production of conidia. In moist weather conidia germinate readily. The disease becomes serious when the season begins with abundant moisture followed by high temperatures.

Control measures. *Crop rotation.* Crop rotation has been proved successful measure to avoid primary infection from conidia that have over-wintered or over-summered in the soil.

Sanitation. The plant debris and dead haulms should be collected and burned immediately after harvest.

Spraying of fungicides. Timely and thorough spraying with copper fungicides of Zineb at 15-day intervcals have given successful results. Weekly spraying of Bordeaux mixture (5 : 5 : 50) has been proved quite effective. The spraying should be done throughout the growing period of the crop.

RUSTS OF WHEAT

Rusts of wheat (*i.e.,* black, brown and yellow) are the most important and destructive of all the plant diseases. They are the potential causes of enormous economic losses in all wheat growing regions of the world. The rusts of wheat are thus a great enemy of the cultivators and often ravage their crops. They are the earliest known disease of crop plants. Early Romans and Greeks knew about the rusts of wheat and barley.

Three different forms of rust attack wheat in India: black or stem rust caused by *Puccinia graminis tritici* (Pers.) Erikss & Henn., leaf, brown or orange rust caused by *Puccinia recondita* Roxb. ex Desm; and yellow or stripe rust by *Puccinia striiformis* West.

Black and orange rusts are practically found all over the world; yellow rust is more restricted, being absent, for instance, from South Africa and Australia.

Black or Stem Rust of Wheat

Pathogen. *Puccinia graminis tritici* (Pers) Erikss & Henn.

Systematic position of pathogen. Class-Basidiomycetes; Order-Uredinales; Family-Pucciniaceae.

Puccinia graminis tritici (Pers.) Erikks. & Henn., usually; does not appear on the wheat crop until late in the season. It is often not seen until March in northern India, time when the wheat is in ear.

Symptoms. The onset of black rust is first marked by an eruption of elongated, brown pustules on the stalk, leaf sheaths and leaves, the stalk being often most attacked. These pustules (uredosori or uredia) may be a quarter of an inch or more in length and frequently run into one another. They very soon burst, exposing a brown powder consisting of thousands of uredospores. The prominent white epidermal fringes appear on the margins of the pustules. Later on teleutosori or telia develop. The teleutospores are often produced in the same sorus as the uredospores, and as they are darker in colour than the latter, one can see the pustules gradually change from brown to black as the season advances. The position of the teleutosori (telia) is similar to that of uredosori (uredia), and they burst through the epidermis in the same manner, exposing a black bed of teleutospores.

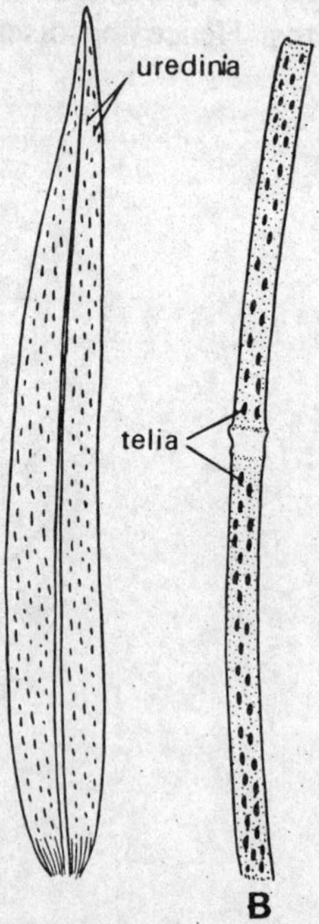

Fig. 19.3. Black or stem rust of wheat (*Puccinia graminis tritici*). Infected culms of wheat showing telial and uredial stages.

The pathogen. Black or stem rust of wheat is caused by *Puccinia graminis tritici.*

Each uredosorus is formed on a limited mycelium. The hyphae of mycelium are about 3.5μ in diameter and extend between the cells of the plant, sending small round or branched haustoria into them to absorb the food material. A mass of hyphae collects under the epidermis and, if early in the season, develops into a uredosorus (uredium). From the base of sorus, numerous short erect stalks arise, and a uredospore develops at the end of each. The growth in size of these spores makes the epidermis rupture and the uredospores are liberated out into the air. Each uredospore is an oval, brown body, measuring 25 to 30 × 17 to 20μ, and consisting of a single cell with a thick wall, provided with minute echines for anchoring the spore to the surface on which it falls. Each uredospore possesses four germ pores on it arranged in an equatorial band. The germ tubes emerge through germ pores during spore germination.

On getting suitable conditions of moisture and temperature for a germ tube capable of developing into a new parasitic mycelium within the plant. A second germ tube is often formed, but soon ceases growth. The germ-tube doesnot enter directly, but the tip swells up into an

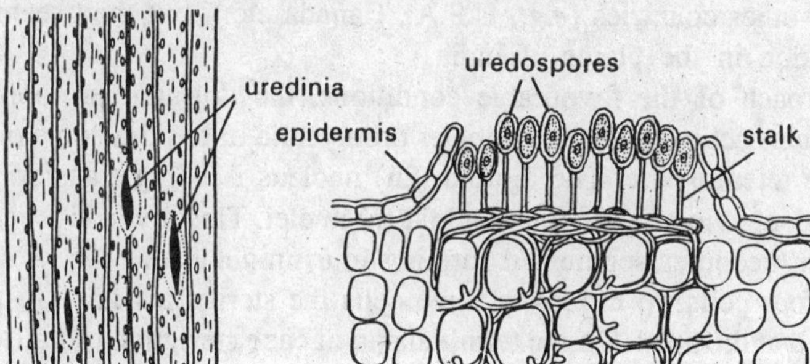

Fig. 19.4. Black or stem rust of wheat (*Puccinia graminis tritici*). A, a part of infected stem showing uredia on leaf sheath; B, V.S. of infected stem showing uredium with uredospores, mycelium and haustoria.

elongated appressorium, measuring about 27 × 29μ. From the appressorium, a narrow branch passes into the stoma and immediately swells up to form a substomal vesicle, all the contents of the germ tube collect in this vesicle and soon after a hypha arises from one end and grows towards a neighbouring cell, into which it sends a haustorium. Infection is now complete and

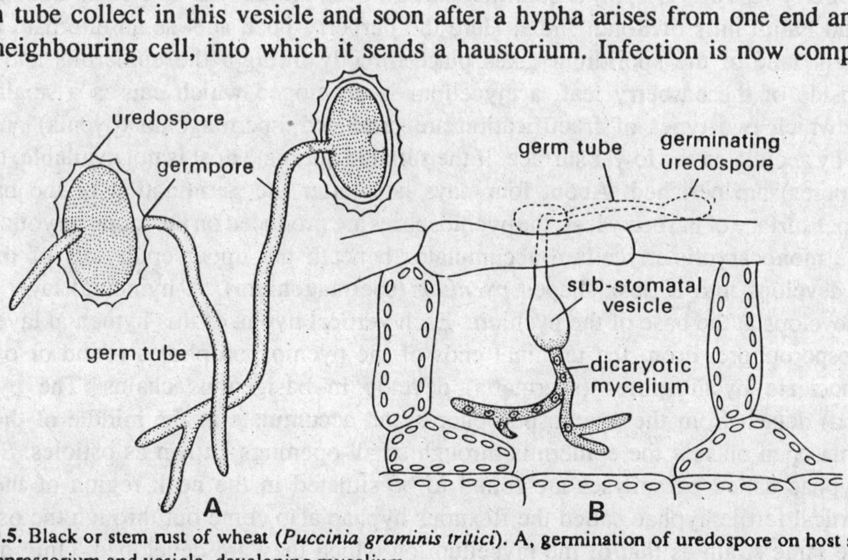

Fig. 19.5. Black or stem rust of wheat (*Puccinia graminis tritici*). A, germination of uredospore on host surface; B, formation of appressorium and vesicle, developing mycelium.

the mycelium grows continuously within the plant. From this mycelium, new pustules are formed within 10 to 15 days from the infection, and thousands of uredospores are formed and liberated out into the air. A single pustule contains hundreds of spores. Each spore is capable in suitable weather of causing a new infection and new pustules, it becomes quite clear how the fungus can multiply and spread through a field, until every plant is infected.

The teleutosori (telia) develop on the same mycelium, in the later part of the season. The teleutospores differ from the uredospores in being firmly fixed on their stalks, and composed of two cells with a thick smooth wall. They are chestnut brown in colour and measure 40 to 60 × 15 to 20μ. The apex of teleutospore is rounded or pointed. Each cell has a germ-pore, that of the upper being at the apex and that of the lower at the side just below the septum. Unlike the uredospores the teleutospores do not germinate immediately after their formation. Prior to germination, they undergo a period of rest of several months. The teleutospores require freezing temperature for a long period of time before germination. Hence the teleutospores are *resting spores* to carry the parasite over to the following season. They get favourable conditions for germination in other countries (*e.g.*, U.S.A., Canada etc.), but they seem to have lost their power of germination in the plains of India.

On the approach of the favourable conditions, the dormant protoplasm of the resting teleutospores becomes activated and the tubular promycelia or basidia come out of the germpores of each cell of the teleutospore. The diploid (2n) nucleus is being transferred in the basidium where it divides twice giving rise to four haploid (n) nuclei. This division is reductional (meiotic) one. Each basidium becomes segmented forming four uninucleate cells. A sterigma comes out from each of the four cells. In the lower three cells the sterigmata arise just beneath the septa and in the upper cell at the apex. On the terminal end of each sterigma a small, rounded sporidium or basidiospore develops. A single basidiospore (sporidium) develops on each sterigma and thus four basidiospores (sporidia) are produced on the basidium; 2 of + strain and 2 of –. The cells of basidium become depleted after the formation of basidiospores. Usually the opposite strained (compatible) nulcei of the basidium are arranged alternately in the segments. The sporidia fall off easily and are blown about. If they fall in a moist place, they germinate. The germ-tube which comes out from a sporidium is unable to infect the wheat plant but can enter the leaf of the barberry (*Berberris* spp.) a common shrub in the Himalayas and other Indian hills, *viz.*, Nilgiri and Palini hills of South India. Here the barberry bush acts as an alternate host. Entry of the germ tube of the sporidium takes place directly through the epidermis and not into a stoma. Inside of the barberry leaf, a mycelium is developed which causes a small yellowish patch on which two types of fructification are produced, spermagonia (pycnia) on the upper followed by aecidia on the lower surface. If the suitable alternate host is not available, the sporidia (basidiospores) are perished. About four days later after the germination of the basidiospore on the upper surface of barberry leaf, the pycniospores are produced on the monocaryotic mycelium.

The monocaryotic mycelium accumulates beneath the upper epidermis of the barberry leaf and develops into a flask-shaped *pycnium* (spermagonium). A hymenial layer of vertical hyphae develops at the base of the pycnium. Each vertical hypha of this hymenial layer is known as pycniosporophore. From the terminal ends of the pycniosporophores round or oval haploid and uninucleate pycniospores (spermatia) develop in basigenous chains. The pycniospores (spermatia) detach from the pycniosporophores and accumulate in the middle of the pycnium. The pycnia open outside the epidermis through small openings known as ostioles. Some of the sterile hyphae called paraphyses are found to be situated in the neck region of the pycnium. Some vertical fertile hyphae called the flexuous hyphae also come out through the ostiole. They are of the same strain as that of the mycelium on which they are developed. Only one strained

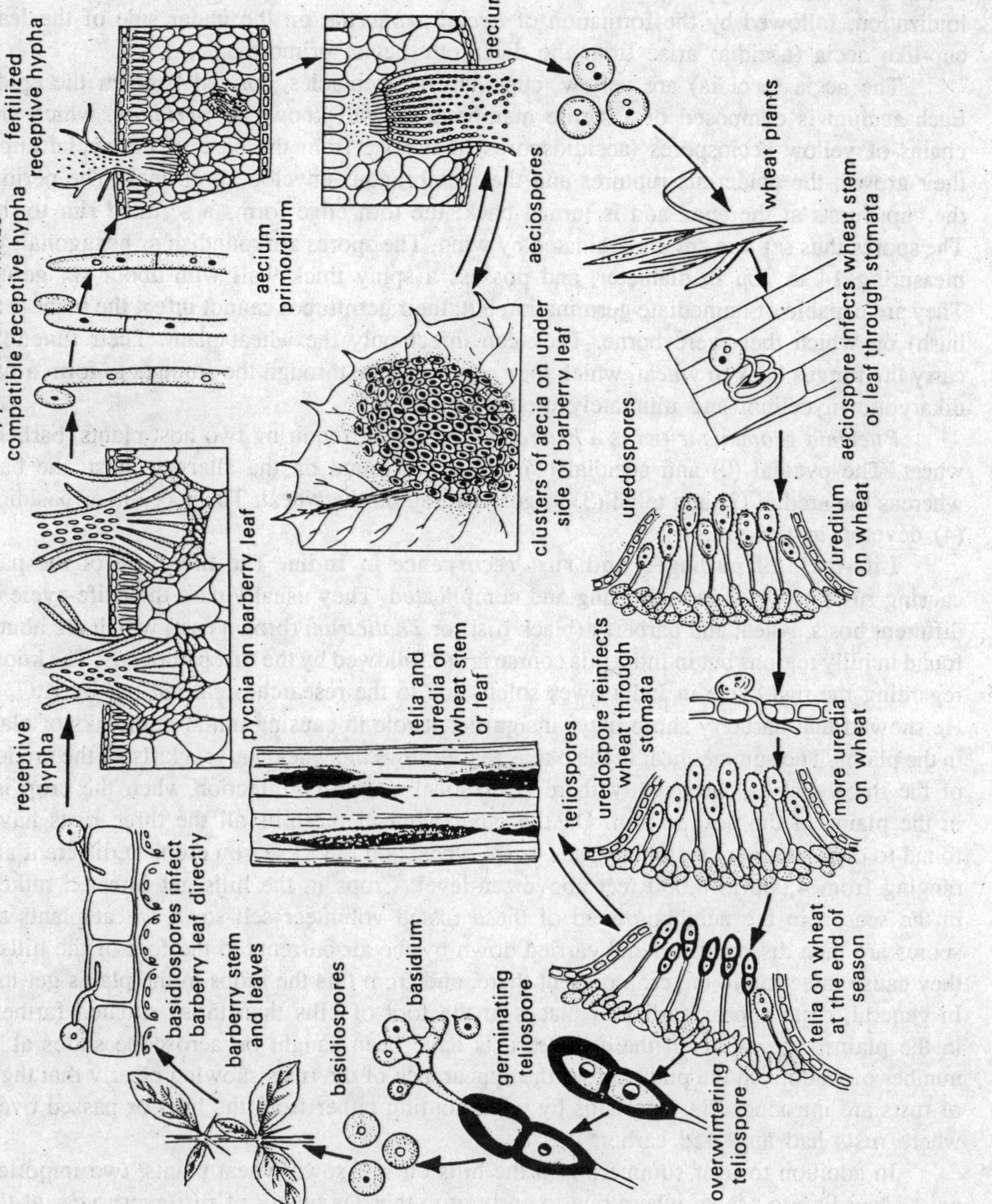

Fig. 19.6. Black rust of wheat caused by *Puccinia graminis tritici*. The life-cycle of fungus is being completed on two different hosts, *i.e.*, wheat (primary) and barberry (alternate or secondary). Diagrammatic disease-cycle.

(+ or −) pycniospores and flexuous hyphae are produced in one pycnium. On the maturation of the pycnium, the nectar oozes out through the ostiole and hundreds of pycniospores (spermatia) are released out along with the nectar. The pycniospores are responsible for the conversion of monocaryotic phase into dicaryotic one by the process of dicaryotization or diploidization. The pycniospores are transferred by insects or other means to flexuous hyphae projecting from pycnia through ostioles. The pycniospores and flexuous hyphae fuse, leading to fertilization and diploidization, followed by the formation of *aecial primordia* on the under side of the leaf. The cup-like aecia (aecidia) arise from the dicaryotic aecial primordia.

The aecia (aecidia) are yellow, cup-shaped receptacles, formed beneath the epidermis. Each aecium is composed of a sterile membranous wall known as *peridium,* which encloses chains of yellow aeciospores (aecidiospores) that arise from the base of the aecial cup. With their growth the epidermis ruptures and the membranous envelope protrudes. The peridium of the cup bursts at the apex and is turned back; the torn edge forms a serrated rim to the cup. The spores thus set free are disseminated by wind. The spores are roundish or hexagonal, yellow, measuring 14 to 26μ in diameter, and possess a spiny thick wall with about six germpores. They are capable of immediate germination but, their germtubes cannot infect the plant (barberry bush) on which they were borne. They can infect only the wheat plant. Their function is to carry the fungus back to wheat, which they can penetrate through the stomata to form a parasitic dikaryotic mycelium and ultimately uredia and telia.

Puccinia graminis tritici is a *heteroecious* fungus, requiring two host plants, barberry and wheat. The pycnial (0) and aecidial (1) stages are found on the alternate host, the barberry, whereas the uredial (2) and telial (3) stages develop on the wheat. The sporidia or basidiospores (4) develop in the soil.

Life-cycle of pathogen and rust recurrence in India. The life-cycle of the pathogen causing rusts of wheat is interesting and complicated. They usually pass their life-cycle on two different hosts, wheat and barberry (black rust) or *Thalictrum* (brown rust) which are abundantly found in hilly regions but in India this course is not followed by the rust pathogens. The knowledge regarding the rust cycle in India owes solely due to the researches carried out by K.C. Mehta. He showed that barberry shrub plays insignificant role in causing initial outbreaks of black rust in the plains. The summer heat in the plains that follows the wheat harvest kills all the uredospores of the three rusts. Consequently there is no local source of infection when the crop is sown in the plains in the next season. On the other hand in the hills all the three rusts have been found to over summer on stubbles, self-sown wheat and out of season crops at different altitudes ranging from 4,000 to 8,000 feet above sea-level. Crops in the hills get infected rather early in the season in the neighbourhood of these rusted volunteer self-sown wheat plants and the spores are then disseminated and carried down by the air currents to the foot of the hills where they cause infection to the crop present there, and from this the crops in the plains get infected. In general, rusts appear earlier in places at the foot of hills than those situated farther away in the plains. Spores of all these three rusts have been caught on aeroscope slides at a large number of stations in the plain before the appearance of the rusts showing clearly that the spores of rusts are introduced in the plains by wind coming either from the hills or passed over areas where rusts had appeared earlier.

In addition to over summering in the hills on self-sown wheat plants, two important foci exist according to Mehta where due to early crop there is plenty of rust every year at the time wheat is sown in the neighbouring plains. These are Central Nepal in the north and the Nilgiri and Palini hills in the south. The infection focus in Nepal is important for Uttar Pradesh as it is the source of disease in the crops of the plain along the Nepal border.

Recent Work. In 1974, L.M. Joshi and his associates reported that black rust develops at an early date in south India which then serves as inoculum reservoir in the form of uredospores for rest of the country.

Brown rust of wheat has two foci of infection, the Himalayas in the North, and Nilgiri and Palini hills in the South. It is the most widely prevalent rust. The uredospores get transported by upper winds from Nilgiris and Palini hills and then are washed down over Central India (Madhya Pradesh) by rains. The northern infection moves slowly southwards until the two populations merge.

The air-borne inoculum of brown rust as well as black rust and its deposition from southern hills (Nilgiri and Palini hills) has been traced by wind trajectories and weather satellite cloud images. From recent investigations of Nagarajan and Singh (1975), it appears that the tropical cyclones have a great bearing on the deposition of spores in Central India (Madhya Pradesh) within a time span of about 70 hours. The cyclonic disturbances occurring in the Bay of Bengal/ Arabian Sea in late October or early November set a pattern of favourable winds which carry the inoculum (uredospores) of black and brown rusts from Southern foci to the target area in Madhya Pradesh along with rain clouds. It has been found that the invisible spore cloud movement can be successfully tagged with the visible cloud movements seen in satellite television cloud photographs. This method has shown that the uredospores are transported from Nilgiris by upper air wind and are deposited over Central India (Madhya Pradesh) along with rain. From these secondary foci, it spreads to other foci making a nation-wide appearance.

Yellow rust is restricted in its distribution and appearance in epidemic form only to north western regions. Normally the rust appears in the foot-hills and plains in December or first fortnight of January, when conditions in plains are favourable and rapid multiplication of inoculum (uredospores) takes place.

Spread of disease. The initial infection of few odd plants in any field in the plains is sufficient to spread the disease. The disease soon spreads from one field to another by the dissemination of spores by air currents. Every rust pustule contains 30,000 to 80,000 spores and each such spore (uredospore) is capable of causing infection. They are easily carried away by wind and lodge on leaf and other green surface of the plant. In presence of moisture, the spores germinate and cause infection. The new pustules are developed within 10-14 days of infection. Usually four or five short cycles are repeated during the season. The greater the number of these short cycles, the greater would be the damage to the crop.

The multiplication and spread of the rusts in the plains depend on the weather conditions specially the rain or heavy dew on the layers of the wheat plants. Heavy dew for a long period or rain, moderately high temperatures and strong wind for dissemination of spores on the susceptible varieties are the important factors for rust epidemics.

Yellow or Stripe Rust of Wheat

Pathogen. *Puccinia striiformis* West.

Distribution. The yellow rust is limited to northern and eastern India, and rarely occurs in peninsular and western India. In comparison to other rust diseases of wheat, it appears earlier. The disease is seen in middle of January and if there are heavy rains it does much damage to the crop.

Symptoms. The uredia are chiefly formed on the leaf blades, but when the attack is severe, they also appear on the leaf sheaths, stalks and glumes as well. Sometimes the rust pustules are also seen on the pericarp and kernels. The green colour of the leaves fades in long streaks, on which rows of small uredo-pustules appear. Each row consists of a series of oval, lemon-yellow pustules arranged end to end and distinct from that above and below. The uredospores eventually break through the epidermis and yellow uredospores are shed.

The telia appear later as dull black patches in long narrow lines like the uredia. The telia are sub-epidermal and remain as flat black crusts.

Uredospores. The uredospores are nearly rounded and not oval or elliptic as in black

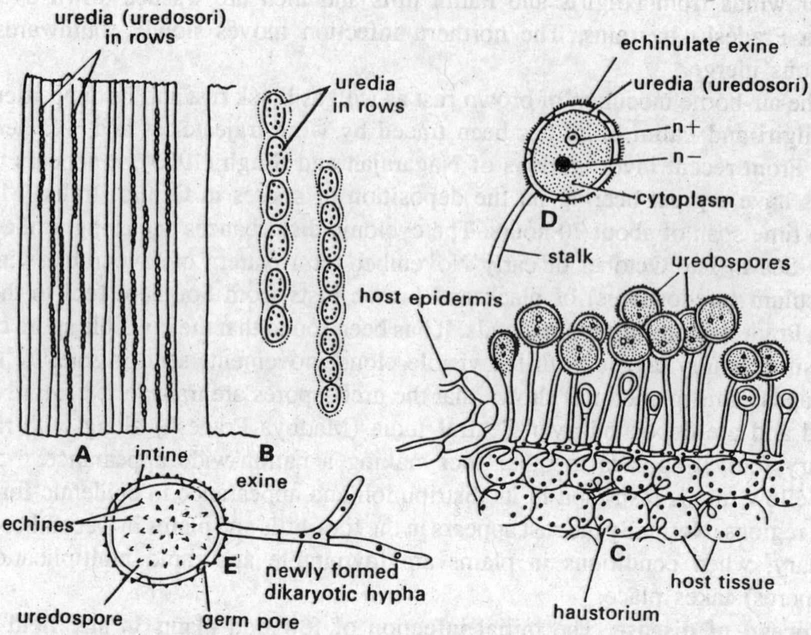

Fig. 19.7. Yellow of stripe rust of wheat. Uredial stage (*Puccinia striiformis*). A, part of infected leaf showing uredia arranged in rows; B, enlarged part of A; C, V.S. of infected leaf through uredium showing mycelium, haustoria and stalked uredospores; D, single uredospore; E, germinating uredospore.

rust. They measure 23-55μ × 20-30μ, and possess a hyaline wall provided with fine spines and with 6-10 scattered germ pores.

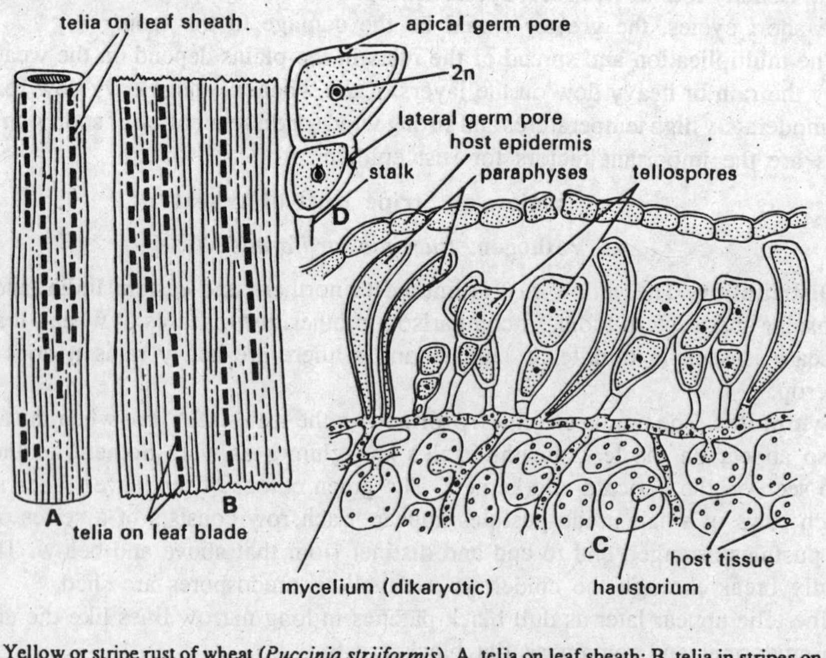

Fig. 19.8. Yellow or stripe rust of wheat (*Puccinia striiformis*). A, telia on leaf sheath; B, telia in stripes on leaf blade; C, V.S. of infected leaf through telium showing; in sub-epidermal state, teliospores, paraphyses, mycelium and haustoria; D, teliospores.

On germination, a small, fragile appressorium is formed over a stoma. The tube of entry swells up to a large, thick-walled, cylindrical sub-stomatal vesicle, upto 19μ broad and placed just below the stomatal opening. From this an infection hypha arises.

Teliospores. The telio-or teleutospores are dark brown, two-celled, often flattened or oblique at the top, and measure 35-63μ × 12-20μ. The teliospores may occupy the complete telium or may be broken up into groups by rows of brown paraphyses.

The yellow rust is heteroecious, but the alternate host is still unknown, and therefore, the pycnial and aecial stages have not been observed.

Nature and recurrence of disease (disease cycle). The disease is air borne. The inoculum (uredospores) causing the annual recurrence is brought from the hills to the plains every year. The uredospores of *Puccinia striiformis* over-summer on the hills at 7,000 feet and above.

Brown, Orange or Leaf Rust of Wheat

Pathogen. *Puccinia recondita* Roxb, ex Desm., Syn. *Puccinia triticina* Pers., *P. rubigo-vera* var. *tritici*.

Distribution. This rust is found throughout the world. Though this rust is found throughout India, yet it is most common in the northern and eastern regions. In the Punjab, Bihar, and Uttar Pradesh this disease causes more damage than stem rust. In Northern regions this disease appears earlier than the other two (black and yellow) rusts. In some districts of the plains of Uttar Pradesh the incidence of this rust takes place in the end of December or beginning of January along with yellow rust and both the diseases take a heavy toll. The disease prevails both in the hills and in the plains, in South India.

Symptoms. The uredo-sori (uredia) appear as a rule on the leaves, being scarce on the stalks and leaf sheaths. The uredia are always scattered on the leaf surface, they are never in rows or stripes. The uredia burst out on the upper surface as points of a bright orange colour.

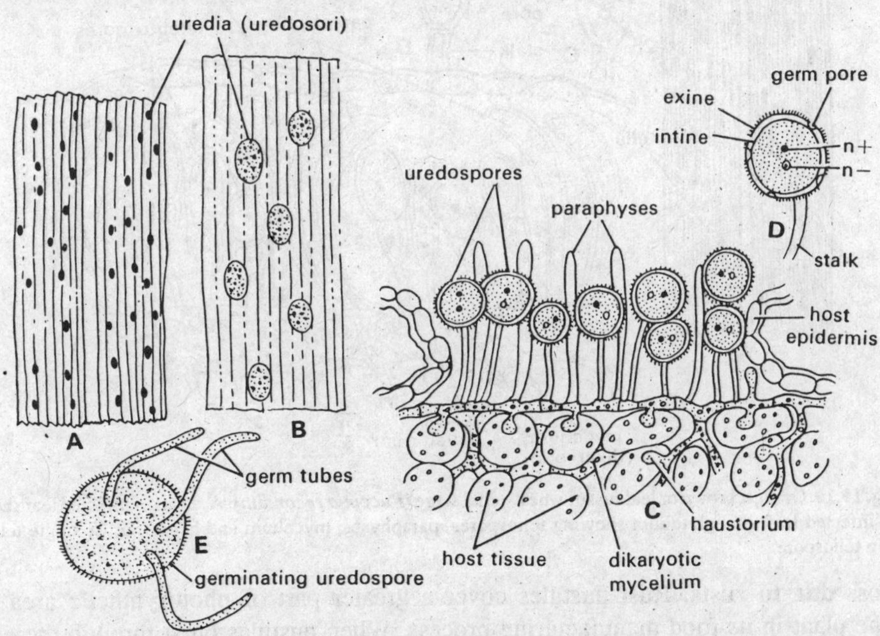

Fig. 19.9. Orange, brown or leaf rust of wheat (*Puccinia recondita*). A, a part of infected leaf with scattered uredia; B, magnified part of the same; C, V.S. infected leaf through uredium showing stalked uredospores, paraphyses, mycelium and haustoria; D, single uredospore; E, germinating uredospore.

The uredia are sometimes grouped in small clusters or irregularly scattered. The scattered uredia and their orange colour form the most characteristic distinguishing features of the brown rust. The uredosori burst early and shed their uredospores.

Telia are rarely formed. Some years they may not be present. In 1904, however, they were quite common and have appeared on several other occasions, (Butler, 1918). If telia are present they are small, oval to linear, black and sub-epidermal.

Uredospores. The uredospores are brown, spherical, minutely echinulate, measuring 20-35μ in diameter and bearing 7-10 germ pores. On germination, the germ tubes emerge through the germpores, which infect the wheat leaf through stomata.

Teliospores. The telia are divided up into several compartments by partitions of paraphyses. The teleutospores are two-celled, smooth, oblong, thick-walled and brown with a rounded apex. The teliospores are slightly constricted at the septum. Each teliospore measures 35-56μ × 12-23μ.

The brown rust is heteroecious. The aecial and pycnial stages of the fungus appear on species of *Thalictrum*. In India, the role of alternate host has not been precisely determined.

Nature and recurrence of disease (disease cycle). The disease is air-borne. Like other rusts of wheat the inoculum (uredospores) survives on the tillers and self-sown plants in the hills. The inoculum survives at 5,000 feet and above. Every year the uredospores are carried over by wind from the hills to the plains, where they cause infection.

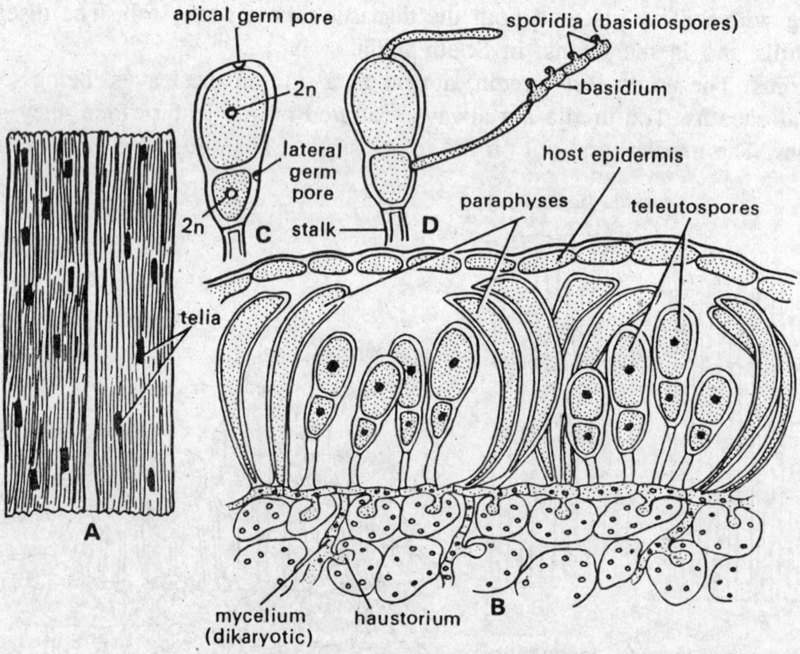

Fig. 19.10. Orange, brown or leaf rust of wheat-telial stage (*Puccinia recondita*). A, a part of infected leaf showing telia; B, V.S. of infected leaf through telium showing teliospores, paraphyses, mycelium and haustoria; C, single teliospore; D, germinating teliospore.

Loss due to rusts. Rust pustules cover a greater part of photosynthetic area and thus hinder the plant in its food manufacturing process. When pustules burst through the epidermis, the water is lost by transpiration resulting in partial sterility, poorly filled ears and shrivelled grains. If rust becomes severe before milk stage of the crop, the losses are always great even resulting in crop failures.

20

Principles of Plant Disease Control

"Diseases exact a heavy toll of crop yields and cause considerable damage to crop year after year. Diverse methods have been adopted from time to time to mitigate the ravages caused by these diseases with varying amounts of success. The acute shortage of food supplies in several countries and the rapid increase in population have, in recent years, brought to the forefront the dire necessity to conserve as much of the crop yields as possible by reducing the losses caused by diseases". This statement of T.S. Ramakrishnan (1961) has become more realistic in this hour of crisis when India's population is reaching to the explosion point.

To check the plant diseases, it becomes necessary to know about the cause of the disease, of the life-history of the causal organism and of the meteorological conditions which influence the host and parasite interaction.

Control measures may be divided into two main groups– (1) *Prophylaxis* and (2) *immunization* or *disease resistance.*

Prophylaxis includes the protection of the host from exposure to the pathogen, from infection or from the environmental factors favourable to disease development.

Immunization or *disease resistance* implies the improvement of resistance of the host to infection and to disease development. This method is generally used as a means of control by the development of strains of the host through hybridization and/or selection, which are more resistant to one or more pathogens.

Prophylaxis is implied to a wide range of control measures. Such variations of control measures are being considered under three sub-groups– (1) *exclusion,* (2) *eradication* and (3) *direct protection.* These methods have been treated separately in the following paragraphs:

EXCLUSION OF THE PARASITE

Under the sub-head *exclusion of the parasite from the host,* the measures are designed to keep the pathogen from entering the area in which the host is growing or to reduce to a minimum the extent to which the pathogen is introduced. These measures include quarantine regulations; inspection and certification etc.

Quarantines

Many plant diseases have been introduced in our country from time to time from other parts of the world. The possibility of the entry of the pathogen in a new area has been increased several fold with the extension of transport facilities at the present time. Sometimes it becomes quite difficult to check the movement of the diseased plant material which transmits the disease. Against this menace most countries have established plant quarantines. In the larger countries similar measures are sometimes taken to prevent the passage of plant diseases from State to State.

The new parasites from other countries, on introduction may upset the biological equilibrium existing between pathogen and host plants and eliminate the susceptible ones. In several agricultural advanced countries, the plant quarantine legislation has been strictly followed to check the movement of diseased plant material or of fungi, bacteria or viruses which are responsible for causing plant diseases. Quarantines have been proved quite effective for preventing the entry of plant diseases in many countries. Under quarantine legislation, the certificates of freedom from disease or from certain specified diseases are being issued by a competent authority acceptable to the importing country.

In India, a "Destructive Insects and Pests Act" was passed by the legislature in 1914, and it has been amended from time to time. Potato tubers are not allowed into India, unless it is certified by the Ministry of Agriculture of the exporting country that the tubers are free from wart disease caused by *Synchytrium endobioticum,* and there was no wart disease within a radius of five miles. Cultures of fungi and bacteria are not allowed to be brought into India unless Head of the Division of Mycology and Plant Pathology, Indian Agricultural Research Institute, New Delhi, is satisfied, that the particular pathogen or organism would not become a parasite in India. No plant can be brought by air, unless issued a special permit. In India, domestic quarantine is in force in the cases of bunchy-top of banana and wart disease of potato. There is complete ban on the transportation of potato tubers from Darjeeling district (West Bengal) to other parts of India, as wart is prevalent in this district of West Bengal.

Sometimes, it is thought that the net gain from this enforcement of quarantine measures is negligible. However, it would be better if the movement of destructive plant diseases and pests is checked at least under favourable conditions, from an infected locality to a non-infected one. Doing so the possibility of the entry of the pathogen is reduced to great extent in a new area. By quarantine legislations some diseases have been successfully confined to their respective countries of occurrence such as Karnal bunt of wheat (India), coffee rust (Eastern Hemisphere), Ufra disease of rice (India), rice dwarf (Japan) etc.

Inspection and Certification

In several agriculturally advanced countries the certification is being done. The certificate must contain that the living plants were thoroughly examined on a date which must be not more than fourteen days prior to shipment and were found to be healthy. In Great Britain for all potatoes a certificate is required that no case of wart disease has occurred on the farm on which they were grown not within two kilometers of it. There is provision for inspection of any consignment and for its treatment or destruction. Compulsory inspection and certification are useful measures to prevent the introduction of disease from a foreign country or from one part of the country to another. Since a large number of diseases are carried on vegetative propagation stocks, a system of inspection and certification is being adopted in many countries.

ERADICATION OF THE PARASITE

Eradication of the pathogen can be done in several ways as- crop rotation, removal of infected parts, elimination of alternate hosts, destruction of wild hosts and weeds, rogueing. For instance, the intensity of the black rust of wheat has been greatly reduced in the United States of America by the systematic removal of the barberry bushes, the alternate host of the black rust. On the other hand sugarcane smut is best controlled by rogueing.

Crop Rotation

It is well known that most of the serious parasitic fungi cannot multiply in the absence of the host plant. They may persist in the soil for some time, but if the proper host plants are absent their number may diminish and they may in due course even go out of existence. A parasite may persist in the soil on diseased plant debris after the crop has been harvested. Many of the organisms survive only so long as the host residue persists as a substrate for their saprophytic existence. In regions where freezing conditions prevail during the winter months, these organisms, commonly persist for 1 or 2 years. In general they can be culminated as source of inoculum, by a 3 or 4 years of rotation with crops which are not hosts.

Removal of Infected Parts

The destruction of diseased parts of plants in the field removes the main *foci* of infection and thus breaks the chain. Citrus canker caused by *Xanthomonas citri,* can be effectively controlled by the removal of affected plant parts. Eradication of infected plant parts may be effectively employed in the control of canker diseases. In the *Koleroga* of arecanut, the pathogen, *Phytophthora arecae* oversummers in tree-tops, and resumes the activity during the monsoon. Destruction of such affected tree-tops and practice of general sanitation by burning all diseased nuts and leaf-sheaths is an effective protection against the breakout of the disease.

Elimination of Alternate Hosts

In some of the destructive diseases in which long-cycled heteroecious rust fungi are concerned, the eradication of alternate host is a possible means of control. The barberry eradication campaign in the control of black rust of wheat in United States, of the buck thorn (*Rhamnus* spp.) in the control of crown rust of oats, of *Thalictrum* spp. in controlling the brown rust of wheat (*Puccinia recondita*), of *Ribes* spp., in the control of white pine blister rust (*Cronartium ribicola*), of red cedar in apple rust (*Gymnosporangium juniperi-virginianae*) have been proved effective.

Destruction of Wild Hosts and Weeds

A large number of diseases, particularly virus diseases, are harboured in wild host and weeds. Removal of such wild hosts is a good method of control. The yellow vein mosaic of *Bhindi* persists on a wild host (*Hibiscus tetraphylus*) in nature and the systematic removal of this wild host has proved successful in combating the disease. Similarly effective control has been obtained in sugarcane against mosaic, by the systematic removal of maize from the neighbouring fields, as the latter acts as a collateral host for the perpetuation of the virus infection chain.

Rogueing

This practice consists of destruction of affected plants from the fields at an early stage by removing *foci* of infection and preventing wide dissemination of the pathogen. This makes one of the routine methods of control of virus diseases in plants. The virus infected plants should be removed and destroyed in early stage to check the spread of virus diseases. The control of yellow mosaic of *Bhindi* and *Katte* disease of cardamom has been obtained through these practices. The whip smut of sugarcane (*Ustilago scitaminea*), loose smut of wheat (*U. tritici*), covered smut of barley (*U. hordei*) are being checked by such practices.

Improved Cultural Practices

Raising of beds. The foot rot of ginger caused by *Pythium myriotylum* occurs in the low bed areas, which are subjected to flooding and are ill-drained and which favour the aquatic pathogen. This disease can be controlled by an improved cultural practice, by planning the crop on raised beds. The raised bed system has removed those conditions which favoured the pathogen.

Change in planting season. The leaf rust of sugarcane (*Puccinia sacchari*) and blast of ragi have been controlled effectively by this method. It is a case of disease escape. The crops are grown during September-October instead of in June-July and thus escape the pathogens. Heavy rust infection may be avoided by early sowing of wheat in the plains of N. India.

Obtaining seed from disease-free localities. For instance, the foot rot of ginger caused by *Pythium myriotylum* is prevalent in South India, which can be controlled by importing seed-rhizomes from disease-free arid zones of Northern India, where the disease is practically absent, because of the dry climate, lighter soils and moderate rainfall.

Proper manuring. Applications of a balanced dose of nitrogen help in the reduction of blast (*Pyricularia oryzae*) and leaf spot (*Helminthosporium oryzae*) of rice. Nitrogenous fertilizers increase the rust incidence of wheat while potassium and phosphatic manures reduce the intensity of rust.

Mixed cropping. The practice of mixed cropping has helped effectively in checking the spread of infectious diseases. The root rot of cotton caused by *Rhizoctonia bataticola* and the wilt of pigeon pea (*arhar*) caused by *Fusarium udum* in Uttar Pradesh, have been successfully overcome by such practice. The growth of an intercrop of *moth* (a leguminous crop), in between rows of cotton tends to keep down the high soil temperatures, which are essential for the development of root rot and thus indirectly reduces the incidence of the disease. On the other hand *arhar* crop is grown mixed with sorghum crop.

Soil hygiene. Field sanitation is an important factor in the healthy and vigorous growth of plants. Uncleaned fields constitute a danger to the well-being of plants, as remnants of previous crops in the field very often harbour disease organisms. Crops grown under such conditions become exposed to attack of diseases and get seriously damaged. Ratoon crops of cotton and sugarcane, generally get easily infected by soil borne diseases. To get rid of disease that perennates in the crop refuge in the soil, the surest method is to collect all parts of diseased plants after harvest and burn them. On no account such debris should be thrown on manure heaps as there is always risk of introducing a disease to the soil by the use of such manure. Wilt disease and root rots render certain fields unfit for growing healthy crops. A large number of soil borne diseases can be checked by devoting attention to good cultivation and observing necessary precautions for keeping out infection.

The incidence of a parasitic organism in the soil can be reduced by keeping the land fallow and planting the non-susceptible crops.

Amendment of soil conditions. When the crop plants are not grown under ideal conditions they are more susceptible to infection and amendment to such factors would control the disease. Soil improvement with a view to controlling diseases includes measures devised to increase host resistance and adjustment of soil temperature, soil moisture, soil texture and soil reaction.

The activity of the organisms which are sensitive to *soil reaction* (pH) can be controlled by adjustment of the reaction of the soil. For instance, the potato scab can be controlled by the addition of sulphur with a view to acidifying the soil. Similarly club root of cabbage which is favoured by acidic soils can be controlled by liming. Addition of sulphur or inorganic acids to soils having a reaction of pH 5.9 or above is recommended. According to Millard, sufficiently liberal dressings of green manure added to the soil will inhibit the disease. This is probably due to the temporary increase in soil acidity, as a result of decomposition of the organic matter by soil fungi, and to an increase in soil moisture.

Soil sterilization and partial sterilization. The soil may be sterilized completely or only partially, whereby not all the organisms are destroyed, but only certain groups. To sterilize a soil it is placed in glass or clay containers and heated under pressure, 15-20 pounds, for 2-3 hours. By using flowing steam for 1-2 hours, on six consecutive days, complete sterilization can also be obtained.

It often appears necessary to partly sterile the soil to destroy certain injurious insects on pathogenic fungi, but not to kill the whole soil population. Such partial sterilization can be brought about by use of heat, as by steam or dry heat, or by means of various volatile or non-volatile antiseptics. The treatments have a selective effect upon the soil microbiological population, affecting particularly the fungi, many of the Protozoa and certain bacteria. Hot weather cultivation and burning trash seems to be a beneficial agricultural practice. The soil sterilization with chemicals cannot be recommended for large-scale application in the field.

Biological control. Several attempts have been made to inoculate the soil with antagonistic organisms for the purpose of controlling plant diseases. To make use of this method it becomes essential to evolve effective ways for checking the activity of a parasite in the soil or for the eradication of the parasite by increasing the activity of the antagonistic soil microflora.

DIRECT PROTECTION
(Use of Fungicides)

The application of the surface of the host plant of substances which prevent the germination of spores or kill the germ tubes before they can enter the tissues is one of the most widely used means of attack on plant pathogens. The above ground parts of plants are sprayed by applications in paste or other convenient forms, seeds are disinfected by immersion in solution of chemicals or by dusting or sprinkling with the compound or mixture. Spraying and dusting have a limited application because they are both troublesome and expensive too.

A good fungicide should be toxic to the parasite and not to the host. It should be reasonably easy to prepare and not too expensive. It should be capable of even distribution from the spraying or dusting machines. It should have good sticking properties so that it is not removed off easily from the surface of the host.

Compounds and mixtures of sulphur and of copper with lime have remained for many years the standard fungicides which fulfil the above-mentioned requirements, except for seed disinfection, where organo-mercurials, formation and other substances are utilized for the purpose.

Following the discovery of Bordeaux mixture by Millardet in France during the last century much attention has been paid to the study of the mode of the action of the fungicide on the pathogen. Many fungicides known as *"insoluble copper"* have been placed on the market as substitutes for Bordeaux mixture.

There are several formulae of preparing Bordeaux mixture;

Bordeaux mixture 4 : 4 : 50 or 5 : 5 : 50 or 2 : 2 : 50

Copper sulphate	4 lbs.
Quick lime	4 lbs.
Water	50 gallons.

Standard 5 : 5 : 50 Bordeaux mixture (5 lb. copper sulphate, 5 lb. lime, 50 gallons water) is made up by dissolving 5 lb. copper sulphate in 25 gallons of water in a wooden container. Five lb. of fresh hydrated lime is pasted in water and then made upto 25 gallons. The two solutions are mixed together while stirring.

One of the big drawbacks of Bordeaux mixture is the time that is spent on its preparation. Today there are several substitutes for Bordeaux mixture that only requires stirring into water before they are ready for use.

Even today Bordeaux mixture is recommended strongly in India and many other parts of the world. In South India the Bordeaux mixture is utilized for the control of leaf rust of coffee, abnormal leaf-fall of rubber, fruit rot of areca etc. Throughout the world the Bordeaux mixture is being utilized for spraying potatoes (early and late blight), grape vines (downy mildew), banana (panama disease) and various vegetables, ornamentals and fruits. There is a great advantage with Bordeaux mixture that its deposit on the leaves acts as persistent protectant not readily washed away by rains.

Dry Bordeaux. It contains 26 per cent copper and is sold as a fine powder in the market. This has been developed as a substitute for Bordeaux mixture and has been used to control many foliage diseases such as leaf spot of beans, beet, peas, potatoes, tomatoes etc. The foliage diseases are being controlled by the application of sprays containing 5 lb, dry Bordeaux per 100 gallons of water.

Insoluble copper. They include compounds like tribasic copper sulphate, copper oxychloride, cuprous oxide, copper phosphate etc. They are utilized as dusts or as miscible spray formulations. However, they are not as tenacious as Bordeaux mixture, and can successfully be utilized only in regions of lower rainfall.

Copper oxychloride. This is a fungicide which has been developed with success as a substitute for Bordeaux mixture. Blister blight of tea, rust of coffee, downy mildew of vines, late blight of potatoes and leaf spot of bananas and tobacco have been controlled effectively by application of this material.

Shell copper fungicide. A Burmah Shell product contains 50 percent metallic copper in the form of copper oxychloride. It is a free-flowing green powder readily dispersible in water.

Cuprous oxide. This material has also been developed as one of the substitutes for Bordeaux mixture. Potato blight, *Alternaria* on tomatoes and downy mildew of onions are being controlled by the applications of this material. Late blight of potatoes, tomato blight, bean rust and anthracnose have been controlled by applications of a 0.4 per cent spray.

Fungimar. A product of Bharat Pulverising Mills Ltd., Bombay. It contains 50 per cent metallic copper as cuprous oxide readily dispersible in water. Used as foliage spray.

Perenox. A product of Plant Protection Ltd., of England. It is a cuprous oxide product containing 50 percent metallic copper. It is a free-flowing reddish brown powder, readily dispersible in water. Used as foliage spray.

Sulphur and sulphur compounds. Next to copper compounds pure sulphur and sulphur compounds (lime sulphur) have been utilized for the treatment of powdery mildews and rusts. Sulphur dust is unique among fungicides in the sense that it need not come into actual contact with the pathogen to exert its fungitoxic effect. It is well known that the fungicidal properties of sulphur are improved by the reduction in the size of the particles of the powder (usually 400 meshes per sq inch). Water miscible sulphur formulations (wettable sulphur) are also available which are used by spraying. Sulphur powder is used for dusting crops against rust and powdery mildews and for seed treatment of sorghum against grain smut.

Processed sulphur containing a mixture of 30 to 40 per cent of talc has been found to be as good as pure sulphur in the control of certain powdery mildews like that on rubber.

Organo-mercury compounds. After World War I, several organo-mercury compounds came into use especially for seed treatment. *Uspulum* and *Germisan,* were among the earliest of these from Germany. These were followed by various other formulations like *Ceresan, Agrosan* etc., and are being used all over the world as seed disinfectants and protectants. Some of these have been employed for field treatment also, against apple scab and rice blast.

The organo-mercurials used as fungicides are ethyl mercury compounds. They are used as dusts or water miscible formulations containing a very low percentage of the active ingredient. As they are poisonous to human beings, the consumption of the treated parts as food should be done only after careful washing of the material.

Organic fungicides. During and after the Second World War several organic fungicides have been developed and placed on the market. These fungicides belong to the group of *carbamates,* *quinones, phenols* etc., Some of them are used for seed-treatment, like *phygon* and *spergon*, while others are employed for field applications, like *captan* and *dithane*. *Nabam* and *zineb* were introduced in the United States of America for the control of the late blight of potato. Formulation of organic nematocides and soil fungicides like *mylone* and *vapum* are also in use.

Phenyl mercury acetate chloride and nitrate. These Phenyl mercury salts (2.5 per cent) are fungicides for use in horticultural crops. They are dispersible powders forming stable suspensions and very readily soluble in water. They are commonly applied for apple scab and pear scab caused by *Venturia inaequalis* and *V. pirina* respectively at the rate of 200 gm. per 100 litres.

Phelam. Phelam is a combination of mercury and a dithiocarbamate. This fungicide makes a good control of apple scab (*Venturia inaequalis*). It is used at the rate of 100 gm. per 100 litres. This can be used at regular intervals as a normal spray.

Sulpham. This has been specially formulated to meet threat of apple mildew in England. It is a formulation which combines phelam with sulphur, to provide a dual purpose fungicide to control both apple scab and apple mildew. It contains 0.6 per cent phenyl mercury dimethyl dithiocarbamate.

Agallol. This is a mercurial fungicide and disinfectant from Bayer. This is a red-coloured compound. The red colour of Agallol solution is due to the presence of a trace dye. This is particularly used in treating sugarcane setts before planting to prevent attack from disease-carrying organisms such as red rot of sugarcane (*Colletotrichum falcatum*). 1 lb. of Agallol in 20 gallons of water, *i.e.*, 0.5 per cent solution is generally used.

Mercurized copper oxychloride (MCO). This is finely divided powder possessing strong eradicant and protectant fungicidal properties. It contains micronized copper oxychloride. It is available in three different formulations, *i.e., dust, dispersible powder* and *oil*. It is used primarily for the control of potato blight (*Phytophthora infestans*); peach leaf curl (*Taphrina deformans*); tomato blight (*Phytophthora infestans*); downy mildew of grapes (*Plasmopara viticola*); leaf rust of coffee (*Hemileia vastatrix*); blister blight of tea (*Exobasidium vexans*) etc.

Captan. This is the common name for N-trichloromethylemercapto-4-cyclohexene-1, 2-dicarboximide. This is a powerful protectant fungicide particularly for foliage applications. It is available as a 50 per cent wettable powder.

Phaltan. This is the common name for N-trichloromethylthiophthalimide. It is used for controlling powdery mildews and other foliage infections. 10 per cent dust and a 50 per cent wettable powder are available.

Thiram. This is the common name for tetramethylthiuram disulphide, the first developed organic fungicide. This material has been developed mainly for seed dressing prior to planting to control damping off of seedlings and seed rot pathogens. Thiram dispersible powder is a stable formulation insoluble in water, but it wets rapidly to form an excellent suspension on addition to water.

Ferbam. This is the common name for a non-volatile organic fungicide, ferric dimethyldithiocarbamate. It has been used successfully to control a large range of diseases. It has been commonly used in controlling disease of fruit foliage. It has also been used successfully as a seed dressing and turf fungicide. Scab and bitter rot of apples have been controlled by using this fungicide. Ferbam is usually sold in 70 and 76 per cent wettable powders.

Apple scab has been controlled by applications of 2lb. of 76 per cent wettable powder in 100 gallons of water.

Damping off of onions has been controlled by treating the seeds with a 0.5 per cent suspension of ferbam.

Zineb. This is the common name for zinc ethylenebisdithiocarbamate. It is used as a protective fungicide for the control of a wide range of diseases of vegetables and fruits. The most widely used formulations are Dithane Z-78 and Parzate. It is practically insoluble in water and is sold as 55 per cent wettable powder and 5-15 per cent dust. Zineb dispersible powder (65 per cent) is a protective fungicide for foliage application. It is a light coloured powder readily dispersible in water forming a stable suspension. The usual rate of spray application is 1.5 - 2 lb. per 100 gallons of water (high volume spraying per acre). It is generally used for controlling downy mildew of onion (*Peronospora destructor*); potato blight (*Phytophthora infestans*); downy mildew of crucifers (*Peronospora parasitica*); downy mildew of vine (*Plasmopara viticola*) etc.

Ziram. This is the common name for zinc dimethyldithiocarbamate. This compound is not effective in the control of late blight of potatoes and tomatoes, but has been proved effective in controlling other diseases of potatoes and tomatoes. It is particularly effective in the control of anthracnose of melons and cucumbers when sprayed at a rate of 2 lb. of 50 per cent wettable powder in 100 gallons of water per acre.

Nabam (dithane D-14). This is the common name for disodium ethylenebisdithiocarbamate. This material is available only in solution. When sprayed in conjunction with zinc sulphate and lime, it has given effective control of late and early blight of potatoes and tomatoes. It is generally used at rate of 2 quarter per hundred gallons.

Maneb (dithane M-22). Maneb is the common name for manganese ethylenebisdithiocarbonate, an organic fungicide similar in properties to zineb. It is generally used at the rate of 1.5 to 2 lb. per 100 gallons of water.

Dichlone. This is an organic fungicide, 2, 3-dichloro 1,4-naphthaquinone, which may be used both as a seed dressing and as a foliage spray. It has been used successfully to control apple scab (*Venturia inaequalis*), leaf curl (viral) and late blight (*Phytophthora infestans*) of potatoes etc. It is sold as 50 per cent wettable powder for spraying, dusting or wet and dry seed treatments.

Tetrachloro para benzoquinone (spergon). This is a nonvolatile organic fungicide which has been used both as a seed dressing and as a foliage spray. Damping off, seed rots, downy mildews and Helminthosporioses are being effectively controlled by its application. It is generally sold in the following formulations: (a) 96 per cent dust for dry seed treatment; (b) 95 per cent wettable powder for use in the slurry treatment of seed and (c) 48 per cent wettable powder for spraying and dusting.

Dinocap. Dinocap, 2,-4 dinitro -6 - (1-methylheptyl) phenylcrotonate, is used as a fungicide. It is available as 25 per cent wettable powder, a 50 percent emulsified liquid and as a dust. It is widely used for the control of powdery mildews of apple, pear, cucumbers etc. It is used both as a protectant and eradicant.

Quintozene. 2,3,4,5,6-pentachloronitrobenzene (Brassicol), is a fungicide for many soil pathogens and seed-borne diseases, including damping off, wheat bunt etc.

Dodine. This is the common name in Great Britain for n-dodecylguanidine acetate. 65 per cent wettable powder is sold in Great Britain under the trade name Melprex.

FUMIGANTS

Chloropicrin. This is an organic fumigant liquid which has been used effectively to control pathogenic fungi which live in the soil.

Carbon disulphide. This is a poisonous and inflammable organic liquid which has been used as a soil fumigant to control *Armillaria* root rot.

Chlorobromopropene. This is a soil fumigant. It is generally sold as a liquid containing 65 per cent of the active material. This material is most effective when the soil temperature is between 50^0 and 70^0F.

ANTIBIOTICS

The antibiotics are those substances which are produced by one microorganism and become toxic to another microoganism. Most of the antibiotics are products of Actinomycetes and some fungi, *e.g., Penicillium.* They are toxic mostly against bacteria but also against some fungi. The chemical formulae of most antibiotics are complex, and not related to each other. Antibiotics used for plant disease control are generally absorbed and translocated systematically by the plant. Among the most important antibiotics in plant disease control are streptomycin, tetracyclines, cycloheximide and griseofulvin. The antibiotics can be antibacterial or antifungal in their activity.

Streptomycin. This is produced by an actinomycete *Streptomyces griseus.* It is marketed as Agrimycin, Phytomycin, Ortho-Streptomycin. It is used as a spray against a broad range of bacterial plant pathogens causing spots, rots etc., *e.g., Erwinia amylovora,* the causal organism of fire blight of pears. Streptomycin is also used as a dip for potato seed pieces against bacterial rots of tubers, and as a seed disinfectant against bacterial pathogens of beans, cotton, crucifers, cereals etc. It is also effective against downy mildews caused by phycomycetous fungi.

Tetracyclines. The tetracyclines are those antibiotics which are produced by various species of *Streptomyces* (Actinomycetes). They are active against several bacteria. Of the tetracyclines Terramycin (oxytetracycline), Aureomycin (chlorotetraycline) and Achromycin (tetracycline) have been used to some extent for plant disease control. Oxytetracycline isolated from *Streptomyces rimosus* is most common. Oxytetracycline has been used to reduce crown gall infections. Tetracyclines have been shown to control certain diseases caused by mycoplasmas (PPLO).

Cycloheximide. Cycloheximide has been isolated from *Streptomyces griseus* (an actinomycete) as a by-product in the production of streptomycin. It is sold as Actidione, Actispray, Actidione PM, Actidione RZ etc. It has been reported to be effective against many pathogenic fungi. It has been used for the control of many turf diseases and of cherry leafspot caused by *Coccomyces hiemalis*. It is also effective against powdery mildews of several crops. However, its high phytotoxicity limits its usefulness to a great extent.

Griseofulvin. Griseofulvin, produced by *Penicillium griseofulvum,* is toxic to several phytopathogenic fungi, such as those causing powdery mildews, rusts, *Botrytis* and others.

It is 7-chloro-4, 6 dimethoxycoumaran-3-one-2-*spiro*-1^1-2^1-(methoxy-6^1-methylcyclohex)-2^1-en-4^1 one. It exhibits true systematic action.

Other antibiotics. Several other antibiotics exhibit activity against several plant pathogens. These antibiotics are–blasticidin, pimaricin, nystatin, rimocidin, filipin, phytoactin, polymyxin, erythromycin and puromycin. Among these blasticidin is effective against the rice blast disease caused by *Pyricularia oryzae*. It is also effective in reducing multiplication of virus in some viral diseases of plants.

GROWTH REGULATORS

Some plant hormones have been reported to reduce infection of plants by certain pathogens, *e.g.*, tomato wilt by *Fusarium* and potato blight by *Phytophthora,* through the increase by these substances of the disease resistance of the host. The root knot nematode, *Meloidogyne,* of tobacco plant is checked, when treated with maleic hydrazide. Treatment of leaves with kinetin reduces virus multiplication, and thus reducing the number and size of lesions. The spray of gibberellic acid also reduces viral infection of several plants.

SYSTEMIC FUNGICIDES

The systemic fungicides were categorically introduced among other fungicides in 1966. The successful use of synthetic systemic fungicides was first demonstrated by von Schemeling and Kulka in1966. They discovered oxathiin fungicides of this series, and thereafter, pyrimidines and benzimidazoles were worked out. When a systemic fungicide is being taken by a plant, it is being translocated within the plant itself, and plant becomes fungitoxic. An ideal systemic fungicide is either toxic to the pathogen or it converts to such a toxicant in the host plant. It may also alter the metabolism of the host so that the biochemical or physical resistance to pathogen may be increased. An ideal systemic fungicide is being absorbed by the plant sufficiently and translocated to the site of pathogen and it should have sufficient stability within the host plant.

Oxathiins. For the first time in 1966 von Schemeling and Kulka developed two products anilides, which were later on known as oxathiins or carboxin and oxycarboxin. These products could control loose smut (*Ustilago nuda*) in barley. These products were 5, 6-dihydro-2-methyl-1, 4-oxathiin-3-carboxamilide (DC MO, carboxin trade, name Vitavax) and 5, 6-dihydro-2-methyl-1, 4-oxathiin-3-carboxamilide-4, 4-dioxide (DCMOD, oxycarboxin, trade name Plantvax). Carboxin (vitavax) is a popular systemic fungicide for seed treatment to control loose smut of wheat (*Ustilago tritici*) and barley (*U. nuda*) at the rate of 250g. per 100 kg. seed. It also gives satisfactory control to bunt (*Tilletia*) and flag smut (*Urocystis*) of wheat. Vitavax and Plantvax are also responsible to check basidiomycetous pathogens. Plantvax is toxic to Basidiomycetes and certain Deuteromycetes such as–*Helminthosporium, Cladosporium, Botrytis, Monilia* etc.

Benzimidazoles. The popular systemic fungicide of this group is benomyl. It is methyl-1-(butylcarbamamoyl)-2-(benzimidazole carbamate), trade name–Benlate. This fungicide is effective against smuts. Benlate has also been found to be effective against the phytopathogens: *Uncinula, Erysiphe, Podosphaera, Sphaerotheca, Venturia, Cercospora, Fusarium, Botrytis, Cladosporium, Monilinia, Gloeosporium* etc. This is a fungicide which has most wide spectrum. It is effective against most Phycomycetes, some Ascomycetes, several Basidiomycetes and many Deuteromycetes. It has been used as seed treatment, soil drench, soil mixture and foliar sprays. As a foliar spray, it controls powdery mildews of apple, cereals and cucurbits. Most commonly it is used as a seed treatment material. Sett dipping reduces the incidence of red rot of sugarcane. Seed treatment of cereals protects the crop against powdery mildew and takes all disease of wheat for more than thirty days. It is also effective against several soil-borne diseases. It also controls wilts of tomato and cucurbits caused by species of *Fusarium*. It is also effective against rust of cereals.

Pyrimidines. One of these compounds, dimethirimol (5-*n*-butyl-2-dimethyl amino-4-hydroxy-6-methyl pyrimidine) was first reported in 1968. This is a specific fungicide for cucurbits and controls powdery mildew caused by *Sphaerotheca fuliginea.* Later on, another compound of this group ethirimol (5-n-butyl-4 ethylamino-5-hydroxy-6-methyl pyrimidine) was added. This systemic fungicide effectively controls powdery mildew of barley caused by *Erysiphe graminis.* It also controls powdery mildew of wheat (*E.graminis tritici*). These systemic fungicides are being translocated from seed and ultimately reach the foliage where they control the powdery mildew. They have been proved more effective as soil or seed treatment rather than as foliar spray. Triarimol (2-4-dichlorophenyl phenyl-5-pyrimidine methanol) is another systemic fungicide which controls the apple scab disease caused by *Venturia inaequalis*. It is also effective against *Ustilago* and *Urocystis.*

Other systemic fungicides. Calixin (N-tridecyl-2, 6-dimethyl morpholine) controls powdery mildew fungus, *Erysiphe graminis.* It also controls powdery mildew of cucurbits caused by *Erysiphe* *cichoracearum*, powdery mildew of peas (*E. polygoni*), leaf spot of banana (*Mycosphaerella musicola*), yellow rust of wheat (*Puccinia striiformis*) and several other diseases of tea, coffee and cereals. Another systemic fungicide is a triazole compound and commercially known as RH 124, which has a remarkable effect in controlling leaf rust of wheat caused by *Puccinia recondita*.

BREEDING FOR DISEASE RESISTANCE

The breeding or selection of resistant varieties of the host is the most important method of control to fight against crop diseases. Resistant varieties against many of the major diseases are now grown in crops such as the cereals, potatoes, beans, peas, cabbage, tomato, cotton, sugarcane and several others. For a breeder, the term *disease* implies any abnormality caused by an upset in the normal functioning of physiological system of the plant. It is not only difficult to induce resistance to a disease with the desired quality of the crop but more complications may be caused by the presence of numerous physiologic races of the parasite, which give rise to new ones.

In breeding for the control of crop diseases, the object may sometimes be attained by breeding for disease escape or disease tolerance, instead for true resistance. Early varieties may escape a disease, sometimes because environmental conditions (temperature etc.) may not be suitable for infection, sometimes because the parasite is not present early in the season in sufficient numbers to cause serious infection. For example, the Indian cereal ragi (*Eleusine coracana*), does not suffer from blast if sown at Coimbatore between October and April, but is heavily infected when sown from June to August.

The ultimate object of all breeding work is to secure a sufficient range of variability in the crop in question to persuit of selection for desirable characters.

The immune types of plants resist further growth and spread of pathogen whereas in the susceptible types the pathogens spread rapidly. Even if the plant is susceptible type, the life cycles of the host and parasite may fall in different seasons of the years and thus the pathogen may not have the ideal conditions for invading the host and the latter thus escapes the disease. Therefore to recognize a truly immune type, all factors relating to both the host and pathogen are being considered and the plant breeder should not judge the plant as immune merely because it is disease-free at the time of observation. The disease resistance may be *partial* or *complete*. The complete resistance is also known as *immunity*. Taking the fungi into consideration, the resistance may be *protoplasmic* or *morphological*. It has been observed that resistance is often due to physiologic incompatibility between the host and the parasite and in such cases the invading pathogen sets up a reaction in the invaded cells. With the result the few invaded cells and the invading fungi may die due to toxic substances on one hand and want of nourishment on the other.

In the morphological type of resistance the plant may have certain morphological features which may make it difficult for the attacking pathogens to cause any damage. For instance, in the case of stem rust of wheat, mycelium develops in collenchyma only and in the case of varieties with reduced layers of collenchyma and large sclerenchyma, rust development is meagre. Such varieties are susceptible at seedling stage but they become resistant when sclerenchyma develops fully.

The other example may be cited of red rot of sugarcane, caused by *Colletotrichum falcatum*. Here the fungus enters the plants through wounds. It enters the vascular bundles and travels up along the xylem vessels. Anatomical features of the resistant and susceptible canes showed that resistance increases with increased sclerenchyma thickening round vascular bundles and fewer number of continuous xylem vessels. The varieties resistant to red rot possess highly lignified vascular sheath and very few continuous xylem vessels.

The internal condition of the plant also affects the extent of resistance to disease. This kind of resistance is known as *protoplasmic resistance*. For example, red gram wilt (*Fusarium vasinfectum*) is being increased by the application of superphosphate manures whereas decreased by green manuring with sunn hemp.

In the case of onion smudge caused by *Colletotrichum circinans*, the white variety of onions is highly susceptible, whereas yellow and red varieties are fairly resistant. It has been shown by biochemical studies that protocatechuic acid which is found in the outer scales of the resistant variety is responsible for resistance.

Immunity. By the term *immunity* we mean the lack of susceptibility of organisms to diseases in relation to parasite infections. Of course the immunity may be of two types; on the one hand *natural* or *congenial* immunity and on the other hand *acquired* immunity produced artificially. But in plants natural immunity has the great significance.

The most widely distributed forms of immunity among plants are generic and specific immunity. In the phenomenon of immunity, two phases have been distinguished in the development of parasites, namely, *the penetration of the parasite into the plant* and *the distribution and the development of the parasite within the tissues of the host plant.*

Environment and immunity. The reactions of immunity are determined by the under-mentioned factors :(1) the heredity of the variety in question, (2) the selectivity or specialization of the species of parasite or its races and (3) the environmental conditions. A change in the environmental conditions may change the immunity reaction to a less or greater extent. The normal infection of tissues and cells by plant parasites to a great extent is determined by the environmental conditions.

The reactions of plants to parasites, may be changed by the conditions of the soil environment, particularly its acidity (pH-value), its physical properties, the presence of various salts, the effects of soil and air temperature and moisture, the effect of light, the quantity of carbonic acid contained in the air and other factors.

Physiologic forms. In fungi attacking the plants there are physiologic forms. However, these forms are morphologically identical but they differ in their pathogenicity. For example, it has been found that the pathogen *Puccinia graminis tritici* has more than 50 physiologic forms. Physiologic forms are definite, genetic entities. Any new variation in pure line cultures of crop plants can arise by *mutation* or *hybridization* with other types. Similarly, in the physiologic forms of fungi, any change in their culture characteristics, can arise by gene mutation or hybridization with other forms.

Laws in the distribution of immunity from infectious diseases in plants. In the breeding for immunity or resistance, it is necessary to consider–(1) the presence of different physiologic races of the distribution of the different physiologic races, (2) varietal differences in reaction toward the different physiologic races, (3) the possibility of combining in a single variety resistant to different parasitic races and (4) the possibility of producing varieties that are resistant to several diseases. Decisive factors in breeding for immunity appear to be the individuality of the parasite against which resistant forms are to be developed, and the individuality of the original variety.

American cottons are susceptible to American form of *Fusarium* and resistant to Indian form in spite of more than hundred years isolation from the former and contact with the latter for the period. These indicate that immunity or susceptibility is a genetically controlled character. The pathogens, may develop new strains that begin to attack the variety of the crop plant that once proved resistant.

The number of genetic factors controlling disease resistance varies in different plants. In the case of wilt of tobacco, tomato, flax and cotton, a complex genetic basis is present. In cabbage, it may be due to a single gene (type A) or may be complex, (type B). In both the types of resistance the host-parasite relation is similar but type B resist parasites at lower temperatures only.

BREEDING PROGRAMME

In case where disease resistance or immunity is governed by a single pair of genetic factors, it is easy to get homozygous types in F_2 of crosses between resistant and susceptible types. In complex cases the recovery of resistant types in recombined forms is more difficult. Disease resistant types may be obtained in the three following ways : (1) introduction, (2) straight selection and (3) hybridization and selection in hybrid progenies.

Introduction. It has been stated that resistance to disease is an inherent characteristic of some plants and occurs in varying degrees throughout the plant kingdom. A very simple and economical way would be to make direct introduction of varieties showing high resistance, into areas affected by a particular disease, in order to eradicate it. Sometimes a newly introduced variety may prove resistant to one disease but may be highly susceptible to another disease. The acclimatization of new introductions to new environment in most cases becomes a difficult problem. For example, wilt resistant American cotton varieties introduced in India, become highly susceptible to rust and black arm diseases. However, successful cases have also been recorded. The introduction into India of early maturing varieties of ground nut from the U. S. A. has successfully arrested the infection of Tikka disease. However, this random sampling method cannot be relied upon.

Straight selection. This method has more chances of success in obtaining disease resistant plants. One important point in any programme for breeding disease resistance type of crops is to select really immune or resistant type. The selected type must not be an escape. Selection must be carried on in optimum conditions of infection. The breeder must be sure that selected types are homozygous for disease resistance and therefore it becomes essential to test the material under controlled epiphytotic conditions before the type is pronounced as disease resistant. Testing of the selection is being done in green houses under conditions of artificial epidemic. In these cases, true protoplasmic resistance seems to be more reliable than the resistance based on morphological characters only. In selecting for disease resistance, it is also to be noted that the primary characters for which the plant is valued, are not lost. For example, in selecting wilt resistant types in cotton, yield and quality of the resistant type should also be maintained. For doing so, the selections may be carried out in the field and thereafter they are being subjected to tests by the pathologist under controlled epidemic conditions in glass house. However, if the material proves heterozygous, further selection becomes necessary. On the other hand, if selection proves homozygous and shows 25 percent resistance it may be released as strain.

Hybridization. This method of developing resistant varieties combined with commercial qualities, though effective and the best, and at the same time needs high technical skill. In this type of development of resistant varieties, first of all the source of resistance is made available. The process of hybridization involves sexual act between two individuals one of which possesses good agronomic qualities but lacks resistance to some specific disease while the other one is the source of resistance but lacks good commercial qualities. The programme of breeding, which normally consists of initial hybridization followed by systematic selection and selfing must be carried out under optimal conditions of environment for the development of disease and standard infection using all the prevailing physiologic races of the pathogen. Such a programme reduces to a minimum the risks involved in the isolation of *disease escapers*.

In general, the following principles are involved in the breeding and development of disease-resistant varieties:

(a) Field selection should be made from heavily infected areas from variable material, either available from natural populations or from segregating generations of crosses. (b) Such plants should be selfed and progenies be obtained. (c) The progenies obtained should be tested for disease resistance under artificial epidemic conditions. (d) All prevailing physiologic races of the pathogen should be employed. (e) All susceptible individuals should be discarded. (f) The selections should be transplanted in disease nursery, especially maintained for the purpose. (g) Desirable cultures should be selfed, and the process should be repeated in subsequent generations until homozygous condition is obtained. (h) Selections should be made, both for commercial qualities and resistance; undesirable individuals should be discarded every time. (i) Ultimately the seeds of the best selections should be multiplied for general distribution.

Hence the process of hybridization has become an established and effective method for obtaining disease-resistant varieties of crop plants. This is being done by effective crosses between varieties as well as species. Inter-specific hybridization has been of great value in introducing desirable resistance from wild types into commercial varieties. For example, successful crossing of wild *Lycopersicon pimpinellifolium* with cultivated tomato *Lycopersicon esculentum* has provided material to develop wilt resistant varieties to tomato. Crossing of wild *Avena strigosa* with cultivated oat *Avena sativa* has resulted in the development of varieties resistant to crown rust. The wild species such as *Saccharum spontaneum* and *S. barberri*, are resistant to sugarcane (*S. officinarum*). Much attention has been paid to crosses between *Solanum demissum* and *S. tuberosum* for obtaining resistant varieties of potato to late blight caused by *Phytophthora infestans*. Sometimes the resistant varieties once again become susceptible after some time because of changing race flora of pathogen. For example Kufri Red and Kufri Neela varieties of potato, were formerly resistant, and later on they were withdrawn, because they again became susceptible.

CONTROL OF PLANT VIRUSES

Viruses attack all forms of plants such as bacteria, fungi, algae, herbaceous plants and trees. The plant diseases caused by them may damage leaves, stems, roots, fruits, seeds and flowers, cause great economic losses by reduction in yield and quality of plant products. Virus diseases are responsible for serious losses to our agricultural crops. They are all the more important in the plantation crops which are propagated vegetatively. It is now a well known fact that the damage they cause probably equals that due to all other disease causing agents. This group of diseases because of their economic importance, has received due attention, and the science of *Virology* has made considerable progress.

As the knowledge about the plant viruses is rapidly increasing, new techniques or procedures have been devised to replace, the existing method of control. However, the best way to control a virus disease is to keep it out of an area through quarantine, inspection and certification systems. The seed certification and the use of virus-free clones of important fruit and vegetatively propagated crops has received wider application. The use of heat and chemotherapeutic treatments has been extended to a number of virus diseases of fruit and other cash crops such as, peach, strawberry, raspberries and sugarcane. The other important methods of preventing disease spread and losses due to them may be categorized as follows:

Eradication. The infected plants and susceptible weeds, and their destruction, checks the possibilities of spread of disease.

Elimination of insects. Plants may be protected against certain viruses by protecting them against the virus vectors. The use of insecticidal dusts and sprays reduce the chances of insect transmission. The possibilities of the use of antibiotics in the control of plant virus diseases are being worked out. The introduction of the systemic insecticides has increased the opportunities of the direct control of insect vectors.

Selection of seeds. It should be made from such fields which were free from infection. Seeds of cucurbits and legumes, setts of sugarcane, tubers, rhizomes and bulbs etc.,should be carefully selected for seed purposes. This is one of the most important measures for avoiding virus diseases of many crops, especially those lacking insect vectors.

Tuber indexing. It is done at the time of digging potatoes. Tubers taken from healthy plants are marked with ink and sown in small insect proof plots. The suspected diseased plants are removed carefully leaving only healthy plants to grow. Thus the healthy seed is multiplied.

Heat treatment. Once inside a plant some viruses can be inactivated by heat. Dormant propagative organs are generally dipped in hot water at 35^0-54^0C for few minutes. By doing so, in many cases the virus becomes inactivated and the plants are completely healthy.

Resistant varieties. Breeding plants for hereditary resistance to virus is of great importance, and many plant varieties resistant to certain virus diseases have already been evolved at various research centres.

21

Methods of Studying Plant Diseases

Methods involved in the study of plant diseases are as varied as diseases themselves, and only a few of them may be generalized. One can study the specific plant diseases, by means of their symptoms, studied either by naked eye or with the aid of a hand lens, while in the field of a particular crop. The symptoms of many diseases are more or less similar in appearance, and sometimes it becomes quite difficult to differentiate a particular disease only on the basis of its external symptoms. For a careful study of plant disease, host-parasite interaction should be studied intensively with the aid of a good microscope. For the study of plant disease, a basic knowledge of botany in the fields of anatomy, taxonomy and physiology becomes essential. The identification of a pathogen of a new disease requires the study of its life cycle as well as the study of its cultural, physiological and biochemical properties. Such type of study includes the isolation of the causal organism from the host, its culturing on culture media or on green house plants and its examination under various conditions of nutrition and environment. For doing all this, one should be familiar with the fundamental procedures of the study of micro-organisms in the laboratory. This includes the laboratory techniques for handling causal organisms, study of their pure culture and the procedures involved in the study of their physiology and biochemistry. The undermentioned procedures have been followed in the investigation of plant diseases in the laboratory and in the field.

Macroscopic Study

In certain plant diseases, the symptoms are so specific that one can immediately establish its identity only by having a glance at it. The symptoms of whip smut of sugarcane, loose smut of wheat, rust of wheat etc., may easily be placed in this category.

Sometimes for the identity of a plant disease, it becomes essential to use a hand lens. By using hand lens, one can observe the ectophytic mycelia, cleistothecia, sclerotia, conidiophores, conidia and other such fruiting bodies; and on the basis of the presence of these characteristic structures the diseases can be identified and confirmed. For example, the red rot symptoms appear on the midrib of sugarcane leaf in the shape of specific lesions; if the black dot-like acervuli are seen with the aid of a hand lens in these lesions, the test becomes confirmatory. In the case of downy mildew of *bajra* and *jowar*, if the conidiophores and conidia are visible on the undersurface of the leaf blade, the disease is confirmed. A critical eye is necessary in the study of field symptoms of plant diseases, and only through a great deal of experience, such study is possible.

Microscopic Study

Just after the study of the lesions or other symptoms with the aid of a hand lens, a careful microscopic examination of sections (both transverse and longitudinal) of the diseased tissues is being done. The sections of the diseased part of the plant are being cut with the help of a hollow ground razor or microtome. Differential staining is being done, so that, the mycelium from the host tissues may be differentiated. To study the host parasite relationship, temporary slides may be prepared. The mycelium of the fungus, its asexual stages, and the fruiting bodies, if present, are studied under different (low power, high power and oil immersion lenses) magnifications of the microscope. In certain cases, only the teasing of the material with the help of a needle is quite useful. The teased material may be examined under the microscope in different magnifications, and the somatic structure, reproductive structures and fruit bodies may be examined (*e.g.*, in downy and powdery mildews, and other diseases of plants).

Only the presence of a fungus within the tissues of a diseased plant does not mean that it is the disease causing parasite. The pathogenicity of the pathogen should be tested experimentally.

In the case of plant diseases caused by pathogens, Koch's postulates must be satisfied to determine the relationship of a particular pathogen to the disease under investigation. These postulates are:

Koch's Postulates

"1. The organism in question must be found constantly associated with a particular symptom.

2. It must be isolated, grown and studied in pure culture.

3. The organism grown in pure culture must be inoculated into a healthy plant to produce the particular disease. The symptom produced in the inoculated plant should be the same as the symptom first observed.

4. The organism must be re-isolated from the inoculated plant and compared with the first culture to be shown to be same as the original culture".

Culture Technique

In order to learn more about the pathogen, it should be cultured. Some of the organisms are obligate parasites (*e.g.*, rusts, mildews etc.) and cannot be cultured in artificial media while

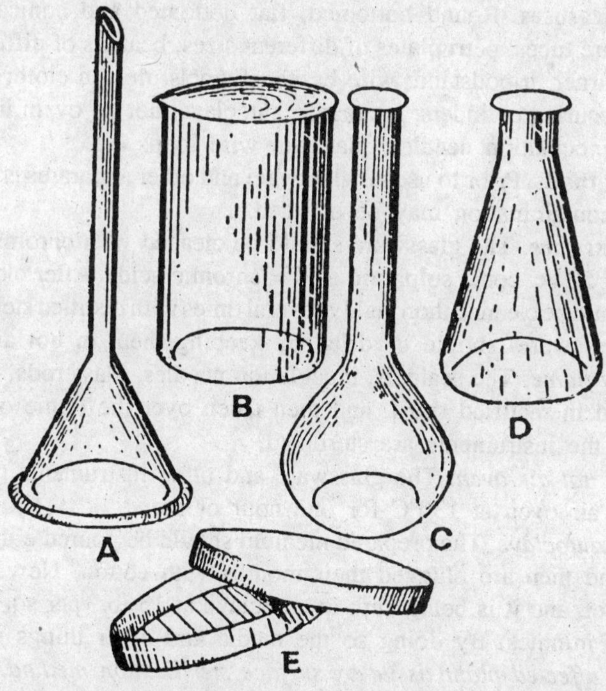

Fig. 21.1. *Glassware.* A, funnel; B, beaker; C, round bottomed flask; D, conical flask; E, petri plates.

others grow readily on such media in the laboratory. In order to understand the pathogenic qualities of the organism, it must be brought into pure culture. For doing so, the pathogen obtained from the affected part of the host plant, is being cultured on the synthetic or natural media in the

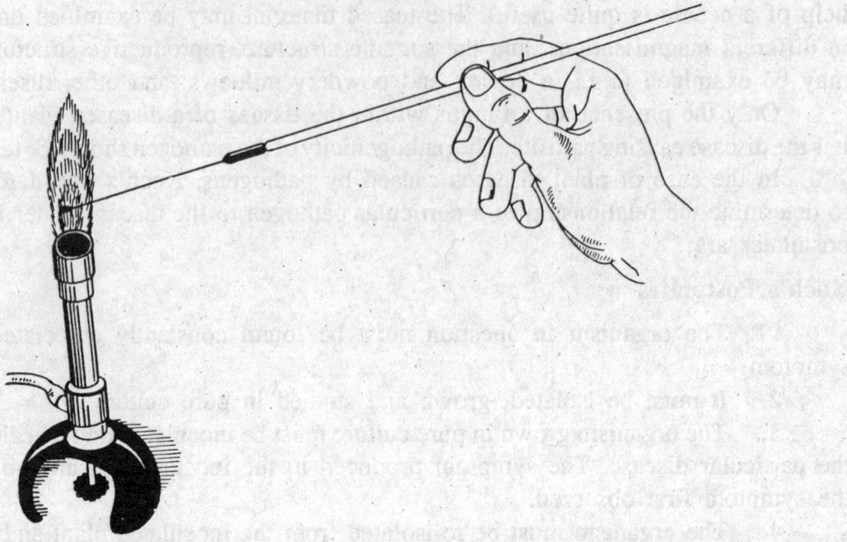

Fig. 21.2. Methods in Bacteriology. Sterilization of inoculating loop. Flame the inoculating loop before and after inoculation.

laboratory. The facultative parasites (*e.g., Pythium, Fusarium*) may readily be grown on these media. The obligate parasites such as *Puccinia, Albugo, Peronospora, Erysiphe* etc., cannot be grown on these media. Such cultures are known as plant cultures.

Required apparatuses. Round bottomed, flat bottomed and conical flasks of various volumes; rimless culture tubes; petri plates of different sizes; beakers of different volumes; glass rods; spirit lamp or burner, tripodstand; wire basket; funnels; muslin cloth; cotton; filter paper; chemical balance; measuring cylinders; incubator; autoclave; hot air oven; inoculation chamber; eye surgery scalpel; inoculation needles; platinum wire loops etc.

Sterilization methods. Prior to use all glassware and other apparatuses should be sterilized, so that any kind of contamination may be avoided.

Cleaning of glassware. The glassware should be cleaned with chromic acid (*i.e.,* 100 cc. potassium chromate + 50 cc. conc. sulphuric acid = chromic acid). After cleaning with chromic acid the glass ware should be cleaned thoroughly several times with distilled sterile water. Following this, the utensils (glass ware) should be dried by keeping them in hot air oven.

Sterilization by flame. The scalpels, inoculation needles, glass rods, platinum wire loops etc., should be dipped in rectified spirit, and then taken over the flame of a spirit lamp or a burner. By doing so the instruments are sterilized.

Sterilization by hot air oven. The glassware and other instruments may be sterilized by keeping them in hot air oven at 130^{0}C for one hour or so.

Sterilization by autoclave. The prepared medium should be poured either in rimless culture tubes or in flasks, and then are plugged their mouths with cotton. Now all these things are placed in a wire basket, and it is being kept in autoclave at 15 lbs. per sq. inch steam pressure at least for 15 to 20 minutes. By doing so the media and other things get sterilized.

Sterilization of affected plant tissue by surface sterilization method. The infected tissue to be used as inoculum should be sterilized as follows:

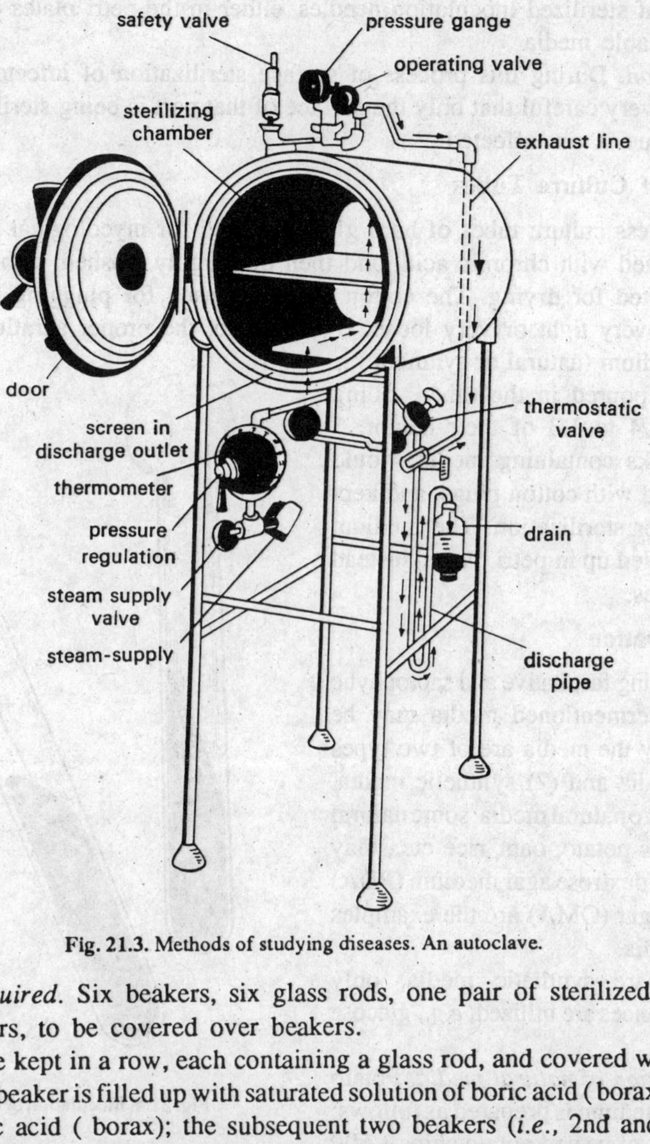

Fig. 21.3. Methods of studying diseases. An autoclave.

Apparatus required. Six beakers, six glass rods, one pair of sterilized petri plates, six sterilized filter papers, to be covered over beakers.

Six beakers are kept in a row, each containing a glass rod, and covered with a filter paper. One-third of the first beaker is filled up with saturated solution of boric acid (borax); the subsequent two beakers of boric acid (borax); the subsequent two beakers (*i.e.,* 2nd and 3rd) are filled up with distilled sterile water, upto the same height (*i.e.,* 1/3 of beaker); the fourth beaker contains 0.1 per cent solution of mercuric chloride; and the remaining 5th and 6th beakers are again filled up with distilled sterile water upto 1/3rd mark of the beakers.

Now a cut part of the infected fruit or leaf is taken. The infected part of the diseased fruit is cut with the help of a sterilized scalpel, and kept in the first beaker, containing saturated borax solution, for ten to fifteen minutes. Thereafter it is taken out of the first beaker with the help of glass rods, and thoroughly washed in the second and third beakers containing distilled sterile water. Now the affected part of the fruit or leaf is being transferred in the fourth beaker containing mercuric chloride solution only for ten to fifteen seconds. Once again the infected material is thoroughly washed in the fifth and sixth beakers containing distilled sterile water. Now, this sterilized inoculum is being transferred in a sterilized petri plate, where it is being cut in small pieces with the help of a sterilized scalpel. These small pieces are being inoculated, with the help of sterilized inoculation needles, either in the petri plates or in the culture tubes, containing suitable media

Precaution. During this process of surface sterilization of infected part of plant tissue, one should be very careful that only the surface of that part is being sterilized, and the pathogen within the tissue is not affected.

Preparation of Culture Tubes

The rimless culture tubes of hard glass are used for mycological work. Prior to use, the tubes are cleaned with chromic acid, and then thoroughly washed with distilled sterile water, and kept inverted for drying. The cotton plugs are used for plugging them. The cotton plug should not be very tight or very loose. By doing so, the proper aeration is maintained. Now the culture medium (natural or synthetic) is prepared, and poured in the tubes, filling them up to 1/4 to 1/3 of their height.

The flasks containing media should also be plugged with cotton plugs, and kept in autoclave for sterilization. The medium may also be filled up in petri plates, instead of culture tubes.

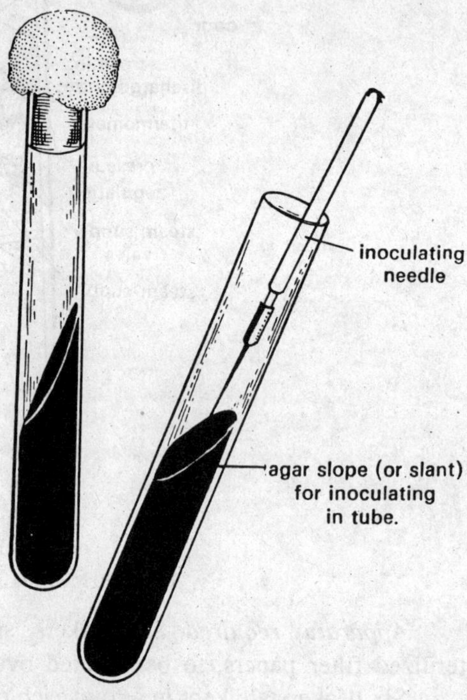

Fig. 21.4. Inoculation of the agar slope with inoculating needle.

Media Preparation

For growing facultative and saprophytic fungi, the undermentioned media may be used. Generally the media are of two types (1) natural media and (2) synthetic media.

To prepare natural media, some natural sources such as potato, oats, rice etc., may be used. Potato dextrose agar medium (PDA) and oat meal agar (OMA) are the examples of natural media.

To prepare synthetic media, only chemical substances are utilized, *e.g.*, glucose agar medium.

Preparation of natural media. Potato dextrose agar medium is prepared as follows:

200 gms. of peeled potato chips + 500 ml. of water are boiled together, so that, the potato tissues are softened. This process takes about 15 minutes. Now this prepared pulp is being sieved through a muslin cloth, 20 gms. of agar and 500 ml. of water are heated together, so that, a solution is prepared. Now, both the solutions are mixed, 20 gms., of dextrose are added to it. Thus, 1,000 ml. of potato dextrose agar medium (P.D.A.) is prepared,

Now this prepared, medium is being poured in several culture tubes. The culture tubes are plugged up with cotton plugs, and then kept in autoclave at the pressure of 15 lbs. per sq. inch, for 15 to 20 minutes. Now the culture tubes are taken out, and placed in slanting position. After some time, the medium is solidified, and the tubes are ready for inoculation.

Oat meal agar medium (O.M.A.). Take 500 ml. water, add 40 gms., oat meal to it, mix them by continuous stirring at 75 to 100°C for few minutes. By doing so, a pulp is prepared which may be sieved through a muslin cloth.

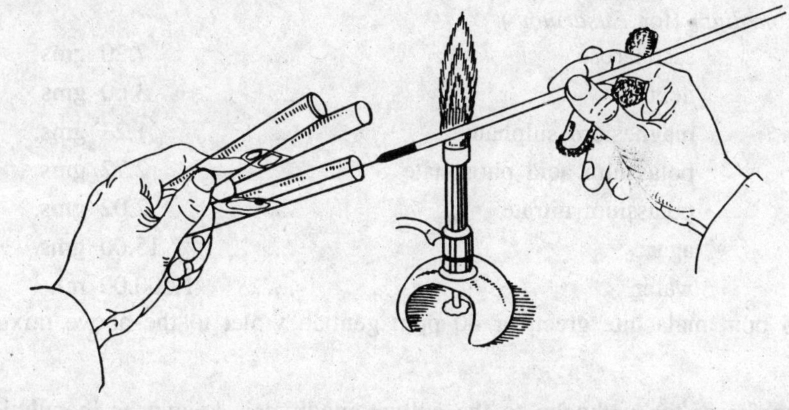

Fig. 21.5. Methods of studying plant diseases. Method for holding tube when cultures are transferred.

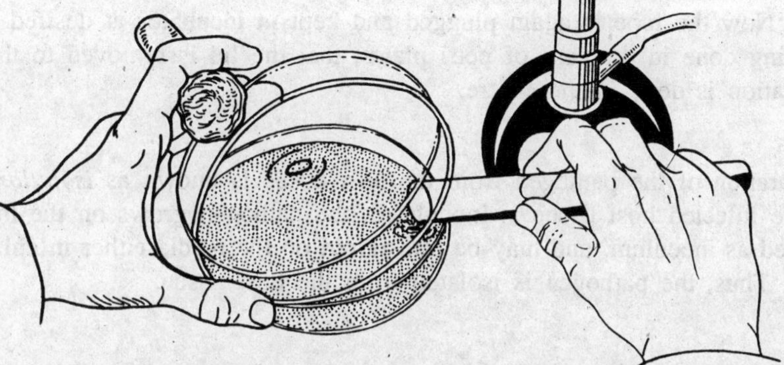

Fig. 21.6. Pouring of agar medium in petri plate.

Dissolve 20 gms. agar in 500 ml. water by warming it for some time. Mix the two and sieve the solution. Now 1,000 ml. O.M.A. is prepared. Pour the medium in several tubes and plug them with cotton plugs. Now autoclave them at 15 lbs. per sq. inch pressure for 15-20 minutes. This brings complete sterilization.

Synthetic medium. Glucose agar medium.

glucose	......	20 gms.
agar	......	20 gms. (in winter)
agar	......	25 gms. (in summer)
water	......	1,000 ml.

Dissolve 20 gms. glucose in 500 ml. water; dissolve 20 gms. agar in remaining 500 ml. water by warming it. Mix both. Thus, 1,000 ml. glucose agar medium is prepared.

Coon's medium (for *Fusarium*)

saccharose	....	7.20 gms.
dextrose	....	3.60 gms
magnesium sulphate	....	1.23 gms.
potassium acid phosphate	....	2.72 gms.
potassium nitrate	....	2.02 gms.
agar	....	15.00 gms.
water	....	1,000.00 ml.

Add 25 ppm malachite green or 40 ppm gentian violet to the above mixture.

Inoculation

The transfer of the pathogen to the culture medium is known as inoculation.

Precautions. All operations concerning inoculation should be done in a completely sterilized chamber. The inoculation chamber fitted with ultra-violet (UV) tube should be used. The hands should be cleaned with toilet soap and then sterilized with rectified spirit. Mouth and nose should be covered with sterilized cloth. All instruments and glassware etc., should be completely sterilized. All precautions should be taken to avoid any kind of contamination.

The culture tubes containing media are kept in slanting position, so that the growing pathogen could get the maximum surface of the medium for its growth. Now with the help of two fingers the cotton plug is being removed, and with the help of sterilized inoculation needle, the inoculum is being transferred in the centre of the medium. Prior to transfer of the inoculum, the medium is scratched in the centre with the help of bent inoculation needle, so that, the pathogen is fitted in the scratch. Now the tube is again plugged and kept in incubator at desired temperature.

So is being done in the case of petri plates, that the lid is removed to the minimum, and the inoculation is done in the centre.

Isolation

The separation of the pathogen from the host tissue is known as *isolation.*

When the infected host tissue is inoculated, the pathogen grows on the medium. This pathogen is used as inoculum, and may be transferred on the media either in culture tubes or in petri plates. Thus, the pathogen is isolated from the host tissue.

Pure Culture

When it is sure that the culture tube contains only one type of pathogen, it is known as *pure culture.* The pure culture may be obtained as follows:

1. *By hyphal tip cut method.* When the fungus grows on the medium in a petri plate, a network of mycelium is formed. Now the plant pathologist examines this network under the field of mycological binoculars; one of the hyphal tips is cut with the help of a sterilized sharp eye surgery scalpel along with the medium. Now this medium block, which contains the hyphal tip of the fungus is transferred in another petri plate containing medium. This hyphal tip grows and a mycelial net is formed, and one gets pure culture of the fungus.

2. *By streak method.* First of all spore suspension is prepared. Thereafter with the help of platinum wire loop a drop of spore suspension is taken. Now a *zig-zag* streak is made with this drop on the surface of medium. The spores are always dense at the origin of the streak, and the density of the spores becomes minimum at the end of this streak. Since there are only few spores in the end part of the streak, one of them may easily be inoculated on the medium of another petri plate, and thus pure culture of the fungus is formed.

Pathogenicity of Leaf-spotting Fungi

- To prove the pathogenicity of leaf-spotting fungi, healthy plants should be raised in pots. When these plants possess four or five leaves, a spore suspension of a particular fungus should

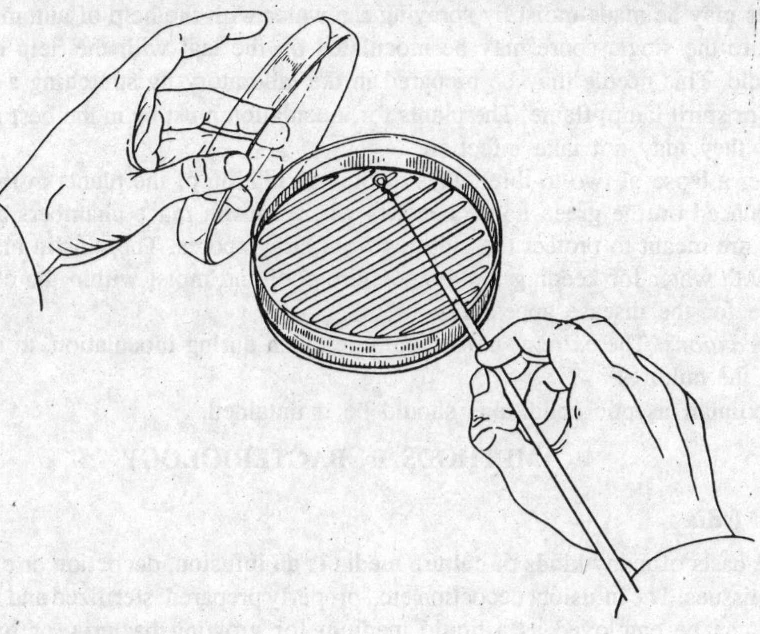

Fig. 21.7. Streaking on agar surface with inoculating loop.

be sprayed on the leaves with the help of an automizer. The pots are then placed in a moist chamber so that the spores may germinate, and the germ-tubes enter the host. Generally the pot plant is covered with a bell jar, which serves as a moist chamber. Polythene covers may be used in place of glass bell-jars. They are convenient to use, and allow gas exchange which glass covers do not. After a day or two, the plants are removed from moist chambers and kept on the green-house bench. By now the spores would have germinated and the germ tubes entered the host plants. Within a few days the disease is manifested. The period in between the spraying on the host with spore suspension and the appearance of the disease symptoms is known as the *incubation period* of the disease.

Precautions. While conducting such pathogenicity tests the undermentioned precautions should be taken:

1. The tests should be conducted in green houses, if available.
2. The variety of the host plant must be the same on which the disease had first appeared.
3. Temperature and humidity conditions in the green house must favour the appearance of the disease.
4. Bright and direct sunlight should be avoided.
5. The soil must be kept moist.

Parasitism of Obligate Parasites

The pathogenicity of obligate parasites such as rusts, downy mildews and powdery mildews can be proved. Koch's postulates cannot be applied to such cases. The experiments can be conducted for the determination of the incubation period of disease, or to study the symptoms of a particular disease or for determining the resistance of a particular host variety. These experiments are being done in spore-proof green houses.

Plants involved in experimentation should be raised in pots containing sterilized soil. When the plants are 3 or 4 leaved, the inoculation is being done. The viable spores should be taken from the rusted (or diseased) plants with a straight-edged scalpel and spread on the moist leaves. The leaves may be made moist by spraying the water with the help of automizer. For obtaining pure culture the single spore may be inoculated on the leaf with the help of a sterilized fine glass needle. This needle may be prepared in the laboratory by stretching a glass rod over the burner's (or spirit lamp) flame. The plants for inoculation must be in the best growing condition, otherwise they may not take infection.

After a lapse of two to three days of the inoculation of the plants in the moist chambers, they are placed on the green house benches where muslin made chambers are provided. Such chambers are meant to protect the cultures from stray spores. The muslin may occasionally be sprayed with water for keeping the temperature cool and moist within the chamber, which are favourable for the disease appearance.

Precautions. The extreme care should be taken during inoculation, to minimize contamination in the cultures.

Maximum aseptic conditions should be maintained.

METHODS IN BACTERIOLOGY

General Media

The basis of many kinds of culture media is an infusion, decoction or extract of vegetable or animal tissues. The infusion, decoction etc., properly prepared, sterilized and adjusted to definite pH value can be employed as a liquid medium for growing bacteria, or by adding agar, for the isolation of bacteria, and also for a growth on a solid substratum.

Culture Media in Bacteriology

Culture Media

- General media for isolation and growth
- Special media for ascertaining the reaction and breakdown products of various organic and inorganic compounds, *e.g.*, sugars, nitrates etc.

Meat-infusion broth or bouillon. This is one of the most useful infusions, and has been derived from lean meat. Take 250 gm. lean meat, remove any fat and mince fine. Place the minced meat in a two-litre flask together with 10 gm. peptone, 5 gm. NaCl and 1 litre of tap water. Put the flesh in the refrigerator and allow to diffuse for 24 hours. Steam for 3 hours and, when cool, strain through muslin and filter through cotton wool. Make up to 1 litre with distilled water and adjust the pH to 7.2. Distribute in 8 ml. quantities into tubes, plug and sterilize in the autoclave at 20 lbs. for 15 minutes.

Meat-infusion agar. Determine the pH of meat-infusion and adjust it to 7.3. Now add 15 gm. powdered agar, melt over the flame, and filter through thick pad of cotton-wool. When cool enough to handle, test the pH reaction against by comparator, as after heating, the medium becomes slightly more acidic. Distribute in tubes, 5ml. for slants, 15 ml. for petri plates, plug and autoclave at 20 lbs, for 15 minutes.

Special Media

Glycerine broth. Most coliform bacteria (*Bacterium* spp.) grow well in this medium. This medium consists of 2 per cent glycerine added to meat-infusion broth. After adjusting the pH to 7.2 the medium is distributed into tubes (8 ml.) and sterilized in the autoclave at 10 lbs. for 15 minutes.

Glycerine agar. Many species of *Pseudomonas* grow well in this medium. This medium consists of 2-5 per cent glycerine added to meat-infusion broth. After adjusting the pH to 7.2 the medium is distributed in tubes containing 8 ml. for slants and 15 ml. for petri plates. The plugged tubes are sterilized in the autoclave at 20 lbs. for 15 minutes.

TECHNIQUES REQUIRED IN INTRODUCTORY BACTERIOLOGY

Media Preparation

All glassware should be thoroughly cleaned with soap and water then dipped in 20% HCl, and finally rinsed in tap water.

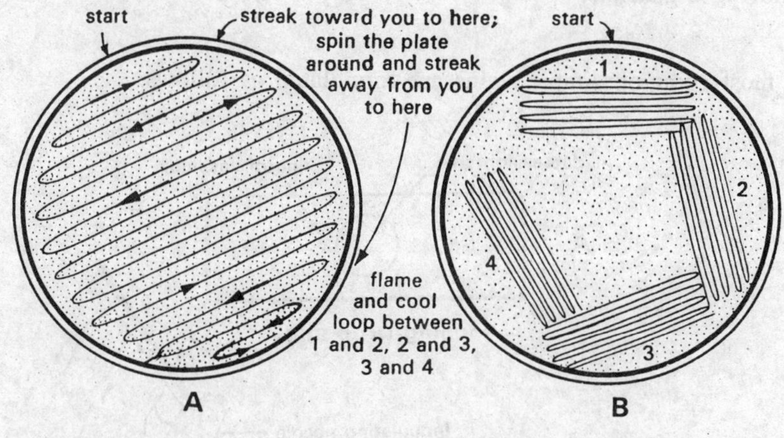

Fig. 21.8. Streak method. Motion of loop in two methods of streaking plates.

Suspend the dehydrated medium in the amount of water specified in the container level and bring to a boil, being careful not to burn the powder which may stick to the bottom of

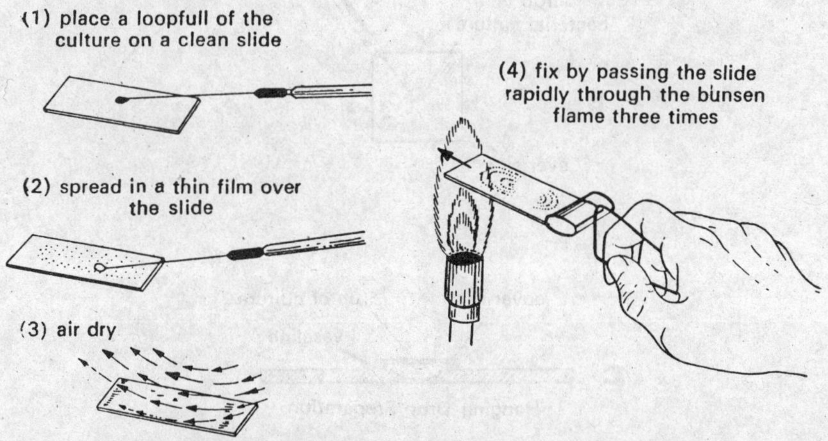

Fig. 21.9. Methods in Bacteriology. Preparing a smear for staining.

the container. After it is in solution, dispense into test tubes. Liquid media should be about two inches deep and agar media one and half inches deep. When pouring the tubes, be careful not to soil the slides near the top.

Plug the mouths of the tubes with cotton to a depth of about one and one-half inches and sterilize in the autoclave at 15 lbs. pressure for 20 minutes. Allow the autoclave to cool until the pressure registers zero, open the exhaust valve, and when steam no longer issues from it, unscrew the lid. To make agar slants, lay the agar tubes on a surface with the mouths of the tubes elevated about three-quarters of an inch. Allow the slants to cool in this position. Test the sterility by incubating random tubes of media at 37°C for 48 hours. Store media in clean, cool place (N.B. agar can be remelted in a water bath at 100°C).

Transfer

Bacteria are usually handled with a platinum wire loop held in either a glass or metal holder. The wire must always be heated to a red glow before and after making transfers or slide preparations. The heated loop may be cooled by plugging it into the butt of the culture before removing organisms.

Staining

The most common simple stains are formulated as follows:

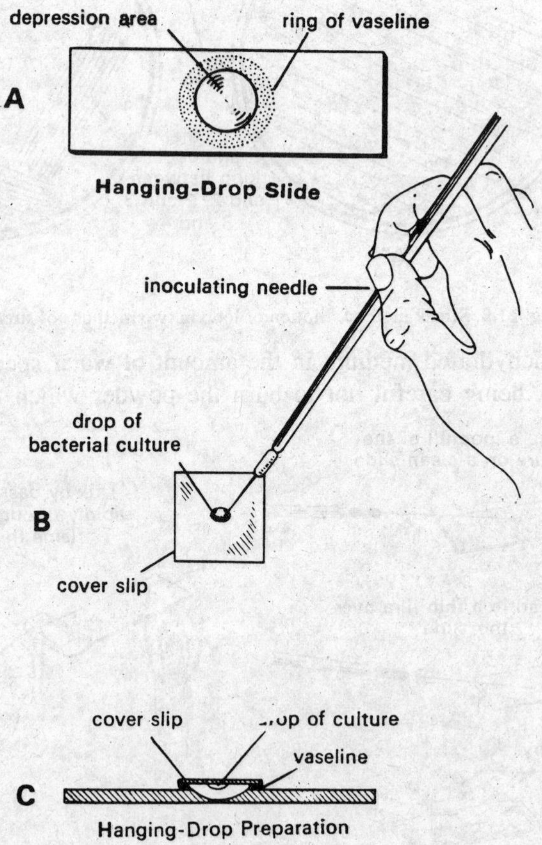

Fig. 21.10. Methods in Bacteriology. Hanging drop preparation (A-C).

Crystal Violet

Crystal violet	....	*3*	*gms.*
Ethyl alcohol (95%)	....	*20*	*ml.*
Dissolve and mix with ammonium oxalate	....	*0.8*	*gms.*
Distilled water	....	*80*	*ml.*

Methylene Blue

Methylene blue	....	*0.3*	*gms.*
Ethyl alcohol (95%)	....	*30*	*ml.*
Dissolve and mix with potassium hydroxide (0.01%) in distilled water	....	*100*	*ml.*

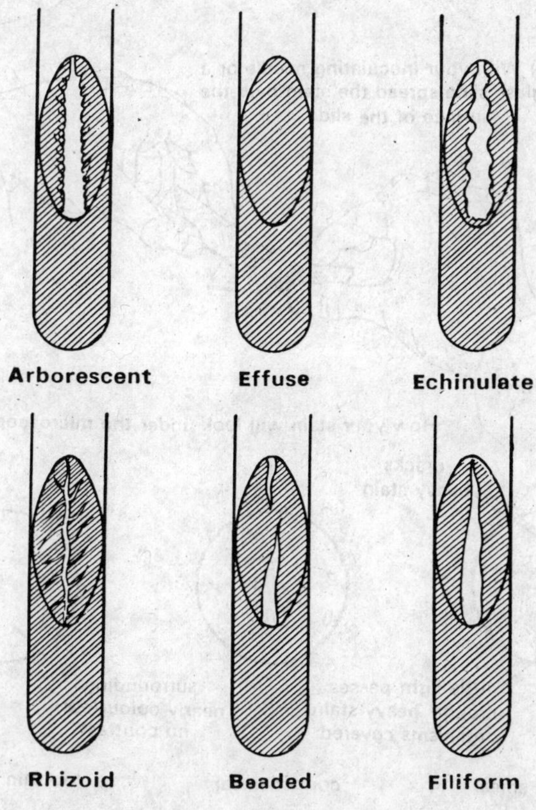

Fig. 21.11. Methods in Bacteriology. Different types of bacterial growth on agar slants.

Safranin

Safranin	....	*0.25*	*gms.*
Alcohol (95%)	....	*10*	*ml.*
Water	....	*100*	*ml.*

Carbon-Fuchsin

Solution A:

Basic fuchsin	....	*0.3*	*gms.*
Ethyl alcohol (95%)	....	*10*	*ml.*

Solution B:

Phenol	....	5	*gms.*
Distilled water	....	95	*ml.*

Mix Solutions A and B,

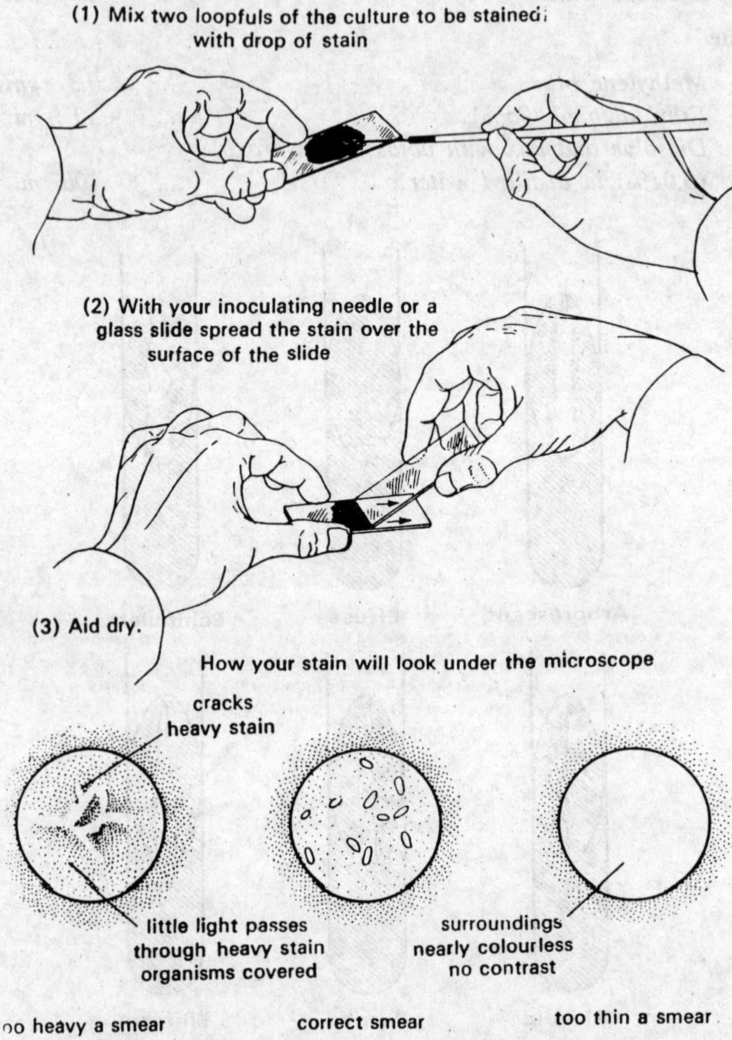

Fig. 21.12. Methods in Bacteriology. The negative or indirect staining.

To stain make a smear on a slide or cover-slip, dry, pass through a flame two or three times, and flood with the desired stain for three minutes. Wash, blot dry, and examine.

Gram's Stain

Gram's stain has long been used to separate bacteria into two groups, the gram-**negative** and **positive** types. The stain and procedure are as follows :

1. Stain one minute in crystal violet.
2. Wash briefly in water.
3. Cover or immerse for one minute in Gram's iodine solution :

Iodine	....	*1*	*gm.*
Potassium iodide	....	*2*	*gms.*
Distilled water	....	*300*	*ml.*

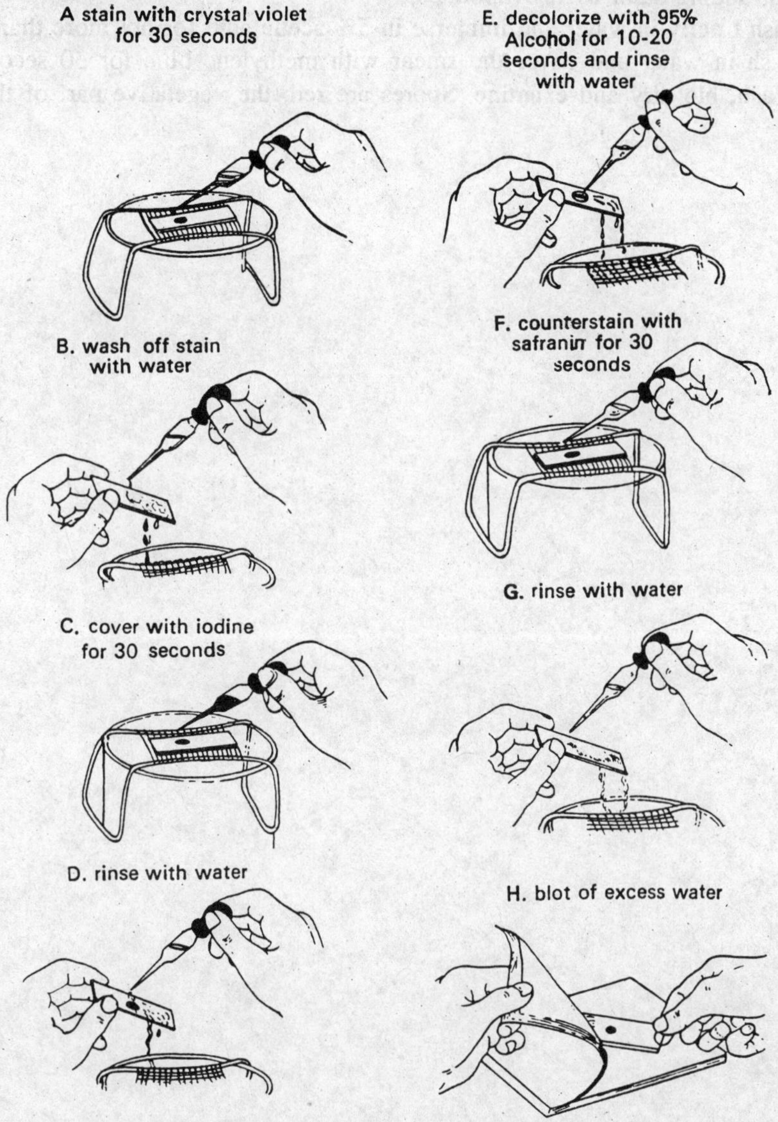

Fig. 21.13. Methods in Bacteriology. Gram staining method (A–H).

4. Wash briefly in water and blot dry.
5. Decolourize in 95% ethyl alcohol for 30 seconds with slight agitation.
6. Wash in water and counterstain with safranin for 10 seconds.
7. Wash, dry, mount and examine.

By this method some bacteria will retain the violet stain and be dark, and other will be dark, and other will be destained and appear red. Until one has had experience, controls of known gram-positive and gram-negative bacteria should be run.

For demonstrating spores, the following methods may be used :

1. Make a smear in the usual manner.

2. Cover with Carbol-fuchsin and heat over a small flame until steam rises. Steam for five minutes, adding stain as it evoporates.

3. Wash briefly in water and immerse in 5% acetic acid for not more than two seconds.

4. Wash in water and cover the smear with methylene blue for 30 seconds.

5. Wash, blot dry and examine. Spores are red; the vegetative part of the cell a blue.

MICROBIOLOGY

22

Bacteria, Mycoplasma, Actinomycetes and Cyanobacteria

BACTERIA

The bacteria are most simple and smallest organisms (0.5 to 50 μ) and may be studied under the high power of light microscope. They were first discovered in 1675, by Anton von Leeuwenhoek. Later on in France, Pasteur and Koch studied several bacteria in the years 1870-76; they also demonstrated that many bacteria cause the human and animal diseases. Koch (1876) had proved that bacteria can cause such diseases as anthrax tuberculosis or Asiatic cholera. Since then several workers are busy in investigations and the science of bacteriology has been established. T.J. Burrill of Illinois, was first to declare that certain bacteria were responsible for disease in plants. He showed that *Micrococcus amylovorus* causes the fire blight of pears. Since then a large number of plant diseases caused by various bacteria have been investigated.

At the time of their discovery, these organisms were supposed to be animals and referred as "animalcules". Later on it was thought that the bacteria had more affinities with plants than

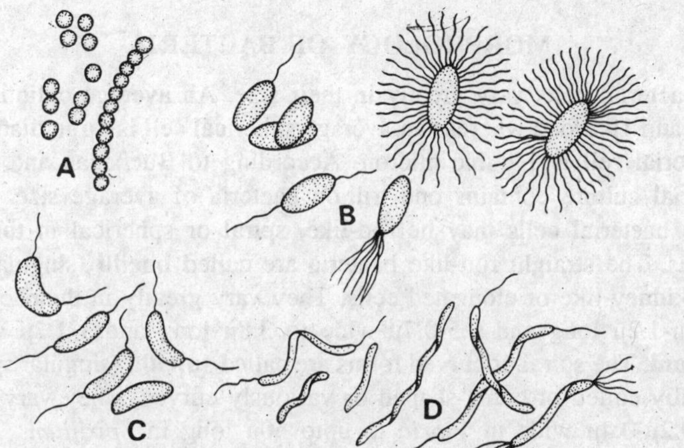

Fig. 22.1. Bacteria. Various forms. A, Coccus; B, Bacillus; C, Vibrio; D, Spirillum.

the animals and then they were included in the Thallophyta of plant kingdom. Some people considered them neither the plants and nor the animals. They adopted the middle way. As majority of the bacteria have more affinities with plants, they are placed in the class Schizomycetes of Thallophyta.

Occurrence. Bacteria are omnipresent. They are found everywhere under all possible natural conditions. They are found in great abundance in tropical and temperate regions. They are found in water, air, soil, on living and dead organic substances. They are very resistant to heat, cold and certain chemicals. They are also found in the intestines of human beings and animals. Certain bacteria may live in the temperature as high as 78°C in hot springs. They are found on the snow as well as in the deep soil. They are found in less number on the snow peaks of the hills, because they lack soil particles which make the seat of bacteria.

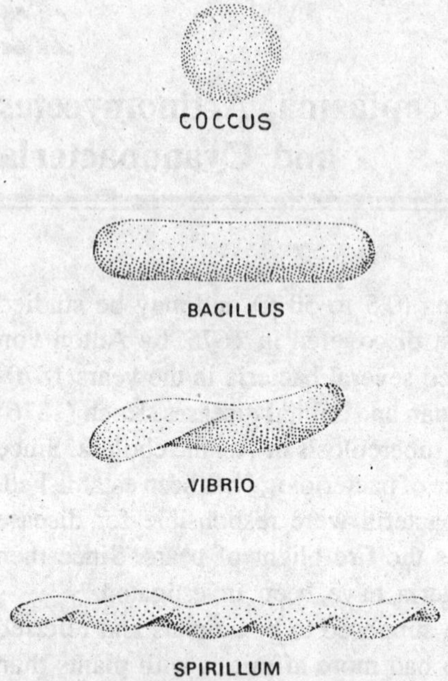

Fig. 22.2. Bacteria. Different types.

General characteristics. The bacteria are the simplest and smallest living organisms of plant kingdom, and may be seen only under the high magnification of the compound microscope. They are devoid of chlorophyll and mostly heterotrophic in nutrition. They reproduce chiefly by fission, sometimes called the *fission fungi* and included in a separate class-Schizomycetes. Majority of the bacteria are unicellular, but the filamentous and colonial forms are quite common. Usually the bacterial cells are embedded in a mucilaginous envelope. Even when bacteria are held together in groups or chains, each individual cell carries on its own metabolic process quite independently; there is no division of labour.

MORPHOLOGY OF BACTERIA

Size. The bacterial cells vary greatly in their size. An average cylindrical bacterial cell measures 3μ long and 1μ broad whereas an average spherical cell is 1μ in diameter. The average volume of a bacterial cell is 1 cubic micron. According to Buchanan and Buchanan (1946), one ml. of bacterial culture contains one trillion bacteria of average size.

Shape. The bacterial cells may be rod-like, spiral or spherical in their shape.

(1) **Bacillus.** The straight rod-like bacteria are called **bacilli** (singular bacillus), which possess rod-like, kidney-like or elongated cells. They vary greatly in their length and diameter ranging from 0.6μ-1.2μ long and 0.5-0.7μ wide to 3.8μ long and 1-1.2μ wide.

(2) **Spirillum.** The spiral or curved forms are called **spirilla** (singular spirillum), in which the cells are spirally coiled or coma-shaped or variously curved. They vary in size from 1.5μ to 4μ long and 0.2μ-0.4μ wide in *Vibrio* to upto 50μ long in *Spirillum.*

(3) **Coccus.** The rounded or spherical forms are called **cocci** (singular coccus) in which the cells are more or less spherical. They are smallest forms among bacteria. After division the cells may either separate from each other or may remain joined together to form groups of two cells in *Diplococcus,* a tetrad of four cells in *Micrococcus tetragenus* and a chain of cells in *Streptococcus.* The cocci range in diameter from 0.5μ-1.25μ.

Under favourable conditions of growth and development, the shape of one species remains constant, whereas under unfavourable conditions, some bacteria, such as the nitrogen fixing species change into at least three distinct forms during a complete life cycle. Under certain conditions some bacteria become very irregular in shape and sometimes abnormally enlarged. These modified cells are known as **"involution forms"**. Many bacteria in young cultures, show a mixture of several integrating forms, besides the original structure of the parent type. This phenomenon is known as **pleomorphism.**

The bacteria, when treated with antibiotic or they are attacked by the bacteriophages or by cold shock they sometimes, develop unusual, soft, protoplasmic forms of various shapes including large spherical or distorted cells. These are known as large bodies or 'L-forms'. This name was given by E. Klienberger (1935). When transferred to the favourable conditions, these L-forms can also revert back to normal shapes of bacteria.

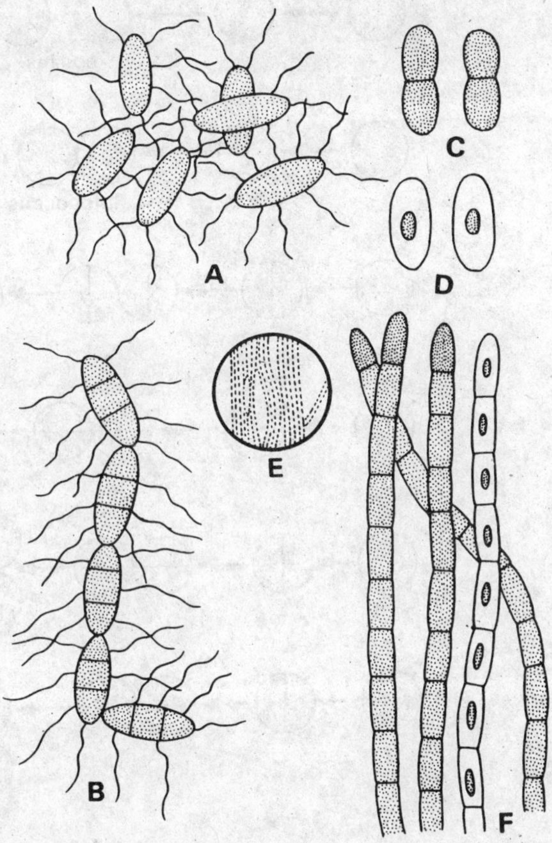

Fig. 22.3. Bacteria. *Bacillus subtilis*. A, vegetative cells; B, chain of cells; C, transverse division; D, endospores; E, zooglea stage; F, chains of endospores.

Flagellation. Many forms of bacteria bear thin, elongated thread-like **flagella** (singular-flagellum) which help in their locomotion. Almost all the spirilla, most of bacilli and some of the cocci, are flagellate. The flagella are fixed on to the protoplast and arise from small basal granules, the **blepharoplasts** situated on the outside of the cytoplasm. The flagella may consist of either a simple filament or 2-3 fibrils coiled helically. In some forms (*e.g., Spirillum*) they twist to form a thick bundle. Bacteria having no flagella are termed **atrichous,** those with only one polar flagellum **monotrichous** (*e.g., Vibrio*), such a group of flagella at one end **lophotrichous** (*e.g., Spirillum*), with a group of flagella at both ends, **amphitrichous** and with flagella uniformly distributed all over the body are termed **peritrichous** (*e.g., Salmonella*)

Flagella and pili. Many bacteria are actively motile, moving at speed of upto 50mμ per second. Such bacteria are normally found to possess flagella.

Bacterial flagella are much smaller than eukaryotic flagella, being about 120-180A° in diameter, they do not show the 9 plus 2 pattern of fibrils, are not enclosed in a membrane and show no ATPase activity.

Bacterial flagella consist essentially of a pure protein called "flagellin". The flagella of motile bacteria are distributed over the surface of the cell in characteristic fashion as described in the preceding paragraph. The flagellum pierces the cell wall and arises from a specialized area of the cytoplasm, sometimes called a blepharoplast by analogy with of higher organisms flagella. Depending upon the arrangement of flagella, they may be atrichous (non- flagellate), monotrichous (single polar flagellum), lophotrichous (a tuft of flagella), amphitrichous (flagella at both the poles) and finally peritrichous (*i.e.,* flagella all round).

The final structures to be considered are the pili or fimbriae. These are straight hair like structures concerned with attachment of the bacterial cell to solid surface and in some cases

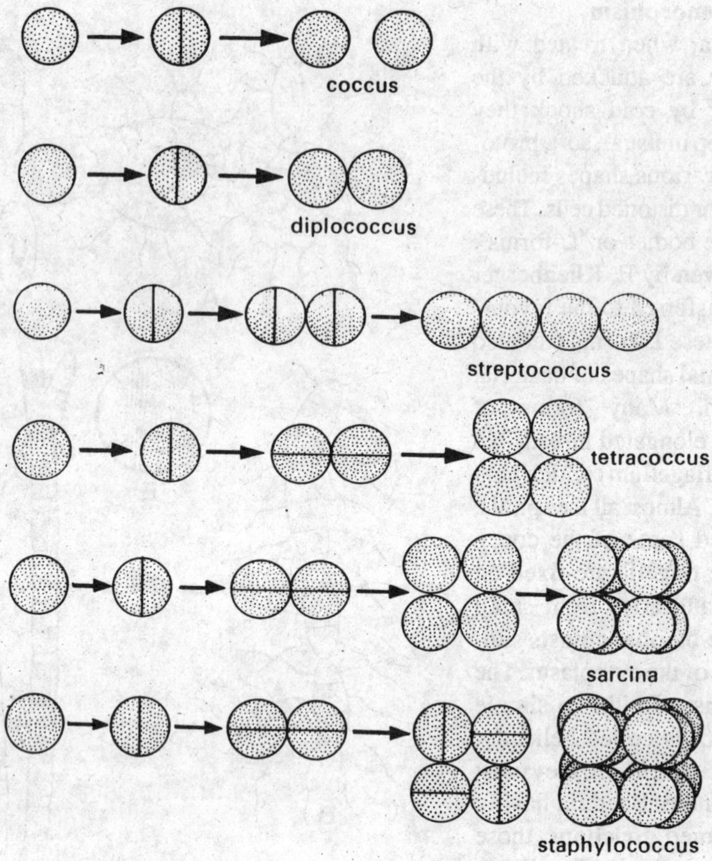

Fig. 22.4. Bacteria. Various forms of coccus bacteria.

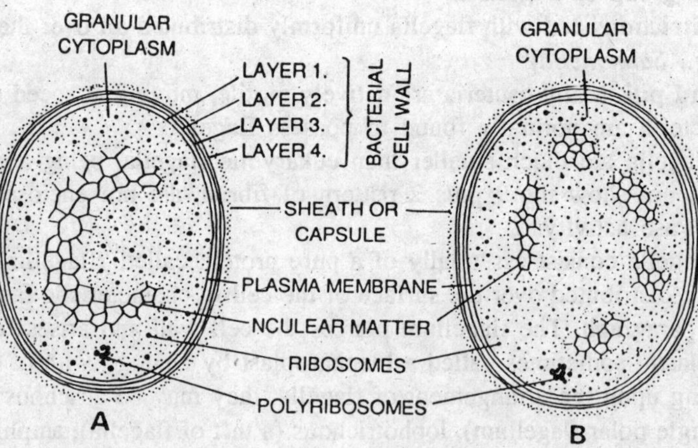

Fig. 22.4 (a). ***Bacteria.*** **Ultrastructure of cocci cells (A–B).**

are known to act as conjugation canals through which DNA passes from one cell to another. Pili are composed of pure protein called 'pilin' and these subunits are helically arranged.

Cell structure. The bacterial cell contains vacuoles, ribosomes and granules of stored food. Water is an important constituent of bacterial cells. As much as 90 per cent of the cell is water. The movement of dissolved materials in and out of the cell is regulated by a cell membrane, formed by the cytoplasm that lies next to the inner of the cell wall. Structurally, the cytoplasm of a bacterial cell is quite similar to cytoplasm found in the living cells of more complex organisms.

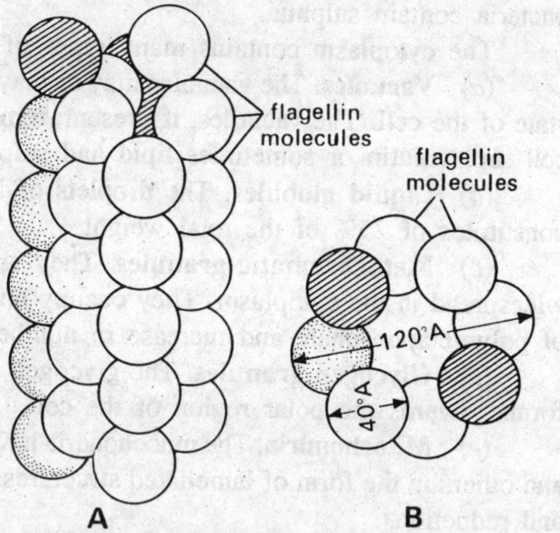

Fig. 22.5. Bacteria. Structure of flagellum. A, eight parallel chains of flagellin molecules to form a hollow cylinder; B, T.S. of a flagellum.

The cytoplasm of bacteria is densely packed with ribosomes of 70 S. Until recent years the cytoplasm of bacteria was thought to be fairly homogeneous and structureless except for ribosomes, granules and nuclear apparatus. However, various types of membranous structures such as mesosomes, photosynthetic vesicles and lamellae have been recently demonstrated.

The cytoplasm of bacterial cells is dense and contains granules of glycogen, proteins and fats but lacks an endoplasmic reticulum. The ribosomes occur free in the cytoplasm and not bound to membrane. The enzymes which are generally found in mitochondria are localized on or near the cell wall. The mitochondria have been reported in certain forms.

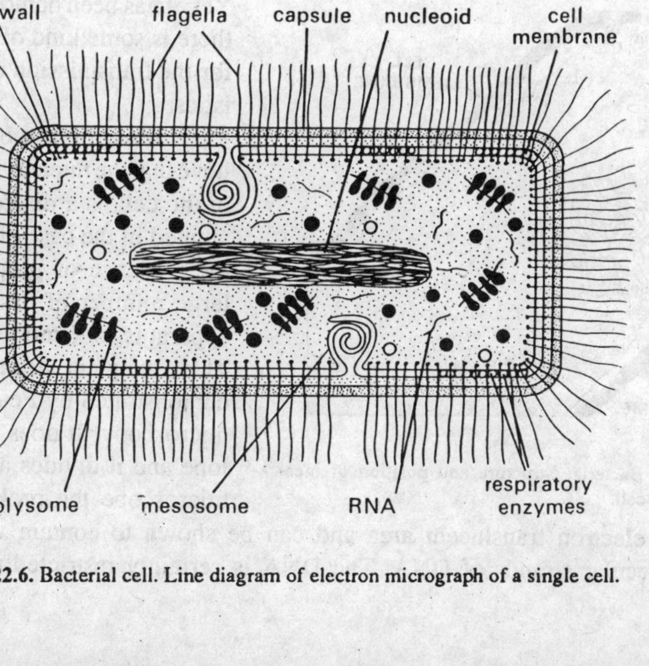

Fig. 22.6. Bacterial cell. Line diagram of electron micrograph of a single cell.

A few bacteria have been shown to have another granular inclusion, **volutin,** an inorganic metaphosphate related to ribonucleic acid, in the cytoplasm and some of the larger sulphur oxidising bacteria contain sulphur.

The cytoplasm contains many types of inclusions:

(*a*) **Vacuoles.** The vacuoles may or may not be present. It depends upon the physiological state of the cell. The vacuoles, if present, remain surrounded by a membrane and may contain cell sap, volutin or sometimes lipid and sulphur.

(*b*) **Liquid globules.** The droplets of liquid occur as refractile globules. Sometimes it constitutes of 25% of the total weight.

(*c*) **Metachromatic granules.** They are also known as 'volutin granules'. They occur widespread in the cytoplasm. They occupy about 40% volume of the cell. They are composed of polymetaphosphate and increase in number towards late in their growth.

(*d*) **Glycogen granules.** The glycogen and other polysaccharide granules occur in some forms towards the polar region of the cell.

(*e*) **Mitochondria.** The mitochondria have been recorded from *Mycobacterium, Streptomyces* and others in the form of lamellated structures. They have been found to be centres of oxidation and reduction.

(*f*) **Chromatophores.** The chromatophores have been reported from the cells of autotrophic bacteria. These photosynthetic pigments are certainly different from those of higher plants.

Mesosomes. The mesosomes arise as invagination of plasmalemma and may become quite a complex whorl of convoluted membranes. The function of mesosomes is a matter of conjecture. It is believed that the mesosomes are active in cell wall synthesis and in the secretion of extracellular substance. It has been shown that transforming DNA taken up by whole cells of *Bacillus subtilis* apparently enters the cell *via* the mesosomes. There is considerable evidence that the bacterial nuclear body is attached to a mesosome.

Nucleus of bacteria (electron microscopic structure). Biologists generally agree that bacteria do not have nuclei of the type found in cells of higher plants and animals. In the cells of these more complex organisms, the nucleus contains a nucleolus or two-is bounded by a visible membrane, and divides by mitosis. Yet, it has been demonstrated repeatedly that there is some kind of mechanism in bacteria for the transmission of hereditary characteristics.

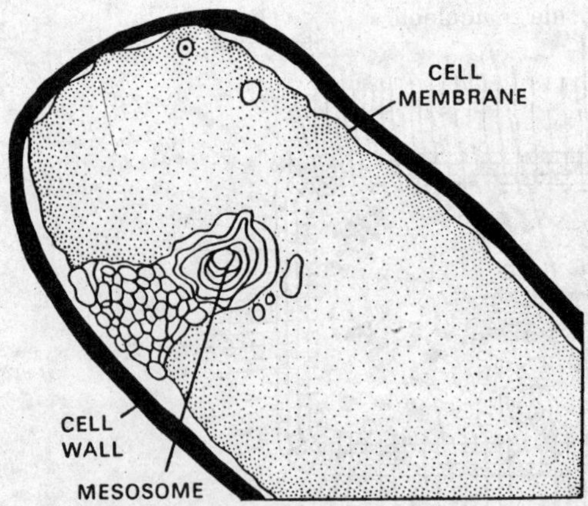

Fig. 22.7. Bacteria. Structure and position of mesosome in bacterial cell.

Most of the bacteriologists now believe that the nucleus in the bacteria is present in the cell as a discrete body. Feulgen tests applied in the case of bacteria have revealed the presence of purple stained bodies in a large number of cases. In bacteria nuclear apparatus is a more rudimentary structure. This incipient form of nucleus can be demonstrated by Feulgen stain and electron microscopy. It does not have nuclear envelope and it divides amitotically. In electron microscope the prokaryotic nuclear region appears as an electron translucent area and can be shown to contain very fine fibrils. These fibrils are molecular strands of DNA. The DNA is certainly restricted to this area of the cell.

Using also radiographic technique, Cairns (1963) has demonstrated the circular DNA of *Escherichia coli.*

It is known that DNA comprises the genetic material of living cells. Some forms of bacteria have their DNA concentrated in one or two deeply staining bodies. Shortly before a bacterium divides, these DNA bodies divide and are equally distributed to the daughter cells. In this way the DNA bodies resemble chromosomes replicating in a dividing cell. More critical observations of bacterial 'chromosomes' have been made by studying ultrathin sections of bacteria under the electron microscope, in which the strands of DNA can be seen packed into a bacterial chromosome. It has been determined for some species of bacteria that the DNA molecule is about 3 millimicrons (mμ) wide and as much 1,200 (μ), or 1.2 mm. long. A bacterial DNA molecule is thus more than 500 times as long as the bacterial cell that contains it. To make these measurements, bacterial chromosomes have been removed from the cell. In this condition the replicating strand of DNA has been observed to be in the form of a circle. Within the cell the circle of DNA appears to be twisted and folded.

The nuclear material of bacteria therefore is similar to and apparently has the same properties as all other organisms. The DNA is present in a distinct nuclear region but there is no nuclear membrane surrounding it. Cocci usually have one nuclear region per cell; rod-like bacilli usually have two or more per cell.

According to Lewis (1941), Robinow (1944) and others it has been advocated for many bacteria that nucleus is present in endospores and vegetative cells. Delameter and Hunter (1951), have demonstrated true mitosis in *Bacillus megatherium.* Knaysi (1951) supported in his statement that nucleus is present in many species of bacteria, *e.g.*, in *Staphylococcus flavo-cyaneus, Bacillus mycoides* and other species.

Cell wall. There is a definite thin cell wall, consisting of a single layer. It is made of a nitrogenous substance **chitin** resembling carbohydrates. The cell wall becomes gelatinous in some cases and appear-like a sheath or capsule. The sheath holds the cells together to form colonies. On stagnant water surface these colonies appear like scum and this scum-like resting stage in the life cycle of bacteria is known as **zooglea stage.** The slimy capsule composed largely of polysaccharides outside the cell wall serves as an additional protective layer.

The cell wall accounts for 20% of the dry weight of the cell. It gives shape and firmness to the cell. It can resist mechanical and chemical injuries and also the attack by other micro-organisms. The chemical composition of cell wall is known as 'muco-complex' which consists of proteins, polysaccharides and lipids.

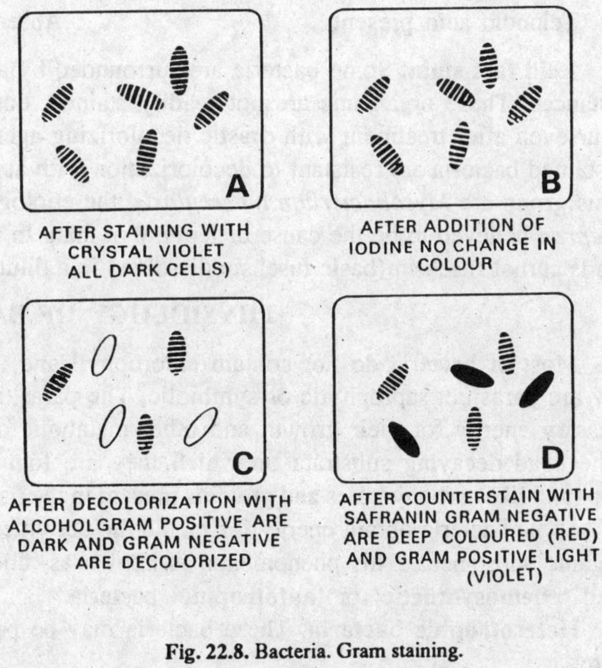

Fig. 22.8. Bacteria. Gram staining.

However, the cell wall can be dissolved in an enzyme called Iysozyme. The cell wall of certain bacteria shows a characteristic reaction to the stain devised by C. Gram. Those bacteria which retain the stain are known as **Gram-positive** and those which do not retain the stain are termed **Gram-negative.** Generally the flagellated bacteria remain covered by a slimy layer whereas, the unflagellated bacteria under certain conditions of growth remain covered by a distinct capsule which is composed of polysccharides or polypeptides.

Just beneath the cell wall there occurs a thin delicate, permeable cell membrane. This membrane surrounds the protoplast which consists of cytoplasm and the nucleus in the form of chromatin body. There is no cytoplasmic streaming in the bacterial cells as it is found in the cells of other higher plants.

The Gram reaction. One of the most important cytological features of bacteria is their reaction to a simple procedure called, after its discoverer, the Gram stain. The procedure involves staining the cells with the dye crystal violet and all bacteria will be stained blue. The bacteria are then treated with an iodine solution and then decolourized with alcohol. Gram positive bacteria retain the stain crystal violet. Gram negative are decolorized. This is a fundamental difference between Gram positive and Gram negative bacteria.

Differences Between Gram Positive and Gram Negative Bacteria

Gram positive bacteria	*Gram negative bacteria*
Cell wall thicker contains only traces of lipids.	Cell wall thinner may contain upto 20% lipids.
Striking simplicity of amino acids.	All the amino acids are present.
Glutamic acid and alanine occur in large amounts.	
Diaminopimelic acid in some.	Diaminopimelic acid in some
Muramic acid more.	Muramic acid less.
Teichoic acid present	Absent.

Acid fast stain. Some bacteria are surrounded by a covering composed of fatty or waxy substances. These organisms are not readily stained, but when stained are able to retain the colour even after treatment with drastic decolorizing agents. They are called acid fast because the stained bacteria are resistant to decolorization with acid alcohol. Two well known members of this group are *Mycobacterium tuberculosis,* the etiological agent of tuberculosis in man and *M. leprae* believed to be the cause of leprosy in man. In the Ziehl-Neilsen method the primary stain is carbol fuschsin (basic fuschsin dissolved in a dilute solution of carbolic acid or phenol).

PHYSIOLOGY OF BACTERIA

Most of bacteria do not contain chlorophyll and, unable to synthesize their own food. They are parasitic, saprophytic or symbiotic. The parasitic and saprophytic bacteria obtain the necessary energy for their growth and other metabolic activities from the tissues of the host or the dead decaying substrata on which they are found, by decomposing complex organic compound like carbohydrates and proteins present in the tissues. Such bacteria are **heterotrophic.**

Some bacteria obtain energy for metabolic activities, from the chemical reactions among inorganic substances. This phenomenon is known as **'chemosynthesis'** and the organisms are called **'chemosynthetic'** or **'autotrophic'** bacteria.

Heterotrophic bacteria. These bacteria may be parasitic, saprophytic and symbiotic in nature.

1. **Parasitic bacteria.** They derive their nutrition from the plants and animals on which they grow. With the result certain enzymes are produced which decompose or kill the protoplasm of the host cells. Such effects of the parasites on the host become visible to naked eye as disease symptoms. Many well known diseases of human beings like typhoid, tetanus, tuberculosis, pneumonia and many others and of plants like 'citrus canker', 'yellow rot of wheat' and 'ring rot of potato' are due to parasitic bacteria. They are also known **pathogenic** bacteria. Some bacteria grow well only in the presence of oxygen, while others grow well in absence of oxygen. The former are known as **aerobes** and the latter **anaerobes.**

2. **Saprophytic bacteria.** They grow on dead and decaying plants and animals, dung, rotten wood, stagnant water and many other decaying substances rich in organic matter. Certain enzymes secreted by the bacteria decompose the complex organic substances of the substrate, converting them into simpler ammonium compounds. They cause decay, and therefore also known as **putrefying** bacteria. The souring of milk, manufacture of cheese, preparation of butter from milk and vinegar from sugarcane juice, are various processes completed by the action of certain specific saprophytic bacteria. *Zygomonas* ferments glucose producing alcohol, lactic acid and carbon dioxide and plays significant role in wine industry. *Acetobacter* oxidises organic compounds to organic acids such as lactic acid thus having a significant role in vinegar industry. *Clostridium aceto-butylicum* forms butyl alcohol from carbohydrates. *Lactobacillus* converts sugars into lactic acid. Canned food is spoiled by *Bacillus stearuothermophilus* and *Clostridium thermosaccharolyticium.*

3. **Symbiotic bacteria.** Some organisms live in close association of other organisms and both partners do mutual benefit. This is termed as **symbiosis.** *Rhizobium* spp. is a striking example of this type. They occur in root nodules of leguminous plants and help in fixing the free nitrogen of the atmosphere in the soil for the plants which in return provide carbohydrates and protection to the bacteria. They are also called **nitrogen fixing bacteria** and add to fertility of the soil.

Azotobacter and *Clostridium* are other examples of nitrogen fixing bacteria. They are found in chalky soil, and obtain energy from the carbohydrates present in the soil. The energy so obtained is used in fixing atmospheric nitrogen into aminoacids in the soil which react with the calcium salts, forming nitrites and thereafter nitrates.

Autotrophic bacteria. They may be chemosynthetic and photosynthetic.

A. Chemosynthetic bacteria. They oxidise inorganic substances and utilize the obtained energy converting the carbon of the carbon dioxide into organic material. On the basis of different inorganic substances oxidised by them, the following forms are recognized.

1. **Nitrifying bacteria.** They occur freely in soil and are of two types. *Nitrosomonas* oxidise the ammonium salts into nitrites and *Nitrobacter* oxidise nitrites into nitrates. They are anaerobic and utilize free oxygen for oxidation.

2. **Denitrifying bacteria.** They are found in oxygen deficient soils such as marshy places. These convert nitrates into nitrites and free nitrogen is liberated. They are anaerobic bacteria (*e.g., Pseudomonas aeruginosa, Micrococcus denitrificans*).

$$NO_3 \longrightarrow NO_2 \longrightarrow N_2O \longrightarrow N_2$$

3. **Sulphur bacteria.** They oxidise sulphurated hydrogen (H_2S-Hydrogen sulphide) to water and free sulphur. This free sulphur is deposited as granules in the cytoplasm. They are aerobic (*e.g., Thiobacillus*).

4. **Iron bacteria.** These oxidise ferrous carbonate to ferric carbonate and the liberated energy is utilized. They are aerobic (*e.g., Ferrobacillus*).

5. Hydrogen bacteria. These oxidise hydrogen to water with the help of some oxides of nitrogen. They are aerobic (*e.g., Hydrogenomonas*).

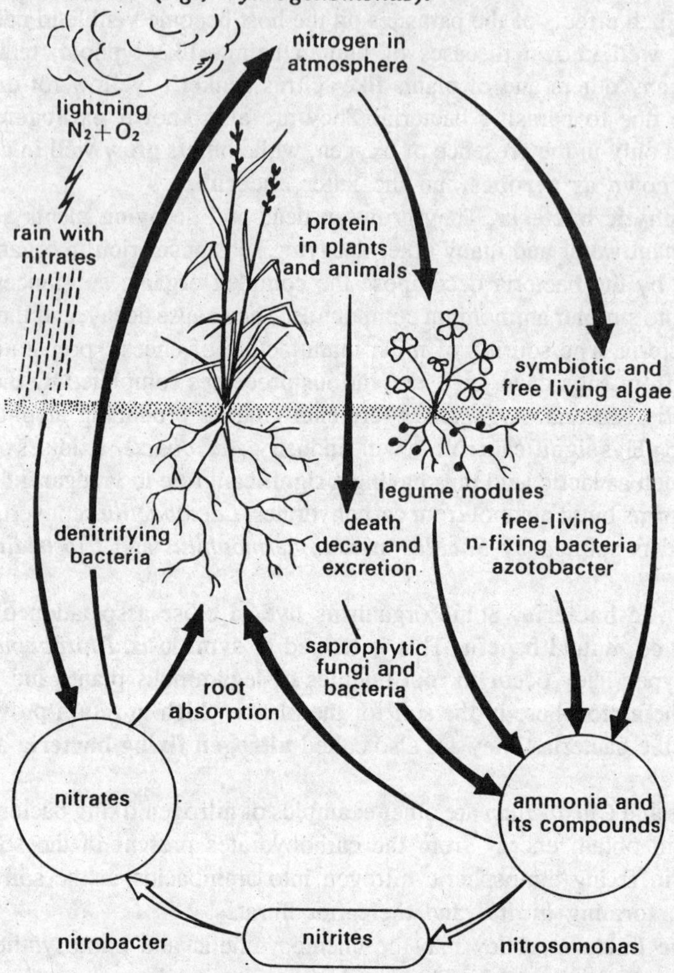

Fig. 22.9. Bacteria. The Nitrogen cycle.

6. Carbon bacteria. These oxidise charcoal and damp-coal into CO_2 in presence of free oxygen. They are aerobic (*e.g., Carboxydomonas*).

7. Methane bacteria. These oxidise methane (CH_4) to (CO_2) and H_2O. They are aerobic (*e.g., Methanomonas*).

B. Photosynthetic bacteria. Very few bacteria contain a red pigment, which help in the synthesis of carbohydrates in presence of sunlight and are therefore known as **photosynthetic bacteria.**

Recently in some bacteria **bacteriochlorophyll** has been observed. It appears to be evenly distributed throughout the cytoplasm. With the aid of the electron microscope the pigment appears to be in minute grana somewhat different from those of the chloroplasts in the higher plants. These bacteria may well be considered independent.

Respiration. Respiration is a process in which energy is liberated as a result of oxidation of organic or inorganic substances. Bacteria oxidise organic and inorganic substances and utilize the liberated energy. Bacteria which can oxidise substances in complete absence of oxygen are known as **anaerobes** while others which require free oxygen for oxidation are known as **aerobes.**

GROWTH AND REPRODUCTION IN BACTERIA

Cell growth. If conditions are favourable, cell division is normally followed by a period of enlargement and growth. Through the absorption of water and food manufactured by the protoplasm the cell enlarges to its original size. Under favourable conditions of moisture, nutrition, pH and temperature some kinds of bacteria, *e.g., E.coli* may double the mass about every 20 minutes, *i.e.,* their generation time. Simple arithmetics will show that enormous numbers could result and if this rate of increase were to continue for even a few days bacteria would occupy the entire earth? However, there are several factors which prevent this. In some cases there may be an exhaustion of the food supply or an accumulation of waste products.

Different bacterial species show various shapes of growth curves depending upon the generation time and the maximum population attainable under the growth conditions that prevail. During a period of one to several hours there may be a *lag phase* in which there is little or no increase in cell numbers. During the first part of the lag phase (which may be called the initial stationary phase) the cells are adapting to the new environment.

When the growing cells begin to divide they usually continue to do so at regular intervals until the maximum growth that can be supported by their environment is approached. This period of rapid cell division is known as the logarithmic phase of growth. The stationary phase occurs when rapid growth is halted by the depletion of nutrients, accumulation of waste products, or other factors. Unless the cells are transformed to new environment capable of supporting continuing growth they will eventually die.

Cell division. Cell division requires the doubling of all cell constituents and their orderly partitioning into the daughter cells. The first step in cell division is the doubling of the DNA complement of the nuclear body, which occurs, by the separation of the two strands and replication along each strand of a new complementary strand. Because of the enormous length of the DNA, the cell faces a problem in partitioning the doubled DNA between the two daughter cells. It is thought that the DNA molecule is attached at some point to the cell membrane and after replication, each one of the double strands while still attached, swings toward one of the two cell halves. Only after this slip has been accomplished can the new cross wall form. At the time the new cross wall, a mesosome of the

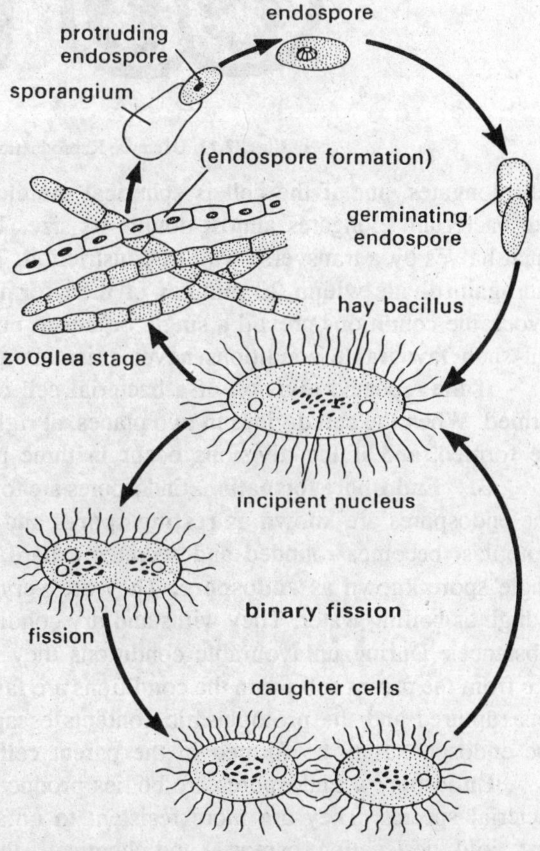

Fig. 22.10. Bacteria. Hay bacillus. Reproduction by endospore formation and binary fission.

membrane can be seen attached to the growing cross wall, and it is likely that this mesosome plays some role in the synthesis of cross wall. The DNA is probably attached to the other end of the same mesosome.

The highly coordinated process, DNA doubling/DNA partitioning/cross wall formation, is the equivalent of the mitotic process in eucaryotic organisms.

Reproduction. In bacteria, asexual and sexual methods of reproduction are known. Sexual reproduction has been investigated recently.

Asexual reproduction. A. Binary Fission. It is the commonest method of reproduction, found in bacteria. The binary fission is simply the multiplication of cells by division. The dividing

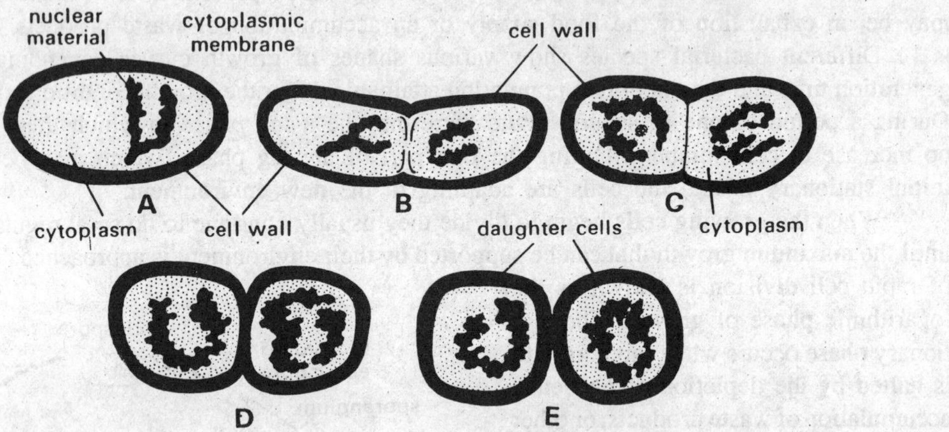

Fig. 22.11. Bacteria. Reproduction by binary fission (A–E).

cell elongates, and if the cell is spherical the elongation is very much restricted, and a rod-like bacterium elongates almost double its size. The protoplasmic mass then divides into two equal halves by a transverse wall or constriction. The two daughter cells soon grow to maturity and again divide within 20 minutes of their formation. This method is very quick and, if the favourable conditions prevail a single organism may produce 16,777,216 cells within 12 hours. But such favourable conditions never exist for a long period in nature.

If the repeated division of a bacterial cell continues to be in one plane only, chains are formed. When the cell divides in two planes, at right angles to each other, flat plate-like colonies are formed, and if the divisions occur in three planes, irregular colonies are formed.

B. Endospore formation. Endospores are formed only in few bacteria in adverse conditions. The endospores are known as **resting spores** and represent the resting stages of bacteria. The protoplast becomes rounded and secretes a hard, resistant wall around it. Each cell forms a single spore known as **endospore.** They are very resistant to temperatures as low as ice and as high as boiling water. They withstand dry conditions and remain alive in poisonous chemical substances. During unfavourable conditions they remain dormant for a long time and are set free from the parent cell when the conditions are favourable. On germination the outer membrane gets ruptured and the protoplasmic contents escape as a bacterial cell. Sometimes more than one endospore may be formed in the parent cell as in *Metabacterium polyspora.*

Endospores. Endospores are bodies produced inside the cells of considerable number of bacterial species. They are more resistant to unfavourable environmental conditions, such as heat, cold, desiccation, osmosis, and chemicals, than the vegetative cells, producing them. The bulk of evidence indicates the existence of a close relationship between spore formation and the exhaustion of nutrients essential for vegetative growth. Sporulation is a defence mechanism to protect the cell when the occasion arises. Spore formation is limited to two genera *Bacillus*

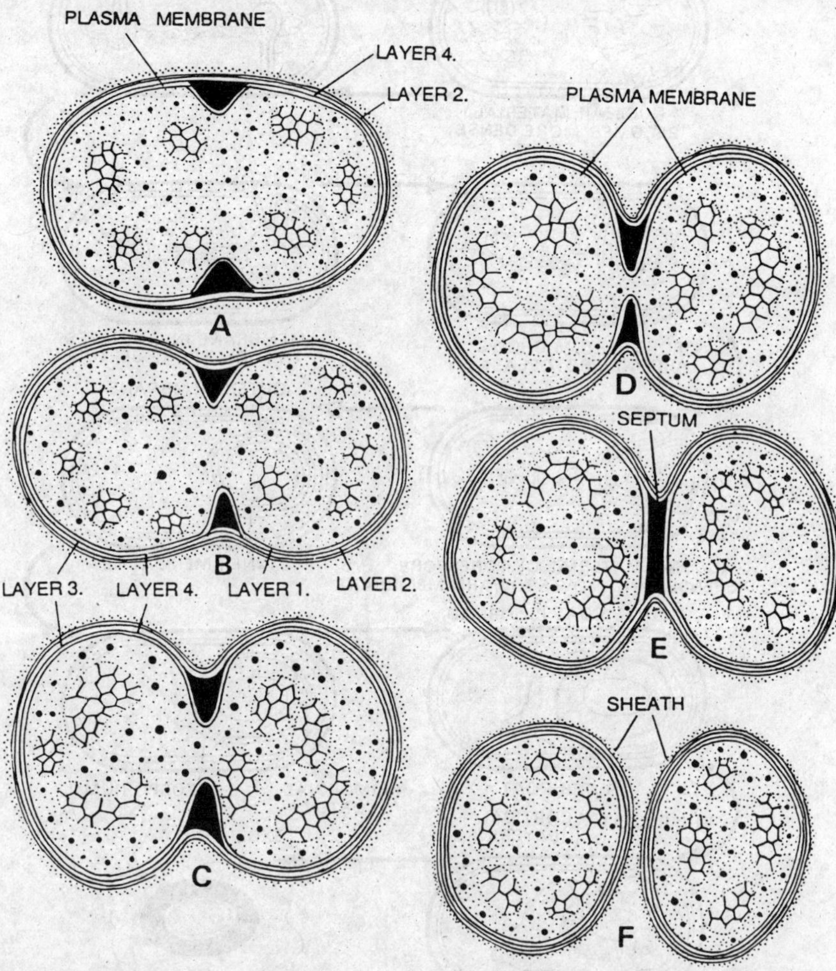

Fig. 22.11 (a). *Bacteria.* A-F, stages in the cell division of a coccus bacterium (ultra structure).

and *Clostridium*. The spore structure is much more complex than that of vegetative cells in that it has many layers. The outermost is the exosporium, a thin delicate covering and within this is the spore coat, which is composed of a layer or layers of wall-like materials; below the spore coat is the cortex, a region consisting of many concentric rings like the cell wall, the cortex is composed of **peptidoglycan.** Inside the cortex are the usual cell wall, cell membrane, nuclear region and other cell components.

SEXUAL REPRODUCTION IN BACTERIA

Cytologic observations and genetic studies indicate something like sexual reproduction, involving the fusion of two different cells and a transfer of hereditary factors occurs in bacteria although infrequently. Genetic recombination occurs in those bacteria that have been carefully

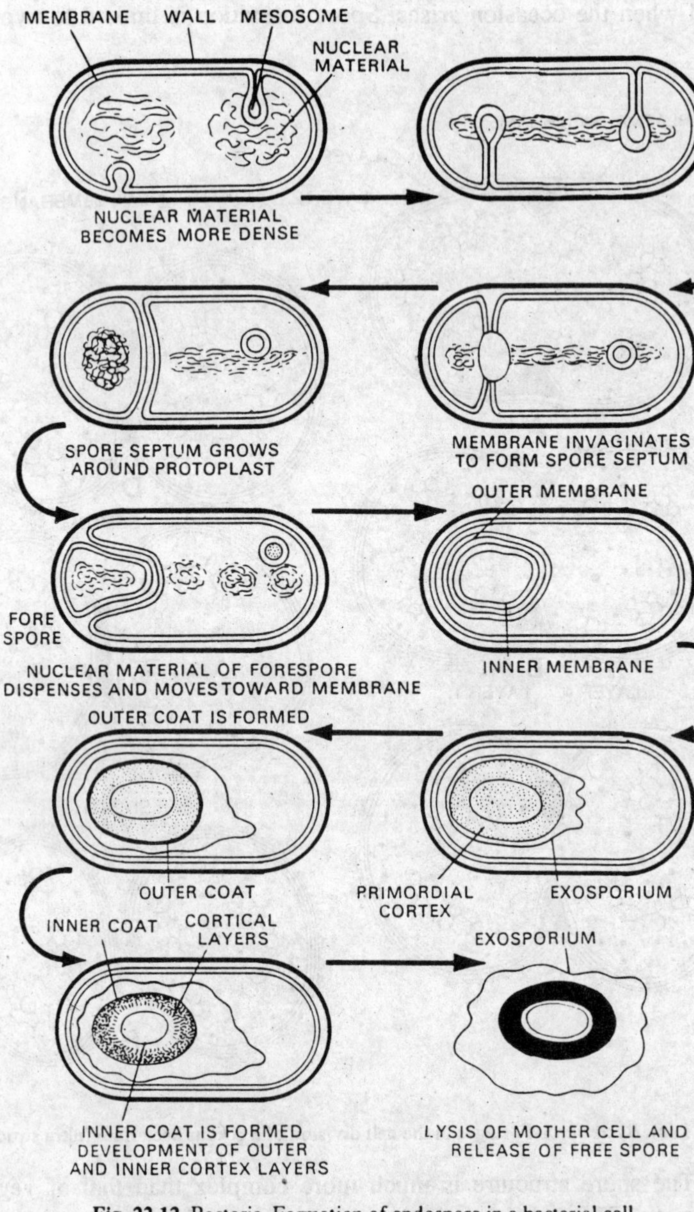

Fig. 22.12. Bacteria. Formation of endospore in a bacterial cell.

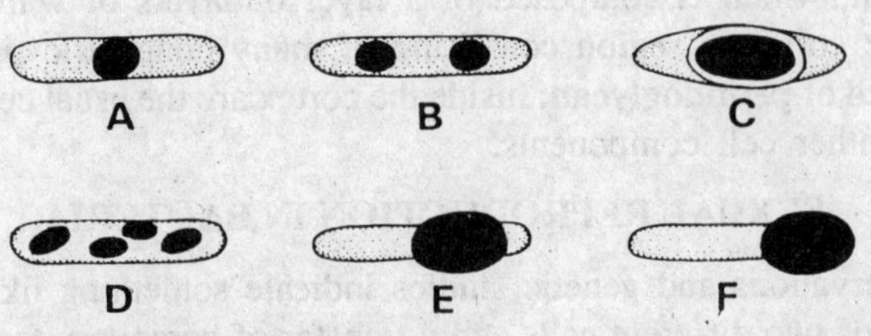

Fig. 22.13. Bacteria. Various stages of endospore formation (A–F).

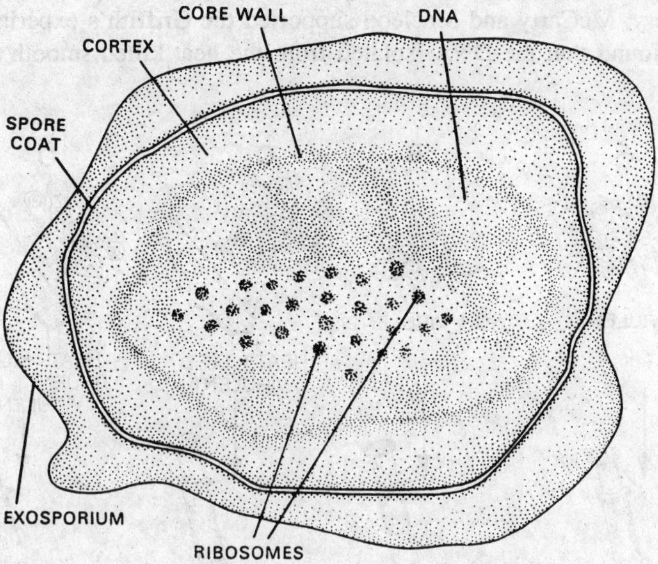

Fig. 22.14. Bacteria. Structure of endospore.

studied and presumably occurs in other species as well. One of the most intensively studied species of bacteria, *Escherichia coli* has been shown to have sex–some act as males and transfer genetic information by direct contact with females. This ability to transfer genes is regulated by a fertility factor F+ which can itself be transferred to a female, thereby converting her into a male.

The usual vegetative bacterial cells are haploid and in sexual reproduction part or all of the chromosome passes from the male cell to the female cell, yielding a cell, *i.e.,* partly or completely diploid. Crossing over then occurs between the female chromosome and the male chromosome or fragment, followed by a process of segregation that yields haploid progeny cells.

1. Bacterial transformation

The genetic transfer in bacteria also occurs by **transformation,** in which the DNA molecule of the donor cell, when liberated by its disintegration, is taken up by another recipient cell and its offsprings inherit some characters of the donor cell. When different strains of bacteria are found in a mixed state either in culture or in nature, some of the resultant offsprings possess a combination of characters of the parent strains. This phenomenon is known as **recombination.**

The phenomenon of transformation was first recorded by Griffith (1928). Avery, Macleod and McCarty (1944) demonstrated that the transforming principle being DNA in the sequence of events in bacterial transformation.

The lines of inquiry that led to an understanding of the chemical nature of genetic material arose from a study of the pestilent organism *Diplococcus pneumoniae*. This bacterium causes pneumonia in males. In 1928, Frederick Griffith found that there are two strains of *D. pneumoniae,* one that forms smooth colonies protected by a capsule, and the other one that formed irregular or rough colonies without a capsule when grown on a suitable medium in petri dishes. When injected into mice (A) only capsulated smooth cells(virulent) produced the disease, but not the non-virulent rough cells (B). On the other hand when the heat killed capsulated (virulent) smooth cells were mixed with non-virulent rough cells (D) and then were injected in the mice the disease was produced. This shows that some factors from the dead capsulated smooth cells, converted the living non-virulent rough cells into living smooth capsulated (virulent) cells.

In 1944, Avery, McCarty and Macleod supported the Griffith's experiment by molecular explanation. They found that the DNA isolated from the heat killed smooth cells, when added

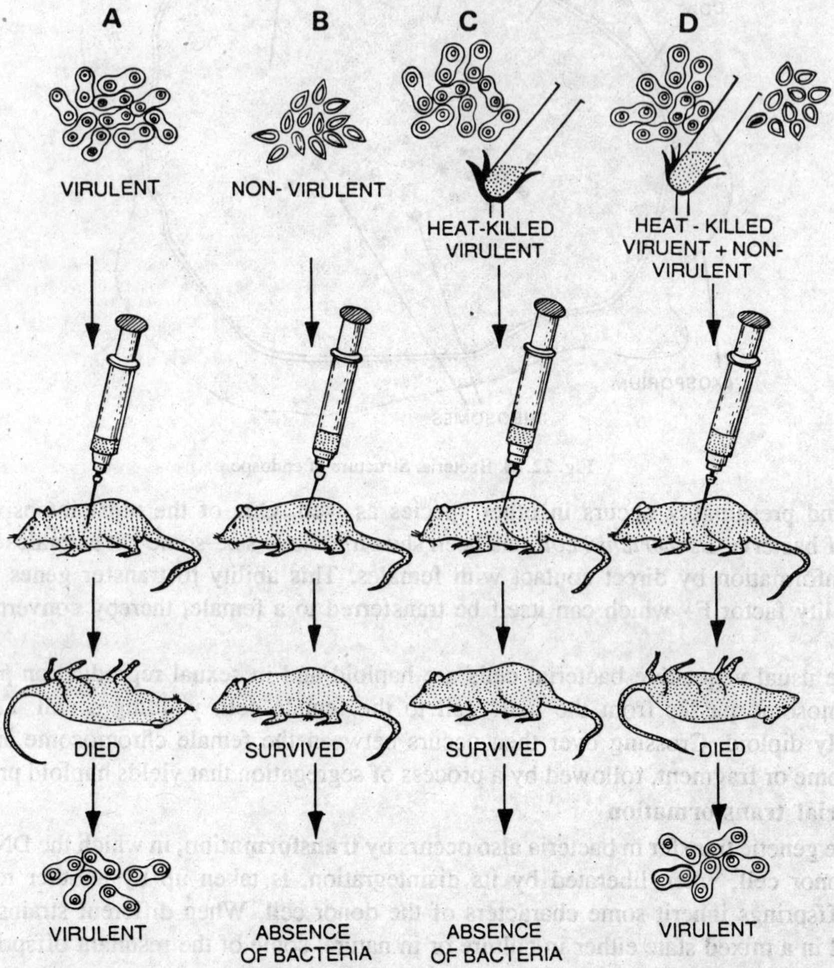

Fig. 22.15. Griffith's experiments with *Diplococcus pneumoniae* and mice.

to rough cells changed their surface character from rough to smooth, and also made them virulent. By this experiment, this was shown that DNA was the genetic material responsible for inducing the smooth character of the cells and their property of virulence in mice. Their experiment proved that bacterial transformation involves transfer of a part of DNA from the dead bacterium (*i.e.*, donor) to the living bacterium (*i.e.*, recipient), that expresses the character of dead cell, and so is known as a **recombinant.**

Viral-infecting agent is DNA

A bacteriophage (T_2 virus) infects the bacterium *Escherichia coli*. After infection, the virus multiplies and T_2 phages are released with the lysis of the bacterial cells. As we know, the

T_2 phage contains both DNA and proteins. Now the question arises, which of the two components has the information to programme for the multiplication of more viral particles.

To solve this problem Hershey and Chase (1952) devised an experiment with two different preparations of T_2 phage. In one preparation they made protein part radioactive and in the other

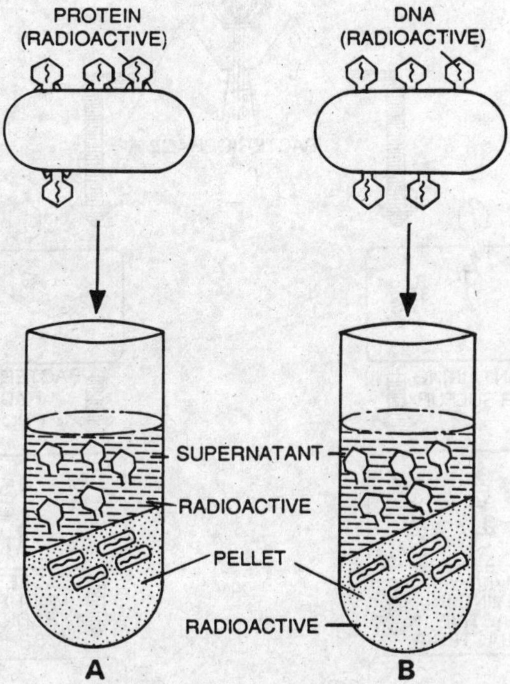

Fig. 22.16. The viral infecting agent is DNA. A, the viral protein coat is radioactive; B, viral DNA is radioactive. The infected bacterial pellet picks up radioactivity only when the viral DNA is radioactive.

preparation the DNA was made radioactive. Thereafter a culture of *E. coli* was made infected by these two phage preparations. Immediately after infection, and before lysis of bacteria the *E. coli* cells were gently agitated in a mixer so that the adhering phage particles were loosened and then the culture was centrifuged. With the result the heavier pellets of infected bacterial cells were settled down in the bottom of tube. The lighter viral particles and those particles which did not enter the bacterial cells were found in the supernatant. It was found that when T_2 phage with radioactive DNA was used to infect *E. coli* in the experiment, the heavier bacterial pellet was also radioactive. On the other hand when T_2 phage with radioactive protein was used, the bacterial pellet had very little radioactivity and most of the radioactivity was found in supernatant. This experiment has proved, that during infection with T_2 phage, it is DNA that actually entered the bacteria when such infected bacterial cells were developed further they lysed and new phage particles were formed. This famous experiment conducted by Hershey and Chase (1952) has proved that it is the viral DNA and not protein that contains information for the production of more T_2 phage particles hence DNA is genetic material. However, in some viruses (*e.g.*, TMV, influenza virus and polio virus) RNA serves as genetic material.

Hershey and Chase conducted two experiments. In one experiment *E. coli* was given in a medium containing the radio-isotope S^{35} and in the other experiment *E. coli* was grown in a medium containing the radio-istope P^{32}. In these experiments *E. coli* cells were made infected with T_2 phage released from *E. coli* cells grown in S^{35} medium have S^{35} in their protein capsid, and those from P^{32} medium had P^{32} in their DNA. When these phages were used to infect new

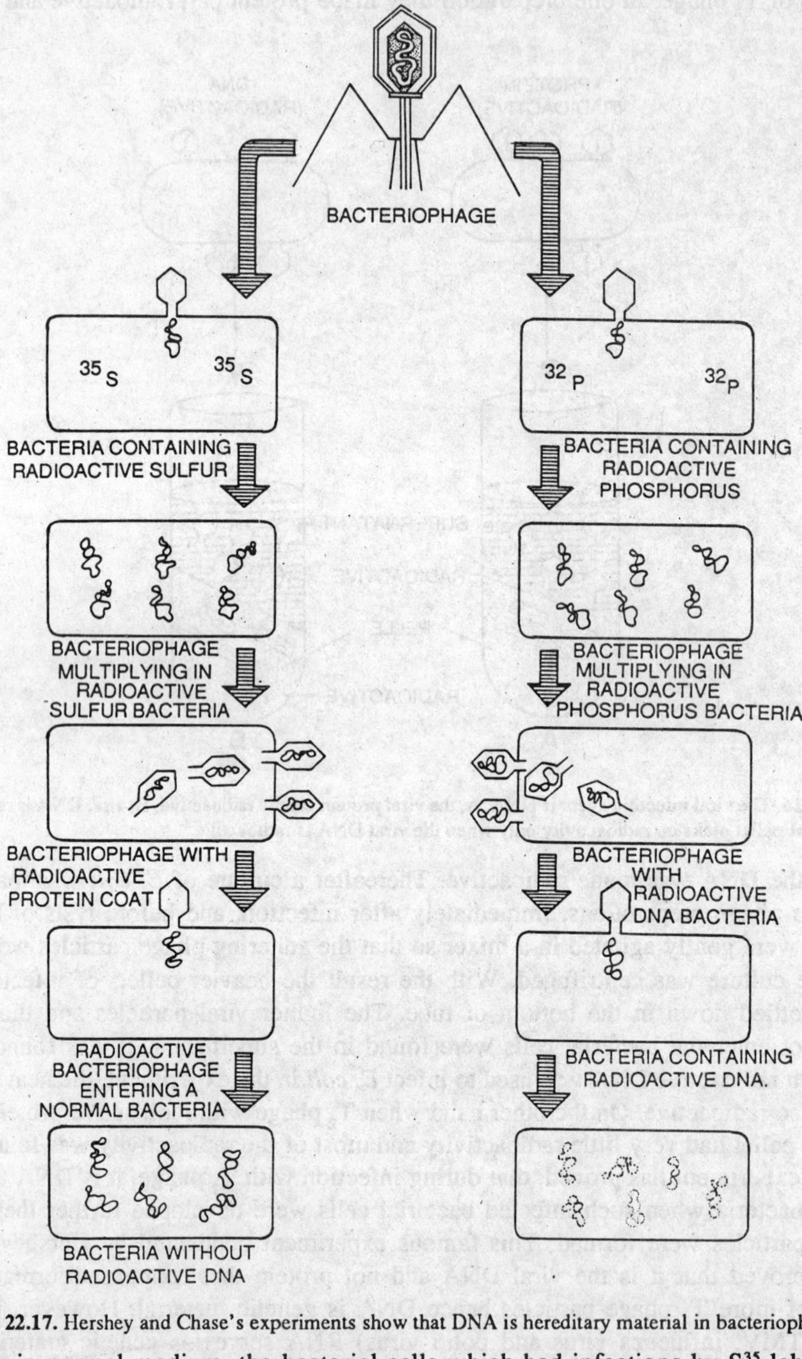

Fig. 22.17. Hershey and Chase's experiments show that DNA is hereditary material in bacteriophages.

E. coli cells in normal medium, the bacterial cells which had infections by S^{35} labelled phages showed the radioactivity in their cell wall and not in cytoplasm. Whereas the bacteria infected with P^{32} labelled phages had shown the reverse condition. Thus it can be said that when T_2 phage infects the bacterial cell, its protein capsid remains outside of the bacterial cell but its DNA enters the cytoplasm of the bacterium. When the infected cells of bacteria get lysed, new complete viral particles (T_2 phages) are formed. This proves, that viral DNA carries the information for synthesis of more copies of DNA and protein capsids. This shows that DNA is genetic material.

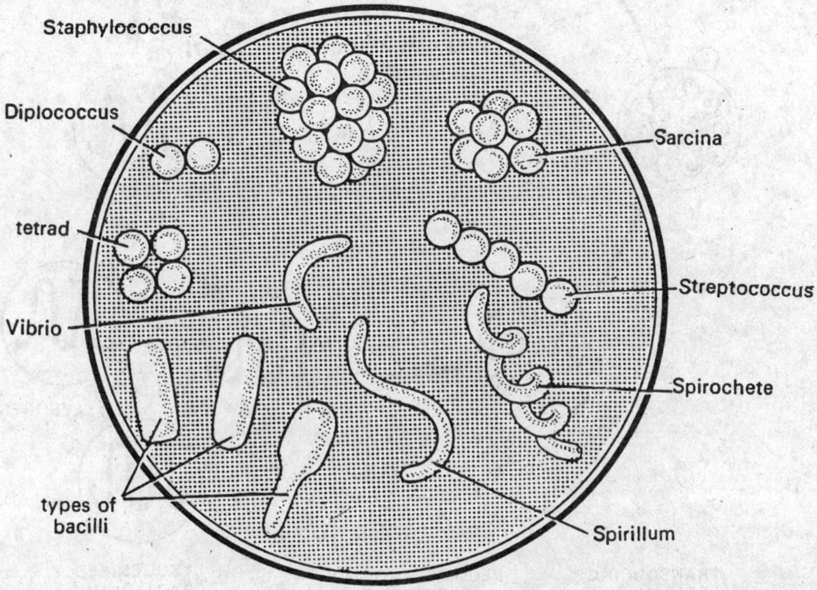

Fig. 22.18. Different types of bacteria.

2. Bacterial transduction

The genetic transfer in bacteria is achieved by a process known as **transduction.** Lederberg and Zinder's (1952) experiment in U-tube *Salmonella typhimurium* indicated that bacterial viruses or phages are responsible for the transfer of genetic material from one to the other lysogenic and lytic phages. Thus the host acquires a new genotype. Transduction has been demonstrated in many bacteria.

In this process, the DNA molecule that carries the hereditary characters of the donor bacterium, is being transferred to the recipient cell through the agency of the phage particle. In this process very few closely linked characters can be transferred by each particle. Thus the bacteriophage brings about genetic changes in those bacteria which survive the phage attack.

When a bacterial cell is being infected with a temperate virus either lytic-cycle or lysogeny starts. Thereafter, host DNA breaks down into small fragments along with the multiplication of virus. Some of these DNA fragments are incorporated with the virus particles becoming transducing one. When bacteria lyse these particles along with normal virus particles are released when this mixture of transducing and normal virus particles is allowed to infect the population of recipient cells, most of the bacteria are infected with normal virus particles and with the result lysogeny or lytic-cycle occurs again. A few bacteria are infected with transducing particles,

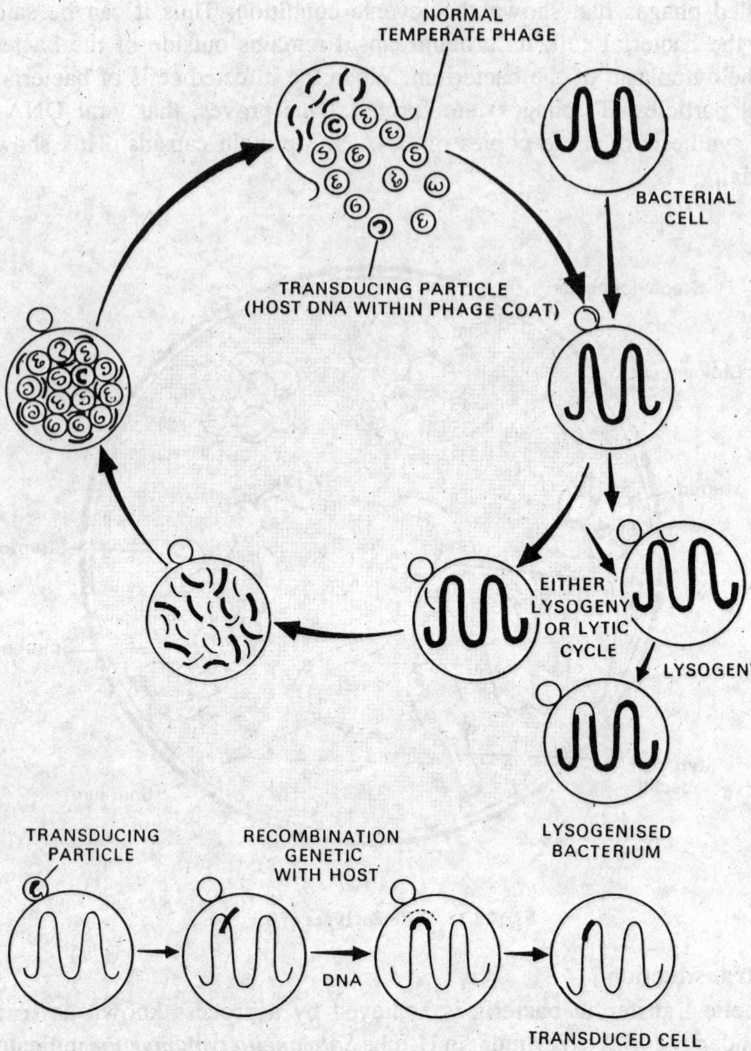

Fig. 22.19. Bacteria. Upper diagram: transduction mechanism where phage particles containing host can be formed. Lower diagram: genetic recombination with transducing particles.

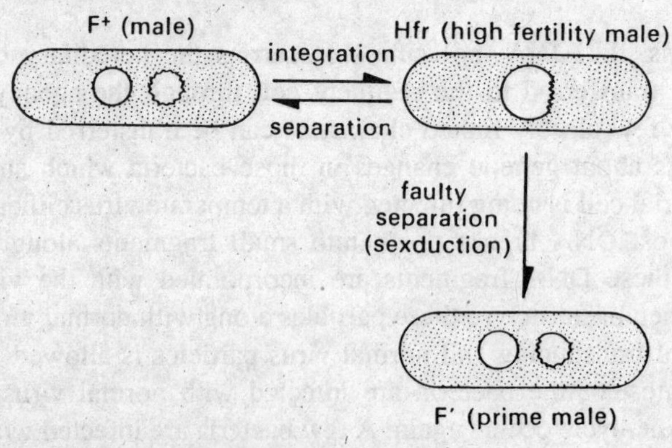

Fig. 22.20. Bacteria, transduction.

transduction takes place and the DNA of virus particles undergo genetic recombinations with the bacterial DNA.

3. Bacterial conjugation

Wollman and Jacob (1956) have described conjugation in which two bacteria lie side by side for as much as half an hour. During this period of time a portion of genetic material is slowly passed from one bacterium which is designated as a male to a recipient designated as a female. This was established that the male material entered the female in a linear series.

The genetic recombination between donor and recipient cells takes place as follows: The Hfr DNA after leaving a part in fragment to recipient cell again reforms in circular manner. In F strain genetic recombination takes place between donor fragment and recipient DNA. Gene transfer is a sequential process and a given Hfr strain always donates genes in a specific order. A single stranded donor DNA (F factor) is integrated in the host chromosome with the help of **nuclease enzyme.**

In bacterial conjugation the transfer of genetic material (DNA) takes place by cell to cell contact of donor and recipient cells. During the process of conjugation large portion of the genome is transferred, while in transformation and transduction only small fragment of DNA is transferred. The process of conjugation was discovered by Lederberg and Tatum (1944) in a single strain of *Escherichia coli.* Conjugation has also been demonstrated in *Salmonella, Pseudomonas* and *Vibrio.*

In conjugation one way transfer of genetic material takes place from donor to recipient strain. The donor and recipient strains are always determined genetically. Recipient strain is designated as F^-, while donor strains are of two kinds and are designated as F^+ and H fr (high frequency of recombination). If the strain donates only a small portion of its genome it is called F^+, and if it donates large amount of genome it is called H fr. These F^+ and H fr factors are called **episomes.**

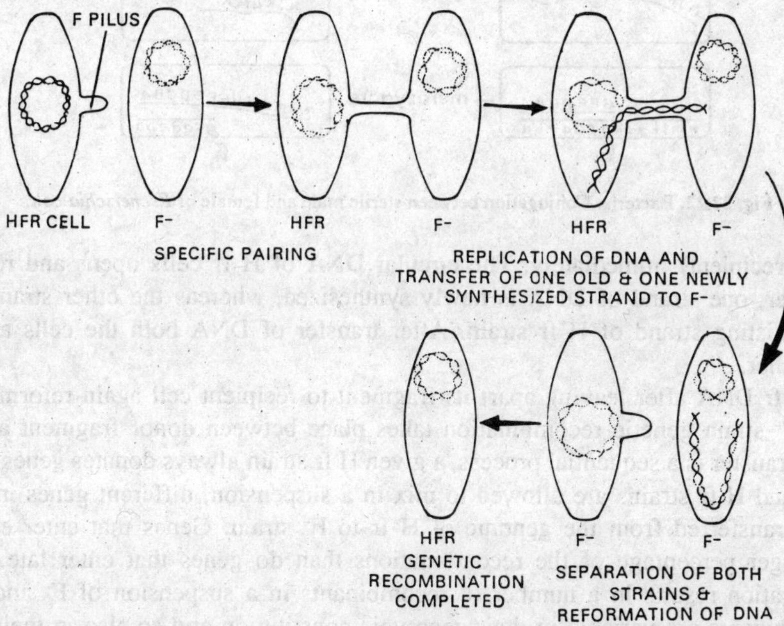

Fig. 22.21. Bacteria, Diagrammatic representation of possible mechanism of conjugation.

Strains F^+ and Hfr are characterised by the presence of specific flagellum like structures, the so called sex pilus. The sex pilus is absent in F^- strains, and is responsible for bacterial mating. Sex pili of F^+ and H fr touch the opposite mating type of cells specifically to transfer the genetic material.

Sex pilus has a hole of 2.5μm diameter which is large enough for a DNA molecule to pass through it lengthwise. At the time of pairing DNA of H fr strain (donor) is transferred

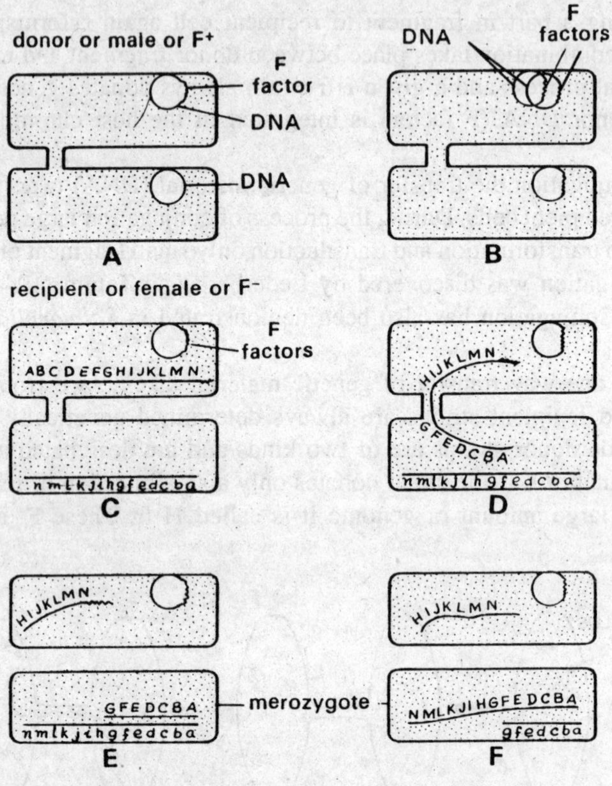

Fig. 22.22. Bacteria. Conjugation between sterile male and female of *Escherichia coli*.

to F^- strain (recipient) immediately. The circular DNA of H fr cells opens and replicates but during transfer, one strand of DNA is newly synthesized, whereas the other strand is derived from a pre-existing strand of H fr strain. After transfer of DNA both the cells are separated from each other.

The H fr DNA after leaving apart its fragment to recipient cell again reforms in circular manner. In F^- strain genetic recombination takes place between donor fragment and recipient DNA. Gene transfer is a sequential process, a given H fr strain always donates genes in a specific order. If F^- and H fr strains are allowed to mix in a suspension, different genes in a sequence of time are transferred from the genome of H fr to F^- strain. Genes that enter early, always appear in larger percentage of the recombinations than do genes that enter late.

Conjugation results in a number of recombinants in a suspension of F^- and H fr cells. These recombinants are variable in their genotypic constitution and so also in their phenotypic expression. These recombinants are entirely new and different from their parents.

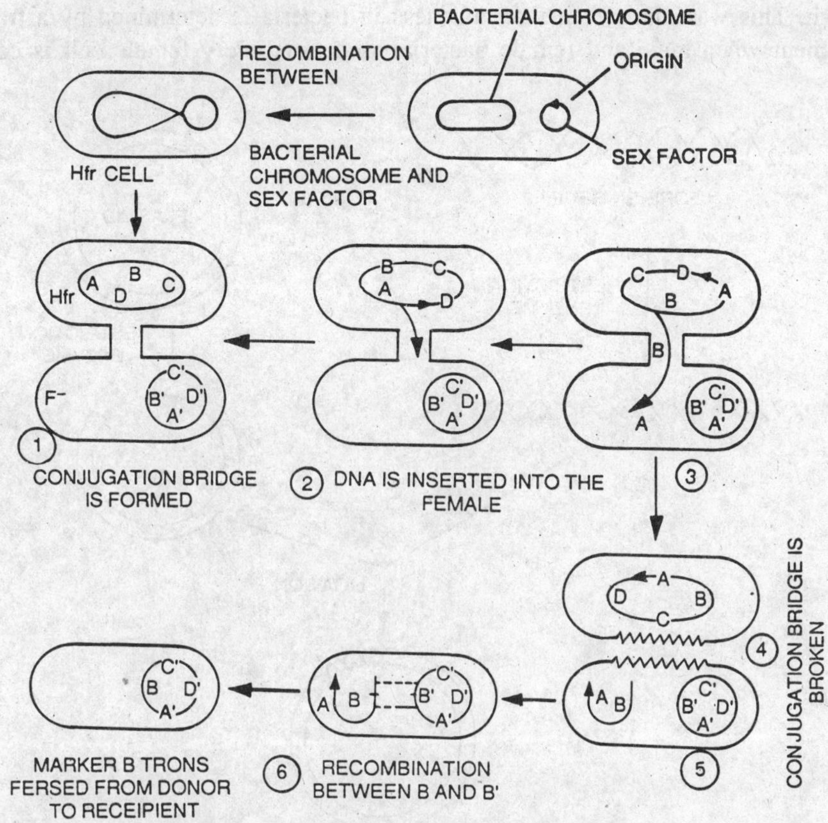

Fig. 22.23. Bacterial conjugation.

PROKARYOTIC CHROMOSOMES

The genetic information of a prokaryotic cell is carried in the nucleoplasm on the structure termed **bacterial chromosome.** It consists of a double helical DNA (deoxyribonucleic acid) molecule, never associated with basic proteins, and has been shown in some prokaryotes to be circular. The bacterial chromosome is consequently not structurally homologous with the nuclear chromosomes of the eukaryotic cell, but rather with the organellar DNA present in the eukaryotic mitochondria and chloroplasts. It is probable, that a single bacterial chromosome (*viz.*, one very long DNA molecule) carries all the genetic information necessary to specify the essential properties of the prokaryotic cell.

Plasmids. Many bacteria can also harbour small, extrachromosomal circular DNA molecules capable of autonomous replication, which are known as **plasmids** so far investigated carry the determinants for such phenotypic characters as resistance to drugs and other antibacterial substances, and for the enzymes which mediate certain metabolic pathways. The amount of DNA in a plasmid is from 0.1 to 5 percent of that in the bacterial chromosome.

This was discovered in *Escherichia coli* that there are two mating types, and during conjugation one partner acts only as **genetic donor,** or **male,** and the other only as **genetic recipient** or **female.** Since the only function of the male is to transfer some of its DNA, it need not remain viable, whereas the female cell must remain viable, so that, the zygote may develop in it. This was discovered that maleness in bacteria is determined by a transmissible genetic element when male and female bacteria conjugate, every female cell is converted to

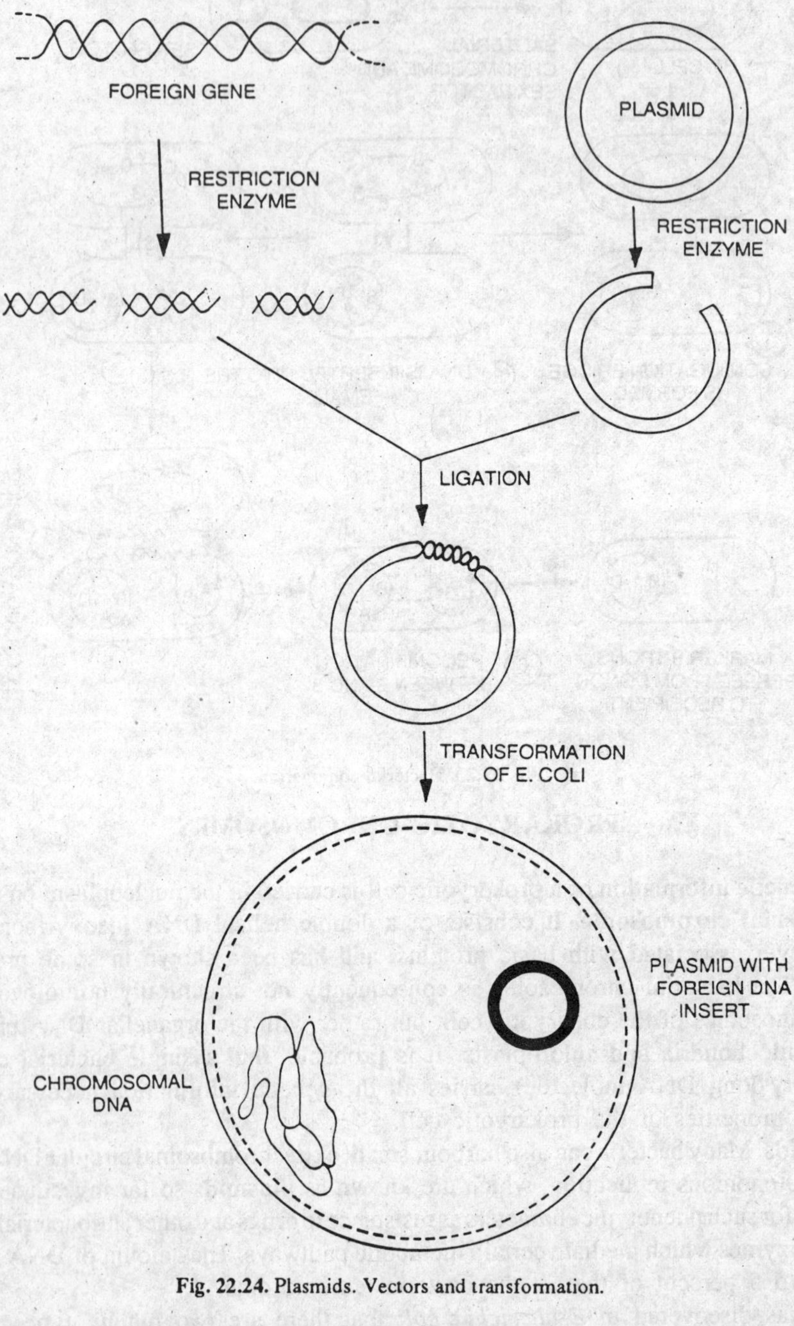

Fig. 22.24. Plasmids. Vectors and transformation.

a male. The genetic element governing the inherited property of maleness is called the **F factor** (F = fertility), it is transmitted only by direct cell to cell contact. In 1952 Lederberg coined the term **plasmid** as a genetic name for all extrachromosomal hereditary determinants, of which

F is an example. It is now known that bacterial plasmids are small, circular molecules of DNA which carry the genes for their own replication. In many cases, they also carry genes which confer new properties on the host cell, such as resistance to drugs or the production of toxins. Many plasmids carry genes that govern the process of conjugation. Thus, conjugation is a mechanism imposed on the bacterial cell by a plasmid, the normal result of which is the transfer of plasmid DNA.

Types of plasmids. Most plasmids have been classified on the basis of host properties. Thus, there are the *R* **factors** (R = resistance) and the *COI* **factors** (COI = Colicinogeny) of the gram-negative bacteria, the **penicillinase plasmids** of *Staphylococcus aureus,* the degradative plasmids of *Pseudomonas,* the **cryptic plasmids** etc.

Properties of plasmids. The structure of all known plasmids consists of circular, double-stranded DNA molecules. Several of them have molecular weights in the range 5×10^7 to 7×10^7. One (an R factor) has a molecular weight of only 1×10^7, and some of the cryptic plasmids are even smaller. Since the amount of DNA required to code for an average polypeptide with a molecular weight of 40,000 is about 6×10^7, F_1 and other plasmids of similar size may contain as many as 100 genes.

Gene Expression in Prokaryotes

Bacterial chromosomes. It has been established now that a bacterial chromosome is always present in the centre of bacterial cell which is not capable of mitotic and meiotic divisions and is not enclosed within a definite nuclear membrane. An average bacterial cell contains one

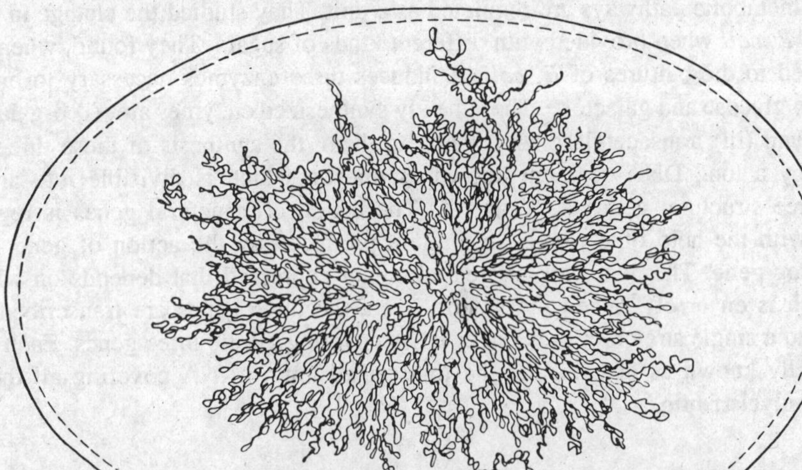

Fig. 22.25. Bacterial chromosome, chromosome of *Escherichia coli.*

thousandth the DNA content of a typical eucaryotic cell. The bacterial chromosome is a thin elongated flexible and circular filament of DNA molecule associated with few proteins. The bacterial cells can divide very rapidly. The cell division is completed by the doubling of all the cell constituents followed by partition of the cell into two daughter cells. The first step in cell division is DNA duplication.

Genetic Recombination in Bacteria

This is a process where genetic materials, contained in two separate genomes, are brought together within one unit. In bacteria the recombination takes place by (1) **transformation,** (2)

transduction and (3) **conjugation.** These phenomena have already been discussed in detail in preceding paragraphs, under the heading 'sexual reproduction in bacteria'.

Induction and Repression

The genetic potential of a virus is limited and it essentially uses the host machinery for its replication. On the other hand, the bacteria can synthesize their constituents from simple salts and sugar. The bacterium, *Escherichia coli* has about 2500 genes on its chromosome. The bacterium maintains its internal economy only by allowing the action of few genes at a time. This means that genes will be turned on or off as per requirement. A set of genes will be switched on when there is necessity to handle and metabolise a new substrate. When the set of these genes is switched on, enzymes are produced, which metabolise the new substrate. This phenomenon is called **induction** and the molecules (metabolites) evoking this phenomenon are **inducers.** On the other hand, when a metabolite needed by the bacterium is supplied in excess from outside, the bacterium inhibits making it and this stops the further production of the metabolite by the bacterium. These inactivated genes are thus named **repressible,** and the phenomenon is known as **repression** or **feed-back repression.** However, some of the genes are constantly expressed to take care of normal cellular activity such as glycolysis. These genes are known as **constitutive,** and the enzymes produced by them are known as **constitutive enzymes,** such as dehydrogenases.

Operon Concept

Francois Jacob and Jacques Monod (1961), while working at the Pasteur Institute, Paris, proposed that metabolic pathways are regulated as a unit. They studied the change in the nature of enzymes of *E. coli* when provided with different kinds of sugars. They found, when the sugar lactose is added to the cultures of *E. coli,* it induces three enzymes necessary to break down the lactose into glucose and galactose. These newly synthesized enzymes are–(i) β-galactosidase, (ii) permease and (iii) transacetylase. According to them, the synthesis of these three enzymes is controlled by a long DNA segment known as **operon** which is divisible into an operator site O and three structural genes Z, Y and A. The action of structural genes is regulated by operator site with the help of a **repressor** protein produced by the action of gene 'i' known as the **regulator gene.** The genes are expressed or not expressed that depends on whether the operator switch is on or off. When the switch is on, the three genes are transcribed by RNA polymerase into a single stretch of messenger RNA covering all the three genes. Each structural gene is generally known as **cistron** and the transcribed long mRNA covering all the cistrons is known as **polycistronic.**

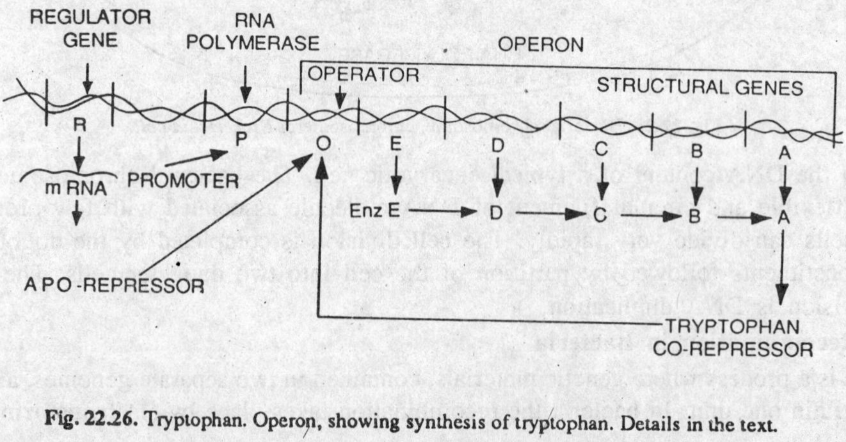

Fig. 22.26. Tryptophan. Operon, showing synthesis of tryptophan. Details in the text.

The switching on or off of the operator switch is achieved by a protein known as **repressor.** When this protein ties together to the operator (O) and blocks it, the switch is turned off and the three genes (Z, Y, A) are not expressed.

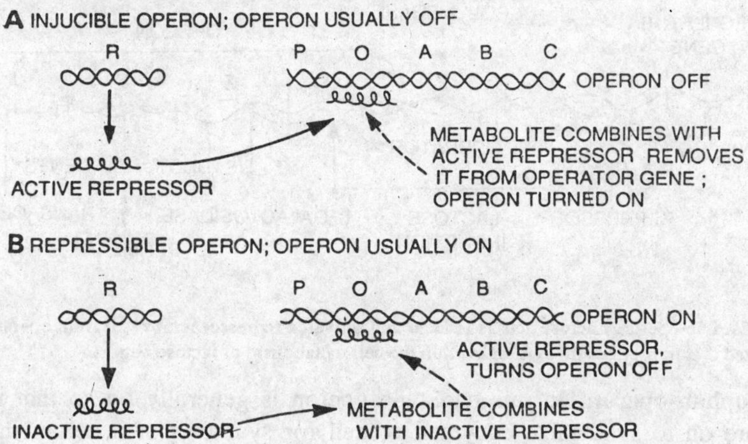

Fig. 22.27. Operons. A, inducible, B repressible. Both the operons become off when operator site is bound by the repressor formed by regulator gene R.

Lac-operon. This is an example of **inducible operon.** A few molecules of lactose are added into the cell by the action of the enzyme permease, a small quantity of which is found even under repressed conditions. These few molecules are then converted into an active form of lactose which binds to the repressor (i gene product) and thus, the repressor cannot bind to the operator switch any more. When the operator is free of repressor RNA polymerase starts

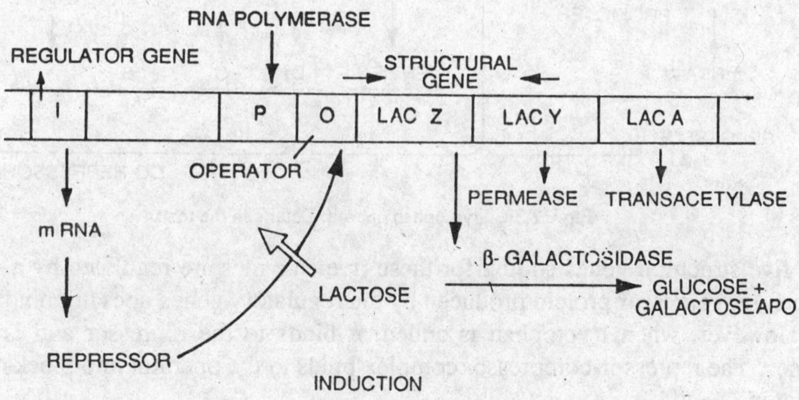

Fig. 22.28. Lac operon. Details in the text.

the transcription of the operon by binding the promotor site P. Messenger RNA corresponding to all the three enzymes is synthesized which gets translated to produce three enzymes-β-galactosidase, permease and transacetylase. With the production of these three enzymes metabolism of lactose begins. The synthesis of enzymes is continued unless and until all lactose molecules are consumed by the cell. When the last molecules of lactose, bound to repressor are also consumed, the inactive repressor becomes active and binds to operator site (O) to switch off the operon as normal.

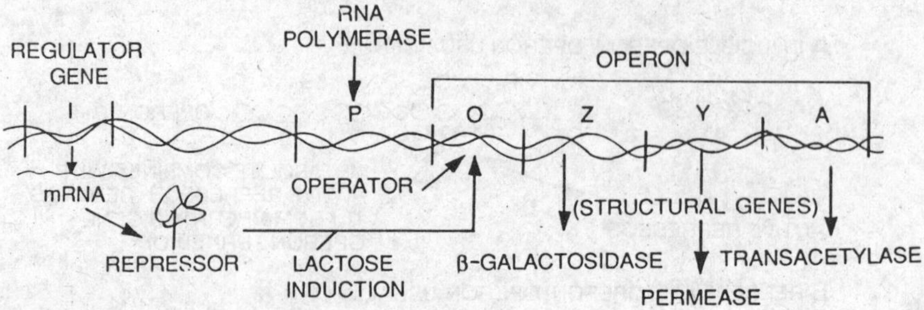

Fig. 22.29. Lac-operon. Lactose acts as inducer and activated repressor removes it from operator site with the result operon is activated that transcribes mRNA and within the cell metabolism of lactose begins.

Tryptophan-operon. In this case, the operon is generally on so that transcription and translation are on to synthesize enzymes needed for synthesis of a certain metabolite by the cell. However, the operon can be switched off when the cell does not require the metabolite or the metabolite has been produced in excess. The tryptophan operon consists of five genes (trp E, D, C, B and A) coding for five enzymes (En_z E, D, C, B, and A) catalysing the synthesis of tryptophan (an amino acid) and thus constituting an anabolic pathway. The presence of tryptophan serves to repress the synthesis of the enzymes responsible for its manufacture.

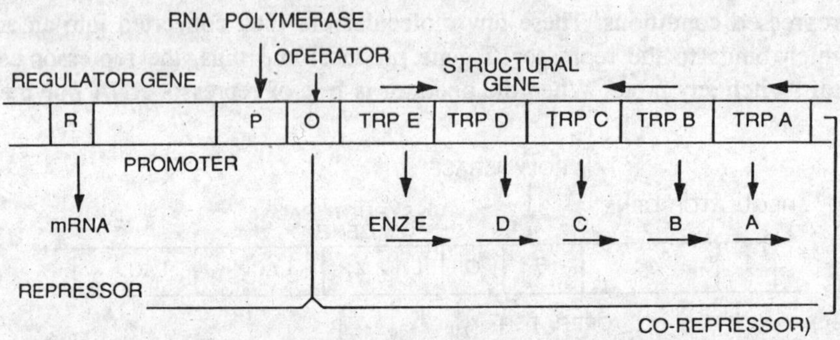

Fig. 22.30. Tryptophan operon. Details in the text.

The five structural genes coding for these five enzymes are regulated by a single operator switch. Here, the repressor protein produced by the regulatory genes does not bind to the operator by itself. However, when tryptophan is added, it binds to the repressor and is known as the **co-repressor.** The repressor-corepressor complex binds to the operator and blocks the expression of this operon.

The structure of the tryptophan operon is more or less similar to that of the lac operon, but has a functional variation. In this case the R gene product is equivalent to the i gene of lac operon. The R gene product produces protein which by itself is unable to bind to operator. This is referred to as **apo-repressor.** In the presence of tryptophan a co-repressor, the functional repressor is formed which now binds to the operator and prevents the transcription of the operon and production of tryptophan. Here the operon model explains both the induction and repression phenomenon in procaryotes.

CLASSIFICATION OF BACTERIA

Because of their simple morphology, bacteria cannot be divided into orders, families, genera and species on the basis of their structure alone. The biochemical, physiological and cultural characters are to be considered for their classification. The scientific world of today accepts the Bergey's classification of Bacteria (1957).

Erwin F. Smith, a pioneer worker in this field at first accepted a system of classification proposed by Migula which was based on the number and arrangement of flagella. It was as follows :

(1) **Bacterium** included all atrichous rod-like forms.
(2) **Pseudomonas** included polar flagellate forms.
(3) **Bacillus** included peritrichous rod-like forms.

In 1905, Smith revised this system with slight modifications in the name of the divisions. Thus the name (*i*) **aplanobacter** was given for atrichous, rod-like bacteria, (*ii*) **bacterium** for polar flagellate bacteria, and (*iii*) **bacillus** for peritrichous bacteria.

The commonly used and more widely accepted divisions of bacteria are:

(1) **Bacterium** or **Bacillus** included all rod-like and kidney-shaped forms.
(2) **Coccus** includes all spherical bacteria.
(3) **Spirillum** includes spiral, comma like and variouly curved bacteria.

Author	Non-motile	Motile with polar flagella	Motile with peritrichous flagella
Migula (1895-1900)	*Bacterium*	*Pseudomonas*	*Bacillus*
Lehmann and Neumann (1897-1927)	Non-spiral Motile or nonmotile *Bacterium*	Sporing motile or non-motile	*Bacillus*
Smith (1905)	*Aplanobacter*	*Bacterium*	*Bacillus*
Bergy (1923-1939)	*Phytomonas*		*Erwinia*
Dowson (1939)		*Pseudomonas* and *Xanthomonas*	*Bacterium*
Bergey (1948)	*Pseudomonas*	*Pseudomonas* *Xanthomonas*	*Bacterium*

BERGEY'S CLASSIFICATION (1957)

Modern schemes for classification of bacteria use a number of properties from, arrangement, Gram stain, motility, various enzymic properties and any other sort of information that can serve to delimit an organism or group of organisms.

A system of classification of Schizomycetes that is used by all bacteriologists and that has an international standing is "Bergey's Manual of Determinative Bacteriology". It represents the collaborative efforts of over 100 of the best qualified microbiologists at the time it was brought together and is a monumental work. It is based on the International Rules of Nomenclature of the Bacteria and Viruses established by the International Committee of Bacteriological Nomenclature in 1947.

As outlined in Bergey's manual the entire group of bacteria (Class-Schizomycetes) comprises some 1500 species. These are divided into 10 orders differentiated from one another primarily on the basis of morphological characters and type of motility.

I. **Pseudomonadales.** Cells rigid, spheroidal or rod-like, straight curved, or spiral, some groups form trichomes; motile species have polar flagella.

II. **Chlamydobacteriales.** Rod-like cells in trichomes, often sheathed, deposit iron hydroxide in sheath; flagella sub-polar when present.

III. **Hyphomicrobiales.** Cells spheroidal or ovoid, connected on stalk or threads, no trichomes; exhibits budding and longitudinal fission; flagella polar when present.

IV. **Eubacteriales.** Typically unicellular spheroidal or rod-like cells, no trichomes, sheath or other accessory structures, motile species have peritrichous flagella.

V. **Actinomycetales.** Cells branch, many species form mycelia and mold like conidiophores and sporangiophores, polar flagellate, sporangiospores in only one species.

VI. **Caryophanales.** Trichomes often very long, peritrichous flagella.

VII. **Beggiatales.** Alga like trichome or coccoid cell, accumulate elemental S, gliding and oscillatory or rolling motion; no flagella.

VIII. **Myxobacteriales.** Cells coccoid, rod-like or fusiform, communal slime, fruiting bodies, cells flexuous, gliding motility in contact with solid surface; no flagella.

IX. **Spirochaetales.** Elongated, spiral cells rotatory and flexing motions and translatory motility; no flagella.

X. **Mycoplasmatales.** PPLO extremely pleomorphic and easily distorted cells without cell walls; complex life cycle; non-motile.

Phylogenetic relationships. The phylogenetic relationships of bacteria are not clear and because of this, their classification has undergone a number of changes. According to recent scheme, the bacteria are placed in the phylum Schizomycophyta in the Sub-kingdom Thallophyta, which include all plants that do not form embryos during development. According to other modern taxonomic systems these organisms have been placed in the kingdom Protista along with algae, fungi and protozoa, or in the kingdom Monera together with blue-green algae.

According to one school of thought, the bacteria have been descended from the blue-green algae, after becoming adapted to a saprophytic or parasitic existence losing their chlorophyll. This view is based on the general similarity of the cell structure of these two forms. According to other investigators, the fact that many bacteria possess flagella indicates that these organisms descended from simple flagellated forms, and perhaps these forms have also given rise to the green algae. There are others who believe that the heterotrophic bacteria of today have been evolved from autotrophic ones. According to these workers, the autotrophic bacteria may have appeared before any of the chlorophyll containing plants. It is also suggested that different groups of bacteria have descended independently from different ancestors. There are still others who believe that bacteria may be a terminal group in evolution that has given rise to no other forms or if they have not descended from the blue-green algae, perhaps the blue-green algae have descended from them.

ECONOMIC IMPORTANCE OF BACTERIA

Bacteria are of great economic value in our daily life. They are useful as well as harmful.

A. Useful bacteria. They do great benefit to the agriculture and industries.

1. Agriculture. Many species of saprophytic and symbiotic bacteria add to the fertility of the soil and provide nitrogen to the plants.

(*a*) **Ammonifying bacteria.** *Bacillus subtilis, B. mycoides, B. ramosus* etc., act upon the dead animal and plant tissues and decompose their complex organic compounds like proteins into ammonium compounds. They are also known as **putrefying bacteria.**

(*b*) **Nitrifying bacteria.** *Nitrosomonas* oxidise the ammonium compounds into nitrites in presence of free oxygen and *Nitrobacter* oxidise nitrites into nitrates in the presence of free oxygen. Thus ammonifying and nitrifying bacteria increase the amount of nitrogenous compounds in the soil. Dead plants, animals and dung etc., are converted into humus by the action of putrefying bacteria. This humus itself acts as fertilizer for plants.

(*c*) **Nitrogen fixing bacteria.** They are *Azotobacter, Clostridium* and *Rhizobium* spp. They fix free nitrogen of the soil and make it available to the plants. The first two bacteria live freely in soil and fix the atmospheric nitrogen in the form of nitrogenous compounds in the soil. The third one is a symbiotic type. They live in the root nodules of leguminous plants, take the free atmospheric nitrogen and fix it within its tissues. These bacteria enable plants to grow in soil where no nitrogenous fertilizers are available. The leguminous plants make the soil rich in nitrogen, and therefore used as green manures.

Nitrogen fixation. The phenomenon of nitrogen fixation takes place by special type of bacteria which fix free atmospheric nitrogen gas into ammonia by means of symbiosis with leguminous plants. The bacteria taking part in this process are *Rhizobium leguminosarum* (Rhizobiaceae) which live in soil. These bacteria produce IAA(Indol-Acetic Acid) due to which the root hairs curl. These rod-like bacteria penetrate through the tip of the root hair forming a continuous 'infection thread' that enters the cortical region within twentyfour hours. During its passage through the root hair, the infection thread gets surrounded by a cellulose wall. This wall is secreted by the host as a reaction to the infection. The infection thread ramifies in the cortical region and the bacterial rods are released in the cytoplasm of the cells which are stimulated. These cells enlarge and multiply to form the characteristic nodules all over the root system. On the outside, the root nodule possesses a cortical layer which is followed by an actively proliferating meristematical region, then the vascular system enclosing in the centre the bacterial zone possessing abundantly the branched rods of *Rhizobium leguminosarum*. These bacteria absorb atmospheric nitrogen and make it available to the host plant in the form of ammonia which is being converted into nitrates. In turn, the bacteria get shelter and carbohydrate-nutrition from the leguminous plant. On the death and decay of root nodules the rhizobia are again set free in the soil; the decomposition of roots adds nitrates into the soil thus increasing fertility of the soil.

Azotobacter is also found in the soil; this fixes the nitrogen gas of the atmosphere in the presence of carbohydrates. This fixation of free nitrogen from the atmosphere through ammonia into free nitrates and again their conversion into ammonia and free nitrogen takes place by means of nitrifying and denitrifying bacteria, along with other organisms. This process is termed nitrogen cycle.

2. **Industry.** A large number of saprophytic bacteria are employed in the manufacture of various industrial products.

(*a*) **Butter making industry.** Saprophytic bacteria such as *Lacto bacilli* popularly known as *starters* make the milk sour and produce various flavours. These bacteria are largely employed in butter industry for ripening milk and producing flavours in butter.

(*b*) **Cheese making industry.** Bacteria are employed in this industry. First the casein of milk is coagulated and then it is ripened by certain bacteria. Bacteria make the casein spongy, soft and give it characteristic taste and flavour.

Pasteurization. Heating milk at 62°C for 30 minutes or at 71°C for 15 seconds.

(*c*) **Vinegar making industry.** *Bacillus aceti* convert the sugar solution into vinegar.

(*d*) **Alcohol and acetone manufacture.** Butyl alcohol and acetone are manufactured by the action of bacteria on molasses.

(*e*) **Tobacco curing.** Crude dry tobacco leaves pass through curing and ripening processes before they are ready for use. Bacteria are employed in both these processes and the peculiar taste and smell in the tobacco is due to the bacterial activity. For this purpose molasses and alcohol are added to tobacco.

(*f*) **Tea curing.** Crude tea leaves are acted upon by certain bacteria. The process is known as curing, which is employed to impart a peculiar taste and flavour to the leaves. For this purpose alcohol is added to tea leaves.

(*g*) **Leather tanning.** The hides and skins after drying, salting and clearing are steeped in fluids containing specific bacteria. The process of fermentation goes on for some time and then they are transferred to tan-pits and are further allowed to be fermented. This whole process is known as tanning and the bacteria employed in the process are obtained from cowdung and the excreta of dogs and poultry.

(*h*) **Fibre retting.** Retting is the process of separating fibres from the plant tissues. Bacteria are employed in this industry, which causes decay of the softer tissues and renders fibres easily separable mechanically. Fibres of flax, hemp, jute, coconut and other fibrous plants are obtained by immersing the specific plant organs in stagnant pond water where bacteria develop and cause retting.

(*i*) **The sewage work.** In order to remove solid and semi-solid constituents of sewage it is allowed to putrify. Putrifying bacteria are allowed to act upon sewage under anaerobic conditions. It gets decayed and liquified. It is now filtered and the liquid is either drained out to the river or used as manure in fields. For this purpose, in the soak pits the horse dung is filled up.

(*j*) **Ensilage.** It is the process of preserving green fodder in pits. Certain bacteria help in the preservation of fodder.

(*k*) **Medicines.** Antitoxins are the chemical substances produced in the host tissues in response to the attack of parasitic bacteria. Different vaccines and serums now prepared from these antitoxins are used in the treatments of specific ailments. The antibiotics such as streptomycin, aureomycin, chloromycetin etc., are obtained from certain actinomycetous bacteria.

B. Harmful bacteria. Many bacteria are harmful to human affairs in many ways.

1. Pathogenic bacteria. These bacteria cause great losses to animal and plant life by causing various diseases in them. Cholera, typhoid, pneumonia, dysentery, tuberculosis, tetanus etc., are more common human diseases. 'Ring disease of potato', 'yellowing rot of wheat,' 'Citurs canker,' 'wilt of cucumber' and 'crown gall' are the common bacterial diseases of plants.

Some common human and plant diseases. *Diplococcus pneumoniae* causes pneumonia. *Streptococcus phyegens* causes sore throat, *Staphylococcus aureus* causes boils. *Vibrio comma* causes asiatic cholera,*Mycobacterium tuberculosis* causes tuberculosis, *Corynebacterium diptheriae* causes diptheria, *Salmonella typhosa* causes typhoid fever, *Heamophilius pertusis* causes whooping cough, *Pastuerella pestis* causes plague, *Pseudomonas solanacearum* causes bacterial wilt of tomato and brown rot of potato, *Xanthomonas citri* causes citrus canker, *Erwinia amylovora* causes fireblight of apples and pears and *Xanthomonas malvacerarum* causes angular leaf spot of cotton.

DISEASES CAUSED BY BACTERIA

In Plants

Name of disease and host	*Causal organisms*
Wilt of potato	*Pseudomonas solanacearum*
Wilt of tomato	*Pseudomonas solanacearum*
Wilt of tobacco	*Pseudomonas solanacearum*
Wilt of pepper	*Pseudomonas solanacearum*
Blight of beans	*Xanthomonas phaseoli*
Black rot of crucifers	*Xanthomonas campestris*
Citrus canker	*Xanthomonas citri*
Ring rot of potato	*Corynebacterium sepedonicum*
Canker of tomato	*Corynebacterium michiganese*
Crown gall of *Rubus* spp.	*Agrobacterium tumefaciens*
Crown gall of apple	*Agrobacterium tumefaciens*
Crown gall of rose	*Agrobacterium tumefaciens*
Crown gall of tomato	*Agrobacterium tumefaciens*
Scab of potato	*Streptomyces scabies*
Fire blight of apple and pear	*Erwinia amylovora*
Soft rot of vegetables	*Erwinia carotovora*
Wilt of cucurbits	*Erwinia tracheiphila*

In Man and Animals

Name of disease	*Causal organisms*
Cholera	*Vibrio cholerae*
Rat-bite fever	*Spirillum minus*
Enteritis in the intestine	*Escherichia coli*
Urinogenital infections	*Klebsiella* spp.
Wound infections	*Proteus* spp.
Enteric fever	*Salmonella* spp.
Bacillary dysentery	*Shigella* spp.
T.B.	*Mycobacterium tuberculosis*
Plague	*Pasteurella pestis*
Whooping cough	*Bordetella* spp.
Undulant fever	*Brucella* spp.
Influenza	*Haemophilis influenzae*
Abscesses	*Staphylococcus*
Gonorrhoea	*Neisseria gonorrhoeae*
Meningitis	*Neissaria meningitides*
Diphtheria	*Corynebacterium diphtheriae*
Pneumonia	*Diplococcus pneumoniae*
Tetanus	*Clostridium tetani*
Anthrax	*Bacillus anthracis*

2. **Food spoilage.** Some saprophytic bacteria grow on unprotected foodstuffs like fruits,

pickles, jams, jellies, bread etc., and spoil them by causing decay. The use of salt, sugar and oil etc., in preservation of pickles and jams, checks the growth of such bacteria. *Clostridium botulinum* produces a very virulent poison in canned foods and many deaths occur due to it.

3. Loss of fertility. Anaerobic bacteria such as *Bacillus denitrificans* reduce the nitrates of the poorly aerated soil to nitrites and then to ammonium compounds, and free nitrogen is liberated. Thus the amount of readily available nitrogen goes to the atmosphere. They are known as denitrifying bacteria.

MYCOPLASMA

(PPLO-Pleuropneumonia like organisms and L-forms)

It has been established now that smallest cell, or free living organisms, is not a bacterium, it is so minute and could not be seen except through an electron microscope. Louis Pasteur

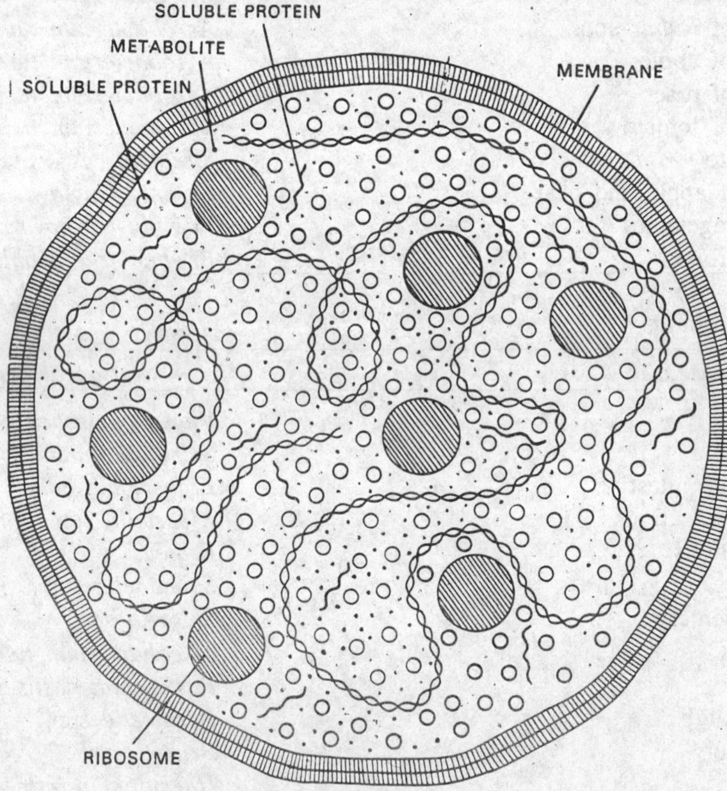

Fig. 22.31. Mycoplasma. Electron micrograph of *Mycoplasma* cell.

discovered the existence of this organism, which is the causative agent of pleuropneumonia, a contagious disease of cattle. But Pasteur could not isolate, culture or see it under a microscope because it was too small. There are several kinds of this organism, but the smallest is about 0.1 micron in diameter and is known as PPLO (Pleuropneumonia like organisms) or *Mycoplasma*. In size these cells are like viruses in that they can pass through a fine-pored filter; then can however, grow in a nonliving medium, as do bacteria. Their internal organization is also bacteria-like. They contain plasma membrane, ribosomes, complete metabolic machinery with some 40

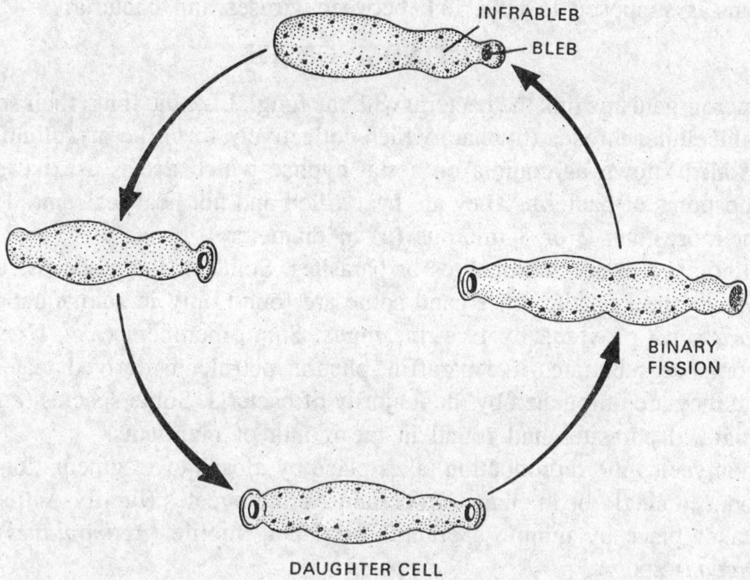

Fig. 22.32. Mycoplasma. Binary fission in *Mycoplasma gallisepticum.*

known enzymes and an ill-defined nuclear apparatus lacking a nuclear membrane.

Mycoplasma and Plant Pathology

Mycoplasma is a new discovery in plant pathology. Before 1967 this was thought that plant diseases were caused by fungi, bacteria, nematodes and viruses. However, in 1967 a team of Japanese workers proved that the plant diseases under the *yellow* group of viruses have been caused by *Mycoplasma,* which possess different characteristics from those of viruses.

For the first time in 1898, Nocard and Roux had discovered *Mycoplasma* as a disease incitant in animals. They also recorded that mycoplasma was similar to virus in size and could be grown in artificial culture. *Mycoplasma mycoides* (causal agent of pneumonia) was cultured by that time.

As mentioned above, mycoplasma causes *yellow* disease in plants. Since 1967 most of the plant diseases of yellow group have been reported to be caused by mycoplasma. Some important mycoplasma diseases occurring in this country have been reported from Indian Agricultural Research Institute, New Delhi. These diseases are: **Little leaf of brinjal; Citrus greening; Sandal spike; Grassy shoot of sugarcane; Rice yellow dwarf; Cotton little leaf** or **Cotton stenosis; Sesamum phyllody** and some others.

Mycoplasma has been isolated in pure cultures from insects, diseased mammals and infected plants. **Mycoplasma is** grown in highly specific culture medium containing sterol.

The **mycoplasma is non**-motile, gram-negative and contains both DNA and RNA. The respective cells of mycoplasma remain surrounded by proteinaceous membranes. Mycoplasma reproduces by budding and binary fission. Mycoplasma varies in its shape. The spherical forms measure 80-150mμ. The pleomorphic forms measure 210-435mμ and the large pleomorphic forms measure upto 1000mμ. The filamentous forms with branching structures have also been reported.

The mycoplasma structures also known as **pleuropneumonia like organisms** (PPLO) or **mycoplasma-like organisms (MLO),** were discovered in the phloem of plants infected with aster yellows and certain other yellow-type diseases. This group of very small, bacteria like microoraganisms is supposed to be a link between viruses and bacteria.

ACTINOMYCETES

These microorganisms link the bacteria with the fungi. Like the fungi their somatic structure consists of multicellular threads (hyphae) which collectively form the mycelium. They produce asexual spores also known as conidia on aerial hyphae which act as asexual spores of fungi and unlike endospores of bacteria. They are heat killed and not heat resistant. Their spores and cells are never more than 2 or 3 microns (μ) in diameter.

The Actinomycetes are saprophytes or parasites. Some of them successfully live in soil (*e.g., Streptomyces* spp.) on the other hand some are found only in semiaquatic habitats (*e.g., Micromonospora* spp.) provided by lacatrine muds. Some members (*e.g., Nocardia* spp.) are known to decompose substrates like paraffin, phenol, petroleum derived materials which are so resistant that they are untouched by the majority of bacteria. Some species (*e.g., Actinomyces* spp.) are specialized parasites and found in the mouth of mammals.

In Actinomycetes the reproduction takes place by means of fragmentation of the hyphae, by conidia produced singly or in chains. In certain Actinomycetes (family-Actinoplanaceae) the reproduction takes place by minute sporangia producing motile (*Actinoplanes*) or non-motile (*Streptosporangium*) spores.

Antibiotics. The genus *Streptomyces* of this group is most important, some species of which produce antibiotic substances of great medicinal value like streptomycin, chlorotetracycline, oxytetracycline, tetracyline, chloramphenicol and erythromycin.

CYANOBACTERIA

There are two main patterns of cellular organization–*prokaryotic* and *eukaryotic*. On the prokaryotic side, there are diverse forms of bacteria and a group generally termed *blue-green algae*. The term algae was applied to these organisms on the basis of their photosynthetic activities before their structural relationship to bacteria was uncovered with the electron microscope; they are, more properly referred to as *blue-green bacteria* or *cyanobacteria*. The cyanobacteria have been included in Volume 3 of Bergey's Manual. According to Bergey's classification they are *oxygenic phototrophic bacteria*.

In cyanobacteria their nuclear material deoxyribo-nucleic acid (DNA), is not delimited from the remainder of the protoplasm by a nuclear membrane, but rather it is dispersed to some degree throughout the cell. The membrane bounded plastids are absent. Large aqueous vacuoles, like those which occur in many green algae are absent from the cells of cyanobacteria or blue-green algae. The cell walls of cyanobacteria show some chemical similarity to those of bacteria. Certain cyanobacteria may be infected with viruses which resemble bacteriophages advocates further similarity, between cyanobacteria and bacteria.

Characteristic Features of Cyanobacteria

1. They are omnipresent, and occur in all possible kinds of habitats.
2. The pigments found in this group are–chlorophyll *a*, β–carotene, Antheraxanthin, Aphanicin, Aphanizophyll, Flavacin, Lutein, Myxoxanthophyll, Oscilloxanthin, Zeaxanthin, Allophycocyanin, Phycocyanin, Phycoerythrin.
3. The storage products are cyanophycean starch and protein.
4. The flagella are absent.
5. They may be unicellular (*e.g., Chroococcus, Tetrapedia, Gloeocapsa*), colonial (*e.g., Aphanocapsa, Nostoc, Aphanothece*) and filamentous (*e.g., Oscillatoria*).

6. The filaments are called trichomes which are generally surrounded by a sheath.

7. Some cyanobacteria live in symbiotic association with other organisms.

8. Many members have the ability to fix the atmospheric nitrogen in the soil.

9. They form a thick stratum on the surface of saline *usar* soils during the rainy season, and can be of use in the reclamation of *usar* lands.

10. In many cases thick walled, sperhical *heterocysts* are found.

11. In some cases the cells of filamentous genera accumulate much of food, become thick walled and called the *akinetes* which face the adverse conditions.

12. They may reproduce asexually by endospore, (*e.g., Dermocapsa*) and exospores (*e.g., Chamaesiphon*).

13. The trichomes of *Oscillatoria* show oscillating movement. In some other cases the trichomes move forward and back within the sheath, such movement is called gliding movement.

14. Some cyanoabacteria live in symbiotic association with protozoans and are called **cyanellae.**

The common examples of cyanobacteria are–*Nostoc, Oscillatoria, Anabanea, Gloeocapsa. Chroococcus, Cylindrospermum, Gloeotrichia, Rivularia* and several others.

23
Viruses

Historical. The **virus** comes from Latin language and means poison. This use of the word goes back to many hundreds of years, long before any one really knew what a virus was, or that it even existed as we know it today. It was generally believed that these 'viruses', or poisons, were carried in the night air and could cause many unexplained diseases. In 1770, a virus disease 'leaf roll' of potato was observed for the first time in England. In 1785, the same disease was reported from Germany. Virus diseases of plants have been described for many years. "Breaking" of tulips, which is now known to be a virus disease was first as early as 1576. Degeneration of potatoes was known in Europe reported in the eighteenth century. Tobacco mosaic virus was recognized by Swieten in Holland in 1887. Adloph Mayer a Dutch investigator working with this disease in Holland was first to point out in 1886 that it was readily transmissible and infectious. Iwanowski a Russain investigator (1892), demonstrated that tobacco mosaic virus would pass through a bacteria proof filter and thereby he distinguished this type of infectious agency from bacteria and from fungi.

This work was confirmed by Beizerink in 1898, who showed further that tobacco mosaic virus will diffuse through an agar agar layer suggested that it was a *"contagium vivum fluidium"*. In 1898, Loeffler and Frosch were the first to show virus of animal origin to be filterable when they demonstrated that the foot and mouth disease of cattle was incited by an entity which passed through bacteria proof filter. Pasteur (1876), investigated a virus disease of insect called 'flacherie'. The 'Sirah' disease of sugarcane caused by a virus was observed in Jawa in 1882, and the methods of its control were also investigated. Mosaic disease of sugarcane, which was then known as 'yellow stripe' disease was also discovered in Jawa in 1890. In 1887, the 'mosaic' of tomato was observed in England, and the disease was studied in detail in America. Mayer (1886), discovered tobacco 'mosaic' in north Europe. He proved that this disease can be transmitted to healthy plants by mechanical means. Iwanowsky (1892), discovered the first virus and thought it to be the small bacterium causing tobacco mosaic. Beijerinck (1898), discarded the Iwanowsky's statement and proposed his theory of *contagium vivum fludium.* In the same year Loeffler and Frosch discovered the animal viruses. In 1901, Takami of Japan, transmitted the dwarf or stunt disease of paddy by an insect *Nephotettix apicalis,* and it was known for the first time that viruses could be transmitted by insects. Hunger (1905) and Freiberg (1917), suggested that the virus diseases were caused by enzymes. Ray Nelson (1923) suggested that a protozoa is responsible for 'bean mosaic'. Later he suggested the causal agent a coccus (a bacterium). Eckerson (1926) suggested the causal agents of 'tomato mosaic' are certain motile micro-organisms. For the first time in 1935, W.M. Stanley isolated the 'Tobacco Mosaic Virus' in paracrystalline form. Green (1935) and Laidlaw (1938) independently put forward the theory that viruses are obligate parasites which have developed parasitism to the highest degree. Bawden and Pirie (1938) isolated a fully crystalline form of the tomato bushy stunt virus. Stanley (1936) and Northrop (1938) suggested that the viruses are autocatalysts and multiply in susceptible cells by activating previously formed inactive precursors. Woods and Du Buy (1943) suggested that plant viruses may have arisen from mitochondria and their derivatives. According to Darlington (1944), the viruses are derived from cell proteins. In his view these undifferentiated proteins may come to acquire the properties of infection.

The discovery of the relationship between viruses and insects was not made in a day and a period of years elapsed between the time when insects were first suspected to transmitting plant viruses and the actual demonstration of this method of transmission. The first to prove experimentally the relationship between an insect and a plant virus seems to have been a Japanese farmer, Hashimoto, who worked in 1894 with the dwarf disease of rice and the leaf hopper *Nephotettix apicalis* var. *cincticeps*. About 1907, three workers in America, Ball, Adams and Shaw suggested that there was some connection between curly top of sugarbeet and the leaf hopper *Eutettix tenella*. Some years later, Smith and Boncquet (1915) confirmed this and showed that a single insect from an infected plant placed on a healthy plant for 5 minutes would produce the disease. The original criterion of a virus was an infectious entity that could pass through a filter with a pore size small enough to hold back all known cellular agents of diseases. However, diseases were soon found that had virus like symptoms not associated with any pathogen visible in the light microscope, but which could not be transmitted by mechanical inoculation. With such disease, the criterion of filterability could not be applied. The infectious nature was established by graft transmission and sometimes by insect vectors. Thus, it came about that certain diseases of the yellows and witches broom type such as aster yellows, came to be considered as due to viruses on quite inadequate grounds. Only very recently, critical examination by electron microscopy and the use of inhibitory drugs have been strong indications that a number of so called virus diseases are really caused by mycoplasma like agents (Doi *et al*, 1967).

During most of the period between 1900 and 1935 attention was focussed on description of diseases. Ineffective attempts were made to refine filtration methods in order to define the size of viruses more closely. There were almost the only aspects of virus diseases that could be studied with the techniques that were available. The influence of various physical and chemical agents on virus infectivity was investigated but methods for assay of infective material were not refined. Holmes (1929) showed the local lesions produced in some hosts following mechanical inoculation could be used for the rapid quantitative assay of infective virus. This technique enabled properties of viruses to be studied much more readily and paved the way for the isolation and purification of viruses a few years later.

In 1926 the first enzyme urease was isolated, crystallised and identified as a protein (Sumner, 1926). The isolation of others soon followed. In the early 1930's workers in various countries began attempting to isolate and purify plant viruses using methods similar to those that had been used for enzymes. Following detailed chemical studies suggesting that the infectious agent of TMV might be protein, Stanley (1935) announced the isolation of this virus in an apparently crystalline form. At first Stanley (1935, 1936) considered that the virus was a globulin containing no phosphorus. Bawden *et al* (1936) described the isolation from TMV infected plants of liquid crystalline nucleoprotein containing nucleic acid of the pentose type. The present concept of the virus particle is that it consists of a protein shell within which is contained a nucleic acid molecule which by its own structure and coding property determined the arrangement of the amino acid sequences in the subunits of the protein cell. The nucleic acid is also the infective agent which as it passes into a healthy cell, dictates a change in the protein metabolism which results in the build up of virus protein usually at the expense of the normal protein.

Introduction. When Louis Pasteur (1822-1895) and Robert Koch (1843-1910) discovered that microbes were the cause of many diseases, they opened up a new field of experiment and research. The word 'virus' which, before their discoveries, was applied to any poisonous substance came to be used for all kinds of infection agents.

As research progressed further, it was found that certain agents were so fine that they could pass through specially designed filters which did not allow even bacteria and other known microorganisms to pass through. Some scientists, unable to conceive their extreme minuteness, hazarded the opinion that these agents were contagious fluids and did not consist of discrete organisms. Finally, when it was established that they consisted of sub-microscopic organisms, organisms which were invisible to the most powerful microscopes of the conventional type, the term virus was restricted to apply only to these 'filter-passing' or filterable sub-micro-organisms.

It was the invention of electron microscope in recent years that has enabled these tiniest of organisms to be identified and photographed. The best of the light microscopes can magnify an object 2,000 times its original size. But the electron microscope gives a direct magnification of 10,000 and can enlarge photographically up to 200,000.

Some of the diseases caused by viruses have been known for a long time. Small-pox for instance, has been known for ages and has caused innumerable deaths. Even in these days it is responsible for thousands of deaths every year. But the nature and cause of these diseases have been understood only recently.

The behaviour of viruses has been a matter of great surprise and speculation; they possess certain characteristics of inorganic substances and they also behave like living organisms. This has led scientists to call them the missing links between dead and living matter.

In 1935, W. M. Stanley, an American biochemist, isolated the tobacco, mosaic virus and was surprised to find that it had all the properties of a crystalline solid. Its chemical constitution lent itself to analysis and produced regular shaped crystals like many chemical salts. In its isolated condition it was incapable of reproduction which is typical of all living organisms. Thus it was not alive in the accepted sense of the word. But as soon as it was brought into contact with a healthy tobacco leaf, it appeared to spring into life, flourishing and multiplying like any primitive living thing.

Chemically, viruses consist of nucleoproteins–a combination of nucleic acid and protein-essential constituents of living matter. The more complex viruses contain some fats in addition. Their extreme simplicity leads one to hope that some day it may be possible to produce them in the laboratory if only for the purpose of producing vaccines.

There are a number of diseases caused by virus infection. Some of these are small-pox, measles, mumps, yellow fever, poliomycilitis (infantile paralysis), usually called polio, chicken pox, rabies, and influenza. It is believed that even common cold is caused by virus infection. In addition there are a number of animal and plant diseases caused by viruses.

The control of virus diseases at present is not adequate. Usually viruses are not affected by antibiotics. It is easier to control pneumonia than the common cold. Viruses can mutate just like other living organisms. By mutation is meant a sudden variation in some well-marked character. This gives rise to new types of viruses. The sudden outbreaks of some epidemics in unexpectedly virulent forms is attributed to such mutations. Naturally it takes some time before the new character is studied and brought under control. The deadly influenza epidemic of 1918 has been cited as a possible example.

Definition. According to Green (1935), 'that they are the smallest units showing the reproductive property considered typical of life.'

Stanely (1938) says, *"We are forced to conclude therefore, that although tobacco mosaic virus (T.M.V.) protein has the ordinary properties of molecules, it also has the ability to reproduce and to mutate, properties not ordinarily ascribed to molecules and hence that T.M.V. protein represents an entity unfamiliar to us."*

The most accepted definition proposed by Bawden (1943), *"the virus is on obligatory parasitic pathogen with at least one dimension of less than 200 millimicrons mμ)."*

Characteristic features. 1. All the viruses are ultramicroscopic.

2. All viruses are obligatory intracellular parasites.

3. The viruses cannot be grown in artificial media in any case and the living cell seems essential for multiplication of viruses.

4. They are crystalline nucleo-proteins of very high molecular weight.

Nature of virus. Viruses are so small that they can not be seen even with the highest magnification of the microscope using visible light. They are recognizable only by their biological behaviour, such as, by the disease they cause. Their exact nature was a mystery for long. They were variously regarded as invisible form of bacteria, protozoa, enzymes, toxins or as unusual products of metabolism of the cells in which they were found. An American biochemist, Stanley in 1935, however isolated by chemical means from the diseased tobacco leaves a material which appeared to be a protein of high molecular weight. He studied this material in detail, and found that it possessed all the properties of a tobacco mosaic virus, which has already been discovered. There are a number of direct, indirect and circumstantial.evidences to show that the material itself is the virus. Stanley, on the basis of the chemical properties, identified the material as **autocatalytic proteins** which can multiply within a living cell only. Bawden purified the tobacco mosaic virus, and found it to be a crystalline nucleo-protein of very high molecular weight, retaining its infectivity even when diluted to a concentration of 1/1,000,000. This virus when examined with the recently developed electron microscope using X-rays, is found to be in the form of bundles of rod-like protein. Such nucleoprotein can not be obtained from healthy plants and is the virus itself. In 1938 the study of potato virus confirmed this. Since then, proteins of high molecular weight possessing all the properties of the respective viruses have been isolated and studied.

Most of the viruses are crystalline and rod-like, but different in size. Tobacco mosaic virus is rod-like in shape, 280 mμ in length and 18 mμ in breadth. 'Bushy stunt' virus of tomato is 274 mμ in diameter and its molecular weight is 8,800,000-12,800,000. Stanley studied the nucleo-proteins of the 'ring spot' virus of tobacco. The virus is rounded with 19 mμ diameter and 3,400,000 molecular weight. Tobacco 'necrosis' virus is smallest of all the plant viruses known so far. It is rounded with 13-20 mμ diameter.

Before 1935 they were believed to be living on the basis of few following properties:

1. That they can live only in a living cell.
2. They can infect healthy plants just like bacteria and fungi.
3. They multiply in number and grow in size, as the living organisms reproduce and grow.
4. They have physiologic specialization in relation to the insect vectors and the plants.
5. They respond to stimuli, such as acids, alkalies, light and temperature.

The supporters of the non-living nature of viruses based their views on the following few properties:

1. They are too small to be observed under visible light.
2. They retain infectivity even in very low concentrations.
3. They can be crystallized like a chemical substance.
4. They can be sedimented like proteins.
5. They can be precipitated by a number of chemical substances.
6. They retain the power of infection even after 31 years in non-living tobacco leaves.

Some workers did not agree with any of the above extreme views and adopted a middle course. They regarded viruses, representing a stage in between living and non-living with the acquired property of multiplication.

At present most of the virologists have agreed that viruses are nucleo-proteins of high molecular weight and have the power of multiplication.

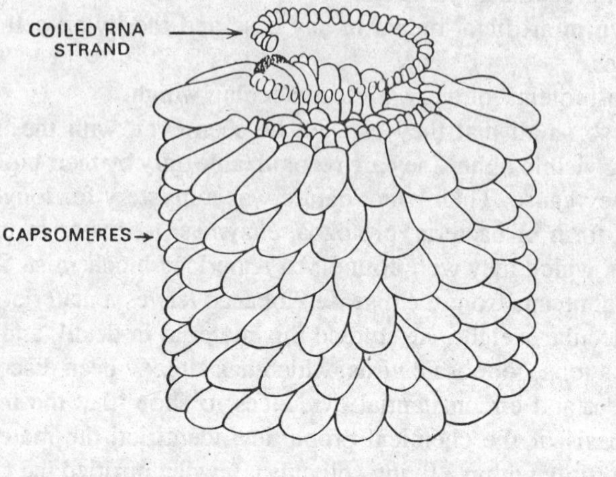

Fig. 23.1. Virus. Structure of tobacco mosaic virus (T.M.V.) a portion of rod of tobacco mosaic virus showing RNA core and protein sheath.

Plant viruses. Plant viruses occur either as spheres or elongated rods. In both cases there is some sort of a ribonucleic acid RNA core surrounded by a protein sheath. The rod forms of tobacco mosaic also contain a central core of RNA as shown in the figure. The elongated rod of tobacco mosaic virus is twisted into uniform spiral to form what appears, in gross form, as a hollow rod.

The life-cycle of a plant virus. There is an incubation period in the body of an insect after it picks up virus particles from an infected plant. There also appears to be an incubation period in the plant cell after its infection with virus particles. Infection may be with viral RNA or with whole virus particles, but in the case of plant body it is always in the form of RNA. The changes of viral RNA reduce or change the

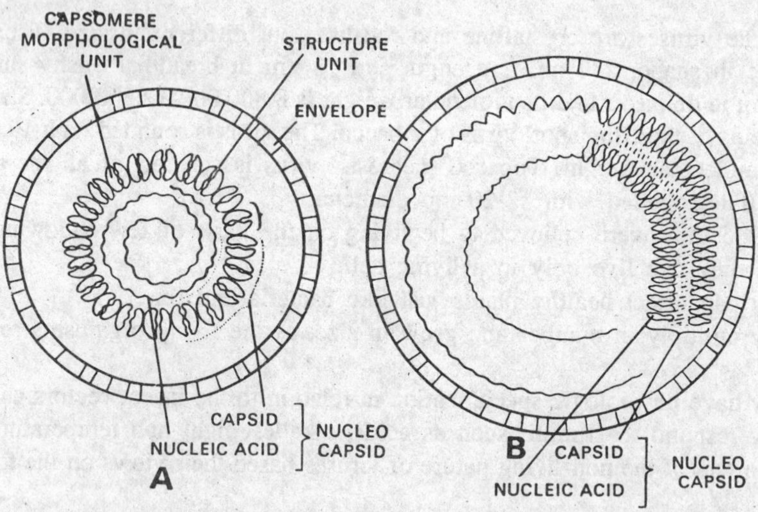

Fig. 23.2. Virus. Diagram showing detailed structure of virus particle.

course of viral infection. There is some evidence that RNA appears in the host nucleus before it appears in the host cytoplasm and that viral RNA is elaborated by the host cytoplasm before the viral protein is formed. The replication of the viral RNA is indeed somewhat of an enigma because current ideas of RNA application and protein synthesis are generally related to information carried in the deoxyribonucleic acid DNA molecule.

Viruses may be divided into three main classes according to the nature of their hosts: Plant viruses, Animal viruses and Bacterial Viruses.

The important plant viruses are Tobacco mosaic virus, Tobacco satellite virus, Turnip yellow mosaic, Rugose mosaic virus. Generally all crystallized plant viruses have been found to consist mainly of ribonucleoproteins.

TMV is the extensively studied virus in plants, discovered by Iwanowski (1892) and obtained in pure state by Stanley (1935). It has a helical symmetry. Tobacco mosaic virus is a cylindrical structure with a molecular weight of 40 millions and dimensions of 160 × 3000 A°. Extensive structural studies of the virus–through X-ray diffraction, electron microscopy at various stages of dissociation, solubility properties as well as studies of the separate protein and RNA components, have yielded the following remarkably detailed and precise model of the virus particle.

The protein coat of the virus consists of 2130 identical protein subunits each with a molecular weight of 18,000. The subunit is composed of a single chain of 158 amino acids of known sequence, the folding of the chain produces an ellipsoid with an axial rotation of 3:1. The RNA of the virus is a single strand of molecular weight of 2.4 million consisting of 6500 nucleotides. The RNA strand forms a helix with a radius of 40 A^0 that is embedded in a helix (radius $85A^0$) of identical pitch ($23A^0$) formed by the protein subunits. Down the middle of the molecule runs a cylindrical hole with a radius of 20 A^0 that can be seen in the electron microscope if special staining technique with phosphotungstate is used.

Animal viruses. Some important animal viruses are Influenza virus, Mumps, Pox virus, Reo virus etc. In structure Influenza virus differs from TMV in that instead of being straight rigid particles, they are apparently more flexible and form loose coils. A further characteristic is that the coils are enclosed in an envelope, the outside surface of which is covered with minute protein particles probably involved in attaching the virus to the surface of host cells.

Bacterial viruses. Viruses attacking bacteria are known as bacteriophages or phages. These are tadpole like in shape T_4 phage attacking the bacterium *Escherichia coli,* is among the most complex of viruses. It consists of a head and a rather complicated tail. The shape of the head has been described as an elongated icosahedron having a length of 1250 A^0 and width of 850 A^0. The major protein of the phage makes up the head membrane or head envelope which is constructed of some 2000 similar subunits. Attached to one of the points of the head, through a neck and collar, is the tail. The naked tail consists of a distal hexagonal base plate attached to an inner hollow cylinder, called the core, through which DNA passes on its way into the host cell. Around the core are the 144 subunits of the contractile sheath also arranged in a hollow cylinder consisting of 24 rays of six subunits each. Joined to the apices of the base plates are six short spikes and six long (1300 A^0) kinked tail fibres. Encapsulated in each head envelope is a linear double stranded DNA molecule, the genetic material of the phage which is 53 μ by 2. The basic problems of virus replication can be put simply, the virus must somehow induce a living cell to make more of the essential components of the virus particle, these components must be assembled in the proper order and the new virus particle must escape from the cell if they are to infect other cells. The various phases of this replication process can be summarized in six stages.

(1) Attachment (adsorption) of virus particle to sensitive cells, (2) penetration into cell of virus nucleic acid, (3) of its replication of the virus nucleic acid, (4) production of protein capsomeres and other essential viral constituents, (5) assembly of nucleic acid and protein capsomeres into new virus particles, (6) release of mature virus particles from the cell.

Properties of viruses. Properties of various plant viruses have been studied in detail. Since the development of virology (science of viruses), tobacco mosaic virus has been the main source for investigations, and most of the virus properties described below are based on it.

1. Viruses are highly infectious. Bawden working on tobacco mosaic virus found it to be infectious even in 1/1,000,000 dilution.

2. Viruses are highly resistant to acids, alkalies and salts. Tobacco mosaic virus is affected by hydrochloric and nitric acids only when 1 gm. of acid is added to 100 c.c. virus solution. They are more affected by alkalies, such as sodium hydroxide and sodium carbonate. Salts like sodium chloride, silver nitrate, and mercuric chloride however do not affect them much, 1gm. copper sulphate in 100 c.c. virus solution, and 4% formaldehyde solution destroy tobacco mosaic virus completely. According to Vinson, acetone and alcohol have no effect on viruses at low temperatures.

3. Viruses are resistant to high temperatures. Tobacco mosaic virus can infect healthy plant even after being kept at 80°C for two days. However, it loses its power of infection within 10 minutes at 85°C–90°C temperatures.

4. Direct sunlight has no effect on viruses. Tobacco mosaic virus is not affected by X-rays and mercury vapours, till the exposures do not exceed half an hour and one hour respectively.

5. Viruses can be filtered through **Brefeld** and **Chamberlain** filters, but according to Mulvania, they can be filtered through collodian membrane also.

6. Viruses can retain the power of infection for long periods., even out of the living cells. Tobacco mosaic virus retains its infectivity in extracted cell sap for 5 years (Dickson, 1925) and according to Valleau and Johns, it remains infectious in dried tobacco leaves for 31 years.

7. Vinson and Petre precipitated viruses with the solution of safranin solution, acetone and ethyl alcohol. The precipitate obtained by safranin solution, has no power of infection but it regains it when ethyl alcohol is added to the precipitate.

8. When the cell-sap contaminated with virus is subjected to a high speed centrifuge, viruses get sedimented like proteins.

9. Viruses increase in number and size within the living protoplasm of cell.

10. They can be transmitted from infected plant to a healthy plant by mechanical and biological means.

11. Insects which transmit viruses are known as vectors. A particular virus can be transmitted only by a particular species of insect and on a definite species of host. This sort of selection of the vector and the host is known as **physiologic specialization.**

The general properties described above are more or less common and the differences are of degree only.

Transmission of viruses. Viruses are transferred from infected plants to healthy ones by a number of agencies described below, and this is known as **transmission** of viruses.

1. **By grafting.** A large number of plants are vegetatively propagated. Grafting is the most common method used in propagating fruit and ornamental plants. When an infected plant is used for grafting with a healthy plant, the virus is transmitted through the cell solutions flowing from the infected part into the healthy parts.

2. **By seeds.** Seed transmission of viruses is not common. Mosaic viruses of cucurbits and legumes are transmitted by seeds. But in the crops which are vegetatively propagated by the use of setts, tubers, rhizomes, bulbs, and corms etc., viruses are transmitted by these organs.

3. **By contact.** Viruses can be transmitted merely by contact or slight rubbing of the infected and healthy plant organs. Such transmission is quite easy in a thickly populated field where one plant is always in close contact with the other and even the slightest movement of the wind can help in rubbing the organs of one with the other. Viruses usually gain entry through

the injuries caused on the plant surfaces.

4. **By air and water.** Unlike fungi and bacteria viruses are not easily transmitted by air and water. The tobacco necrosis virus has been observed to be transmitted by both air and water.

5. **By soil.** Tobacco mosaic virus lies in the soil with the plant debris after the harvest of the crop, and infects the new crop, when sown in the same field.

6. **By tools and agricultural operations.** At the time of agricultural operations such as topping, pruning, weeding, rogueing or irrigation, the agricultural tools and the hands of the worker may get contaminated by the juice of an infected plant if it gets injured. These tools and the hands of the workers transfer the viruses to the healthy plants, the contact with which cannot be avoided ordinarily.

7. **By smokers.** Tobacco mosaic virus remains infective in dry tobacco leaves for as long as 31 years. This virus is very resistant to high temperatures. It can spread by the fingers of the smokers, by the smoke and the unburnt pieces of cigarettes, cigars and biris. Tobacco chewers sputum can also transmit virus if it is there in the tobacco leaves.

8. **By store house.** Viruses, such as tobacco mosaic virus is transmitted to the new stock of tobacco, when it is stored in the same store house, where the infected leaves were stored.

9. **By insects.** In nature, viruses are ordinarily transmitted by aphids, jassids and white flies which are the sucking insects. Most of the crop diseases viruses are transmitted by insects, and for this simple reason some virologists believe that there would have been no virus diseases if there were no insects. One virus can be transmitted by several species of insects and *vice versa.*

Insect vectors taking part in transmission, first suck juice from the infected plant. Now if it visits a healthy plant, the virus may be transferred and the new plant becomes infected. But in some cases a vector fails to infect a healthy plant soon after it has fed upon a diseased plant but it can infect the plant after some time. This period taken by the virus in developing infectivity within the vector is known as **incubation period.** Incubation period is different for different viruses and varies from hours to days. In such cases the insect vectors act as alternate hosts, in which the viruses undergo some changes before infecting the real or say, the primary host.

All the insect vectors cannot transmit different viruses indiscriminately. Curly top virus of beet-root is transmitted only by a leaf hopper *Eutettix tenellus,* and cannot be transmitted by any other sucking insects found on beet-root leaves. Mosaic virus of beet-root is transmitted only by 'peach aphid'. Stunt virus of paddy is transmitted only by a leaf hopper *Nephotettix apicalis.* From the plants, simultaneously infected with a mixture of tobacco mosaic and cucumber mosaic viruses, only tobacco mosaic virus is transmitted by needle prick, whereas cucumber mosaic virus is transmitted by aphids alone.

The above-mentioned examples show that there exists some close relationship between the virus and its insect vector. Though this relationship is not properly understood in some cases, it is not very difficult to comment upon it. All the species of insect vectors differ to a lesser or greater extent in their habit, morphology, anatomy and physiology. An insect which feeds on the pollen grains will not suck the sap, and one feeding on the leaves may not feed on the stems, or other organs. Viruses are sometimes present only in the cells of deeper tissues and as such they can be sucked up only by the insects having long proboscis. Surface feeders cannot transmit such viruses. Similarly the vectors feeding on the deeper tissues do not feed on the surface tissues.

In case, where there is a definite incubation period, the virus passes through the entire alimentary canal and coelome of the vector, then enters into the salivery glands and can go out with the saliva through the proboscis of the insect when it punctures into the host tissue. In passing through this long way it has to come in contact with several intestinal secretions. Some viruses multiply and grow while passing through the body of the vectors and others pass out as such without undergoing any change. Such viruses are favoured by the physiological activities of the vectors and pass out of it, retaining their infectivity. Physiological activities of a particular vector cannot suit all the viruses and therefore this differential adaptation of viruses to the vector is also related with the transmission of a particular virus and the reason for this is also related to their physiological behaviour.

Viruses can be recognized easily by the symptoms they produce on the host. Sometimes the same virus can cause widely different symptoms on different host plants, and the symptoms may vary in the same plant according to its age, nutrition and other environmental factors. Symptoms may sometimes be produced by a mixture of two or more viruses on the same plant. A few more common and easily detectable symptoms are given here:

1. **Chlorosis.** Due to the presence of viruses the chlorophyll of the green organs disappears at places, leaving yellowish spots, this is known as chlorosis. The presence of yellow spot at places, in the green tissue appears like a 'mosaic' pattern and therefore, the diseases with such symptoms are known as 'mosaic' diseases.

2. **Yellows.** When the chlorophyll disappears completely from the host tissue, the organs turn yellow and the symptom is knowm as 'yellows'.

3. **Vein clearing and vein banding.** The disappearance of chlorophyll along the veins of the leaves is known as **vein clearing** and when chlorophyll surrounding the veins disappears the symptom is known as **vein banding.**

4. **Necrosis.** The brownish spots due to the death and ultimate drying of the tissue are known as necrotic spots and the phenomenon is known as necrosis. Necrotic spots are also known as lesions.

Ring spots, bunchy top, galls, hypertrophy, atrophy, rolling, curling, crinkling of leaves, stunting and dwarfing of plants are various other symptoms usually produced on the hosts by viruses.

Control. The easy methods of preventing disease spread and losses due to them are as follows :

1. **Eradication.** The destruction of infected plants and susceptible weeds, lessen the possibilities of the spread of disease.

2. **Elimination of insects.** The use of insecticidal dusts and sprays reduces the chances of insect transmission.

3. **Selection of seeds.** It should be made from such fields which were free from infection. Seeds of cucurbits and legumes, setts of sugarcane, tubers, rhizomes and bulbs etc., should be carefully selected for seed purposes.

4. **Tuber indexing.** It is done at the time of digging potatoes. Tubers taken from healthy plants are marked with ink and sown in small insect proof plots. The suspected diseased plants are removed carefully leaving only the healthy plants to grow. Thus the healthy seed is multiplied.

5. **Resistant varieties.** They are evolved at various research centres, and offer the best method for growing healthy crops.

Tobacco Mosaic Virus (TMV)

Symptoms. On the younger leaves of tobacco plants the veins may show a clearing and later this may be followed by mottling. As the leaves enlarge, abnormally dark green spots appear which develop into irregular crumpled blister-areas while the remainder of the tissue becomes more and more chlorotic. Plants are stunted in various degrees. The diseases characterized by mottling or variegation of leaves are referred to as 'mosaics'.

The virus. Typical tobacco mosaic virus.
Tobacco virus I.
Nicotiana virus 1 K.M. Smith.
Marmor tabaci Holmes.

The rod forms as illustrated by tobacco mosaic contain a central core of RNA, this elongated rod is twisted into a uniform spiral to form, in gross form, as a hollow rod. The RNA core

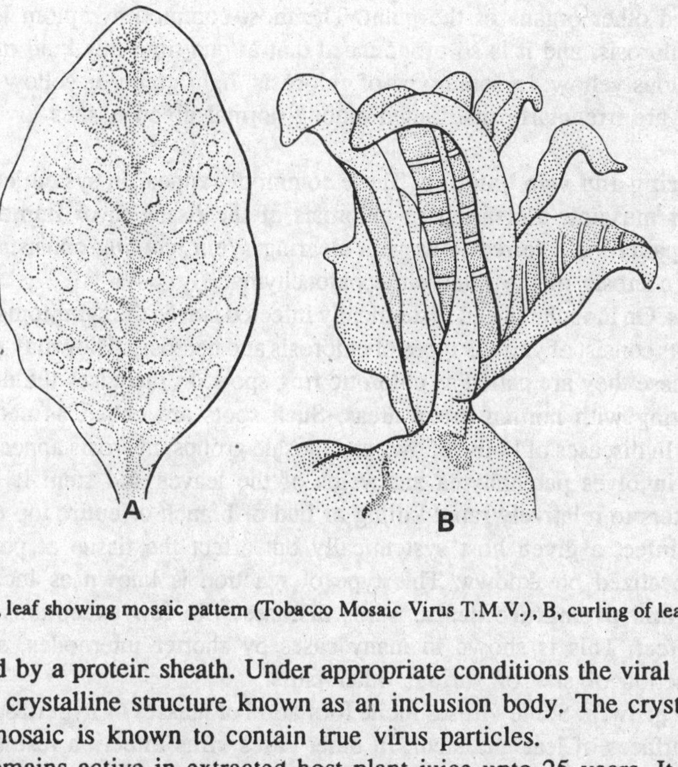

Fig. 23.3. Virus. A, leaf showing mosaic pattern (Tobacco Mosaic Virus T.M.V.), B, curling of leaves of tobacco.

remains surrounded by a protein sheath. Under appropriate conditions the viral particles induce the formation of a crystalline structure known as an inclusion body. The crystalline inclusion body of tobacco mosaic is known to contain true virus particles.

The TMV remains active in extracted host plant juice upto 25 years. It is infectious in dilutions upto 1 : 1,000,000 and withstands heating upto 90°C for 10 minutes.

Transmission. Dissemination of TMV from plant to plant takes place through mechanical transmission. This virus is so very infectious that this may be carried from one plant to another by almost any sort of contact. Workers in the tobacco field may carry tobacco virus from one plant to another on their hands or clothing. The TMV is not destroyed in the manufacture of smoking tobacco. Thus, should cigarettes or biris made from virus infected leaves be smoked by a field worker, he may easily carry the virus on his hands to healthy plants.

Control measures. (1) One should avoid infested soil and the use of tobacco refuge on land on which tobacco is to be grown.

(2) Seed beds should be steam sterilized and well removed from tobacco ware-houses.

(3) One should avoid contamination of hands with the virus from tobacco products. Though washing with soap is an effective practical means of cleaning hands between operations.

Virus Symptoms in Plants

Plant viruses on being introduced into the appropriate host produce characteristic symptoms. The presence of viruses can easily be recognized by the symptom picture they produce on the host, but symptoms as a basis of identifying specific viruses are not reliable. The same virus can cause widely different symptoms in different host plants, and symptoms may vary in the same plant with variation in age, nutrition and environmental conditions of growth. A host plant may also be attacked by a large number of viruses and similar symptoms can be caused by different viruses.

The most striking effects of virus infection are general reduction in growth, vigour and cropping power of the plant. Diseased growth is usually accompanied by certain distinct changes in the leaves and other organs of the plant. The most common symptom is change in colour of the leaves–chlorosis, and it is so pronounced that at one time this kind of virus disease was known as infectious yellow. In some type of chlorosis, light green or yellow patches of varying sizes and shape are irregularly distributed among normal green tissues giving a characteristic mosaic pattern.

Vein clearing and vein banding. These commonly appear in systemically infected leaves before mottle or mosaics, a clearing or chlorosis of the tissue in or immediately adjacent to the veins. This pattern is referred to as vein clearing. Vein banding consists of a broader band of chlorosis or necrosis in the interveinal parenchyma.

Ring spots. On inoculated and systemically infected leaves the symptoms appear in localized spots. These spots consist of various types of chlorosis and necrosis. They may be circular chlorotic areas in which case they are called as chlorotic ring spots. In the cases the necrosis may appear in rings alternating with normal green areas. Such spots are called as necrotic ring spots.

Necrosis. In diseases of both yellows and mosaic groups, necrosis appears in various forms. When necrosis involves parenchyma and veins of the leaves and stem it is called as streak. Top necrosis refers to relatively rapid killing of bud or branch or entire top of the plants. Some viruses do not infect a given host systemically but affect the tissue at points of inoculation by causing a localized breakdown. This type of reaction is known as local necrosis.

Stunting and premature death. Virus diseases with few exceptions are hypoplastic in their general effect. This is shown in many cases by shorter internodes, smaller leaves, and fruits, and reduction of size of various other parts.

Excessive growth. Some viruses incite formation of masses of hypertrophied tissue, known as enation of surfaces of leaf and stem. In other cases virus infection results in stimulation of dormant buds, hyperplastic tissue and unusual differentiation. Spindle tuber of potato is example of such distorted growth. An extreme example of a typical growth is found in the extensive stimulation of numbers of buds in the potato witches broom disease.

Masked symptoms and symptomless carriers. There are many instances in which the virus is present in the infected plant but no distinguishable symptoms appear. This may be due to a particular set of environmental conditions under which the symptoms appear. Under such conditions the plant is referred to as having masked symptoms. In some diseases the virus infects a green host and increases therein but no visible signs appear over the entire range of environmental conditions to which the host is usually exposed and there is no obvious sign of the diseases as in latent mosaic of potato in many varieties of potato. Such an infected host plant is known as symptomless carrier.

Synergistic effect. There are numerous cases in which symptoms shown by the infected plant are due to the synergistic or combined action of two or more viruses. For example rugose mosaic of potato is due to infection by two viruses, namely, Potato virus X and Potato virus Y.

CLASSIFICATION OF VIRUSES

There are two general ways in which viruses may be classified. One is the classical monothetic hierarchial system applied by Linnaeus to plants and animals. This is a logical system in which divisions are made as to the relative importance of different properties which are then used to place a taxon in a particular phylum, order, family, genus, etc. An alternative system was proposed by Adanson (1763). He suggested that all known information should be used and that all characters should be considered equally important. There are at present proposals and proponents for both these approaches to virus classification (Lwoff, 1967, Gibbs and Harrison, 1968).

Lwoff *et al,* (1962) proposed a system in which the kind of nucleic acid in the particle (DNA or RNA) the architecture and symmetry of the virus particles, the presence or absence of an envelope, the number of morphological subunits (inicosahedral viruses), or the diameter of rod-shaped viruses were considered the most competent characters (in descending order) in making major subdivisions. Their system was supported in the proposals and recommendations of the Provisional Committee for Nomenclature of various groupings down to family level for the first three groupings.

Phylum	*Subphylum*	*Class*
Vira	Deoxyvira	Deoxyhelica
		Deoxycubica
		Deoxybinala
	Ribovira	Ribohelica
		Ribocubica

Adansonial classification. Adanson (1763), considered that taxa were best derived by considering all available characters and giving equal weight to each. The method is labourious and has not been much used until recently. The availability of computer has renewed interest in this kind of classification.

Nomenclature. One of the main reasons why a Latin binomial system of nomenclature for viruses is inappropriate at the present time is that such names attempt to provide both a label and some information about the virus being labelled. In the present stage of knowledge or lack of it for most viruses, such names would be found to require changing frequently in the future. In an attempt to overcome this problem, Gibbs and his colleagues (Gibbs *et al,* 1966, Gibbs and Harrison, 1968) have suggested a two part system in which the first part of virus name is an unchanging label (the current vernacular name) and the other is a codified information store which can be readily adopted and changed as facts accumulate about the viruses. Each virus consists of four pairs of symbols as follows :

1st pair Type of nucleic acid/Strand of nucleic acid.
2nd pair Molecular weight of nucleic acid/Percent of nucleic acid in infective particle.
3rd pair Outline of particle/Outline of nucleo capsid.
4th pair Kinds of host infected/Kinds of vector.

For example, tobacco mosaic virus (R/1 : 2/5 : E/E :S*)

* This property of the virus is not known.

BACTERIOPHAGES

The group of viruses which attacks bacteria was first described in 1915 by the British scientist Twort and more fully studied about in 1917 by the French investigator De Herelle.

De Herelle noticed that some invisible agent was destroying his cultures of dysentery bacilli. Like other viruses, bacteriophages are filterable and will grow only in the presence of living

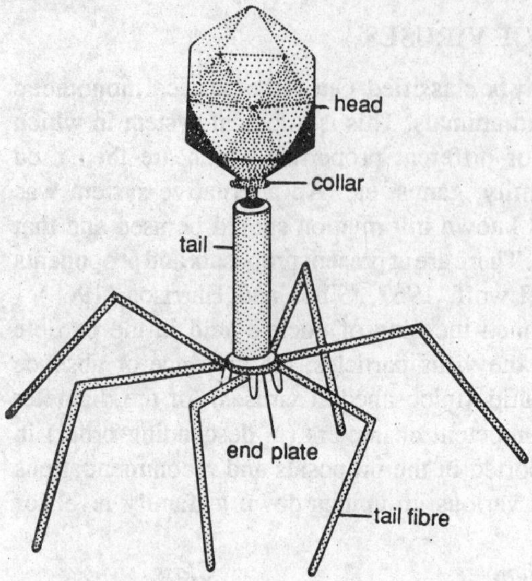

Fig. 23.4. Bacteriophage. Structure.

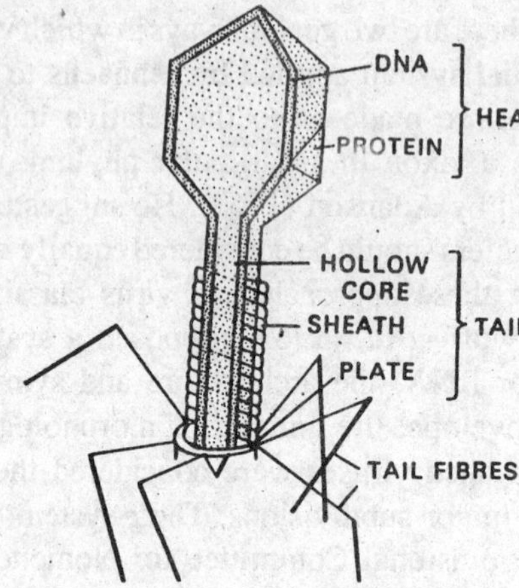

Fig. 23.5. Bacteriophage. Details of a phage particle.

cells in bacteria, which they cause to swell and dissolve. The bacteriophages (viruses) are found in nature wherever bacteria occur. They are especially found in abundance in the intestines of man and other animals.

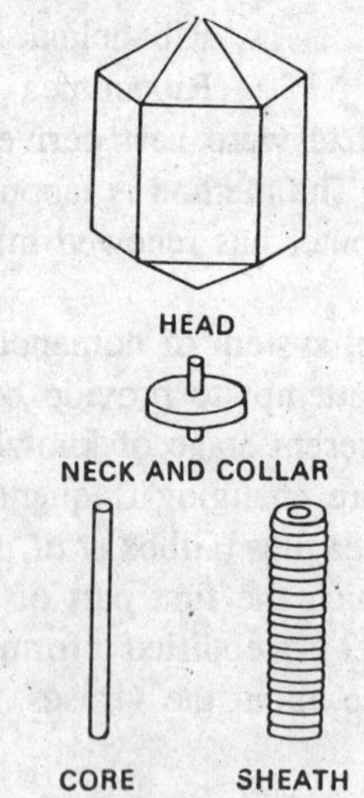

Fig. 23.6. Bacteriophage. Different components of a phage particle.

There are several varieties of bacteriophages. Usually each kind of bacteriophage will attack only one species or even only one strain of bacteria.

Electron micrographs revealed that the bacteriophages may be spherical or comma shaped or may have a tail. They are about 5mμ in diameter.

The initial step in viral reproduction is the attachment of the virus to the bacterial cell by means of its protein tail. An enzyme is found in the tail digests part of the bacterial cell wall and the deoxyribonucleic acid (DNA) is found in the core of virus passes into the bacterial cell. Hershey and Chase have shown that only the DNA of the virus is injected into the bacterium while the protein coat of the head and tail does not enter.

The inference is that the DNA contains all the genetic information for the synthesis of the complete virus particle. The DNA directs the biosynthetic system of the host cell to produce viral DNA and viral protein.

In the first 10-15 minutes increasing number of viral particles accumulate, and some 30 minutes after infection the bacterial cell bursts and several hundred newly formed viral particles are released, ready to attack new bacterial cells.

Multiplication of viruses. Viruses are regarded as "regressed parasites", that must take advantage of the biochemical machinery of the host cell within which it reproduces. In viruses most of the work has been done on bacterial viruses (bacteriophages). The bacteriophage attaches to the bacterial surface by its tail and then releases its nucleic acid into the bacterial cytoplasm. An independent synthesis of the viral components occurs within the cell followed by an assembly of those components into complete virus particles. After a well defined period the bacterial cell bursts and releases the newly formed virus particles. The middle part of this sequence appears to be general for all types of virus infections.

An interesting modification of this life cycle occurs when a certain type of bacteriophage, termed temperate, infects certain types of bacteria. In this instance genetic material of the temperate

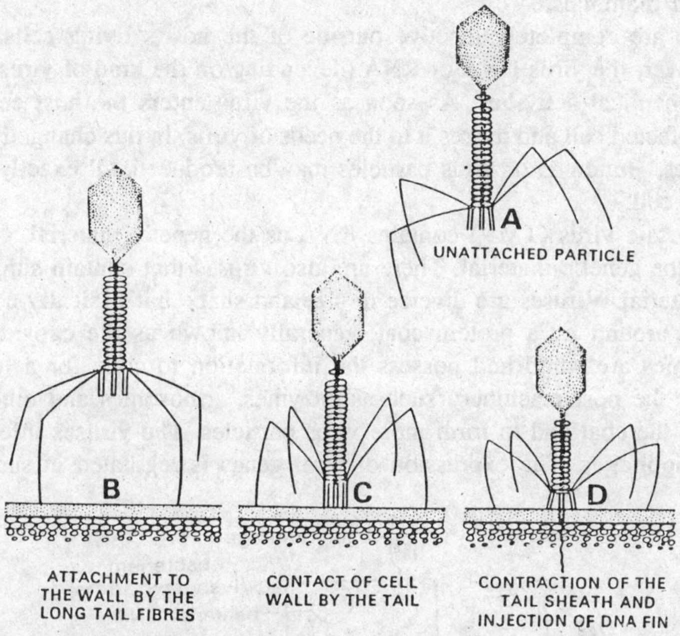

Fig. 23.7. Bacteriophage. Diagram showing adsorption and penetration of virus (phage) particle.

viruses attaches itself to a bacterial chromosome in a manner which is not understood. The bacterium shows no immediate sign of infection and continues to grow and divide nothing had

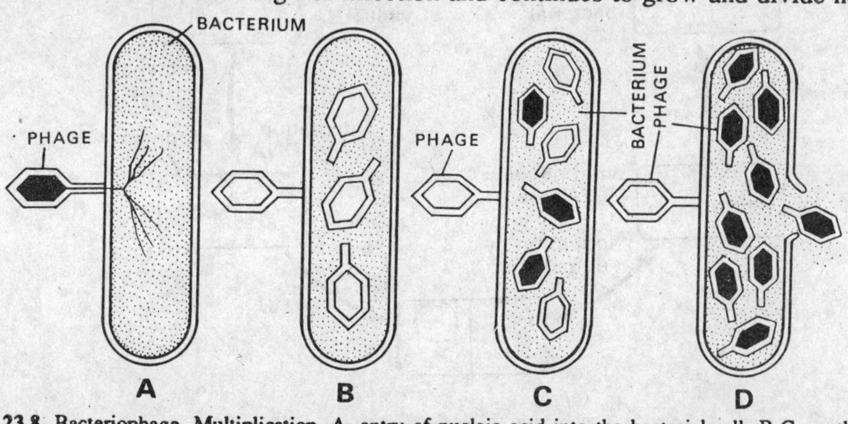

Fig. 23.8. Bacteriophage. Multiplication. A, entry of nucleic acid into the bacterial cell; B-C, synthesis of viral components in the cell; D, lysis of bacterial cell and liberation of phage particle.

happened. Such a bacterium is termed lysogenic. Occasionally this bacterium will spontaneously start making viral components and these components will be assembled into mature virus particles.

Biological importance of bactertiophages. The fact that bacteriophages can destroy bacteria suggest of course, that they might be used to combat bacterial diseases. Many bacteriophage preparations have been given, without much effect, to patients suffering from dysentery and staphylococcus infections. But the bacteriophages are ineffective in the presence of blood, pus or fecal matter and this fact has led to the abandonment of their use for therapeutic purposes.

Viral Genes

Viruses are submicroscopic entities which multiply only inside living cells and possess the ability to cause diseases to all forms of living organisms, from single-celled plants or animals to large trees and mammals.

The viruses are completely inactive outside of the host's living cells. Once inside the host's cells, however, the virus DNA or RNA (depending on the kind of virus) assumes control of the cell's biochemical activities. As soon as the virus enters the host cell, it changes the activities of the infected cell and makes it to the needs of virus. In this changed cell environment, the virus replicates. Hundreds of virus particles may be produced, all exactly like the one that infected the host cell.

Tobacco mosaic virus (TMV) contains RNA as the genetic material. Other viruses may contain DNA as the genetic material. There are also viruses that contain single stranded DNA as the genetic material. Viruses are diverse in size and shape but basically contain the genetic material wrapped around by a protein coat, generally known as the **capsid.**

Viral genomes are small and possess the information to code for a few proteins only. Thus, viruses use the host machinery such as enzymes, ribosomes and other components to replicate, to form the coat and to form more virus particles. The viruses infecting bacteria are known as **bacteriophages.** The expression of viral genes is regulated in such a way that the

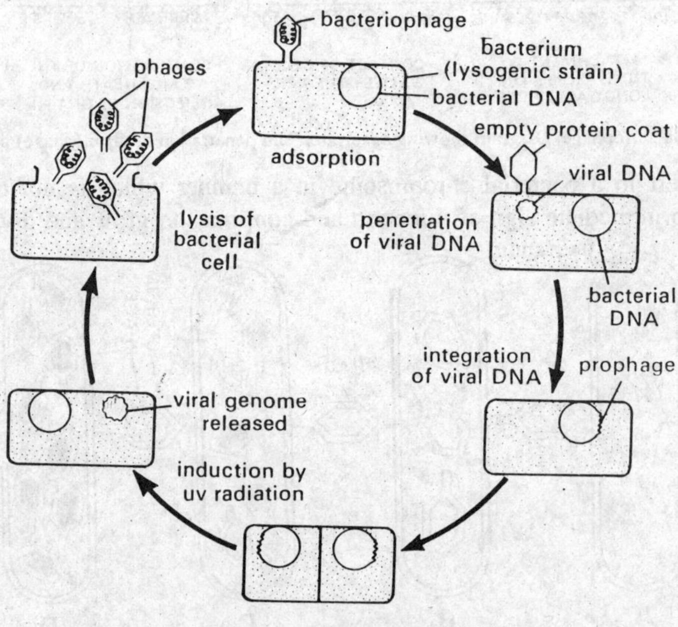

Fig. 23.9. Bacteriophage-life cycle.

lysis of the host cells is caused. Thereafter many virus particles (**lytic**) are liberated which can infect new host cells to repeat the **lytic-cycle.** In some viruses after infection of the host cells viral particles get integrated with the host chromosome (DNA) and replicate along with it (**lysogeny**).

Lytic-cycle

Bacteriophages are the best understood viruses in terms of their gene structure and expression. For example T_2-bacteriophage infects *Escherichia coli* and causes lytic cycle. This phage has a double stranded circular DNA enclosed in a hexagonal proteinaceous head, cylindrical hollow tail and six tentacles for attachment to the host. The phage gets attached to bacterial wall by its tentacles. The lysozyme found at the tip of the tail dissolves the host cell wall to form a pore. The tail now contracts and injects the viral DNA into the host cell. Thereafter the viral DNA synthesises an enzyme known as nuclease which degrades the host DNA. Only after few minutes the host DNA is destroyed by nuclease. On the other hand, the viral DNA is resistant to nuclease because its cytosine residues are methylated. Now the viral genes make use of host ribosomes for multiplication. First of all the replication of viral DNA takes places. Thereafter, the proteins of head tail and tentacles are synthesized. An independent synthesis of viral components occurs within the cell followed by an assembly of those components into complete virus particles. After a well defined period the bacterial cell bursts and releases the newly formed virus particles. The liberated virus particles again infect the bacterial cells and the lytic cycle is repeated.

Lysogenic Cycle

An interesting modification of lytic cycle occurs when a certain type of bacteriophage, termed temperate, infects certain types of bacteria. In this instance genetic material of the temperate viruses attaches itself to a bacterial chromosome in a different manner. Here the viral DNA gets attached to bacterial DNA, becomes inactive and is known as **prophage** or **provirus.** The inactivity of phage DNA is because of the synthesis of repressor protein by phage DNA that causes repression of all the phage-genes. Thereafter as the bacterial cell divides, phage DNA also replicates with it and is inherited by all the bacterial cells of following generations. In the other option, DNA or viral gene integrates with the bacterial *(E. coli)* chromosomal DNA and gives rise to a prophage. Here, the phage replicates along with the host. At times, the prophage may be activated due to altered environmental conditions. This inhibits the repressor protein synthesis, and results in the expression of lytic genes. Now the prophage becomes a lytic phage and resumes the lytic cycle. Here the bacterial cell *(E. coli)* shows no immediate sign of infection and continues to grow and divide as nothing had happened. Such a bacterium is termed **lysogenic**, and the cycle involved, the **lysogenic cycle.** Occasionally this bacterium will spontaneously start making viral components and these components will be assembled into mature virus particles.

Reverse Transcription

This phenomenon was studied by Temin and Baltimore (1972), and thus known as Teminism. While studying the activity of double stranded RNA containing Rous sarcoma virus (RSV) in the cancerous tissue, they found that viral RNA synthesized DNA complementary to its strands. As soon as the RNA of RSV comes in contact of the cytoplasm of host cell, it synthesizes the enzymes **reverse transcriptase** that catalyses the conversion of RNA to DNA copy and exhibits a reverse phenomenon of the normal process. Such phenomenon is known as reverse transcription or Teminism. Once the DNA complementary to viral RNA is synthesized it follows the normal *rule and synthesizes viral* RNA and viral proteins as depicted in the figure. The central dogma says that the flow of information is unidirectional, *i.e.*, DNA———>RNA——

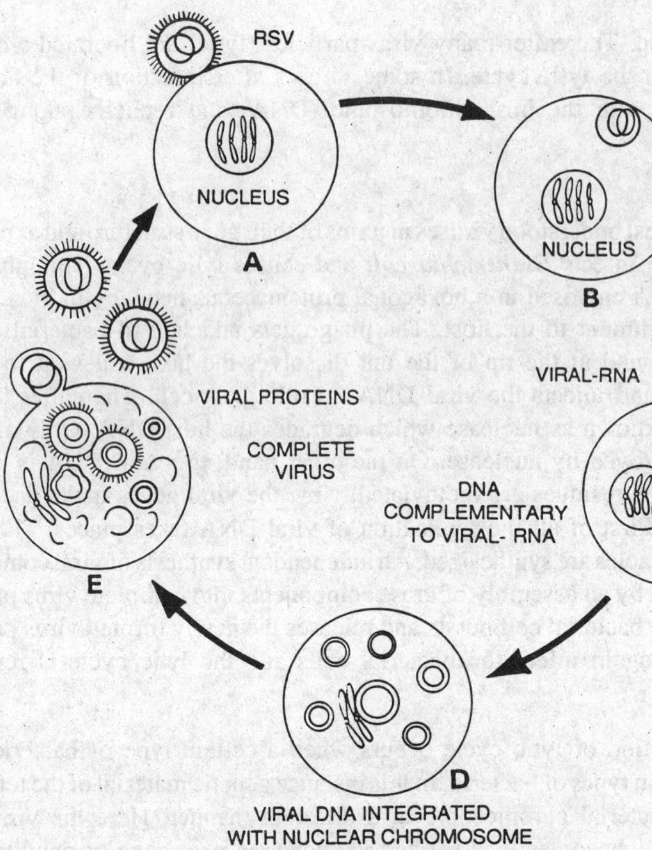

Fig. 23.10. Multiplication of Rous Sarcoma Virus (RSV). A-E, showing different stages.

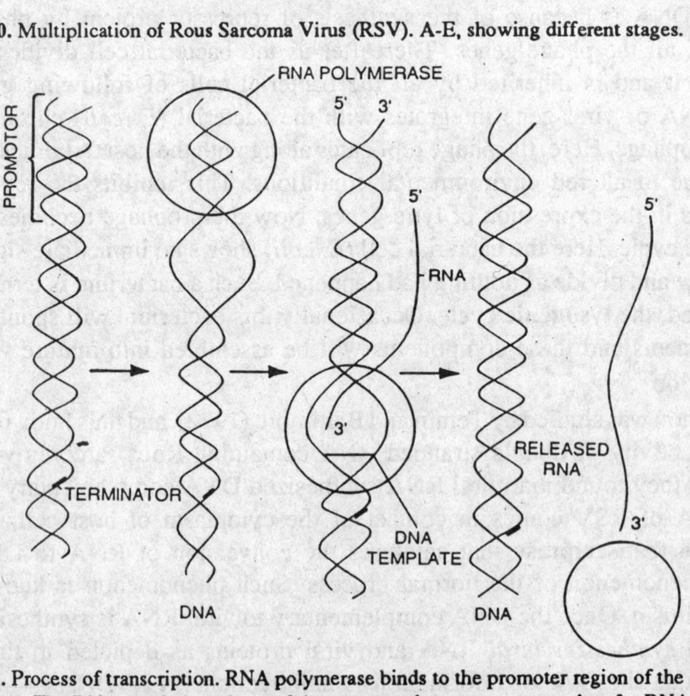

Fig. 23.11. Process of transcription. RNA polymerase binds to the promoter region of the DNA and starts the transcription process. The DNA unwinds and one of the two strands serves as a template for RNA synthesis, and a complementary copy of RNA is formed on the template strand.

—>protein. However, with the discovery of enzyme reverse transcriptase, it becomes clear that RNA can also go back to DNA as represented here :

DNA====RNA———>Protein.

This is a characteristic of **retroviruses,** and this course is not followed by other RNA viruses. The virus HIV-III (human immuno deficiency virus III) which is responsible for causing AIDS disease is also a retrovirus. About twenty viral genes have been identified which are responsible for triggering cancer in cells. On the other hand, slightly modified versions of these genes are also present in normal cells which are known as **protooncognes or cellular oncogenes.** Most of the cellular oncogenes code for growth factors or for protein required for growth factor action such as receptors. The origin of cancer is a complex phenomenon, where viral oncogenes or activated cellular oncogene products are responsible for uncontrolled growth of cells.

24

Human Diseases: by Bacterial, Viral and Fungal Pathogens

COMMUNICABLE HUMAN DISEASES

The word **disease** is a very broad term. It covers such a variety of conditions that we can speak of almost any deviation of the human body from normal as a disease. In other words any deviation from normal health leads to disease. A disease can also be defined as a disorder of the mind or body. It is opposed to health. It is not easy to classify all the human diseases. However, they can be broadly divided into congenital and acquired diseases. **Congenital diseases** are present right from the birth and may result from metabolic disorder or defect in the development. **Acquired diseases** are those which develop after birth.

CLASSIFICATION OF COMMUNICABLE DISEASES

Communicable diseases may also be classified, according to the nature of the causative organism, such as diseases caused by bacteria, diseases caused by virus, diseases caused by Protozoa, diseases caused by helminthes and diseases caused by fungus.

Diseases Caused by Bacteria

The important bacterial diseases to be discussed here are tuberculosis, typhoid, leprosy, cholera, diphtheria, and tetanus. Some of these diseases are quite common, while some occur rarely. Some break out in the epidemic form while others do not.

Tuberculosis. Tuberculosis is responsible for the loss of an enormous number of lives every year, being especially common among people who live in dingy, congested parts of large cities. Tuberculosis is caused by a small rod-shaped bacterium, *Mycobacterium tuberculosis,* spread by sputum from infected persons. The bacteria of tuberculosis invade any part of the body, multiply rapidly and destroy the tissues. Lungs are the favourite site of infection where small tubercles are formed. They release a toxin called **tuberculin.** The disease spreads mostly by the throat and nose discharges from a person suffering from an active stage of disease. The symptoms of pulmonary tuberculosis are fever, cough, sputum containing blood, pain in the chest and loss of body weight. The incubation period is quite variable. These bacteria are so widespread that most persons develop a tubercular infection of their lungs at some time during their life usually during youth. Most people overcome minor infections without knowing they had the disease; but if resistance is low, the infection may spread and damage the lung tissue extensively.

The diagnosis of tuberculosis is made on the basis of positive tuberculin test, chest X-rays, positive sputum, gastric analysis, etc. Tuberculosis is not a hereditary disease. The modern treatment of tuberculosis is based on the six main factors : namely, rest, diet, drugs, surgery, rehabilitation and health education. Vaccination against tuberculosis with **BCG vaccine** provides considerable protection against the disease. The vaccine is injected into the skin. There are also other measures in effective operation for the control of the disease. Medical and public health experts have cautioned that BCG vaccination should be used to supplement rather than replace other measures of control. To check the spread of the disease it is important that every patient is located and treated. Various government and private organizations are working for the eradication of tuberculosis in India. Tuberculosis is a disease that requires treatment in its early stages for best results. Young people, specially young women, between the ages of 17 and 25 years are most susceptible. Those who are exposed to tuberculosis, *i.e.*, resident physicians, medical students, nurses and hospital employees should be immunized against tuberculosis.

Typhoid. Typhoid is an acute infection of the intestines. It is characterized by continued fever, often with delirium, slow pulse, abdominal tenderness and a rose-coloured eruption or rash. The causative agent of typhoid fever is *Salmonella typhi*. These are rod-shaped, motile organisms, from 1 to 3.5 microns long. Although *S. typhi* do not produce entotoxin, they contain an endotoxin which is released on disintegration of the microbial bodies. Typhoid fever is spread by intestinal discharges. Any person carrying the typhoid fever germs in his intestinal tract can spread the disease to others even though the person himself may not be suffering from the disease. These persons are known as **healthy carriers.** In addition, any person who suffers from the disease is likely to spread it to others. The principal means of spread are contaminated food and water.

The incubation period averages two weeks, but it may be short as seven days or as long as twenty-one to twenty-three. Its duration depends mainly on the individual organism. In most patients prodromal symptoms are displayed for several days toward the end of the incubation period in the form of mild malaise, increased fatigability, irritability and poor appetite. The fever lasts for two or three weeks and it may relapse when other parts of the body like bone marrow, spleen or gall-bladder are infected through the blood stream. Death may occur due to haemorrhage or puncturing of the intestine.

Diagnosis of typhoid fever is made through pathological detection of the germ which causes the disease in the intestinal discharge of the patient. In recent years attempts to cure typhoid carriers have been made by surgical removal of the gall-bladder in which the germs appear to be concentrated and by treatment with antibiotics such as **chloromycetin.**

The prevention of typhoid fever is based on proper community sanitation, protection of water supply, protection of food from contamination of flies and by personal cleanliness. Vaccination or immunization against typhoid fever is advisable at any age during an epidemic of the disease or during a natural catastrophe such as floods or hurricanes. Vaccination is also useful when there has been an exposure to a known carrier of the disease.

Leprosy. Leprosy is a chronic communicable disease. It is caused by leprosy bacillus. The disease is characterized by skin lesions including the peripheral nerves so that the infected area becomes benumbed. The other symptoms of the disease include ulcers, nodules, scaly scabs, deformities of fingers and toes; and wasting of body parts. The disease is communicated only after long and close contact with infected individuals. Children isolated from leper parents early in life grow into normal and healthy persons. Leprosy is a far dreaded disease than most communicable diseases because of the social stigma attached to it. Even after the patient has been cured of the disease, it is very difficult to rehabilitate him. It is very essential to educate the public about the actual nature of the disease. This disease is prevalent mostly in Africa and Asia. At places of pilgrimage in India it is common sight to find flocks of lepers begging for alms.

Cholera. Cholera exists in several forms. The type called Asian cholera has persisted in this country since thousands of years and breaks out periodically. It has caused great sufferings to the mankind. During floods and after floods and other natural calamities, epidemic cholera breaks out in our country. The causative organism is *Vibrio comma,* a **gram-negative** bacterium. The cholera bacteria spread through contaminated food and water. The symptoms include vomiting, acute diarrhoea and muscular cramps. The stool becomes very thin and has rice water appearance. The symptoms result in dehydration, loss of minerals and in some severe cases death may occur. The fatality rate of infected persons used to be 30-50 per cent. The incubation period, *i.e.*, the period between the entry of the organism inside the body and the appearance of the symptom generally from a few hours to two or three days.

The important preventive measures are heating of food, boiling of drinking water, proper disposal of waste and protection as well as purification of drinking water. Vaccination may be quite useful for the protection from cholera. It is always advisable to take the vaccine, particularly before travelling to a region known to be infested with the disease or during the outbreak of an epidemic. However, proper sanitation is a better control measure because immunization is effective only for a short period.

Diphtheria. Diphtheria specially is a serious disease of children, but the disease can attack adult also. The disease is caused by a rod-shaped bacterium, *Corynebacterium diphtheriae.* The bacteria grow in a membrane on the wall of the throat and block the air passage by their excessive growth. A severe general reaction to the disease is the body's response to the toxin produced by the organism causing the disease. The disease is spread by discharges from the throat of an infected person. The incubation period is from 2 to 5 days. The early symptoms of the disease may not be severe, such as mild fever, sore throat and a general feeling of indisposition. However, in the latter period the symptoms become very severe. Several complications arise. Among these are difficulty in breathing due to obstruction in the throat by the formation of the membrane, general swelling and inflammation. If such complications arise, surgery becomes essential. Sometimes the toxins produced by the organism cause weakness, high fever and damage to the heart and nervous system and death occurs due to choking.

Treatment for this disease is very effective if started early. Diphtheria antitoxin, when given within the first 12 to 24 hours of the appearance of the symptoms, completely neutralizes the toxin produced and saves the patient from the damage. If given after 24 hours, even the strongest dose may not save the patient from severe illness or even death. The antitoxin is given by injection, usually in a single dose. Although antibiotics may be helpful, the primary treatment is given by injecting antitoxin. When children are immunised against diphtheria, the immunity does not last for a life time. It has now become customary to immunise against diphtheria along with tetanus and whooping cough. The vaccine used for the immunization of diphtheria, tetanus and whooping cough is called triple vaccine or triple antigen. This triple antigen is used for the simultaneous immunization of children against these three diseases. Vaccination or immunization and serum inoculation have greatly reduced the infection of diphtheria.

Tetanus. Tetanus is a very serious and fatal disease. This disease is caused by *Clostridium tetani* which usually gains entrance into body tissues through deep wounds. It has an incubation period of from four days to three weeks. The bacterium grows in the intestine of many animals without doing any harm. Horses are excellent breeders of it; the number of cases of tetanus has greatly diminished with the decline of the horse as a means of transportation. Tetanus is highly fatal; death results from most cases. The symptoms are painful contraction of muscles, usually of the neck and jaw, followed by the paralysis of the thoracic muscles. Very often death may result. Because of this symptom it is also called lock jaw. Infection may occur through a wound or an abrasion of the skin. Children are usually infected as a result of injuries sustained in the home or street; the newly born may be infected through the navel. This disease is not transmitted from man to man and infection occurs only on direct contact. Treatment is possible by injecting the **tetanus antitoxin.** It is always advisable to take an anti-tetanus toxoid injection (ATS) in the case of an injury in road accident or cut contaminated with soiled objects like animal faecal matter or street dust, etc. It has now become a common practice to immunize the children by triple antigen or triple vaccine against tetanus, diphtheria and whooping cough. Immunization is very essential after every three to five years.

Diseases Caused by Viruses

There are numerous diseases which are caused by different viruses. A few important diseases caused by viruses are described below :

Chickenpox. Chickenpox is caused by a virus. It is usually spread or transmitted by contact with sores or by skin of an infected person or by contact with clothings or other articles soiled with discharges from an infected person. The incubation period is from two to five weeks. It is a common, comparatively mild disease of childhood. Susceptibility to chickenpox is very high, practically universal. Chickenpox is very rare in children after 10 years of age or in adults. Stable life-long immunity follows some attack, second attacks are extremely rare. The primary symptoms are rise in temperature and general discomfort. Skin eruptions appear first. All the eruptions do not appear at once, but in stages. The length and severity of the disease is dependent upon the number of eruptions produced. In severe cases, almost the whole body is covered. The preventive measure includes isolating the patient. The patient's bed and clothing should be kept neat and clean. Patient should be kept away from all public places until all crusts have fallen off. Some suitable lotion may be applied on the eruptions in order to check the itching in the skin.

Measles. Measles is also a common childhood disease. It is caused by a virus, *Polynosa morbillorum,* which is very unstable and perishes rapidly outside the human organism. The source of infection in measles is a sick person. The virus is spread by discharges from nose and throat. The incubation period is from 12 to 14 days. The symptoms are fever, inflammation of the respiratory mucous membranes, sensitivity of the eyes to the light, loss of appetite, vomiting and a rash eruption of the skin. Patients are likely to contact pneumonia as a secondary infection.

Properly organized hygienic conditions for the patient, careful nursing and protection from secondary infection are of immense significance for the treatment of measles and prevention of complications. One attack of measles gives permanent immunity.

Rabies. Rabies is also known as **hydrophobia.** It is a very dreadful disease transmitted to man by the bite of mad rabid dogs through the saliva. The incubation period ranges from about 1 to 6 months. It is a viral disease. The virus first stimulates and then destroys the cells of the brain and spinal cord. The symptoms of the disease include severe headache, high fever with alternating stages of excitement and depression. The patient has difficulty in swallowing even liquid and develops severe muscular spasm in the throat and chest. The patient dies a painful death following restlessness, choking, convulsions and inability to swallow liquids. The disease is not transmitted from man to man, but only through bite of rabid dogs. The long incubation period from 1 to 6 months makes it possible for a rabies vaccination after a bite to develop immunity and prevent the disease from occurring. Death results from almost every case of the disease that develops in animals including man.

The treatment of rabies is one of Pasteur's greatest contributions to the mankind and is known as Pasteur's treatment. It consists of a series of injections given daily for 14 days. The injection is prepared from fixed virus. The injections induce the formation of anti-bodies in the patient. Any person bitten by a stray dog should take this treatment as a preventive measure

Disease Caused by Fungi

Fungi cause many diseases, most common amongst them are ringworm, athlete's foot and deep mycoses which are described here.

Ringworm, athlete's foot etc. The dermatophytes are fungi which cause diseases of the skin of man, animals or both. Some of them survive in the soil, which thus becomes a source of infection. The diseases they cause are grouped under the general term **dermatomycoses** (Gr. *derma*=skin) and are commonly known as ringworm, athlete's foot etc.

Of the four form genera–*Epidermophyton, Keratinomyces, Microsporum* and *Trichophyton*- to which the dermatophytes belong, the first two are monotypic, *i.e.,* consist of but a single form species. *Epidermophytom floccossum* is one of several **dermatophytes** causing chronic infections commonly called **athlete's foot.** It produces large multiseptate, club-shaped hyaline conidia on the somatic hyphae. There are no special conidiophores.

The form-genus *Microsporum* produces very small conidia (microconidia) on its hyphae, but in addition it produces large, multiseptate, spindle-shaped macroconidia. Five species of this form-genus are recognized. *Microsporum* generally infects the scalp of children, more rarely of adults, causing a condition called by medical personnel *tinea capitis.*

The form-genus *Trichophyton,* also a cause of athlete's foot and other skin ailments, is the largest of the form-genera of dermatophytes, and contains some thirteen form species variously distributed over the world. The microconidia and macroconidia are produced. The microconidia are more common. The macroconidia are hyaline and multiseptate.

Deep mycoses. These are diseases of the human body which affect tissues below the outer skin and which are usually chronic and serious in their effects. The fungi responsible for causing these diseases are mentioned here. The form-genera of the Moniliaceae (class-Deuteromycetes), which include serious human pathogens are–*Blastomyces, Histoplasma, Geotrichum* and *Sporotrichum.*

Blastomyces dermatitidis causes North American blastomycosis. There are two forms of the infection; a localized form of mild skin disease and a severe gneralized form of a pulmonary nature. The latter damages the lungs and sometimes shows symptoms similar to those of tuberculosis.

Histoplasma capsulatum is the cause of histoplasmosis, a very widespread and serious disease which is often fatal. *Histoplasmȧ capsulatum* is a polymorphic organism exhibiting a mycelial and yeast-like phase of growth. Emmons (1949) has repeatedly isolated the organism from the soil, and it is now well established that the soil is an important source of infection, not only for this ailment but for many mycoses.

Certain form species of *Geotrichum* are known to be pathogenic to man. Conant *et al* (1954) state that four forms of geotrichosis have been described–oral, intestinal, bronchial and pulmonary.

Sporotrichum schenkii is the cause of sporotrichosis in man and animals. The organism is normally a saprobe on plant material but becomes pathogenic to the human body it enters through a wound.

25

Industrial Uses of Micro-organisms

INDUSTRIAL MICROBIOLOGY

Industrial microbiology is that portion of microbiological science which deals with the possible utilization of micro-organisms in industrial processes, or in processes in which their activities may become of industrial or technical significance. For several decades it has been known that numerous kinds of yeasts, moulds and other lower fungi, and several types or groups of bacteria have direct relation, either favourable or unfavourable, to certain types of economic processes carried out in connection with industrial or factory operations such as brewing, wine making, cheese making etc., which have grown up from small-scale or family arts. Knowledge in this field has greatly extended, as research in many countries and in many lines has been carried out. The scale of operations has greatly enlarged and concentrated in manufacturing plants. These changes have made it evident not only that industrial microbiology is an exceedingly interesting branch of study but that it has already become a distinctly important branch of applied science, and one with even greater potentialities. On the more positive side, it is clearly advantageous to know the biological and biochemical characteristics of the many types of organisms that are the prime and direct causes of chemical transformation of materials into desired products. Here one utilizes the micro-organisms capable of producing, by fermentation processes, relatively of large quantities of chemical substances of usefulness and economic value. It becomes quite evident that industrial microbiology should include in its scope the study (i) of the numerous fermentation processes in which the production of alcohols, organic acids, glycerol, acetone and other substances are end products; (ii) of certain aspects of food-manufacturing processes, such as baking and making of the cheese, butter, and pickles, in which microbic agencies take a significant and important accessory part; (iii) of food-conservation methods, such as canning and preserving, refrigeration, quick freezing and drying; and (iv) of the microbiological problems concerned with textile and commercial fibres. Obviously in the processes grouped under (ii) and (iii) and in a part of those under (i) industrial microbiology is intimately associated with food technology.

FERMENTATION

The micro-organisms of fermentation include yeasts, moulds and bacteria. These micro-organisms are unable to manufacture their own food by the ordinary process of photosynthesis since they lack chlorophyll and are classified in fungi. Certain of the Ascomycetes (sac-fungi) and of the Phycomycetes (algal-fungi), and a large number of species of the bacteria are the principal micro-organisms that are directly concerned.

From the biochemical standpoint, fermentation is the name given the general class of chemical changes of decompositions produced in organic substrates through the activity of living micro-organisms. Thus there may be many kinds of fermentation falling within this category depending on the type of the organisms involved, the type of substrate or even the conditions imposed, such as pH or oxygen supply. The word *fermentation* is a term that has undergone numerous changes in meaning during the past hundred years. According to the derivation of the term, it signifies merely a gentle bubbling or boiling condition, and the term was first applied when the only known reaction of this kind was in the production of wine. Even then no knowledge existed about the cause. Thus in an active ethyl alcohol fermentation, as in a wine or cidar fermentation, carbon dioxide is always liberated in the form of bubbles of gas, which at the height of reaction may cause a marked agitation or movement of the liquid medium, especially in a large vat or tank; sufficient to give to it the appearance of a boiling liquid. This interpretation of the word was the accepted one for several thousand years. After Gay-Lussac studied the process the meaning was changed to signify the breakdown of sugar into alcohol and carbon dioxide. With the increase in knowledge following Pasteur's researches into the cause of this change in the nature of the material fermenting, the word became associated with micro-organisms and still later with enzymes, which are the biologically produced reagents by which microbes work. Although fermentation is frequently or even generally associated with the evolution of gas caused by the action of living cells neither gas evolution nor the visible presence of living cells is today regarded as an essential criterion of fermentation. In certain fermentations, for example, some of the lactic fermentations, only gas is liberated.

A *fermentation*, in the broad sense in which the term is now used, may be defined as *a process in which chemical changes are brought about in an organic substrate through the action enzymes elaborated by micro-organisms*. Although fermentation generally takes place in the presence of the living cells, it may, in some cases, occur in their absence, for example, in the production of dextran.

Carbohydrates are often regarded as being essential materials for fermentation, but it must be clear that organic acids (including amino acids) and their salts, proteins and their derivatives, fats, sterols, alcohols, esters and other organic compounds are fermentable under certain conditions by selected micro-organisms.

Industrial fermentations are those in which chemical products of value are manufactured.

The conversion of sugars into alcohol and carbon dioxide is termed alcoholic fermentation. The alcohol forming yeasts that grow at the top of the fermenting liquid are known as 'top yeasts'. The other yeasts which grow in the lower portions are known as 'bottom yeasts'. Though yeasts grow in less supply of oxygen yet fermentation does not take place in total absence of oxygen and most of the yeasts are intermediate between aerobic and anaerobic types. During fermentation besides the production of alcohol and carbon dioxide other substances like glycerol, ethers, fatty acids, acetic acid and succinic acid are also produced in small quantities.

The important fermenting yeasts are–the wine yeast (*Saccharomyces ellipsoides*); the beer and bread yeasts (*S. cerevisiae*); the ginger beer yeast (*S. piriformis*); the sake wine yeast (*S. sake*); African beer yeast (*S. pombe*) etc.

ALCOHOL

'One of the most important and best known industrial fermentations is that in which ethyl alcohol is produced from sugars by yeasts. The chemical manufacturer, the brewer, the distiller, the baker, the vinegar manufacturer, the scientist, the housewife and many others depend in one way or another on the ability of the yeast to convert sugars to alcohol, carbon dioxide, and other end products'. From the time immemorial the man has exploited the natural process of fermentation, and used its products for his own pleasure. In all ages, he has celebrated the occasions with alcoholic beverages. Today the alcoholic beverages are consumed all over the world. Alcohol is a poison, and when taken to excess, produces hazardous effects on the human system. The alcoholic beverages bring about cerebral excitation, followed by depression, and may produce the complete, though temporary, suppression of the functions. The evils of excessive drinking are known all over the world.

Manufacture of ethyl alcohol. Generally the ethyl alcohol is manufactured from molasses. The molasses mash is adjusted to the desired sugar concentration and temperature by the addition of water and to the desired pH by the addition of a measured quantity of acid. A yeast 'starter' is mixed with the mash in the fermentation tank, which is usually covered. Streams of the adjusted mash and the starter flowing simultaneously into the fermenter may be caused to converge on a baffle board located in the upper part of the tank. The mash and starter become well mixed as they spatter and fall to the bottom of the tank. The fermentation rapidly becomes vigorous with the evolution of large quantities of carbon dioxide. In the modern plant, this gas is collected, purified and used for the manufacture of dry ice or for other purposes. Within 50 hours or less, the fermentation is complete. The fermentation molasses, is distilled in a continuous still to separate the alcohol and other volatile constituents from the mash. The alcohol is purified by means of rectifying columns and then stored in a bonded warehouse.

There are two distinct categories of alcoholic beverages : 1. The fermented beverages, where the alcohol is formed by the fermentation of sugar and 2. the distilled beverages which are obtained by the distillation of some alcoholic liquor.

Fermented Beverages : Beer

Brewing. 'Brewing' or the production of malt beverages, is the name given to the combined process of preparing beverages from infusions of grains that have undergone sprouting (malting), and the fermenting of the sugary solution by yeast, whereby a portion of the carbohydrate is changed to alcohol and carbon dioxide. It is an ancient industry and was probably invented by the Egyptians.

Composition of beers. The substance found in a beer depends largely upon the nature and the quality of the raw materials, the treatment of the sprouted grain or malt used in mashing, and the character of the ensuing fermentation, but storage and finishing operations affect the final composition. In normal beer carbohydrates–such as dextrin, maltose and glucose–and protein derivatives–such as peptones, amino acids and amides are present. The products are produced mainly as the result of the action of the enzymes of the malt. Hops contribute bitter substance–such as resins, essential oils and tannins. As a result of alcoholic fermentation the sugars of the wort are being converted, in part to ethyl alcohol and carbon dioxide. Some of the amino acids are being transformed to higher alcohols and acids. Salts and traces of oil are always found. The finished beer contains 85 to 92 per cent water by volume.

The brewing process. The process of brewing alcoholic beverages from cereals is very old. Millet was perhaps the first to be so used, and it is still fermented in India. Rice, maize and rye have been used on a small scale, but barley has always been the chief source. The important steps in the manufacture of beer or ale include the following : cleaning, grinding and weighing of the malt; grinding and weighing of malt adjuncts; mashing of the malt and processing of the malt adjuncts; filtering of the mashed materials to separate the soluble material (the wort) from the insoluble material (the spent grain); boiling of the wort with hops; separation of the wort from hop residues and protein precipitates, cooling of the wort fermentation of the wort, clarification, attenuation, and maturing of the malt beverage during storage chillproofing and carbonation, filtration packing, pasteurizing, labelling, inspecting and stamping of the cases.

The commercial manufacture of beer involves two distinct processes–*malting and brewing*. The malting is done for the conversion of the starch present in the grains into sugar. This is brought about through the agency of an enzyme, diastase, which is produced during the process of germination. Large, fresh, perfect, light-coloured barley grains are used. The barley grains are steeped in water from one to four days. During this time the grains soak the water, they are spread out on malting floor in a temperature of 50 to 60^{0}F, and are constantly turned over. The germinated barley grains are then kiln dried for twelve hours. The colour of the dried product, the malt depends on the degrees of heat.

The subsequent process is brewing. Now the malt is crushed or coarsely ground in a roller mill and is mixed with water heated to 170^{0}F. The sugar dissolves out and the infusion or wort is drawn off. This process of mashing is repeated several times. The wort is then boiled with hops for two hours. The hops impart the bitter flavour and tonic properties. The liquid is then cooled rapidly and yeast is added to bring about the fermentation of the sugar. Precaution must be taken to keep an optimum temperature for enzyme action. The beer is then drained off and strained and allowed to cool in wooden casks. A slow fermentation goes on, that increases the alcoholic content and results in the formation of carbon dioxide which is responsible for the foaming of the beer. Beer contains 3-8 per cent alcohol.

Wine

Wine is the product made by the normal alcoholic fermentation of the juice of sound ripe grapes (*Vitis vinifera*). Relatively small amounts of wine are made from apples, raisins, black berries, peaches, cherries, oranges, currants, apricots, grapefruit, pomegranates, raspberries, pears, honey and strawberries. The wine made from the fruit is named after the fruit, for example "apple wine".

Wine making areas. A large part of the world's wine is made in the countries located near the Mediterranean Sea. France leads the world in wine making, followed by Italy, Spain, Algeria, Portugal, Romania, Argentina, Russia, Hungary, Yugoslavia, United States, Chile, Greece, Bulgaria, South Africa, Germany and other countries.

In France the region around Bordeaux produces most of the wine. This district is the most outstanding single wine growing area in the world. Burgundy wines are produced in the hilly country of the Cote d' Or in east central France. Champagnes are produced in the vicinity of Reims and Epernay. Only wines made in this Champagne region have a right to the name. Black and red grapes are used and the manufacture involves a series of elaborate processes which extend over a period of six or seven years.

Making of red wine. Selected grapes of the proper maturity are crushed and stemmed, treated with sulphur dioxide, or a sulfite, or pasteurized, and inoculated with a starter containing a pure culture of yeast. After a short fermentation period the wine is drawn off placed in storage tanks for further fermentation, racked, stored for aging and packaged.

Wines vary considerably in their characteristics. The alcoholic content varies from 7 to 16 per cent. The sugar content of the grapes is from 12 to 18 per cent. Fermentation of the fruit juice is carried on in vats, usually with the aid of selected yeasts (strains of *Saccharomyces cerevisiae*). The optimum temperature is 68^{0}F. The aroma and flavour are due to various aromatic principles present in the fruit. The characteristic bouquet develops only after the wine has been aged from four or five years to several decades.

White wines are made from white grapes or expressed juice. Red wines are made from coloured grapes and derive their own colour from the pigments present in the skins of the fruits. In dry wines the fermentation is stopped before all the sugar is being converted and at least 1 per cent is still present. In sparkling wines, the wine is bottled before fermentation is complete. The still wines have a higher alcoholic content due to the addition of wine, brandy or alcohol.

Other important wines are : The dry *Rhine wines* of Germany, *Chianti*, *Astl* and other wines of Italy; *tokay*, a golden yellow wine of Hungary; *sherry*, a dry wine fortified with brandy of Spain; *port* of Portugal; *champagne* of France and California; *sherry* of California.

Distilled Beverages

Whisky. Whisky is an alcohol distillate from a fermented mash of grains. Whisky is obtained by distillation from a fermented mash of malted or unmalted cereals or potatoes. After several distillations of the mash the "low wines" are resulted. Further distillation yields the high wines. A mixture of water and high wines makes straight whisky. At first several principles are present which make whisky harsh and unpalatable. It must be aged to allow these principles to disappear. The whiskies are aged in charred oak containers. At first the whisky is colourless, the colour develops during the aging process. A continued distillation of high wines results in the formation of neutral spirits which are used in blended whiskies and cordials.

The Scotch whisky is prepared from barley malt. Irish whisky is made from malt or unmalted grains of barley, oats and maize. The Russian Vodka is made from fermented wheat mash. The Vodka it not aged and bottled immediately after distillation and therefore, it remains colourless.

Rum. Rum is an alcoholic distillate from the fermented juice of sugarcane, sugarcane syrup, sugarcane molasses or other sugarcane by-products. Rum is manufactured in general in those countries which grow sugarcane or import molasses or other sugarcane products. It possesses a characteristic flavour, aroma, and colour. The flavour and aroma, improve with aging. Rum contains about 40 per cent alcohol. Rum is usually aged in charred whiteoak barrels. Rum may be used in the preparation of ice cream candies and mincemeat; in the curing of tobacco; as a beverage; and as medicinal.

Brandy. Brandy is distilled only from wine. It is also distilled from the fermented juice of various fruits. The best brandy is made in France in the Charente district. Only this product is known as *cognac*. The other French brandies are known a *armagnac*. The finest grades of brandy are made from white wines. The brown colour of brandy develops when it is stored in wooden casks. Sometimes the brandy is coloured with caramel. It contains about 65 to 70 per cent alcohol. Apple brandy is known as applejack.

Gin. It is obtained by distillation from a fermented malt or raw grain. The finest gin is distilled from the malt of barley and rye. It requires several distillations. The flavour of gin and any medicinal value are due to oil of juniper.

ANTIBIOTICS

Introduction. The term *antibiosis* means antagonism between microbes competing for existence in any given medium.

Antibiotic. A substance produced by bacteria, actinomycetes or fungi which inhibit the growth of micro-organisms, particularly which are pathogenic.

Now, a few of them are also synthetically produced, *e.g.*, chloramphenical and cycloserine. The essential nucleus of penicillin has been isolated and by adding various side-radicals to its biosynthetically reduced nucleus, a number of semi-synthetic penicillins have been produced.

The antibiotics while in action against the pathogenic organisms meet resistance also. Most gram negative bacilli are *naturally resistant* to benzyl-penicillin, spirochaetes to streptomycin and some others to chlorotetracycline.

While other bacterial strains develop acquired resistance, *e.g.*, staphylococci to penicillin and *Mycobacterium tuberculosis* to streptomycin. Because staphylococci produce penicillinase to counter attack the penicillin, the bacillus is able to shield itself against the attack of the penicillins. This is a sort of physiological mutation in the bacterial cell. But this phenomenon has led to the production and use of mixed antibiotics known as synergids.

The indiscriminate use of antibiotics has also been responsible for the resistance acquired by the pathogens.

The subject of fungi in medicine has attained great importance since 1929 when Alexander Fleming reported his observation on lysis of Streptococci in agar plate cultures contaminated by *Penicillium notatum* Westling. Chain *et al* showed in 1940 that an active antibacterial substance could be extracted from culture media in which *Penicillium notatum* was grown and that it could be preserved for appreciable periods. Since then progress has been rapid and several active principles, antibiotics as they are called, have been isolated from specific fungi and some of them have been used in the treatment of diseases.

Penicillin. It is now widely employed in the treatment of a variety of bacterial diseases in man. It is the metabolic product of a number of moulds generally referred to as *Penicillium notatum–chrysogenum* series. High yielding strains of *Penicillium* adapted for submerged culture and producing specific penicillins or increased general yield of penicillin, are selected for commercial production of this antibiotic. They are cultured in suitable media under aeration.

Penicillins are bacteriostatic and, in sufficient concentrations, bactericidal against a wide range of common pathogenic bacteria. Gram-negative bacteria are also susceptible. Among the conditions which have been successfully treated with Penicillins of wounds and fractures, boils, carbuncles, abscesses, acute tonsillites, pneumonia, peritonitis, pericarditis, subacute bacterial endocarditis, acute osteomyelitis, otitis media, mastoiditis, meningitis, ocular infections, gonorrhoea and syphilis. Penicillins are administered orally or through intramuscular, intravenous or thoracic injections.

Polyporin. This is obtained from the culture filtrates of *Polystictus sanguineus* Fr. The crude antibiotic is active against typhoid, cholera and dysentery organisms (*i.e., Staphylococcus aureus* and *Escherichia coli*). It is completely non-toxic to animals and is also stable.

Other fungal antibiotics. Clitocybine is extracted from *Clitocybe gigantea* Fr. It has not been extracted in pure form. It is highly bacteriostatic. It prevents the growth of a number of Gram-negative and acid-fast organisms. It inhibits the growth of *Mycobacterium tuberculosis.*

The other fungal antibiotics which have been studied in some detail are as follows–Aspergillic acid from *Aspergillus flavus;* avenacin from *Fusarium avenaceum* Sacc; candidulin from *Aspergillus candidus* Link; chaetomin from *Chaetomium cochlioides* Palliser, citrinin from *Penicillium citrinum* and other species of *Penicillium;* and *Aspergillus;* clavacin from *Aspergillus clavatus* and *Penicillium* spp; fumigacin from *Aspergillus fumigatus;* fuscine from *Oidiodendron fuscum* Robak; geodin from *Aspergillus terreus;* gladiolic acid from *Penicillium gladioli* Machacek; javanicin from *Fusarium javanicum* Koord; lactaroviolin from *Lactarius deliciosus* Fr; lycomerasmin from *Fusarium* spp., oregonensin from *Canoderma oregonense* Murrill; penicilic acid, from *Penicillium* spp. and *Aspergillus* spp.; spinulsin from *Penicillium spinulosum* Thom., and *Aspergillus fumigatus.*

List of common antibiotics

Antibiotics	*Producing organism*	*Sensitive organisms*
1. Penicillin	*Penicillium notatum*	Gram-positive bacteria; *Neisseria;* Spirochaete; actinomycetes: clostridia; *Corynebacterium diphtheriae*
2. Streptomycin	*Streptomyces griseus*	Gram-positive and Gram-negative

		bacteria; *Mycobacterium tuberculosis*; actinomycetes.
3. Becitracin	*Bacillus licheniformis*	Gram-positive bacteria; clostridia; *Treponema; Histoplasma capsulatum*
4. Chlorotetracycline	*Streptomyces aureofaciens*	Gram-positive; and Gram-negative bacteria; rickettsiae and large viruses.
5. Erythromycin	*Streptomyces erytheraeus*	Gram-positive bacteria; some Gram-negative bacteria; rickettsiae and large viruses.

APPLICATIONS OF MICROBIOLOGY

Microorganisms because of their enzymatic activities, are like miniature chemical factories. They are capable of synthesizing a large number of chemical compounds. Industrial processes based on the application of microbial action are of various types.

(1) **Fermented milk products.** By the application of dairy microbiology desirable changes can be brought about in milk products.

(a) Butter. It is made by churning the cream that has been soured by lactic acid bacteria. Two species of bacteria are added *Leuconostoc citrovorum* to impart the flavour and *Streptococcus lactis* for lactic acid production.

(b) Butter milk. Produced by adding *Leuconostoc citrovorum* and *S. cremoris* to the milk.

(c) Cheese. Unripened cottage cheese is prepared from the pasteurised skim milk inoculated with *Streptococcus lactis, S. cremoris, Leuconastoc citrovorum, L. dextraniaum,* Roquefort cheese is ripened by the blue, green mold *Penicillium roqueforti*, while the camembert cheese is manufactured by the help of *P. camemberti*. Certain bacteria and yeasts grow on the surface of yeast and penetrate into it to produce enzymes which produce the flavours, softening and aroma in the cheese.

(d) Curdling of milk. Caused by *Streptococcus lactis, S. cremoris, Lactobacillus casei, L. fermentis, L. bulgaris* etc.

(2) **Alcoholic fermentation.**

(a) Ethyl alcohol. It is produced from the fermentation by yeasts, *e.g., S. cerevisiae*. Molasses are used as mash.

$$C_6H_{12}O_6 \xrightarrow{\text{Yeast}} 2C_2H_5OH + 2CO_2$$

The CO_2 is converted into solid CO_2, It is also used for carbonating beverages.

(b) Wine. It is produced by the action of yeast on the fruit juices; yeast fermentation of diluted honey, sugar cane juice and other sugary solutions give rise to number of beverages related to wine.

(c) Beer. It is prepared from starchy foods. Starch is converted into sugar by the action of *Aspergillus oryzae*. Sugar is converted into alcohol by yeast.

Distillation of wine, beer etc. produce brandy, whisky and rum.

(d) Production of vinegar. This process involves two biochemical changes by *Azotobactor* (i) Alcoholic fermentation of carbohydrates (ii) Oxidation of alcohol to acetic acid.

(3) **Baking industry.** *S. cerevisiae* is helpful in the baking industry.

(4) **Microbial production of vitamins.** They are produced as :

(1) Primary growth products. (2) As by-products in certain microbial reactions.

(a) Riboflavin : Growth product of mold *Achyla.*

(b) Vitamin B : By-product of antibiotic synthesis by *Streptomyces.*

(5) **Microbial production of enzymes.**

(a) Diastase. Produced by *Aspergillus oryzae* and *A. niger.*

(b) Proteases. Produced by *A. oryzae* and *Bacillus subtilis.*

(c) Pectinases. From *Penicillium frequens, Saccharmyces.*

(d) Invertase. From *S. cerevisiae.*

(e) Glucose Oxidase. From *A. niger.*

(f) Penicillinase. By *B. subtilis.*

(g) Gibberellin. It is a growth hormone produced by *Gibberella fujikuroi.*

(6) **Production of antibiotics.** They are the chemical substances of microbial origin used against the micro-organisms. Different species of Actinomycetes, Bacteria and fungi are used in the manufacture of antibiotics.

(7) **Production of organic acids.**

(a) Lactic Acid : Microbes are used for the fermentation of carbohydrates to produce lactic acid. These are the species of *Lactobacillus, Leuconostoc, Streptococcus* and some molds like *Rhizopus.*

(b) Citric acid. It is a mold fermentation product *Aspergillus niger* is the mold used.

(c) Gluconic acid, is produced by the action of *Aspergillus niger*

(d) Fumaric acid. Here, *Rhizopus nigricans* is the fermenting agent.

(8) **Micro-organisms as food.**

(a) Yeast. Brewer's yeast is the source of vitamin B complex and protein.

(b) Chlorella. This green alga is rich in proteins which can be used as food.

(9) **Retting of fibres.** This involves the use of naturally occurring microbial cultures. *Clostridium pectinivorum* is the main organism that helps in decomposition of pectin.

(10) **Sewage disposal.**

(11) **Biological control.**

(12) **Bioassay**–Assay of antibiotics, vitamins and amino acids etc.

(13) **Biological warfare.**

(14) **Space research.**

Question Bank

FUNGI AND PLANT PATHOLOGY

Long Answer Type

1. Trace the progressive degeneration of sexuality in the members of Ascomycetes and Basidiomycetes.
2. Distinguish between conidia, ascospores, and basidiospores. What role is played by these spores in the life-cycle of Ascomycetes and Basidiomycetes?
3. Discuss the origin and evolution of Ascomycetes.
4. Describe the significance of the role played by plasmogamy, karyogamy and meiosis in the life-cycle of Basidiomycetes.
5. List any five resemblances and five differences between the Basidiomycetes and Ascomycetes.
6. Give a comparative account in a tabulated form of the rusts and the smuts with reference to structure and reproduction.
7. Give an illustrated account of the life-history of *Claviceps purpurea*. What are its economic uses ?
8. "A knowledge of the biology of a pathogen is of great importances in devising measures to control it". Comment on this statement with special reference to smuts and rusts.
9. (a) What are the different types of sporangia produced by *Allomyces* ?
   (b) Describe the behaviour of each type of sporangium after its formation.
   (c) What leads to the formation of gametophytic thallus ?
10. Describe five different ways in which dikaryotic mycelium is formed. Give the cytological significance of dikaryotic phase in the life-cycle of Basidiomycetes.
11. In what ways do the Ascomycetes find their place in industries ? Taking the examples included in your syllabus describe in which particular areas of industry they find place.
12. Describe the life-history of the fungus that causes 'wart disease of potato'. (Kanpur, 1981)
13. Give a comparative account of asexual reproduction in *Achlya* and *Mucor*. (Kanpur, 1981)
14. Describe briefly the structure and development of an ascus. How does an ascus differ from basidium ? (Kanpur, 1981)
15. Give a brief illustrated account of the life-history of a smut fungus. Discuss various kinds of its infection and possible methods of controlling it. (Kanpur, 1981)
16. Give a comparative account of sexual reproduction in *Cystopus* and *Mucor*. (Kanpur, 1981)
17. Give botanical names of two edible fungi along with their classification. Describe the structure and method of reproduction in any one of them. (Rohilkhand, 1979)
18. Describe the habitat, structure and methods of reproduction in *Cystopus candida*. Give methods of its control. (Rohilkhand, 1979)
19. Describe the structure and method of reproduction in *Ustilago*. Give methods of its control also. (Rohilkhand 1979)
20. Describe the method of asexual reproduction in *Albugo*. Name the disease caused by this fungus. (Rohilkhand, 1980)
21. How does the reproduction take place in *Penicillium*. What is its economic importance ? (Rohilkhand, 1980)
22. Describe the life-history of *Puccinia graminis tritici*.
23. Describe the life-history of *Puccinia* on alternate host (secondary host). Name three diseases caused by this fungus on wheat plant. (Rohilkhand, 1981)
24. Describe the life-history of *Morchella*. (Rohilkhand, 1981)
25. Describe the reproduction in yeasts. (Rohilkhand, 1981)
26. Differentiate loose smut and covered smut. Give an account of life-cycle of *Ustilago*. (Rohilkhand, 1982)
27. Describe life-cycle of gills bearing fungus of your course. Also describe structure of its basidiocarp. (Rohilkhand, 1982)
28. Describe sexual reproduction of the fungus which causes, "white rust". Also explain symptoms of this disease. (Rohilkhand, 1983)
29. Give an account of thallus, structure and sexual reproduction of *Aspergillus*. What light does it throw on the degeneration of sex ? (Rohilkhand, 1983)

30. Write an essay on annual recurrence of "wheat rust" in India. Also explain heteroecism. (Rohilkhand, 1983)

31. Describe structure of the mycelium and reproduction of a 'smut fungus' studied by you. (Rohilkhand, 1983)

32. Give the different biological categories of fungi based on their modes of nutrition. Write brief notes on each, mentioning at least one example of each. (Kumaon, 1983)

33. Give the life-history and economic importance of *Saccharomyces* (yeast). (Kumaon, 1983)

34. What material (host plant) will you collect for studying any five of the following genera ? (a) *Synchytrium*, (b) *Albugo*, (c) *Ustilago*, (d) *Puccinia*, (e) *Erysiphe*. Give the symptoms of the diseases caused by at least one species of the above genera. (Kumaon, 1983)

35. Give a brief account of the different types of somatic structure in fungi. (Kumaon, 1984)

36. Describe the methods of infection and control measures of the different species of *Ustilago*. Discuss how are they interlinked. (Kumaon, 1984)

37. With the help of labelled diagrams only describe the life-cycle of *Puccinia graminis tritici*. (Kumaon, 1985)

38. Give a comparative account of cleistothecium, perithecium, and apothecium with suitable examples. (Kumaon, 1986)

39. On *Puccinia graminis tritici* both heterothallic and heteroecious conditions occur. Illustrate your answer with suitable sketches. (Kumaon, 1987)

40. Write about the reproduction of a fleshy fungus of the class Basidiomycetes. (Rohilkhand, 1984)

41. Describe the life-history of *Ustilago* or *Agaricus*. (Rohilkhand, 1985)

42. Give systematic position, habit and habitat of *Penicillium*. How does the reproduction take place in it and what is its economic importance ? (Rohilkhand, 1986)

43. Write an essay on annual recurrence of 'wheat rust' in India. Also explain heteroecism. (Rohilkhand, 1986)

44. Give an illustrated account of the life-history of *Synchytrium*. (Kanpur, 1989)

45. Give botanical names of two edible fungi along with their classification. Describe the life-history of any one of them. (Rohilkhand, 1987)

46. What is damping-off disease? Describe the life-cycle of the causative organism.

47. What are the different rusts of-wheat ? What are their distinguishing features ? Explain the annual recurrence of rusts in the plain of Northern India.

48. Name any three important plant diseases occurring in India. Mention their symptoms, pathogenicity, and control measures.

49. What measures would you adopt to control the powdery mildew of peas and red rot of sugarcane and why?

50. Give a clear and illustrated account of the life-history of *Phytophthora* and explain its mode of perennation in the late blight disease of potato.

Short Answer Type

1. Give the structure of mycelium during somatic phase in the case of *Rhizopus*.
2. Draw the T.S. of a *Cystopus* infected leaf of *Brassica* showing the manner in which conidia are produced.
3. Give three modifications of fungal mycelium and mention their uses if any.
4. What type of ascocarp is produced in *Penicillium*. Give at least two chief characters of such a structure?
5. Bring out the differences between oidia, chlamydospores, rhizomorphs and sclerotia.
6. The mycelium of *Erysiphe* is found to be only on the surface of leaves. What is the name given to such a parasite? How does it obtain nourishment ?
7. Draw a neat labelled diagram of the L.S. of gill in *Agaricus*.
8. Very often people talk about the 'fairy rings' they most commonly see in the forests. What are they? how do you account for their appearance?
9. Illustrate the degeneration of sexuality in the fungi with example.
10. Describe the external and internal structure of the basidiocarp of *Lycoperdon*.
11. Describe the sexual reproduction in *Mucor*.
12. Where are the yeasts found in nature? Mention their economic importance ?
13. In what essential respects to the apothecium, perithecium and cleistothecium differ from each other ?
14. Write illustrated notes on :
    (a) Clamp connection. (Kanpur, 1981)
    (b) Buller's phenomenon (Kanpur, 1981)
    (c) Mushroom's fairy rings (Kanpur, 1981)
    (d) Heterothallism (Kanpur, 1981)
    (e) Aecidial cup in *Puccinia* (Kanpur, 1981)
15. Point out three differences between each of the following pairs. (Kanpur, 1981)
    (i) Prosenchyma and pseudoparenchyma; (ii) Sporangiophore and conidiophore; (iii) Zygospore and oospore.
16. Explain the following terms with the help of suitable diagrams. (a) Symbiotism, (b) Parasitism, (c) Saprophytism. (Kanpur, 1982)

17. Draw suitable diagrams of – (a) stage O of *Puccinia*, (b) V.S. of *Morchella* ascocarp, (c) sexual stage of wart disease. (Kanpur, 1982)

18. How will you distinguish between ? (a) rust and smut, (b) *Morchella* and *Agaricus* fructifications, (c) Cleistothecium, apothecium and perithecium. (Kanpur, 1982)

19. Give the systematic position of *Achlya, Cystopus, Saccharomyces, Aspergillus, Morchella, Synchytrium, Puccinia, Agaricus, Mucor, Ustilago*. (Kanpur, 1983)

20. How will you distinguish the following diseases in the field ? (a) Wart disease, (b) white rust disease, (c) brown rust disease, (d) early blight of potato. (Kanpur, 1983)

21. Write short notes on – (a) Mushroom cultivation, (b) algal origin of fungi. (Kanpur, 1983)

22. Give the life-cycle of any holocarpic fungus. (Kanpur, 1983)

23. Draw well-labelled diagrams of the sections passing through– (a) *Brassica* leaf infected with white rust disease, (b) potato leaf infected with early blight disease, (c) wheat leaf infected with brown rust. (Kanpur, 1984)

24. Explain the following terms with the help of suitable examples– (a) Heterothallism, (b) autoecious and heteroecious forms, (c) fungi as test organism. (Kanpur, 1984)

25. Draw the symptoms and write the specific names of causal organisms of the following plant diseases – (i) wart disease of potato, (ii) loose smut of wheat, (iii) black rust of wheat, (iv) early blight of potato. (Kanpur, 1985)

26. Distinguish between each of the following pairs– (a) parasitism and saprophytism, (b) rust and smut, (c) annual recurrence of rust on wheat in India. (Kanpur, 1986)

27. What are imperfect fungi ? Describe the structure and reproduction of *Alternaria solani*. Write the name and symptoms of the disease caused by it. (Kanpur, 1986)

28. Distinguish between each of the following pairs– (a) parasitism and saprophytism, (b) rust and smut, (c) hypertrophy and hyperplasia. (Kanpur, 1986)

29. Where do you expect to find the following in nature ? (i) *Achlya*, (ii) *Aspergillus*, (iii) *Saccharomyces*, (iv) *Alternaria*. (Kanpur, 1987)

30. Write note on : Economic importance of fungi. (Kanpur, 1988)

31. Write main identifying characters of the following giving their diagrams and importance– (a) *Saccharomyces*, (b) *Aspergillus*. (Kanpur, 1988)

32. Distinguish between any two of the following– (a) Heterothallism and heteroecism, (b) oospore and zygospore. (Kanpur, 1988)

33. Write about the asexual reproductive structure of the following– (a) *Achlya*, (b) *Alternaria*, (c) *Synchytrium*. (Kanpur, 1988)

34. Describe the characteristic features of Ascomycotina. (Kanpur, 1989)

35. Write notes on– (i) Early blight of potato, (ii) fruit body of *Morchella*.

36. Why are Myxomycetes placed under fungi ?

37. Write short notes on sex organs of *Pythium*.

38. Give a brief account of human disease caused by fungi.

39. Comment on – gleba of *Lycoperdon*.

40. Comment on – asexual reproduction of *Penicillium*.

41. Make labelled outline figures of the following. Spore producing organs of fungi.

42. By means of simple and labelled drawings, explain the structure of the reproductive organs in *Aspergillus*.

43. Describe the reproductive organs in *Saprolegnia*.

44. Give the labelled diagram of teleutospores of *Puccinia graminis* as seen in a L.S. of stem of infected wheat.

45. Why do mushrooms frequently appear in circles are called fairy rings ?

46. Write critical notes on– (a) *Colletotrichum*, (b) *Fusarium*, (c) *Claviceps*, (d) *Lycoperdom*, (e) *diplanetism*.

47. What evidence is their to prove that Myxomycetes are fungi ?

48. Trace the nuclear changes in the life-cycle of a macrocyclic rust.

49. During which process does the dikaryotization of the hyphae in *Puccinia* take place and mention the name of host in which it occurs.

50. Write short notes on the following : (i) Smut disease, (ii) cleistothecium, (iii) symptoms of white rust, (iv) clamp connection. (Rohilkhand, 1984)

51. Give well labelled diagrams of– (a) *Synchytrium*–sexual stage, (b) *Aspergillus*–asexual reproduction, (c) a section through the teleutosorus, (d) ascocarp of *Morchella* (Rohilkhand 1986)

52. Write short notes on the following– (a) Smut disease, (b) economic importance of fungi, (e) ascocarp of *Morchella*. (Rohilkhand, 1987)

53. Write short notes on the following– (a) Ascospore, (b) basidiospore, (c) oospore, (d) zygospore. (Kumaon, 1983)

54. How will you distinguish the following ? (a) Zoospore and aplanospore, (b) oospore and zygospore, (c) ascospore and basidiospore, (d) uredospore and teliospore, (e) conidium and sporangiospore. (Kumaon, 1984)

55. Discuss the mode of nutrition in any five of the following– (a) *Stemonitis*, (b) *Synchytrium*, (c) *Saprolegnia*,

(d) *Saccharomyces,* (e) *Erysiphe,* (f) *Morchella,* (g) *Puccinia,* (h) *Agaricus,* (i) *Alternaria.* (Kumaon, 1985)

56. Write short notes on the following : (a) Basidium, (b) Ascus, (c) Sporangium, (d) Zoosporangium. (Kumaon, 1986)

57. Compare and contrast sexual reproduction in the following pairs of genera– (a) *Rhizopus* and *Albugo,* (b) *Aspergillus* and *Erysiphe,* (c) *Synchytrium* and *Saprolegnia,* (d) *Mucor* and *Phytophthora.* (Kumaon, 1986)

58. Give names of the fungi which cause following : (a) Wart disease of potato, (b) early blight of potato, (c) loose smut of wheat, (d) late blight of potato, (e) white rust of crucifers. (Kumaon, 1987)

Multiple Choice

1. *Erysiphe* causes the disease. (i) powdery mildews, (ii) downy mildews, (iii) covered smut, (iv) late blight of potato.
2. The coprophilic fungi inhabit. (i) Dung substratum, (ii) dead wood, (iii) decaying leaves, (iv) food articles.
3. Mycotrophy is the symbiosis of a fungus with (i) Bacteria, (ii) algae, (iii) bryophytes, (iv) other fungi.
4. The process of self-fertilization in fungi is known as. (i) Automixis, (ii) amphimixis, (iii) spermatization, (iv) somatogamy.
5. Diplanetism is exhibited by. (i) *Phytophthora,* (ii) *Saprolegnia,* (iii) *Mucor,* (iv) *Albugo.*
6. The position of the antheridium in connection with the oogonia in *Albugo* is called as paragynous when the antheridium. (i) grows beside the oogonium, (ii) encircles the oogonium, (iii) remains at the base of the oogonium, (iv) grows on the oogonial wall.
7. The fertile portion in the fruiting body of *Lycoperdon* is called (i) Gleba, (ii) peridium, (iii) hymenium, (iv) gills.
8. Macrocyclic rust is the name given to some fungi, (i) which produces bigger spores, (ii) where all the five spore stages are produced, (iii) which completes its life-cycle on a single host, (iv) which selects many hosts to complete its life-cycle.
9. What is the fruit body of *Penicillium* called (i) Perithecium, (ii) cleistothecium, (iii) apothecium, (iv) stroma.
10. *Rhizopus* multiplies by the production of. (i) zoospores, (ii) conidiospores, (iii) sporangiospores, (iv) chlamydospores.
11. Sclerotium is a perennating and vegetatively reproducing body, the structure of which has (i) hyphae aggregated to form strands, (ii) loosely interwoven hyphae which have not lost their identity, (iii) compactly interwoven hyphae which have lost their individuality, (iv) thick-walled hyphae giving a rounded or irregular configuration.
12. The obligate parasitic fungi absorb their nourishment from the host cells through: (i) the surface, (ii) haustoria, (iii) appressoria, (iv) rhizoids.
13. Biological specialization is a term used for fungus which : (i) can infect differential hosts, (ii) shows host specialization, (iii) can grow in a variety of substrata, (iv) are biologically useful.
14. Sporangial proliferation in *Saprolegnia* will be characterized by the: (i) development of secondary sporangium into the primary sporangium, (ii) the primary sporangium cuts off spores from its apex, (iii) production of new sporangia from the vegetative hypha, (iv) germination of spore into a mycelium.
15. Which of the following depicts the position of antheridium in *Penicillium* in connection with the ascogonium would be: (i) coils loosely around the ascogonium, (ii) grows besides the ascogonium, (iii) remains at the base of the ascogonium, (iv) approaches the ascogonium only at its tip.
16. The fungus which is so important for its use in genetic studies is : (i) *Aspergillus,* (ii) *Rhizopus,* (iii) *Penicillium,* (iv) *Neurospora.*
17. White rust of crucifer is caused by : (i) *Puccinia,* (ii) *Ustilago,* (iii) *Cystopus,* (iv) *Peziza.*
18. Microconidia are found in : (i) *Claviceps,* (ii) *Neurospora,* (iii) *Rhizoctonia,* (iv) *Pyricularia.*
19. In *Agaricus,* the cell in which reduction division takes place is known as : (i) basidiospore, (ii) basidium, (iii) chlamydospore.
20. Coprophilous fungi are growing in : (i) grasses, (ii) dung, (iii) animals, (iv) wood.
21. Stroma is : (i) compact somatic hyphae with fruit bodies, (ii) loosely interwoven hyphae, (iii) a small hyphal branch, (iv) a group of spores.
22. Somatogamy is the : (i) fusion of gametes, (ii) fusion of vegetative cells, (iii) contact between two gametangia, (iv) copulation between two gametangia.
23. Fungus *Alternaria solani* belongs to class : (i) Ascomycetes, (ii) Deuteromycetes, (iii) Schizomycetes, (iv) Oomycetes.
24. The protective covering of sterile hyphae around an ascocarp is termed as : (i) periderm, (ii) peridium, (iii) appendages, (iv) epiderm.
25. In *Penicillium* conidia are produced : (i) in sori consisting of several conidiophores, (ii) in branched conidiophores, (iii) on unbranched conidiophores, (iv) on both branched or unbranched conidiophores.
26. A haustorium of a fungus is meant for: (i) fixing up to the mycelium to the host, (ii) increasing the spread of the disease, (iii) reproduction of the fungus, (iv) absorbing nourishment from the host.

27. The sexual reproduction of *Puccinia graminis* is of the type known as : (i) somatogamy, (ii) dikaryotization, (iii) spermatisation, (iv) automixis.

28. In *Agaricus* the fruiting body is made up of : (i) tertiary mycelium, (ii) primary mycelium, (iii) secondary mycelium, (iv) diploid mycelium.

29. In the Ascomycetes karyogamy occurs within the : (i) ascogonium, (ii) antheridium, (iii) ascus, (iv) ascogenous hypha.

30. Haustoria are produced in the case of mycelium which is : (i) both intracellular and endoparasitic, (ii) ectoparasite, (iii) both intercellular and endoparasite, (iv) either ectoparasitic or intercellular.

31. Perfect stage of fungus means : (i) when the fungus is perfectly healthy, (ii) when it reproduces asexually, (iii) when it reproduces sexually, (iv) when it forms perfect resting spores.

32. Penicillin was discovered by : (i) Alexander Fleming, (ii) Edward Jenner, (iii) Louis Pasteur, (iv) Ian Fleming.

33. In the fruit body of *Agaricus* basidia are produced on the : (i) gills, (ii) pileus, (iii) stipe, (iv) rhizomorph.

34. A macrocyclic fungus is the one which (i) needs two different hosts to complete its life-cycle, (ii) produces many types of spores to complete the life-cycle, (iii) does not show any asexual reproduction, (iv) has a prolonged life-cycle.

35. The gametes taking part in the sexual reproduction of *Rhizopus* are : (i) uninucleate, (ii) binucleate, (iii) multinucleate, (iv) dikaryotic.

36. The classification of the fungi is based mainly on : (i) The structure of vegetative mycelium, (ii) the asexual stage, (iii) the sexual reproductive stage, (iv) both the mycelial structure and sexual stages.

37. A phragmo-basidium means : (i) an entire basidium which is fully reproductive, (ii) a septate basidium which for all purposes is one structure, (iii) a septate basidium where only one cell is reproductive, (iv) a septate basidium where both cells are reproductive.

38. The phenomenon of heterothallism was first discovered in Mucorales by : (i) Charles Bessey, (ii) Gaumann, (iii) Blakeslee, (iv) Alexopoulos.

39. The dikaryotic mycelium of heterothallic forms is characterized by having in each of its cells : (i) single 2 n nucleus, (ii) two diploid nuclei belonging to opposite strains, (iii) two halpoid nuclei belonging to opposite strains, (iv) two haploid nuclei of similar strains.

40. A sclerotium refers to a modified mycelium which is : (i) an underground structure, (ii) a hard resting body, (iii) mainly a food storing organ, (iv) easily carried off by wind.

41. In *Phytophthora* the asexual reproductive bodies behave as : (i) conidia, (ii) sporangia, (iii) conidiosporangia, (iv) both conidia and conidiosporangia.

42. The azygospores produced in Mucorales are formed from : (i) zygotes, (ii) unfertilized gametangia (iii) vegetative myceluim, (iv) the female sex organ.

43. Early blight of potato is caused by : (i) *Albugo candida*, (ii) *Phytophthora infestans*, (iii) *Alternaria solani*.

44. The phenomenon of heterothallism was observed for the first time in the order : (i) Erysiphales, (ii) Mucorales, (iii) Ustilaginales, (iv) none of above.

45. Tikka disease of groundnut is caused by : (i) *Aspergillus*, (ii) *Puccinia*, (iii) *Cercospora*, (iv) *Fusarium*.

46. The name 'smut diseases' is given to those produced by *Ustilago* because : (i) its mycelium is black in colour, (ii) it parasitizes cereals, (iii) the host becomes completely black, (iv) the fungus produces black sooty spore masses.

47. White rust of crucifers is a pseudo-rust because : (i) the disease is not caused by basidiomycetous members, (ii) the colour of the pustule is not red, (iii) the disease is seen on crucifers, (iv) the disease is not seen on wheat.

48. Wilt of arhar is caused by : (i) *Pythium*, (ii) *Alternaria*, (iii) *Colletotrichum*, (iv) *Fusarium*.

49. The whip smut of sugarcane is caused by : (i) *Ustilago maydis*, (ii) *Ustilago hordei*, (iii) *Ustilago scitaminea*, (iv) *Ustilago nuda*.

50. Downy mildews are caused by the members of : (i) Erysiphales, (ii) Taphrinales, (iii) Ustilaginales, (iv) Peronosporales.

51. The rusts are caused by : (i) Ustilaginales, (ii) Peronosporales, (iii) Uredinales, (iv) Erysiphales.

52. The wall of hyphae of *Rhizopus* is made up of : (i) cellulose, (ii) callose, (iii) pectin, (iv) chitin. (C.P.M.T. 1978)

53. *Rhizopus* resembles a moss in the both develop : (i) mycelia, (ii) hyphae, (iii) archegonia, (iv) spore. (C.P.M.T. 1978)

54. Penicillin was extracted by : (i) Flemming, (ii) Huxley, (iii) Lamarck, (iv) Brown. (C.P.M.T. 1979)

55. Yeast is an important source of : (i) vitamin C, (ii) riboflavin, (iii) sugar, (iv) protein. (C.P.M.T. 1979)

56. Fungi occurring on wood are : (i) epibiotic, (ii) eucarpic, (iii) epixylic, (iv) epigean. (C.P.M.T. 1979)

57. Which is an edible fungus : (i) *Rhizopus*, (ii) *Mucor*, (iii) *Agaricus*, (iv) *Polyporus*. (C.P.M.T. 1979)

58. Gibberelin was first extracted from : (i) Bacteria, (ii) Fungi, (iii) virus, (iv) algae. (C.P.M.T. 1979)

59. The mushroom is : (i) a plant consisting of fine green threads, (ii) an edible fungus, (iii) a bryophyte devoid of root, (iv) a flowering plant. (C.P.M.T. 1979)

60. The brown gills of the mushroom : (i) have no function to perform, (ii) are meant for its respiration, (iii)

help the plant to float in water after heavy rains, (iv) bears spores which help in reproduction. (C.P.M.T. 1979)

61. Toadstools cannot manufacture their own food because : (i) they do not have roots, (ii) they do not have leaves, (iii) they do not have chlorophyll, (iv) they do not need food for their growth. (C.P.M.T. 1979)

62. Reproduction in 'fairy rings' occurs by means of : (i) seeds, (ii) spores, (iii) flowers, (iv) gills. (C.P.M.T. 1979)

63. Fungi are always : (i) parasitic, (ii) saprophytic, (iii)autotrophic, (iv) heterotrophic. (C.P.M.T. 1980)

64. An organism which is normally a saprophyte, but can also become a parasite is called : (i) facultative saprophyte, (ii) partial saprophyte, (iii) facultative parasite, (iv) partial parasite. (C.P.M.T. 1981)

65. Which of the following is a good example of heterothallism : (i) *Pteris*, (ii) *Rhizopus*, (iii) *Cycas*, (iv) castor bean. (C.P.M.T. 1981)

66. Why zygospores are not generally formed in a culture of *Rhizopus* developed from a single spore : (i) due to lack of light, (ii) due to shortage of oxygen, (iii) due to absence of plus (+) and (-) strains of mycelium. (C.P.M.T. 1981)

67. Columella is present in the sporangium of : (i) *Spirogyra*, (ii) yeast, (iii) *Ulothrix*, (iv) *Rhizopus*. (C.P.M.T. 1982)

68. A mushroom is : (i) saprophyte, (ii) photosynthetic organism, (iii) facultative parasite, (iv) obligate parasite. (C.P.M.T. 1982)

69. What is the mode of nutrition in *Rhizopus*, (i) autotrophic, (ii) parasitic, (iii) symbiotic, (iv) saprophytic. (C.P.M.T. 1983)

70. Which of the following diseases is caused by a fungus : (i) cholera, (ii) rust of wheat, (iii) T.B., (iv) tetanus. (C.P.M.T. 1983)

71. Mycology is the study of : (i) Algae, (ii) Fungi, (iii) Bryophytes, (iv) Pteridophytes. (C.P.M.T. 1985)

72. Which of the following is an edible fungus : (i) *Rhizopus*, (ii) *Penicillium*, (iii) *Mucor*, (iv) *Agaricus*. (C.P.M.T. 1985)

73. Which of the following diseases is caused by a fungus : (i) small-pox, (ii) tuberculosis, (iii) cancer, (iv) black rust of wheat, (C.P.M.T. 1985)

74. Which of the following is a good example of heterothallism : (i) *Spirogyra*, (ii) *Rhizopus*, (iii) *Pinus*, (iv) castor bean. (C.P.M.T. 1985)

75. In which of the following, respiration in absence of oxygen too takes place : (i) man, (ii) yeast, (iii) potato, (iv) *Spirogyra*. (C.P.M.T. 1985)

76. Gills are seen in : (i) bacteria, (ii) *Osscillatoria*, (iii) *Ulothrix*, (iv) *Agaricus*. (C.P.M.T. 1986)

77. The zygospore of *Mucor* is thick-walled and its colour is : (i) blue, (ii) white, (iii) green, (iv) black. (C.P.M.T. 1986)

78. The vegetative cells of the *Saccharomyces* are recognised by the presence of : (i) chloroplasts, (ii) a large vacuolated nucleus, (iii) a small nucleus without a nuclear membrane, (iv) a distinct cell wall. (C.P.M.T. 1986)

79. Heterothallism was discovered by : (i) Bessey, (ii) Blakeslee, (iii) Alexopoulos, (iv) Leuwenhoek. (C.P.M.T. 1986)

80. The structure in which the ascospores are formed in : (i) basidium, (ii) sporangium, (iii) ascus, (iv) gametangium. (C.P.M.T. 1986)

81. Fungal hyphae penetrate hard cell wall of their host with the help of : (i) enzymes, (ii) hormones, (iii) sharp tips, (iv) haustoria. (C.P.M.T. 1987)

82. Loose smut of wheat is caused by : (i) *Ustilago tritici*, (ii) *Cystopus*, (iii) *Puccinia*, (iv) *Aspergillus*. (C.P.M.T. 1987)

83. Obligate parasites are those organisms which : (i) are essentially saprophyte can become parasite, (ii) are essentially parasite but can also become saprophyte, (iii) live only in dead and decaying organic matter, (iv) live only in living hosts. (C.P.M.T. 1987)

84. Fermentation of sugar occurs by : (i) *Mucor*, (ii) *Saccharomyces*, (iii) *Rhizopus*, (iv) *Penicillium*. (C.P.M.T. 1987)

85. Fungal spores produced asexually at the tip of hypha are called : (i) conidia, (ii) sporangiophores, (iii) spores, (iv) arthrospores.

86. Mushroom is : (i) plant consisting of fine green threads, (ii) an edible fungus, (iii) bryophytes, (iv) flowering plants. (C.P.M.T. 1988)

87. Same haploid structures of *Rhizopus* include the : (i) mycelia, sporangia and spores, (ii) hyphae, zygote and sporangia, (iii) mycelia, zygospore and spores, (iv) mycelia, zygospore and suspensor. (C.P.M.T. 1988)

88. Eucarpic fungi are those: (i) in which the habitat is saprophytic, and mycelium coenocytic, (ii) in which reproductive organs arise from a part of thallus while rest carries out of somatic function, (iii) in which entire thallus may be converted into reproductive structure so that somatic and reproductive phases do not occur in some individual. (C.P.M.T. 1990)

89. Fungal spores produced asexually at tips or side of hyphae are called: (i) Sporangiospores, (ii) Arthrospores,

(iii) Conidia (iv) Spores. (C.P.M.T. 1990)

90. When two host species are required for completion of parasitic fungi life-cycle, this condition is described as: (i) autoecism, (ii) autotrophic, (iii) heteroecism, (iv) heterokaryotic. (C.P.M.T. 1990)

91. Mycorrhiza is a term to indicate: (i) fungus association with stem, (ii) bacteria association with root, (iii) fungi association with root, (iv) study of fungi. (C.P.M.T. 1990)

92. After fusion of sexual gametes in *Mucor* the resultant structure is known as : (i) oospore, (ii) cleistothecium, (iii) zygospore, (iv) zygote. (C.P.M.T. 1990)

93. Heterothallism was discovered by : (i) Blakeslee, (ii) Faraday, (iii) Alexopoulos, (iv) Gaumann. (C.P.M.T. 1990)

94. Clamp connections are very common in : (i) Ascomycetes, (ii) Basidiomycetes, (iii) Phycomycetes, (iv) Deuteromycetes. (C.P.M.T. 1990)

95. Haplo-diplo-biontic life-cycle is exhibited by (i) yeast, (ii) *Mucor,* (iii) *Penicillium,* (iv) *Aspergillus.* (C.P.M.T. 1990)

96. The worker associated with mycology : (i) S.R. Kashyap, (ii) A.J. Eames, (iii) A.F. Blakeslee, (iv) Y. Bhardwaja.

97. Heterothallism in Mucorales was discovered in : (i) 1904, (ii) 1918, (iii) 1927, (iv) 1931.

98. Sort out the father of Indian mycology and plant pathology : (i) K.C. Mehta, (ii) B.P. Pal, (iii) E.J. Butler, (iv) B.B. Mundkur.

99. The aseptate mycelium is found in : (i) lower fungi, (ii) higher fungi, (iii) fungi imperfecti, (iv) none of above.

100. The mycelium of *Erysiphe* is : (i) aseptate, (ii) septate, (iii) both (i) and (ii), (iv) none of above.

101. *Neurospora sitophila* is known as : (i) Black mold, (ii) red mold, (iii) blue mold, (iv) green mold.

102. The spermatization takes place in (i) *Neurospora,* (ii) *Penicillium,* (iii) *Peziza,* (iv) *Erysiphe.*

103. One of the following represents cup fungi : (i) *Peziza,* (ii) *Morchella,* (iii) *Agaricus,* (iv) *Amanita.*

104. *Peziza* is a member of : (i) Phycomycetes, (ii) Ascomycetes, (iii) Basidiomycetes, (iv) Deuteromycetes.

105. The basidiospores are : (i) exogenous spores, (ii) endogenous spores, (iii) both (i) & (ii), (iv) none of above.

106. Black rust of wheat is caused by : (i) *Puccinia graminis,* (ii) *Puccinia recondita,* (iii) *Puccinia striiformis,* (iv) *Puccinia glumarum.*

107. The sexual reproduction lacks in : (i) Ascomycetes, (ii) Basidiomycetes, (iii) Phycomycetes, (iv) Deuteromycetes.

108. Only asexual reproduction is found in : (i) Ascomycetes, (ii) Basidiomycetes, (iii) Oomycetes, (iv) Deuteromycetes.

109. *Alternaria solani* causes : (i) late blight of potato, (ii) wart of potato, (iii) early blight of potato, (iv) leaf curl of potato.

110. 'Target board effect' is caused by : (i) *Alternaria,* (ii) *Colletotrichum,* (iii) *Pyricularia,* (iv) *Helminthosporium.*

ANSWERS

1 (i), 2 (i), 3 (iv), 4 (iv), 5 (i) 6 (i), 7 (i), 8 (ii), 9 (ii), 10 (iii), 11 (iv), 12 (ii), 13 (ii), 14 (i), 15 (iv), 16 (iv), 17 (iii), 18 (ii), 19 (ii), 20 (ii), 21 (i), 22 (ii), 23 (ii), 24 (ii), 25 (ii), 26 (iv), 27 (ii), 28 (iii), 29 (iv), 30 (iv), 31 (iv), 32 (i), 33 (i), 34 (ii), 35 (iii), 36 (iv), 37 (ii), 38 (iii), 39 (iii), 40 (ii), 41 (ii), 42 (ii), 43 (iii), 44 (ii), 45 (iii), 46 (iv), 47 (i), 48 (iv), 49 (iii), 50 (iv), 51 (iii), 52 (iv), 53 (iv), 54 (i), 55 (iv), 56 (iii), 57 (iii), 58 (ii), 59 (ii), 60 (iv), 61 (iii), 62 (ii), 63 (iv), 64 (iii), 65 (ii), 66 (iii), 67 (iv), 68 (i), 69 (iv), 70 (ii), 71 (ii), 72 (iv), 73 (iv), 74 (ii), 75 (ii), 76 (iv), 77 (iv), 78 (ii), 79 (ii), 80 (iii), 81 (iv), 82 (i), 83 (iv), 84 (ii), 85 (iv), 86 (ii), 87 (i), 88 (iii), 89 (ii), 90 (iii), 91 (iii), 92 (iii), 93 (i), 94 (ii), 95 (i), 96 (iii), 97 (i), 98 (iii), 99 (i), 100 (ii), 101 (ii), 102 (i), 103 (i), 104 (ii), 105 (i), 106 (i), 107 (iv), 108 (iv), 109 (iii), 110 (i).

BACTERIA, VIRUSES, LICHENS AND MYCOPLASMA

Long Answer Type

1. Describe the habit, structure and reproduction of a lichen collected by you. State the relationship between its components.
2. What is symbiosis? 'Lichens are the best example of symbiosis'. Justify this statement. (Kanpur, 1981)
3. Give the distinguishing features of fungi, bacteria, virus, lichens and mycoplasma. (Kanpur, 1983)
4. "Bacteria are both good and bad associates of human civilisation". Justify the statement. (Kanpur, 1983)
5. Discuss briefly what you know about PPLO and bacteriophage. (Kanpur, 1983)
6. Explain the various methods of reproduction found in bacteria. (Kanpur, 1983)
7. Write an essay on food value of fungi, bacteria and lichens. (Kanpur, 1983)
8. Briefly describe the ultra-structure of a fungal cell, a bacterium, TMV and bacteriophage. (Kanpur, 1984)

9. Describe the characteristics of mycoplasma. How are they different from bacteria and viruses? Mention some of the plant diseases caused by PPLO. (Kanpur, 1984)
10. Give the structure and reproduction of lichens. (Kanpur, 1984)
11. What are lichens? Describe their methods of reproduction and economic importance. (Kanpur, 1985)
12. Describe the ultra-structure of tobacco mosaic virus (TMV) and bacteriophage. (Kanpur 1985)
13. Describe the forms and internal features of lichen. Explain, how are they ecologically and economically important. (Kanpur, 1986)
14. "Lichens are the best example of symbiosis". Justify this statement. Give an account of various methods of reproduction in lichens. (Kanpur, 1987)
15. Describe the structure and economic importance of bacteria. (Kanpur, 1988)
16. Give an account of the structure and economic importance of lichens. (Kanpur, 1988)
17. Give an account of the structure and nature of plant viruses. (Kanpur, 1989)
18. Write an essay on the economic importance of bacteria. (Kanpur, 1989)
19. Give an account of symptoms of viruses. Describe their nature also. (Rohilkhand, 1982)
20. Write about the methods of reproduction in bacteria. (Rohilkhand, 1983)
21. Describe internal structure of lichen thallus. Also describe structures attached with the thallus. (Rohilkhand, 1984)
22. Describe the methods of reproduction in lichens or bacteria. (Rohilkhand, 1985, 1987)
23. What are viruses? Are they living or non-living agents? Give the methods of their transmission. (Rohilkhand, 1986)
24. What are lichens? Give habit and habitat, structure, vegetative and asexual reproduction and economic importance of lichens. (Rohilkhand, 1986)
25. What are the procaryotic and eucaryotic cells? Which of the two is more primitive cells type and why? (Kumaon, 1983, 1987)
26. Give an account of multiplication of plant viruses. (Kumaon, 1983)
27. "The beneficial effects of bacteria outweigh the harmful ones". Justify the above statement and mention the part played by bacteria in the economy of nature. (Kumaon, 1983, 1987)
28. Describe the structure and reproduction in a typical bacterium. How does it differ from a blue-green alga? (Kumaon, 1984, 1986)
29. Give an account of structure and reproduction of lichers with special reference to *Parmelia*. (Kumaon, 1985)
30. How are plant viruses transmitted? Give the control measures for a typical plant viral disease. (Kumaon, 1985)

Short Answer Type

1. In what ways do viruses differ from fission plants and fungi.
2. Given an apothecium, how will you identify whether it belongs to Ascomycetes or lichen.
3. Comment on the relationship between alga and fungus in a lichen.
4. Write the important differences between a procaryote and a eukaryote. Name one example of each.
5. Which algae and fungi are usually associated in lichens?
6. Why are not lichens found in Delhi?
7. Lichens are rare or absent in cities. What conclusions can you draw from this as to the physiology of lichens.
8. Write note on economic importance of lichens.
9. Write a note on organisation of thallus in lichen.
10. Write critical notes on fruticose lichen.
11. Write explanatory notes on: reproduction in lichen.
12. Discuss the comparative advantages gained by the fungus and the alga in a lichen.
13. Write critical notes on the isidia of lichens.
14. Write illustrated notes on the following : (i) nature of viruses, (ii) mycoplasma. (Kanpur, 1981)
15. Write short notes on the following : (i) Tobacco Mosaic Virus (TMV), (ii) bacterial cell, (iii) fruticose lichens. (Kanpur, 1981)
16. Describe the following : (i) nitrogen fixing bacteria, (ii) economic importance of lichens. (Kanpur, 1981)
17. Write short notes on the following : (i) life-cycle of a bacteriophage, (ii) conjugation in bacteria. (Kanpur, 1982)
18. Give the distinguishing features of fungi, bacteria, virus, lichens and mycoplasma. (Kanpur, 1983)
19. Write short notes on the following : (a) economic importance of lichens, (ii) antibiotics from bacteria. (Kanpur, 1984)
20. Write notes on : (a) nitrogen fixing bacteria, (b) virus disease problems in India. (Kanpur, 1984)
21. Write notes on the following : (i) mycoplasma, (ii) antibiotics. (Kanpur, 1985)

22. Give the symptoms of (i) citrus canker, (ii) mosaic disease of tobacco.
23. Write notes on the following : (i) bacteriophage, (ii) citrus canker. (Kanpur, 1986)
24. Describe the following : (i) Tobacco mosaic virus, (ii) role of bacteria in industry. (Kanpur, 1987)
25. Write notes on the following : (i) nitrogen fixing bacteria, (ii) nature of virus. (Kanpur, 1987)
26. (a) What is he biological status of virus? (b) How do plant viruses multiply in a cell? (Kanpur, 1988)
27. Write notes on the following : (a) tobacco mosaic virus, (ii) reproduction in bacteria. (Kanpur, 1988)
28. Write notes on : (i) nitrogen fixing bacteria, (ii) bacteriophage. (Kanpur, 1989)
29. Describe the following : (i) reproduction and economic importance of bacteria, (ii) structure of thallus in lichens. (Rohilkhand, 1981)
30. Explain the following : (a) structure of virus, (b) role of bacteria, (c) symbiosis. (Rohilkhand, 1987)
31. Write about the following : (a) that the viruses are living organisms, (ii) when a bacteriophage infects a bacterial cell, what part of it is left outside, (iii) what type of nucleic acid is present in a phage. (Kumaon, 1982, 1984)
32. Write short notes on the following : (a) bacteriophage, (b) nature of plant viruses. (Kumaon, 1986)
33. Write short notes on : (i) symbiotic relationship in lichens, (ii) the lichen acids. (Kumaon, 1987)
34. Give the distinguished characteristics of the following types of lichens : (a) crustose lichen, (b) foliose lichen, (c) fruticose lichen. (Kumaon, 1987)
35. Classify the bacteria on the basis of their flagellation.
36. Give the ultra-structure of a bacterial cell.
37. Write a note on chemosynthetic bacteria.

Multiple Choice

1. The bacterial cell wall consists of : (i) chitin, (ii) lignin, (ii) cellulose, (iv) pectose.
2. Bacteria were first discovered by (i) Pasteur, (ii) Koch, (iii) T.J. Burill, (iv) Anton von Leeuwenhoek.
3. Bacteria were first discovered in : (i) 1575, (ii) 1675, (iii) 1775, (iv) 1875.
4. The bacteria are : (i) unicellular, (ii) bicellular, (iii) multicellular, (iv) filamentous.
5. The bacterium with a group of flagella at both ends is : (i) lophotrichous, (ii) peritrichous, (iii) amphitrichous, (iv) none of above.
6. Which of the following is not found in bacterial cell : (i) glycogen, (ii) proteins, (iii) fats, (iv) endoplasmic reticulum.
7. Sort out nitrogen fixing bacteria : (i) *Azotobacter*, (ii) *Pseudomonas*, (iii) *Xanthomonas*, (iv) *Salmonella*.
8. Scientist concerned with classification of bacteria : (i) Alexopoulos, (ii) Hutchinson, (iii) Bergey, (iv) Rendle.
9. Typhoid fever is : (i) viral disease, (ii) bacterial disease, (iii) mycoplasma disease, (iv) none of above.
10. Tetanus is : (i) viral disease, (ii) bacterial disease, (iii) mycoplasma disease, (iv) none of above.
11. The bacteria are : (i) eukaryotic, (ii) prokaryotic, (iii) mesokaryotic, (iv) none of above.
12. The microorganisms found in the leguminous roots are : (i) *Nitrosomonas*, (ii) *Azotobacter*, (iii) *Rhizobium*, (iv) *Xanthomonas*.
13. Sort out the bacterial disease : (i) typhoid, (ii) cholera, (iii) tuberculosis, (iv) all the above.
14. A virulent poison is produced in canned foods by : (i) *Xanthomonas*, (ii) *Pseudomonas*, (iii) *Rhizobium* sp., (iv) *Clostridium* sp.
15. The nitrogen-fixing bacteria are : (i) *Azotobacter*, (ii) *Rhizobium*, (iii) *Clostridium*, (iv) all the above.
16. Sort out the ammonifying bacteria : (i) *Bacillus subtilis*, (ii) *Bacillus mycodes*, (iii) *Bacillus ramosus*, (iv) all the above.
17. Nitrogen fixation is done by : (i) soil fungi, (ii) bacteria, (iii) green algae, (iv) virus.
18. The bacteria belong to : (i) Bacillariophyceae, (ii) Myxophyceae, (iii) Schizomycetes, (iv) Myxomycetes.
19. The common method of reproduction in bacteria is : (i) budding, (ii) fragmentation, (iii) fission, (iv) hormogone formation.
20. The bacteria-like algae are : (i) Chlorophyceae, (ii) Phaeophyceae, (iii) Myxophyceae, (iv) Rhodophyceae.
21. Sort out the sulphur bacteria : (i) *Ferrobacillus*, (ii) *Thiobacillus*, (iii) *Hydrogenomonas*, (iv) *Carboxylomonas*.
22. Sort out the bacterial disease : (i) late blight, (ii) early blight, (ii) leaf curl of potato, (iv) ring rot of potato.
23. Pleuropneumonia of cattle is caused by : (i) virus, (ii) fungus, (iii) mycoplasma, (iv) bacteria.
24. The mycoplasma is : (i) eukaryotic, (ii) prokaryotic, (iii) multicellular, (iv) none of above.
25. The membrane found around mycoplasma is : (i) single-layered, (ii) double-layered, (iii) three-layered, (iv) none of above.
26. The nuclear membrane in mycoplasma is : (i) single-layered, (ii) double-layered, (iii) nuclear membrane lacking, (iv) nuclear membrane well-defined.
27. The diameter of smallest mycoplasma is : (i) 1μ, (ii) 5μ, (iii) .05μ, (iv) .1μ.
28. Little leaf of brinjal is caused by : (i) mycoplasma, (ii) fungi, (iii) virus, (iv) bacteria.

29. The mycoplasma contains : (i) only DNA, (ii) only RNA, (iii) both RNA and DNA, (iv) none of above.

30. Little leaf symptom is produced by : (i) fungi, (ii) algae, (iii) mycoplasma, (iv) virus.

31. Milk spoilage is due to : (i) *Aspergillus*, (ii) *Peudomonas*, (iii) *Lactobacillus*, (iv) *Staphylococcus*. (C.P.M.T. 1977)

32. Tobacco mosaic virus was first crystallized by : (i) F.C. Bawden, (ii) K.M. Smith, (iii) W.M. Stanley, (iv) V. Ivanowski. (C.P.M.T. 1978)

33. A free living bacterium capable of fixing atmospheric nitrogen is : (i) *Clostridium*, (ii) *Rhizobium*, (iii) *Staphylococcus*, (iv) *Streptococcus*. (C.P.M.T. 1978)

34. Sort out the bacterial disease, (i) red rust of tea; (ii) white rust, (iii) citrus canker, (iv) athlete's foot.

35. In nitrogen-cycle the bacteria which change, proteins to NH_2 are known as : (i) bacteria of decay, (ii) denitrifying bacteria, (iii) nitrate bacteria, (iv) nitrogen fixing bacteria. (C.P.M.T. 1978)

36. The leguminous plants are important in agriculture because : (i) they are disease resistant (ii) four crops of legumes can be produced in a year, (iii) they require very little irrigation, (iv) they help in nitrogen economy of nature. (C.P.M.T. 1978)

37. Small pox is caused by : (i) virus, (ii) bacteria, (iii) housefly, (iv) mosquito. (C.P.M.T. 1979)

38. Bacteria that are responsible for fermentation of dairy milk and plant product : (i) *Lactobacillus*, (ii) *hay bacillus*, (iii) *Acetobacter*, (iv) *Rhizobium*. (C.P.M.T. 1979)

39. Nitrogen-fixing bacteria are concerned with family : (i) Leguminosae, (ii) Cruciferae, (iii) Gramineae, (iv) Malvaceae.

40. Bacteriophage is made up of : (i) protein, (ii) DNA, (iii) nucleoprotein, (iv) lipid and protein. (C.P.M.T. 1979)

41. In nitrogen-cycle, which of the following play an important role : (i) *Rhizopus*, (ii) *Mucor*, (iii) *Nitrobacter*, (iv) *Spirogyra*. (C.P.M.T. 1979)

42. Bacteria cannot survive in a highly salted pickle because : (i) they become plasmolysed and consequently killed, (ii) they do anaerobic respiration, (iii) water is not available to them, (iv) all the above. (C.P.M.T. 1980)

43. The organisms which participate most actively in nitrogen cycle in nature are : (i) saprophytic angiosperms, (ii) parasitic fungi, (iii) bacteria, (iv) legumes. (C.P.M.T. 1980)

44. Which of the following is bacterial disease : (i) small pox, (ii) influenza, (iii) T.B., (iv) rabies. (C.P.M.T. 1980)

45. A bacterial cell divides once every minute. It takes an hour to fill a cup. How many minutes will it take to fillhalf the cup : (i) 59, (ii) 49, (iii) 30, (iv) 29. (C.P.M.T. 1981)

46. A free-living anaerobic bacterium capable of fixing nitrogen is : (i) *Azotobacter*, (ii) *Clostridium*, (iii) *Rhizobium*, (iv) *Streptococcus*. (C.P.M.T. 1981)

47. A bacterial cell differs from eukaryotic cell due to : (i) green algae, (ii) red algae, (iii) heterochromatin, (iv) rigid cell wall. (C.P.M.T. 1982)

48. Which of the following disease is caused by bacteria : (i) arthritis, (ii) amoebic dysentery, (iii) beri-beri, (iv) dipthería. (C.P.M.T. 1982)

49. Lichens are composite organs, consisting of algae and : (i) mosses, (ii) protozoa, (iii) fungi, (iv) bacteria. (C.P.M.T. 1982)

50. The bulk of nitrogen in nature is fixed by : (i) lightning, (ii) symbiotic bacteria, (iii) denitryfying, (iv) chemical industries. (C.P.M.T. 1982)

51. True nucleus is absent in : (i) mosses, (ii) green algae, (iii) soil fungi, (iv) bacteria. (C.P.M.T. 1984)

52. Nodules with nitrogen fixing bacteria are present in : (i) mustard, (ii) wheat, (iii) gram, (iv) cotton. (C.P.M.T. 1984)

53. Bacteria have cell membrane made up of (i) protein, (ii) cellulose, (iii) fat, (iv) chitin. (C.P.M.T. 1984)

54. Bacteriophage consists of : (i) carbon and nitrogen, (ii) DNA, (iii) nucleoproteins, (iv) proteins only. (C.P.M.T. 1984)

55. Bacteria cannot survive in a highly salted pickle because : (i) salts inhibit reproduction, (ii) bacteria do not get enough light for photosynthesis, (iii) they become plasmolysed and killed, (iv) pickle does not contain nutrients necessary for bacteria to live. (C.P.M.T. 1984)

56. One of the interesting features of the viruses is that they : (i) multiply only in host cytoplasm, (ii) behave as if they were plants, (iii) are made of proteins only, (iv) occur only inside bacteria. (C.P.M.T. 1984)

57. Virology is the study of : (i) viruses, (ii) bacteria, (iii) fungi, (iv) algae. (C.P.M.T. 1984)

58. Microbiology is the study of : (i) lower organisms with microscope, (ii) micro-organisms, (iii) bacteria, (iv) protozoa. (C.P.M.T. 1985)

59. The free living nitrogen fixing bacteria belong to the genus : (i) *Pseudomonas*, (ii) *Azotobacter*, (iii) *Rhizobium*, *Xanthomonas*. (C.P.M.T. 1985)

60. The production of nitrates from ammonia through *Nitrosomonas* is called : (i) nitrification, (ii) ammonification, (iii) nitrogen fixation, (iv) denitrification. (C.P.M.T. 1985)

61. The bacteria which in association with some plant roots fix atmospheric nitrogen are called : (i) *Pseudomonas* (ii) *Bacillus*, (iii) *Salmonella*, (iv) *Rhizobium*. (C.P.M.T. 1985)

62. *Escherichia coli* is the common inhabitant of : (i) human intestine, (ii) soil, (iii) water, (iv) decaying fruits. (C.P.M.T. 1986)

63. Name of bacteria is first proposed by : (i) Anton von Leeuwenhock, (ii) Linnaeus, (iii) Watson, (iv) Ehrenberg. (C.P.M.T. 1987)

64. Polymorphism is found in : (i) *Micrococcus*, (ii) *Diplococcus*, (iii) *Azotobacter*, (iv) *Clostridium*. (C.P.M.T. 1987)

65. In nitrogen cycle which of the following plays an important role : (i) *Rhizopus*, (ii) *Mucor*, (iii) *Nitrobacter*, (iv) *Spirogyra*. (C.P.M.T. 1987)

66. The nucleus absent in : (i) green algae, (ii) fungi, (iii) lichens, (iv) bacteria.

67. The nitrogen present in atmosphere : (i) is utilized by plants through micro-organisms, (ii) no use to plants, (iii) it is injurious to plants, (iv) none (C.P.M.T. 1988)

68. Viruses cause : (i) dysentery, (ii) malaria, (iii) pneumonia, (iv) small pox.

69. Mitochondria are absent in : (i) yeast, (ii) fungi,, (iii) bacteria, (iv) green algae. (C.P.M.T. 1989)

70. Transfer of genetic material from one bacterium to another by virus is called : (i) transduction, (ii) transformation, (iii) conjugation, (iv) lysogeny. (C.P.M.T. 1989)

71. In the nitrogen cycle, nitrite is converted to nitrate by : (i) *Azotobacter*, (ii) *Rhizobium*, (iii) *Nitrosomonas*, (iv) *Nitrobacter*. (C.P.M.T. 1989)

72. The most abundant protein in the plant world is found in : (i) root hairs, (ii) mitochondria, (iii) chloroplasts, (iv) viruses. (C.P.M.T. 1989)

73. Some diseases caused by bacteria are : (i) measles, mumps, malaria, (ii) tetanus, typhoid, tuberculosis, (iii) small pox, sleeping sickness, syphilis, (iv) pneumonia, polio, ring worm. (C.P.M.T. 1989)

74. Citrus canker caused by : (i) *Xanthomonas citri* (ii) *Azotobacter*, (iii) *Pseudomonas*, (iv) *Erwinia*. (C.P.M.T. 1990)

75. Virus is first isolated by : (i) Stanley, (ii) Miller, (iii) Iwanowsky, (iv) Schwann. (C.P.M.T. 1990)

76. Vibrio is : (i) Virus, (ii) bacteria, (iii) lichen, (iv) angiosperm. (C.P.M.T. 1990)

77. In majority of lichens the fungal partner is : (i) member of Ascomycetes, (ii) member of basidiomycetes, (iii) member of Oomycetes, (iv) none of above.

78. A group of algal cells imprisoned in a fungal mycelium and which is used for vegetative multiplication of a lichen is : (i) isidium, (ii) soredium, (iii) cephalodium, (iv) helotism.

79. The mode of life of lichen is : (i) saprophytic, (ii) parasitic, (iii) symbiotic, (iv) autotrophic.

80. A bacteriophage virus can be recognized by its : (i) extremely irregular shape, (ii) beautifully rounded shape, (iii) tadpole shape, (iv) rhomboidal shape.

81. Viruses are found to be consisting of : (i) purely proteins, (ii) purely nucleic acids, (iii) nucleoproteins, (iv) phosphates and sugars.

82. Among different kinds of water which of the following is free from bacteria : (i) deep well water, (ii) rain water as it falls down, (iii) sea water, (iv) water of hot springs.

83. A viral disease of potato : (i) brown rot, (ii) late blight, (iii) early blight, (iv) leaf roll.

84. A disease in cattle caused by viruses : (i) yellow fever, (ii) foot and mouth disease, (iii) anthrax, (iv) brucellosis.

85. The first person to use the Latin term virus in its current sense : (i) D. Iwanowski, (ii) M. Beijirinck, (iii) A. Meyer, (iv) W.M. Stanley.

86. The condition where the flagella are distributed all over the body of the bacterium is : (i) atrichous, (ii) monotrichous, (iii) amphitrichous, (iv) peritrichous.

87. A term meaning 'bacterium eater' : (i) cyanophage, (ii) coliphage, (iii) bacteriocide, (iv) bacteriophage.

88. A virologist who discovered that T.M.V. can be crystallized : (i) Beijerinck, (ii) W.M. Stanley, (iii) Iwanowski, (iv) Adolf Meyer.

89. That part of the virus which gives it hereditary integrity : (i) capsomere, (ii) capsid, (iii) nucleic acid, (iv) nucleotide.

90. A viral disease of plants : (i) citrus canker, (ii) brown rot of potato, (iii) pea mosaic, (iv) angular leaf spot of cotton.

91. Cocci arranged in cubes with eight or more cells : (i) tetrads, (ii) streptococci, (iii) Diplococci, (iv) Sarcinae.

92. In bacteria the respiratory enzymes are situated in the : (i) cell membrane, (ii) cytoplasm, (iii) mitochondria, (iv)ribosomes.

93. One of the following bacterial characters is a plant character(i) presence of flagella, (ii) prokaryotic nucleus, (iii) rigid cell wall, (iv) heterotrophic nutrition.

94. The first bacteriologist : (i) Pasteur, (ii) Leeuwenhoek, (iii) Jenner, (iv) Robert Koch.

ANSWERS

1 (i), 2 (iv), 3 (ii), 4 (i), 5 (iii), 6 (iv), 7 (i), 8 (iii), 9 (ii), 10 (ii), 11 (ii), 12 (iii), 13 (iv), 14 (iv), 15 (iv), 16 (iv), 17 (ii), 18 (iii), 19 (iii), 20 (iii), 21 (ii), 22 (iv), 23 (iii), 24 (ii), 25 (iii), 26 (iii), 27 (iv), 28 (i), 29 (iii), 30 (iii), 31 (iii), 32 (iv), 33 (i), 34 (iii), 35 (ii), 36 (iv), 37 (i), 38 (i), 39 (i), 40 (iii), 41 (iii), 42 (i), 43 (iii), 44 (iii), 45 (i), 46 (ii), 47 (iii), 48 (iv), 49 (iii), 50 (ii), 51 (iv), 52 (iii), 53 (iv), 54 (iii), 55 (iii), 56 (i), 57 (i), 58 (ii), 59 (ii), 60 (i), 61 (iv), 62 (i), 63 (i), 64 (ii), 65 (iii), 66 (iv), 67 (i), 68 (iv), 69 (iii), 70 (i), 71 (iii), 72 (iii), 73 (ii), 74 (i), 75 (iii), 76 (ii), 77 (i), 78 (ii), 79 (iii), 80 (iii), 81 (iii), 82 (ii), 83 (iv), 84 (ii), 85 (i), 86 (iv), 87 (iv), 88 (iii), 89 (iii), 90 (iii), 91 (ii), 92 (i), 93 (iii), 94 (ii).

References

Books

Agrios, G.N. 1969. *Plant Pathology.* Academic Press, N.Y.

Ahmadjian, V. 1967. *The Lichen Symbiosis.* Waltham, Mass : Blaisdell.

Ainsworth, G.C. 1952. *Medical Mycology.* Pitman, London.

Ainsworth, G.C. 1971. *A Dictionary of the Fungi.* Commonwealth Mycological Institute, Kew, Surrey.

Ainsworth, G.C. and K. Sampson, 1950. *The British smut fungi (Ustilaginales).* Kew, Surrey.

Alexopoulos, C.J. 1962. *Introductory Mycology.* John Wiley & Sons, Inc., N.Y.

Altman, J. 1966. *Phytopathological Techniques. Laboratory Manual.* Colorado.

Anonymous, 1953. *Plant Diseases.* U.S. Dept. Agr. Year book.

Arthur, J.C. 1934. *Manual of Rusts in the United States and Canada,* Indiana.

Barnes, E.H. 1968. *Atlas and Manual of Plant Pathology* Appleton, New York.

Bessey, E.A. 1950. *Morphology and Taxonomy of Fungi.* The Blakiston Co., Philadelphia.

Bisby, G.R. 1955. *An introduction to the taxonomy and nomenclature of fungi.* Kew, England.

Brown, W.H. 1935. *The Plant Kingdom.* Ginn & Company.

Butler, E.J. 1918. *Fungi and Disease in Plants Thacker Spink & Co. Calcutta.*

Bulter, E.J., and G.R. Bisby. 1931. *The Fungi of India.*

Butler, E.J., and S. G. Jones. 1949. *Plant Pathology.* Macmillan & Co., Ltd. London.

Chester, K.S. 1946. *Cereal Rusts.* Chronica Botanica Co., Waltham Mass.

Chopra, G.L. 1934. *Lichens of the Himalayas Part I.* Lahore.

Christensen, C.M. 1951. *The molds and man.* Minneapolis.

Christensen, C.M. 1955. *Common fleshy fungi.* Minneapolis.

Chupp, C. and A.F. Sherf, 1960. *Vegetable Diseases and their control.* Ronald Press, New York.

Cochrane, V.W. 1958. *Physiology of Fungi.* John Wiley & Sons, Inc., New York.

Dickson, J.G. 1956. *Diseases of Field Crops.* McGraw Hill, New York.

Duddington, C.L. 1957. *The Friendly Fungi.* London.

Fink, B, 1960. *The Lichen flora of the United States.* University of Michigan Press, Ann Arbor.

Fischer, G.W. and C.S. Holton. 1957. *Biology & Control of the Smut Fungi.* Ronald Press, New York.

Fitzpatrick, H.M. 1930. *The lower fungi, Phycomycetes.* McGraw Hill, New York.

Foster, J.W. 1949. *Chemical activities of fungi,* Acad. Press, New York.

Garett, S.D. 1944. *Root disease fungi.* Chronica Botanica Co., Waltham Mass.

Gaumann E.A. 1950. *Principles of plant infection.* Crosby Lockwood & Son, Ltd. London.

Gaumann, E.A. 1952. *The Fungi.* Hafner Publishing Co., New York.

Gaumann, E.A. and C.W. Dodge. 1928. *Comparative morphology of fungi.* McGraw Hill, New York.

Gray, W.D. 1959. *The Relation of Fungi to Human Affairs.* New York.

Gwynne-Vaughan, H.C.I., and B. Barnes. 1937. *The structure and development of the fungi.* Cambridge University Press.

Hale, M.E. Jr. 1961. *Lichen handbook.* Washington D.C.

Hale, M.E. Jr. 1967. *Biology of the lichens.* Edward Arnold, London.
Hawker, L.E. 1950. *Physiology of Fungi.* Univ. London Press Brickley, England.
Hawker, L.E. 1967. *The physiology of reproduction in fungi.* Cambridge University Press.
Heald, F.D. 1933. *Manual of plant diseases.* McGraw Hill, New York.
Heald, F.D. 1943. *Introduction to Plant Pathology.* McGraw Hill, New York.
Horsfall, J.G. 1956. *Principles of fungicidal action.* Chronica Botanica, Waltham, Mass.
Ingold, C.T. 1953. *Dispersal in fungi.* Oxford.
Kamat, M.N. 1961. *Handbook of mycology.* Prakash Publishing House, Poona.
Kamat, M.N. 1953. *Practical plant pathology.* Poona.
Kamat, M.N. 1956. *Introductory plant pathology.* Poona.
Karling, J.S. 1942. *The Plasmodiophorales.* New York.
Karling, J.S. 1964. *Synchytrium.* Acad. Press, London.
Lilly, V.G. and H.L. Barnett. 1951. *Physiology of the fungi.* McGraw Hill, New York.
Martin, C.W, and C.J. Alexopoulos, 1969. *The Myxomycetes,* lowa.
Mehrotra, B.S. 1976. *The Fungi.* Oxford & IBH,
Mehrotra, R.S. 1980. *Plant Pathology.* Tata McGraw Hill, New Delhi.
Mehta, K.C. 1940. *Further Studies on Cereal Rusts in India* Vols. I & II, I.C.A.R. New Delhi.
Melhus, I.E. and G.C. Kent. 1948. *Elements of plant pathology.* The Macmillan Co., New York.
Mukandan, T.K. 1964. *Plant Protection Principles and Practice.* Asia Publ. House, Bombay.
Mundkur, B.B. and M.J. Thirumalachar. 1952. *Ustilaginales of India.* Kew, England.
Mundkur, B.B. 1967. *Fungi and Plant Disease.* 2nd Ed. Macmillan and Co., Ltd. London.
Pandey, B.P. 1982. A text book of plant pathology–*Pathogen and Plant Disease.* S. Chand & Co. Ltd. New Delhi.
Pandey, B.P. 1980. *Kavak.* S. Chand & Co., Ltd. New Delhi.
Pandey, B.P. 1981. *Kavak tatha padap rog vigyan.* S. Chand & Co. Ltd, New Delhi.
Ramsbottom, J. 1923. *A handbook of the larger British fungi.* The British Museum, London.
Ramsbottom, J. 1929. *Fungi, An Introduction to Mycology.* London.
Ramsbottom, J. 1953. *Mushrooms and Toadstools.* Collins, London.
Raper, K.B. and D.I. Fennel. 1965. *The genus Aspergillus.* Baltimore.
Rawlins, T.E. *Phytopathological and Botanical Research Methods.* John Wiley, New York.
Singh, R.S. 1979. *Plant Diseases.* 4th Ed. Oxford & IBH, New Delhi.
Singh, R.S. 1979. *Introduction to Principles of Plant Pathology,* 2nd. ed. Oxford & IBH, New Delhi.
Smith, A.L. 1926. *A monograph of the British Lichens.* British Museum, London.
Smith, G. 1969. *An Introduction to Industrial Mycology.* Edward Arnold & Co., London.
Smith, G.M. 1955. *Cryptogamic Botany,* Vol. I 2nd. ed. McGraw Hill, New York.
Sparrow, F.K. 1960. *Aquatic Phycomycetes.* University of Michigan Press, Ann. Arbor.
Stakman, E.C. and J.G. Harrar. 1957. *Principles of Plant Pathology.* Ronald Press, New York.
Stevens, F.L. 1925. *Plant disease fungi.* The Macmillan Co., New York.
Stevens, N.E. and R.B. Stevens. 1952. *Disease in Plants.* Waltham, Massachusetts.
Talbot, P.H.B. 1971. *Principles of fungal taxonomy.* The Macmillan Press, London.
Vasudeva, R.S. 1960. *The fungi of India* I.C.A.R. New Delhi.
Vasudeva, R.S. 1963. *Indian Cercosporae.* I.C.A.R. New Delhi.
Walker, J.C. 1968. *Plant Pathology,* 3rd ed. McGraw Hill, New York.
Wheeler, B.E.J. 1969. *An Introduction to plant diseases.* John Wiley, London.
Westcott, Cynthia. 1960. *Plant Disease Handbook.* 2nd ed., Van Nostrand, Princeton, New Jersey.
Wolf. F.A., and Wolf, F.T. 1947. *The Fungi.* Vols. I & II. John Wiley & Sons, Inc., New York.

Glossary

Acervulus. A subepidermal, saucer-shaped, asexual fruiting body producing short conidiophores and conidia (*e.g., Colletorichum* spp.).

Actinomycetes. A group of microorganisms apparently intermediate between bacteria and fungi (*e.g., Streptomyces* spp).

Aeciospore. A binucleate rust spore produced in an aecium (*e.g., Puccinia graminis tritici* on *Berberris* leaf).

Aecium. A cup-shaped fruiting body of the rust fungi which produces aeciospores (*e.g. P. graminis tritici* on *Berberris* leaf).

Aerobic. A microorganism which lives in the presence of molecular oxygen (*e.g.*, certain bacteria).

Agar. A gelatin-like substance obtained from seaweed (red algae-*Gracilaria, Gelidium* etc.). and used to prepare culture media on which microorganisms are grown for study.

Agglutination. A serological test in which viruses or bacteria suspended in a liquid collect into clumps.

Alternate host. One of two kinds of plants on which a parasitic fungus (*e.g.*, black rust of wheat caused by *Puccinia graminis tritici*) must develop to complete life-cycle.

Anaerobic. A microorganism that lives in the absence of molecular oxygen (*e.g.*, certain bacteria).

Angstrom (Å). A unit of length equal to 1/10 μ or 1/10,000μ.

Annulation. A series of transverse depressions on the cuticle of a nematode.

Anthracnose. A leaf spot or fruit-spot type of a disease caused by fungi that produce their asexual spores in an acervulus (*e.g.*, disease symptoms produced by *Colletotrichum* spp.).

Antibiotic. A chemical compound produced by one microorganism which inhibits the growth of other organisms.

Apothecium. An open cup or saucer-shaped ascocarp of Ascomycetes.

Appendage. A hyphal or rigid structure for attachment of perithecium to or from mycelium, varying in structure and function in different Ascomycetes.

Appressorium. The swollen tip of a hypha or germ tube that facilitates attachment and penetration of the host by the fungus (*e.g., Erysiphe graminis tritici*).

Ascocarp. The fruiting body of Ascomycetes which contains asci.

Ascomycetes. A group of fungi producing their sexual spores, ascospores, within asci.

Ascospore. A sexually produced spore borne in an ascus.

Ascus. A membranous spore sac, as of Ascomycetes.

Aseptate. Without any septum.

Autoecious fungus. A parasitic fungus which completes its entire life cycle on the same host (*e.g., Melampsora lini*).

Bacillus. A rod-shaped bacterium.

Bactericide. A chemical compound that kills bacteria.

Bacteriology. The science dealing with bacteria.

Bacteriophage. A virus that infects specific bacteria and usually kills them.

Bacteriostatic. A chemical or physical agent that prevents multiplication of bacteria without killing them.

Bacterium. A unicellular microscopic plant that lacks chlorophyll and multiplies by fission.

Basidiomycetes. A group of fungi producing their sexual spores, basidiospores, on basidia.

Basidiospore. A sexually produced spore born on a basidium.

Basidium. A club-shaped structure on which basidiospores are borne.

Biflagellate. Having two flagella.

Biotype. A subgroup within a species usually characterized by the possession of a single or few characters in common.

Blight. A disease characterized by general and rapid killing of leaves, flowers and stems (*e.g.*, late blight and early blight of potato).

Blotch. A disease characterized by large, and irregular in shape, spots or lesions on leaves, shoots and stems.

Budding. The production of buds (*e.g.*, in *Saccharomyces*).

Bursa. Lateral cuticular extension present at the posterior end of males of some nematodes.

Canker. A necrotic or sunken lesions on a stem, branch or fruit of a plant (*e.g.*, Citrus canker caused by *Xanthomonas citri*).

Capitate. Enlarge or swollen at tip.

Capsid. The protein coat of viruses which forms the closed shell that contains the nucleic acid and consists of protein subunits capsomeres.

Capsomere. A small protein molecule that is the structural and chemical unit of the protein coat (capsid) of a virus.

Capsule. A relatively thick layer which surrounds some kinds of bacteria.

Cellulase. An enzyme that breaks down cellulose.

Cellulose. A carbohydrate forming main part of plant cell walls $(C_6H_{10}O_5)$ n.

Chemotherapy. Control of a plant disease with chemicals that are absorbed and are translocated internally.

Chlamydospore. A thick-walled asexual spore formed by the modification of a cell of a fungus hypha.

Chlorosis. Yellowing of green tissue due to chlorophyll destruction.

Chronic symptoms. Symptoms that appear for a long period of time.

Circulative viruses. Viruses that are acquired by their vectors through their mouthparts, accumulate internally, then are passed through their tissues and introduced into plants again through the mouthparts of the vectors.

Clamp connection. Swellings on certain dikaryotic hyphae for passage of a daughter nuclei to cell below with subsequent septum formation; also occurring in whorls, for distribution of nuclei to hyphal branches (*e.g.*, *Ustilago* spp).

Clavate. Club-shaped; thickened at one end (*e.g.*, sporangiophore of *Albugo*).

Cleistothecium. An ascocarp which remains closed and produces spores internally (*e.g.*, *Erysiphe graminis*).

Cloaca. A chamber in male nematodes into which the digestive and reproductive systems enter which empties through the anus.

Coccus. A spherical bacterium.

Coenocytic. Aseptate and multinucleate mycelium (*e.g.*, Phycomycetes–the lower fungi).

Columella. A vegetative prolongation into sporangium or sorus.

Concentric. Forming one circle around another with a common centre (*e.g.*, target-board effect, produced by *Alternaria* spp).

Conidiophore. A specialized hypha on which one or more conidia are produced.

Conidium. A fungal spore asexually produced by constriction of sterigma or of part of a hypha;

spore formed from the end of the conidiophore.

Crosier. Hook formed by terminal cells of ascogenous hyphae.

Cross protection. The phenomenon in which plant tissues infected with one strain of a virus are protected from infection by other strains of the same virus.

Culture. The cultivation of microorganisms or tissues in prepared media.

Culture medium. The prepared food material on which microorganisms are cultured.

Cyst. An encysted zoospore (*e.g.* in fungi); in nematodes, the carcass of dead adult females which may contain eggs.

Damping off. Destruction of seedlings near the soil line, resulting in the falling of seedlings on the ground (characteristic infection by *Pythium* spp).

Detoxification. The inactivation or destruction of a toxin by breakdown of the toxic molecule.

Dichotomous. Characterized by dichotomy.

Dichotomy-Branching which results from division of growing point into two equal parts; repeated forking.

Dieback. Progressive death of shoots and roots generally starting at the tip.

Dikaryon. A pair of compatible nuclei (+ –), as in cells of Basidiomycetes.

Dikaryotic. Mycelium or spores containing two sexually compatible nuclei (+ –) per cell, as in Basidiomycetes.

Dimorphic. Having two different forms.

Dimorphism. State of having reciprocally transformable unicellular and filamentous types, as in some bacteria and fungi.

Dioecious. Having sexes (male and female) separate.

Diplanetism. Condition of having two periods of mobility in one life history, as of zoospores in some Phycomycetes.

Diploid. Having a double set of chromosomes; two haploid (n) nuclei make of diploid (2n) nucleus after fusion.

Disease. Any disturbance of a plant that interferes with its normal structure, function or, economic value.

Disease cycle. The chain of events involved in disease development, including the stages of development of pathogen and the effect of the disease on the host.

Disinfectant. A physical or chemical agent that frees a plant or organ from infection.

Disinfestant. An agent that kills or inactivates pathogens in the environment or on the surface of the plant, prior to infection.

Disjunctor. Intercalary cells, and zone of separation between successive conidia.

Dissemination. Dispersal of inoculum from its source to healthy plants.

Downy mildew. A plant disease in which the mycelium and spores of the fungus appear as a downy growth on the host surface, caused by Peronosporaceae.

Ectoparasite. A parasite that lives on the exterior of an organism (*e.g., Erysiphe graminis*).

Egg. A female gamete. In nematodes, the first stage of the life cycle containing a zygote or a larva.

Enation. Malformation or outgrowth induced by certain virus infections.

Encyst. To form a cyst.

Endogenous. Originating within the organism.

Endoparasite. A parasite that enters the host and feeds from within.

Endospore. An endogenous spore.

Enzyme. A protein by living cells that can catalyze a specific organic reaction.

Epidemic. A widespread and severe outbreak of a disease.

Epiphytotic. A widespread and destructive outbreak of a disease of plants.
Eradicant. A chemical substance that destroys a pathogen at its source.
Eradication. Control of plant disease by eliminating the plants that carry the pathogen.
Esophagus. The portion of the digestive system of a nematode between the stomach and the intestine.
Exclusion. Control of plant disease by excluding the pathogen or infected plant material from disease free areas.
Exudate. Liquid discharge from plant tissue.
Facultative. Having the power of living under different conditions.
Facultative parasite. An organism that is usually saprophytic but which under certain conditions may become parasitic.
Facultative saprophyte. An organism that is usually parasitic but which may also live as a saprophyte.
Fertilization. The union of male and female nuclei.
Fertilization tube. Process of an antheridium, penetrating oogonial wall, for passage of male gamete in certain fungi.
Filamentous. Thread-like; filiform.
Filifom. Thread-like; filamentous.
Fission. Cleavage of cells asexually (*e.g.,* in bacteria).
Flagella. Plural of flagellum.
Flagellate. Furnished with flagella.
Flagellum. The lash-like process of many motile bodies, and functions as an organ of locomotion.
Flagging. The loss of rigidity and drooping leaves and tender shoots preceding the wilting of a plant.
Free-living. A microorganism that lives, freely, unattached; or a pathogen living in the soil, outside its host.
Fructification. Fruit body.
Fruiting body. A complex fungal structure containing spores.
Fumigant. A toxic gas or volatile substance that is used to disinfest certain areas from various pests.
Fumigation. The application of fumigant for disinfestation.
Fungal. Pertaining to fungi.
Fungicide. A compound toxic to fungi.
Fungistatic. A compound which prevents fungal growth without killing fungus.
Fungus. An undifferentiated plant lacking chlorophyll and conductive tissues.
Gall. A swelling produced on a plant as a result of infection by certain pathogens.
Geniculate. Bent like a knee joint (*e.g.* in mycelium of Deuteromycetes).
Genus. A group of closely related species, in classification of plants and animals.
Germ pore. The exit pore of a germ tube in the spore integument.
Germ tube. Short filamentous tube put forth by a germinating spore.
Germination. The beginning of growth of a spore or seed.
Giant cell. A multinucleate mass of protoplasm formed by coalescence of several adjacent plant cells. Found in plants infected by certain nematodes.
Globose. Spherical.
Growth inhibitor. A natural substance that inhibits the growth of a plant.
Gum. Complex polysaccharide formed by cells in reaction to wounding or infection.
Gummosis. Production of gum by plant tissue.

Haploid. Having single (n) complete set of chromosomes.

Haplont. An organism having haploid (n) somatic nuclei.

Haustorium. A projection of hyphae into host cells which acts as a penetration and absorbing organ.

Heteroecious. Passing different stages of life history in different hosts. Pertaining to rust fungi.

Heterothallic fungi. Fungi producing compatible male and female gametes on the same mycelium.

Host. A plant that is invaded by a parasite and from which the parasite obtains its nutrients.

Host range. The various kinds of host plants that may be attacked by a parasite.

Hyaline. Clear, transparent.

Hybridization. The crossing of two individuals different in one or more heritable characters.

Hydrolysis. The enzymatic breakdown of a compound through the addition of water.

Hyperplasia. Excessive development due to increase in number of cells.

Hypersensitivity. Excessive sensitivity of plant tissues to certain pathogens. Affected cells are killed quickly, blocking the advance of obligate parasites.

Hypertrophy. Excessive growth due to increase in size of cells.

Hypha. The thread-like filament of vegetative mycelium of a fungus or a single branch of a mycelium.

Hypoplasia. Underdevelopment of a tissue or plant due to decreased cell division.

Hypotrophy. Underdevelopment of a tissue or plant due to abnormally reduced cell enlargement.

Immune. Exempt from infection by a given pathogen.

Immunity. The state of being immune.

Imperfect fungus. Fungus lacking the sexual spore stage.

Imperfect stage. The part of the life cycle of a fungus in which no sexual spores are produced.

Incubation period. Period between infection and appearance of symptoms induced by parasitic organisms.

Indexing. A procedure to determine whether a given plant is infected by a virus.

Indicator. A plant that reacts to certain viruses or environmental factors with production of specific symptoms and is used for detection and identification of these factors.

Infection. Invasion, or condition caused by endoparasites.

Infectious disease. A disease that is caused by a pathogen which can spread from a diseased to a healthy plant.

Infested. Applied to a plant surface or soil contaminated with bacteria, fungi etc.

Inoculate. To bring a pathogen into contact with a host plant or plant organ.

Inoculation. Transfer of a pathogen to the host.

Inoculum. The pathogen that can cause disease.

Intercalary. Inserted between others.

Intercellular. Among or between cells.

Intine. The inner covering membrane of spore.

Intracellular. Within or through the cells.

Invasion. The spread of pathogen into the host.

In vitro. Outside the host; outside the lab.

In vivo. In the host; in the lab.

Isolation. The separation of pathogen from its host and its culture on a nutrient medium.

Larva. The life stage of a nematode between the embryo and the adult.

Latent infection. The state in which a host is infected with a pathogen but does not show any symptoms.

Latent virus. A virus that does not induce symptoms in its host.

Leaf spot. A self-limiting lesion on a leaf.

Lesion. A localized area of discoloured, diseased tissue.

Lysis. Dissolution of cells by enzymes or viruses.

Macroconidium. A comparatively large conidium (*e.g., Fusarium udum*).

Macrocyclic. Having a long life cycle (*e.g.,* in *Puccinia graminis tritici*–black rust of wheat).

Macroscopic. Visible by the naked eye.

Malignant. A cell or tissue that divides and enlarges autonomously and its growth can not be controlled by the organism on which it is growing.

Mechanical inoculation. Inoculation of a plant with a virus through transfer of sap from o virus-infected plant to healthy plant.

Microbiology. Biology of microscopic organisms.

Microconidium. A comparatively small conidium (*e.g., Fusarium udum*).

Microcyclic. Short cycle with haplophase stage only.

Micron (µ). A unit of length equal to 1/1000 of a millimeter.

Microscopic. Can be seen only with the aid of light microscope.

Mildew. A plant disease caused by a fungus in which the mycelium and spores are seen as a whitish growth on the host surface.

Millimicron (mµ). A unit of length equal to 1/1000 of a micron (µ).

Millimeter (mm). A unit of length equal to 1/10 of centimeter (cm).

Mold. Profuse fungus growth on damp or decaying matter.

Monokaryotic. Containing one nucleus of a definite strain (+ or –).

Mosaic. Symptom of certain viral diseases of plants characterized by intermingled patches of normal and light green or yellowish colour.

Mottle. An irregular pattern of indistinct light and dark areas.

Mycelium. Mass of hyphae which make the body of a fungus.

Mycology. That part of botany which deals with fungi.

Mycoplasma. A group of very small bacteria-like microorganisms, intermediate between viruses and bacteria.

Mycorrhiza. A symbiotic association of fungus with the roots of a plant.

Natural openings. Stomata; lenticels and hydathodes.

Necrosis. The death of cells or of tissues.

Necrotic. Dead and discoloured.

Nematocide. A chemical compound that kills nematodes.

Nematode. Microscopic, wormlike animals that live as saprobes in water or soil or as parasites of plants and animals.

Neutralization. A serological test in which a virus in suspension is neutralized by specific antibodies added to the suspension and loses its infectivity.

Noninfectious disease. A disease caused by an environmental factor, and not by pathogen.

Nonseptate. Aseptate; without cross walls.

Nucleic acid. An acid substance containing pentose, phosphorus and pyrimidine and purine bases. Nucleic acids determine genetic properties of organisms.

Nucleoprotein. Consists of nucleic acid and protein; referring to viruses.

Nucleoside. The combination of sugar and base molecule in a nucleic acid.

Nucleotides. The building blocks of DNA and RNA.

Nucleus. The dense protoplasmic body found in all cellular organisms and essential in all synthetic and developmental activities of a cell.

Obligate parasite. A parasite that in nature can grow and multiply only on living organisms; a parasite which can not exist independently of host.

Oogonium. A female gametangium of some Phycomycetes.

Oosphere. An egg before fertilization.

Oospore. A sexual spore produced by the union of two morphologically different gametangia (oogonium and antheridium).

Order. In classification, group of organisms closely allied, ranking between family and class.

Ostiole. A porelike opening in perithecia and pycnidia through which the spores escape from the fruiting body.

Pandemic. Very widely distributed; referring to plant diseases.

Papilla. A small projection as on the sporangium of *Phytophthora*.

Papillate. With papilla.

Paraphysis. A slender filamentous epidermal outgrowth occurring among sporogenous organs; plural-paraphyses.

Parasexuality. A mechanism whereby recombination of hereditary properties is based on mitosis.

Parasite. An organism living with or within another to its own advantage in food.

Parasitic. An organism living at expense of another, and in or on it.

Parasitism. The parasite living on its host.

Parasitology. The science treating of plant and animal parasites.

Pathogen. Any disease causing agent or organism.

Pathogenicity. The relative capacity of pathogen to cause disease.

Pectin. A methylated polymer of galacturonic acid found in the middle lamella and the primary cell wall.

Pectinase. An enzyme that breaks down pectin.

Penetration. The initial invasion of a host by a pathogen.

Perennial mycelium. Mycelium overwintering as such on or in a host plant.

Perfect. Complete; fungi producing sexual spores.

Peridium. The external covering of certain fruiting bodies of some fungi.

Periplasm. The region of an oogonium outside the oosphere in fungi.

Perithecium. The spherical or flask-like ascocarp of Pyrenomycetes, having an ostiole.

Phage. A virus that attacks bacteria; also known as bacteriophage.

Phasmid. One of a pair of lateral caudal swellings of a nematode believed to be chemoreceptive.

Phenolic. Applied to phenolic compounds (*e.g.,* common phenolics).

Phycomycetes. A group of fungi; the mycelium has no cross walls.

Physiologic race. One of a group of microorganisms like in morphology but unlike in certain cultural, physiological, pathological or other characters.

Phytoalexin. A substance that inhibits the development of a fungus on hypersensitive tissue, formed only when host plant cells come in contact with the parasite.

Phytopathogenic. A microorganism that can incite disease in plants.

Phytotoxic. Toxic to plants.

Polysaccharide. A large organic molecule consisting of many units of a simple sugar.

Polymorphism. Occurrence of different forms of spores, in same individual at different periods (*e.g., Puccinia graminis*).

Primary infection. The first infection of a plant by the perennating pathogen.

Proliferation. A rapid and repeated production of new cells, tissues or organs (*e.g.,* green-ear disease of *bajra–Sclerospora graminicola*).

Promycelium. The short hypha produced by the teliospore; the basidium.

Propagative virus. A virus that multiplies in its insect vector.

Protectant. A substance that protects an organism against infection by a pathogen.

Protein. A high molecular weight compound consisting of aminoacids. It may be a structural protein or an enzyme.

Protein subunit. A small protein molecule that is the structural and chemical unit of the protein coat of a virus; a capsomere.

Protoplasm. Living cell substance.

Purification. The separation of virus particles in a pure form free from cell components.

Pustule. Small blister-like elevation of epidermis as spores emerge (*e.g.*, White rust of crucifers-*Albugo candida*).

Pycnidium. An asexual flask-like fruiting body lined inside with conidiophores and producing conidia.

Pycniospore. A spermatium; a spore produced in a pycnium.

Pycnium. A fruiting body of the rust fungi that produces small spores, pycniospores or spermatia which can not infect plants but function as gametes or gametangia; a spermagonium.

Quarantine. Control of export and import of plants to prevent spread of diseases and pests.

Race. A genetically distinct mating group within a species; also a group of pathogens with distinct pathological or physiological characteristics.

Receptive hypha. A specialized hypha protruding out of a pycnium and functioning as a female gamete; also known as flexuous hypha.

Resistance. The ability of an organism to overcome, completely or partially the effect of a pathogen.

Resistant. Possessing qualities that inhibit the development of a given pathogen.

Resting spore. An inactive stage of a fungus, usually a thick-walled spore that is resistant to unfavourable conditions, and often germinates after a rest period.

Rhizoid. A short, thin hypha growing like a root toward the substrate.

Rhizomorph. A root-like strand of hyphae in certain fungi.

Rhizosphere. The soil near a living root.

Ring spot. A circular area of chlorosis with a green centre; symptom of many virus diseases.

Root nodules. Small swellings on roots of leguminous plants and containing nitrogen fixing bacteria.

Rosette. Short, bunchy habit of plant growth.

Rot. The softening, discolouration, and disintegration of a succulent plant tissue as a result of fungal or bacterial infection.

Russet. Brownish roughened areas on fruit skin.

Rust. A disease of grasses and other plants giving a rusty appearance to the plant and caused by Uredinales (rust fungi).

Sanitation. The removal and burning of infected plant debris.

Saprophyte. An organism which lives on dead and decaying organic matter.

Scab. A rough, crust-like diseased area on the surface of a plant organ. A disease in which such areas are formed.

Sclerotium. Resting, dormant, or winter stage of some fungi when they become a mass of hardened mycelium.

Scorch. Burning of leaf margins as a result of infection or unfavourable environmental conditions.

Secondary infection. Any infection caused by inoculum produced as a result of a primary infection; and infection caused by secondary inoculum.

Secondary inoculum. Inoculum produced by infections that took place during the same growing seasons.

Septate. Divided by partitions.

Septum. A cross wall; a partition separating cells.

Shot hole. A symptom in which small diseased fragments of leaves fall off and leave small holes in their place.

Sign. The pathogen seen on a host plant.

Smut. A disease caused by Ustilaginaceae; characterized by masses of dark, powdery spores.

Sorus. A compact mass of spores or fruiting structure found especially in rusts and smuts.

Spermatogonium. A flask-like fruiting body of the rust fungi in which the spermatia or pycniospores are produced, also known as pycnium.

Spermatium (pycniospore). The male gamete of rust fungi.

Sporangiophore. A stalk-like structure bearing sporangia.

Sporangium. A spore case in which asexual spores are produced.

Spore. A highly specially reproductive cell of plants.

Sporidium. The basidiospore of the smut fungi.

Sporodochium. A hemispherical aggregate of conidiophores.

Sporophore. A spore bearing structure, in fungi.

Sporophyte. The diploid ($2n$) spore producing phase in alternation of plant generations.

Sterigma. slender filament arising from basidium or conidiophore giving rise to spores by abstriction; plural-sterigmata.

Sterile fungi. A group of fungi that do not produce any kind of spores.

Sterilization. The elimination of pathogens from soil by means of heat or chemicals.

Stroma. Tissues of hyphae or of fungus cells with host tissue, in or upon which spore bearing structures may be produced (*e.g., Claviceps purpurea*).

Stylet. A long, slender, hollow feeding structure of nematodes and some insects.

Stylet borne. A virus borne on the stylet of its vector.

Suscept. Any plant that can be attacked by a specific effect of a pathogen; a host plant.

Susceptibility. The inability of a plant to resist the effect of a pathogen.

Swarm spore. Zoospore.

Symbiosis. A condition in which two plants live in mutually beneficial partnership.

Symptom. The external and internal alterations of a plant as a result of a disease.

Synergism. The concurrent parasitism of a host by two pathogens in which the symptoms or other effects produced are of greater magnitude than the sum of the effects of each pathogen acting alone.

Systemic. Throughout the plant body, referred to a pathogen or a chemical.

Teliosorus. Telium.

Teliospore. The sexual, thick-walled resting spore of the rust and smut fungi.

Telium. The fruiting structure in which teliospores are formed.

Toxin. A compound produced by a microorganism and being toxic to a plant or animal.

Transmission. A malignant overgrowth of tissue.

Uredium. The sorus of the rust fungi in which uredospores are produced.

Uredospore. Reddish spores borne on sporophores of rust fungi; a binucleate spore of Uredinales.

Variability. The ability of an organism to change its characteristics from one generation to the other.

Vector. An insect able to transmit a pathogen.

Vegetative. Asexual, somatic.

Veinbanding. Bands of green tissue along and veins while the tissue between the vein has become chlorotic.

Veinclearing. Destruction of chlorophyll in the vein tissue, as a result of infection by a virus or other pathogen.

Vesicle. A hyphal swelling, produced by a zoosporangium and in which the zoospores are released.

Virescent. A white or coloured tissue that develops chloroplasts and becomes green.

Viron. A complete virus particle.

Virulence. Degree of pathogenicity of a pathogen.

Virulent. Strongly pathogenic.

Viruliferous. Avector containing a virus and can transmit it.

Virus. An ultramicroscopic obligate parasite which consists of nucleic acid and protein.

Vulva. The external opening of the female reproductive system of nematode.

Wilt. Loss of rigidity and drooping of plant parts wholly or partially.

Witches broom. Broomlike growth.

Yellows. Yellowing and stunting of host plant; mycoplasma disease symptom.

Zoosporangium. A sporangium, which contains zoospores.

Zoospore. Swarm spore bearing flagellia; capable of moving in water.

Zygospore. A resting spore of Zygomycetes formed by conjugation of similar gametangia.

Zygote. Cell formed by union of two gametes; fertilized ovum.

INDEX

BRYOPHYTA

1 Introduction

There are 960 genera and 24,000 species of bryophytes.

From the point of view of their evolution the bryophytes stand at level higher than that of thallophytes but lower than that of pteridophytes and phanerogams. The plants belonging to algae are commonly found in water and rarely on the land whereas the bryophytes are land-inhabiting plants. The water is still needed for the movement of the gametes of bryophytes and in their vegetative structure they have adapted themselves to a terrestrial life. The bryophytes are known as **amphibians** of the plant kingdom. Some of the bryophytes are inhabitants of water, *e.g., Riccia fluitans.* The other bryophytes like the swampy muddy shady and humid places for their survival. Most of the bryophytes are land inhabitants. In our country the bryophytes are very commonly found in the hilly regions of the Himalayas. They are also quite common in the hills of South India, whereas on the other hand certain species of *Riccia, Marchantia, Anthoceros* and *Funaria* are quite common in the plains.

Distribution. The bryophytes are cosmopolitan in distribution. They are found in all places where plants can live except in the sea. They are quite commonly found in the moist mountain forests of tropical regions as well as in the sub-tropical regions of Arctic Tundra. Some of the bryophytes have been recorded at altitudes as high as 18,000 to 20,000 feet a.s.l. in the Himalayas. A moss plant, *Aongstroemia julacea* has been recorded from an altitude of 19,800 feet a.s.l.

Many members of Jungermannineae (acrogynous Jungermanniales), Musci (mosses) and all species of *Dendroceros* are epiphytes and found in tropical rain forests. Certain small species are epiphyllous and grow on the surface of leaves (*e.g., Radula protensa*).

Most of the bryophytes are autotrophic but a few exceptions are there. For example, *Buxbaumia aphylla* and *Mnium hornum* are more or less saprophytic and grow upon organic matter such as rotten wood.

Characteristic features. The most characteristic features of the bryophytes are as follows:

The bryophytes occupy the position in between algae on one hand and the pteridophytes on the other.

With the exception of few aquatic forms they are truly land-inhabiting plants. They are found in humid and shady places. As water is indispensable for the act of fertilization they are treated to be the **amphibians** of the plant kingdom.

They are quite small and inconspicuous organisms. The gametophyte is highly developed and differentiated than that of a complex alga. It is independent plant at maturity. It consists of a flattened thallus (*e.g., Riccia, Marchantia*) or an erect plant body (*e.g., Funaria, Polytrichum* etc.).

The true roots are always absent. Instead of true roots the unicellular or multicellular hair-like **rhizoids** develop from the thalli. The rhizoids absorb the nutrients from the moist soil.

They lack typical vascular tissue, *i.e.,* xylem and phloem from their gametophytes and sporophytes.

They are **homosporous.** It means, that the spores of a species are morphologically similar in size and form.

The spore germinates into a filamentous or thalloid green **protonema** which later on gives rise to the thallus (gametophyte).

The sexual reproduction is of oogamous type, *i.e.,* it takes place by means of gametes. The male gametes are motile and known as **antherozoids;** the female gametes are non-motile and known as **eggs** (oosphere). The gametes are produced within the sex organ known as **antheridium** (male) and **archegonium** (female).

The antheridia are usually club shaped. Each antheridium is surrounded by a single layer of protective sterile jacket cells. Within the jacket there are **antherozoid mother cells** or **androcytes.** Each androycyte metamorphoses into a motile biflagellate antherozoid.

The archegonia are usually flask-like. Each archegonium consists of a **venter** and a **neck.** The venter is basal swollen portion and the neck is elongated. Within the neck and the venter there is an axial row of cells surrounded by sterile jacket cells. This axial row consists of a few **neck canal cells, a ventral canal cell** and an **egg** or **oosphere.**

The water is essential for the act of fertilization. The motile ciliated antherozoids swim in the film of water and reach to the neck of an archegonium. The antherozoid enters the neck and ultimately approaches the egg. The antherozoid penetrates the egg and fertilization is effected. With the result of fertilization the zygote is formed. The zygote begins to develop into a multicellular embryo just after the act of fertilization without going under any resting period. The embryo remains within the venter of the archegonium and liberated as in the case of algae. The venter wall enlarges along with the developing embryo to form the protective envelope known as **calyptra.**

Ultimately the **sporogonium (sporophyte)** develops. The sporogonium consists of a **foot, seta** and **capsule.** In the case of bryophytes the sporogonium is completely dependent for its nourishment upon the gametophyte. The foot of the sporophyte remains embedded in the tissues of gametophyte and acts as haustorium.

The **spore mother cells** are produced within the sporogonium. The spore mother cells are diploid (2n) and they represent the last stage of the sporophyte generation. The spore mother cells undergo the reduction division (meiosis) and the tetrads of the haploid (n) spores are formed. The spores represent the beginning of the gametophyte generation.

SUMMARY OF A TYPICAL BRYOPHYTE

Habitat

1. The bryophytes grow frequently in humid and shady places. With the exception of few aquatic forms (*e.g., Riccia fluitans, Ricciocarpos natans* and *Riella* spp). They are truly land inhabiting plants. They may grow in bogs (*e.g., Sphagnum* spp.), and in xeric conditions (e.g., many mosses); some are epiphyllous (*e.g., Frullania* spp., *Radula* spp. etc.), and some are saprophytes (*e.g., Buxbaumia* spp). *Porella plathypylloidea* grows on barks of trees and rocks and can face adverse desiccation.

Structure of Gametophyte

2. They have sharply defined heteromorphic alternation of generations in which the diploid (2n) asexual generation (*i.e.,* sporophyte), although morphologically distinct from the haploid (n) sexual generation (*i.e.,* gametophyte), is attached to it and never becomes an independent free living plant.
3. The gametophytic phase is the dominant one of the life cycle and generally the term 'plant body' is used to denote this stage.
4. The gametophyte is always an independent plant at maturity and is nutritionally self-sufficient

because of the presence of chloroplasts within it.

5. In many cases the gametophyte is a thallus (*e.g., Riccia, Marchantia, Pellia* etc.), that is, a plant body without differentiation into root, stem and leaf. In many mosses the plant body is externally differentiated into stem and leaves, but there are no roots and instead only one-celled or multicellular rhizoids (absorptive in function) are present.

6. The thalli of primitive forms remain attached to the substratum, by unicellular unbranched rhizoids (*e.g.,* in *Riccia, Marchantia* etc.), whereas in higher forms they remain attached by branched multicellular rhizoids (*e.g.,* in mosses).

7. In some bryophytes (*e.g., Riccia* and *Marchantia*) the purple coloured multicellular scales are present.

8. As regards the internal structure, the plant body consists of simple parenchymatous cells. They donot possess xylem and phloem. The parenchynia may be differentiated into **chlorophyllous** and storage cells (*e.g.,* in *Riccia* and *Marchantia*).

Reproduction

In bryophytes, the reproduction takes place by means of vegetative (asexual) and sexual methods.

Vegetative Reproduction

9. Bryophytes largely multiply by means of vegetative reproduction. This takes place by death of older parts, e.g., in *Riccia, Marchantia, Anthoceros, Notothylas;* by branch tips as in several species of *Riccia;* by adventitious branches, as in several species of *Riccia, Marchantia* and *Anthoceros;* by gemmae as in the species of *Marchantia, Lunularia, Funaria* etc., by tubers as in species of *Riccia, Anthoceros* etc., by primary and secondary protonema as in species of *Funaria* and other mosses.

Sexual Reproduction

10. All bryophytes are oogamous. The spermatozoids (male gametes) are motile and small while the eggs (female gametes) are large and non motile.

11. The gametes (male and female) are produced within multicellular sex organs (antheridia and archegonia) in which there is an outer sterile layer of jacket cells.

12. The antheridium (male organ) consists of a central mass of androcytes enclosed by a single layer of sterile jacket cells. Each androcyte metamorphoses into a biflagellate spermatozoid.

13. The archegonium (female organ) is a multicellular flask-like structure. The basal swollen portion is venter and contains an egg (oosphere) in it. The elongated neck contains neck canal cells.

Fertilization

14. The water is essential for the act of fertilization. The motile flagellate spermatozoid swims to the neck of archegonium and ultimately approaches the egg effecting the fertilization. With the result the zygote (2n) is formed.

The Sporophyte

15. The zygote divides repeatedly immediately after fertilization. There is no resting period.

16. The first division of zygote is transverse and the embryo develops from the upper cell. Such emboryogeny is known as **exoscopic embryogeny.**

17. The embryo remains within the venter of the archegonium. The venter wall enlarges along with the developing embryo to form the protective envelope known as **calyptra.**

18. Generally, the sporongonium consists of **foot, seta** and **capsule.**

19. Here the sporogonium is completely dependent for its nourishment upon the gametophyte.

20. The spore mother cells are developed in the sporogonium. They are diploid (2n) and represent the last stage of the sporophytic generation. The spore mother cells (2n) undergo meiosis and the tetrads of haploid (n) spores are formed. All bryophytes are homosporous.

The Young Gametophyte

21. The spores (n) represent the beginning of the gametophyte generation.
22. The spores are cutinized and dispersed by means of wind.
23. The spores may germinate directly into the new gametophyte (*e.g.*, in *Riccia* and *Marchantia*) while in mosses they germinate to produce filamentous protonema from which buds are produced to develop into new plants (young gametophytes).

ALTERNATION OF GENERATIONS

The life-cycle of a bryophyte shows regular alternation of gametophytic and sporophytic generations. This process of alternation of generations was demonstrated for the first time in 1851 by Hofmeister. Thereafter in 1894 Strasburger could actually show the periodic doubling and halving of the number of chromosomes during the life-cycle.

The haploid phase (n) is the gametophyte or sexual generation. It bears the sexual reproductive organs which produce gametes, *i.e.*, **antherozoids** and **eggs**. With the result of gametic union a zygote is formed which develops into a sporophyte. This is the diploid phase (2n). The sporophyte produces spores which always germinate to form gemetophytes. During the formation of spores, the spore mother cells divide meiotically and haploid spores are produced. The production of the spores is the beginning of the gametophytic or haploid phase. The spores germinate and produce gametophytic or haploid phase. The spores germinate and produce gametophytes which bear sex organs. Ultimately the gametic union takes place and zygote is resulted. It is diploid (2n). This is the beginning of the sporophytic or diploid phase. This way, the sporophyte generation intervenes between fertilization (syngamy) and meiosis (reduction division); and gametophyte generation intervenes between meiosis and fertilization.

In bryophytes, where the two generations are morphologically different, the type of alternation of generations is known as **heteromorphic.**

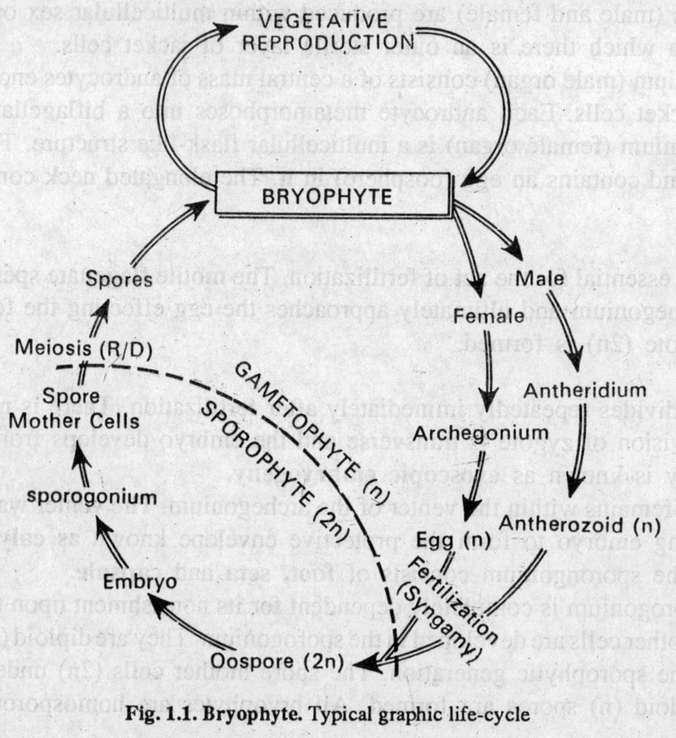

Fig. 1.1. Bryophyte. Typical graphic life-cycle

In the case of bryophytes the gametophyte generation is conspicuous and longer-lived phase of the life-cycle in comparison to that of sporophyte generation. Here, the gametophyte is quite independent whereas the sporophyte is dependent somehow or other on the gametophyte for its nutritive supply. The gametophyte gives rise to sporophyte and sporophyte to the gametophyte and thus there is regular alternation of generations.

Resemblances of Bryophytes with Algae

In many ways the bryophytes resemble with algae in their morphology and physiology. More probably they are near to green algae. The main resemblances are as follows :

1. The plant body is thallus-like.
2. The plants are autotrophic, *i.e.*, similar in mode of nutrition.
3. The pigments (*i.e.*, chlorophyll, carotene, leutin, violaxathin and zeaxanthin) are similar in both.
4. Reserve food material is starch in both cases.
5. The vascular tissues are absent in both.
6. Roots are absent in bryophytes as well as in algae.
7. The cell wall is made up of cellulose in both.
8. The gametophyte is dominant both in bryophytes and algae.
9. Spermatozoids are motile and flagellated in bryophytes and many algae (mostly Chlorophyceae).
10. The spermatozoids are biflagellate and both the flagella are of whiplash type.
11. Water is required for fertilization.
12. The protonema, during early stage of development in many bryophytes resemble with the filamentous green algae.

The above mentioned similarities put the bryophytes akin to the green algae. This gives support to the view that bryophytes have evolved from algal ancestors.

Resemblances of Bryophytes with Pteridophytes

1. They are terrestrial in habit.
2. The primitive root-less and leafless sporophyte of Psilotales (pteridophytes) can be compared with sporophytes of the bryophytes.
3. In both cases the development of embryo stage after gametic union is similar.
4. The structure of archegonium is fundamentally similar in both cases and the oosphere (egg) remains protected by a layer of sterile cells.
5. In both cases the androcytes or antherozoid mother cells remain enclosed in a single layer of sterile jacket cells.
6. Antherozoids (spermatozoids) are flagellated.
7. Water is essential for fertilization.
8. Sexual reproduction is oogamous.
9. In bryophytes, as well as in pteridophytes a sharply defined heteromorphic type of alternation of generations is present.
10. Cuticle is present in both cases.
11. The stomata are present except in the liverworts.
12. The multicellular sporangia are present.

Points of Differentiation

1. In pteridophytes the plant body is sporophyte, while in bryophytes it is gametophyte.
2. In pteridophytes the sporophyte is independent and the dominant phase of life cycle whereas

in bryophytes the sporophyte is dependent on gametophyte.

3. The plant body (*i.e.*, sporophyte) of a pteridophyte consists of root, stem and leaves while in bryophytes the plant body (*i.e.*, gametophyte) is thalloid.
4. In pteridophytes the vascular tissues are well developed whereas in bryophytes they are not developed.

DIFFERENCES BETWEEN THALLOPHYTES AND BRYOPHYTES

Thallophyta (Algae)	Bryophyta
1. They are mostly aquatic	1. Mostly terrestrial and prefer damp and shady places.
2. The thallus consists of a single cell to well developed uniseriate or branched filaments.	2. The thalles is not filamentous except in protonema stage. It is made up of parenchymatous cells.
3. There is no or ill defined tissue differentiation.	3. There is well defined tissue differentiation.
4. In each cell one or few chloropasts are present. In other cases instead of chloroplasts, the chromatophores are present.	4. In each chlorophyllous cell many well developed chloroplasts are present.
5. The stomata or pores are not present.	5. The pores or stomata are present.
6. Generally rhizoids are not present and if present they are of simple type.	6. The rhizoids are present. They may be smooth walled, teberculate or obliquely septate. The scales are also present.
7. Every cell is capable of growth and development.	7. Only the special cells are capable of growth and development.
8. Asexual reproduction takes place by means of zoospores or aplanospores. In many cases vegetative reproduction is commonly found.	8. Asexual reproduction is absent. Vegetative reproduction is common.
9. Sexual reproduction may be isogamous, anisogamous or oogamous.	9. Sexual reproduction is only oogamous.
10. The sex organs are unicellular, and when multicellular every cell forms a gamete. There is no jacket of sterile cells.	10. The sex organs are multicellular and remain protected by a jacket of sterile cells.
11. The female sex organ is single-celled oogonium. It is not covered by any sterile jacket layer.	11. The female sex organ is flask-shaped, multicellular archegonium which remains covered by a sterile jacket layer. Neck canal cells, ventral canal cell and egg are found within archegonium.
12. The zygote is liberated from the plant and passes into the resting stage.	12. The zygote is not liberated from the plant and does not undergo any resting period.
13. No embryo is formed after fertilization.	13. In all bryophytes the embryo is developed after fertilization.
14. They show ill defined homologous type of alternation of generations.	14. They show well defined heteromorphic type of alternation of generations.
15. The gametophyte and sporophyte are independent.	15. The sporophyte is dependent on gametophyte for its nutrition.

ORIGIN OF BRYOPHYTES

Origin of the Gametophyte

The bryophytes are quite soft and delicate and, therefore, they lack fossil records. There are no known fossil bryophytes more primitive than the forms of to-day. However, there are two schools of thought about their origin. According to one school of thought they are evolved from the green thallophyta the algae; and according to the other school they have been descended from the pteridophytes. Majority of the workers support their origin from the algal ancestors.

Origin from algae. This view of the origin of bryophytes has been supported by most of the bryologists. Though there is no fossil connection between algae and bryophytes yet there are so many points in support of this view, such as-the necessity of water for the act of fertilization; their amphibian nature and the presence of ciliated antherozoids. These points support the view that they have been originated from aquatic ancestors. Lignier in 1903, pointed out that the algae gave rise to a connecting link known as **'prohepatics'** and thereafter bryophytes originated from this connecting link on one hand and the pteridophytes on the other. Bower (1908) also supported this view and said that the Archegoniatae have been evolved from the aquatic ancestors, *i.e.*, the algae. The bryophytes resemble in many respects the green algae, *i.e.*, Chlorophyceae, and Fritsch (1916, 1945) has advocated that the Chaetophorales gave rise to the bryophytes.

There seems no apparent relation between the antheridium and the archegonium of the bryophytes and the antheridium and the oogonium of the algae. In none of the algae the egg is surrounded by any cellular jacket as it is always enclosed within a protective layer (jacket layer) in the case of bryophytes.

According to many workers the sex organs of the bryophytes have been evolved from those of the algae as follows: According to this view the antheridium and archegonium of bryophytes originated from gametangia of a type similar to that of *Ectocarpus*. In *Ectocarpus* (Phaeophyceae) the gametangium consists of a number of cells, each of which gives rise to a gamete. As soon as the migration from the water to land took place, there arose the necessity for the protection of the gametes from desiccation. With the result the outer layer of the cells of the gametangium became sterile and functioned as a protective layer. This way, the antheridium has been derived from the algal gametangium. For the derivation of the archegonium from such structure, it has been suggested that after the formation of the protective wall, further sterilization took place, and in the centre an axial row of cells developed. According to this view the neck canal cells were originally female gametes, which later on lost their walls and cytoplasm. The ventral canal cell is the sister cell of the oosphere and very rarely it may be fertilized. However, *Ectocarpus* is not a member of Chlorophyceae, but it is presumed that bryophytes have been originated

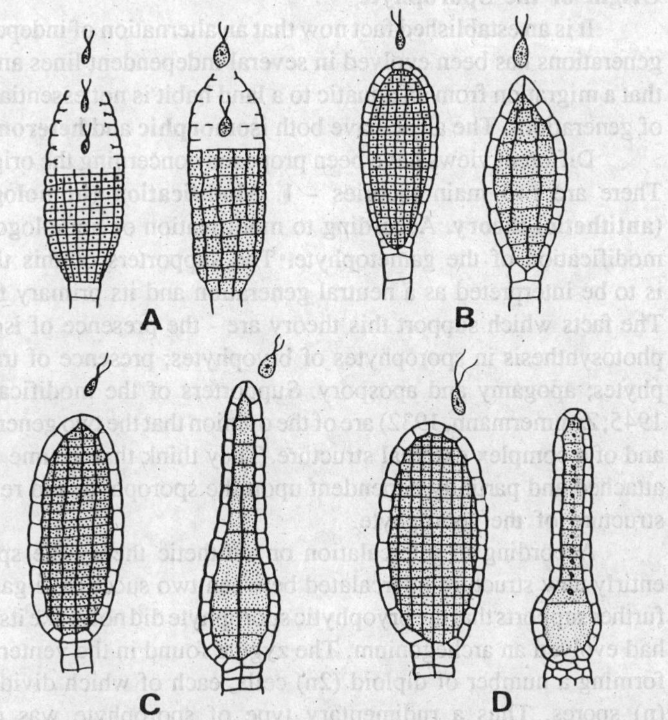

Fig. 1.2. Origin of bryophytes. Diagrams (A-D) illustrating the hypothetical origin of the antheridium and archegonium from the plurilocular sporangium of certain Phaeophyceae (*Ectocarpus*).

from green algae. According to Smith (1938) the reproductive cells of *Schizomeris* and antheridia of *Chaetonema* are quite alike to that of the gametangia of *Ectocarpus*.

According to Church (1919), the bryophytes have been originated from the marine ancestors and not from the fresh water ancestors. This theory could not get general support because of the lack of evidences from palaeobotany and geology. According to majority of workers the bryophytes have been originated from Chlorophyceae which are commonly found in fresh waters and rarely in sea waters.

Origin from pteridophytes. According to other school of thought the bryophytes have been originated (descended) from pteridophytes by means of reduction. Though this view could not get general support yet several workers postulated the evidences in support of this view. According to Lang (1917), Kidston and Lang (1917), Scott (1923), Halle (1936), Haskell (1949) and Christensen (1954) the bryophytes have been descended by the process of reduction from pteridophytes. Kashyap (1919) also supported the view, because of common resemblances of the two groups. Similarities between sporangia of some members of Psilophytales (*Rhynia, Horneophyton* and *Sporogonites*) with capsules of Anthocerotales, *Sphagnum* and *Andreaea* led to conclude this hypothesis. The Psilophytales are the oldest pteridophytes in which the sporophytes were rootless, leafless and dichotomously branched with terminal sporangia. Such sporophytes resemble the bryophytes, especially the members of Anthocerotales and are thought to have evolved by progressive reduction. Proskaeur (1960), thinks that if bryophytes are polyphyletic in origin, at least Anthocerotales originated from Psilophytales like *Horneophyton*. According to Kashyap (1919), "bryophytes represent a degenerate evolutionary line of pteridophytes or in more correct term, the bryophytes are descendents of pteridophytes."

Origin of the Sporophyte

It is an established fact now that an alternation of independent gametophytic and sporophytic generations has been evolved in several independent lines among aquatic algae. It is also thought that a migration from an aquatic to a land habit is not essential for the appearance of an alternation of generations. The algae have both **isomorphic** and **heteromorphic alternation of generations.**

Different views have been proposed concerning the origin of the sporophytes of bryophytes. There are *two* main theories - 1. **Modification (homologous) theory** and 2. **Intercalation (antithetic) theory.** According to modification or homologous theory the sporophyte is a direct modification of the gametophyte. The supporters of this theory advocate that the sporophyte is to be interpreted as a neutral generation and its primary function is the production of spores. The facts which support this theory are - the presence of isomorphic alternation in some algae; photosynthesis in sporophytes of bryophytes; presence of tracheids in gametophytes of pteridophytes; apogamy and apospory. Supporters of the modification theory (Church, 1919; Fritsch, 1945; Zimmermann, 1932) are of the opinion that the two generations were isomorphic, independent and of a complex external structure. They think that in time the sporophyte became permanently attached and partially dependent upon the sporophyte and resulted in a reduction in the complex structure of the sporophyte.

According to intercalation or antithetic theory the sporophyte has been interpreted as a entirly new structure intercalated between two successive gametophytic generations. This theory further supports that the bryophytic sporophyte did not make its appearance until after a gametophyte had evolved an archegonium. The zygote found in the venter of archegonium divided mitotically forming a number of diploid (2n) cells, each of which divided meiotically to form four haploid (n) spores. Thus a rudimentary type of sporophyte was developed in which all cells were sporogenous. Further evolution of the sporophyte took place as a result of sterilization of sporogenous tissue and foot, seta and capsule were differentiated. According to this theory there was a progression from a simple to a more complex sporophyte by a progressive sterilization of sporogenous tissue (also see chapter 12 - General Discussion).

Evolution Among Bryophyta

The major lines (*i.e.*, Hepaticopsida, Anthocerotopsida and Bryopsida) have been considered among bryophytes. According to G.M. Smith (1955) the primitive bryophytic gametophyte was

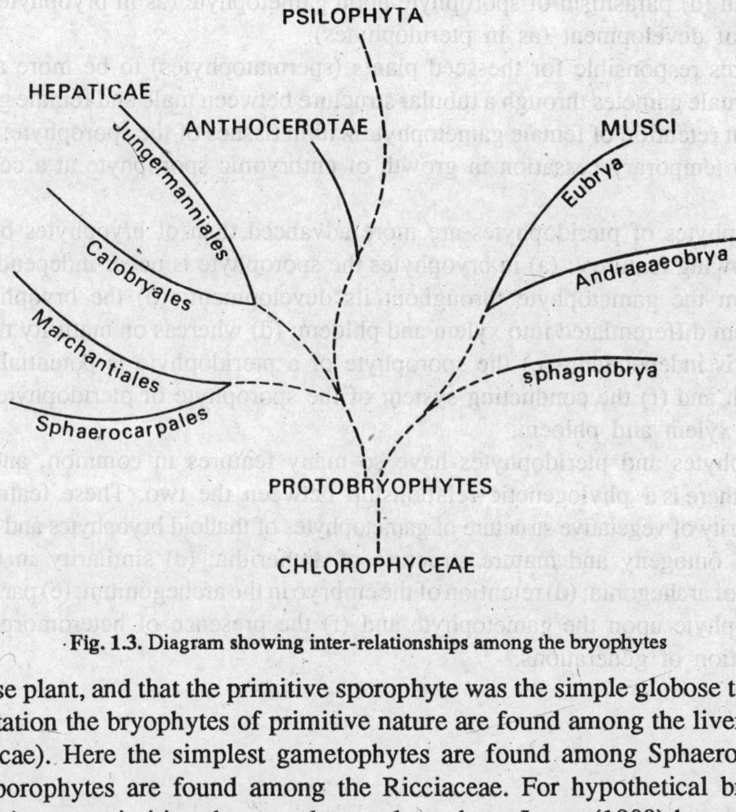

Fig. 1.3. Diagram showing inter-relationships among the bryophytes

a simple thallose plant, and that the primitive sporophyte was the simple globose type. According to this interpretation the bryophytes of primitive nature are found among the liverworts (Hepaticopsida-Hepaticae). Here the simplest gametophytes are found among Sphaerocarpaceae, and the simplest sporophytes are found among the Ricciaceae. For hypothetical bryophytes (*i.e.*, protobryophytes) more primitive than any known bryophyte, Lotsy (1909) has suggested a type combining the simple gametophyte of *Sphaerocarpos* with the simple sporophyte of Ricciaceae to form the imaginary genus ***Sphaero-riccia***. The Marchantiales of Hapaticae is one characterized by gametophytes of external simplicity but internal complexity. Features in ontogeny of sex organs indicate that relationships of Jungermanniales and Calobryales with other Hepaticae are rather remote. According to Smith (1955) these orders are of an advanced type among the Hepaticae. No matter what the evolutionary order of their interrelationships the Hepaticae seem to constitute a blindly ending evolutionary side line. The mosses (Bryopsida) also make a blindly ending evolutionary side line. Their gametophytes are externally complex and most of them have sporophytes with greater internal differentiation of tissues. The mosses are sometimes thought to have been evolved from leafy Hepaticae (*i.e.*, Jungermanniales and Calobryales). On the other hand the gametophytes of Anthocerotales, except for their embedded sex organs resemble those of thallose Hepaticae. However, the anthocerotean sporophyte is of a much more advanced type than is found in any Hepaticae or Bryopsida (moss). Because of their similarities in gametophytes, the Anthocerotae may be considered a series which departed from primative Hepaticae.

Bryophytes and Pteridophytes
(Evolutionary Tendencies)

1. The bryophytes and the pteridophytes remain at an evolutionary level higher than that of algae, but lower than that of spermatophytes (seed plants).
2. The features which keep the bryophytes and pteridophytes at a higher evolutionary level than algae are (a) multicellular sex organs with an outer jacket layer of sterile cells; (b) permanent retention of the zygote within the archegonium; (c) retention of the embryonic sporophyte within archegonium; and (d) parasitism of sporophyte upon gametophyte (as in bryophytes) for at least in early stages of development (as in pteridophytes).
3. The features responsible for the seed plants (spermatophytes) to be more advanced are: (a) migration of male gametes through a tubular structure between male and female gametophytes; (b) the permanent retention of female gametophyte within tissues of the sporophyte; (c) formation of seeds and (d) temporary cessation in growth of embryonic sporophyte at a certain stage in development.
4. The sporophytes of pteridophytes are more advanced than of bryophytes because of the presence of following features : (a) in bryophytes the sporophyte is never independent and takes its nutrition from the gametophyte throughout its development; (b) the bryophytes have no conducting system differentiated into xylem and phloem; (d) whereas on maturity the sporophyte of pteridophyte is independent; (e) the sporophyte of a pteridophyte is potentially capable of unlimited growth and (f) the conducting system of the sporophyte of pteridophyte remains differentiated into xylem and phloem.
5. The bryophytes and pteridophytes have so many features in common, and therefore it is thought that there is a phylogenetic relationship between the two. These features include - (a) general similarity of vegetative structure of gametophytes of thalloid bryophytes and pteridophytes; (b) similarity in ontogeny and mature structure of antheridia; (c) similarity in ontogeny and mature structure of archegonia; (d) retention of the embryo in the archegonium; (e) partial parasitism of mature sporophyte upon the gametophyte and (f) the presence of heteromorphic life cycle showing alternation of generations.

2

Classification of Bryophytes

For the first time Braun in 1864 gave the name Bryophyta to this group of plants. However, he included algae, fungi, lichens and mosses in his Bryophyta. Now, it is an established fact that algae, fungi and lichens comprise the group thallophyta and the mosses are included in Bryophyta. Thereafter Schimper in 1879 gave the name Bryophyta which is used in full sense for the plants included in this group. Eichler in 1883 divided Bryophyta into two groups-Hepaticae and Musci. Engler (1892) divided the class Hepaticae into three orders-Marchantiales, Jungermanniales, and Anthocerotales. However, Bower (1935), Wettstein (1935), Bessey, Fritsch (1929), Evans (1938, 1939) and other bryologists still follow the same old system. Underwood (1894) and Gayeh (1897) however, withdrawn the order, Anthocerotales from class-Hepaticae.

According to Campbell, Smith, Takhtajan and others, the Bryophvta has been divided into three classes-Hepaticae, Anthocerotae and Musci.

In 1951, Rothmaler changed the class names. He recognized Hepaticae as Hepaticopsida; Anthocerotae as Anthoceropsida and Musci as Bryopsida. The above given classes have been also recognized by the international code of botanical nomenclature, 1956. Proskauer (1957) however changed the name Anthocerospida to Anthocerotopsida and thus, the Bryophyta may be classified as follows.

Division.	**Bryophyta**
Class 1.	Hepaticopsida (Hepaticae)
Class 2.	Anthocerotopsida (Anthocerotae)
Class 3.	Bryopsida (Musci)

Class 1. **Hepaticopsida.** There are 4 orders, 9 familles, 225 genera and 8,500 species.

1. The gametophytes are dorsiventrally differentiated. They may be thalloid (thallose) or differentiated into leaves and stem (foliose).
2. In foliose types the leaves are arranged in two or three rows on the axis and are always without mid-rib.
3. The sex organs develop from superficial cells on the dorsal side of the thallus, except when they are terminal in position.
4. The sporophyte may be simple, or differentiated into foot and capsule, or into a foot, seta and capsule.
5. The sporogenous cells develop from the endothecium of sporogonium.
6. The sporophyte is completely dependent on gametophytes for its nutritive supply.
7. The wall of sporogonium is one to several layered thick. The stomata are not present on the wall of sporogonium.
8. The dehiscence of sporogonium is irregular.

The class Hepaticopsida is further divided into several orders - (1) Sphaerocarpales; (2) Marchantiales; (3) Metzgeriales; (4) Jungermanniales; (5) Calobryales and (6) Takakiales.

Order-Sphaerocarpales (3 genera)-two families.

1. Family-Sphaerocarpaceae - *Sphaerocarpos* (seven species) and *Geothallus* (**single** species).

2. Family-Riellaceae-*Riella* (17 species).

The characteristic features of the order are as follows :

1. Vegetative structure of gametophyte is similar to that of order-Metzgeriales, but in which development and structure of sex organs, as well as the structure of sporophyte are similar to those of order-Marchantiales, and because of this the genera are placed in separate order Sphaerocarpales.

2. The main diagnostic feature by which the order is recognized is the presence of globose or a flask-like envelope or involucre around each of the sex organs (*i.e.*, antheridia and archegonia).

Order-Marchantiales (32 genera; 400 species)

The characteristic features are as follows :

1. The ribbon-like, dichotomously branched and dorsiventral thalli grow prostrate upon suitable substrata.

2. Excluding *Dumortiera, Monoselenium* and *Monoclea,* the rest of the genera possess internally differentiated air chambers on the dorsal side of the thallus, such chamber opens outside by an air pore of a particular design.

3. The ventral portion of the thallus consists of parenchyma which acts as storage tissue; oil and mucilage cells may be present in this region.

4. The scales and rhizoids are present on the ventral side of the thallus; the rhizoids are of two types (smooth-walled and tuberculate).

5. The antheridia and archegonia may be found directly on the dorsal surface of the thallus or they may be present on the special branches known as antheridiophores and archegoniophores respectively.

6. In most of cases the capsules of the sporophytes posses single layered jacket.

7. The capsule may be simple as in *Riccia* or it may be differentiated into foot, seta and capsule as in *Marchantia.*

8. The elaters may or may not be present. According to Campbell (1940). There are *five* families in this order. The characteristic features of *two* families are given here :

I. Family-Ricciaceae (3 genera; 140 species)

1. The gametophyte consists of a rosette-like dichotomously branched thallus.

2. In the thallus, the dorsal portion consists of chlorophyllous strips which may or may not have air canals among them; the ventral portion of the thallus is parenchymatous and acts as storage tissue.

3. The sex organs (antheridia and archegonia) are found in the longitudinal groove on the dorsal side from the growing apex to backward in basipetal succession.

4. The sporogonium consists of a simple capsule which is not differentiated into foot, seta and capsule.

5. Elaters not present.

6. The archesporium produces only the spores.

The important genera are-*Oxymitra, Ricciocarpus* and *Riccia.*

II. Family-Marchantiaceae (23 genera; 250 species)

1. The thallus is dorsiventral; it has distinct assimilatory and storage regions.

2. The assimilatory region remains divided into several chambers and each chamber contains branched assimilatory filaments.

3. The pores of the thallus may be simple or barrel-shaped.

4. The archegonia are borne upon special erect, stalked, vertical branches, the archegoniophores.

5. The antheridiophores may or may not present; however, in *Marchantia*, the antheridia are borne upon these erect, stalked antheridiophores.

6. The typical sterile elaters are found in the sporogonium mixed with tne spores. The important genera are - *Conocephalum, Cryptometrium, Lunularia, Marchantia* etc.

Order-Metzgeriales (23 genera; 550 species).

The characteristic features of this order are as follows :

1. The gametophyte may be thalloid or differentiated into stem and lateral leaves.
2. In most cases the gametophytes are without internal differentiation of tissues but certain genera have a central strand of thick-walled cells.
3. The ventral surface of a gametophyte bears smooth-walled rhizoids.
4. The sex-organs are found to be scattered on dorsal surface of thallus.
5. The archegonia arise from the young segments cut off by the apical cell.
6. The mature sporophytes lie some distance back from the growing apex of a gametophyte.
7. The sex organs (antheridia and archegonia) are produced on any branch of the gametophyte or only on special branches.

Family-Pelliaceae (Three genera- *Pellia, Noteroclada* and *Calycularia*).

1. The thallus is prostrate, dorsiventral and very often lobed by irregular incisions.
2. The rhizoids are simple, non-septate, smooth and thin-walled. The scales are absent.
4. The sex organs (antheridia and archegonia) remain scattered on the dorsal surface of the thallus.
5. The archegonial cluster always remains surrounded by an involucre which is an outgrowth of the thallus.
6. The capsule (sporogonium) is globose or oval in shape. It possesses a basal elaterophore.

Family-Riccardiaceae (two genera).

1. The gametophytes are wholly thallose or have thallose terminal branches
2. The cells of thallus possess finely segmented oil bodies.
3. The sex organs (antheridia and archegonia) are borne on short lateral branches.
4. A well-developed calyptra is present but there is no involucre.
5. A distal elaterophore is present to which some elaters are attached.
6. The capsule is ovoid to cylindrical and dehisces longitudinally into four parts extending to the base.

Family-Fossombroniaceae (4 genera; *Fossombronia, Simodon, Petalophyllum* and *Sewardiella).*

1. Thallus is distinctly foliose.
2. The thallus is dorsiventral and prostrate.
3. The stem is branched. Growth of the main axis and of its branches is by means of an apical cell with two cutting faces.
4. The leaf is thin, one cell-thick except the basal portion which is 2 or 3 cells in thickness.
5. Antheridia develop in acropetal succession singly or in small groups.
6. Archegonia occur in small groups.
7. Young sporophyte remains surrounded by a calyptra and which is ensheathed by a cuplike involucre.
8. The mature sporophyte is surrounded and protected by a bell-shaped sheathing perianth.
9. Important genus-*Fossombronia.*

Order-Jungermanniales (220 genera; 8,500 species).

The characteristic features of this order are as follows:

1. The gametophyte is differentiated into stem and leaves; the leaves are borne in a

regular spiral succession along the stem.

2. The apical cell is pyramid-like with three cutting faces.

3 The stem generally bears three rows of leaves; two rows are lateral and consist of leaves of normal size; the third row consists of the under leaves which are generally smaller than the lateral leaves.

4. The archegonia are always restricted to the apices of the axis and its branches.

5. The sporophytes are always terminal in position.

6. The antheridia are borne singly or in groups in the axis of leaves.

Family-Porellaceae (single genus-*Porella*).

1. The leaves are arranged in three rows on the stem; ventral leaves are well developed and usually decurrent at the base; dorsal leaves are incubuous; postical lobe distinct.

2. The rhizoids are scarce and arise from the lower side of the stem in tufts generally near the base of underleaves (ventral leaves).

3. The archegonia are borne in terminal cluster on small lateral branches; the archegonia remain surrounded by a large inflated perianth.

4. The spherical capsule dehisces by four valves which split only to half way down.

Family-Frullaniaceae (three genera; important genus *Frullania*).

1. The thallus is pinnately branched and differentiated into stem and leaves.

2. The leaves are arranged in three rows two laterals unequally lobed and a ventral lobule.

3. The ventral leaves are bifid and trumpet-shaped.

4. The archegonia develop in a group.

Order-Calobryales 2 genera-*Calobryum* (8 spp.) and *Haplomitrium* (single spp.)

The characteristic features are as follows :

1. They possess erect leafy gametophytes with leaves in three vertical rows.

2. The leaves are dorsiventrally flattened.

3. They have a pale, subterranean, sparingly branched rhizome from which arise erect leafy branches.

4. Erect branches bearing sex organs have the uppermost leaves close together and in more than three rows.

5. They are devoid of rhizoids.

6. The antheridia are ovoid, stalked, and borne at the apex of the stem.

7. The jacket of the neck of archegonium has only four vertical rows of cells.

8. The sporophyte bears an elongate capsule whose jacket layer is only one cell in thickness except at the apex.

9. The number of chromosomes is-n=9.

Since there is single family Calobryaceae the characters are similar to that of the order. Two genera-*Calobryum* and *Haplomitrium*.

Order-Takakiales (1 genus; 2 species)

The characteristic features are as follows :

1. They possess cylindrical, rhizomatic and erect gametophores.

2. They are devoid of rhizoids.

3. They possess copious beaked or non-beaked mucilage hairs on them.

4. They possess terete bifid-trifid-quadrifid leaves or phyllids.

5. The gametophores are about 1 to 1.5 cm. in height.

6. The leafless branches facing downward known as 'flagella' or 'stolons' may present.

7. Asexual reproduction is not known.

8. Only female (archegonial) shoots are known. They bear conspicuous pedestalled archegonia.

9. The male (antheridial) shoots and the sporophytes are not known.

10. They have lowest chromosome number (*i.e.*, n=4).

11. They are supposed to be most primitive and sometimes known as living fossil. There is one family Takakiaceae, and one genus *Takakia*.

Class II. **Anthocerotopsida.** There are 1 order, 1 or 2 families, 6 genera and 301 species.

1. The gametophyte is thalloid and dorsiventral, bearing simple and smooth-walled rhizoids; tuberculate rhizoids and ventral scales are altogether absent.
2. The tissues of the thallus are undifferentiated; air chambers and air pores are absent; each cell bears a large chloroplast and a conspicuous pyrenoid within it.
3. The sex organs are found to be embedded in the gametophytic tissue.
4. The antheridia arise from the hypodermal cells of the thallus on the dorsal side of it; they develop within the antheridial chambers, singly or in groups on the dorsal side of the thallus.
5. The archegonia are found in sunken conditions on the dorsal side of the thallus, they develop from superficial cells.
6. The elongated and cylindrical sporogonium arises from the dorsal side of the thallus.
7. The sporogonium consists of foot, meristematic region and capsule; the meristem is intercalary and continues its growth throughout the growing season.
8. The wall of sporogonium contains chlorophyll.
9. The central sterile portion of sporogonium is columella, which remains surrounded by sporogenous tissue and spores; the elaters are also present.
10. The sporogenous mass develops from amphithecium and arches over the columella.

The class Anthocerotopsida includes a single order, the Anthocerotales with the same characters. There are two families 1. Anthocerotaceae and 2. Notothylaceae.

Family–Anthocerotaceae (4 or 5 genera; important genus *Anthoceros*).

1. The capsule is linear and vertical.
2. The stomata are present on the wall of capsule.
3. The archesporium develops from amphithecium.
4. The elaters are four-celled, smooth or thick-walled; thickening band may or may not present.

Family–Notothylaceae (single genus-*Notothylas*)

1. The capsule is cylindrical and horizontal.
2. The stomata are not found on the wall of capsule.
3. Archesporium arises from endothecium and amphithecium.
4. Elaters are short and stumpy; they have irregular thickening bands.

Class III. **Bryopsida.** There are 3 orders, 28 families, 660 genera and 15,504 species.

1. The gametophyte consists of prostrate, thalloid, branched protonema and erect leafy gametophore.
2. The gametophytic plant body consists of the stem, spirally arranged leaves and the sex organs (antheridia and archegonia) at its apical portion.
3. The rhizoids are multicellular, branched and obliquely septate.
4. The sex organs (antheridia and archegonia) develop from the superficial cells of the gametophore.
5. The sporophyte is differentiated into foot, seta and capsule.

6. The capsular wall remains interrupted by stomata at several places.

7. The archesporium or sporogenous mass develops from outer layer of endothecium which in addition forms columella.

8. The elaters are not present in the sporogonium.

The class Bryopsida (Musci) has been divided into *three* sub-classes (1) Sphagnobrya (Sphagnidae); (2) Andreaeobrya (Andreaeidae) and (3) Eubrya (Bryidae).

I. Sub-class. Sphagnobrya. This sub-class has a single order, the Sphagnales and a single family, the Sphagnaceae. (single genus *Sphagnum* with 326 species). The characteristic features are as follows :

1. They are called 'bog mosses' or 'peat mosses'.
2. The protonema is broad and thallose; it produces one gametophore; the leaves of gametophores lack mid-rib and usually composed of two types of cells- (i) the narrow living green cells and (ii) large hyaline dead cells.
3. The branches arise in lateral clusters in the axis of the leaves borne on the stem.
4. The antheridia are borne in the axis of leaves on the antheridial branch.
5. The archegonia are terminal and formed acrogynously.
6. The sporogenous tissue of a sporophyte develops from the amphithecium.
7. The sporogonium remains elevated above the gametophyte due to elongation of a stalk of gametophytic tissue, the pseudopodium.

II. Sub-class. Andreaeobrya. This sub-class has a single order, the Andreaeales, and a single family, the Andreaeceae. The important genus is *Andreaea*.

The characteristic features are as follows :

1. The gametophores are brittle, and can easily be broken.
2. There is practically no tissue differentiation in plant body.
3. The leaves are generally large, erect and convolute.
4. The archesporium and columella develop from the endothecium.

III. Sub-class. Eubrya. (650 genera; 14,000 species). This sub-class has been further divided into *three* cohorts and *fifteen* orders. The true mosses are included in this sub-class. The characteristic features are as follows :

1. The leaves of the gametophores are more than one cell in thickness and possess mid-rib on them.
2. The protonema are filamentous.
3. The sporophyte bears a well differentiated, elongated seta which pushes out the capsule from the gametophore.
4. The sporogenous tissue is derived from the endothecium.
5. The archesporium doesnot overarch the columella; the columella continues upto the apex of the capsule; both columella and archesporium have been derived from the endothecium.
6. In between spore sac and columella, the partitioned air spaces are present.
7. The mature capsule possesses the complex structure made of many tissues.
8. The capsule opens at its apex by an operculum; the spore dispersal is regulated by a teeth like apparatus, the persistome.

Order-Funariales (26 genera; 356 species).

Characteristic features.

1. The plants are terrestrial; they are small in size and may be annual or biennial.
2. The leaves possess distinct mid-ribs and arranged in rosettes at the apex of the gametophyte.

3. The capsule is wide and provided with an unbeaked operculum.

4. The peristome of the capsule is double and consists of inner and outer peristomes called endostome and exostome respectively.

5. There are *five* families in this order, of which Funariaceae is most important.

Family-Funariaceae (9 genera; 200 species).

1. The leaves are one cell in thickness except at the mid-rib region.

2. The small mosses form the velvety appearance on the surface of the substratum.

3. The calyptra are soon detached from the opercula of the capsules; the calyptra are provided with long beaks.

4. The capsules are pyriform and situated on the long, elongated setae.

Order-Polytrichales

Characteristic features.

1. The gametophyte is perennial and tall.

2. The leaves are narrow and possess longitudinal lamellae on the upper surface of the midrib.

3. The capsule is terminal.

4. The single annular series of cells gives rise to a peristome in the inner zone of the amphithecium.

5. There are 32 to 64 pyramidal teeth in peristome; the tips of the peristome teeth remain joined above to a thin membrance, the epiphragm covers the mouth of the capsule.

6. There is a single family, the Polytrichaceae in this order; the important genera of this family are-*Polytrichum* and *Pogonatum*.

3

Hepaticopsida

Order-Marchantiales

This class includes 4 orders, 9 families, about 225 genera and 8,500 species (Smith, 1955). The Latin word *hepatica* means liver and there from the members of Hepaticopsida are popularly known as liverworts. The most characteristic features of the class are as follows :

The gametophytes are dorsiventrally differentiated. The vegetative plant body (gametophyte) may be either a thallus (thallose) or a leafy axis, *i.e.*, differentiated into leaves and stem (foliose). In foliose types the leaves are arranged in two or three rows on the axis and are always without mid-rib.

The interior of the gametophyte is either simple or composed of various tissues. The assimilatory cells contain numerous chloroplasts which are devoid of pyrenoids.

The sex organs are always developed from superficial cells on the dorsal side of the thallus, except when they are terminal in position.

The sporophyte (sporogonium) may be simple, or differentiated into foot and capsule, or into a foot, seta and capsule. In each case the sporogenous cells develop from the endothecium of an embryo.

The sporophyte is completely dependent on gametophyte for its nutritive supply.

Classification. According to Engler (1892), the class Hepaticopsida had only two orders: Jungermanniales and Marchantiales. Cavers in 1910 isolated the family Sphaerocarpaceae from the order Jungermanniales and gave it the rank of order, *i.e.*, Sphaerocarpales. This way according to Cavers there are three orders in the class-Sphaerocarpales, Jungermanniales and Marchantiales. Campbell (1936) raised another family Calobryaceae of Jungermanniales to the rank of order, *i.e.* Calobryales. Thus the classification of Hepaticopsida is as follows (Smith, 1955):

Class. **Hepaticopsida**

Order 1. Sphaerocarpales
Order 2. Marchantiales
Order 3. Jungermanniales
Order 4. Calobryales.

In the present text, however, *six* orders have been recognized in class-Hepaticopsida. They are as follows :

Order 1. Sphaerocarpales
Order 2. Marchantiales
Order 3. Metzgeriales
Order 4. Jungermanniales
Order 5. Calobryales
Order 6. Takakiales.

ORDER-MARCHANTIALES

There are about 32 genera and 400 species in this order. The ribbon shaped, dichotomously branched and dorsiventral gametophytes of this order grow prostrate upon the suitable substrata. Excluding *Dumortiera, Monoselenium* and *Monoclea* the rest of the genera posses internally differentiated air chambers on the dorsal side of the thallus, such chamber opens outside by an air pore of a particular design. The ventral portion of the thallus consists of parenchyma which acts as storage tissue. Sometimes the oil and mucilage cells are also found in this region of parenchyma. Usually the scales and rhizoids are found on the ventral side of the thallus. Commonly the rhizoids are of two types. The antheridia and archegonia may be found directly on the dorsal surface of the thallus or they may be present on the special branches designated antheridiophores and archegoniophores respectively. The capsules of the sporophytes of most of the Marchantiales possess single layered jacket. The capsule may be simple as in *Riccia* or it may be differentiated into foot, seta and capsule as in *Marchantia*. The elaters may or may not be present.

Classification. Different bryologists have put forward the various systems of classification from time to time. The bryologists, such as Von Wettstein (1908), Kashyap (1919), Verdoorn (1932) and Evans (1939) supported the view of retrogression in Marchantiales from the complex type *Marchantia* to the simple type *Riccia*. This view was supported and put forward by Goebel (1910).

Verdoorn (1932) divided the order Marchantiales into six families. They are, (1) Marchantiaceae; (2) Operculatae; (3) Astroporae; (4) Targioniaceae; (5) Corsiniaceae and (6) Ricciaceae. Evans (1939), however, also recognized the six families. They are (1) Marchantiaceae; (2) Rebouliaceae; (3) Sauteriaceae; (4) Targioniaceae; (5) Corsiniaceae and (6) Ricciaceae.

Campbell (1940), has divided the order into five families. He followed the progression of the complexity from Ricciaceae to Marchantiaceae. The five families recognized by him are, (1) Ricciaceae; (2) Corsiniaceae; (3) Targioniaceae; (4) Monocleaceae and (5) Marchantiaceae.

The Campbell's classification has been followed by various authors of the different books. Gilbert M. Smith has followed the same classification in his text book Cryptogamic Botany Vol II. In the present text, the Campbell's classification has been followed.

Family-Ricciaceae

There are three genera and about 140 species in this family. These three genera are-*Oxymitra, Ricciocarpos* and *Riccia.*

The gametophyte consists of a rosette-like, dichotomously branched thallus. In the gametophyte, the dorsal portion consists of chlorophyllous strips which may or may not have air canals among them. The ventral portion is parenchymatous and acts as storage tissue.

The sex organs are found in the longitudinal groove on the dorsal side from the growing apex to backward in basipetal succession.

The sporogonium consists of a simple capsule which is not differentiated into foot, seta and capsule. The elaters are also not found. The archesporium produces only the spores.

Genus RICCIA

There are about 130 species in this genus. However, Reimers (1954) has reported about 200 species of *Riccia.* About 30 species of *Riccia* have been reported from India by various workers. The pioneer Indian worker S.R. Kashyap recorded a number of species from Himachal Pradesh (then Punjab), Kashmir and other regions of Western Himalayas.

About all the species are terrestrial plants which grow on the damp soil of moist rocks. Some species may withstand the drought condition and grow on the surface of the soil in exposed conditions. The species have been recorded from the hills as well as from the plains. *Riccia himalayensis* has been recorded even from the altitude of 9,000 feet in the Himalayas. *R. crystallina* occurs in Western Himalayas at fairly high altitude upto 14,000 feet. *R. gangetica* and *R. pandei* are endemic to India.

Riccia fluitans and an allied species *Ricciocarpos natans* are aquatic in nature, and found in free floating condition on the surface of the water. These species may also grow on soil, and on soil their shapes become so much changed that they cannot be recognized.

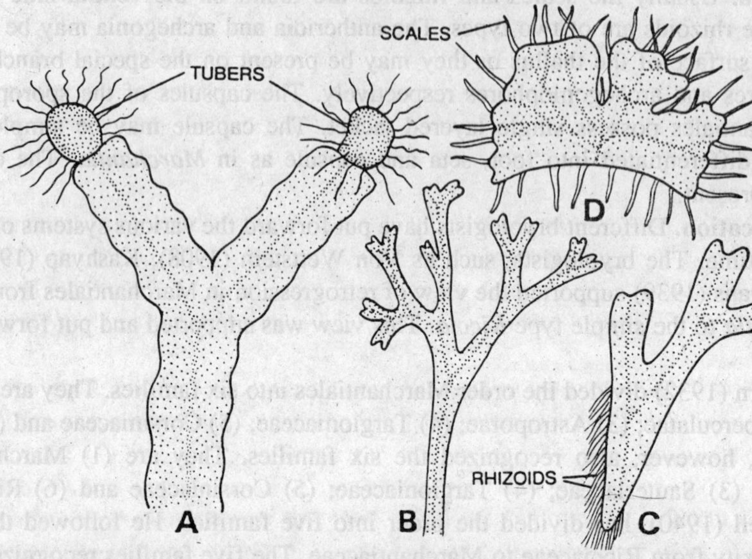

Fig. 3.1. External features of the thalli. A, *Riccia billardieri*; B, *R. fluitans*-water form; C, *R. fluitans*-land form; H, *Ricciocarpos natans*. (A, after Udar).

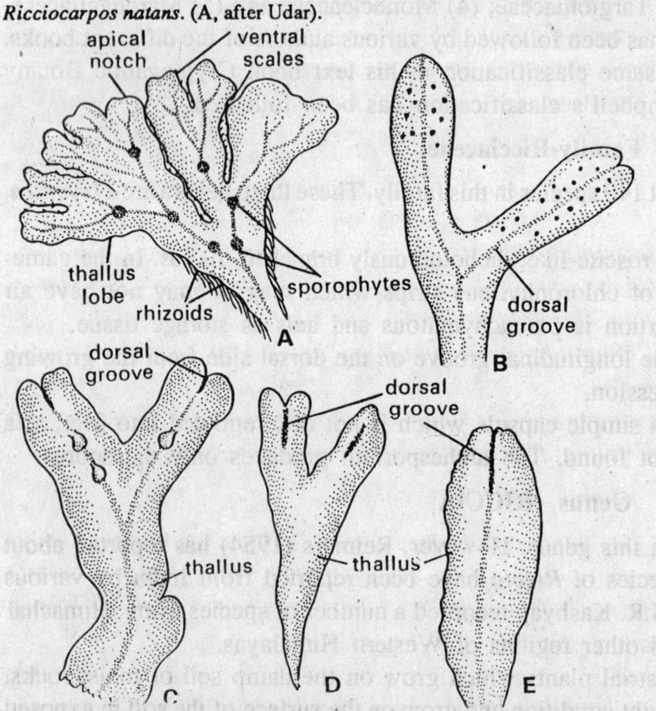

Fig. 3.2. *Riccia* . Thalli of different species showing external structure: A, *Riccia* spp. thallus showing apical notch, ventral scales, rhizoids,sporophytes etc.; B, thallus of *R. gangetica* showing dorsal groove; C, thallus of *R. pathankotensis*; D, thallus of *R. melanospora* and E, thallus of *R. discolor*.

Though the genus is cosmopolitan in distribution, yet most of the species are confined to the Southern Hemisphere.

According to Udar (1958-70) the distribution of the genus in India is as follows :

12 species are found in East Himalayan Territory. They are-*R. ciliata*; *R. discolor*; *R. glauca*; *R. beyrichiana*; *R. sorocarpa*; *R. gangetica*, *R. billardieri*; *R. frostii*; *R. crystallina*; *R. heubeneriana*; *R. attenuata* and *R. fluitans*.

11 species are found in West Himalayas Territory. They are-*R. melanospora*; *R. hirta*; *R. pathankotensis*; *R. discolor*; *R. sorocarpa*; *R. aravelliensis*; *R. gangetica*; *R. billardieri*; *R. crystallina*; *R. pandei* and *R. fluitans*.

16 species have been recorded from Central zone of India. They are-*R. melanospora*; *R. pa-*

thankotenis; R. discolor; R. aravelliensis; R. reticulaiula; R. pimodic; R. tuberculata; R. billardieri; R. gangetica; R. curtisii; R. frostii; R. plana; R. cruciata; R. crystallina; R. heubeneriana and *R. fluitans*.

11 species have been recorded from South India. They are-*R. melanospora; R. warnstrofii; R. crozalsii; R. tuberculata; R. discolor; R. billardieri; R. gangetica; R. heubeneriana; R. plana; R. cruciata* and *R. frostii*.

R. discolor (*R. himalayensis*), *R. gangetica*, *R. billardieri* and *R. melanospora* are commonly found in the Indian plains especially during rainy season, *i.e.*, from July to October whereas *R. crystallina*, *R. cruciata* and *R. frostii* are found in abundance from October to March. However, *R. reticulata* shows xerophytic characters.

THE GAMETOPHYTE

External structure of the thallus (adult gametophyte). The adult terrestrial gametopnyte is prostrate, rosette-like, dichotomously branched, dorsiventral, deep green and found upon suitable substratum of damp soil. The aquatic species however, possess light green, thin membranous dichotomously branched thallus. The dichotomous branchings of the thallus are found quite close to each other and thus a rosette-like appearance is attained. A conspicuous median longitudinal groove is found on the dorsal side of each branch of the thallus. A notch is found on the terminal end of each branch, and on the dorsal side of each branch of the thallus. The growing point is situated in this notch. The ventral surface of the thallus bears a row of the one-celled thick scales. The scales are violet coloured, multicellular and are arranged closed to each other towards the apex of the branch. But on the contrary, away from the notch, the scales are quite apart from each other. The scales are found in one row towards the apex of the branch, whereas they are found in two rows in the portion away from the apex. This means that the older parts of the thallus bear two rows of the scales. In *Riccia crystallina*, the scales are either absent or rudimentary. The rhizoids are also found on the ventral surface of the thallus. The rhizoids absorb the nutrients and water from substratum, and, in this way they perform the function of the roots. The rhizoids are of two types, *i.e.*, smooth walled and with tuberculate walls. In each case the rhizoids are unicellular. The tuberculate rhizoids possess the peg-like infoldings peeping into the lumen of the rhizoids. The simple or smooth walled rhizoids have no such infoldings.

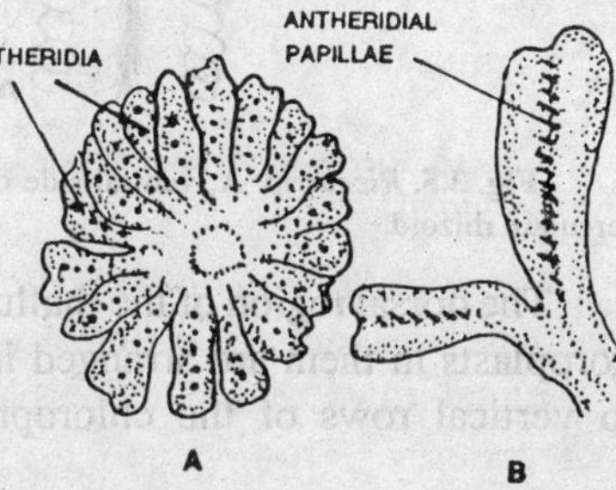

Fig. 3.3. *Riccia* spp. Male thalli: A, male thallus of *R. frostii*; B, male thallus of *R. discolor*.

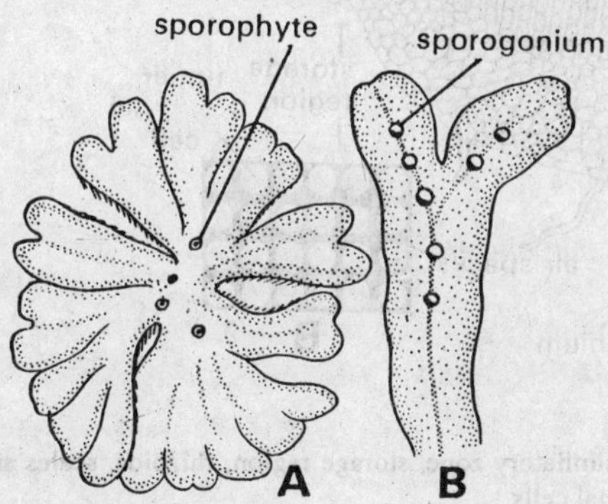

Fig. 3.4. *Riccia* spp. Female thalli: A, *Riccia frostii* with sporophyte; B, *R. discolor* with sporophyte.

Internal structure of the thallus (anatomy). To study the anatomy of the adult thallus of *Riccia*, one has to cut the thin vertical sections of the thallus. From the point of view of the anatomy the thallus may be differentiated into two regions. The ventral region of the thallus consists of simple parenchyma, which is colourless. However, the intercellular spaces are not found. The cells of this region make the storage tissue and are filled up with starch grains. From the single layered epidermis of the ventral surface several unicellular rhizoids (smooth walled or tuberculate) and multicellular scales are given out.

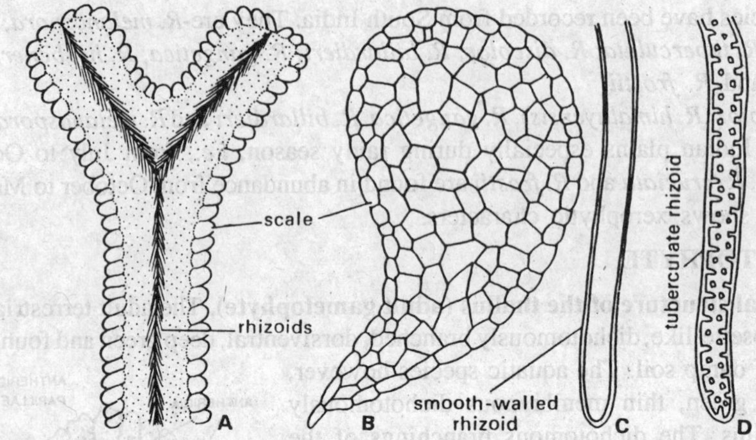

Fig. 3.5. *Riccia* sp. A, ventral side of thallus showing scales and rhizoids; B, scale; C, smooth walled rhizoid; D, tuberculate rhizoid.

The dorsal region of the thallus consists of the chlorophyllous cells. These cells with discoid chloroplasts in them are arranged in vertical rows. There are regular air canals in between each two vertical rows of the chlorophyllous cells. This region is photosynthetic and assimilate

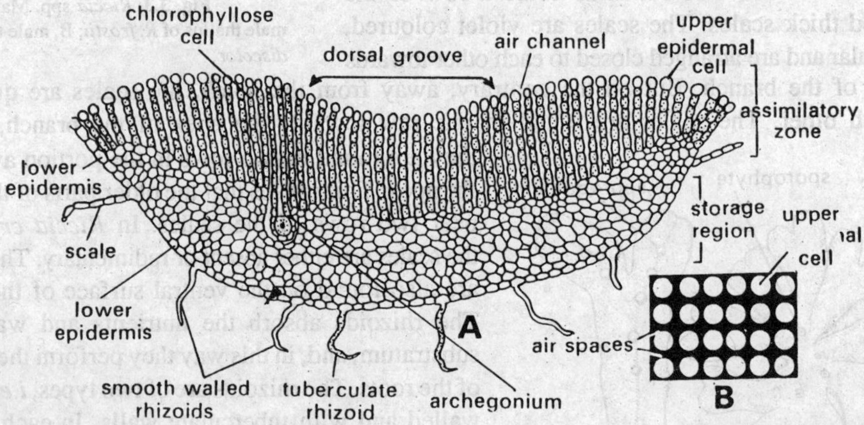

Fig. 3.6. *Riccia* spp. A, vertical section of thallus showing assimilatory zone, storage region, rhizoids, scales and archegonium; B, surface view of thallus showing air spaces and epidermal cells.

carbohydrates. The epidermis of the dorsal surface of the thallus is discontinuous and opened outside at several places by the opening of the air canals. The epidermis is single layered. However, the epidermis is continuous in aquatic species, *i.e., R. fluitans*. The exchange of gases takes place through the air canals.

Apical growth. In *Riccia*, the apical growth of the thallus takes place by means of a row of 3 to 5 apical cells situated in the notch of the branch. Each such cell cuts off derivatives alternately on its dorsal and ventral faces. Sometimes the segments are cut off from lateral face of the apical cell. According to Pietsch (1911), from the segments of the dorsal surface the dorsal chlorophyllous region is derived. The segments of the ventral face, give rise to the region

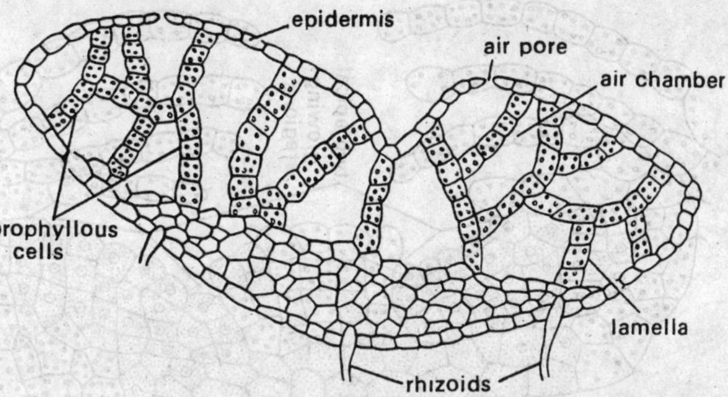

Fig. 3.7. *Riccia fluitans*. Transverse vertical section of thallus of a land form. (After Parihar).

of the ventral surface, rhizoids and scales. The derivatives from the outer daughter cell give rise to the epidermis and the air canals.

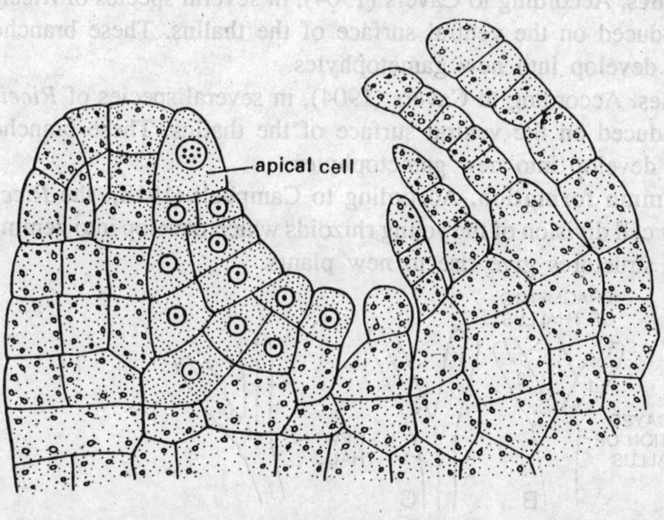

Fig. 3.8. *Riccia* sp. Apical growth of thallus. Longitudinal vertical section through the growing point of thallus. (After Black).

Air chamber formation. According to Lietgeb (1879), Hirsch (1910) and Black (1913) the air chambers develop by the cessation of the growth of the tissue of the thallus in surface area at several points, and the parts around these points grow vigorously upward. With the result, these depressions become quite deep and narrow, and called the air chambers. According to the other view, which is widely accepted and proposed by Barnes and Land (1907), Pietsch (1911), Black (1913) and Orth (1943) the air chambers develop schizogenously like intercellular spaces of the higher plants.

Formation of dichotomous branches. In the young thallus, one or more cells in the centre of the row of apical cells stop to divide with the result that the original row of apical cells becomes separated into two sets of initial cells. Each new set of initial cells continuously grows and develops the tissue of the thallus which is found between the two groups of initial cells. With the result the two apical growing regions are further separated from one another. Each of these growing points forms a separate branch and each branch possesses its own row of apical cells. This process continues in each of the branches thus developed, and the new rosette is formed.

Reproduction. The reproduction in *Riccia* takes place by means of (1) vegetative and (2) sexual methods.

(1) Vegetative reproduction. This type of reproduction takes place by several ways.

(a) By the death and decay of the older parts of the thallus. Sometimes a part of the thallus, dichotomously branched decays from the posterior end, and this way the terminal ends of the branches remain unaffected, which may grow separately into new thalli.

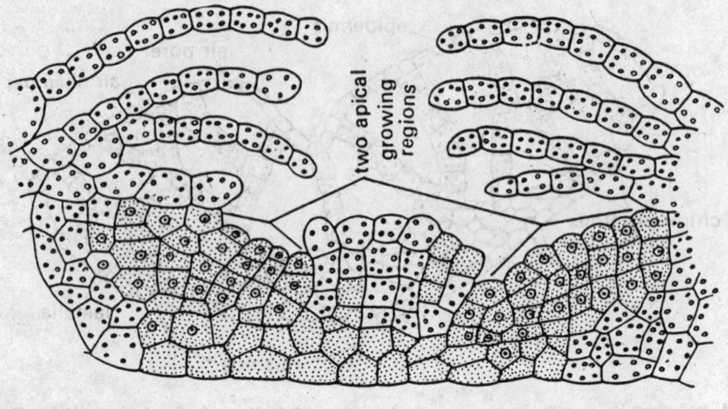

Fig. 3.9. *Riccia* sp. Dichotomous branching; transverse section through the growing end of thallus showing dichotomous branching. (After Black).

(b) By adventitious branches. According to Cavers (1904), in several species of *Riccia*, the adventitious branches are produced on the ventral surface of the thallus. These branches get detached from the thalli and develop into new gametophytes.

(c) By adventitious branches. According to Cavers (1904), in several species of *Riccia*, the adventitious branches are produced on the ventral surface of the thallus. These branches get detached from the thalli and develop into new gametophytes.

(d) By cell division or gemma formation. According to Campbell (1918), the *Riccia* may also reproduce vegetatively by cell division of the young rhizoids which develop into gemma-like structure of the cells. These structures give rise to new plants.

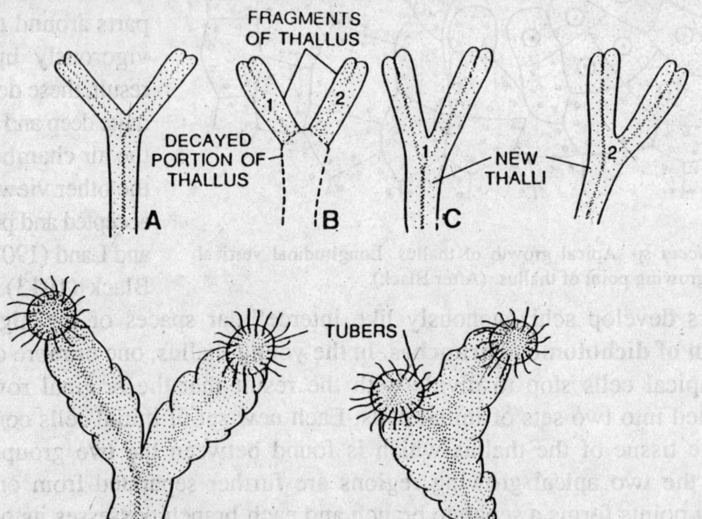

Fig. 3.10. *Riccia* sp. Vegetative reproduction, A-C, by the death and decay of the older parts of the thallus; D-E, by tubers. (D, *R. billardieri*; E, *R. discolor*–After Udar).

(e) By tubers. In the species, such as, *R. discolor*. *R. vesicata*, *R. bulbifera* and *R. perennis*, the vegetative structure, called the tubers, develop at the apices of the branches of the thallus which face adverse conditions, and develop into new plants on the approach of favourable conditions.

(f) By thick apices. In certain species like *R. himalayensis* and others in the end of the growing season the apex of the thallus grows downward into the soil and becomes thick. This thick apex survives in the soil and develops into a new plant on the approach of favourable conditions.

2. Sexual reproduction. Majority of the species of *Riccia* are homothallic (monoecious), *i.e.*, antheridia and archegonia are borne upon the same thallus. The important species of this type are *R. glauca, R. gangetica, R. crystallina* and many others. The heterothallic (dioecious) species are also common. In such species the antheridia and archegonia develop separately on different thalli. The important species of this type are *R. himalayensis* (*R. discolor*), *R. bischoffii* (*R. ciliifera*), *R. frostii, R. personii* and *R. curtisii.* According to MacAllister (1916, 1928), at the time of the formation of spores, there is genotypic type of sex determination, *i.e.*, two spores of a tetrad develop into female and two into the male gametophytes.

The sex organs are produced in the groove situated on the dorsal surface of the mature gametophyte in acropetal succession. In a homothallic species the alternate groups of antheridia

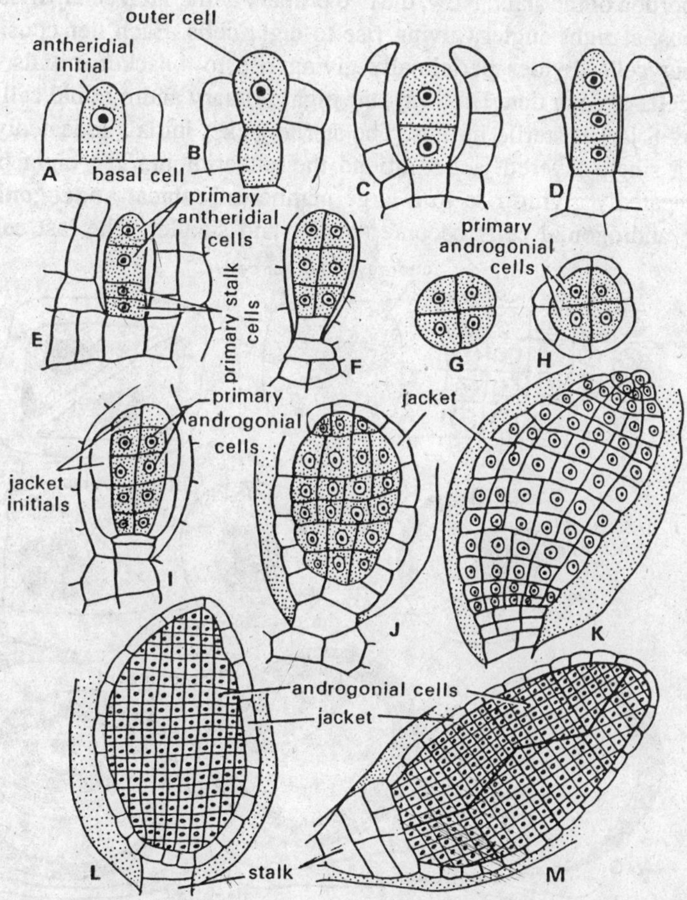

Fig. 3.11. *Riccia* sp. Development of antheridium. A, antheridinal initial; B, transverse division of antheridial initial; C-L, successive stages in the development of antheridium; M, mature stalked antheridium (After Lewis).

and archegonia are found at a sufficient distance from the growing point. The antheridia and archegonia are found in groups separately in the median longitudinal grooves of different thalli. Both the antheridia and archegonia develop singly on the dorsal surface of the thallus. They develop successively for a long time simultaneously from the segments of the apical cell. As there is no particular time for the development of the sex organs, one can detect all the development stages at one time in different sections of the same thallus.

Development of antheridium. The antheridium develops from a superficial dorsal cell called the **antheridial initial** which is situated two or three cells back of the spical cell. The stages of the development of the antheridium in *Riccia* were worked out by Black (1913), and Campbell (1918). They are as follows :

The antheridial initial soon divides, giving rise to two cells. The upper one is called **outer cell** and the lower one the **basal cell.** The outer cell projects somewhat outside the thallus. The basal cell remains embedded in the thallus and develops into the embedded portion of the stalk of the antheridium. The outer cell, however, develops into the main antheridium. The outer cell further divides by transverse septa and a vertical file of three cells is resulted. The two upper cells of this vertical file are called the **primary antheridial cells,** which produce the proper antheridium. The lowermost cell of the file is called the **primary stalk cell** which produces the projecting portion of the stalk. Now, the two primary antheridial cells, divide by two successive vertical divisions, at right angles, giving rise to eight cells. Each tier consists of 4 cells. Now each tier of four cells divides periclinally giving rise to 4 jacket initials, which encircle the 4 androgonial cells of each tier. This way, the eight primary androgonial cells are formed, which are encircled by 8 jacket sterile initials. The sterile jacket initials repeatedly divide anticlinally giving rise to a single layered jacket around the antheridium. The eight primary androgonial cells divide repeatedly giving rise to a large number of cubical **androgonial cells.** By further divisions these androgonial cells become smaller and smaller. The last cell generation of the

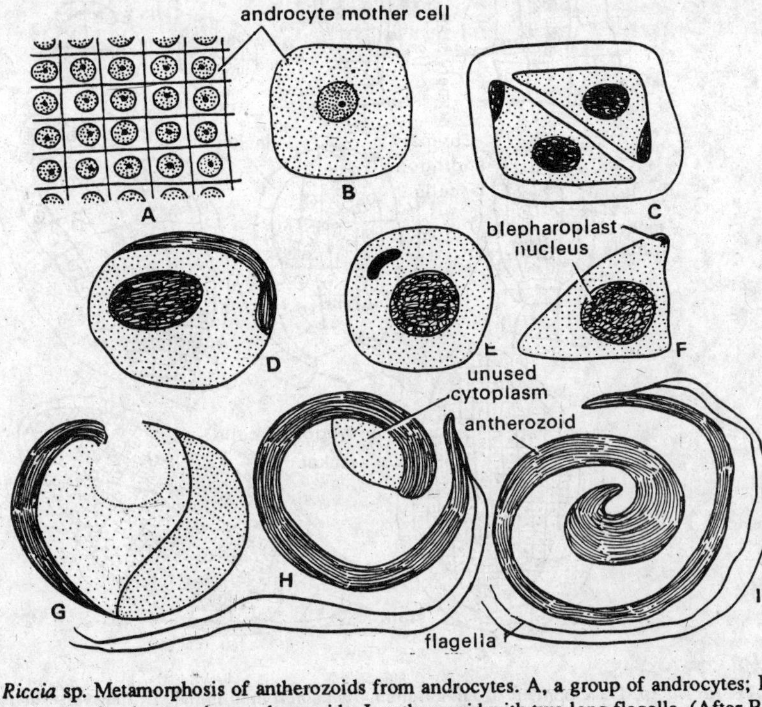

Fig. 3.12. *Riccia* sp. Metamorphosis of antherozoids from androcytes. A, a group of androcytes; B-H, successive stages in the metamorphosis of androcytes into antherozoids; I, antherozoid with two long flagella. (After Black).

androgonial mother cells consists of the **androcyte mother cells.** Each androcyte mother cell divides diagonally (Nevins, 1933) giving rise to two **androcytes.**

Formation of antherozoid from androcyte. Soon after the formation of androcytes they are metamorphosed into **antherozoids.** The process of metamorphosis is as follows :

The androcytes are somewhat triangular in shape. Each androcyte possesses a big, promient nucleus. An extra nuclear granule, the **blepharoplast** appears in the cell. The granule becomes somewhat large in size, elongates and develops into a cord like body adhering the plasma membrance (Nevins, 1933). Very soon the two flagella arise from the anterior end of the blepharoplast. During the metamorphosis of androcyte into antherozoid the androcyte becomes rounded. The nucleus becomes crescent-shaped and shifts towards the blepharoplast and becomes united with it firmly. The elongated cord-like blepharoplast extends about three fourth of the cell. During the process of metamorphosis the internal cell walls of the jacket layer of the antheridium become disintegrated and produce a liquid substance in which the antherozoids lie in nonmotile condition. The metamorphosis of androcytes into antherozoids was worked out by Black (1913).

Liberation of antherozoids. The jacket layer of the fully developed antheridium gelatinizes and the antherozoids are discharged by the imbibition of the water by the gelatinized mass within the antheridium. The antherozoids lie free in the antheridium embedded in the viscous substance. Though the actual process of the liberation of the antherozoids from the antheridium is yet to be discovered, yet, according to Cavers (1903), it takes place by explosive mechanism as in other Marchantiaceae. According to Anderson (1931) they are exudated in a gelatinous mass. The mature antheridium is found in an **antheridial chamber** which is connected to the outer atmosphere through a small opening. The antherozoids mixed with gelatinous substance come out of the antheridium, and then through the opening of the antheridial chamber, they come to the dorsal surface of the mature gametophyte.

Structure of mature antherozoids. The main body of a mature antherozoid mainly consists of nucleus portion. The elongated blepharaplast adhered to the nucleus bears two flagella at its anterior end. With the help of the flagella, the antherozoid moves here and there in the water. One flagellum of the antherozoid helps in propulsion and the other helps in rotating the body. Sometimes, small unused portion of cytoplasm remains attached to the posterior end of the antherozoid in the form of a vesicle.

Structure of a mature antheridium. The mature antheridium remains embedded in the antheridial chamber, which opens by a ostiole on the dorsal side of the thallus. The mature antheridium consists of a few celled stalk and the antheridium proper. The antheridium proper may be rounded or somewhat pointed at its apical end. A sterile single layered jacket-layer encircles the antheridium and protects it. The mature antheridium contains androcytes within the jacket layer. Each androcyte metamorphoses into an antherozoid.

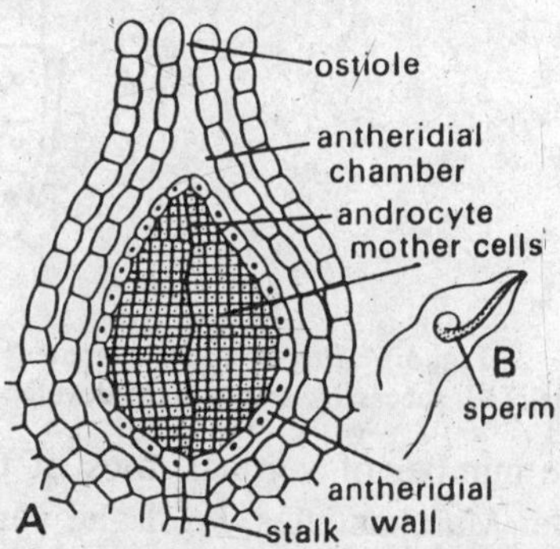

Fig. 3.13. *Riccia* sp. A, antheridium (male sex organ) in sectional view; B, biflagellate spermatozoid.

Development of archegonium. It develops from a superficial cell which lies two or three cells away from the apex of the thallus. This cell is called the **archegonial initial.** As worked out by Black (1913) and Campbell (1918), the further development stages are as follows: The archegonial initial divides by a transverse wall into two cells. The lower cell is the **basal cell** and the upper cell is the **outer cell.** From the basal cell, the lowermost portion of the archegonium is produced. Whereas, the outer cell produces the main body of the archegonium. The outer cell divides vertically producing a peripheral initial, and it is followed by two more such divisions, giving rise to three cells in total. These cells are peripheral initials. The three cells are situated upon a **primary axial cell.** The three peripheral initials divide vertically resulting in six **jacket initials.** All the six cells surround the central cell. Soon after each jacket initial divides by a transverse division producing six **neck initials** which are arranged in a tier. The tier of six neck cells is situated above the tier of six **venter initials.** By several transverse divisions, the neck initials give rise to a neck of archegonium 6 to 9 cells in length and six-celled in perimeter.

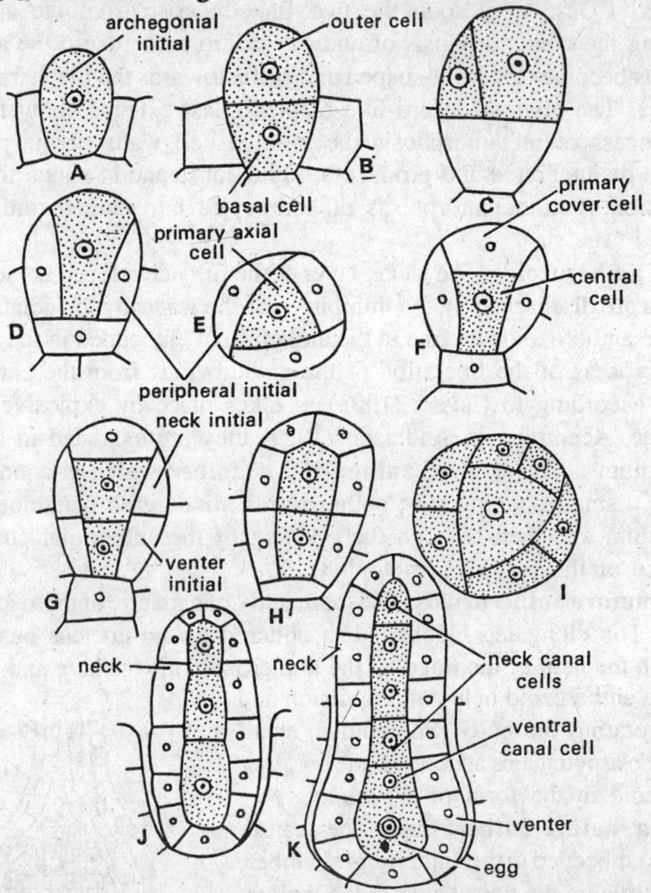

Fig. 3.14. *Riccia* sp. Development of archegonium. A, archegonium initial; B, transverse division of archegonial initial; C-J, successive stages in the development of archegonium; K, young archegonium. (After Lewis).

The number of vertical rows of the cells of which the archegonium consists of, is six in the order Marchantiales. From the venter intitials the jacket of the venter is developed. The initials of the jacket of venter are somewhat different from the neck cells in division. The neck initials divide only by transverse divisions producing daughter cells, whereas, the venter initials divide both ways, transversely and vertically producing the bulbous venter jacket. The jacket of the venter is 12 to 20 cells in perimeter.

The primary axial cell divides by an unequal transverse division producing a **primary cover cell** and a **central cell.** The primary cover cell divides twice vertically producing four cover cells at the apex of jacket layer. Eventually, the central cell divides by a transverse wall producing an **upper canal cell** and a **lower canal cell.** The upper canal cell divides twice giving

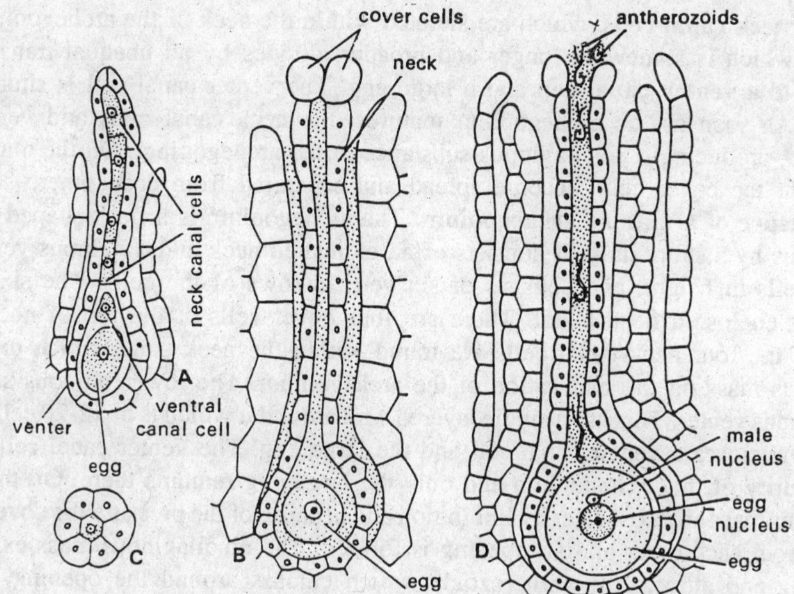

Fig. 3.15. *Riccia* sp. A, young archegonium; B, mature archegonium; C, transverse section of archegonium; D, fertilization.

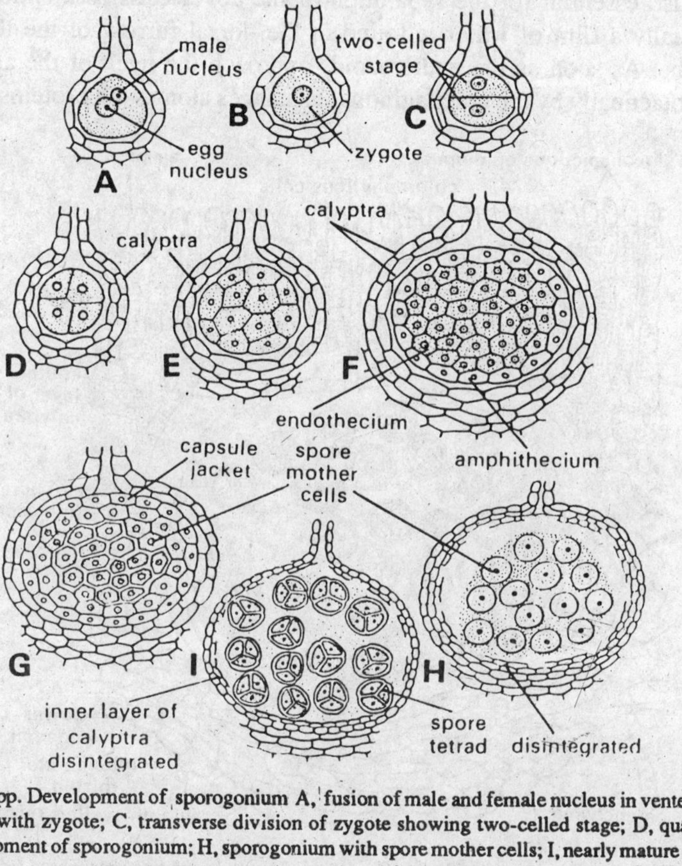

Fig. 3.16. *Riccia* spp. Development of sporogonium A, fusion of male and female nucleus in venter of archegonium; B, venter of archegonium with zygote; C, transverse division of zygote showing two-celled stage; D, quadrant stage; E-G, further stages in the development of sporogonium; H, sporogonium with spore mother cells; I, nearly mature sporogonium with spore tetrads.

rise to four **neck canal cells,** which are situated within the neck of the archegonium. The lower canal cell, which is somewhat longer and broader, divides by an unequal transverse division giving rise to a **venter canal cell** and a large **egg.** The venter canal cell is situated above the large egg. As soon as the archegonium matures, the neck canal cells and venter canal cell desintegrate, producing a mucilaginous substance in the archegonium. On the maturation of the archegonium the cover cells become spread and separated from each other.

Structure of a mature archegonium. The archegonium is a flask-shaped body attached to the thallus by a short stalk. It consists of an elongated neck and a bulbous venter. The neck is 6 to 9 cells in height, and consists of six vertical rows of the cells. The six vertical rows of the cells enclose a neck canal. There are four cover cells at the top of neck canal. Prior to maturity the four neck canal cells are found within the neck canal which disintegrate into mucilaginous mass on the maturation of the archegonium. The lower bulbous structure of the archegonium is venter. This has a single layered wall around it which is of 12-20 cells in perimeter. The venter encloses a venter canal cell and the large egg. The venter canal cell disintergrates on the maturity of the archegonium and only the large egg remains there. On the maturity the mucilaginous mass absorbs water by imbibition and because of the pressure the cover cells become separated from each other and an opening is formed. The mucilaginous mass extrudes through this opening and attracts the antherozoids, which enmass around the opening.

Fertilization or syngamy. The water is indispensable for the process of fertilization. The antherozoids reach to the mouth of the neck of archegonium through the medium of water. The water is also essential for the separation of the cover cells as mentioned in the preceding paragraph. Usually a film of water is found in the dorsal furrow of the thallus. This film acts as capillary tube. As soon as the antherozoids approach the neck of the archegonium, they are attracted chemotactically by the mucilaginous substances along with proteins and certain inorganic

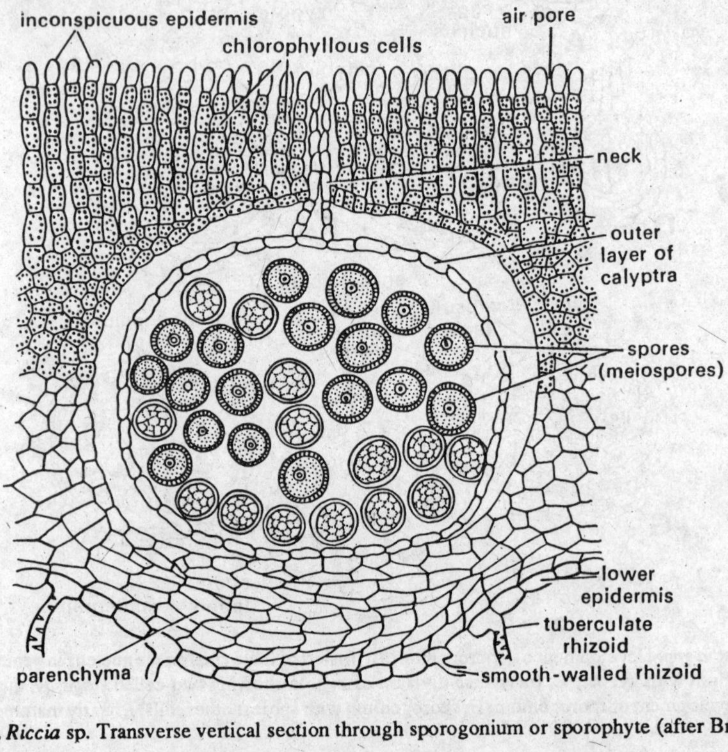

Fig. 3.17. *Riccia* sp. Transverse vertical section through sporogonium or sporophyte (after Brown).

salts; oozing out through the mouth of the archegonium. The antherozoids enter the mouth of the archegonium travel through the neck and reach in the vicinity of the egg. One of the antherozoids penetrates egg cell and the fertilization is effected. The details of the gametic fusion have not been worked out so far. However, Black (1913) and Pande (1933) have seen the male nucleus lying in the close vicinity of the egg. Ultimately, by the union of the nuclei of male and female gametes, syngamy takes place, and the zygote is formed. The zygote contains 2n number of chromosomes.

THE SPOROPHYTE

Development of embryo. Soon after the fertilization, the zygote secretes a wall around it, enlarges in size and nearly fills the cavity of the venter. The venter cells are stimulated by the process of fertilization, they divide periclinally and the wall of the venter becomes two-celled in thickness. Thereafter, the venter cells divide anticlinally and ultimately a two layered calyptra is formed inside which the developing embryo is situated.

According to Campell (1918), Pagon (1932) and Pande (1923) the first division of the zygote is transverse. With the result of this division two approximately equal cells are formed. In most of the species these two cells (epibasal and hypobasal) divide vertically and a four celled embryo of quadrant type is resulted. But according to Garber (1904) and Lewis (1906)

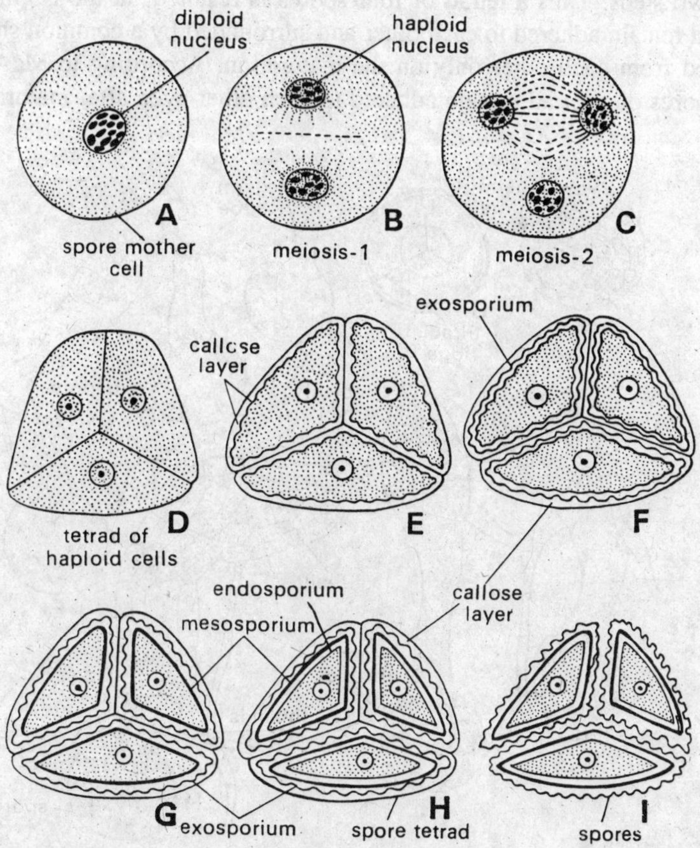

Fig. 3.18. *Riccia* spp. Stages in sporogenesis. A, spore mother cell; B-C, meiosis in spore mother cell; D-H, formation of spore tetrad; I, haploid spores.

in some of the species, from the two celled embryo the four celled filamentous type embryo is formed. Sometimes both the types of embryo may be formed in the same genus. This four celled embryo divides by a vertical wall and the eight celled embryo (octant stage) is formed.

The octant stage is followed by several irregular divisions and a 20 to 30 celled embryo is formed. At this stage there are periclinal divisions, and the embryo is differentiated into two regions. The outer layer is **amphithecium** and the inner mass of cells is **endothecium.** The amphithecium is protective in nature, whereas, the endothecium divides repeatedly giving rise to mass of sporogenous cells. All the cells of the last generation of sporogenous tissue are called the **sporocytes** or **spore mother cells.** But according to Pagon (1932) in *R. crystallina* the sporogenous tissue eventually differentiates into **sporocytes** and **nurse cells.** The sporocytes consist of dense granular cytoplasm. Whereas, the nurse cells are with thin vacuolate cytoplasm. Pagon considers the nurse cells as forerunners of the elaters of *Marchantia.* The nurse cells and the inner jacket cells disintegrate giving rise to a mucilaginous mass, in which the sporocytes remain suspended. During the process of meiosis the sporocytes receive the nourishment from this mucilaginous fluid. Eventually, the walls of the spore mother cells disintegrate, and prior to their reduction division, they lie free in the sporogonium. The functional spore mother cells become rounded.

Beer (1906) and Lewis (1906) have recorded the meiotic division of the nucleus of spore mother cell in two steps. Thus a tetrad of four spores is resulted. In the beginning all the four spores of a tetrad remain adhered to each other and surrounded by a common sheath. The spores become separated from each other only on the maturation. According to McAllister (1916) in *R. curtisii* the spores of a tetrad remain adhered to each other even after maturation. The spores are haploid (n).

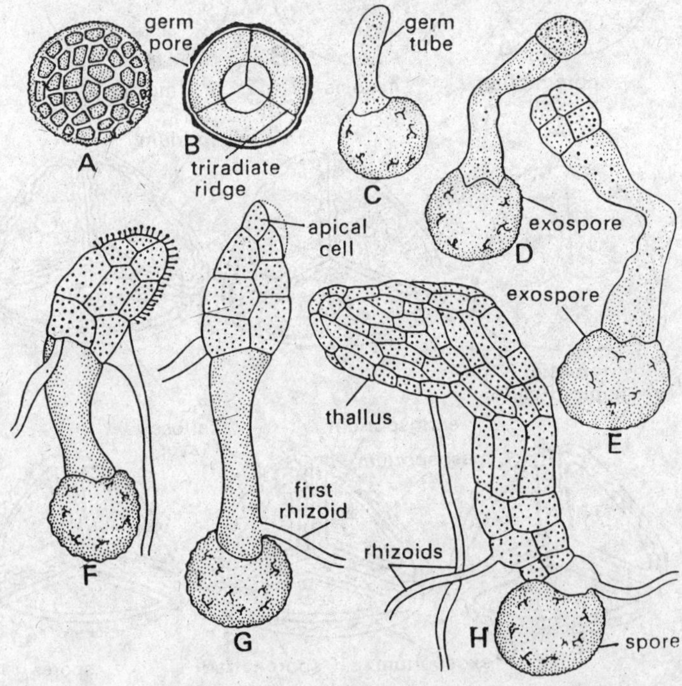

Fig. 3.19. *Riccia* spp. Spore germination and development of gametophyte (thallus). A, spore; B, sectional view of spore; C, germinating spore with germ tube; D, differentiation of a terminal cell and formation of rhizoidal cell; H, newly formed thallus and rhizoids.

The spores of *Riccia* are not disseminated by any special method. On the death and decay of the thallus the spores get free from the sporogonium. This is a long process. The spores are not liberated immediately after their maturation. Sometimes, they remain within the sporogonium even for a year or more.

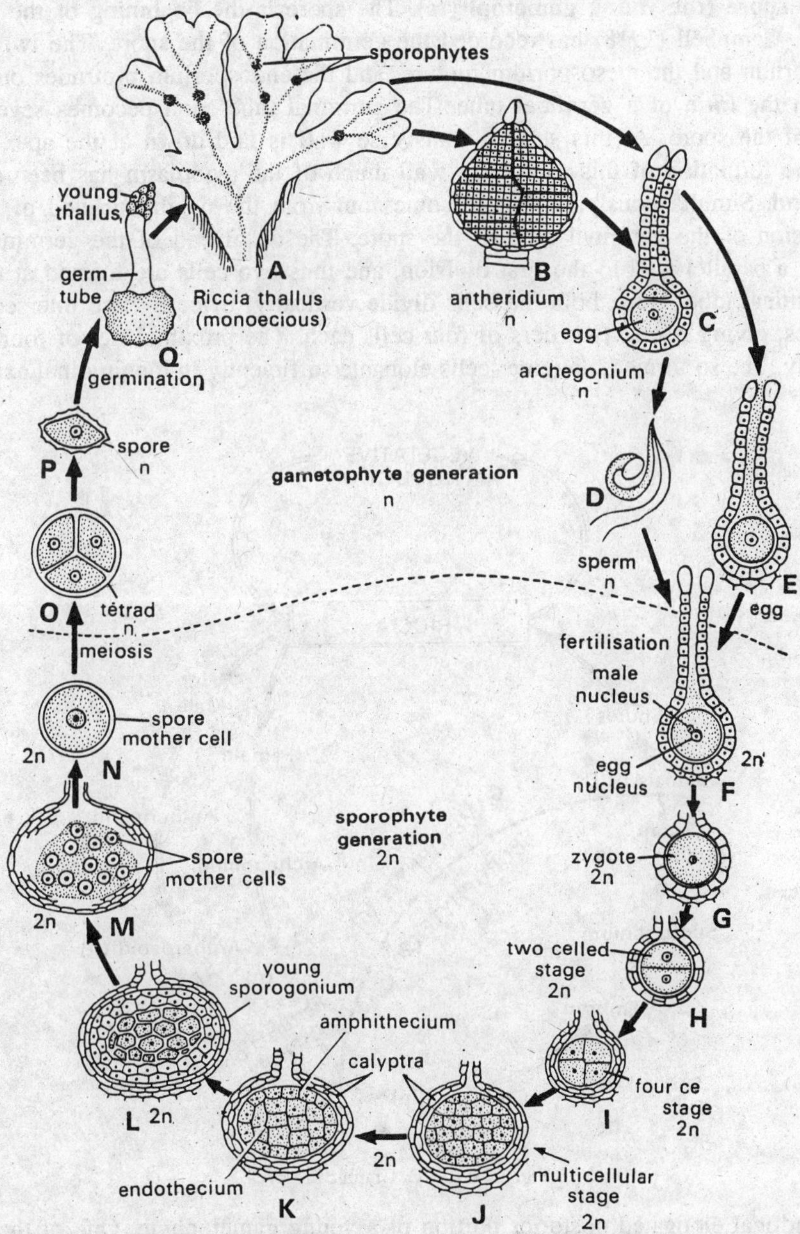

Fig. 3.20. *Riccia* spp. Diagrammatic life-cycle. A, thallus; B, antheridium; C, archegonium; D, sperm; E, egg; F, fertilization; G, zygote; H, two-celled stage of embryo; I, four-celled embryo; J, multicellular embryo; K-M, young sporogonium; N, spore mother cell; O, meiosis and formation of spore tetrad; P, spore; Q, spore germination and development of young thallus.

Structure of spore. The mature spore is three layered. The outermost cutinized layer is **exosporium.** The middle layer is **mesosporium,** which is thick walled and consists of three concentric zones. The innermost layer is **endosporium.** According to Beer (1906) the endosporium is composed of callose and pectose. The complete spore wall which surrounds the spore is thick and irregularly thickened.

The spore (the young gametophyte). The spore is the beginning of the gametophytic generation. Campbell (1918) has recorded the germination of the spore. The two outer layers, the exosporium and the mesosporium rupture, and the endosporium protrudes out through the opening in the form of a germinal tube. The germinal tube soon becomes several times the diameter of the spore. At this stage a transverse wall is laid down at the apex of this tube. Prior to the formation of this transverse wall much of the cytoplasm has been shifted in the terminal end. Simultaneously, a rhizoid comes out from the neighbourhood of the region of the protrusion of the germinal tube of the spore. The distal end of the germinal tube again divides by a parallel wall to the first division, and thus two cells are formed at the distal end of the germinal tube. Now, both the cells divide vertically, twice by two intersecting walls at right angles, giving rise to two tiers of four cells each. The proximal tier of four cells divides transversely. The so formed, daughter cells elongate sufficiently in longitudinal axis, giving rise

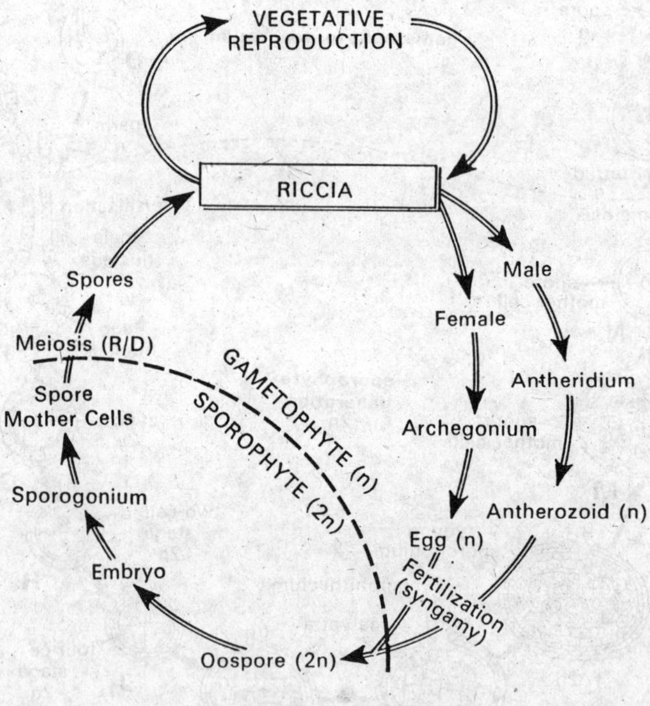

Fig. 3.21. *Riccia*. Graphic life-cycle.

to the cylindrical elongated posterior portion of a young gametophyte. One of the cells of the four celled distal tier of the octant stage acts as an apical cell. This apical cell possesses two cutting faces. It cuts cells repeatedly from its left and right faces, giving rise to a multicellular young thallus. The rest three cells of the distal tier divide once or twice. However, the new young thallus is formed from the single celled spore.

Systematic position. Division-Bryophyta
Class-Hepaticopsida (Hepaticae)
Order-Marchantiales
Family-Ricciaceae
Genus-*Riccia*.

Family-Marchantiaceae

There are 23 genera and about 250 species in this family. The archegonia of this family borne upon special erect, stalked, vertical branches, the **archegoniophores.** The male branches, the **antheridiophores** may or may not present. In *Marchantia* the antheridia are borne upon these erect, stalked antheridiophores.

The typical sterile **elaters** are found in the sporogonium mixed with the spores.

The Marchantiaceae are separated into three sub-families, but according to Evans (1923, 1939) they are treated as separate families.

Genus MARCHANTIA

Occurrence and distribution. This genus comprises of about 65 species. They are cosmopolitan. *Marchantia polymorpha* the best known species, is widely distributed. According to R.S. Chopra (1943) there are about eleven Indian species. They are mostly confined in the Himalayas. Only one or two species have been recorded from the plains.

According to Udar (1970) six species are found in the Himalayas. The common Himalayan species are-*M. palmata, M. nepalensis, M. polymorpha, M. simalana* and *M. indica*. The common species of the Indian plains are *M. polymorpha* and *M. indica*. These two species are also found in the hills of South India. Brandis reported *M. simalana* from the hills of Simla. *M. polymorpha* grows luxuriantly at 8,000 feet on Himalayan and South Indian hills on moist rocks and banks of streams. The thalli with gemma cups are found throughout the year whereas the plants with sex organs occur abundantly during February-March in Himalayas and October-November in the hills of South India.

The thalli of *Marchantia* commonly thrive upon moist soil found on the rocks in shady places, in open wood lands or near the banks of streams. This genus grows best in the burnt

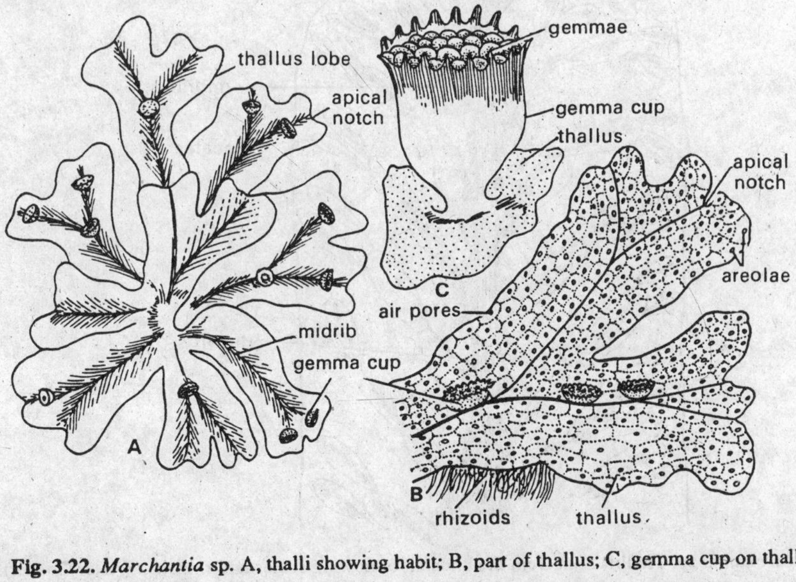

Fig. 3.22. *Marchantia* sp. A, thalli showing habit; B, part of thallus; C, gemma cup on thallus.

soil. They commonly grow after the forest fires in the burnt soil. According to Richards (1958) this is perhaps because of the nitrification of the soil due to the fire.

THE GAMETOPHYTE

External structure of the thallus (adult gametophyte). The thallus of *Marchantia* is prostrate, dichotomously branched and dorsiventral. Comparatively, the dorsal surface is deeper

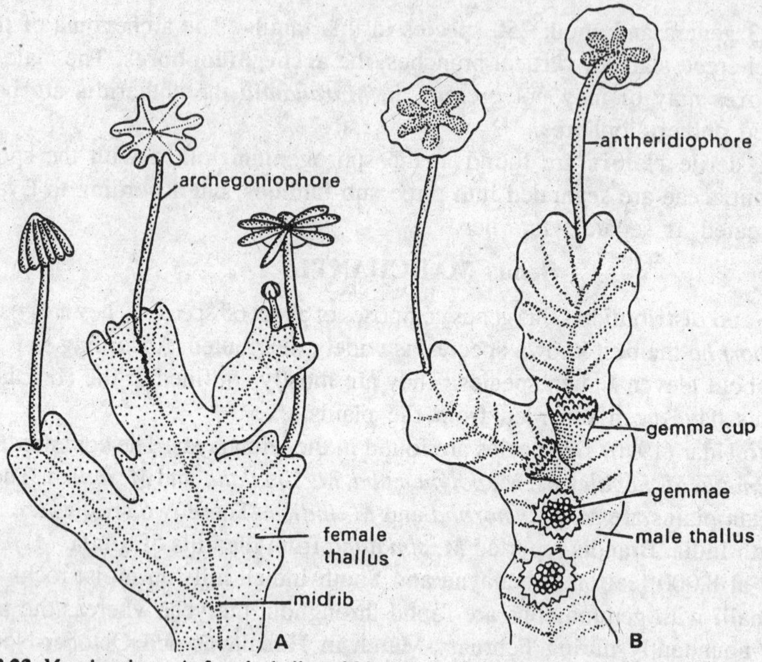

Fig. 3.23. *Marchantia* sp. A, female thallus of *M. palmata*; B, male thallus of *M. polymorpha*.

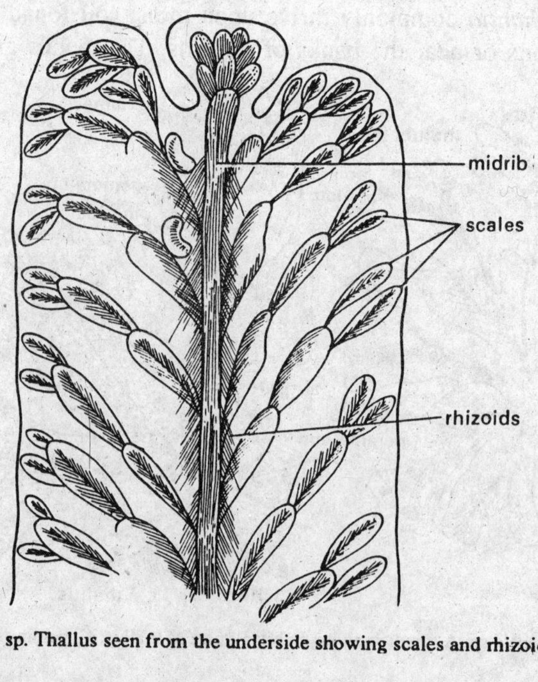

Fig. 3.24. *Marchantia* sp. Thallus seen from the underside showing scales and rhizoids. (After Goebel).

green than the ventral one. The rhombiodal or polygonal small areas are found on the dorsal surface of thallus. Each such small area is provided with a small pore in its centre. The apex of each branch of the thallus bears a notch in which the growing point is situated. The thallus reaches to the length of 2 to 10 cm. On maturity the margin of the thallus is somewhat wavy.

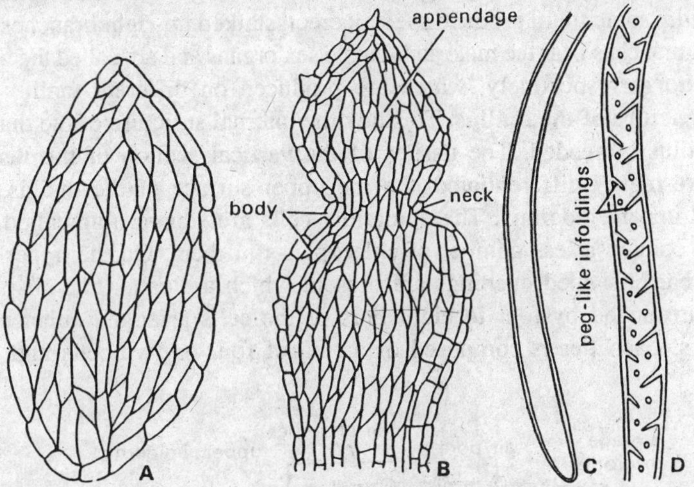

Fig. 3.25. *Marchantia* sp. A, simple scale; B, appendiculate scale; C, smooth-walled rhizoid; D, tuberculate rhizoid.

The thallus bears a conspicuous mid rib, which is well recognizable on the dorsal surface by the presence of a groove and on the ventral surface by presence of a ridge.

On the ventral surface of the plant gametophytes, on either side of the mid-rib two or more rows of the pinkish, multicellular scales are present, which protect the growing points.

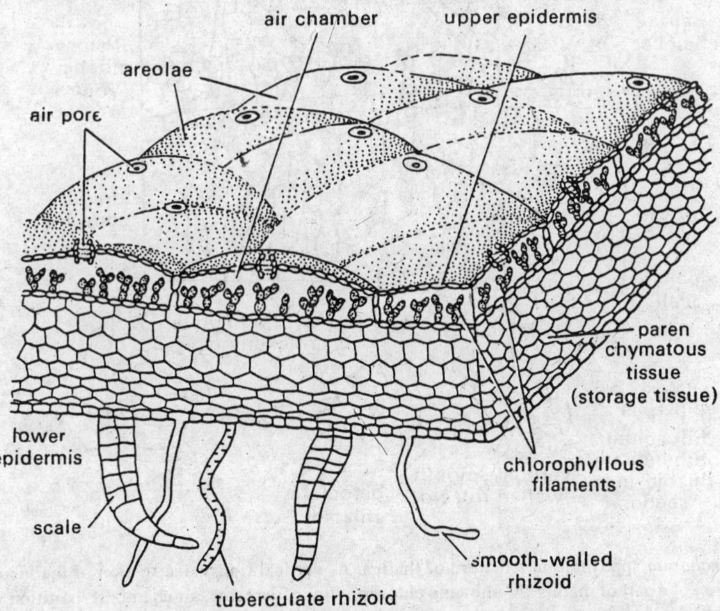

Fig. 3.26. *Marchantia* sp. Three dimensional diagram of a part of thallus (After Goebel).

The simple and tuberculate rhizoids are also found on the ventral surface, which are absorptive in nature. The thallus remains attached to the substratum by means of these rhizoids.

On the dorsal surface of the plant gametophytes, the **gemma cups** are found. The gemma cups are usually found along the mid-ribs. The margins of the gemma cups are cut. The gemma cups contain the vegetative bodies, the **gemmae.** Such structures give rise to new plant gametophytes.

In *Marchantia,* some thalli produce special, erect, stalked up-right branches at their growing apices. The special branches bear the male and female sex organs and are called the **antheridiophores** and **archegoniophores** respectively, which are produced on different thalli.

Internal structure of the thallus. To study the internal structure of the thallus, the vertical section of the thallus is needed. The tissues of the vertical section of the thallus seen under the microscope are highly differentiated. On the upper surface of the thallus there is a clear cut single layered upper epidermis. The epidermal cells are square, thinwalled, arranged close to each other and contain a less number of chloroplasts in them. On the upper epidermis, here and there certain barrel-shaped openings are present which are called the air-pores. Each such pore is usually surrounded by four to eight tiers of the cells arranged either superimposed or in concentric rings. Each tier is composed of a ring of four or five cells and thus in total 16

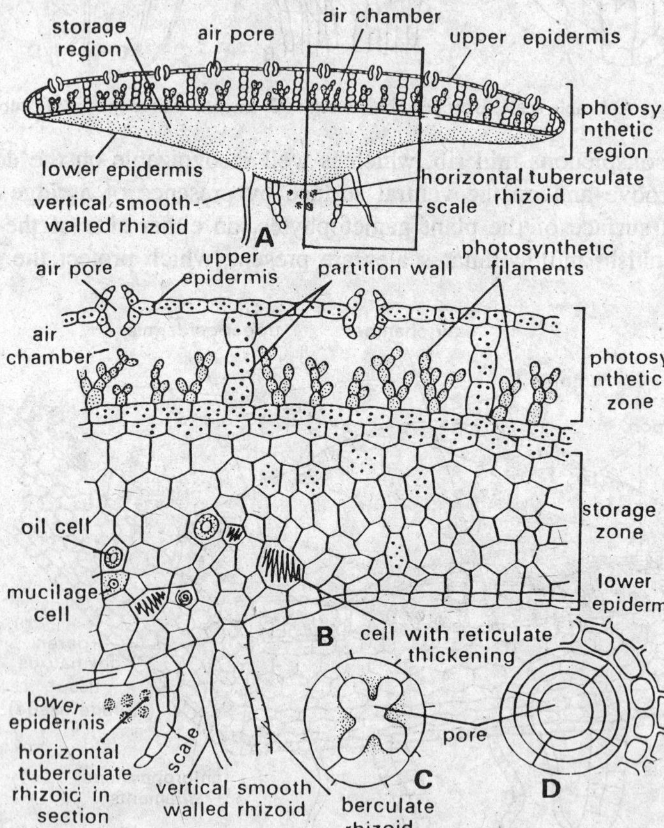

Fig. 3.27. *Marchantia* spp. Internal structure of thallus. A, vertical transverse section of thallus-outline sketch; B, vertical transverse section of a part of thallus 'A' showing chlorophyllous filaments, air chambers, partition walls, air pores on the upper surface, tubercled and simple rhizoids and scales on the lower epidermis; C, air pore as seen from below; D, air pore as seen from the upper surface.

to 40 cells are there around a pore arranged in a collar. Sometimes, the cells of the innermost tier project inward in the pore, and the opening of the pore looks starlike in its surface view. Just beneath the upper epidermis, the air chambers are present. The air chambers are found

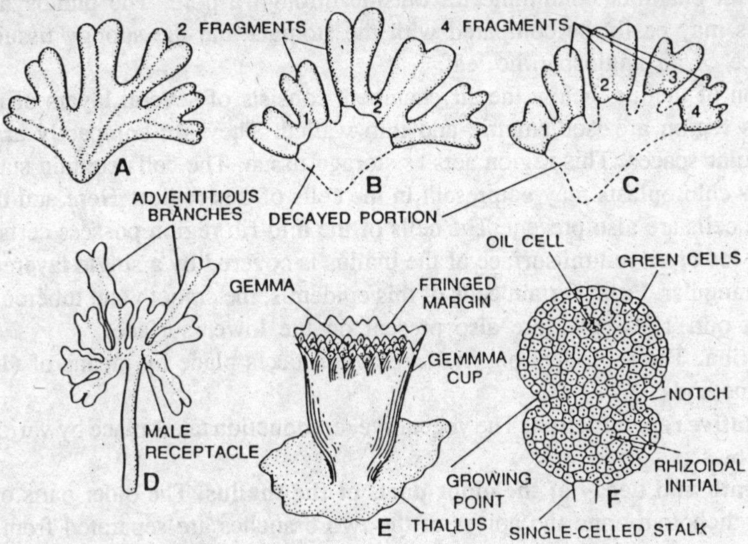

Fig. 3.28. *Marchantia* sp. Vegetative reproduction. A-C, by death and decay of the older parts of the thallus; D, by adventitious branches; E-F, by gemmae.

in a single horizontal layer. The exchange of gases takes place through the air pores which communicate with the air chambers. The air chambers are separated from each other by single

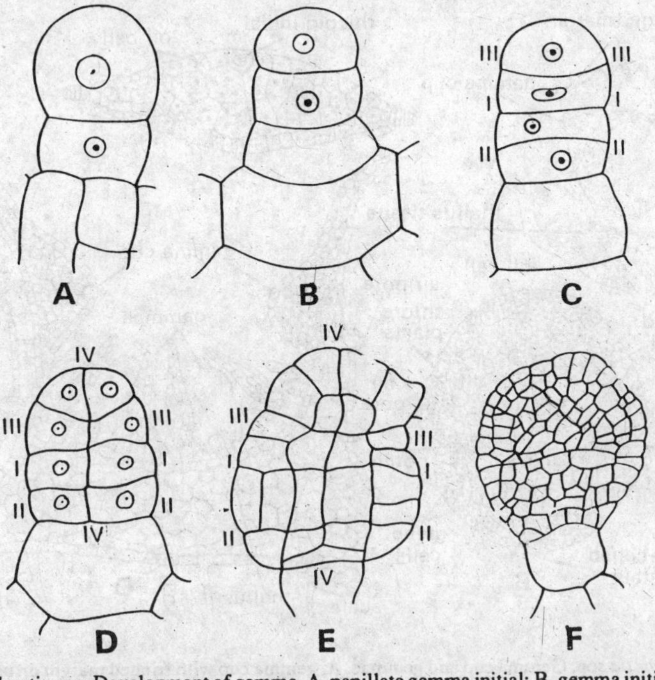

Fig. 3.29. *Marchantia* spp. Development of gemma. A, papillate gemma initial; B, gemma initial divides transversely; C, both cells divide transversely forming four cells; D-E, these four cells divide vertically and horizontally; F, further irregular divisions form the gemma.

layered partition walls. These partitions are two to four celled in height. These cells also contain chloroplasts. The air chambers contain the branched photosynthetic filaments, which arise from the floor of the chamber. A great number of chloroplasts is found in the cells of photosynthetic filaments. Each air chamber communicates outside through a pore. The photosynthetic tissue and the air pores may easily be compared with the stomata and the spongy tissue present on the lower surface of an angiospermic leaf.

The portion of thallus, below the air chambers consists of several layers of parenchyma. The cells of this region are isodiametric and thin walled. They are compactly arranged, and, thus no intercellular spaces. This region acts as storage tissue. The cells contain starch in them. Sometimes a few chloroplasts may be present in the cells of this region. Here and there, certain oil and mucilage cells are also present. The cells of the mid-rib region possess certain reticulate thickenings. The lower or ventral surface of the thallus is covered by a single layered epidermis. The cells are rectangular. From certain cells of this epidemis, the smooth and tuberculate rhizoids have been given out. The scales are also present on the lower surface.

Reproduction. The reproduction, in *Marchantia,* takes place by means of (1) vegetative and (2) sexual methods.

1. Vegetative reproduction. The vegetative reproduction takes place by various methods. They are as follows :

(a) By death and decay of the older parts of the thallus. The older parts of the thallus decay below the dichotomy and the apices of the two branches are separated from each other. On the advent of the favourable conditions these apices grow into the new thalli.

(b) By adventitious branches. Certain adventitious branches develop from the ventral surface of the thallus, which detach from the thalli of the parent plants and give rise to new thalli.

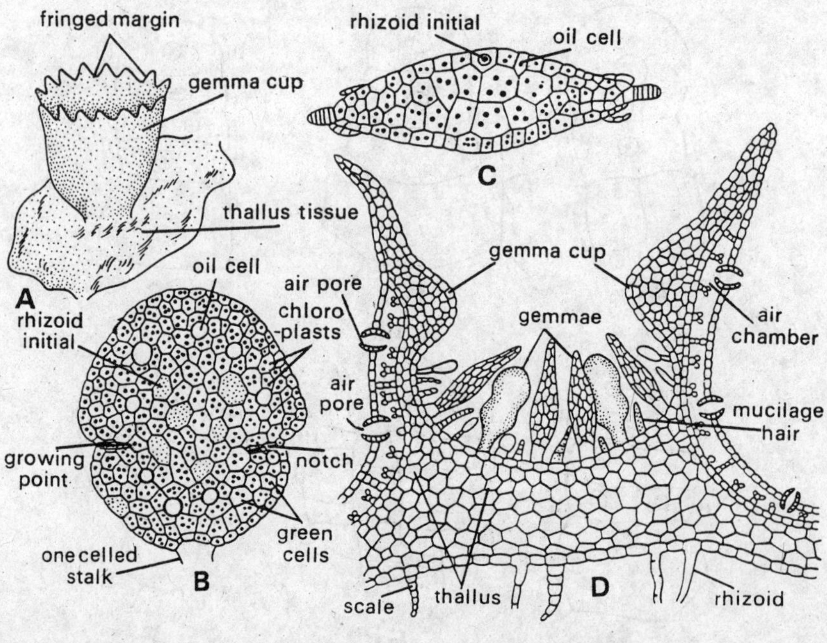

Fig. 3.30. *Marchantia* spp. Gemma cup and gemmae. A, gemma cup with fringed margin on upper surface of thallus; B, single gemma; C, transverse section of a mature gemma; D, vertical transverse section of thallus passing through a gemma cup.

(c) By gemmae. The most common method of the vegetative reproduction in *Marchantia* takes place by means of especially designed vegetative bodies, the **gemmae,** in the cup like structures, the **gemma cups,** found on the dorsal surface of the thallus (plant gametophyte). The gemma cups have fringed margins. Each gemma cup contains a large number of gemmae in it.

Development of gemma. Each gemma develops from a single superficial cell present on the floor of the gemma cup. Any of the superficial cells protrudes out from the floor and acts as a **gemma initial.** This initial divides twice transversely producing three cells. The basal cell, the stalk cell and the upper primary cell which changes into gemma proper. The stalk cell does not divide further and changes into a single celled stalk. The primary cell divides further by transverse, longitudinal and periclinal divisions giving rise to the gemma proper. In the beginning the gemma is flat and one cell in thickness, but in later stages, due to further periclinal divisions, it becomes three or four celled in thickness in the centre.

Structure of mature gemma. The mature gemma is found attached by a single celled stalk to the floor of the gemma cup (cupule). It is disciform and few celled thick in its centre, and quite thin at its margins. It is somewhat dump-bell like. There are two depressions or notches situated on the lateral margins opposite to each other. The notches are growing points. A marginal row of apical cells is situated in each notch. About all the cells of the gemma contain chloroplasts in them. A few superficial cells are colourless which are somewhat larger in size than the other cells. There are certain isolated cells, here and there on the gemma, which contain oil in them and called the oil cells.

Mixed with the gemmae, certain mucilage cells are found on the floor of the cupule. These small mucilage cells discharge mucilage from them. This fluid absorbs water by imbibition,

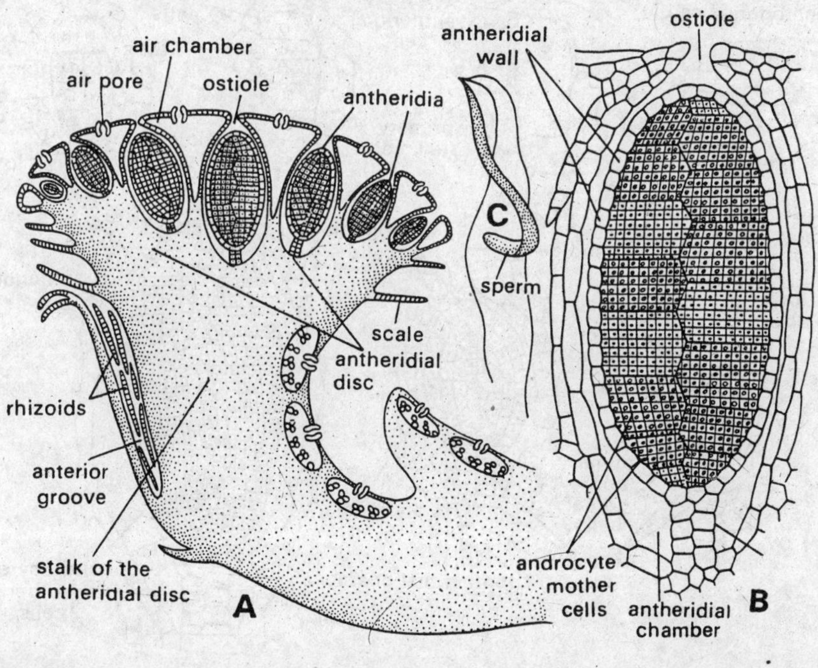

Fig. 3.31. *Marchantia* spp. Male sex organs. A, longitudinal section of antheridiophore with antheridia; B, a mature stalked antheridium covered by a jacket; C, a mature biflagellate sperm or antherozoid.

which helps, however, in detaching the gemmae from their stalks. The colourless cells, described in preceding paragraph are also called the **rhizoidal cells,** and the rhizoids come out from these cells at the time of germination.

Germination of gemma. As soon as the gemma falls on the soil, and if the suitable conditions for its germination prevail, it germinates. The rhizoids come out first from the rhizoidal cells and penetrate the soil. The marginal rows of the apical cells situated in the two notches of the gemma become activated and begin in function in normal way. From each growing point, a young thallus develops. This way, two young thalli develop in opposite directions from a single gemma. Evenaually, the central part of gemma dies and the two thalli are separated, which grow in opposite directions.

2. Sexual reproduction. In *Marchantia,* the sex organs are antheridia and archegonia, which are borne upon the special erect stalked branches, called the antheridiophores and archegoniophores, respectively. These branches are the modified prostrate branches. This fact may be proved by the morphology of the reproductive branch. The ventral side of an archegoniophore possesses rhizoids and scales situated in one or two longitudinal furrows. The dorsal side of it possesses the usual air chambers with photosynthetic filaments. The development of the reproductive branches depends upon several environmental and climatic factors. In *Marchantia,* the male (antheridiophores) and female (archegoniophores) reproductive branches develop on different thalli, *i.e.*, the genus is strictly heterothallic (dioecious). The upright sexual branches consist of a stalk and horizontal discs at their apical ends, in each case.

The structure of antheridiophore. The antheridiophore consists of a two to three centimetres long stalk, and a flattened, usually eight lobed disc at its apical end. As mentioned in the preceding paragraph the antheridiophore is a modified branch of the prostrate thallus.

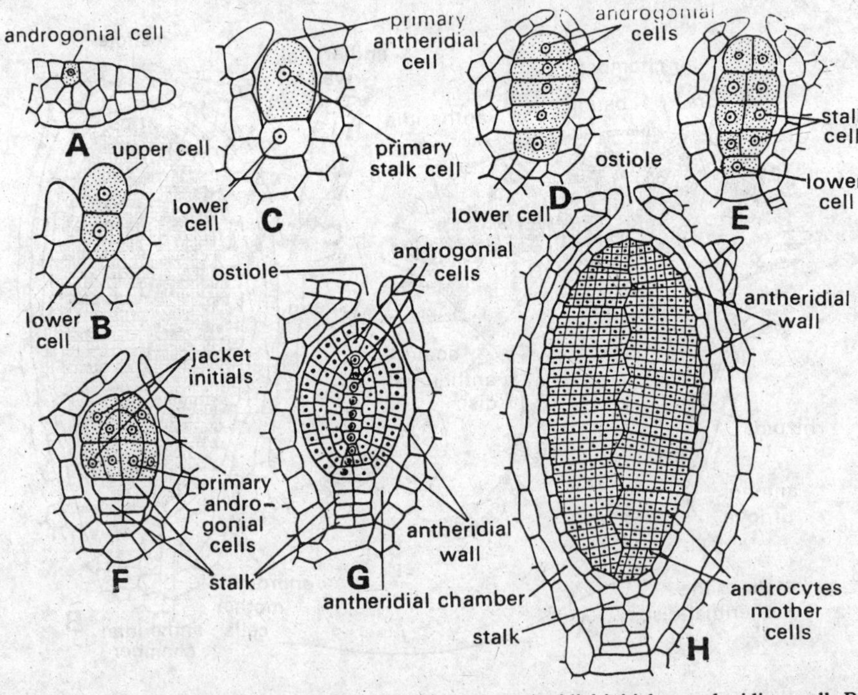

Fig. 3.32. *Marchantia* spp. Development of antheridium. A, antheridial initial or antheridium cell; B, transverse division of antheridial initial; C-G, successive stages in the development of antheridium; H, a stalked antheridium with androcytes.

The terminal disc of the thallus shows a well developed branch system. Each lobe represents a branch. At the tip of each lobe a growing point is situated. Sometimes, in certain species, the number of lobes is reduced to four. The rhizoids and scales are present in the two grooves situated on the ventral surface of antheridiophore.

The disc of antheridiophore is somewhat convex at its upper face. The upper epidermis is interrupted by several usual barrelshaped air pores. These pores open in the air chambers, containing photosynthetic filaments in them. The flask like cavities are also found among and in the neighbourhood of these air chambers. Such flask-like cavities are developed by the rapid growth of the tissues surrounding them. Each flask-like cavity contains a stalked antheridium within it, which partially or wholly fills up the cavity. The antheridial cavities open outside through small openings, the **ostioles.**

Development of antheridium. The antheridium develops from a superficial dorsal cell called the **antheridial initial** which is found two or three cells back of the apical cell. The stages of the development of the antheridium in *Marchantia* are as follows :

The antheridial intial divides, and two cells are formed. The upper one is called the **outer cell** and the lower one the **basal cell.** The outer cell protrudes somewhat out of the thallus. The basal cell remains embedded in the thallus and develops into the embedded portion of the stalk of the antheridium. The outer cell develops into the main antheridium. Now the outer cell further divides transversely and a vertical file of three cells is formed. The two upper cells of this vertical file are called the **primary antheridial cells,** which make the antheridium proper.

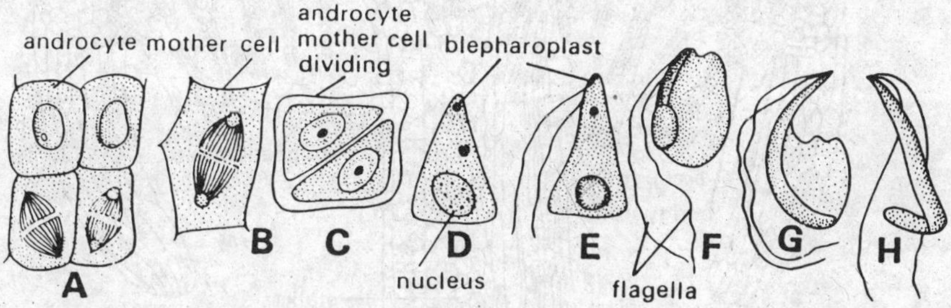

Fig. 3.33. *Marchantia* spp. Spermatogenesis. A, androcyte mother cell; B-C, androcyte mother cell dividing diagonally into two androcytes; D-G, formation of antherozoid; H, single antherozoid.

The lowermost cell of the file is called the **primary stalk cell** which makes the projecting portion of the stalk. Now, the two primary antheridial cells, divide by two successive vertical divisions, at right angles, giving rise to eight cells. Each tier consists of four cells. Now each tier of four cells divides perclinally giving rise to four jacket initials, which encircle the four androgonial cells of the each tier. Thus, the eight primary androgonial cells are formed, which are encircled by eight jacket sterile initials. The sterile jacket initials divide repeatedly anticlinally giving rise to single layered jacket around the antheridium. The eight primary androgonial cells divide repeatedly giving rise to a large number of cubical **androgonial cells.** By further divisions these androgonial cells become smaller and smaller. The last cell generation of the androgonial mother cells consists of the **androcyte mother cells.** Each androcyte mother cell divides diagonally giving rise to two **androcytes.**

Soon after the formation of androcytes they are metamorphosed into **antherozoids.**

Structure of mature antheridium. The mature antheridium consists of a short stalk and a rounded structure above it. The antheridium proper is surrounded by a single layered jacket. Inside the jacket layer a large number of androcytes are filled up.

Discharge of antherozoids from antheridium. In usual cases, the antherozoids come out from the antheridia in the cavities, and thereafter they come outside of the cavity through the ostiole. However, the water enters the antheridial cavity through the ostiole, the jacket cells of the upper part of the antheridium become gelatinized, and the antheridium gives way. The androcytes are liberated from the antheridium in a long smoke-like column. As soon as, the mass of androcytes comes out, it breaks up into individual androcytes. Very soon, the antherozoids are liberated from the androcytes.

Structure of antherozoid. Each antherozoid is elongated, rod-like, uninucleate and biflagellate. The antherozoids move in the water with the help of their flagella.

Structure of archegoniophore. The archegoniophore as already stated is a modified branch of the prostrate thallus. This develops by an upward bending of a prostrate branch. According to Cavers (1904), there is a dichotomy of the young archegoniophore. The forked apex divides

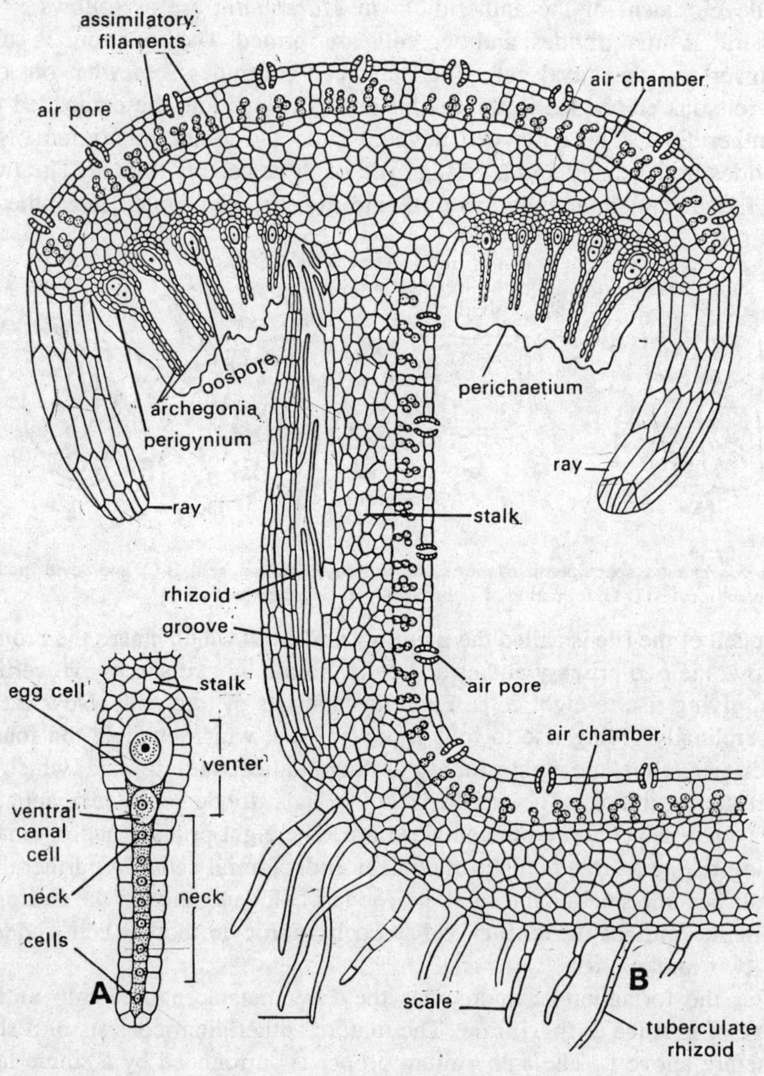

Fig. 3.34. *Marchantia* spp. Female sex organs. A, longitudinal section of archegoniophore; B, a mature archegonium.

again giving rise to a four-lobed structure. This is followed by another dichotomy resulting in a eight lobed rosette-like disc. As soon as, the apical branching of archegoniophore stops, the archegonia are developed on dorsal side of it acrogenously. The fertilization takes place in this stage. As soon as the fertilization is over, the marginal portion of the disc becomes inverted and the archegonia become up side down, *i.e.,* their necks become downward. Now, the oldest archegonia are situated towards periphery of the disc and youngest towards the stalk. In many cases, the discs posses nine rays.

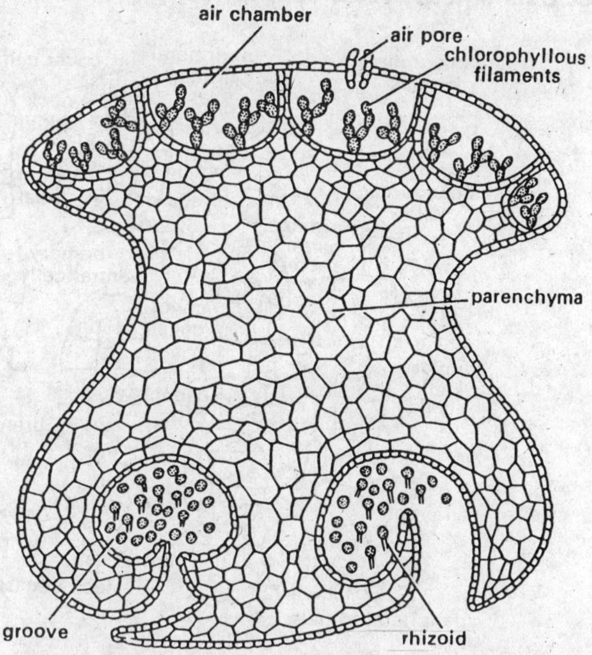

Fig. 3.35. *Marchantia* sp. T.S. of the stalk of archegoniophore.

After being curved of the margin of the disc a single layered plate of tissue develops on either side of the groups of archegonia. In this way, each group of 12 to 15 archegonia is enclosed in a single layered fringed **perichaetium**. In many cases the archegonial lobes elongate further in the green cylindrical rays. In *M. polymorpha* there are nine rays coming out from the disc. The disc looks stellate in appearance from the upper side, because of the presence of these stout, cylindrical rays.

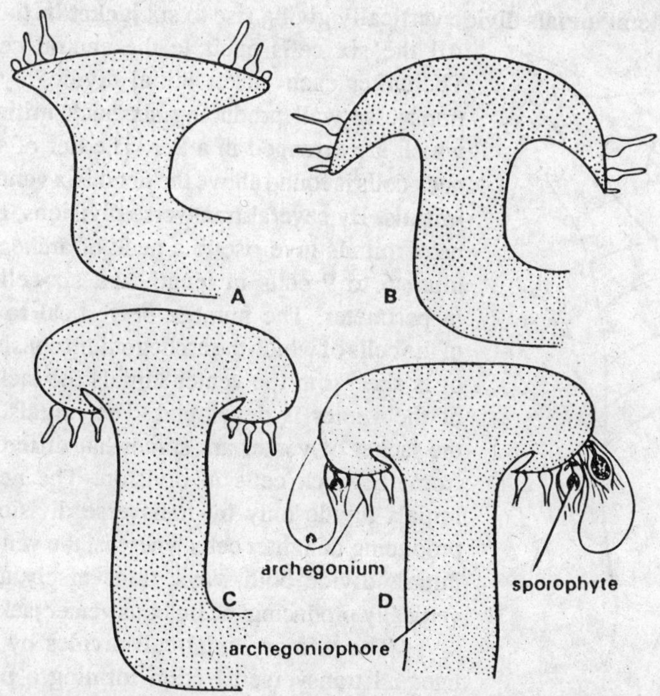

Fig. 3.36. *Marchantia polymorpha*–A–D, diagrams of vertical longitudinal sections of stages in development of archegoniophore (After G.M. Smith).

Development of archegonium. The archegonium develops from a superficial cell which lies two or three cells back from the apex of the thallus. This cell is called the **archegonial initial.** Now the archegonial initial divides by a transverse wall into two cells. The lower cell is the **basal cell** and the upper cell is the **outer cell.** From the basal cell, the lowermost portion of the archegonium is developed. Whereas the outer cell produces the main body of the archegonium. The outer cell divides vertically producing a peripheral initial, and it is followed by two more such divisions, giving rise to three cells in total. These cells are peripheral initials. The three cells remain situated upon a

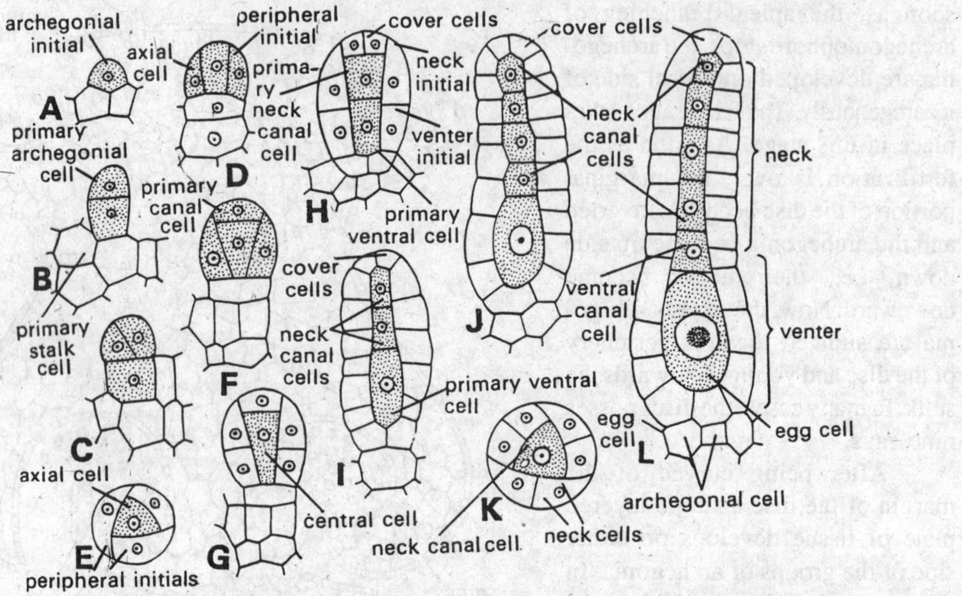

Fig. 3.37. *Marchantia* spp. Development of archegonium. A-K, early stages of development; E and K, transverse sections of archegonium; L, a nearly mautre archegonium with venter and neck, the venter contains an egg and the neck contains canal cells.

primary axial cell. The three peripheral initials divide vertically giving rise to six **jacket initials.** All the six cells encircle the central cell. Thereafter each jacket initial divides by a transverse wall producing six **neck initials** which are arranged in a tier. The tier of six neck cells is found above the tier of six **venter initials.** By several transverse divisions, the neck initials give rise to a neck of archegonium 6 to 9 cells in length and six-celled in perimeter. The number of vertical rows of the cells of which the archegonium consists of is six. From the venter initials the jacket of the venter is developed. The initials of the jacket of venter are somewhat different from the neck cells in division. The neck initials divide only by transverse divisions producing daughter cells whereas, the venter initials divide both ways, transversely and vertically producing the bulbous venter jacket.

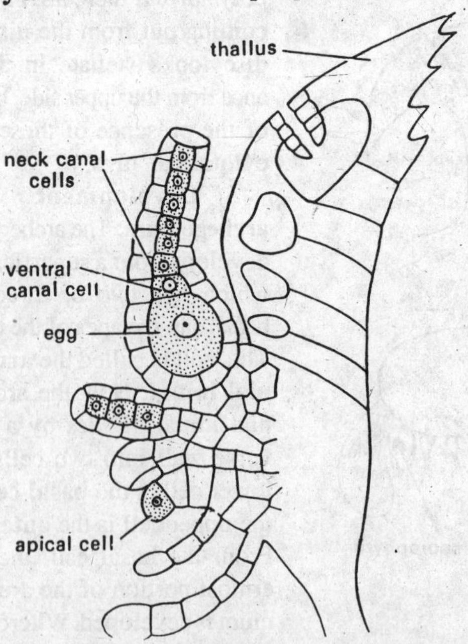

Fig. 3.38. *Marchantia polymorpha.* L.S. through a young archegoniophore showing archegonia originating on the upper surface of the disc. (After Goebel).

The primary axial cell divides by an unequal transverse division forming a **primary cover cell** and a **central cell.** The primary cover cell divides twice vertically producing four cover cells at the apex of jacket layer. Eventually, the central cell divides by a transverse wall producing an **upper canal cell** and a **lower canal cell.** The upper canal cell divides twice forming four **neck canal cells,** which are found within the neck of the archegonium. The lower canal cell, which is somewhat longer and broader, divides by an unequal transverse division forming a **venter canal cell** (ventral canal cell) and a large **egg.** The ventral canal cell is situated above the large egg. On the maturation of the archegonium, the neck canal cells and ventral canal cell disintegrate, and produce a mucilaginous substance in the archegonium. When the archegonium attains maturity, the cover cells become spread and separated from each other.

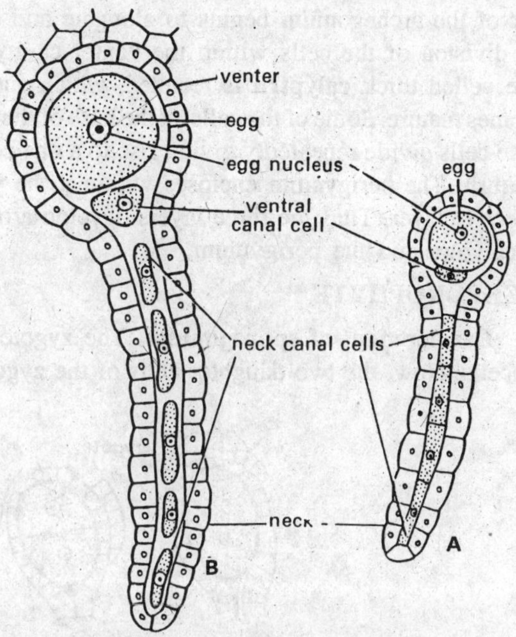

Fig. 3.39. *Marchantia polymorpha*. A, young archegonium; B, mature archegonium.

Structure of archegonium. In *Marchantia,* the flask like archegonium is found attached to the lobe of the disc by a small stalk. The archegonium consists of an elongated neck and a bulbous venter. The neck consists of the jacket cells arranged in six vertical rows. Four or more neck canal cells are found in the neck canal. The venter is surrounded by a single layered jacket. It is somewhat dialated and contains a large egg and a venter canal cell situated above the egg cell. The egg is also called **oosphere.** At the top of the neck there are four or five cover cells, which give way for the entrance of the antherozoids at the time of fertilization by their disintegration.

Transference of the antherozoids to the archegoniophore and fertilization. On the maturation of the antheridia, the disc of the antheridiophore receives a drop or two of water, which spread over it. The antherozoids, liberated from the antheridia, by the gelatinization of the upper portion of the latter, come above in the drop of water. As the rain drops fall on the concavities of the antheridiophores, the antherozoids are disseminated from these on the discs of the archegoniophores coming out from the neighbouring thalli. The disc of mature archegoniophore is somewhat convex. The antherozoids travel downward through the medium of water and come in contact of the mature archegonia.

The fertilization takes place only in the presence of water. The free-swimming antherozoids are attracted towards the mouth of the archegonium, because of the presence of certain chemicals, which ooze out from the mouth. In other words the antherozoids are positively chemotactic to these chemical substances. These chemical substances are certain proteins and inorganic salts of potassium. At the time of the fertilization the archegonia have their necks directing upward and the archegoniophore is quite young in its developmental stage.

The cover cells of the archegonium become disintegrated and an opening is created. The neck canal cells have also been disintegrated by this time. The antherozoids enter the mouth of the archegonium, travel through the neck and reach in the close vicinity of the egg (oosphere).

One of the antherozoids penetrates the egg and fertilization is effected. As reported by Anderson (1929), the union of the nuclei of the two gemates may take a long time. With the result of the fertilization the zygote (oospore) is formed, which contains 2n number of chromosomes.

Post-fertilization stages. As soon as the fertilization is over the fertilized egg begins to enlarge in size, secretes a cellulose wall, around it, and ultimately fills the cavity of the venter. This structure is called the **zygote or oospore.** After fertilization many changes take place. The stalk of the archegonium begins to elongate and ultimately becomes 3 or 4 centimetres long. The division of the cells within the venter cavity is stimulated by fertilization and a two or more celled thick **calyptra** is resulted, which surrounds the sporophyte unless and until this becomes mature. Some of the cells, at the base of the venter also become stimulated by fertilization. These cells divide repeatedly giving rise to a one celled thick collar-like **perigynium** or **pseudo-perianth.** The perigynium encloses within it the young sporogonium. The perigynium acts as protective layer. Thus the three layers develop around the sporogonium, *viz.*, the perichaetium, the calyptra and the perigynium.

THE SPOROPHYTE

Development of sporogonium. The zygote divides by a transverse wall, giving rise to two cells. Now, the two daughter cells of the zygote divide vertically giving rise to a quadrant

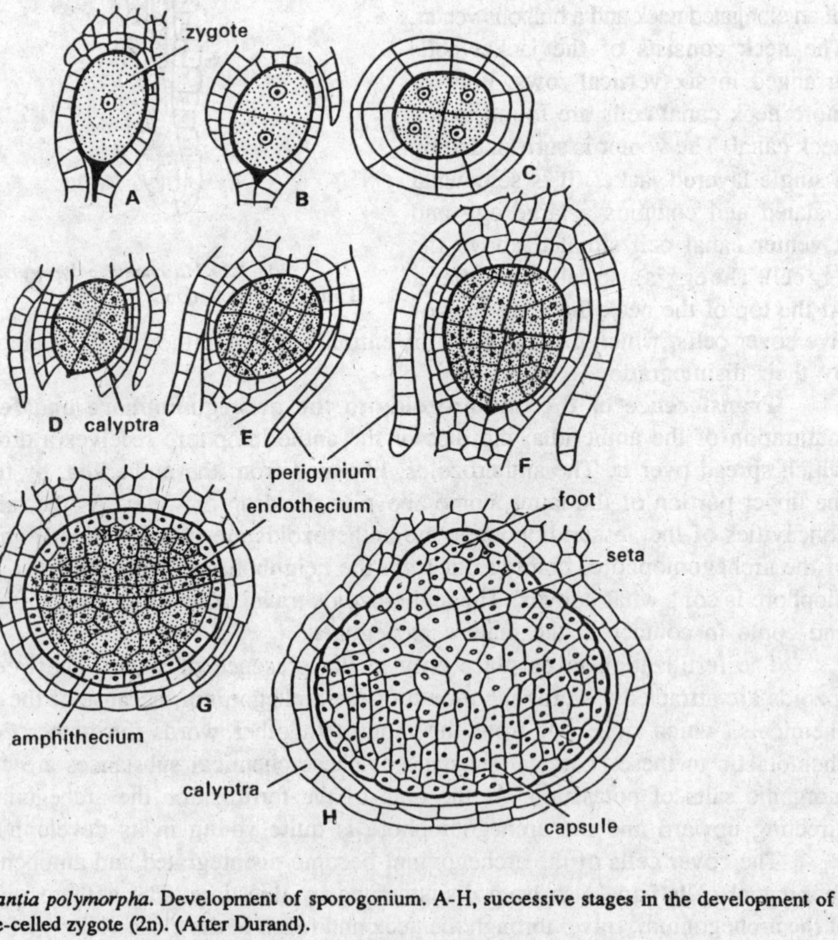

Fig. 3.40. *Marchantia polymorpha.* Development of sporogonium. A-H, successive stages in the development of sporogonium from a single-celled zygote (2n). (After Durand).

type fourcelled embryo. The hypobasal half of the embryo gives rise to foot and seta, whereas the epibasal half develops into the main sporophyte the capsule.

The four-celled embryo divides further by vertical walls intersected at right angles, giving rise to eight celled embryo, *i.e.*, the **octant stage.** Now, the embryo elongates to some extent. The cells of both the epi and hypobasal regions divide irregularly giving rise to many cells in both the regions. The cells of the hypobasal region divide repeatedly giving rise to a parenchymatous tissue. The cells of the posterior region of the parenchyma, ultimately develop into bulbous mass of cells, the **foot.** The foot anchors the sporophyte to the gametophyte and absorbs food materials for the former from the latter. Next to the foot the **seta** is developed. The cells of the seta are arranged in vertical rows. The cells divide few times and thus the seta remains somewhat short in structure. But at the time of the sporogenesis, the cells of seta divide many times transversely. These cells elongate, thus an elongated seta is resulted which pushes the capsule, out of the three layers, *viz.*, the calyptra, perigynium and perichaetium.

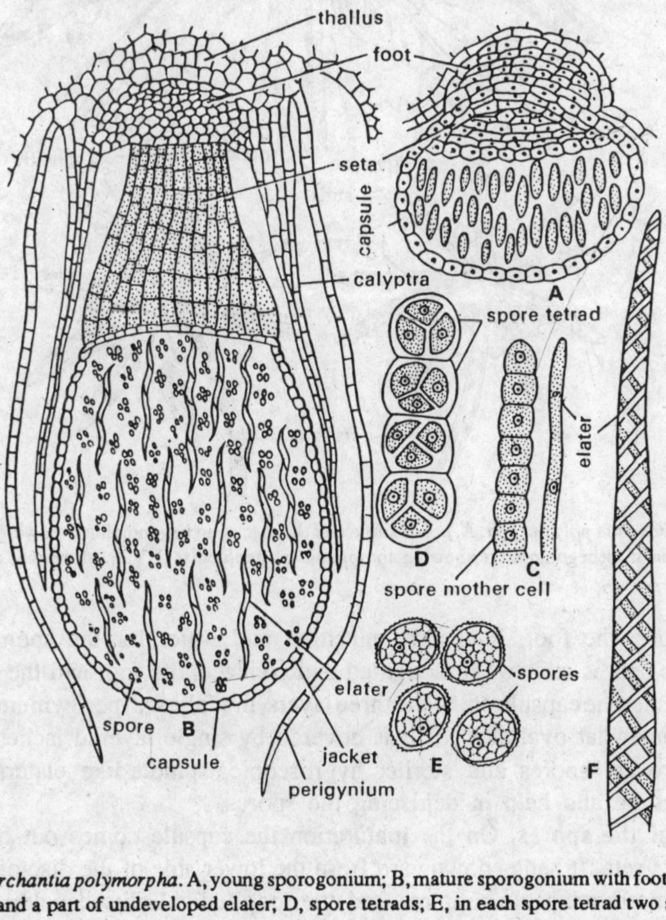

Fig. 3.41. *Marchantia polymorpha.* A, young sporogonium; B, mature sporogonium with foot seta and capsule; C, row of spore mother cells and a part of undeveloped elater; D, spore tetrads; E, in each spore tetrad two spores are male and two female; F, a part of elater.

The cells of the upper part of the sporogonium divide periclinally, giving rise to well differentiated regions the **amphithecium** and the **endothecium.** The amphithecium gives rise to a single jacket layer of the capsule. The endothecium develops into the **archesporium.** The cells of this region divide repeatedly giving rise to sporogenous tissue. Eventually, about half of the sporogenous cells divide many times transversely giving rise to the vertical rows of the **spore mother cells or sporocytes.** According to O'Hanlon (1926) each sporogenous cell divides five times resulting in a vertical file of 32 spore mother cells (sporocytes). Half of the sporogenous cells, which do not divide become elongated and give rise to sterile **elaters.** The elaters are tapering at both the ends and possess spiral thickenings on their walls. Each spore mother cell divides meiotically producing 4 spores. In *Marchantia polymorpha* to each elater there are 32 sporocytes, which give rise to 128 spores. This way, there are 128 spores to each elater. Usually in most of the species the elaters and spores are evenly distributed in the capsule.

According to O'Hanlon (1930), in *Marchantia* the output of spores from a single capsule is about 300,000 spores.

Structure of mature sporogonium. The mature sporogonium is differentiated into three regions, *viz.*, the foot, seta and capsule. Towards the base of the archegonium, there is a bulbous,

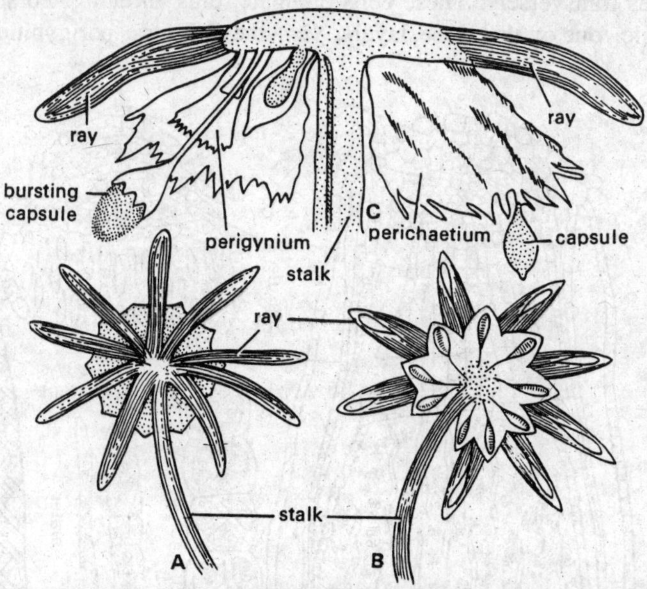

Fig. 3.42. *Marchantia polymorpha*. A, upper surface of the disc of archegoniophore showing rays and involucres; B, undersurface of the disc of archegoniophore showing sporogonia in involucres; C, V. S. of the disc of archegoniophore. (A, B after Kny).

absorptive structure, the foot. It absorbs nutrition and water for the sporogonium from the gametophyte. The seta is somewhat elongated and connects the foot and the capsule. As stated before, the seta pushes the capsule out of the three layers, the calyptra, perigynium and perichaetium. The capsule is somewhat oval shaped. It is covered by single layered jacket layer. Within the jacket layer, there are spores and sterile, hygroscopic, spindle-like elaters. The elaters are hygroscopic in nature and help in dehiscing the spores.

Dispersal of the spores. On the maturation the capsule comes out of the three layers with the help of its seta. It hangs downward from the lower side of the disc of archegoniophore. The wall of the mature capsule ruptures and the longitudinal slits develop about half of the length of the capsule, giving rise to several teeth like lobes rolling backward. The elaters are hygroscopic in nature. In dry atmosphere, they lose water to the atmosphere and become twisted. This action of the elaters help in the release of the spores from the capsule. As soon as, the spores are released and they come out of the capsule, they are dispersed by wind.

Structure of spore. The spores are small and spherical. They range from 12 μ to 30 μ in diameter. Each spore is covered by a thin coat, differentiated into two layers. The outer layer of the coat is **exospore** and the inner one is **endospore.** The exospore is somewhat thick and the endospore is thin and smooth. Each spore contains a small amount of granular cytoplasm and a nucleus within it.

Spore germination and development of young gametophyte. As soon as the spores fall on the soil, and if the other conditions are favourable, they germinate immediately. After coming in contact of moist soil, the spore enlarges at least double of the original and thereafter it germinates (Menge, 1930; O'Hanlon, 1926). The germinating spore immediately produces a long irregular filament of 6 to 8 cells. At the apex it is two cells wide. One of the cells acts as an apical

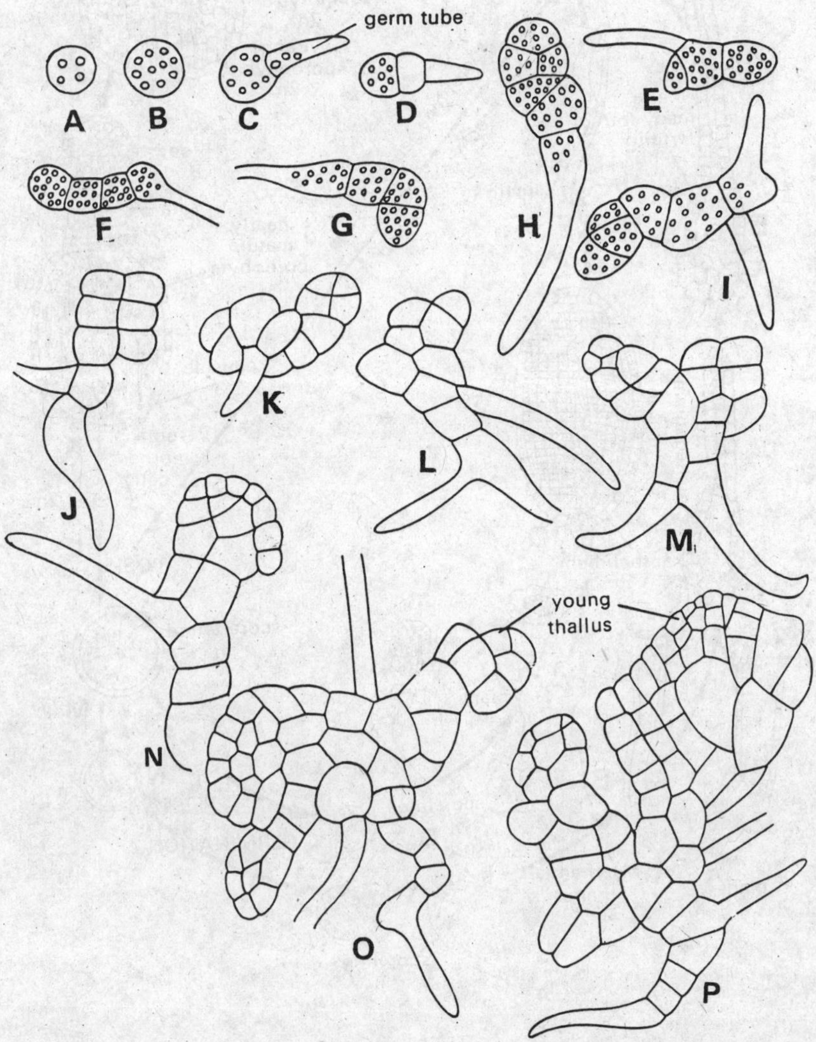

Fig. 3.43. *Marchantia* spp. Spore germination and development of thallus (gametophyte). A-B, different stages of spore; C, germinating spore; D-N, successive stages in the development of gametophyte (thallus); O-P, young gametophyte (thallus) with rhizoids.

cell with two cutting faces. This cell cuts alternately 5 to 7 segments both on right and left faces. This division continues. The derivatives of the first formed segments divide twice or thrice, but the derivative of the later-formed segments divide again and again producing a large number of cells. After cutting off a few cells, the two-faced apical cell itself divides repeatedly giving

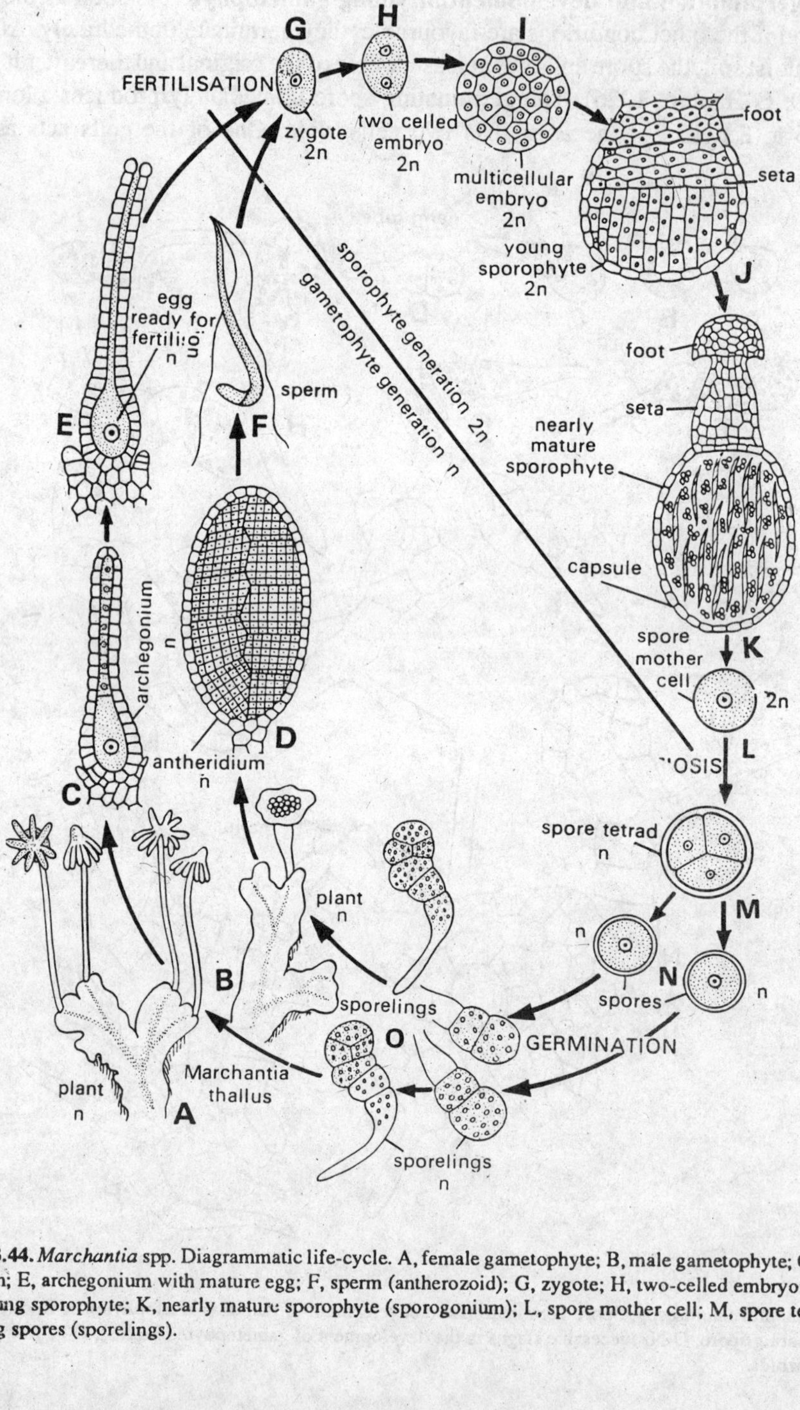

Fig. 3.44. *Marchantia* spp. Diagrammatic life-cycle. A, female gametophyte; B, male gametophyte; C, archegonium; D, antheridium; E, archegonium with mature egg; F, sperm (antherozoid); G, zygote; H, two-celled embryo; I, multicellular embryo; J, young sporophyte; K, nearly mature sporophyte (sporogonium); L, spore mother cell; M, spore tetrad; N, spores; O, germinating spores (sporelings).

rise to a sheet of a large number of cells. In this sheet, a transverse row of the apical cells characteristic of the adult gametophyte of *Marchantia* develops. When the young gametophyte becomes 30 to 40 celled, the notch appears in the apical portion of it.

Systematic position. Division. Bryophyta
Class. Hepaticospida (Hepaticae)
Order. Marchantiales
Family. Marchantiaceae

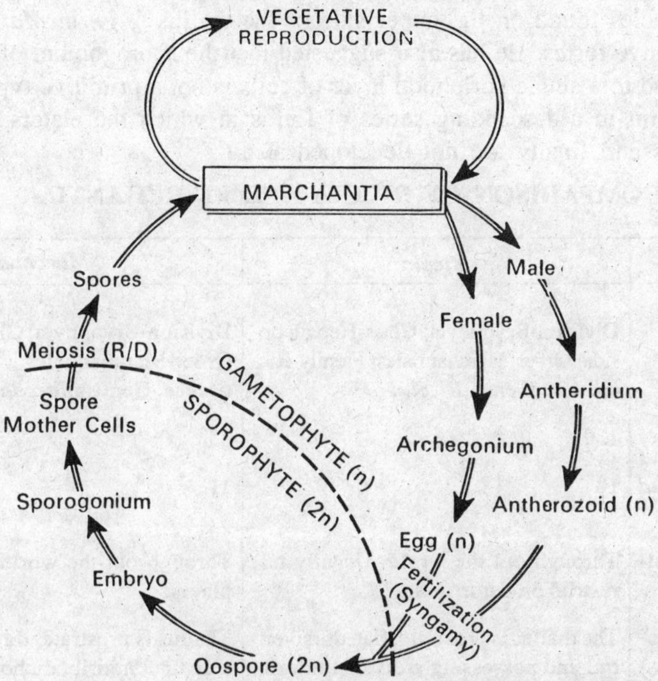

Fig. 3.45. *Marchantia*. Graphic life-cycle.

PHYLOGENY OF MARCHANTIALES

In the order Marchantiales, starting from *Riccia,* there is a general advancement in the elaboration of vegetative organs, the aggregation of the sexual organs into complex gametophores, and a progressive differentiation of the sporogonium. This is known as **progressive evolution.** Schiffner, Cavers, Campbell, Bower, Fritsch, Smith are the chief supporters of this view.

The simplest thallus structure is seen in most species of *Riccia,* where the upper tissue is made up of the chlorophyllous filaments separated by narrow air spaces. In higher Marchantiales the structure of thallus is more advanced and differentiated into air chambers which contain the chlorophyllous filaments. The elaborated pores (*e.g.,* in *Marchantia*) remain surrounded by a single ring of cells, forming a barrel-like structure. The elaboration of the thallus took place independently in several distinct lines.

In *Riccia,* the sporophyte is the simplest known among the Hepaticopsida (Hepaticae). It is simply a sac of spores and incapable of self-nutrition. It doesnot possess foot and seta. The wall of capsule consists of one layer of cells in thickness. On the other hand the sporophyte of *Marchantia* is complex one and is completely dependent on the gametophyte for its nutrition. It consists of foot, seta and capsule. There is gradual and progressive sterilization of the fertile cells of the sporogenous tissue in the sporophyte.

The above mentioned theory of **progressive sterilization** was first proposed by Bower and later supported by Cavers. According to this theory *Riccia* has been considered as primitive and *Marchantia* as a highly evolved or advanced genus.

The opposing view, according to which the Marchantiales show reduction, starting from *Marchantia* and culminating in the genus *Riccia*. Here *Riccia* represents not a primitive form but the lowest member in a descending series of reduction forms. This view has been supported by Goebel. According to him those members of the Marchantiales in which the sexual organs are borne in receptacles found on the upper side of the thallus (*e.g.*, in *Marchantia*), are reduced and not primitive forms. He has also suggested that the sporogonium of *Riccia* in which sterilization is limited to a single peripheral layer of cells is not a primitive type of sporophyte, but is the lowest term in a descending series of forms in which the elaters become reduced to short sterile cells and finally are not developed at all.

COMPARISON OF RICCIA AND MARCHANTIA

	Riccia	*Marchantia*
Systematic position	Division-Bryophyta; Class-Hepaticopsida; Order-Marchantiales; Family-Ricciaceae, Genus-*Riccia*.	Division-Bryophyta, Class-Hepaticopsida, Order-Marchantiales, Family-Marchantiaceae, Genus-*Marchantia*.
Total number of species	130	65
Number of species found in India	18	11
Distribution and habitat	Through out the world. Usually terrestrial on damp soil.	Through out the world. Usually in moist places.
External features of gametophyte (thallus) plant body	The thallus is prostrate, flat, dorsiventral and possessing a distinct midrib, dichotomous branching rhizoids, smoothwalled and tuberculate (*i.e.*, of two types), unicellular, scales arranged in single row, apparently two rows one near each lateral margin.	Thallus is prostrate, flat, dorsiventral with a distinct midrib, dichotomous branching, rhizoids of two kinds, smooth-walled and tuberculate (*i.e.*, of two kinds), unicellular, scales arranged in two to four rows on each side of the midrib, *ligulate* and *appendiculate* (*i.e.*, of two kinds).
Internal structure of thallus	Pores, rudimentary, simple intercellular spaces bounded by 4 to 8 epidermal cells, narrow vertical canals or large air chambers present; the photosynthetic tissue consists of vertical columns of chlorophyll-containing cells, or one-celled thick lamellae separating the air chambers; the ventral region of thallus makes the storage tissue which is composed of compact, colourless parenchyma.	Pores, compound, barrelshaped, composed of 4 to 8 superimposed tier of cells, each tier consists of 4-5 cells, there is single horizontal layer of air chambers separated by partitions, the photosynthetic tissue consists of single or branched filaments of chlorophyllous cells arising from the floor of air chambers, the storage tissue is made up of the ventral region of the thallus which is composed of compact, colourless parenchyma.
Apical growth	The apical growth takes place by transverse row of 3-5 apical cells each with two cutting faces which cut of segments from dorsal and ventral faces.	As in *Riccia*.

	Riccia	*Marchantia*
Sex organs	Monoecious (*e.g., R. crystallina, R. glauca, R. billardieri, R. gangetica* or dioecious (*e.g., R. discolor, R. frostii, R. curtisii* etc.).	*Marchantia* is dioecious as the antheridiophores and archegoniophores are borne on different thalli.
Antheridia	The antheridia are situated on dorsal surface of thallus and remain immersed in antheridial chambers; the stalk of antheridum is short and few celled, jacket of antheridium is singlelayered; antherozoids biciliate.	The antheridia are borne in groups on the upper surface of the disc of antheridiophore, and remain immersed in antheridial chambers; the antheridial stalk, short and few celled; antheridial jacket, singlelayered; antherozoids biciliate.
Archegonia	The archegonia are found to be situated on dorsal surface of thallus; the archegonia are protected by archegonial chambers; the stalk of archegonium is short, the neck of archegonium consists of six vertical rows of cells, the venter is single-layered in thickness, four cover cells at the tip of neck, usually four neck canal cells.	The archegonia are situated on the disc of stalked archegoniophore; the archegonia are protected by perichaetium, rays and disc of the archegoniophore; archegonial stalk short; the neck consists of six vertical rows of cells; the venter is single-layered thick; there are 4 cover cells at the tip of neck; generally 4-6 neck canal cells are present.
Sporophyte	The jacket of sporophyte is developed by *amphithecium;* the *endothecium* gives rise to archesporium; archesporium gives rise to sporocytes and abortive nurse cells; the foot is altogether absent; the seta is also absent; the shape of sporophyte is globose; the wall of sporophyte is single-layered and abortive; the elaters are absent; the spores are liberated by the decay of thallus tissue; the sporophytic phase is completely dependent (parasitic) on the gametophyte plant.	The *amphithecium* gives rise to the jacket of capsule; the *endothecium* gives rise to archesporium; the archesporium gives rise to sporocytes and elaters; the foot is bulbous or broad-spreading; the long seta elongates rapidly after the maturity of spores; the capsule is nearly spherical structure at the distal end of the sporogonium; the wall of capsule is single-layered and persistent; long, narrow, spindle-shaped elaters with two spiral thickenings; the wall of capsule splits longitudinally into a number of lobes and the elaters become helpful in spore dispersel; sporophyte is dependent on gametophyte.
Young gemetophyte	The spore is surrounded by 3 wall layers; the size of spore varies from 0.05 to 0.12 mm; on the germination of the spore, a germ tube is formed; there is differentiation of an apical cell in a cell plate at the end of germ tube.	The spore is surrounded by 2 wall layers; the size of spore varies from 0.012 to 0.03 mm; on germination of spore, a cell filament is formed directly; thereafter a many-celled tissue is developed, in which the apical cell is differentiated.

4

Hepaticopsida

Order-Metzgeriales

The characteristic features of this order are as follows:

The gametophyte may be thallose or differentiated into stem and lateral leaves. Mostly the gametophytes are without internal differentiation of tissues but certain genera have a central strand of thick walled cells. The ventral surface of a gametophyte bears smooth-walled rhizoids. Growth of a gametophyte is initiated by a single apical cell.

The members of this order do not have the apical cells developing into archegonia, and because of this feature, mature sporophytes lie some distance back from the growing apex of a gametophyte. The archegonia arise from the young segments cut off by the apical cell. Sex organs are borne laterally and on the dorsal face of a thallus. The sex organs are produced on any branch of the gametophyte or only on special branches.

This order includes about 23 genera and 550 species.

Classification. According to Evans (1937) there are seven or eight families in this order. They are: Treubiaceae; Fossombroniaceae; Pelliaceae; Blasiaceae; Pallaviciniaceae; Metzgeriaceae; Riccardiaceae and Monocleaceae.

Family-Pelliaceae

Characteristic features. The thallus is prostrate and dorsiventral. It is often lobed by irregular incisions. The rhizoids are simple, unseptate, smooth and thin walled. The scales are not present. The antheridia and archegonia remain scattered on the dorsal surface of the thallus. The archegonial cluster always remains surrounded by an involucre which is an outgrowth of the thallus. The capsule is globose or oval in shape. It possesses a basal elaterophore.

There are two or three genera in this family. Here the genus *Pellia* has been discussed in detail.

Genus **PELLIA**

Occurrence. This genus occurs commonly by the sides of streams, in damp woods, springs, ditches and under the hedges. Sometimes it appears on old humus laden sand dunes. Occasionally it appears on moist rocks and sometimes actually under water. *Pellia epiphylla* and *P. fabbroniana* occasionally occur submerged under flowing water, but the aquatic forms usually remain sterile.

This genus includes four species, *i.e., P. epiphylla, P. fabbroniana, P. neesiana* and *P. columbiana.* The last species has been described by Krajina and Brayshaw (1951) from British Columbia. The first three species have been reported by Kashyap (1929) from our country. Kashyap reported that *P. fabbroniana* is quite common in the Western Himalayas and Kumaon hills from 5,000 to 8,000 feet. According to him *P. epiphylla* is commonly found in Eastern Himalayas and Sikkim regions. *P. neesiana* is not common.

Jones (1958) has recognized a fifth species known as *Pellia borealis.*

THE GAMETOPHYTE

External structure. The gametophyte plant body is a small, simple and dorsivental thallus. It is thin, prostrate, flat and dichotomously branched. The margins, of the thalli are sinuous.

The lobed thallus branches repeatedly and the lobes often overlap one another. Since many plants generally grow together, it may cover quite large area of ground. The upper surface of the thallus

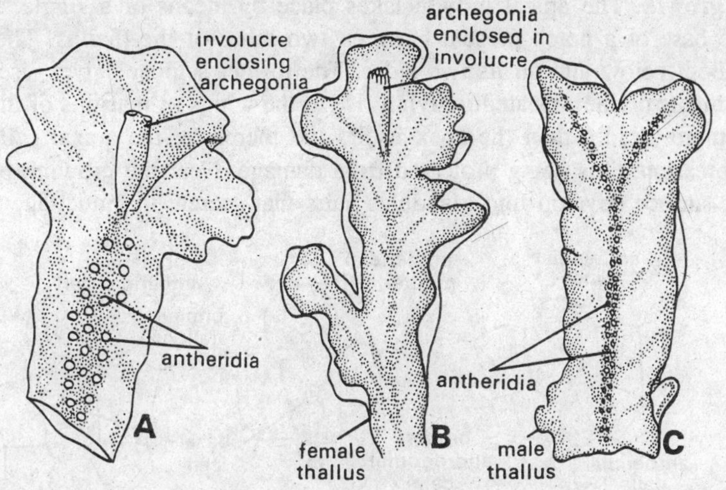

Fig. 4.1. *Pellia* sp. Thalli of different species. A, monoecious thallus of *Pellia epiphylla*; B, female thallus (dioecious) of *P. calycina*; C, male thallus (dioecious) of *P. calycina*.

is comparatively darker green than the lower. The thallus bears a purplish-coloured midrib. The thallus bears numerous rhizoids on its underside in the region of midrib and the plants remain attached to the ground by means of these rhizoids. All rhizoids are smooth walled. Tuberculate rhizoids and scales are not found. Each lobe of the thallus bears a terminal notch. A growing point remains situated in the bottom of this notch.

Internal structure (anatomy). The internal structure of the thallus is simple, and usually consists of polyhedral cells which form a uniform tissue known as parenchyma. The thallus is composed of layers of cells joined together in a honey comb like manner. The midrib is many layered which projects below and merges gradually with the single layered thick margins. The cells of the marginal regions and the upper layer of the midrib contain numerous chloroplasts while the cells of the lower region of midrib contain few or no chloroplasts but the starch grains occur in all the cells of the thallus. These starch grains constitute the reserve food material resulting from carbon assimilation. Some of the cells of thallus contain oil. In certain species (*e.g.*, *P. epiphylla* and *P. neesiana*) the cells are elongated and the cell walls possess interlacing thicken-

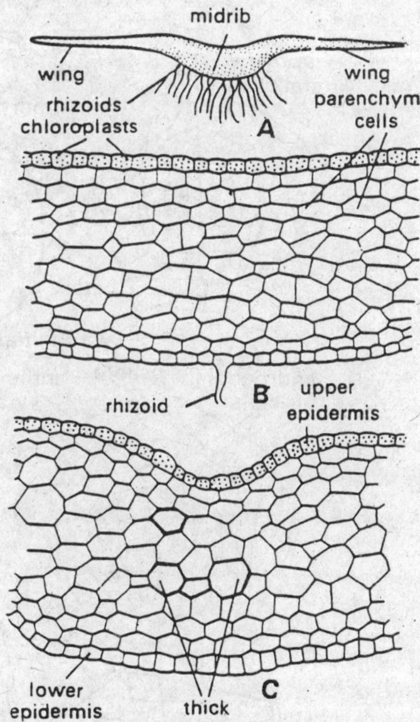

Fig. 4.2. *Pellia* sp. Internal structure of thallus. A, *P. epiphylla* - vertical transverse section of thallus (outline sketch); B, *P. calycina* - vertical transverse section of thallus (detailed structure); C, *P. epiphylla* - vertical transverse section of thallus (detailed structure)

ings forming a network throughout the tissue of the thallus. The layer of the cells covering the upper and lower surface of the thallus is called the epidermis.

Apical growth. The apical growth takes place by means of a single, large, apical cell situated at the base of a notch present between two lobes of the thallus. The apical cell cuts off segments both below and on its two sides. The former segment gives rise to midrib while the lateral segments divide repeatedly giving rise to the wings or margins of thallus. The lateral tissue grows more rapidly than the apex itself, and therefore, the apical cell remains always in a slight depression, thus being protected from damage. Near the growing point some of the cells of lower surface develop into glandular hairs that secrete the mucilage and this protects

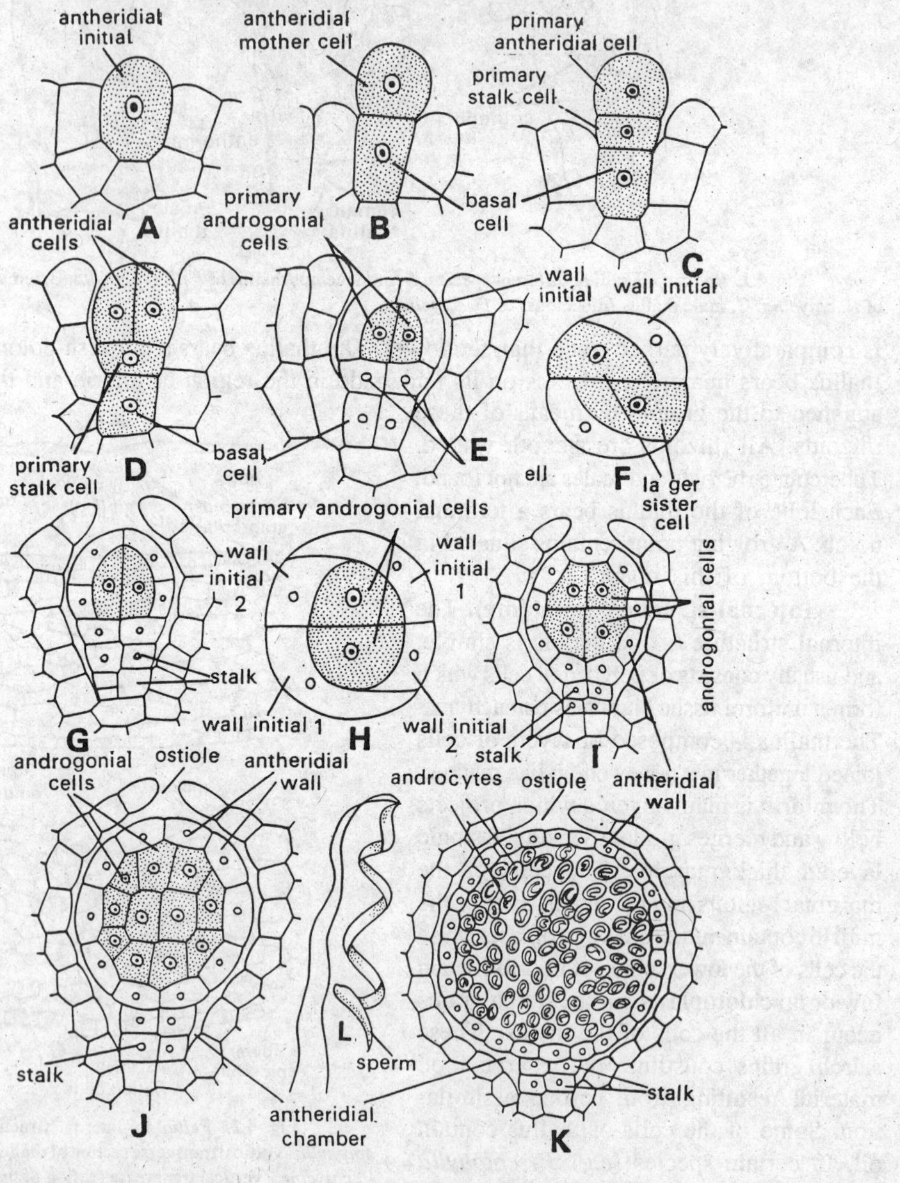

Fig. 4.3. *Pellia* sp. Development of antheridium. A, antheridial initial; B-J, successive stages in the development of antheridium; F and H in transverse sections; K, mature antheridium; L, sperm (antherozoid).

the apical cell from becoming desiccated. The thallus divides dichotomously. At the beginning of dichotomy the apical cell divides longitudinally into two, thereafter both apical cells cut off segments in the similar way as before.

Reproduction. The reproduction takes place by means of vegetative and sexual methods.

Vegetative reproduction. It often bears adventitious buds which develop on the dorsal surface of the thallus from the superficial cells. On being detached these adventitious buds on shoots give rise to new independent thalli. In many species the decay and disintegration in the posterior region of the thallus leads to the separation of the lobes from the parent thallus. Each such lobe develops into an independent thallus.

Sexual reproduction. The thallus is gametophyte and bears the sex organs. They consist of **antheridia** and **archegonia,** the male and female sex organs respectively.

The antheridium and its development. The antheridia are found to be present on the dorsal surface of the gametophyte (thallus) along the midrib. Their position is indicated by circular wart like porjections scattered on the upper surface of the thallus. Each such projection marks the **antheridial chamber** in which lies a single antheridium. The antheridial chamber opens outside on the upper surface of the thallus by a small opening, the **ostiole.**

The antheridium develops from a single superficial cell which lies on the upper surface of the thallus just behind the apical cell. This antheridial initial forms a papillate prorrusion and divides transversely by a cross wall into a **basal cell** and an **outer cell.** The basal cell remains embedded into the tissue of the thallus while the outer cell protrudes out of the surface of thallus. Thereafter the outer cell divides transversely forming a lower **primary stalk cell** and upper **primary antheridial cell.** The primary stalk cell gives rise to the stalk of antheridium, while the primary antheridical cell divides longitudinally into daughter cells of equal size. By this time, the dorsal cells of thallus that surround the antheridium divide again and again forming a ring-like involucre which opens on the dorsal surface of the thallus.

Each of the two daughter cells developed from the primary antheridial cell divides by a periclinal wall into two unequal cells. This way two outer **jacket initials** and two inner **primary androgonial cells** are formed. The two jacket initials are unequal in size, the smaller one is the first and the larger one is the second jacket initial.

The two primary androgonial cells divide again and again forming a large number of androgonial cells. The last cell generation of the androgonial cell is called the **androcyte mother cell.** Each androcyte mother cell divides diagonally forming two **androcytes.** Each androcyte

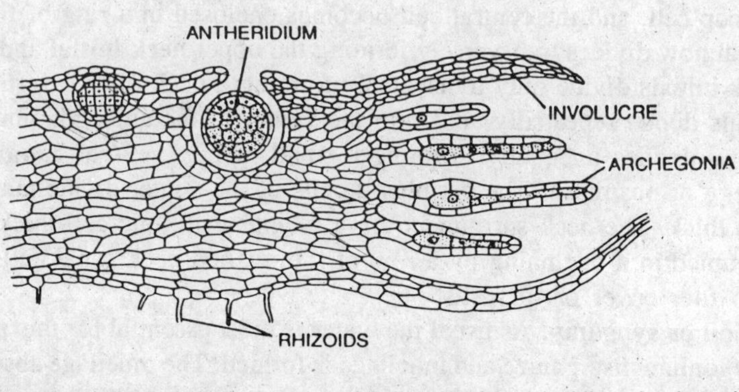

Fig. 4.4. *Pellia.* Longitudinal section of thallus showing antheridia and archegonia.

metamorphoses into an antherozoid. Simultaneously the jacket initials divide anticlinally again and again forming a single layered jacket around the antheridium.

A single antherozoid consists almost entirely of the nucleus and two long flagella. The body of the antherozoid is tapered and spirally coiled and the flagella remain attached to the thinner end. The antherozoids liberate out by dissolution of the mother cells and the opening of the antheridial wall at the apex.

The archegonium and its development. The archegonia are produced in groups on the upper surface of the thallus lobes just behind the apical cell. All the archegonia in the cluster are found to be situated on a slightly raised transverse ridge of tissue known as **receptacle.** A delicate membrane arising from the top of the ridge covers the archegonia as in a pocket. This membranous cover is known as **involucre.** The involucre is protective in function. The involucre is cylindrical in *P. neesiana,* tubular in *P. fabbroniana* and flap-like in *P. epiphylla.* The archegonia almost lie horizontally. The archegonia are found in the groups of four to twelve.

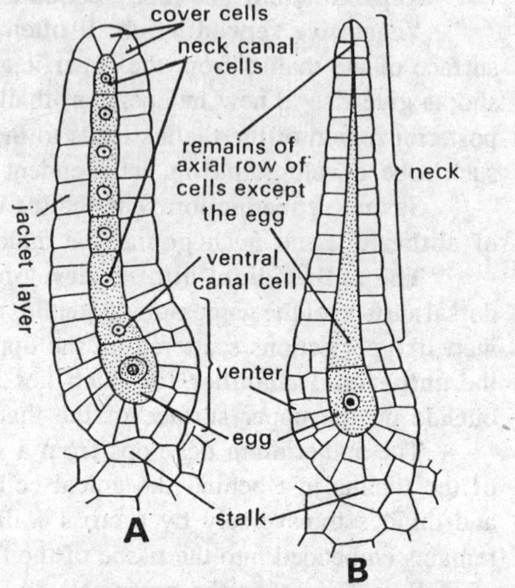

Fig. 4.5. *Pellia* sp. Archegonia. A, nearly mature archegonium; B, mature archegonium with egg ready for fertilization.

A mature archegonium is flask shaped. It has a short multicellular stalk, a dialated venter and a long neck. The venter consists of two layers of cells. It contains the egg and a ventral canal cell. The neck consists of five longitudinal rows of cells. It contains 6 to 9 neck canal cells.

The archegonia arise from a group of cells on the upper surface of the thallus lobes. These cells act as archegonial initials. The archegonia are not formed in a regular sequence. The young and old archegonia remain irregularly distributed on the upper surface of the thallus.

Any superficial cell may act as an **archegonial initial.** The archegonial initial enlarges and divides by a transverse wall forming a lower **basal cell** and an **upper cell.** The archegonium is produced from the upper cell. This cell divides by three vertical walls which form three peripheral cells, leaving a central cell in the middle. Of the three peripheral cells one is much smaller and usually does not divide by a vertical wall while the remaining two larger peripheral cells divide by vertical walls forming five **jacket initials.** The central cell divides by a transverse wall forming a cap cell, and the central cell becomes enclosed in a ring of five jacket initials. Each jacket initial now divides transversely forming the upper **neck initial** and the lower **venter initial.** The neck initials divide only transversely forming a neck of five vertical rows of cells. The venter initials divide repeatedly and form the venter of the archegonium. The central cell of the venter now divides unequally, forming a small, upper, **ventral canal cell** and a large lower cell, the **egg** or **oosphere.** The peripheral cells of the venter divide tangentially forming a wall two cells thick. The neck surrounded by a tubular wall, one cell thick, encloses a long **neck canal,** occupied in a beginning by a row of thin walled neck canal cells. Finally the cap cell divides into four cover or **lid cells.**

Fertilization or syngamy. As usual the water is most essential for this process. The axial cells of the archegonium disorganize and mucilage is formed. The mucilage absorbs water, swells and thus forces open the neck of the archegonium by separating the cover cells. Meanwhile the cells of the antheridium take up water, swell and eventually burst the wall, liberating the antherozoids. These antherozoids make their way in the water film and enter the neck of the archegonium. One of the antherozoids penetrates the oosphere and thereafter loses its flagella. The fertilization is effected by the union of the nucleus of one antherozoid with that of the

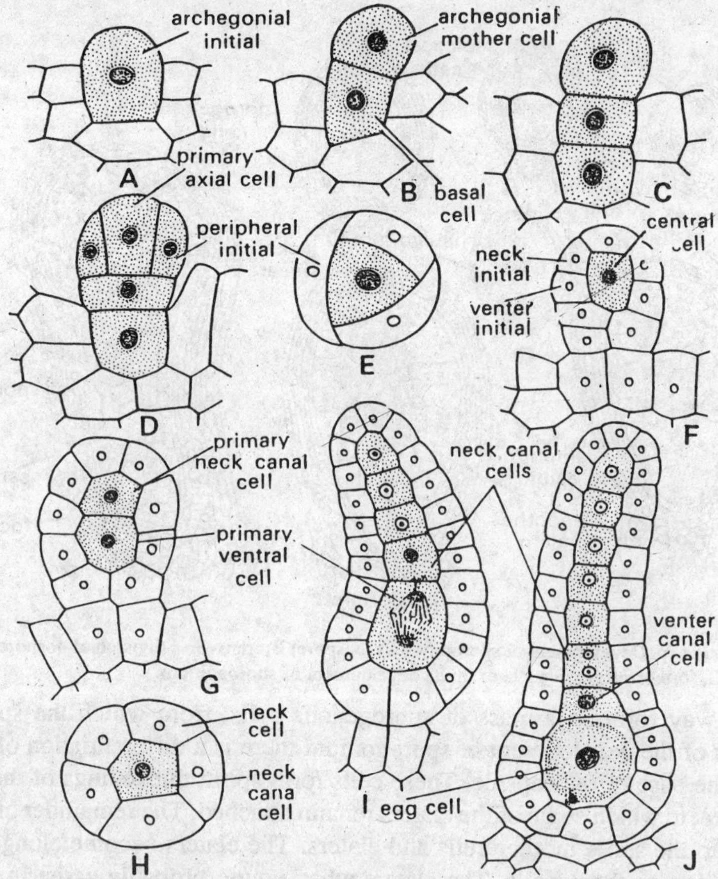

Fig. 4.6. *Pellia* sp. Development of archegonium. A, archegonial initial; B-I, successive stages in the development of archegonium; E and H, transverse sections; J, mature archegonium containing egg, ventral canal cell and neck canal cells.

oosphere. The fertilized oosphere secretes a wall around it and is now called the **zygote** or the **oospore.** The zygote contains 2n number of chromosomes.

THE SPOROPHYTE

The oospore enlarges in size. The cells of the venter divide repeatedly forming a **calyptra,** which usually encloses the young sporogonium until the capsule is nearly mature.

Development of the sporogonium. The enlarged zygote divides by a transverse wall into two cells. The upper one is divided by a transverse wall into two cells. The upper one is known as **epibasal cell** and the lower one as **hypobasal cell.** The hypobasal cell forms a suspensor which acts as a **haustorium.** It does not contribute to the embryo proper.

All the important changes and divisions take place in the epibasal cell. The entire sporogonium and its parts, *i.e.*, foot, seta and capsule have been derived from the epibasal cell. In the epibasal cell the first division is by a vertical wall and then by one at right angles to it. These four cells are now divided by vertical walls forming the two tiers of four cells each. The four lower cells divide and redivide forming the seta and the foot. The seta at its lower end develops a conical foot, with a flange projecting upwards, in outline like an arrow head. The four upper cells divide periclinally thus separating the central **endothecium** from the peripheral **amphithecium.** The endothecium gives rise to archesporium. The cells of archesporium divide and redivide

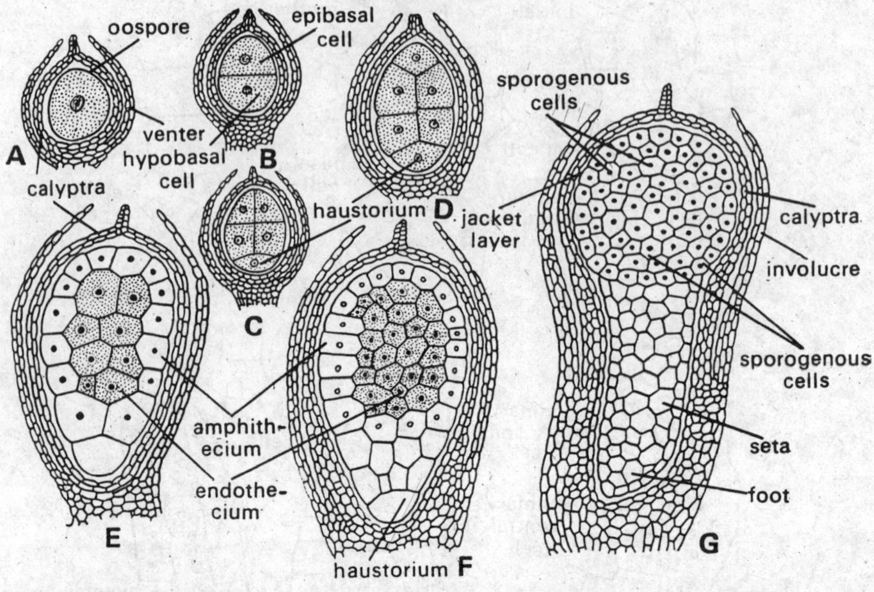

Fig. 4.7. *Pellia* sp. Development of sporophyte. A, oospore; B, transverse division of oospore forming epibasal and hypobasal cells; C-G, further successive stages in the development of sporogonium.

in an irregular way forming a mass of sporogenous cells, from which the spores are formed. In earlier stages of the development of sporogonium there is a differentiation of a mass of larger sterile cells at the base of the capsule. These cells form spiral thickenings of their walls forming the **elaterophore,** to which some of the elaters remain attached. The remainder of the sporogenous cells, give rise to the spore mother cells and elaters. The elaters become elongated and develop spirical thickenings on their walls. The elaters when young probably assist in transferring food

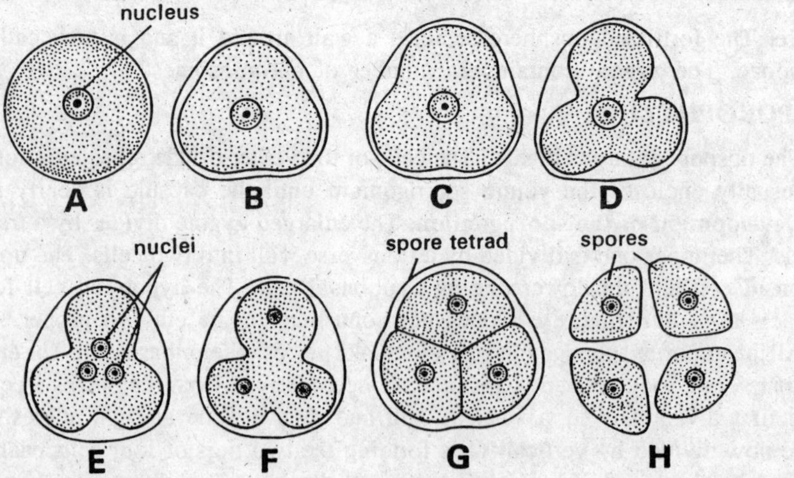

Fig. 4.8. *Pellia* sp. Sporogenesis. A, spore mother cell (2*n*); C-F, formation of four-lobed structure; G, spore tetrad;H,spores (*n*).

material from the seta to the spores, but on the maturity of the capsule they help in the dissemination of the spores.

Sporogenesis. During this process the spores are formed from spore mother cells (2n) by meiosis. The spore mother cells become deeply four lobed. The lobes being arranged in tetrahedral fashion. The diploid nucleus divides meiotically forming four daughter nuclei and one of the daughter nuclei passes into each lobe. Finally these lobes are separated by cell walls in between them and a tetrad of haploid spores is formed. It remains surrounded by a common sheath. The sheath ruptures and the ripe spores separate from each other.

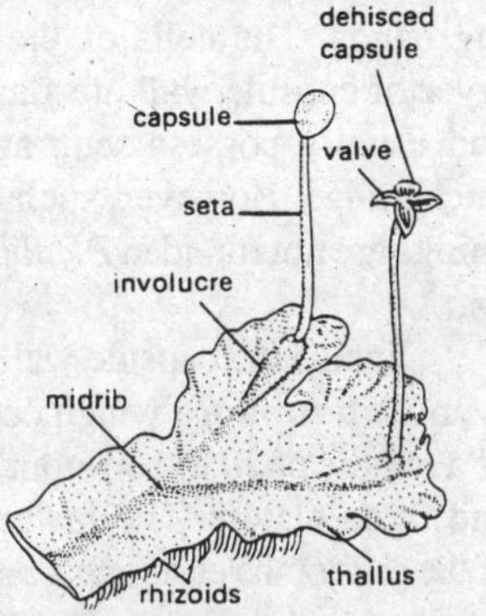

Fig. 4.9. *Pellia* sp. Thallus with mature sporogonia.

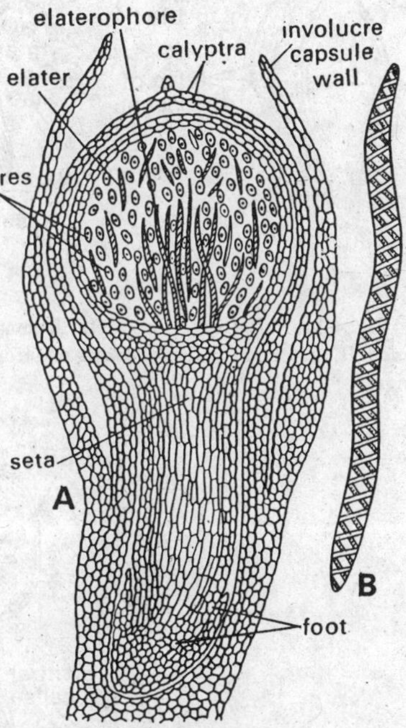

Fig. 4.10. *Pellia* sp. Sporophyte. A, mature sporogonium in longitudinal section showing foot, seta, elaterophore, elaters and spores; B, single elater with double spiral thickening.

It is notable that all the developmental changes take place within the venter of the archegonium, which has therefore enlarged rapidly, keeping pace with the development of the sporogonium. It forms a complete envelope, the **calyptra** around the sporogonium. After its development the sporogonium remains dormant for considerably a long period, within the calyptra. Thereafter the seta elongates rapidly from the base upwards. With the result the calyptra is ruptured which remains as a torn membrane round the base of the stalk. During a period of three or four days the seta grows to 2 or 3 inches long.

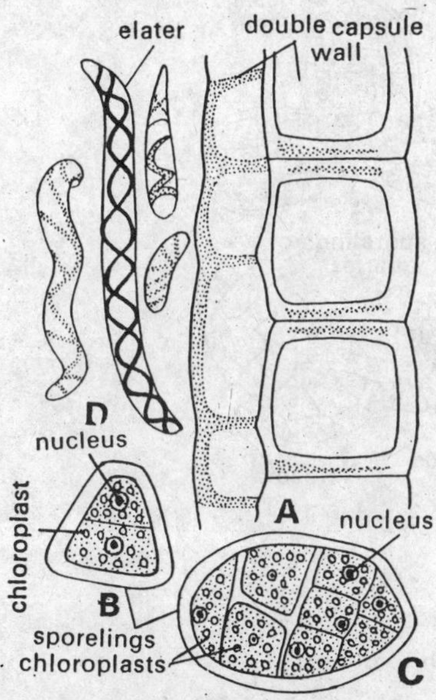

Fig. 4.11. *Pellia* sp. A, a part of the wall of the capsule; B-C, sporelings with nuclei and chloroplasts;

Structure of mature sporogonium. The mature sporogonium consists of a **foot, seta** and **capsule.** The foot forms a conical basal absorbing organ of the sporogonium. Its edges project upwards forming a collar like structure around the base of the seta. It consists of parenchymatous cells. By means of foot the sporogonium remains firmly embedded in the thallus.

The seta is elongated, slender, white and almost transparent in appearance. It consists of regular longitudinal rows of cells which usually contain starch. On maturation the cells of seta become very much elongated and lack starch grains.

A dark green or black capsule which resembles a large black pin head is found on the terminal end of seta. The outer jacket of capsule is composed of two or more cell layers. The outer layer of the capsule wall consists of polygonal cells, and their radial walls posses brown thickening bands. The cells of the inner layer of capsule wall are flattened and usually possess semi-angular thickenings. However, such thickenings are not found in *P. fabbroniana.*

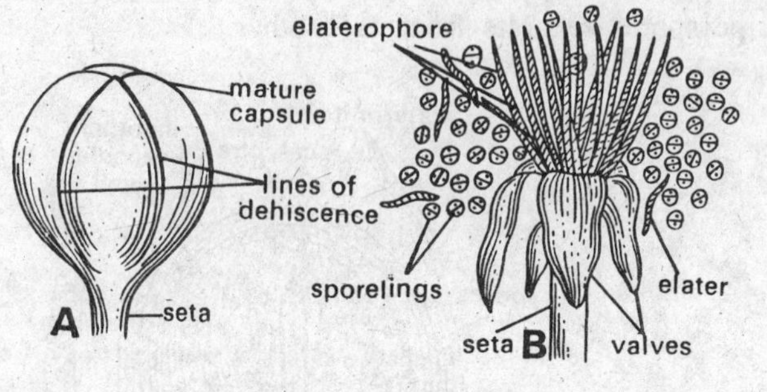

Fig. 4.12. *Pellia* sp. Sporophyte. A, mature capsule with lines of dehiscence; B, dehisced capsule showing elaterophore, elaters, valves and sporelings.

Inside the capsule wall there is an **elaterophore** which consists of a bundle of 20 to 100 stout, erect and fixed elaters. The lower ends of the cells of the elaterophore remain attached to the floor of the capsule

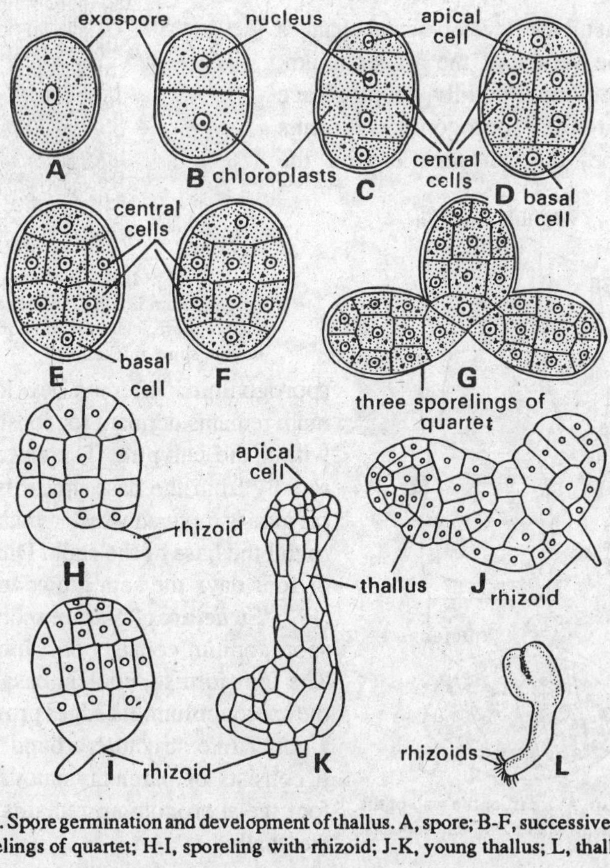

Fig. 4.13. *Pellia* sp. Spore germination and development of thallus. A, spore; B-F, successive stages in the development of sporeling; G, three sporelings of quartet; H-I, sporeling with rhizoid; J-K, young thallus; L, thallus with rhizoids.

cavity. The upper free ends of the cells of the elaterophore are found to be radiating into the cavity of capsule intermingled with spores and free elaters. The spores are quite large and begin to germinate even before they are shed. The elaters are long, slender spindle like and each of them is provided with 2 to 3 spiral thickened bands.

Dehiscence of the capsule. On maturation of the sporogonium the capsule bursts and the spores are dispersed in the atmosphere. The dehiscence of the capsule takes place by the elongation of the seta. The seta elongates rapidly, ruptures the calyptra and carries the capsule up in the air. The ruptured calyptra remains as a torn membrane round the base of the stalk. Under favourable conditions the capsule bursts; the wall of capsule splits forming four petal-like valves that spread out horizontally. By this process the spores are liberated. The separation of spores from one another is assisted by the elaters. The elaters are hygroscopic; they coil and uncoil according to the degree of atmospheric humidity. During this process the elaters twist and turn rapidly and by means of this they stir up the spores and separate them from the exposed spore mass. The flicking movement of the elaterophore assists in the gradual shedding of the free spores. The elaterophore persists even after shedding of the spores, in the form of a bundle of many long, thread-like spirally thickened cells.

Germination of spore. The germination of spore begins while the spores are retained within the capsule, and they may consist of several cells. Each cell contains a chloroplast and a nucleus so that spore in fact is a minute thallus. On liberation these multicellular spores begin to germinate immediately. They do not require any resting period.

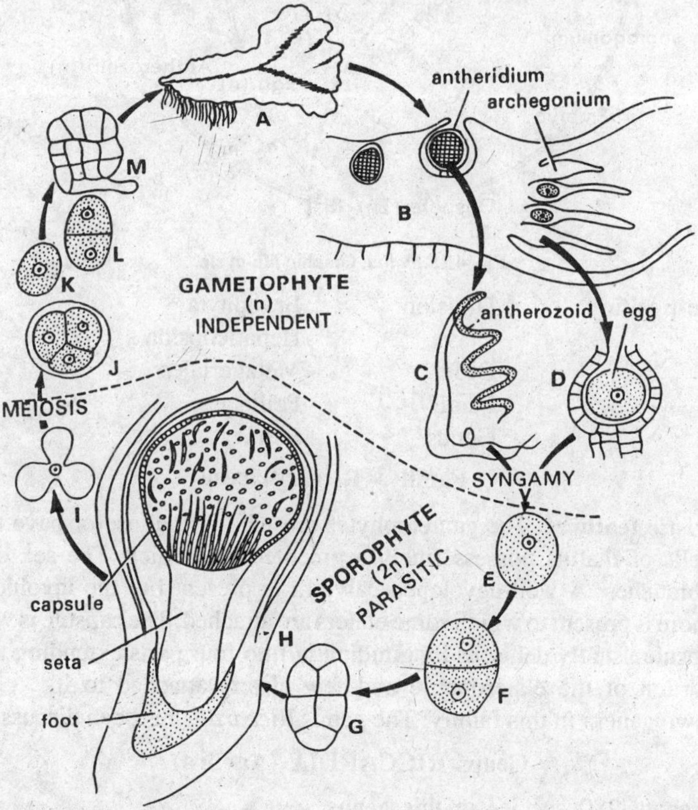

Fig. 4.14. *Pellia* sp. A-M, diagrammatic life-cycle. (modified after Parihar).

The unicellular spore first divides transversely forming two cells. Each of these cells again divides, by transverse wall and this way a row of four cells is formed. The lowermost cell contains less cytoplasm and fewer plastids. The next division is vertical and occurs simultaneously in the two central cells. The spore is usually shed from the capsule when it is six to nine celled. On falling on moist soil, the basal cell grows into a small rhizoid while the cells of the upper region divide again and again forming a new thallus.

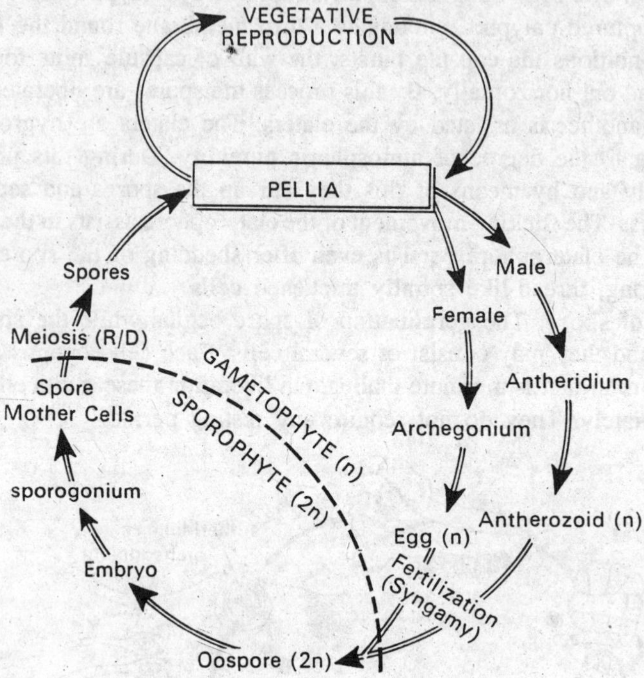

Fig. 4.15. *Pellia*. Graphic life-cycle.

Systematic position.

	Division.	Bryophyta
	Class.	Hepaticopsida
	Order.	Metzgeriales
	Family.	Pelliaceae
	Genus.	*Pellia*

Family – Riccardiaceae

Characteristic features. The gametophytes are wholly thallose or have thallose terminal branches. The cells of thallus possess finely segmented oil bodies. The sex organs are borne on short lateral branches. A well-developed calyptra is present but the involucre is not found. A distal elaterophore is present to which some elaters are attached. The capsule is void to cylindrical in shape. The capsule usually dehisces longitudinally into four parts extending to the base. Each part carries a portion of the elaterophore and few elaters attached to it.

There are two genera in this family. The genus *Riccardia* has been discussed here in detail.

Genus RICCARDIA (Aneura)

There are about 280 species in this genus.

Occurrence and distribution. The genus is cosmopolitan in its distribution. The species are commonly found in the tropical and subtropical regions. About ten species of *Riccardia* have been reported from our country. These species are-*Riccardia sikkimensis, R. villosa, R. levieri, R. foreauana, R. cardoti, R. indica, R. multifida, R. pinguis, R. decolyana* and *R. palmatiformis. Riccardia* grows on various habitats. It grows on moist rocks, in or near streams, wet soil, moist sandy soil, ditches, pools and low land marshes. Many species are epiphytic.

THE GAMETOPHYTE

External structure. The gametophytes are wholly thallose or they possess thallose terminal branches. The thallus is dichotomously branched. According to Evans (1921) there is unequal growth of dichotomies, and therefore, it results in a gametophyte in which the branches appear

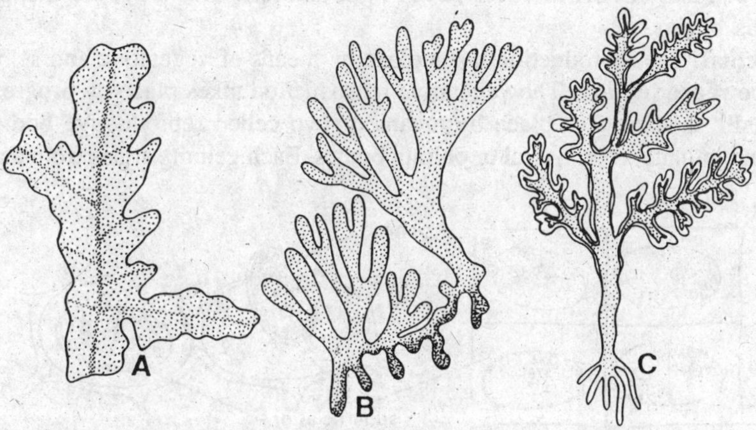

Fig. 4.16. *Riccardia,* A, thallus of *R. indica*; B, thallus of *R. bogotensis*; C, thallus of *R. eriocaulis.*

to be lateral appendages. The gametophyte of *R. pinguis* is wholly prostrate. It is rarely differentiated into a midrib and lateral wings. The prostrate thalli may be slightly branched, *e.g.*, in *R. indica* and *R. pinguis. R. levieri* possess brownish thalli which are irregularly pinnately branched twice or thrice. A prostrate creeping axis with two types of branches on its both sides is found in *R. bogotensis.* The main axis and its lower branches are cylindrical, while the upper branches are erect, spreading and flattened found in *R. eriocaulis* and *R. fucoides.* The lobes of these species possess distinct midrib and lateral wings. In certain other species, the margins of the branches are strongly incurved forming water sacs (*e.g.*, in *R. hymenophylloides*).

Internal structure. A cross-section of the thallus shows a very simple structure. *R. pinguis* and other related species do not show internal differentiation of tissues. Many partially erect

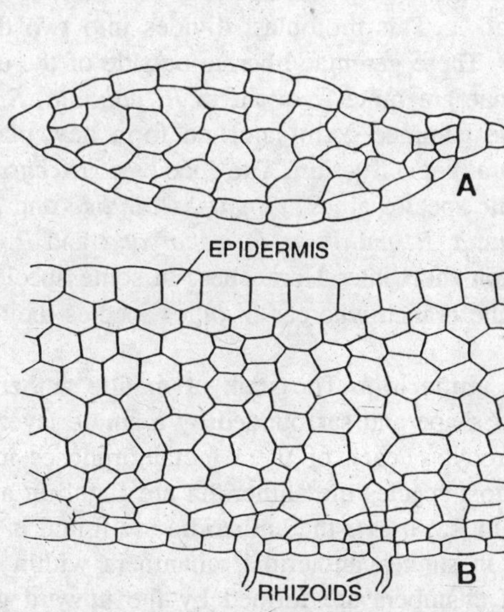

Fig. 4.17. *Riccardia.* A transverse section of thallus of *R. muitifida;* B, transverse section of *R. indica.*

species possess a well defined system of elongate thick-walled cells. The cell contains chloroplasts and oil bodies. The ventral surface of a thallus possess smooth-walled rhizoids and mucilage hairs. The young rhizoids contain chloroplasts while the old rhizoids lack them.

Apical growth. The apical growth of the thallus takes place by means of a wedge shaped apical cell with two cutting faces which cut off primary segments on both sides alternately right and left. The apical cell is found to be situated in a depression at the anterior end of a branch. Two or more apical cells are found in each depression. The primary segments formed from an apical cell divide in the same way as a two faced apical cell, but these segments cut off the segments above and below and not right and left. A segment formed from a apical cell occasionally cuts of three or four derivatives above and below and thereafter it begins to act as a true apical cell and cut off the derivatives right and left. This way, the dichotomy on the branch of thallus begins.

Reproduction. The reproduction takes place by means of vegetative and sexual methods.

Vegetative reproduction. The vegetative reproduction takes place by progressive growth and death of thalli. It also takes place by means of two celled reproductive bodies known as **gemmae.** They are minute, round, oval or oblong bodies. Each gemma arises from any superficial

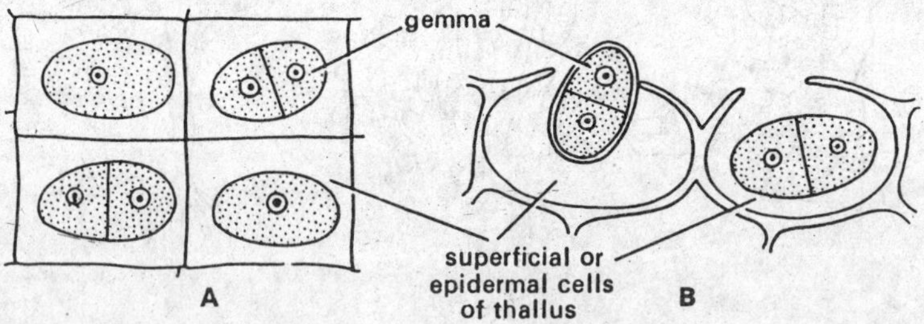

Fig. 4.18. *Riccardia multifida*. Vegetative reproduction. A, stages in the formation of gemmae; B, two fully formed gemmae.

cell of a thallus. The protoplast of a gemma mother cell becomes rounded and secretes a new wall around it. This protoplast divides into two daughter cells which remain firmly unite to each other. These gemmae liberate outside of the original cell wall by means of gelatinization. The gemmae are quite frequent in *R. palmata, R. multifida, R. palmatiformis, R. levieri* and others. The gemmae germinate and form new plants.

Sexual reproduction. The species of *Riccardia* may be heterothallic or homothallic. The heterothallic species are-*R. pinguis, R. indica* and *R. palmata* whereas the homothallic species are-*R. sinuata, R. multifida, R. decolyana* and *R. latifrons*. In both the cases the sex organs are borne on short lateral branches. In some species the sex organs are borne along the entire length of the branch whereas in other species they are restricted to the terminal portion of the branch.

The antheridia. The stalk of mature antheridium is two to three cells in length. It is globular in shape and surrounded by a single layered jacket. The mature antheridium contains many androcytes, each of them metamorphoses into a biflagellate antherozoid.

In most species the antheridia are found in a double row on the dorsal side of a branch. However, in *R. pinguis* the antheridia are found in three or four irregular rows. The antheridia are found in sunken antheridial chambers within the tissue of the antheridial branches. The antheridial chambers are formed by the upward growth of adjoining vegetative cells of the antheridial branch.

Development of antheridium. According to Clapp (1912) and Showalt . (1923) the development of an antheridium is in the manner characteristic of Metzgeriales as already has been described earlier in *Pellia* on pages 59-60.

The mature antheridium. The stalk of a mature antheridium is two or three cells in length. The body of antheridium is globular and remains surrounded by a one layered jacket. Inside the jacket there are many androcytes each one of which develops into a biciliate antherozoid.

Development of archegonium. The archegonia develop on the archegonial branch. The branches bearing archegonia are generally shorter than those bearing the antheridia. The arrangement of archegonia on the archegonial branches is irregular. Each successive segment cuts off by the apical cell develops into an archegonium. Development of an archegonium is in the manner characteristic of Metzgeriales as already has been described in *Pellia* on page 60.

The mature archegonium. Typical five vertical rows of neck cells and four to six neck canal cells are formed. One minor difference is there that the primary venter cell divides early into an egg and venter canal cell. Moreover, the jacket cells divide periclinally so that the mature archegonia may have a two celled thick neck and a venter two or three celled thick. This is a massive archegonium with little external differentiation into the neck and venter.

Fertilization. The fertilization takes place in the usual manner for Hepaticopsida. Water is indispensable for fertilization. The neck of archegonium opens by absorbing water. The antherozoids try to enter the neck of the archegonium. One of the antherozoids enters the neck, and finally the male nucleus fuses with tne female resulting into the formation of an oospore or zygote.

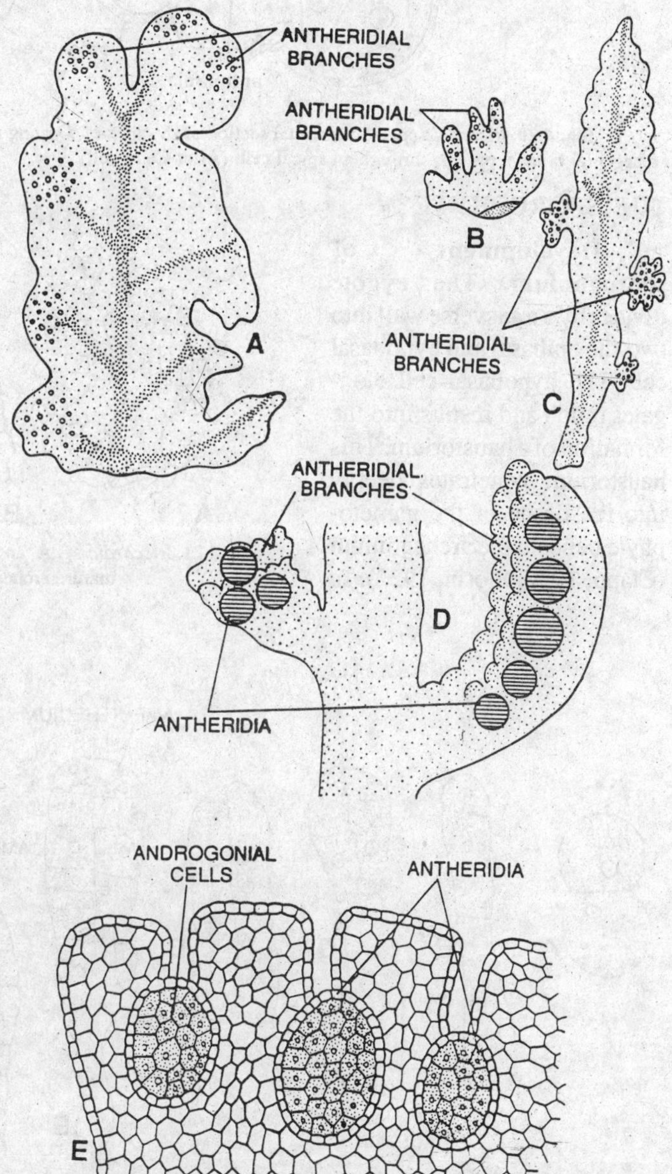

Fig. 4.19. *Riccardia*. A, male thallus of *R. indica* with antheridia on lateral branches; B, antheridial branches of *R. multifida;* C, male thallus with antheridial branches of *R. pinguis;* D, part of a thallus with two antheridial branches; E, sectional view of thallus with antheridia.

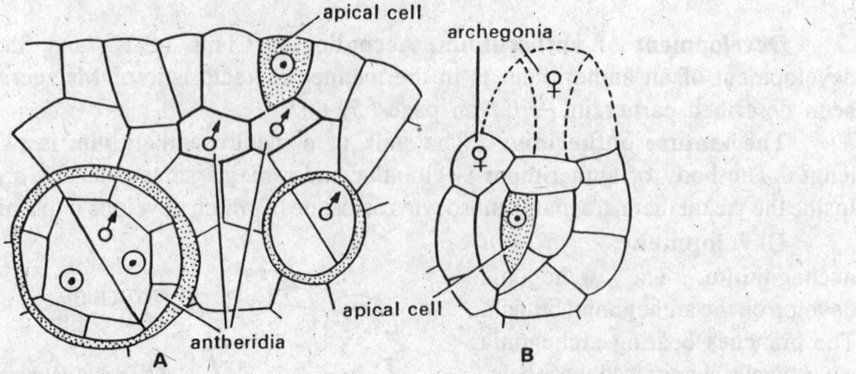

Fig. 4.20. *Riccardia* sp. A, horizontal section of the apex of a young antheridial branch; B, transverse section of an archegonial branch, passing through an apical cell. (After Campbell).

THE SPOROPHYTE

Development of sporogonium. The zygote divides by a transverse wall into two-the epibasal and hypobasal cell. The hypobasal cell elongates much and results into the formation of a haustorium. This haustorium penetrates deeply into the tissue of the gametophyte beneath the archegonium (Clapp, 1912; Florin, 1922). In

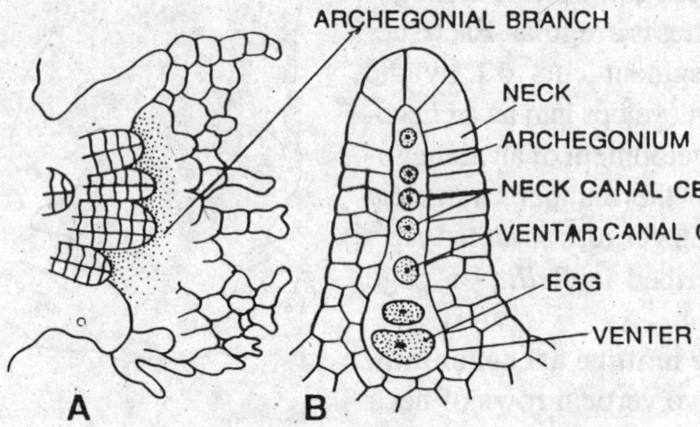

Fig. 4.21. *Riccardia* sp. A, an archegonial branch of *R. sinuata;* B, nearly mature archegonium. (After Campbell).

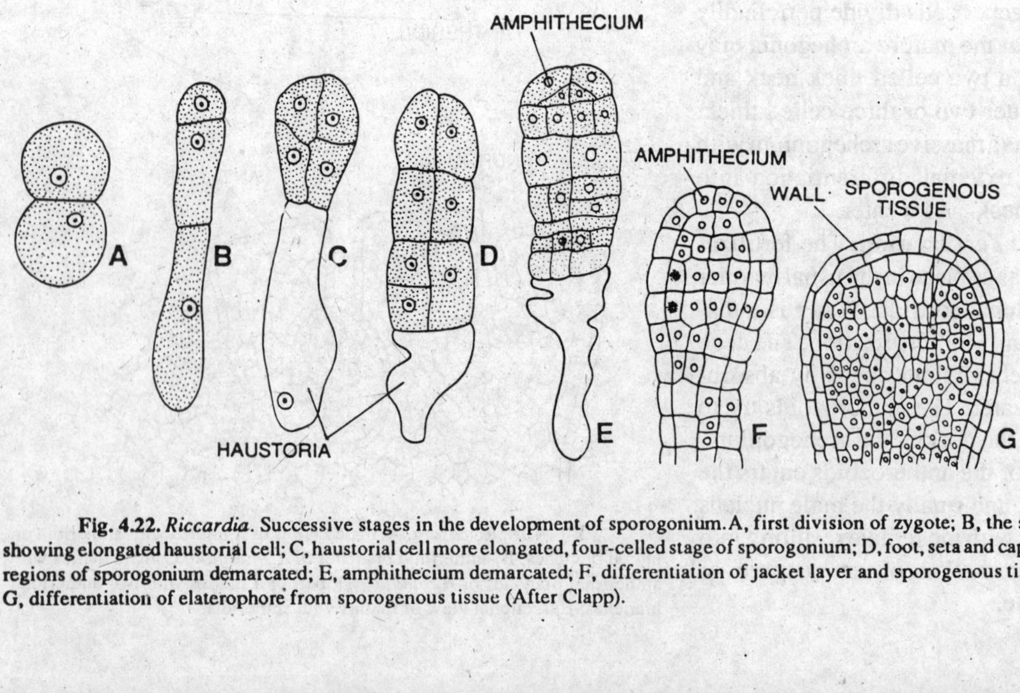

Fig. 4.22. *Riccardia*. Successive stages in the development of sporogonium. A, first division of zygote; B, the same showing elongated haustorial cell; C, haustorial cell more elongated, four-celled stage of sporogonium; D, foot, seta and capsule regions of sporogonium demarcated; E, amphithecium demarcated; F, differentiation of jacket layer and sporogenous tissue; G, differentiation of elaterophore from sporogenous tissue (After Clapp).

many cases there is no division of the haustorial cell. Except for the haustorium practically the whole sporogonium develops from the upper epibasal cell. The epibasal cell divides transversely and thereafter the upper daughter cell soon divides transversely and three cells are formed. These three superimposed cells develop, respectively, into foot, seta and capsule of the sporogonium. The cells which are to develop into foot and seta first undergo two successive vertical divisions and thereafter the vertical and transverse divisions take place in irregular way. The cell which is to develop into a capsule also undergoes two successive vertical divisions forming four cells. Each of these four cells divides transversely. This way two tiers of four cells each are formed. Each cell in these two four-celled tiers divides periclinally demarcating the peripheral amphithe-

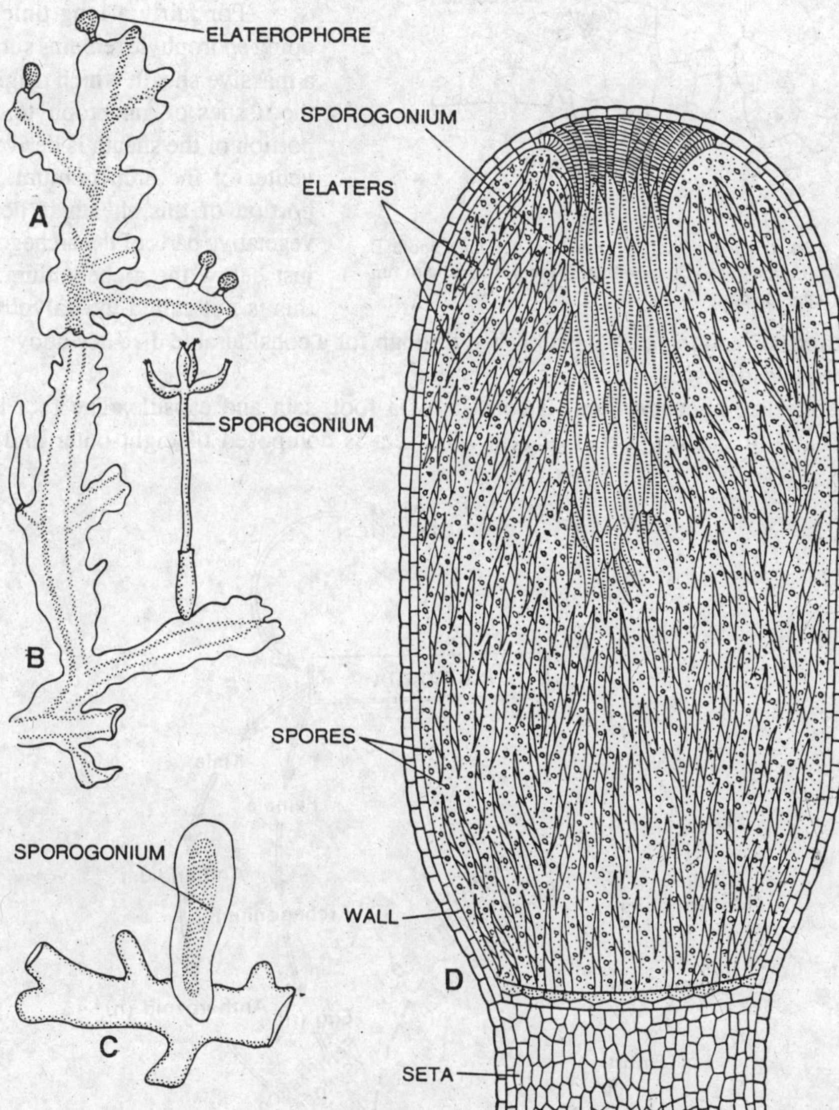

Fig. 4.23. *Riccardia*. A, female thallus of *R. india* with sporogonia; B, female thallus of *R. pinguis* with sporogonia; C, female thallus of *R. multifida* with sporogonium; D, longitudinal section of a mature capsule of *R. pinguis* (A, after Kashyap and Pande; B, after Velenovsky; C, after Pearson; D, after Goebel).

cium from the axial endothecium. The amphithecium forms the jacket of the capsule, two cells in thickness. The endothecium represents the archesporium. The cell of archesporium (sporogenous cells) divide in an irregular sequence, but rather early there is a differentiation of an apical mass of elongated cells, the **elaterophore.** The sporogenous cells which do not develop into the elaterophore eventually give rise to spore mother cells (sporocytes) and elaters. Each spore mother cell finally divides meiotically forming four spores.

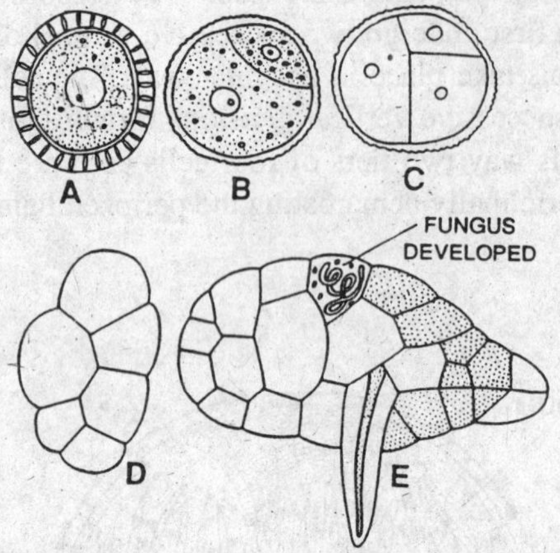

Fig. 4.24. *Riccardia*. Spore germination. A, mature spore; B, first stage of germination; C-D, sporeling; E, older thallus with fungus-present (After Clapp).

For fairly a long time the developing sporophyte remains surrounded by a massive sheath which originates from the tissues of gametophyte. The apical portion of the sheath is derived from the venter of the archegonium. The major portion of this sheath is derived from vegetative parts of the archegonial branch just below the archegonium. Therefore this is not called the calyptra. Later on the seta elongates and the capsule is pushed through for a considerable distance above the sheath, and the capsule dehisces.

The mature sporogonium. It consists of a foot, seta and capsule. The foot is club like swelling found at the lower end of seta. The seta is composed of eight outer and four inner

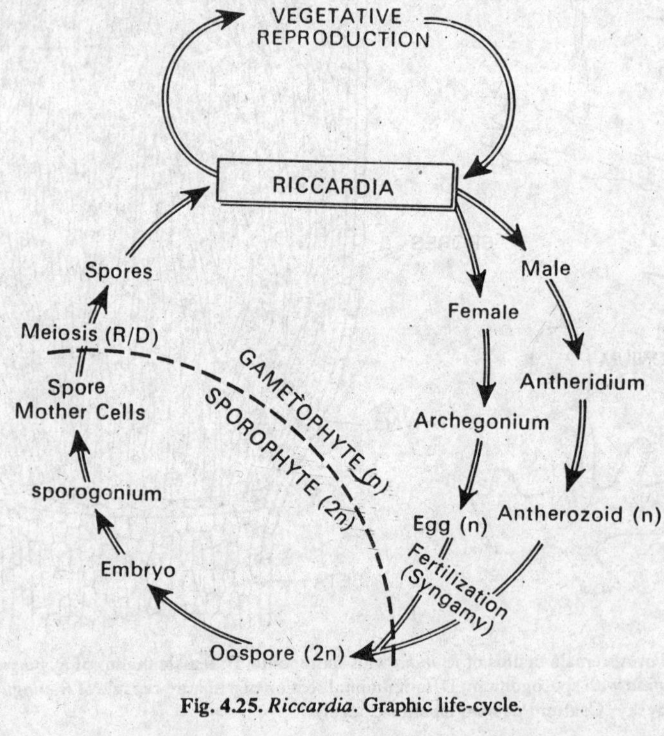

Fig. 4.25. *Riccardia*. Graphic life-cycle.

cell rows. The capsule remains surrounded by a two-celled thick jacket. The walls of the cells of the two layers of the jacket possess thickenings, except in four vertical strips of cells which make the future lines of dehiscence of the capsule. There is an apical elaterophore consisting of elongated cells which hangs downwards in the cavity of the capsule. There are two types of elaters found within the capsule-the **fixed elaters** which **radiate out from the elaterophore and remain fixed to it**, the others are **free elaters** which **remain scattered in the capsule** and they are pointed at both ends. Each free elater possesses **a broad** brown spiral band of thickening.

Dehiscence begins at the apex of a capsule and the four parts into which the capsule remains divided, each with a portion of the elaterophore, bend back with a jerk, expelling out the spores and elaters.

The spore and its germination. The spores are small and with two wall layers the outer wall layer is exine and the inner one is intine. The exine is nearly smooth, echinulate or granulose whereas the intine is always thin and smooth. The spore is uninucleate and possesses chloroplasts within it.

According to Showalter (1925) the germination of the spore is as follows-the spores germinate immediately after they are shed. It divides by a transverse wall into two cells, one large and the other small. The large cell does not divide further whereas the small cell divides again by a diagonally vertical wall forming a wedge shaped apical cell which initiates the formation of a new thallus immediately. Rhizoids appear quite early on the germling. They are borne towards the posterior end of it.

Systematic position. Division. Bryophyta
Class. Hepaticopsida
Order. Metzgeriales
Family. Riccardiaceae
Genus. *Riccardia.*

Family-Fossombronianceae

The gametophyte is distinctly foliose, *i.e.*, the gametophyte remains differentiated into stem and leaves. There are four genera-*Fossombronia, Simodon, Petalophyllum* and *Sewardiella.* Of these the genus *Fossombronia* is best known and widely distributed. The representative genus *Fossombronia* of this family has been described here in detail.

Genus FOSSOMBRONIA

Fossombronia, a widely distributed genus with some 50 species, of which *F. indica* and *F. himalayensis* are found in India. *F. indica* is found in Pachmari (M.P.) and South India, whereas *F. himalayensis* is common in the Himalayas (5000-7000 feet above sea level). Two other species namely *F. cristula* and *F. foreauii* have also been reported from India by Udar and Srivastava (1969) and Udar and Srivastava (1972) respectively.

THE GAMETOPHYTE

External structure. The gametophyte is distinctly foliose and remains differentiated into stem and leaves. The thallus is almost wholly prostrate and with a profuse branching. A branch is made up of a well-defined distinct stem which bears a single row of leaves along both lateral margins. The midrib is somewhat flattened on the upper side and convex on the lower side. In some species the leaves near the growing apex are vertically inserted whereas the margins of the lower leaves show overlapping where each leaf overlaps the anterior margin of the next older leaf, (*e.g.*, in *F. intestinealis*). In other species the leaves are convoluted, (*e.g.*, in *F. longiseta*).

Smooth walled, unicellular violet-coloured or hyaline rhizoids arise from the ventral face of the stem. The rhizoids anchor the plant to the substratum and absorb the food material from it. Near the apex of the plant there are multicellular mucilage hairs which overarch and protect the apical region. However, such hairs are not found on older parts of the stem. The tuberculate rhizoids and ventral scales are also not found.

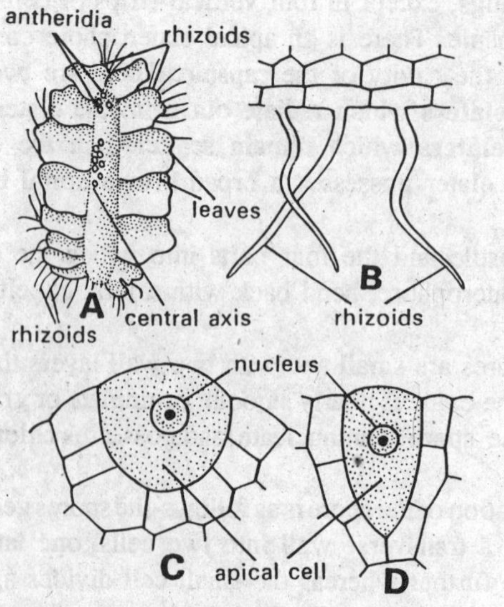

Fig. 4.26. *Fossombronia* sp. A, male plant (thallus) having antheridia, rhizoids and two lateral rows of leaf-like structures; B, smooth-walled rhizoids developed from lower epidermis of the central axis (mid-rib); C, apical cell with two cutting faces; D, lateral view of the apical cell.

The basal portion of a leaf is two or three cells in thickness, whereas in other parts it is one cell in thickness.

Internal structure of stem. It consists of isodiametric thin-walled parenchymatous cells. The sectional view of old thallus of *F. himalayensis* exhibits mycorrhiza.

Apical growth. The apical growth of the main axis and of its branches takes place by means of an apical cell. This apical cell has two cutting faces which cut off the segments alternately to left and right. As seen in vertical longitudinal section the apical cell is semicircular in outline, whereas in horizontal longitudinal section it appears triangular in outline. The first division in a segment cut off by an apical cell is horizontal and thus two daughter cells are formed. The ventral daughter

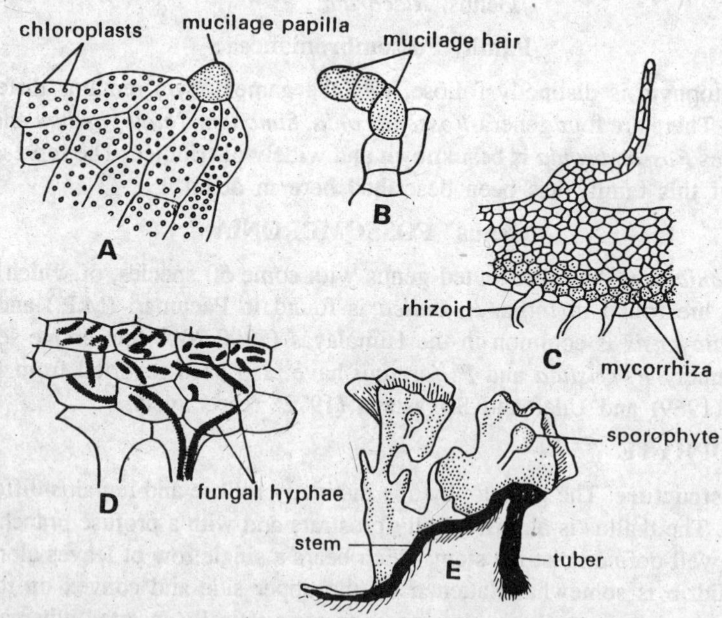

Fig. 4.27. *Fossombronia* sp. A, leaf cells with chloroplasts and a mucilage papilla; B, mucilage hair; C, sectional view of thallus showing rhizoids and mycorrhiza; D, part of thallus with few cells containing fungal hyphae (mycorrhiza); E, female plant with sporophyte, tuber and stem.

cell gives rise to the ventral portion of the stem. The dorsal daughter cell gives rise to the dorsal portion of the stem and to a leaf. This cell also divides horizontally, the upper daughter cell acts as the initial of a dorsal portion of the stem and the lower daughter cell acts as the initial cell of a leaf. However, branching does not take place by a vertical division of the apical cell into two cells, and therefore, true branching is not there. Instead a second apical cell is differentiated in a young segment derived from the apical cell. Thus, combined growth from the original apical cell and the newly formed one results in a false dichotomy, but appears as to be a true dichotomy.

Reproduction. The reproduction is *Fossombronia* takes place by means of vegetative and sexual methods.

1. Vegetative reproduction. It takes place by means of regeneration and tuber formation. In *F. himalayensis* sometimes a part of thallus decays from the posterior end, and the terminal or middle parts remain unaffected which grow separately into new thalli. The mucilage cells and the nucilage papillae help in withstanding the desiccation.

Some species of *Fossombronia* (*i.e., F. himalayensis* and *F. tuberifera*) develop tubers on them. The tubers develop at the apices of the branches of the thallus which face adverse conditions, and develop into new plants on the approach of favourable conditions.

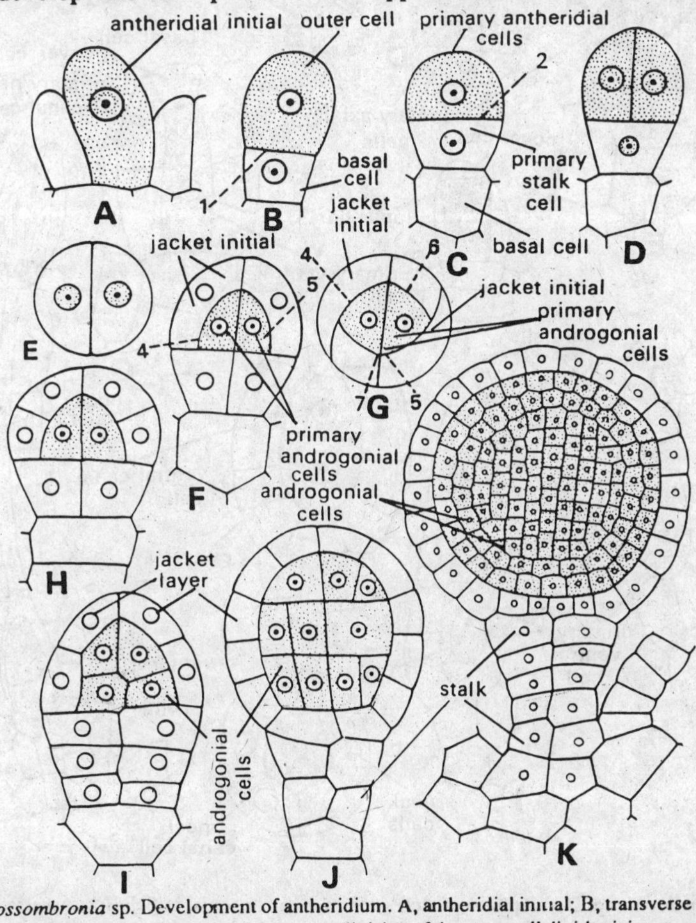

Fig. 4.28. *Fossombronia* sp. Development of antheridium. A, antheridial initial; B, transverse division of antheridial initial forming outer cell and basal cell; C, a second transverse division of the outer cell divides it into two equal upper and lower cells; D-J, further successive divisions in the development of antheridium; E and G, transverse divisions at different stages; K, nearly mature stalked antheridium surrounded by a jacket layer and containing androcytes.

2. Sexual reproduction. Majority of the species of *Fossombronia* (*e.g.*, *F. cristula*, *F. longiseta* etc.) are monoecious, *i.e.*, antheridia and archegonia are borne on the same thallus. The sex organs (*i.e.*, antheridia and archegonia) develop in acropetal succession on the dorsal side of the midrib. The sex organs occur scattered or in groups. Each sex organ develops from a single superficial cell found behind and quite near to the apical cell. The antheridia and archegonia develop simultaneously or one after other.

The antheridium. A mature antheridium of *Fossombronia* possesses a stalk and globular body. The stalk is composed of four rows of cells usually 4 or 5 cells high. The body of antheridium remains surrounded by a single layered jacket. The androcytes are found within the jacket. Each

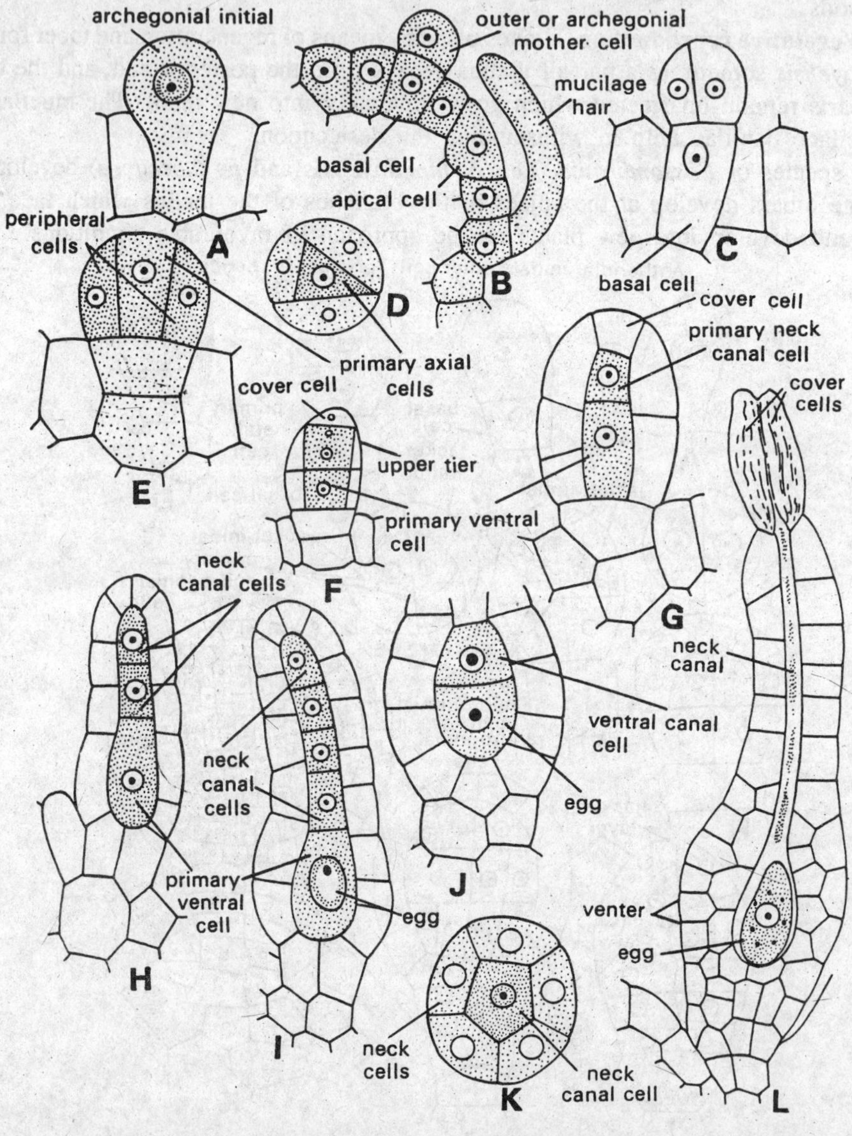

Fig. 4.29. *Fossombronia* sp. Development of archegonium. A, archegonial initial; B, transverse division of archegonial initial; C, first vertical division; D, cross-section of E; E, second and third vertical divisions; F, formation of cover cell; G, young archegonium having primary ventral cell, primary neck canal cell and cover cell; H-J, further development in archegonium; K, transverse section of archegonium; L, mature archegonium ready for fertilization

androcyte metamorphoses into a biciliate antherozoid. The antherozoids are relatively large and have the two flagella inserted at different points near the anterior end (Showalter, 1926). The antheridium bursts suddenly on its maturity, but this is not accompanied by an explosive discharge of the antherozoids.

Development of antheridium. The antheridium develops from a single superficial cell known as **antheridial initial.** This cell is derived from the lateral segment of the apical cell and is situated behind and quite close to it. The antheridial initial divides transversely forming two cells-the upper cell and the basal cell. Thereafter there is a second transverse division takes place in the outer cell forming two upper and lower equal daughter cells. The upper daughter cell acts as the **primary antheridial cell** while the lower one acts as the **primary stalk cell.** The third median vertical division takes place in both the cells and thus two terminal segments are derived from the primary antheridial cell. These cells look hemispherical in shape when seen in cross section. Each of these two daughter cells divides by a periclinal wall into two unequal cells. Thus two outer **jacket initials** and two inner **primary androgonial cells** are formed.

The two primary androgonial cells divide repeatedly forming a large number of **andro**-gonial cells. The last cell generation of the androgonial cells consists of the **androcyte mother cells.** Each androcyte mother cell divides diagonally forming two **androcytes.** **Each androcyte** metamorphoses into a biflagellate **antherozoid.** Simultaneously the jacket initials **divide anti**-clinally again and again forming a single layered jacket around the antheridium.

The primary stalk cell divides repeatedly and gives rise to the stalk of antheridium.

The archegonium. The archegonia are produced in groups on the upper surrace of the midrib near the apical cell protected by the young leaves. At the base of each such leaf the archegonia develop. A mature archegonium possesses six to eight neck canal cells surrounded by five vertical rows of neck cells. The venter of an archegonium is only slightly broader than the neck and has a jacket layer two cells in thickness.

Development of archegonium. Any superficial cell may act as an **archegonial initial.** It lies very near to apical cell. The archegonial initial enlarges, becomes papillate and divides by a transverse wall forming two cells-a **lower basal cell** and an **upper cell.** A second transverse division takes place in the basal cell and not in the upper cell. The upper cell acts as an **archegonial mother cell** and produces archegonium. This cell divides by three vertical walls which forms three peripheral cells, and an axial cell. Of the three peripheral cells one is much smaller and usually does not divide by a vertical wall while the remaining two larger peripheral cells divide by vertical walls forming five **jacket initials.** The central cell divides by a transverse wall forming a cap cell, and the central cell becomes enclosed in a ring of five jacket initials. Each jacket initial now divides transversely forming the

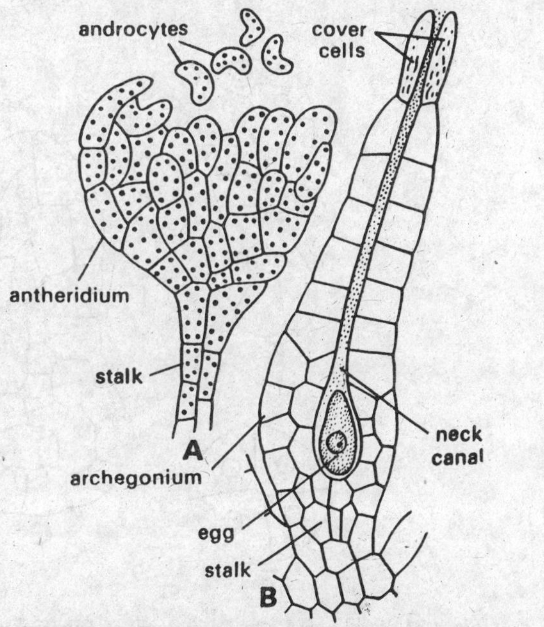

Fig. 4.30. *Fossombronia* **sp. Sex organs. A, dehiscence of antheridium, releasing out androcytes; B, mature archegonium, ready for fertilization.**

upper **neck initial** and the lower **venter initial.** The neck initials divide transversely forming a neck of five vertical rows of cells. The venter initial divides repeatedly forming the venter of the archegonium. The central cell within the venter now divides asymmetrically forming a small upper **ventral canal cell** and a large lower cell, the **egg** or **oosphere.** The peripheral cells of the venter divide tangentially forming a wall two cells in thickness. The neck surrounded by a tubular wall, one cell in thickness, encloses a long **neck canal,** occupied in the beginning by a row of thin walled neck canal cells. In the end, the cap cell divides into four **cover** or **lid cells.**

Fertilization or syngamy. As usual the water is essential for this process. The axial cells of the archegonium disorganize and mucilage is formed. The mucilage absorbs water, swells and thus forces open the neck of the archegonium by separating the cover cells. Meanwhile the cells of the antheridium take up water, swell and eventually burst the wall, liberating the antherozoids. The antherozoids make their way in the water film and enter the neck of the archegonium. One of the antherozoids penetrates the oosphere and thereafter loses its flagella. The fertilization is effected by the union of the nucleus of one antherozoid with that of the oosphere. The fertilized oosphere secrets a wall around it and in now called the **zygote** or **oospore.** The oospore contains 2n number of chromosomes. From the zygote onward the sporophytic stage begins.

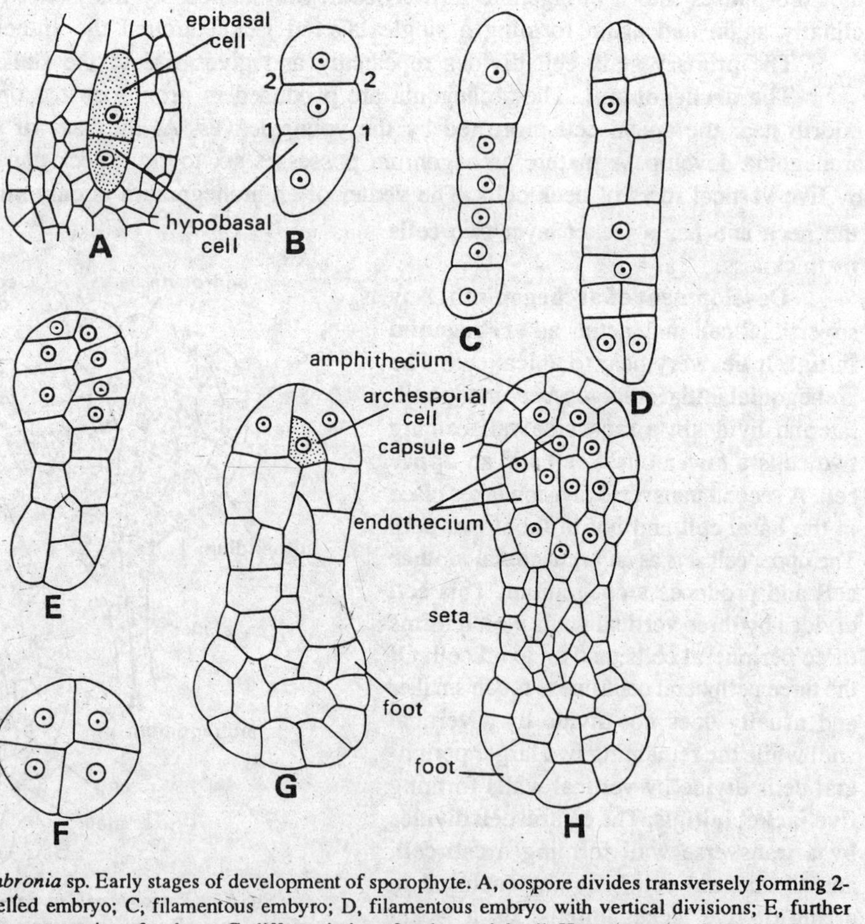

Fig. 4.31. *Fossombronia* sp. Early stages of development of sporophyte. A, oospore divides transversely forming 2-celled embryo; B, three-celled embryo; C, filamentous embyro; D, filamentous embryo with vertical divisions; E, further development of embryo; F, cross-section of embryo; G, differentiation of archesporial cell; H, young sporophyte showing the formation of foot, seta and capsule.

THE SPOROPHYTE

The oospore enlarges in size. The cells of the venter divide repeatedly forming a **calyptra,** which usually encloses the young sporogonium until the capsule is nearly mature.

Development of sporophyte (sporogonium). The enlarged oospore divides by a transverse wall into two cells. The **epibasal cell** and the **hypobasal cell.** The epibasal cell is somewhat larger than the hypobasal cell. The hypobasal cell eventually develops into the **foot** of a mature sporophyte. It does not contribute to the embryo proper. All the important changes and divisions take place in the epibasal cell. The entire sporogonium and its parts, *i.e.,* foot, seta and capsule are derived from the epibasal cell. Usually the epibasal cell divides transversely. The upper daughter cell eventually develops into the **capsule** and the lower one into the **seta** of a mature sporophyte (Chalaud, 1929-1931). However, in certain species there may be a vertical division of epibasal and hypobasal cells and then a transverse division of their daughter cells (Showalter, 1927). These four cells are now divided by vertical walls forming the two tiers of four cells each. The four lower cells divide and redivide to form the seta and the foot. The seta of the sporophyte remains about a millimeter in length until the spores are mature. Then it elongates rapidly and pushes the capsule through a calyptra to a considerable distance above the **perianth.**

On the other hand four upper cells divide periclinally thus separating the central **endothecium** from the peripheral **amphithecium.** The endothecium gives rise to **archesporium.** The cells of archesporium divide and redivide in an irregular way forming a mass of **sporogenous cells,** from which the **spores** are formed. Soon afterward the jacket layer becomes two-celled thick, and there may be further periclinal divisions in the apical portion of the jacket. Differentiation into elaters and sporocytes does not take place until the formation of last cell generation of

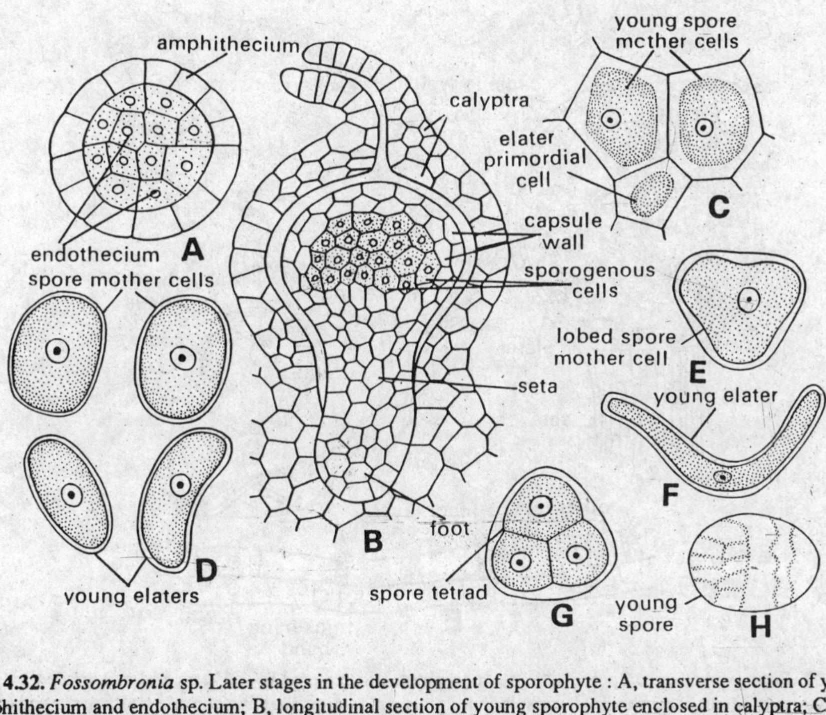

Fig. 4.32. *Fossombronia* sp. Later stages in the development of sporophyte : A, transverse section of young capsule showing amphithecium and endothecium; B, longitudinal section of young sporophyte enclosed in calyptra; C, young spore mother cells and elater primordial cells; D, spore mother cells and young elaters; E, lobed spore mother cell; F, young elater; G, spore tetrad; H, young spore.

sporogenous tissue. The sporogenous tissue becomes differentiated into two types of cells-the **spore mother cells and elater primordial cells.** The protoplasts of the sporogenous cells withdraw from the cell walls and become somewhat spherical, whereas the young elaters become somewhat elongated. Both develop their new walls. Elaters of *Fossombronia* have unusual characteristics that the thickening on their walls may be laid down in five to nine rings instead of usual two or three longitudinal spirals in other genera of the order. An elaterophore, if at all present is quite indistinct in structure.

Structure of sporophyte. The sporophyte of *Fossombronia* consists of foot, seta and capsule. The foot is haustorial in function. In some species the seta is short while in others it is long. The mature capsule is more or less spherical in shape. The wall that surrounds the capsule is two cells in thickness except at its apical end where it may be three cells in thickness. The spore chamber of the capsule contains spores and elaters. The elaterophore is absent. The mature sporophyte remains covered by a sheathing organ, the **perianth.** The young sporophyte is surrounded by a **calyptra.** The remnants of the calyptra may be seen within the perianth of mature sporophyte.

Sporogenesis. During the process of sporogenesis the spores are formed from **spore mother cells** (2n) by meiosis. The spore mother cells become four lobed. The lobes are arranged in tetrahedral way. The diploid (2n) nucleus divides meiotically forming four daughter nuclei and

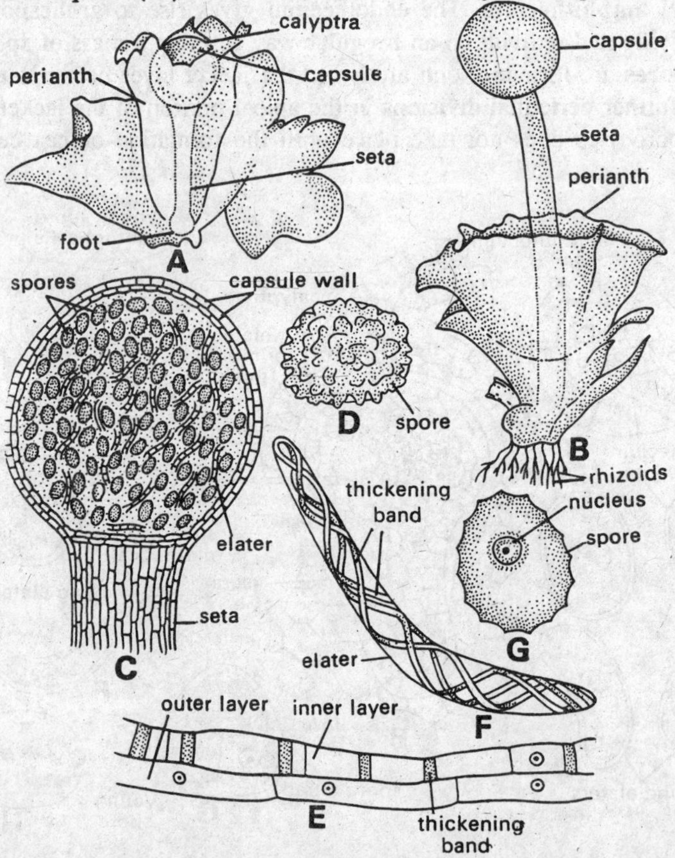

Fig. 4.33. *Fossombronia* sp. Sporophyte. A, sporophyte still covered by calyptra and surrounded by perianth; B, mature sporophyte coming out of perianth; C, capsule in longitudinal section showing capsule wall,spores and elaters within it; D, mature spore with rough surface having ridges and furrows; E, cpsule wall in longitudinal section showing thickening bands; F, an elater with three thickening bands; G, a nearly mature spore.

one of the daughter nuclei passes into each lobe. Ultimately these lobes are separated by cell walls in between them and a tetrad of haploid spores (n) is formed. It remains surrounded by a common sheath. The sheath ruptures and the ripe spores are separated from each other. The spore (n) denotes the beginning of the gemetophytic generation.

Dehiscence of the capsule. On maturity of the sporophyte the capsule bursts and the spores are dispersed. The dehiscence of the capsule takes place by the elongation of the seta. The seta elongates, ruptures the calyptra and carries the capsule up in the air. The wall of the capsule bursts forming four valves that spread out horizontally and the spores are liberated out. The separation of spores from one another is assisted by the hygroscopic nature of the elaters. During this process the elaters twist and turn rapidly and by means of this they stir up the spores and separate them from the exposed spore mass.

Germination of spore. The germination of a spore results in the formation of a protonema consisting of 2 to 12 cells in which the cells nearest the old spore wall often bear rhizoids. Thereafter the distal cell of protonema divides irregularly forming a globose mass of cells, one of which soon acts as an apical cell with two cutting faces (Chalaud, 1929-1931), which cut off segments right and left. For some time the segments cut off by the apical cell develop into a thalloid structure without any differentiation into stem and leaves. However, in the later formed portions of the thallus, the derivatives of each segment cut off by the apical cell differentiate into a leaf and a portion of the stem.

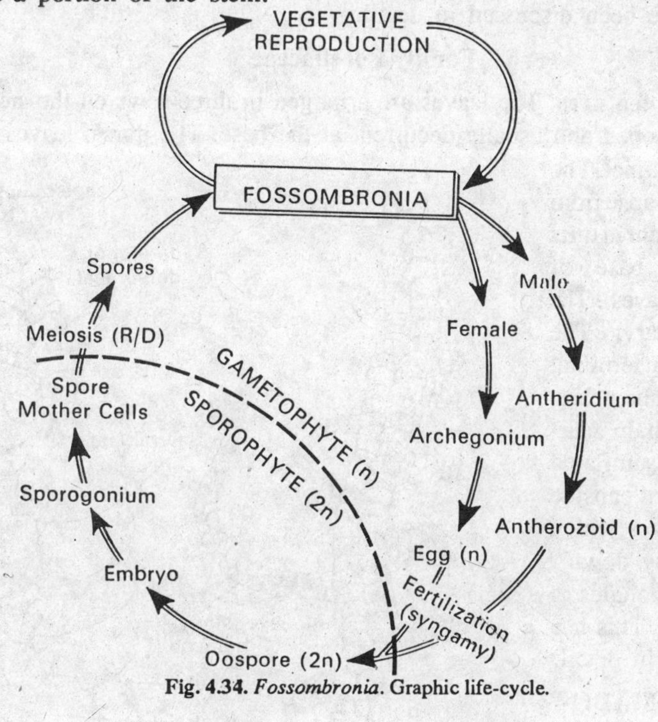

Fig. 4.34. *Fossombronia*. Graphic life-cycle.

Systematic position.	Division.	Bryophyta
	Class.	Hepaticopsida
	Order.	Metzgeriales
	Family.	Fossombroniaceae
	Genus.	*Fossombronia.*

5

Hepaticopsida

Order-Jungermanniales

The characteristic features of the order are as follows: The gametophyte is differentiated into stem and leaves. The leaves are borne in a regular spiral succession along the stem. The apical cell is pyramid-like with three cutting faces. The stem usually bears three rows of leaves. Two rows of leaves are lateral and consisting of leaves of normal size. The third row of leaves consists of the under leaves which are commonly smaller than the lateral leaves. The archegonia are always restricted to the apices of the axis and its branches. The last formed archegonium is developed from the apical cell itself. With the result of this acrogynous formation of archegonia, the sporophytes remain always terminal in position. The antheridia are borne singly or in groups in the axils of leaves.

There are about 220 genera and 8500 species in this order. According to Evans (1938) this order consists of seventeen families. Here the genus *Porella* of family Porellaceae and *Frullania* of Frullaniaceae have been discussed in detail.

Family-Porellaceae

Characteristic features. The leaves are arranged in three rows on the stem. The ventral leaves are well developed and usually decurrent at the base. The dorsal leaves are incubuous. The postical lobe is distinct. The rhizoids are scarce and arise from the lower side of the stem in tufts generally near the base of underleaves (ventral leaves). The antheridia are solitary. The archegonia are borne in terminal cluster on small lateral branches. The archegonia remain surrounded by a large, inflated perianth. The spherical capsule dehisces by four valves which split only to half way down.

This family includes a single genus *Porella*. This has been discussed here in detail.

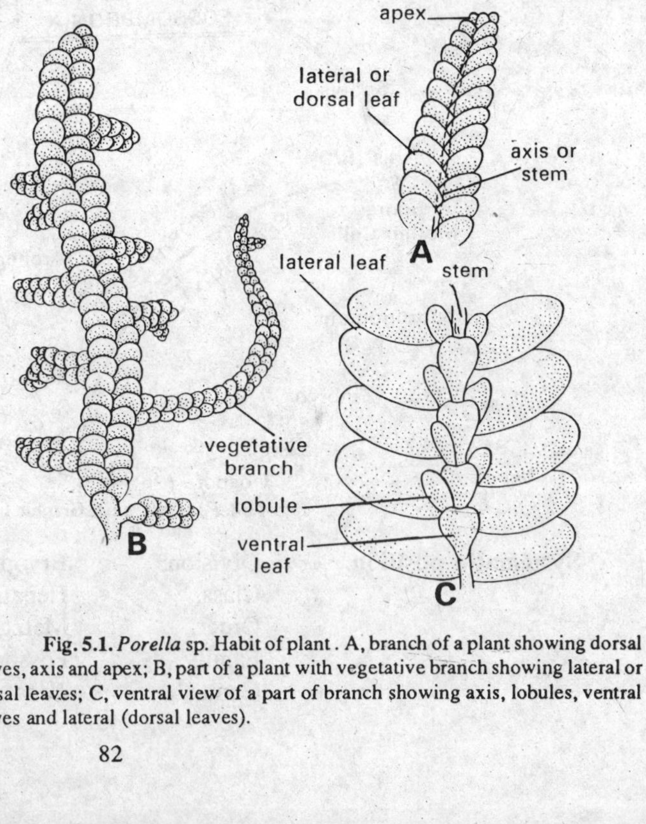

Fig. 5.1. *Porella* sp. Habit of plant. A, branch of a plant showing dorsal leaves, axis and apex; B, part of a plant with vegetative branch showing lateral or dorsal leaves; C, ventral view of a part of branch showing axis, lobules, ventral leaves and lateral (dorsal leaves).

Genus PORELLA (MADOTHECA)

Occurrence and distribution. There are about 180 species in this genus. These species are mainly distributed in tropical regions, but many of them are also found in temperate zones. *Porella platyphylla* is most widely distributed species and is found in Europe, America, Asia and India. About 34 species have been reported from our country. Of these twenty one species have been reported from Himalayas by Kashyap, and a few from South India (Chopra, 1943). *Porella* usually grows in moist and shady places. It grows on rocks, stones, on the bark of tree, trunks and sometimes even on soil. Occasionally they are found so abundantly that they cover the entire substratum on which they grow.

THE GAMETOPHYTE

Structure. The plant body is large, greenish and leafy. It is 15cm. or sometimes even more long. The plants grow in compact flat greenish patches covering the substratum. The plant body of gametophyte is dorsiventral. It consists of a branched central axis bearing leaves. The branching in *Porella* is monopodial. The stem bears three rows of leaves. There are two rows

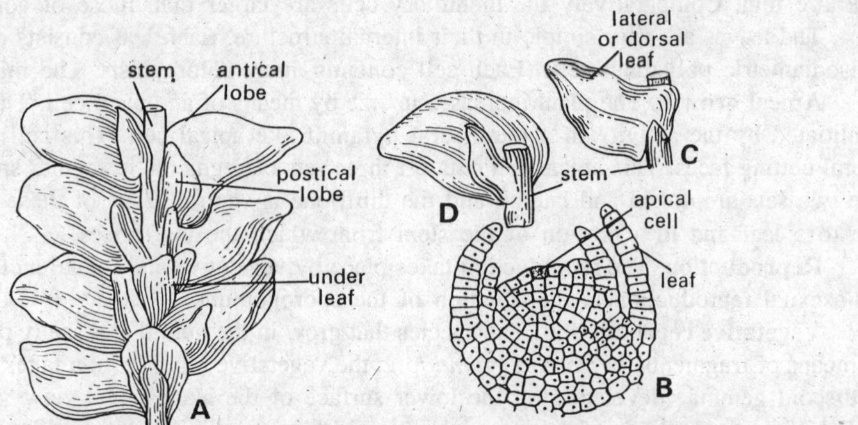

Fig. 5.2. *Porella* sp. Incubous leaves. A, incubous leaves seen from ventral side showing the under leaves and the antical and postical lobes of dorsal leaves; B, vertical section of shoot apex showing leaf and apical cell; C, lateral or dorsal leaf attached to the stem as seen from the above; D, lateral or dorsal leaf attached to the stem as seen from the ventral side.

of dorsal leaves and one row of ventral leaves. The dorsal leaves closely overlap each other and this way they cover the stem from above. The anterior edge of each leaf covers the posterior edge of the leaf next above it, when seen from above; such an overlapping arrangement of

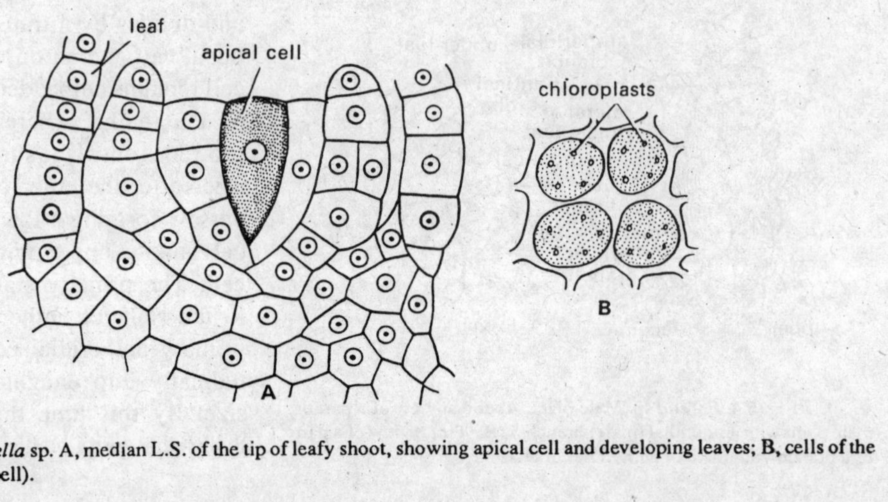

Fig. 5.3. *Porella* sp. A, median L.S. of the tip of leafy shoot, showing apical cell and developing leaves; B, cells of the stem. (A, after Campbell).

the leaves is known as incubous arrangement. Each dorsal leaf is bilobed and the lobes are unequal in size, of the two lobes the larger (antical) lobe is usually ovate and possesses a rounded apex. The much smaller postical lobe is known as **lobule;** it is narrow and acute at the apex; it appears like a separate leaf. The postical lobe (lobule) remains more or less parallel to the stem and frequently decurrent at the external base. The small leaves of the ventral row are designated as **amphigastria.** The amphigastria resemble the postical lobe (lobule) of the dorsal leaves but they are broader and frequently decurrent on both the sides at the base.

A larger number of rhizoids are found to be scattered on the lower side of the stem. The main function of the rhizoids is to anchor the plant to the substratum. The absorption of water takes place directly through the leaf and stem cells.

Anatomy. The young stem of *Porella* is very simple in its structure and shows little differentiation of tissues. The cell walls of cortical cells are thick; and the cell walls of medullary cells are thin. Comparatively the medullary cells are larger than those of cortical cells.

The leaves are very simple in their internal structure. Each leaf consists of the thin plate of isodiametric polygonal cells. Each cell contains many chloroplasts. The midrib is lacking.

Apical growth. The plant increases in size by means of an apical cell. The apical growth is initiated by the activity of a tetrahedral pyramid like apical cell. This cell possesses three lateral cutting faces. This apical cell cuts off three sets of segments in regular spiral succession. The two sets are dorsal and lateral, and the third one is ventral. Each of these segments gives rise to a leaf and to a portion of the stem from which the leaf arises.

Reproduction. The reproduction takes place by vegetative and sexual methods. However, the asexual reproduction is the function of the sporogonium.

Vegetative reproduction. The species that grow in the humid and shady places reproduce by means of fragments. In *Porella rotundifolia* the vegetative reproduction takes place by means of discoid gemmae developed on the lower surface of the leaves; this view was propounded by Schiffner on the basis of the material collected from Brazil; but later on Degenkolbe (1938) did not find the gemmae in Schiffner's material and he concluded that these thin walled discoid bodies were blue green algae and not gemmae.

Sexual reproduction. *Porella* is dioecious. The male and female plants are easily recognizable. The male plants are smaller than the female ones. The antheridia and archegonia are borne on short side branches. The male branches arise at right angles from the main stem.

Development of antheridium. Each antheridium develops from a superficial dorsal cell which functions as an **antheridial initial.** The antheridial initial forms a papillate protrusion and divides by a transverse wall into a **basal cell** and an **outer cell.** The basal cell remains embedded within the tissue of the thallus whereas the outer cell protrudes out of the surface of the thallus. Thereafter the outer cell divides transversely forming a lower **primary stalk cell** and the upper **primary antheridial cell.** The primary stalk cell gives rise to the stalk of antheridium, while the primary antheridial cell divides longitudinally into daughter cells of equal size. By this time the dorsal cells of thallus that surround the antheridium divide

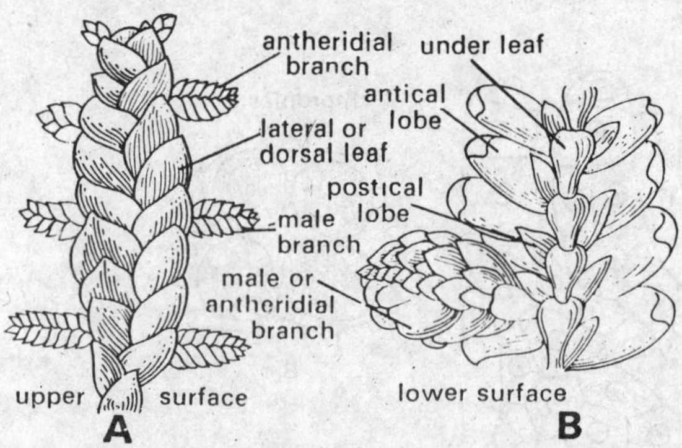

Fig. 5.4. *Porella* sp. Male plant. A, dorsal view of a part of male plant with antheridial (male) branches; B, ventral view of a part of a branch with male or antheridial branch.

again and again forming a ring-like involucre which opens on the dorsal surface of the thallus.

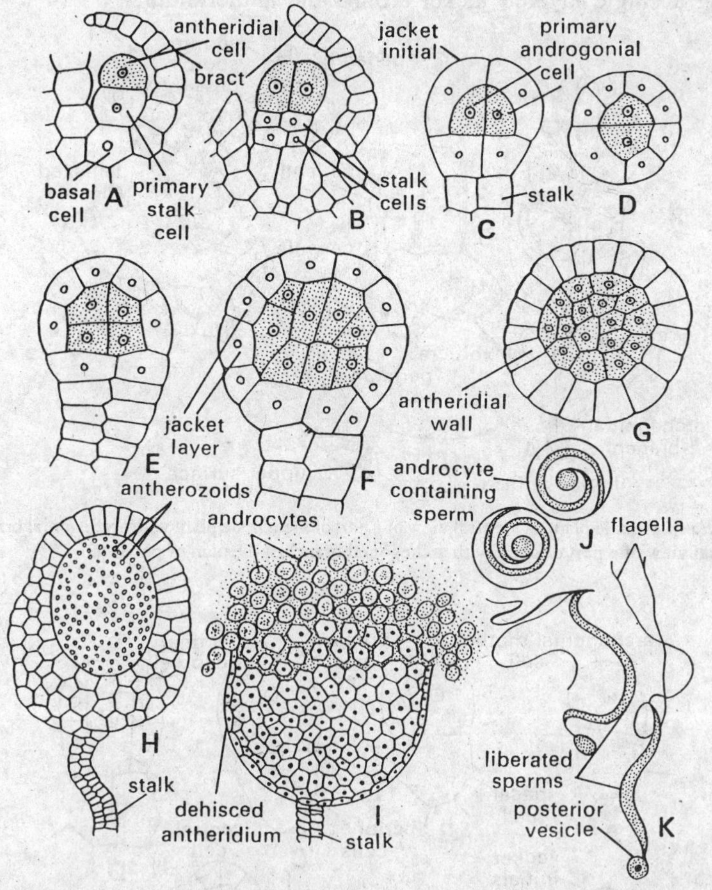

Fig. 5.5. *Porella* sp. Development of antheridium. A, antheridial initial and stalk cell; B-G, further successive stages in the development of antheridium; D and G, cross sections of developing antheridium at different stages; H, mature antheridium; I, dehisching antheridium; J, androcyte containing sperm; K, liberated biflagellate sperms.

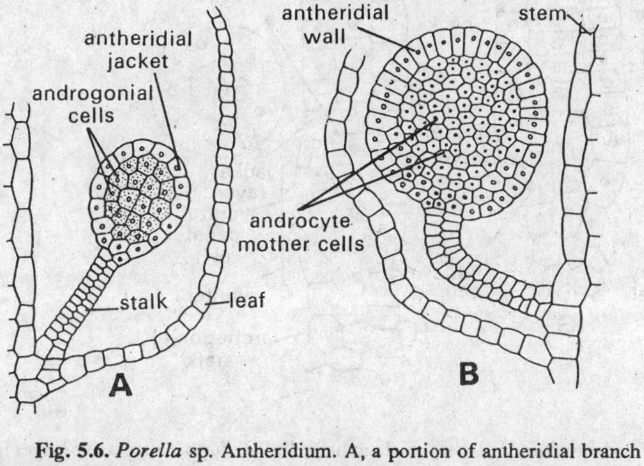

Fig. 5.6. *Porella* sp. Antheridium. A, a portion of antheridial branch showing young antheridium in the axil of leaf; B, a nearly mature antheridium in the axil of leaf.

Each of these two daughter cells developed from the primary antheridial cell divides by a periclinal wall into two unequal cells. This way, the outer **jacket initials** and two inner **primary androgonial** cells are formed.

The two primary androgonial cells divide again and again resulting in a large number of androgonial cells. The last cell generation of the cells is called the **androcyte mother cell.** Each androcyte mother cell divides diagonally forming two **androcytes.** Each androcyte metamorphoses into an antherozoid. Simultaneously the jacket initials divide anticlinally again and again forming a single layered jacket around the antheridium.

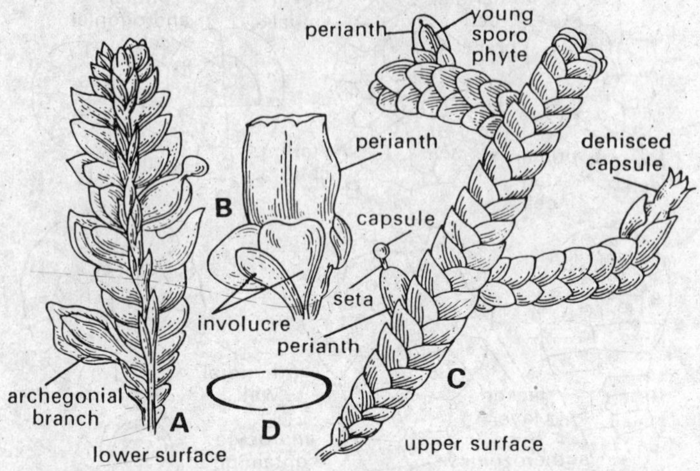

Fig. 5.7. *Porella* sp. Female plant. A, ventral view of a part of the female plant with archegonial branches; B, enlarged female branch; C, dorsal view of a part of plant with archegonial branches; D, plan of perianth.

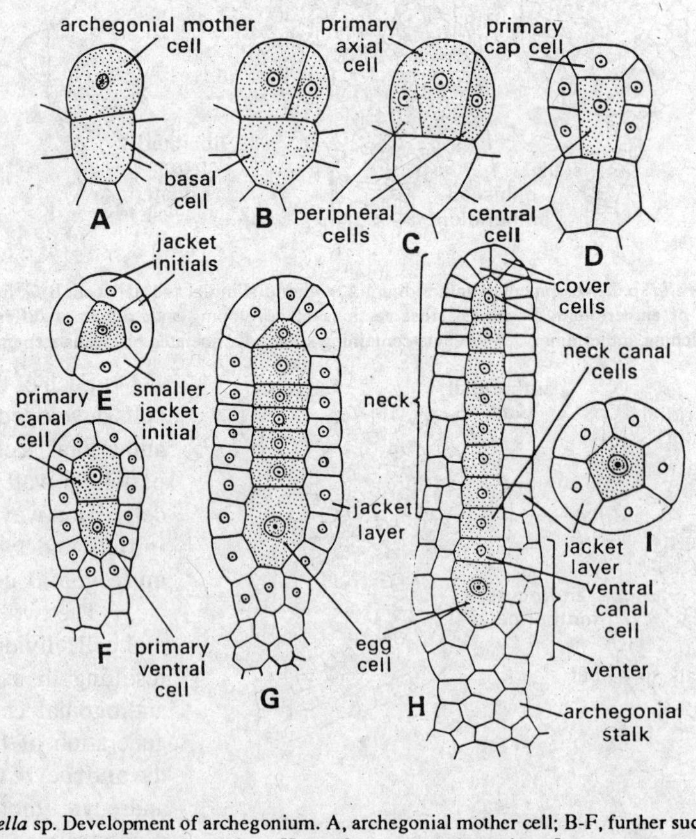

Fig. 5.8. *Porella* sp. Development of archegonium. A, archegonial mother cell; B-F, further successive stages in the development of archegonium; G, young archegonium; H, nearly mature archegonium; I, transverse section of archegonium.

Structure of mature antheridium. A mature antheridium of *Porella* possesses a long stalk and globular body. The stalk is composed of two rows of cells. The body of antheridium remains surrounded by a single-layered jacket in its upper part while 2 to 3 layered jacket in its basal part. The androcytes are found within the jacket. Each androcyte metamorphoses into a biciliate antherozoid.

The mature antheridium dehisces in a very characteristic manner. The upper part of the antheridial jacket is thinner than that of the basal part. On access of water the upper part of antheridium bursts open by a number of irregular lobes which curl back strongly. The whole mass of androcytes is escaped out into the water that causes the rupture. Thereafter the antherozoids liberate from the androcytes and swim to the water with the help of their cilia.

The archegonial branch. The archegonia are produced on the lateral branches of plants other than antheridial branches. These branches are much less distinct than the antheridial branches. The archegonia remain situated at the apex of the archegonial branch. There are four or five leaves on each archegonial branch. The apical cell of an archegonial branch cuts off two or three segments in the same manner as in the vegetative branch; these segments develop leaves. Thereafter each segment cut off by an apical cell divides into an inner (basal) and outer (distal) cell. The distal cell acts as the mother cell of the archegonium. The first formed few archegonia arise in acropetal order and ultimately the apical cell of the branch also acts as an archegonial initial and this way the further growth of archegonial branch is checked.

Development of archegonium. The development of archegonium is in a manner characteristic of the Jungermanniales as described in *Pellia* on page 60.

Structure of mature archegonium. The mature archegonium possesses a neck which is composed of five vertical rows of cells. The neck contains within it 6 to 8 neck canal cells. The wall of venter is two-layered. It encloses the small oosphere (egg) and a ventral canal cell.

Fertilization. On the access of water the mature archegonium opens at its tip and the cover cells separated from each other. The antherozoids from the antheridia of male plants are carried to the archegonia of the female plants through the agency of water. To facilitate this process the male and female plants grow in close vicinity in the dense patches closely covering the substratum. The antherozoid reaches the egg and fertilization takes place. This process results in the formation of zygote (oospore).

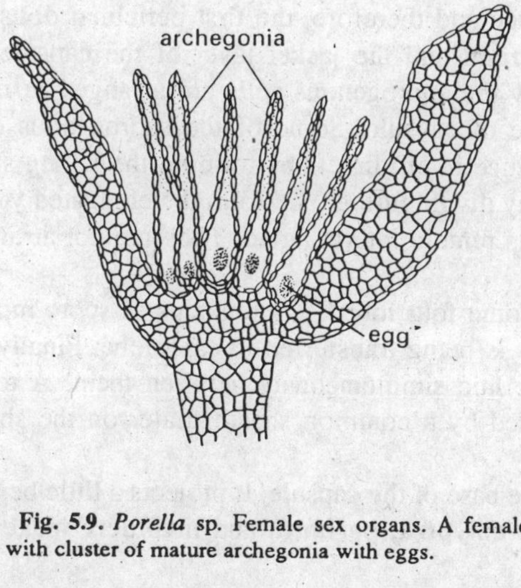

Fig. 5.9. *Porella* sp. Female sex organs. A female branch with cluster of mature archegonia with eggs.

THE SPOROPHYTE

Development of sporogonium. The zygote secrets a wall and increases in size. It divides by a transverse wall into two halves. The upper cell is called **epibasal cell** and lower cell the **hypobasal cell.** Thereafter the epibasal cell again divides by a transverse wall resulting into two cells. At this stage the young embryo is composed of three cells. The hypo-basal cell does not divide anymore and develops into a **haustorium or suspensor.** The whole sporogonium develops from the two cells formed by the transverse division of cell. Subsequently the vertical and transverse divisions take place in these two cells. These divisions are in irregular sequence and, therefore, the limits of the primary segments are less distinct. It is also difficult to demarcate between seta and capsule and the number of segments which make the capsule cannot be known with certainty. Campbell reports that in the terminal segments of the embryo the first periclinal

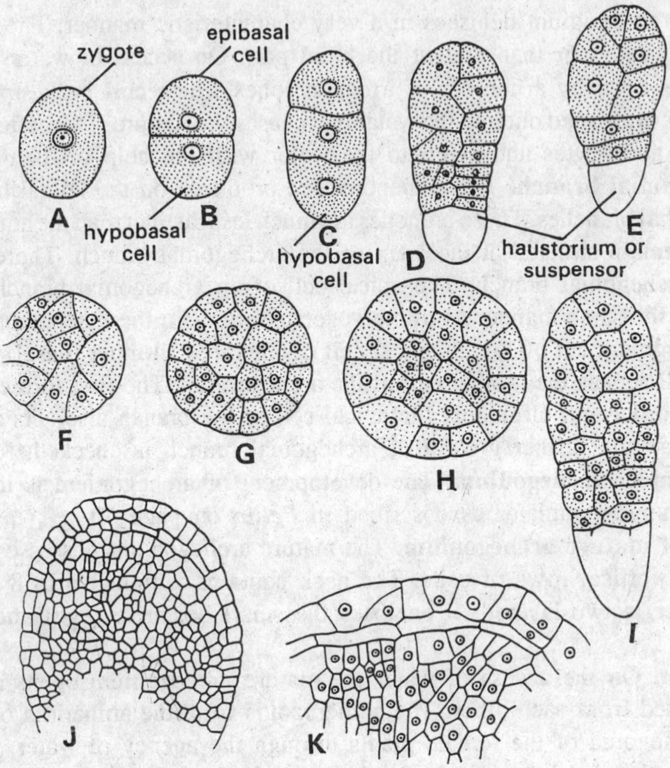

Fig. 5.10. *Porella* sp. Development of sporophyte. A, zygote; B, transversely divided zygote with epibasal and hypobasal cells; C-I, further successive stages in the development of sporophyte; F-H, cross sections at different stages; I, embryo with a mass of undifferentiated cells; J-K, further advanced stages of development of embryo (sporophyte)

walls appear at different distances from the surface and therefore, the first periclinal divisions do not determine differentiation of the archesporium and the jacket layer of the capsule. At a later stage these regions are well defined. Now the sporogenous cells are arranged in more or less marked rows radiating out from the base of capsule. Some of the sporogenous cells do not divide further and grow in a regular sequence in all directions forming the young spore mother cells. The remaining sporogenous cells may divide further and form the elongated young elaters. The spore mother cells and the elater cells remain intermingled. They are not arranged in a definite or regular order.

Prior to meiosis the spore mother cells become four lobed. The nucleus of spore mother cell divides meiotically and one daughter nucleus is being transferred to each lobe. Finally the lobes are being separated by cell wall which are laid simultaneously between them. A tetrad of haploid spores is formed. It remains surrounded by a common sheath. Later on the sheath breaks and the ripe spores are separated.

The seta is short. It merges gradually into the base of the capsule. It projects a little beyond the surrounding protective sheath. In *Porella,* the **calyptra, perianth** and **involucre** make this protective sheath. The calyptra is several-layered thick. The perianth is developed by the coalescence of two distal bracts just below the cluster of archegonia. The involucre is formed by

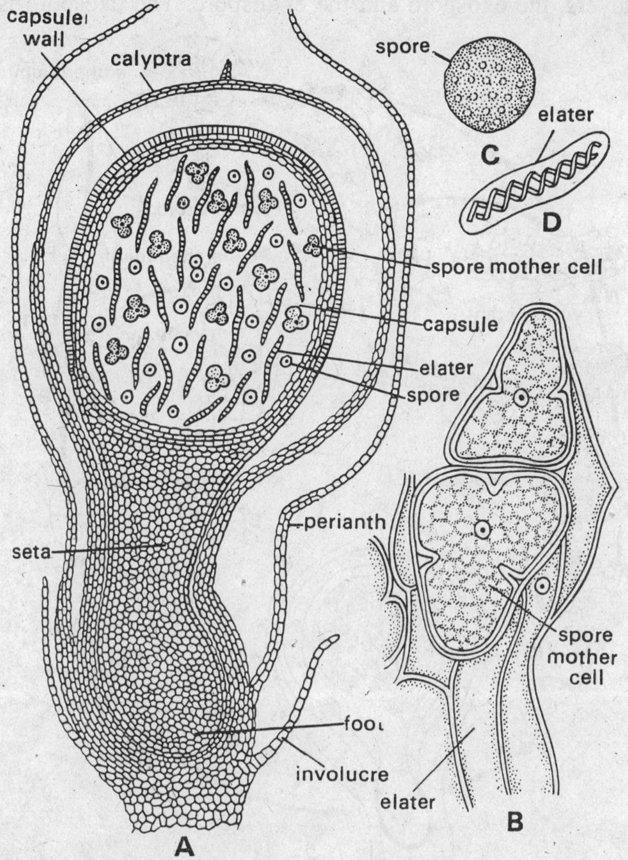

Fig. 5.11. *Porella* sp. Sporophyte. A, longitudinal section of nearly mature sporogonium showing foot, seta and capsule; B, enlarged lobed spore mother cells and elater cells within sporogonium; C, single mature spore; D, single elater showing double spiral band.

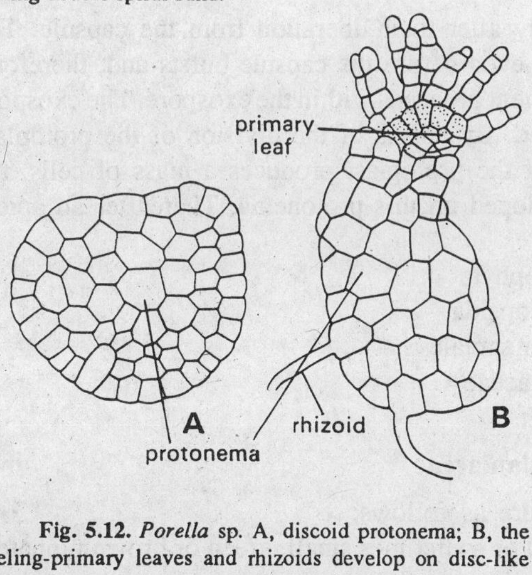

Fig. 5.12. *Porella* sp. A, discoid protonema; B, the sporeling-primary leaves and rhizoids develop on disc-like protonema.

the enlarged bracts which surround the base of the perianth. The foot is inconspicuous and is simply a somewhat enlarged portion of the seta.

Structure of mature sporogonium. The sporogonium consists of an inconspicuous foot, short seta and a globular capsule. The jacket of capsule is two to four-layered thick. The capsule contains within it short elaters and the spores.

Dehiscence of the capsule. On the maturity of the spores the seta elongates, and with the result, the protective sheath consisting of calyptra, perianth and involucre, ruptures. The capsule then ruptures by four valves releasing the spores outside. The hygroscopic movements of the elaters help in thrusting away the spores to some distance.

The spore and its germination. The spores are .03 to .05 mm in diameter. The spore wall consists of two layers, the exospore and the endospore. The exospore is either smooth or echinulate.

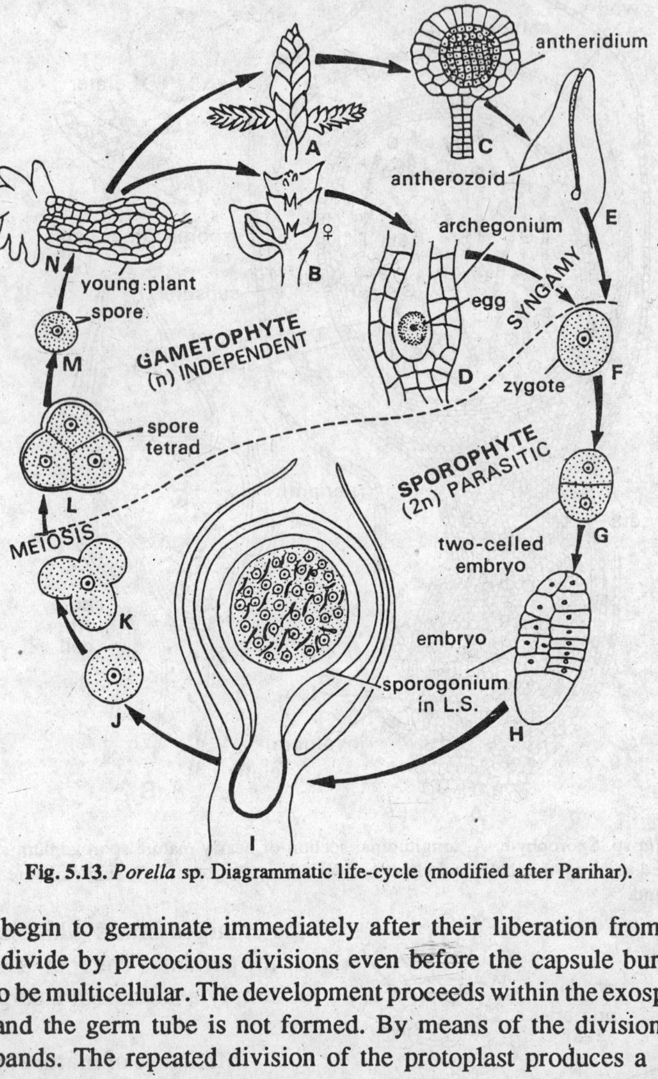

Fig. 5.13. *Porella* sp. Diagrammatic life-cycle (modified after Parihar).

The spores begin to germinate immediately after their liberation from the capsule. The spores of *Porella* divide by precocious divisions even before the capsule bursts and, therefore, the spores appear to be multicellular. The development proceeds within the exospore. The exospore does not rupture and the germ tube is not formed. By means of the division of the protoplast the endospore expands. The repeated division of the protoplast produces a mass of cells, the **protonema.** One or more rhizoids may be developed on this protonema. Thereafter an apical cell is formed at the edge of the protonema.

Systematic position. Division. Bryophyta
Class. Hepaticopsida
Order. Jungermanniales
Family. Porellaceae
Genus. *Porella.*

Family-Frullaniaceae

The characteristic features of the family are as follows:

1. The family comprises of medium-sized or sometimes small, green or brown pinnately

branched foliose liverworts.

2. The leaves are arranged on the stem in three rows. The two rows consist of dorsolateral leaves. The leaves do not have any midrib, and they are only one cell in thickness. The third row consisting of small leaves is found on the ventral side of the stem; they are called amphigastria or underleaves. The lateral leaves are arranged quite close to each other; they are imbricate,

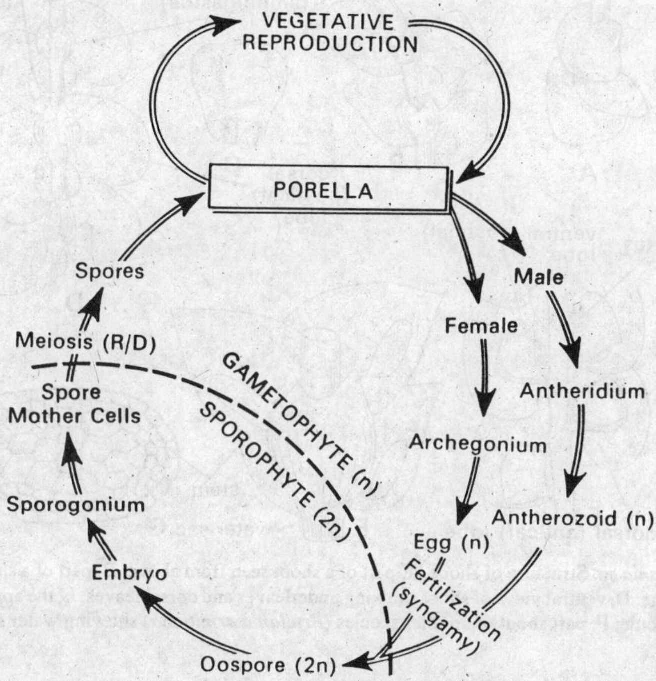

Fig. 5.14. *Porella*. Graphic life-cycle.

incubous and bi-lobed; the upper large lobe is called antical lobe, and the lower small lobe is known as lobule.

3. The unbranched, single-celled and smooth walled rhizoids are developed from the base or middle part of the underleaf.

4. The antheridia are situated on short lateral branches known as male branches or androecia. The archegonia are found in groups at the apices of short lateral branches; the cluster of archegonia remains covered by a protective envelope, the perianth.

The best known genus of this family is *Frullania*.

Genus FRULLANIA

This genus includes about 700 species, of which 39 species have been recorded from India (R.S. Chopra, 1943).

Distribution and habitat. Most of the species are found in tropical and sub-tropical regions. They may grow on wet soil (terrestrial species), on moist rocks, on moist tree trunks (epiphytes) or on leaf surfaces (epiphyllophytes). They grow quite close to each other and form brown, reddish brown or dark brown mats.

THE GAMETOPHYTE

External structure of the thallus (adult gemetophyte). The gametothallus of *Frullania* is a dorsiventral, pinnately branched leafy axis. The axis is pinnately or bipinnately branched. The leaves on the axis are being arranged in three rows-two dorsolateral rows and a row of ventral underleaves, the amphigastria. The dorsolateral leaves are unequally bilobed, and photosynthetic in function. The lateral leaves are incubously arranged. Each lateral leaf is bilobed. The dorsal

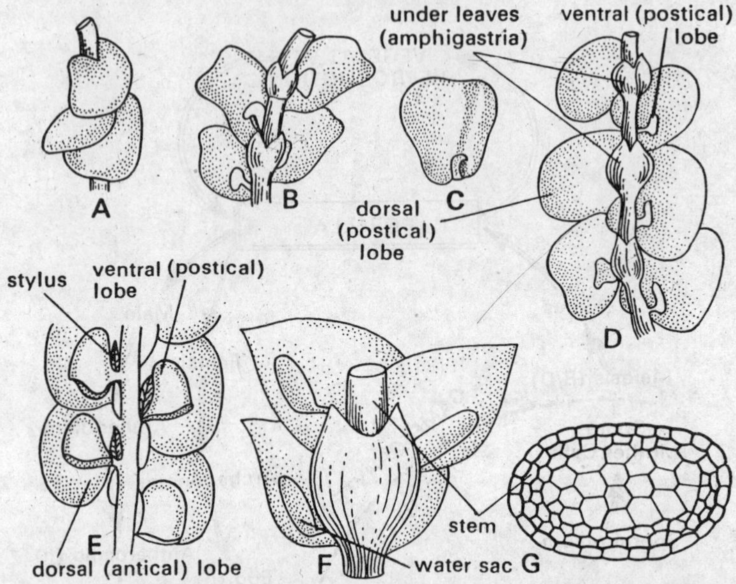

Fig. 5.15. *Frullania* sp. Structure of shoot. A, part of a shoot seen from above; B, part of a shoot seen from below; C, dorsal leaf with appendage; D, ventral view of shoot showing underleaves and dorsal leaves; E, the appendage known as stylus lies between stem and lobule; F, part shoot of another species (*Frullania armitiana*) showing water sacs on lateral leaves; G, cross section of stem.

lobe is known as antical lobe while the small ventral lobe is called ventral or postical lobe (lobule). The two lobes are free from each other. The antical or larger lobe is somewhat ovate or suborbicular in shape. This is without any midrib. The small postical lobe or lobule is hood-shaped. In certain species the lobules assume the different shapes such as saccate or bladder like. Thus the lobules can retain water in them and face the drought conditions. In some species each lobule (postical lobe) bears a membranous stylus at the junction between the lobule and the axis. The stylus is one cell in thickness and consists of several rows of cells.

Generally the amphigastria are smaller than the leaves. Each amphigastrium is provided with a rounded or cordate base and a retuse or bifid apex. The amphigastria and the stylus together make some capillary spaces which retain water in them. The smoothwalled, unicellular and unbranched rhizoids arise from the midbase of the amphigastria, which anchor the gametothallus to the substratum. There is typical branching which is called *Frullania* type. The branch develops from the apical cell of the lateral segment of the lobule.

Internal Structure

Anatomy of stem. The internal structure of axis is quite simple. The cells of the outer region are small, brown and thickwalled, which make the cortex. The epidermis is not very well distinguished. The cells of the central region of the axis are large and thinwalled, and make the medulla. The cells of medullary region do not have any pigments. There is no central strand or conducting tissue in the axis.

Anatomy of leaf. The leaves are unistratose, and consist of one row of cells. The cells contain several chloroplasts and 3-8 spherical or globular oil bodies. In some species (*e.g., F. tamarisci* and *F. asagrayana*), the hyaline large cells known as **ocelli** are found in a row on the lobe. The leaf has no midrib.

Apical growth. The apical growth of the plant takes place by the activity of a tetrahedral apical cell. The apical cell has three cutting faces. Two segments are dorsal and the third is ventral. The derivatives of the segment on the ventral surface form amphigastria and the derivatives of the dorsal segments form portion of axis and lateral leaves.

Reproduction

Reproduction takes place by means of vegetative and sexual methods.

Vegetative reproduction. By the death and decay of older parts of the thallus, the **fragments** are formed, each fragment develops into a new plant.

In certain species (*e.g., F. dilatata*) 4-6 celled gemmae develop on the margin of leaves. Each such gemma gives rise to a new plant.

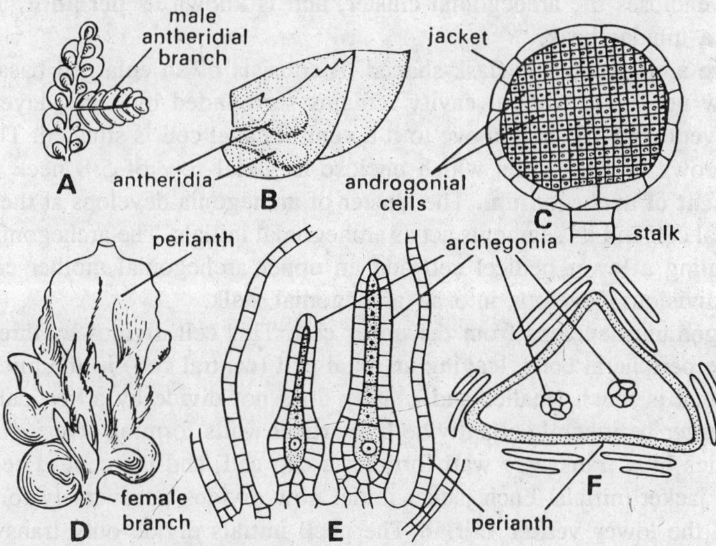

Fig. 5.16. *Frullania* sp. Sex organs. A, part of a male plant with antheridial branch; B, antheridia arising in the axil of a perigonial bract; C, nearly mature antheridium in longitudinal section; D, female branch with perianth as seen ventrally; E, longitudinal section of perianth with archegonia; F, transverse section of perianth with two archegonia.

In certain species (*e.g., F. brittoniae, F. reparia* and *F. plana*) the vegetative reproduction takes place by means of caducous leaves and adventitious branches. In *F. fragilifolia* the propagules are formed. Each propagule develops into a new plant.

Sometimes in *F. dilatata* one to several celled tubercula are developed on the surface of perianth. Each such outgrowth develops into a new plant on shedding.

Sexual reproduction. The species of *Frullania* may be monoecious or dioecious. The antheridia and archegonia develop on separate special lateral branches. All monoecious species are autoicous where the male and female sex organs are borne on separate branches of the same plant.

The leaves associated with the sex organs are known as **bracts.** The bracts found on the male branch are called the **perigonial bracts** while that present on the female branch are **perichaetial bracts.**

The antheridia. The antheridia develop in the axil of concave, close set perigonial bracts. Each male branch bears 2-5 pairs of perigonial bracts. The perigonial bracts are bilobed. Both lobes are almost equal in size. The branches of limited growth on which the antheridia occur are known as **androecia.** Generally two antheridia are developed in the axil of each perigonial bract.

The mature antheridium consists of a long stalk and a spherical body. The stalk is made up of two rows of cells. The body of antheridium has a single sterile layer that encloses a mass of **androcyte mother cells.** Each androcyte mother cell divides diagonally into two **androcytes.** Each androcyte metamorphoses into a biflagellate antherozoid.

The development of antheridium is similar to that of *Porella.*

The archegonia. The archegonia develop in groups at the apices of short lateral branches. Two to four archegonia are found in a cluster. The archegonial cluster remains surrounded by 2-5 pairs of perichaetial bracts. The perichaetial bracts are dentate and larger than the foliage leaves. The uppermost perichaetial bracts become fused together forming a common protective envelope which encloses the archegonial cluster, and is known as **perianth.** The apex of the perianth makes a tubular beak.

The mature archegonium is flask-shaped. It consists of an enlarged basal venter and an elongated narrow neck. The ventral cavity remains surrounded by a two-layered wall. There is an egg in the venter cavity, and above to it a ventral canal cell is situated. The neck consists of five vertical rows of neck cells which enclose an axial row of 5-8 neck canal cells.

Development of archegonium. The cluster of archegonia develops at the apex of female branch. The apical cell and its segments act as archegonial initials. The archegonial initial divides transversely forming a lower pedicel cell and an upper archegonial mother cell. The pedicel cell by further divisions develops into an archegonial stalk.

The archegonium develops from the upper cell. This cell divides by three vertical walls which form three peripheral cells, leaving an axial cell (central cell) in the middle of the three peripheral cells one is much smaller and usually does not divide by a vertical wall while the remaining two larger peripheral cells divide by vertical walls forming five **jacket initials.** The central cell divides by a transverse wall forming a cap cell, and the central cell gets enclosed in a ring of five jacket initials. Each jacket initial now divides transversely forming the upper **neck initial** and the lower **venter initial.** The neck initials divide only transversely forming a neck of five vertical rows of cells. The venter initials divide repeatedly and form the venter of the archegonium. The central cell of the venter now divides unequally, forming a small, upper **ventral canal cell** and a large lower cell, the **egg** or **oosphere.** The peripheral cells of the venter divide tangentially forming a wall two cells thick. The neck surrounded by a tubular wall, one cell thick, encloses a long **neck canal,** occupied in the beginning by a row of thin walled 5-8 neck canal cells. Finally the cap cell divides into four cover or **lid cells.**

Fertilization or syngamy. As usual the water (rain or dew) is essential for this process. The axial cells of the archegonium disorganise and mucilage is formed. The mucilage absorbs water, swells and thus forces open the neck of the archegonium by separating the cover cells. Meanwhile the cells of the antheridium take up water, swell and eventually burst the wall, liberating the antherozoids. These antherozoids make their way in the water film and enter the neck of the archegonium. One of the antherozoids penetrates the oosphere and thereafter loses its flagella. The fertilization is effected by the union of the nucleus of one antherozoid with that of the oosphere. The fertilized oosphere secrets a wall around it and is called the **zygote or oospore** the zygote contains 2n number of chromosomes.

THE SPOROPHYTE

Development of sporogonium. The zygote divides by a transverse wall into two cells- an upper **epibasal** half and a lower **hypobasal** half.

The epibasal half divides twice by transverse walls whereas the lower half (hypobasal) divides by a vertical wall. The epibasal cells divide successively by two vertical divisions at right angles to each other, forming three tiers of four cells each in the epibasal half. The two hypobasal cells divide again by a vertical wall at right angles to the first. Thus the hypobasal half consists of a tier of four cells. At this stage the young sporophyte consists of four tiers of cells; each tier is made up of four cells. The main **capsule** is derived from the upper epibasal tier; the **seta** is derived from the median epibasal tier and the **foot** from the lower epibasal tier. The cells of the hypobasal tier divide repeatedly in irregular manner producing a haustorium. The foot is haustorial and derives food from the gametophytic tissue. The cells of the middle tier divide repeatedly forming a broad seta and upper portion of foot. The cells of the upper tier divide periclinally and the outer four cells are known as **amphithecium** which enclose the four inner cells called the **endothecium** and which act as **archesporium.** The amphithecial cells first divide anticlinally and then periclinally in each cell forming a two-layered wall of the capsule. The wall of capsule remains incomplete, and it makes an arched structure, thus the capsule remains half spherical. The cells of outer layer possess rod-like thickening and that of inner layer have sheet-like thickening band.

The cells of endothecium (*i.e.*, archesporium) divide again and again longitudinally producing the sporogenous tissue which consists of a lens-shaped mass of elongated cells. This sporogenous mass is generally made up of two hundred cells. Here the central cells are longer than the peripheral cells. The sporogenous cells become differentiated into two kinds of cells. About half of these cells remain sterile and form elaters, and known as **elater mother cells,** whereas the cells of the other half are fertile and form the **spore mother cells.** Each elater mother cell elongates

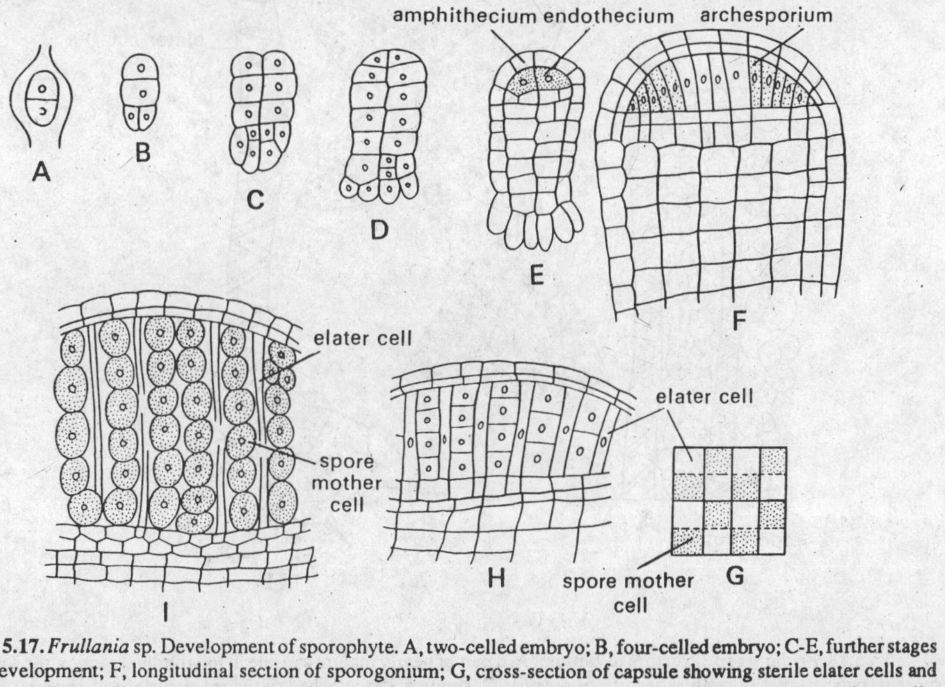

Fig. 5.17. *Frullania* sp. Development of sporophyte. A, two-celled embryo; B, four-celled embryo; C-E, further stages in the early development; F, longitudinal section of sporogonium; G, cross-section of capsule showing sterile elater cells and fertile spore mother cells; H, transverse section of capsule (a part) ; I, later stage showing spore mother cells and elater cells.

to develop into a trumpet-shaped elater. Each elater has a single spiral thickening band and remains attached to the floor and the inner surface of the wall of capsule. The fertile cells (*i.e.*, spore mother cells) on maturity separate from each other and undergo the reductional division (*i.e.*, meiosis), each forming four haploid spores. Each spore is somewhat rounded and ranges from 0.025 to 0.056 mm in diameter.

The spore wall consists of two layers-the outer one is **exospore** and the inner **endospore.** The exospore is rough and tuberculate, while the endospore is thin and smooth. There is some amount of cytoplasm, single nucleus and some chloroplasts within the spore.

Simultaneously the venter of archegonium makes a multilayered calyptra which encloses the sporogonium till its maturity. Surrounding the calyptra a pyriform perianth is also found. The cells of the wall of capsule remain unthickened at four vertical strips, which make the lines of dehiscence.

Structure of mature sporogonium. The mature sporogonium consists of **foot, seta** and **capsule.** The foot is not much differentiated and acts as haustorium. It obtains its food from the gametophytic tissue. The seta is broad, short 8-9 cells in thickness. It is not sharply distinguished from capsule. The wall of capsule is two-layered. The cells of outer layer possess rod-like thickenings at the angles and that of inner layer possess sheet-like thickenings. The spore tetrads and the elaters are arranged linearly in alternate rows. The elaters remain firmly attached at both the ends or may be attached at one end after breaking. The sporogonium remains covered by a multicellular calyptra followed by a perianth.

Dehiscence of capsule. On the maturity of the sporogonium the short seta rapidly elongates, and thus the calyptra ruptures and the globose, dark brown capsule is pushed above the ensheathing perianth. The torned calyptra remains at the base of sporogonium as a membranous sheath. The

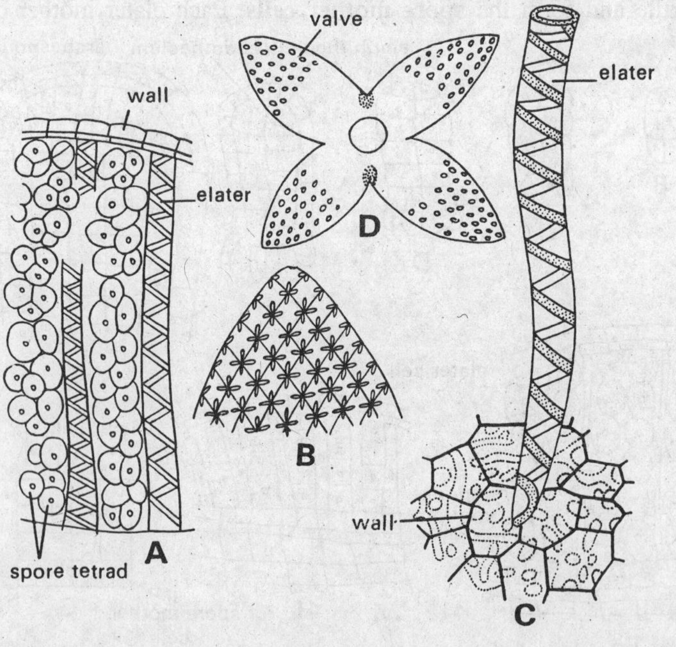

Fig. 5.18. *Frullania* sp. Structure of capsule. A, a part of nearly mature capsule in longitudinal section showing elaters and spore tetrads; B, part of capsule seen from outside; C, single elater attached to the inner surface of capsule; D, opened capsule-four valves showing arrangement of elaters.

wall of capsule dries up; the outer layer of cells shrinks and the inner layer is exposed out. Thus, the tension is set up and the capsule wall splits suddenly into four values. The slits between the valves run down from the top of the capsule to two-third of its length. Due to stretching strain, the lower ends of the elaters get detached and swing into the air causing the flicking

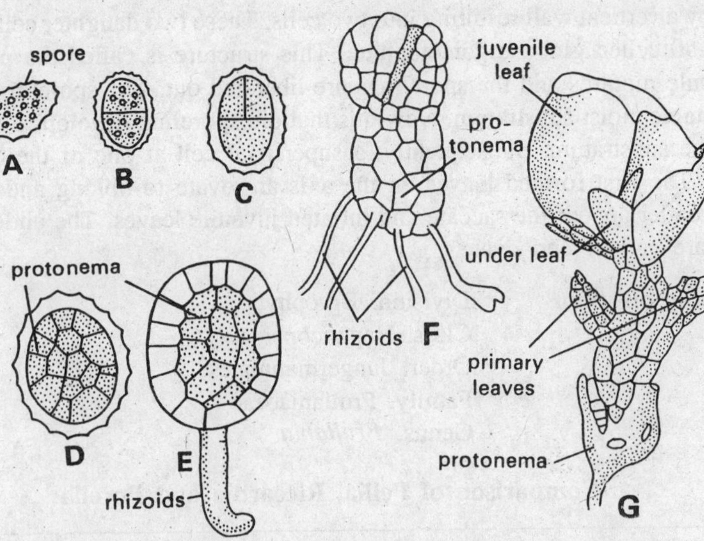

Fig. 5.19. ***Frullania*** **sp. A, Germination of spore; B-E, stages in the development of protonema within exospore; F, a sporeling; G, later stages of sporeling with juvenile and primary leaves.**

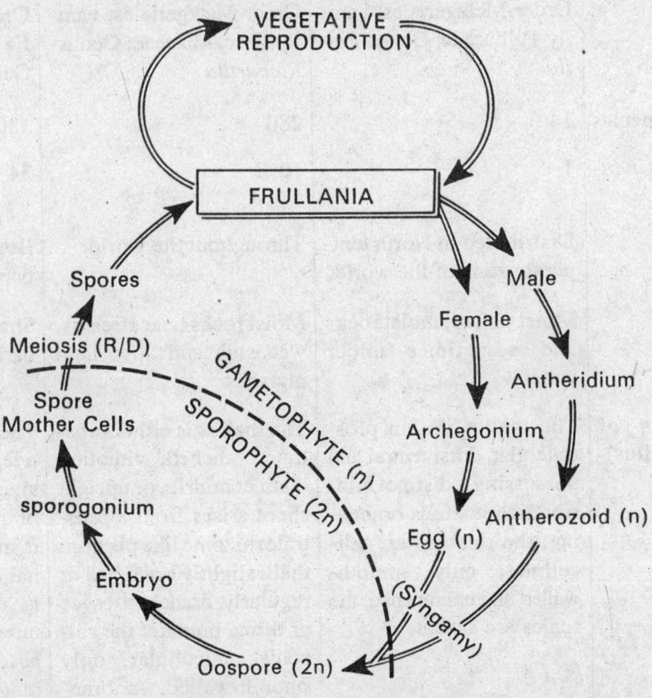

Fig. 5.20. ***Frullania*****. Graphic life-cycle.**

of the spores in the air to a short distance a few inches. This sling-like action of elaters expels the spores out of capsule. This is called **spiral spring mechanism** dispersal of spores.

Germination of spore. The germination of spore begins while the spores are retained within the capsule. Each spore contains a few chloroplasts and a nucleus so that spore in fact is a minute thallus. First division is transverse, and two cells are formed. The upper cell divides immediately by a vertical wall resulting into two cells. These two daughter cells divide repeatedly forming a 40-50 celled globose gametophyte. This structure is called the **protonema.** At this stage the capsule ruptures and the sporelings are liberated out. The sporeling develops rhizoids reaching a suitable moist substratum. Now this thalloid sporeling develops a few rhizoids which anchor it to the substratum. Subsequently, a superficial cell at one of the ends develops into a leafy shoot. The first formed leaves on the axis are ovate to oblong and 2-4 cells broad at the base. Thereafter appear the saccate and inflated juvenile leaves. The underleaves developed at this stage are narrow and ovate.

Systematic position.
Division. Bryophyta
Class. Hepaticopsida
Order. Jungermanniales
Family. Frullaniaceae
Genus. *Frullania*

Comparison of Pellia, Riccardia and Porella

	Pellia	*Riccardia*	*Porella*
Systematic position	Division-Bryophyta; Class-Hepaticopsida; Order-Metzgeriales; Family-Pelliaceae; Genus-*Pellia.*	Division-Bryophyta; Class-Hepaticopsida; Order-Metzgeriales; Family-Riccardiaceae; Genus-*Riccardia,*	Division-Bryophyta; Class-Hepaticopsida; Order-Jungermanniales; Family-Porellaceae; Genus-*Porella,*
Total number of species	14	280	180
No. of species found in India	1	10	34
Distribution	Distributed in North temperate zone of the world.	Throughout the world.	Both in tropical and temperature regions.
Habitat	Moist places, moist rocks and sometimes under water.	Moist rocks near streams, wet soil and low land marshes.	Shaded rocks, stones or bark of trees.
External features of gametophyte (thallus)-Plant body	The thallus is thin prostrate, flat, dorsiventral and possessing a distinct midrib; dichotomous branching; the rhizoids are unicellular, only smooth-walled and unbranched; the scales are absent.	The thallus is either prostrate branched, without a distinct midrib, or upright shoot arises from a prostrate rhizome like portion; thalli slightly branched or regularly branched twice or thrice pinnate; the rhizoids, unicellular, only smooth-walled, unbranched; scales absent.	The plant body possesses a leafy axis which is dorsiventral prostrate and branched; the branching is monopodial and terminal; rhizoids are unicellular, only smooth-walled and unbranched; the scales are absent; the leaves are arranged in 3 rows, 2 rows of dorsal, lobed, larger

	Pellia	Riccardia	Porella
			leaves and a ventral row of small under leaves (amphigastria); all leaves are single-layered.
Internal structure	Photosynthetic cells of the wings and upper layer of the midrib; all cells of thallus act as storage tissue; either a cuneate apical cell with four cutting faces or a lenticular cylindric cell.	All cells of the thallus contain chlorophyll at sometime; all cells of the thallus act as storage tissue. Wedge-shaped apical cell with two cutting faces.	Cortical cells small, thick walled; no distinct central cylinder-the inner (medullary) cells are large and thin walled. Single tetrahedral apical cell with three cutting faces.
Sexual Organs	Monoecious and dioecious; antheridia are on dorsal surface of thallus, immersed in antheridial cavities, stalk is short, few-celled, body jacket of antheridium single-layered, antherozoids biciliate, archegonia at the anterior end of the thallus on the dorsal surface. Protection of archegonia by involucre, stalk is short, neck is made up of 5 vertical rows of cells, venter is two-layered thick, cover cells are four, neck canal cells are usually 6 to 8.	Monoecious and dioecious; dorsal surface of antheridial branch sunk in antheridial chambers, stalk is short, 2-3 cells in length, body jacket of antheridium is single-layered, antherozoids biciliate; archegonia on the dorsal surface of an archegonial branch, protection of archegonia by the tissue of the archegonial branch, stalk is short, neck is made up of 5 vertical rows of cells, venter is two to three-layered thick, cover cells are four, neck canal cells are usually 3-6.	Dioecious only; antheridia are in the axis of bracts of an antheridial branch, stalk is long, 2 celled broad, body jacket of antheridium is single-layered in the upper part, but 2 to 3-layered in the lower part, antherozoids biciliate; archegonia at the tip of the archegonial branch, protection of archegonial branch, protection of archegonia by perichaetial bracts, stalk is short, neck is made up of 5 vertical rows of cells venter is two layered thick, cover cells are four, neck canal cells are usually 6 to 8.
Sporophyte	Amphithecium gives rise to jacket of capsule; endothecium gives rise to archesporium; archesporium gives rise to sporocytes, elaters and elaterophores; foot is conical; seta is long, elongates rapidly after the spores are mature; capsule is globose; capsule wall is two or more-layered, persistent; elaters are long, narrow with 2 to 3 spiral thickened bands, elaterophores basal; columella is absent; wall splits longitudinally into four valves,	Amphithecium gives rise to jacket of capsule; endothecium gives rise to archesporium; archesporium gives rise to sporocytes, elaters and elaterophore; foot is club-shaped; seta is long, elongates rapidly after the spores are mature; capsule is ovoid; capsule wall is two-layered, persistent; elaters are long, pointed with onespiral thickened band, elaterophores apical; columella is absent; wall splits longitudinally into four valves,	Amphithecium gives rise to jacket of capsule; endothecium gives rise to archesporium; archesporium gives rise to sporocytes and elaters; foot is slightly bulbous, seta is long and elongates rapidly after the spores are mature; capsule is globose; capsule wall is two-or more-layered, persistent; elaters are long, narrow with 2 to 3 spiral thickened bands; columella is absent wall splits longitudinally into four valves, elaters help in spore dis-

	Pellia	*Riccardia*	*Porella*
	elaters help in spore dispersal.	elaters and elaterophore help in spore dispersal.	persal.
Young Gametophyte	Spore with two wall layers; spore is 0.068-0.076 mm in length, 0.035-0.042 mm in breadth. While spore germination, the cell division starts while the spore is still inside the capsule, formation of an ovoid cell mass, in which the apical cell develops either at one end or in the middle.	Spore with two wall layers; spore size is 0.012 to 0.025 mm; formation of a 3 to 4 celled structure on germination of spore, in which a 2 sided apical cell is differentiated which begins to function immediately.	Spore with three-wall layers; spore size is 0.03 to 0.05 mm; at the time of spore germination, it undergoes precocious divisions before the capsule opens, formation of an ovoid cell mass (protonema) within the exospore, an outer cell of the protonema becomes an apical cell.

6

Hepaticopsida

Order-Calobryales.

The order Calobryales consists of a single family the Calobryaceae with *two* genera-*Calobryum* and *Haplomitrium*. *Calobryum* includes eight species of which *Calobryum blumii* is best known. *Haplomitrium* is represented by a single species *H. hookeri*.

The more important characteristic features of the order are as follows:

The members of this order possess erect leafy gametophytes with leaves in three vertical rows. The leaves may be **isophyllous** or **anisophyllous.** In the latter case, the row of smaller leaves is dorsal.

The leaves are dorsiventrally flattened and towards the base are 2-4 stratose, while remaining unistratose in the terminal portion.

They have a pale, subterranean, sparingly branched rhizome from which arise erect leafy branches.

Erect branches bearing sex organs have the uppermost leaves close together and in more than three rows. Such branches have a strong superficial resemblance to the erect gametophores of mosses.

They are devoid of rhizoids.

The antheridia are ovoid, stalked and borne at the apex of the stem.

Archegonia differ from those of other members of Hepaticopsida in that the jacket of the neck has only four vertical rows of cells.

The sporophyte bears an elongate capsule whose jacket layer is only one cell in thickness except at the apex. The number of chromosomes is-n=9.

These liverworts are frequently placed among the Jungermanniales and either as a family of Jungermannineae or as a separate suborder. The older bryologists placed these two genera (*i.e., Haplomitrium* and *Calobryum*) in the order Jungermanniales. However, Campbell (1940) and Jones (1958) placed them in a separate order Calobryales.

Genus CALOBRYUM

There are *eight* species in this genus. Of all the eight species so far recorded *C. blumii* is the best known. The species are chiefly known from the tropics. In India, *C. indicum* has been recorded from Darjeeling district (Udar and S. Chandra, 1965); the other important species *C. blumii* has been recorded from Jawai (Assam) (Udar *et.al.,* 1968); and the third species *C. denundatum* (Kumar and Udar, 1976). They are shade and moisture loving plants. They occur on forest floor and steep clay banks. They are either hygrophytes or mesophytes. They cannot withstand drought conditions.

Gametophyte. The plant body consists of a pale, subterranean, sparingly branched rhizome from which arise erect leafy branches. The erect branches possess leaves in three vertical rows. All leaves may be of the same size (**isophyllous**) and shape, or those of one row may be slightly smaller than those of the other two (**anisophyllous**). The leaves are simple, entire, dorsoventrally flattened and without a midrib. According to Grolle (1964) all species of *Calobryum* are anisophyllous. According to smith the smaller leaves are thought to be homologous with underleaves of Jungermannineae, and the side of the stem bearing them is considered the morphologically ventral side, rhizoids are lacking on both the rhizoids and erect portions of the stem.

Branches of a rhizome are intercalary in origin. A newly formed branch grows horizontally for a time, then grows upwards and develops leaves.

The erect branches that bear sex organs possess the uppermost leaves close together and in more than three rows. Such branches superficially resemble the erect gametophores of mosses.

As regards their anatomy the leaves vary in structure in different species. In *C. blumii* the leaves are polystratose in their basal portions. The leaf cells are thin-walled, parenchymatous and possess chloroplasts and oil bodies in them.

Superficial cells anywhere on the stem may develop into short two-or three-celled mucilage hairs (slime papillae) in which the terminal cell is clavate. They secrete mucilage.

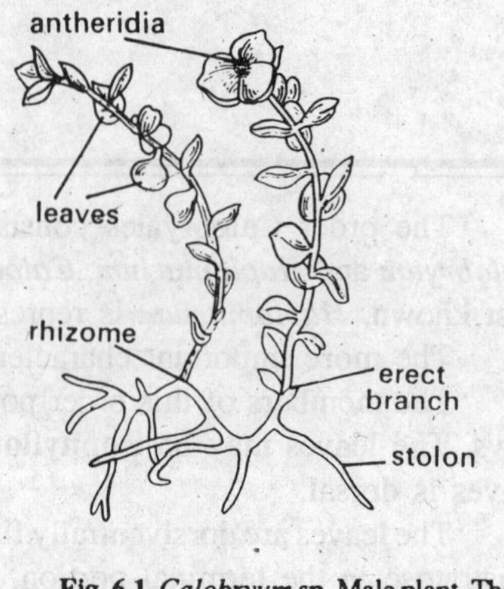

Fig. 6.1. *Calobryum* sp. Male plant. The branches possess terminal antheridia and lateral leaves.

The transverse section of the axial portion of the stem shows a sharply delimited conducting tissue (central strand) 10 to 15 cells in diameter and a surrounding cortex. The cortex has large parenchymatous cells in which there are numerous starch grains. The peripheral cortical cells generally develop into 2-3 celled mucilage papillae (hairs) which secrete mucilage. In *C. gibbsiae*, abundant oil drops are found in the cortical cells (Campbell, 1959).

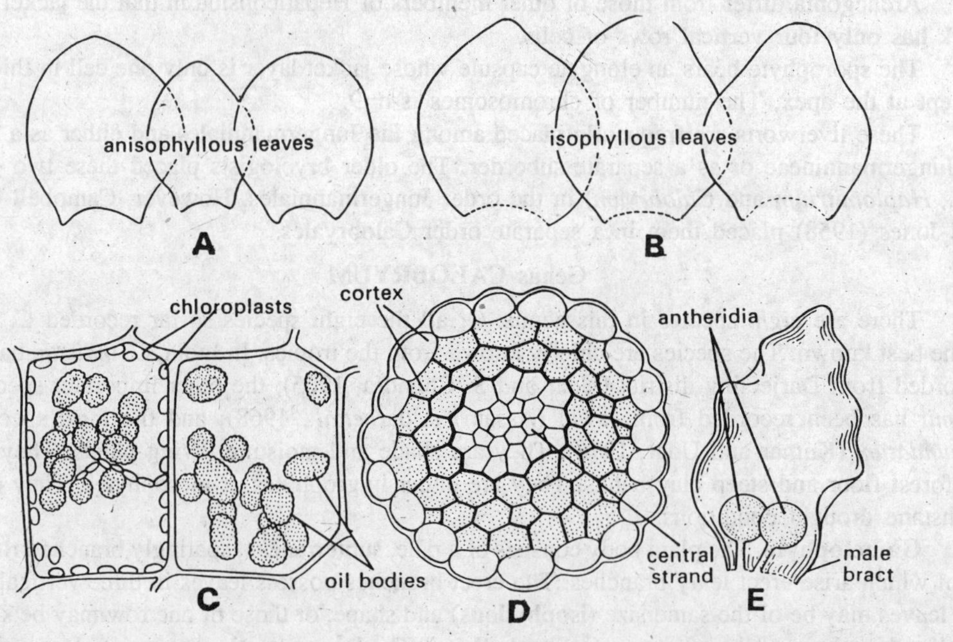

Fig. 6.2. *Calobrym* sp. A, three anisophyllous leaves in a single cycle ; B, isophyllous leaves in a single cycle; C, the cells of leaf having chloroplasts and oil bodies ; D, cross section of stem showing central strand and cortex ; E, male bract with antheridia.

Apical growth. The apical growth in a branch of *Calobryum* takes place due to a pyramidal apical cell with three cutting faces, one slightly narrower than the other two. This narrower face gives rise to the ventral file of leaves by subsequent divisions.

Reproduction. Asexual reproduction is not known in *Calobryum.*

Sexual reproduction. *Calobryum* is heterothallic, *i.e.*, the gametophytic plants are of two types, male and female. The sex organs (male and female) are produced in abundance on flattened apices of leafy branches of different plants.

Antheridia. The antheridia are produced in abundance on flattened tips of leafy branches. They are orange-yellow in colour. The leaves that surround the antheridia of male plants are larger than the others. As a result these male fertile branches resemble gametophores of mosses.

The mature antheridium consists of an ovoid body situated on a long stalk made up of several superimposed tiers of four cells each. The antheridial body remains covered by a jacket layer of cells that encloses a central mass of androgonial cells. The cells that give rise to antherozoids are called **androcyte mother cells.**

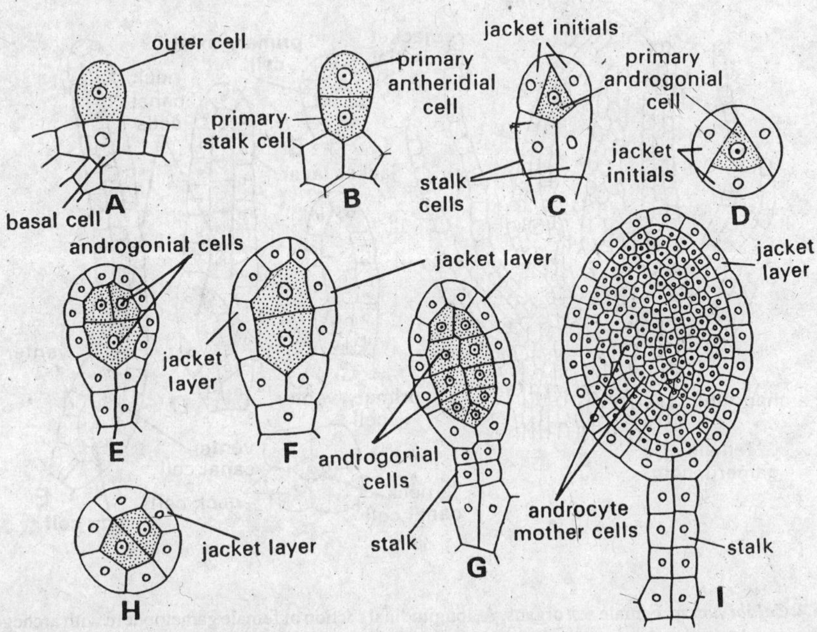

Fig. 6.3. *Calobryum* sp. Development of antheridium. A, transversely divided antheridial cell having outer cell and basal cell ; B, outer cell divides transversely forming primary antheridial cell and primary stalk cell ; C, primary antheridial cell divides by three successive oblique vertical walls forming jacket initials and primary androgonial cell ; E-G, further successive divisions in the development of antheridium, D and H, cross sections of developing antheridium at different stages; I, nearly mature stalked antheridium containing androcyte mother cells.

The details of antheridial development have been worked out in *C. blumii.* They are as follows: the antheridial initial cell divides transversely into a **basal cell** embedded in the thallus, and an **outer cell,** which projects above the thallus. The outer cell then divides transversely into **a primary antheridial cell** and a **primary stalk cell.** In most cases there then follow three successive vertical divisions of the primary antheridial cell. This results in the formation of three **jacket initials** completely enclosing a single **primary androgonial cell.** The first division of the primary androgonial cell is transverse. Thereafter the two daughter cells divide transversely and longitudinally. The primary stalk cell develops into a stalk composed of several superimposed tiers of four cells each. The upper and lower androgonial cells divide vertically thus forming four **androgonial cells.** The four androgonial cells divide several times transversely and longitudinally forming a central mass of **androcyte mother cells.** Each androcyte mother cell divides mitotically forming two **androcytes.** Now each androcyte metamorphoses into a biflagellate **sperm** or **antherozoid.**

Archegonia. An expanded receptacle develops on the tip of the female branch of gametophyte. About thirty or more archegonia are formed in a cluster on the flat, dilated, terminal disc and remain surrounded by the bases of three large perichaetial leaves.

The archegonium possesses a stalk and a long twisted neck. The neck is composed of four rows of neck cells that enclose a row of many (16-20) **neck canal cells.** The **venter** is somewhat broader than the **neck.** The venter contains an **egg** (oosphere) and a **ventral canal cell** above it.

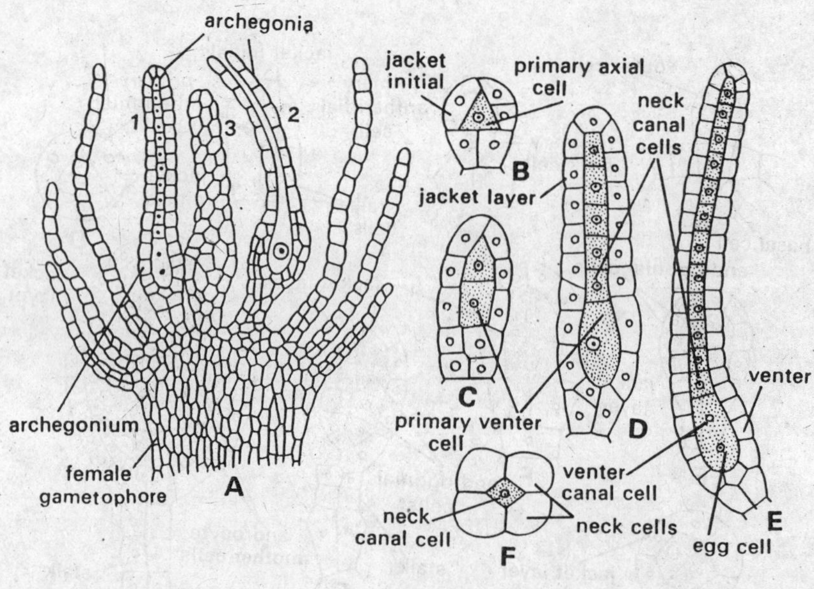

Fig. 6.4. *Calobryum* sp. Female sex organs. A, longitudinal section of female gametophore with archegonia in different views ; B-E, successive stages in the development of archegonium ; E, transverse section of archegonium.

The development of archegonia is as follows: The archegonia are developed from about a half dozen recently formed segments from the apical cell and then the apical cell itself develops into an archegonium, and thus, *Calobryum* is **acrogynous.** Whereas *Haplomitrium* is **anacrogynous** and there is no disappearance of the apical cell when the archegonia are developed. In *Calobryum blumii* usually three vertical divisions of the primary archegonial cell take place and thus three jacket initials are formed which surround a primary axial cell. In most cases the jacket initials intersect one another and completely enclose the primary axial cell. With the result the primary axial cell acts directly as a central cell and without cutting off a primary cover cell. Now the central cell divides by a transverse division into two cells-the upper primary canal cell and lower primary ventral cell. The primary canal cell divides again and again giving rise to a row of 16-20 neck canal cells. On the other hand the primary ventral cell divides to form an egg and an upper ventral canal cell. On maturity of the archegonium the venter becomes 2-3 cells in thickness. The archegonia are naked and not covered by any perianth sheath.

The fertilization takes place in usual manner. The water is indispensable for the process of fertilization. The antherozoids enter the mouth of archegonium and reach the egg. One of the antherozoids penetrates the egg effecting fertilization. Ultimately the zygote (2n) is formed.

Sporophyte. The zygote secretes a wall around it, enlarges in size and nearly fills the cavity of the venter. Now the zygote divides transversely giving rise to two cells (epibasal and hypobasal). These cells divide further repeatedly giving rise to epibasal and hypobasal portions. The hypobasal portion of the embryo develops into a haustorium whereas the epibasal portion gives rise to foot, seta and capsule of the mature sporophyte.

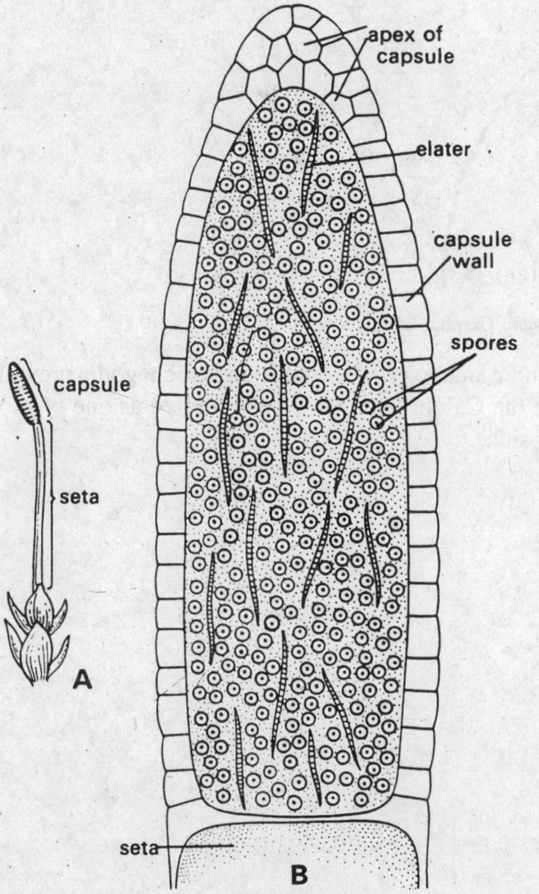

Fig. 6.5. *Calobryum* sp. Sporophyte: A, female gemetophore with mature sporophyte ; B, longitudinal section of capsule containing spores and elaters.

The mature sporophyte bears a cylindrical capsule, a long seta, and an acuminate foot. Except for the apical portion, the jacket layer of the capsule is one cell in thickness. The cell walls of the jacket layer are thickened in a median annular band perpendicular to the surface of the capsule.

The capsule opens by the four valves and dehiscence of spores takes place.

Sporogenous tissue within the young capsule has an early differentiation into elaters and the spores. The elaterophore is not formed.

A massive long, fleshy, green to yellowish green, brittle calyptra surrounds the developing sporophyte. Sometimes it is termed the 'shoot calyptra'.

Phylogeny of Calobryales.

According to Smith (1955) the Calobryales are a group that arose along the same evolutionary line as the Jungermanniales but it departed quite early from that line. The gametophytes of Calobryales show a combination of advanced and primitive features. As far as the external and internal structures are concerned the gametophytes are quite complex. However, the sex organs are not so much evolved. There is similarity in the early ontogeny of antheridia and archegonia which shows that they are homologous structures. This is an evidence for the primitiveness. The early ontogeny of the sex organs shows that the Calobryales are the most primitive of any in the Hepaticopsida.

According to Mehra (1969) the Calobryales and foliose Jungermanniales are offshoots from ancesters like Takakiales but at the diploid level. The Calobryales still retain in their leaves some likeness of a phyllid structure in their multicellular base. They are relatively primitive is shown by the organization on antheridia and archegonia from a three-sided apical cell.

It has been interpreted by Grubb (1970) and Watsan (1974) that the smaller leaves of third row in Calobryales represent the dorsol row, and therefore, cannot be equated with the amphigastria of Jungermannineae, separate Calobryales from the latter which are exclusively acrogynous. The

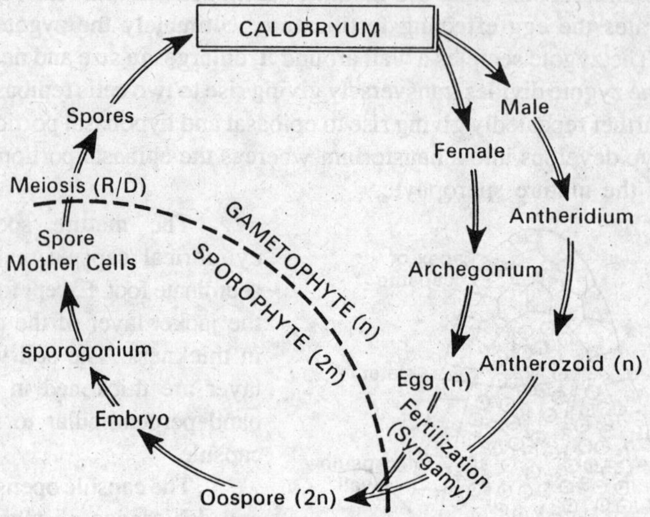

Fig. 6.6. *Calobryum.* **Graphic life-cycle**

Calobryales appear closer to the Metzgerinae where anacrogynous condition of archegonia prevails. However, we can follow Mehra (1969) where the Calobryales have been treated as one of most primitive group among Hepaticae (Hepaticopsida).

7

Hepaticopsida

Order-Takakiales

The order Takakiales consists of a single family the Takakiaceae and a single genus *Takakia* with *two* known species *T. ceratophylla* (recorded from Sikkim, India) and *T. lepidozioides*.

The characteristic features of the order are as follows:

Both the species possess cylindrical, rhizomatic and erect gametophores.

They are devoid of rhizoids.

They possess copious mucilage hairs (beaked or non-beaked) on them.

They possess terete, bifid-trifid-quadrifid leaves (**phyllids**).

The gametophores are about 1-1.5 cm in height.

The leafless branches facing downward known as **'flagella'** or **'stolons'** may present.

The gametophores cannot withstand drought.

Asexual reproduction in not known.

Only female shoots (archegonial) are known. They bear conspicuous pedestalled archegonia.

The male shoots (antheridial) and the sporophytes are not known.

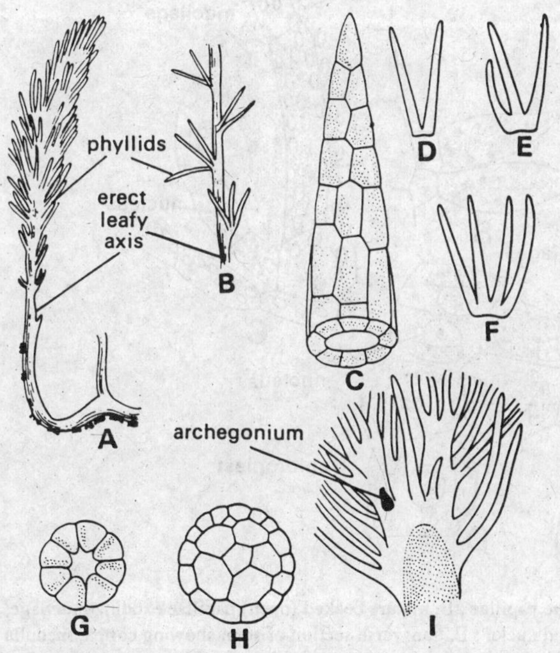

Fig. 7.1. *Takakia* sp. A, rhizomatous gametophore with phyllids ; B, portion of gametophore with phyllids ; C, single enlarged undivided phyllid ; D, bifid phyllid ; E, trifid phyllid ; F, quadrifid phyllid ; G, transverse section of simple phyllid; H, transverse section of complex phyllid ; I, archegonial shoot with archegonium.

Since there are single family and single genus they have the characters similar to that of the order.

They have lowest chromosome number (*i.e.*, n=4).

They are supposed to be most primitive and sometimes called living fossil.

Genus TAKAKIA

Distribution. An interesting species *Takakia ceratophylla* has been recorded from Sikkim (11,000 feet a.s.l.), eastern Himalayas (Grolle, 1963). It belongs to the monogeneric order Takakiales. This species is very similar to *T. lepidozioides*, the only other earlier known species from Japan, South-west Canada and North Borneo. *T. ceratophylla* has also been recorded from the Aleutian islands growing on moist soil in ditches and on the banks of streams.

Gametophyte. The species of *Takakia* (*i.e.*, *T. ceratophylla* and *T. lepidozioides*) possess cylindrical rhizomatic and erect gametophores. They are devoid of rhizoids and have copious **mucilage hairs** on them. They have terete, bifid-trifid-quadrifid multistratose leaves (**phyllids**) arranged triseriately and nearly isophyllous. The gametophores are about 1-1.5 cm tall. In certain cases a newly developed branch from the rhizome grows horizontally for a short distance and then bends up giving rise to an erect leafy axis, the **gametophore.** Sometimes from the base of erect gametophore may arise downward leafless branches known as **'flagella'** or **'stolons'**. According to Grubs (1970) these structures are called **'roots'**. The gametophore is always fleshy, soft and thick, and therefore, cannot withstand drought.

Each leaf is forked into two, three or four segments from its base. According to Hattori and Mizutani (1958) each independent segment of leaf is considered a **'phyllid'.** These terete segments or phyllids are multistratose, solid and fleshy, and each of them tapers towards the apex and ends in a short, blunty conical cell. Excepting the tip region each segment is 3-5 celled in thickness. These cells are parenchymatous and have chloroplasts in them. The transverse section of the upper and the middle part of the leaf segment shows one big medullary cell which remains surrounded by a layer of cortical cells (**cortex**). However, in the lower part of the leaf segment 2-5 medullary cells are found which remain surrounded by a single-layered cortex.

The transverse section of the stem of *Takakia* shows two specific zones-the outer **cortical region** surrounding the inner **medullary region.** The cortical region consists of chlorophyllous cells. The cortex is 1-2 stratose thick. It consists of slightly thick-walled cells with brown walls. The medullary region consists of a small central strand of small-celled tissue which remains surrounded by a somewhat large-celled medulla.

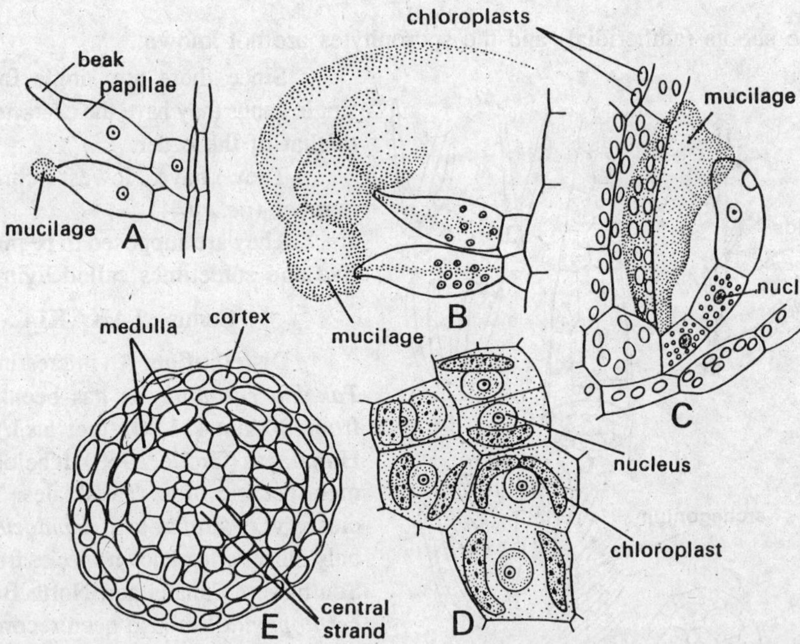

Fig. 7.2. *Takakia* sp. A, beaked (open) nearly mature papillae ; B, mature beaked (open) papillae exuding mucilage; C, stalked closed papilla ; D, leaf cells with chloroplasts and nuclei ; E, transverse section of stem showing cortex, medulla and central strand.

The slime or mucilage papillae are found on the axis of *Takakia.* These papillae may be non-beaked or beaked in structure. In *T. ceratophylla* the non-breaked slime papillae consist of a 2-celled filament. The lower cell is called the stalk-cell while the terminal one oozes out the mucilage. The mucilage is secreted by the wall of the upper cell. The beaked slime papillae occur in clusters on the leafy and leafless axes. Each beaked slime papilla consists of a slender, flask-shaped upper cell. It is found on a two or more-celled stalk. The beak possesses a distal pore through which the mucilage is secreted and oozed out.

Reproduction. Only female (archegonial) shoots are known. They hear conspicuous pedestalled archegonia. The male shoots (antheridial) and the sporophytes are not known. The archegonium is naked, large, green when young and stalked. The neck consists of six rows of neck cells (Inoue, 1961). The venter is fleshy and 2-stratose just before fertilization. The sporophytes are not known. Asexual reproduction is not known.

Phylogency. According to Mehra (1967, 1968, 1969) "Takakiales are the most primitive as indicated by their simple body structure, with the 'leaves' undifferentiated from the branch systems, and the iowest chromosome number (*i.e.*, n=4) yet recorded in the group. These are truly at the haploid level and represent relics of a race that seems to have died out. The genus *Takakia* is a living fossil in the Hepaticae". He further states, "The Calobryales and foliose Jungermanniales are offshoots from ancestors like Takakiales but at the diploid level". The other important primimitive features of *Takakia* are – their disjunct distribution, polymorphous leaves, lack of drought resistance; absence of rhizoids; presence of slime papillae; antheridium and sporophyte not known and presence of primitive type of archegonium.

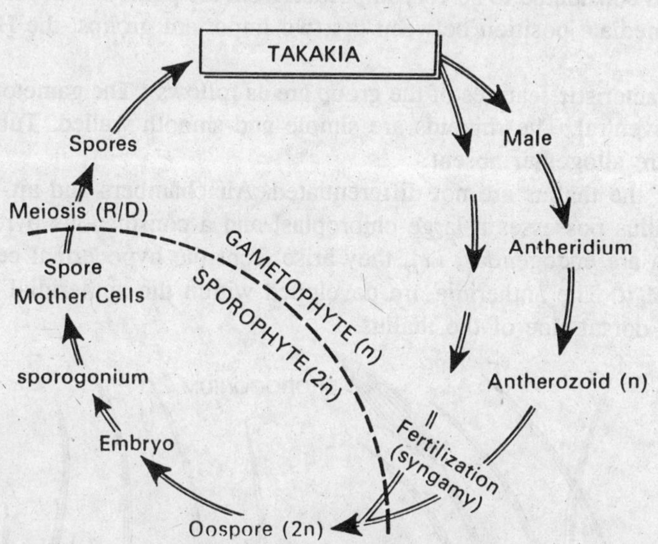

Fig. 7.3. *Takakia*. Graphic life-cycle.

Systematic position.

Division. Bryophyta
Class. Hepaticopsida
Order. Takakiales
Family. Takakiaceae
Genus. *Takakia*.

8

Anthocerotopsida

Order-Anthocerotales

The class Anthocerotopsida (Anthocerotae) consists of à single order, the Anthocerotales and a single family, the Anthocerotaceae, 6 genera and 301 species. According to Muller (1940), Reimers (1954) and Proskauer the order Anthocerotales includes two families, (i) Anthocerotaceae and (ii) Notothylaceae. The latter includes a single genus, *i.e., Notothylas.* However, according to top bryologists, there is only one family, *i.e.,* Anthocerotaceae. About five or six genera are included in this family.

These genera are–*Anthoceros, Phaeoceros, Aspiromitus, Notothylas, Dendroceros* and *Megaceros.* Four genera are universally recognised. they are–*Anthoceros, Megaceros, Dendroceros* and *Notothylas.* This group differs in many respects from the other Bryophyta. However, the group is placed intermediate between Hepaticopsida (Hepaticae) and Bryopsida (Musci). The group is considered to be very important from the point of view of its morophology, because of its intermediate position between the two important groups, the Hepaticopsida and Bryopsida.

The most characteristic features of the group are as follows : The gametophytic plant body is thalloid and dorsiventral. The rhizoids are simple and smooth walled. Tuberculate rhizoids and ventral scales are altogether absent.

The tissues of the thallus are not differentiated. Air chambers and air-pores are absent. Each cell of the thallus possesses a large chloroplast and a conspicuous pyrenoid within it.

The antheridia are endogenous, *i.e.,* they arise from the hypodermal cells of the thallus on the dorsal side of it. The antheridia are developed within the antheridial chambers, singly or in groups on the dorsal side of the thallus.

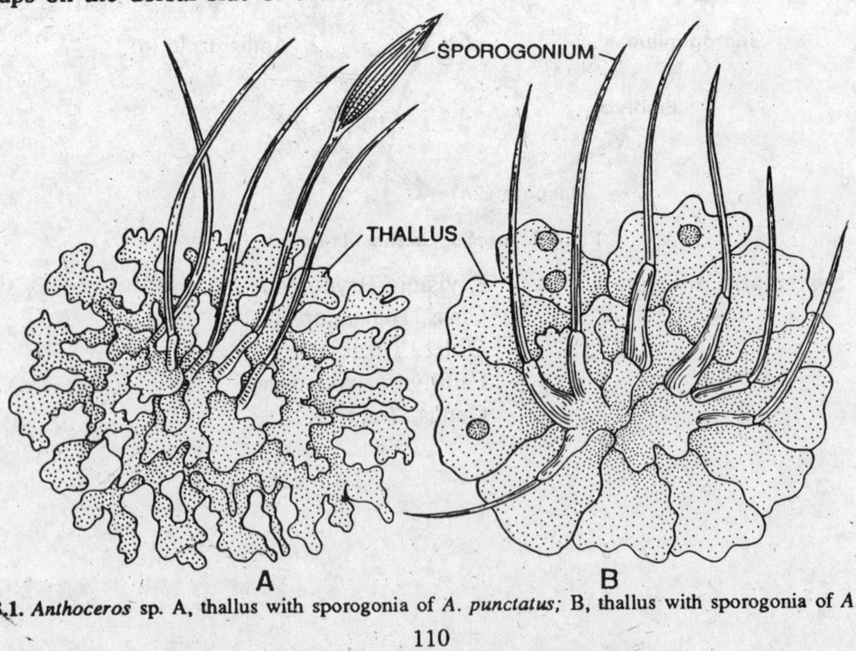

Fig. 8.1. *Anthoceros* sp. A, thallus with sporogonia of *A. punctatus;* B, thallus with sporogonia of *A. laevis.*

The archegonia are found in sunken condition on the dorsal side of the thallus.

The sporogonium arises from the dorsal side of the thallus. It is elongated and cylindrical in structure. It consists of foot, meristematic region and capsule. It possesses intercalary meristem,

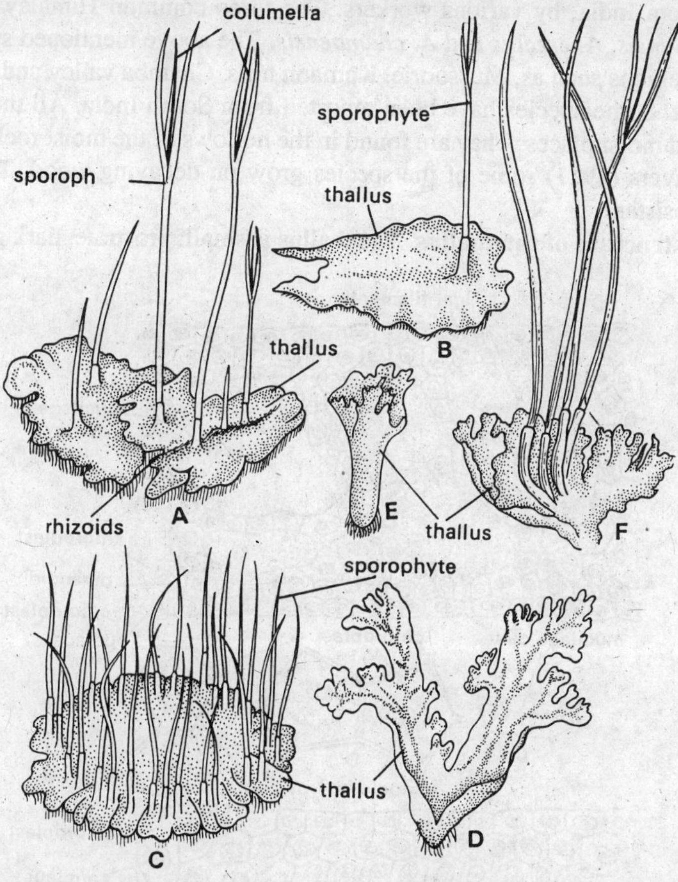

Fig. 8.2. *Anthoceros* sp. Gametophyte and sporophyte. A, gametophyte (thallus) bearing rhizoids and mature and immature sporophytes; B, part of a thallus with opened sporophyte; C, thallus of *Anthoceros crispulus* with several elongated horny sporophytes; D and E, thalli of (sterile) *A. erectus* without sporogonia; F, thallus (fertile) of *A. fusiformis* with one opened and three unopened sporophytes.

and continues its growth throughout the growing season. The wall of sporogonium contains chlorophyll. The central sterile portion is columella, which is surrounded by sporogenous tissue and spores. The elaters are also present.

The sporogenous mass develops from amphithecium and arches over the columella.

Family-Anthocerotaceae.

There are *five* genera (*i.e., Anthoceros, Phaeoceros, Aspiromitus, Dendroceros* and *Megaceros*) in this family.

Characteristic features. The sporogonium (capsule) is linear and vertical. Generally the stomata are present on capsule wall. The archesporium arises from amphithecium. The elaters are four-celled, smooth or thick-walled and with or without thickening bands. The genus *Anthoceros* has been discussed here in detail.

Genus ANTHOCEROS

Habitat and distribution. About 200 species of this genus are founa uiroughout the world in temperate and tropical regions. The species are moist and shade loving. About 25 species have been reported from India, by various workers. The three common Himalayan species are, *Anthoceros himalayensis, A. erectus* and *A. chambensis.* The above mentioned species are common in various hilly regions such as, Mussoorie, Kumaon hills, Chamba valley and other places, 5,000 feet to 8,000 feet. Some species have been reported from South India. All the species are found in very shady and moist places. They are found in the hollows of the moist rocks in dense patches. According to Cavers (1911) some of the species grow on decaying wood. The species, are not at all drought resistant.

External structure of the thallus. The thallus is small, prostrate, dark green and dorsiventrally differentiated. The thallus is lobed and the lobes are somewhat divided. The mid-rib is not found. The dorsal surface of thallus of *A. laevis* is smooth, whereas it is velvet like in *A. crispulus* (Bhardwaj, 1950) or it may be with spines and ridges as in *A. fusiformis.* In every case the smooth walled, simple rhizoids are found. The ventral scales and tuberculate rhizoids are altogether absent. The thalli are dark green, because of the presence of the *Nostoc* colonies, which may be easily seen with the help of lens from the underside of the thallus

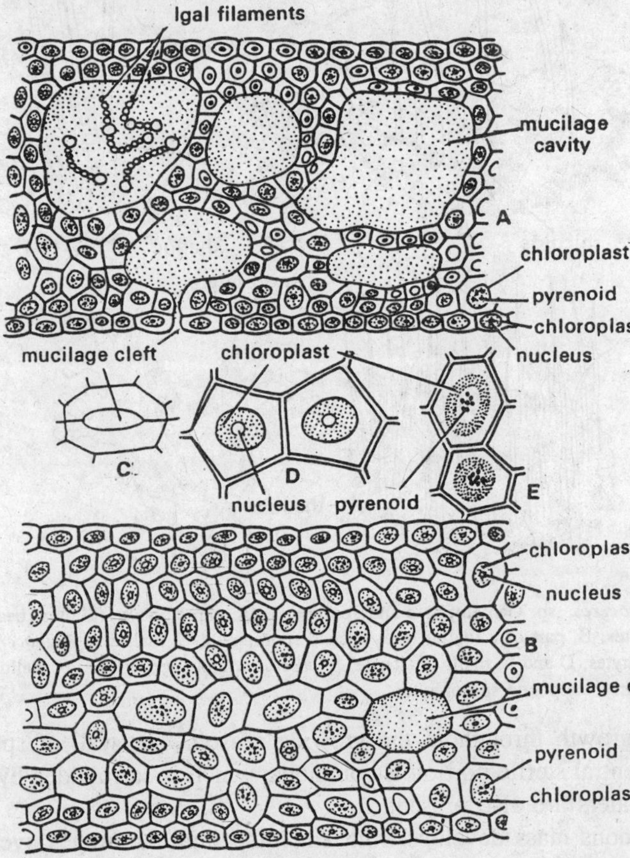

Fig. 8.3. *Anthoceros* sp. A, portion of a section of thallus of *A. punctatus;* B, portion of a section of thallus of *A. laevis;* C, mucilage cleft from the ventral surface of thallus; D–E, cells of thallus enlarged.

Internal structure of the thallus. The anatomy of the thallus is quite simple. Internal to the upper and lower epidermis there are simple, parenchymatous cells. The cells of parenchyma are isodiametric and uniform. Air chambers and air pores are absent. Each cell contains a big chloroplast which possesses a single pyrenoid in its centre. The chloroplasts are lens shaped. The chloroplasts of the superficial cells are longer than the chloroplasts of the other cells. According to McAllister (1914, 1927) the pyrenoids of *Anthoceros* are quite different in structure from those of Chlorophyceae. On the ventral side of the thallus certain intercellular **mucilage cavities** are found. These cavities open by small openings, the **slime pores** on the ventral surface of the thallus. Sometimes, the colonies of blue green algal form-*Nostoc,* are found in the mucilage cavities. There is no symbiotic relationship between these *Nostoc,* colonies, and thalli. According to Peirce (1960) these colonies, however, do harm to the thalli. The nucleus lies in the close vicinity of the chloroplast, near the pyrenoid. Sometimes the chloroplast enfolds the nucleus within it.

Apical growth. The apical growth of *Anthoceros* is a controversial topic, whether it takes place by a single apical cell or by a group of apical cells. According to Smith (1955) the apical growth of the thallus is initiated by a single apical cell. According to Leitgeb (1879) the apical growth in this genus takes place by several marginal apical cells. According to Mehra and Handoo (1953) the apical growth in *Anthoceros erectus* and *A. himalayensis* takes place by a group of cells situated in the depression at the apex of the thallus.

Reproduction. The reproduction takes place by means of (1) vegetative and (2) sexual methods.

1. **Vegetative reproduction.** The vegetative reproduction takes place by various ways.

(a) **By progressive growth and death of thallus.** The vegetative propagation takes place by progressive growth and death of the older part of the thallus reaching dichotomy. But this method is not so common in *Anthoceros* as in *Riccia* and *Marchantia.*

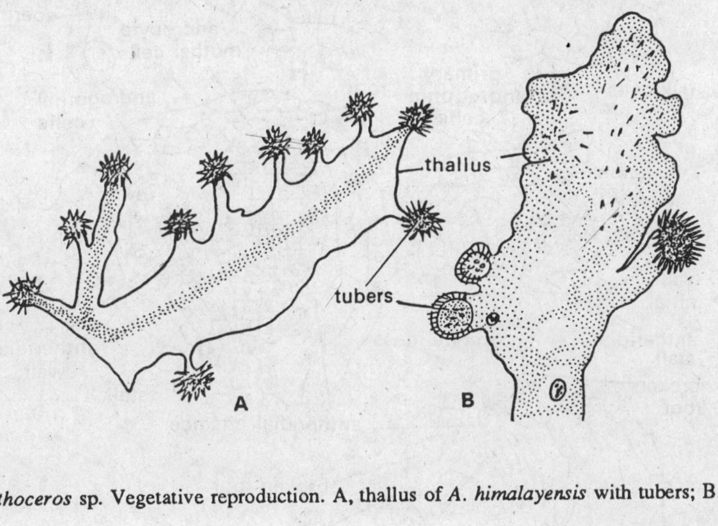

Fig. 8.4. *Anthoceros* sp. Vegetative reproduction. A, thallus of *A. himalayensis* with tubers; B, thallus of *A. laevis* with tubers.

(b) **By tubers.** In certain species of *Anthoceros,* the thallus becomes thickened at several places on the margins. Such marginal thickenings are called, the **tubers.** These tubers are perennating structures. They survive in the drought conditions. On the advent of the favourable conditions, they develop into new thalli. The tubers are formed in *A. laevis, A. tuberosus, A hallii, A. pearsoni* and *A. himalayensis.*

(c) **By gemmae.** In some of the species of *Anthoceros,* the gemmae have been found.

The gemmae have been recorded from the species, *A. glandulosus*, *A. formosae* etc. Each such gemma develops into a new thallus.

(d) **By persistent growing apices.** According to Campbell the thalli of the species *A. pearsoni* and *A. fusiformis* become completely dried up in summers, leaving growing apices with adjacent tissues. These apices face the drought conditions. On the approach of favourable conditions, these apices develop into new thalli.

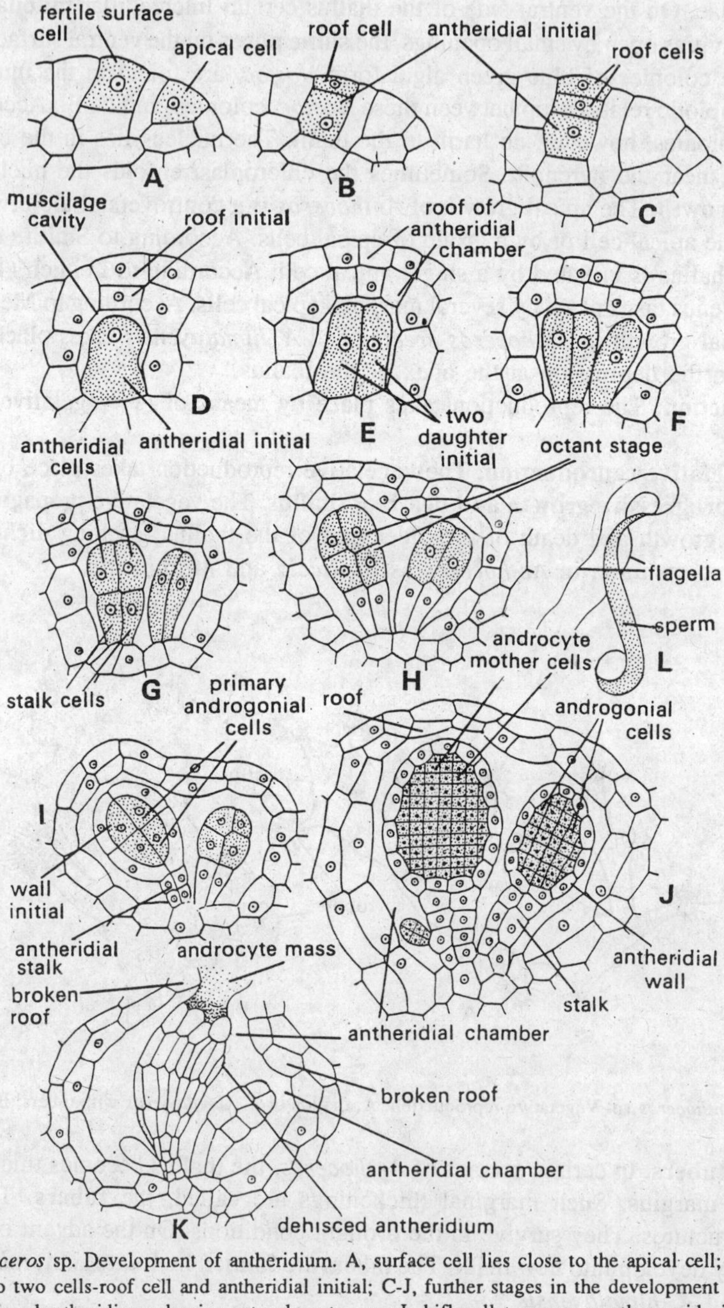

Fig. 8.5. *Anthoceros* sp. Development of antheridium. A, surface cell lies close to the apical cell; B, surface cell divides periclinally into two cells-roof cell and antheridial initial; C-J, further stages in the development of antheridium and roof; K, mature dehisced antheridium releasing out androcyte mass; L, biflagellate sperm or antherozoid with long anterior flagella.

2. Sexual reproduction. The species of *Anthoceros* may be homothallic (monoecious) or heterothallic (dioecious). Some of the homothallic species are- *A. fusiformis, A. punctatus,* Kashyap (1915, 1929) has recorded, *A. himalayensis* as a dioecious (heterothallic) species, but Mehra and Handoo (1953) have reported the same as monoecious (homothallic) but protandrous. The heterothallic species are, *A. pearsoni, A. halli. A. erectus* and others. The sex organs, *i.e.,* antheridia and archegonia are found embedded in the tissues of the dorsal side of the thallus.

Development of antheridium. The antheridia are produced singly or in groups in the antheridial chambers. The development is endogenous. Though the antheridium develops from a superficial cell, yet it is enclosed within the antheridial chamber which does not open out by any opening.

A dorsal superficial cell of the thallus, situated near the growing apex divides periclinally giving rise to two daughter cells. According to Cavers, Campbell and Haupt the superficial cell divides transversely and not periclinally. The upper daughter cell acts as **roof initial** and the lower one as **antheridial initial.** Eventually, a mucilage filled space appears in between the roof initial and antheridial initial. This mucilage cavity enlarges in size and ultimately becomes the **antheridial chambers.** The roof initial is nothing to do with the development of the antheridium. It divides and redivides several times anticlinally and periclinally giving rise to a two layered roof of the antheridial chamber. Simultaneously, the antheridial initial develops into a single antheridium or in a group of antheridia. A single antheridium develops in *A. pearsoni* and sometimes

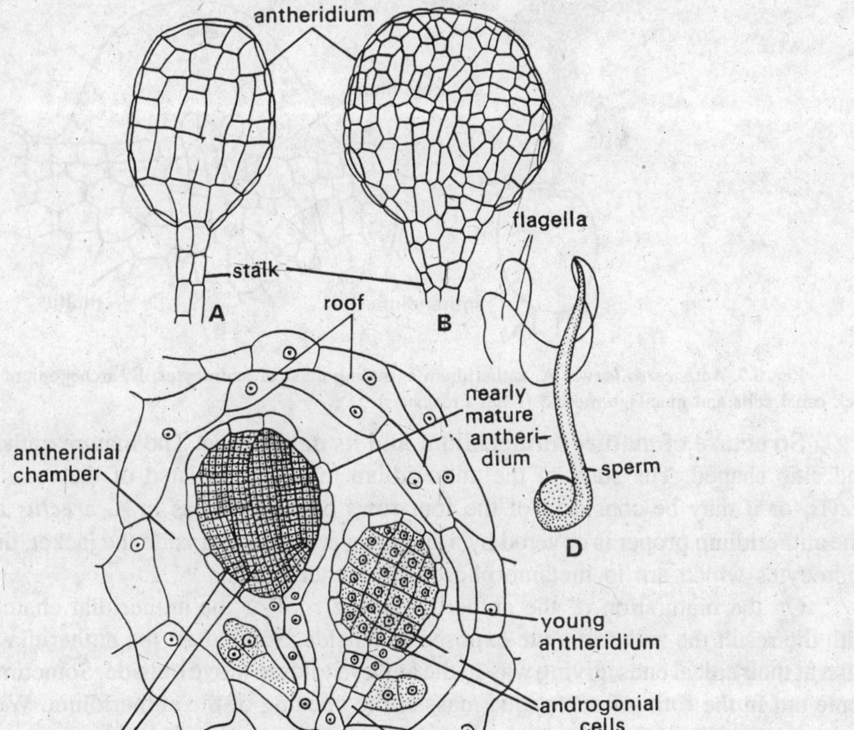

Fig. 8.6. *Anthoceros* sp. Male sex organs. A and B, stalked mature antheridia of *A. crispulus* and *A. laevis* respectively; C, young and mature antheridia inside the antheridial chamber, secondary budded antheridia are seen on the stalks of primary antheridia; D, biflagellate sperm or antherozoid.

in *A. himalayensis*. According to Mehra and Handoo (1953), in *A. erectus* a number of antheridia develop in an antheridial chamber. Here, the antheridial initial divides many times anticlinally producing many cells, and each cell thus produced, develops into an antheridium. The further development is as follows:

The antheridial initial divides twice by vertical walls intersecting each other at right angles, giving rise to four cells. This is followed by another transverse division giving rise to two tiers of four cells each. The four cells of the upper tier divide transversely giving rise to eight cells, the octant stage. All of the cells of octant stage divide periclinally giving rise to eight outer **primary jacket cells** and eight inner **primary androgonial cells.** The four cells of the lower tier develop into a stalk of the antheridium consisting of the four rows of the cells. The so formed androgonial cells divide repeatedly. The last generation of these cells are androcyte mother cells. According to Bagchee (1924) each androcyte mother cell divides diagonally producing two **androcytes.** Each androcyte metamorphoses into a spindle like biciliate antherozoid.

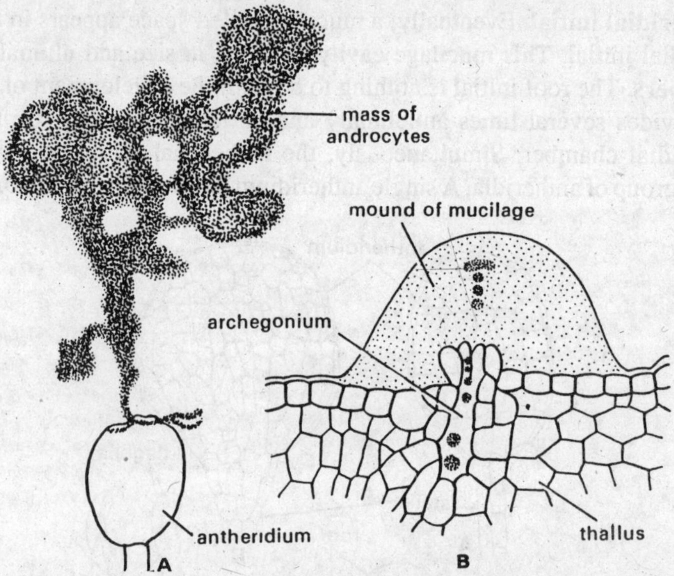

Fig. 8.7. *Anthoceros laevis.* A, antheridium extruding mass of androcytes; B, archegonium showing extrusion of neck canal cells and mucilage mound (After Proskauer).

Structure of mature antheridium and its dehiscence. The mature antheridium is stalked and club shaped. The stalk of the antheridium may be consisted of the mass of cells, *e.g., A. laevis,* or it may be consisted of the four rows of the cells, as in *A. erectus* and *A. punctatus.* The antheridium proper is covered by a single layered jacket. Inside the jacket, there are numerous androcytes which are to metamorphose into antherozoids.

On the maturation of the antheridium, the roof of the antheridial chamber disintegrates, with the result the antheridia are exposed to outside. Soon after, the antheridia absorb water and burst at their apical ends, giving way to the antherozoids to move outside. Sometimes the androcytes come out in the form of an opaque mass at the opening of the antheridium. Within few minutes they metamorphose into the antherozoids.

The antherozoid. The antherozoid is spindle like and biciliate. The cilia are attached to the anterior end of the body. Sometimes just near the attaching point of the flagella to the body, the blepharoplast is visible. The antherozoids swim in the water by the lashing moment of their flagella.

Development of archegonium. The archegonia are found embedded in the thallus. They remain in direct contact of the vegetative cells of the tissue of the thallus lateral to them. They do not possess jacket sterile cells around them. The development of archegonium begins from a single superficial cell. This cell becomes prominent and acts as **archegonial initial.** According to Mehra and Handoo (1953), this has been established now, that the archegonial initial functions directly as a **primary archegonial cell.** Formerly it was believed (Campbell) that it divides, and

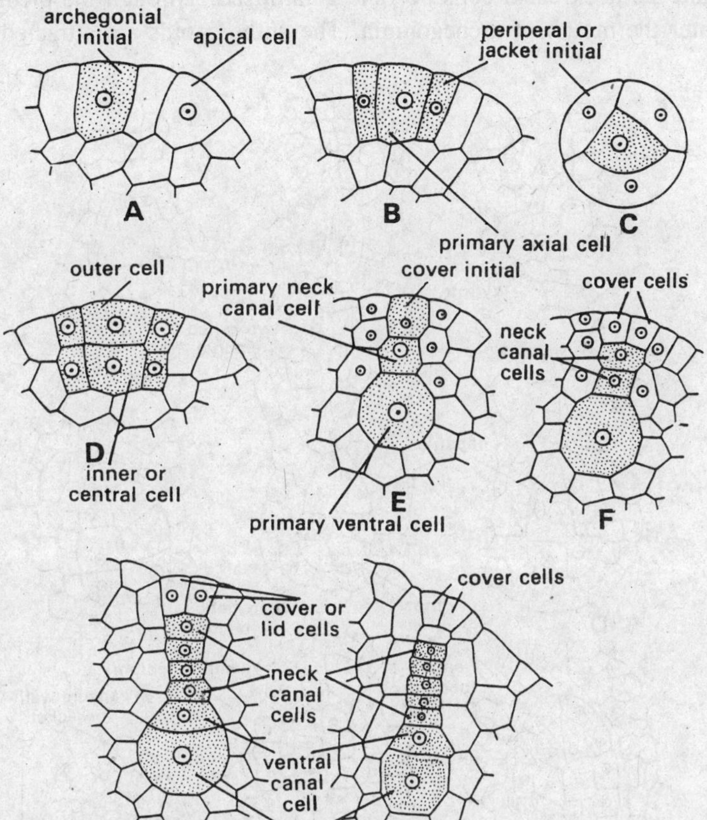

Fig. 8.8. *Anthoceros* sp. Development of archegonium. A, archegonial initial; B, differentiation of primary axia. cell in L.S.; C, same in T.S.; D, division of axial cell into inner and outer cell; E, development of cover initial, primary neck canal cell and primary ventral cell; F, archegonium with egg, ventral canal cell, two neck canal cells and cover cells; G, nearly mature archegonium; H, mature archegonium (After Campbell).

produces two cells, the primary archegonial cell and primary stalk cell. The archegonial initial first divides vertically, producing three **jacket initials** which surround an **axial cell.** The axial cell divides transversely, producing a **cover initial** and a **central cell.** Thereafter, the central cell divides by a transverse wall, giving rise to a **primary canal cell** and a **primary venter cell.** The primary canal cell divides repeatedly, producing a linear file of 4-6 neck canal cells. The primary venter cell divides once transversely, giving rise to two cells, a **ventral canal cell** and an **egg** (oosphere). Comparatively, the neck canal cells are narrower than the venter canal cell and the egg. Eventually, the three jacket initials also divide by transverse walls. The further development of the jacket layer is not at all clear. Since the cells on the lower face of the egg have been derived from the archegonial initial they cannot be treated as a part of archegonium.

Structure of archegonium. On the maturation of the archegonium, the venter canal cells and neck canal cells become gelatinized. Thus a mature archegonium is flask-like in shape, without neck canal cells and with an egg (oosphere) in its venter. At the top of the neck of the archegonium there are four cover cells, which become separated from the archegonium, as soon as the gelatinization of the venter and neck canal cells is over.

Fertilization (syngamy). Prior to fertilization, the cover cells become detached from the archegonium, and the neck canal cells become gelatinized. Through the medium of water, the antherozoids enter the mouth of archegonium. The antherozoids are attracted chemotactically.

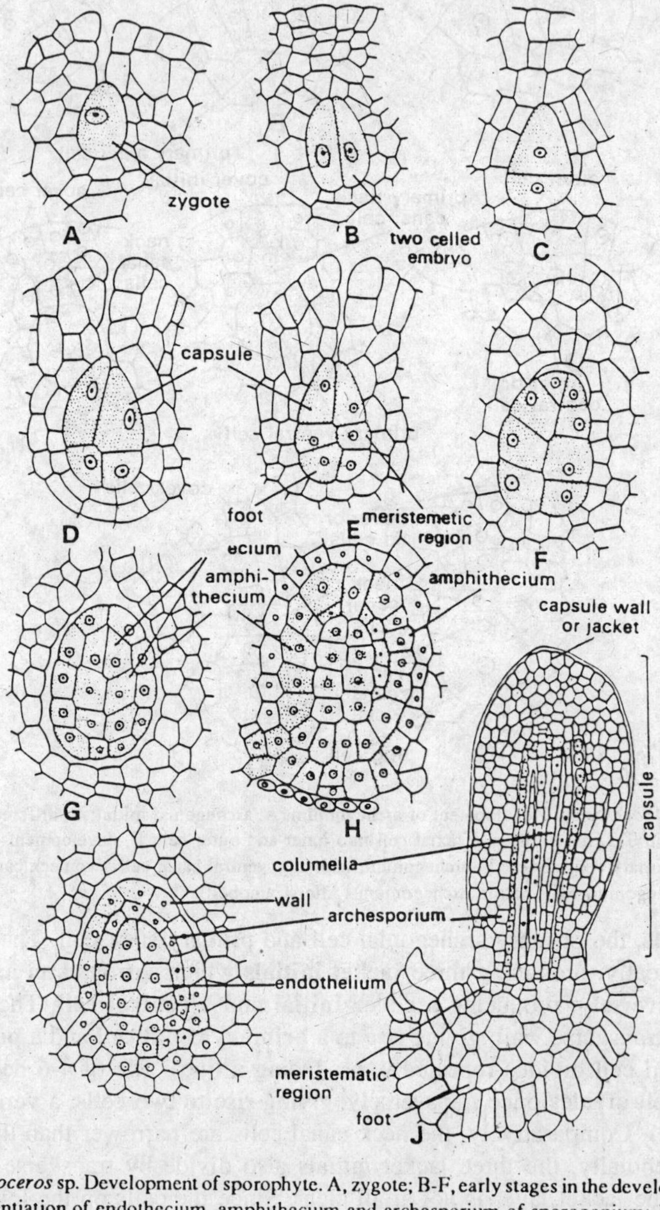

Fig. 8.9. *Anthoceros* sp. Development of sporophyte. A, zygote; B-F, early stages in the development of sporophyte; G-I, stages of the differentiation of endothecium, amphithecium and archesporium of sporogonium; J, longitudinal section of sporophyte showing capsule wall, capsule, archesporium, columella, meristematic region and foot.

Ultimately, one lucky antherozoid penetrates the egg, and the fertilization is effected. The male and female nuclei unite to each other, producing a zygote (oospore), zygote is 2n, and this is the beginning of the sporophytic stage.

Development of sporogonium. After fertilization, the zygote secretes a cellulose wall around it and enlarges in size till it completely fills the venter of the archegonium. The first division of the zygote is vertical. But according to Pande (1932) and Bhardwaj (1950), in certain cases this divides transversely. With the result of the first vertical division, the daughter cells are produced, which are subjected to a transverse division producing four cells of equal or unequal size. When the cells are unequal in size, definitely, the cells towards the neck of the archegonium are larger cells. These cells again divide vertically, developing eightcelled embryo, four cells in each tier. The upper tier of four cells divides transversely. This way the three tiers of four cells each have been produced. The lowermost tier produces the **foot,** the middle tier produces partly the foot and mainly the **seta** and the upper-most tier produces the **capsule.**

The cells of the lowermost tier divide regularly or irregularly many times, producing the bulbous foot. The foot is haustorial in nature, which absorbs food from the tissue of the gametophyte.

The uppermost tier of four cells, divides once or twice transversely, producing two or three tiers of cells. Now the cells divide periclinally, giving rise to an outer layer the **amphithecium** and the central mass of cells the **endothecium.** In the young sporogonium, the columella consists of four vertical rows of the cells, but later on it is made up of sixteen rows of cells. According to Bhardwaj (1958) in *A. gemmulosus* the columella consists of 36 to 49 vertical rows of the cells. The amphithecium divides periclinally producing the outer sterile layer of the **jacket initials** and an inner sporogenous tissue, the **archesporium.** The jacket initials divide again and again periclinally producing the 4 to 6 layered wall of the capsule. The outermost layer develops into the single layered epidermis. The epidermal cells are cutinized. The stomata may or may not develop on the epidermal layer. The rest of the layers, beneath the epidermis develop in normal chlorenchyma. These chlorophyllous cells, however, help in synthesizing the food.

The layer of archesporium developed by periclinal division overarches the columella. The sporogenous layer may be one to four celled in thickness in its further development. In *Anthoceros hawaiensis* it remains one celled in thickness; in A. *pearsoni* and *A. himalayensis* it may become two, three or even four cells in thickness. In younger stages all the cells of sporogenous tissue remain somewhat rectangular in shape. Later on, the sporogenous tissue becomes differentiated into two types of cells, *i.e.,* (i) the **sporocytes** (spore mother cells) and (ii) the **sterile cells** (pseudoelaters).

The sporocytes or spore mother cells undergo the reduction division, each producing a tetrad of four spores. These spores are haploid. The spores, which develop in the upper part of the capsule, mature first. Each spore contains a nucleus and a chloroplast.

The sterile cells soon divide obliquely or transversely producing three to five celled pseudoelaters. On maturity, the pseudoelaters lose their protoplasm. The walls of the elaters may be smooth, irregularly thickened or with spiral thickenings. Such thickenings, vary from species to species. The pseudoelaters help in the dehiscence of the spores and behave like true elaters. In earlier stages their function seems to be nutritive.

The sporogonium and its dehiscence. The capsules arise from the thalli in the form of small horny structures. Usually they are two to three centimeters long. But in some species they range even from five to fifteen centimeters in their height and because of their horny appearance, the species are called 'hornworts'. The mature sporogonium consists of a bulbous foot and a projecting, slender and erect capsule. There is a meristematic zone above the foot, instead of seta. The bulbous foot consists of parenchyma. It remains penetrated in the thallus and acts as haustorium. The superficial cells of the foot are palisade like. The space in between the foot and the capsule is occupied by a meristematic zone. The cells of this zone divide throughout unless and until the food is completely exhausted. This way, the capsule increases in length. The capsule increases in height even after maturation. The cells developing from the meristem become differentiated into jacket layer, columella and archesporium. This way, the upper part of the sporogonium matures first, and the basal part remains young. The capsule does not mature at the same rate in all parts of it. The mature spores liberate from the upper part of the capsule whereas, in the basal part still the cells are in embryonic condition.

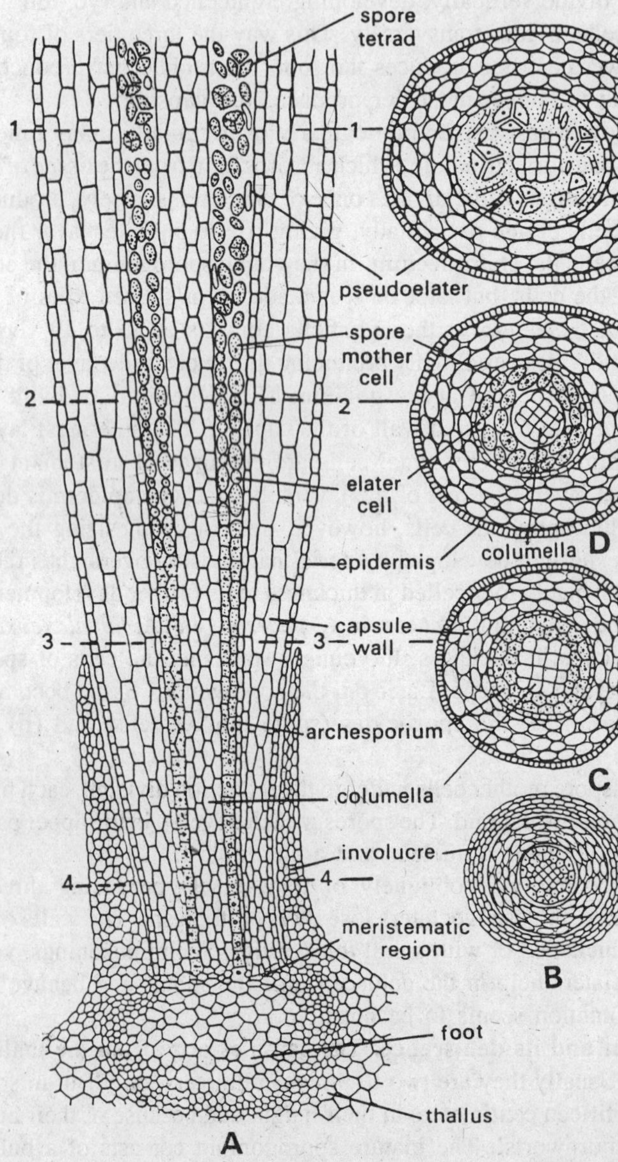

Fig. 8.10. *Anthoceros* sp. A, longitudinal section of sporogonium; B, cross section of sporophyte (A) at 4-4; C, cross section of sporophyte (A) at 3-3; D, cross section of sporophyte (A) at 2-2; E, cross section of sporophyte (A) at 1-1.

Fig. 8.11. *Anthoceros* sp. T.S. of sporogonium.

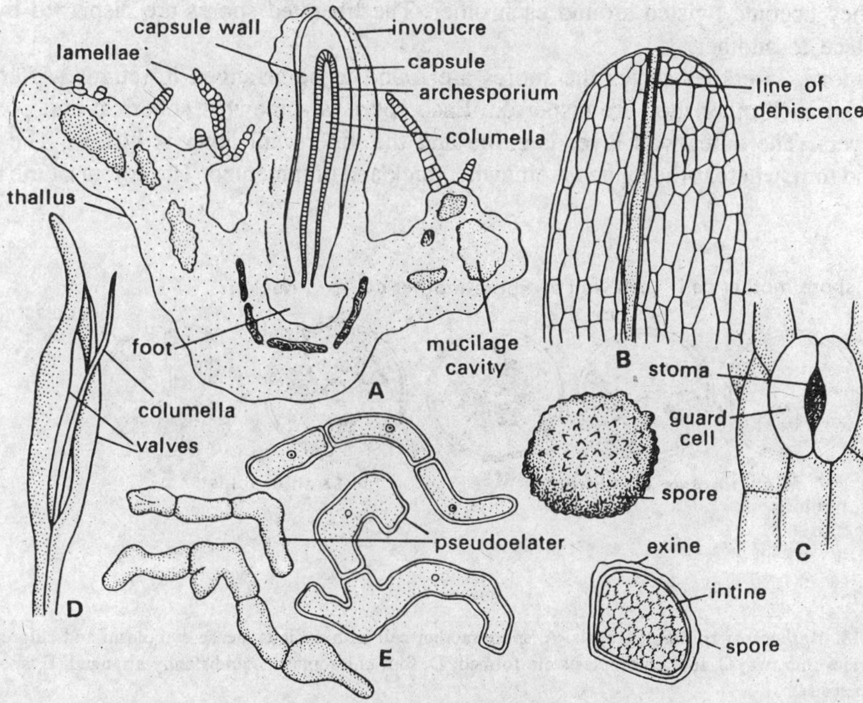

Fig. 8.12. *Anthoceros* sp. A, vertical longitudinal section of thallus with sporophyte enclosed within involucre; B, apical or terminal portion of sporophyte with line of dehiscence; C, stoma with guard cells on the surface of capsule; D, dehiscing capsule showing columella and valves; E, pseudoelaters of different irregular shapes.

The main capsule consists of many important parts. The central region of the capsule is occupied by a sterile columella. According to Campbell (1924), in *A. fusiformis* the columella acts as water conducting tissue. However, this function of columella in other species is not very certain. The main function of columella is to give the mechanical support to the sporogonium. It also helps in the dispersal of the spores.

The columella remains surrounded by sporogenous tissue. In the region just above the foot the archesporium is single layered and too young. The tip region of the sporogonium possesses mature spores and elaters. The wall of the capsule consists of the four to six layers of the parenchymatous cells. The outermost layer is epidermis, which is interrupted by stomata at several places. The epidermal cells are cutinized. The stomata open in the intercellular spaces of the chlorophyllous cells. Usually each cell possesses two chloroplasts. The process of photosynthesis takes place by means of chloroplasts and stomata. This way, the organic food is synthesized for the sporogonium. However, the sporogonium remains dependent upon the thallus for the supply of water and other nutrients throughout its life.

On maturation, the tip of the sporogonium becomes black or dark-brown in colour. The capsule divides at this stage. The tip of the capsule shrivels up by losing water. The dehiscence of the capsule is more or less dependent upon the loss of water. This way the dry atmosphere helps in the dehiscence of the capsule. The dehiscence begins from the tip region of the capsule. At first a small longitudinal slit appears, which widens and enlarges. The pseudoelaters are hygroscopic in nature. They begin to twist after the exposition of the internal mass the outside. Due to this twisting of the pseudoelaters the pressure is exerted on the jacket layer, and it bursts liberating the spores in the atmosphere. According to species, the dehiscence takes place by means of one to four longitudinal slits. The valves of the capsule curve backward and ultimately, on drying up they become twisted around each other. The liberated spores are dispersed by wind from one place to another.

The spore. In earlier stages the spores are found to be arranged in tetrads. After being separated from each other they are dispersed. Each spore is somewhat spherical and possesses two wall layers. The outer wall layer is **exine** and the inner wall layer is **initine.** The initine is smooth and thin, whereas the exine is somewhat thick and ornamented. The colour of the mature

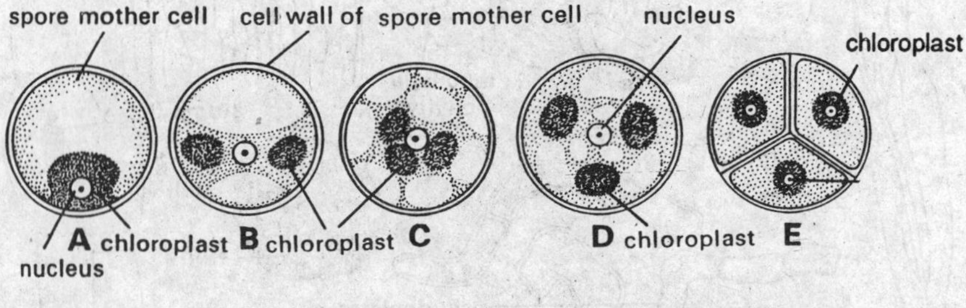

Fig. 8.13. *Anthoceros* sp. Sporogenesis. A, spore mother cell with nucleus, dense cytoplasm and chloroplast; B, chloroplast divides into two; C, four chloroplasts are formed; D, four chloroplasts equidistantly arranged; E, spore tetrad formed after meiosis.

spores varies from species to species, this may be yellow, brown, darkbrown or black. Each spore possesses a single nucleus, a colourless plastid, few oil droplets and food material within it.

Germination of spore. After their liberation from the sporogonium the spores undergo a period of rest prior to germination which ranges from few weeks to few months. The exine of the spore ruptures, and the intine comes out in the form of a germinal tube or protonema of variable length.

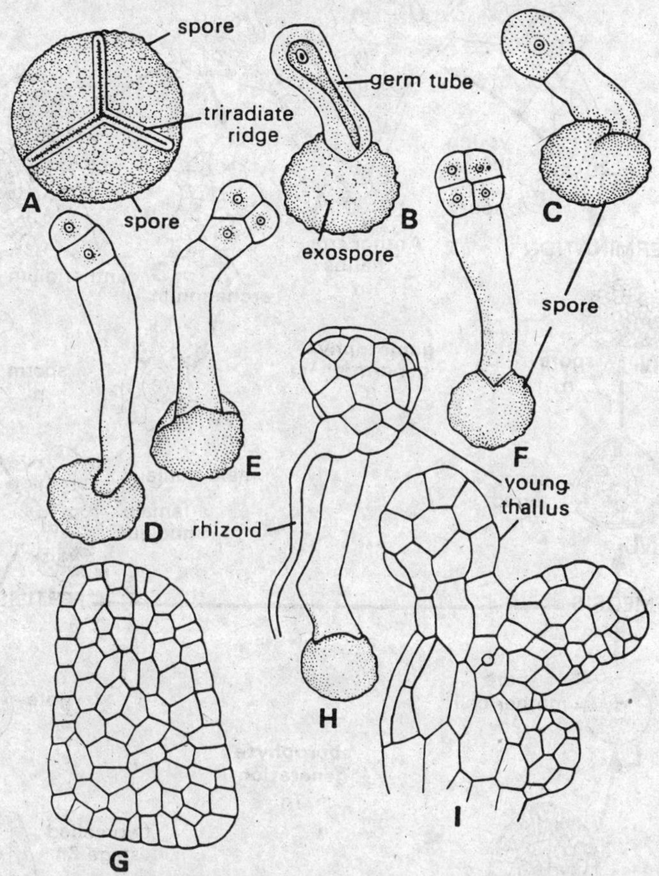

Fig. 8.14. *Anthoceros* sp. Spore and its germination. A, spore with triradiate ridge; B, germinating spore producing germ tube; C-F, further stages of spore germination; G-I, formation of young gametophyte (thallus) and rhizoids.

Development of young gametophyte. The chlorophyll present in the chloroplast of the spore passes in the germinal tube along with oil droplets and food material. Thereafter the germinal tube divides transversely at its apical end. This division is followed by another transverse division. Soon after, the so formed two cells divide by longitudinal intersecting walls and the quadrants are resulted. At the terminal end a growing point with an apical cell appears which by producing several segments develops into the young gametophyte. Soon after a mucilage slit develops on the ventral side of the thallus. Some of the marginal cells of the young thallus develop into smooth walled rhizoids. The *Nostoc* sp. penetrates the thallus through the mucilage slits, which later on form the colonies of the same.

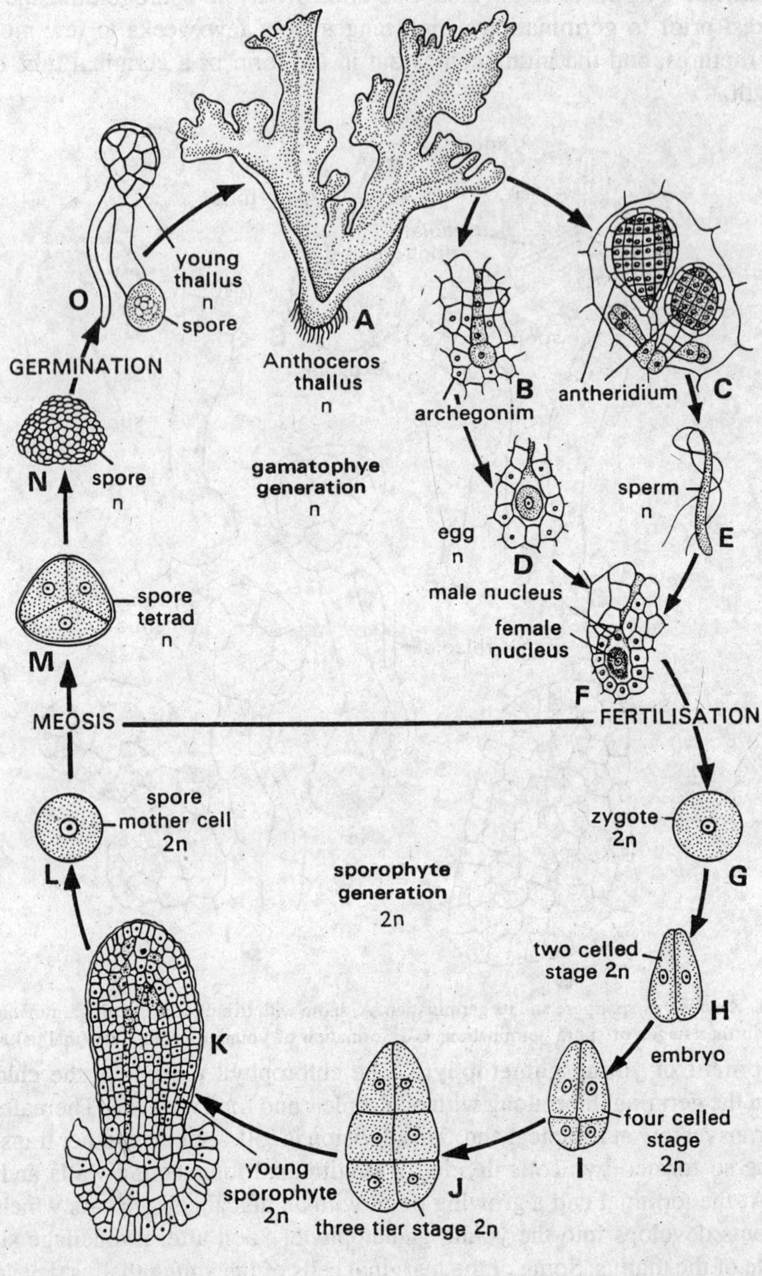

Fig. 8.15. *Anthoceros* sp. Diagrammatic life-cycle. A, thallus; B, archegonium; C, antheridium; D, egg within venter; E, sperm or antherozoid; F, male and female nuclei are in close vicinity; G, zygote (2n); H, two-celled embryo; I, four-celled embryo; J, three tier stage; K, young sporophyte in L.S.; L, spore mother cell; M, spore tetrad; N, spore (n); O, germination of spore and development of young thallus.

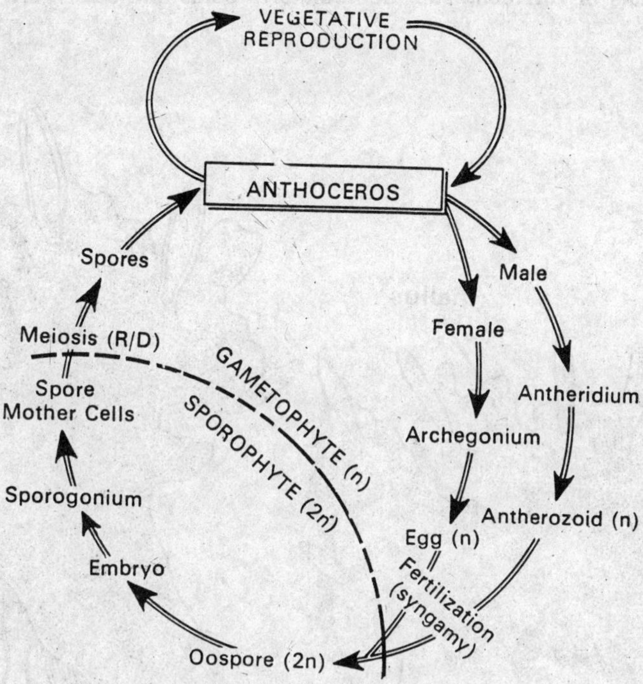

Fig. 8.16. *Anthoceros.* Graphic life-cycle.

Systematic position.

Division. Bryophyta
Class. Anthocerotopsida (Anthocerotae)
Order. Anthocerotales
Family. Anthocerotaceae
Genus. *Anthoceros.*

Family-Notothylaceae

There is a single genus (*i.e., Notothylas*) in this family.

Characteristic features. The capsule (sporogonium) is cylindrical and horizontal. There are no stomata on capsule wall. Archesporium may be endothecial and amphithecial in origin. The elaters are short and stumpy having irregular thickening bands.

Genus NOTOTHYLAS

Occurrence and distribution. There are eleven species in this genus. Three of them are found in our country. They are- *Notothylas indica, N. levieri* and *N. chaudhurii.* As usual this genus is also found in moist and shady places. The species are found on moist rocks or earth or on the walls. It is found both in temperate and tropical regions.

THE GAMETOPHYTE

External structure. The gametophytes are thallose, somewhat lobed or radially dissected. The gametophyte is prostrate, thin and delicate. The orbicular or suborbicular thallus is light green or yellowish in colour. The gametophytes are always dorsiventrally differentiated and possess numerous smooth-walled rhizoids on the ventral surface. The thallus remains attached to the substratum by means of rhizoids. The tuberculate rhizoids and scales are altogether absent.

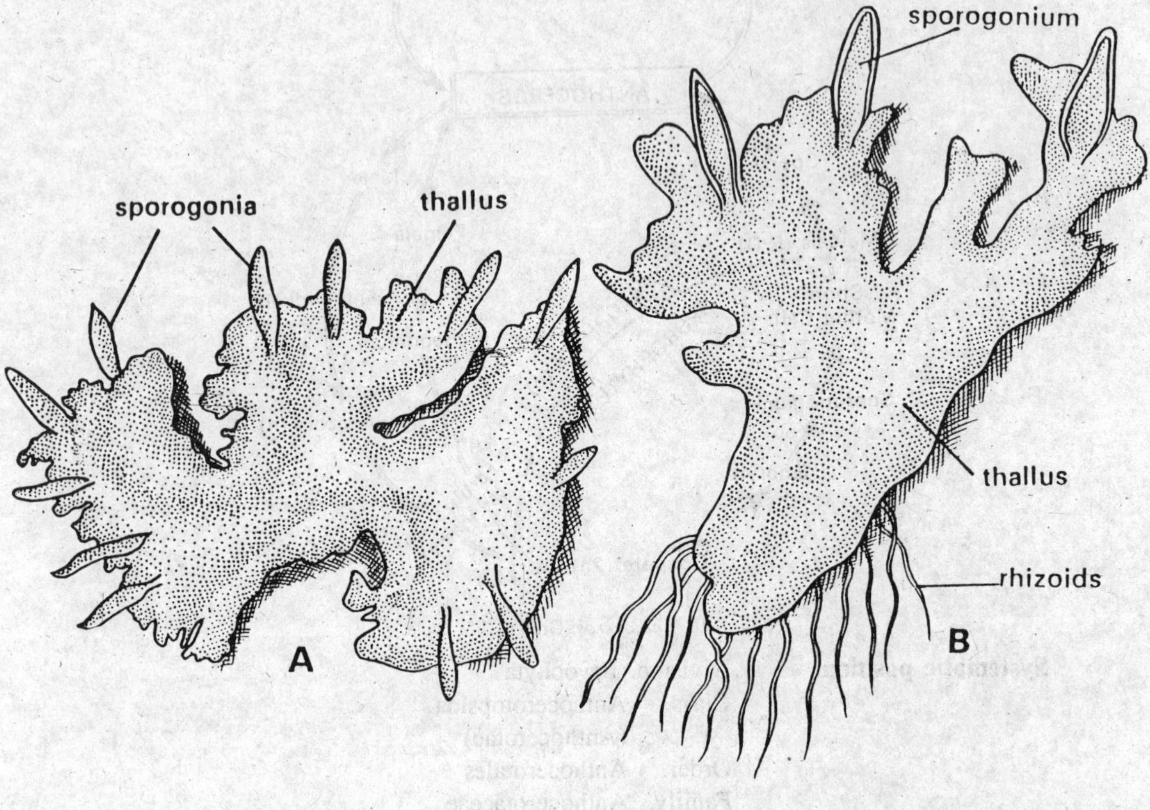

Fig. 8.17. *Notothylas indica*. A, gametophyte with many sporogonia; B, gametophyte (thallus) with few sporogonia and rhizoids.

Internal structure. The thallus, when examined in its cross section shows no internal differentiation of tissues. The ventral portion of a thallus possesses mucilage-filled intercellular cavities on the dorsal side and opening to the surface by narrow slits. Very often these mucilage cavities contain *Nostoc* colonies. However, the thallus of *Notothylas javanicus* is solid and does not contain any colonies of blue green alga.

In the middle, the thallus is 6 to 8 cells in thickness. The lateral margins are 1 to 3 cells in thickness. The internal cells are twice as big as the cells of the upper and lower epidermal layers.

The cells usually contain a single large chloroplast. The chloroplasts of superficial cells are usually larger than those in other cells and are lens shaped. Each chloroplast possesses a single large pyrenoid.

Apical growth. The apical growth of a thallus is initiated by a single apical cell. This cell gives rise to a transverse row of cells by a series of vertical divisions. A cell near each end of the row begins to function as an apical cell and this way, the two growing points separate farther and farther from each other as growth continues. A compact rosette like thallus is being resulted by continuous repeated dichotomous branching.

Reproduction. It takes place by means of vegetative and sexual methods.

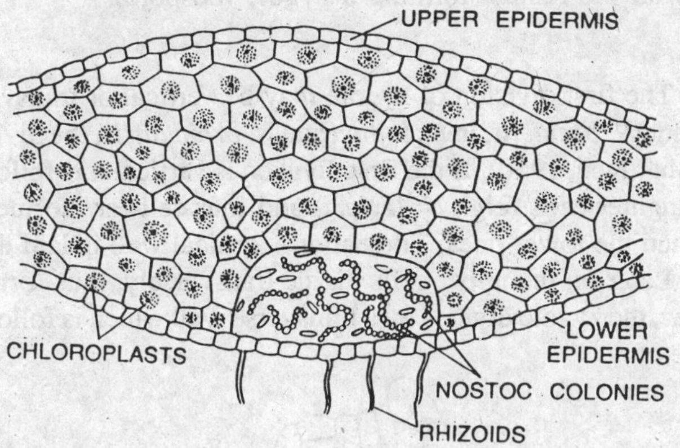

Fig. 8.18. *Notothylas indica*. Cross section of thallus showing algal cavity with *Nostoc* colonies and smoothwalled rhizoids.

Vegetative reproduction. The vegetative reproduction is found less frequently. It takes place by progressive growth and death reaching dichotomies. Sometimes the margins of the gametophytes become thickened and the superficial cells develop into a corky layer. These structures are called 'tubers' which remain viable during drought period when other portions of a thallus die. On the approach of favourable conditions each such tuber develops into a new thallus.

Sexual reproduction. The species may be homothallic or heterothallic. All the three Indian species, *i.e., N. indica, N. levieri* and *N. chaudhurii* are homothallic and protandrous. However, Kashyap (1929) has described both *N. indica* and *N. levieri* as heterothallic.

Antheridium and its development. Each antheridium possesses a short stalk. Three or four antheridia are found in each antheridial chamber, but sometimes as many as six antheridia are met with in each chamber. The antherozoids are uninucleate and biciliate.

The antheridia develop endogenously as in *Anthoceros* and these are formed near the growing point. The development of antheridium in *Notothylas* is essentially similar to that of *Anthoceros.*

Archegonium and its development. The structure of archegonium in *Notothylas* is similar to that of *Anthoceros* with minor differences. Comparatively the neck canal is usually wider in *Notothylas* and usually contains 3 to 5 neck canal cells.

The development of archegonium is essentially similar to that of *Anthoceros*. (See fig. 8.8; description on pp. 117).

Fertilization. At the time of fertilization an egg does not completely fill the venter of an archegonium. The water

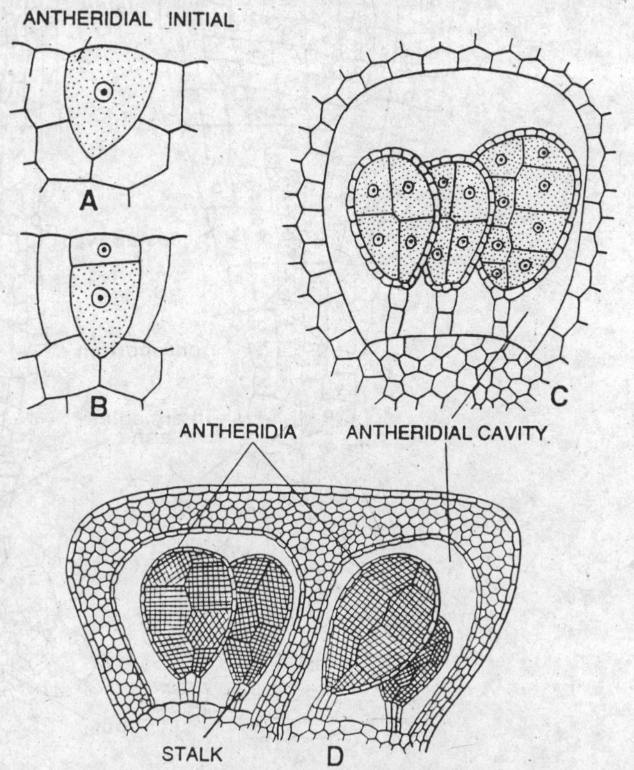

Fig. 8.19. *Notothylas*. Development of antheridium. A, antheridial initial; B, dividing antheridial initial; C, young antheridia; D, nearly mature antheridia in the antheridial cavities.

is indispensable for fertilization. Through the medium of water, the antherozoids enter the mouth of the archegonium. Ultimately one of the antherozoids penetrates the egg and the fertilization is effected. The male nucleus fuses with the female forming a zygote (oospore).

THE SPOROPHYTE

Development of sporogonium. The first division of zygote may be vertical or transverse. It is vertical in *N. javanicus*, *N. levieri* and *N. breutelli*. In *N. indica* and *N. orbicularis*, the division of zygote is transverse (Pande, 1932; Bhardwaj, 1950). If the first division is vertical it is followed by a transverse division of the two daughter cells (*e.g.*, *N. levieri*) and four cells are formed of which the two upper cells are larger than the lower ones. Thereafter a vertical wall is laid down and an eight celled embryo is formed. Later on the upper cells divide transversely, thus forming three tiers of four cells each. In *N. indica*, the zygote divides by a transverse wall which is followed

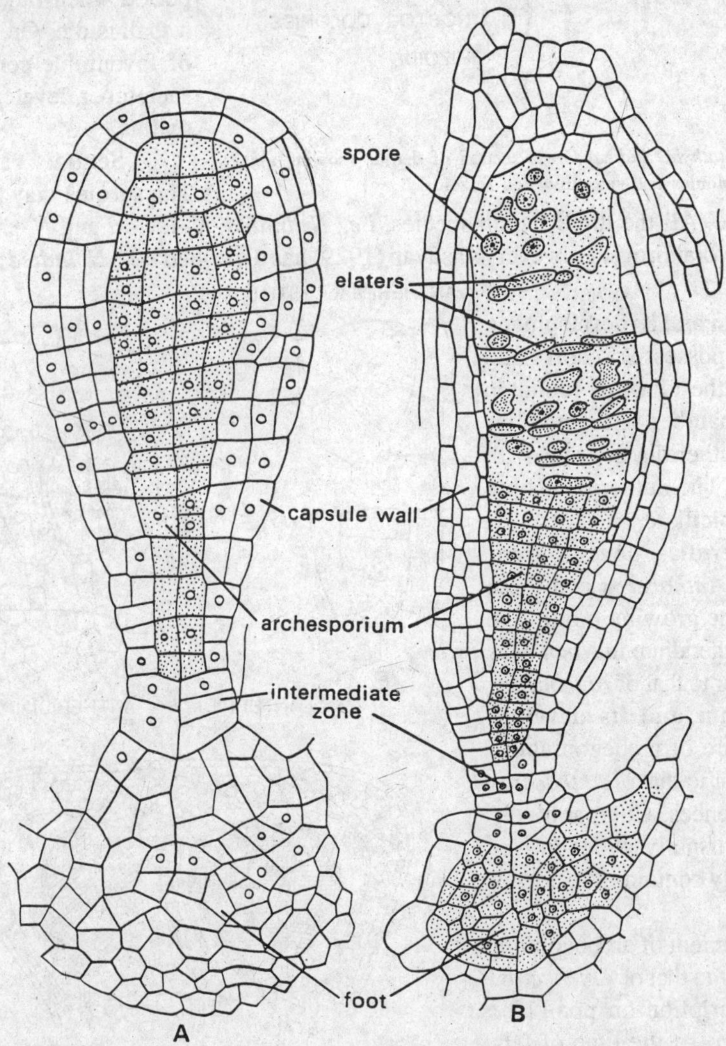

Fig. 8.20. *Notothylas* sp. Sporophyte. A, longitudinal section of young sporogonium; B, longitudinal section of mature sporogonium containing spores and elaters. (After Pande).

by two succeeding vertical divisions, at right angles to each other and to the primary wall and this way an eight celled embryo is resulted. The upper cells of this embryo divide transversely forming three tiers of four cells each.

In both types, of the three tiers the lower two tiers produce the foot and the uppermost tier forms the capsule and seta. The cells of the uppermost tier divide periclinally and a central **endothecium** and the peripheral **amphithecium** are being differentiated.

In *N. indica,* and many other species the amphithecium divides periclinally forming an inner and outer layer. The inner layer forms the **archesporium** and the outer layer gives rise to the wall of capsule. The entire endothecium gives rise to the **columella.** This way, in *N. indica* the sporogenous tissue develops exclusively from amphithecium like that of *Anthoceros.*

However in *N. breutelli* the endothecium instead of producing the columella, gives rise to the archesporium. However, in many cases the endothecium forms sterile tissue towards the end of the development. Campbell has reported an intermediate condition in *N. javanicus* where the columella may be well developed, but in some cases the columella is much smaller and the upper portion gives rise to spores. In some species, *e.g., N. levieri* and *N. chaudhurii* the columella is altogether absent. Here the entire endothecium forms the archesporium, while the whole amphithecium forms the wall. In *N. indica* and *N. orbicularis* where the columellae exist the archesporium is usually four cells thick and there are alternating bands of fertile spore mother cells and sterile cells. In *N. levieri,* where columella does not exist, the alternating bands of spore mother cells and sterile cells extend across the capsule. The spore mother cells divide meiotically forming the tetrads of the haploid spores.

Structure of mature sporogonium. The fully mature sporogonium is cylindrical and 2 to 3 mm. long. The sporogonia are found along the margin of the thallus in between the lobes. They are tapering at both the ends and usually found horizontally on the thallus. The sporogonia may remain completely surrounded by the thin membranous involucres, *e.g.,* in *N. indica* and

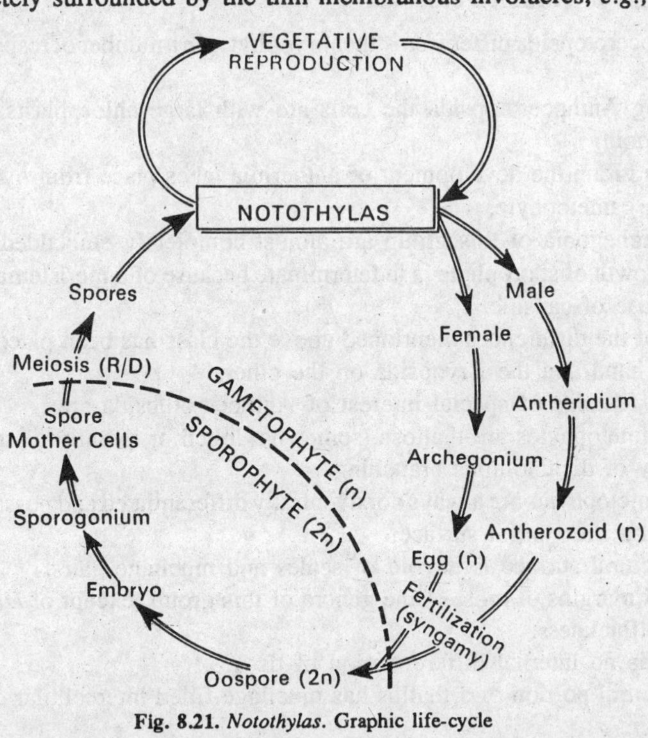

Fig. 8.21. *Notothylas.* Graphic life-cycle

N. levieri. In *N. javanicus* and sometimes in *N. indica* the capsules project beyond the involucres. The sporogonium consists of a foot, a meristematic zone and a capsule. The foot is more or less triangular and much smaller than that of *Anthoceros*. The columella may or may not present. It is found in *N. indica* and *N. orbicularis* where as it is absent in *N. levieri* and *N. chaudhurii*. An intermediate condition of columella is found in *N. javanicus*. The wall of capsule is composed of four layers of cells. The stomata are absent. The elaters are unicellular, short and irregular in shape.

Dehiscence of sporogonium. The capsule ruptures lengthwise, generally by one suture only. But in some cases they may dehisce along both sutures. In *N. orbicularis*, the capsule divides by two to four valves.

The spore and its germination. The spores are dark brown and minutely granular. Each spore remains surrounded by two wall layers-a thin endospore and thick exospore.

In *N. indica*, the spores go under rest prior to germination. On germination the exospore ruptures and the endospore comes out in the form of a small papilla. Two oblique walls are laid down in this papilla and thus an apical cell is established, the apical cell cuts off several segments and the young gametophyte (thallus) is formed.

Systematic position. The genus *Notothylas* is often placed in the family Anthocerotaceae. However, according to Muller (1940), Proskauer and Reimers (1954) this genus has been placed in a separate family, the Notothylaceae, including a single genus, *Notothylas*.

Systematic position. Division. Bryophyta
Class. Anthocerotopsida
Order. Anthocerotales
Family. Notothylaceae
Genus. *Notothylas*

Interrelationships of Anthocerotopsida

The Anthocerotopsida differ from other bryophytes in a number of respects. These differences are :

(a) Among Anthocerotopsida the cells are with large chloroplasts and each chloroplast contains a pyrenoid.

(b) In this group the development of antheridia takes place from hypodermal cells on the dorsal side of a gametophyte.

(c) The archegonia of this group are almost completely embedded in the gametophyte.

(d) The growth of sporophyte is indeterminate because of a meristematic region continually adding to the base of capsule.

Because of the differences mentioned above the class has been placed in between Hepaticopsida on one hand and the Bryopsida on the other.

The other features of special interest of Anthocerotopsida are :

(a) The gametophytes are thallose, somewhat lobed or radially dissected, and sometimes show a tendency of dichotomous branching.

(b) The gametophytes are always dorsiventrally differentiated and possess numerous smooth-walled rhizoids on the ventral surface.

(c) The ventral surface is devoid of scales and mucilage hairs.

(d) Lateral margins of most of the genera of this group (except of *Dendroceros*) are more than one cell in thickness.

(e) There is no internal differentiation of tissues.

(f) The ventral portion of a thallus has mucilage-filled intercellular cavities on the dorsal side and opening to the surface by narrow slits. These cavities generally contain *Nostoc* (a blue-green alga) colonies in them.

(g) The pyrenoids of Anthocerotopsida are not homologous with those of green algae (Chlorophyceae) since they consist of a crowded mass of 25 to 300 disc or spindle shaped bodies (McAllister, 1914, 1927).

(h) The growth of a thallus is initiated by a single apical cell with two cutting faces (except in *Dendroceros* where there are three cutting faces).

(i) The vegetative reproduction by death and decay of thalli is less frequent in this group than in Hepaticopsida. However, tuber formation is frequent in this group.

(j) Most of the species are homothallic, but some are heterothallic (Proskauer, 1948). In heterothallic species the sex determination is genotypic, that is, two spores of a tetrad develop into male and two into female gametophytes.

(k) Anthocerotopsida and Hepaticopsida are fundamentally different in the fact that in the former an antheridial initial is the inner daughter cell produced by periclinal division of a superficial daughter cell of the gametophyte. This suggests that Anthocerotopsida are derived from ancestors in which antheridia developed from superficial dorsal cells.

(l) In *Anthoceros* and some other genera of this group, the antheridial initial may divide vertically into two or four daughter cells, each of which develops into an antheridium.

(m) The development of the primary antheridial cell into the antheridium proper is similar as in Sphaerocarpales and Marchantiales.

(n) In Anthocerotopsida, the spermatogenesis is much like that of other bryophytes and involves a metamorphosis of androcytes into biflagellate sperms or antherozoids.

(o) In Anthocerotopsida the archegonial initial functions directly as a primary archegonial cell instead of dividing into primary archegonial cell and primary stalk cell as found in other bryophytes.

(p) The first division of a zygote is vertical but cases have been found (Bhardwaj, 1950; Pande, 1932) where the transverse division occurs.

(q) The amphithecium divides periclinally, where the outer layer functions as the initial layer of the jacket and the inner layer as the archesporium.

(r) One unique feature of Anthocerotopsida is that cells of a capsule do not mature at the same rate and that cells in the basal portion of a capsule remain embryonic even after those in the apical portion are fully mature. This feature is not found in other bryophytes.

Affinities of Anthocerotopsida

This group exhibits similarities with green algae, Hepaticopsida (liver worts), bryopsida (mosses) and Psilophytales of Pteridophyta.

(A) Features common with green algae

The green algae (Chlorophyceae) have been considered a group from which the bryophytes and pteridophytes are believed to have originated.

(i) Usually each cell of gametophyte has a single large chloroplast of a definite shape.

(ii) The pyrenoids are present in the chloroplasts of the cells of gametophyte. The presence of pyrenoids is the characteristic of cells of green algae only

(iii) The pyrenoids of Anthocerotopsida and green algae are similar in function and form starch grains in their peripheral region.

(iv) The outline and branching of the gametophyte is similar in both cases.

(v) The presence of biciliate or biflagellate (both flagella of whiplash type) antherozoids.

(B) Features common with liverworts (Hepaticopsida)

Many taxonomists include Anthocerotales in Hepaticae.

(i) The gametophyte is thallus-like.

(ii) The smooth-walled rhizoids are found in the members of Anthocerotopsida as well as in the members of Jungermanniales of Hepaticopsida.

(iii) The apical growth of thallus is similar in both.

(iv) Archesporium giving rise to spores and sterile cells in both groups. The sterile cells with spiral bands are found in *Megaceros* of Anthocerotopsida which exhibit the similarity with many members of Hepaticopsida.

(v) Differentiation of the amphithecium and endothecium by periclinal walls is similar to that of many Hepaticae.

(C) Features common with the Bryopsida (mosses)

(i) Presence of central columella in both groups.

(ii) Large reduction of the sporogenous tissue in both Anthocerotopsida as well as Bryopsida groups.

(iii) Presence of functional stomata (*e.g.*, in *Funaria*).

(iv) Differentiation of archesporium from the inner amphithecium as in Sphagnales. This feature shows link between Anthocerotopsida and Bryopsida.

(v) The developmental stages of embryo are quite similar. The early divisions are very much alike.

(D) Features common with the Pteridophyta

(i) The presence of sunken sex organs is common in both groups.

(ii) The presence of similar vegetative structure of the gametophyte in *Anthoceros* and Fern.

(iii) The presence of highly developed sporogonium with photosynthetic tissue indeterminate growth and functional stomata.

The above mentioned facts support that the Anthocerotopsida are a distinct but **synthetic group** of plants. It forms a connecting link with liverworts and mosses on one hand and with pteridophytes on the other. There is also a remote connection with green algae (Chlorophyceae). Campbell (1928) suggested, "The fact that the primary sporogenous tissue in the Anthocerotales always arises from the amphithecium, while in all other liverworts it is developed from the endothecium, would seem to be a radical difference". Campbell is also of opinion that the sporophyte of *Anthoceros* with its assimilatory system with stomata and continued growth shows the close alliance to the independent, rootless dichotomously branched sporophyte of the primitive fossil group, Psilophytales. Mehra (1957) suggested that both Anthocerotopsida and Psilopsida arose from the common Anthorhyniaceae stock.

Biological significance of Anthocerotopsida

The sporophytes of Anthocerotopsida exhibit probable lines of biological progress as follows:

(i) The presence of elaborate ventilated assimilatory system suggests the beginning of the physiological independence of the sporophyte.

(ii) The discontinuation of continuous sporogenous tissue by the growth of sterile cells between the spore mother cells which suggests the beginning of the formation of sporangia.

(iii) The establishment of a well developed sterile columella from the central endothecium suggests the beginning of the formation of conducting system, and the initial stage in the formation of superficial sporangia.

(iv) The presence of intercalary meristematic zone suggests the beginning of the indeterminate and continuous growth of the sporophyte.

Comparison of Anthoceros and Notothylas

	Anthoceros	*Notothylas*
Systematic position and Distribution	Division-Bryophyta; class Anthocerotopsida (Anthocerotae); Order-Anthocerotales; Family-Anthocerotaceae; Genus-*Anthoceros.* 25 species are found in India; cosmopolitan in distribution.	Division-Bryophyta; class Anthocerotopsida (Anthocerotae); order-Anthocerotales; Family-Notothylaceae; Genus-*Notothylas* only 3 species are found in India. Its distribution is confined to tropical and temperate regions.
Habit: external features	Moist shaded places. Thallus thin, dorsiventral with a broad indistinct mid rib; tendency towards dichotomous branching; rhizoids-unicellular, only smooth walled; unbranched scales are absent.	Damp, shady places. Thallus thin, prostrate delicate without midrib; branching is same as in *Anthoceros;* rhizoids-smooth walled, absent in mature gametophore; scales are absent.
Internal structure	All cells photosynthetic; apical growth is either by a single apical cell or a group of apical cells.	As in *Anthoceros;* single apical cell is there.
Sexual organs	Monoecious and dioecious; antheridia-endogenous, inside closed antheridial cavities on the dorsal surface of thallus, stalk is long, either slender or massive, body jacket is single layered, antherozoid is biciliate; archegonia-embedded in the dorsal surface of the thallus, neck is made up of 6 vertical rows of cells, venter is single layered thick, cover cells are 2 to 4, neck canal cells are usually 4.	Monoecious and dioecious; antheridia-as in *Anthoceros* stalk is short, body-jacket is single layered, antherozoids biciliate; archegonia as in *Anthoceros,* neck is made up of 6 vertical rows of cells, venter is single-layered thick, cover cells are 4 ncek canal cells are usually 3 to 5.
Sporophyte	Amphithecium gives rise to jacket of capsule and archesporium; endothecium gives rise to columella; archesporium gives rise to sporocytes and pseudoelaters; foot here is bulbous; seta is absent; capsule is long and cylindrical and its wall is four to six-layered and persistent; pseudoelaters without thickenings; columella present, arched over by spore sac; dehiscence of spores occur when capsule wall splits into 1 to 4 valves, which remain united at the tip, pseudoelaters help in spore dispersal.	Amphithecium gives rise to either to jacket of the capsule and archesporium; endothecium gives rise to either columella or archesporium; archesporium gives rise to sporocytes and elaters; foot, here, is triangular; seta is absent; capsule is cylindrical and its wall is four-layered and persistent; elaters unicellular, with short curved thickened bands; columella is present or absent; dehiscence along one suture or along both sutures or by 2 to 4 valves.
Young gametophyte	Two spore wall layers; size of spore is 0.025 to 0.05 mm; germinal tube forms at the time of spore germination.	Two spore wall layers; size of spore is approximately 0.036 mm; a short germinal tube is formed at the time of spore germination.

9

Bryopsida (Musci)

Order-Sphagnales

This is the third and the largest group of Bryophyta. It comprises of 3 orders, 28 families, about 660 genera and 14,504 species. The most characteristic features of the group Bryopsida are as follows:

There are two stages of gametophyte (i) prostrate, thalloid branched protonema and (ii) erect, leafy gametophore. The gametophytic plant body consists of the stem, spirally arranged leaves and the sex organs, *i.e.*, antheridia and archegonia. The rhizoids are multicellular, and obliquely septate.

The tissue of the stem are mainly differentiated into two regions. The outer thin walled cells constitute the cortex whereas the central thick walled cells form the conducting tissue. However, xylem and phloem are absent.

The sex organs develop from the superficial cells of the gametophore (gametophytic plant).

The sporogonium (sporophyte) is differentiated into foot, seta and capsule. The capsular wall is interrupted by stomata at several places. The spores produced in the sporogonium are the beginners of the gametophytic stage. On germination, the spores produce protonema, which are to develop into gametophytic plants. However the elaters are not present in the sporogonium. The central columella remains surrounded by archesporium which gives rise to spore mother cells, and ultimately the spores. The archesporium or sporogenous mass develops from outer layer of endothecium which in addition forms columella.

Classification of Bryopsida (Musci). Various classifications have been proposed by various workers from time to time.

Bower (1935), Wettstein (1935) and Campbell (1940) have subdivided this large group into three orders, *i.e.*,

(1) Sphagnales
(2) Andreaeales
(3) Bryales

However, Smith (1955) divided this group into three subclasses. They are-

(1) Sub-class-Sphagnobrya
(2) Sub-class-Andreaeobrya
(3) Sub-class-Eubrya.

Engler, Werdermann and Reimers (1954) have divided the class Bryopsida (Musci) into five sub-classes. They are-

(1) Sub-class-Sphagnidae
(2) Sub-class-Andreaeidae
(3) Sub-class-Bryidae
(4) Sub-class-Buxbaumiidae
(5) Sub-class-Polytrichidae.

However, Parihar has divided the class Bryopsida (Musci) into three sub-classes.

(1) Sub-class-Sphagnidae
(2) Sub-class-Andreaeidae

(3) Sub-class-Bryidae.

In the present text the classification proposed by G.M. Smith (1955) has been followed.

Sub-class-SPHAGNOBRYA

The characteristic features of this sub-class are as follows. They are known as bog mosses or peat mosses. All species of *Sphagnum* grow in ponds, swamps and other moist places. The compact mass of dead gametophytes together with the remains of other plants is known as **peat.**

The protonema is broad and thallose. It produces one gametophore. The leaves of gametophores lack midrib and usually composed of two types of cells – the narrow living green cells and large hyaline dead cells. The branches arise in lateral clusters in the axis of the leaves borne on the stem.

The antheridia are borne in the axils of leaves on the antheridial branch. The archegonia are terminal in position. They are formed acrogynously.

The sporogenous tissue of a sporophyte develops from the amphithecium. The sporogonium remains elevated above the gametophyte because of the elongation of a stalk of gametophytic tissue, the **pseudopodium,** rather than to an elongation of a seta, as found in higher Bryopsida.

Classification. This sub-class has a single order Sphagnales. This single order contains but one family, the Sphagnaceae. There is single genus *Sphagnum* in this family. This genus includes about 336 species. The genus *Sphagnum* has been discussed here in detail.

Genus SPHAGNUM

Occurrence. This genus includes about 336 species. This is world-wide in distribution. The species of *Sphagnum* extend from tropics north and south through temperature zones to sub-arctic and extensive masses on boggy and peaty soils, where they often make the greater part of the plant covering. They are very commonly met with in swampy place, and on very wet rocks of hills. They build up certain types of wet peat that the term **'sphagnum bog'** is used in Plant Ecology. Some species grow as sub-merged aquatics in peaty pools. About 10 to 17 species are found in our country. They are commonly known as **bog moss, turfmoss** and **peat moss.**

Structure. The species of *Sphagnum* are among the largest mosses in point of size. The aquatic species may attain length of several feet. The young plants are differentiated into rhizoids, stem and leaves. On the maturity of the plants, the rhizoids disappear. The stem bears several lateral branches which arise from leaf axils.

On germination the spore produces a **protonema,** which is thalloid and lobed. In poor light the protonema may be filamentous but when light intensity is much the protonema, becomes thalloid. The thalloid structure is one cell in thickness. It remains attached to its substratum by means of multicellular rhizoids. The leafy gametophyte plant arises from the margin of the thalloid protonema, as in other mosses. The gametophyte develops with the result of the formation of a three-sided apical cell from one protonemal cell, which by its rapid divisions builds up the leaf bearing axis.

Stem. The leafy gametophyte is perennial and bears an upright stem. The mature plant consists of an upright stem which has practically indefinite power of growth. When the plants grow in deep water the stem may reach a length of several feet. On land, however, the lower parts decay and, therefore, the living stems are only a few inches long. Branching is normally lateral, from the leaf axils. Near the apex of the stem the branches are short and of limited growth. These branches are clustered together closely to form conspicuous compact head also known as **coma.** The coma is formed because of the shortened internodes between the branchtufts near the apex. Elongated additional branches are borne lower down on the stem. In the species which grow out of water the branches are of two types-**divergent** and **drooping** branches. The divergent branches are usually short, stout and grow upwards. The drooping branches are long, slender and drooping. They are found loosely arranged around the main stem. These elongated branches act as water conductors.

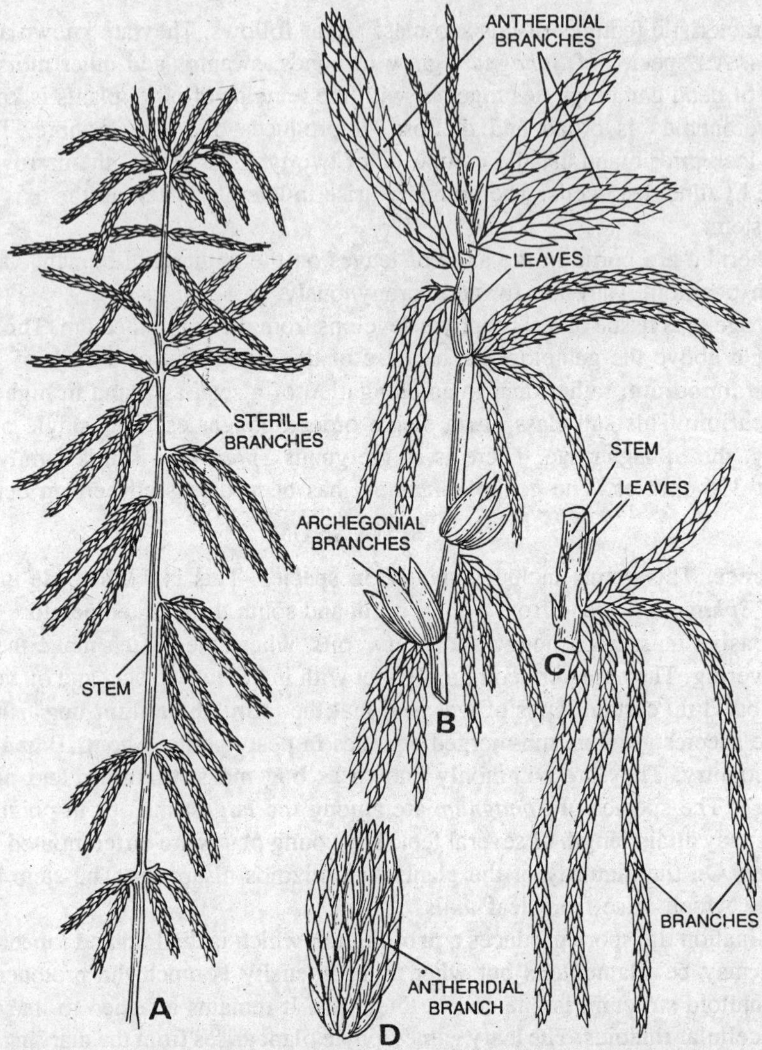

Fig. 9.1. *Sphagnum*. A, gametophyte with stem, sterile branches and fertile branches at the top; B, part of gametophore bearing male (antheridial) and female (archegonial) branches; C, portion of a plant showing a tuft of branches; D, an antheridial branch.

Anatomy of stem. The anatomy of the axis is somewhat variable. Typically the stem in transverse section shows three zones. The outermost zone consists of a layer of **spongy cortex or hyalodermis.** The cells of which are dead and empty. In the beginning it is single layered but later on this becomes multi-layered. In lateral branches it is always one cell in thickness. In mature stem the cells of cortex possess pores in their walls and sometimes spiral thickenings too. Like velamen in orchids, this tissue actively absorbs water by capillary action and takes the place of rhizoids which are not found in mature plants. In certain species such as *S. tenellum* and *S. molluscum,* the side branches, though not the main axis possess the cells of the outer layer which are found at the points of leaf insertion, elongated and flask-shaped, with the open neck

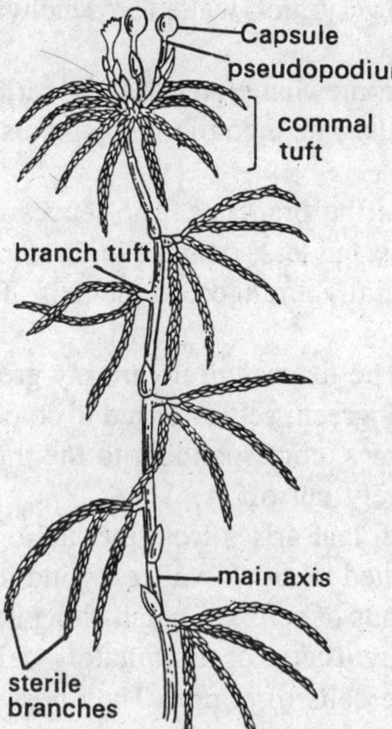

Fig. 9.2. *Sphagnum* sp. Gametophyte bearing sporophyte. A leafy gametophore bearing tufts of branches on main axis, and a terminal cluster of sporogonia, each sporogonium is situated at the end of a pseudopodium.

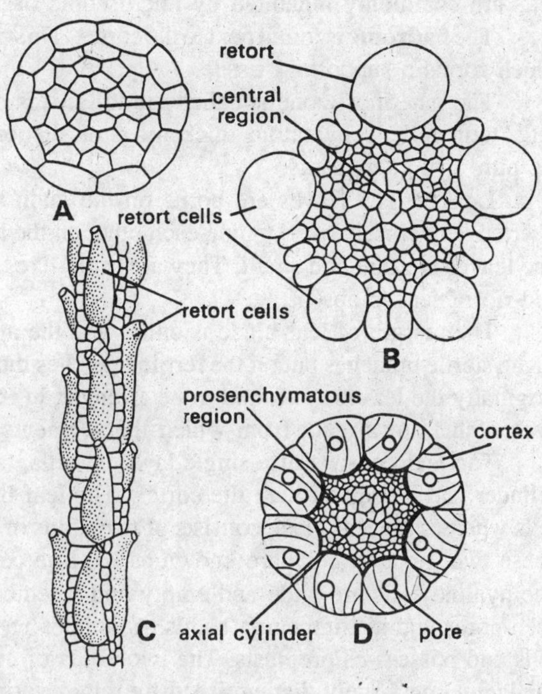

Fig. 9.3. *Sphagnum* sp. Internal structure of stem. A, transverse section of a young branch; B, transverse section of stem with large retort cells; C, portion of a stem after removal of leaves showing retort cells; D, transverse section of an old branch of *Sphagnum palustre*.

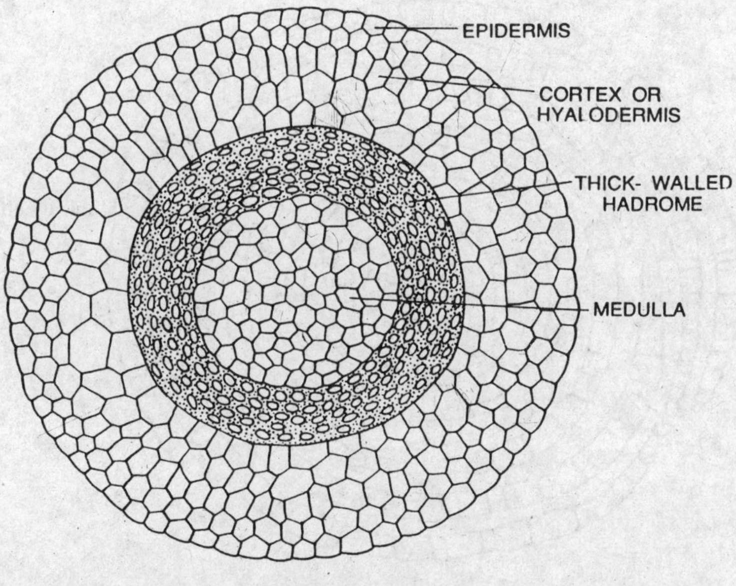

Fig. 9.4. *Sphagnum acutifolium.* Transverse section of older stem.

turned outwards. These flask-like cells are also known as **retort** cells. These specialized absorption cells are commonly inhabited by microscopic organisms.

The **hadrome** is found next to the cortex. This zone consists of very thick-walled prosenchyma which forms a supporting tissue.

The innermost zone is called **medulla.** It is compound of somewhat elongated, colourless cells, with collenychymatous thickenings on the longitudinal walls. The medulla corresponds to the pith of higher plants.

Leaves. The leaves are borne on the main axis as well as the branches. The leaves are inserted very closely overlapping each other on the lateral branches, but less so on the main stems. The leaves are thin and small. They are scale-like, sessile and spirally arranged on the axis. The mid-rib of leaf is absent.

The margin of leaf blade is entire and the apex is acute. The leaves are invariably green on the sterile branches but on the fertile branches they become dark green, yellow or red in colour. Originally the leaves are found to be arranged in three vertical rows, corresponding to the three sides of the apical cell, from which the segments are successively cut off.

The leaf consists of a single layer of cells, the base of each leaf arises from the hadrome cylinder and passes through the cortex. The leaf base is constituted of thick-walled cylindrical cells whereas the leaf blade consists of two kinds of cells. Both kinds of cells are much elongated. These two kinds of cells are known as **hyaline cells** and **photosynthetic** or assimilatory cells. The hyaline cells are wide and empty and resemble those of the cells of cortex. They possess open pores and strengthening bands of cuticle. The photosynthetic cells are very narrow living cells and possess chloroplasts. The two kinds of cells alternate with each other. The species of *Sphagnum* are largely distinguished by minor variations of this structure, but on the whole the leaf of *Sphagnum* is of unique type. The green cells of the leaf are all joined together and form a network with curving walls, each rhomboidal mesh is being occupied by one of the dead hyaline cells. The green narrow cells make the assimilatory tissue whereas the large hyaline cells are

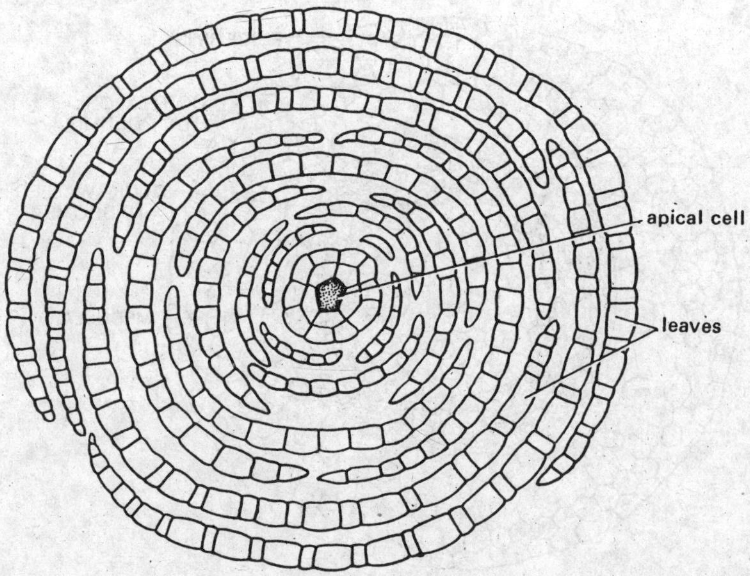

Fig. 9.5. *Sphagnum* sp. T.S. of growing point of stem showing the apical cell and its segments. (After Cavers).

hygroscopic and help in the absorption and retention of water like a sponge. The water accumulates in the hyaline cells. Sometimes these cells hold water as much as twenty times the weight of the plant.

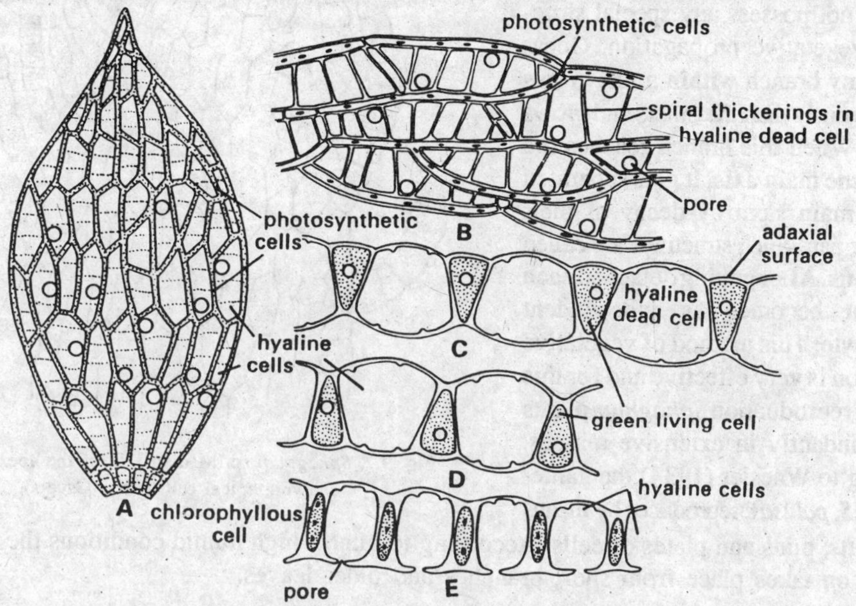

Fig. 9.6. *Sphagnum* sp. Structure of leaf. A, surface view of a leaf; B, some cells of leaf in surface view (magnified); C, D and E, cross sections of the leaf of different species of *Sphagnum*.

Physiology of absorption and conduction of water. The mature *Sphagnum* plant does not possess rhizoids and, therefore, it directly absorbs water through its leaves and stem. The spongy cortex, of the stem; branches which constitute of dead empty cells with porous walls and the large, hyaline, empty capillary cells of leaves are concerned with this process. The cells of both the stem and leaves absorb and retain water by the capillary action of these cells. These cells hold a large amount of water like a sponge. The ascent of the water upto the apex in the stem takes place in two different ways. In the species where the porous elements of the cortex of stem are present (*i.e., S.palustre*) these porous elements of cortex serve as capillary apparatus to raise the water to the apex of the stem. But in other species where porous elements of cortex are not found in the stem, the water is drawn up by capillary action of drooping branches which hang down and form a loose covering round the stem. The spaces found in the thick loose covering of the drooping branches act as a capillary apparatus.

Apical growth. The leafy shoot and the branches of the gametophyte grow by means of a tetrahedral apical cell with three cutting faces. Each segment parallel to its flat face divides periclinally forming an outer and inner cell. The outer cell divides repeatedly and develops the cortex of the stem and a single leaf, whereas the inner cell gives rise to the stem. This way the segments derived from the apical cell give rise separately to a leaf and the subtending portion of the stem.

The young leaf also grows by means of an apical cell. The leaf possesses two cutting faces. The segments are cut off parallel to flat faces. This way, a young leaf develops which consists of a single layer of cells.

Reproduction. The plants of *Sphagnum* reproduce by means of vegetative and sexual methods.

Vegetative reproduction. The plants do not possess any special structure for vegetative propagation. Occasionally any branch within a tuft grows more vigorously than the others and grows upwards. When this branch reaches the height of tne main axis, it gets separated from the main stem by decay of their basal older part. Such structures are called **innovations.** After getting detached each innovation becomes as independent gametophyte. This method of vegetative propagation is very effective and for this method of reproduction *Sphagnum* plants occur abundantly in extensive masses. According to Waesler (1934) the gametophyte of *S. palustre* reproduces by means of filaments, buds and plates of cells. According to him in high humid conditions the vegetative reproduction takes place from short branches and older leaves.

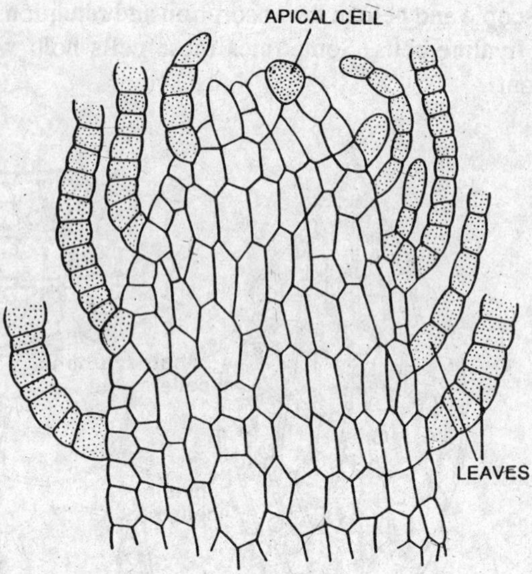

Fig. 9.7. *Sphagnum* sp. Median L.S. of the apex of stem showing apical cell. (After Cavers).

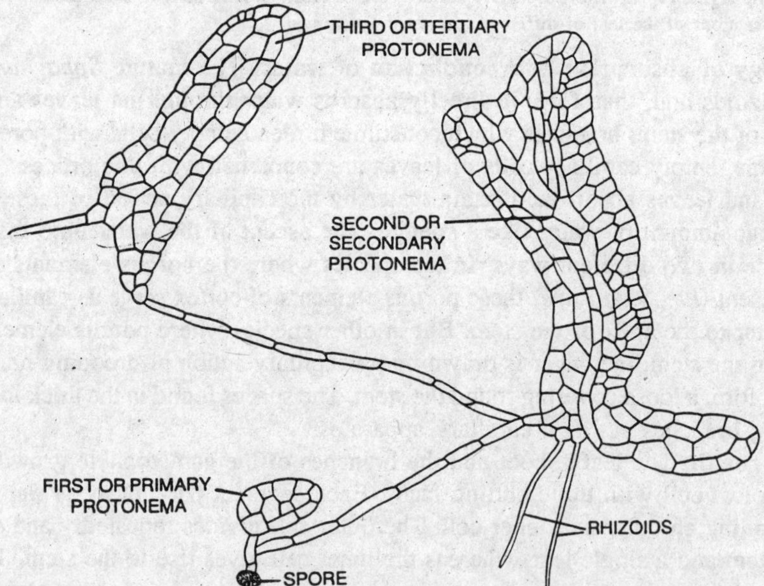

Fig. 9.8. *Sphagnum* sp. Vegetative reproduction by multiplication of protonemal stage.

Sexual reproduction. The sexual reproduction takes place by means of antheridia and archegonia. The gametophytic plants may be **monoecious** or **dioecious.** In monoecious plants the antheridia and archegonia are borne on the same plant but on two different branches, whereas in dioecious plants the male and female sex organs are found on two different plants. The plants are protandrous. The sexual branches are either found in the cluster of terminal branches, the **coma** or lower down on the stem.

The antheridial branch. The antheridial branches arise near the apex of the main shoot. These branches are catkin-like in appearance. The leaves present on the antheridial branch are

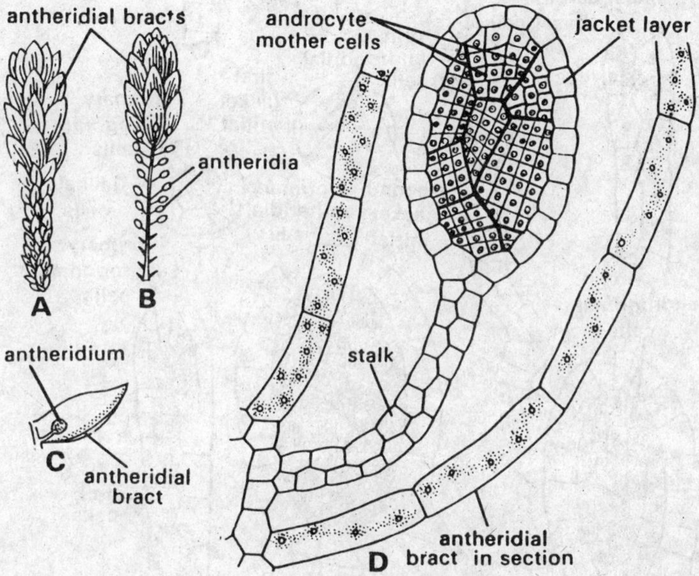

Fig. 9.9. *Sphagnum* sp. Male sex organs. A, antheridial branch; B, antheridial bracts removed to expose stalked antheridia situated on the antheridial branch; C, antheridium in the axil of protective antheridial bract; D, stalked, nearly mature antheridium arising between antheridial bracts (leaves).

just like the foliage leaves but in comparison they are usually shorter. These leaves are brightly coloured, commonly yellow, purple, brown, bright red or dark green. A single antheridium is found to be situated in the axil of each leaf. This way the position of antheridium is axillary (*i.e.*, the position where a lateral vegetative branch normally develops). The antheridia are produced in acropetal succession.

Development of antheridium. Each antheridium develops from a single superficial cell of the stem. This cell is known as the **antheridial initial.** The antheridial initial divides several times transversely forming a small filament of cells. The terminal cell of the filament acts as an apical cell. This apical cell possesses two cutting faces. This cuts of derivatives on both right and left sides till the young antheridium of 12 to 15 cells is developed. Now, each of the last 2-5 segments derived from the apical cell, divides vertically forming a **jacket initial** and a larger sister cell. The larger sister cell now again divides by a vertical division forming another **jacket initial** and a **primary androgonial cell.** At this stage the young antheridium consists of 2 to 5 primary androgonial cells which remain enclosed within a layer formed of jacket initials. Thereafter, the primary androgonial initials repeatedly giving rise to a large number of **androgonial cells.** Simultaneously the jacket initials also divide thus forming a single-layered jacket. The remaining lower cells of the filament, which do not take part in the formation of antheridium, divide by transverse and longitudinal divisions resulting in the formation of a long stalk consisting

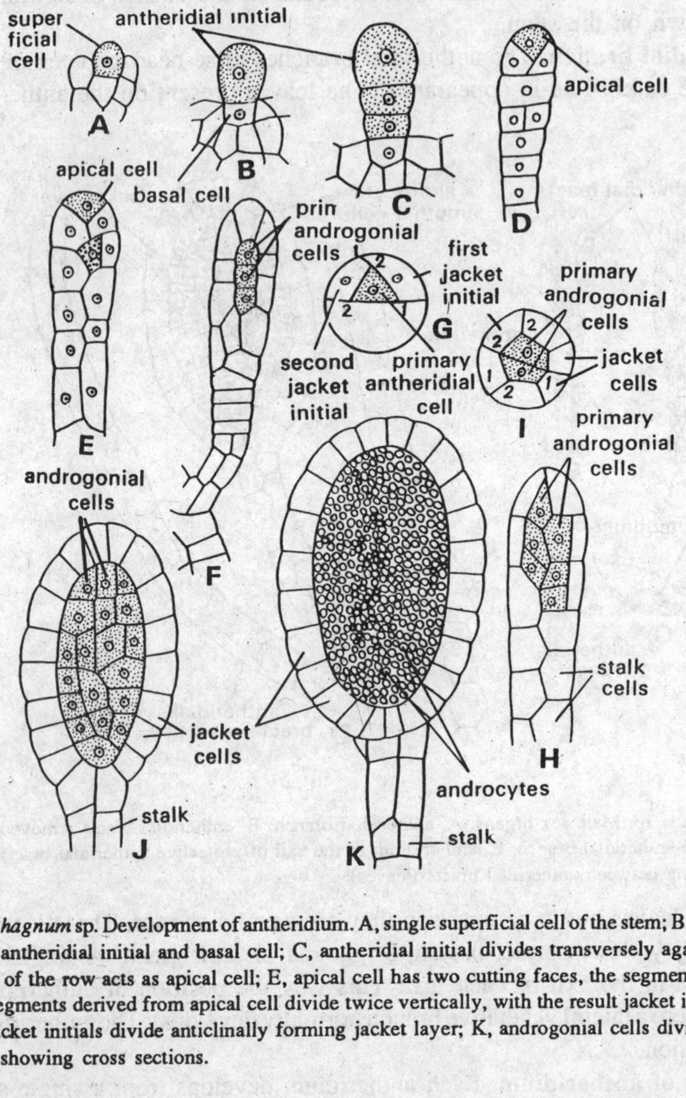

Fig. 9.10. *Sphagnum* sp. Development of antheridium. A, single superficial cell of the stem; B, superficial cell divides transversely into two-antheridial initial and basal cell; C, antheridial initial divides transversely again producing a row of cells; D, terminal cell of the row acts as apical cell; E, apical cell has two cutting faces, the segments are cut off right and left; F-I, two to five segments derived from apical cell divide twice vertically, with the result jacket initials and androgonial cells are formed; J, jacket initials divide anticlinally forming jacket layer; K, androgonial cells divide repeatedly forming androcytes; G and I, showing cross sections.

of 2 to 4 rows of cells.

Structure of mature antheridium. The antheridium consists of a long stalk and a spherical or broadly oval body. The stalk may be as long as the body of the antheridium. It consists of 2-4 rows of cells. The spherical body of antheridium remains surrounded by a single layered jacket. Inside the jacket there are a large number of androcytes. Each androcyte metamorphoses into an antherozoid.

The antherozoids are uninucleate and biciliate.

Dehiscence of antheridium. On the maturity of the antheridium, it absorbs water and with the result the cells at the apex of the jacket swell, and the body of the antheridium bursts at the apex by a number of irregular lobes turning backwards. The mass of androcytes ejects out of the antheridium through this opening. The antherozoids liberate out from the androcytes and swim in the water with the help of their flagella.

The archegonial branch. The archegonia occur at the apex of archegonial branches. These female branches are short, green and bud-like in appearance. These branches bear much larger leaves than the normal ones. These possess abundant chlorophyll in the green cells. In comparison to branch leaves they possess few fibres in the hyaline cells. These large-sized leaves surround and protect the archegonia and later on the young sporogonia and make a **perichaetium**. The archegonial branches are somewhat globular. The number of archegonia on each branch varies from one to five but usual number is three. One archegonium is primary while the rest of them are secondary.

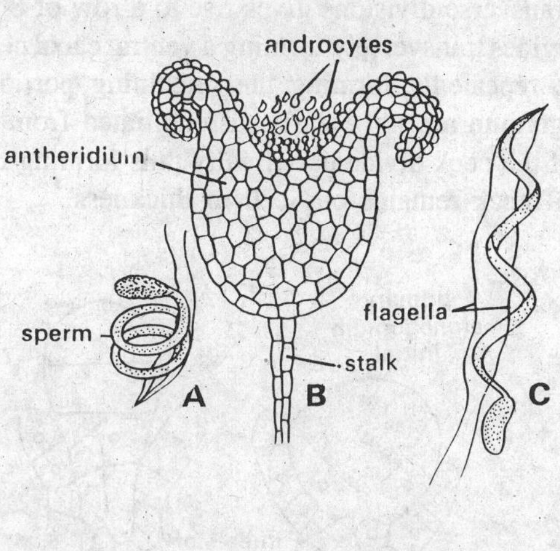

Fig. 9.11. *Sphagnum* sp. A, biflagellate coiled sperm or antherozoid; B, dehisced antheridium liberating androcytes; C, uncoiled elongated biflagellate sperm or antherozoid.

Development of archegonium. In both primary and secondary archegonia, first of all a short filament of 4 to 5 cells is formed. In case of the primary archegonium it is formed either by the successive transverse divisions of the terminal cell or by means of apical cell with two cutting faces. During the development of secondary archegonium the apical cell with two cutting faces is never being differentiated. Here the filament is being formed by means of transverse divisions of the terminal cell. In both cases of archegonia the further development is quite similar. When the filament consisting of 4-6 cells is being formed; the terminal cell divides by three vertical oblique walls forming three peripheral **jacket initials** which surround the **primary axial cell.** Thereafter, the primary axial cell divides transversely forming an outer and an inner cell. The outer cell is known as **cover initial** and the inner one as **central cell.** Further, the cover initial divides vertically

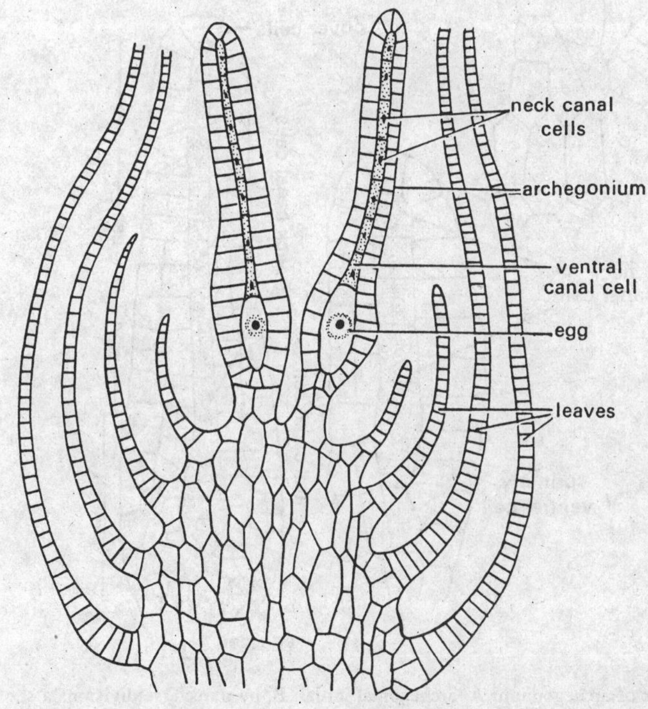

Fig. 9.12. *Sphagnum compactum.* L.S. of the archegonial branch showing two archegonia (After Cavers).

thus forming a rosette of cells. This rosette consists of eight or more cells which develop the terminal jacket portion of the neck of the archegonium. The central cell divides transversely giving rise to a **primary neck canal cell** and **primary ventral cell.** The neck canal cell by successive transverse divisions gives rise to a row of 8 or 9 neck canal cells while the primary ventral cell divides transversely forming a ventral canal cell and an egg. The three peripheral jacket initials divide repeatedly forming the remaining portion of the jacket. The neck and venter of the archegonium are not clearly differentiated from each other. The cells of the venter and lower part of the neck divide periclinally thus forming two or three layers of cells. However, the upper part of neck remains one cell in thickness.

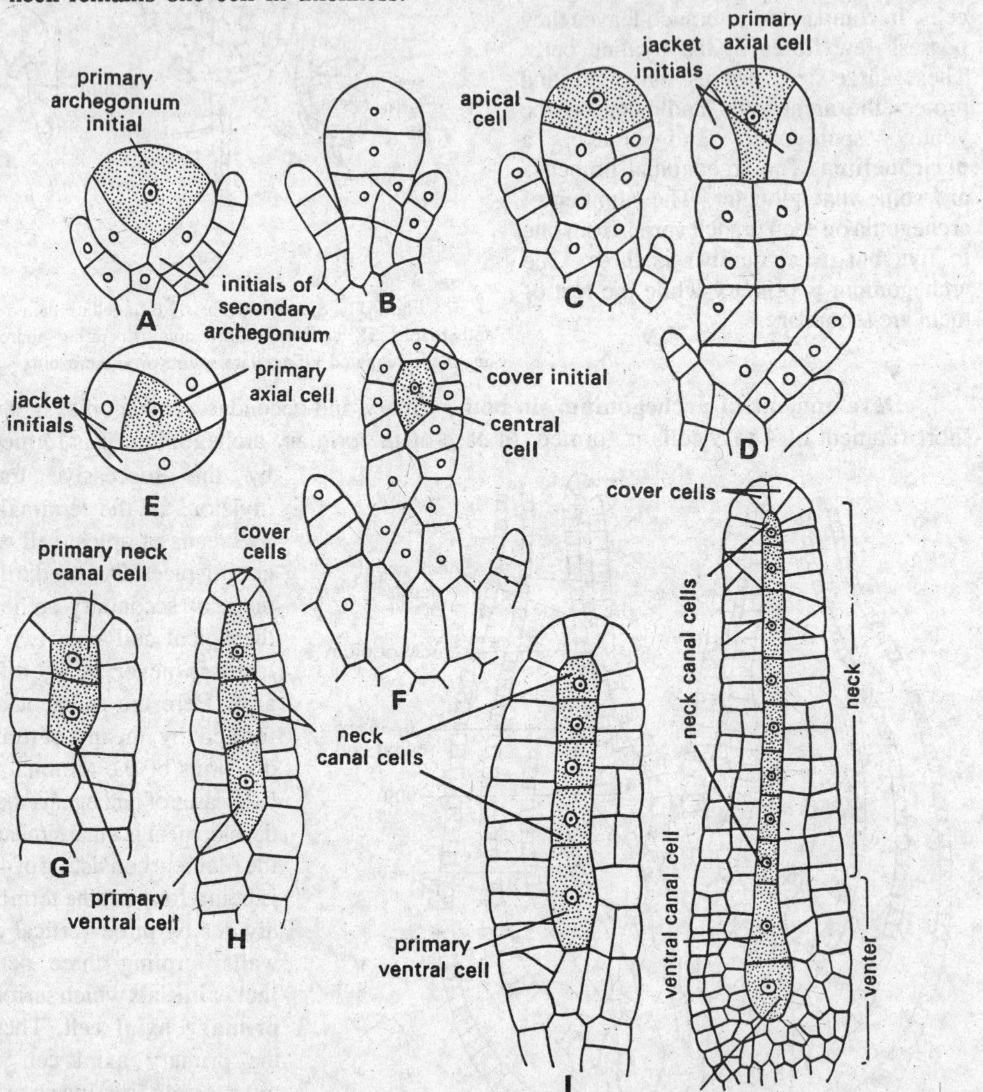

Fig. 9.13. *Sphagnum* sp. Development of archegonium: A, archegonial initial; B, by transverse divisions a short filament of cells is formed; C, terminal cell of filament acts as apical cell; D, apical cell divides by three oblique vertical walls; E, transverse section of D; F, primary axial cell divides transversely forming outer and inner cells, outer acts as cover initial and inner as central cell; G-I, further stages in the development of archegonium; J, nearly mature archegonium containing egg, ventral canal cell and neck canal cells.

Structure of mature archegonium. The mature archegonium possesses a long stalk. The venter of archegonium is massive, and the long neck is twisted. The neck is composed of six vertical rows of neck cells. There are 8 to 9 neck canal cells, one ventral canal cell and an egg in the axial row of archegonium.

Fertilization. The water is indispensable for fertilization. This process is similar to that in other bryophytes. The antherozoids swim in the film of water and reach to the neck of the archegonium. The neck canal cells disorganize and finally the nucleus of one antherozoid fuses with egg nucleus thus forming a zygote (oospore).

The Sporophyte

Development of sporogonium. The sporophytic phase starts with the formation of the zygote within the venter. The zygote enlarges in size and secretes a wall around it. The zygote divides transversely into two approximately equal cells. According to Bryan (1920) more transverse divisions occur forming a 5-12 celled embryo. The upper part of the filament consisting of 3 or 4 cells gives rise to the capsule, middle portion develops into a foot and seta while the lowermost region gives rise to the haustorium. Each cell of the upper region divides into equal quadrants by two vertical divisions. Periclinal divisions take place in each tier of four cells thus forming the outer **amphithecium** and the central **endothecium.** The cells of endothecium divide repeatedly giving rise to a bulky mass of central sterile tissue known as **columella.** The amphithecium divides by periclinal divisions and gives rise to an inner fertile layer, the **archesporium** and an outer sterile layer. The archesporium forms a semicircular arch over the columella like a dome and later on this divides forming a sporogenous tissue two to four layers of cells in thickness. All sporogonous cells become spore mother cells. Each spore mother cell divides meiotically forming a tetrad of four haploid spores. A large number of spores are found in the spore sac.

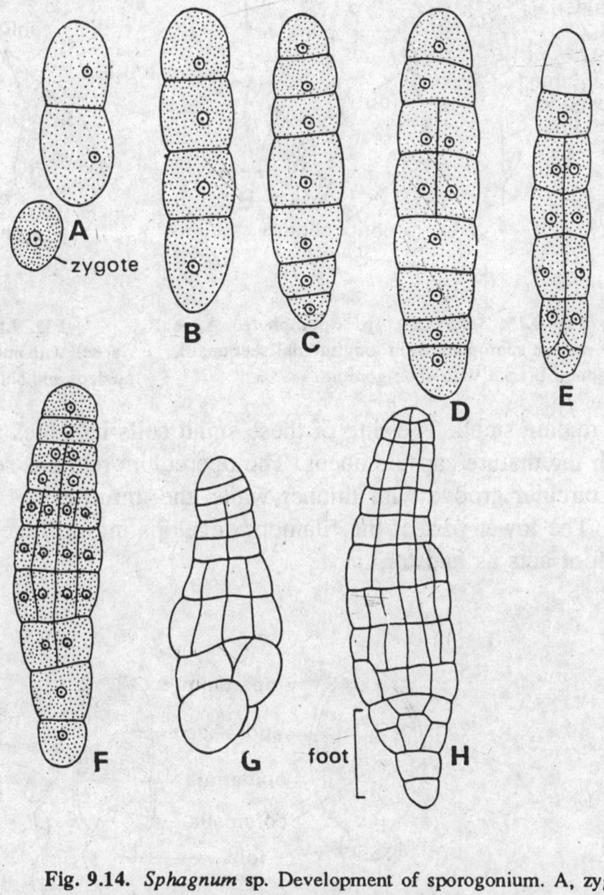

Fig. 9.14. *Sphagnum* sp. Development of sporogonium. A, zygote and two-celled embryo; B, 4-celled embryo; C, seven-celled embryo; D-E, formation of vertical walls in embryo with eight primary segments; F, formation of vertical walls in embryo with ten primary segments; G, embryo with bulbous base; H, young sporogonium with foot.

The capsule wall develops from the cells of the outer layer of the amphithecium by means of periclinal division. This wall is composed of 3 to 7 layers of cells. The outermost layer of the capsule wall is known as epidermis. Several non-functional rudimentary stomata are found upon this epidermis. The epidermal cells become thick-walled in the mature capsule. The cells of the wall inner to the epidermis are thin-walled and without intercellular spaces between them. These cells contain chlorophyll in them. As the spores mature within the spore sac a ring-like groove is differentiated out in the upper portion of capsule. The epidermal cells of this ring grow less actively than the neighbouring cells, and thus these

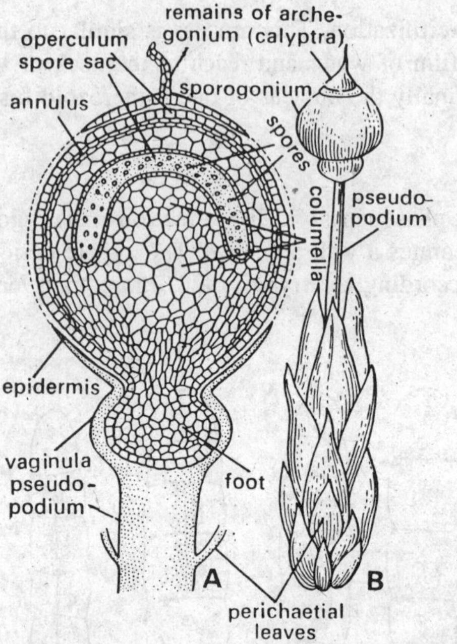

Fig. 9.15. ***Sphagnum*** **sp. Sporophyte. A, a nearly mature sporogonium in longitudinal section; B, archegonial branch with sporogonium.**

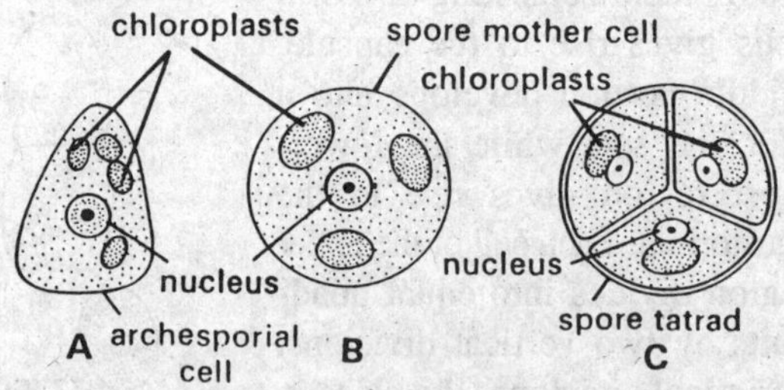

Fig. 9.16. ***Sphagnum*** **sp. Sporogenesis. A, archesporial cell with nucleus and chloroplasts; B, spore mother cell with nucleus and chloroplasts; C, spore tetrad formed after meiosis.**

cells remain small. The ring of these small cells indicates the limit of the lid or **operculum** by which the mature capsule opens. The operculum remains separated from the rest of the capsule by a circular groove with thinner walls, the **annulus.**

The lower part of the filament develops into a large bulbous foot and a very short seta. The foot acts as haustorium.

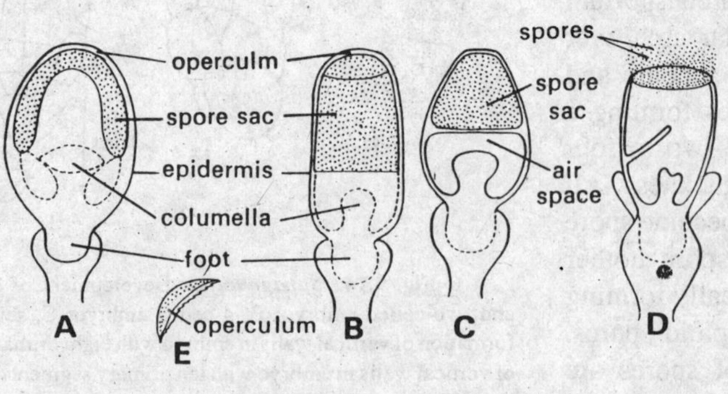

Fig. 9.17. ***Sphagnum*** **sp. Dehiscence of sporogonium (capsule). A, an undehisced capsule before drying; B-C, capsule after drying but before dehiscence; D, lid blown off and forcible ejection of spores; E, lid or operculum.**

The seta never elongates and the whole capsule remains, until mature, enveloped in a **calyptra** developed by the archegonial wall, the lower part of which forms a sac enclosing the foot, which

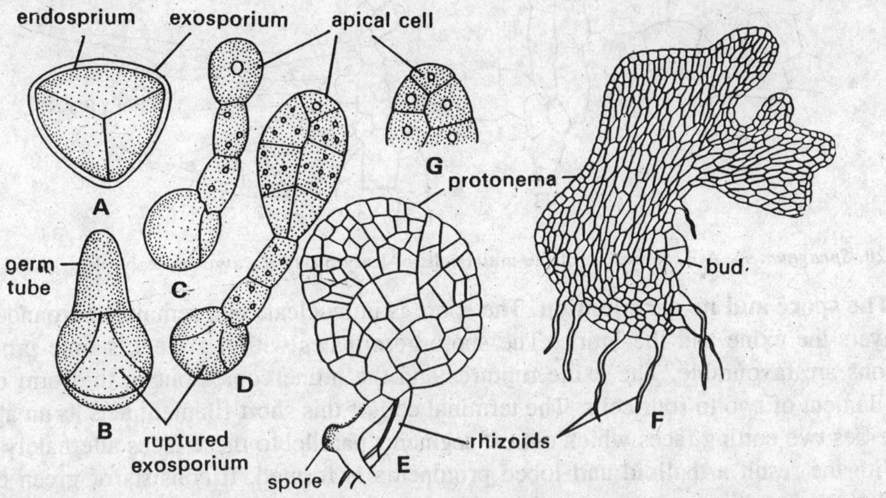

Fig. 9.18. *Sphagnum* sp. Spore, spore germination and development of gametophyte. A, spore with triradiate ridge; B, germinating spore with germ tube; C, the terminal cell of filament acts as apical cell; D, apical cel! has two cutting faces, segments are cut right and left; E, flat green protonema is formed; F, protonema becomes irregularly lobed, green plate one cell in thickness, bud develops into gametophore; G, apical cell (tetrahedral) of the bud.

is known as the **vaginula.** The neck of the archegonium dries up. The calyptra is very delicate and is torn irregularly by the growth of the capsule. On the maturation of the capsule the top of the gametophyte axis rapidly elongates, emerging from between the leaves of the archegonial branch and carrying up the whole sporophyte, with the foot still embedded in the vaginula, on a leafless stalk, the **pseudopodium.** As already mentioned the seta remains suppressed and the function of seta is performed by the **pseudopodium.** As the pseudopodium elongates it carries the sporogonium at its top beyond the perichaetial leaves.

Dehiscence of the capsule. When the capsule is ripe, the thinwalled columella shrivels up leaving an air space between the spore layer. The outer walls go on shrinking unless and until the capsule becomes cylindrical. This puts considerable pressure on the contained air, which cannot escape because there are no stomatal apertures. The thickened cells of the operculum resist this shrinkage and, therefore a strain is caused at the rim. The air pressure over-comes all this, and an explosion occurs which throws away the lid to a distance of several feet and the spores are ejected out of

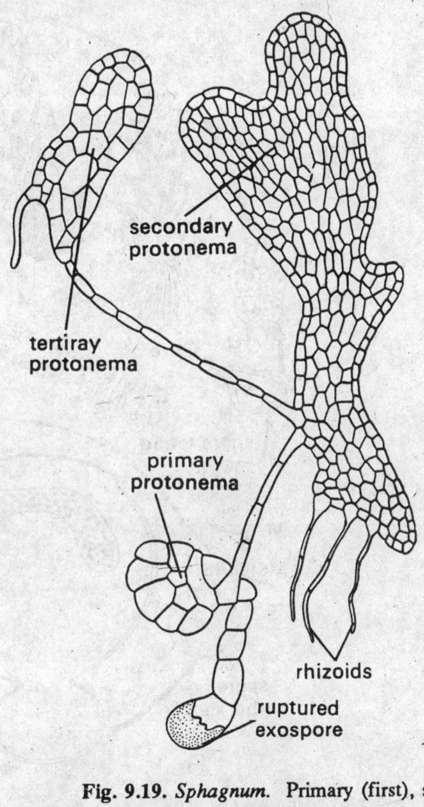

Fig. 9.19. *Sphagnum.* Primary (first), secondary (second) and tertiary (third) protonema. (After Noguchi).

the capsule. The above mentioned mechanism of the dehiscence of the capsule was explained by Nawaschin (1897).

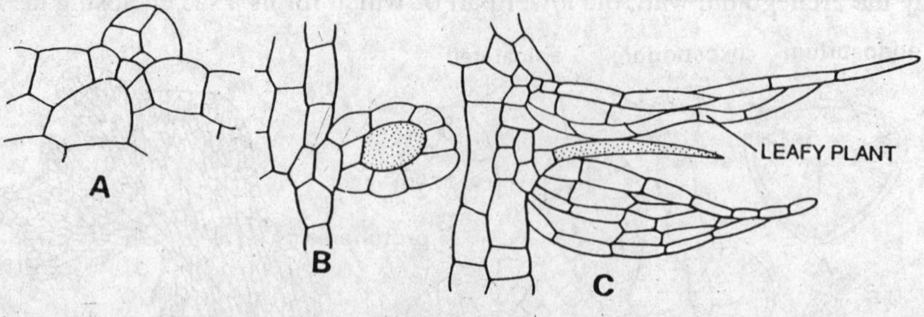

Fig. 9.20. *Sphagnum* sp. A-B, formation of the initial cells of leafy plants; C, a young leafy plant. (After Noguchi).

The spore and its germination. The spore is uninucleate and remains surrounded by two wall layers-the exine and the intine. The spore germinates within a week's time provided the conditions are favourable. The exine ruptures and the intine comes out in the form of a short green filament of two to four cells. The terminal cell of this short filament acts as an apical cell. It possesses two cutting faces which cut off segments parallel to these faces alternately right and left. With the result a thalloid and lobed protonema is formed. It consists of green cells. The cells are found to be arranged in a plate of one cell in thickness.

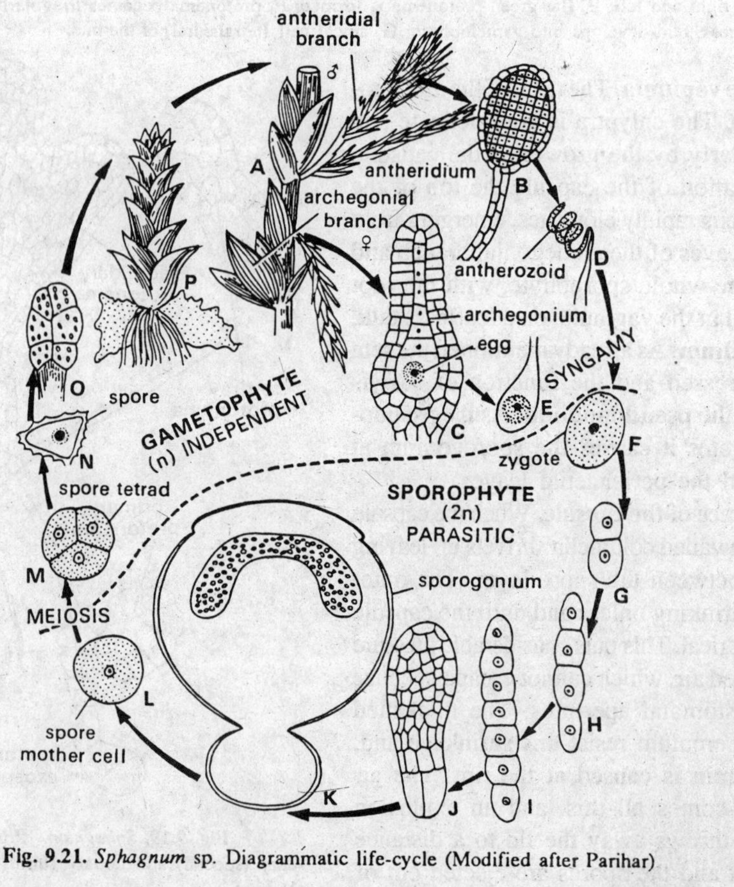

Fig. 9.21. *Sphagnum* sp. Diagrammatic life-cycle (Modified after Parihar)

To bring further growth the apical cell becomes less active and begins to divide consequently the protonema becomes irregularly lobed. This is still one celled thick and remains attached to its substratum by means of multicellular rhizoids given out from the cell of the posterior portion of protonema. Any marginal cell of the thalloid protonema may become meristematic. By growth and segmentation this develops into a septate marginal filament. Later on the apical portion of these filamentous structures become thalloid and are known as **secondary protonema.** According to Noguchi (1958) in certain species (*e.g., S. girgensohnii*) secondary and tertiary protonemata are being derived from the primary protonema. This way the thalloid protonema reproduces vegetatively. One of the marginal cells near the base of thalloid protonema forms a bud by growth and segmentation. This bud develops into a leafy gametophore.

Ecological importance. The *Sphagnum* plants are of great ecological importance. When these plants establish themselves in some lake or other areas full of water, sooner or later they cover the whole surface of the water. Due to deposition of plant debris the surface may be raised. The *Sphagnum* plants along with other hydrophytes form a dense surface covering over the water below. This covering gives the appearance of solid soil from the surface. These areas are known as **quacking bogs.** Later on these bogs are converted into swamps. Ultimately these swamps are replaced by the forest growth of mesophytic type.

Economic importance. The peat mosses or *Sphagnum* plants are the most important bryophytes from the view point of their direct economic importance. Dried peat may be used as fuel. In Ireland, Scotland and other European countries the peat is used for fuel. The peat is also a potential source of coal. The *Sphagnum* plants are slightly antiseptic and possess superior absorptive power. On account of these properties they may be used for filling absorbent bandages in place of cotton, in the hospitals. The plants absorb and hold water in them. For these prop-

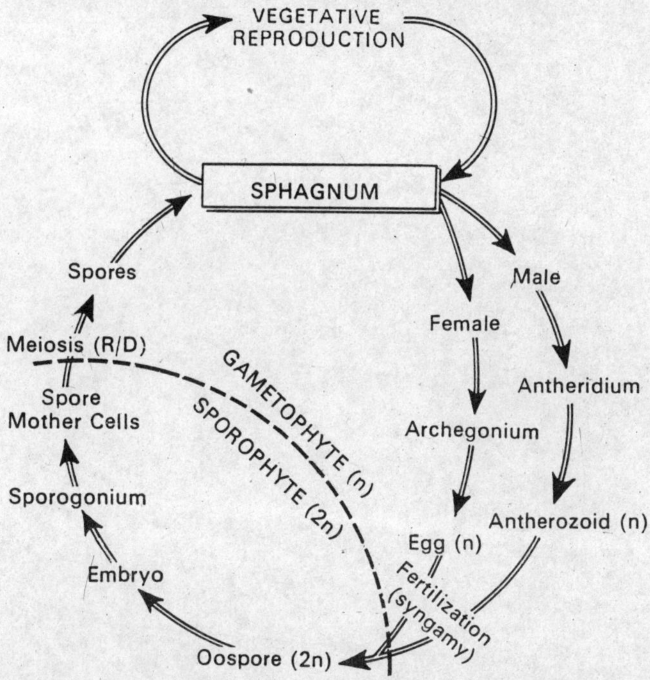

Fig. 9.22. *Sphagnum*. Graphic life-cycle.

erties they are used in seed beds and green houses to root cuttings. They are also used to maintain high soil acidity required by certain plants.

Systematic position. Division. Bryophyta
Class. Bryopsida
Sub-class. Sphagnobrya
Order. Sphagnales
Family. Sphagnaceae
Genus. *Sphagnum*

10

Bryopsida (Musci)

Order-Funariales

Sub-class EUBRYA

The Eubrya are called the true mosses. This group consists of a great majority of the mosses. There are about 650 genera and 14,000 species. The characteristic features of the true mosses are as follows.

The leaves of the gametophores are more than one cell in thickness and possess mid-rib on them.

The protonema are filamentous.

The sporophyte possesses a well differentiated, elongated seta which pushes out the capsule from the gametophore.

The sporogenous tissue is derived from the endothecium. The archesporium does not overarch the columella. The columella continues upto the apex of the capsule. Both columella and archesporium have been derived from the endothecium.

In between spore sac and columella, the partitioned air spaces are present.

The mature capsule possesses the complex structure. It is made of many tissues.

The capsule opens at its apex by an operculum. The spore dispersal is regulated by a teeth like apparatus, called the peristome.

Classification. According to Bortherus (1924-1925) there are 80 families in this sub-class. According to Schaffner (1938) and Sharp (1939), the families have been grouped into seven orders. According to Brotherus (1924-1925) and Dixon (1932) there are fourteen orders in this sub-class. They have taken both gametophytic and sporophytic characters in grouping the families into orders. In the present day, the classification of Eubrya (Bryidae), proposed by Fleischer, Dixon and Wettstein has been followed. This is as follows-

Sub-class (*Unterclasse*)-**Bryidae**

I.	Cohort (*Reihengruppe*)	.	Eubryiidae
1.	,, ,,	-	Fissidentales
2.	,, ,,	-	Dicranales
3.	,, ,,	-	Pottiales
4.	,, ,,	-	Grimmiales
5.	,, ,,	-	Funariales
6.	,, ,,	-	Schistostegales
7.	,, ,,	-	Tetraphidales
8.	,, ,,	-	Eubryales
9.	,, ,,	-	Isobryales
10.	,, ,,	-	Hookeriales
11.	,, ,,	-	Hypnobryales
II.	Cohort (*Reihengruppe*).		Buxbaumiidae
12.	Order (*Reihe*)	-	Buxbaumiales
13.	,, ,,	-	Diphysciales

III. Cohort (*Reihengruppe*). Polytrichiidae
14. Order (*Reihe*) - Polytrichales
15. ,, ,, - Dawsoniales

ORDER FUNARIALES

The most characteristic features of this order are as follows-There are about 26 genera and 356 species. Usually the plants are terrestrial. They are quite small and may be annual or biennial. The leaves are with distinct mid-ribs and arranged in rosettes at the apex of the gametophyte. The capsule is wide. It is provided with an unbeaked operculum. The peristome of the capsule is double. It consists of inner and outer peristomes which are called **endostome** and **exostome** respectively.

The other **Funariales** has been further sub-divided into *five* families. They are as follows:

1. Gigaspermaceae
2. Funariaceae
3. Disceliaceae
4. Oedipodiaceae
5. Splachnaceae.

The genus *Funaria* is of family Funariaceae. In the present text, this genus has been discussed in detail.

Family-**Funariaceae**

The outstanding features of the family are as follows-This family includes about 9 genera and 200 species. The leaves are one cell in thickness except at the mid-rib region. This family includes the small mosses which form the velvety appearance on the surface of the substratum. The calyptra are soon detached from the opercula of the capsules. The calyptra are provided with long beaks. The capsules are pyriform in structure. They are situated on the long, elongated setae.

Genus **FUNARIA**

Habitat and distribution. This genus is cosmopolitan in its distribution. It includes about 117 species. Bruhl (1931) has recorded about 15 species of *Funaria* from our country. The species

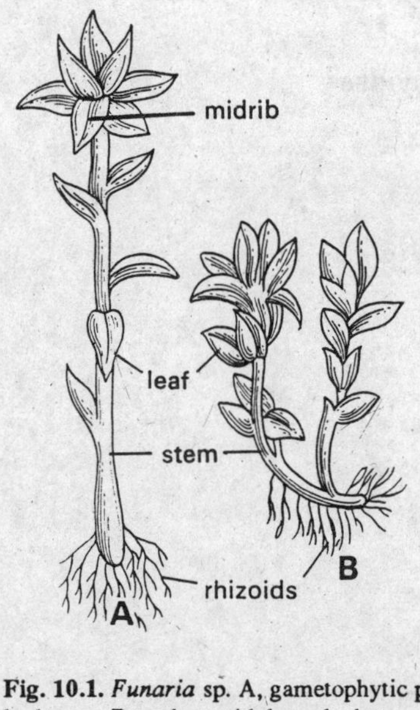

Fig. 10.1. *Funaria* sp. A, gametophytic plant with unbranched stem; B, a plant with branched stem.

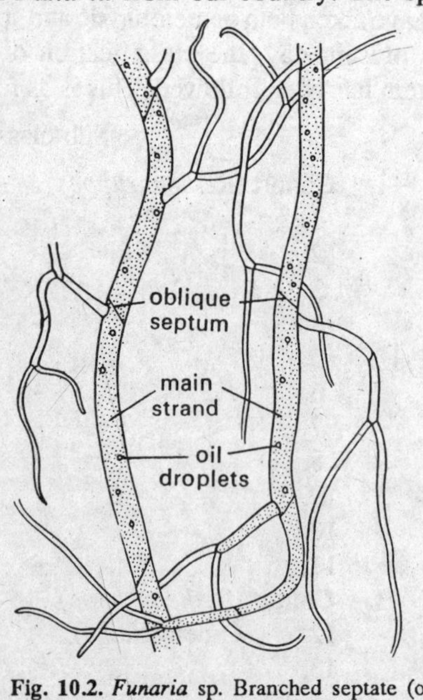

Fig. 10.2. *Funaria* sp. Branched septate (oblique septa) rhizoids containing oil droplets.

Funaria hygrometrica is best known among the mosses and found throughout the world. The mosses may grow luxuriantly in humus soil and on the soils burnt by fire. Sometimes they occur on the rocks and damp walls in the form of velvety mat. The green protonemata of the mosses appear in the recently ploughed fields. Some mosses are epiphytic in habitat and grow upon the trunks of the trees.

External structure. The small green moss plants may easily be collected from the damp walls after the rains, where they are found in velvety mats. The small, erect, green gametophytic plant arises from a prostrate alga-like filament the protonema. The gametophytic plant of *Funaria* may easily be differentiated into the rhizoids, stem and leaves. The gametophytic plant may also be called the gametophore, as it bears the sex organs at its apex.

The gametophytic plants are green, erect and one to three centimetres in height. As mentioned above, each plant consists of rhizoids, leaves and stem. Usually the stem is branched. The branching is of monopodial type.

At the base of the gametophytic plant the **rhizoids** are found. The rhizoids are branched, multicellular and thread-like. The septa of the rhizoids are oblique. In earlier stages the rhizoids are hyaline or whitish in colour whereas, in later stages they become brown or pink in colour. The rhizoids absorb the water and nutrients from the soil for gametophytic plants as well as they help in anchoring the plants to their substrata. They usually contain oil in them, but if exposed to the light, develop chlorophyll in them and help in assimilation.

The **leaves** are small, ovate, bright green and spirally arranged on the stem. Each such leaf possesses a distinct mid-rib. The upper leaves are somewhat larger in size and crowded at the apex of the plant, whereas the lower leaves are smaller and scattered on the stem. The leaves are sessile, ovate and with broad bases at the point of attachment to the stem.

The **stem** is upright erect, green and monopodially branched. Sometimes, this may or may not be branched.

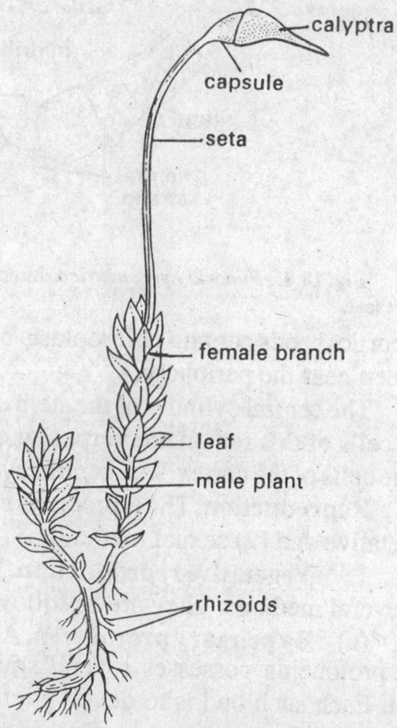

Fig. 10.3. *Funaria hygrometrica*. Moss plant with male and female shoots showing autoicous condition.

Internal structure-the leaf. To study the internal structure (anatomy) of the leaf, one has to cut the leaf in vertical sections. The leaf possesses a distinct mid-rib and wings. The mid-rib is several celled in thickness whereas the wing on either side is single layered. There is central strand in the centre of the mid-rib. The cells of the wings contain chloroplasts in them which facilitate the carbon assimilation. The chloroplasts continuously divide again and again. This process goes on even after the maturity of the leaves.

The stem. The internal structure of the stem may easily be understood by studying the transverse section under the microscope. It is mainly consisted of three parts, (1) the epidermis, (2) the cortex and (3) the central cylinder.

The epidermis is single layered. It is the outermost layer consisting of thinwalled, compactly arranged cells with chloroplasts. This layer is assimilatory in function. It is devoid of cuticle and stomata. Sometimes, at certain places the epidermis becomes double layered.

The cortex is multilayered and consists of thinwalled parenchymatous cells. In earlier stages

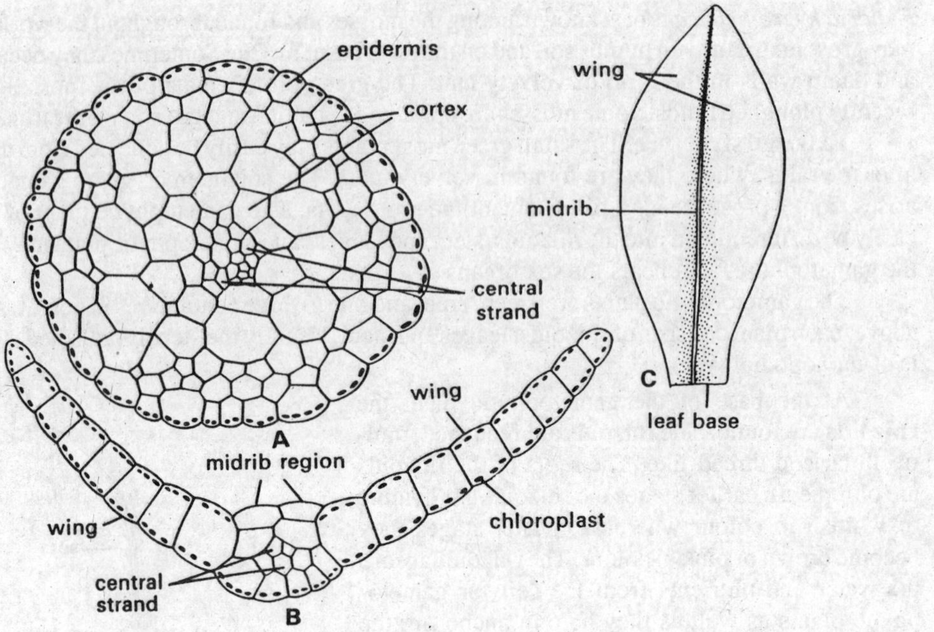

Fig. 10.4. *Funaria hygrometrica*. Internal structure. A, transverse section of stem; B, transverse section of leaf; C, entire leaf.

the cortical cells contain chloroplasts but later on they disappear. The diagonal leaf traces may also be seen near the periphery.

The central cylinder of the stem consists of somewhat thick walled, compactly arranged cells. The cells of this region are vertically elongated and comparatively of smaller diameter than those of the cells of the cortex. The central cylinder acts as conducting tissue. It helps in water conduction.

Reproduction. The reproduction in *Funaria hygrometrica* chiefly takes place by means of (1) vegetative and (2) sexual methods.

1. Vegetative reproduction. In mosses, the vegetative multiplication takes place by means of several methods. They are as follows-

(a) By primary protonema. After germination, the spore develops into primary protonema. The protonema possesses several small buds on it. Each such bud is to develop into a new moss plant. The protonema breaks up and propagates vegetatively. Each such small fragment of the protonema develops into a new plant.

(b) By secondary protonema. The protonema which develop from the other parts of the moss plant are called the secondary protonema. Such protonema resemble the primary protonema in their function and behaviour. The secondary protonema may develop from any detached part of the plant gametophyte, such as leaf, stem, antheridium, paraphyses and even from the exposed rhizoids. Such protonema may also occur from the wounded portions of the moss plants. Each protonema develops into a new plant.

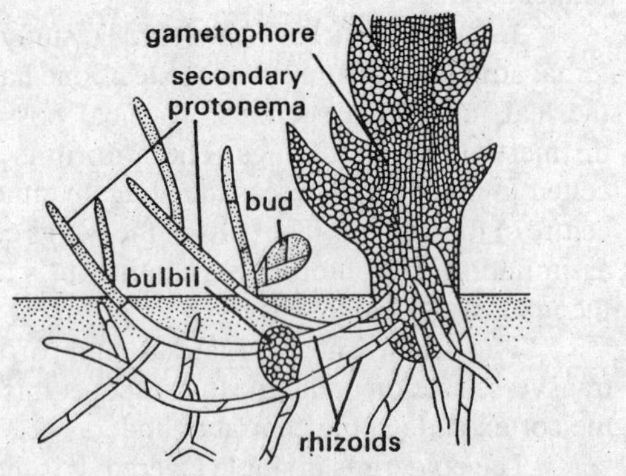

Fig. 10.5. *Funaria hygrometrica*. Vegetative reproduction. Rhizoids with oblique septa developing from lower part of gametophore; outside the substratum secondary protonema bears buds; the bulbil is seen on the rhizoids within substratum.

(c) By gemmae. Many mosses produce small, multicellular gemmae, in groups at the apices of the leaves. Sometimes, solitary gemmae may be produced on the rhizoids. Subterranean gemmae, produced on the rhizoids are called the bulbils. On the advent of the favourable conditions, each such gemma or bulbil develops into a new moss plant.

(d) By death and decay of prostrate system. The prostrate branches of the gametophyte are rhizoids. After death and decay of such branches each erect branch behaves like an independent plant.

(e) Apospory. Sometimes, the wounds are developed on the sporophytic tissue. From these wounds the protonema arise which later on develop into new plants. So, here the reproduction or multiplication takes place by means of sporophytic tissue and not by the spores.

Sexual reproduction. Formerly this was believed that *Funaria hygrometrica* is a dioecious species. But now this has been proved by Boodle (1906) and Miss Brown (1919) that the species is strictly monoecious and autoicous. The term autoicous means that the male and female sex organs develop on the two separate branches of the same plant. The main shoot of the gametophytic plant bears the male sex organs whereas the lateral branch bears the female sex organs. Sometimes the lateral branch even grows higher than the main shoot. On maturation the male branches become brownish in colour whereas the female branches remain green.

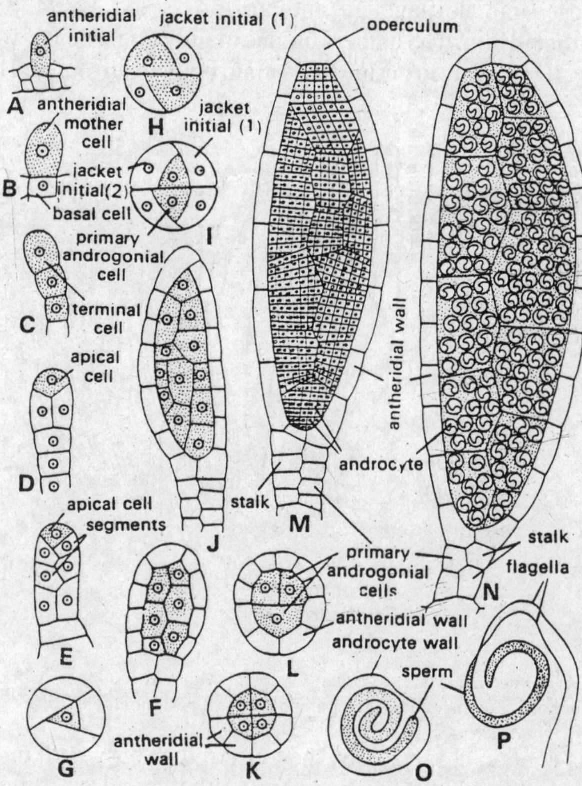

Fig. 10.6. *Funaria hygrometrica.* Development of antheridium. A, antheridial initial; B, antheridial initial divides transversely forming antheridial mother cell and basal cell; C, antheridial mother cell divides transversely forming a 2 or 3 celled filament; D, apical cell developed having two cutting faces; E-M, further successive stages in the development of antheridium; G,H,I and L, cross sections at different stages; N, antheridium containing androcytes; O, single androcyte; P. single biflagellate sperm or antherozoid.

Development of antheridium. At the apex of the male branch a single superficial cell acts as an **antheridial initial.** This cell may be distinguished by its papillate and projecting nature. The antheridial initial divides first transversely, giving rise to two cells. The outer daughter cell gives rise to the complete main antheridium whereas the lower cell develops into the embedded portion of the stalk. The outer daughter cell divides twice or thrice transversely producing a filament consisting of two or three cells. The terminal cell of the filament acts as an apical cell with two cutting faces. The apical cell cuts off the segments on its both cutting faces, and this way 5-7 or more regularly arranged segments are cut off.

Sometimes, even before all the segments are formed by the cell, the fourth or fifth segment begins to divide and further this division proceeds in the remaining segments from base to apex. Each segment divides first diagonally. This way the segment divides into two unequal cells. The smaller daughter cell acts as **jacket initial.** The larger daughter cell divides again giving rise to two cells, the peripheral cell called the peripheral initial and the inner one the **primary androgonial cell.** In cross section the primary androgonial cell appears to be triangular. This way, each segment gives rise to three cells, two jacket initials, and one primary androgonial cell. The primary androgonial cell of each segment divides further in all planes producing numerous **androcyte mother cells.** Simultaneously the jacket initials also divide repeatedly giving rise to a single-layered **jacket** of the antheridium. From each androcyte mother cell, two androcytes are produced. Later on each androcyte metamorphoses into a biflagellate antherozoid.

Structure of antheridium. The antheridium is mainly consisted of two parts a short massive stalk and the main body. It is clavate in outline. The main body is surrounded by a single layered outer

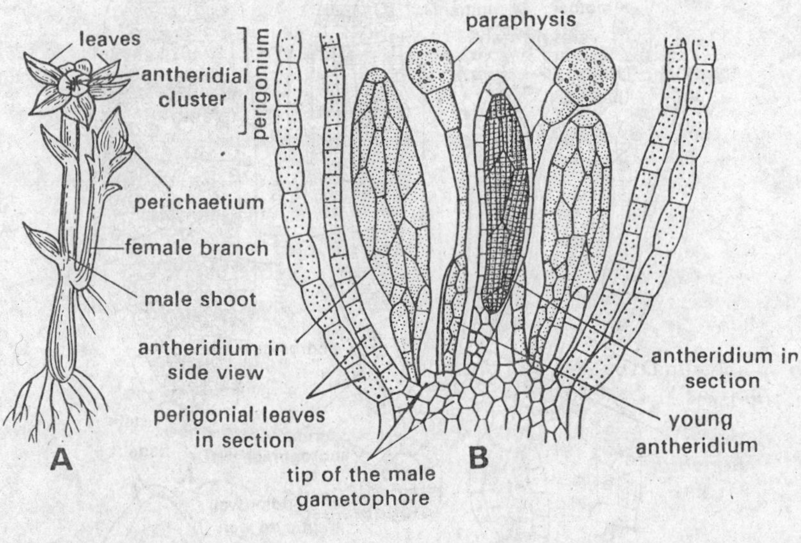

Fig. 10.7. *Funaria hygrometrica*. Male sex organs. A, plant with male and female branches; B, longitudinal section of the tip of the male gametophore showing antheridia, paraphyses and perigonial leaves.

jacket. The jacket cells contain chloroplasts, they turn red or brown on maturity. The jacket laye surrounds, the central dense mass of androcytes. At the apical end of the male branch of the gametophore the antheridia are intermingled with several sterile **paraphyses.** They are hair-like in structure. Each paraphysis is multicellular and consists of 4 to 5 cells arranged in a uniseriate row. The lower cells of the paraphysis are elongated and the terminal cells are globular. The function of these paraphyses is not very definite. It is assumed that they hold water among them which is needed for the developing antheridia.

Dehiscence of antheridium. The water is essentially required for the dehiscence of the antheridium. At the time of the dehiscence the rain water or dew is collected at the apical end of the male branch of the gametophore in a cupular structure developed by perichaetial leaves. On the approach of water the opercular distinctive cell of the antheridium becomes mucilaginous and somewhat swollen. The inner wall of the opercular cell disintegrates and it is soon followed by the disintegration of the upper wall of the cell, thus, giving rise to an apical pore, the mass of androcytes squeezes out through this pore. As soon as this mass comes in contact of the water collected in the cup of perichaetial leaves, the androcytes become separated and spread out in the film of water. They become motile, biflagellate antherozoids which swim here and there in the film of water.

Development of archegonium. The development of the archegonium in *Funaria hygrometrica* is as follows. According to Campbell the archegonial initial divides transversely giving rise to two cells, a basal cell and a terminal cell. The terminal cell, which is also designated as the mother cell

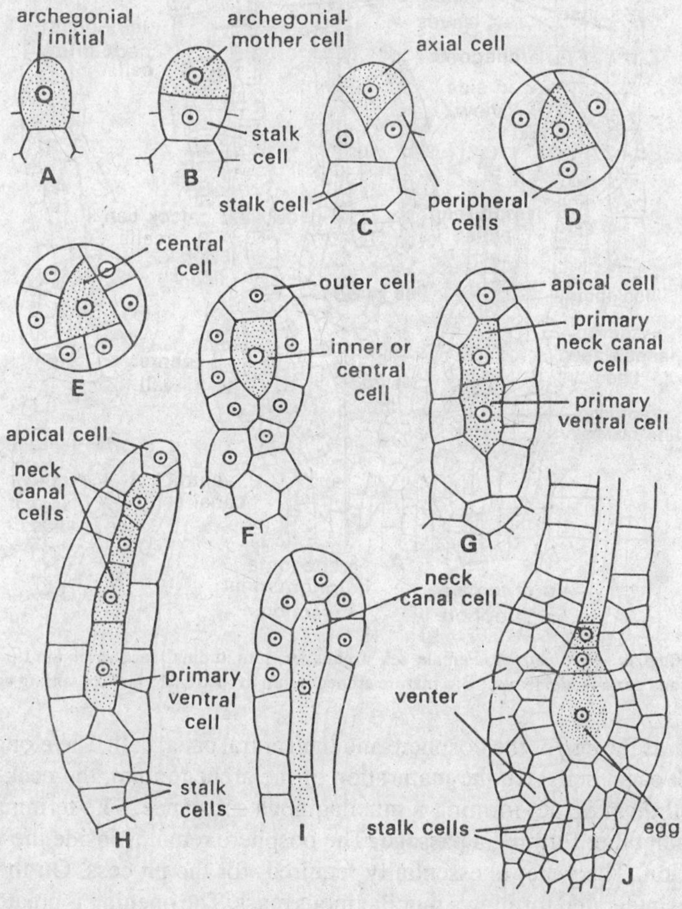

Fig. 10.8. *Funaria hygrometrica.* Development of archegonium. A archegonial initial; B, archegonial initial divides transversely forming archegonial mother cell and stalk cell; C-D, archegonial mother cell divides by three oblique walls forming three peripheral cells surrounding the central axial cell; D and E, cross sections of the same; F-H, further successive stages in the development of archegonium; I, neck of nearly mature archegonium; J, venter containing egg of mature archegonium.

of the archegonium divides by three oblique walls successively. These walls do not reach the basal cell. With the result, three peripheral cells surround a central polyhedral cell. The three peripheral cells develop the wall of the venter which later on becomes two layered.

The surrounded tetrahedral cell therefore, divides transversely giving rise to two cells. The upper cell is known as the **primary cover cell** and the lower one is the **central cell.** The central cell divides and redivides, giving rise to the primary neck canal cell, ventral canal cell and the egg or oosphere. The primary cover cell acts as an apical cell. It cuts off three segments from its lateral faces. The three rows of the segments developed from the three lateral segments divide vertically and the six rows of the jacket cells of the neck are produced. The row of neck canal cells develops from the row of basal segments.

Structure of archegonium. Comparatively, the stalk of archegonium is longer than that of antheridium. The archegonium is flask-like. It possesses a massive stalk, the venter and the neck. The bulbous venter possesses a two-layered jacket, whereas the jacket of the neck is single-layered.

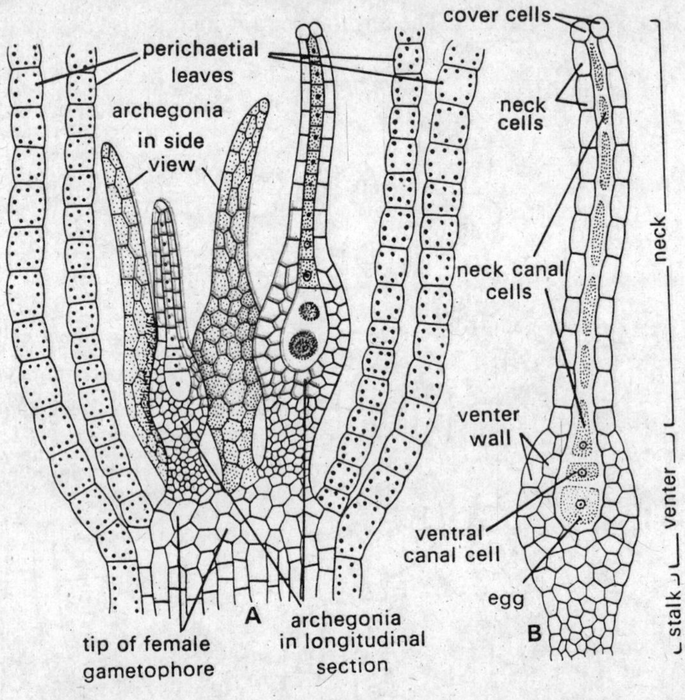

Fig. 10.9. *Funaria hygrometrica.* Female sex organs. A, longitudinal section of the tip of female gametophore showing archegonia and perichaetial leaves; B, a mature archegonium in sectional view containing egg, ventral canal cell and neck canal cells.

The venter contains the egg or the oosphere and the ventral canal cell. The elongated neck contains six or more neck canal cells. On the maturation of the archegonium, the neck canal cells and the ventral canal cell disintegrate forming a mucilaginous substance. The terminal cells of the neck separate from each other forming a passage. The oosphere remains inside the venter.

Fertilization. The water is essentially required, for the process. On the maturity the neck canal cells are disintegrated forming a mucilaginous mass. The opening is created by the separation of the apical cells of the neck. The antherozoids are attracted towards the mouth of the archegonium by its secretions. The antherozoids are chemotactic. Certain sugars ooze out through the opening which attract the antherozoids. Some of the antherozoids enter through the clear passage and reach to the oosphere. Ultimately the single antherozoid penetrates the egg and the fertilization is effected. The rest of the antherozoids within the venter, disintegrate. The male nucleus of the antherozoid fuses with female nucleus of the egg and the **oospore** is resulted.

The sporophyte. As soon as the fertilization is over, the zygote increases in size and begins to secrete a wall around it. Thereafter the zygote divides transversely giving rise to two cells. The upper cell is epibasal cell, and the lower one is hypobasal cell. In the epibasal cell, two oblique intersecting walls are formed successively, giving rise to a two-faced apical cell. In the same manner another two-faced apical cell is formed in the hypobasal cell. This way, the two growing points are established in the earlier stage of the development of the sporogonium, in its upper and lower cells respectively. The upper two-faced apical cell cuts off the segments to the right and left alternately and in the end the derivatives assemble in the form of a capsule and the upper part of the seta. The lower apical cell, also cuts off cells, but not so regularly as the upper one. The derivatives ultimately give rise to the lower part of the seta and the foot of the capsule.

Development of the sporogonium (capsule). The capsule of the sporophyte develops from the segments successively cut off right and left by the apical cell in the epibasal region of the young embryo. The first division of the segment is vertical. This is soon followed by a transverse division,

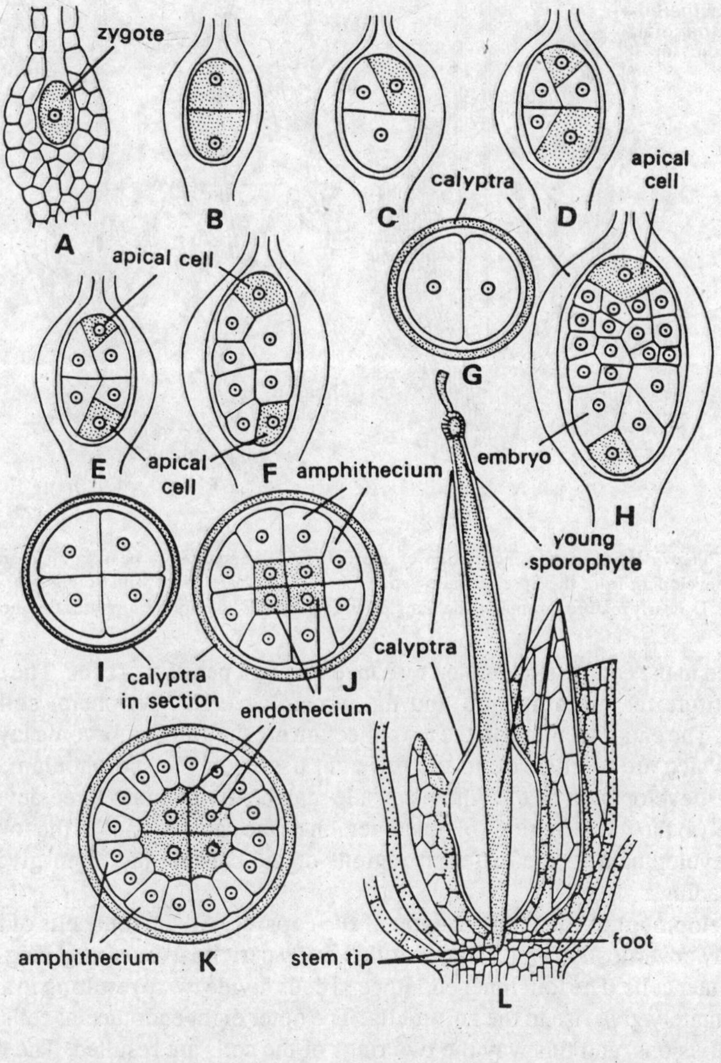

Fig. 10.10. *Funaria hygrometrica.* Development of young sporophyte. A, zygote within venter; B, transverse division of zygote; C-L, further successive stages in the development of young sporophyte; G,I,J and K are cross sections at different stages; rest are longitudinal sections.

giving rise to a quadrant stage. Now each of the quadrants divides vertically in such a way that one of the daughter cells is approximately triangular and the other is approximately rectangular when seen in transverse section. Thereafter, each quadrant divides periclinally and this way, the four cells

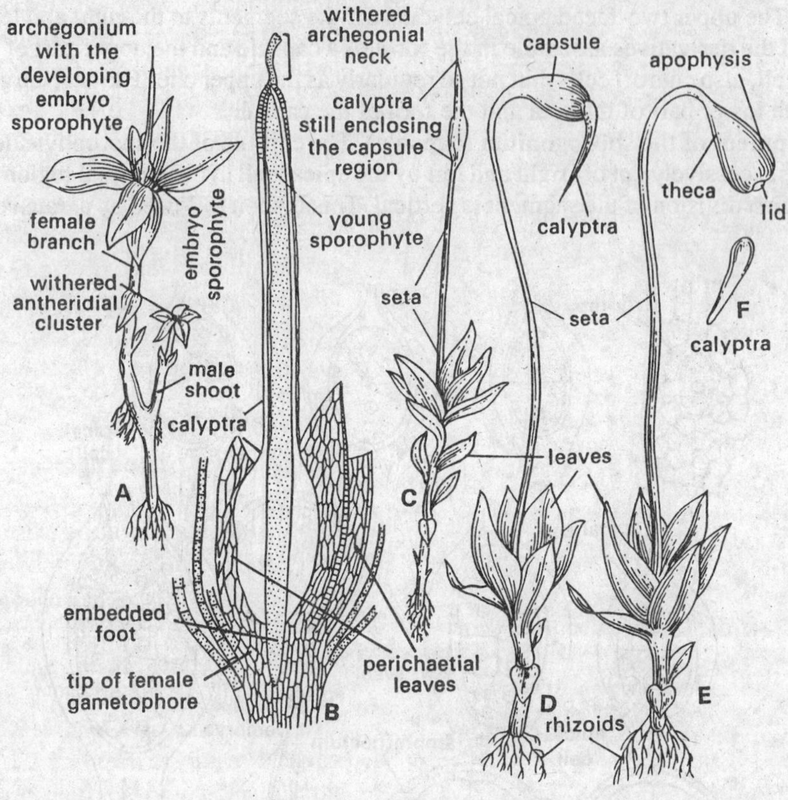

Fig. 10.11. *Funaria hygrometrica.* Formation of sporophyte A, gametophore bearing male and female shoots, B, young sporophyte developing from the tip of female gametophore; C, female shoot with young sporophyte; calyptra still encloses the capsule; D, nearly mature sporophyte on female gametophyte; E, mature sporophyte after the removal of calyptra; F, calyptra.

are differentiated in the centre, surrounded by a layer of eight peripheral cells. The centrally located four cells constitute the **endothecium** and the remaining eight, peripheral cells constitute the **amphithecium.** The endothecium and the ampithecium are the chief embryonic layers of the young sporogonium, which are to give rise to the different tissues of the sporogonium. For the sake of convenience the development of the whole capsule may be divided into three development zones. These zones are-(a) the fertile region (b) apical region of the capsule and (c) the lower region of the capsule. The development in the different regions of the capsule has been given below, under separate sub-headings.

(a) Development of the fertile region of the capsule. All the four cells of the endothecium divide diagonally or vertically, which is soon followed by periclinal division giving rise to four inner cells and eight outer cells. The four inner endothecial cells divide twice resulting in a group of sixteen cells which ultimately give rise to the **columella.** The outer eight endothecial cells divide by radial and periclinal divisions, and this way the two rings of the cells are resulted. The cells of the outer layer divide once again radially, and the **archesporium** is resulted. The cells of the inner layer, adjacent to the columella develop into the **inner spore sac.** The archesporium may be one or two layered. The cells of the archesporium are spore mother cells. They divide by reduction division giving rise to haploid spores. In the earlier stage of the development, the spores are arranged in tetrads.

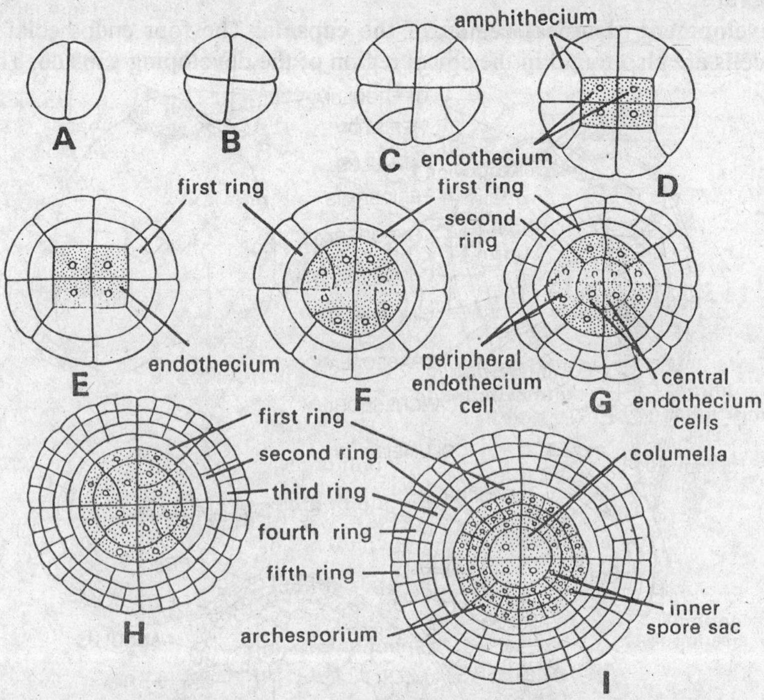

Fig. 10.12. *Funaria hygrometrica*. Developmental stages of capsule in cross sections. A-D, successive stages in the differentation of amphithecium and endothecium; E-I, further successive stages in the differentation of five rings of cells from the amphithecium.

The cell division of the amphithecial cells is very regular and takes place in a definite pattern. According to Goebel, this definite pattern of division of the amphithecium is called the **grundquadrat.** The amphithecial cells divide by periclinal division, giving rise to two concentric layers. The inner layer may be designated as **first ring.** This layer consists of eight cells. The cells of the outer concentric layer divide anticlinally giving rise to sixteen cells. This layer of sixteen cells divides periclinally forming two concentric layers. Each such layer consists of sixteen cells. The inner layer of these two layers is designated as **second ring.** The outer layer of these two layers divides anticlinally giving rise to thirty two cells. These 32 cells divide periclinally giving rise to two layers of 32 cells each. The inner layer of these two layers may be referred as the **third ring.** The outer layer, consisted of 32 cells, divides periclinally, giving rise to two layers of 32 cells each. The inner layer of 32 cells may be referred as **fourth ring** and the outermost layer of the same number of cells is the **fifth ring.** These five rings give rise to the different parts of the fertile region.

The cells of the first ring divide anticlinally giving rise to thirty-two cells. These cells again divide periclinally and a three-layered **outer spore sac** is formed. These cells lack chloroplasts.

The 16 celled second ring develops chloroplasts in them and elongate radially; thus giving rise to lacunae or air spaces. The cells become separated from each other. Each cell divides transversely twice or thrice giving rise to a filament of 3 or 4 cells. Such filaments connect the outer spore sac to the wall of the capsule.

The third ring which consists of 32 cells, remains one cell in thickness, and the chloroplasts develop in the cells on their maturation.

The fourth ring also consists of 32 cells. These cells divide periclinally giving rise to two or three concentric layers of cells without chloroplasts.

The fifth ring also possesses 32 cells. The cells of this ring divide anticlinally and develop into a distinct epidermis.

(b) Development of apical region of the capsule. The four endothecial and the eight amphithecial cells are also found in the apical region of the developing capsule. The endothecial

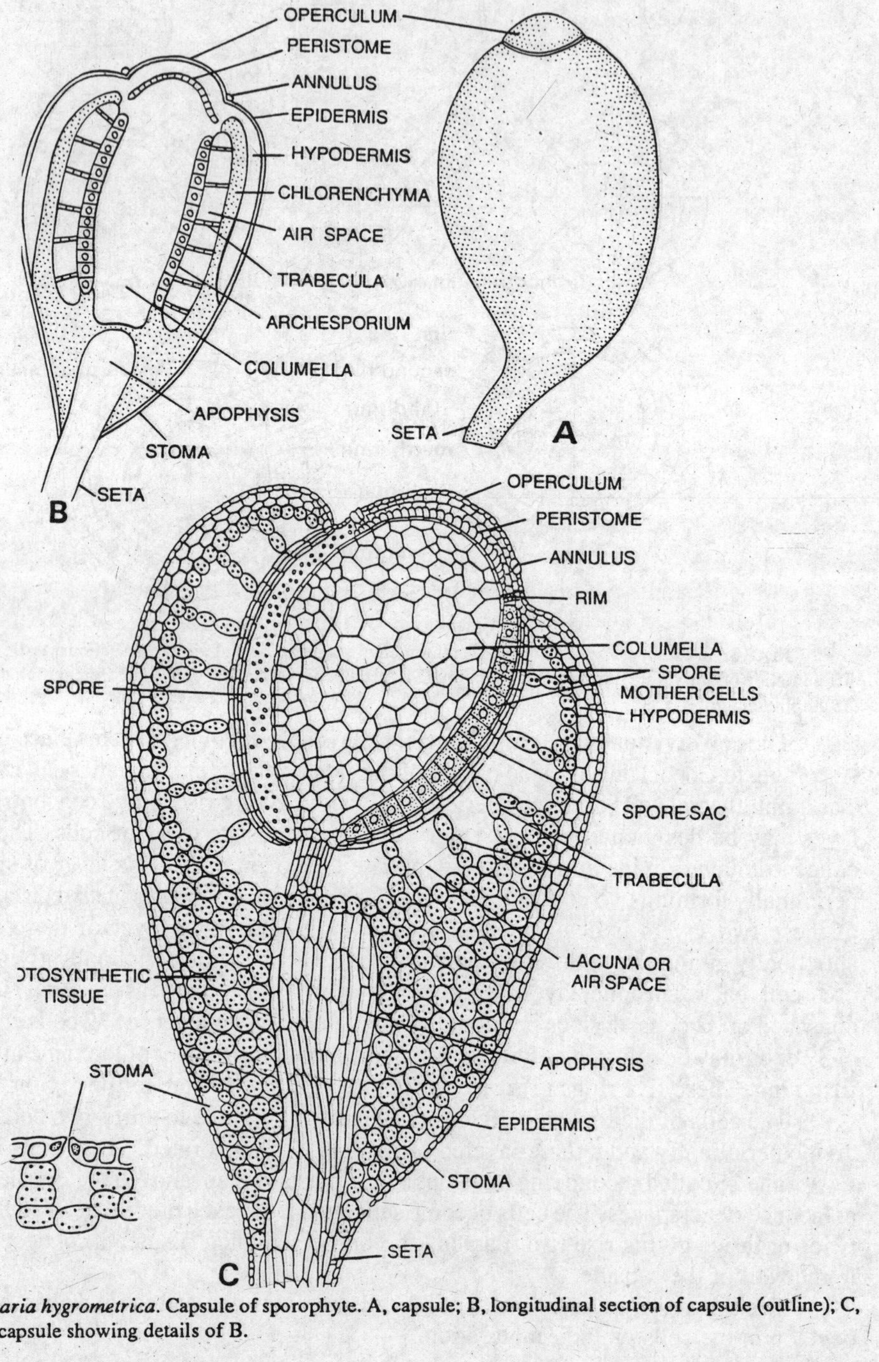

Fig. 10.13. *Funaria hygrometrica*. Capsule of sporophyte. A, capsule; B, longitudinal section of capsule (outline); C, longitudinal section of capsule showing details of B.

cells divide again and again continuously giving rise to thin walled parenchyma in continuation of the columella of the capsule. The eight cells of amphithecium divide alternately periclinally and anticlinally, giving rise to five usual concentric rings of the cells. Each concentric ring consists of twice as many cells as the next inner ring. The operculum and peristome, are, however, developed from the cells of these rings.

The peristome develops from the first and second rings. The first ring consists of 32 cells and forms the **inner peristomial layer,** whereas the second ring consists of 16 cells and forms the **outer peristomial layer.** The cells of these two inner and outer peristomial layers are so arranged that one cell of the inner layer is covered by the two cells of the outer layer. On maturation, the wall material is added to the peristomial layers and a double set of the teeth of peristome is developed. In each series (set) of the peristome, there are sixteen teeth or clefts. The teeth are somewhat curved, narrow and triangular in outline. The teeth are attached to the rim of the mouth of the capsule. This complete structure, consisting of the two sets of the teeth is called the **peristome.**

External to the peristome, third to fifth rings of the amphithecium give rise to the operculum of the capsule. The third and fourth rings give rise to a three celled thick tissue. However, the fifth ring derived from the amphithecium, develops into the epidermis of the operculum. The epidermal cells at the base of the operculum enlarge radially and form a ring of **annulus.** The annulus is constituted of 5 to 6 layers of the cells of the epidermis. This is the broadest region of the operculum. The upper superimposed layers of the epidermal cells of the annulus are narrow and thickwalled whereas the cells of the lowermost two layers of the annulus are thin walled.

(c) Development of the lower region of capsule. In the later stages of the development of sporophyte the seta and the capsule are differentiated. There is a conducting region of apophysis in between seta and capsule. The tissues in this region are developed in the same way as they are developed in the fertile region, only with the difference that they lack archesporium and spore sac layers. The endothecial cells in this region give rise to the conducting strand of the seta. The amphithecium forms the spongy chlorenchyma and the epidermis. The epidermis is interrupted by stomata here and there.

Structure of mature sporogonium. The sporophyte consists of a foot, seta and capsule.

The foot is a small, conical structure embedded in the apical portion of the female branch of the gametophore. This is a poorly developed structure. It absorbs water and nutrients from the gametophyte for the development of the sporogonium.

The seta is an elongated slender and thread like structure which bears the capsule at its apical end. The cells of the tissue of seta are elongated. The tissue helps somewhat in the conduction of water but mainly its function is mechanical.

The outline of a mature capsule is pear shaped. In the beginning, an irregular calyptra is found as a cap-like structure at the apical end of the capsule, but very soon this is blown off. The main parts of the capsule are as follows:

The apophysis. The elongated seta expands at its apical end to form the apophysis. This is assimilatory region. The stomata may be seen here and there in the epidermis. The stomata are meant for gaseous exchange. The cells with chloroplasts possess intercellular spaces among them. The central conducting strand consists of colourless cells. This strand is continuous with the conducting strand of seta. This region is assimilatory in function and makes the capsule self-sufficient in nutrition to some extent.

The theca. The central fertile region of the capsule is known as the theca proper. This region consists of many layers of the cells. The outermost layer is the epidermis, which lies in continuation of the epidermis of the apophysis of the capsule. Just below the epidermis, there is one or two layered hypodermis. The cells of the hypodermal region are colourless. Just next to the hypodermis there is one or two layered chlorenchyma tissue. The cells of this layer contain chloroplasts and act as photosynthetic tissue. This chlorenchymatous layer becomes several layered in the region of apophysis. Just beneath the chlorenchymatous layer there is a big air space, traversed by several **trabeculae.** Each trabecula consists of 3 or 4 green cells. These filiform structures act as connections

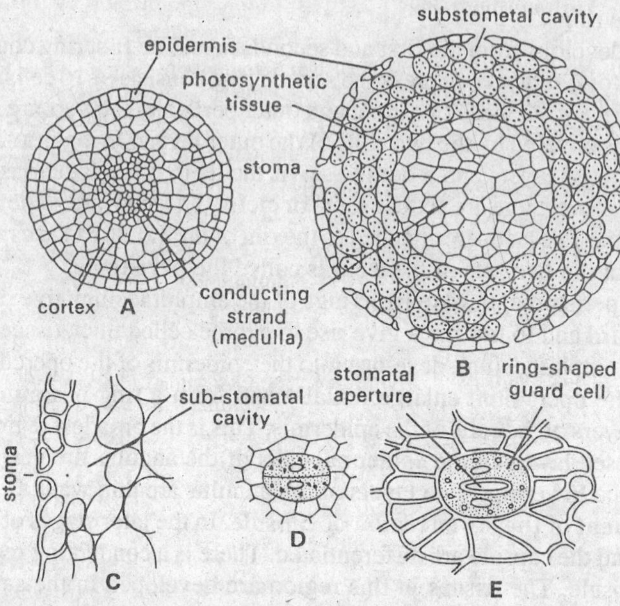

Fig. 10.14. *Funaria hygrometrica.* Anatomy of different parts of sporophyte. A, transverse section of seta showing cortex and conducting strand; B, transverse section of capsule through apophysis showing photosynthetic tissue, conducting, strand and epidermis with stomata; C, enlarged portion of B, showing epidermis, stoma and sub-stomatal cavity; D, young stoma in surface view; E, mature stoma in surface view; stomata confined to apophysis region only.

between chlorenchymatous layer and the outer spore sac of the capsule. The central region of the theca is occupied by a pith like solid cylinder of parenchyma, called the **columella.** The columella is narrow at its base and broad at its apical end. It is connected to the conducting strand of the apophysis of the capsule at its base. The columella is surrounded by the spore sac. The spore sac is barrel shaped. The spore sac has an inner single layered wall called the inner spore sac. The outerwall of the spore sac is 3 or 4 layered and known as the outerspore sac. In between these inner and outer spore sacs there are spore mother cells. As usual each spore mother cell develops into a spore tetrad of four spores. The first division is the reductional one.

The upper region. The upper region of the capsule consists of operculum and peristome. It is differentiated from the theca proper by a well marked constriction. The lid of the capsule is somewhat obliquely placed upon it. The lid or operculum is 4 or 5 layeres in thickness. The outermost layer of it is epidermis. The epidermis consists of the cells of greatly thickened walls. The next 3 or 4 layers of the cells consist of thin walled parenchymatous cells. Just beneath the constriction there is a 2 or 3 layered rim of radially elongated cells. The rim is found in the form of a circular edge. It stretches inward from the epidermis and this way connects the peristome to the epidermis of the capsule.

The peristome lies just beneath the operculum. It consists of two sets of incurved teeth known as inner and outer peristome. Each set of teeth consists of sixteen incurved, triangular teeth. The teeth are spirally twisted towards left. The teeth of the outer peristome are red and of inner peristome are colourless. The inner teeth are shorter than the outer ones.

The annulus is found just above the rim. It consists of 5 or 6 layers of epidermal cells. The structure of annulus has already been described in foregoing pages.

The mouth of the capsule remains closed by means of lid or operculum.

Dehiscence of the capsule. The capsule begins to dry up on its maturation. The columella and the outer thin walled tissues of the capsule lose water and shrink up. This way, the spore containing space is teared off. The annulus breaks, and the operculum is thrown off. As soon as the operculum is detached from the capsule the peristome teeth move outward hygroscopically, and help in throwing away the operculum. The hygroscopic movements of the peristome teeth help in the gradual dispersal of the spores from the capsule. On becoming wet the outer layer of each tooth becomes long

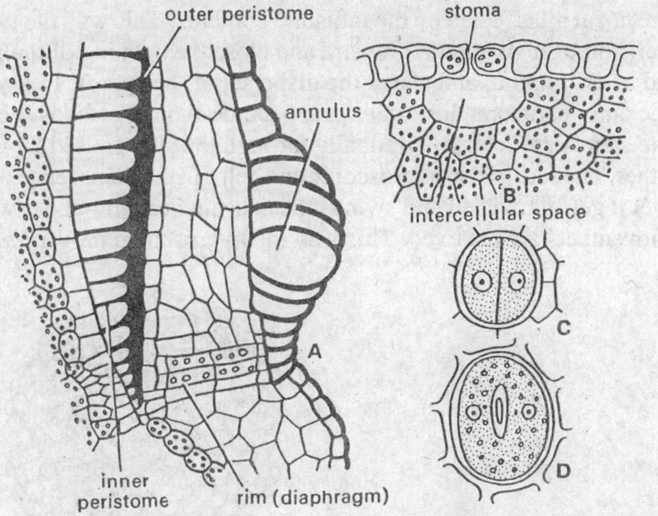

Fig. 10.15. *Funaria hygrometrica*. A, a portion of L.S. through operculum and upper part of theca exhibiting relationship of peristome and rim; B, T.S. through apophysis showing stoma; C, young stoma in surface view; D, mature stoma in surface view.

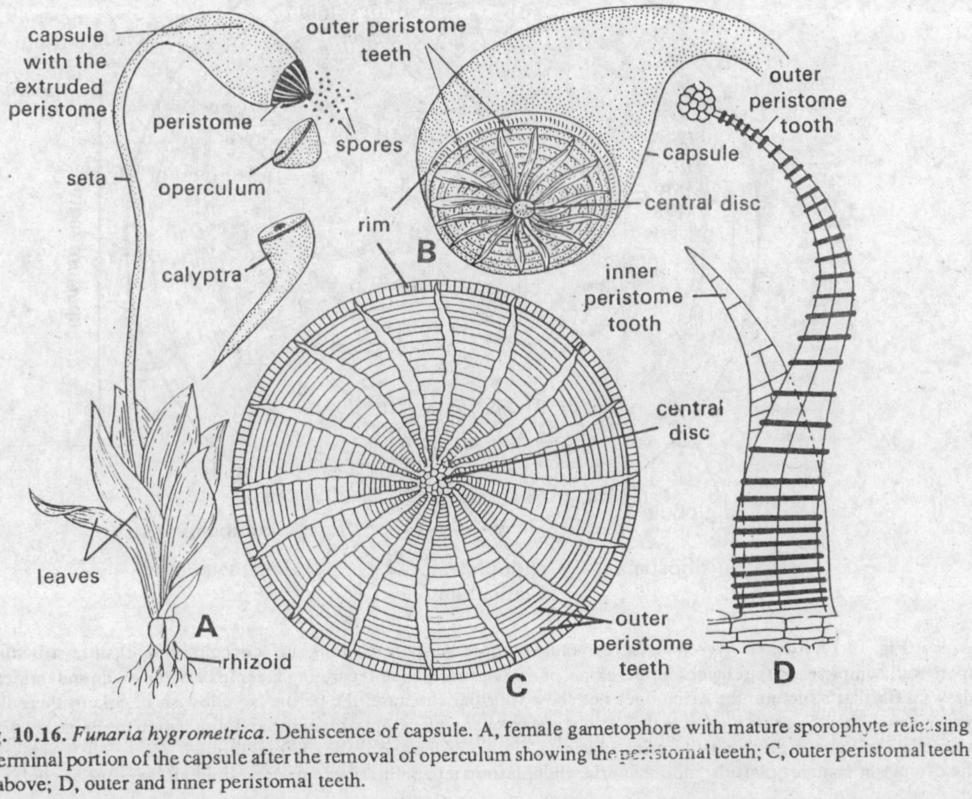

Fig. 10.16. *Funaria hygrometrica*. Dehiscence of capsule. A, female gametophore with mature sporophyte releasing spores; B, terminal portion of the capsule after the removal of operculum showing the peristomal teeth; C, outer peristomal teeth seen from above; D, outer and inner peristomal teeth.

and on becoming dry each tooth becomes short. However, the inner layer of the teeth is not affected by the changing conditions of the moisture. The outer layers of the teeth of the outer peristome absorb water on the removal of the operculum and the teeth increase in length than the inner teeth which are not at all affected by the moisture contents. This way the two sets outer and inner of teeth of the peristome curve together inward and close the opening of the capsule caused by the removal of the lid or operculum, and check the dispersal of the spores. In dry weather outer layers of the teeth of the outer peristome lose water and become short. This way the teeth curve outwards with jerks and the spores are released gradually through the slits caused by the separation of the teeth from each other. The seta is also hygroscopic and helps in the dehiscence of the capsule. When the seta becomes wet it gets untwisted and swings the capsule in round-about way. On becoming dry of the seta the movements are reserved. This way the hygroscopic movements of the peristome and seta assist in

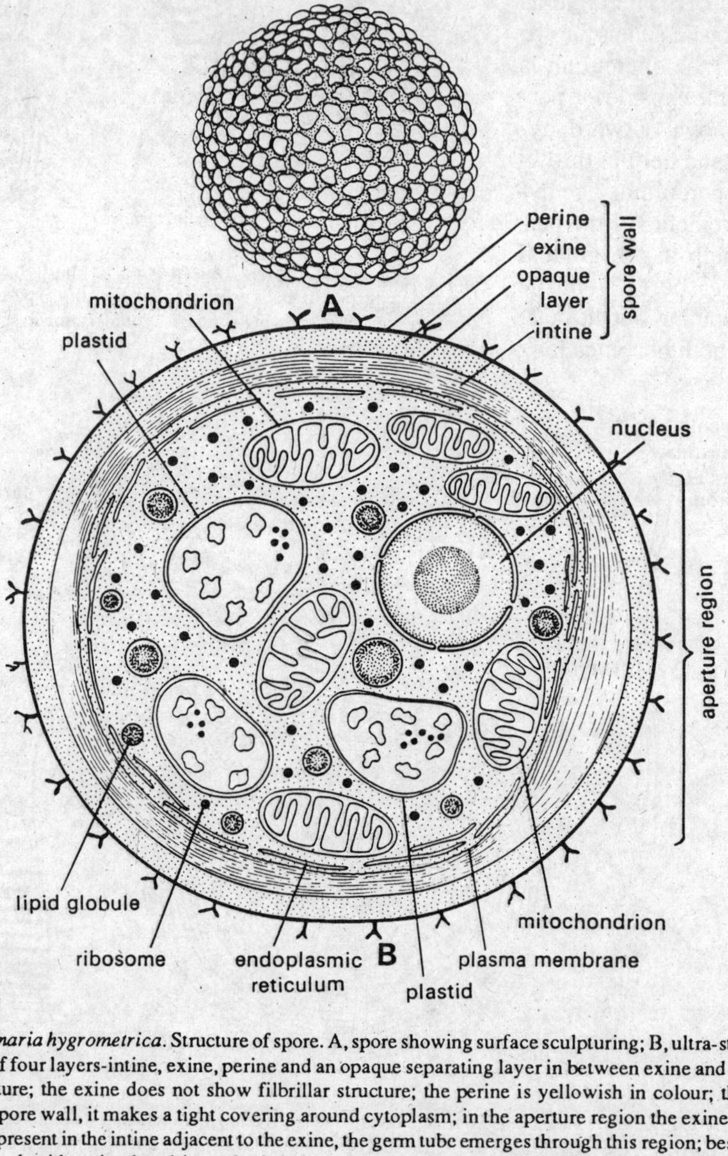

Fig. 10.17. *Funaria hygrometrica.* Structure of spore. A, spore showing surface sculpturing; B, ultra-structure of spore, spore wall comprises of four layers-intine, exine, perine and an opaque separating layer in between exine and intine; the intine shows a fibrillar structure; the exine does not show filbrillar structure; the perine is yellowish in colour; there is a plasma membrane within the spore wall, it makes a tight covering around cytoplasm; in the aperture region the exine is quite thin and a lamellate structure is present in the intine adjacent to the exine, the germ tube emerges through this region; besides the nucleus the cytoplasm contains plastids, mitochondria, endoplasmic reticulum, ribosomes and lipid globules; no vacuoles.

the dispersal of the spores from the capsule. The spores are released gradually from the capsule for a long period. The spores are carried from one place to another by wind and other suitable agencies.

Structure and germination of spore. The spores are more or less spherical. Each spore possesses a covering wall of two layers. The outer layer is somewhat coloured, smooth and known as exosporium. The inner layer is colourless, smooth and known as endosporium. The spore contains within it, a nucleus, oil globules and chloroplasts.

Usually the spore does not germinate immediately after its shedding from the capsule. If the spore gets favourable conditions after it has been shed from the capsule, it germinates within a few days. According to Heitz (1942), in certain species the spores remain viable even for two years. According to Malta (1922), Meyer (1941), in certain other species, the spores may germinate even after 8 to 16 years of their shedding.

The germinating spore increases somewhat in size, the exospore ruptures and the endospore protrudes out in the form of one or two germ tubes. A cross wall appears in the germ tube near its point of emergence from the exosporium. The cell formed by this cross wall gives rise to a multicellular filament called the **primary protonema.** The protonema further grows strictly by the division of the apical cell. According to Correns (1899), Muller (1874) and Sironval (1947) the primary protonema is differentiated into two kinds of branches, known as **chloronema or chlorone-**

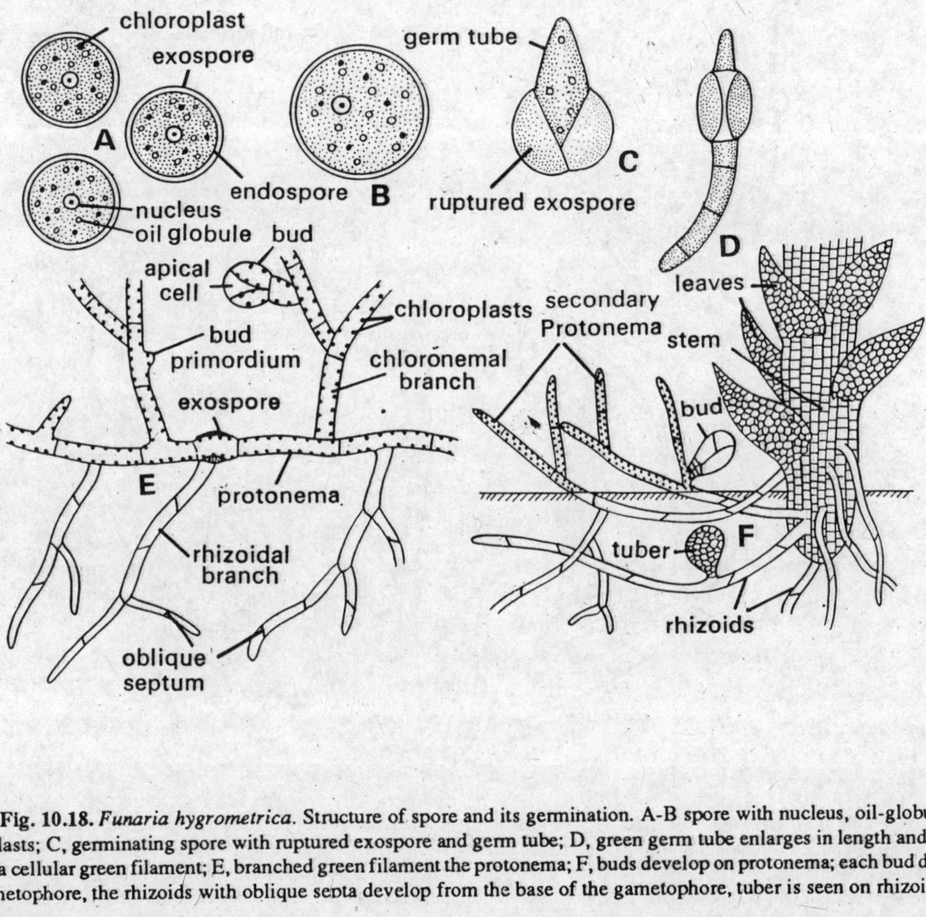

Fig. 10.18. *Funaria hygrometrica.* Structure of spore and its germination. A-B spore with nucleus, oil-globules and chloroplasts; C, germinating spore with ruptured exospore and germ tube; D, green germ tube enlarges in length and divides to form a cellular green filament; E, branched green filament the protonema; F, buds develop on protonema; each bud develops in a gametophore, the rhizoids with oblique septa develop from the base of the gametophore, tuber is seen on rhizoid.

mal branches and rhizoids or rhizoidal branches. The chloronemal branches are aerial and prostrately upon the surface of the substratum, whereas, the rhizoidal branches or rhizoids grow downward and penetrate the substratum. The chloronemal branches are thick, possessing hyaline cell walls, with transverse cross walls forming right angles to the lateral walls, and containing

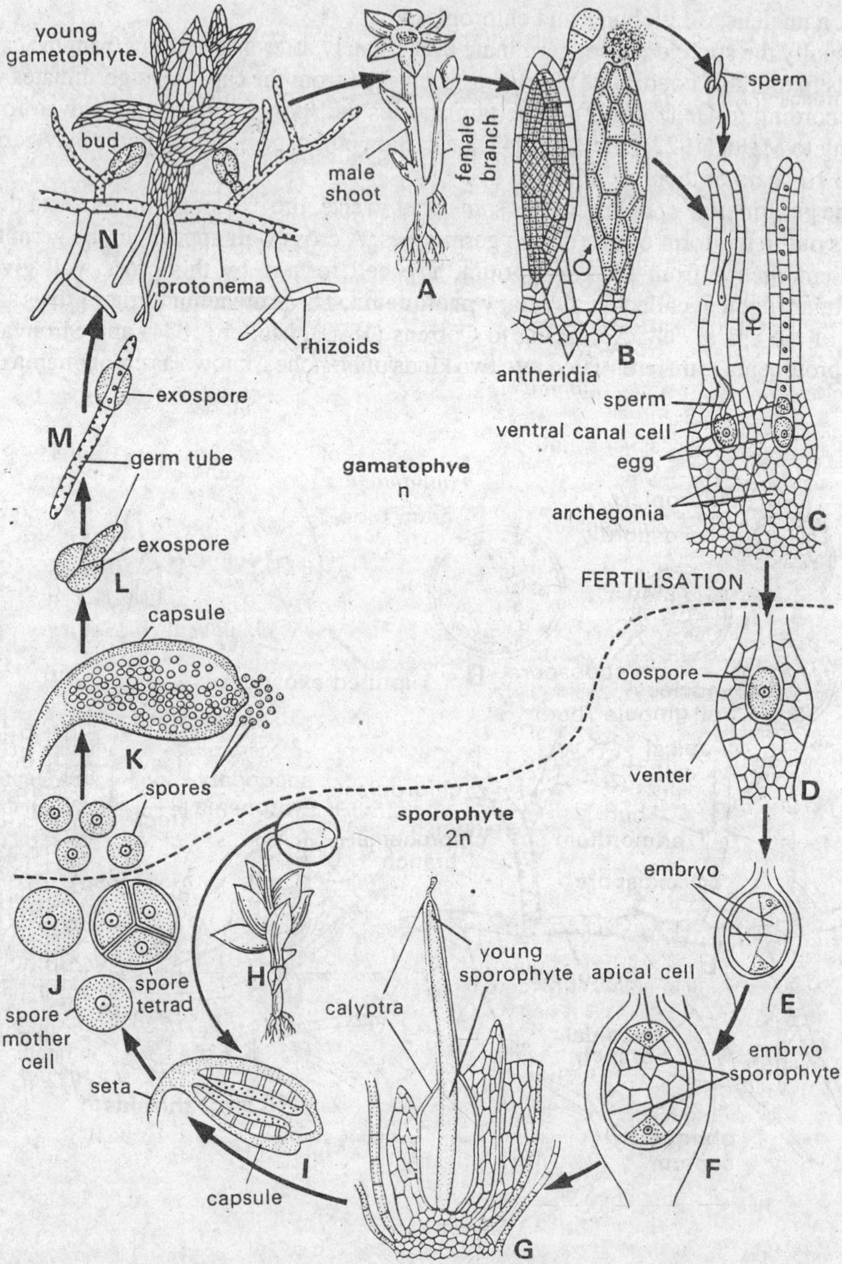

Fig. 10.19. *Funaria hygrometrica.* Diagrammatic life-cycle. A, gametophore with male and female shoots; B, antheridia; C, archegonia; D, venter containing oospore (2n) after fertilization, E-G, successive stages in the development of young sporophyte; H, gametophore bearing sporophyte; I, longitudinal section of sporogonium (outline sketch); J, spore mother cell (2n) and spore tetrad (n); K, spores (n); L-N, germination of spore and development of young gametophyte.

numerous chloroplasts in them. The rhizoidal branches are relatively thin, brown and with diagonal cross walls. They possess inconspicuous small chloroplasts or leucoplasts in them. Some of the rhizoidal branches which, however, grow in the light are provided with hyaline walls, conspicuous chloroplasts and cross walls at the right angles to the lateral walls. And, this way, the rhizoidal and chloronemal branches may mainly be differentiated on the basis of environmental conditions. In earlier stages the rhizoids act as absorbing organs but later on they perform the function of the attachment of the plants to the substratum. The chloronemal branches are photosynthetic.

According to Sironval (1947), in *Funaria hygrometrica,* in the older portions of the primary protonema, the gametophore initials are produced in the lowermost cell of the lateral branch. Such gametophore initials are formed on a profusely branched portion of the protonema called the **caulonema.** The caulonema possesses oblique cross walls in it. The buds of the leafy gametophores are formed only on the caulonema. Van Andel (1952) does not support the presence of caulonema in *Funaria hygrometrica*. Allsopp and Mitra (1958) however, could not see the two distinct stages the 'chloronema' and 'caulonema'. According to Allsopp and Mitra, the germinating spore produces a filamentous structure with cross walls at right angles to the long axis, hyaline cell walls and numerous discoid chloroplasts in it. This structure resembles to that of a typical chloronema and may be designated as chloronemal branches. These branches grow horizontally on the surface of the substratum. This structure develops the heterotrichous protonema with two types of branches. The upright and prostrate branches are provided with discoid conspicuous chloroplasts, hyaline cell walls, and cross walls at the right angles of the lateral walls. They are chloronemal branches. The branches which go downward (rhizoidal branches) possess incospicuous chloroplasts or leucoplasts, oblique cross walls and somewhat brownish walls. Finally the buds appear on the protonema. The buds usually appear just behind the cross walls. Each such bud develops into a new gametophyte. As soon as the leafy gametophores with few leaves and rhizoids have been established in the soil

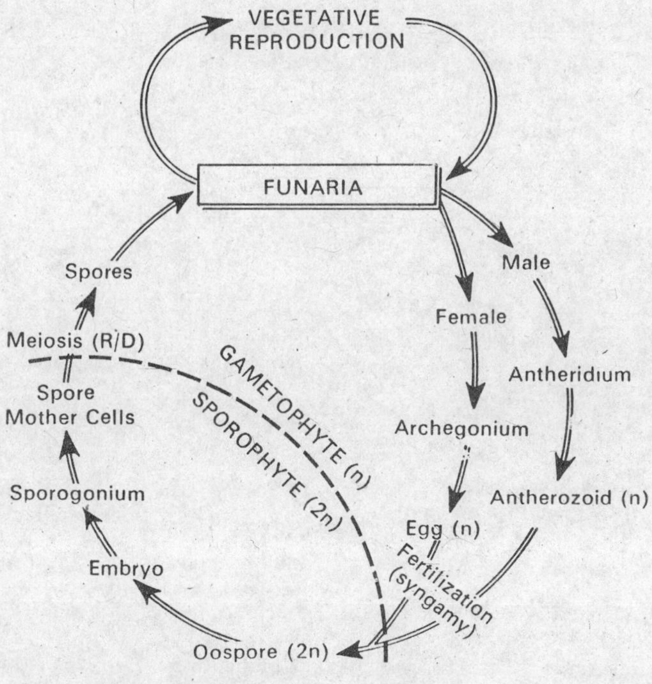

Fig. 10.20. *Funaria hygrometrica*. Graphic life-cycle.

(substratum), the primary protonema disintegrates and disappears, and the gametophores are separated from each other and become independent.

Alternations of generations. The moss plants are gametophytes (gametophores). These gametophores bear antheridia and archegonia on the separate branches of the same plant. The antherozoids are produced from the antheridium, and the egg is produced within the venter of the archegonium. They are haploid. Soon after fertilization, an oospore is produced. Here, the male and female nuclei are fused, and thus the oospore becomes diploid in nature. The oospore is the first phase of the sporophytic generation. Later on the sporophyte is produced, which is differentiated into foot, seta and capsule. In the capsule the spore mother cells are produced. They represent the last phase of the sporophytic (2n) generation. The spore mother cells divide meiotically and tetrads of the spores are produced. The spores are haploid and they represent the beginning of the gametophytic generation. This way, there is alternation of generations. The gametophyte is independent and gives rise to a parasitic sporophyte upon it. The sporophyte produces spores, and the spores again give rise to gametophytic plants after their germination. Here, the two generations (gametophytic and sporophytic) alternate with each other, and this is called the alternation of generations.

Systematic position. Division. Bryophyta
Class. Bryopsida (musci)
Sub-class. Bryidae
Cohort. Eubriidae
Order. Funariales
Family. Funariaceae
Genus. *Funaria*.

11

Bryopsida (Musci)

Order-Polytrichales

The characteristic features of this order are as follows. The gametophyte is perennial and tall. The leaves are quite narrow and possess longitudinal lamellae on the upper surface of the midrib. The capsule is terminal. The single annular series of cells gives rise to a peristome, in the inner zone of the amphithecium. There are 32 to 64 pyramidal teeth in peristome. The tips of the peristome teeth remain joined above to a thin membrane, the epiphragm covers the mouth of the capsule.

There is a single family, the Polytrichaceae in this order. This family includes about 15 genera and 350 species. Genera *Polytrichum* and *Pogonatum* have been discussed here in detail.

Genus POLYTRICHUM

Occurrence and distribution. There are about ninety two species in this genus. It is cosmopolitan in its distribution. It is mainly found in cool temperate and tropical regions. Like other mosses it is also found in cool and shady places. They may be found growing in bogs and marshes, on soil of firm or loose texture, on rocks and cliffs, and as epiphytes on trunks of trees. In India it is commonly found on the hills. Bruhl (1935) has reported three species from our country-*Polytrichum densifolium, P. juniperinum* and *P. xanthopilum.*

Polytrichum is one of the most highly developed types of Moss. In size it varies very considerably according to the environment. Sometimes when it grows among long grass on a damp marshy place, it may reach 30 cms. or more in length.

The Gametophyte

External structure. The gametophyte is differentiated into rhizoids, the underground **rhizome** the erect **stems** and **leaves.**

The young leaves at the apex of a stem are arranged in a definite manner. The arrangement of leaves is directly correlated with the number of cutting faces of the apical cell of the stem. In *Polytrichum,* the apical cell is with three cutting faces, and therefore, the young leaves being spirally arranged in three vertical rows. Each leaf possesses a broad colourless membranous sheath at its base. The leaf becomes narrow upwards. The upper portion of the leaf is expanded which is green or brownish in colour. Each leaf possesses a broad midrib. The midrib remains covered on its upper surface by means of longitudinal cell plates which contain chlorophyll and are known as lamellae.

Numerous rhizoids are found on the rhizome of gametophyte. The rhizoids are long and thickwalled. They possess oblique septa in them. The rhizoids form a tuft or twisted mass which looks like a string. It is sometimes as thick as the rhizome itself. The rhizoids give mechanical support to the plants, the water rises in rhizoids by external capillarity, and therefore, the plants even at dry places flourish well. The rhizoids also help vegetative reproduction.

Internal structure (anatomy). Here the anatomy of rhizome, aerial stem and leaf has been considered in details.

Anatomy of rhizome. The outline of rhizome is broadly triangular. The cortex is divided by three **radial strands.** These strands penetrate into the central cylinder, giving it a three-lobed outline.

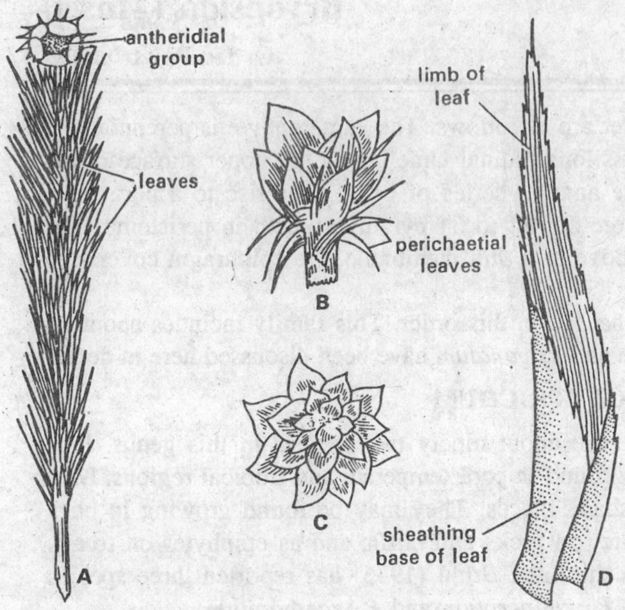

Fig. 11.1. *Polytrichum.* A, male plant; B, female head; C, male head; D, leaf of *P. commune.*

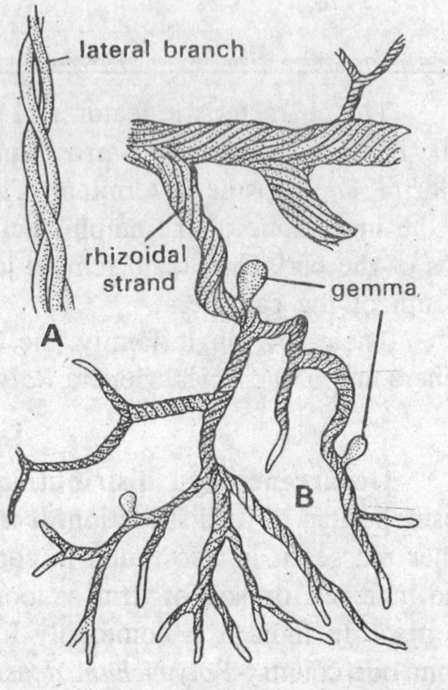

Fig. 11.2. *Polytrichum* sp. Rhizoids. A, lateral branch of rhizoidal strand showing detailed structure; B, rhizoidal strand bearing gemmae.

The **cortex** consists of three to four layers of cells of which the outermost layer is strongly suberized. The innermost layer of the cortex consists of very large cells with thin suberized walls, known as the **endodermis.**

Two or three-layered primitive **pericycle** is found just beneath the endodermis. This pericycle does not make continuous band. It surrounds the **central cylinder.** The greater part of the central cylinder is made up of thick-walled, somewhat elongated cells, which form the **sterome,** among which there are scattered groups of empty, elongated cells, the **hydroids.**

The three radial strands start from groups of thick-walled cortical cells, while their inward ends which remain embedded in the central cylinder, consist of thin walled **leptoids** corresponding to the **leptome** in the aerial stem.

The inner groups of leptoids is separated from the tissue of the central cylinder by a single layer of small cells containing starch, called the **amylome.**

Anatomy of aerial stem. The outline of the transverse section of aerial stem is irregular due to the insertion of the leaves. The **superficial layer** or **epidermis** is inconspicuous. The aerial stem is differentiated into a cortex and a central conducting tissue.

Inside the superficial layer is the **cortex.** The outer cortex is extensive and thick-walled while the inner cortex is thin-walled. The cells of the cortex commonly contain starch in them. The leaf **traces** are seen in the cortical region which pass through it and join the central cylinder.

Inside the inner cortex there is **rudimentary pericycle.** The pericyclic band is not complete and remains interrupted by leaf traces.

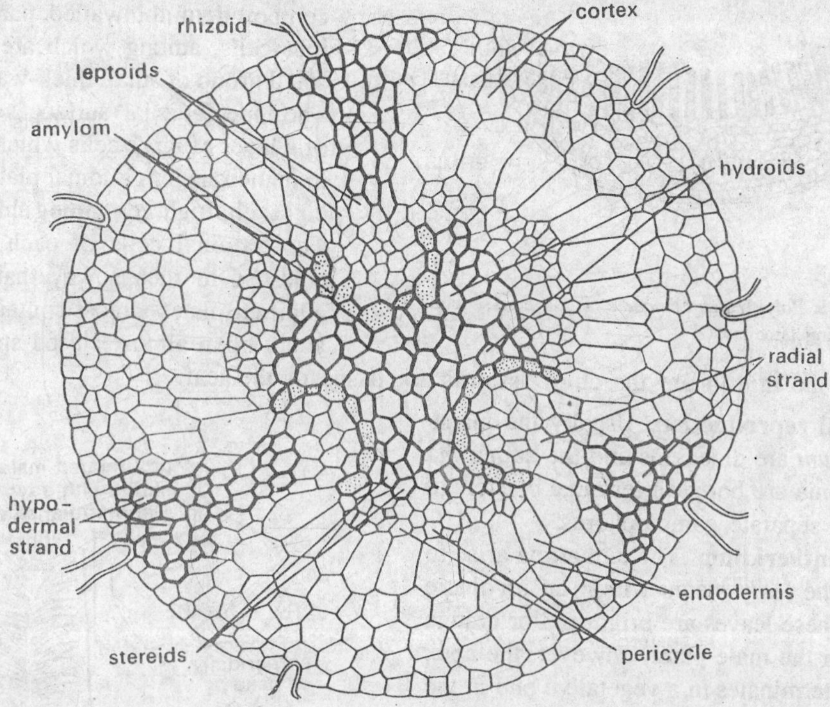

Fig. 11.3. *Polytrichum* sp. Transverse section of rhizome showing detailed cellular structure.

Inside the rudimentary pericycle there is a **leptom mantle.** This is similar to the phloem of higer plants.

Internal to the leptom mantle there is **hydrom sheath** which is also known as **amylom layer.** It consists of one or two layers of cells. The cell walls are suberized and the cells contain starch.

Inside the amylom layer there is the **hydrom mantle.** It consists of thinwalled cells. In the centre of the stem there is **hydrom cylinder** which is composed of thick-walled cells. This plays an important role in the conduction of water. This tissue is equivalent to xylem of higher plants.

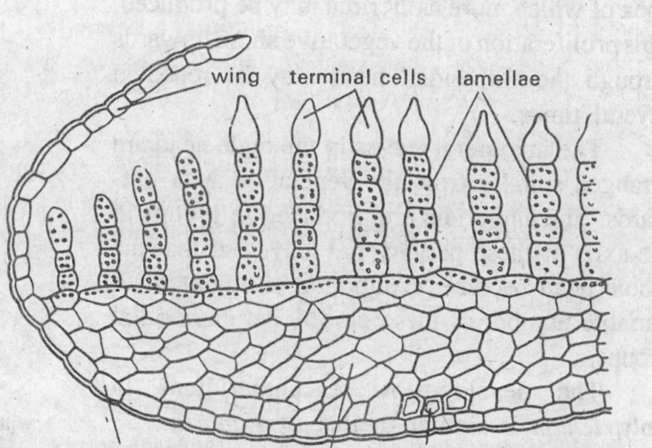

Fig. 11.4. *Polytrichum juniperinum.* Transverse section of a leaf showing lamellae.

Anatomy of the leaf. The broad midrib is several cells thick in the centre and gradually merges into the so called lamina at the margins. On the lower surface there is a well-marked **epidermis** composed of large cells whose outer walls are thickened. Inside the epidermis there are one or two layers of very small cells with very thick walls. The central tissue of the leaf is composed of thinwalled parenchymatous cells, among which are scattered small group of small thick-walled cells. The upper (adaxial) surface is composed of a layer of large cells which give rise to numerous longitudinal plates, five to eight cells high, containing chloroplasts. The terminal cells of each plate are enlarged in such a way that those of adjacent plates almost containing cells about upon almost closed spaces. The lamellae of the midrib are the chief assimilatory tissue of the leaf.

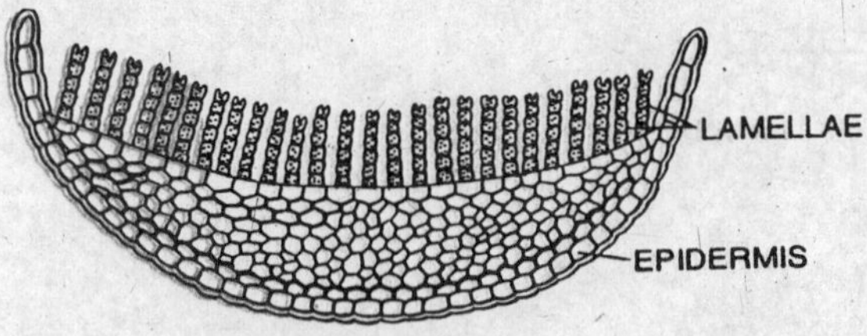

Fig. 11.5. *Polytrichum commune*. Transverse section of a leaf showing lamellae.

Sexual reproduction. Usually the plants of *Polytrichum* are dioecious and the antheridia and archegonia are borne in terminal clusters at the apex of separate gametophores.

The antheridium. The antheridia arise to the top of the leafy stems within an involucre of leaves. These leaves are bright red or orange in colour. In the male plant, however, the apex of the stem terminates in a vegetative bud in the middle of the antheridial head, which, after the development of the antheridia may grow out in the following year through the antheridial group and produce a fresh shoot (proliferation), at the apex of which more antheridia may be produced. This proliferation of the vegetative shoot upwards through the antheridial head may be repeated several times.

The involucral leaves in the male head are arranged spirally from the vegetative apex outwards. The antheridia are produced in groups in the axils of these perichaetial leaves so that the whole head becomes compound and contains a variable number of these closely set antheridial groups.

The development of antheridium in *Polytrichum* is similar to that of *Funaria*.

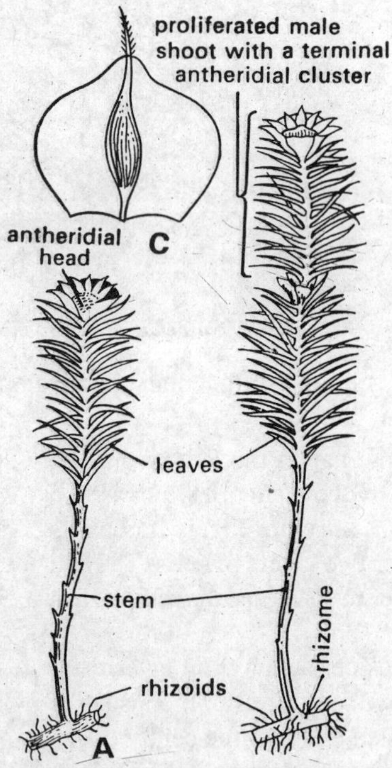

Fig. 11.6. *Polytrichum* sp. A, male plant with antheridial head; B, male plant with proliferated male shoot and terminal antheridial head; C, perigonial leaf of *Polytrichum juniperinum*.

The mature antheridium is composed of a stalk and a clavate body. The club shaped body remains surrounded by a single layered jacket. Inside the jacket there are androcytes within the antheridium. The antheridia are intermingled with paraphyses. Some paraphyses are simple and filament-like while the others are broadened at their tips.

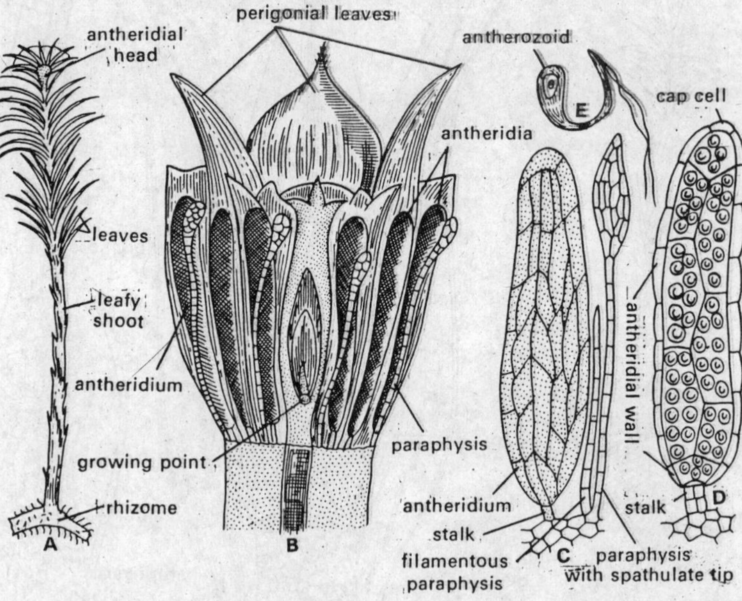

Fig. 11.7. *Polytrichum*. A, male plant; B, L.S. through the apex of male gametophore; C, antheridium with two types of paraphyses; D, L.S. of mature antheridium; E, antherozoid with two flagella.

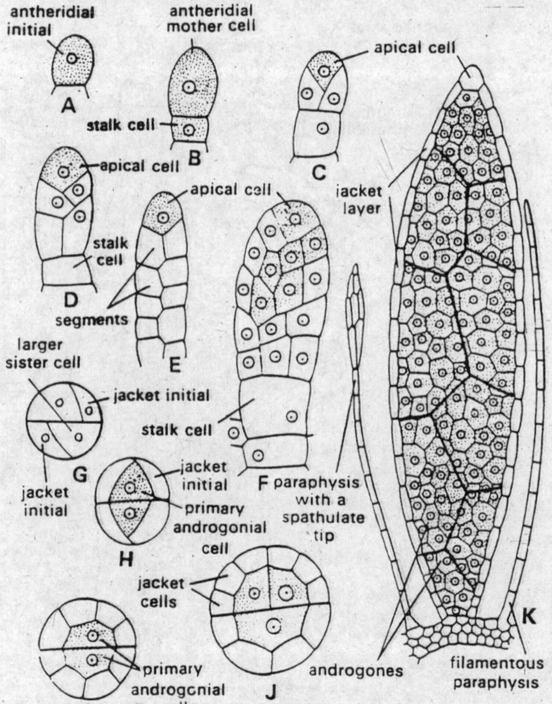

Fig. 11.8. *Polytrichum* sp. Development of antheridium. A, antheridial initial; B, antheridial initial divides transversely forming stalk cell, and antheridial mother cell; C, antheridial mother cell divides by two oblique walls forming peripheral cells and an apical cell; D, apical cell cuts right and left segments; E, 13 to 15 segments are cut off; F, periclinal divisions take place and young antheridium is formed; G,H,I and J, cross sections at different stages; K, longitudinal section of nearly mature antheridium covered with jacket layer; the androgones (androcytes) develop into sperms or antherozoids.

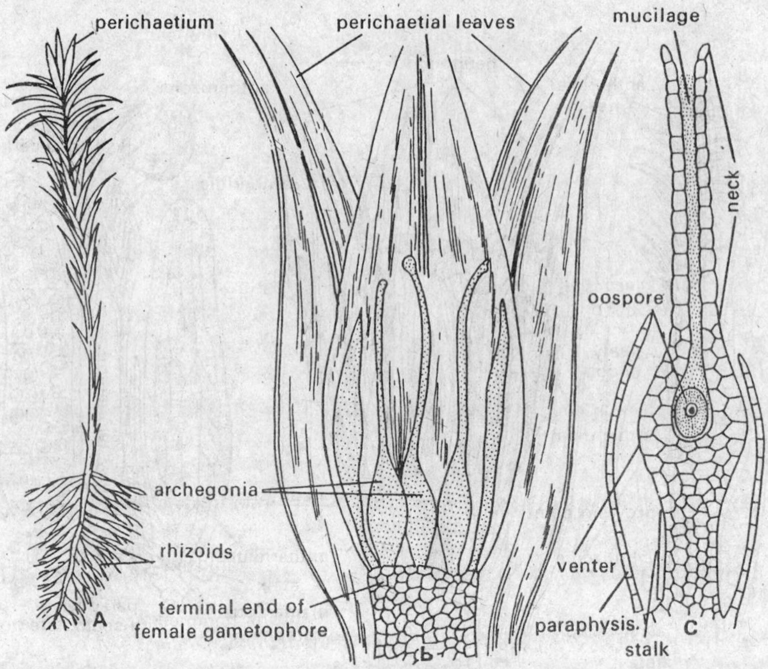

Fig. 11.9. *Polytrichum.* A, female plant; B, longitudinal section through the apex of female gametophore; C, mature archegonium.

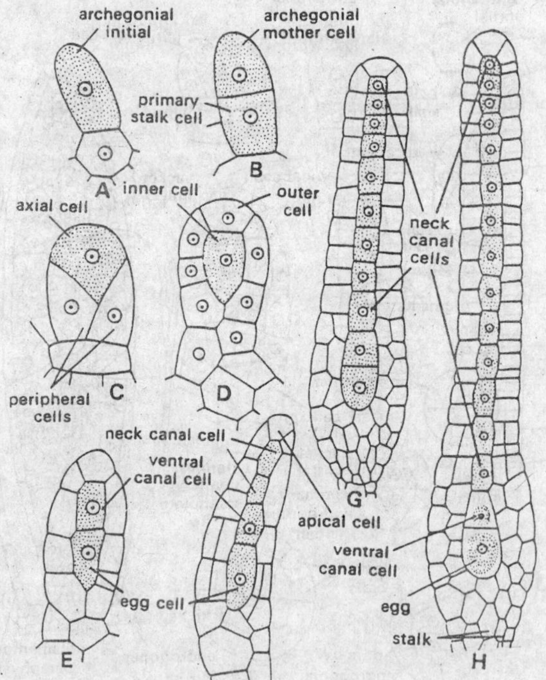

Fig. 11.10. *Polytrichum* sp. Development of archegonium. A, archegonial initial; B, transverse division of archegonial initial forming primary stalk cell and archegonial mother cell; C, archegonium mother cell divides by three oblique walls forming three peripheral cells and an axial cell; D, axial cell divides transversely forming inner central cell and an outer cell; E-F, further development of archegonium; G, young archegonium; H, nearly mature archegonium having egg within venter, ventral canal cell and neck canal cells within neck canal.

The archegonia. The archegonia arise at the top of the leafy stems within an involucre of leaves. The apical cell of the leafy shoot itself forms the initial of an archegonium with the result the growth of the female branch stops with the formation of a sporogonium. Usually three archegonia are found in an archegonial head. The structure and development of archegonium is similar to that of *Funaria.*

Fertilization. The water is essential for the antherozoids to swim upto the archegonium. After the antherozoids reach near the archegonium, they are attracted towards the neck of the archegonium chemotactically. Many antherozoids enter the archegonium through the fluid remains of the neck canal cells and ventral canal cell, but only one fuses with the egg.

The Sporophyte

The development of sporogonium in *Polytrichum* is more or less similar to that of *Funaria.*

The mature sporogonium consists of a **foot, seta and a capsule.** The foot remains embedded in the tissue of an archegonium. It consists of thin-walled parenchymatous cells.

Just above the foot and continuous with it there is a long slender seta which supports the capsule at its terminal end. The seta may reach a length of several inches. The seta and apophysis are considerably larger; the stomata on the apophysis have, however, no pore opening and appear to be functionless.

In transverse section the capsule is square instead of being round. The wall of the capsule consists of several layers of chlorophyllous cells. The outermost layer represents the epidermis. In the mature capsule the sporogenous tissue forms a tube around the **columella** and is separated from it by air spaces which are traversed by filaments of assimilatory cells. A similar assimilatory tissue is also developed between the spore mass and the wall of the capsule. This additional assimilatory tissue, or **aerenchyma,** enables the capsule to obtain more carbohydrate material from the air by means of photosynthesis. All cells of sporogenous tissue give rise to spores.

At the apex of the capsule, the **calyptra** remains attached for a considerable time. The calyptra develops a brown colour, and grows after its separation from the basal part of the archegonium, forming a shaggy, hairy cup which covers the whole capsule and because of this feature sometimes the species of *Polytrichum* is known as 'hair moss'.

At the top of the capsule there is an **operculum** which appears as a lid. The operculum is conical, with a long beak or **rostrum,** and there is no well marked annulus, though the thickened **diaphragm** (rim) is present.

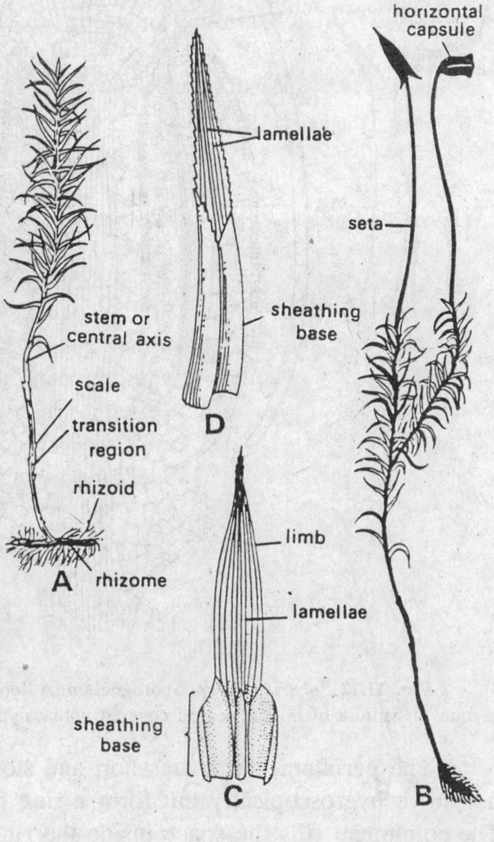

Fig. 11.11. *Polytrichum* sp. A, a leafy gametophore with stem, scales, rhizoids and rhizome; B, the branches of leafy gametophore bearing sporophytes (sporogonia); C and D, leaves of *Polytrichum juniperinum* and *P. commune* respectively.

At the base of operculum there is a thin membranous tissue which constitute the **epiphragm.** In other words, the top of the columella is expanded into a flat disc, the epiphragm.

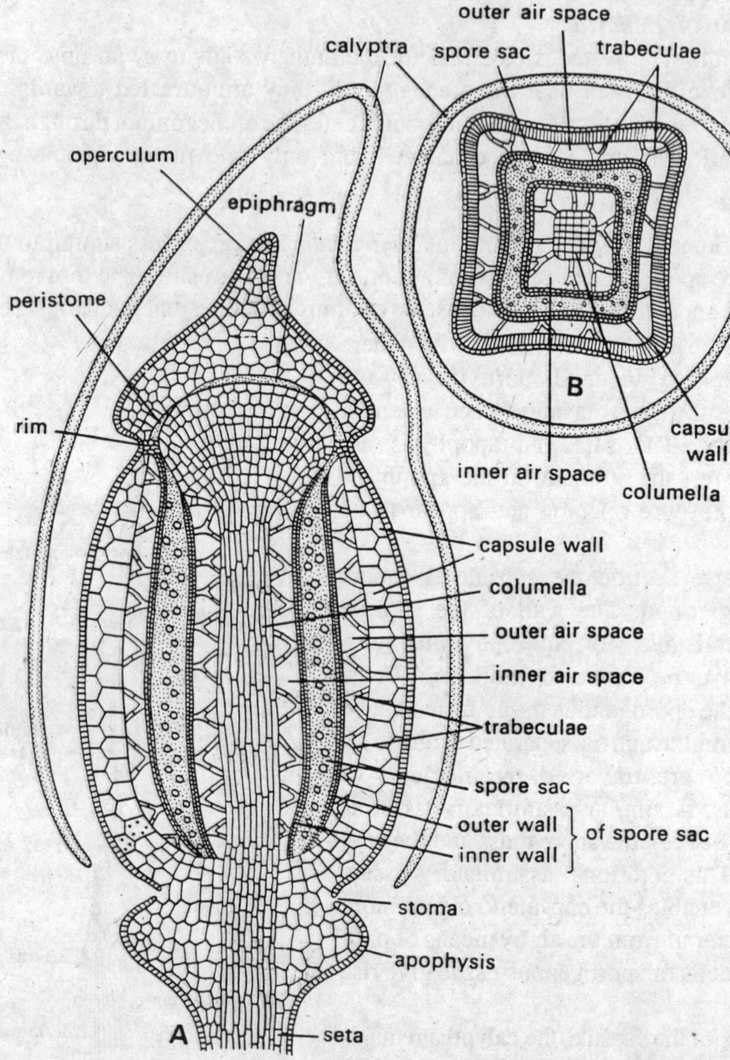

Fig. 11.12. *Polytrichum.* sp. Sporogonium. A, longitudinal section of capsule covered with calyptra; B, transverse section of capsule of middle region covered with calyptra.

The **peristome** teeth are short and stout, formed of a group of sclerotic cells. These do not move hygroscopically but form a ring of rigid teeth when the operculum has fallen off. The epiphragm fills the space inside the ring of peristome teeth and is attached to their tips. At maturity the peristome consists, of 32 or 64 teeth. The openings between the teeth form a ring of pores and the spores are dispersed through these pores by the force of the wind shaking the sporogonium. The pores remain opened by the drying and subsequent shrinkage of the interior columella tissue.

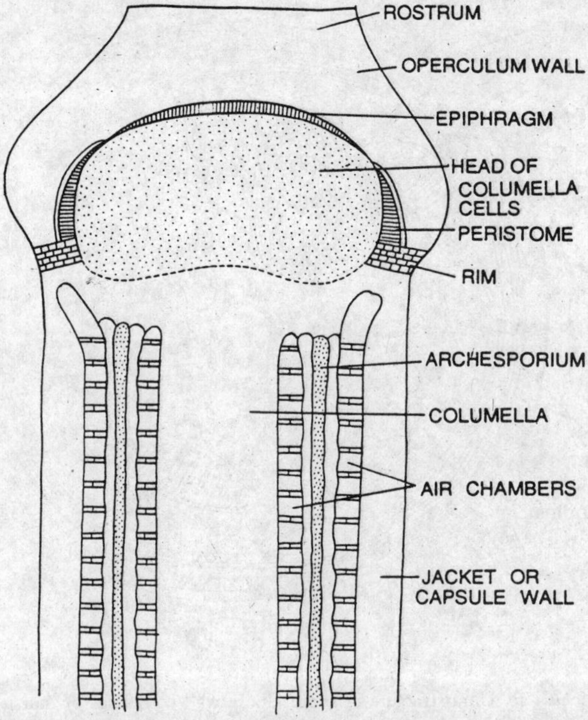

Fig. 11.13. *Polytrichum.* Longitudinal section of the upper part of the capsule.

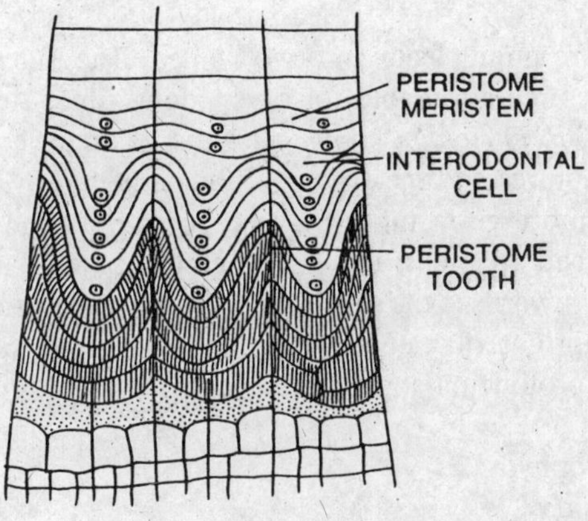

Fig. 11.14. *Polytrichum.* Tangential section of the operculum showing peristome teeth.

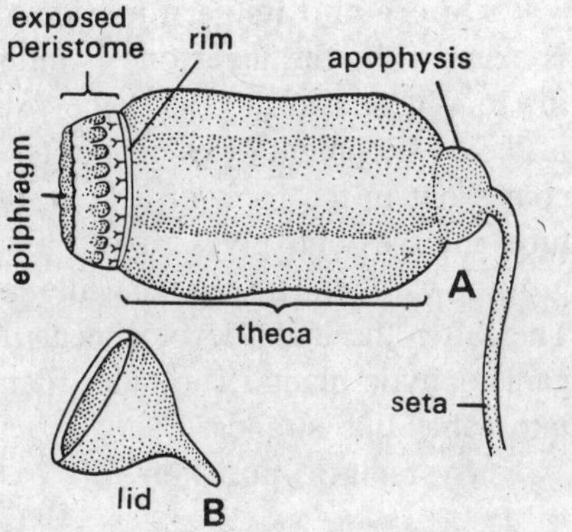

Fig. 11.15. *Polytrichum* sp. A, capsule without lid; B, lid; the lid separates from the capsule at the time of dehiscence of spores.

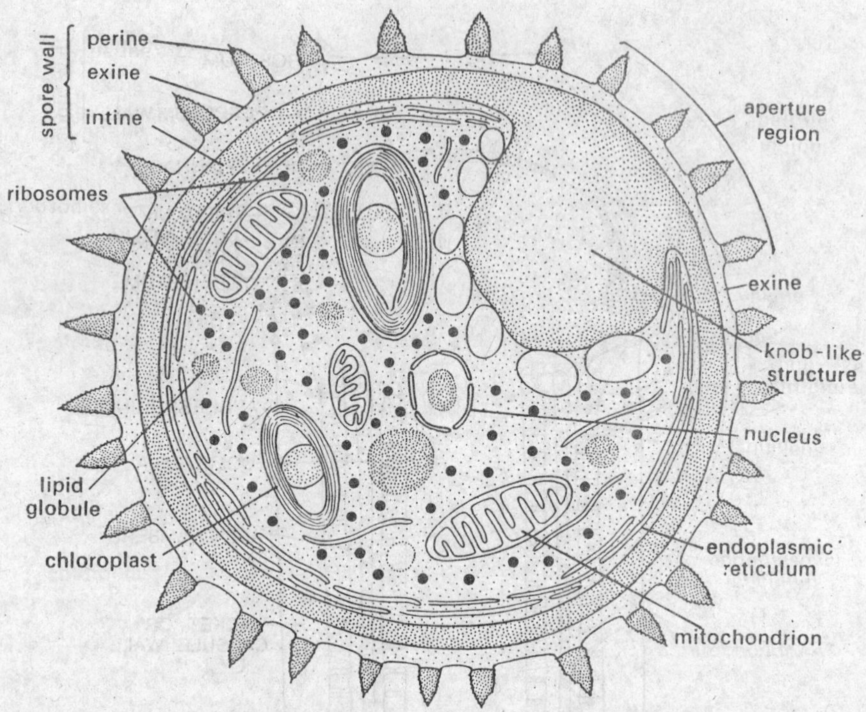

Fig. 11.16. *Polytrichum* sp. Ultra-structure of spore. Spore wall comprises of four layers-intine, exine, perine and a separating layer in between intime and exine; intine shows a conspicious disc-shaped thickening; there lies a knob-like structure in between disc-shaped intine thickening and the plasma membrane; the exine extends into the perine; in the aperture region, the exine is quite thin, and at the time of germination the germ tube comes out of this region; besides the nucleus the cytoplasm contains-endoplasmic reticulum, mitochondria, lipid globules, ribosomes and chloroplasts; no vacuoles.

Spore and its germination. The spores are uninucleate and two walled. The outer wall is exine while the inner one is intine. The spores remain viable for a very long time. According to Wigglesworth (1947) the yellow spore of *Polytrichum commune* turns to green because of the development of chloroplasts. The exine ruptures and the spore protoplast bound by intine comes out in the form of a germ tube. One or more germ tubes may be given out. The germ tube enlarges and gives rise to a septate branched filament, the **protonema.** Some filaments grow upwards and turn green while some grow downwards to the substratum and remain colourless. Thereafter the buds develop near the base of upright filaments. These buds give rise to new gametophytic plants. The older filaments of the protonema sometimes become twisted together into cable like strands.

Systematic position.

Division. Bryophyta
Class. Bryopsida
Sub-class. Eubrya
Order. Polytrichales
Family. Polytrichaceae
Genus. *Polytrichum*

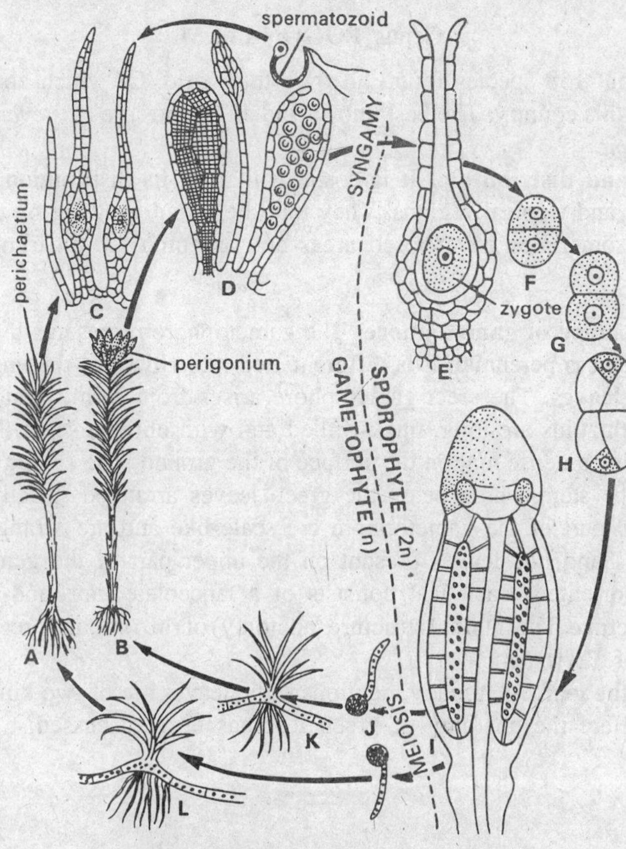

Fig. 11.17. *Polytrichum.* Diagrammatic life-cycle.

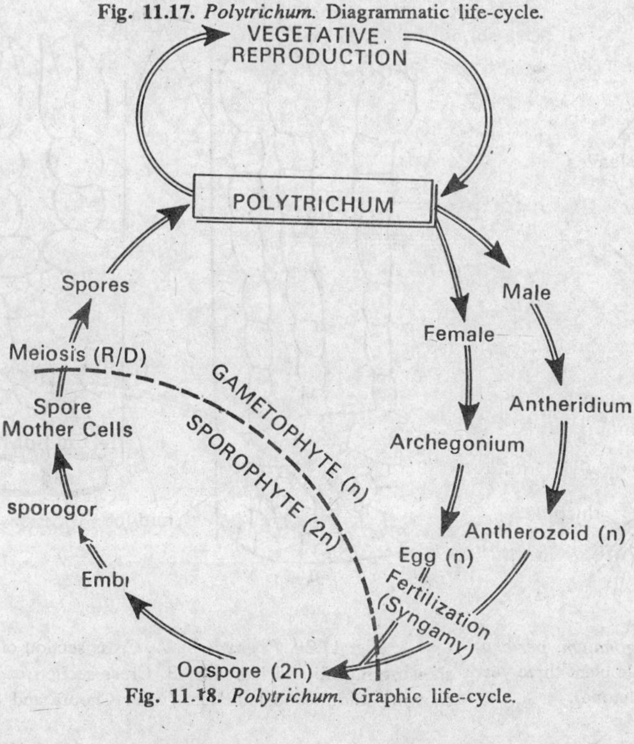

Fig. 11.18. *Polytrichum.* Graphic life-cycle.

Genus POGONATUM

There are about 158 species found all over the world. Of which about 23 species have been recorded from this country. The best known Indian species are-*P. stevensii, P. perichaetiale* and *P. microstomum.*

Occurrence and distribution. It is cosmopolitan in its distribution. It is mainly found in cool temperature and tropical regions. They may be found growing on damp soil, on moist rocks, in swamps, sometimes on exposed areas and as epiphytes on trunks of trees.

The Gametophyte

External structure of gametophore. The gametophore represents the adult stage of this robust moss. The plant is perennial. It is differentiated into **rhizoids,** the underground **rhizome,** the erect **stem** and **leaves.** The erect gametophore arises from a rhizomatous portion covered with rhizoids. The rhizoids are long, thick-walled and with oblique septa. Many gametophores grow together forming a dense mat on the surface of the ground. The erect gametophore consists of a central axis, the stem which bears the green leaves arranged spirally on it. The leaves present on the basal part of the gametophore are scale-like and are arranged in three vertical rows. On the other hand, the leaves present on the upper part of the gametophore are thick, green and densely oriented. Each leaf consists of a lanceolate limb and a sheathing base.

Internal structure. The internal structure (anatomy) of rhizome and erect stem of *Pogonatum* is similar to that of *Polytrichum.*

Anatomy of the leaf. As already mentioned, the leaves are of two kinds, *i.e.,* scale leaves and green leaves. Here the anatomy of green leaf has been discussed.

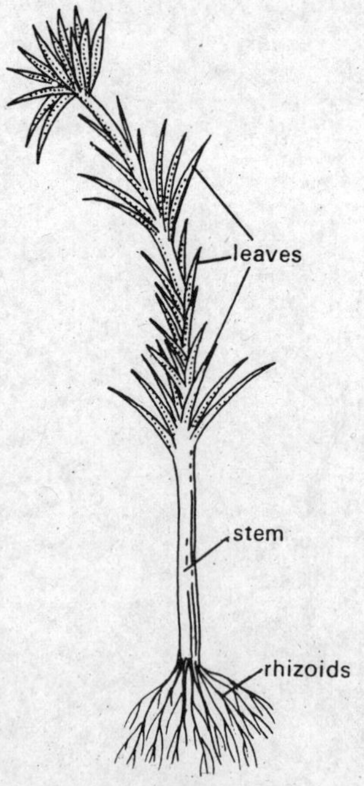

Fig. 11.19. *Pogonatum perichaetiale.* A proliferated male plant-three year old. (After Chopra and Sharma).

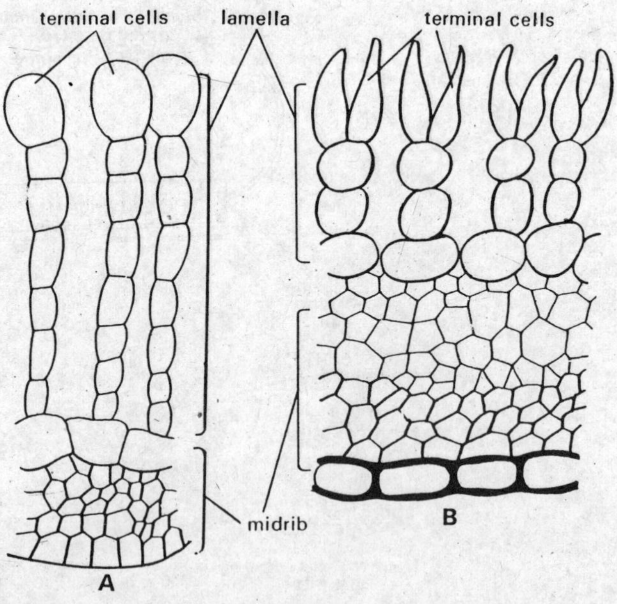

Fig. 11.20. *Pogonatum.* A, Cross section of leaf of *P. perichaetiale* showing midrib and lamellae; B, Cross section of leaf of *P. microstomum* showing midrib and lamellae. (After Chopra and Sharma).

The leaf-sheath is made up of green thick-walled cells. In cross section, the leaf lamina shows several cells thick midrib in the centre which merges into the wings gradually. A distinct lower epidermis is made up of large cells whose outer walls are thickened. The lower epidermis is followed by few layers of cells having thickened walls. The central mass of leaf blade is constituted of parenchyma. On the upper side, the central parenchymatous mass is delimited by a layer of large cells which gives rise to numerous vertical lamellae. Each lamella is made up of 4-8 cells containing chloroplasts and jointed in longitudinal chain. The upper most cell of the chain is wider or papillose and hyaline. The green lamellae are so closely placed that their terminal cells almost touch each other. In *P. microstomum* the uppermost cells of the lamellae are divided into two conical cells.

Sexual reproduction. Most of the species are dioecious (*e.g., P. perichaetiale, P. stevensii*) but *P. microstomum* is monoecious.

The antheridial heads. The antheridia are formed in groups on the position of lateral buds under the leaves. The apical growth of shoot continues through the antheridial head which remains surrounded by leaves. There may be upto three antheridial heads present in a male plant.

Structure of mature antheridium. The mature antheridium is composed of a stalk and a clavate body. The club-shaped body is surrounded by a single-layered jacket. Inside the jacket there are androcytes within the antheridium. The antheridia are intermingled with paraphyses. Each paraphysis is multicellular and consists of several cells arranged in a uniseriate row.

Development of antheridium. At the apex of the male gametophore a single superficial cell acts as an **antheridium initial.** It divides first transversely, giving rise to two cells. The

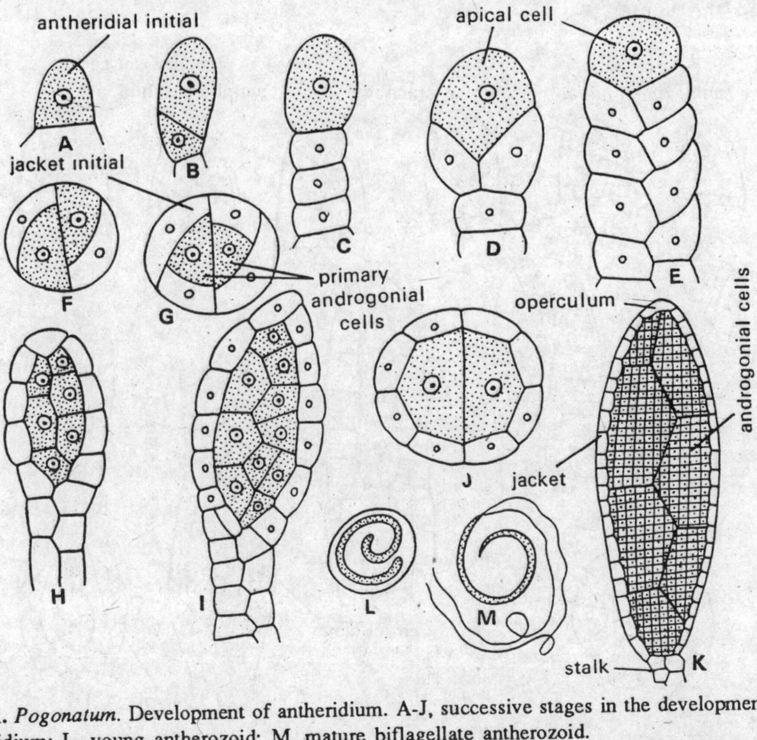

Fig. 11.21. *Pogonatum.* Development of antheridium. A-J, successive stages in the development of antheridium; K, mature antheridium; L, young antherozoid; M, mature biflagellate antherozoid.

outer daughter cell gives rise to the complete main antheridium while the lower cell develops into the stalk. The outer daughter cell divides twice or thrice transversely forming a filament consisting of two or three cells. The terminal cell acts as an apical cell with two cutting faces. The apical cell cuts off the segments on its both cutting faces, and thus 5-7 or more, regularly arranged segments are cut off. Sometimes, even before all the segments are formed by the cell, the fourth or fifth segment begins to divide and further this division proceeds in the remaining segments from base to apex. Each segment divides first diagonally. Thus the segment divides into two unequal cells. The smaller daughter cell acts as **jacket initial.** The larger daughter cell divides again giving rise to two cells, the periphery cell called the peripheral initial and the inner one the **primary androgonial initial.** Thus, each segment gives rise to three cells-two jacket intials and one primary androgonial cell. The primary androgonial cell of each segment divides further in all planes producing numerous **androcyte mother cells.** Simultaneously the jacket initial also divides repeatedly giving rise to a single-layered **jacket** of the antheridium. Each androcyte mother cell gives rise to two androcytes. Each androcyte metamorphoses into a biflagellate antherozoid.

The archegonial cluster. The archegonia are produced in cluster of 3-6 terminally at the apices of gametophore. The archegonial cluster remains surrounded by the overlapping perichaetial leaves. The filamentous paraphyses are found among the archegonia.

Structure of archegonium. The archegonium is flask-like. It possesses a massive stalk, the venter and the neck. The neck is made up of 6 tiers of cells. The bulbous venter possesses a two-layered jacket, while the jacket of the neck is single-layered. The neck contains 6-9 neck canal cells. The venter contains the large egg and a ventral canal cell. On the maturation of the archegonium, the neck canal cells and the ventral canal cell disintegrate forming a mucilaginous substance. The terminal cells of the neck separate from each other forming a passage. The egg remains within the venter.

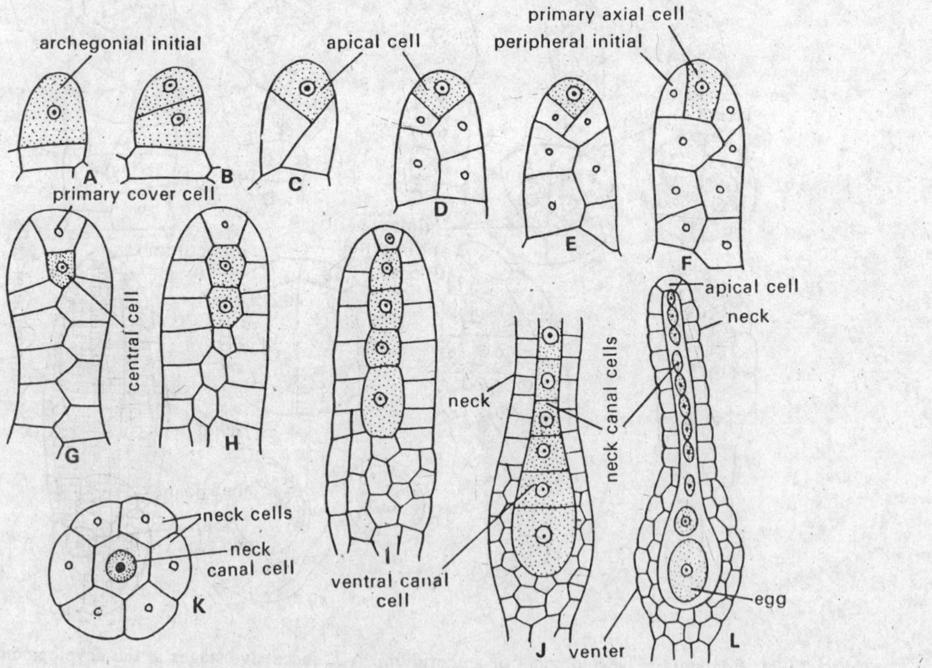

Fig. 11.22. *Pogonatum.* Development of archegonium. A-I, successive stages in the development of archegonium; J, young archegonium in longitudinal section; K, young archegonium in transverse section; L, mature archegonium in longitudinal section.

Development of archegonium. Any apical superficial cell of the female gametophore may act as an **archegonial initial.** Now the archegonial initial divides transversely giving rise to two cells-a basal cell and a terminal cell. The terminal cell, also known as archegonial mother cell, divides by three oblique walls successively. These walls do not reach the basal cell. With the result, three peripheral cells surround a central polyhedral cell. The three peripheral cells give rise to the wall of the venter which later on becomes two-layered. Thereafter, the surrounded tetrahedral cell divides transversely giving rise to two cells. The upper cell is known as the **primary cover cell** and the lower one is the **central cell.** The central cell divides and redivides, giving rise to the primary neck canal cell, ventral canal cell, and the egg. The primary cover cell acts as an apical cell. It cuts off three segments from its lateral faces. The three rows of the segments developed from the three lateral segments divide vertically, and with the result the six rows of the jacket cells of the neck are produced. The row of neck canal cells develops from the row of basal segments.

Fertilization. The water is essential for this process. On the maturity of the archegonium, the neck canal cells disintegrate and a mucilaginous mass is formed. The apical cells of the neck are separate from each other, and an opening is developed. The sugars ooze out through the opening which attract the antherozoids. The antherozoids are chemotactic. Several antherozoids enter through the clear passage and reach to the oosphere. Ultimately the single antherozoid penetrates the egg and the fertilization is effected. The male nucleus fuses with the female one and the **oospore** ($2n$) is formed.

The Sporophyte

Development of embryo. The zygote enclosed within the venter secretes a wall and begins to increase in size. The zygote divides transversely into an upper epibasal cell and a lower

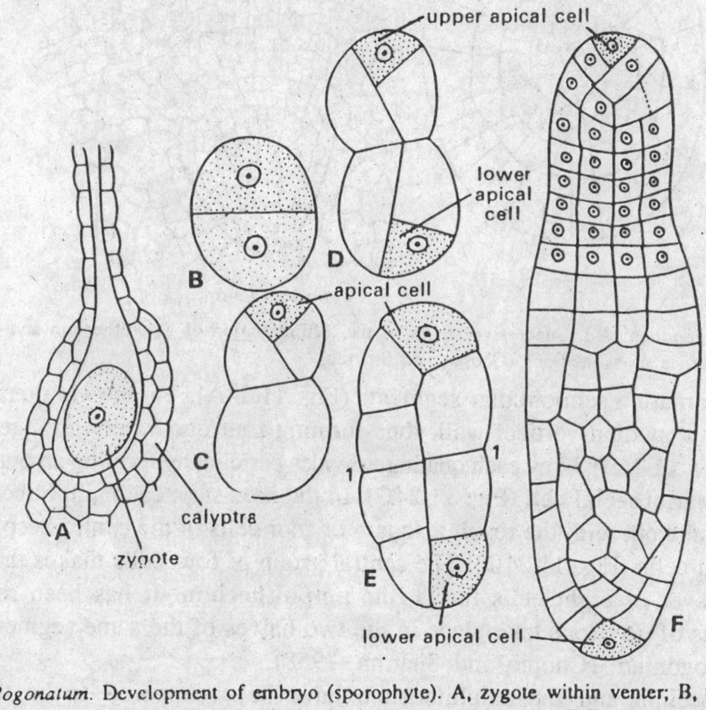

Fig. 11.23. *Pogonatum.* Development of embryo (sporophyte). A, zygote within venter; B, transversely divided oospore; C, formation of upper cell; D, formation of upper and lower apical cells; E-F, young embryo with upper and lower apical cells.

hypobasal cell. In the upper cell two successive oblique intersecting walls are laid down, thus forming a two-sided apical cell. An apical cell is differentiated in the lower cell also, in exactly the same manner as in the upper cell. Thus two growing points are established in the opposite directions of the developing embryo. The upper apical cell regularly cuts off segments right and left alternately, and ultimately the derivatives of the upper apical cell make the capsule and the upper part of the seta. The lower apical cell is less active and the segments derived from this cell ultimately form the foot and the lower part of the seta.

Development of the capsule. The alternating segments formed by the upper apical cell make the tissue of the capsule in the upper region of the embryo. In a cross section, the young sporogonium just beneath the apex, appears as a circle divided into two parts, which represent

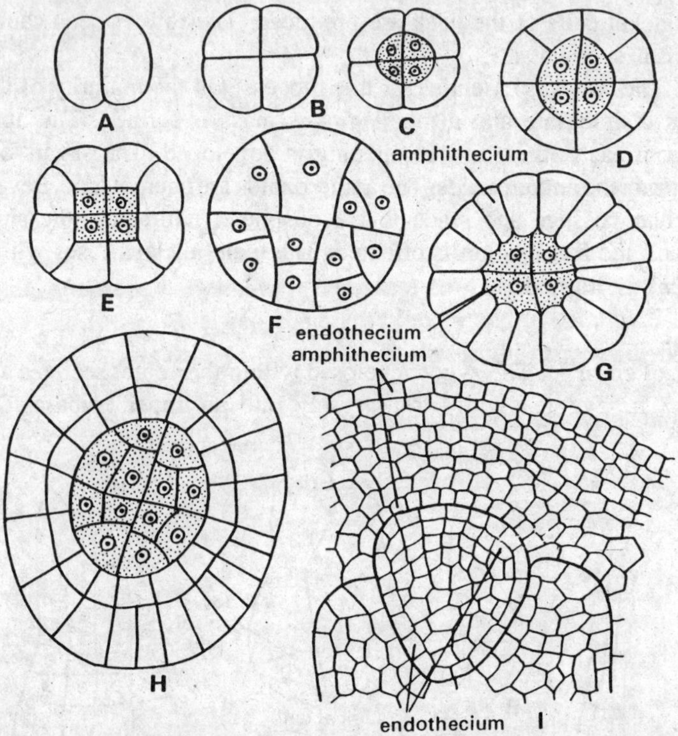

Fig. 11.24. *Pogonatum.* A-I, Successive stages of the differentiation of amphithecium and endothecium in the development of capsule, in cross sections (Chopra and Sharma).

the two young alternating semicircular segments (Fig. 11.24A). These two alternating segments divide radially by a median vertical wall, thus forming four quadrately arranged cells, as seen in cross section (Fig. 11.24B). Now each quadrant divides periclinally forming an outer **amphithecial cell** and an inner **endothecial cell** (Fig. 11.24C). In the next step, each amphithecial cell divides into two by a radial wall, with the result a square of four cells in the centre becomes surrounded by a layer of eight cells (Fig. 11.24D). The central group of four cells makes the **endothecium,** while the outer layer of eight cells forms, the **amphithecium.** It has been reported that the two different types of divisions take place in the two halves of the same segment (Fig. 11.24F) in the same sporogonium (Chopra and Sharma, 1958).

The endothecium and the amphithecium have been supposed to be the fundamental embryonic layers, which give rise to different types of tissues in the different parts of the capsule. Both amphithecial cells of the young sporogonium divide repeatedly in a regular sequence and definite pattern. The divisions in the amphithecium are always periclinal and radial and with the result about seven concentric rings of the amphithecial cells are formed (Fig. 11.24I) . The cells of endothecium, however, divide in all the planes, in such a manner that four sectors of endothecium are formed (Fig. 11.24H).

The three outer concentric rings of the cells of amphithecium give rise to the wall of capsule, which later becomes 4 to 5 cells in thickness by more divisions of the cells of the capsule wall. The cells of the fourth and fifth concentric rings give rise to the trabeculae as the outer air space develops. The sixth and seventh concentric layers of the amphithecium develop the outer wall of the spore sac. The peripheral layer of the endothecium gives rise to archesporium. The other two inner layers of the endothecium give rise to the inner wall of the spore sac, and the following two layers of the endothecium develop in the trabeculae of the inner air space. The central cells of the endothecium give rise to the columella.

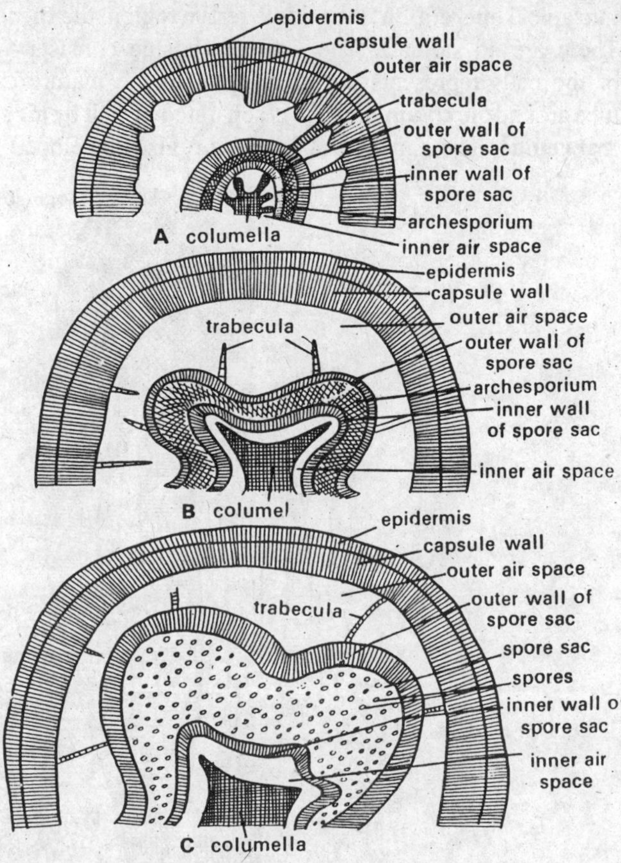

Fig. 11.25. *Pogonatum.* A-C, Cross sections of the successive stages of development of capsule (After Chopra and Sharma).

The apical portion of the capsule develops from amphithecial as well as endothecial cells. These cells enlarge and give rise to the opercular region of the capsule. The peristome develops in the lower inner part of this region. The peristome remains covered by the surface layers of the operculum. The thin-walled parenchymatous tissue of the columella extends into the base of the operculum, which makes a fan-shaped epiphragm. An annular ring (annulus) is developed at the lower margin of the operculum.

The peristome of *Pogonatum microstomum* is made up of a ring of 32 short, pyramidal teeth, which arise from the rim of the capsule. These teeth are not hygroscopic.

Structure of sporogonium (sporophyte). The sporogonium is differentiated into **foot, seta** and **capsule.**

The foot is a parenchymatous mass and remains embedded in the apex of female gametophyte. The function of the foot appears to be absorptive.

Just above the foot and continuous with it there is a long slender seta which supports the capsule at its terminal end. The seta may reach a length of several centimetres. A cross section of seta exhibits the following structures-The epidermis consists of thick-walled cells, the outer cortex consists also of thick-walled cells; the inner cortex is made up of thin-walled cells with intercellular spaces; the cortex is followed by lepton mantle, which remains differentiated into leptoids and parenchymatous cells; the central cylinder contains hydroids.

The capsule in transverse section is somewhat circular in outline. The capsule is differentiated into apical **operculum,** the middle fertile region, the **theca** and the basal sterile part, the **apophysis.** There are no stomata. The wall of capsule consists 4-5 layers of cells. The outermost layer of the cells represents the epidermis. In the mature capsule the sporogenous tissue makes a tube around the **columella,** and is separated from it by **air spaces** which are traversed by filamentous **trabeculae.** The similar trabeculae are also developed in the air space, between the spore sac

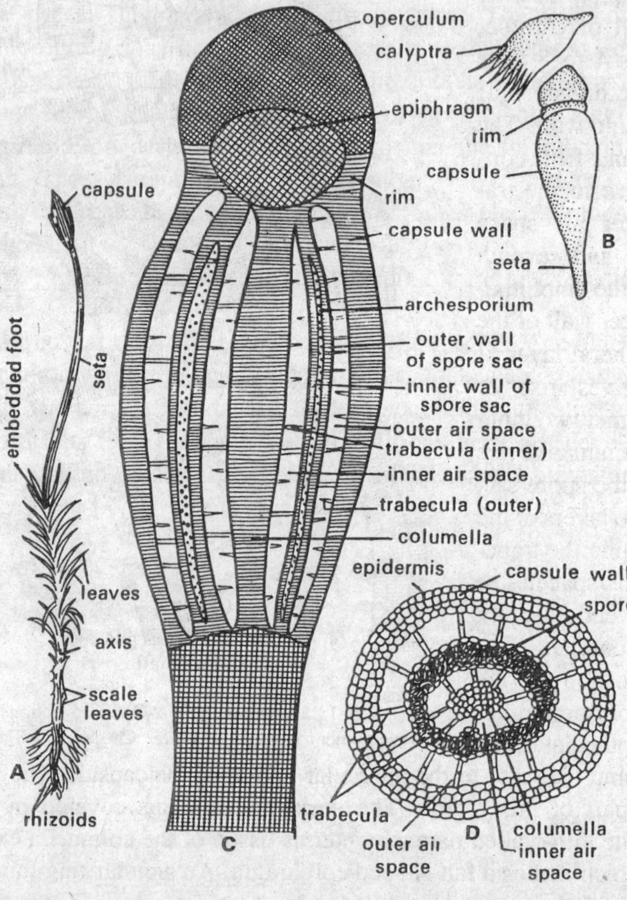

Fig. 11.26. *Pogonatum.* A, leafy female gametophore bearing terminally a sporophyte; B, sporophyte showing seta, capsule, operculum and calyptra; C, longitudinal section of capsule (sporophyte); D, transverse section of capsule through middle region.

and the wall of the capsule. The trabeculae are responsible for holding the spore sac in proper position. The outer and inner walls of spore sac are about two-cell in thickness. The sporogenous cells of the last cell generation in the spore sac are known as **spore mother cells.** As usual each spore mother cell develops into a spore tetrad of four spores by meiotic division.

The upper part of the capsule develops into **operculum** and **peristome.** The number of segments or **teeth** comprising the peristome is 32 or 16 (*e.g.*, in *P. perichaetiale*). The peristome teeth regulate the rate of the discharge of spores. Since the peristome teeth are joined to the margin of the **epiphragm,** the spore discharge is regulated by its up and down movements.

Dehiscence of capsule. On the maturation of the capsule, the calyptra is being removed, and the capsule becomes dry. The loosened operculum also drops off, and the peristome becomes exposed. The peristome teeth are not hygroscopic. The minute spores are released out through the small pores found among the teeth. The discharge of the spores is regulated by the movements of the epiphragm.

Spores. The minute spores are spherical and smooth. Each spore remains surrounded by two layers, the outer **exospore** and the inner **endospore.** The cytoplasm of the spore contains a nucleus, chloroplasts and oil globules. Since the spores are haploid (n), they give rise to the gametophytes.

Germination of spore. Generally the spore does not germinate immediately after its shedding from the capsule. If the spore gets favourable conditions after it has been shed from the capsule, it germinates within a few days. The germinating spore increases somewhat in size, the exospore ruptures and the endospore protrudes out in the form of one or two germ tubes. A cross wall

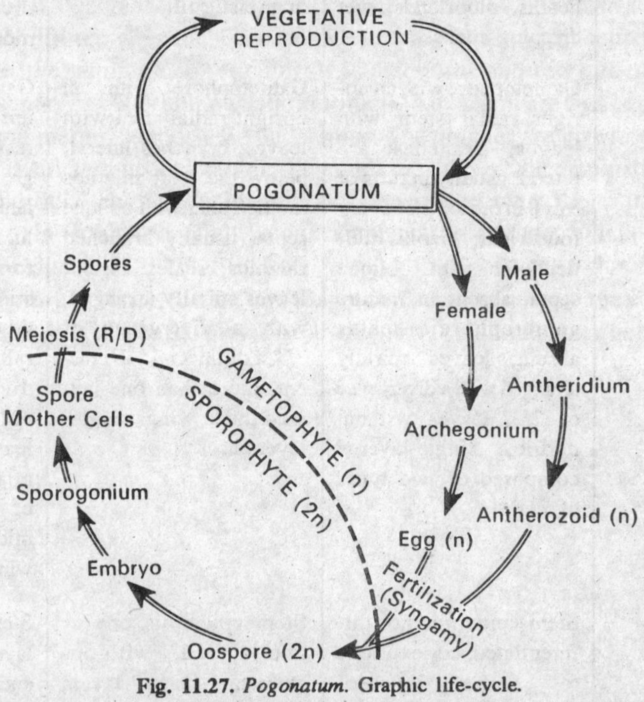

Fig. 11.27. *Pogonatum.* Graphic life-cycle.

appears in the germ tube near its point of emergence from the exosporium. The cell formed by this cross wall, gives rise to a multicellular filament called the **primary protonema.** The protonema further grows strictly by the division of the apical cell. The primary protonema becomes differentiated into two kinds of branches, known as **chloronemal branches** and **rhizoidal branches.** The chloronemal branches are aerial and develop prostrately upon the surface of the substratum, whereas the rhizoidal branches grow downward and penetrate the substratum. The leafy phase of the gametophyte develops as a lateral bud on the chloronemal branches. Later on the adult gametophytes are developed.

Systematic position. Division. Bryophyta
Class. Bryopsida
Sub-class. Eubrya
Order. Polytrichales
Family. Polytrichaceae
Genus. *Pogonatum*

Comparison of Sphagnum, Funaria and Polytrichum.

	Sphagnum	*Funaria*	*Polytrichum*
Systematic position and distribution	Division-Bryophyta; Class-Bryopsida (Musci); Order-Sphagnales; Family-Sphagnaceae. Genus Sphagnum; 17 species found in India; cosmopolitan in distribution.	Division-Bryophyta; Class-Bryopsida (Musci); Order-Funariales; Family-Funariaceae. Genus-*Funaria;* 15 species found in India; cosmopolitan in distribution.	Division-Bryophyta; Class-Bryopsida (Musci); Order-Polytrichales; Family-Polytrichaceae. Genus-*Polytrichum;* 3 species found in India; cosmopolitan in distribution.
Habitat	Lives in bogs, moist heaths, moorlands, wet dripping rocks.	Lives on rocks, walls or in moist soil.	Lives on sandy ground, dry stony places, marshy moors, damp soils.
External features	Gametophore with an upright radial stem with leaves; branches are lateral, usually in tufts of 3 or 8 in the axils of every fourth leaf; rhizoids multicellular with oblique septa, absent in mature gametophore; scales absent; leaves spirally arranged with a divergence of 2/5, leaves without midrib, single-layered composed of two types of cells.	Gametophore with an upright radial stem with leaves; branches lateral, below the leaf; rhizoids multicellular with oblique septa, usually branched rhizoids; scales absent; leaves spirally arranged, with a divergence of 3/8, a distinct midrib present, more than one-layered thick, wings single-layered.	Gametophore with an upright radial stem with leaves, and an underground portion; branches lateral; rhizoids multicellular with oblique septa-form wick like strands; scales absent; green leaves on the aerial portion spirally arranged with a divergence of 3/8, colourless scale-like leaves on the lower part of axis with a divergence of 1/3, leaf with broad midrib and a rudimentary wing; lamellae present.
Internal structure	Stem epidermis not differentiated; cortex is one to many-layered, colourless in some species with spiral thickenings and pores; no distinct central conducting strand; single-tetrahedral apical cell with three cutting faces.	Stem epidermis one or two-layered, with-out stomata; many layers usually thickwalled; central cylinder consisting of long, narrow thin walled colourless cells without protoplasm; as in *Sphagnum.*	Stem epidermis single-layered both in rhizome and aerial portion, without stomata, cortex in rhizome, many-layered, partly; parenchymatous and partly sclerenchymatous, cortex in aerial stem-prosenchymatous (outer cortex), and parenchymatous (inner cortex); central cylinder differentiated into "hydrom" and "lepton"; as in *Sphagnum.*
Sexual organs	Monoecious and dioecious; antheridia in the axils of leaves of an	Monoecious and dioecious; antheridia at the apex of an antheridial	Dioecious; antheridia at the apex of the gametophore, stalk short, body-

	Sphagnum	*Funaria*	*Polytrichum*
	antheridial branch stalk long, body-jacket single-layered; antherozoids biciliate; archegonia, at the tip of the archegonial branch, long stalk, neck made up of 6 vertical rows of cells venter 2 to 3-layered thick, cover cells 8 or more, neck canal cells usually 8 to 9.	branch, stalk long, body jacket single layered; antherozoids biciliate; archegonia, at the tip of the archegonial branch, long stalk, neck made up of 6 vertical rows of cells venter 2-layered thick, single cover cell which acts as an apical cell with 4 cutting faces, neck canal cells usually 8 to 10.	jacket single layered; antherozoids biciliate; archegonia, at the tip of the gametophore, long stalk, neck made up of 6 vertical rows of cells, venter 2-layered thick, cover cell as in *Funaria*, neck canal cells usually 8 to 10.
Sporophyte	Amphithecium gives rise to jacket of capsule and archesporium; endothecium gives rise to columella; archesporium gives rise to sporocytes; bulbous foot; seta absent; globose capsule; capsule four to six layered, persistent; elaters absent; columella present, arched over by spore sac; dehiscence takes place by the separation of operculum; peristome absent.	Amphithecium gives rise to the jacket of capsule; endothecium gives rise to columella and archesporium; archesporium gives rise to sporocytes; small, conical foot; seta long and elongates gradually; pyriform (pear-shaped) capsule; capsule wall more than four-layered, persistent; elaters absent; columella present, penetrates the spore sac; dehiscence takes place by separation of operculum; peristome present.	Amphithecium gives rise to the jacket of capsule; endothecium gives rise to columella and archesporium; archesporium gives rise to sporocytes; small conical foot; seta, long elongates gradually; angular capsule; capsule wall several layers of cells thick, persistent; elaters absent; columella present, penetrates the spore sac; dehiscence takes place by separation of operculum; peristome and epiphragm present.
Young gametophyte	Spore with two wall-layers; spore size approximately 0.02 mm.; spore germination by formation of a thalloid protonema.	Spore with two-wall layers; spore size approximately 0.012 to 0.015 mm.; spore germination by formation of a branched filamentous protonema.	Spore with two wall layers; spore size approximately 0.005 to 0.01 mm; spore germination by formation of a branched filamentous protonema.

12

General Discussion

VEGETATIVE PROPAGATION IN BRYOPHYTES

Most of the bryophytes propagate vegetatively. The vegetative reproduction takes place in favourable conditions for the vegetative growth. The vegetative reproduction takes place by various means and methods. Certain bryophytes, such as *Bryum* reproduces exclusively by vegetative methods, but most of the bryophytes reproduce both by sexual and vegetative methods. Some of the important methods of vegetative propagation are quoted below:

1. By death of older parts. This method of vegetative propagation is commonly found in many bryophytes. In *Riccia, Marchantia, Anthoceros, Notothylas* and others the progressive death and decay of older parts reach to the dichotomy and two branches are resulted, each of such branches may develop into a new plant.

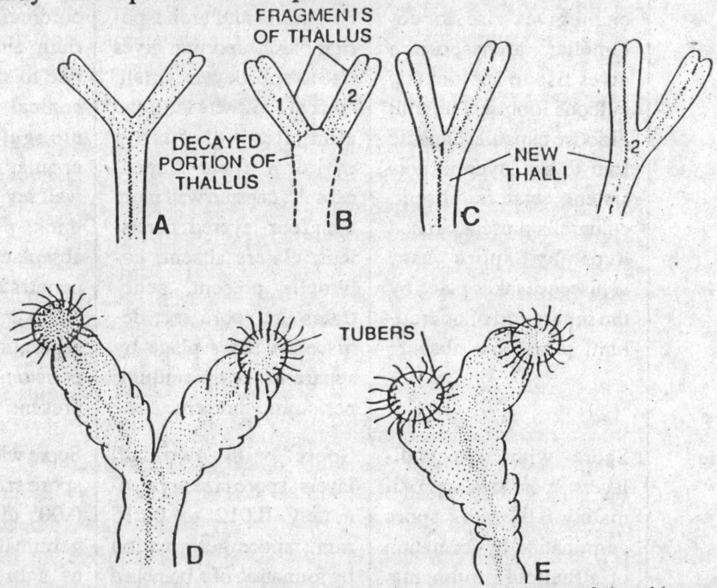

Fig. 12.1. Vegetative reproduction in *Riccia*. A-C, by the death and decay of the older parts of the thallus; D-E, by tubers.

2. By branch tips. According to Smith, in the regions of prolonged drought, all parts of a gametophyte but the branch tips are killed. Each such branch tip is capable to give rise to a new plant on the approach of favourable conditions. This method is quite common in *Riccia*.

3. By adventitious branches. According to Cavers (1904) several species of *Riccia* produce adventitious branches from the ventral surface of gametophyte ; these branches on being detached may result in the formation of new gametophytes. Such adventitious branches have also been recorded from other bryophytes, *e.g., Marchantia, Anthoceros* sp.

4. By Gemmae. According to Campbell (1918) even in *Riccia glauca*, the cell division takes place in the apices of young rhizoids resulting in gemma-like structures which later on develop into new thalli.

In *Marchantia* and *Lunularia* the gemmae are produced in gemma cups situated on the dorsal surface of the gametophyte. Many gemmae are found in each gemma cup. On being

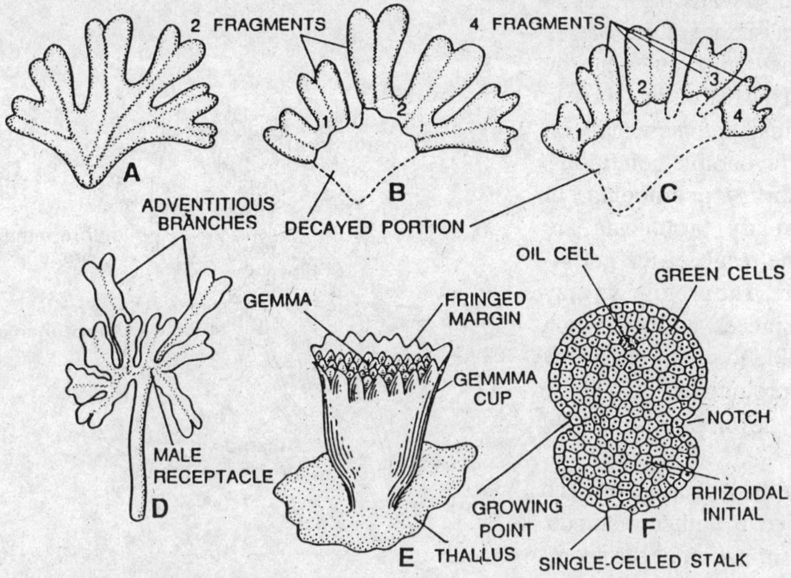

Fig. 12.2. Vegetative reproduction in *Marchantia*. A-C, by death and decay of the older parts of the thallus; E-F, by gemmae.

detached from the cup, each gemma gives rise to a plant. The gemma cups are circular in *Marchantia* and crescent-shaped in *Lunularia*.

In *Anthoceros glandulosus* and some other species the gemmae develop on the margin and dorsal surface of the thallus. Each gemma germinates into a new plant.

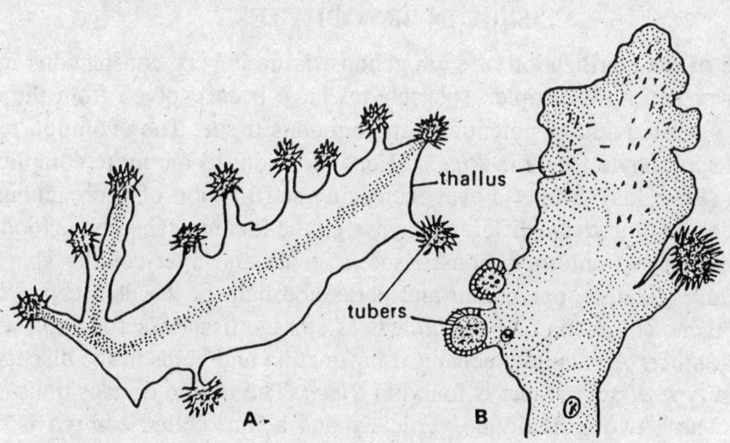

Fig. 12.3. Vegetative reproduction in *Anthoceros* by tubers in A. *himalayonsis* (A) and A. *laevis* (B).

In *Funaria*, small, multicellular, linear green gemmae are borne at the leaf apices, shoot apex and on the rhizoids. Such gemmae also develop on the protonema of *Funaria hygrometrica*. Each gemma is capable to give rise to a new plant. The underground gemmae are known as bulbils.

5. By tubers. Many bryophytes reproduce vegetatively by means of tubers. The tubers are formed on the margins of the thalli of *Riccia discolor, R. billardieri, Anthoceros halli, A. pearsoni*. The tubers are borne upon stalks on the ventral surface of *Anthoceros himalayensis*. They are found near the growing points of the thallus in *A. laevis*. The tubers germinate into new thalli on the approach of favourable conditions.

6. By primary protonema. In *Funaria* the primary protonema are produced with the result of the germination of the spore. The protonema may break into small pieces; and each such fragment is capable to grow into a new protonema. The protonema bears many buds. Each bud develops into a new plant.

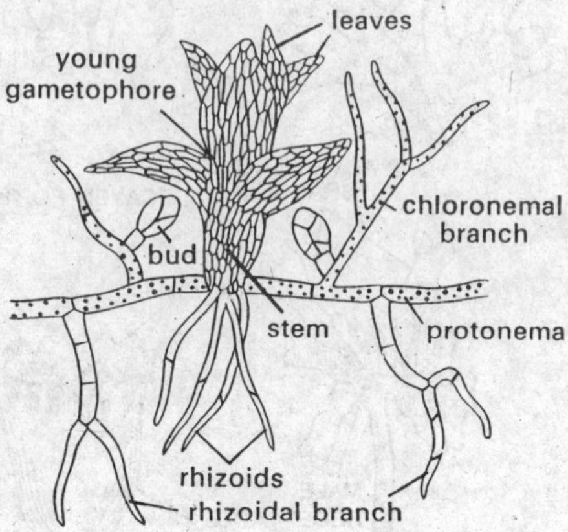

Fig. 12.4. Vegetative reproduction by primary and secondary protonema in *Funaria hygrometrica* (moss).

7. By secondary protonema. The protonema formed by other methods, than from the germination of the spore, are known as secondary protonema. Morphologically they are quite alike to primary protonema. The secondary protonema may develop from the exposed rhizoid or any other detached living part of the gametophyte. These protonema also produce buds which develop into gametophytes. This method of vegetative reproduction is very common in *Funaria hygrometrica*.

PROGRESSIVE STERILIZATION OF SPOROGENOUS TISSUE IN BRYOPHYTES

The process of the sterilization of sporogenous tissue is very conspicuous in bryophytes. According to Bower the more complex sporophytes have been evolved from the simpler ones by the progressive sterilization of potentially sporogenous tissue. The evolution may be traced from the simplest sporophyte found in *Riccia* (Hepaticopsida) to the more complex sporophyte found in *Funaria* (Bryosida). There is ever increasing sterilization of sporogenous tissue. The so formed sterile tissues function in different ways, *e.g.*, the foot may absorb the food and perform the function of anchorage ; chlorophyllous tissue, stomata and inter-cellular spaces are meant for food manufacture ; elaters, operculum and peristome help in the dehiscence of the spores somehow or the other ; columella of *Funaria* acts as storage tissue for food and water whereas the columella of *Anthoceros* is quite mechanical in function and helps in the dispersal of spores.

The simplest type of sporophyte is found in *Ricca*. The zygote divides transversely giving rise to two cells. These two cells divide vertically and a four celled embryo is formed. This is followed by several irregular divisions and a 20 to 30 celled embryo is formed. At this stage there are periclinal divisions and the embryo is differentiated into **amphithecium** and **endothecium.** The amphithecium is protective layer and the endothecium develops into sporogenous tissue by repeated divisions. Here, the sterilization of sporogenous tissue is negligible. However, in *R. crystallina* Pagon in 1932 recorded that the sporogenous tissue differentiates into sporocytes and **nurse cells.** Pagon considers the nurse cells as forerunners of the **elaters** of *Marchantia.*

In *Sphaerocarpos,* some cells of the sporogenous tissue become sporocytes which form spores by meiotic division. Other cells of the sporogenous tissue develop into sterile **nurse cells** which supply food to the spores. Here the sterilization of sporogenous tissue has progressed to some extent.

In *corsinia,* the last generation of the sporogenous tissue differentiates into **soporocytes** and **sterile cells** which persist until the maturity of the spores.

In *Targionia,* about half of the cells of the last generation in the sporogenous tissue become

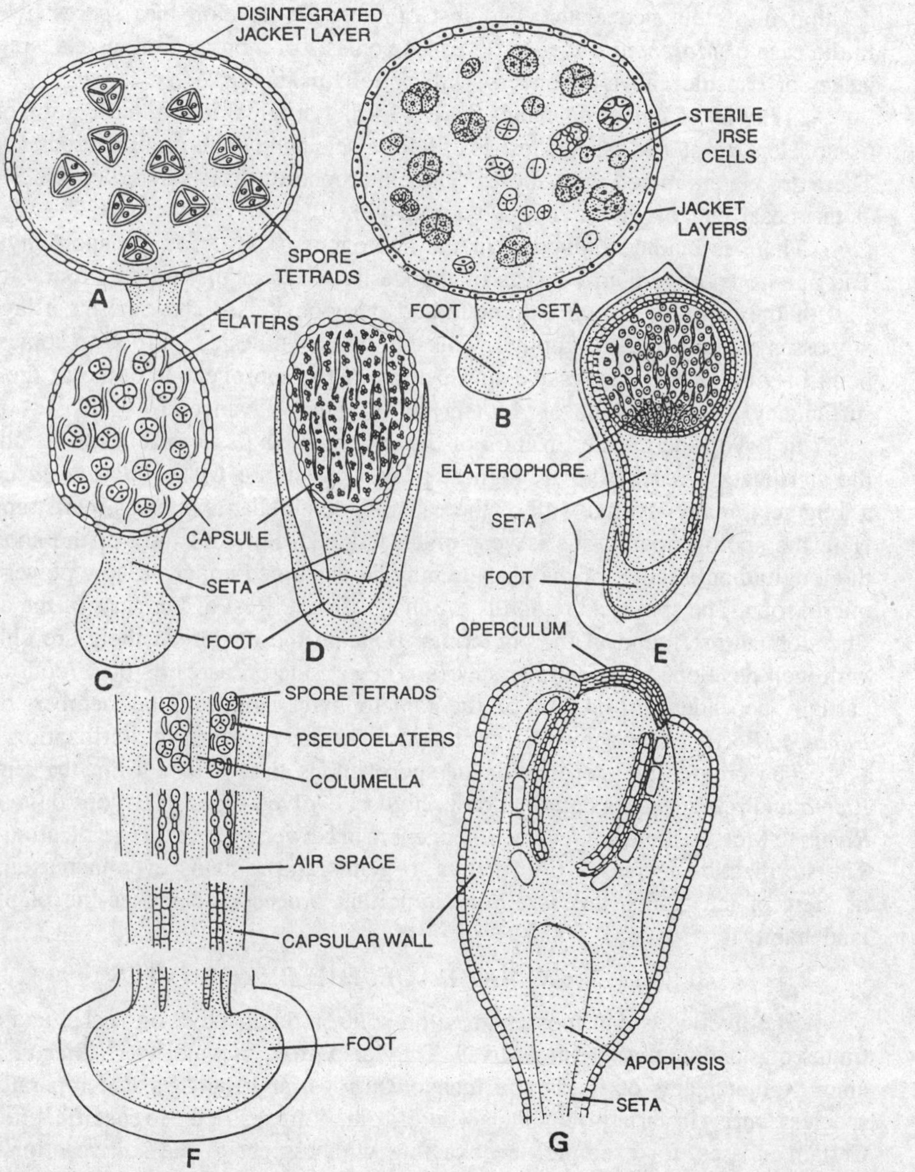

Fig. 12.5. Progressive sterilization of sporogenous tissue in bryophytes. A, sporophyte of *Riccia*; B, sporophyte of *Sphaerocarpos* sp.; C, sporophyte of *Targionia* sp.; D, sporophyte of *Marchantia* sp.; E, sporophyte of *Pellia* sp.; F, sporophyte of *Anthoceros*; G, sporophyte of *Funaria hygrometrica*.

sporocytes while the rest half of the cells elongate greatly and mature into **elaters.** In *Targionia* the sporophyte consists of a broad foot, a seta and a single layered jacket of the capsule. Here, the sterilization of the sporogenous tissue shows an advance over that of *Riccia.*

In *Marchantia,* the zygote divides-transversely and thereafter vertically resulting into a four-celled embryo. The lower half of the embryo develops into foot and seta while the upper half develops into the capsule. The capsule portion soon differentiates into amphithecium and endothecium. The amphithecium develops into one celled thick protective jacket layer. The cells of endothecium divide repeatedly forming sporogenous tissue. Some of the sporogenous cells develop into elongated elaters and rest of the cells develop into spores by meiotic division. In the case of *Marchantia* the sterile tissue consists of a broad foot, a seta, single layered sterile jacket of capsule and long elaters with spiral thickenings.

In *Pellia,* of Jungermanniales there is further progress in the sterilization of the sporogenous tissue. Here the sterile tissue consists of a foot, seta and two to multilayered jacket of the capsule. There are elaters mixed with spores. The elaterophore (massive sterile tissue) is found attached at the basal end of the cavity of the capsule.

There is marked reduction in the sporogenous tissue of the sporophyte of *Anthoceros.* The mature sporogonium consists of the sterile tissue of the bulbous foot, four to six layered wall of the capsule, central columella and pseudoelaters. The outermost layer of the capsule possesses stomata and chlorophyll. This can photosynthesize its food to some extent. From this point of view of the progressive sterilization of the sporogenous tissue of the capsule and self-sufficiency the sporophyte of *Anthoceros* is highly advanced.

In Bryopsida the sterilization of the sporogenous tissue reaches to its climax. In *Funaria,* the sterilization reaches to its highest peak. The sterile tissue in *Funaria* consists of a foot, a long seta, many-layered wall of the capsule, columella, apophysis, peristome, operculum etc. Here the sporogenous tissue is very much reduced. For the study of the spore sac and spores the longitudinal section of the capsule may be examined under the low power of the compound microscope. The spore sac region is too insignificant. Rest of the parts of the capsule are sterile. The stomata are found in the epidermis. Beneath the epidermis there are chlorophyllous cells with well developed intercellular spaces. The capsule prepares its own food to some extent and partially dependent for its food on the gametophyte. This way, the members of Bryopsida, *e.g., Funaria, Polytrichum* show the culmination in the progressive sterilization.

The progressive sterilization of sporogenous tissue starts from the simplest types, *e.g., Riccia* and reaches to its culmination in highest evolved types of Bryopsida, *e.g., Funaria.* From *Riccia* to Mosses, there are several other genera in between where the sterilization is ever increasing. The sterilization increases from genus to genus and remains ever increasing. From the point of view of the plants, this is a very important process and makes the plants well suited for land habit.

ECOLOGY OF THE BRYOPHYTES

The liverworts and mosses grow on soil, on damp sand, on rocks, and on the trunks and trunks of standing and prostrate tress. They also grow in water (*e.g., Ricciocarpos natans)* and among other plants of fields and meadows, bogs, and marshes in temperate countries. Some species flourish in variety of habitats whereas others are restricted to specific, limited environments. Certain mosses, for example, are exacting with respect to the soil reaction and are confined either to acid or alkaline soils. In general, the bryophytes are more tolerant of shade than are higher form of plant life. The mosses include many xerophytic forms as well as mesophytes and hydrophytes. Bryophytes are likewise adopted to great extremes of temperature, for they range from the arctic zone to the tropics and grow in the vicinity of hot springs. They reach their greatest development in cool, moist forests in temperate countries and the mountains of the tropical countries.

The bryophytes are an important component of the flora of the earth and play a significant role in the economy of nature. This is partly the result of the great number of individual plants produced by vegetative propagation. Mosses are so prolific that they form great masses or carpets covering the soil. Another characteristic of ecological importance is the ability of mosses to hold water, which is trapped among the leaves and stems. Many woodland mosses and species of *Sphagnum* absorb water through their leaves. By their structures and their mode of life, mosses contribute in many ways to the modification of their own environment.

The significance of mosses as solid formers following lichens or other lower forms of plant life on bare rock surfaces is of much importance in the succession of vegetation. Lichens are followed by mosses, which, like lichens, are able to survive in a dry environment. The mosses shade the lichens and successfully compete with them for water and nutrients. The death and decay of older mosses often produce a mat over the rock surface. As this mat becomes thicker and develops a water-holding capacity a new stage in the plant succession follows. This stage consists of annual and perennial herbs. The retention of water by mosses of leafy liverworts and mosses growing on fallen trees and other organic material hastens the processes of decomposition and hence the organic enrichment of the soil. Absorbing but little water from the substratum, they do not dry out the soil but protect it from desiccation. As a result of their ability to retain water, natural beds of mosses undoubtedly act as seed beds for herbaceous and woody flowering plants and for conifers.

One of the roles of the bryophytes is in the retardation of erosion. Carpets or felt like mosses possess a greater water retaining power than do layers of dead leaves. They therefore slow down the rapid run off rain water and melted snow. In addition to this, dense strands of moss collect and hold particles of soil. Insignificant as the individual plants of this group may appear, they play a part, together with other and more advanced forms of plant life, in making and changing man's environment.

BRYOLOGY IN INDIA

Researches on the Indian bryophytes begin with the publications of Hooker (1818,1820) on mosses and on liverworts of India and Nepal (Lindenberg and Lehman, 1832). Royle (1839) reported 113 species of mosses from India and Nepal. Later on Gottsche, Lindenberg and Nees (1844, 1847) recorded some Indian liverworts from the Himalayas. Griffith (1849) contributed a lot to Indian bryology in its early days. Mitten (1859) published a comprehensive account of Indian mosses (85 genera; 800 species). Mitten (1860, 1861) also published an account of the Indian liverworts. C. Muller (1878) wrote several articles on the Indian mosses. Brotherus (1898) described the mosses of the North-western Himalayas and in 1899 he also published an account of the mosses of South India.

Our present knowledge of Bryophytes is the result of the pioneering efforts of Professor S.R. Kashyap. The more urgent task in our country is the preparation of a country-wide flora of bryophytes.

This was year 1914 when Kashyap published the first paper on some liverworts from Western Himalayas. Prior to this, contributions had been made by foreign workers. Kashyap's work was published in two volumes (Kashyap, 1929 ; Kashyap and Chopra, 1932). He discovered three well recognized genera-*Aitchinsoniella, Sewardiella* and *Stephensoniella*-all of which are monotypic and endemic to India.

Since Kashyap initiated researches on liverworts numerous contributions have been made by Indian workers on various aspects of the life of these plants (Pande, 1958 ; Pande and Bhardwaj, 1952 ; Pande and Srivastava, 1957 ; Maheshwari and Kapil, 1963). Apart from detailed descriptions of a number of plants several taxa unrecorded from India have been discovered. Significant among these are the discovery of *Riella vishwanathai* (Pande et al., 1955), *Takakia ceratophylla* (Grolle, 1963) and the order Calobryales represented by *Calobryum indicum* (Udar and S. Chandra, 1965), *C. blumii* (Udar *et al.*, 1968) and *Haplomitrium hookeri* (Udar and V. Chandra, 1965). The vegetation of Pachmari has been described by Pande and Srivastava (1952) and of Mount Abu by Bapna and Vyas (1962). Parihar (1961-62) has presented a census of Indian hepatics.

Detailed morphological investigations have also been carried out on a number of genera. Some of these have provided relevant details for inter-relationships and phylogenetic considerations. From his study of *Notothylas* it has been clearly shown by Pande (1932, 1934) that *N. levieri* deviates from other members of Anthocerotales is showing endothecial archesporium, indicating close relationship and affinity of the Anthocerotales with the Hepaticae. Mehra and Handoo (1953) consider Anthocerotales and Rhyniaceae to have been derived from the same ancestral stock, the Anthorhyniaceae, in the pre-Devonian. This stock originated from a still earlier proliverwort stock which must have had its origin in some of the Chlorophyceae that migrated to land. The study on *Petalophyllum* by Mehra and Vashisht (1950) led to the development of a new concept on the origin of the thallus and phylogeny of Marchantiales by Mehra (1957, 1968). Contrary to the views of Kashyap, Mehra believes that the Hepaticae have their ultimate ancestry in the green algae belonging to or allied to the Chaetophorales.

In recent years emphasis has been also laid on study of spore morphology for considerations in taxonomy and phylogeny. Spore characteristics have been found to be helpful in segregating *Riccia himalayansis*-complex into three species-*R. discolor*, *R. billardieri* and *R. gangetica* (Udar, 1957). In the complex of species of *Cyathodium*, exine ornamentation has been found to be useful in determining the status of various species (Udar, 1964). Bhardwaj (1960) has shown that it is possible to use spore characters in the identification of the species of the genus *Anthoceros*. Mehra (1968) has supported his theory of the phylogeny of Hepaticae on palynological considerations.

Some conditions have also been made on liverwort enzymology. Udar and Chandra (1960) extracted twelve enzymes from the thalli of *Ricia discolor* which show physiological similarity to higher plants. The male plants were found to have greater enzymatic activity than the female plants.

The study of mosses has received much less attention as compared to that of liverworts. Since the publication of the 'Census of Indian Mosses by Bruhl (1931), the plants found in the country have been mainly listed *viz.*, mosses of Mussoorie by R.S. Chopra *et al.*, (1956), Mosses of Nainital by N. Chopra (1960), Mosses of Kumaon by Srivastava (1966) and Mosses of Palni Hills by Foreau (1961, 1963). Illustrated taxonomic accounts have been given by Gangulee for mosses of Eastern India dealing with Fissidentales (Gangulee, 1957) and Discranales (Gangulee, 1959, 1960, 1963). Later on Gangulee (1964) published illustrated account of five new species of *Fissidens*, one each of *Dicranella*, *Campylopus*, *Bryoerythrophyllum* and *Semibrabula* from Eastern India and adjacent regions. In a detailed taxonomic investigation of mosses of the same region, Gangulee (1969) has published a monograph dealing with Sphagnidae, Andreaidae and Nematodontae (Buxbaumiidae and Polytrichiidae).

Morphological investigations have been pursued on some genera. The most extensively worked out order is Polytrichales through a series of publications on *Pogonatum* by R.S. Chopra and Sharma (1958) on *Atrichum* by R.S. Chopra and Bhandari (1959), on *Oligotrichum* by R.S. Chopra and Sharma (1959) and on *Lyellia* by Sharma and Chopra (1964). In an evolutionary context the Polytrichales are held to be primitive. A significant observation in this connection has been made by R.N. Chopra *et al.*, that in *Splachnobryum* the archegonia are borne individually and laterally along the axis. Such a distribution of archegonia recalls a similar condition in the primitive liverwort *Takakia*.

Among recent additions to the bryoflora of India. Udar *et al.*, (1970) have reported *Buxbaumia* from Western Himalayas (Deoban: altitude a. s. l. 10,500 feet). This plant, highly significant in its morphology and nutrition has been shown to approach *B. minakatae* of Japan in its taxonomic features.

ECONOMIC IMPORTANCE OF BRYOPHYTES

A few bryophytes are economically important.

Ecological importance. The liverworts, mosses and lichens are supposed to be the pioneers in establishing vegetation where other vegetation seems to be practically impossible. They colonize the barren rocks and exposed areas of hills, and make them suitable for growing angiospermic and other plants by depositing humus soil and plant debris. In the beginning the forms and grasses grow, and ultimately shrubs and trees also establish, and the whole area converts into dense wood.

However the *Sphagnum* plants are of great ecological importance. When these plants establish themselves in some lake or other areas full of water, sooner or later they cover the whole surface of the water. Due to deposition of plant debris the surface may be raised. The *Sphagnum* plants along with other hydrophytes form a dense surface covering over the water below. This covering gives the appearance of the soil from the surface. These areas are known as quacking bogs. Later on these bogs are converted into swamps. Ultimately these swamps are replaced by the forest growth of mesophytic type.

A few bryphytes play an important role in checking the soil erosion. They are capable of holding the soil by their extensive carpets, and prevent the soil erosion to some extent. (Also see page 196 'ecology of bryophytes').

Packing material. Most of the mosses are used as packing material after being dried. They make a fairly good packing material in the case of glass ware and other fragile goods. Especially the dried peat mosses (*Sphagnum* spp.) are used to pack bulbs, cuttings and seedlings for shipment.

Used in seed beds. Since the peat mosses have remarkable power to absorb and hold water like a sponge, they are extensively used in seed beds and green houses to root cutting. The peat mosses (Sphagna) are also used to maintain high soil acidity required by certain plants.

As a source of fuel. The peat is also a potential source of coal. Dried peat may be used as fuel. In Ireland, Scotland and other European countries the peat is used for fuel. In colder parts of the world where peat reaches its greatest development, the lower layers of peat become carbonized, and after the ages have passed, becomes available to human kind in the form of coal.

Absorbent bandages. The *Sphagnum* plants are slightly antiseptic and possess superior absorptive power. On account of these properties they may be used for filling absorbent bandages in place of cotton, in the hospitals.

PHYLOGENY OF BRYOPHYTES

There are *two* theories : (1) The first theory is known as **up-grade or progressive evolution theory.** (ii) and the second one is called **down-grade or regressive evolution theory.** According to these theories the evolution in bryophytes is as follows :

Progressive (Up-Grade) Evolution Theory

According to this theory there is progressive evolution which means that it starts with simple forms and terminates in complex forms. Cavers (1910), Campbell (1940), and Smith (1955) supported this view. According to them the primitive gametophytes possessed simple, dorsiventral, prostrate thallus showing simplicity in their external and internal structures. According to this theory the first evolved bryophyte was *Sphaero - Riccia*, a hypothetical type which combined the present day genus *Sphaerocarpos* (Proskauer, 1954). Contrary to it Campbell considered *Ricccardia* and *Metzgeria* as primitive bryophytes. However, Cavers (1910) proposed progressive theory and showed a phylogenetic line of evolution in bryophytes.

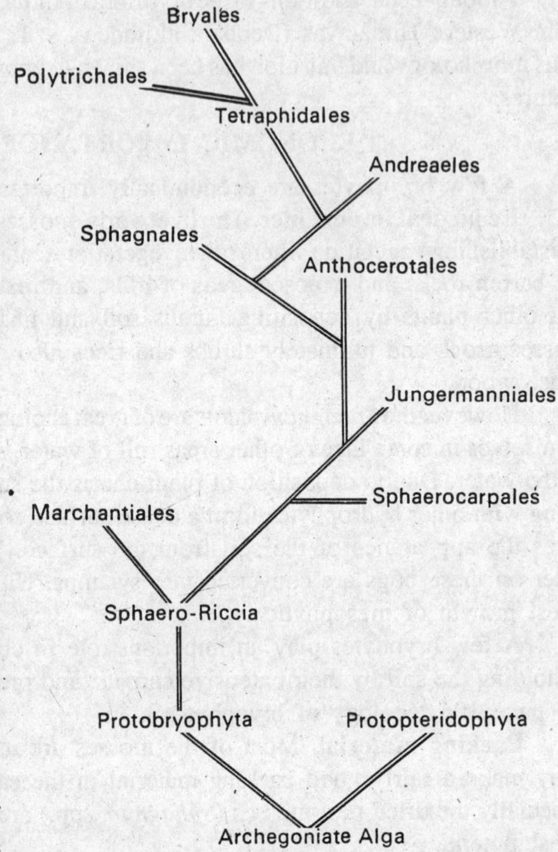

Fig. 12.6. Phylogeny of Bryophytes (Cavers)

According to the first line of evolution the primitive plants proceeded upto Marchantiales where the tissue differentiation in thallus took place in the form of epidermis, pores and air-chambers with chlorophyllous filaments in the sex-organs (antheridia and archegonia) in definite receptacles. The second line culminated in Jungermanniales and retained the simplicity in the thallus (gametophyte) without air pores but with lateral expansions known as wings or leaves. On the ventral surface of the thallus the multicellular filaments developed which later on converted into scales or under leaves with chlorophyll. On the other side, the thallus developed a distinct mid-rib and thin wings. Later on these wings divided up into definite segments and became leafy in structure. The Anthocerotales developed as one line from the Jungermanniales by elaboration of sporophyte while retaining the simple gametophyte. The Musci (*i.e.*, Sphagnales, Polytrichales, Bryales) arose from Anthocerotales.

Regressive (Down-Grade) Evoloution Theory

According to this theory the primitive bryophytes were mass-like in appearance. They had erect leafy shoot with radial symmetry like that of mosses. From mosses the evolution proceeded through Acrogynous Jungermanniales, Anthocerotales and Marchantiales. This view has been supported by Wettstein (1908), Kashyap (1919), Church (1919), Evans (1930), Mehra (1957), Pande (1960), Praskauer (1960), Fulford (1965), Zimmermann (1966), Udar (1970) etc. Mehra (1957) proposed a common origin of Anthocerotales and Psilophytales through Antho-rhyniaceae stalk.

On the basis of his **'condensation theory'** Mehra (1957) explained the course of evolution in Bryophytes. According to him it is after the regressive deviation of Marchantiales, a line of progressive evolution terminates in Marchantiaceae and both Marchantiaceae and Ricciaceae are the extreme forms in evolution in two different lines. Here the thallose forms originated

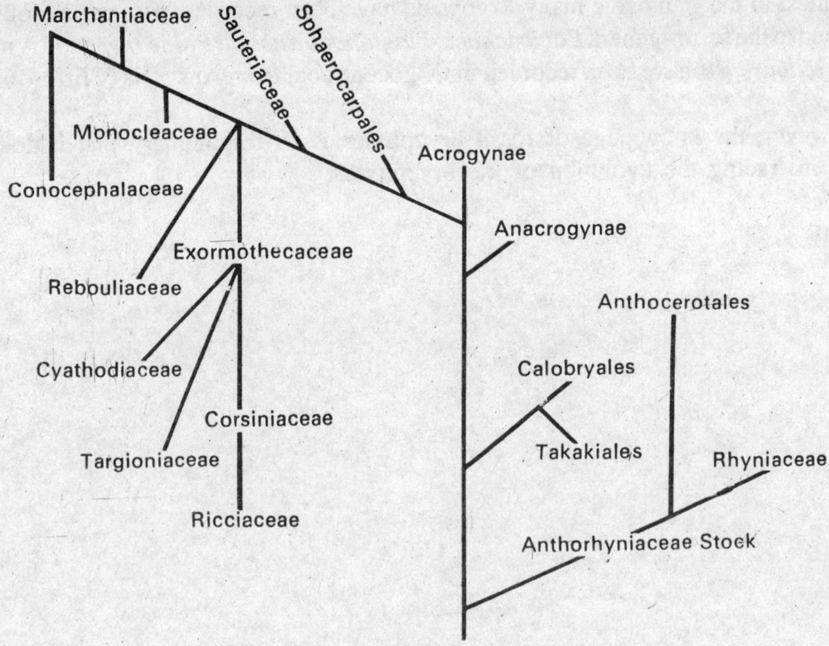

Fi.g 12.7. Phylogeny of Bryophytes (Mehra's view)

from foliose forms in Metzgerineae. According to Mehra the Anthocerotales have not arisen from Hepaticeae but from the separate stock called Antho-rhyniaceae stock which splitted into Rhyniaceae and Anthocerotales.

FOSSIL BRYOPHYTES

Compared with the pteridophytes the known number of fossil bryophytes is small because of the relatively fragile nature of the plant body. The stems and thalli of bryophytes possess neither lignified vascular tissues and nor cutinized epidermis. The leaves of this group of plant kingdom are rarely more than one layer of cells in thickness.

Fossil Hepaticopsida. The oldest known fossils have been recorded from the upper Carboniferous (Walton, 1925). All these fossils are assigned to the form-genus *Hepaticites,* which resemble Hepaticopsida. The other fossils of this period are referable to Metzgeriales, and among them are species resembling such modern genera as *Aneura* and *Treubia*. The genera referable to the Marchantiales have been found as far back as the lower Cretaceous (Steere, 1946). Fertile gametophytes of *Naiadita* with archegonia and mature sporophytes have been found (Harris, 1938) in abundance in Jurassic deposits. Harris (1938) is of opinion that *Naiadita* is quite close to the Reillaceae of Sphaerocarpales, but there are arguments which consider them to be closer to the Calobryales. In the New world the earliest record of the form-genus *Marchantites* is from the Lower Cretaceous. In the upper Cretaceous besides *Marchantites,* form-genus *Jungermannites* has also been described (Berry, 1919). Berry (1920, 1929) has described *Marchantites blairmorensis* and *M. sewardi* from North America, while Lundblad (1954) has reported and described *M. hallei* from South America.

Fossil Bryopsida. The form-genus *Muscites* with two species *M. bertrandi* and *M. polytrichaceus* have been recorded and described from the upper Carboniferous. *M. polytrichaceus* shows numerous stems and many universal leaves. It can be compared with *Polytrichum* of Polytrichales. In the Cainozoic many Bryopsida have been recorded. The mosses of the Miocene are assigned to the form - genera *Polytrichites, Plagiopodopsis* and *Palaeohypnum.* A moss capsule, *Muscites yellourensis* have been recorded in Oligocene coal from Australia (Clifford and Cookson, 1953).

However, the knowledge of fossil bryophytes is so fragmentary that it does not throw any light in tracing the evolution of the bryophytes.

Question Bank

Long Answer Questions (15 minutes; 15 marks)

1. Discuss the evolutionary advancement of Musci over Liverworts.
2. Trace the evolution of the sporophyte in the various members of Bryophytes.
3. Describe the various views on the origin of Bryophytes in Plant Kingdom.
4. Explain the theory of "progressive sterilization of the potentially sporogenous tissue" in Bryophytes.
5. Give comparative account of the position and structure of the archegonia of *Riccia, Marchantia, Anthoceros* and Moss.
6. By means of outline labelled diagrams only, illustrate the chief events in the life history of *Sphagnum*.
7. Describe the antheridiophore and archegoniophore of *Marchantia*.
8. Compare the vegatative thalli of *Riccia, Marchantia* and *Anthoceros* and give the importance of the various structures found in them.
9. What are bryophytes ? What are their features of advancement over algae and how far they lag behind the pteridophytes? (Kumaon , 1981, 1983, 1985).
10. Compare the sporophytes of *Marchantia, Pellia* and *Anthoceros* on the basis of (a) origin of sporogenous tissue, (b) capsule wall and (c) extent of dependency on the gametophyte. (Kumaon, 1983).
11. Give an account of the classification of the bryophytes and the criteria used. (Kumaon, 1986).
12. Describe the typical life-cycle pattern of bryophytes. How does it differ from that of pteridophytes? (Kumaon, 1987).
13. Compare the sporophyte of *Marchantia* and *Anthoceros* (Kanpur, 1981).
14. Describe briefly the life-cycle of *Pellia* (Kanpur, 1981, 1983).
15. Draw the life-cycle of moss with the help of diagrams alone. (Kanpur, 1981).
16. Describe the vegatative reproduction in bryophytes. (Kanpur, 1981).
17. Illustrate the differences between the gametophytes of *Riccia, Marchantia, Pellia* and *Anthoceros* with the help of neat and labelled diagrams alone. (Kanpur, 1982).
18. Describe in brief the life-cycle of *Anthoceros*. (Kanpur, 1982. 1984).
19. Describe briefly the characteristic features and classification of liverworts. How do they differ from mosses ? (Kanpur, 1983).
20. Describe the structure of gametophyte of *Riccia* with the help of suitable diagrams. (Kanpur, 1984)
21. Write an illustrated account of the progressive development of sporophytes in bryophytes. (Kanpur, 1984).
22. Draw neat and labelled diagrams of (a) L.S. of sporophyte of *Funaria,* (b) L.S. of sporophyte of *Marchantia*. (Kanpur, 1984).
23. Describe the characters of bryophytes and give an outline of their classification. (Kanpur, 1984).
24. With the help of suitable diagrams compare the internal structure of the thallus of *Riccia, Pellia* and *Anthoceros*. (Kanpur, 1985).
25. Describe the structure and position of sex organs in different genera of bryophytes studied by you. (Kanpur, 1985).
26. With the help of labelled diagrams only illustrate the life-cycle of *Marchantia*. (Kanpur, 1985).

27. Give a comparative account of structure of sporophytes of *Riccia* and *Pellia*.

Short Answer Questions (5 minutes ; 5 marks)

1. Why are air pores in *Marchantia* not called stomata.
2. Is the sporophyte of *Riccia* wholly dependent for its nutrition on the gametophyte? Justify your answer.
3. Draw neat and labelled sketches of the following T.S. of *Marchantia* thallus.
4. Write what you know about : Vegetative reproduction in the Hepaticopsida.
5. Show with the help of properly labelled diagrams only the microscopic structures of the following Internal structure of *Riccia* thallus.
6. Show with the help of properly labelled diagrams only, the microscopic structure of the following: V.S. mature capsule of *Anthoceros*.
7. Show with the help of properly labelled diagrams only, the microscopic structures of the following : V.S. antheridiophore of *Marchantia*.
8. Draw neat labelled diagram of the following : T.S. mature sporoganium of *Anthoceros*.
9. Describe the thallus of *Anthoceros*.
10. Draw the structure (L.S.) of sporogonium of *Riccia* and label the parts.
11. Describe the structure of gemma-cup in *Marchantia*.
12. Draw the T.S. of *Marchantia* thallus and label the parts.
13. Describe the structure of mature archegonium of *Marchantia*.
14. Describe the leaves in *Porella*.
15. Mention any two differences between *Riccia* and *Marchantia* with reference to sporophytes.
16. Describe the gametophytes of *Porella*.
17. Explain the post-fertilization changes in *Riccia*.
18. Describe the structure and development of antheridia in *Anthoceros*.
19. Describe the structure of sporogonium in *Porella*.
20. Draw neat labelled diagrams representing the haploid phase (n) of *Anthoceros*.
21. Describe the female receptacle in *Marchantia* after the formation of mature archegonia.
22. Describe the internal structure of *Anthoceros* thallus, point out the significance of mucilage cavities.
23. Taking the sporogenous tissue into consideration do you consider sporophyte of *Anthoceros* to be more advanced than the sporophyte of *Marchantia*. Give at least two reasons.
24. Compare the gametophytes of *Riccia* with that of *Marchantia* taking the external morphology.
25. Describe the behaviour of gemmae when they get detached from the parent plant of *Marchantia*.
26. Differentiate between *Pellia* and *Porella*.
27. Draw a section cut parallel to the upper surface of the thallus of *Marchantia* and passing through the air chambers.
28. Comment briefly on the morphological nature of the male and female receptacles of *Marchantia*.
29. By mistake the materials of the following pair got mixed up. What are the criteria you will use to separate the components : Sterile thalli of *Anthoceros* and *Pellia*
30. Among the sporogonia of *Riccia* and *Anthoceros* which is more primitive and why ?
31. Write short note on : Experimental studies on the gemmae of *Marchantia*.
32. "In their general habits and adaptations the liverworts are comparable to the amphibians of animal kingdom". Comment upon this statement.
33. Describe the modes of perennation in the liverworts studied by you.

33\. Give reasons for the inclusion of *Riccia* under Bryophytes, Hepaticeae, Marchantiales and Ricciaceae.

34\. Discuss the evolutionary importance of the sporophytic generation of *Anthoceros*.

35 Draw labelled diagrams only : T.S. mature capsule of *Pellia* at the level of elaterophore.

36 Draw labelled diagrams only : T.S. of the archegonial necks of *Riccia, Anthoceros* and *Pellia*.

37 Draw labelled diagrams of the following : T.S. capsule of *Marchantia* along with the calyptra and perigynium.

38. Draw labelled diagrams of the following : V.S. fertile thallus of *Riccia* parallel to the longitudinal axis.

39. Draw labelled diagrams of the following : T.S. capsule of *Pellia* at the level of elaterophore.

40. Draw labelled diagrams of the following : Lower surface view of the negatative thallus of *Madotheca*.

41. Briefly write about the following : Thallus of *Marchantia*.

42. Distinguish between : Rhizoid of a liverwort and root hair of an angiosperm.

43. In which habitat is *Anthoceros* found ?

44. Describe the T.S. of the thallus of *Riccia*.

45. Describe the structure of mature sporophyte of *Anthoceros* which has started spore dispersal.

46. Write notes on : (a) peristome of *Funaria*, (b) rhizoids in bryophytes, (c) scales of *Marchantia*. (Kanpur, 1985).

47. Give an account of vegetative reproduction in bryophytes. (Kanpur, 1986).

48. Write notes on : (a) archegoniophore, (b) capsule of *Funaria*, (c) pseudoelaters. (Kanpur, 1986).

49. Write notes on : (a) archegoniophore, (b) rhizoids in bryophytes, (c) scales of *Marchantia*. (Kanpur, 1987).

50. Write notes on : (a) antheridiophore of *Marchantia*, (b) paraphysis, (c) dehiscence of moss capsule. (Kanpur, 1988).

51. Write short notes on : (a) archesporium, (b) archegoniophore of *Marchantia* (c) operculum. (Kanpur, 1989).

52. Write short notes on : (i) rhizoids in bryophytes, (ii) liverworts, (iii) *Nostoc* cavity. (Kanpur, 1989).

53. Write notes on (a) function of elaters in bryophytes, (b) differences between liverworts and moss, (c) function of peristome in moss. (Kanpur, 1981).

54. Write short notes on any three of the following : (a) peristome, (b) gemmae, (c) alternation of generations, (D) elaters. (Kanpur, 1982).

55. Describe in any three of the following : (a) structure and function of scales in *Marchantia*, (b) mechanism of spore dispersal in *Pellia*, (c) methods of vegatative reproduction in *Funaria*, (d) economic importance of bryophytes. (Kanpur, 1982).

56. Draw neat and labelled diagrams of (a) V.L.S. of *Riccia* thallus passing through dorsal furrow with antheridia, (b) *Marchantia* gemma structure and germination, (c) V.S. *Anthoceros* thallus passing through mucilage cavity. (Kanpur, 1983).

57. Write notes on : (a) vegetative reproduction in *Marchantia*, (b) structure of sex organs of *Pellia*. (Kanpur, 1984).

58. Write short notes on any four (a) calyptra, (b) protonenia, (c) peristome, (d) paraphysis, (e) apophysis. (Rohilkhand, 1980).

59. Discuss the following : (a) evolutionary significance of *Anthoceros*, (b) mechanism of spore-dispersal in moss. (Rohilkhand, 1981).

59. Draw neat and labelled diagrams of (i) V.S. of *Anthoceros* thallus passing through archegonium, (ii) L.S. of female branch of *Funaria*, (iii) V.S. of leaf of *Funaria*. (Rohilkhand, 1983).

60. Draw neat and labelled diagrams of (a) V.S. of antheridiophore of *Marchantia*, (b) L.S. of moss capsule (Rohilkhand, 1984).

61. Name five important evolutionary features which enabled the plants to establish themselves successfully on land through the ages.

62. Write notes on the following : Elaters and Pseudoelaters.

63. Describe the external structure of the gametophyte of *Sphagnum*.

64. Give reasons : *Sphagnum* grows in water or marshy land and yet it shows xerophytic features.

65. By means of outline labelled diagrams (cellular details are not required) only, illustrate the following : L.S. gametophyte of *Sphagnum*.

66. Briefly write about the following : Biological importance of *Sphagnum*.

67. How do you distinguish a protonema of moss from a filamentous green alga ?

68. By mistake the materials of the following pair got mixed up. What are the criteria which you will use to separate the components : Gametophores of *Funaria* and *Sphagnum*.

69. Write short note on : Mechanism of spore dispersal in mosses.

70. The stem of *Pogonatum* is said to be comparable to that of a vascular plant in function but not in structure. Why ?

71. Draw labelled diagrams only : T.S. capsule of *Funaria* at the level of apophysis.

72. Draw labelled diagrams of the following : T.S. capsule of *Funaria* at the level of spore sac.

73. What are the taxonomic significance and function of peristomal teeth ?

74. Does protonema suggest the ancestry of mosses ? Comment.

75. Make well labelled sketches of the following : L.S. Moss capsule.

76. Write note on the following : Apophysis.

77. Write explanatory notes on the following : Moss flowers.

78. Write brief note on : Bud formation in protonema of mosses.

79. Write short note on : Spore dispersal in *Sphagnum*.

80. Why the mosses are not considered as ancestors to the Pteridophyta in preference to the Anthocerotae.

81. Describe the stages of development in the amphithecial and endothecial regions of the "theca zone" of Moss capsule.

82. Describe the mechanism by which spores are dispersed from the capsule of Moss.

83. Write short note on the following : Peristome.

84. Describe the external structure of an adult 'Moss plant' bearing capsule.

85. What is the significance of protonemal stage in the life-cycle of a moss ?

86. How would you distinguish a true moss from a club moss.

87. List out the distinctive anatomical features of Moss stem.

88. Write short notes on any three : (a) economic importance of *Sphagnum*, (b) alternation of generations in bryophytes, (c) gemmae, (d) elaters, (e) peristome. (Awadh, 1980).

89. Write short notes on any three : (a) protonema, (b) economic importance of *Sphagnum*, (c) peristome, (d) gemmae, (e) sporophyte of *Anthoceros*. (Awadh, 1981).

90. Describe the important features of *Sphagnum*. (Awadh, 1982).

91. Write short notes on any three (a) archegoniphore, (b) structure of leaf of *Pogonatum*, (c) sporophyte of *Riccia*, (d) characteristic features of Bryophyta, (e) elaters, (Awadh Univ. 1982).

92. Write short notes on any three of the following : (a) sporophyte of *Pellia*, (b) vegetative reproduction in Bryophyta, (c) economic importance of bryophytes, (d) elaters, (e) structure of leaf of *Sphagnum*. (Awadh Univ. 1983).

93. Write short notes on : (a) sporophyte of *Anthoceros*, (b) protonema, (c) classification of bryophytes, (d) gemmae, (e) alternation of generations in bryophytes. (Awadh Univ. 1984).

94. How would you distinguish with a hand lens : (a) *Riccia* plant from that of *Marchantia*, (b) antheridiophore from archegoniophore of *Marchantia*, (c) sporophyte of *Pellia* from that of *Anthoceros*. (Awadh Unive 1985).

95. How would you distinguish the following : (a) thallus of *Anthoceros* and *Pellia*, (b) thallus of *Riccia* and green leaves of *Pogonatum* (in a T.S.), (c) elaters and pseudoelaters. (Awadh Univ. 1986).

96. If you are on a botanical tour, how would you differentiate *Riccia*, *Marchantia* and *Anthoceros* in their habitat. (Rohilkhand, 1987).

97. Write short notes on : (a) gemma cup, (b) peristome, (c) rhizoids, (d) scales. (Rohilkhand, 1986).

98. Write a brief account on any two : (a) elaters, their types and function in bryophytes, (b) vegetative propagation in bryophytes, (c) habit and habitat of bryophytes. (Rohilkhand, 1985).

Constant Alternative Questions (1 minute; 1 mark)

1. The sporophytic generation of Bryophyta is more dominant than the gametophytic generation.
True False
2. Apospory is development of gametophyte directly from sporophyte without formation of spores
True False
3. The sporogonium of *Riccia* consists of foot, seta and capsule.
True False
4. The gametophores are the prolongations of the thallus in *Marchantia.*
True False
5. *Porella* is strictly dioecious.
True False
6. Assimilatory filaments are present in *Porella.*
True False
7. In *Anthoceros* the antherida develop endogenously.
True False
8. *Anthoceros* consists of disc-shaped chloroplasts.
True False
9. Some liverworts form tubers, when they are exposed to desiccation.
True False
10. Vegetative propagation in *Marchantia* takes place by the formation of gemmae spores.
True False
11. Mature archegonium of *Anthoceros* resembles some of the Pteridophytes.
True False
12. *Porella* is dioecious.
Yes No
13. In *Riccia* sex organs are borne on special sexual branches of the thallus.
True False
14. In *Marchantia* archesporium is derived from the amphithecium.
True False
15. In *Riccia* the sporophyte produces peristomic teeth that help in the liberation of spores.
True False
16. The columella of *Anthoceros* sporophyte corresponds to the vascular tissue of higher plants..
True False
17. In mosses the sporophyte is differentiated into stem and leaves.
True False
18. The protonema, rhizoids, gemmae, archegonia and calyptra of a moss belong to the gametophytic (haploid) generation.
True False
19. The hyaline cells are present in *Polytrichum* leaves.
True False
20. Apophysis is present in the capsule of *Polytrichum.*
True False
21. The entire sporogenous tissue in *Funaria* develops into the spore mother cells.
True False
22. The sporophyte is simple and not well distinguished in moss.
True False
23. In moss apophysis is limited by a single layer of cells bearing stomata.
True False
24. In *Funaria* spores are released in instalments.
True False

25. In *Riccia* the sporophyte consists of foot, seta and capsule.
True False
26. In *Marchantia*,the gemmae are found on archegoniophores.
True False
27. In moss the rhizoids are aseptate.
True False
28. In *Anthoceros* pseudoelaters are found in sporogonium.
True False
29. A bryophyte has multicelled sex organs with a sterile jacket and lacks vascular tissues.
True False
30. Rhizoids of *Funaria* are multicellular with oblique septa.
True False
31. In *Riccia* the sporophyte has foot, seta and capsule.
True False
32. The antheridium of *Riccia* is a unicellular structure.
True False
33. In bryophytes the gametophyte is predominent.
True False
34. In *Funaria* stomata are found on capsule.
True False
35. In *Funaria* antheridia and archegonia are found on different plants.
True False

Completion Questions (1 minute; 1 mark)

1. Hyaline cells are present in the leaves of the bryophyte member........................
2. *Nostoc* colonies are recorded inside the thallus of........................
3. The entire .... gives rise to columella in *Anthoceros*.
4. In *Marchantia* asexual reproduction is brought about by special bodies called................
5. In *Marchantia* specialized branch systems of the thallus bearing sex organs are called.........
6. The smaller leaves of the ventral row in *Porella* are called........................
7. The nurse-cells are present in the sporogonium of......................
8. In mosses, calyptra develops from........................
9. The tissue of the calyptra grows out to form a covering called........................ in *Marchantia*.
10. The elaters are hygroscopic in nature and so serve in the dispersal of........................

Multiple Choice Questions (1 minute; 1 mark)

1. Development of a sporophyte directly from the sporophytic tissue is called (a) Apospory, (b) Parthenogenesis, (c) Apogamy, (d) Syngamy.

2. The simplest known sporophyte among the Bryophyta is seen in (a) *Riccia*, (b) *Funaria*, (c) *Marchantia*, (d) *Anthoceros*.

3. The theory of progressive sterilization of potentially sporogenous tissue was first proposed by (a) Campbell, (b) Bower, (c) Smith, (d) Cavers.

4. The advanced sporophyte is seen in (a) *Riccia*, (b) *Porellà*, (c) *Sphagnum*, (d) *Anthoceros*.

5. Epiphragm is seen in (a) Archegonium, (b) antheridium, (c) gametophyte, (d) sporophyte.

6. In archegonium the cell above the egg cell is (a) Neck-canal cell, (b) Neck-cell, (c) Cover-cell, (d) Ventral-canal cell.

7. Calyptra is seen in (a) Gametophyte, (b) Sporophyte, (c) archegoniophore, (d) antheridiophore.

8. Perichaetium is seen in (a) archegoniophore, (b) antheridiophore, (c) sporogonium, (d) none of the above.

9. Spore mother cell in Bryophytes is (a) haploid in nature, (b) diploid in nature, (c) triploid in nature, (d) tetraploid in nature.

10. Elaters are seen in (a) antheridium, (b) archegonium, (c) sporogonium, (d) none of the above.

11. Nourishing tissue surrounding the spore producing tissue in a young sporangium is (a) archesporium, (b) tapetium, (c) spore mother cells, (d) sporocytes.

12. In *Polytrichum* the spore liberation is regulated by (a) operculum, (b) columella, (c) peristome, (d)annulus.

13. Elongated cylindrical sporogonium is seen in (a) *Anthoceros*, (b) *Polytrichum*, (c) *Marchantia*, (d) *Porella*.

14. Trabeculae are seen in the sporogonium of (a) *Sphagnum*, (b) *Polytrichum*, (c) *Anthoceros*, (d) *Riccia*.

15. In *Anthoceros* the meristematic tissue is present (a) at the apex of sporogonium, (b) at the base of sporogonium above the foot, (c) in the middle of sporogonium, (d) none of the above.

16. In *Marchantia* the chloroplast is (a) cup-shaped, (b) disc-shaped, (c) star-shaped, (d) ribbon-shaped.

17. In *Anthoceros* the sporogenous tissue is derived from (a) amphithecium tissue, (b) endothecium tissue,(c) gametophytic tissue, (d) columella tissue.

18. Peristomes are present in (a) *Marchantia*, (b) *Polytrichum*, (c) *Sphagnum*, (d) *Porella*.

19. In *Marchantia* the archegonia are situated (a) on the disc, (b) below the disc, (c) in the middle of the disc, (d) on the sides of the disc.

20. The most primitive type of sporogonium is seen in (a) *Anthoceros*, (b) *Marchantia*, (c) *Porella*, (d) *Riccia*.

21. The nurse cells are present in the sporogonium of (a) *Riccia*, (b) *Marchanitia*, (c) *Porella*, (d) *Anthoceros*.

22. Stomata are present on capsule wall of (a) *Marchantia*, (b) *Anthoceros*, (c) *Porella*, (d) *Riccia*.

23. In *Riccia* (a) smooth rhizoids are present, (b) pegged rhizoids are present, (c) multicellular scales are present, (d) both smooth and pegged rhizoids present.

24. In which of the following plants, sporophyte is completely dependent on gametophyte (a) *Riccia*, (b) *Funaria*, (c) Angiosperms, (d) None of above.

25. Obliquely septate rhizoids are found in (a) *Riccia*, (b) *Marchantia*, (c) *Funaria*, (d) *Anthoceros*.

26. Columella is absent in (a) *Anthoceros*, (b) *Funaria*, (c) *Riccia*, (d) *Anthoceros himalayensis*.

27. The gametophyte is leafy shoot in (a) *Riccia*, (b) *Marchantia*, (c) *Funaria*, (d) *Anthoceros*.

28. The sporophyte grows continuously for a long period due to basal meristem in (a) *Funaria*, (b) *Anthoceros*, (c) *Riccia*, (d) *Marchantia*.

29. Pseudoelaters are found in the sporophyte of (a) *Riccia*, (b) *Funaria*, (c) *Marchantia*, (d) *Anthoceros*.

30. Elevated areolae are present on the upper surface of the gametophytic thallus of (a) *Funaria*, (b) *Riccia*, (c) *Marchantia*, (d) *Anthoceros*.

31. In *Riccia* growth of the thallus takes place by the activity of a (a) group of intercalary initials, (b) group of apical initials, (c) single apical cell, (d) basal meristem.

32. Female sex organs in *Marchantia* are borne on (a) an elaterophore, (b) a rhizophore, (c) an antheridiophore, (d) an archegoniophore.

33. A dioecious gametophyte is seen in the case of (a) *Funaria*, (b) *Riccia*, (c) *Marchantia*, (d) *Anthoceros*.

34. A sporophyte of *Marchantia* is enveloped by (a) two protective sheaths, (b) one protective sheath, (c) three protective sheaths, (d) four protective sheaths.

35. An endophytic alga is present in the thallus of (a) *Anthoceros*, (b) *Riccia*, (c) *Funaria*, (d) *Marchantia*.

36. The true elaters are found in sporophyte of (a) *Riccia*, (b) *Anthoceros*, (c) *Marchantia*, (d) *Funaria*.

37. Spores are liberated from the sporogonium only by the decay of gametophyte in (a) *Marchantia*, (b) *Riccia*, (c) *Funaria*, (d) *Anthoceros*.

38. Leptoids are present in (a) *Sphagnum*, (b) *Polytrichum*, (c) *Anthoceros*, (d) *Marchantia*.

39. In *Sphagnum* the spore-sac is (a) spindle-shaped, (b) arc-shaped, (c) dome-shaped, (d) disc-shaped.

40. In *Sphagnum* the zygote first divides (a) Transversely, (b) Longitudinally, (c) Obliquely, (d) Irregularly.

41. Gametophyte is predominant in (a) *Cycas*, (b) pea, (c) moss, (d) fern. (C.P.M.T. 1977)

42. In *Funaria* the stomata are present (a) in the epidermis of leaf, (b) in the epidermis of stem, (c) in the epidermis of capsule wall, (d) in none of these. (C.P.M.T. 1978).

43. In *Funaria* stomata are found on : (a) leaves, (b) stem, (c) archegonia, (d) capsule. (C.P.M.T. 1980)

44. In *Funaria*, antheridia and archegonia are found on : (a) different plants, (b) different branches of the same plant, (c) different branches of plant but separately, (d) the same branches of a plant in inner middle condition. (C.P.M.T. 1980)

45. The bryophyte of considerable economic importance is : (a) *Funaria*, (b) *Sphagnum*, (c) *Marchantia*, (d) *Riccia*. (C.P.M.T. 1981)

46. In *Funaria* stomata are present on the : (a) leaf, (b) stem, (c) upper part of capsule, (d) lower part of capsule. (C.P.M.T. 1981)

47. When moss spores germinate, they form (a) leafy gametophyte directly, (b) capsule directly, (c) first protonema, then from bud a leafy gametophyte, (d) protonema which bears archegonia and antheridia. (C.P.M.T. 1982.)

48. The fern differs from a moss in having : (a) an independent gametophyte, (b) an independent sporophyte, (c) swimming antherozoids, (d) archegonia. (C.P.M.T. 1984)

49. Multicellular and jacketed sex organs are present in : (a) *Funaria*, (b) *Spirogyra*, (c) *Saccharomyces*, (d) *Hibiscus*. (C.P.M.T. 1984.)

50. The antherozoids of moss are : (a) motile, coenocytic and multiciliate, (b) motile, uninucleate and uniciliate, (c) motile, uninucelate and biciliate, (d) non-motile and without cilia. (C.P.M.T. 1985).

51. Xylem and phloem donot form the conducting strand of : (a) *Pinus*, (b) *Cycas*, (c) *Brassica*, (d) *Funaria*. (C.P.M.T. 1985).

52. Bryophytes include : (a) liverworts and ferns, (b) mosses and ferns, (c) mosses and liverworts, (d) none of the above. (C.P.M.T. 1986.)

53. In *Riccia* the sporophyte has : (a) foot, seta and capsule, (b) seta only, (c) capsule only, (d) foot only. (C.P.M.T. 1986).

54. The antheridium of *Riccia* is a: (a) unicellular structure, (b) multicellular structure, (c) structure having 20 cells, (d) structure having 60 cells. (C.P.M.T. 1986)

55. Plants of *Funaria* grow in tufts and are : (a) thallose, (b) foliose, (c) thallose and foliose, (d) found in the hot springs of Rajgiri. (C.P.M.T. 1986).

56. Rhizoids of *Funaria* are : (a) unicellular, (b) green coloured, (c) unicellular with septa, (d) multicellular with oblique septa. (C.P.M.T. 1987)

57. Cortex cells of the young stem of *Funaria* are (a) chlorenchymatous, (b) collenchymatous, (c) parenchymatous, (d) sclerenchymatous. (C.P.M.T. 1987).

58. The spores of moss on germination give rise to : (a) protenema, (b) primary protonema, (c) secondary protonema, (d) operculum.

59. *Riccia* is a bryophyte because it : (a) occurs mostly on land and has motile sperms, (b) has heteromorphic alternation of generations, (c) has multicellular sex organs with a sterile jacket and lacks vascular tissues, (d) none. (C.P.M.T. 1988)

60. Which one of the following statements is not true of Bryophyta : (a) they lack tracheids and sieve tubes, (b) they are photosynthetic, (c) their zygote undergoes meiosis and then produces the sporophyte, (d) their spores germinate, producing gametophytes. (C.P.M.T. 1989)

61. Rhizoids of *Funaria* are : (a) unicellular, (b) green coloured, (c) unicellular with septa, (d) multicellular with oblique septa. (C.P.M.T. 1990).

ANSWERS

1(a), 2(a), 3(b), 4(c), 5(d), 6(d), 7(b), 8(a), 9(b), 10(c), 11(b), 12(c), 13(a), 14(b), 15(b), 16(b), 17(b), 18(b), 19(d), 20(d), 21(a), 22(b), 23(d), 24(b), 25(d), 26(c), 27(c), 28(b), 29(d), 30(b), 31(c), 32(d), 33(c), 34(b), 35(a), 36(c), 37(b), 38(b), 39(c), 40(a), 41(c), 42(c), 43(d), 44(b), 45(b), 46(d), 47(c), 48(a), 49(a), 50(c), 51(d), 52(c), 53(c), 54(b), 55(b), 56(d), 57(c), 58(b), 59(c), 60(c), 61(d).

Simple Questions (1 minute; 1 mark)

1. What is an operculum ?
2. By what type of division does a spore mother cell give rise to spores ?
3. After fertilization which part of the archegonium gives rise to calyptra ?
4. Which organ in the sporogonium of *Polytrichum* controls the spore liberation ?
5. By what type of succession the sex organs are developed in *Riccia*?
6. What is the principal function of a pegged rhizoid ?
7. What type of branching is found in *Riccia* plant ?
8. Mention the shape of chloroplast in *Marchantia* .
9. Name the tissue in *Anthoceros* which gives rise to spore mother cells.
10. How many rows of leaves are there in *Porella*.

Rearrangement Questions (2 minutes ; 2 marks)

1. Arrange the following layers of sporogonium in *Marchantia* from outside to inside (a) capsule wall ; (b) perigynium and (c) calyptra.
2. Arrange the following portions from base to apex in the sporogonium of *Polytrichum*. (a) operculum ; (b) seta ; (c) foot and (d) capsule
3. Arrange the following cells in the archegonium of bryophytes from base to apex. (a) neck-canal cells ; (b) cover cells ; (c) ventral canal cell and (d) egg cell.

Further Reading

Bower, F.O. 1935. Primitive Land Plants. Macmillan and Co. London.

Bruhl, P. 1931. *A Census of Indian Mosses*. Records of Botanical Survey of India, Vol. 13, Nos. 1-2.

Campbell, D.H. 1918. *The structure and development of mosses and ferns*. 3rd ed. New York.

Campbell, D.H. 1940. *The evolution of land plants* (Embryophyta). Stanford University Press, California.

Cavers, F. 1911. *The inter-relationships of the Bryophyta*. Church, A.H. 1919. *Thalassiophyta and the subaerial transmigration*. Oxford Bot. Mem. No. 3. 1-95.

Dixon, H.N. 1924. *The students hand book of British mosses*. London.

Doyle, W.T. 1964. *Nonvascular plants, Form and Function*. California.

Doyle, W.T. 1970. *The Biology of Higher Cryptogams*. The Macmillan & Co. London.

Evans, A.W. 1923. *Marchantiales*. New York.

Evans, A.W. 1939. *The classification of Hepaticae*. Bot. Rev. 5 : 48-96.

Ingold, C.T. 1939. *Spore discharge in land plants*. Oxford.

Ingold, C.T. 1965. *Spore liberation*. Oxford.

Kashyap, S.R. 1929. *Liverworts of the Western Himalayas and the Punjab Plain*. Lahore.

MacVicar,S.M. 1926. *The students hand book of British Hepatics*. 2nd ed. London.

Pande, S.K. 1960. *The Anthocerotales, some aspects of their systematics and morphology*. 47th, Ind. Sc. Cong.

Parihar, N.S. 1967. *An Introduction to Embryophyta*. Vol. I. Central Book Depot, Allahabad.

Smith, G.M., *et. at.* 1953. *A text book of general botany*. 5th. ed. New York.

Smith, G.M., *et. at.* 1953. *A text book of general botany*. 5th ed. New York.

Smith G.M. 1955. *Cryptogamic Botany*. Vol.II. *Bryophytes and Pteridophytes*. 2nd. ed. New York.

Srivastava, K.P. 1964. *Bryophytes of India*. I. *Ricciaceae*. Bull. Nat. Bot. Gardens. Lucknow.

Udar, R. 1976. *Bryology in India*. Chronica Britanica Co. New Delhi.

Watson, E.V. 1955. *British mosses and liverworts*. Cambridge.

Watson, E.V. 1971. *The structure and life history of bryophytes*. 3rd. Edn. Hutchinson & Co. London.

Selected References

Abheywickrama, B.A. 1945. The structure and life history of *Riccia crispatula* Mill., *Ceylon Jour. Sci. A. Bot.*, **12** : 145-153.

Ahmad, S. 1912. Three new species of *Riccia* from India. *Curr. Sci.* **11** : 433-434.

Allen, C.E. 1917. Spermatogenesis of *Polytrichum juniperinum. Ann Bot* **31** : 433-434.

Allen, C.E. 1945. The Genetics of Bryophtes. *II Bot. Rev* **II** : 260-287.

Allsopp, A. and G.C. Mitra, 1958. The morphology of protonema and bud formation in the Bryales. *Ann. Bot.* **22** :95-115.

Andersen, E.N. 1929. Morphology of sporophyte of *Marchantia domingensis*. *Bot. Gaz.* **88** : 150-166.

Andersen, E.N. 1931. Discharge of sperms in *Marchantia domingensis*. *Bot. Gaz.* **65** : 66-84.

Bagchee, K.D. 1924. The spermatogenesis of *Anthoceros laevis*. *Ann. Bot.* **38** : 105-111.

Bapna, K.R. and P. Kachroo, 1975. Further studies in the genus *Riccia* in India. *Jour. Ind. Bot. Soc.* **54** : 219-224.

Bartlett, E.H. 1928. A comparative study of the development of the sporophyte of Anthcerotaceae with special reference ot the genus *Anthoceros*. *Ann. Bot.* **42** : 409-430.

Beer, R. 1906. On the development of spores of *Riccia glauca*. *Ann Bot.* **20** : 277-291.

Berkley, E.E. 1941. Gemmae of *Funaria hygrometrica*. *Trans. Illi. State Acad. Sci.* **24**: 102-104.

Berrie, G.K. 1963. Cytology and Phylogeny of liverworts. *Evolution.* **17**: 347-357.

Bhardwaj, D.C. 1950. Studies in Indian Anthocerotaceae. I. On the morphology of *Anthoceros crispulus*. *J. I.B.S.* **29** : 145-163.

Bhardwaj, D.C. 1958. Studies in Indian Anthocerotacece II. The morphology of *Anthoceros gemmulosus*. *Jour. Ind. Bot. Soc.* **37** : 75-92.

Black, C.A. 1913. The morphology of *Riccia frostii Ann. Bot.* **27** : 511-532.

Blaikley, N.M. 1933. the structure of the foot in certain masses and in *Anthoceros laevis Trans. Roy. Soc.* Edinburgh. **57** : 699-709.

Bold, H.C. 1938. The nutrition of the sporophyte in the Hepaticae. *Amer. Jour. Bot.* **25**: 511-557.

Bold, H.C. 1948. The prothallium of *Sphagnum palustre*. *Bryologist.* **51** : 55-63.

Bopp, M.E. 1963. Development of the protonema and bud formation in mosses. *Jour. Linn. Soc. (Bot.)* **58** : 305-309.

Brown, M.M. 1919. The development of the gametophyte and the distribution of sexual characters in *Funnaria hygrometrica*. *Amer. Jour. Bot.* **6** : 387-400.

Bryan, G.S. 1915. Archegonium of *Sphagnum*. *Bot. Gaz.* **59** : 40-56.

Bryan, G.S. 1920. Early stages in the development of the sporophyte of *Sphagnum subsecundum*. *Amer. Jour. Bot.* **7** : 269-303.

Burr, F.A. 1970. Phylogenetic transitions in the chloroplast of the Anthocerotales I. The number and ultrastructure of the mature plastids. *Amer. Jour. Bot.* **57** (1) : 97-110.

Campbell, D.H. 1924. A remarkable development of the sporophyte in *Anthoceros fusiformis*. *Ann. Bot.* **38** : 473-483.

Campbell, D.H. 1925. The relationships of the Anthocerotaceae. *Flora.* 118-119 : 62-74.

Campbell, D.H. 1936. The relationships of the Hepaticae. *Bot Rev.* **2** : 53-66.

Cavers, F. 1903. On sexual reproduction and regeneration in Hepaticae. *New Phytol.* **2**: 121-133; 155-165.

Chavan, A.R. and T.S. Mahabale, 1945. Distribution of liverworts in Gujarat. 32nd *Ind. Sci. Cong.* 70.

Chopra, R.N. and Ram Udar, 1957. Cyto-taxonomic studies in the genus *Riccia* I *R. billardieri* and *R. gangetica*. *Jour. Ind. Bot. Soc.* **36** : 191-195.

Chopra, R.N. and Ram Udar, 1957. Cyto-taxonomic studies in the genus *Riccia* II *R. crystallina* and *R. cruciata*. *Jour Ind. Bot. Soc.* **36** : 535-538

Chopra, R.S. 1943. A census of Indian Hepaticae. *Jour. Ind. Bot. Soc.* **22** : 237-259.

Chopra, R.S. 1967. Relationships between liverworts and Mosses. *Phytomorphology* **17**: 70-77.

Chopra, R.S. and P.D. Sharma, 1958. Cytomorphology of genus *Pogonatum. Phytomorphology.* **8** : 41-50.

Christensen, T. 1954. Some considerations on the phylogeny of the Bryophyta. *Bot. Tidsskr.* **51** : 53-58.

Clee, D.A. 1939. The morphology and anatomy of *Pellia epiphylla* considered in relation to the mechanism of absorption and conduction of water. *Ann. Bot.* **3** : 106-111.

Cribbs, J.E. 1918. A columella in *Marchantia polymorpha Bot. Gaz.* **65** : 91-96.

Durand, E.J. 1908. The development of the sexual organs and sporogonium of *Marchantia polymorpha. Bull. Torrey. Bot Club.* **35** : 321-325.

Evans, A.W. 1939. The classification of Hepaticae. *Bot. Rev.* **5** : 49-96.

Favoli, M.A. and M. Bassi, 1973. Seta ultrastructure in *Polytrichum commune. Nova Hedgwigia.*

French, J.C. and D.J. Paolillo, 1975. On the role of calyptra in permitting expansion of capsule in the moss *Funaria. The Bryologist.* **78** : 438-446.

French, J.C. and D.J. Paolillo, 1976. Effect of light and other factors on the capsule expansion in *Funaria hygrometrica. The Bryologist.* **79** (4) : 457-465.

Fulford, M. 1944. Vegetative reproduction in *Porella pinnata. The Bryologist.* **47** : 78-81.

Fulford, M. 1948. Recent interpretations of the relatioships of the Hepaticae. *Bot. Rev.* **14** : 127-173.

Fulford, M. 1965. Evolutionary trends and convergence in the Hepaticae. *The Bryologist.* **68** : 1-30.

Fulford, M. 1976. Recent advances and trends in Hepaticae. *Recent advances in Botany.*

Galatis, B. and P. Apostokalos, 1977. On the fine structure of differentiating mucilage papillae of *Marchantia. Can. J. Bot.* **55** : 772-795.

Greenwood, H. 1911. Development of *Pellia epiphylla. The Bryologist,* **14** : 59-70, 77-83, 93-100.

Grolle, R. 1963. *Takakia* in the Himalayas. *Ost. Bot. Zeitschr.* **110** : 444-447.

Grubb, P.J. 1970. Observations on the structure and biology of *Haplomitrium* and *Takakia,* Hepatics with roots. *New Phytol.* **69** : 303-326.

Harvey-Gibson, R.J. and D. Miller Brown, 1927. Fertilization of Bryophyta. *Polytrichum commune Ann. Bot.* **41** : 190-191.

Haberlein, E.A. 1929. Morphological notes on a new species of *Marchantia. Gaz.* **88**: 427

Haskeil, G. 1949. Some evolutionary problems concerning the Bryophyta. The Bryologist **52** : 49-57.

Hattori, S. and Inoue, 1958. Preliminary report on *Takakia lepidozioides.* Jour. *Hatta. Bot. Lab.* **19** : 133-137.

Hattori, S., Z. Iwatsuki, M. Mizutanc and K. Yamacha. 1973. The genus *Takakia* in East Nepal. *Jour. Jap. Bot.* **48** : 1-9.

Haupt, A.W. 1920. Life history of *Fossombronia cristula.* Bot. Gaz. **67** : 318.

Hausmann, M.K. and D.J. Paolillo Jr. 1977. On the development and maturation of antheridia in *Polytrichum. The Bryologist* **80** (1) : 143-148.

Hoffman, G.R. 1966. Observations on the mineral nutrition of *Fumaria hygrometrica. The Bryologist.* **69** : 182-192.

Harner, H.T., N.R. Lerston and C.C. Brown, 1966. Spore development in the liverwort *Riccardia pinguis. Amer. Jour. Bot.* **53** : 1048-1064.

Horne, A.S. 1909. Discharge of antherozoids in *Fossombronia. Ann. Bot. XXIII* : 159-160.

Hutchinson, A.H. 1915. Gametrophyte of *Pellia epiphylla. Bot. Gaz.* **60** : 134-143.

Inoue, H. 1960. Studies in the spore germination and earlier stages of gametophyte development in the Marchantiales. *Jour Hattori Bot. Lab.* **23** : 148-191.

Kachroo, P. 1950. A note on the morphology of some species of *Riccia. Bryologist.* **58**: 134-136.

Kachroo, P. 1954. Studies in Assam Hepaticae, II. On a new species of *Anthoceros* and *Riccia Sci. & Cul.* **20** : 98-101.

Kachroo, P., Bapna, K.R. and G.L. Dhar, 1977. Hepaticae of India. Taxonomic survey and census V. Fossombroniaceae through the Anthocerotaceas. *Jour. Ind. Bot. Soc.* **56** : 62-86.

Kamimura, M. 1961. A monograph of Japanese Frullaniaceae. *Jour. Hottari Bot. Lab.* **24** : 1-190

Kashyap, S.R. 1915. Morphological and biological notes on new and little known west Himalayan liverworts. *New Phytol.* **14** : 1-18.

Kashyap, S.R. and N.L. Datt, 1925. Two Indian species of genus *Notothylas.* Proc. Lahore *Phil. Soc.* **4** : 49-56.

Kumar, D.S. and R. Udar, 1976. *Calobryum denundatum* Kumar et Udar. Sp. nov. : a new species of *Calobryum* from Indian. J.I.B.S. **55** : 23-30.

Lang, W.H. 1907. On the sporogonium of *Notothylas. Ann. Bot.* **21** : 201-210.

Lewis, C.E. 1906. The embryology and development of *Riccia lutescens* and *R. crystallina. Bot. Gaz.* **41** : 109-138.

Manning, F.L. 1914. Life history of *Porella platyphylla Bot. Gaz.* **57** : 320-323.

McAllister, F. 1927. The pyrenoids of *Anthoceros* and *Notothylas* with special reference to their presence in the spore mother cells. *Amer Jour. Bot.* **14** : 246-257.

McClymont, J.W. and D.A. Larson, 1964. An electron microscopic study of spore wall structure in the Musci. *Amer. Jour. Bot.* **51** (2) : 195-200.

Mc Naught, H.L. 1929. Development of sporophyte of *Marchantia chenopoda. Bot Gaz.* **88** : 400-416.

Mehra, P.N. and O.N. Handoo, 1953. Morphology of *Anthoceros erectus* and *A. himalayensis* and the phylogeny of Anthocerotales. *Bot. Gaz.* **114** : 371-382.

Mehra, P.N. and S. Sood, 1969. Studies on the spore morphology of some Western Himalayan Hepatics and Anthocerotes. *Bull. Res. Pun. Uni.* **20** : 71-73.

Mehra, P.N. 1967. Phyletic evolution in the Hepaticae *Phytomorphology.* **17** : 47-58.

Mehra, P.N. 1967-70. Evolutionary trends in the Hepaticae with particular reference to Marchantiales. *Phytomorphology.* **19** (3) : 203-218.

Naidu, T.R. 1973. Occurrence of androgynous receptacles in *Marchantia polymorpha. The Bryologist.* **76** : 428-430.

Nehira, K. 1974. Phylogenetic significance of the sporeling pattern in Jungermanniales. *Jour Hattori Bot. Lab.* **38** : 151-160.

Nirula, R.L. 1949. Embryogeny of *Notothylas chaudhurii* and its theoretical significance. *Proc. Ind Sci. Cong.* **36** (4) : 4-5.

Noguchis, A. 1958. Germination of spores in two species of *Sphagnum. Jour. Hattori Bot. Lab.* **19** : 71.

O'Hanlon, S.M.E. 1926. Germination of spores and early stages in the development of gametophyte of *Marchantia polymorpha. Bot. Gaz.* **82** : 215-222.

Obsen, P. and G.S. Magensen, 1978. Ultrastructure histochemistry and notes on germination stages of spores in selected mosses. *The Bryologist.* **81** (4) : 493-516.

Pagen, F.M. 1932. Morphology of the sporophyte of *Riccia crystallina. Bot. Gaz.* **93** : 71-84.

Pande, S.K. 1932. On the morphology of *Notothylas indica. J.I.B.S.* **11** : 169-177.

Pande, S.K. 1933. On the morphology of *Riccia robusta. J.I.B.S.* **12** : 110-121.

Pande, S.K. 1934. On the morphology of *Notothylas levieri. Proc. Indo. Acad. Sci. B.* **5** : 205-217.

Pande, S.K. and D.C. Bhardwaj, 1949. On the morphology of *Anthoceros jackii. Proc. 35th, Ind. Sci. Cong.*

Pande, S.K., T.S. Mahabale, Y.B. Raje and K.P. Srivastava, 1954. Studies in Indian Metzgerineae. *Fossombronia himalayensis* Kash. *Phytomorphology.* **4** : 365-378.

Pande, S.K. and R. Udar, 1957. Genus *Riccia* in India. I. A reinvestingation of taxonomic status of Indian species of *Riccia. J.I.B.S.* **36** : 564-579.

Pande, S.K. and K.P. Srivastava, 1958. The genus *Riccurdia* in India, *J.I.B.S.* **37** : 417-421.

Pande, S.K. 1960. The Anthocerotales, some aspects of their systematics and morphology. *Presidential address, Bot. Sec.* 47th, *Ind. Sci. Cong.*

Paolillo, D.J. Jr. 1977. Release of sperms in *Funaria hygrometrica. The Bryologist.* **80**: 619-624.

Paolillo, D.J. Jr. 1975. The release of sperms from the antheridum of *Polytrichum juniperinum. New Phytologist.* **74** : 287-293.

Paolillo, D.J. Jr. and F.A. Bazar, 1968. Photosynthesis in the sporophytes of *Polytrichum* and *Funaria. The Bryologist.* **71** : 335-343.

Parihar, N.S. and Jagdish Lal, 1972. Anomalous Carpocephala in *Marchantia* and their phyletic significance. *The Bryologist.* **75** : (1)

Peirce, G.J. 1906. *Anthoceros* and its *Nostoc* colonies. *Bot. Gaz.* **42** : 55-59.

Proskaeur, J. 1948. Studies on the morphology of *Anthoceros,* I. *Ann. Bot.* **12** : 237-265.

Proskaeur, J. 1948. Studies on the morphology of *Anthoceros,* II. *Ann. Bot.* **12** : 427-440.

Proskaeur, J. 1951. Studies on the Anthocerotales, III. *Bull. Torrey Bot. Club.* **78** : 331-349.

Proskaeur, J. 1953. Studies on the Anthocerotales, IV. *Bull. Torrey Bot. Club.* **80** : 65-75.

Proskaeur, J. 1957. Studies on the Anthocerotales. V. *Phytomorphology.* **7** : 113-135.

Proskaeur, J. 1960. Studies on the Anthocerotales, VI. *Phytomorphology.* **10** : 1-19.

Proskaeur, J. 1962. On *Takakia,* especially its mucilage hairs. *Jour. Hattori Bot. Club* **25** : 217-223.

Proskaeur, J. 1967. Studies on the Anthocerotales, VII. *Phytomorphology.* **17** : 61-70.

Reese, W.D. 1955. Regeneration of some moss paraphyses. *The Bryologist.* **58** : 239-241.

Scheirer, D.C. 1972. Anatomical studies in the Polytrichaceae I. *The Bryologist,* **74** : 458-463.

Sane, P.V. 1942. Observations on some species of *Anthoceros* Lind, from Poona and neighbouring hills of the Western Ghats. *Jour. Univ. Bom.* **10** : 5.

Schuster, R.M. 1967. Studies on Hepaticae XIV Calobryales. *Nova Hedgwigia.* **13** : 1-63.

Sharma, A.K. 1949. Indian Sphagnums. *Bull. Bot. Soc. Bengal.* **3** : 99-111.

Showalter, A.M. 1923. Studies in the morphology of *Riccardia pinguis*. *Amer. Jour. Bot.* **10** : 148-166.

Showalter, A.M. 1925. Germination of the spore of *Riccardia pinguis* and *Pellia fabbroniana*. *Bull Torrey Bot. Ciub.* **52** : 157-166.

Srinivasan, K.N. 1939. The developmental morphology of Androgynous receptacles in *Marchantia palmata*. *Proc. Ind. Acad. Sci.* **10B** : 88.

Srinivasan, K.N. 1940. On the morphology, life history and cytology of *Riccia himalayensis* *Jour. Madras Univ.* **5** : 59-80.

Srinivasan, K.N. 1944. The developmental morphology and cytology of *Marchantia palmata*. *Jour. Madras Univ.* **12** : 101-133.

Srivastava, K.P. 1957. Spermatogenesis in *Notothylas levieri*. *Jour. Ind Bot. Soc.* **36** : 302-305.

Srivastava, K.P. 1960. Studies in Indian Metzgerineae IV. *Riccardia levieri*. *J.I.B.S.* **39**: 537-547.

Srivastava, K.P. 1964. Bryophytes of India. I. Ricciaceae. *Bull Nat. Bot. Gar.* Lucknow.

Udar, R. 1950. Studies in Indian Ricciacae. I. *Proc.* 37th *Ind. Sci.* Cong. 40.

Udar, R. 1956. On two species of *Riccia* new to Indian flora, *Curr. Sci.* **25** : 232-233.

Udar, R. 1957. Cultural studies in the genus *Riccia* I sporeling Germination in *R. billardieri*. *Jour. Ind. Bot. Soc.* **36** : 46-50.

Udar, R. 1965a. On a new species of *Calobryum, C. indicum* Udar et Chandra from Darjeeling, India. *Rev. Bryol. et. Lichenol* (Paris) **33** : 555-559.

Udar, R. and S Chandra, 1968. *Calobryum brumii* Nees. A taxon new to Indian flora. *Ibid.* **37** : 265.

Van Andel, O.M. 1952. Germination of the spores and development of primary protonema and secondary protonema of *Funaria hygrometrica*. *Trans. Brit. Bryol. Soc.* **20** : 74-81.

Verdoorn, Fr. 1932. Classification of Hepatics. In *Manual of Bryology,* Chapter **15** : 413-422. *The Hague.*

Wallis, T.E. 1910. Note on *Pellia epiphylla*. *New Phytol.* **10** : 347-348.

Walton, J. 1943. How the sperm reaches the archegonium in *Pellia epiphylla*. *Nature.* **152** : 51.

Wilson, M. 1911. Spermatogenesis in Bryophyta. *Ann. Bot.* **25** : 415-459.

Wolfson, A.M. 1928. Germination of the spores of *Pellia epiphylla* and *P. neesiana*. *Amer. Jour Bot.* **15** : 179-184.

Zerov, D.K. 1966. The Problem of phylogeny of liverworts (Hepaticopsida). *Bot. Zhurn Acad. Nauk. U.S.S.R.* **51** : 3-14.

Glossary

Abaial-The surface of any structure which is truned away from the axis.

Acrogenous-Increasing in growth at apex.

Acropetal-Ascending, *e.g.*, leaves, flowers or roots, developing successively from an axis so that youngest arise at apex.

Adaxial-Turned towards the axis.

Adherent-Attached to some substratum.

Adventitious-Found in an unusual place, *e.g.*, adventitious roots.

Aerenchyma-Aerating cortical tissue in floating plants.

Alteration of generations-The occurance in one life history of two or more different forms differently produced, usually an alternation of sexual with an asexual form.

Alveolus-A small pit or depression.

Amphibian-Adapted for life either on land or water.

Anacrogynous-Certain liverworts in which female reproductive bodies do not arise at or near apex of shoot.

Anatomy-The science which treats of the structure of plants.

Androcyte-A cell arising by grwoth from an antheridium and giving rise to antherozoid.

Annulus-Any ring like structure; special ring in fern sporangium, by action of which sporangium bursts.

Anterior-Nearer head end.

Antheridia-Plural of antheridium.

Antheridiophore-A gametophore bearing antheridia.

Antheridium-Male gametangium in which male sexual cells are produced in many cryptogams.

Antherozoids-Male sexual cells in antheridia.

Anticlinal-Line of division of cells at right angles to surface of apex of a growing point.

Apical-Cell at tip of growing point.

Apogamy-Reproduction without intervention of sexual organs.

Apophysis-Small protuberance at apex of ovuliferous scale in pine.

Apospory-Production of a diploid gametophyte from a sporophyte without intervention of spore formation.

Aquatic-Liying in water.

Archegoniophore-Gametophore bearing archegonia, *e.g.*, *Marchantia*.

Archegonium-A female gametangium in which oospheres are formed, and in which the young plant begins development.

Archesporium-A cell or mass of cells dividing to form spore mother cells and elater forming cells.

Asexual-Having no sexual organs.

Asymmetrical-Having two sides disproportionate.

Autoecous-Bearing antheridia and archegonia on the same plant but different branches, *e.g.*, *Funaria.*

Axial-Pertaining axis or stem.

Axillary-Growing in axil, as buds.

Basal-Near the base.

Basipetal-An order of development of organs in which the youngest structures are at the base and the oldest at the apex.

Biennial-Lasting for two years.

Biflagellate-Having two flagella.

Blepharoplast-A basal granule which gives rise to the cilia of antherozoid.

Botany-The branch of biology dealing with plants.

Bulbous-Like a bulb.

Calyptra-Tissue enclosing developing sporogonium in liverworts.

Capsule-A sac containing spore; sporogonium in Bryophta.

Cauline-Belonging to stem.

Chloroplast-A plastid containing chlorophylls a and b.

Columella-A prolongation of stalk into sporogonium.

Cortex-The extrastelar fundamental tissue of the sporophyte.

Cosmopolitan-World wide in distribution.

Cryptogam-A plant without apparent reproductive organs.

Cuneate-Wedge shaped.

Cupule-The gemmae bearing cup of *Marchantia.*

Decumbent-Lying on the ground but rising at apex.

Dehiscence-The spontaneous opening of an organ releasing spores etc.

Development-The changes undergone by an organism from its beginning to maturity.

Dichotomy-Repeated forking.

Dioecious-Having male and female sexes on different individuals.

Diploid-Having a double set of chromosomes (2n).

Dorsal-Upper surface of thallus or prothallus.

Dorsiventral-With upper and lower surfaces distinct.

Egg-Oosphere, mature female germ cell.

Elater-One of the cells with a spiral thickening which assists in dispersing spores from capsule in liverworts, *e.g., Marchantia.*

Elaterophore-Tissue bearing the elaters, in some liverworts, *e.g., Pellia.*

Embryo-A young organism in early stages of development.

Endospore-Inner coat of spore; intine.

Endosporium-Inner coat of spore; wall.

Endothecium-The central region of an epibasal octant of oospore of liverorts and mosses.

Entire-With continuous margin.

Epidermis-The outermost protective layer of stems.

Erect-Directing upwards.

Evolution-The gradual development of organisms from pre-existing organisms since the dawn of life.

Exine-Outer layer of spore wall; exospore, exosporium.

Fertilization-The union of male and female nuclei.

Foot-An embryonic structure in vascular cryptogams through which nourishment is obtained from prothallus or thallus; basal portion of sporophyte in mosses.

Fossil-Petrified plant portion found in rocks.

Gametangium-A structure producing sexual cell.

Gametes-Sexual cells.

Gametogenesis-Gamete formation.

Gametophyte-The gamete forming phase in alternation of plant generation; sexual generation of plants.

Gemma-A bud or outgrowth of a plant which develops into a new organism, *e.g., Marchantia, Funaria* etc.

Gemma-cup-Cupule containing gemmae, *e.g., Marchantia.*

Genera-Plural of genus.

Genus-A group of closely related species, in classification of plants.

Germ tube-Short filamentous tube put forth by a germinating spore.

Germination-Process of initial development.

Groove-Furrow or depression.

Ground tissue-Conjunctive parenchyma.

Growing point-A part of plant body at which cell division is localized generally terminal and composed of meristematic cells.

Habitat-The locality or external environment in which a plant lives.

Haploid-having n number of chromosomes.

Haplont-An organism having haploid somatic nuclei.

Hepatic-Liverworts.

Hypobasal-The lower segment of a developing zygote.

Internode-The part between two successive nodes.

Intine-The inner covering membrane of a pollen grain or of a spore.

Karyogamy-Union of nuclei after cyptoplasmic fusion (plasmogamy)

Lacuna-A space between cells.

Life-cycle-The various phases through which an individual species passes to maturity.

Mesophyll-The internal parenchyma of a leaf; chlorophyllous cells.

Metamorphosis-Change of form and structure, *e.g.,* the formation of antherozoid from an androcyte.

Mid-rib-The large central vein of a leaf.

Monoecious-With sex organs on one gametophyte; hermaphrodite.

Morophology-The science of form and structure of plants.

Neck-canal-The hollow within the elongated part of an archegonium.

Node-The joint of a stem at which leaves arise.

Nurse cells-Cells providing nourishment to the developing spores in the sporogonium.

Octant-One of the units in eight celled stage in segmentation of ovum.

Oosphere-An egg before fertilization.

Oosphore-The zygote or fretilized egg cell.

Operculum-A lid or covering flap at apex of capsules of mosses.

Order-In classification, group of organisms closely allied, ranking between family and class.

Palaeobotany-Botany of fossil plants and plant impressions.

Paraphysis-A slender filamentous epidermal outgrowth occuring among sex organs, *e.g., Funaria.*

Parthenogenesis-Reproduction without fertilization by a male element.

Peduncle-Stalk.

Perichaetium-One of membranes enveloping archegonia of bryophytes, *e.g., Marchantia.*

Periclinal-System of cells parallel to surface of apex of a growing point.

Perigynium-Membranous envelope of archegonium in liverworts, *e.g., Marchantia.*

Peristome-The region surrounding mouth; term used in connection with moss capsule.

Posterior-Situated behind.

Primitive-Of earliest origin.

Protonema-The filamentous thallus of mosses from which the moss plant buds.

Pseudoelater-One of the chains of cells of sporogonium of liverworts.

Rachis-The axis bearing leaflets.

Receptacle-A sporophore; terminal disc of mosses.

Rhizoid-A root-like outgrowth of thallus, *e.g.*,liverworts, mosses, ferns; unicellular hairs on lower side of prothallus.

Rhizome-A thick horizontal stem, partly along and partly underground, sending out shoots above and roots below, *e.g.*, Ferns.

Root-Descending portion of plant, fixing it in soil, and absorbing moisture and nutrients.

Segments-A division formed by cleavage of an ovum.

Septa-Plural of septum.

Septum-A partition separating two cavities of tissue.

Seta-Sporophore of liverworts and mosses.

Sexual cell-Ovum or sperm.

Spermatozoid-An antherozoid; a free swimming male gamete.

Spore-A highly specialized reproductive cell of plants.

Spore-mother-cell-Sixteen cells produced by repeated division of an archesporium, each in turn dividing into four spores.

Sporogenesis-Spore formation.

Sporogenous-Spore producing.

Sporophyte-The diploid (2n) spore-producing phase in alternation of plant generations.

Syngamy-Sexual reproduction; fertilization.

Terminal-Situated at the end.

Tetrad-A group of four spores formed by meiotic division of spore mother cells.

Thallus-A combination of cells presenting no differentiation of leaf and stem.

Theca-A spore-case.

Trabeculae-Plants of sterile cells extend across cavities of pteridophytes.

Vertical-Standing upright; lenghthwise in direction of axis.

Zone-An area characterized by similar flora.

Zygote-Cell formation by union of two gametes or reproductive cells.

INDEX